Frederick County, Maryland

Estate Docket Index Book

Volume 4: Combined Compiled Index 1815–ca 1950

Trudie Davis-Long

HERITAGE BOOKS
2022

HERITAGE BOOKS
AN IMPRINT OF HERITAGE BOOKS, INC.

Books, CDs, and more—Worldwide

For our listing of thousands of titles see our website
at
www.HeritageBooks.com

Published 2022 by
HERITAGE BOOKS, INC.
Publishing Division
5810 Ruatan Street
Berwyn Heights, Md. 20740

Heritage Books by the author:

1889 List of Taxpayers of Frederick County, Maryland

Abstracts of the Wills and Estate Records of Granville County, North Carolina, 1833–1846 by Zae Hargett Gwynn

Abstracts of the Wills and Estate Records of Granville County, North Carolina, 1846–1863 by Zae Hargett Gwynn

Abstracts of the Wills and Estate Records of Granville County, North Carolina, 1863–1902 by Zae Hargett Gwynn

Frederick County, Maryland Estate Docket Index Book, Volume 1: A to G, 1815–ca 1950

Frederick County, Maryland Estate Docket Index Book, Volume 2: H to R, 1815–ca 1950

Frederick County, Maryland Estate Docket Index Book, Volume 3: S to Z, 1815–ca 1950

Frederick County, Maryland Estate Docket Index Book, Volume 4: Combined Compiled Index, 1815–ca 1950

International Standard Book Number
Paperbound: 978-0-7884-2578-3

TABLE OF CONTENTS

A Little History, Maryland Testamentary Laws, Settling an Estate,
Estate Docket Books at the Frederick Courthouse, Administration Accounts,
List of Register of Wills.
Notes from the Transcriber i

Index 1

A Little History

The General Assembly, by an act of February, 1777, established the Orphans' Court, to be held by not less than three justices of the peace. This court was empowered to take all probate of wills, grant letters of administration and letters testamentary, also warrants to appraisers in cases where there was no dispute, and in every respect had the same power, jurisdiction, and authority in connection with the register of wills that the deputy commissary had before that time in connection with the County Court. This court was authorized to bind out as apprentices orphan children, the profits of whose estates were not sufficient for their maintenance, the children of beggars, illegitimate children, and the children of parents out of the State, where a sufficient support was not afforded. By the act of 1798 the Governor, by and with the advice and consent of the Council, had authority to appoint and commission three men of integrity and judgment to be justices of the Orphans' Court, and to hold their offices until their successors were appointed. Under the constitution of 1838 and legislative enactments in pursuance thereof, the judges held office for four years.
The first court was held Oct. 13 and 14, 1777.[1]

When the Federal government was organized after the Revolutionary War, papers held by the Prerogative Court were sent to the counties to be recorded.

From 1817, the Register of Wills was empowered to receive inventories and accounts of sales, and to state guardians', executors' and administrators' accounts subject to review by the court. He was authorized to take probate of wills in 1832 and he was also directed to retain the originals of all wills probated in his office."' It is interesting to note also that from 1806 until the Civil War, the Register was authorized to grant certificates of freedom to Negroes and was required to keep a record of those he issued.[2]

The number of Orphans' Court Justices commissioned in each county was reduced to three in 1790 and beginning in 1847, the person who was to be Chief Judge was so designated in the commission issued by the Governor. The Justices and the Registers of Wills were appointed to serve during good behavior until 1838 when their terms were limited to seven years. The Constitution of 1851 made both offices elective and reduced the term of office of the Justices to four years and that of the Registers to six years. The terms of both Justices and Registers were fixed at six years under the Constitution of 1864.[3]

Maryland Testamentary Laws [4]

REGISTER OF WILLS—	**Section**	**Article**	**Page**
to give bond and penalty of, how approved and where recorded	253	93	675
penalty for neglect to execute	254	93	675
copy to be sent to comptroller	255	93	675
to act as clerk to orphans' court	256	93	675
to attend office daily	257	93	676
to file and record papers	257	93	676
to receive inventories and accounts of sale	258	93	676
to state accounts	258	93	676
may take probate of accounts	259	93	676
may pass accounts, end of what amount	260	93	676
to keep record of claims passed	260	93	676
may take probate of wills	261	93	676
may grant administration	261	93	676
not to receive fee for advice	262	93	676

---

[1]Scharf, J. T. (1968). *History of Western Maryland: Being a History of Frederick, Montgomery, Carroll, Washington, Allegany, and Garrett Counties from the earliest period to the present day, including biographical sketches of their representative men.* (Vol. 1). Clearfield Co. pg 480

[2]Radoff, Morris L. *The Old Line State A History of Maryland 1956 Library of American Lives Vol 1: Source Edition Recording the Early and Contemporary History of Maryland Through the Medium of Extensive Research and the Life Histories of its most constructive Members—Chronicling the Backgrounds and Activities of its Prominent Families and Personages with Emphasis on Their Accomplishments in making Maryland one of America's Greatest States.*. Hopkinsville, KY: Historical Record Association. page 348

[3]Ibid.

[4]Otho Scott, Hiram M'Cullough, compilers. *The Maryland Code: Public General Laws and Public Local Laws.* (Baltimore: John Murphy & Co., 1860). p 798

not to act as attorney	263	93	677
[not to act as attorney]	16	11	55
to grant and register certificate of freedom	264	93	677
second certificate, how obtained	265	93	677
when to act as auditor, and fees for	266	93	677
to pay over surplus emoluments	267	93	678
office expenses, how ascertained	268, 271	93	678
penalty for false swearing in relation to	269	93	678
bond liable for surplus emoluments	270	93	678
how payment of public money by enforced	19	22	124
fees of	26	38	297
to produce books in suit against	70	75	532
to enter claims against decedent, and how	114	93	644

Settling an Estate

If the estate is TESTATE (WILL)
1. Will is presented to Court by the executor. If the will is valid, it is accepted or probated.
2. An inventory of property is completed.
3. Certain household articles exempt from execution and money are set off to the widow.
4. Executor compiles lists of debts and credits called Accounts and exhibits them to the Court.
5. Court orders the distribution according to the will.
6. If the will is invalid, the estate becomes intestate.
7. Guardians are appointed for minor children.

If there is no will the decedent died INTESTATE
1. Court appoints an administrator or grants letters of administration.
2. Articles exempt from execution and money are set off to the widow before accounts are drawn.
3. Inventory taken, usually not by administrator.
4. Guardians are appointed for minor children.
5. Administrator compiles lists of debts and credits as Accounts and exhibits them to the Court. Court determines if the estate is solvent or insolvent. If solvent, debts are paid in full and assets (personalty and/or land) are distributed to the heirs at law.

Estate Docket Books at the Frederick Courthouse

The large three-volume estate dockets (A-G, H-R, S-Z) on top of the counter are the indexes to all estate papers. The original implementation was in 1815. The current set of books run through 1950, but there are individual data additions after 1950 to estates that had not be completely finalized. The names are alphabetical by initial letters of the surname, then the given name, according to the Campbell system described under Land Records. Names are chronological down the left side of the left page.

The books are listed in chronological order starting with the initials of the clerk who was Register at the time the records were presented to the court.

Typed into the book is the following:

Historical

This book was completed September 29, 1935, being a copy with additions of the General Indexes completed January 15, 1896. The work being done by Oscar C Sponseller and Rollins J Atkins, Deputies under John Hershberger, Register of Wills. Work was started May 1, 1935 and was done each night until completed.

Columns are provided for the following information:

Decedent
Administrator or executor
Bonds: date and reference
Bondsmen
Inventory or sale of personal property, date and reference
Inventory of current money and debts due, date and reference
Inventory of stocks, bonds, real estate, date and reference

Sale of real estate, date and reference
First account, final account, dates and references
Remarks (often say "2nd and fl- meaning second and final)

The index books contain many errors, additions and attempts to correct errors. The only way to verify the information is to pull the referenced source and check it yourself. With or without a will the process was similar.

Administration Accounts

Final account filings should not be ignored..

The administrator or executor of an estate included in his accounts the amount of the inventory and settled all the accounts. If the estate proved to be insolvent, creditors were paid a percentage, although all debts due doctors and funeral expenses and the widow's portion were not discounted. If the estate was solvent, a distribution of the assets was made to the legal heirs. This valuable list is usually included in the accounts, but often is missing.

Some estates required the Equity court to become involved for settlement .

List of Register of Wills

The number of books created by each Register of wills varies depending on how long they held the office.

Henry Steiner [HS]	1815-1825
George M Eichelberger [GME]	1825-1845
Thomas Sappington [TS]	1845-1851
George Hoskins [GH]	1851-1857
Absalom P Kessler [APK]	1857-1863
Thomas L McLean [TLMc]	1863-1867
S G Cockey [SGC]	1867-1873
John R Rowzer [JRR]	1873-1879
James P Perry [JPP]	1879-1885
Hamilton Lindsay [HL]	1885-1891
James K Waters [JKW]	1891-1897
Charles E Sayler [CES]	1897-1903
William B Cutshall [WBC]	1903-1909
Samuel D Thomas [SDT]	1909-1915
Albert M Patterson [AMP]	1915-1921
George E Smith [GES]	1921-1927
Russell E Lighter [REL]	1927
Charles E Butts [CEB]	1927-1929
Charles E V Myers [CEM]	1929-1930
Melvin F Shepley [MFS]	1930-1934
John Hershberger [JH]	1934-1938
Roy L Leatherman [RLL]	1938-1946
Harry D Radcliff [HDR]	1946-1958
Thomas Eichelberger [TE]	1958-1990
Virginia P Fifer [VPF]	1990-2014

Notes from the Transcriber

This index is a combination of all indexes from the 3 docket books. This includes names, places and businesses found in all 3 docket books.

The book and page number reflect the **original** page in the docket itself and not the page in the transcribed books.

The format is name, page and volume number. For any one spelling that person can show up 3 times in the list; one for each volume they are listed in.

Additions to the docket indexes did continue into the 1990's.

Original scanned images of individual pages can be found at

Estate docket index, A-G, 1816-1950
https://www.familysearch.org/ark:/61903/3:1:3QSQ-G9S1-VHKR?mode=g&cat=1876656

Estate docket index, H-R, 1816-1950
https://www.familysearch.org/ark:/61903/3:1:3QSQ-G9S1-V83H?mode=g&cat=1876656

Estate docket index, S-Z, 1816-1950
https

Name Page[s] Vol

*New Amsterdam
Casualty Co 18 2
, Franklin B 294 2
, Frederick W 221a 2
?, Alvie 79 3
?, Charles E 28, 43 3
?, Chas B 91 3
?, Christopher T 176 3
?, Effie M 102 3
?, Mary Ann 70 3
?, Thomas H 81 3
?anney, John W 111 3
[sic], John L 101 1
Aab, Conrad 4 1
Aaskey, William A 160 3
Abb, Calvin L 4 1
Abb, Dorthy 213 2
Abb, Minnie M 19 1
Abbott, Henry H 56 3
Abbott, John H 185 2
Abbott, Julia 14 1
Abell, Geo 54 3
Abell, John 13 1
Abell, Mary H 54 3
Abey, Annie 1 1
Abney, Mary Francis 19 1
Abott, John H 14 1
Abrahams, Cora 4 1
Abrahams, Grace E 22 1
Abrahams, Harry W 4 1
Abrahams, Romeo A 22 1
Abrecht, Ada B 284 2
Abrecht, Clyde S Jr 284 2
Abrecht, Daisy G 6 1
Abrecht, Earl E 8 1
Abrecht, George 10 1
Abrecht, George F 10, 23 1
Abrecht, George T 178 2
Abrecht, Gertrude 10 1
Abrecht, James E 14 1
Abrecht, John D 6 1
Abrecht, John W 10, 14 1
Abrecht, Louise W 8 1
Abrecht, Luther W 23 1
Abrecht, Niles A 25 1
Abrecht, Rhoda C 14 1
Abrecht, Sarah E 14, 23 1
Abrecht, Wm 14 1
Abrecht, Wm H 25 1
Acaleer, Hugh 71 1
Adam, Ann M 25 1
Adam, Ann Mary 25 1
Adam, John S 14 1
Adam, John W 14, 25 1
Adam, Margaretha E 14 1
Adam, Margaretha E 106 2
Adam, W H 25 1
Adam, Wilhelm 25 1
Adam, Wm 25 1
Adam, Wm H 25 1
Adams, Abraham T 1 1
Adams, Andrew 1 1
Adams, Annie M 1, 13 1
Adams, Carter 59 1
Adams, Catherine 1, 4 1
Adams, Charles Edmund 15 1
Adams, Chas D 156 1
Adams, Clarence C 4 1
Adams, Dorsey C 8 1
Adams, E C 106 1
Adams, Ed E 8 1
Adams, Edw E 8 1
Adams, Edw E 119 2
Adams, Edward E 20 3
Adams, Edward J 1, 8 1
Adams, Eliza 8 1
Adams, Elizabeth 8 1
Adams, Fannie E C 9, 24, 25
1
Adams, George 1 1
Adams, Gladys V 14 1
Adams, J D 6 3
Adams, J H 55 3
Adams, J H 19 1
Adams, J Paul 14 1
Adams, Jacob 25 1
Adams, James 13 1
Adams, James 81 3
Adams, James 101 2
Adams, John 201 1
Adams, John F 13 1
Adams, Kate 15 1
Adams, Leona 18 1
Adams, Letha 18 1
Adams, Lydia 13, 18 1
Adams, Mallie V 253 1
Adams, Margaret 19 1
Adams, Margaret 210a 2
Adams, Mary T 19 1
Adams, Sarah 19 1
Adams, Sarah A 23 1
Adams, Thomas 23, 24 1
Adams, Thomas H 24 1
Adams, Valenten [sic] 18 1
Adams, Valentine 24, 244 1
Adams, Valentine 113 3
Adams, Wilhelm 217 3
Adams, William 55 3
Adams, William R 71 1
Adams, Wm 14, 25 1
Adams, Wm Clinton 253 1
Adams, Wm E 25 1
Adams, Wm H 19 1
Adams, Wm H H 24, 25 1
Addelsperger, John 184 3
Addelsperger, Michael 231 2
Addesburger, James 254 2
Addison, Chas W 166 3
Addison, Frank R 13, 19, 25
1
Addison, John 181 2
Addison, John D 19 1
Addison, Martha C 13 1
Addison, Martha H 19 1
Addison, Mary B 19 1
Addison, Mary N 166 3
Addl 41 2
Adellsperger, Michael 7 2
Adelsberger, Francis A 166 1
Adelsberger, Francis M 88 1
Adelsberger, Jennie M 9 1
Adelsberger, Maria I 9 1
Adelsberger, Mary E 19 1
Adelsberger, Michael 27 2
Adelsperger 19 1
Adelsperger, AP 169 2
Adelsperger, Cahterine 24 1
Adelsperger, D G 9 1
Adelsperger, Elizabeth 19 1
Adelsperger, Francis 8 1
Adelsperger, Jacob 9 1
Adelsperger, James F 186 1
Adelsperger, John 205, 220,
219a 2
Adelsperger, John 8, 13, 70
1
Adelsperger, Joshua 13. 169 1
Adelsperger, Joshua 197 2
Adelsperger, Joshua E 110 1
Adelsperger, M C 13 1
Adelsperger, Mary E 13 1
Adelsperger, Michael 13 1
Adelsperger, Michael 238 2
Adelsperger, Michael C 19 1
Adelsperger, Thomas 256 1
Ader, Stacy 24 1
Adkins, Chas M 23 1
Adkins, E M 20 3
Adkins, Ida E 4 1
Adkins, Keefer E 12 1
Adkins, Samuel 4 1
Adler, L M 84 2
Adlum, John 23 1
Adlum, John Sr 13 1
Adlum, Joseph 13 1
Adlum, Mary 13 1
Aetna accident & Liability Co 13
1
Aetna Accident & Liability Co 113
3
Aetna Accident & Liability Co of Con
96 2
Aetna Casualty & Indemnity Co 199
2
Aetna Casualty & Surety Co 51
3

Aetna Casualty & Surety Co 3, 268 2
Aetna Casualty & Surety Co, The 65, 223, 272 1
Aetna Casualty & Surety Company 119 2
Aetna Casualty and Inse Co 235 1
Aetna Casualty Surity Co 267 2
Aetna Indemnity Co, The 119 1
Affleck, L H 93 2
Agneio, Margaret 148 1
Agnew, D 209, 224 3
Agnew, David 6, 19 1
Agnew, David 22, 39 2
Agnew, David 106, 205 3
Agnew, John 11 2
Agnew, Margaret 110 1
Aguilla, Alfred 6 1
Ahalt, Albert M 1, 14 1
Ahalt, Alberta M 88 1
Ahalt, B S 1 1
Ahalt, Barbara 85 1
Ahalt, Benjamin S 96 1
Ahalt, Benjamin S 3, 19 1
Ahalt, C W 68 1
Ahalt, Carlton E 4 1
Ahalt, Carlton P 13, 14, 23, 37 1
Ahalt, Chas 102 2
Ahalt, Chas P 4 1
Ahalt, Clarence L 4, 18 1
Ahalt, Clifford 18 1
Ahalt, Cora E 18 1
Ahalt, Earl M 16 2
Ahalt, Earl M 22 1
Ahalt, Elsie F 8 1
Ahalt, Fannie E 14 1
Ahalt, Grace 32 2
Ahalt, Harriet J 11 1
Ahalt, Harry R 4 1
Ahalt, Helen H 22 1
Ahalt, Henry 11 1
Ahalt, Huffer 1 1
Ahalt, Huffer J 11 1
Ahalt, J 81 3
Ahalt, J Guy 11 1
Ahalt, Jacob 70, 106, 185 3
Ahalt, Jacob 187 2
Ahalt, Jacob 11, 13, 88, 189, 228, 249 1
Ahalt, Jacob B 13 1
Ahalt, Jacob L 18, 19 1
Ahalt, Jeanette 179 3
Ahalt, John 8, 214 2
Ahalt, John 14 1
Ahalt, John D 23, 24, 244 1
Ahalt, John M 14 1
Ahalt, John V 179 3
Ahalt, John W O 13 1
Ahalt, Joshua 14, 88 1
Ahalt, Joshua 9 3
Ahalt, Joshua 106, 115, 205, 282 2
Ahalt, Joshua D 22, 96, 264 1
Ahalt, Josiah 223 3
Ahalt, L C 169 2
Ahalt, Lester 18 1
Ahalt, Lester R 19 1
Ahalt, Lewis H 13, 18 1
Ahalt, Lola E 4 1
Ahalt, Lorena 18 1
Ahalt, Luther 202 2
Ahalt, Luther M D 8 1
Ahalt, M Foster 18, 19 1
Ahalt, Mae A 32 2
Ahalt, Margaret A 18 1
Ahalt, Margaret L 68 1
Ahalt, Mary 19 1
Ahalt, Mary M 19 1
Ahalt, Mathias 46 2
Ahalt, Mathias 19, 219 1
Ahalt, Mathias S 19 1
Ahalt, Matthias 22, 58 1
Ahalt, Paul R 22 1
Ahalt, Phobe 22 1
Ahalt, Ralph 4 1
Ahalt, Rosa A 11 1
Ahalt, Russel M 4 1
Ahalt, Samantha J 14, 23 1
Ahalt, Saml 6 1
Ahalt, Samuel 13, 19, 23, 30, 37, 79, 91, 195 1
Ahalt, Samuel 18, 64 3
Ahalt, Samuel 39, 101, 205, 211, 264 2
Ahalt, Samuel P W, 4 1
Ahalt, Walter L J 18 1
Ainsworth, Catherine E 217 1
Ainsworth, Chas R 4 1
Ainsworth, David A 217 1
Ainsworth, David Andrew 6 1
Ainsworth, John E 4 1
Ainsworth, Margie Alice 6 1
Akers, E M 44 1
Alabugh, T S 72 3
Albaugh, A 64 3
Albaugh, A Ridgely 14 1
Albaugh, Abraham 1 1
Albaugh, Ann Catherine 1 1
Albaugh, Azariah N 1 1
Albaugh, Catherine 23, 219 1
Albaugh, Catherine L 8 1
Albaugh, Catherine S 12 1
Albaugh, Chas D 14 1
Albaugh, Chas E 21, 22, 254 1
Albaugh, Chas F 4 1
Albaugh, Cora J 1, 8 1
Albaugh, Cordelia G 21 1
Albaugh, Daniel 6 1
Albaugh, David 6 1
Albaugh, E Guy 25, 52 1
Albaugh, E H 19 3
Albaugh, E V 68, 244 1
Albaugh, Edgar G 4 1
Albaugh, Edna E 8 1
Albaugh, Elias 8, 23 1
Albaugh, Elias R 171 3
Albaugh, Elias V 71, 171 3
Albaugh, Elias V 194, 205 1
Albaugh, Ella 8 1
Albaugh, Emma J 10 1
Albaugh, Emma L 6 1
Albaugh, Ephraim 8, 176, 217 1
Albaugh, Ephriam 112 2
Albaugh, Geo W 13 1
Albaugh, George M 10 1
Albaugh, George W 13 1
Albaugh, Gertrude W 10, 12 1
Albaugh, H C 22 1
Albaugh, Harry E 11 1
Albaugh, Hattie M 24 1
Albaugh, Henrietta 11 1
Albaugh, Henrietta E 13 1
Albaugh, Henry C 24 1
Albaugh, Herbert J 11 1
Albaugh, Horace J 188 3
Albaugh, Howard 46 2
Albaugh, Howard M 21, 28 3
Albaugh, Irving 199 2
Albaugh, Irving C[?] 12 1
Albaugh, Irving S 12, 14, 68, 73, 140, 184 1
Albaugh, Irving S 21, 46, 68 3
Albaugh, Irving S 134 2
Albaugh, Isaac 213 3
Albaugh, Isaac 280 2
Albaugh, Isaac A 7 2
Albaugh, Isaac A 12, 14, 24, 197 1
Albaugh, Isaac H 1 2
Albaugh, Isaac I 12 1
Albaugh, J P S 203 3
Albaugh, J V 14 1
Albaugh, J Valentine 282 2
Albaugh, J W 81 3
Albaugh, James S 14, 23 1
Albaugh, Jasper 13, 14, 33 1
Albaugh, Jeremiah W 25, 96, 188 1
Albaugh, Jermiah 171 3
Albaugh, John 13 1
Albaugh, John 1, 202 3
Albaugh, John 28, 276, 282 2
Albaugh, John H 14, 23, 25, 184 1
Albaugh, John of D 13 1
Albaugh, John of Daniel 13 1

Albaugh, John Thomas S 12 1
Albaugh, John W 51 2
Albaugh, John W 12, 14 1
Albaugh, Joseph S 22 1
Albaugh, Joshua 28, 138, 153 2
Albaugh, Joshua 24, 41, 60, 125 1
Albaugh, Joshua V 14 1
Albaugh, Kathryn 14 1
Albaugh, Katie S 11 1
Albaugh, Lewis 171 3
Albaugh, Lewis 138 2
Albaugh, Lewis 25, 139 1
Albaugh, Lucrecia 282 2
Albaugh, Luther A 11 1
Albaugh, M j 6 1
Albaugh, M J 3, 21, 210 3
Albaugh, Mary 14 1
Albaugh, Mary A 255 2
Albaugh, Mary A 8 1
Albaugh, Mary E 19, 41 1
Albaugh, Maurcie J 19, 55, 92, 144, 119, 166, 172, 186, 205 1
Albaugh, Maurice 209 2
Albaugh, Maurice J 21, 51, 154, 176, 188 3
Albaugh, Melville E 25 1
Albaugh, Morris J 12 1
Albaugh, N H 172 2
Albaugh, N J 102 2
Albaugh, Nicholas 21 1
Albaugh, Nicholas H 290 2
Albaugh, Nicholas R 22 1
Albaugh, Paul E 14 1
Albaugh, Rachel 22 1
Albaugh, Rachel R 14 1
Albaugh, Rebecca 22 1
Albaugh, S Laura H 23 1
Albaugh, Samuel 280 2
Albaugh, Sarah 23 1
Albaugh, Sarh C, 14 1
Albaugh, Singleton 23 1
Albaugh, Susan 23 1
Albaugh, Susannah 6, 25 1
Albaugh, T F 2 2
Albaugh, T S 87 3
Albaugh, Thomas 10 3
Albaugh, Thomas S 75 3
Albaugh, Thomas S 23. 24 1
Albaugh, Thos 253 1
Albaugh, Thos L 24 1
Albaugh, Truman G 11 1
Albaugh, V A 24 1
Albaugh, Valentine A 25, 139 1
Albaugh, Valentine S 203 3
Albaugh, W V 100 1
Albaugh, W V 60 1
Albaugh, William 286 2
Albaugh, William A 1 1
Albaugh, William A 171, 203 3
Albaugh, William H 64 3
Albaugh, Wm 11 2
Albaugh, Wm 205 3
Albaugh, Wm 245 1
Albaugh, Wm A 25 1
Albaugh, Wm H 14 1
Albaugh, Wm H 38 2
Albaugh, Wm U 65 3
Albaugh, Wm V 25, 119 1
Albert, Herman 19 1
Albert, Ida M 179 1
Albert, Marjorie 239 2
Albert, May 19 1
Albin, James R 21 1
Albin, Nellie E 21 1
Albsugh, William A 70 1
Alcock, James 13 1
Aldelspergere, Josiah 167 3
Alder, Albert G 1 1
Alder, F E 107 2
Alder, Frank E 1, 9 1
Alder, Lucy E 8 1
Aldersberger, John 135 3
Aldridge, David 184 2
Aldridge, David C 9, 19, 272 1
Aldridge, E J 8 1
Aldridge, Geo 260 1
Aldridge, Geo W 21 1
Aldridge, John L S 19 1
Aldridge, Lewis A 21, 191 1
Aldridge, Margaret A 19 1
Aldridge, Mary Ellen 19 1
Aldridge, Oliver P 21 1
Aldridge, Singleton J 205 3
Alexander, Andrew 163 3
Alexander, Andrew 1 1
Alexander, Andrew S 1 1
Alexander, Armstead T 1 1
Alexander, Arstead T M 11 1
Alexander, Ashton 206, 120 3
Alexander, C 18 1
Alexander, Carvel L 1 1
Alexander, Catherine 4 1
Alexander, Catherine 107 2
Alexander, Cornelia 4 1
Alexander, Effie E 79 3
Alexander, Elizabeth A 8 1
Alexander, Elizabeth Ann 1 1
Alexander, Elizabetha 8 1
Alexander, Frank 19 1
Alexander, George F 10 1
Alexander, Henry 11 1
Alexander, Jacob 13 1
Alexander, John 14, 18 1
Alexander, Lawson 71 1
Alexander, Lawson 87 2
Alexander, Mary 19 1
Alexander, Mary M 14 1
Alexander, Matilda 19 1
Alexander, Meredith H 14 1
Alexander, Orpha M 62 3
Alexander, Tilghman 24 1
Alexander, A S 1 1
Algire, Harry C 14 1
Algire, Joseph P 14 1
Alison, Robert 222 2
Allnutt, Elizabeth D 8 1
Allbright, Charles P 4 1
Allen, C C 4 1
Allen, Chas A 4 1
Allen, Clarence G 255 2
Allen, Delia C 22 1
Allen, Delia K 6 1
Allen, Edw E 171 1
Allen, Elizabeth C 8 1
Allen, Francis J 25 1
Allen, Harry B 11 1
Allen, James 38 2
Allen, James 13, 56 1
Allen, James E 260 1
Allen, James F 6 1
Allen, Jennie Borders 14 1
Allen, Margaret E 186 1
Allen, Martha J M 255 2
Allen, Mary F 244 1
Allen, Patrick J 22 1
Allen, Russell E 22 1
Allen, Theresa E 25 1
Allen, Wm 25 1
Allgire, William 10 3
Allison, Chas B 4 1
Allison, John G 22 1
Allison, Matilda 22 1
Allison, Robert 22, 195 1
Allison, Robert B 22 1
Allison, Robert R 22 1
Allnut, John H 9 1
Allnut, Wm P 58 1
Allnutt, Elizabeth D, 10 1
Allnutt, Franklin 9 1
Allnutt, George S 10, 14 1
Allnutt, J H 62 3
Allnutt, James N 13 1
Allnutt, John H 9, 13 1
Allnutt, John H 218 2
Allnutt, John T 14 1
Allnutt, John T 19 1
Allnutt, Mary M 19 1
Allnutt, William P 9 1
Allnutt, Wm P 13, 19, 117, 129 1
Alnutt, John T 218a 2
Alnutt, W Thomas 8 1
Alnutt, William P 58 1
Alnutt, William P 218a 2
Alt, Gertrude G 189, 248 1

Althalt, A 124 3
Althoff, Aloysius 11 1
Althoff, Elsie E 9 1
Althoff, Flora M 10 1
Althoff, Fred 9 1
Althoff, Henry 11, 196 1
Althoff, Wm A 11 1
Altman, Ann M 14 1
Altman, Geo P 14 1
Altman, Jacob G 14 1
Altman, John M 13 1
Altman, Thos J 14 1
Alvey, Annie Ridgely 14 1
Alvey, James 283 2
Alvey, James M 24, 30 1
Alvey, Mary Isabelle 14 1
Alvey, Thos Frederick 24 1
Ambercrumbie, Sarah 25 1
Ambercrumbie, Sarah A 25 1
Ambercrumbie, Wm 25 1
Ambrose, Alinda S 25 1
Ambrose, Carl M 6 1
Ambrose, David E 6, 21 1
Ambrose, Geo E 42 1
Ambrose, Geo H 84 1
Ambrose, George H 10 1
Ambrose, J 19 2
Ambrose, Jacob 13 1
Ambrose, John C 14 1
Ambrose, Lena R 42 1
Ambrose, Leonard S 18 1
Ambrose, Malissa 6 1
Ambrose, Marshall F 14 1
Ambrose, Matilda 10 1
Ambrose, Melvin W 21 1
Ambrose, Nellie Y 52 1
Ambrose, Nora 21 1
Ambrose, Rosie M 23 1
Ambrose, Sterling L O 23 1
Ambrose, W C 193 2
Ambrose, Walter C 25 1
Ambrosius, Daniel 6 1
Ambrosius, Henry 6, 11 1
Ambrosouis, Mary 19 1
Ambush, Agnes Barton 14 1
Ambush, Florence 22 1
Ambush, James Labrosia 14 1
Ambush, Labrosia 76 1
Ambush, Patrick 22 1
Amer Bonding C of Balto 6 3
Amer Bonding Co of Baltimore 231, 294 2
Amer Bonding Co of Balto 2, 27, 51 3
Amer Bonding Co of Balto 32, 268 2
Amer Surety Co of N Y 278 1
Amer Surety Co of N Y 23, 140 2
Amer Surety of N Y 113 1
American & Trust Co of Baltimore 160 3
American Banking and Trust Co 30 1
American Bond Co of Baltimore 112 1
American Bondin Company 265 2
American Bonding & Tr Co of Baltimore City 30 2
American Bonding & Trust Co of Baltimore City, The 30 1
American Bonding C of Balto 82 3
American Bonding Co 119, 124, 155, 192, 243, 254 1
American Bonding Co 18, 32, 68, 72, 80, 222 2
American Bonding Co 3, 68, 91, 124, 221 3
American Bonding Co Baltimore 84 2
American Bonding Co of Balitmore 28, 38, 72, 92, 106, 126, 139, 140, 165, 172, 183, 186, 223, 230, 235, 239, 250, 265, 276 1
American Bonding Co of Balt 202 2
American Bonding Co of Baltimore 11, 45 3
American Bonding Co of Baltimore 5, 8, 9, 23, 32, 67, 81, 150, 154, 161, 166, 177, 195, 202, 227, 210a 2
American Bonding Co of Baltimore MD 161 2
American Bonding Co of Balto 2, 56, 72, 91, 129, 149, 169, 172, 174, 3
American Bonding Co of Balto 32, 36, 140 2
American Bonding Co of Montpilier, Vt 172 1
American Bonding Co of Vt 113 3
American Bonding Co oof Balto 107 3
American Bonding Company 11, 57 3
American Bonding Company 1 1
American Bonding Company 35, 84, 199 2
American Bonding Company of Bal, The 230 1
American Bonding Company of Bal, The 34 1
American Bonding Company of Bal, The 215 1
American Bonding Company of Baltimore 122 2
American Bonding Company of Baltimore 21 3
American Bondsmen Co 119 1
American Casualty Co of Reading 87 2
American Casualty Co of Reading, Pa 223a 2
American Casualty Co of Reading, The 266 1
American Fidelity & Deposit Co of Mont. Vt 227 1
American Fidelity & Mutual Co 62 1
American Fidelity Co 223, 245 1
American Fidelity Co 217 3
American Fidelity Co 227a 2
American Fidelity Co of Montpelier, Vt 257 2
American Fidelity Co of Texas 199 2
American Fidelity Co of Vt 102 3
American Fidelity Co, Montpelier Vt 82 1
American Fiedlity Co of Vt 31 2
American Security Co of N Y 76 2
American Suerty Co of N Y 246 2
American Suerty Co of N Y 259 2
American Surety Co of MD 182 2
American Surety Co of N Y 4, 57, 116, 124, 166, 167, 180, 121, 228 3
American Surety Co of N Y 34, 163, 175 2
American Surety Co of N Y 144, 179, 189, 192, 257, 279 1
American Surety Company 34 1
American Surety Company of N Y 280 2
American Surety Company of New York 250 1
American Surety Company of New York 265 2
Amsburg, John R 165 2
Amsperger, Lawrence 18 1
Anders, A Eugene 1 1
Anders, A H 126 1
Anders, A R 72 3
Anders, Aaaron R 1 1
Anders, Aaron 23, 49, 68, 181, 189

2
Anders, Aaron 6 3
Anders, Aaron 1, 40, 58, 91, 164, 244 1
Anders, Aaron B 1 1
Anders, Aaron R 28, 56, 196 3
Anders, Aaron R 226, 290 2
Anders, Aaron R 1, 4, 126, 140 1
Anders, Abraham 192, 283 1
Anders, Adam 1 1
Anders, Adam H 4 1
Anders, Alice V 1 1
Anders, Alma B 3 2
Anders, Andrew 225, 244 1
Anders, Andrew 27 2
Anders, Ann 10 1
Anders, Annie M 1 1
Anders, Aron 197 1
Anders, C B 198 2
Anders, C E 14 1
Anders, Calvin 1 1
Anders, Calvin B 1, 4 1
Anders, Catherine 1 1
Anders, Charles C 4 1
Anders, Charles K 145 2
Anders, Charles K 11, 21 1
Anders, Chas V 80, 113 2
Anders, Claressa E 4 1
Anders, E A 207 1
Anders, E E 19 1
Anders, Emma A 126 1
Anders, Emma M 72 3
Anders, Erin 5 2
Anders, Fegunies 72 3
Anders, Frank 179 1
Anders, George 10 1
Anders, George W 10 1
Anders, Grayson H 14 1
Anders, Guy 207 3
Anders, Guy 200, 206 2
Anders, Guy 44 1
Anders, Harry T 72 3
Anders, Harry T 4 1
Anders, Hugh M 11 1
Anders, Jacob 13 1
Anders, Jesse 72 2
Anders, Jesse B 18, 240 1
Anders, Jesse V 214 1
Anders, John W 14 1
Anders, Lillian R 1, 18 1
Anders, Louise G 19, 126 1
Anders, Melvin J 166, 248 1
Anders, Michael 1, 10, 13, 19, 240 1
Anders, Moses 19, 28 2
Anders, Nina C 19 1
Anders, Orra W 21 1
Anders, Rosa M 25 1
Anders, Sadie D 240 1
Anders, Susan 23 1
Anders, Susannah 1 1
Anders, Thomas 58 1
Anders, Thomas 23 3
Anders, Virginia Burke 36 2
Anders, W H B 113, 151 2
Anders, William 1 1
Anders, William H B 63 1
Anders, Wm 51 1
Anders, Wm C 25 1
Anders, Wm H 1 1
Anderson, A 205 2
Anderson, Aden 1, 13, 19 1
Anderson, Aden 78 2
Anderson, Albert 24, 25 1
Anderson, Albert L 22 1
Anderson, Alice Thomas 1 1
Anderson, Allen 43 2
Anderson, Alma B 3 1
Anderson, Alvin A 1 1
Anderson, Ann 1, 22 1
Anderson, Ann H 1, 24 1
Anderson, Asa 167 3
Anderson, Barbara E 3 1
Anderson, Clayton A 4 1
Anderson, Edward 8 1
Anderson, Ellen 106 1
Anderson, Elsie M 4 1
Anderson, Fannie 9 1
Anderson, Florence V 22 1
Anderson, H B 106 1
Anderson, Harriet B 11 1
Anderson, Harry E 4 1
Anderson, James R 14 1
Anderson, James W 22 1
Anderson, James W Jr 161 3
Anderson, Jesse T 14 1
Anderson, Joe H 184 2
Anderson, Mary 19, 22 1
Anderson, Mary A 24 1
Anderson, Myra Urban 134 3
Anderson, Otis A 3 1
Anderson, Philemon 67 3
Anderson, Philemon 22, 137 1
Anderson, Philemon S 22 1
Anderson, Richard L 22 1
Anderson, Robert 22 1
Anderson, Robert A 22 1
Anderson, Sadie N 22 1
Anderson, T H 22 1
Anderson, Thomas 1, 24, 25, 183 1
Anderson, Thomas 67, 171 3
Anderson, Thomas A 9 1
Anderson, Thomas J 24 1
Anderson, Thompson 19 1
Anderson, Thos 22, 24, 277 1
Anderson, Thos 167 3
Anderson, Thos T 24 1
Anderson, Thos W 24 1
Anderson, William T 67 3
Anderson, Wm 22, 24 1
Anderson, Wm 137 2
Anderson, Wm P 237 2
Anderson, Wm P 19, 24, 25 1
Anderson, Wm S 218 3
Anderson, Wm Y 166 2
Anderson, Zephaniah 24, 25 1
Andes, Andrew 19 1
Andes, Andrew 57 2
Andes, Joseph D 19, 25 1
Andes, Mary 19 1
Andes, Wm 25 1
Andrew, George W 10 1
Andrew, Rose Edith 10 1
Andrews, George J 10 1
Andrews, J Mortimer 10 1
Andrews, Thomas 67 3
Angel, Alverda 4 1
Angel, Andrew 10, 57, 96 1
Angel, Andrew 124 2
Angel, Andrew 18 3
Angel, Charles 4 1
Angel, David 6 1
Angel, Edgar S 8 1
Angel, George 10 1
Angel, Isaac 38 2
Angel, Jacob 184 3
Angel, Margaret 10 1
Angel, Michael 207 1
Angel, Phebe I 22 1
Angel, Polly J 22, 104 1
Angelberger, David S 6 1
Angelberger, Lewis 6 1
Angelberger, Louisa 35 2
Angelberger, Wm D 35 2
Angell, Abbie B 18 1
Angell, Artie B 24 3
Angell, Chas L 14 1
Angell, James 14 1
Angell, James A 18 1
Angell, John 244 1
Angell, Lester W 18 1
Angell, Samuel 192 3
Angell, Samuel 152 1
Angell, Sarah V 23 1
Angevine, Catherine B 4 1
Angevine, Frank 4 1
Angevine, Joseph Roth 14 1
Angleberger, Chas 23 1
Angleberger, Chas J 22 1
Angleberger, Daisy E 21 1
Angleberger, Dennis 6 1
Angleberger, Edw I 8 1
Angleberger, Elizabeth 13 1
Angleberger, Geo 11 1
Angleberger, Geo 185, 224

3
Angleberger, George 10 1
Angleberger, George W 10 1
Angleberger, Grayson C 13, 22, 111
1
Angleberger, Howard F 11 1
Angleberger, Jacob 13 1
Angleberger, Joseph 13 1
Angleberger, Louise 10 1
Angleberger, Lydia A 18 1
Angleberger, Margaret A 19 1
Angleberger, Mary C 11 1
Angleberger, Millard 19 1
Angleberger, Nettie F 21 1
Angleberger, Philip J 22 1
Angleberger, Sahar[?] 22 1
Angleberger, Sarah J 23 1
Angleberger, Sidney 19 1
Angleberger, W R 8 1
Angleberger, Ward A 21 1
Anna, Roberthy 22 1
Annan, Andrew 1, 14, 54, 138, 159,
195, 222 2
Annan, Andrew 106, 171, 176, 195
3
Annan, Andrew 22, 23, 26, 95, 139,
193, 266, 278, 283 1
Annan, Andrew A 1 1
Annan, Andrew Dr. 169 2
Annan, E L 12 1
Annan, E L 166 3
Annan, E L 134 2
Annan, E L Jr 21 3
Annan, Edgar L 40, 209 2
Annan, Edgar L 96 3
Annan, Edgar L 12, 61, 100 1
Annan, Helen E 21 3
Annan, Henry C 40, 81 3
Annan, Hessie McN B 22 1
Annan, Hy C 13 1
Annan, I F 58 2
Annan, I S 12, 19, 22 1
Annan, I S 107 3
Annan, Isaac 169, 265, 278 1
Annan, Isaac 138, 148, 153, 198, 209
2
Annan, Isaac L 12 1
Annan, Isaac M 22 1
Annan, Isaac M 197 3
Annan, Isaac S 30, 268, 280 2
Annan, Isaac S 22, 23, 169 1
Annan, J F 175 2
Annan, J S 1, 252, 265 1
Annan, J Stewart 40, 178, 205, 209,
220a 2
Annan, J Stewart 1, 12, 13, 22. 27, 61,
72, 96, 169, 1
Annan, James C 19, 257 1
Annan, John 22 1
Annan, Julia L 12 1
Annan, Luella 1 1
Annan, Luella M 197 3
Annan, Luella White 1, 18, 19
1
Annan, R L 12 1
Annan, Robert 22, 32, 252 1
Annan, Robert 1, 252, 294 2
Annan, Robert 26, 40 3
Annan, Robert L 22, 208, 283 1
Annan, Robet 224a 2
Annan, Robt 81 3
Annan, Robt 129, 197, 214 2
Annan, Rose J 13 1
Annan, S 45 2
Annan, Samuel 137 2
Annan, Samuel E 23 1
Annan, William 221a 2
Annan, Wm 49 2
Annon, Robert 210a 2
Ansberger, William A 277 2
Anthony, Hester 11 1
Anthony, Robert 22 1
Anthony, Stelio 28 3
Apple, Jacob Sr 125 1
Apple, Joseph H Jr, 19 1
Apple, Miriam R 19 1
Appleby, B Carter 19 1
Appleby, Grace B 14 1
Appleby, J R 22 1
Appleby, James 175 2
Appleby, James W 14 1
Appleby, Margaret E 19 1
Appleby, Martha A 22 1
Appleby, Rufus H 22 1
Appleman, Elizabeth 13 1
Appleman, John 13, 22, 23 1
Appleman, Josephine Lane 23
1
Appleman, Nancy 13 1
Appleman, Philip 22 1
Appleman, Sadler Philip 23 1
Appleman, Susan 23 1
Appler, Jacob Sr 38 2
Archibald, Edward 8 1
Arledge, Virginia L 24 1
Armacost, Margaret R 19 1
Armor, James W 13 1
Armstead, Clara A 4 1
Armstrong, Eliza 25 1
Armstrong, Isaac 13 1
Armstrong, James 13 1
Armstrong, Nora V 23 1
Armstrong, Samuel 23 1
Armstrong, Wm 25 1
Arnest, Peter 22 1
Arnest, Solomon 1 1
Arnold, Andrew D 1, 22 1
Arnold, Annie 1, 14, 25 1
Arnold, Anthony H 25 1
Arnold, Ariana McElfresh Belt 27
1
Arnold, Augustine 245 1
Arnold, Averal C 1 1
Arnold, Charles G 4 1
Arnold, Charles J 4 1
Arnold, Charles J 36 2
Arnold, Chas J 109 1
Arnold, Daniel 6 1
Arnold, David 6, 8, 13, 19, 23, 252,
264, 271 1
Arnold, David 113, 203 2
Arnold, David J 1 1
Arnold, David Jr 6 1
Arnold, David Sr 6 1
Arnold, Edith 8 1
Arnold, Elizabeth 13, 25 1
Arnold, Ezra 101 2
Arnold, Ezra 8 1
Arnold, Geo V 10, 24, 44 1
Arnold, Geo V etc 58 3
Arnold, George 190 2
Arnold, George V 10, 126 1
Arnold, J Claude 13 1
Arnold, Jacob 13, 14 1
Arnold, James A 24, 230 1
Arnold, James Alfred 13 1
Arnold, John 93, 219a 2
Arnold, John 9, 96 3
Arnold, John 8, 13, 14 1
Arnold, Joshua 14, 240 1
Arnold, Laura B 25 1
Arnold, Laura B 163, 197 3
Arnold, M Portia 10 1
Arnold, Mahlon 19 1
Arnold, Margaret 19 1
Arnold, Martin 19 1
Arnold, Mary 19 1
Arnold, Mary S 51 2
Arnold, Nettie F 21 1
Arnold, Otis 51 2
Arnold, Ottis 19 1
Arnold, Peer 6 1
Arnold, Peter 13, 22 1
Arnold, Peter 18, 31, 64, 70 3
Arnold, Peter 264 2
Arnold, R Claude 22 1
Arnold, Sarah 23 1
Arnold, Sarah Grace 8 1
Arnold, Thelma M 25 2
Arnold, Thomas 6, 10, 23, 24 1
Arnold, Thos 14, 24 1
Arnold, Thos 220 3
Arnold, Thos V 19, 24 1
Arnold, W R 198 2
Arnold, W Weiner 25 1
Arnold, William A 14 1
Arnold, Wm 25 1

Arnold, Wm W 6 1
Arnsparger, Annie R 1 1
Arnsparger, G N[?] 25 1
Arnsparger, Russell W 25 1
Arnsparger, W A 25 1
Arnsparger, W Russell 1 1
Arnsparger, Wm 25 1
Arnsparger, Wm A 25 1
Arnsparger, Wm A 15 2
Arrington, B F 58 3
Arthur, Barbara 6 1
Arthur, Daniel 6, 9, 106 1
Arthur, Daniel 9 1
Arthur, Frederick 9, 179 1
Arthur, Hiram 9, 21 1
Arthur, John 7, 22, 89, 100 2
Arthur, John 174, 207 3
Arthur, John 13, 23, 79, 238, 240 1
Arthur, Joshua 13 1
Arthur, Josiah 13 1
Arthur, Michael 19 1
Arthur, Nancy C 21 1
Arthur, Peter 22 1
Arthur, Samuel 23 1
Artzberger, J Harry 14 1
Arvin, Annie Rebecca 14 1
Arvin, John W 14 1
Aserman, John 96 3
Ash, Gorgon Monges 10 1
Ash, Nannie Drill 159 1
Ashbaugh, Aquilla 1 1
Ashbaugh, Chas G 172 3
Ashbaugh, George H 11 1
Ashbaugh, Herbert M 11, 41 1
Ashbaugh, Herbert M 172 3
Ashbaugh, Jacob H 1 1
Ashbaugh, John 13 1
Ashbaugh, Margaret 19 1
Ashbaugh, Mary J 19 1
Ashbaugh, Rosie May 22 1
Ashbaugh, Wm E 172 3
Ashby, Georgiana 10 1
Asherman, David 50 3
Ashford, John 13 1
Ashford, Margaret 13 1
Ashley, Harley V 132 3
Ashman, Nancy 21 1
Askin, George 10 1
Askin, Nancy 10 1
Atkins, Harry E 12 1
Atkins, John J 13 1
Atkinson, Emma S 102 2
Atkinson, Fannie 9 1
Atkinson, Jacob 13 1
Atkinson, Justus B 14 1
Atkinson, Rollins 180 3
Atkinson, Rollins J 14 1
Atkinson, Sarah 13 1
Atlee, James 65, 205 2
Atley, James C 1 3
Attick, Albert S 1 1
Attick, Clemmia A 1 1
Attick, John 159 2
Attick, John 9 3
Attick, John 13 1
Attick, Martha J 13, 19 1
Atwood, John 75 2
Atwood, Teresa 13 1
Aubert, Alfred H 1, 24 1
Aubert, Henrietta 1 1
Aubert, Jacob 13 1
Aud, Edgar T 8 1
Aud, Ena M 8 1
Augenbaugh, M A 160 3
Augenbaugh, Margaret A 186 3
Aughenbaugh, M A 160 3
Ault, Edgar T 22 1
Ault, Edgar Theodore 8 1
Ault, Emma E 22 1
Ault, Mary C 19 1
Ault, Nellie Florence 8 1
Ault, Rudolph T 22 1
Aumen, Rebecca M 22 1
Ausheerman, John 13 1
Ausherman, Ann C 1 1
Ausherman, C C 72, 126 1
Ausherman, C C 50 3
Ausherman, C C 198 2
Ausherman, C F 18 1
Ausherman, Chas G 75 3
Ausherman, David 126, 272 1
Ausherman, David 32, 167 3
Ausherman, Effie L 19 1
Ausherman, Helen 11 1
Ausherman, Henry 11, 131 1
Ausherman, Ira D 1 1
Ausherman, John 11, 13 1
Ausherman, John 238 1
Ausherman, John 210a 2
Ausherman, John 31 3
Ausherman, John Sr 13 1
Ausherman, Lydia 18 1
Ausherman, Milton K 19 1
Ausherman, Samuel 190 2
Ausherman, T T 205 3
Ausherman, Tilghman 13 1
Ayers, Dorothy G 288 2
Ayers, Harry W 11 1
Ayers, Margaret C 89 3
Ayres, Grace D 11 1
Babcock, Giulia W 189 3
Babel, George A 60 1
Babel, J C 60 1
Babel, John C 60 1
Babel, Mary J 60, 72 1
Babylon, Andrew 176 3
Babylon, Andrew 171 2
Babylon, Philip 186 2
Bachman, Catherine 32 1
Bachman, Frederick 38 2
Backman, Frederick 171, 186 2
Bacon, Sophia T 85, 88 1
Bacon, Sophia T 238 2
Bacon, T S 249 1
Bacon, Thomas S 88 1
Bade, Robert T 40 3
Bader, John G 58 1
Baer, Alice H 28 1
Baer, Annie S 27 1
Baer, Annie T 28, 34, 76 1
Baer, Annie V 62 1
Baer, Anthony 118 1
Baer, C D 61 1
Baer, Catherine R 33 1
Baer, Charles J 47, 33 1
Baer, Charlotte 33 1
Baer, Charlotte C 33, 91 1
Baer, Chas 27 1
Baer, Chas D 34 1
Baer, Chas J 41, 58 1
Baer, David 58, 59 1
Baer, David H 38 1
Baer, Elizabeth W 40 1
Baer, Ezra 41, 56 1
Baer, Geo 69, 165, 213 2
Baer, Geo 202 3
Baer, Geo of W 47 1
Baer, George 47, 116 1
Baer, George Jr 56, 91 1
Baer, George of Wm 91 1
Baer, Harriet 91 1
Baer, Harry 52 1
Baer, Harry L 52 1
Baer, Henry 52, 56, 208 1
Baer, Ida M 82 1
Baer, Ira G 28 1
Baer, J H 61 1
Baer, J H 44 3
Baer, J Howard 62 1
Baer, J W 58 1
Baer, Jacob 129 3
Baer, Jacob 41, 58, 59, 60, 116, 163 1
Baer, Jacob 87, 185 2
Baer, Jacob F 62 1
Baer, Jacob MD 118 1
Baer, Jacob S 59 1
Baer, Jacob Sr 58 1
Baer, John 58 1
Baer, John 154 2
Baer, John H 58, 61 1
Baer, John R 62 1
Baer, John S 63 1
Baer, John Sr 56 1

Baer, Joseph G P 58 1
Baer, Lillie M 51 3
Baer, Mary M 56 1
Baer, Michael 52, 58 1
Baer, Nellie M 70, 83 1
Baer, Nicholas P B 76 1
Baer, Norman C 26 1
Baer, Peter 76, 79 1
Baer, Philip 79 1
Baer, R W 63 1
Baer, Ray S 135 3
Baer, Ridgely W 28 1
Baer, Robert H 82 1
Baer, Robert L 83 1
Baer, Rose 33 1
Baer, Rose Schley 82 1
Baer, S Stella 59 1
Baer, Sallie Ann 62, 85 1
Baer, Sally Ann 85 1
Baer, Sarah 47 1
Baer, Solome 85 1
Baer, Thomas E 76 1
Baer, William 91, 102 1
Baer, William 229a 2
Baer, Wm 91 1
Baer, Wm C 76 1
Bagby, D P 241 2
Bagent, Andrew C 28 1
Bagent, Earl J W 63 1
Bagent, James Earl 63 1
Bagley, Rebecca L 140 1
Baightel, Emmet E 40 1
Baightel, Mary A 40 1
Baightel, Mary Ann 72 1
Baightell, Noah 89 2
Bail, Michael 197 2
Bail, Peter 37 1
Baile, Abraham 79, 116, 203 1
Baile, Abraham 211 2
Baile, David 37 1
Baile, David 195 3
Baile, Jesse 5 2
Baile, Jesse 60 1
Baile, Ludwick 88 1
Baile, Michael 70 1
Baile, Peter 79 1
Baile, William 79 1
Bailey, Abraham 152 1
Bailey, Ellen Viola 63 1
Bailey, John 181 2
Bailey, John 113 3
Bailey, John W 63 1
Bailey, R Shaffer 267 2
Baille, Wm 169 2
Bair, Bessie V 51 3
Baker 139 2
Baker, A J 175, 188 2
Baker, A W 27 1
Baker, Aaron 37, 44, 58, 125 1
Baker, Adam 26 1
Baker, Alfred 28, 196 1
Baker, Alice 227 2
Baker, Alice May 28 1
Baker, Amanda E 28 1
Baker, Amelia J 27 1
Baker, Andrew 208 2
Baker, Andrew J 52, 135 1
Baker, Andrew W 71 1
Baker, Ann C 26 1
Baker, Anna Barbara 27 1
Baker, Annie E 53 1
Baker, Annie E 85 2
Baker, Asa 26 1
Baker, Aug C 76 1
Baker, Augustus 253 1
Baker, Augustus C 28 1
Baker, B E 67 2
Baker, Basil 30, 155, 214, 228, 271 1
Baker, Basil 14 2
Baker, Benjamin 30 1
Baker, Brooke 30, 271 1
Baker, Brooke 26, 213, 214 3
Baker, C Clarence 32 1
Baker, Caroline M 165 2
Baker, Catherine 57, 86 1
Baker, Celia Grim 34 1
Baker, Charlotte 32 1
Baker, Chas D 67 1
Baker, Chas E 67, 172 1
Baker, Christopher 86 1
Baker, Conrad 32 1
Baker, D 23 1
Baker, D 129 3
Baker, D A 39 2
Baker, Daniel 19, 87, 100, 106, 113, 120, 129, 219, 227 3
Baker, Daniel 58, 82, 119, 131, 156, 223 1
Baker, Daniel 39, 69, 101, 132, 138, 181, 211, 242 2
Baker, Daniel 15 2
Baker, Daniel F of F 38 1
Baker, Daniel G 118 1
Baker, Daniel Jr 146 1
Baker, Daniel of F 37 1
Baker, Daniel Sr 42 3
Baker, David 87 2
Baker, David A 38, 41, 48, 92, 123, 182, 238 1
Baker, David A 84, 242 2
Baker, David A 54, 196 3
Baker, Dorothy 37 1
Baker, Edw 153 2
Baker, Edw 27, 37, 44, 52, 125 1
Baker, Edw L 62 1
Baker, Edward 41 1
Baker, Edward L 42 1
Baker, Elegene L F 42 1
Baker, Elizabeth 41 1
Baker, Ellen E 44, 61 1
Baker, Fannie M 73, 84, 92 1
Baker, Frank L 32, 86 1
Baker, Frederick 6, 37 3
Baker, Frederick 37, 44, 70, 79, 84, 120, 194, 270 1
Baker, G W 283 1
Baker, Geo 47 1
Baker, Geo Jr 47 1
Baker, Geo L 41 1
Baker, Geo W 62 1
Baker, George F 48 1
Baker, George H 49 1
Baker, George W 48 1
Baker, Geraldine Frost 53 1
Baker, Greenbury W 48 1
Baker, Guy 81 2
Baker, Guy E 220 2
Baker, Guy E 22 1
Baker, H 24, 28, 112, 156 1
Baker, H D 160 3
Baker, H Josephine 72 1
Baker, Hannah 51 1
Baker, Hannah M 52 1
Baker, Harvey D 85 2
Baker, Harvey G 22 1
Baker, Helen V 151 3
Baker, Henry 7, 22, 80, 202, 208, 290 2
Baker, Henry 22, 51, 53, 58, 70, 84, 91, 96, 115, 117, 156, 171, 203 1
Baker, Henry 81, 100, 144, 184, 207 3
Baker, Henry A 27 1
Baker, Henry Jr 51 1
Baker, Holmes D 124 3
Baker, Holmes D 53, 63, 86, 90 1
Baker, Imogene 42 1
Baker, Isabell M 76 1
Baker, Isaiah 55 1
Baker, J B 72 1
Baker, J D 32, 43, 98, 160 3
Baker, J D 128 2
Baker, J E 44 1
Baker, J Edgar 92 1
Baker, J Edward 61 1
Baker, Jacob 57 1
Baker, James 61, 156 1
Baker, James 57 2
Baker, James E 82 1
Baker, James H 61 1
Baker, James H P 30 1
Baker, James H T 70 3
Baker, James W 26 1
Baker, Jesse T 234 2
Baker, John 44, 56, 57, 58, 61, 91,

159 1
Baker, John 43, 64, 69, 84, 87, 154, 186, 214, 221, 294 2
Baker, John 87, 163 3
Baker, John A 30, 58, 203 1
Baker, John D 60 1
Baker, John D 19 3
Baker, John E 63 1
Baker, John H 20, 124 3
Baker, John H 72, 86, 92 1
Baker, John Jr 57 1
Baker, John M 61 1
Baker, John M 217 3
Baker, John W 61, 62, 146 1
Baker, John W 227 2
Baker, Joseph 63 2
Baker, Joseph D 61, 63, 135 1
Baker, Joseph D 223 3
Baker, Joseph D 189 2
Baker, Joseph G 91, 100 1
Baker, Julia C 61 1
Baker, Julian 62 1
Baker, Laura S 67 1
Baker, Lawrence E 53 1
Baker, Lee Anna 48 1
Baker, Lewis P 51 1
Baker, Liberius 68 1
Baker, Lydia Amelia 51 1
Baker, Margaret O 234 2
Baker, Mary 67, 70, 71 1
Baker, Mary E 72 1
Baker, Mary J 67 2
Baker, Mary M 61 1
Baker, Mary S 27, 73 1
Baker, Mildred L 72 1
Baker, Morris A 30 1
Baker, Nason 113 2
Baker, Nathan 73, 76, 159, 176, 228 1
Baker, Nathan G 28 1
Baker, Nathan T 9 1
Baker, Nicholas 101 2
Baker, Nicholas 76, 88 1
Baker, O M 3 3
Baker, Philip 51 1
Baker, Quincy May 254 1
Baker, Ralph 73 1
Baker, Roy E 48 1
Baker, Ruben 82 1
Baker, Rufus 165 1
Baker, S Ella 30 1
Baker, Samuel 84, 86 1
Baker, Sarah C 51 1
Baker, Sarah E 86 1
Baker, Sophia 26 1
Baker, Susan M 86 1
Baker, Susanna 84 1
Baker, T 179 3
Baker, Thomas 195 3
Baker, Thomas 88 1
Baker, Thomas M 62 1
Baker, Thomas of T 179 3
Baker, Thos F 57 1
Baker, Thos G 82 1
Baker, Thos M 82, 119 1
Baker, Virginia M 28 1
Baker, W G 19 2
Baker, W G 160 3
Baker, W Snader 44, 63, 90 1
Baker, Wilbur 92 1
Baker, Wilbur W 220 2
Baker, Wilhelmina C 58 1
Baker, William 92, 120 1
Baker, William 215a 2
Baker, William 53 3
Baker, William B 82 1
Baker, William D 196 3
Baker, William G 72 1
Baker, William G 215a 2
Baker, William G 19, 42, 75, 160 3
Baker, William H 26 1
Baker, Wm 1, 39, 72 2
Baker, Wm 27, 51, 71, 91, 131, 140, 253 1
Baker, Wm D 38, 92, 182, 186 1
Baker, Wm G 15, 138, 208, 214, 225 2
Baker, Wm G 87, 98, 106, 224, 205, 219 3
Baker, Wm G 41, 92, 100, 129 1
Baker, Wm G Jr 92 1
Baker, Wm H 51, 92, 146 1
Balch, L P 185 2
Balch, L P W 57 1
Balch, L P W 87 2
Balch, Louis W P 195 3
Balch, S P 57 1
Balck, Catherine 32 1
Baldeoin, Daniel 37 1
Balderson, John 58 1
Balderson, Margaret 71 1
Balding, Grace 47 1
Baldner, Mary C 70, 71 1
Baldner, Michael 71, 71 1
Baldner, Michael Sr 56 1
Baldwin, John 57, 70 1
Baldwin, Samuel 88 1
Baldwin, Thomas 88 1
Baldwin, Tyler 88 1
Baldwin, Wm 91 1
Ball, Carrie Briant 34 1
Ball, Garnett C 255 2
Ball, Geo 178 2
Ball, Horatio 34 1
Ball, Irving O 55, 56 1
Ball, J F 51 2
Ball, John 56 1
Ball, John L 62 1
Ball, John R 61 1
Ball, Louis W 85 1
Ball, Mary E R 61 1
Ball, Mary V 62 1
Ball, Notlee 76 1
Ball, Robert L 225 1
Ball, S M 85 1
Ball, Sarah R 62 1
Ball, Sarah Reich 255 2
Ball, Thomas S 51 2
Ball, Wm M 91 1
Balle, Em [sic] 139 1
Ballenger, Mary 82 1
Ballenger, Richard 82 1
Ballinger, Cassandra 32 1
Ballinger, Elizabeth 82 1
Ballinger, Mary 70 1
Bally, Ada C 145 2
Balmer, Alice R 93 1
Balmer, Geo B 58 3
Balmer, Walter J Theo 93 1
Balsh, L P W 76 1
Balt, M D 219 1
Baltzel, Geo 213 1
Baltzell, Aaron H 26 1
Baltzell, Amanda M 92 1
Baltzell, Annie E 28 1
Baltzell, Charles 32 1
Baltzell, Charles W 8, 34 1
Baltzell, Chas 139, 234 1
Baltzell, Chas 50 3
Baltzell, Edith F 8 1
Baltzell, Edw 40 1
Baltzell, Geo 18, 38, 100, 144, 149, 171, 186 2
Baltzell, Geo 40, 47, 88, 115, 152, 225, 234, 256, 260, 263, 279 1
Baltzell, George 47, 279 1
Baltzell, George 1, 8, 14, 31, 37, 38, 39 3
Baltzell, George 257 2
Baltzell, J F McC 61 1
Baltzell, J M 166 2
Baltzell, James W 61, 67 1
Baltzell, Jay K 56 1
Baltzell, John 196, 229 1
Baltzell, John 31 3
Baltzell, John 19 2
Baltzell, John Dr. 58 1
Baltzell, Josephine 224 2
Baltzell, Josephine B 217 2
Baltzell, Josephine V 92 1
Baltzell, Lawrence 26 1
Baltzell, Levi 67 1
Baltzell, Lewis 32 1
Baltzell, Mary F 67 1
Baltzell, Michael 32 1
Baltzell, Michael 171 2

Baltzell, Raymond W 34 1
Baltzell, Ruth 58 1
Baltzell, Susannah 26 1
Baltzell, Wm 92 1
Baltzell, Wm 217 2
Baltzell, Wm H 92 1
Baltzell, Wm W 56 1
Bangs, James 57 2
Banker, Isaac 149 2
Banker, J 149 2
Banker, John 32, 61 1
Banker, John of J 149 2
Banker, Peter 56, 70 1
Bankerd, Alfred 59 1
Bankerd, John 59 1
Bankert, John 287 2
Banks, Elizabeth 40 1
Banks, John W 171 3
Banks, Thomas W 40 1
Bantx, Gideon Jr 64 3
Bantz, Ann M 26 1
Bantz, Annie E 27 1
Bantz, F Marion 47 1
Bantz, G 187 2
Bantz, G 152 1
Bantz, G Ernest 13 1
Bantz, Gideon 43, 46, 57, 115, 118, 129, 163, 177, 186, 245, 264, 282 2
Bantz, Gideon 41, 50, 71, 81, 185, 195 3
Bantz, Gideon 13, 26, 40, 47, 57, 91, 116, 118, 139, 186, 213, 222, 237, 264 1
Bantz, Gideon Jr 37, 47, 51, 271 1
Bantz, Gideon Sr 64 3
Bantz, Gideon Sr 40, 47, 51, 264 1
Bantz, Gideon Sr 46 2
Bantz, Harry 70 1
Bantz, Henry 51 1
Bantz, Henry 91, 179 3
Bantz, Henry 137 2
Bantz, Henry Sr 51 1
Bantz, Julia A 61 1
Bantz, Nimrod 51 1
Bantz, Nimrod 197 2
Bantz, Nimrod 111 3
Bantz, T Marion 27 1
Bantz, Uriah 51 1
Bantz, Uriah S 264 1
Bantz, WF 69 2
Bantz, William 106 3
Bantz, William S 195 3
Bantz, Wm 25, 225 2
Bantz, Wm 264 1
Bantz, Wm B 96 3
Bantz, Wm F 40 1
Bantz, Wm S 1 2
Bantz, Wm S 195 3
Bantz, Wm S 47, 51, 91, 234, 264, 277 1
Barber, Ann E 290 2
Barber, Charles 290 2
Barber, Johnsey 96 1
Barbour, Johsey 61 1
Barbour, Jonsey 85, 117 1
Barbour, Sarah R 59 1
Barclay, Joseph 56 1
Bare, Charles E 34 1
Bare, Eleanore May 113 2
Bare, Elizabeth M 249 1
Bare, Ella M 34 1
Bargee, Thos 5 2
Barger, Alta May 28 1
Barger, Bertha May 42 1
Barger, Edw D 42 1
Barger, G W 72 1
Barger, J Frederick 63 1
Barger, Laura E 34 1
Barger, Laura V 78 1
Barger, McKinley H 68 1
Barger, Otho U 78 1
Barger, Thomas F 49 1
Barkdoll, George W 49, 88 1
Barkdoll, James H 49 1
Barker, Agnes A 61 1
Barker, Carrie Virginia 34 1
Barker, Edw A 41 1
Barker, Ezra C 42 1
Barker, Hilda 239 2
Barker, Hilda D 34 1
Barker, Ida M 61 1
Barker, Isabella R 41 1
Barker, John H 61 1
Barker, Mary Elizabeth 61 1
Barker, Minnie M 74, 166 1
Barker, Turner T 88 1
Barker, Vernon H 88 1
Barker, William M 93 1
Barkman, David 260 1
Barkman, David 107 2
Barmon, Hugh 52 1
Barnard, Bessie M 52 1
Barnard, Daniel P Jr 28 1
Barnard, Harry A 52 1
Barnbarger, Arnold 253 1
Barner, Charles R 63 1
Barnes L Amidee 68 1
Barnes, Annie M 28, 85 1
Barnes, Archibald 38 2
Barnes, Carrie V 1 1
Barnes, Charles R 86 1
Barnes, Darius H 104 1
Barnes, Dora M 78 1
Barnes, E E 18 1
Barnes, Eliza J 41 1
Barnes, Emma J 42, 68 1
Barnes, Evelyn Kinsey 113 2
Barnes, F W 67 1
Barnes, Florence E 4 1
Barnes, Florence E 107 2
Barnes, Frances W 221 2
Barnes, Francis W 85, 88, 150 1
Barnes, G 144 2
Barnes, Harry T 86 1
Barnes, Henry H 52 1
Barnes, Hugh 154 2
Barnes, Hugh N 53 1
Barnes, Irvin E 55 1
Barnes, J Vernon 10 3
Barnes, James H 72 1
Barnes, James Peter 59 1
Barnes, Jesse V 85 1
Barnes, John F 67 1
Barnes, John T 41, 59 1
Barnes, John W 59, 62, 63, 86 1
Barnes, L Victor 76 1
Barnes, Lester E 173 2
Barnes, Levi 159 1
Barnes, Levi A 58 1
Barnes, Levi Z 28 2
Barnes, Levi Z 62, 67, 135 1
Barnes, Levin 67 1
Barnes, Lewis E 1 1
Barnes, Lucy 67 1
Barnes, M Elizabeth 73 1
Barnes, M Gertrude 72 1
Barnes, Mary A 72 1
Barnes, Mary C 53 1
Barnes, Mary E 55, 59 1
Barnes, Mary M 106 2
Barnes, Minnie N 52 1
Barnes, Noah 76 1
Barnes, Noah 187 3
Barnes, Nola C 262 2
Barnes, Percy S 72 1
Barnes, R M 154 2
Barnes, Raymond H 51 1
Barnes, Samuel 63, 91, 117, 176, 196 1
Barnes, Samuel 276 2
Barnes, Samuel F 86 1
Barnes, Samuel T 86 1
Barnes, Silas J 70 1
Barnes, Susannah 85 1
Barnes, T E 59 1
Barnes, Thomas A 38 1
Barnes, Thomas E 88 1
Barnes, Thos & 19 2
Barnett, Annie B 52 1
Barnett, Hager D 52 1
Barnford, John W 58 1
Barnhard, Michale 37 3
Barnhart, Jacob 70 1
Barnhart, Michael 70, 194 1
Barnhart, Philip 78 1
Barnhouse, Jacob N 63 1

Barnhouse, Jessie A 37 1
Barnitz, M 38 2
Barnitz, Michael 147 2
Barnover, David 56, 63 1
Barnover, John 56 1
Barns, Joshua 58 1
Barns, Matthias 70 1
Barns, Samuel 1 3
Barrett, Geo W 48 1
Barrett, John 57 1
Barrett, Sarah C 48 1
Barrick Geo W 72 1
Barrick Wm 47 1
Barrick, A L 184 2
Barrick, A Lamar 73 1
Barrick, A Lamar 16, 175, 190 2
Barrick, A Lamar 29, 46 3
Barrick, A Lorene 44 1
Barrick, A M 225 2
Barrick, Alice M 63 1
Barrick, Ann M 26 1
Barrick, Barbara A 58 1
Barrick, Barbara Ann 30 1
Barrick, C J 32 1
Barrick, C W 116 2
Barrick, Catherine 32, 47, 92 1
Barrick, Catherine E 33, 48 1
Barrick, Charles L 34 1
Barrick, Chas 225 2
Barrick, Chas J 32, 48, 61, 72, 275 1
Barrick, Christian 32, 201 1
Barrick, Clarence W 34, 76, 101 1
Barrick, Clarence W 132 2
Barrick, Cora H 34, 44 1
Barrick, Cora V 91, 186, 217 1
Barrick, Cornelius P 32 1
Barrick, D M 210 1
Barrick, Daniel 32, 253 1
Barrick, David M 38 1
Barrick, David Martin 32, 74 1
Barrick, E 91 3
Barrick, Edw 41, 93 1
Barrick, Edward 41 3
Barrick, Eliza 79 1
Barrick, Elizabeth 41 1
Barrick, Elizabeth 231 2
Barrick, Elizabeth G 41, 84 1
Barrick, Emma L 145 2
Barrick, Enos 32 1
Barrick, Ezra 26, 40 1
Barrick, Ezra 274 2
Barrick, Ezra E 96 3
Barrick, Ezra E 41, 84, 117, 125, 139, 219 1
Barrick, F D 48 1
Barrick, Florence E 44 1
Barrick, Frank S 44 1
Barrick, Frederick 47, 57, 61, 116 1
Barrick, Frederick D 44 1
Barrick, Geo 192 1
Barrick, Geo D 34, 48 1
Barrick, Geo P 32, 47, 48, 152 1
Barrick, Geo T 64 3
Barrick, Geo W 47, 48, 271 1
Barrick, George 57, 60, 70, 91 1
Barrick, George D 33 1
Barrick, Grover E 145 2
Barrick, Harry 51 1
Barrick, Harry W 24 3
Barrick, Henry 51, 86 1
Barrick, Hester 51 1
Barrick, Hettie 82 1
Barrick, J W 195 3
Barrick, Jacob 78 1
Barrick, Jacob of J 57 1
Barrick, James I 63 1
Barrick, John 46, 163 2
Barrick, John 79 1
Barrick, John 15 3
Barrick, John of C 58 1
Barrick, John of P 57 1
Barrick, John W 57, 58 1
Barrick, John W 14 3
Barrick, Julia Ann 61 1
Barrick, K J 68 1
Barrick, L E 172 2
Barrick, Leonard C 68 1
Barrick, Lewis E 84, 85 1
Barrick, Lucy Ann 72 1
Barrick, Mamie A 73 1
Barrick, Mamie Alice 74 1
Barrick, Mamie I 3 3
Barrick, Marie S 24 3
Barrick, Mary 70 1
Barrick, Mary A 72 1
Barrick, Mary C 72 1
Barrick, Mary S 32 1
Barrick, Nancy 76, 84 1
Barrick, Nannie I 68 1
Barrick, Nellie M 76 1
Barrick, Nellie M 132 2
Barrick, Nora 76 1
Barrick, Olive H 275 1
Barrick, Oscar 32 1
Barrick, Peter 78, 79, 86 1
Barrick, Presley J 79 1
Barrick, R D 71 3
Barrick, R G 19 2
Barrick, Randolph 237 2
Barrick, Randolph G 47 1
Barrick, Randolph J 30 1
Barrick, Robert 30 2
Barrick, Robert 82, 197, 237 1
Barrick, Robt 8 2
Barrick, Rudolph B 215 3
Barrick, Samuel D 84 1
Barrick, Samuel W 86 1
Barrick, Sarah 84, 85, 1
Barrick, Simon 44, 84 1
Barrick, Solomon 237 2
Barrick, Solomon 78, 84, 85 1
Barrick, Susan E 84 1
Barrick, William D 73 1
Barrick, William David 40 1
Barrick, Wm 44, 93 1
Barrick, Wm 100 2
Barrick, Wm R 61, 91 1
Barringer, George F 49 1
Barritz, Michael 165 3
Barroll, Eleanora H 159 1
Barroll, Hope H [sic] 159 1
Barron, Fred B 44 1
Barron, Fred B, Senior 44 1
Barry, Hester 52, 59 1
Barry, John 59 1
Barry, John 197, 237 2
Barry, Thomas 294 2
Barry, Thos 102 3
Bartgis, A W 68 1
Bartgis, Alice W 52 1
Bartgis, Benjamin F 70 1
Bartgis, Dewitt C 37 1
Bartgis, E James 70 1
Bartgis, Georgianna 71 1
Bartgis, Helen L 11 3
Bartgis, Hiram 73, 91, 100 1
Bartgis, Hiram 203 3
Bartgis, James 152, 282 1
Bartgis, James 152 1
Bartgis, James 19, 46 2
Bartgis, John A 139 2
Bartgis, Lewis G 73 1
Bartgis, Loretta F 40 1
Bartgis, M E 68, 133 1
Bartgis, M E 96, 151, 165 3
Bartgis, M E 57 2
Bartgis, Margaret 71 1
Bartgis, Mary 73 1
Bartgis, Mary E 37 1
Bartgis, Mary E 139 2
Bartgis, Mathias 73, 152, 245 1
Bartgis, Mathias 202 3
Bartgis, Mathias 100, 148, 213 2
Bartgis, Mathias E 92 2
Bartgis, Mathias E 70 1
Bartgis, Mathias E 87 3
Bartgis, Matthias 87 2
Bartgis, Matthias 26, 70, 72, 147 1
Bartgis, Matthias E 137, 189 1
Bartgis, Wm 91 1

Bartgiss, Mathias E 1 3
Barthalow, John 59 1
Barthalow, John B 59 1
Barthalow, P J 133 1
Barthalow, Sarah A 59 1
Barthelow, John 22, 166 2
Barthelow, Sarah A 166 2
Barthlow, Harry W 62 1
Barthlow, John 14 3
Barthlow, John H 62 1
Barthlow, Wm H 92 1
Bartholow, Clara 46 2
Bartholow, Geo 47 1
Bartholow, Harry S 273 1
Bartholow, John 47 1
Bartholow, John 205 3
Bartlett, Carrie S 96, 113 3
Bartlett, Elmer C 96, 113 3
Barton, Bertie E 31 1
Barton, Catherine G 46 3
Barton, Charles Edw, 34 1
Barton, Charles Edward 34 1
Barton, Charles T 34 1
Barton, Greenbury 47 1
Barton, Isaac N 55 1
Barton, Isaac N 213 3
Barton, Rose E Mrs 62 1
Barton, W A 241 2
Basford, Albert 115, 233 1
Basford, Howard 52 1
Basford, Jacob 62 1
Basford, James C 93 1
Basford, John T 60 1
Basford, John W 58 1
Basford, Marion 62 1
Basford, Norman C 93 1
Basford, Vernon 60 1
Basford, William E 93 1
Basford, Wm E 62 1
Bash, Catherine 70 1
Bash, John 70 1
Bash, Michael 70 1
Bassford, Alfred 26 1
Bassford, Eleanore 40 1
Bassford, John T 40 1
Bast, Charles E 72 1
Bast, Elias 79 1
Bast, Henry 51 1
Bast, John 116 1
Bast, John H 79 1
Bast, Joseph 72 1
Bast, Margaret 72, 84 1
Bast, Maria B 70 1
Bast, Mary M 72 1
Bast, Micahel [sic] 234 1
Bast, Polly 79 1
Bast, Sidney 84 1
Bast, Susanna 51 1
Bateler, Wm C 50 3
Bateman, Adrianna 27 1
Bateman, Maria E 227a 2
Batesoll, Daniel 56 1
Batesoll, John 56 1
Batholow, Elizabeth 47 1
Batman, Maria 280 2
Bauer, Adam 70 3
Bauer, Stephen 184 3
Baugh, Jacob 263 1
Baugh, Jacob 100 2
Baugher, Alexius O 26 1
Baugher, Annie 27 1
Baugher, Catherine 32 1
Baugher, Chas H 71 1
Baugher, Daniel 32 1
Baugher, Daniel B 37, 84 1
Baugher, Elizabeth 84 1
Baugher, Elwood E 42 1
Baugher, Harry W 55 1
Baugher, Isaac 57, 73, 82, 164, 177, 263 1
Baugher, Isaac 51, 165, 214 2
Baugher, Isaac 91 3
Baugher, Isaac & 69 2
Baugher, James 55 1
Baugher, James 35 2
Baugher, James W 144 2
Baugher, James W 55 1
Baugher, John 67 3
Baugher, John 59 1
Baugher, John D 61, 271 1
Baugher, John M 26 1
Baugher, Joseph 26 1
Baugher, Joseph 26 2
Baugher, Joseph 61, 164 1
Baugher, Joseph & 57 2
Baugher, Mary Ann E 92 1
Baugher, Mary E 202 2
Baugher, Michael 73 1
Baugher, Mildred A 42 1
Baugher, Rhoda 73 1
Baugher, Samuel B 84 1
Baugher, Samuel Sr 61 1
Baugher, Sarah L 84, 85 1
Baugher, Susannah 37 1
Baugher, Wm H 61, 92 1
Baughman, Adam 26, 56, 59 1
Baughman, Andrew 68 2
Baughman, Annette H 27 1
Baughman, C Francis 62 1
Baughman, E Austin 42 1
Baughman, Ethel Grimes 257 1
Baughman, Frederick 228a 2
Baughman, Helen Abell 52 1
Baughman, J W 160 3
Baughman, J William 196 3
Baughman, J William 59, 62 1
Baughman, John W 22 2
Baughman, John W 179 3
Baughman, John W 72, 104, 234 1
Baughman, L C 165 1
Baughman, L V 192, 209 3
Baughman, L Victor 92 1
Baughman, Mary J 59 1
Baughman, Mary Jane 72, 73 1
Baughman, Sarah A 26 1
Baughman, William 274 2
Baught, James W 282 2
Baughter, Isaac 70 1
Baughter, Issac 226 2
Baumgardner, Adelle 61 1
Baumgardner, Barbara 30 1
Baumgardner, Bernard R 88 1
Baumgardner, Carl Wm 74 1
Baumgardner, Catherine 32 1
Baumgardner, Chas 96 2
Baumgardner, Clarence M 88 1
Baumgardner, Daisy r 88 1
Baumgardner, Edw T 52 1
Baumgardner, Edward T 4 1
Baumgardner, Elizabeth 40 1
Baumgardner, Emma D 4 1
Baumgardner, Florence C 44 1
Baumgardner, Florence E 45 1
Baumgardner, Geo 182 3
Baumgardner, Geo T 56 3
Baumgardner, Geo T 44 1
Baumgardner, Geo T 226 2
Baumgardner, George J 62 1
Baumgardner, Geroge T 48 1
Baumgardner, Grace A 49, 93 1
Baumgardner, Grace A 44 1
Baumgardner, H D 166 3
Baumgardner, Hattie L 48, 51 1
Baumgardner, Henry 32, 52, 53, 67, 71 1
Baumgardner, Henry 14, 153, 221a 2
Baumgardner, Jacob 67, 87 3
Baumgardner, Jacob 44, 61, 79, 88, 116, 152, 225 1
Baumgardner, Jacob Jr 51 1
Baumgardner, John 30, 32, 56, 62, 71, 79, 88, 99, 106, 116, 225 1
Baumgardner, John 83, 220a 2
Baumgardner, John H 34, 52, 62, 271 1
Baumgardner, John S 30 1
Baumgardner, John S Jr 56 3
Baumgardner, Joseph W 44, 52, 62, 86, 1
Baumgardner, Josiah 71 1
Baumgardner, L Ann G 96 2
Baumgardner, Luther A 56 3

Baumgardner, Luther A 18 2
Baumgardner, Margaret 79, 88 1
Baumgardner, Mary Nina 74, 88 1
Baumgardner, Moses P 219 1
Baumgardner, Nettie E 86 1
Baumgardner, Oscar H 78 1
Baumgardner, Richard B 49 1
Baumgardner, Robert E 20 2
Baumgardner, Robert E 51 1
Baumgardner, Samuel 267 2
Baumgardner, Samuel 53, 263 1
Baumgardner, Samuel 81, 167 3
Baumgardner, Samuel J 86 1
Baumgardner, Thomas 113, 124 3
Baumgardner, Thomas 88 1
Baumgardner, Thomas H 88 1
Baumgardner, Thos 265 1
Baumgardner, Wm D 44, 62, 93 1
Baumgartner, John 159 2
Baus, Henry 51 1
Bausen, Eva L 65 3
Baust, Cornelius 70 1
Bawden, Lambert 58 1
Baxter, Barbara Ann 31 1
Baxter, Harry U 52 1
Baxter, Mabel A 189 3
Baxter, Norma A 52 1
Baxter, Russell N 52 1
Baxton, Amy C 27 1
Baxton, Brooker 27 1
Baxton, Frank E 215 2
Baxton, Julian 58 1
Bayard, Stephen A 86 1
Bayer, Jacob 57 1
Bayer, Jacob 1 2
Bayer, Laura V 68 1
Bayer, Lewis 68 1
Bayer, Michael 70 1
Bayley, Hezekiah 51 1
Bayley, John 116, 162 1
Bayley, John 69 2
Bayly, Elizabeth 41 1
Bayne, James 57 1
Bayne, John G 57, 70, 79 1
Bayne, Michael 57 1
Be rd, Martin L 213 3
Beach, Philip S 27 1
Beachley, Albert C 28, 38, 79 1
Beachley, Alvie L 57 3
Beachley, Ann R 38 1
Beachley, Anna R E 72 1
Beachley, Athene C 28 1
Beachley, Austin L 42 1
Beachley, Barbara 30 1
Beachley, Blanche H 15 2
Beachley, Blanche Hammett 31 1
Beachley, Catherine C 34 1
Beachley, Chas E 44 1
Beachley, Chas W, 8 1
Beachley, Clyde H 53 1
Beachley, Cora A 34 1
Beachley, D V 37 1
Beachley, D Vincent 3 3
Beachley, Daniel 58, 59, 71, 153 1
Beachley, Daniel 14, 53, 64 3
Beachley, Daniel 138 2
Beachley, Daniel H 38 1
Beachley, Daniel J 38 1
Beachley, Dorothy E 31 1
Beachley, E Walter 88 1
Beachley, Edna E 57 3
Beachley, Elmer 44 1
Beachley, Elmer E 42 1
Beachley, Ezra 14, 122 2
Beachley, Ezra 37 1
Beachley, Ezra 19 3
Beachley, Florence S 34 1
Beachley, Franklin E 42 1
Beachley, G Dewey 68 1
Beachley, H D 143 2
Beachley, Helen F 53 1
Beachley, Henry 37 1
Beachley, Jacob 30 1
Beachley, John 58, 59, 260 1
Beachley, John O 38, 62 1
Beachley, Jonas 61 1
Beachley, Jonas E 37 1
Beachley, Joseph 248, 252, 260 1
Beachley, Joseph 148, 253 2
Beachley, Katherine 28 1
Beachley, Laura V 38 1
Beachley, Lizzie M 59, 62 1
Beachley, Martin 167 3
Beachley, Martin 290 2
Beachley, Martin H 68, 72, 213 1
Beachley, Mary K 48 3
Beachley, Mehrle F 34 1
Beachley, Sarah S 8 1
Beachley, Tobitha O 88 1
Beacht, Claude N 76 1
Beacht, Freda P 76 1
Beacht, Jacob 56 1
Beacht, Joseph 57 1
Beacht, Nellie 76 1
Beacht, Norman 76 1
Beachtol, John 220a 2
Beackley, Milton 13 1
Beahey, Joseph 249, 256, 263 1
Beahey, Joseph 134 2
Beahey, Joseph 263 1
Beahey, Joseph [sic] 256 1
Beakey, Joseph 58 1
Beakley, Ezra 52 1
Beakley, Hannah 52 1
Beakley, Henry 51 1
Beakley, Jacob 56 1
Beakley, John 56 1
Beakley, John D 221a 2
Beakley, John Henry Sr 56 1
Beakley, John W 52 1
Beakley, Jonas E[?] 52 1
Beakly, Conrad 32 1
Beakly, Ezra 32 1
Bealer, Charles E 35 3
Beall, Adam T 28 1
Beall, Albert T W 28 1
Beall, Alexander O 30 1
Beall, Arthur L 72 1
Beall, Augusta Ann 28 1
Beall, Benj 51 2
Beall, Benjamin 30 1
Beall, C H 72 1
Beall, Cassandra 32 1
Beall, Charles E 33 1
Beall, Chas H 85 1
Beall, Daniel 37 1
Beall, E D 67 1
Beall, Elijah 40 1
Beall, Elinore 41 1
Beall, Eliza 40 1
Beall, Elizabeth 41 1
Beall, Elizabeth E 67 1
Beall, Emily M 41 1
Beall, Emory K 48 1
Beall, Francis 44 1
Beall, Fred R 23 2
Beall, Geo 57 2
Beall, Geo W 76 2
Beall, Geo W 32, 48, 71, 92 1
Beall, George W 40, 47, 48, 139 1
Beall, Horace H 41 1
Beall, I W 241 2
Beall, Ira W 73 1
Beall, Ira W 23 2
Beall, Ira W 188 3
Beall, J W 41 1
Beall, James F 61, 71 1
Beall, James H 59 1
Beall, Janette 61 1
Beall, Jeanette 61 1
Beall, John 30 1
Beall, John H 60, 120 1
Beall, Josephine Ann Lavinia C 59 1
Beall, Levin 129 2
Beall, Levin C 67 1
Beall, Marcellus 72, 85, 92 1
Beall, Margaret 41 1
Beall, Martha E 73 1
Beall, Mary 71 1
Beall, Mary Alice 71 1
Beall, Mary Ann 72, 92 1

Beall, Mary H 70 1
Beall, Millard T 124 1
Beall, Murphy A 74 1
Beall, Nancy 76 1
Beall, Nova M 225 1
Beall, Pearl May 61 1
Beall, R Edgar 72, 80 1
Beall, Rezin 82 1
Beall, Richard 33 1
Beall, Robert L 82, 83 1
Beall, Rosa B 41 2
Beall, Rosa W 140 1
Beall, Rose M 74 1
Beall, Sophia 106 3
Beall, Stonewall J 92 1
Beall, Theodore 88 1
Beall, Thomas 88 1
Beall, W R 72 1
Beall, Wallace R 73, 85, 86 1
Beall, Wallace R 23, 160 2
Beall, Washington E 92 1
Beall, William S 61 1
Beall, Wm 43, 72, 96, 189, 205, 211 2
Beall, Wm 40, 263 1
Beall, Wm C 92 1
Beall, Wm H 32 1
Beall, Wm H 50 3
Beall, Wm M 91, 92, 117 1
Beall, Wm M 19, 118, 175, 177, 181, 208 2
Beall, Wm M 106 3
Beall, Wm T 92 1
Beam, Jacob 194 1
Beam, Nicholas 76 1
Beam, Wm 139 1
Beamer, Henry 51 1
Bean, William 254 2
Bean, Wm 70 2
Beaner, David 37 1
Beaner, Frederick V 44 1
Beaner, Mary 107 3
Beaner, Matilda 44 1
Beans, Harry M 73 3
Beans, Hyett T 73 3
Beans, Melinda R 124 1
Bear, Anthony 195 3
Bear, Christian 33 1
Bear, Davisd H 196 3
Bear, Eliza 41 1
Bear, Geo W 47 1
Bear, George 47 1
Bear, George Sr 47 1
Bear, James E 62, 86 1
Bear, Peter 79 1
Bear, Salome 79 1
Bear, Simon 86 1
Bear, Welzie M 26 1
Beard, Abraham 32, 33 1
Beard, Barnhart 30 1
Beard, Catherine 32, 58, 79 1
Beard, Chas 243 1
Beard, Claude H 113 2
Beard, Emma L 53 1
Beard, George W 61 1
Beard, Grace G 48 1
Beard, Henry B 53 1
Beard, Henry Jr 53 1
Beard, Jacob 58, 79 1
Beard, Jacob 81, 64 3
Beard, Jacob 144 2
Beard, Jacob Jr 39 3
Beard, James C 58 1
Beard, James P 11 3
Beard, John 58, 101 1
Beard, John E 254 1
Beard, John Philip 30 1
Beard, John T 61, 85 1
Beard, Joseph 8 1
Beard, Joseph H 32, 59, 79 1
Beard, Julianna 59 1
Beard, Keller J 80 2
Beard, Loretta R 267 2
Beard, M L 216 3
Beard, M L Rev 264 2
Beard, Martin L 72 1
Beard, Mary 71 1
Beard, Mary A 58 1
Beard, Mathias 39 3
Beard, Mathias 214, 229, 234 1
Beard, Mathias 58, 71 1
Beard, Matthias 71 1
Beard, Myrtle M 26 1
Beard, Paul S 21 3
Beard, Peter 115 2
Beard, Peter 81 3
Beard, Peter 32, 79, 101 1
Beard, Peter A I 79 1
Beard, Philip 58, 79 1
Beard, Solomon 58, 85 1
Beard, Solomon 19 3
Beard, Wm H 72 1
Beaton, Harriet 52 1
Beattty, Sarah 40 1
Beatty, A P 51, 90 1
Beatty, Charles E 24 3
Beatty, Edward J 222 2
Beatty, Elijah 40 1
Beatty, Emma L 42, 93 1
Beatty, Geo W 48 1
Beatty, J E 3 3
Beatty, John 56 1
Beatty, John M 56 1
Beatty, John W 224a 2
Beatty, Joseph E 234 2
Beatty, Thomas 88 1
Beatty, Thomas A C 88 1
Beatty, Thomas, Sr 88 1
Beatty, William A 93, 107 1
Beatty, William A 222a 2
Beatty, Wm A 97 1
Beatty, Wm C 93 1
Beaumont, Pastal 79 1
Bechley, Ann R E 27 1
Bechley, Henry 19 1
Becht, Joseph 70 1
Becht, Michael 184, 214 3
Bechtol, Daniel 47 1
Bechtol, John 67 1
Bechtol, Lewis 67 1
Beck, Adam 26 1
Beck, Ann 26 1
Beck, Ann R 27, 78 1
Beck, Charles R R 33 1
Beck, E Gertrude 42 1
Beck, Edw 40 1
Beck, Elizabeth 27, 42, 48 1
Beck, Fannie O 42, 44, 90 1
Beck, Fanny 162 1
Beck, Gertrude 162 1
Beck, Grover J 48 1
Beck, James M 61 1
Beck, John 58 1
Beck, John F P 78 1
Beck, Michael 70 1
Beck, Nicholas 58 1
Beck, Osborne 78 1
Beck, Osbourn 87 2
Beck, Upton B 90 1
Beckenbaugh, Geo 53, 79 3
Beckenbaugh, Geo 47 1
Beckenbaugh, George 40, 56, 79, 117 1
Beckenbaugh, George 282 2
Beckenbaugh, Jacob 56 1
Beckenbaugh, John 56, 70 1
Beckenbaugh, Michael 70, 71 1
Beckenbaugh, Peter A 79 1
Beckenbaugh, Sarah 85 1
Beckenbaugh, Susanna 84 1
Becker, Catherine 51 1
Becker, Christopher 51 1
Becker, Henry 51 1
Becker, Lewis P 51 1
Beckinbaugh, Geo 253 1
Beckinbaugh, Geo 57, 137 2
Beckinbaugh, George 40 1
Beckinbaugh, George 87, 106 3
Beckles, Sarah 84 1
Beckley, Anna L 28 1
Beckley, Annie M 27 1
Beckley, E L 27, 67 1
Beckley, Edwin L 42, 119 1
Beckley, Gabriel 165 2
Beckley, Laura V 67 1
Beckley, Regina E 82 1
Becraft, Almira 79 1

Becraft, P M 79 1
Becraft, Peter 79 1
Bedheimer, Ferdinand 44 1
Bedheimer, Geo 44 1
Bedheimer, Geo J 48 1
Beekinbaugh, George 116 3
Beihl, Martin L 85 1
Beihle, Susan M 85 1
Beiller, Samuel L J 28 2
Beimbrink, Geo M 187 3
Beinbrink, Geo H 48 1
Beinbrink, Henry 59 1
Beirlein, F Geo 98 3
Beirlein, Geo 125 1
Beitler, C Eva A 21 3
Beitler, Ethel G 52 1
Beitler, Eva A 21 3
Beitler, Henry C 52, 84 1
Beitler, Jesse 84 1
Beitler, Samuel 84 1
Beitler, Samuel J 84 1
Beleke, Casper K 117 1
Beler, John R 201 1
Belknop, Catherine 58 1
Belknop, James 58 1
Bell, Alice E 86 1
Bell, Alice L 28 1
Bell, Amy T 255 2
Bell, Benjamin F 30 1
Bell, Carrie C 75 3
Bell, Carrie V 23 2
Bell, Charles A 34 1
Bell, Charles W 34 1
Bell, Charles William 74 1
Bell, Chas A 34 1
Bell, Chas L 60 1
Bell, Chas W 33 1
Bell, Emma F 30 1
Bell, Ephriam G 61 1
Bell, G Frank 68 1
Bell, Geo A 253 1
Bell, Howard N 255 2
Bell, Irving A 189 2
Bell, Jacob 28 1
Bell, Jacob 70 3
Bell, James C 23 2
Bell, James U 57, 86 1
Bell, John 61 1
Bell, John H 71, 91 1
Bell, John M 61 1
Bell, Louisa 68 1
Bell, Margaret 70 1
Bell, Markham W 224 3
Bell, Marshall W 83 3
Bell, Mary 70, 71 1
Bell, Mary B 74, 92 1
Bell, Mary E 288 2
Bell, Mary E 165 1
Bell, Mary V 28, 86 1
Bell, Orman T 74 1
Bell, Samuel H 86 1
Bell, Sophia T 85 1
Bell, Susan F 86 1
Bell, Thomas 88 1
Bell, Tiney 101 1
Bell, W A R 206 2
Bell, Wm 91 1
Bell, Wm D 92 1
Belleson, George W 165 3
Bellwood, Edward 40 1
Belt, Alfred 26 1
Belt, Alfred 195 2
Belt, Alfred M 26, 59, 60, 85 1
Belt, Anne Remsen 28 1
Belt, Ariana Teresa Trail 27 1
Belt, Emma V 41 1
Belt, Emos W 40 1
Belt, Enos W 67 1
Belt, Harry D 235 1
Belt, James R 56 1
Belt, Jeremiah 56, 57, 58 1
Belt, John 26, 60 1
Belt, John L 60, 85 1
Belt, John L 203 2
Belt, John L Jr 59 1
Belt, John L Sr 59 1
Belt, John Lloyd 60 1
Belt, Julia 63, 67 1
Belt, Lloyd C 67, 73 1
Belt, Margaret 70 1
Belt, Margaret Ann 88 1
Belt, Margaret Ford 235 1
Belt, Mary 70 1
Belt, McG 60 1
Belt, McGill 73, 85, 99, 172 1
Belt, McGill 139, 195 2
Belt, Norman A 16 2
Belt, Sarah 70 1
Belt, Sarah E 85 1
Belt, Thomas A 26 1
Belt, Tobias 56, 88, 243 1
Belt, Tobias 56 1
Belt, Townsend 88 1
Belt, Wm H 91 1
Beltz, Samuel 248 1
Bender, John 124 2
Benner, Alonza 27 1
Benner, Chas 25 1
Benner, Florence V 44 1
Benner, Frank P 45 1
Benner, John W 27 1
Benner, Martin L 44 1
Bennet, Alton I 133 1
Bennett, A Y 85, 259 2
Bennett, A Y 18 1
Bennett, Alton Y 21, 28, 29, 46, 72, 83, 167, 174, 180, 210 3
Bennett, Alton Y 32, 40, 49, 59, 140, 173, 175, 178, 182, 190, 196, 203, 268, 283 2
Bennett, Alton Y 28, 31, 38, 42, 53, 68, 83, 111, 113, 148, 157, 177, 193, 246, 254, 270 1
Bennett, Annie Hartman 221 3
Bennett, Benjamin 30 1
Bennett, Burtis 119 2
Bennett, Burtis 30, 96 1
Bennett, Burtix 215 3
Bennett, Elisha 30 1
Bennett, Elizabeth 40 1
Bennett, Francis W 112 1
Bennett, H L 62 1
Bennett, H W 85 3
Bennett, Hallie M 52 1
Bennett, Harry L 166 3
Bennett, Helen Reid 53 1
Bennett, Henry L 53 1
Bennett, John H 60, 62, 67 1
Bennett, Julia A 60 1
Bennett, L H 60 1
Bennett, Lewis H 67 1
Bennett, Mary E 85 1
Bennett, Mary P 48 1
Bennett, Nehemiah H 76 1
Bennett, Nellie B 48 1
Bennett, O P 52, 92 1
Bennett, O P 5 2
Bennett, O P 179 3
Bennett, Oliver P 78 1
Bennett, Perry 82 1
Bennett, Purtes 214 3
Bennett, R A 73 3
Bennett, R A 52 1
Bennett, Rachel 82 1
Bennett, Raymond L 76 1
Bennett, Robert A 42, 83, 92 1
Bennett, Robert A 32, 70, 148, 190, 203 2
Bennett, Robert A 28, 96 3
Bennett, S B 197 3
Bennett, Samuel B 86 1
Bennett, Sara V 53 1
Bennett, Sarah V 107 1
Bennett, Sarah V 49 2
Bennett, Sidnor 179 3
Bennett, Stella S 197 3
Bennett, Sybelle M 92 1
Bennett, Sydnor H 48 1
Bennett, William B 37, 53, 85 1
Bennison, H 107 2
Benson, Chas W 245 1
Benson, Chas W 71 1
Benson, Jonathan B 67 1
Benson, Lloyd 67 1
Bentel, Andreas 26 1

Bentel, Christopher	26	1
Bentel, Maria E	26	1
Bentley, Ann	26	1
Bentley, George	47	1
Bentley, Israel	25	2
Bentley, Mary	70	1
Bently, Caleb	40	1
Bently, Eli	40	1
Benton, Benjamin	30	1
Benton, Elizabeth A	84	1
Benton, Elizabeth E	41	1
Benton, Maria	30	1
Benton, Samuel S	83	2
Benton, Samuel S	27, 84	1
Bentz, Alice V	27, 60, 146	1
Bentz, Ann M	27	1
Bentz, Anna M E	28, 60	1
Bentz, Arthur	28, 38	1
Bentz, Catherine	32	1
Bentz, Catherine A	33	1
Bentz, Catherine E	33, 52	1
Bentz, Catherine M	33	1
Bentz, Charles	32	1
Bentz, Charles E	33	1
Bentz, Charlotte S	65	3
Bentz, Chas	111	2
Bentz, Chas E	32, 60	1
Bentz, Daniel	41	2
Bentz, Daniel	37, 60	1
Bentz, Daniel K	37	1
Bentz, Daniel W	38	1
Bentz, David	42	1
Bentz, Edward	9, 202	2
Bentz, Edward	57, 67, 70	1
Bentz, Elizabeth	40	1
Bentz, Ezra	184	3
Bentz, Ezra	28	1
Bentz, Florence	44, 47	1
Bentz, Francis H	37	1
Bentz, Geo	175	2
Bentz, George	47, 56	1
Bentz, H W	47	1
Bentz, Harry	33	1
Bentz, Henry	33, 52, 165	1
Bentz, Horatio W	33, 52, 56, 70, 210, 214	1
Bentz, Jacob	59, 234	1
Bentz, Jacob Jr	60	1
Bentz, Jacob M	60, 63	1
Bentz, Jacob Sr	63	1
Bentz, John	32	1
Bentz, Julia Anna	62	1
Bentz, L	185	3
Bentz, Laurence E	42	1
Bentz, Lawrence	67, 131	1
Bentz, Lewis	67, 207	1
Bentz, Lewis	221a	2
Bentz, Lydia	67, 229	1
Bentz, Margaret	70	1
Bentz, Mary E	37	1
Bentz, Rebecca	82	1
Bentzel, Arthur H	28	1
Bentzel, Calvin I	28, 73	1
Bentzel, Ivan N	215a	2
Bentzel, John H	62	1
Bentzel, Mary J	92	1
Bentzel, Mary P	73	1
Bentzel, William E	93	1
Bentzel, Wm H	92	1
Bentzell, Emma E	62	1
Berbard, Solomon	111	2
Berch, Elizabeth	88	1
Berch, Thomas	88	1
Bere, Lee	68	1
Berely, George K	47	1
Berger, Aleine	42	1
Berger, Anna	27	1
Berger, Edmund	42	1
Berger, Elizabeth	14	2
Berger, Frank	27	1
Berger, Frank A	41, 58	1
Berger, Frederick	44	1
Berger, Jacob	46, 57, 132	2
Berger, Jacob	58	1
Berger, Leah Frances	192	3
Berger, Mary	14	2
Berger, Mary M	58	1
Berger, Peter	31	3
Berglite, Daniel	214	1
Berlin, Geo	229	1
Bernard, Grafton	67	1
Bernard, Luke	67	1
Bernard, M	7	2
Bernard, Malachi	159	1
Berry, Edith Bantz	42	1
Berry, George	47	1
Berry, Jerome C	76	1
Berry, Mary A	47	1
Berry, Thos	89, 190	2
Berry, Wm H	92	1
Besant, Catherine B	42	1
Besant, Emily F M	42	1
Besant, G M	166	3
Besant, G M	199	2
Besant, G Mantz	48, 52, 78, 92	1
Besant, G Mantz	79, 92	2
Besant, H R	109	1
Besant, Harry R	113	3
Besant, Henry R	37	1
Besant, James	213a	2
Besant, James H	288	2
Besant, James H	52, 67, 117	1
Besant, Wm H	116	2
Besant, Wm T	92	1
Best, Arie N	78	1
Best, Catherine	33	1
Best, David	37, 159	1
Best, Elizabeth C	92	1
Best, Flora C	48	1
Best, Geo W	48, 99, 135	1
Best, Geo W	22	2
Best, George R	33	1
Best, George Z	83	2
Best, George Z	92	1
Best, Hester Preston	53	1
Best, J T	61	1
Best, John	187	2
Best, John F	57	1
Best, John N G	30	1
Best, John T	81	3
Best, John T	51	2
Best, John T	37, 72, 78, 171	1
Best, John T, Jr	53	1
Best, John T, Sr	61	1
Best, Lizzie A	37	1
Best, Margaret J	72	1
Best, Oliver D	78	1
Best, William O	37	1
Best, Wm H	53, 92	1
Best, Wm H	81	3
Best, Wm H	8	2
Betson, Casper Frost	68	1
Betson, Catharine A	38	1
Betson, Catherine Amanda	38	1
Betson, Dora M	68	1
Betson, Lewis Edgar	68	1
Betson, Susan	85	1
Betts, A B	82	1
Betts, Annie N	61	1
Betts, D S	61	1
Betts, Josiah	82, 85	1
Betts, L D	82	1
Betts, Noah J	76	1
Betts, Samuel	85	1
Betts, Samuel	195	2
Betzenberger, Joanna S	59	1
Betzendanner, Jacob	50	3
Bevan, John	57	1
Bevan, John H	57	1
Bevan, Johnathan	141	3
Bevans, Chas A	154	2
Beyer, Detrick	37	1
Beyer, Margaret	88	1
Beyer, Theodore E	88	1
Bickel, Harry S	52	1
Bickel, Harvey C	33	3
Biddinger, Adam	71	1
Biddinger, Chas W	62	1
Biddinger, Emory N	42	1
Biddinger, John A	62, 63	1
Biddinger, John D	61	1
Biddle, Geo W	201, 206	3
Biddle, John H	58	1
Biddle, Jonathan	58	1
Biddle, Sarah E	91	1
Biddle, William M	96	3

Biddle, Wm R 91 1
Bidel, Caniel C 33 1
Bidel, Christopher 33 1
Bidel, John A 33 1
Bidle, Alma 227 2
Bidle, Bertha J 34 1
Bidle, Charles E 92, 93 1
Bidle, Chas M 72 1
Bidle, D C 115 2
Bidle, Daniel C 72 1
Bidle, Daniel C of A 38 1
Bidle, Eileen G 154 2
Bidle, Eyster 63 1
Bidle, Geo H 48 1
Bidle, Geo W 174 3
Bidle, Guy W 93 1
Bidle, J Clifford 61 1
Bidle, John A 62, 63, 72 1
Bidle, Keefer M 61 1
Bidle, Mary C 72 1
Bidle, Raymond 227 2
Bidle, Raymond L 62 1
Bidle, Ruth A 38 1
Bidle, Sallie B 34 1
Bidle, William A 93 1
Bidle, Wm A 92 1
Biehl, David 37 1
Biehl, David 57 2
Biehl, Jacob 58, 228 1
Biehl, John 214, 238 2
Biehl, John 37 1
Biehl, John 28 2
Biehl, Martha (Mattie L) 73 1
Biehl, Wm M Jr 116 2
Biehle, David 228 1
Bielfeld, J J 62 1
Bielfeld, J J 172 3
Bielfeld, Jonathan B 219 1
Bierlein, F G 195 2
Bierlein, F George 195 3
Bierley, Charles E 34 1
Bierley, Jacob 38 3
Bierley, Mehrl E 34 1
Bierley, William H 34 1
Bierly, John 40 3
Biggers, Mary Lavinia 85 1
Biggers, Solomon 85 1
Biggs, Amon S 161 3
Biggs, Andrew J 26 1
Biggs, Anna W 26 1
Biggs, Augustus A 26 1
Biggs, Benjamin 66, 165 2
Biggs, Benjamin 27, 30, 56, 70 1
Biggs, Benjamin D 30 1
Biggs, Benjamin of B 30, 91 1
Biggs, C M 33 1
Biggs, Calvin M 48, 61 1
Biggs, Catherine 91 1
Biggs, David M 79 1
Biggs, E F 227 3
Biggs, E H 100 1
Biggs, Edw S 161 3
Biggs, Elbridge F 55, 73, 120 1
Biggs, Frederick 56 1
Biggs, Ida C 55 1
Biggs, Irma V 55 1
Biggs, J 38, 57, 118, 186 2
Biggs, J S 30 1
Biggs, Jacob 30, 48, 56, 70, 91, 193 1
Biggs, Jacob 18, 37, 53, 184 3
Biggs, Jacob 100, 118, 186, 254 2
Biggs, James 181 2
Biggs, James S 56, 60, 61, 79, 92, 201 1
Biggs, James W 61 1
Biggs, jno 179 3
Biggs, John 56 1
Biggs, John J 60 1
Biggs, Joseph 32 1
Biggs, Joshua 60, 91, 106 1
Biggs, Joshua 28, 57, 87, 101, 119, 198, 296 2
Biggs, Joshua 40 3
Biggs, Josiah 224 3
Biggs, Julia 60 1
Biggs, Laura L 33 1
Biggs, Martha 26 1
Biggs, Mary A 73 1
Biggs, Mary E 27 1
Biggs, Mary I 26 1
Biggs, Milton B 30 1
Biggs, Phoebe 181 2
Biggs, Phoebe S 60 1
Biggs, Robert 181, 296 2
Biggs, Robert 61, 79, 193 1
Biggs, Sophia E 23 1
Biggs, William 37, 184 3
Biggs, Wm 30, 60, 61, 91, 117 1
Biggs, Wm 96 2
Biggs, Wm H 30, 60, 79, 91, 240 1
Biggs, Wm of B 72, 91 1
Biggs, Wm of J 38, 57, 118, 186 2
Biggs, Wm of J 91, 234 1
Biggus, Solomon 86 1
Bigham, Armor 26 1
Bigham, James 26 1
Billman, Chester A 211 2
Billman, E I 211 2
Billmyer, Cordelia Ann 59 1
Billmyer, John 59 1
Binger, Abraham col'd 26 1
Binnie, Clothworthy 80 2
Birch, James 179 3
Bird, Anna C 30 1
Bird, Belle W 30 1
Birelein, John G 59 1
Bireley, Cath D 67 1
Bireley, David 39, 40 3
Bireley, Elizabeth 40 1
Bireley, Ellis 45 3
Bireley, Eveline H 90 1
Bireley, Ewos 47 1
Bireley, George 47, 67 1
Bireley, J Wm 99 1
Bireley, Jacob 47 1
Bireley, Lewis A 67 1
Bireley, Mary E 67 1
Bireley, Valentine 90 1
Bireley, Wm 91 1
Birely, A D 101 2
Birely, A D 4, 27 1
Birely, Adam D 26, 44 1
Birely, Ann E 47, 60 1
Birely, Barbara A 30 1
Birely, Belva A E 85 1
Birely, Bertha B 74 1
Birely, Catherine D 32 1
Birely, Charles E 42 1
Birely, Charlotte 32 1
Birely, Chas S 34 1
Birely, D 47 1
Birely, D O 155 1
Birely, Daniel 37 1
Birely, Daniel O 192 3
Birely, David 37, 40, 41, 84, 191 1
Birely, David 81 3
Birely, David 113, 226, 276 2
Birely, Edw 149 2
Birely, Elizabeth 27, 40, 57 1
Birely, Elmer 195 2
Birely, Elmer B 40, 60 1
Birely, Elmer E 42 1
Birely, Eveline H 90 1
Birely, F 47 1
Birely, Frances 203 2
Birely, Frances H 44 1
Birely, Frederick 44, 191 1
Birely, Frederick 202 2
Birely, Geo 61 2
Birely, Geo 32 1
Birely, Geo Jr 165 2
Birely, Geo K 47, 70, 183 1
Birely, George 48, 144 1
Birely, H C 210 3
Birely, H P C 104 1
Birely, Hannah M 60 1
Birely, J W 29, 124, 249 2
Birely, J W 59, 100 1
Birely, J W 41, 71, 81, 209 3
Birely, J William 195, 222 3
Birely, J Wm 40, 60, 135, 152, 165,

257 1
Birely, J Wm 55 3
Birely, J Wm 153 2
Birely, Jacob 202, 226 2
Birely, Jacob 44, 47, 57, 60, 205, 253 1
Birely, Jacob M 60 1
Birely, John 7, 63, 137 2
Birely, John 32, 60, 61, 263 1
Birely, John T 131 2
Birely, John W 78 2
Birely, John W 44, 112, 131, 264 1
Birely, John W 55 3
Birely, John Wm 87 2
Birely, John Wm 164 1
Birely, Joseph 57 1
Birely, Katheryn E 42 1
Birely, Katheryne E 33 1
Birely, Kathryne E 195 2
Birely, L F 36 2
Birely, L S 20, 72, 153, 188, 192 3
Birely, L S 62, 65, 72, 92, 123, 148 1
Birely, L S 169, 238 2
Birely, Leslie 1, 133 1
Birely, Leslie 132 2
Birely, Leslie S 174, 219 3
Birely, Lester 134 2
Birely, Lester S 26, 28, 97, 254, 260 1
Birely, Lester S 2, 12, 49, 81 2
Birely, Lewis 40, 70, 156, 194, 253, 257 1
Birely, Lewis 38, 70, 205 3
Birely, Lewis 28, 116, 132, 137, 267 2
Birely, Lewis A 26 1
Birely, Lewis E 44, 47, 48, 61, 68, 137, 183 1
Birely, Lillian E 68 1
Birely, Lillie M 68 1
Birely, Lillin S 34 1
Birely, Louisa 60, 68 1
Birely, M A 244, 282 1
Birely, M Ella 60 1
Birely, M Rose 73 1
Birely, Margaret Ellen 73, 93 1
Birely, Martha E 61 1
Birely, Martha Ellen 60 1
Birely, Mary R 72, 73 1
Birely, Maurice 132 2
Birely, Maurice A 38 1
Birely, Morris A 30, 74, 254 1
Birely, Morris A 45 3
Birely, Morris A 215, 284 2
Birely, P H 60 1
Birely, P H C 38, 79 1
Birely, P H C 192 3
Birely, P H C 124 2
Birely, Philip 203 2
Birely, Philip C H 26 1
Birely, Samuel 10, 40, 57, 73, 84 1
Birely, Samuel 26, 64 3
Birely, Samuel M 9, 32, 187, 206 3
Birely, Samuel M 12, 30, 38, 55, 85, 99, 100, 116, 224 1
Birely, Samuel M 160, 254 2
Birely, Samuel W 52 1
Birely, Susan 60 1
Birely, T F 13 1
Birely, Valentine 40, 44, 47, 90, 264 1
Birely, Valentine 38, 70 3
Birely, Valentine 203 2
Birely, Victor M 2 2
Birely, W C 192 3
Birely, W C 44 1
Birely, W F 245 1
Birely, William 228a 2
Birely, William C 93 1
Birely, William C 23, 192 3
Birely, William K 93 1
Birely, Wm 38, 131, 139 1
Birely, Wm 89, 124, 149 2
Birely, Wm 55 3
Birely, Wm C 60, 72, 73, 104, 252, 257 1
Birely, Wm C 210 3
Birely, Wm C 23, 139, 142, 149 2
Birely, Wm F 23 2
Birely, Wm H 68 1
Birely, Wm M 32 1
Bireman, Geo H 47 1
Bireman, George F 47 1
Birley, M A 196 3
Birley, William C 196 3
Birrs, Catherine W 32 1
Biser, Adam 79 1
Biser, Albert C 86 1
Biser, Arbenia E 27 1
Biser, C C 80, 93 2
Biser, C T 52 1
Biser, Carrie E 34 1
Biser, Carrie M 34 1
Biser, Catherine 30 2
Biser, Catherine 33 1
Biser, Chas C 27, 61 1
Biser, Chas C 181 2
Biser, Chas C 55 3
Biser, Clarence S 34 1
Biser, Cyrus T 11 1
Biser, Cyrus T 277 2
Biser, D 64 3
Biser, Dan el 15 3
Biser, Daniel 33, 37, 58, 59 1
Biser, Daniel 275 2
Biser, Daniel 26 3
Biser, Daniel G 37, 84 1
Biser, Daniel S 84 2
Biser, Daniel S 96 3
Biser, Daniel S 38, 40, 57, 71, 84 1
Biser, Daphne K 83 2
Biser, David C 169 2
Biser, David C 40 1
Biser, Elizabeth 41, 55 1
Biser, Emma A 42 1
Biser, Emma A E 129 3
Biser, Emma E 48 1
Biser, Enos 144, 164 1
Biser, Erie C 55 1
Biser, Esla M 72 1
Biser, Frederick 70, 79 1
Biser, Frederick 31 3
Biser, Geo 176 3
Biser, Geo C 113 3
Biser, Geo Cost 119 2
Biser, Geo E 48 1
Biser, George C 57 1
Biser, Gladys 82 3
Biser, H 100 3
Biser, H C 68 1
Biser, H E 192 3
Biser, H H 160 3
Biser, H M 160 3
Biser, Henrietta 52 1
Biser, Henry 48, 52, 55, 58, 71 1
Biser, Henry 276 2
Biser, Henry C 41, 51 1
Biser, Henry H 51, 52, 84 1
Biser, Ira B 55 1
Biser, Ira E 55 1
Biser, Irene C 55 1
Biser, Irving S 55 1
Biser, J 37 1
Biser, J G 186 2
Biser, Jacob 40, 52, 57, 59, 79, 110, 125, 263 1
Biser, Jacob 37, 160, 202 3
Biser, Jacob 237 2
Biser, James K P 244 1
Biser, James P 38 1
Biser, Jennie 63 1
Biser, Jennie 153 2
Biser, Jennie I 37, 230 1
Biser, Jennie I 82, 166 3
Biser, John 57, 58, 88, 137 1
Biser, John 100, 185, 208 2
Biser, John 65, 160, 185, 202, 215 3
Biser, John C 84 1
Biser, John G 137, 271 1
Biser, John J 62 1
Biser, John of F 58 1
Biser, John W 101 2

Biser, Johnothan 65 3
Biser, Jonas 58 1
Biser, Jonathan 58, 61, 119 1
Biser, Jonothan 41, 91, 124, 171 3
Biser, Joshua 59 1
Biser, Joshua D 58 1
Biser, Lloyd 250 1
Biser, Lydia 67 1
Biser, M A 119 1
Biser, M A E 194, 203, 229, 234, 253, 260, 279 1
Biser, M A E 15, 40, 65, 68, 80, 150, 198, 238, 294 2
Biser, M A E 55, 72, 77 3
Biser, M E A 72 3
Biser, Margaret 71 1
Biser, Mary J 80 2
Biser, Maurice 202 2
Biser, Maurice V 34, 52 1
Biser, Melvin 30 2
Biser, Melvin A 19 1
Biser, Melvin A E 27, 33, 72, 112, 230, 279 1
Biser, Melvin A E 9, 75, 87 3
Biser, Melvin A E 20, 189 2
Biser, Melvin E 230 1
Biser, Melvin E A 67 3
Biser, Melvyn A E 119 1
Biser, Mildred 63 1
Biser, Nervin M 63 1
Biser, Peter 54 2
Biser, Peter 79 1
Biser, Richard C 55 1
Biser, Rosanna 82, 88 1
Biser, Roseni 19 3
Biser, S Ethel Routzahn 33 1
Biser, Sarah A R 86 1
Biser, Silas T 84 1
Biser, Sophia 84, 85 1
Biser, Sophie E 86 1
Biser, T 270 1
Biser, T H 27 1
Biser, T M 110 1
Biser, T M 153, 224, 225 2
Biser, T M 2 3
Biser, Thad M 50, 55 3
Biser, Thad M 92 2
Biser, Thad M 33 1
Biser, Thaddeus 68 2
Biser, Thaddeus M 61, 88, 230, 272 1
Biser, Thomas 88 1
Biser, Thos B 37 1
Biser, Tilghman 5 2
Biser, Tilghman 38, 57, 67 1
Biser, William T 86 1
Biser, Wm T 27 1
Bisers, Melvin A E 15 3
Bishop, Charles A 33 1
Bishop, Degrey R 222 2
Bishop, Elijah 38, 45 2
Bishop, Geo S 48 1
Bishop, Jacob 57, 88, 123 1
Bishop, John 56 1
Bishop, John 53 3
Bishop, Mabel Lowell 70 1
Bishop, Mark 74, 129, 179, 271 1
Bishop, Mary 70 1
Bishop, Sophia C 28 1
Bitler, Albert S 48, 63, 148, 200 1
Bitler, Albert S 168, 271 2
Bitler, Charles O 28 1
Bitler, Ozella K 26, 78 1
Bitsenberger, Abraham 57, 78 1
Bitsenberger, Abram 57 1
Bitsenberger, John 57 1
Bittinger, Daniel 29 2
Bittinger, Geo W 10 3
Bittle, Amanda 181 1
Bittle, Catherine 92 1
Bittle, Charles J 34 1
Bittle, Chas J 2 2
Bittle, Chas J 92 1
Bittle, Clay L 42, 92 1
Bittle, D Edgar 23 2
Bittle, D Edgar 34, 48 1
Bittle, D Edgar 35 3
Bittle, Eleanor R 262 2
Bittle, Eleanor Ricketts 257 2
Bittle, Emily C 107 1
Bittle, Emma K 42 1
Bittle, G W 274 2
Bittle, Geo 47 1
Bittle, Geo 32, 58, 66, 195, 209 2
Bittle, Geo & 189 2
Bittle, Geo F 61 1
Bittle, Geo W 11, 166 3
Bittle, Geo W 61, 82, 92, 166, 250, 272 1
Bittle, Geo W 232, 265 2
Bittle, George 47 1
Bittle, George W 23, 108, 190, 235, 267 2
Bittle, George W 48, 52, 250, 252 1
Bittle, George W 167, 176, 197 3
Bittle, Henry 139 1
Bittle, J Thos 166 3
Bittle, John H 19, 82 1
Bittle, Jonathan 47 1
Bittle, L F 34 1
Bittle, Lawson F 68, 147 1
Bittle, Loulie A 68 1
Bittle, Mary 42 1
Bittle, Rachel 82 1
Bittle, Silas D 92 1
Bittle, T J 264 1
Bittle, Thomas 6 1
Bittle, Thomas F 234 2
Bittle, Thos F 277 2
Bittle, Wm C 92 1
Bittle, Wm E 82 1
Bittle, Wm M 92, 147 1
Bitzemberger, Wm 91 1
Bitzenberger, Abraham 26 1
Bitzenberger, Arthur 91 1
Bitzenberger, Joanna 26 1
Bitzer, Annie E 28 1
Bitzer, Meredith R 28 1
Bitzer, Ralph C 28 1
Bixler, Emanuel 113, 282 2
Bixler, Peter 113 2
Black, Abraham 39 2
Black, Abraham A 68, 234 1
Black, Adam 26 1
Black, Annie 27 1
Black, C H 215, 217 3
Black, C H 19 2
Black, Catherine 32 1
Black, Chas V 34 1
Black, Chester 34 1
Black, Cornelia C 61 1
Black, Cornelius H 33 1
Black, Cornelius H 267 2
Black, E E 234 1
Black, E E 177 2
Black, Elizabeth 40 1
Black, Elizabeth A 58 1
Black, Elmer 14 1
Black, Elmer 228a 2
Black, Elmer 32 3
Black, Elmer E 91, 159 3
Black, Elmer E 30, 92, 210, 239 1
Black, Elmer E 277 2
Black, Eva 32 1
Black, Frederick 40, 44 1
Black, Frederick 81, 106 3
Black, Frederick, Jr 44 1
Black, Frences Irene 51 1
Black, Henry 26, 57, 63 1
Black, Henry 38, 40, 87 3
Black, Henry 26, 132, 147 2
Black, J B 61 1
Black, James B 32, 110 1
Black, Jeremiah 40, 92 1
Black, Jeremiah 234 2
Black, John 51, 57, 58, 163 1
Black, John B 33 1
Black, John W 63 1
Black, Lucilia 67 1
Black, Marian A 27 1
Black, Mary E 34, 72 1
Black, Mary J 239 2
Black, Morris G 93 1
Black, Peter 79 1
Black, Polly 79 1

Black, Rebecca 82 1
Black, Roy C 63 1
Black, S P W 156 1
Black, Sarah 79 1
Black, T J 229 1
Black, Thos J 52 1
Black, W Geyer 93 1
Black, William 220a, 221a 2
Black, William 57 1
Black, William 40 3
Black, William J 9, 187 3
Black, William R 205 3
Black, Wm 91, 223, 264 1
Black, Wm 224 3
Black, Wm 39, 101, 187 2
Black, Wm H 215 3
Black, Wm H 33 1
Black, Wm J 43, 166, 167, 179, 187 3
Black, Wm J 177 2
Black, Wm J 92, 96, 106, 110, 118, 175, 229, 234, 239, 272 1
Black, Wm K 205 3
Blackborn, Wm & 57 2
Blackson, Rebecca 82 1
Blacksten, Eliza A 42 1
Blacksten, Eliza Ann 42 1
Blacksten, Geo W 61 1
Blacksten, John H 61 1
Blacksten, Margaret E 8 1
Blackston, Benjamin H 30 1
Blackston, Bernard 30 1
Blackston, Clara C H 34 1
Blackston, Eva 215 1
Blackston, Henry 210 1
Blackston, Herman 215 1
Blackston, John 57 1
Blackston, Margaret E 4 1
Blades, Mary 27 1
Blair, Anna E 34, 266 1
Blair, Catherine 210a 2
Blair, Charles F 34 1
Blair, Florence 63 1
Blair, George W 27 1
Blair, John A 63 1
Blair, Joseph 63 1
Blair, Mary Alice 92 1
Blair, Samuel 84 1
Blair, Wm G 92, 96 1
Blake, Chas G 82 1
Blake, Franklin 44 1
Blake, Julia 44 1
Blake, Rebecca Ellen 82 1
Blake, W 37 1
Blakeley, David 37 1
Blakeley, David 214 1
Blandford, Reeves H 108 2
Blandford, Regenia M 113 3
Blane, John P 22 1
Blank, Bertie Mrs 68 1
Blank, Dorothy V 68 1
Blank, Elmer E 259 2
Blank, Harriet V 52 1
Blank, John 59 1
Blank, John H 59 1
Blank, John Henry 52 1
Blank, L F 52 1
Blank, Lewis F 68 1
Blank, Lloyd F 68 1
Blank, Wilfred G 68 1
Blank, William E Sr 93 1
Blank, Wm E Jr 93 1
Blant, Roberta C 162 1
Blave, William J 27 3
Blentinger, A T 41 1
Blentinger, Wm 41 1
Blentlinger, A T 112 1
Blentlinger, Adam T 28 1
Blentlinger, Ira E 55 1
Blentlinger, Laura Jane 68 1
Blentlinger, Nannie W 76 1
Blentlinger, Pearl M 55 1
Blentlinger, Rosa E 89 2
Blentlinger, W Sheridan 28 1
Blentlinger, William H 68 1
Blentlinger, Wm H 66 2
Blentlinger, Wm H 92 1
Blenttinger, Charles C 33 1
Blenttinger, Rosa E 33 1
Blenttinger, Wm H 33 1
Blessing, A 89 3
Blessing, Abraham 26 1
Blessing, Abraham of G 26 1
Blessing, Adam 26 1
Blessing, Benjamin L 30, 47, 58, 211 1
Blessing, Christian 56 1
Blessing, Eliza 40 1
Blessing, Elizabeth 57 1
Blessing, Emma S 40 1
Blessing, Eve 41, 42 1
Blessing, Francis T 71 1
Blessing, Frank 234 2
Blessing, Frank L 26, 88 1
Blessing, Ge 89 3
Blessing, Geo 159 2
Blessing, Geo 40, 42, 196 1
Blessing, Geo 91 3
Blessing, Geo W 37 1
Blessing, George 207 3
Blessing, George 41, 47, 71, 76, 84 1
Blessing, George P 56, 79 1
Blessing, George Sr 47 1
Blessing, J 122 3
Blessing, Jacob 57 1
Blessing, John 79, 84 1
Blessing, Joshua 47 1
Blessing, Julianna 47 1
Blessing, Lydia A 56, 68, 213 1
Blessing, Marie 42 1
Blessing, Marie M 71 1
Blessing, Mary 84, 88 1
Blessing, Mary 91 3
Blessing, Mary A 72 1
Blessing, Mary C 90 1
Blessing, Mary M 26 1
Blessing, Neri 91, 111 3
Blessing, Neri 26, 76 1
Blessing, Philip 79, 279 1
Blessing, Philip 64 3
Blessing, Philip 282 2
Blessing, Philip N R 79 1
Blessing, Rhoda E 211 1
Blessing, Sarah 84 1
Blessing, Solomon 26, 79, 84, 186 1
Blessing, Susan 85 1
Blessing, T L 68 1
Blessing, Tilghman 14 1
Blessing, Tilghman L 234 2
Blessing, Tilghman L 30, 88, 230 1
Blessing, Valletta S T 71 1
Blessing, Wm H 90, 91 1
Blickenstaff, Clinton H 48 1
Blickenstaff, Cyrus O 37 1
Blickenstaff, D W 19 2
Blickenstaff, Daniel 38 1
Blickenstaff, Daniel W 55, 219, 253 1
Blickenstaff, Elias 169 2
Blickenstaff, Elias 41 1
Blickenstaff, G W 8 2
Blickenstaff, Geo M 48 1
Blickenstaff, Geo R 48 1
Blickenstaff, Geo W 41 1
Blickenstaff, J 60 1
Blickenstaff, Jacob 40 1
Blickenstaff, Jno 167 3
Blickenstaff, John 60 1
Blickenstaff, Margaret C 73 1
Block, C H 167 3
Block, Wm H 217 3
Blondell, Lewis 188 2
Bloom, Adam 26 1
Bloom, John Jr 58 1
Bloom, John Sr 58 1
Blowers, Richard 56 1
Blubaker, John 58, 82, 100 1
Bluer, James 57 1
Blum, Bertha M 30 1
Blum, Elsie 76 1
Blum, H W 135 3
Blum, Nicholas 76 1
Blume, John 159 2

Blume, Michael 91 1
Blume, Wm H 91 1
Blumenauer, Annie C 47 1
Blumenauer, Catherine 33 1
Blumenauer, Chas 34 1
Blumenauer, Frederick A 44, 76 1
Blumenauer, G A 44 1
Blumenauer, George 47 1
Blumenauer, George W 47 1
Blumenauer, Georgia A 76 1
Blumenauer, John 178 2
Blumenauer, John N 76 1
Blumenauer, Margaret E 47 1
Blumenauer, Mary K 34 1
Blumenauer, N 1 1
Blumenauer, Nicholas 47, 76 1
Blumenauer, Nicholas 268 2
Blumenauer, Sallie M R 47 1
Blumenauer, Sarah A 47 1
Blunenauer, Mary C 44 1
Boblitz, E L 206 3
Boblitz, E L 230 1
Boblitz, Ellen B 53 1
Boblitz, Emma J 41 1
Boblitz, Ephm L 41 1
Boblitz, Harriet D 53 1
Boblitz, Lucy D 53 1
Boblitz, Nellie B 41 1
Bobst, Elizabeth A 19 3
Bobst, Leslie E 175 2
Bobst, Mary 71 1
Body, Andrew 115 2
Boetler, Basil S 169 1
Boetler, George W 13 1
Boetler, Henry 163, 165 2
Bogan, Magdalea 70 1
Bogner, John 237 2
Bohn, Carrie O 85 2
Bohn, Claude Solomon 34 1
Bohn, Derward A 37 1
Bohn, Fannie Stoner 45 1
Bohn, Frederick R 82 1
Bohn, George I 34 1
Bohn, Harry E 52 1
Bohn, Harvey S 53 1
Bohn, James 60 1
Bohn, James F 63 1
Bohn, Marry E Wilson 73 1
Bohn, Mary Rebecca 73 1
Bohn, Noma K 52 1
Bohn, Richard S 72, 82 1
Bohn, Shirley W 73 1
Bohn, William 73 1
Bohn, Wm M 13 1
Bohr, John 165 2
Bohrer, Eliza E 42 1
Bohrer, I I 42 1
Bohrer, Ira I 55 1
Bohrer, William I 55 1
Boileau, Chas E 33 1
Boileau, Mary G 73 1
Boileau, Mary G 267 2
Boileau, O C 33 1
Boileau, W G 33 1
Boileau, Wm G 180 1
Boisneuf, Payen 78 1
Boist, Chas T 33 1
Boist, Ruth J 33 1
Boland, Fannie J 245 1
Boleyn, Lester E 73 1
Boleyn, Mary C 73 1
Bollar, Effie 23 2
Bollenbrocker, Amelia 26 1
Boller, Anna I 52 1
Boller, Anson E 4 1
Boller, C N 230 1
Boller, Cassandra 33 1
Boller, Catherine 32 1
Boller, Clarence G 34 1
Boller, Effie Mae 230 1
Boller, Guy W 53 1
Boller, Harry 31 2
Boller, Harry R 53 1
Boller, Henry 52 1
Boller, Henry A 33, 55 1
Boller, Isaiah W 52, 55 1
Boller, Isarael 59 1
Boller, Isiah N 62 1
Boller, Isiah W 85 1
Boller, Israel 55 1
Boller, John R 171 3
Boller, John R 59, 62 1
Boller, Margaret S 83 1
Boller, Rena E 85 1
Boller, Ross M 83 1
Boller, Sarah W 4 1
Boller, Savilla 52 1
Boller, Sherman T G 55. 85 1
Boller, Susan C 55 1
Boller, Virginia A 34 1
Boller, William Jr 32 1
Boller, Wm 26, 64 3
Boller, Wm 84 1
Boller, Wm & 197 2
Boller, Wm H 14 2
Boller, Wm H 91 1
Bollinger, Christian 32 1
Bollinger, Fannie 44, 45 1
Bollinger, Jacob 60 1
Bollinger, L A 60 1
Bollinger, Mary C 74 1
Bollinger, Rachel 32 1
Bollinger, Theodore J 44, 45 1
Bolly, Frederick 44 1
Bond, Andrew 71, 164 1
Bond, Charles 135 1
Bond, Chas 51 1
Bond, Cornelius 59, 79 1
Bond, Dora E 143 2
Bond, Elijah 14, 159, 186, 197 2
Bond, Elijah 196 1
Bond, Elisha 225 2
Bond, Elizah 88 1
Bond, Henry 51 1
Bond, J A E 265 1
Bond, James 56 1
Bond, John H 79 1
Bond, Julia A 51 1
Bond, Peter 59, 79 1
Bond, Rosella 72 3
Bond, Thomas 88 1
Bond, Thomas 159 2
Bond, Thomas D 88 1
Bond, Thomas J 88 1
Boner, G H 72 3
Bonsack, Nathaniel 27 2
Bonsall, J S 91 1
Bonsall, Jesse S 218 2
Bonsall, Jesse S 59 1
Bonsall, Susan R 30 1
Boogher, Baalis C 59, 76 1
Boogher, Elizabeth 40 1
Boogher, Nicholas 76 1
Booke, Richard 213a 2
Booker, Henry 51 1
Booker, Jacob 38 3
Booker, Jacob 51, 59 1
Booker, Sarah 59 1
Bookfelter, Margaret 58 1
Boon, Geo W 70 1
Boon, Martin 70 1
Boon, Solomon 70 1
Boone, (Bohn) Harvey S 53 1
Boone, A Willetta 28 3
Boone, Adam 26 1
Boone, Alexius 26 1
Boone, Anna M 26 1
Boone, Arthur C 26 1
Boone, Benedict 26, 28, 70, 117, 164, 263 1
Boone, Benedict 56, 76, 75, 76, 107 2
Boone, Benedict 23 3
Boone, Benjamin 163 3
Boone, Catherine F 82 1
Boone, Elsie Gertrude 53 1
Boone, Geo W 26 1
Boone, Grace 48 1
Boone, H W 52 1
Boone, Harriet 51 1
Boone, Harry W 68 1
Boone, Harry W 172 2
Boone, Henry 52 1
Boone, Henry 8 2
Boone, J 47 1
Boone, J W 88 1
Boone, Jacob 57 1

Boone, Jennie L 88 1
Boone, Jeringham 82 1
Boone, Jerningham 51 1
Boone, Joseph 82 1
Boone, Lester LeRoy 52 1
Boone, Louisa 68, 76 1
Boone, M D 119 2
Boone, Maria 70 1
Boone, Marshall D 72 1
Boone, Mary M 71 1
Boone, Michael 70 1
Boone, Naomi 76 1
Boone, Nellie Whipp 76 1
Boone, Nicholas 76, 244 1
Boone, Nicholas 113, 202 2
Boone, R 217 1
Boone, R 226 2
Boone, R Sanchez 32 3
Boone, Richard S 47 1
Boone, Robert 163 3
Boone, Robert 49, 107 2
Boone, Robert 47, 51, 68, 70, 72, 82, 88 1
Boone, Robt 159, 165, 187, 197 2
Boone, Roy 20 2
Boone, S Ida 86, 133 1
Boone, Sarah 84 1
Boone, Solomon 26 1
Boone, Thomas W 88 1
Boone, W E 88 1
Boone, William 231 2
Boose, Mary 70 1
Booth, Charles A 95 1
Booth, Zachary T 95 1
Booze, Edw 40 1
Booze, Jacob 70 1
Boozer, John 181 2
Bopst, Alvin W 76 1
Bopst, Bion E 31 1
Bopst, Daniel 38 1
Bopst, G K 3 3
Bopst, Georgette 48 1
Bopst, Leslie E 93 1
Bopst, Milton B 27 1
Bopst, Nettie J 3 3
Bopst, W M 33, 38 1
Bopst, William M 93 1
Bopst, Wm M 41 1
Borders, Lewis N 14 1
Borger, John Peter 59 1
Born, John 56 1
Born, Margaret 56 1
Borne, Elizabeth 40 1
Borne, U G Dr 101 1
Bortel, Christian 32 1
Bosley, Charles B 166 1
Bosley, Matilda 71 1
Boslus, Stephen R 71 1
Bossard, Samuel 85 1
Bost, Cornelius 80 2
Bost, Henry 165 3
Bost, John 196 1
Bostain, Elizabeth 1 1
Bostian, Andrew 26, 41, 51 1
Bostian, Andrew 22 2
Bostian, Andrew 53 3
Bostian, Anthony 26 1
Bostian, C Alton 34 1
Bostian, Charles E 34 1
Bostian, Cora 6 3
Bostian, David T 38 1
Bostian, Elizabeth 41, 55 1
Bostian, Florence 45 1
Bostian, Henry 51 1
Bostian, Henry 53 3
Bostian, Isaac 55 1
Bostian, Jacob 60, 61 1
Bostian, Jacob A 61 1
Bostian, James L 62, 63 1
Bostian, James M 61 1
Bostian, James M 113 2
Bostian, James W 55 1
Bostian, Jesse A 60, 61 1
Bostian, John 62, 156, 205, 214, 219, 240 1
Bostian, John I 62 1
Bostian, John J 41 1
Bostian, John of A 71 1
Bostian, M Roberta 63 1
Bostian, Martha C 61 1
Bostian, Nellie R 38 1
Bostian, Philip 275 2
Bostian, Samuel G 84 1
Bostian, Sarah A 61 1
Bostian, William 1 1
Bostian, William 275 2
Bostian, Wm 51, 60, 91, 163 1
Bostion, John W 82 1
Bostion, Rebecca 82 1
Boteler, Alice V 26 1
Boteler, Arthur 26, 58 1
Boteler, Augustus L 27, 51 1
Boteler, Basil D 85 1
Boteler, Clingan 40 1
Boteler, Edw 26, 112 1
Boteler, Edw L 40, 51 1
Boteler, Edw L 40 1
Boteler, Elias 57 1
Boteler, Elias W 40 1
Boteler, Elias W 209 3
Boteler, Elizabeth 40 1
Boteler, Elizas W 51 1
Boteler, Ellen 171 2
Boteler, Henry 51, 67, 106, 234, 253, 270 1
Boteler, Henry 29, 144, 171, 181, 229a 2
Boteler, Henry A 51 1
Boteler, Hezekiah 51, 52, 82, 72, 95 1
Boteler, Israel 39 2
Boteler, James 91 1
Boteler, Jefferson O 58 1
Boteler, John E 61 1
Boteler, John M 72, 82 1
Boteler, L H 71 1
Boteler, Laura 51 1
Boteler, Lillie S 67 1
Boteler, Lillie S 112 2
Boteler, Lingan 92, 195 1
Boteler, Lingan 38, 229a, 231 2
Boteler, Lucy J 51 1
Boteler, M L 33 1
Boteler, Margaret 71, 72, 82 1
Boteler, Margaret A 71 1
Boteler, Margaret E 85 1
Boteler, Margaret Elizabeth 73 1
Boteler, Maria Sidney 71 1
Boteler, Mary 71 1
Boteler, Mary Lee 74 1
Boteler, Robert H 82, 95 1
Boteler, Rose Etta 27 1
Boteler, S Margaret 85 1
Boteler, Sarah 67 1
Boteler, Saraha S 27, 84 1
Boteler, Silas 51, 84, 85 1
Boteler, Thomas 67 1
Boteler, Thomas 229a 2
Boteler, W E, Dr 71 1
Boteler, William 231 2
Boteler, William L 92 1
Boteler, Wm 51 1
Boteler, Wm E 71, 91 1
Boteler, Wm E 29 2
Boteler, Wm H 84, 92, 112 1
Boteler, Zachariah B 95 1
Boteler, Zachariah G 84 1
Boteler, Zacharias 271 1
Botler, Lingan 184 3
Botler, Winnie T 92 1
Boub, Henry 235 2
Boucher, Daniel 106 3
Bouic, Robert B H 82 1
Bouldin, Alice 28 1
Bourke, Eleanor 254 1
Bourn, U G 235 1
Bourne, G Dr 172 2
Bourne, U G 18, 65, 75, 154 2
Bourne, U G 91 3
Bourne, U G 146, 275 1
Bourne, U G Dr 192 3
Bourne, U G Dr Jr 28 1
Bourne, U G Sr 214a 2
Bourne, U G Sr, 28, 131 1

Bourne, U G, Dr 97 1
Bourne, U S G 129 3
Bourne, Ulysses G 92 1
Bourne, Ulysses G Sr 259 2
Bousall, Susan R 85 1
Bowden, Lambert 67 1
Bowen, Cyrus 59 1
Bowen, Henrietta 51 1
Bowen, James 59 1
Bowen, John 56 1
Bowen, William A/k/a Brown, Willima 27 1
Bower, Adam 67, 91 1
Bower, C C 262 2
Bower, Christian 51 2
Bower, Daniel 56, 70, 84 1
Bower, David 37 1
Bower, Henry 225 2
Bower, Jacob 56 1
Bower, Joseph 70 1
Bower, L 11 2
Bower, Lawrence 67 1
Bower, Margaret 56 1
Bower, Stephen 70 1
Bower, Susanna 84 1
Bowers, Ada A S 73 1
Bowers, Adam 27 1
Bowers, Adam 14, 54 3
Bowers, Allen S 73 1
Bowers, Andrew P 52 1
Bowers, Anna I 73, 214 1
Bowers, Annie I 28 1
Bowers, Barbara 30 1
Bowers, Barbara A 30 1
Bowers, C C 9 2
Bowers, Charles W 33 1
Bowers, Charles W 283 2
Bowers, Charlotte E 34, 91 1
Bowers, Chester G 48, 76 1
Bowers, Clara Jane 48 1
Bowers, Clarence 34 1
Bowers, Clarence C 48, 82, 230 1
Bowers, D A 72 1
Bowers, D Washington 37 1
Bowers, Daniel 37, 59, 72, 135, 228, 234 1
Bowers, Daniel 11, 101 2
Bowers, Daniel 195 3
Bowers, Daniel A 38 1
Bowers, David 5 2
Bowers, David W 38 1
Bowers, Elizabeth 40 1
Bowers, Elizabeth E 151 2
Bowers, Emily 41 1
Bowers, Emily J 42 1
Bowers, Emma Kate 42 1
Bowers, Flora V 170 2
Bowers, Francis 44 1
Bowers, G E 169 1
Bowers, Geo 23 2
Bowers, Geo O 48 1
Bowers, Geo T 48 1
Bowers, Geo W 34 1
Bowers, George Raymond 48 1
Bowers, George W 48 1
Bowers, Glattice M R 48 1
Bowers, Grayson 214 1
Bowers, Grayson 166 2
Bowers, Grayson E 110 1
Bowers, H W 72 1
Bowers, H W 89 2
Bowers, Harrient L 252 2
Bowers, Harriet L 252 2
Bowers, Harriet M 252 2
Bowers, Harriet W 33 1
Bowers, Harry W 52, 91, 110, 169, 214 1
Bowers, Harry W 15 3
Bowers, Henry 34 1
Bowers, Hilda E 52, 68 1
Bowers, Isaac F 55 1
Bowers, Isaac S 55 1
Bowers, J Edw 91 1
Bowers, J H 27, 159 3
Bowers, J H 37, 59 1
Bowers, Jacob H 34, 60, 67, 265 1
Bowers, Jacob H 19 3
Bowers, James E 42, 229 1
Bowers, John 50 3
Bowers, John H 52, 63, 68 1
Bowers, John H 20, 139 2
Bowers, John S 60, 189 1
Bowers, John V 62 1
Bowers, John W Jr 62 1
Bowers, John William 62 1
Bowers, Jonathan 59 1
Bowers, Joseph E 33 1
Bowers, Laura L 68 1
Bowers, Laura M 34 1
Bowers, Lemuel 170 2
Bowers, Lemuel 67 3
Bowers, Lemuel 230 1
Bowers, Leslie L 42 1
Bowers, Lillian S 190 3
Bowers, Lillian S 198 1
Bowers, Lilly A 67 1
Bowers, Lulu M 188 3
Bowers, Mahlon A 73 1
Bowers, Margaret A 195 3
Bowers, Margaret S 72 1
Bowers, Mary A 71 1
Bowers, Mary L 72 1
Bowers, Michael 71 1
Bowers, Michael B 73 1
Bowers, Milton 52 2
Bowers, Milton D 34 1
Bowers, Nettie G 73, 76 1
Bowers, Paul J 58 3
Bowers, R R 169 1
Bowers, Reuben I 71 1
Bowers, Rosa E 63 1
Bowers, Rosa M 82 1
Bowers, Ruth C 62 1
Bowers, S P 45, 63, 136, 192 1
Bowers, S P 41, 106 2
Bowers, Samuel N 92 1
Bowers, Sherman 193, 198 1
Bowers, Sherman 85 2
Bowers, Sherman 197 3
Bowers, Sherman P 3, 12, 20, 32, 41, 52, 56, 70, 73, 115, 122, 129, 155, 173, 175, 190, 203, 209, 215, 228a, 242, 250, 255, 259, 260, 265, 284 295 2
Bowers, Sherman P 8, 19, 28, 31, 34, 48, 63, 76, 86, 90, 97,107, 113, 127, 136, 145, 148, 153, 177, 192, 198, 220, 223, 231, 235, 240, 257 1
Bowers, Sherman P 3, 10, 11, 16, 21, 28, 33, 35, 45, 46, 48, 51, 58, 73, 87, 96, 152, 190, 192, 102, 206 3
Bowers, W D 214 2
Bowers, William D 19 1
Bowers, Wm 101 2
Bowers, Wm D 15 2
Bowers, Wm D 28, 37, 91 1
Bowers, Wm H 92 1
Bowersock, Chrisitan 32 1
Bowersock, George Adam 32 1
Bowersock, Jacob 32, 47 1
Bowersock, John 47 1
Bowersox, E T 51 1
Bowersox, Emily J 67 1
Bowersox, George 165 3
Bowersox, George 90 1
Bowersox, Henry 8, 165 3
Bowersox, Henry 51 1
Bowersox, Jacob 70 1
Bowersox, John 70 1
Bowersox, Magdalena 70 1
Bowersox, Valentine 90 1
Bowersox, Valentine 165 3
Bowey, Dennis 37 1
Bowey, James Edw 37 1
Bowhan, Elizabeth 48 1
Bowhan, Geo 106 1
Bowhan, Geo W 47 1
Bowhan, George 47. 48 1
Bowhan, Julia H 58 1
Bowhan, S Angeline 58 1
Bowhan, Sarah Angelina 85 1
Bowhan, Thomas J 88 1
Bowie, Calvin 68 1
Bowie, Elizabeth 41 1

Bowie, Grace L 48 1
Bowie, Grover C 48 1
Bowie, Henry 51 1
Bowie, James 41 1
Bowie, Juliet 60 1
Bowie, Nettie E 76 1
Bowie, Richard 82 1
Bowler, James L 63 1
Bowler, Leo J 63, 68 1
Bowler, Leo James 200 1
Bowles, David 184 3
Bowles, Edw 72 2
Bowles, Geo W 26 1
Bowles, George 64 3
Bowlus, Adam 186 3
Bowlus, Adam 32, 100, 125, 164, 197 1
Bowlus, Alta L 28 1
Bowlus, Andrew 26 1
Bowlus, Ann 26, 47 1
Bowlus, Ann C 27 1
Bowlus, Ann S 27 1
Bowlus, Asa 84 1
Bowlus, Asa 15 2
Bowlus, Asa 19 3
Bowlus, Carrie G 32 1
Bowlus, Catherine 32, 34, 56 1
Bowlus, Charles U 34 1
Bowlus, Charlotte S 32 1
Bowlus, Chas N 92 1
Bowlus, Chas U 89 2
Bowlus, Chas W 68 1
Bowlus, D A 32 1
Bowlus, David 106, 129, 176 3
Bowlus, David 37, 47, 91, 125, 257, 263 1
Bowlus, David 1, 26, 137, 181, 237 2
Bowlus, E 271 2
Bowlus, E M 271 2
Bowlus, Edgar 33 1
Bowlus, Edw 111 3
Bowlus, Edw 41, 83, 85, 100, 279 1
Bowlus, Edw 11, 15, 134, 153 2
Bowlus, Edw S 14 2
Bowlus, Edw S 41 1
Bowlus, Edward 19 3
Bowlus, Edward 85 1
Bowlus, Elizabeth 57 1
Bowlus, Emert R 1 1
Bowlus, Emmert R 96, 215 3
Bowlus, Emmert R 3, 178, 200, 227a, 229a 2
Bowlus, Emmert R 24, 34, 86, 241 1
Bowlus, Emory M 65 3
Bowlus, Esther 40 1
Bowlus, Etta M 42 1
Bowlus, Frank L 44 1
Bowlus, Franklin 27 1
Bowlus, Franklin L 22, 44, 51, 230 1
Bowlus, Franklin L 264 2
Bowlus, G Grayson 227a 2
Bowlus, Geo 51, 56, 85, 139, 163, 201, 214, 228, 238 1
Bowlus, Geo 165, 175, 197 2
Bowlus, Geo 53 3
Bowlus, Geo A 89 2
Bowlus, Geo A 68, 92 1
Bowlus, Geo Jr 189 1
Bowlus, Geo W 47 1
Bowlus, Geo W 41 3
Bowlus, George 235 2
Bowlus, George 47, 91, 219 1
Bowlus, George 1 3
Bowlus, George A 28 1
Bowlus, George Jr 37 3
Bowlus, George S 28 1
Bowlus, George Sr 47 1
Bowlus, George W 48 1
Bowlus, Grayson W 48 1
Bowlus, Henry 47 1
Bowlus, Henry 8, 37, 214 3
Bowlus, J 39 2
Bowlus, Jacob 37 1
Bowlus, Jacob 138 2
Bowlus, Jennie 63 1
Bowlus, Jennie E 26 1
Bowlus, John 32, 37, 47, 56, 57, 58, 62, 219, 239, 263 1
Bowlus, John 163 3
Bowlus, John 186 2
Bowlus, John A C 44 1
Bowlus, John A C 144 2
Bowlus, John S 62, 68, 230 1
Bowlus, John S 46 3
Bowlus, John S 167 2
Bowlus, John W 73 1
Bowlus, Jonathan 57 1
Bowlus, Joseph 27, 60 1
Bowlus, Joseph 29, 112 2
Bowlus, Joshiah 84 2
Bowlus, Katie E 227a 2
Bowlus, L H 33, 150 1
Bowlus, L H 205 2
Bowlus, L H 2 3
Bowlus, L Pearce 145 2
Bowlus, L Pearce 27, 83, 102, 109 1
Bowlus, L Pearce 68 3
Bowlus, Lewis H 27, 44, 68, 85 1
Bowlus, Lewis J 41 1
Bowlus, Loretta C 67, 68 1
Bowlus, M C H 91 1
Bowlus, Mahala 71 1
Bowlus, Martha 134 2
Bowlus, Martha A 41 1
Bowlus, Mary 72, 73 1
Bowlus, Mary 134 2
Bowlus, Mary A 213 3
Bowlus, Mary Ann 85, 91 1
Bowlus, Mary E 72 1
Bowlus, Mary Ellen 72 1
Bowlus, Mattie M 171 3
Bowlus, Maurice 73 1
Bowlus, Maurice C H 262 2
Bowlus, Muarice A 73 1
Bowlus, Nicholas 76 1
Bowlus, Noah 84, 104 1
Bowlus, Noah 19, 42 3
Bowlus, Noah 15 2
Bowlus, Ruby May 83 1
Bowlus, S R 51 1
Bowlus, Sallie 32 1
Bowlus, Samuel 143, 267 2
Bowlus, Samuel 27, 67, 76, 84, 86, 131 1
Bowlus, Samuel 1 3
Bowlus, Samuel L 52, 62, 86, 164 1
Bowlus, Sarah 85 1
Bowlus, Sarah Ellen 40 1
Bowlus, Sophia 84, 86 1
Bowlus, Stephen 34 1
Bowlus, Stephen 214 2
Bowlus, Stephen R 26, 84, 249 1
Bowlus, Steven R 15 3
Bowlus, Thos H 47, 85 1
Bowlus, W H 42 3
Bowlus, Walter H 68, 91 1
Bowlus, Wilbur 85 1
Bowlus, Wm 22 2
Bowlus, Wm 91, 169, 219 1
Bowlus, Wm D 171 3
Bowlus, Wm E 92 1
Bowlus, Wm F 41 1
Bowlus, Wm H 26, 91 1
Bowlus, Wm H 186 3
Bowlus, Wm H 144 2
Bowman, Augustus 229 1
Bowman, Charlotte 56 1
Bowman, Daniel 38 1
Bowman, Jacob 56 1
Bowman, James F 57 1
Bowman, John M 167 3
Bowman, Margaret 71 1
Bowman, Robert 82 1
Bowman, S H 91 1
Bowman, William H 40 3
Bowman, Wm 91 1
Bowman, Wm H 91, 171 1
Bowman, Wm H 28 2
Bownsock, Henry 240 1

Bowr, Isaac 80 2
Bowrs, Harriet M 53 1
Bowser, James E 49 2
Bowsticks, Dilly 26 1
Boyd, Andrew 37, 51, 71 1
Boyd, Andrew 70, 100, 106, 120, 185, 186 3
Boyd, Andrew 28, 29 2
Boyd, Belle S 170 2
Boyd, Benjamin 30 1
Boyd, Caroline 26 1
Boyd, David 1, 26, 75, 100, 177 2
Boyd, David 37, 40, 57, 210, 234 1
Boyd, David 70, 81, 185 3
Boyd, Francis 138 2
Boyd, H B 170 2
Boyd, Hamilton 37 1
Boyd, John 51 1
Boyd, John 49 2
Boyd, John H 63 1
Boyd, John J 185 3
Boyd, Mary 71 1
Boyd, Melvin P 277 1
Boyd, Nelson 70 3
Boyd, Ruth 170 2
Boyd, William H A 197 3
Boyd, Wm R 51 1
Boyden, Ella W 42 1
Boyden, Peter M 26 1
Boyer, Adam 32 3
Boyer, Adam 30, 51 2
Boyer, Adam 27, 32, 79 1
Boyer, Addie A 33 1
Boyer, Albert A 34, 62, 78 1
Boyer, Albert A 294 2
Boyer, Albert H 27 1
Boyer, Ann Mary 26 1
Boyer, Basil E 41 1
Boyer, Benjamin F 30 1
Boyer, Catherine 32 1
Boyer, Catherine A 33, 79 1
Boyer, Charles S 34 1
Boyer, Chas W 34 1
Boyer, Christiana 32 1
Boyer, Clara H 61 1
Boyer, Clara Z 42 1
Boyer, Columbus W 33 1
Boyer, Cora H 30 1
Boyer, Daniel 32, 37, 42, 53 1
Boyer, Daniel 186 3
Boyer, Eldridge C 52, 68, 222 1
Boyer, Eliza M 59 1
Boyer, Elizabeth A 41, 48 1
Boyer, Ella V 42 1
Boyer, Emory E 62, 72 1
Boyer, Foster A 45 1
Boyer, Geo 163 2
Boyer, Geo L 48 1
Boyer, Grace M 12, 161 3
Boyer, Greenbury 48, 165 1
Boyer, H H 42, 60 3
Boyer, Hanson 52 1
Boyer, Helen 21 1
Boyer, Helen S 52, 86, 92, 93 1
Boyer, Henry 30 2
Boyer, Henry 27 1
Boyer, Henry H 53, 55, 273 1
Boyer, Henry L 51 1
Boyer, Herman A 27 1
Boyer, Isabella R 42, 55 1
Boyer, Isabelle R 32 3
Boyer, J Russell 16 2
Boyer, J T 60 1
Boyer, James 33, 70, 79 1
Boyer, James A 61, 79 1
Boyer, James D 62 1
Boyer, John C 65 3
Boyer, John C 61 1
Boyer, John H 12, 24, 65, 161 3
Boyer, John H 62, 83 1
Boyer, John L 84 1
Boyer, John Mrs 61 1
Boyer, John R 60 1
Boyer, John W H 61, 62 1
Boyer, Jonathan 58 1
Boyer, Laten H 71, 84 1
Boyer, Latin H 37 1
Boyer, Laura J 93 1
Boyer, Laura P 62 1
Boyer, Leonard C 42 1
Boyer, Leslie S 61, 68 1
Boyer, Leslie W 52, 92 1
Boyer, Lester W 73, 210 1
Boyer, Lewis 219 3
Boyer, Malinda 70 1
Boyer, Martha M 72 1
Boyer, Mary 33 1
Boyer, Mary J R 70, 73 1
Boyer, Mary M 71 1
Boyer, Mary M V 71 1
Boyer, Michael 100 3
Boyer, Michael 72, 142 1
Boyer, Missouri 71 1
Boyer, N Gertrude 21 1
Boyer, Nicholas 71 1
Boyer, Norman D 259 2
Boyer, Oliver 76, 78 1
Boyer, Paul W 26 1
Boyer, Peter 7, 19, 80, 169, 247 2
Boyer, Peter 32, 37, 42, 78, 79, 177 1
Boyer, Peter 209 3
Boyer, Rachel 51 1
Boyer, Ralph W 83 1
Boyer, Rebecca A 210 1
Boyer, Robert D 93 1
Boyer, Robert L 83 1
Boyer, Roy L 45 1
Boyer, Salome Lee 84 1
Boyer, Samuel 84, 86 1
Boyer, Samuel L 37 1
Boyer, Silas C 84, 85 1
Boyer, Solomon 78 1
Boyer, Solomon 137 2
Boyer, W E 78 1
Boyer, W Ernest 21 1
Boyer, William B 53, 86, 273 1
Boyer, William E 34, 93 1
Boyer, William E 27 3
Boyer, Willis 27, 55, 61, 79, 93, 192 1
Boyer, Wm E 33, 34, 92 1
Boyer, Wm Ernest 27 1
Boyer, Wm H 92 1
Boyle, Cordelia D 33 1
Boyle, Daniel 37, 56, 82 1
Boyle, Elizabeth 79 1
Boyle, Harry S 32 3
Boyle, Henry 67 2
Boyle, Henry 32 3
Boyle, Henry S 33 1
Boyle, J Brooke Sr 63 1
Boyle, John 67, 137 2
Boyle, John & 203 2
Boyle, John B 37 1
Boyle, John Brooke 62 1
Boyle, John D 33 1
Boyle, Lenore O 63 1
Boyle, Peter 79 1
Boyle, Peter 37 3
Boyle, Sarah 84 1
Boyley, Elizabeth 154 2
Boyley, John 57 1
Boyley, May M 140 1
Bradford, Jane 91 1
Bradford, Martha 73 1
Bradford, Wm 76 1
Bradlee, Newton 76, 91 1
Bradley, B J 199 2
Bradley, B J 30 1
Bradley, Bernard J 62, 217 1
Bradley, Patrick 78 1
Bradley, Patrick 282 2
Bradley, Wm 197 2
Bradsaw, F L 82 1
Bradshaw, Austin L 34 1
Bradshaw, Charles W 34 1
Bradshaw, Earl S 34 1
Bradshaw, G W 82 1
Bradshear, Osborn 78 1
Brady, Anne Eliza 138 2
Brady, David 106 3

Brady, Eliza 59 1
Brady, Geo 91 3
Brady, Geo A 113 2
Brady, George A 118 3
Brady, Jacob 59, 60 1
Brady, James 58 1
Brady, Maggie 234 2
Brady, Medora [?] 192 1
Brady, Richard 82 1
Brady, Robert W 84 1
Brady, Susan 84 1
Bragonier, Jacob 59 1
Brahsear, George T[?] 30 1
Brandan, C August H 32 1
Brandan, Helena 32 1
Brandan, Wm A 52 1
Brandeburg, J Robert 62 1
Brandeburg, Lemuel 195 3
Brandenberg, C U 85 1
Brandenburg, A R 92 1
Brandenburg, Alice 27 1
Brandenburg, Alvey 245 1
Brandenburg, Amos 27 1
Brandenburg, Amos W 79 1
Brandenburg, Andrew J 28 1
Brandenburg, Barbara 30 1
Brandenburg, Barbara C 30 1
Brandenburg, Bradley J 31, 60 1
Brandenburg, C W 87 3
Brandenburg, Catherine 48 1
Brandenburg, Charlotte 33 1
Brandenburg, Chas 27 1
Brandenburg, D 112 1
Brandenburg, Daniel 38, 55 1
Brandenburg, Daniel 264 2
Brandenburg, E 198 2
Brandenburg, Eli 41, 51 1
Brandenburg, Eli 186 3
Brandenburg, Eli 264 2
Brandenburg, Elmer 228a 2
Brandenburg, Emma D 72 1
Brandenburg, Estella 245 1
Brandenburg, Ethel E 41 1
Brandenburg, Ezra 67, 254 1
Brandenburg, Frederick 44, 70 1
Brandenburg, G Floyd 33 1
Brandenburg, G M 48, 60, 67 1
Brandenburg, G N 110 2
Brandenburg, Garrison M 55 1
Brandenburg, Geo K 72 1
Brandenburg, Geo W 41 1
Brandenburg, Geo W 113 2
Brandenburg, H L 30 1
Brandenburg, Henry 51, 52 1
Brandenburg, Ida A 55 1
Brandenburg, Isaac 176, 213, 217 3
Brandenburg, Isaac 55, 63 1
Brandenburg, J Roger 63 1
Brandenburg, Jacob 33 1
Brandenburg, Jesse 57, 58, 60, 67 1
Brandenburg, Joel 59 1
Brandenburg, John 287 2
Brandenburg, John 54 3
Brandenburg, John 51 1
Brandenburg, John A 84 1
Brandenburg, John D 61 1
Brandenburg, John N 13 1
Brandenburg, John N 81 3
Brandenburg, John W 63 1
Brandenburg, John W 52 2
Brandenburg, Joseph H 62 1
Brandenburg, Lemuel 67 1
Brandenburg, Lewis H 85 1
Brandenburg, Lloyd R 52 1
Brandenburg, Lydia A 67 1
Brandenburg, M G 91 1
Brandenburg, Margaret E 41 1
Brandenburg, Marion G 41 1
Brandenburg, Martin R 72 1
Brandenburg, Mary 71 1
Brandenburg, Matthias 70, 85 1
Brandenburg, Maurice 38, 67 1
Brandenburg, Melissa 55, 59 1
Brandenburg, Nicie 31 1
Brandenburg, Peter 79 1
Brandenburg, Raymond R 28 1
Brandenburg, Samuel 81 3
Brandenburg, Samuel 58, 71, 73, 84, 85 1
Brandenburg, Samuel C 65 2
Brandenburg, Samuel E 84, 86, 92 1
Brandenburg, Samuel T 86 1
Brandenburg, Stewart J 166 1
Brandenburg, Susanna C 85 1
Brandenburg, Virginia B M 107 1
Brandenburg, Walter L 86 1
Brandenburg, William H 61 1
Brandenburg, Wilmer H 86 1
Brandenburg, Wm 57 1
Brandenurg, B J 48 1
Brandon, Helena 52 1
Brandt, G Milton 33 1
Brandt, Hallie 24 3
Brandt, Hallie M 93 1
Brandt, Wm B 93 1
Brane, Chas M 33 1
Brane, John 177 1
Brane, Sarah E 33 1
Brane, Sarah E 57 3
Brane, Sarah F 86 1
Braner, Lizzie 68 1
Brangle, Mary 62 1
Brant, Christian 32 1
Brant, Wm 91 1
Brantner, J T 23 2
Brantner, Z T 49, 280 2
Brantner, Z T 233 1
Brantner, Z T 166 3
Brantner, Zacharia T 282 1
Branwer, Wm 91 1
Brashear, Ambrose L 30 1
Brashear, Ann D 27 1
Brashear, Bessie M 30 1
Brashear, C T 27 1
Brashear, Christian 139 1
Brashear, Cornelius 78 1
Brashear, Eli 40 1
Brashear, H A 78 2
Brashear, Harry A 20 2
Brashear, J J 27 1
Brashear, J W 26 1
Brashear, Leonard E 68 1
Brashear, Lillie M 68 1
Brashear, Mary 70 1
Brashear, Owen D 82 1
Brashear, Richard 82 1
Brashear, Richard J 78 1
Brashear, Thomas C 26 1
Brashears, Ann 30, 88 1
Brashears, Belt 30, 70 1
Brashears, Belt D 30 1
Brashears, Fanny M 44 1
Brashears, John H 59 1
Brashears, Norman E 102 1
Brashears, Thomas C 26, 30 1
Brashears, Thomas E 30, 110 1
Brasher, Mary Jane 72 1
Braun, Elsie 44 1
Braun, Frederick A 44 1
Brawner, Edw 40 1
Brawner, Elizabeth 40 1
Brawner, George 91 1
Brawner, Henry 40 1
Brawner, Ignatius 40, 51 1
Brawner, Ignatius 282 2
Brawner, J B 119 1
Brawner, James 79 1
Brawner, James M 60, 91 1
Brawner, John B 55 3
Brawner, John B 32, 91 1
Brawner, Joseph 60, 62 1
Brawner, Mary 70, 71 1
Brawner, Rebecca 70 1
Brawner, William 40 1
Brawner, Wm 40, 91 1
Brawner, Wm 84 2
Breachner, Alexander 26 1
Breachner, Anthony 26 1
Bready, Annie E 27 1
Bready, David 47, 56, 176 1
Bready, David F S 27 1
Bready, E T 72 1

Bready, Eleven Tobias 42 1
Bready, Geo A 122 3
Bready, George 47 1
Bready, Guy P 42, 72 1
Bready, Jacob 147 1
Bready, John 56 1
Bready, Luther Roy 76 1
Bready, Mary T 72 1
Bready, Nannie C 76 1
Brean, John 81 3
Breckenridge, Alberta C 67 1
Breckenridge, Lemuel 67 1
Breckenridge, Martha 70, 82 1
Breckenridge, Robert 82 1
Breckenridge, Roger D 67 1
Breckenridge, William 70 1
Breckenridge, Wm 82 1
Breedon, Lester V 68 1
Breedon, Loma Katherine 68 1
Breighner, Daniel 38 1
Breighner, Nettie 76 1
Brein, Luke T 67 1
Brenaman, Cora L 92 1
Brenaman, Wm C 27 1
Brendle, Alice S 222 3
Brengle, Alexander 67, 92, 125 1
Brengle, Alexander 220 2
Brengle, Alexander 26 1
Brengle, Alexander 54 3
Brengle, Alfred F 165 2
Brengle, Alfred F 57, 67, 71 1
Brengle, Amelia Ann 26 1
Brengle, Annie 27 1
Brengle, Caroline 91 3
Brengle, Caroline 258 2
Brengle, Caroline E 32 1
Brengle, Christian 184 3
Brengle, Christian 44, 51, 163 1
Brengle, Christian 84 2
Brengle, Clarence E 137 1
Brengle, D M 37 1
Brengle, Daniel 37, 67, 225 1
Brengle, David 27 1
Brengle, David M 37, 38 1
Brengle, Eliza 40 1
Brengle, Elizabeth 41, 48 1
Brengle, Emma V 42 1
Brengle, Ezra 138 2
Brengle, Ezra M 41 1
Brengle, Ezra M 67 3
Brengle, Fanny C 27 1
Brengle, Florence J 221 3
Brengle, Francis 44, 79, 137 1
Brengle, Francis 22 2
Brengle, Frank E 32 2
Brengle, Geo L 47, 146 1
Brengle, Geo W 48 1
Brengle, George 47 1
Brengle, George Elmer 189 3
Brengle, J 287 2
Brengle, J L 57 1
Brengle, Jacob 18, 122 3
Brengle, Jacob 59, 79, 116, 125, 139, 225 1
Brengle, Jacob 245 2
Brengle, James J 41 1
Brengle, James S 56 1
Brengle, John 41, 57, 67 1
Brengle, John 87, 132 2
Brengle, John 38, 221, 222 3
Brengle, John N 44, 139 1
Brengle, John N 176 3
Brengle, John W 61, 92 1
Brengle, John W 119, 258 2
Brengle, L J 125, 194 1
Brengle, L J 14 2
Brengle, L J 113 3
Brengle, Laura E 67 1
Brengle, Lawrence 137 2
Brengle, Lawrence 39 3
Brengle, Lawrence I 37 1
Brengle, Lawrence J 113, 222 3
Brengle, Lawrence J 37, 40, 47, 57 1
Brengle, Lewis A 47, 67, 125 1
Brengle, Lewis A Jr 67 1
Brengle, M 287 2
Brengle, Margaret J L 27 1
Brengle, Maria 44, 71, 92 1
Brengle, Mary 71, 72, 76 1
Brengle, Mary C 71 1
Brengle, Mary M 26 1
Brengle, Nicholas 37, 42, 56, 57, 76, 79 1
Brengle, Nicholas 222 3
Brengle, Nicholas 29, 96, 128, 229a 2
Brengle, Peter 163 3
Brengle, Peter 61, 139, 159, 163, 189, 191 1
Brengle, Peter 84, 92 2
Brengle, Robert 82, 196 1
Brengle, Robert 91 3
Brengle, Robt 44 1
Brengle, Samuel B 42 1
Brengle, Virginia 91 3
Brengle, William 19 3
Brengle, Wm D 72 1
Brengle, Wm H 92 1
Brenneisen, Frank P 44 1
Brenner, Charles F 19 1
Brenner, Isaac 191 1
Brenner, Jesse Iet al 21 3
Brenner, Josephine 19 1
Brenner, Lewis 50 3
Brenner, W M I 188 3
Brenner, Wm 91 1
Bressler, H Bond 51, 58 3
Brien, Ann 27 1
Brien, Henry A 57 1
Brien, John 57 1
Brien, John 165, 186, 214 2
Brien, Robert C 81 3
Briggs, Edgar 119 2
Briggs, G D 119 2
Briggs, Mary C 72 1
Briggs, R B 119 2
Brighner, Joseph I 38 1
Bright, Edwin D Rev 31 1
Bright, Robert S 83 1
Brighton, Eliza 42 1
Brighton, Marie 42 1
Brightwell, Carl P 34 1
Brightwell, Margaret E 73, 85 1
Brightwell, Susannah 84 1
Brightwell, W H 159 2
Brightwell, Wm H 85, 92 1
Brightwell, Wm M 92 1
Brimmerman, Frederick W 91 3
Brinebrink, Henry 218a 2
Brining[?], Ernest R 282 1
Briscoe, George W 160 3
Briscoe, John 57 1
Briscoe, Mary 71 1
Briscoe, Sallie 84 1
Brish, Adam 159 2
Brish, Barbara 30 1
Brish, Daniel 113 2
Brish, Devilla C 224 3
Brish, Devillo C 74 1
Brish, Harriet 51 1
Brish, Henry 32 1
Brish, Henry 18 3
Brish, Henry C 51, 76 1
Brish, Henry H 224 3
Brish, John 163 1
Brish, John 35 2
Brish, John 51 1
Brish, John M 207 3
Brish, John M 57, 116, 163 1
Brish, Margaret S 165 3
Brish, Margaret S 91 1
Brish, Minnie H 74 1
Brish, Murray 91 1
Brish, Murray 22 2
Brish, Wm H 91 1
Brislin, Michael 70 1
British, John M 14 2
Britner, Isabella J 61 1
Britner, Joseph N 61 1
Brittain, Elizabeth R 53 1

Brittain, Harry L 33 1
Broadrup, Charles 53, 71 1
Broadrup, Charles 18, 31 3
Broadrup, Chas 110, 171, 194 1
Broadrup, Chas 31 3
Broadrup, Mary E 33 1
Broadrup, S M 71 1
Brockee, Ignatius 55 1
Brockley, Bruce W 42 1
Brockley, Elizabeth 42 1
Bromer, Isaac 8 1
Brometts, Michael 71, 91 1
Bromett, Michael 129 3
Bromett, Michael 57, 159 2
Bromwell, Frances R R 44 1
Bromwell, John H 60 1
Bromwell, Louisa E 30, 60 1
Brooke, Basil 56, 67, 82 1
Brooke, Clotilda 32 1
Brooke, George R 56 1
Brooke, Jane 82, 86 1
Brooke, John R 70 1
Brooke, John Thompson 82 1
Brooke, Mary A 70 1
Brooke, Mary Ann 82 1
Brooke, Raphael 82, 84 1
Brooke, Richard 91 3
Brooke, Richard 82 1
Brooke, Robert 89 2
Brooke, Roger 82 1
Brooke, Roger C 82 1
Brooke, Samuel B 84 1
Brooke, Samuel W 86 1
Brooke, T 222 2
Brookey, Albert H 79 1
Brookey, Anna G 254 1
Brookey, Annie 88 1
Brookey, Annie V 28 1
Brookey, Ellen V 42, 79 1
Brookey, Peter 71, 79 1
Brookey, Theodore 88, 165 1
Brookover, Thomas 88 1
Brookover, Wm 88 1
Brooks, Basil 253 1
Brooks, C S 235 1
Brooks, Catherine J 34 1
Brooks, Charles H 33 1
Brooks, Chas S 41 1
Brooks, Chas S 129 3
Brooks, Edna Elizabeth 172 2
Brooks, Ella S 60, 68 1
Brooks, Eugenia 41 1
Brooks, Homer C 76 1
Brooks, James W 60 1
Brooks, John L 60, 73 1
Brooks, John R 41 1
Brooks, Julia E 61 1
Brooks, Lottie 68 1
Brooks, Maria 33, 73 1
Brooks, Nathaniel 76 1
Brooks, Noah S 76 1
Brooks, O W 195 3
Brosius, C T Jr 272 1
Brosius, Chares J, Jr 34 1
Brosius, Genevive D 34 1
Brosius, J W 40 2
Brosius, John 72 2
Brosius, John W 106 3
Brosius, John W 91 1
Brosius, John William Jr 63 1
Brosius, John Wm, Sr 63 1
Brosius, Louise Davis 63 1
Brosius, Margaret M A 70 1
Brotherton, Jeannette 97 1
Brough, Maria C 71 1
Brower, Emmanuel 40 1
Brower, Emmanuel Jr 40 1
Brower, Emmanuel Sr 40 1
Brower, Isaac 51, 55 1
Brower, Isaac 247 2
Brower, Issac 160 3
Brower, Jacob 139 1
Brown, A M 212 3
Brown, A S 31, 49, 70, 172, 209 2
Brown, A S 13, 85, 111, 126, 183 1
Brown, Adam 26, 266 1
Brown, Albert 182, 222a 2
Brown, Albert J 28 1
Brown, Albert Marion 27, 90 1
Brown, Albert S 27, 28, 85 1
Brown, Albert S 56, 141 3
Brown, Albert S 25, 116, 125, 131, 206 2
Brown, Alexander H 40, 153 1
Brown, Alfred 67 1
Brown, Alfred 188 3
Brown, Amelia P K 27 1
Brown, Andrew J 27, 28 1
Brown, Anna Mae 83 1
Brown, Anna V 28 1
Brown, Annie M 56 3
Brown, Anthony 39 2
Brown, Arthur T 28 1
Brown, B P 91 1
Brown, Benjamin 30 1
Brown, Benjamin F 30, 90, 96 1
Brown, Bernice M 68 1
Brown, Bessie M 34 1
Brown, Bridget Teresa 30 1
Brown, C H 40 2
Brown, C H 52 1
Brown, C S 139 2
Brown, Caroline 33 1
Brown, Caroline Eliza 35 1
Brown, Catherine 57 1
Brown, Charles A 34 1
Brown, Charles H 34 1
Brown, Chas 30 1
Brown, Chas 182 2
Brown, Chas A 2 2
Brown, Chas H 61 1
Brown, Clara E 85 1
Brown, Clara M 85, 90 1
Brown, Clarissa 32 1
Brown, Claude H 35, 63 1
Brown, Clifford H 62 1
Brown, Cyrus R 37 1
Brown, Daisy F 91 3
Brown, Daniel 37, 38, 41 1
Brown, David 47, 57 1
Brown, Dorsey 91 1
Brown, E H 229 1
Brown, E L 225 1
Brown, E Lincoln 209 3
Brown, E Peyton 42 1
Brown, Eleanor S 25 2
Brown, Eli 40 1
Brown, Elizabeth 41, 240 1
Brown, Elizabeth D 40 1
Brown, Elizabeth J 41 1
Brown, Ellen A 41 1
Brown, Ellen R 62 1
Brown, Emma M 52 1
Brown, Emma P 28 1
Brown, Emma Pope 42 1
Brown, Etta 30 1
Brown, Evelyn R 274 2
Brown, Ezra 41 1
Brown, Florence I 227a 2
Brown, Francis L 44 1
Brown, Frank F 44 1
Brown, Frederick 44 1
Brown, Frederick H 45 1
Brown, Geo & Thomas 88 1
Brown, Geo J 91 1
Brown, Geo W 37 1
Brown, George A 47 1
Brown, George W 85 1
Brown, Grafton Lee 202 3
Brown, Harry 52 1
Brown, Helen S 51 1
Brown, Henry 167, 171, 205 3
Brown, Henry 51, 52, 57, 93 1
Brown, Henry C 53, 234 1
Brown, Herman M 83 1
Brown, Hezekiah P 41 1
Brown, Ignatius 55, 58, 71, 88 1
Brown, Ignatius 264 2
Brown, Irving W 55 1
Brown, Isaac 143 3
Brown, Isaac 57, 275 2
Brown, J 60 1
Brown, J B 19 2
Brown, J L 79 1

Brown, Jacob 258 2
Brown, Jacob 84, 144 1
Brown, James 67 1
Brown, James A 41, 52, 72 1
Brown, James D 61 1
Brown, James E 62, 90 1
Brown, James H 59 1
Brown, James Peter 59 1
Brown, Jennie 61, 62 1
Brown, Jennie 264 2
Brown, Jeremiah 34, 67 1
Brown, Jesse J 82, 205 1
Brown, Jesse W 28, 62 1
Brown, Jessie W Jr 172 1
Brown, Joel 55 1
Brown, John 57, 62, 79 1
Brown, John 163, 179 3
Brown, John H 167, 188 3
Brown, John H 61, 63, 67, 72, 91 1
Brown, John L 58 1
Brown, John of W 58 1
Brown, John W 41 1
Brown, Joseph 59, 61, 71, 91, 156, 159 1
Brown, Joseph 31, 70 3
Brown, Joseph 39, 51, 138, 214, 258, 264 2
Brown, Joseph A 6 1
Brown, Joseph B 57, 61 1
Brown, Joseph T 179 3
Brown, Joshua 59, 61 1
Brown, Julia M 52 1
Brown, Laura R 68 1
Brown, Lenious J 37 1
Brown, Levi 67, 68 1
Brown, Lewis W 86 1
Brown, Lottie M 42 1
Brown, Lydia Keith 82 1
Brown, Magdalena 70 1
Brown, Mahalia 26 1
Brown, Malinda 58 1
Brown, Margaret 60, 71 1
Brown, Margaret (col'd) 73 1
Brown, Margaret A 92 1
Brown, Martha C 37 1
Brown, Martin L 33, 51, 73 1
Brown, Mary 71, 72, 91 1
Brown, Mary A 28 1
Brown, Mary Alice 73 1
Brown, Mary C 39 2
Brown, Mary C (col'd) 71 1
Brown, Mary Evelyn 163 2
Brown, Mary Jeanette 72 1
Brown, Matthew 70 1
Brown, Matthew 80 2
Brown, May Etta 65, 75 2
Brown, Myrtle M 68 1
Brown, N H 165 3
Brown, Nettie J 34 1
Brown, Nettie L 61 1
Brown, Newton L 67 2
Brown, Nicholas 234 1
Brown, Nicholas 37 3
Brown, Oscar F 28 3
Brown, Pauline A 294 2
Brown, Pauline A 55 1
Brown, Peter 79, 84 1
Brown, Peter 11 2
Brown, Peter H 87, 217a 2
Brown, Peter H 70 1
Brown, Peter W 79 1
Brown, R 1 2
Brown, Ralph M 28 1
Brown, Raymond George 83 1
Brown, Richard B 35 1
Brown, Robert H 63, 82 1
Brown, Rosa E 28 1
Brown, Roscoe P 34, 82, 92 1
Brown, Roscoe P 224a 2
Brown, Rose C 79 1
Brown, Russell N 52 1
Brown, S Elmer 45, 160 3
Brown, S Elmer 82, 85 1
Brown, S Elmer 35, 265 2
Brown, S Elmer of W 92 1
Brown, Samuel 35, 258 2
Brown, Samuel E 201 1
Brown, Samuel H 62 1
Brown, Samuel H 129 3
Brown, Samuel M 148 3
Brown, Samuel W 85, 86 1
Brown, Sarah A 85, 86 1
Brown, Sarah E 27 1
Brown, Sarah J 85 1
Brown, Sophia 82 1
Brown, Stewart Hobbs 140 2
Brown, Stewart Hobbs 4, 210 3
Brown, Susan R 44 1
Brown, Susanna 84 1
Brown, Thomas 88, 112 1
Brown, Upton B 90 1
Brown, Victor 28 1
Brown, Vitus Viola 90 1
Brown, W H 52, 92 1
Brown, W T 92 1
Brown, Washington 75 2
Brown, Wilbur 91 1
Brown, William 55 1
Brown, William T 91 1
Brown, Wm 92, 93, 112, 156, 253 1
Brown, Wm 22, 58 2
Brown, Wm 53 3
Brown, Wm A 47 1
Brown, Wm B 91, 92 1
Brown, Wm D 57 1
Brown, Wm F 41 1
Brown, Wm H 51, 71, 92 1
Brown, Wm H 89, 210 3
Brown, Wm J 91 3
Brown, Wm O 92 1
Brown, Wm Sr 91 1
Brown, Wm T 201 1
Brown, Zilpha E 186 1
Browner, John D 230 1
Browning, A D 177 1
Browning, Addie 27 1
Browning, Amanda M 61, 82 1
Browning, Avery 82 1
Browning, Charles E 33 3
Browning, D M 72 1
Browning, Daniel M 60 1
Browning, Eunice M 154 2
Browning, F D 154 2
Browning, Ferdinand D 160 2
Browning, H M 67 1
Browning, J 192 3
Browning, J M 67 1
Browning, J Thomas 57 1
Browning, J Thos 203 2
Browning, Jeremiah 61, 82, 196 1
Browning, John W 58 1
Browning, Jonathan 58, 60 1
Browning, Jonathan 160 3
Browning, Jonathan of A 58 1
Browning, Jonothan 6 3
Browning, Lindsay L 28 1
Browning, Lindsay L 83 3
Browning, Luther H H 67 1
Browning, Lynn 27 1
Browning, Maria 60 1
Browning, Mary A 71, 72 1
Browning, Ralph 82, 166 1
Browning, Ralph 44 3
Browning, Reverdy 27, 61 1
Browning, Richard 82 1
Browning, Richard 110 2
Browning, Samuel H 84 2
Browning, Wm 91 1
Brrick, E Ruth 33 3
Brubaker, Francis A 44 1
Brubaker, Luther R 44 1
Brubaker, Wm A 44 1
Bruce, Alice K 106 2
Bruce, Emma L 42 1
Bruce, F D 22 1
Bruce, Frederick D 283 2
Bruce, Frederick D 72, 82 3
Bruce, Frederick D 42, 83 1
Bruce, Harry 51 1
Bruce, Harry C 42 1
Bruce, Henry 52 1
Bruce, R T 82 3
Bruce, Rachel 42 1
Bruce, Richard T 51, 83 1

Bruchey, Betty L 63 1
Bruchey, Charles E 73 1
Bruchey, Chas E 48 1
Bruchey, Chas Edgar 44 1
Bruchey, Edw Eli 192 3
Bruchey, Ethel M 48 1
Bruchey, Fannie A 44 1
Bruchey, Geo W 48 1
Bruchey, Georgiana F 48 1
Bruchey, Harry C 11 3
Bruchey, Ira C 48 1
Bruchey, James 84 1
Bruchey, John M 63 1
Bruchey, Joseph 59 1
Bruchey, Minnie R 73 1
Bruchey, Norma E 178, 215 2
Bruchey, Norma E 166 1
Bruchey, Viola 90 1
Bruckey, Adam D 28 1
Bruckey, Fannie A 44 1
Bruestle, Bertram G 93 1
Bruestle, Mildred B 93 1
Brum, Peter 184 3
Bruner, Catherine M 91 1
Bruner, Elizabeth C 42 1
Bruner, Emanuel 41 1
Bruner, Geo 239 1
Bruner, Geo W 48 1
Bruner, James 152 1
Bruner, James H 72 1
Bruner, James M 42 1
Bruner, Jeanette C 63 1
Bruner, John H 59 1
Bruner, John H 71 3
Bruner, John R 72 1
Bruner, John W 63 1
Bruner, Lewis 71 3
Bruner, Margaret A 72 1
Bruner, Mary Ellen 48 1
Bruner, V 196 3
Bruner, Val S 111 3
Bruner, Valentine 113 3
Bruner, Virginia 72, 73 1
Bruner, Wm 91 1
Brunner Ann Rebecca Sophia 27 1
Brunner, Allen L 28 1
Brunner, Ann S 55 1
Brunner, Ann Sophia 26 1
Brunner, Anna S 27 1
Brunner, Annie R 28 1
Brunner, Barbara 30 1
Brunner, Benjamin 137 2
Brunner, Benjamin 30, 32, 56 1
Brunner, Catherine 26, 56 1
Brunner, Edw A 27, 32, 41, 79 1
Brunner, Elias Jr 40 1
Brunner, Elias Jr 31 3
Brunner, Elizabeth 41, 56, 59 1
Brunner, Ezra 40 1
Brunner, Frances 102 2
Brunner, Frances M 28 1
Brunner, Frances M 87 2
Brunner, Francis M 44, 93 1
Brunner, Geo H 79 1
Brunner, Grayson E 41 1
Brunner, H 51 1
Brunner, Henry 32, 51, 55 1
Brunner, Henry 31, 41 3
Brunner, Isaac 52, 55 1
Brunner, Issac 195 3
Brunner, J 57, 184 2
Brunner, J 56 1
Brunner, Jacob 56, 57, 263 1
Brunner, Jacob 1, 46 2
Brunner, Jacob of J 56 1
Brunner, Jacob of John 4 1
Brunner, James 7, 19, 28, 46, 67, 198, 225, 212a, 249 2
Brunner, James 39 3
Brunner, James 32, 37, 56, 57, 58, 59, 164 1
Brunner, Jasper L 227a 2
Brunner, John 56, 152, 156, 205, 210, 253, 260 1
Brunner, John 26, 27, 87, 92 2
Brunner, John 219, 222 3
Brunner, John H 60 1
Brunner, John H 1 2
Brunner, John J 56 1
Brunner, John Jr 60, 260 1
Brunner, John Jr of J 56 1
Brunner, John of H 13 1
Brunner, John of J 57, 184 2
Brunner, John of J 47, 51, 56, 57 1
Brunner, John of J B 51, 84 1
Brunner, John of Jacob 51 1
Brunner, John of S 56, 84 1
Brunner, John R 41 1
Brunner, John Sr 32 1
Brunner, John W 182 3
Brunner, Jonathan 57, 58 1
Brunner, Jonothan 14 3
Brunner, Joshua 59, 60 1
Brunner, Joshua 195 3
Brunner, Josiah 187 3
Brunner, Lewis 234, 271 1
Brunner, Lewis 38, 144, 159, 254 2
Brunner, Lewis 15, 40 3
Brunner, Louis 1, 14 2
Brunner, Maggie W 60 1
Brunner, Margaret J 52 1
Brunner, Margaret M 59, 72 1
Brunner, Mary E 71, 90 1
Brunner, Milton O 73 1
Brunner, Peter 79 1
Brunner, Sophia 79, 84 1
Brunner, Stephen 56 1
Brunner, Susanna 84 1
Brunner, Susannah 85 1
Brunner, Theodore S 88 1
Brunner, V 179 3
Brunner, V J 176 1
Brunner, V S 165 3
Brunner, V S 41, 193 1
Brunner, V S 205 2
Brunner, Val 35 2
Brunner, Val F 8 2
Brunner, Val S 40, 207 1
Brunner, Valentine 40, 56, 57, 90, 140 1
Brunner, Valentine 18, 87, 185, 246 2
Brunner, Valentine 18, 222 3
Brunner, Valentine J 1 2
Brunner, Valentine J 57, 116 1
Brunner, Valentine J of J 51 1
Brunner, Valentine of J B 51,56 1
Brunner, Valentine S 57, 85, 90, 91, 118 1
Brunner, Valentine S 31 3
Brunner, Valentine S 169, 280 2
Brunner, Virginia 90 1
Brunner, Virginia 75 2
Brunner, Wm 163 1
Brunnet, John 37 3
Brust, A T 67 2
Brust, August F 28 1
Brust, August T 28 1
Brust, Augustus 18 1
Brust, Casper 33 1
Brust, Charles L 33 1
Brust, George 48 1
Brust, Georgiana 48 1
Brust, Guy V 265 2
Brust, Myrtle Eliz 129 3
Brust, Priscella C 33 1
Brust, Priscilla C 79 1
Brust, Sarah 33 1
Brust, Wm S 79 3
Brutner, Z T & 155 3
Bryan, John 213 2
Buch, Amelia C T M 27 1
Buch, Edmond C 27, 30 1
Buch, Eugene W 30 1
Buch, Frank W 27 1
Buch, Justin 27 1
Buch, Minnie H 30 1
Buchaman, Edna J 280 2
Buchanan, John 57 1
Bucher, Catherine 32 1
Bucher, Elizabeth 32 1

Bucher, Henry 1 3
Bucher, Nicholas 70 3
Buchheimer, Catherine L 92 1
Buchheimer, Mary A 92 1
Buchheimer, Wm H 92 1
Buchie, Joseph 91 1
Buchman, Frederick 26 3
Buck, James 91 1
Buck, Wm 32 1
Bucker, Mary 137 2
Buckey, Charlotte 32, 91 1
Buckey, D E 222 2
Buckey, D H 38, 42, 48, 68, 82, 92, 120, 144, 169, 189, 200, 235, 240, 244, 245, 254 1
Buckey, D P 15, 20, 31, 35, 47, 116, 189, 209, 215, 222, 222a, 228a 2
Buckey, D P 3, 6, 28, 57, 68, 72, 75, 82, 151, 172, 188, 203, 216 3
Buckey, D P 257 1
Buckey, D Princenton 4, 8, 38, 62, 67, 73, 101, 113, 120, 137, 150, 166, 183, 193, 219, 222, 245, 246, 266, 270, 273, 278, 280 1
Buckey, D Princeton 11, 21, 24, 45, 107, 113 3
Buckey, D Princeton 2, 3, 10, 16, 20, 23, 36, 40, 41, 43, 62, 67, 68, 85, 89, 96, 99, 113, 116, 119, 122, 132, 154, 160, 181, 196, 206, 215, 222a, 247, 252, 295 2
Buckey, D Princeton[?] 47 1
Buckey, Daniel 48, 52, 162, 163 1
Buckey, Daniel 69, 84, 96, 225, 250 2
Buckey, Daniel 70 3
Buckey, Daniel E 217, 229 1
Buckey, Daniel E 41 3
Buckey, Daniel E 30 2
Buckey, Daniel G 37 1
Buckey, David 37, 47, 56 1
Buckey, David 11, 275 2
Buckey, E D 220 2
Buckey, E D 48 1
Buckey, E E 71 3
Buckey, Earl l 49 1
Buckey, Edw 117, 271, 245 1
Buckey, Edw 218 2
Buckey, Edw D 41 1
Buckey, Edward 40, 42, 55, 79 1
Buckey, Eli 57, 90 1
Buckey, Eli 197 2
Buckey, Eli 159 3
Buckey, Emma 29 2
Buckey, Ethel C 97 1
Buckey, Ezra 70 3
Buckey, Ezra 40 1
Buckey, Ezra C 82 1
Buckey, Fannie 192 3
Buckey, G William 40 1
Buckey, G Wm 58, 67 1
Buckey, Geo 75, 178, 159 2
Buckey, Geo Jacob 26 1
Buckey, Geo P 40, 47, 48, 57, 70, 84, 88, 112, 229 1
Buckey, Geo P 77 3
Buckey, Geo P 69 2
Buckey, Geo W 22 2
Buckey, Geo W 32, 47, 48, 118 1
Buckey, Geo W 23, 50 3
Buckey, Geo Wm 176, 192 1
Buckey, George 47 1
Buckey, George 247 2
Buckey, George H 139 3
Buckey, George P 32, 48 1
Buckey, George P 41, 57 3
Buckey, George P Jr 49 1
Buckey, George W 262 2
Buckey, H A 48 1
Buckey, Herman 227 2
Buckey, Herman A 220 2
Buckey, Herman A 42, 52, 62 1
Buckey, Herman H 62 1
Buckey, J H 1 1
Buckey, J M 56 1
Buckey, J M 39 3
Buckey, Jacob 58, 176 1
Buckey, Jacob 107, 112 2
Buckey, Jacob M 84 2
Buckey, Jacob M 131 1
Buckey, John 56 1
Buckey, Kemp 19 1
Buckey, Lou E 71 3
Buckey, Mary 70 1
Buckey, Mary E 56 1
Buckey, Michael 245, 258, 275 2
Buckey, Michael 74, 90, 191, 208, 228 1
Buckey, Peter 79, 90 1
Buckey, Peter 31 3
Buckey, Richard R 40 1
Buckey, Susan 56, 82 1
Buckey, Susannah 84 1
Buckey, T P 48 1
Buckey, Thomas G 180, 215 3
Buckey, Thomas G 47, 101, 250 1
Buckey, Valentine 226, 268 2
Buckey, Valentine 56, 90, 92, 110, 131, 228 1
Buckey, W Maynard 44, 52 1
Buckey, William A 93 1
Buckey, Wm A 92 1
Buckfelder, John 58 1
Buckias, John Sr 56 1
Buckingham, Beall 30 1
Buckingham, Benjamin 201 1
Buckingham, Geo 40 1
Buckingham, Margaret 70 1
Buckingham, Noah M 257 1
Buckingham, Richard P 82 1
Buckingham, Wm 185 3
Buckinham, Maurice 100 3
Bucky, Wm 135 1
Buddy, Philip 18 3
Budy, Philip 276 2
Buesing, Amelia F 91 1
Buesing, Frederick 44 1
Buesing, Mattie M 83 2
Buesing, Theo A 44 1
Buesing, Theodore A 88 1
Buesing, Wm F 91 1
Buffington, Abraham 26 1
Buffington, Alexander 57, 67, 253 1
Buffington, David 228 1
Buffington, Jacob 57 1
Buffington, Jacob 81 3
Buffington, John E 63 1
Buffington, Jonah 56, 196 1
Buffington, Joshua 56 1
Buffington, Leah 67 1
Buffington, M C 253 1
Buffington, Mary Ann 26 1
Bufington, Lavia A E 28 1
Buheman, W A 165 3
Buhrman, Albert L 33, 61 1
Buhrman, Alfred 51 1
Buhrman, Alfred J 28 1
Buhrman, Cecelia Ann 33 1
Buhrman, Chas D 33 1
Buhrman, Clyde A 42 1
Buhrman, Cora M 72 1
Buhrman, Cornelia 67 1
Buhrman, D 212 3
Buhrman, Daniel 37 1
Buhrman, David 38 1
Buhrman, Elden E 28, 42 1
Buhrman, Emory 41 1
Buhrman, G 212 3
Buhrman, George 51, 58, 91 1
Buhrman, Grover 245 1
Buhrman, Harry 214 1
Buhrman, Harry S 120 3
Buhrman, Harvey 208 2
Buhrman, Harvey M 51 1
Buhrman, Henry 52, 67 1
Buhrman, Isaiah H 55 1
Buhrman, J L 67 1
Buhrman, Jacob 58 1
Buhrman, Jane E 61 1

Buhrman, John 58 1
Buhrman, John 87 2
Buhrman, Joseph L 67 1
Buhrman, Joshua 55 1
Buhrman, Leah 67 1
Buhrman, Levi 67 1
Buhrman, Martin L 72 1
Buhrman, Mary 37 1
Buhrman, R Paul 55, 86 1
Buhrman, Russell P 28 1
Buhrman, Sida 33 1
Buhrman, Sida H 61, 85 1
Buhrman, Silas 67, 85 1
Buhrman, Silas 208 2
Buhrman, Upton 41 3
Buhrman, Upton 51 1
Buhrman, Vernon A L 92 1
Buhrman, W E 189 1
Buhrman, W Elmer 120 1
Buhrman, W Elmer Mrs 120 1
Buhrman, Wm 58 1
Buhrman, Wm H 37 1
Buhrman, Wm L 85 1
Buhrman, Wm L 89 3
Bulkley, Olcott 67 2
Bunn, A S 72 3
Bunting, John A 16 2
Burall, Henry O 85 1
Burall, S 33 1
Burall, Samuel 85 1
Burall, Sophia P 33 1
Burall, W Edgar 92 1
Burall, Walter E 199 2
Burbin, Wm 192 3
Burch, Ernest W 4 1
Burch, Mary S 67 1
Burck, Ann Catherine 67 1
Burck, Caroline 33 1
Burck, Ernest 33 1
Burck, George A 48, 219 1
Burck, James T 88 1
Burck, John 54 2
Burck, Kate Lee 67 1
Burck, Lewis A 67 1
Burck, Mary Stecket 72 1
Burck, Milton G 73 1
Burdette, Basil B 12 3
Burdette, Chas M 33 1
Burdette, E L 140 2
Burdette, Edgar 232 2
Burdette, Fannie C 21 3
Burdette, Fannie C 45 1
Burdette, Florence Irene 45, 111 1
Burdette, Frank 44 1
Burdette, Geo L 107 1
Burdette, Ira L 21 3
Burdette, Ira Lansdale 63, 200 1
Burdette, James T 63, 111 1
Burdette, Jeremiah 63 1
Burdette, Jeremiah L 68, 237 1
Burdette, John J 79 1
Burdette, Luther M 68, 172 1
Burdette, Melvin W 68 1
Burdette, Monroe 147 1
Burdette, Perry G 79 1
Burdette, Roberta E 20 2
Burdette, Rufus 83 1
Burdette, Rufus H 83, 119 1
Burdette, Vivia C 63 1
Burdette, W L 69, 161, 190 2
Burdette, W L 107 1
Burdette, W V 35 2
Burdette, Willie L 191 2
Burdette, Willie L 124 1
Burdette, Wm E 33 1
Burdette, Wm H 79 1
Burdner, Andrew 27 1
Burdner, Sarah 27, 28 1
Burgee, Amon 140, 259 2
Burgee, Amon 72, 86 1
Burgee, Clara E 33 1
Burgee, Clyde E 104 3
Burgee, Eli T 40 1
Burgee, Frederick L 40 1
Burgee, Frederick U 139 2
Burgee, Grafton 44, 47, 152 1
Burgee, Grafton 184 3
Burgee, Grafton 38 2
Burgee, Grafton & 137 2
Burgee, Howard 72 1
Burgee, Ida 72 1
Burgee, Isaac 55 1
Burgee, J Thomas 141 3
Burgee, J Thomas Dorsey 67 1
Burgee, James T 44 3
Burgee, James Thos 59 1
Burgee, Jane 84, 120 1
Burgee, L Ray 28 1
Burgee, Lethe Ellen 67 1
Burgee, Lewis 67 1
Burgee, Lydia 198 2
Burgee, Lydia M 67, 79 1
Burgee, Margaret A 44 1
Burgee, Marrietta 71 1
Burgee, Mary E 28 1
Burgee, McSherry 33, 73 1
Burgee, Miel 72, 144 1
Burgee, Miel 119 2
Burgee, Miel E 72 1
Burgee, Mile 70 1
Burgee, Nettie J 73 1
Burgee, Polly 79 1
Burgee, Ralph M 73 1
Burgee, Singleton 84, 88 1
Burgee, Singleton 63 2
Burgee, Thomas 70 1
Burgee, Thomas 63, 198 2
Burgee, Thomas H 96 1
Burgee, Thomas Sr 88 1
Burgee, Thos 196 1
Burgee, Thos 163 3
Burgee, Thos 18 2
Burgee, Thos A 135 1
Burgee, Thos H 40 1
Burgee, W 171 3
Burgee, Wash 185 3
Burger, Anna M 92 1
Burger, Anna Mary 27 1
Burger, Annie M 48 1
Burger, Charles E 34 1
Burger, Chas E 52 1
Burger, Edmund 42 1
Burger, Elizabeth 41 1
Burger, Geo Philip 48 1
Burger, Henry C 52 1
Burger, Jacob 13 1
Burger, Mary A 52 1
Burger, Mary H 74 1
Burger, Mary S 11 3
Burger, W H 59 1
Burger, W L 24 3
Burger, W Leslie 34 1
Burger, Wm A 92 1
Burger, Wm H 92, 118 1
Burgess, Arthur P 42 1
Burgess, B W W 9 3
Burgess, Bayard C 48 1
Burgess, Brice W W 30 1
Burgess, Caleb 32 1
Burgess, Edward E 42 1
Burgess, Geo W 48 1
Burgess, John 56, 57 1
Burgess, John E 37 1
Burgess, John E F 246 2
Burgess, John E F 60 1
Burgess, John W 62 1
Burgess, Louisa 140 1
Burgess, Lucretia 62 1
Burgess, Lucretia M 68 1
Burgess, M Louisa 123 1
Burgess, Margaret Louise 73 1
Burgess, Nancy 30 1
Burgess, Nettie L 60 1
Burgess, Olan 91 1
Burgess, Owen 78 1
Burgess, Rachel 32, 91 1
Burgess, Samuel 84, 139 1
Burgess, Sarah E 56 1
Burgess, Washington 56, 57, 85 1
Burgess, Washington 209 3
Burgess, West 68 2
Burgess, West 91 1
Burgess, William 42 1
Burget, Frederick 44 1
Burhman, Ekie I 120 3
Burhman, Geo 54 3

Burhman, Geo & 101 2
Burhman, S H 122 2
Burhman, Wm L 92 1
Burk, Daniel 186 1
Burk, Hazel 51 1
Burke, Annie C 62 1
Burke, Annie L 68 1
Burke, Eugina L 88 1
Burke, Franklin G 44 1
Burke, Harry C 52 1
Burke, Henry 72 2
Burke, Howard A 62 1
Burke, Isaac N 55 1
Burke, J Edw 132, 160 2
Burke, J Edward 72 1
Burke, James Edward 62 1
Burke, Jesse D 62 1
Burke, John E 45 3
Burke, John E 62 1
Burke, John F 60 1
Burke, Joseph R 52, 68 1
Burke, Joseph Roy 44 1
Burke, L C 145 3
Burke, Leonard F 63, 68 1
Burke, Lewis A 67 1
Burke, Luther C 68 1
Burke, Mary A E 71 1
Burke, Mary LC 169 3
Burke, Michael 55 1
Burke, Milton 72 2
Burke, Milton 70, 72 1
Burke, Perry M 68 1
Burke, Thomas J 88 1
Burke, W H 44 1
Burke, Willianna 55, 72 1
Burke, Willieanna 92 1
Burke, Wm 92 1
Burket, Amelia 28 1
Burket, Amelia 56 3
Burket, Amelia F 123, 159, 201 1
Burket, Margaret 44 1
Burket, Mary E 72 1
Burket, P F 108 2
Burket, Peter 199 2
Burket, Peter 28 1
Burket, Peter F 56, 107 3
Burket, Peter F 61, 72, 123, 159, 266, 280 1
Burket, Peter F 10, 23, 102, 184 2
Burket, T F 166 1
Burkett, A W 171 3
Burkett, Amelia F 102 2
Burkett, Ezra 37 1
Burkett, Henry 40, 51, 57 1
Burkett, John 57 1
Burkett, P F 203 1
Burkett, P F 52 1
Burkett, P F 18 2
Burkett, Peter 210a 2
Burkett, Peter F 186, 201, 202 1
Burkett, Peter F 43, 199 3
Burkett, William F 2 3
Burkhard, A W 9 3
Burkhart, A W 18 1
Burkhart, A W 31, 50, 65, 203 3
Burkhart, A W 15, 212a 2
Burkhart, Albert W 220 3
Burkhart, Albert W 150 2
Burkhart, Albert W 27, 28 1
Burkhart, C H 224 2
Burkhart, Charles 31, 86 3
Burkhart, Charles J 31 3
Burkhart, Charles N 70 3
Burkhart, Charlotte C 88 1
Burkhart, Chas 10, 110 1
Burkhart, Chas 187 2
Burkhart, Chas H 11 2
Burkhart, Chas H 18, 112, 139, 223 1
Burkhart, Chas H 31, 220 3
Burkhart, Elizabeth 41 1
Burkhart, Ezra 181 1
Burkhart, Frederick 41 1
Burkhart, James Henry 62 1
Burkhart, John 57 1
Burkhart, Theodore L 88 1
Burkhart, W A 99 1
Burkhart, Wm T 91 1
Burkit, P F 11 1
Burkley, John 58 1
Burlando, James F 59 1
Burman, C M 80 2
Burman, H M 171 3
Burman, John 106 3
Burman, S H 171 3
Burns, Clifton W 172 3
Burns, Daniel 37 1
Burns, E Fielder 293 2
Burns, Ellen 41 1
Burns, Ellen A 3 3
Burns, Etta M 14 1
Burns, Etta M (also Etta Young) 42 1
Burns, Geo 248 1
Burns, Harvey C 86 1
Burns, Henry 51 1
Burns, Ida D 86 1
Burns, Jmaes 184 3
Burns, Richard Rudy 42 1
Burns, Rudy 14 1
Burns, Silas B 86 1
Burrall, Cameron E 33 1
Burrall, Jesse M 91 3
Burrall, Jesse M 63 1
Burrall, Jesse W 96 3
Burrall, Mary E 73 1
Burrall, Samuel 219 1
Burrall, W E 107 3
Burrall, Walter E 96 3
Burrall, Walter E 63 1
Burrall, Wm E 147 1
Burras, Charles T 52 1
Burras, Helen E 52 1
Burras, Helen R (E was mother's initial) [addition] 52 1
Burrier, A E 34 1
Burrier, Adam 26 1
Burrier, Albert W 34, 62 1
Burrier, Allen Z 28 1
Burrier, Amanda E 62 1
Burrier, Barbara 30 1
Burrier, C S 33 1
Burrier, Calvin S 208 2
Burrier, Calvin S 38, 125 1
Burrier, Catherine 33 1
Burrier, Charles D 33 1
Burrier, Chas 101 2
Burrier, Chas L 34 1
Burrier, Daniel 32, 129, 224 3
Burrier, Daniel 101, 208 2
Burrier, Daniel 38, 58, 99, 125 1
Burrier, Darwin D 182 2
Burrier, Eli 224 3
Burrier, Elmer L 73 1
Burrier, Emerson D 28 1
Burrier, Emma J 85 1
Burrier, Emma Jane 33 1
Burrier, Flora C 44, 48 1
Burrier, Geo M 48 1
Burrier, Grayson D 44 1
Burrier, Harry F 52 1
Burrier, Howard M 44 1
Burrier, Ira E 26, 198 1
Burrier, J Howard 220 3
Burrier, Jacob 30, 60, 67 1
Burrier, Jacob 42 3
Burrier, Jacob S 62 1
Burrier, Jacob Sr 58 1
Burrier, John E 62, 73 1
Burrier, John William 62 1
Burrier, Jonas L 48 1
Burrier, Katie E 65 1
Burrier, Laura C 67 1
Burrier, Mary C 52 1
Burrier, Mary E 73 1
Burrier, Mary S 73 1
Burrier, Nevin S 38, 44 1
Burrier, Philip 138 2
Burrier, Ray L 73 1
Burrier, Simon E 85 1
Burrier, Solomon 26, 243 1
Burrier, Sophia 84 1
Burrier, Susannah 84 1
Burrier, William H 93 1
Burrier, Wm 73 1
Burrier, Wm H 99, 120, 223 1
Burris, Carie S 33 1

Burris, Henry J 33 1
Burt, Fannie E 189 3
Burton, James 57 1
Burton, John W 57 1
Burton, Wm H 101 1
Busa, Christopher 32 1
Busby, Rachel 95 1
Busby, Zachariah H 95 1
Buser, Annie 28 1
Buser, Edward 28 1
Busey, Kenneth I 73 1
Busey, Mary A 73 1
Bush, Arthur 199 3
Bush, David 199 3
Bush, John 199 3
Bush, Justin 60 1
Bush, Marion P 227a, 229 2
Bushey, Augusta 59, 67, 76 1
Bushey, Charistian A 33 1
Bushey, J M 2 3
Bushey, J M 181 2
Bushey, J W 54, 101 2
Bushey, Jacob M 59, 91 1
Bushey, Jacob M 113 2
Bushey, Jacob M 41, 129 3
Bushey, John 220 2
Bushey, Virginia 33 1
Bushman, Alfred 40 3
Bushman, Thomas 274 2
Business B & O RR 129 3
Bussard, Albert L 107 1
Bussard, Albert L 23 2
Bussard, Ann S 27 1
Bussard, Bertha V 31, 48 1
Bussard, Catherine A 79 1
Bussard, Charles E 34 1
Bussard, Charles F 33 1
Bussard, Clarence 124, 172 2
Bussard, Clarence A 38, 63, 79 1
Bussard, D Albert 37 1
Bussard, Daniel 57 3
Bussard, Daniel 37, 38 1
Bussard, Daniel L 38 1
Bussard, David 38, 79 1
Bussard, David F 38 1
Bussard, E A C 32 3
Bussard, Earl W 42 1
Bussard, Elsie F 92 1
Bussard, Emma M 38 1
Bussard, Enos 40 1
Bussard, Erma E 173 1
Bussard, Evelyn I 42 1
Bussard, Florence R 44 1
Bussard, G 44 1
Bussard, Gideon 181 2
Bussard, Gideon 48, 104 1
Bussard, Gideon 42 3
Bussard, Gideon A 48 1
Bussard, Hattie V 52 1
Bussard, Henry 61 2
Bussard, J Elmer 62 1
Bussard, J H 40 2
Bussard, J H 87 3
Bussard, J M 38 1
Bussard, J O 139 2
Bussard, James O 62, 123, 265 1
Bussard, Joanna May 38 1
Bussard, John 63, 70, 79 1
Bussard, John 58 2
Bussard, John L 38 1
Bussard, John M 62 1
Bussard, John M 119 2
Bussard, John M 10 3
Bussard, John S 63 1
Bussard, John W 79, 82, 85, 277 1
Bussard, John W 26 3
Bussard, John W 280 2
Bussard, Jos H 50 3
Bussard, Jos H 160 2
Bussard, Joseph 124, 166, 172 2
Bussard, Joseph 33 1
Bussard, Joseph H 48, 63, 266 1
Bussard, Joseph H 176, 224 3
Bussard, Joseph H 189 2
Bussard, Katie A 34 1
Bussard, Luther D 173 1
Bussard, Margaret 70 1
Bussard, Peter 79 1
Bussard, Peter E 38 1
Bussard, Peter E 33 3
Bussard, Peter E 282 2
Bussard, Peter H 51, 79, 85 1
Bussard, Raymond 225 1
Bussard, Roy L 86 1
Bussard, Samuel 6, 63, 138 2
Bussard, Samuel 8 3
Bussard, Samuel 1, 176 1
Bussard, Samuel D 63, 79, 86 1
Bussard, Samuel M 85 1
Bussard, Sarah 84 1
Bussard, Sarah E 38, 86 1
Bussard, Susan C 85 1
Bussard, Susannah C 38 1
Bussard, T Hamilton 31 1
Bussard, T T 27 1
Bussard, Thaddeus T 48, 52 1
Bussard, Wm 91 1
Bussard, Wm 202 2
Bussard, Wm H 59 1
Bussey, Julia P 60, 92 1
Buston, Hallie B 34 1
Buston, John T 30 1
Butcher, Geo G 47 1
Butcher, Jacob 59 1
Butcher, Louisa 67 1
Butcher, Michael 71 1
Butcher, Robert 82 1
Buthaupt, Chas F 31 3
Butler, Aarabelle S 33 1
Butler, Albert T 27 1
Butler, Arabella 27 1
Butler, Arabella S 38 1
Butler, Benjamin H 30 1
Butler, Carrie E 33 1
Butler, Charles col'd 32 1
Butler, Charles J 122 3
Butler, Crinond 82 1
Butler, David 37 1
Butler, David S 38 1
Butler, Harriet[?] 51 1
Butler, Isaac C 55 1
Butler, Isaac C, Jr 55 1
Butler, James 56, 59 1
Butler, John B 63 1
Butler, John D 63 1
Butler, John M 60 1
Butler, John Sr 56 1
Butler, Josephus 59 1
Butler, Kennedy H 268 2
Butler, Lewis O 59 1
Butler, Marie W 63 1
Butler, Mary A 63 1
Butler, O F 150 2
Butler, Richard 59 1
Butler, Sarah E 268 2
Butler, Thomas 82, 88, 106 1
Butler, Thos 83, 111 2
Butler, Tobias 27 1
Butler, Tyler 33, 37, 38, 88 1
Butt, M D 62 1
Butts, Benjamin 31 1
Butts, Charles R 31 1
Butts, Chas H 150 2
Butts, Clarence J 34 1
Butts, Fannie Virginia 44 1
Butts, Frank 44 1
Butts, M D 265 1
Butts, Vernie L 262 2
Butz, Carrie 34 1
Buxton, Basil 55 3
Buxton, Basil D 30 1
Buxton, Brook 30 1
Buxton, Brooke 30, 88, 100 1
Buxton, Carrie B 41 1
Buxton, Carrie V 30 1
Buxton, Charles A 33 1
Buxton, Charles W 30 1
Buxton, Emma J 34, 41 1
Buxton, F E 62 1
Buxton, fl 30 1
Buxton, Frank E 10 3

Buxton, Frank E 41, 62 1
Buxton, Frank V 85 1
Buxton, Geo N 47 1
Buxton, Hallie 52 1
Buxton, J E 85 1
Buxton, J L 119 1
Buxton, James 62 1
Buxton, James L 15 2
Buxton, Jennie 62 1
Buxton, John 15 2
Buxton, John E 33 1
Buxton, John S 63 1
Buxton, John T 60 1
Buxton, Mary Ann 47 1
Buxton, Milton G 96 2
Buxton, Milton G 72 1
Buxton, Mollie 85 1
Buxton, Samuel T 85 1
Buxton, Sarah 85 1
Buxton, Thomas S 88 1
Buxton, William O 60 1
Buxton, William P 63 1
Buxton, Wm H 33 1
Buxton, Wm O 85 1
Buzard, Samuel 120 3
Buzzard, David 37 1
Buzzard, John W 58 1
Buzzard, Joseph H 1 1
Buzzard, Samuel 191 1
Buzzard, Samuel Jr 84 1
Buzzard, Samuel Sr 84 1
Buzzell, Margaret A 107, 111 1
Byerly, Charles 34 1
Byerly, Charles Jr 202 1
Byerly, George 47 1
Byerly, Lester 113 1
Byerly, Lewis 31 3
Byerly, Lewis 218 2
Byerly, Mamie 74 1
Byerly, Mary 73 1
Byerly, Regina E 34 1
Byerly, Susannah 47 1
Byers, Calvin Herman 34 1
Byers, David 0 38 1
Byers, David A 38 1
Byers, Dennis O 34 1
Byers, Edw 42 1
Byers, Edw M 42 1
Byers, Elinor 41 1
Byers, Ezra 42 1
Byers, Gabriel 47 1
Byers, Jno A 133 3
Byers, John A 47 1
Byers, John R 38 1
Byers, Jos 50 3
Byers, Joseph 60 1
Byers, Joseph 64 3
Byers, Joseph 29, 83, 134, 138, 188, 198 2
Byers, Ruth M 34 1
Byers, Selina Jane 86 1
Byme, Michael 59 1
Byrd, Margaret C 126 3
Byrne, Annie E 140 2
Byrne, Joseph 71, 82 1
Byrne, Michael 205 3
Byrne, Michael 76, 171, 176, 252 1
Byrne, Michael 203 2
Byrne, Michael & 129 2
Byrne, Terence 59 1
C T Co 102 3
Cadow, Elizabeth 107 1
Cadow, Laura V 107 1
Cadow, Robert E 123 1
Cahill, Philip I 159 2
Cahill, Philip J 27, 57 2
Cain, Anna D 96, 117 1
Cain, Catherine 100 1
Cain, Ellen 118 1
Cain, Ephriam 106 1
Cain, James I 79 1
Cain, John 117 1
Cain, John T 100, 279 1
Cain, Joseph 106, 117, 118, 245, 257 1
Cain, Joseph E 140 1
Cain, Joseph G 96 1
Cain, Joseph J 15, 238 2
Cain, Joseph J 117, 119, 135 1
Cain, Joseph J 139 1
Cain, Joseph P 27 1
Cain, Joshua 106, 117 1
Cain, Lydia 106 1
Cain, Margaret C 119 1
Cain, Ruth A 133 1
Cain, Sarah E 117 1
Cain, Wm 135, 139 1
Cain, Wm 106 1
Cain, Wm J 139 1
Cain, William J 140 1
Calder, Mary P 126 1
Calderon, Guadeloupe 110 1
Caldwell, Francis L 109 1
Caldwell, Joseph D 109 1
Caldwell, Winona May 140 1
Calhoun, Vera P 140 1
Calhoun, Wm H 140 1
Call, Catherine 100 1
Callahan, Florence J 119 1
Callahan, Fred S 119 1
Callahan, James W 119 1
Callahan, Mary Louise 197 3
Calliflower, Agnes C 97 1
Camden, Wilson Lee 288 2
Camillo, Ruby I 245 2
Camp, Christian 96 2
Camp, Gilbert 116 1
Campbell, A 96 1
Campbell, Abner 146, 196, 205 1
Campbell, Abner 14, 25, 65, 111 2
Campbell, Albert 107 1
Campbell, Annie 97 1
Campbell, Bernard W 125 1
Campbell, Clinton 100 1
Campbell, Edw 106 3
Campbell, Edw 106, 282 1
Campbell, Edwin M 135 1
Campbell, Emma L Beard 107 1
Campbell, Everett 139 1
Campbell, F J 83, 113, 182 3
Campbell, F J 81, 102 2
Campbell, Frances J 108 2
Campbell, Francis T 109 1
Campbell, Frank J 170, 108 2
Campbell, James 116 1
Campbell, John 262 2
Campbell, John Jr 116 1
Campbell, John Sr 56 1
Campbell, Randolph 165, 209 3
Campbell, Randolph 116, 133 1
Campbell, Richard C 133 1
Campbell, Robert 133 1
Campbell, Robert H 96 1
Campbell, Robert L 107 1
Campbell, Sophia E 56 1
Campbell, William H 294 2
Campbell, Wm 135, 139, 196 1
Campbell, Wm 209 3
Campell, Jane 117 1
Camper, Elizabeth 100 1
Cannon, A C 133 1
Cannon, Aoarilla 150 2
Cannon, Elizabeth J 120 1
Cannon, Irving V 115 1
Cannon, Isaac D 115 1
Cannon, J B 150 2
Cannon, J William 120 1
Cannon, Mary E 35 3
Cannon, Mary E 127, 133 1
Cannon, Mary E A K A Stone, Ida A 127 1
Cannon, Roy B 133 1
Cannon, T V L 115 1
Cannon, Wm 133 1
Cantwell, Howard W 146 1
Capelin, Samuel 224a 2
Carbaugh, Bessie V 225 2
Carbaugh, Grace M 196 2
Carbaugh, Nicholas J 8 2
Carble, Jane 117 1
Carbyle, Susanna 135 1
Care, Ida L 115 1
Care, Wm L B 115 1

Carey, Carrie V 120 1
Carey, Emily L 106 1
Carey, Harriet V 113 1
Carey, Harriett V C 113 1
Carey, Helen V 136 1
Carey, James 100 3
Carey, James K 120 1
Carey, Jesse H 30, 120 1
Carey, John 215 2
Carey, John 117, 166 1
Carey, Lawrence 163 2
Carey, Lester L 163 2
Carey, Louise 215 2
Carey, Louise A 124 1
Carey, Mary 125 1
Carey, Michael 163 2
Carey, Minnie B 140 1
Carey, Robt H 120 1
Carey, Ruth S 120 1
Carey, Sheley 136 1
Carey, William P 140 1
Carl, John D 120 1
Carl, Rosie M 120 1
Carleton, Thomas 169 1
Carleton, Thomas 96, 139 3
Carleton, Thos 53, 195, 199 3
Carleton, Thos 38, 84 2
Carlin, A C 97 1
Carlin, Ann C 109 1
Carlin, Charles C 100 1
Carlin, Charles F 101 1
Carlin, Chas L 126 1
Carlin, David 104 1
Carlin, David J 101 1
Carlin, Evan & Kenneth 101 1
Carlin, F B 115 1
Carlin, Francis B 109 1
Carlin, Frank S 109 1
Carlin, Henry 112 1
Carlin, James 26 2
Carlin, James 184, 203 3
Carlin, James 131, 137 1
Carlin, Jane 100 1
Carlin, John Q 117 1
Carlin, Joseph 100 1
Carlin, Kenneth 101 1
Carlin, Martha E V 126 1
Carlin, Matilda 117 1
Carlin, Priscilla 131 1
Carlin, Rachel 100 1
Carlin, Thomas 137 1
Carlisle, A M 100 1
Carlisle, Annabelle 111 1
Carlisle, Armistead 96 1
Carlisle, C E 205 1
Carlisle, C Edw 192 1
Carlisle, Charles 227a 2
Carlisle, Charles 100 1
Carlisle, Charles A 101 1
Carlisle, Charles C 100 1
Carlisle, Charles W 111 1
Carlisle, Eugene C 107 1
Carlisle, Guy E 111, 189 1
Carlisle, Helen V 107 1
Carlisle, Katherine G 101 1
Carlisle, Mary A 96 1
Carlisle, Robert B 100, 126, 133 1
Carlisle, Sarah E 133 1
Carlotn, Thomas [sic] 106, 171 1
Carlton, John 116 1
Carlton, Mary 125 1
Carlton, Mary E 32 1
Carlton, Thomas 76, 84, 99, 106, 109, 137, 171, 225, 228 1
Carlton, Thomas 37, 87, 151 3
Carlton, Thomas 25, 57, 111, 137, 208 2
Carlton, Thomas C 116 1
Carlton, Thos 19, 148, 149, 177, 197, 205, 213 2
Carlton, Thos 131, 163, 271 1
Carlton, Wm 139 1
Carlyle, C A 188 3
Carmack, Caroline 100 1
Carmack, Ellen 106 1
Carmack, Ephriam 32 1
Carmack, Ephrian [sic] 91 1
Carmack, Epraim [sic] 123 1
Carmack, Evan 57 2
Carmack, Evan 38, 81 3
Carmack, Evan 191 1
Carmack, Isabella 115 1
Carmack, Izabella 40 1
Carmack, John 47, 117, 135, 147, 214 1
Carmack, John 38, 184 3
Carmack, Lizzie 123 1
Carmack, Paul 8, 37, 38, 40, 50, 79, 184 3
Carmack, Paul 63 2
Carmack, Paul 214, 228, 263, 283 1
Carmack, Pauline E 3, 32 2
Carmack, Salome 51 1
Carmack, Sam 129 3
Carmack, Samuel 38, 81 3
Carmack, Samuel 11, 27, 92 2
Carmack, Samuel 135, 139, 191, 214, 271 1
Carmack, Sarah 135 1
Carmack, Thos 139 1
Carmack, Wilson T 26 1
Carmack, Wm 135, 139, 140 1
Carmack, Wm 27 2
Carmack, Wm 71 3
Carmack, Wm E 140 1
Carmick, Paul 70 3
Carn, Ezra 264 1
Carnahan, Barbara A 99 1
Carnahan, Barton R 99 1
Carnes, Authur C 97 1
Carnes, Bessie V 97 1
Carnes, Roy C 97 1
Carns, Nancy 129 1
Carns, W H 40 2
Caroline, Ann C 89 2
Caroline, Martin 23 3
Carpenter, A E 125 1
Carpenter, A J 125 1
Carpenter, Andrew 96 1
Carpenter, Andrew J 118 1
Carpenter, Annie E 97 1
Carpenter, Charles H 124 1
Carpenter, Evan L 96 1
Carpenter, Grover M 97 1
Carpenter, Grover N 113, 131 1
Carpenter, Hattie V 113 1
Carpenter, Ida C 124 1
Carpenter, Jake 195 1
Carpenter, John 282 2
Carpenter, John C 118 1
Carpenter, Lafayette 188 3
Carpenter, Lafayette C 56 3
Carpenter, Lafayette L 124 1
Carpenter, M Mrs 96 1
Carpenter, Margaret 125 1
Carpenter, Mary 96 1
Carpenter, Peter J 56 3
Carpenter, Peter J 118, 125, 131 1
Carper, James S 110 1
Carr, Allen Bowie 97 1
Carr, Arthur R 97 1
Carr, John H 44 1
Carr, Matilda 125, 137 1
Carr, Nannie D 97 1
Carr, Oscar B 117 1
Carr, Thomas 11 2
Carr, Thomas 130, 137 1
Carr, Thos 201, 264 1
Carr, Warren E 130 1
Carr, Wm H C 139 1
Carr, Wm T 125 1
Carrey, John 117 1
Carroll, D H 26 1
Carroll, Daniel 104 1
Carroll, M Caroline 14 2
Carroll, Maria E 50 3
Carroll, Osborne 100 3
Carrott, Erasueus 26 1
Carskaden, Thomas 214 1
Carson, Clara F 119 1
Carson, George 110 1

Carson, Isabella 118 1
Carson, Jacob E 119 1
Carson, John 118 1
Cartee, Frisber G 109 1
Cartee, James 117 1
Cartee, John Sr 116 1
Cartee, Laura C 96 1
Carter, Albert 99, 109 1
Carter, B Virginia 100, 125 1
Carter, Charity 100, 112, 126 1
Carter, Chas A 101 1
Carter, Dessie M 104 1
Carter, Elizabeth A 107, 112 1
Carter, H B 134 2
Carter, Henry 125, 171, 181 1
Carter, Henry 7, 225, 215a 2
Carter, Isabella 129 1
Carter, Janie 120 1
Carter, John Milton 99, 153 1
Carter, Lena E 124 1
Carter, Lillian 123 1
Carter, Louis 124 1
Carter, Louis C 101 1
Carter, M C 38 1
Carter, Milton 57, 262 2
Carter, Milton 2, 43, 71, 192 3
Carter, Milton 71, 112, 118, 125, 126, 164 1
Carter, Myrtie L 107, 126 1
Carter, Noah E 129 1
Carter, Nora 198 2
Carter, Wesley 139 1
Cartney, M M 179 1
Carty, Annie W 188 3
Carty, C C 48, 210, 263 1
Carty, C C 20, 87, 100, 188 3
Carty, C C 2, 30, 40, 75, 148 166 2
Carty, Chas C 72, 101, 219 1
Carty, Chas P 181 2
Carty, Clarence 89 2
Carty, Clarence C 100, 107, 113, 169 1
Carty, Clarence C 21 3
Carty, Clarence C 96, 148, 245 2
Carty, Dorothy Riordan 153 1
Carty, Dorthy R 113 1
Carty, Elizabeth M 35 2
Carty, Elizabeth M 100, 113 1
Carty, Hallie W 161 3
Carty, Hallie W 101, 113 1
Carty, Harry 160 2
Carty, Harry E 35, 160 2
Carty, Harry E 89 3
Carty, Harry E 107, 113 1
Carty, Harry L 147 3
Carty, J L 255 2
Carty, J W L 9, 20, 24, 71, 87, 180 3
Carty, J W L 72, 75, 85, 96, 175, 268 2
Carty, J W L 68, 126, 129, 146, 210, 245 1
Carty, J Walker 161 3
Carty, J Walker 19 1
Carty, Jos W L 89 2
Carty, Joseph W L 2, 30, 265 2
Carty, Joseph W L 100, 101, 118, 172 1
Carty, Mary M 118 1
Carty, Nannie C 129 1
Cartzendafner, David 228 1
Cartzendafner, Joseph 174 3
Cartzendofner, Joseph 81 3
Carver, Jacob 117 1
Cary, Wm 139 1
Case, Daniel E 104 1
Case, Francis P 109 1
Case, Robert D 109 1
Casey, Mary E 125 1
Cash, E O 215 2
Cash, Edw O 61 1
Cash, John 141 3
Cash, Lewis 32 3
Cash, Louis 203 2
Cashour, W C 96 1
Cashour, Albert 96, 133 1
Cashour, Annie M & [sic] 140 1
Cashour, Basil David 99 1
Cashour, C Kemp 101 1
Cashour, Charlotte E 99 1
Cashour, Chas F 110 1
Cashour, Chas W F 101 1
Cashour, Edward 96 1
Cashour, Everett G 115, 133 1
Cashour, Geo A 96 1
Cashour, Ida L 115 1
Cashour, J 89 3
Cashour, Martha 139 1
Cashour, Maude S 21 3
Cashour, Ruth A 133 1
Cashour, William T 140 1
Cashour, Wm 139 1
Caskery, John 167 3
Cassel, Chas E 120 1
Cassel, David 254 2
Cassel, George 8 3
Cassell, Charles E 1 3
Cassell, David 26, 226 2
Cassell, Geo 76 1
Cassell, Henry 226 2
Cassell, Henry 116 1
Cassell, Isaac 26, 38 2
Cassell, Isaac 76 1
Cassell, J Howard 120 1
Cassell, Jacob 116 1
Cassell, Jacob 80 2
Cassell, John 211 2
Cassell, John 116 1
Cassell, Rosanna 133 1
Cassin, John 130 1
Cassin, Olivia E 130 1
Cast, Geo 51 1
Castel, Daniel of T 124 3
Castel, T 124, 160 3
Castle, Abraham H 38 2
Castle, Albert B 97, 99 1
Castle, Ann T 97 1
Castle, Anna Rebecca 96 1
Castle, Barbara 99 1
Castle, Barbara E 99 1
Castle, C A 72 1
Castle, C Bess 127 1
Castle, C Phillips 101 1
Castle, Charles A 101, 104 1
Castle, Charles F 101 1
Castle, Chas A 104 1
Castle, Chas E 1 1
Castle, Cleantha D 100 1
Castle, Daniel 2, 165, 202, 224 3
Castle, Daniel 71 1
Castle, Daniel of T 160 3
Castle, Daniel of T 177 2
Castle, Daniel of T 99, 104, 137 1
Castle, Daniel T 104 1
Castle, Daniel W 97 1
Castle, David 160, 287 2
Castle, David A 104 1
Castle, David A 245 2
Castle, Donald 240 1
Castle, E C B 119 1
Castle, E Glenmore 107 1
Castle, Elizabeth P 107 1
Castle, Ellen C 107 1
Castle, Emory C 96 1
Castle, Florence V 140 1
Castle, Franceller J 264 2
Castle, Franceller J 109 1
Castle, Frank A 127 1
Castle, Frank J 101 1
Castle, Geo 20 2
Castle, Geo E 35 2
Castle, George C 111 1
Castle, George H 111 1
Castle, Georgianna M 110 1
Castle, Grace A 111 1
Castle, Harriet D 112 1
Castle, Harry C 111 1
Castle, Henry 112 1

Castle, Ida A 115 1
Castle, Ida A 126 1
Castle, J C 217 3
Castle, Jacob 152 1
Castle, James 193, 205 1
Castle, James 19, 100, 237, 257 2
Castle, James 203 3
Castle, James & 27 2
Castle, James E 117 1
Castle, James H 111 1
Castle, James Sr 117 1
Castle, James T 117 1
Castle, John 93, 188 2
Castle, John A 97 1
Castle, John C 120 1
Castle, John C 197 3
Castle, John W 165 3
Castle, John W 119 1
Castle, Joseph E 133 1
Castle, K T 81 3
Castle, Kenderson D 125 1
Castle, Kenderson T 123 1
Castle, Laura A 123 1
Castle, Leona D 157 1
Castle, Lewis O 104 1
Castle, Martin A 100, 126 1
Castle, Mary B 86 1
Castle, Mary C 180 3
Castle, Mary E 127 1
Castle, Mary J 126 1
Castle, Maude R 111 1
Castle, Melinda C 125 1
Castle, Nannie C 112 1
Castle, Rebecca 129, 133 1
Castle, Resin J 133 1
Castle, Silas C 136 1
Castle, Susan 57 1
Castle, T 177 2
Castle, T 160 3
Castle, Thomas 84, 104, 110, 137 1
Castle, Thomas F 126, 137 1
Castle, Thomas S 100 1
Castle, Thos 125 1
Castle, Thos 197 2
Castle, Wm L 140 1
Catlett, George D 111 1
Catlett, Mary B 127 1
Catlett, Mary P 111 1
Catzendafner, David 104 1
Catzendafner, Mary L 125 1
Cauffman, James C 96 1
Cauliflower, J T 217 3
Cavell, Jonathan 118 1
Cavell, Jonathan F 118 1
Cavell, Joshua 118 1
Cavell, Lydia 118 1
Cavell, Nellie E 129 1
Cavell, Norman M 129 1
Cavell, Wm M 129 1
Ceaser, Bessie L 99 1
Ceaser, Harry K 99 1
Cecil, Anna 46, 287 2
Cecil, Anna 96 1
Cecil, C C 119 1
Cecil, Charles C 101 1
Cecil, Chas C 115 1
Cecil, Christopher C 100 1
Cecil, Florence 172 2
Cecil, George W 111 1
Cecil, Hamadathea 112 1
Cecil, Ida A R 115 1
Cecil, James N. 100 1
Cecil, John T 119 1
Cecil, Lena 101 1
Cecil, Lona C 124 1
Cecil, Margaret E 126 1
Cecil, Nettie E 119 1
Cecil, Otho M 135 1
Cecil, Ralph E 111 1
Cecil, Samuel 46, 287 2
Cecil, Samuel 135 1
Cell, Peter 15 3
Central Tr Co 76 2
Central Tr Co 42 1
Central Tr Co of Md 9, 31, 189, 193, 195, 211, 213, 2
Central Tr Co of Md 230, 233, 280 1
Central Tr Company 178 2
Central Tru Co of Md 1 1
Central Trust Co 222, 234 2
Central Trust Co 10, 96, 206 3
Central Trust Co of Md 62, 76, 79, 82, 123, 186, 192, 147, 260 1
Central Trust Co of Md 129, 218a, 221a, 277 2
Central Trust Co of Md 57, 96, 201 3
Centrust Co of Md 113 2
Century Indemnity Co 72 2
Chamberlain, James 117 1
Chambers, Adelaide 125 1
Chambers, Ann Eliza 96 1
Chambers, Ann M 96 1
Chambers, Anthony S 63 1
Chambers, Benj D 80 2
Chambers, Benjamin D 73, 85, 97, 99 1
Chambers, Clara V 96 1
Chambers, Elinor M 99 1
Chambers, Emily F 107 1
Chambers, Florence A 96 1
Chambers, Geo M 96 1
Chambers, George F 111 1
Chambers, George M 110 1
Chambers, Greenburg 110 1
Chambers, James A 110 1
Chambers, Mary 113, 125 1
Chambers, Mary C 99 1
Chambers, Mazie C 259 2
Chambertain, George W 110 1
Champer, Christian 100 1
Chandler, John 116, 117 1
Chaney, America 96 1
Chaney, Caroline R 100 1
Chaney, Charles 100 1
Chaney, Elizabeth 106 1
Chaney, Nathan E 129 1
Chaney, Norman E 136 1
Chaney, Sarah A 136 1
Chaplain, Thomas A 214 3
Chaplane, Thomas A 82 1
Chaplin, Harry E 82, 127 1
Chaplin, T A 35 2
Chaplin, Thos A 85, 110, 120 1
Chapline, Chas 73 1
Chapline, Geo M 45 3
Chapline, George 137 1
Chapline, Harry E 224 3
Chapline, Harry E 113 1
Chapline, Mary B 159 3
Chapline, Mary B 3, 172 2
Chapline, Mary Byerly 73 1
Chapline, T A 60, 172 3
Chapline, T A 58, 166, 172, 189 2
Chapline, Thomas A 45, 65 3
Chapline, Thomas A 190 2
Chapline, Thomas A Jr 137 1
Chapline, Thomas H 56 3
Chapline, Thos 137 1
Chapline, Thos A 3, 31 2
Chapline, Thos A 189, 223, 224 3
Chapman, James W Jr, 25 1
Chapman, Kate 123 1
Chapman, Page H 131 1
Charity, Mahala 126 1
Charlton, David E 118 1
Charlton, David E 198 2
Charlton, John 260 1
Charlton, John W 118 1
Charlton, John W 290 2
Chase, Abraham 96 1
Chase, Carlos 133 1
Chase, Carlos T 123 1
Chase, Helen Stirling 113 1
Chase, Henry 112 1
Chase, Jeremiah 117 1
Chase, Lloyd T 123 1
Chase, Robert S 133 1
Chase, Thomas 137 1
Chatman, Harry L 113 1
Cheney, Geo L 23 2
Cheney, Louis 106 1
Cheney, Nathan E 60 1
Chew, Charles E 101, 102, 111 1

Chew, Chas E 111, 113 1
Chew, George L 113, 135 1
Chew, Joseph E 131 1
Chew, Pearl Eva 131 1
Chew, Samuel 135 1
Chew, Thomas 101 1
Chew, Thomas H 137 1
Chew, W 179 3
Chew, Wm 84 1
Chew, Wm 205 3
Chick, Elsie 121 1
Chick, Jesse W 121 1
Chick, W Milo 58 1
Chilcote, Richard 19 3
Chilcote, Richard 121, 177 1
Chilcote, Richard 290 2
Chilton, Cecelia E 100 1
Chilton, Wm F 100, 140 1
Chipley, Charles L 124 1
Chipley, Lillie May 124 1
Chiswell, Daisy L 199 3
Chiswell, Eugenia G 120 1
Chiswell, Howard G 67 3
Chiswell, J N 163 2
Chiswell, J N 106, 124 3
Chiswell, John A 120 1
Chiswell, Joseph N 120 1
Chiswell, Joseph W 118 1
Chiswell, Mary 254 1
Chiswell, Mary C 120 1
Chiswell, Virginia 118 1
Chiswell, Wm T 124 3
Chrisholm, John N 116 1
Chrisiner, Edwin 76, 123, 201 1
Chrismer, Edwin 108 2
Chrismer, John Everett 284 2
Christ, Ann 96 1
Christi, Milton 127 1
Christis, George 127, 146 1
Christis, Marie (Christie) 127 1
Christis, Milton 127 1
Christner, John M 117 1
Church, Anna L 97 1
Churchner, John A 118 1
Churchner, Margaret 118 1
Chylinski, Stephen J 10 1
Clabaugh, Annie E 140 1
Clabaugh, Charles B 101 1
Clabaugh, D C 129 1
Clabaugh, Francis 109 1
Clabaugh, Frank G 20 2
Clabaugh, G M 129 1
Clabaugh, Henry F 112 1
Clabaugh, Jacob 109 1
Clabaugh, James 195 3
Clabaugh, James 116, 117 1
Clabaugh, John 46 2
Clabaugh, John 27 1
Clabaugh, John 195 3
Clabaugh, John T 116, 136 1
Clabaugh, Mary E 126 1
Clabaugh, Melvin J 20 2
Clabaugh, Minerva 112 1
Clabaugh, Norman B 129 1
Clabaugh, Sallie M 206 3
Clabaugh, Samuel S 136 1
Clabaugh, Wm F 140 1
Clabaugh, Wm R 140 1
Clabuagh, John 119 2
Clagett, Samuel 125, 137 1
Clagett, Samuel 160 2
Clagett, Thos & 165 2
Claggett, Ann 96 1
Claggett, Anna P 96 1
Claggett, Catherine 100 1
Claggett, Charles H 101 1
Claggett, Elizabeth, 135 1
Claggett, Grafton A 117 1
Claggett, H M 96 1
Claggett, Henry 54, 228a 2
Claggett, Henry H. 101, 113 1
Claggett, Horatio 112, 137 1
Claggett, Jeanette E 135 1
Claggett, Joan F 120 1
Claggett, John H M 120 1
Claggett, L B Keene 112 1
Claggett, Mary 125, 135 1
Claggett, Mary L 137 1
Claggett, Mary S 126 1
Claggett, Minnie J 113 1
Claggett, Rebecca 133 1
Claggett, Rebecca Miss 135 1
Claggett, Salomia V 33 1
Claggett, Samuel 101, 112, 135, 234, 270 1
Claggett, Samuel 171 3
Claggett, Samuel 250 2
Claggett, Samuel M 135 1
Claggett, Sinphia 135 1
Claggett, T W. 136 1
Claggett, T West 135 1
Claggett, T West Jr 169 3
Claggett, Thomas 137 1
Claggett, Thomas H 96 1
Claggett, Thomas J 100, 112, 137 1
Claggett, Thomas Jr 137 1
Claggett, Thos 51, 264 2
Claggett, Thos W 120 1
Claghorn, John 116 1
Clantice, Peter 58 1
Clapham, Dorcas 104 1
Clapham, Thos 198 2
Claphum, Elizabeth M 172 1
Clapp, R E 15 2
Clapp, Robert E Jr 112 1
Clappen, Hiram 112, 133 1
Clappen, Mary J 112 1
Clarey, Amos 96 1
Clarey, Henry 96 1
Clarey, Reuben 104 1
Clark, Anna M 161 2
Clark, Anna M 109, 127 1
Clark, Cecile Smith 68 3
Clark, Effie R 57 3
Clark, Frank 109 1
Clark, George V 126 1
Clark, J Milla See Milla Clark 120 1
Clark, J Miller 119, 125 1
Clark, James 175 2
Clark, James Avery 161 2
Clark, James Avery 116 1
Clark, John 119, 127 1
Clark, John H 47, 119 1
Clark, John W 61, 119 1
Clark, Joshua H 120 1
Clark, Lewis T 67 3
Clark, Maggie 127 1
Clark, Maggie 127 1
Clark, Margaret E 126 1
Clark, Milla 120 1
Clark, Philip 131 1
Clark, Raymond S 22 1
Clark, Samuel 136 1
Clark, Verva M 131 1
Clarke, Benjamin H 99 1
Clarke, C S 119 1
Clarke, Desire N 67 3
Clarke, Edith Eaton 58 3
Clarke, George H 120 1
Clarke, Horace W 112 1
Clarke, James C 119 1
Clarke, Janie 96 1
Clarke, Jas T 67 3
Clarkin, Eliz A 145 2
Clarkson, Mary A 63 2
Clary, Aaron 97, 99, 120 1
Clary, Amos 156 1
Clary, Amos 148 2
Clary, Annie R 112 1
Clary, Burgess N 99, 117 1
Clary, Clara Smith 101 1
Clary, Claude N 195 2
Clary, Claude N 101 1
Clary, Cornelius 139 1
Clary, Daniel 104 1
Clary, Dora 119 1
Clary, Elizabeth 106 1
Clary, Frederick S 34 1
Clary, Hammond 9, 16, 25, 85, 110, 113, 160, 172, 220, 242, 249, 283, 286 2
Clary, Hammond 16, 20, 57, 83, 176 3

Clary, Hammond 19, 68, 101, 109, 177, 179, 192, 205, 235, 260 1
Clary, Hanson 112 1
Clary, Henry 112, 118 1
Clary, Henry M 112 1
Clary, J E 119 1
Clary, James 270 1
Clary, James A 82, 109, 135 1
Clary, James B 135, 150 1
Clary, Jesse 117 1
Clary, Jesse T 119 1
Clary, John 154 2
Clary, John E 148 2
Clary, John F 119 1
Clary, John H 118 1
Clary, John M 101 1
Clary, John M 195 2
Clary, John N 58, 214a 2
Clary, John N 235 1
Clary, John W 119 1
Clary, Laura V 112 1
Clary, Lina 119 1
Clary, Lycurgus 140 1
Clary, M G 135 1
Clary, Mary A 125 1
Clary, Mary T 126 1
Clary, Moses 133 1
Clary, Moses 27 2
Clary, Nathan 129 1
Clary, Nathan M 130 1
Clary, Nathaniel H 106 1
Clary, Oliver M 57, 130 1
Clary, Reuben 133, 140 1
Clary, Reuben T 99 1
Clary, Samuel 57 2
Clary, Sarah 99, 106 1
Clary, Solomon 117, 135 1
Clary, Sophia 135 1
Clary, Vachel L 139 1
Clary, W H H 106 1
Clary, Weden 125, 129, 133 1
Clary, Weeden 140 1
Clary, Weedon 140 1
Clary, Wm 138 2
Clary, Wm H H 112, 118 1
Claudy, Edgar W 178 2
Clay, Albert J 97 1
Clay, Calvin E 101, 110, 126 1
Clay, Carl D 97 1
Clay, Ciney M 97, 102 1
Clay, Fannie C 109 1
Clay, Fannie M 120 1
Clay, Geo H 123 1
Clay, Geo M 118 1
Clay, Geo W 140 1
Clay, George 110 1
Clay, Grafton 110 1
Clay, Howard R 109 1
Clay, Izabelle 115 1
Clay, James O 119 1
Clay, Jesse 115, 120, 197 1
Clay, Jessie 120 1
Clay, John H 118 1
Clay, John N 119 1
Clay, John Nelson 110 1
Clay, Lemuel 120, 123 1
Clay, Louisa Johnson 123, 197 1
Clay, Mary M 126 1
Clay, Mary M 2, 50 3
Clay, Sarah 120 1
Clay, Weden 253 1
Clay, Wm 140 1
Clay, Wm 198 2
Clay, Wm P 140, 253 1
Clay, Zebluon 87 3
Clay, Zenbulon 88 1
Claybaugh, J 271 1
Clayton, L S 87 3
Clem, Chester G 120 1
Clem, Adam 203 2
Clem, Adam 96 1
Clem, Ann Maria 96 1
Clem, Bradley E 120 1
Clem, Catherine 100, 110 1
Clem, Catherine E (Katie) 101 1
Clem, Charles M 102, 120 1
Clem, Chester G 142, 235 1
Clem, Chester, Mrs 142 1
Clem, Eliza 106 1
Clem, Ellen N 101 1
Clem, Enos W 101 1
Clem, Ersie F 102, 140 1
Clem, Eve 117 1
Clem, Geo A 110 1
Clem, George 102, 110, 117 1
Clem, Graydon F 140, 156 1
Clem, J W 187 2
Clem, Jacob Sr 117 1
Clem, Jacob W 169 2
Clem, John A 132 1
Clem, John H 120 1
Clem, Julia M 120 1
Clem, Peter 110 1
Clem, Peter Jr 131 1
Clem, Peter Sr 131 1
Clem, Queen May 132 1
Clem, Samuel 135, 249 1
Clem, Samuel 192 3
Clem, Susan Elizabeth 136 1
Clem, Susie E Bitler 136 1
Clem, Thomas W 142 1
Clem, William U G 140 1
Clem, Zoa A 142 1
Clemments, Leonard 123 1
Clemson, Abraham 214 1
Clemson, Andrew 76 2
Clemson, Clarence L 241 2
Clemson, Clarence L 120 1
Clemson, D D H 126 1
Clemson, Dennis D H 112 1
Clemson, H 67 3
Clemson, Hanson 187 2
Clemson, Hanson T 116, 117, 125 1
Clemson, Henson T 118 1
Clemson, J H 51 2
Clemson, J H. 57 1
Clemson, James 116, 126 1
Clemson, James 282 2
Clemson, James H 59 1
Clemson, James H 42 3
Clemson, James H 51 2
Clemson, John 185 3
Clemson, John 117, 118 1
Clemson, John D 43, 49 2
Clemson, John H 116, 169 1
Clemson, John Jr 117, 120, 125 1
Clemson, John Sr 117 1
Clemson, Mary 125 1
Clemson, Mordecai 125 1
Clendenin, Sophia A 116 1
Clepham, Elizabeth 198 2
Clevenger, Leslie E 137 1
Clevenger, Lulu L 137 1
Clevenger, Thomas W 137 1
Clevenger,Thos W 137 1
Clever, Edw B 96 1
Cline, Absalom 106, 110 1
Cline, Adam 96 1
Cline, Ann 96 1
Cline, Annie A 97, 129 1
Cline, Annie F 140 1
Cline, Benjamin 99 1
Cline, C E 57, 82, 83 3
Cline, C E 9, 16, 23, 65, 149, 160, 172, 253, 259, 265 2
Cline, Casper 159, 220 2
Cline, Casper 14, 100, 101, 112, 135 1
Cline, Casper E 41 2
Cline, Casper E 11, 35, 57, 163, 276, 213 3
Cline, Casper E 34, 55, 97, 179, 186, 202, 203, 239 1
Cline, Casper E 25, 41, 110, 124, 163, 160, 175, 232, 242, 280 2
Cline, Casper E Jr 41, 163 2
Cline, Casper E Jr 55, 202, 245 1
Cline, Casper E Jr 45, 57, 73 3
Cline, Casper E Sr 45, 57, 111 3
Cline, Casper E Sr 199 2
Cline, Charles L 101 1
Cline, Chas 182 2

Cline, Chas C 123 1
Cline, Chas L 140 1
Cline, Corvilla 100 1
Cline, Corville 100 1
Cline, Elias 131 1
Cline, Ellen 107 1
Cline, Geo 80 2
Cline, George 110 1
Cline, George T (col) 110 1
Cline, Grover C 9 2
Cline, Hezekiah 131 1
Cline, Isabelle M 208 3
Cline, Jacob E 143 2
Cline, John 277 1
Cline, Lawson 131 1
Cline, Lawson 41 3
Cline, Lawson H 19 1
Cline, Lewis 123 1
Cline, N O 100 1
Cline, Nicholas O 100, 106, 129 1
Cline, Nicholas O 163 3
Cline, Nicholas O 171 2
Cline, Oscar F 107 1
Cline, Oscar F 85 2
Cline, Philip 131 1
Cline, Wade F 140 1
Cline, Wilbur J 143 2
Cline, Wm H 140 1
Clingan, Annie 111 3
Clingan, Archibald 96 1
Clingan, C C 111 3
Clingan, Charles E 101 1
Clingan, Charles Edgar 101 1
Clingan, Charles Wm 111 3
Clingan, Ella S 94 3
Clingan, Emma I 110 1
Clingan, George F 110 1
Clingan, John F 27, 118 1
Clingan, L S 41, 71, 76, 110, 139 1
Clingan, L S 100, 104 3
Clingan, Lewis 40, 87 2
Clingan, Lewis S 27, 118, 123, 125, 135, 140 1
Clingan, Lewis S 72, 188 3
Clingan, Lewis S 52, 80 2
Clingan, Maria L 126 1
Clingan, Minerva E 123 1
Clingan, S S 61 1
Clingan, Sophia 135, 139 1
Clingan, Winchester 139 1
Clingan, Wm M 139 1
Clink, C M 32 1
Clipp, Edna Beachley 58 3
Clipp, Frances A 140 1
Clipp, Wm A 140 1
Clobaugh, N N [sic] 26 1
Clominger, Mary M 125 1
Cloninger, Philip 131 1
Cloninger, Philip Sr 97 1
Close, A B 129 2
Close, A B 43 3
Close, Adelaide L 60, 131 1
Close, Albert B 97, 106, 110 1
Close, Christian 100 1
Close, Elizah 106 1
Close, Jesse 100 1
Close, John 220 3
Close, John 119 1
Close, Mary A 126 1
Close, Mary Ann 25 1
Clover, Wm of Y 25, 119 1
Clunt, Jacob 116 1
Clutz, Hazel Boller 53 1
Coale, James 118 1
Coale, James M 133 1
Coale, Richard 13, 133, 139 1
Coale, Richard 38 2
Coale, Richard 8 3
Coale, William 249 2
Coale, William 184 3
Coale, Wm 133, 139, 256, 264 1
Coates, Chas B 101 1
Coates, Harriet 113 1
Coates, John 101 1
Coates, William H 113, 146 1
Coats, Harriett 137 1
Coats, Isaac 115 1
Coats, Thomas 137 1
Coats, Wm Judson 97 1
Cobean, Alexnader 96 1
Cobean, Annie E 97 1
Cobell, Ann 96 1
Cobell, Joel 96 1
Cobelntz, E L 224 3
Coberly, Emerentienne V 116 1
Coblentz, A M 3 3
Coblentz, Albert M 176 3
Coblentz, Albert M 126 1
Coblentz, Albert N 63 1
Coblentz, Alliance 164 1
Coblentz, Alta G 106 1
Coblentz, Andrew 198 2
Coblentz, Annie 192 3
Coblentz, Barbara 99 1
Coblentz, Byron G 102 1
Coblentz, C Frank 101 1
Coblentz, C H 14 1
Coblentz, Calvin 87 2
Coblentz, Calvin P 116 2
Coblentz, Calvin R 67, 101, 106, 112 1
Coblentz, Catherine 19 1
Coblentz, Charlotte E 100, 101, 123 1
Coblentz, Chas C 198 2
Coblentz, Chas C 101, 133 1
Coblentz, Chas H 101 1
Coblentz, Clara E 102, 110, 127, 208 1
Coblentz, Clara S 106 1
Coblentz, D 47 1
Coblentz, D P 92 1
Coblentz, Daisy M 32 1
Coblentz, Daniel 26, 123 1
Coblentz, Danson 166 3
Coblentz, David 39, 143 2
Coblentz, David 76, 104, 117, 125 1
Coblentz, E F 118 1
Coblentz, E Frank 106 1
Coblentz, E Franklin 1 1
Coblentz, E L 6, 10, 15, 20, 27, 43, 50, 55, 56, 65, 72, 82, 83, 91, 100, 107, 109, 111, 124, 126, 166, 167, 182, 188, 206, 215, 216, 221 3
Coblentz, E L 23, 27, 61, 62, 72, 85, 92, 99, 101, 131, 135, 153, 166, 177, 179, 183, 222, 230, 249, 254, 257, 260, 265, 272 1
Coblentz, E L 2, 9, 30, 46, 49, 52, 62, 65, 70, 80, 93, 102, 112, 124, 129, 134, 139, 145, 150, 154, 160, 166, 169, 172, 175, 181, 189, 195, 198, 209, 214, 220, 218a, 222a, 234, 238, 241, 254, 265, 277, 283, 290 2
Coblentz, Edw F 58 1
Coblentz, Edw L 26, 106, 131 1
Coblentz, Edward F 67 3
Coblentz, Edward L 163 3
Coblentz, EL 160 3
Coblentz, Elias 101, 116 2
Coblentz, Elias 100, 106, 214, 253, 272 1
Coblentz, Eliza 106 1
Coblentz, Elizabeth 106, 125 1
Coblentz, Elizabeth C 106 1
Coblentz, Ellen F 126 1
Coblentz, Emma Frances 4 1
Coblentz, Emory 172 2
Coblentz, Emory L 19, 28, 35, 43, 44, 56, 67, 196, 206 3
Coblentz, Emory L 2, 8, 12, 15, 25, 30, 40, 54, 66, 70, 76, 84, 89, 102, 113, 115, 144, 160, 172, 242, 255, 268, 271, 277, 283, 286, 290, 2
Coblentz, Emory L 8, 9, 14, 19, 23, 27, 33, 38, 41, 42, 52, 61, 63, 67, 72, 73, 85, 86, 96, 97, 100, 101, 106, 110, 112, 119, 123, 126, 133, 135, 140, 144, 152, 172, 183, 189, 194, 203, 210, 219, 229, 230, 234, 249, 253, 272, 279, 280

1
Coblentz, George G 110 1
Coblentz, H B 259 2
Coblentz, H J 71 1
Coblentz, Hamilton N 112 1
Coblentz, Harry B 55 1
Coblentz, Henry 51, 177, 268 2
Coblentz, Henry 112, 118, 127 1
Coblentz, Henry 9 3
Coblentz, Henry of J 112 1
Coblentz, Herman J 120 1
Coblentz, Horace B 101 1
Coblentz, J 247 2
Coblentz, J C 71 3
Coblentz, J C 118, 135 1
Coblentz, J V 207 1
Coblentz, J V 107 3
Coblentz, J Vernon 40 1
Coblentz, J Vernon 72 2
Coblentz, Jacob 19, 43, 51, 169 2
Coblentz, Jacob 217, 218 3
Coblentz, Jacob 78, 84, 115, 123 1
Coblentz, James H 116 1
Coblentz, John 32, 47, 117, 118, 228 1
Coblentz, John 70 3
Coblentz, John C 19 3
Coblentz, John C 58 1
Coblentz, John of P 118, 120 1
Coblentz, John of P 264 2
Coblentz, John of T 54 3
Coblentz, John of T 106 1
Coblentz, John P 137 2
Coblentz, John Philip 117 1
Coblentz, John Sr 176 3
Coblentz, Joseph D 101 1
Coblentz, Julia A 106 1
Coblentz, L N 57, 96, 113, 167 3
Coblentz, L N 220 2
Coblentz, L Phillip 33 1
Coblentz, Leslie 91 3
Coblentz, Leslie 107, 166, 169, 203 2
Coblentz, Leslie H 166 3
Coblentz, Leslie M 23, 123 1
Coblentz, Leslie N 3, 102, 107, 122, 208 3
Coblentz, Leslie N 3, 52, 66, 89, 227a, 255, 262, 291 2
Coblentz, Leslie N 42, 48, 73, 101, 110, 115, 123, 124, 126, 146, 183, 189, 205, 207, 235, 240, 254, 272 1
Coblentz, Lewis P 112 1
Coblentz, Lloyd E 101 1
Coblentz, Louis P 123 1
Coblentz, Lucinda E M 123 1
Coblentz, Luther H 123 1
Coblentz, M C 112 1
Coblentz, M R 83 3
Coblentz, M Virginia 126 1
Coblentz, Magdalene 125 1
Coblentz, Martin C 126 1
Coblentz, Mary A 127 1
Coblentz, Mary Wyand 124 1
Coblentz, O B 239, 270 1
Coblentz, O B 56 3
Coblentz, Oliver P 130 1
Coblentz, Oliver P 197 2
Coblentz, Oscar B 106 1
Coblentz, Oscar B 67 3
Coblentz, Oscar B 30, 283 2
Coblentz, Oscar P 30 1
Coblentz, P 138, 264 2
Coblentz, Peter 76, 101, 123, 125, 131 1
Coblentz, Peter 1 3
Coblentz, Peter Jr 32, 76, 131 1
Coblentz, Peter Sr 32 1
Coblentz, Philip 19, 163, 215 3
Coblentz, Philip 87, 100, 101 2
Coblentz, Philip 118, 125, 131, 228 1
Coblentz, Rebecca 198 2
Coblentz, S B 131 1
Coblentz, S C 106, 131 1
Coblentz, S Calvin 126, 135 1
Coblentz, Sarah 135 1
Coblentz, Silas 112 1
Coblentz, Stephen B 112, 130 1
Coblentz, T 54 3
Coblentz, Vernon J 146 1
Coblentz, W L 166 2
Coblentz, Walter B 53 1
Cochran, Anna M 96 1
Cochran, Chas R 100 1
Cochran, Clifford 100 1
Cochran, Cornelius 100, 112, 133 1
Cochran, Daniel 104 1
Cochran, Elanor 118 1
Cochran, Eleanor 76 1
Cochran, Henry 106, 112, 117 1
Cochran, Hugh 117 1
Cochran, James 118 1
Cochran, James B 126 1
Cochran, John 118 1
Cochran, John 150 2
Cochran, John W 71 1
Cochran, Lewis R 225a 2
Cochran, Louis 112 1
Cochran, Margaret 126 1
Cochran, Margaret C. 100 1
Cochran, Mary Jane 126 1
Cochran, Perry J 96 1
Cochran, R Clifford 219 1
Cochran, Reuben F 133 1
Cochran, Zora Carlton 142 1
Cochrane, Laura C 124 1
Cochren, Elizabeth A 106 1
Cochren, L R 106 1
Cock, Samuel 106 1
Cockerly, Lewis C 262 2
Cockey, Elizabeth S 135 1
Cockey, Ellen 116 1
Cockey, Henrietta 116 1
Cockey, J G 117, 139 1
Cockey, J Paul 125, 139 1
Cockey, James C 135 1
Cockey, John 117 1
Cockey, John 37 3
Cockey, John C 98, 222 3
Cockey, John C 116 1
Cockey, John C 205 2
Cockey, Joseph 37 3
Cockey, Joseph C 171 2
Cockey, Joshua 116 1
Cockey, Joshua 254 2
Cockey, Joshua Jr 116 1
Cockey, M Elizabeth 125 1
Cockey, M Elizabeth 171 2
Cockey, Mary C 125 1
Cockey, O S 135 1
Cockey, S G 214 2
Cockey, S G 110, 139 1
Cockey, S Graff 129 3
Cockey, S Graff 137 1
Cockey, S Sprigg 135 1
Cockey, Sebastian G 135 1
Cockey, Sebastian G 7 2
Cockey, Sebastian S 106 1
Cockey, Sebatian 76 2
Cockey, T F 214 2
Cockey, Theodore F 137 1
Cockey, Wm 139 1
Cockey, Wm 7 2
Coe, Basil 116 1
Coe, Benjamin 116 1
Coe, Catherine 116, 133 1
Coe, Jesse 116 1
Coe, John 116 1
Coe, John Sr 116 1
Coe, Joshua 116 1
Coe, Rebecca 133 1
Coepnhaver, Jacob 116 1
Coffman, Andrew 96 1
Coffman, Basil S Jr 197 3
Coffman, Elizabeth 133 1
Coffman, James 262 2
Coffman, Russell 96 1
Coghlan, Wm 137 2
Colbert, Andrew J 28, 133 1
Colbert, Charles T 120, 144 1

Colbert, J A 96 1
Colbert, John A 120 1
Colbert, Mary M 96 1
Colbert, W R 144 1
Colbert, Wm T 96 1
Cole, Ava R 215 2
Cole, Beatrice M 115 1
Cole, C E 85 1
Cole, Charles 84, 100 1
Cole, Charles E 170 2
Cole, Chas 100, 223 1
Cole, Chas 50 3
Cole, Chas 14, 169 2
Cole, David 84 2
Cole, Frank W 33 1
Cole, Geo 195 2
Cole, Geo A 176 1
Cole, Ida M 115 1
Cole, James M 67 2
Cole, James R 67 2
Cole, John 117 1
Cole, Lewis M 268 2
Cole, Louis M 117 1
Cole, Mary C 127 1
Cole, Richard 23 3
Cole, Sallie 60 1
Cole, Thomas C 82 1
Cole, William L 215 2
Cole, Wm 137, 223 1
Coleburger, Francis 171 2
Coleburn, Geo R 150 1
Colegate, Edw 245 1
Colegate, Harriett 21 1
Colegate, John 21 1
Coleman, Betty F 99 1
Coleman, Catherine 223 3
Coleman, David 104 1
Coleman, Henry 112 1
Coleman, Jacob 112 1
Coleman, Wm 139 1
Colgate, Geo 133 1
Colgate, George 70 1
Colgate, John 110, 133 1
Colgate, Mary 110 1
Colgate, Richard 133 1
Coll, Chas D 34 1
Coll, Mary C 125 1
Colleberry, Elizabeth R 109 1
Colleberry, Francis 109 1
Collenberry, Cordelia 117 1
Collenberry, Jacob 115 1
Colliberry, Israel 117, 135 1
Colliberry, Sallie 115 1
Colliberry, Susanna 135 1
Collier, Joseph P 59 1
Colliflower, B 99, 117 1
Colliflower, B 85, 174 3
Colliflower, Bernard 19, 93, 177
2
Colliflower, Bernard 9, 94 3
Colliflower, Bernard 119, 140,
156, 234, 253, 264119, 1
Colliflower, Ella Jane 239 1
Colliflower, F 38 1
Colliflower, Geo 263 1
Colliflower, George 110 1
Colliflower, Hannah 112 1
Colliflower, Howard E 282 1
Colliflower, Howard F 113 1
Colliflower, Howard S 113 1
Colliflower, J 234 1
Colliflower, J 93 2
Colliflower, J T 94 3
Colliflower, J T 93 2
Colliflower, Jago 85 3
Colliflower, Jago 19, 177 2
Colliflower, Jago 99 1
Colliflower, James A 119 1
Colliflower, Jennie E 119 1
Colliflower, John 52 2
Colliflower, John 174 3
Colliflower, John A 140 1
Colliflower, John F 35 2
Colliflower, John F 189 1
Colliflower, John T 177 2
Colliflower, John T 99 1
Colliflower, Lewis 110 1
Colliflower, Michael 125 1
Colliflower, Samuel 185 2
Colliflower, Vernon 113 1
Colliflower, Walter R 113, 175
1
Colliflower, Wm D 140 1
Colliflower, Wm H 140 1
Collins, Alcelia 97 1
Collins, Ann 96 1
Collins, Asenath 96 1
Collins, Catherine 100, 101
1
Collins, Chas A 88, 118 1
Collins, Daniel 96 1
Collins, Ellen 96, 112, 137 1
Collins, Ellen V 107 1
Collins, Ephriam 112 1
Collins, Frances M 101 1
Collins, Henry 112 1
Collins, John 118 1
Collins, Lydia A 135 1
Collins, Nicholas 129 1
Collins, Samuel 135, 152 1
Collins, Sylvia D 136 1
Collins, Tabitha 137 1
Collmus, A B 172, 240 1
Colon, Victor F 202 2
Colonial Trust Co 189 2
Colonial Trust Co of Baltimore 189
2
Colson, Edw 106 3
Colston, Edward 120 3
Coltrane, Katherine 68 3
Combash, Joseph W 119 1
Combs, Floyd G 109 1
Combs, Helen R 109 1
Combs, Henry 112 1
Combs, Raphel 133 1
Comer, Nellie I 61 2
Commercial Casualty Co of N J 116
2
Commercial Casualty Ins Co 295
2
Compher, Alice C 23 2
Compher, Atlee Sr 113 2
Compher, Bessie 107 1
Compher, Burns 189 3
Compher, Burns W 113, 120
1
Compher, Edw A 107 1
Compher, Edw C 126 1
Compher, Ella 126 1
Compher, Everett C 130 1
Compher, Henry 113 1
Compher, James W 120 1
Compher, Joseph H T 119 1
Compher, Mary C 126 1
Compher, Millard T 107 1
Compher, Otho E 130 1
Compher, Samuel W 136 1
Compher, W W 126 1
Compher, Wesley M 136 1
Compher, Williard T 189 3
Compler, Samuel P [sic] 119 1
Compton, Alice Mae 48 3
Compton, Cora N 220 2
Compton, Edward L 107 1
Compton, Parmelia 131 1
Compton, Peter V 131 1
Compton, Robt A 131 1
Conard, L Louise 124 1
Conden, Wesley 75 3
Condon, A S 166 3
Condon, A W 94 3
Condon, Albert W 97, 113 1
Condon, Caroline R 118 1
Condon, Charlie E 9 2
Condon, Charlie E 107 1
Condon, Edw E 107 1
Condon, Fannie 117 1
Condon, Fannie E 46 3
Condon, John 185 3
Condon, John 97, 142, 248 1
Condon, John H 135 1
Condon, Joseph 118 1
Condon, Susanna 100 1
Condon, Zacharia 198 2
Condon, Zachariah 118, 135, 142
1
Condry, Harold S 198 2

Conlan, Vincentia S 3 3
Conley, C H 102 2
Conley, C H 99 1
Conley, C H 189 3
Conner, Blanche W 113, 265 1
Conner, Catherine 100 1
Conner, Creighton 101 1
Conner, Emma 106 1
Conner, Harriet R 112 1
Conner, Harvey P 106 1
Conner, Henry 226 2
Conner, James 106, 112, 113, 117 1
Conner, James T 112 1
Conner, James T 117 1
Conner, Julia A 120 1
Conner, Margaret H 177 2
Conner, Mary 137 1
Conner, Mary M 181 2
Conner, Thomas 137 1
Conner, Thos 75 2
Conner, Thos 163 1
Conrad, Elizabeth 120 1
Conrad, Elizabeth L 107 1
Conrad, Geo 228 1
Conrad, Henry 82 1
Conrad, James 117 1
Conrad, John 119 1
Conrad, John 148 2
Conrad, John D 120 1
Conrad, Joseph M 117 1
Conrad, Mary 54 3
Conrad, Richard N 148 1
Conradt, D M 27 2
Conradt, Geo 46 2
Conradt, Geo M 92 2
Conradt, George M 23 3
Constan, George 110 1
Constance, Louisa 118 1
Contee, John 118 1
Contee, John 123, 129 1
Conway, Betty E 133 1
Conway, Bridget K 118 1
Conway, J G 133 1
Conway, John 118 1
Conway, Julia G 227 2
Conway, Julia G 129 1
Conway, M E 133 1
Conway, Nona E 129 1
Conway, Richard O 133 1
Cook, Abraham 96 1
Cook, Baltzer 112 1
Cook, Barton 99 1
Cook, Catherine Ida 35 3
Cook, Charlotte 119 1
Cook, Charlotte C 100 1
Cook, Charlotte T 100, 101 1
Cook, Ellen M 110 1
Cook, Ellen Minerva 107 1
Cook, Florence A 110 1
Cook, George E 110 1
Cook, George W 110 1
Cook, Henry 112 1
Cook, J Carlton 13 1
Cook, James 137 2
Cook, James 118, 133 1
Cook, Jesse 217 2
Cook, John 118, 228 1
Cook, John 14, 72, 229a, 249 2
Cook, John & 209 3
Cook, John R 118 1
Cook, John W 119, 120 1
Cook, John W E 107 1
Cook, Lillian 107 1
Cook, Mary 126 1
Cook, Mary A 126 1
Cook, Melissa B 100 1
Cook, Millard F 126, 130 1
Cook, Newton S 82 3
Cook, Oscar R 130 1
Cook, Otho 188 2
Cook, Otho T 91 3
Cook, Rachel F 133 1
Cook, Zena 142 1
Cookerley, Lewis C 135 1
Cookerley, Rosanna 133 1
Cookerley, Sarah E 116 1
Cookerly, George 101 2
Cookerly, Jacob 125, 135, 163 1
Cookerly, Jacob C 135 1
Cookerly, John N 70 2
Cookerly, Lewis 187 2
Cookerly, Lewis C 29 2
Cookerly, Lewis C 51 1
Cookerly, Margaret 125 1
Cookerly, Mary A R 126 1
Cookerly, Michael 205 3
Cookerly, Minnie E 25 1
Cookerly, Wm 116, 126, 139, 159 1
Cookson, Samuel 184 3
Cool, George J 136 1
Cool, Samuel David 136 1
Coole, James M 133 1
Cooley, Caroline R 101 1
Cooley, Frederick G 81 2
Cooley, John J 101, 140 1
Cooley, Millard I 81 2
Cooley, Wm L 140 1
Coomes, Joseph 211 2
Coomes, Joseph W 118 1
Coon, George 110 1
Coon, John 185 3
Coon, John 28 2
Coon, John W 1 2
Coones, Raphael 135 1
Cooney, Sarah E 135 1
Coons, Abraham 112 1
Coons, Henry 112 1
Coons, Jacob 112 1
Coons, John Sr 116 1
Cooper, Charles H 101 1
Cooper, Chas 264 1
Cooper, Ellen E 140 2
Cooper, Ellen E 101 1
Cooper, Emanuel 106 1
Cooper, Fanny M 133 1
Cooper, G W 89 2
Cooper, Glenn 113 1
Cooper, Herbert E 113 1
Cooper, Howard 113 1
Cooper, James 117 1
Cooper, James Gen'l 118 1
Cooper, James Jr 214 2
Cooper, Jane M 214 2
Cooper, Jane M 118 1
Cooper, John 11 2
Cooper, Joseph 179 3
Cooper, Joshua 117 1
Cooper, Lavinia 123 1
Cooper, Myrtle I 222 2
Cooper, Roy S 133 1
Cooper, W H 79 3
Cooper, Wilbur 113 1
Copelan, Rose 10 3
Copeland, Charles 100 1
Copelin, Elizabeth 106,135 1
Copelin, Samuel B 135 1
Copeline, Samuel 205 3
Copenhaver, Jacob 133 1
Copenhaver, John 116 1
Copenhaver, Wm 57 2
Coppersmith, Abraham 96 1
Coppersmith, Lewis 39 3
Coppersmith, Lewis F 125, 197 1
Coppersmith, Lewis T 222 3
Coppersmith, Mary M 125 1
Corberly, John R 116 1
Corbet, Lola R 243 1
Corbett, Charles H 74 1
Corbett, Mary A 126 1
Corbett, Wm J 126 1
Corbin, W W 148 1
Corbitt, Charles M 101 1
Corbitt, Wm J 101 1
Cordell, Harvey W 121 1
Cordell, Helen V 121 1
Cordell, Jacob 120 1
Cordell, Joseph W 121 1
Corell, Wm 96 2
Cornel, Ellen 106 1
Cornelius, James 119 1
Cornell, Benjamin 99 1
Cornell, Jane 99 1

Cornell, Margaret 125 1
Cornell, William 26 3
Cornell, Wm 210 1
Cornpropst, Harry E 113 1
Cornpropst, Margaret S 113 1
Cornwell, Caroline 41 1
Cornwell, Jacob 35 2
Correll, Christian 100 1
Correll, Mary E 126, 139 1
Corrick, Andrew 96 1
Corrick, Joshua 96 1
Corrick, Joshua 181 2
Corry, A B 107 3
Corry, Anna B 97 1
Corry, Jane F 107 3
Corry, Martha J 97, 131 1
Corry, P J 107 3
Corry, Paul J 131 1
Corum, Chas W 140 1
Corum, John W 120 1
Corum, Sarah E, 140 1
Corum, Virginia C 110 1
Corum, Wm A 140 1
Corun, Calvin 101 1
Corun, Carrie 101 1
Corun, Chas A 115 2
Corun, George C 110 1
Corun, I Edgie 101 1
Corun, W E 101 1
Cosgrave, William D 254 2
Coskery, John 100 2
Cost, Ann Maria 110 1
Cost, Bennedictor 99 1
Cost, Christian 202 3
Cost, Christian 100 1
Cost, Elias 106 1
Cost, Elizabeth 110 1
Cost, Geo 110 1
Cost, George 57, 110, 249 1
Cost, Henry 99, 110, 112, 116, 271 1
Cost, Henry 27, 111, 203, 227a, 237 2
Cost, Henry 106, 202, 207 3
Cost, Jacob 116, 196, 244 1
Cost, John 202 3
Cost, John 229a 2
Cost, Mary A S 112 1
Cost, Mary Ann 100 1
Costelle, Caroline 101 1
Costello, Thomas 137 1
Coster, William 139 1
Coster, Wm 116 2
Costley, Annie 97 1
Costley, Grafton 110 1
Costley, Grafton 160 3
Costley, Louis P 123 1
Costley, Walker 140 1
Costly, Daniel 104 1
Costs, Mary E 125 1
Cotter, Mary 125 1
Couch, George 110 1
Coughlan, Clifton Y 133 1
Coughlan, Hannah M 133 1
Coughlan, Helen E 133 1
Coughlan, M Virginia 133 1
Coughlan, Richard T 133 1
Coughlan, William T 133 1
Coughlin, Clifton Y 113 1
Coughlin, Hannah Matilda 113 1
Courtney, Mary 126, 137 1
Courtney, Thomas 137 1
Couston, George A 110 1
Covall, Edmiah 106 1
Covell, Aann [sic] 96 1
Covell, Elizabeth 106 1
Covell, Emma L 119 1
Covell, Forrest D 119 1
Covell, Frederick 109 1
Covell, J F 61 1
Covell, Jonathan 116 1
Covell, Jonathan F 119 1
Covell, Mabel E 16 2
Cover, Amis 187 2
Cover, Amos N 159 2
Cover, Anna M 96 1
Cover, Anna R 268, 280, 284 2
Cover, Anna R 97 1
Cover, Charles 100 1
Cover, Curits [sic] 120 1
Cover, Cyrus 132, 150 2
Cover, Daniel 26 2
Cover, Daniel 167 3
Cover, Emos M 106 1
Cover, Ephraim 58 1
Cover, Ephriam of J 106 1
Cover, Frank C 115 1
Cover, Harry C 112 1
Cover, Harry C 9 3
Cover, Hattie L 112 1
Cover, Irene M 115 1
Cover, J B 106 1
Cover, J H 106 1
Cover, J H 222 3
Cover, J Henry 117 1
Cover, Jacob 120, 142 1
Cover, Jacob Jr 78 1
Cover, Jacob Sr 120 3
Cover, Jacob Sr 116 1
Cover, Jacob Sr 134 2
Cover, James B 91 1
Cover, John 1, 28, 118 2
Cover, John 91, 106, 116, 142, 228 1
Cover, Joseph 142, 150, 159, 164, 183 1
Cover, Joseph 26, 275 2
Cover, Margaret 125 1
Cover, Margaret A 58 1
Cover, Mary 125 1
Cover, Susan 135 1
Cover, Susannah 135 1
Cover, Thomas F 100, 135 1
Cover, Thomas T 32 3
Cover, Thos 198 2
Cover, Thos F 119 2
Cover, Tobias 46 2
Cover, Tobias 137, 271 1
Cover, William H 96 1
Cover, Wm of Y 50 3
Cover, Y 50 3
Cover, Yost 142 1
Cowan, Margaret 125 1
Cowman, Gerard 43 2
Cox, Addie C 119 1
Cox, Addie E 97 1
Cox, Audrey B 66 2
Cox, Chas B 44 1
Cox, Elizabeth 106 1
Cox, Esther L 119 1
Cox, Geo 195 3
Cox, Geo E 119 1
Cox, George 110 1
Cox, George E 111 1
Cox, Georgie C 119 1
Cox, James 202 3
Cox, James L 119, 140 1
Cox, John P 119 1
Cox, John R 110 1
Cox, Joseph B 27 3
Cox, Joseph B 119 1
Cox, Margaret 140 1
Cox, Mary C 140 1
Cox, Mary E 126 1
Cox, Mary L 140 1
Cox, Wm G 140 1
Cox, Wm M 140 1
Cozens, Maggie C 129 1
Cozens, Wm M 129 1
Crabbs, Benjamin 184 3
Crabbs, Frederick 14 2
Crabbs, Frederick 56 1
Crabbs, Geo 217 1
Crabbs, John 7 2
Crabbs, Margaret 101 1
Crabill, Charles L 102, 125 1
Crabill, Raymond L 101 1
Crable, Jane 117 1
Crabs, Frederick 27 2
Crabs, Frederick 100 3
Crabs, Joseph 100 3
Crabster, Abraham 96 1
Crabster, Alice M 118 1
Crabster, Augustus W 96 1
Crabster, Basil 116 1

Crabster, Basil D 118 1
Crabster, James W 116 1
Crabster, John 116, 118 1
Crabster, John 64 2
Crabster, Margaret 125 1
Craft, Frederick 109 1
Craft, Wm E 139 1
Crall, Daniel 116 1
Crall, David 115 1
Crall, Isaac 115 1
Cramer, Ada M 107, 120, 123 1
Cramer, Albert J 96 1
Cramer, Amanda C 96 1
Cramer, Amos 96, 97 1
Cramer, Andrew G 96 1
Cramer, Andrew N 97, 131 1
Cramer, Andrew N 241 2
Cramer, Anna Barbara 96 1
Cramer, B E 20 3
Cramer, Barbara 99 1
Cramer, Bessie 30 1
Cramer, Bradley 91 3
Cramer, Bradley 107, 109, 165 1
Cramer, Bradley T 99 1
Cramer, C A 29 2
Cramer, C A 245 1
Cramer, C H 119 1
Cramer, Caroline S 100 1
Cramer, Carrie 112 1
Cramer, Carrie M 100 1
Cramer, Catherine A 100, 101 1
Cramer, Charles G 101, 110 1
Cramer, Chas C 205, 206 3
Cramer, Chas M 125, 140, 230, 234 1
Cramer, Clarence S 100 1
Cramer, Columbus A 100, 107 1
Cramer, Cora D 150 1
Cramer, Cora Strine 34 1
Cramer, Cordelia A 100, 101 1
Cramer, Cornelius 116, 119 1
Cramer, D J 112 1
Cramer, Daniel 104 1
Cramer, David 104, 119 1
Cramer, David 205 3
Cramer, David 23 2
Cramer, David J 104 1
Cramer, E Catherine 106 1
Cramer, E K 205 2
Cramer, E L 87 2
Cramer, E Virginia 107, 137 1
Cramer, E Virginia 2 3
Cramer, Edna A 99 1
Cramer, Edna A 288 2
Cramer, Edw 107 1
Cramer, Eili 30, 96, 100, 106, 107 1
Cramer, Eli 53 3
Cramer, Elizabeth C 117, 119 1
Cramer, Ella D 28 3
Cramer, Ella K 3 3
Cramer, Ella K, 129 1
Cramer, Ella Kate 107 1
Cramer, Ellen Virginia 107 1
Cramer, Ernest Eugene 8 1
Cramer, Etta V 264 2
Cramer, Ezra 70, 104, 106, 116, 120, 125, 159, 171, 228 1
Cramer, Ezra 31, 227 3
Cramer, Ezra 57, 218, 268, 275 2
Cramer, Ezra D 106 1
Cramer, Ezra L 107 1
Cramer, Ezra L 42 3
Cramer, Ezra L Sr 112 1
Cramer, Ezra L, Jr 112 1
Cramer, Fannie 109 1
Cramer, Fannie F 101 1
Cramer, Fannie M 166 3
Cramer, Florence May 109 1
Cramer, Frederick W 72 1
Cramer, Frederick W 39 3
Cramer, G W 85 1
Cramer, G W 102 3
Cramer, Geo 119 2
Cramer, Geo L 110, 119 1
Cramer, Geo W 125, 131, 186, 194, 264 1
Cramer, Geo W 205 2
Cramer, George 110 1
Cramer, George H 110 1
Cramer, George L 242 2
Cramer, George T 207 3
Cramer, George T 1, 97 1
Cramer, George W 110, 124 1
Cramer, Grayson D 56 3
Cramer, Grayson D 119, 123 1
Cramer, H D 112, 129 1
Cramer, H M 57 3
Cramer, H R 110 1
Cramer, Hallie C 140 1
Cramer, Harry E 107, 113 1
Cramer, Harry E 16, 271 2
Cramer, Harry M 112, 120, 148 1
Cramer, Harry M 207 3
Cramer, Harvey R 9, 268 2
Cramer, Henrietta 47, 124 1
Cramer, Henry 99, 113 1
Cramer, Henry D 124 3
Cramer, Henry D 112, 135 1
Cramer, Herbert L 104 1
Cramer, Ira D 112, 115 1
Cramer, J C 33 1
Cramer, J H 87 2
Cramer, J Henry 119, 125 1
Cramer, J Henry 42 3
Cramer, J P 59 1
Cramer, J W 30, 133, 237 1
Cramer, Jacob 37, 53, 150, 222, to 27 3
Cramer, Jacob 197, 294 2
Cramer, Jacob 32, 57, 112, 116, 117, 118, 125, 139, 156, 183 1
Cramer, Jacob W 73 1
Cramer, Jacob W 96 3
Cramer, James 3 2
Cramer, James H 88, 107, 119 1
Cramer, James H 16 2
Cramer, Jeremiah C 96 1
Cramer, Jeremiah H 106 1
Cramer, Jeremiah Henry 116 1
Cramer, John 117, 123 1
Cramer, John 7 2
Cramer, John A 119 1
Cramer, John A 92 2
Cramer, John B 119, 120 1
Cramer, John B 56 3
Cramer, John D 107, 131 1
Cramer, John D 205 3
Cramer, John E 97, 119, 123, 150 1
Cramer, John F 97 1
Cramer, John H 120 1
Cramer, John of H 117 1
Cramer, John William 120 1
Cramer, Joseph 118 1
Cramer, Joseph C 120 1
Cramer, Julian 119 1
Cramer, Katharine L 129 2
Cramer, L Glenn 123 1
Cramer, Laura C 123 1
Cramer, Lauretta V 124 1
Cramer, Leslie E 110 1
Cramer, Lewis 28 2
Cramer, Lewis 123 1
Cramer, Lizzie McD 120 1
Cramer, Lucy C 113 1
Cramer, Lydia A 117 1
Cramer, M C 272 1
Cramer, M E 101 1
Cramer, M J 233 1
Cramer, Mae 165 1
Cramer, Mae Smith 101 1
Cramer, Margaret C 112, 126 1
Cramer, Martin O 106 1
Cramer, Mary 112, 125 1
Cramer, Mary B 110 1
Cramer, Mary E 110, 126 1
Cramer, Mary O 115 1

Cramer, Minnie H 117, 125 1
Cramer, Moses 125, 127 1
Cramer, Murray W 104 1
Cramer, N E 234 2
Cramer, N Z 67 3
Cramer, Naoh E [sic] 110 1
Cramer, Newton C 107 1
Cramer, Nina 57 1
Cramer, Noah 76, 99, 101, 115, 117, 129 1
Cramer, Noah E 3, 28 3
Cramer, Noah E 119, 129, 133, 135, 152 1
Cramer, Noah E 15, 72, 144, 242, 282 2
Cramer, Nora E 205 2
Cramer, Oscar 106 1
Cramer, Peter 27 2
Cramer, Peter 1, 117, 120, 131 1
Cramer, Philip 40, 205 1
Cramer, Philip H 131 1
Cramer, Raymond J 104 1
Cramer, Rebecca 133 1
Cramer, Rebecca E 133 1
Cramer, Robert 166 3
Cramer, Robert 165 1
Cramer, Robert L 99 1
Cramer, Robt 166 2
Cramer, S C 101, 107, 137 1
Cramer, S Clinton 100, 107, 125, 135 1
Cramer, Samuel 135 1
Cramer, Sarah 104 1
Cramer, Silas H 115, 125 1
Cramer, Stieiner L 106 2
Cramer, Sue I 24, 118 1
Cramer, Susan 135, 136 1
Cramer, Susan Ann 118 1
Cramer, Susan N 109 1
Cramer, T F 96 3
Cramer, T L 110, 135 1
Cramer, Thomas L 169 1
Cramer, Victoria E 139 1
Cramer, W Glenn 120 1
Cramer, W L 125 2
Cramer, William L 126 1
Cramer, Wm 33 1
Cramer, Wm A 100, 139, 140 1
Cramer, Wm B 92 2
Cramer, Wm C 119 1
Cramer, Wm G 101 1
Cramer, Wm H 119, 133 1
Cramer, Wm J 59, 96, 106, 140 1
Cramer, Wm J 171 3
Cramer, Wm J 14 2
Cramer, Woodrow W 288 2
Crammer, Frederick W 87 2
Crampton, Alice 97 1
Crampton, Ann 228a 2
Crampton, Anna M 97 1
Crampton, B P 198, 228a 2
Crampton, Benjamin P 99 1
Crampton, C A 101 1
Crampton, Clarence A 96 3
Crampton, Clarence A 139, 248 1
Crampton, Clinton F 100 1
Crampton, Douglas I 107 1
Crampton, Earl H 107 1
Crampton, Eleanora 107 1
Crampton, Eleanore 125 1
Crampton, Emma H 119 1
Crampton, Erie A 89 2
Crampton, Exie 102 2
Crampton, Exie A 101 1
Crampton, Exie A 83 2
Crampton, Exie Kemp 107 1
Crampton, Harry C 97 1
Crampton, Henry D 99 1
Crampton, Henry H 112 1
Crampton, J W 56 2
Crampton, James F 119 1
Crampton, John C 40, 119 1
Crampton, John W 70, 112, 117, 119 1
Crampton, Joseph M 120, 130, 217, 233, 270 1
Crampton, Joshua 119 1
Crampton, Keefer R 23 1
Crampton, Mary 56 2
Crampton, O P 86, 99, 117 1
Crampton, Oscar 253 1
Crampton, Oscar 228a 2
Crampton, Oscar P 71, 137 1
Crampton, Oscar T 84 1
Crampton, Thomas 231, 250, 275 2
Crampton, Thomas 84 1
Crampton, Thomas 137 1
Crampton, Thomas 70, 84, 137 1
Crampton, Thos 7, 28 2
Crampton, Thos 40, 225 1
Crampton, Violetta G 139 1
Crapster, Basil 225a 2
Crapster, G W 187 2
Crapster, John 203, 225a 2
Crapster, W W 214 2
Crapster, William 35 3
Crapster, William W 2 3
Craver, Agnes 117 1
Craver, Caroline 100 1
Craver, Chas P 100 1
Craver, Elizabeth 118 1
Craver, Geo W 118 1
Craver, George W 110 1
Craver, Harriet E 100 1
Craver, Jacob 137 2
Craver, Jacob 116 1
Craver, John 117, 118 1
Craver, Joshua 113 2
Craver, Joshua 118 1
Craver, Joshua N 100 1
Craver, Laura V 123 1
Craver, Lewis I 124 1
Craver, Peter 57 1
Craver, Peter 113 2
Craver, Rosa L 135 1
Craver, Samuel S 118 1
Craver, Simon P 113 2
Craver, Simon P 135 1
Craver, Wm 139 1
Crawford, Alfred 101 1
Crawford, Charles F 101, 179 1
Crawford, Chas H 6 1
Crawford, David 8, 11, 15, 22, 40, 61, 101, 169 2
Crawford, David 104, 126 1
Crawford, David 265 1
Crawford, David H 29 2
Crawford, Edgar S 101 1
Crawford, Edna N 124 1
Crawford, Ella D 72 2
Crawford, George H 110 1
Crawford, L C 25 1
Crawford, L D 61, 92 1
Crawford, L D 35 2
Crawford, Laura B 6 1
Crawford, Lewis 8, 11, 15, 22, 29, 169, 181, 187 2
Crawford, Lewis 160 3
Crawford, Lewis 84, 101, 123, 194 1
Crawford, Lewis D 124 1
Crawford, Lewis D 140 2
Crawford, Louis 110 1
Crawford, Louis 203 2
Crawford, Lydia 123 1
Crawford, Mary E 126 1
Crawford, Robert 87 3
Crawford, Robert 56 1
Crawford, Robert 221 2
Crawford, Samuel 123 1
Crawford, Thos 279 1
Crawford, Wm 163 1
Crawl, Isaac 129 1
Crawl, Nicholas 129 1
Crawley, Richard 133 1
Crawmer, Daniel 131 1
Crawmer, Helper 118 1
Crawmer, James K P 119 1
Crawmer, John 118 1
Crawmer, John H L 119 1
Crawmer, Peter 131 1
Crawmer, Philip 131 1

Crawner, James L 120 1
Crawner, John Moss 120 1
Crawner, Levi 123, 260 1
Crawner, M A Mrs 125 1
Creager, Adam 125, 135 1
Creager, Amanda 97 1
Creager, Amanda E 97 1
Creager, Ann Matilda 96 1
Creager, Annie F 96 1
Creager, Chambers I 96, 126 1
Creager, Charles E 100 1
Creager, Charles F 101 1
Creager, Chas W 140 1
Creager, Clarence 140 1
Creager, Clayton 72 1
Creager, Daniel 135 1
Creager, Effie G 119 1
Creager, Eliza 106 1
Creager, Ellen 104 1
Creager, Esau D 106, 107 1
Creager, Florence 123 1
Creager, Geo 163 1
Creager, Geo 79 3
Creager, Geo W 137 1
Creager, Georgie C 133 1
Creager, Harry T 112 1
Creager, Henry 127, 179 1
Creager, Henry of J 116 1
Creager, J Wesley 206 3
Creager, J Wesley 119 1
Creager, Jacob 117 1
Creager, James 117 1
Creager, John David 118 1
Creager, John Sr 116 1
Creager, John W Jr 120 1
Creager, John William 118 1
Creager, Julia A 120 1
Creager, Laura C 123 1
Creager, Lawrence 123 1
Creager, Leo M 123 1
Creager, Levi 123 1
Creager, Lewis 123 1
Creager, Lewis 75 2
Creager, M L 210 3
Creager, M L 8, 223 1
Creager, M L 190, 262 2
Creager, M Luther 58, 213 3
Creager, M Luther 274 2
Creager, M Luther 53, 65, 126, 127, 133, 136, 147, 230, 235, 276 1
Creager, Maggie C 85 2
Creager, Manasaha 64 3
Creager, Manassas 57 2
Creager, Mannasseh 125 1
Creager, Margaret C 126 1
Creager, Mary 125 1
Creager, Mary A 125 1
Creager, Mary Abbie 101, 127 1
Creager, Mary Ann 123 1
Creager, Mary F G 126 1
Creager, Mary H 127 1
Creager, Noble 175 2
Creager, O C 134 2
Creager, Raymond [?] 230 1
Creager, Raymond E 106, 140, 142, 172 2
Creager, Raymond E 101, 233 1
Creager, Richard M 96, 127 1
Creager, Robert E 127, 133 1
Creager, Roy 235 1
Creager, Russell L 120 1
Creager, S Amanda 106 1
Creager, Sarah E 125 1
Creager, Simon 135 1
Creager, Soloman 222 3
Creager, Solomon 135 1
Creager, Sophia 112 1
Creager, Thaddeus 126 1
Creager, Theodore L 137, 140 1
Creager, William 167 3
Creager, William T 140 1
Creager, William T 161 3
Creager, Winfield T 137 1
Creager, Wm 139 1
Creager, Wm E 140 1
Creager, Wm H 139 1
Creager, Wm L 139 1
Creagh, John 116 1
Createn, James 96 1
Creatin, Andrew 96 1
Creating, Nancy 129 1
Crebbs, David 104 1
Crebbs, Eve 104 1
Crebbs, Frederick 106, 109, 176 1
Crebbs, George 116 1
Crebbs, John 116 1
Creed, Virdie M 219 1
Creeger Mary 214a 2
Creeger, Carroll C 101 1
Creeger, Chambers S 257 1
Creeger, Clarence C 101 1
Creeger, Clarence E 161 2
Creeger, Daniel 104 1
Creeger, Elias 101 2
Creeger, Elsie M 107 1
Creeger, Ephrian 262 2
Creeger, George 18 3
Creeger, George 258 2
Creeger, George W 110 1
Creeger, J Howard 101 1
Creeger, James 119 1
Creeger, John 263 1
Creeger, John M 265 2
Creeger, M L 15 3
Creeger, M L 120 1
Creeger, M Luther 199 2
Creeger, M Luther 119 1
Creeger, Manassah 26 3
Creeger, Mary 210a 2
Creeger, Mary A 101 1
Creeger, Roy 101 1
Creeger, Soloman 1 3
Creeger, William 165 3
Creeger, Wm 32 1
Creeger, Wm 50 3
Creeger, Wm E 110 1
Creeger, Wm H 245 1
Creezer, Esan D 48 1
Creighton, Samuel 135 1
Creps, William J 140 1
Cress, Jacob 25 1
Cress, Jacob 25 2
Cress, John 25 1
Cress, John 25 1
Cretin, Alexius 70, 71 1
Cretin, Anderw [sic] 40 1
Cretin, Andrew 186 1
Cretin, Andrew 19 2
Cretin, Ann 96 1
Cretin, Charles C 51 3
Cretin, Emily E 91 1
Cretin, James 27, 144 2
Cretin, James 91, 117, 119 1
Cretin, John 70 1
Cretin, John F 11, 71, 96 1
Cretin, John H 96, 117 1
Cretin, John T 160, 209 3
Cretin, John T 119 1
Cretin, Joseph A 119 1
Cretin, Mary Ann 117 1
Creton, Alexius J 96 1
Creton, Josph A 160 3
Crider, Henry 112 1
Crider, Margaret C 126 1
Crim, Emily 101 1
Crimm, Emily 83 2
Crimmins, J D 126 1
Crimmins, J Daniel 140 1
Crimmins, Mary 126 1
Crimmins, Robt 126 1
Crimmins, Wm M 140, 223 1
Criner, Michael 1 3
Crise, Daniel 112 1
Crise, George 110 1
Crise, Henry 112 1
Crise, Valentine 97 1
Crist, Anna B O 110, 139 1
Crist, David M 97, 104 1
Crist, Elizabeth A 97 1
Crist, G Bruce 104, 119 1
Crist, George B 111 1

Crist, George W 110 1
Crist, Grafton B 116 1
Crist, Jacob 119, 129, 219 1
Crist, Joseph 118 1
Crist, Matilda A 123 1
Crist, Michael C 97 1
Crist, Myrtle G 110, 179 1
Crist, Myrtle Gesey 111 1
Crist, Nathan 129 1
Crist, Wm H 119 1
Critzer, Jacob 116 1
Croft, E F 107 3
Croft, Elizabeth 106 1
Croft, John 106 1
Croft, John 203 2
Cromwell, A 131 1
Cromwell, Annie M 96 1
Cromwell, Arthur 97, 129, 140 1
Cromwell, Arthur 72 2
Cromwell, Arthur H 97, 131 1
Cromwell, Arthur R 113, 135 1
Cromwell, C C 3 3
Cromwell, C Merhl 102 1
Cromwell, Carlton 96 1
Cromwell, Caroline 133 1
Cromwell, Christianna W 96 1
Cromwell, Clara B 102 1
Cromwell, Curtis A 123, 140 1
Cromwell, Edgar 218a 2
Cromwell, George W 111 1
Cromwell, Harriet E 113 1
Cromwell, J M 7 2
Cromwell, J M 123 1
Cromwell, James M 8 1
Cromwell, James M 82 3
Cromwell, John 156 1
Cromwell, John 64 3
Cromwell, John C 123 1
Cromwell, Joseph 37 3
Cromwell, Joseph E 89 3
Cromwell, Laura A 133 1
Cromwell, Lucie E 236 2
Cromwell, Luther O 123 1
Cromwell, Mary 125 1
Cromwell, Nicholas 129, 131 1
Cromwell, P C 131 1
Cromwell, Philemon 131, 150 1
Cromwell, Philemon C 51 1
Cromwell, R 131, 133 1
Cromwell, Rachael 26 1
Cromwell, Richard 133, 135 1
Cromwell, Richard 26, 75, 96, 100, 124 2
Cromwell, Richard 31 3
Cromwell, Richard N 111 2
Cromwell, Robert E 133 1
Cromwell, Scott 113 1
Cromwell, Stephen C 135 1
Cromwell, Susannah 135 1
Cromwell, Thomas T 137 1
Cromwell, W 11 2
Cromwell, W W 140 1
Cromwell, William H 8 2
Cromwell, Windfield S 139 1
Cromwell, Wm H 139 1
Cromwell, Zacharias T 142 1
Crone, Carleton H 106 1
Crone, Catherine 118 1
Crone, Charley E 100 1
Crone, Conrad 100, 101 1
Crone, Eliza Ann 100, 106 1
Crone, Garfield 57 3
Crone, Harry H 100 1
Crone, Henry 100, 101, 112, 118 1
Crone, Jacob 100, 125 1
Crone, John 100, 106, 118 1
Crone, John E 118, 152 1
Crone, Joseph 118 1
Crone, Lee A 215 2
Crone, Margaret 125, 126 1
Crone, Mary E 4 1
Crone, Sam'l C 118 1
Crone, Samuel D 215 2
Crone, Susan 51 3
Cronise, Adele A 96, 97 1
Cronise, Anna 107, 109 1
Cronise, Anna M 109 1
Cronise, Benjamin F 58 1
Cronise, C J 181 2
Cronise, Catherine 100 1
Cronise, Chas L 118, 119 1
Cronise, Clara A 100 1
Cronise, E Margaretta 119 1
Cronise, Eleanor M 107 1
Cronise, Elizabeth 106 1
Cronise, Frederick 109, 110, 133, 163 1
Cronise, Frederick 71, 185, 202 3
Cronise, Frederick 137, 290 2
Cronise, George W 110 1
Cronise, Gideon D 26 1
Cronise, Isaac 110, 115, 271 1
Cronise, Isaac 1, 41, 81, 195 3
Cronise, Isaac 198, 202 2
Cronise, J 100, 109 1
Cronise, J 64 3
Cronise, J Calvin 6 1
Cronise, Jacob 57, 144 2
Cronise, Jacob 71 3
Cronise, Jacob 40, 96, 109, 115, 117, 118 1
Cronise, James 30, 214 2
Cronise, John 38, 100, 185 2
Cronise, John 8, 184 3
Cronise, John 119, 120, 135, 219 1
Cronise, John & 26 2
Cronise, John Calvin 119, 196 1
Cronise, John F 26, 115 1
Cronise, Joseph 8, 14, 29, 35, 84, 89, 106, 138, 177, 208, 222, 227, 238, 252 2
Cronise, Joseph 26, 27, 33, 41, 52, 59, 67, 100, 109, 115, 117, 118, 119, 125, 142, 186, 201, 205, 234, 243, 252 1
Cronise, Joseph 26, 41, 55, 71, 75, 202, 196, 199, 203, 227 3
Cronise, Josephine 118 1
Cronise, Lillie R 226 3
Cronise, Lillie R 100 1
Cronise, Lilly R 124 1
Cronise, Mary E 210a, 215a 2
Cronise, Minnie M 125 1
Cronise, Samuel 117, 135 1
Cronise, Samuel 93 2
Cronise, Sarah R 13 1
Cronise, Simon 110, 118, 135 1
Cronise, Simon 236, 268 2
Cronise, Wilbert E 271 2
Crookerly, Lewis 87 2
Crooks, Robert 164, 177 1
Cross, Belle 36 2
Cross, Catherine 100 1
Cross, Henry 112 1
Cross, Lewis 18 2
Cross, Lewis 56 1
Crothers, Charles R 74 1
Crothers, Daisy A 140 1
Crothers, Robert B 267 2
Crothers, Wm J 140 1
Crouch, James 116 1
Crouse, Abraham 37 1
Crouse, Ada B 259, 267 2
Crouse, Blanche K 99 1
Crouse, Eliza 125 1
Crouse, Geo 113 3
Crouse, George 47 1
Crouse, George S 110 1
Crouse, George S 267 2
Crouse, George W 110 1
Crouse, Harry S 113 1
Crouse, Isaac 110 1
Crouse, J Calvin 2 3
Crouse, Jacob 37 3
Crouse, James 30 2
Crouse, James B 119 1
Crouse, James M 110, 119 1

Crouse, John 23, 37 3
Crouse, John H 113 3
Crouse, Joseph 110 1
Crouse, Joseph 27 3
Crouse, Lewis M 161 2
Crouse, Lewis W 99 1
Crouse, Michael 110. 125 1
Crouse, Michael 287 2
Crouse, Michael 26, 113 3
Crouse, Rudolph W 190 2
Crouse, Sarah A 119 1
Crouse, Thomas 52 1
Crouse, Valentine 139 1
Crouse, Wm A 140 1
Crow, Matilda 125 1
Crowl, David 19 2
Crowl, George 135 3
Crowl, Jim 87 2
Crowl, John 135 3
Crown, Oscar F 130 1
Crown, S C 130 1
Crum Edw L 106 1
Crum G A 110 1
Crum, Albert W 62 1
Crum, Alice B 135 1
Crum, Alice K 123 1
Crum, Annie M 104 1
Crum, C W R 101 1
Crum, Casper 100 1
Crum, Charles V 101 1
Crum, Chas 87 3
Crum, Chas Edw 101 1
Crum, Chas V 119 1
Crum, Chas W 110 1
Crum, Chas W 145 2
Crum, Claude R 192, 205 1
Crum, David O 104 1
Crum, Elizabeth 106 1
Crum, Elizabeth A 106 1
Crum, Ellen S 107 1
Crum, Ellen S 171 3
Crum, Emma J 118 1
Crum, Florence M 109 1
Crum, Florence W 101 1
Crum, Frank P 242 2
Crum, Frederick 70 3
Crum, Frederick 109, 125 1
Crum, G W 138 2
Crum, G W 100 3
Crum, Geo 129, 150 2
Crum, Geo 229 1
Crum, Geo B 25 1
Crum, Geo H S 106 1
Crum, Geo W 110, 117, 118, 123, 249, 26 1
Crum, Geo W 70, 111, 171 3
Crum, Geo W 1, 9, 113, 276 2
Crum, George 129 2
Crum, George H 110 1
Crum, George H Jr 71 1
Crum, George W 110, 112 1
Crum, George W 276 2
Crum, George W S 110 1
Crum, George W Sr 110 1
Crum, Glenn R 211 2
Crum, Grace E 211 2
Crum, H E 120 1
Crum, Harriet 101 1
Crum, Harry C 101, 109, 112 1
Crum, Hattie D 113 1
Crum, Hazel May 112, 192 1
Crum, Henry 112, 119, 205 1
Crum, Henry 18 3
Crum, Henry 69, 154 2
Crum, Henry H 115, 131 1
Crum, Isaac 116, 119 1
Crum, J C 125 1
Crum, J E 120 1
Crum, J H 138 2
Crum, J L 135 1
Crum, Jacob L 120 1
Crum, James C 120 1
Crum, James H 100 1
Crum, John 107, 116, 117, 119 1
Crum, John D 119 1
Crum, John D 159 3
Crum, John E 140 2
Crum, John E 19 1
Crum, John Henry 71 1
Crum, John W 106, 118, 119 1
Crum, Judge P 119 1
Crum, LeRoy Irvin 131 1
Crum, Lewis 123 1
Crum, M D 237 1
Crum, Magdalena 119 1
Crum, Margaret 110 1
Crum, Margaret E 126 1
Crum, Margaret L 126 1
Crum, Martha 125 1
Crum, Mary A 125 1
Crum, Mary C 278 2
Crum, Mary W 126 1
Crum, Millard 189 1
Crum, Pansy I 131 1
Crum, Phoebe A 62 1
Crum, R S 72, 82, 126, 131, 230, 238 1
Crum, R S 58, 70 2
Crum, R S 134, 206 3
Crum, Reada 255 2
Crum, Reno S 126 1
Crum, Roy L 113 1
Crum, Solomon 135 1
Crum, Solomon C 135 1
Crum, Stephen B 135 1
Crum, Sterley E 126 1
Crum, Virginia C 110 1
Crum, W R 110 1
Crum, Walter C 140 1
Crum, Walter C 255 2
Crum, William 171 3
Crum, William H 229a 2
Crum, Wm H 126 1
Crum, Wm T 187 3
Crum, Wm T 60 1
Crum, Evelyn Virginia 131 1
Crumbacker, Abraham 96 1
Crumbacker, James 96 1
Crumbaker, Elizabeth 106 1
Crumbaug, Gideon D 112 1
Crumbaug, Gideon D [sic] 159 1
Crumbaugh, G D 117 1
Crumbaugh, Geo F B 84 1
Crumbaugh, George 54 3
Crumbaugh, John 171 3
Crumbaugh, John 118, 126 1
Crumbaugh, John D 23, 67 3
Crumbaugh, John D 136 2
Crumbaugh, John D 135, 229 1
Crumbaugh, Margaret C 84 1
Crumbaugh, Simon 126, 135 1
Crumbaugh, Simon 197 2
Crumbaugh, Susan E 126 1
Crumitt, Frederick M 120 1
Crumitt, James E 120 1
Crumlish, Catherine 101 1
Crumlish, John J 101 1
Crumlish, John J Jr 120 1
Crumlish, John J Sr 120 1
Crummit, Mabel 196 2
Crummitt, George W 111 1
Crummitt, Lena M 111 1
Crummitt, Lula May 124 1
Crummitt, Mabel 124 1
Crummitt, Mehrl C 124 1
Crust, Baylor U 73 1
Crutchley, Annie C 113 1
Crutchley, Bernard A 106 1
Crutchley, C Marion 83 3
Crutchley, Elias 116, 188 1
Crutchley, Elva J 83 3
Crutchley, Harry E 113 1
Crutchley, Helen F 213a 2
Crutchley, Milton C 126 1
Crutchley, Rachael 133 1
Cubits, Barbara 99 1
Cubits, George 99 1
Culberson, James 13 1
Culbertson, J 81, 122 3
Culbertson, Joseph 205 3
Culburtson, Joseph 210a 2

Cullen, Margaret Eva 127 1
Cullen, Thos F 127 1
Cullen, Victor F 210, 265 1
Cullen, Victor F 190, 215a, 232 2
Cullen, Victor F Dr 204 1
Culler, Amanda 96 1
Culler, Anna M 97 1
Culler, Annie E 113, 120 1
Culler, Annie M 97 1
Culler, C K 15 2
Culler, Catherine R 52 2
Culler, Charles K 101 1
Culler, Chas 32 3
Culler, Chas K 119 1
Culler, D Milton 104 1
Culler, Daniel 104 1
Culler, Daniel 192, 220 3
Culler, Daniel 112 1
Culler, Daniel 104 1
Culler, Daniel 14 2
Culler, David 125, 200 1
Culler, Edgar P 219 1
Culler, Ella E 120 1
Culler, Ella Mary 107 1
Culler, Ella V 126, 130, 240 1
Culler, Ellen E 97 1
Culler, Emma F 107 1
Culler, George C 110 1
Culler, George W 111 1
Culler, Grace Myer 120 1
Culler, Grace R 133 1
Culler, H 81 3
Culler, Harman F 112 1
Culler, Harriet L 112, 113 1
Culler, Harry C 11 1
Culler, Henry 100, 112, 113, 116, 125, 165, 207, 228 1
Culler, Henry 29, 58, 287 2
Culler, J H 192 3
Culler, J H 35 2
Culler, J Harmon 104 1
Culler, J J 94, 196, 219 3
Culler, J J 67, 118 1
Culler, J J 46, 171 2
Culler, Jacob 96, 117, 125, 222 1
Culler, Jacob 100 2
Culler, Jacob 79 3
Culler, Jacob A 117 1
Culler, John 104, 117, 118, 120, to 29 1
Culler, John 58 2
Culler, John 41 3
Culler, John David 120 1
Culler, John H 119, 150 1
Culler, John H 27, 41 3
Culler, John J 96 3
Culler, John J 287 2
Culler, John J 119 1
Culler, John Jacob 55, 120 1
Culler, John M 119, 120 1
Culler, John W 113, 136 1
Culler, Jullia Ann 117 1
Culler, Kurdy[?] E 126 1
Culler, L C 124 3
Culler, Lester M 62, 107 1
Culler, Lillie Pearl 97 1
Culler, Lloyd 189 2
Culler, Lloyd C 101, 111, 112, 120 1
Culler, Lucinda C 123 1
Culler, Luther B 104 1
Culler, M A 15 2
Culler, Margaret A 73, 124 1
Culler, Mary A 120, 126 1
Culler, Mary A 280 2
Culler, Mary E 112 1
Culler, Michael 120, 125, 264 1
Culler, Mildred R 113 1
Culler, Millard 126 1
Culler, Millard F 283 2
Culler, Minnie C 101 1
Culler, O D 96 1
Culler, Oscar D 119, 126 1
Culler, Paul Z 117, 130 1
Culler, Paul Z 280 2
Culler, Peter 41, 224 3
Culler, Peter 117, 164, 270 1
Culler, Philip 179 1
Culler, Philip David 112 1
Culler, Philip L 133 1
Culler, Ralph 133 1
Culler, Ralph E 119 1
Culler, Roger P 110 1
Culler, Rose L 133 1
Culler, Rose L 133 1
Culler, S M 15, 154 2
Culler, Samuel L 112 1
Culler, Samuel M 126, 136 1
Culler, Sarah A 135 1
Culler, Sarah A 264 2
Culler, Sarah A V 136 1
Culler, Sarah Ann 119 1
Culler, Silas H 123 1
Culler, Susie B 68 1
Culler, V I 189 3
Culler, Victor F 136, 219 1
Culler, Wilbur D 140 1
Culler, William 14 3
Culler, William L 140 1
Culler, William L 113 3
Culler, William Walter Jr 193 2
Culler, Wm 39 2
Cullet, Henry 275 2
Culp, Geo 231 2
Cumiskey, C Jos 177 3
Cummings, George D 111 1
Cummings, John 116 1
Cummings, Lavinia 123 1
Cummings, Nellie K 108 2
Cummings, Robert 57 1
Cummings, Robert C 133 1
Cummings, Ruth E 111 1
Cunningham, B A 106 3
Cunningham, B A 99 1
Cunningham, B A 69, 211 2
Cunningham, B Amon 39, 120, 185 3
Cunningham, B Amos 118 1
Cunningham, B Amos 242 2
Cunningham, Catherine 100 1
Cunningham, Chas 40 1
Cunningham, Daniel 139 1
Cunningham, Daniel T 104 1
Cunningham, James 116 1
Cunningham, James J 119 1
Cunningham, John 40 3
Cunningham, John A 118 1
Cunningham, John A H 118, 171 1
Cunningham, Martha C 125 1
Cunningham, Mary Louise 126 1
Cunningham, Mary S 125 1
Cunningham, Wm C 100 1
Curd, Thomas J 137 1
Curfman, Barbara 116 1
Curfman, Jacob 116 1
Curfman, John 116 1
Curfman, Peter 116, 131, 222, 257, 263 1
Curfman, William D 140 1
Curfman, William H 140 1
Curley, Thomas 99 1
Curley, Wm R 123, 200 1
Curran, Wm 139 1
Curren, James 116 1
Currens, Elijah 139 1
Currens, Wm 139, 228 1
Currey, James Sr 116 1
Currey, Jeremiah 116 1
Currey, Wm 116 1
Curry, Alice L 169 1
Curry, Eleanor 106 1
Curry, Elizabeth E 140 1
Curry, F A 56 1
Curry, Jeremiah 139, 169 1
Curry, Jeremiah 237 2
Curry, John 118 1
Curry, Martha 106 1
Curry, W R 144 1
Curry, William 56 1
Curry, Wm 85, 139 1
Curry, Wm 124, 218 2
Curry, Wm R 140, 228, 272 1
Curtis, Erma 20 2
Curtis, Ida C L 79 1

Curtis, John R 179, 184, 195 3
Curtis, John R 117, 123, 135 1
Curtiss, John D 53 3
Curtiss, John R 6, 31, 38, 53 3
Curtiss, John R 234 2
Cushing, Thomas 32 1
Custard, Adam 38 2
Custard, Adam 185, 186, 223 3
Custard, Adam 96, 106, 125, 223, 233 1
Custard, Adam & 211 2
Custard, Elizabeth 106 1
Custard, Geo W 96 1
Cutsail, James A 120 1
Cutsail, Ann R 96 1
Cutsail, Clarence LeRoy 102 1
Cutsail, Emma S 102 1
Cutsail, Etta 110 1
Cutsail, Etta M 107 1
Cutsail, Fannie A 110 1
Cutsail, George H 110, 111 1
Cutsail, George W 110 1
Cutsail, Helen Crampton 48 3
Cutsail, Hiram S 96, 112 1
Cutsail, Hiram S 160 3
Cutsail, Horace E 112, 124 1
Cutsail, Ida C 115, 120 1
Cutsail, J H 96 1
Cutsail, James 102 2
Cutsail, James A 124 1
Cutsail, James H 35 2
Cutsail, James H 120 1
Cutsail, John J 119 1
Cutsail, Joseph M 120 1
Cutsail, Lydia A 124 1
Cutsail, Maude L 182 3
Cutsail, Noah E 96 1
Cutsail, Noah E 160 3
Cutsail, Peter 131 1
Cutsail, Roy C 115 1
Cutsail, Roy W 120 1
Cutsail, Susan R 119 1
Cutsail, Walter A 124 1
Cutshall, 13 1
Cutshall, Catherine E 140 1
Cutshall, Gail L 140 1
Cutshall, Henrietta J 112 1
Cutshall, J H 209 2
Cutshall, John 76 1
Cutshall, John 46, 294 2
Cutshall, John H 119, 123, 131 1
Cutshall, Louisa S 123 1
Cutshall, Philip 183 1
Cutshall, Philip 131 1
Cutshall, Philip 96 2
Cutshall, Sarah L 22 1
Cutshall, W B 79, 139, 160, 220a 2
Cutshall, W B 45, 179 3
Cutshall, W B 38, 63, 112, 140, 169 1
Cutshall, W D 22 1
Cutshall, William B 140 1
Cutshall, William B 52 2
Cutshall, Willie B 76 1
Cutshall, Wm 4, 123, 131, 225 1
Cutshall, Wm B 56, 68, 82, 199 3
Cutshall, Wm B 24, 41, 119, 147 1
Cutshall, Wm B 9, 58 2
Cutshall, Wm[?] B 189 1
Cutujian, Avac 97 1
Cutujian, Frances c 97 1
Cutujian, Frances Catharine 127 1
Cutujian, Margaret R 127 1
Cyphers, Joseph 131 1
Cyphers, Peter 100 1
Dade, Columbus 131, 147 1
Dade, Columbus 129 2
Dade, J M 147 1
Dade, Mary V 172 1
Dade, Maurice J 75 2
Dade, R L 62 1
Dadisman, J 149 3
Dadisman, Susanna 179 1
Dadysman, Ezra 225, 263 1
Dagenhart, Jay L 169 1
Dagenhart, Lulu Irene 169 1
Dahoff, Joseph 276 2
Dailey, Zachariah 185 1
Daily, Benjamin 146 1
Daily, Henry 165 1
Daily, Jane 165, 171 1
Daily, John H 165 1
Dal, Ida M 162 1
Daley, Mary Ann 106 1
Dall, James 2 2
Dall, James A 165, 171 1
Dall, M O 171 1
Dalwick, George W 188 3
Damuth, C A 283 1
Damuth, C A 159, 166 2
Damuth, Chas 171 3
Damuth, Chas 39, 188 2
Damuth, Chas 165 1
Damuth, Chas A 147 1
Damuth, David 81 3
Damuth, Harriet E 159 1
Damuth, Henry 137, 264 2
Damuth, Henry 159, 165 1
Damuth, Henry Jr 137 2
Damuth, Howard R 165 1
Damuth, James A 179, 184 1
Damuth, John 192 1
Damuth, Lester B 147 1
Damuth, Sarah Ann 72 1
Damuth, Stanley 134 2
Damuth, Stanley R 147, 179 1
Damuth, Warren K 134 2
Damuth, Warren K 179, 184 1
Dangerfield, William 38 3
Daniel, Emma Rebecca Doll 48 3
Daniel, J J 165 1
Daniel, Richard P 165 1
Daniel, Wm A 183 1
Daniell, Isabelle K 162 1
Daniels, Annie C 150 1
Daniels, Dennis M 150 1
Daniels, Dennis M Jr 150 1
Daniels, Harry S 150, 172, 254 1
Daniels, Mary A 172 1
Daniels, Mary Anna 144 1
Danner, Abraham 150, 171 1
Danner, Anna 145 1
Danner, Benjamin G 146 1
Danner, Carrie E 264 2
Danner, D Raymond 135 1
Danner, Daniel 146, 150 1
Danner, E D 159 1
Danner, Ed L 150 1
Danner, Edw D 150, 152, 156, 283 1
Danner, Edw L 152 1
Danner, Edw L 72, 179, 188 3
Danner, Edward G 146 1
Danner, Edward L 153 1
Danner, Franklin A 175 1
Danner, Geo 177 1
Danner, George 156 1
Danner, Halley M 146 1
Danner, Harriet 159 1
Danner, Hazel M E 175 1
Danner, J W 62 3
Danner, Jacob 106, 163 3
Danner, Jacob 164 1
Danner, Jaseph 96 1
Danner, Joel B 160, 186 3
Danner, John 125, 156 1
Danner, John 287 2
Danner, Joseph 164 1
Danner, Joseph 177 2
Danner, Joseph 64, 205 3
Danner, Joseph H 166 1
Danner, Lena M 166, 183 1
Danner, Lillie M 45 1
Danner, Lola I 283 2
Danner, Mark S 146 1
Danner, Norman Edward 175 1
Danner, Rachel 177 1

Danner, Rachel A 177 1
Danner, Thomas L 181 1
Danner, W E 44 3
Danner, William 62 3
Danner, William P 183 1
Danner, Wm H 144 1
Dannhower, Washington 119 1
Dansberger, G Wm 177 1
Dansberger, George W 172 1
Dansberger, Mary F 172 1
Dansberger, Russell Y 177 1
Daper, Thomas 51 1
Darbey, Walter 14 3
Darby, Helen 293 2
Darby, John 56, 82, 156 1
Darby, Perry 53 3
Darcus, Henry Sr 153 1
Dare, Elizabeth M 159, 179 1
Dare, John 260 1
Dare, John 19, 128 2
Dare, Susan M 179 1
Darkes, Anna 150 1
Darkes, David 150 1
Darkes, Jacob 150 1
Darkes. David 150 1
Darkis, Margaret 171 1
Darn, James 217a 2
Darner, Alta M 148 1
Darner, Altie M 145 1
Darner, C B 153 1
Darner, Carrie E 147, 148 1
Darner, Carrie E 23 3
Darner, Catherine 163 1
Darner, Charles B 148 1
Darner, Cicero J 147 1
Darner, Edw 31, 124, 154 2
Darner, Edward L 10 3
Darner, Elizabeth 152 1
Darner, Elizabeth E 153 1
Darner, Geo F 23 3
Darner, George 112 1
Darner, H J 164 1
Darner, Henry 183 1
Darner, Henry J 159 1
Darner, J W 51 1
Darner, Jacob 163, 164 1
Darner, James C 166 1
Darner, John 71 1
Darner, John 287 2
Darner, John W 215 3
Darner, Joseph 116, 164, 233, 263 1
Darner, Joseph 18 2
Darner, Joseph W 169 1
Darner, Louis S C 148 1
Darner, Lydia E 169 1
Darner, Lydia E 169 1
Darner, Mary M 159 1
Darner, Naomi E 183 1
Darner, Nora E 219 3
Darner, Paul 152 1
Darner, Samuel M 152, 153, 179 1
Darner, Sarah W 179 1
Darner, Thomas A 107 1
Darner, Wm E 147, 153, 183 1
Darner, Z Preston 179 1
Darnes, Francis 35 2
Darr, (or Tarr) Philip 44 1
Darr, Jacob 44, 176 1
Darr, Jacob 120 3
Darr, John 38 2
Darr, John 163, 164, 176 1
Darr, Luther B 170 2
Darr, Norval 175 1
Darr, Phillip 164 1
Darrell, Robert & 184 3
Daugherty, John 209 3
Davenport, Alexander 179 1
Davenport, Susie 179 1
Daver, Henry P 100 1
Davidge, Margery (Mannix) 177 1
Davidge, Robert Harold 177 1
Davidson, Daniel 30 2
Davidson, Florence Trail 100 3
Davidson, H Bradley 126 1
Davidson, Louise A 126 1
Davidson, Patrick 176 1
Davie, George W 157 1
Davies, Wm 183 1
Davis, A Winson 6 3
Davis, Aaaron 91 3
Davis, Aaron 144 1
Davis, Alexander 144 1
Davis, Alfred W 144 1
Davis, Amanda B 260 2
Davis, Ann R 181 1
Davis, Anna 165 1
Davis, Antonia 144 1
Davis, Aubrey G 177 1
Davis, Austin O 145 1
Davis, Bernard M 177 1
Davis, Bernard M Sr 177 1
Davis, Bertha Beckley 146 1
Davis, Carrie B 147 1
Davis, Catherine 147, 162 1
Davis, Catherine A 147 1
Davis, Charles Wm 148 1
Davis, Charlotte E 148 1
Davis, Charolette E 148 1
Davis, Chas E 189 3
Davis, Chas T 34 2
Davis, Clara P 147 1
Davis, Clarence E 146 1
Davis, D F 209 2
Davis, D P 222 2
Davis, David F 147, 150, 155 1
Davis, Edith 148 1
Davis, Edw T 144 1
Davis, Eli 152, 164 1
Davis, Eli 185 3
Davis, Eli 214 2
Davis, Eli R 152 1
Davis, Elias 88 1
Davis, Elizabeth 152, 175 1
Davis, Elizabeth G 164 1
Davis, Elsie R 153 1
Davis, Emily 164 1
Davis, Ephriam 152 1
Davis, Evelyn A 153 1
Davis, Everett W 104 1
Davis, Florida M 191 2
Davis, Franklin H 152, 155 1
Davis, G Vernon 230 1
Davis, Geo 83 2
Davis, Geo P 156 1
Davis, Geo S 156 1
Davis, Geo W 101 1
Davis, Geo Wilson 165 1
Davis, George 156 1
Davis, George L 227a 2
Davis, George W 19 1
Davis, Gilbert 63, 93, 275 2
Davis, Gilbert 156, 157, 181, 183, 283 1
Davis, Harry C 260 2
Davis, Harry Cassell 159 1
Davis, Henrietta 144 1
Davis, Henry L 222 2
Davis, Hettie V 179 1
Davis, Howard Samuel 162 1
Davis, Ignatius 162, 177, 180 1
Davis, Ignatius 75 2
Davis, Ira L 96 1
Davis, Isaac 83, 188 2
Davis, Isaac 112, 135, 147, 152, 177 1
Davis, Isaac 40 3
Davis, Isaac T 152 1
Davis, J L 125 1
Davis, J Lynn 165 1
Davis, J W 40 2
Davis, Jacob 152 1
Davis, Jacob H 166 1
Davis, James 47 1
Davis, James 87 2
Davis, James B Mrs 222 2
Davis, James L 129 3
Davis, James L 118, 147, 152, 164, 165, 171 1
Davis, James L 27, 205 2
Davis, James M 147, 152 1
Davis, James N 165 1
Davis, Jas L 64, 106, 113 3

Davis, Jas M 176 3
Davis, Jas N 87 3
Davis, Jesse 144 1
Davis, Joab W 165 1
Davis, Joab W Jr 144 1
Davis, John 188 2
Davis, John 157, 166 1
Davis, John F 259 2
Davis, John F 157 1
Davis, John M 164 1
Davis, John W 166 1
Davis, John W Jr 40 2
Davis, John W Jr 152 1
Davis, Joseph 187 2
Davis, Joseph 41 3
Davis, Luke 155, 163, 166 1
Davis, M A Rebecca 172, 181 1
Davis, Mahlon 117 1
Davis, Mahlon Jr 171 1
Davis, Mahlon Sr 147 1
Davis, Margaret B 189 3
Davis, Merdith 212 3
Davis, Meredith 39, 67, 113, 118, 124 3
Davis, Meredith 66 2
Davis, Meredith 171, 234, 283 1
Davis, Mildred N 222 2
Davis, Nannie H 125 1
Davis, Nathan 175 1
Davis, Norvel R 145 1
Davis, O O 166 1
Davis, R Lee 100 3
Davis, Rachel Morsell 177 1
Davis, Ray M 153 1
Davis, Remus Charles Sumner 184 1
Davis, Resin 106 1
Davis, Richard 177 1
Davis, Robert Lee 177 1
Davis, Robert Leslie 177 1
Davis, Ronald 179 1
Davis, Rufus 188 2
Davis, Rufus 164 1
Davis, Rufus H 60 3
Davis, S Eugenia 179 1
Davis, S P 33 1
Davis, S R 72 3
Davis, Samuel H 166 1
Davis, Samuel Howard 180 1
Davis, Samuel T 147 1
Davis, Sarah R 179 1
Davis, Solomon 177 1
Davis, Stella M 179 1
Davis, Susan M 203 3
Davis, Thomas 181 1
Davis, Thomas J 70 1
Davis, Thomas J 38 3
Davis, Thos 147, 162, 181 1
Davis, Thos 69 2
Davis, Thos E 210 3
Davis, Thos J 27 2
Davis, Thos S 181, 257 1
Davis, Ursula B 30 1
Davis, Walter 183 1
Davis, Walter H 172 1
Davis, Warren 122 2
Davis, William H 166 1
Davis, William H T 184 1
Davis, William Thomas 87 3
Davis, Wm H 144 1
Davis, Wm K 165 1
Davis, Wm M 152 1
Dawson, Margaret E 172 1
Dawson, Oliver E 172 1
Dawson, Patrick 176 1
Dawson, Pauline T 100 3
Dawson, Philip 176 1
Dawson, Wm 186 2
Day 139 2
Day, Addison S 144 1
Day, Adison L 48 1
Day, American S 177 1
Day, Ann Mary 147 1
Day, Annie E 144 1
Day, C W 52 2
Day, Columbs W 63 1
Day, Daisy M 144, 169 1
Day, Ellen 169 1
Day, Geo F 87 3
Day, Henry 159 1
Day, James 226 2
Day, James D 110 1
Day, James S 166 1
Day, James T 82 1
Day, Jas T 87 3
Day, Jesse D 169 1
Day, L W 41 1
Day, L W 197 3
Day, L W 189 2
Day, Langdon S 172 1
Day, Latimer E 177 1
Day, Latimer W 169 1
Day, Laura M 144 1
Day, Laura V 166, 169 1
Day, LaUra W 169 1
Day, Lorenzo T 169 1
Day, Luanah T 169 1
Day, Mary F 166 1
Day, Mary Frances 169 1
Day, Maud O 172 1
Day, Murray 144 1
Day, Murray D 144 1
Day, Murray O 166, 169, 172 1
Day, Myrtle L 177 1
Day, Nettie 166 1
Day, Polly 176 1
Day, R K 67 1
Day, R K 209 3
Day, Raymond F 147 1
Day, Robert J 169 1
Day, Rufus A 144, 177 1
Day, Rufus K 177 1
Day, Titus G 177 1
Day, W L 48 1
Day, Washington L 169, 183 1
Dayhoff, Anne 153 2
Dayhoff, Annie M 138 2
Dayhoff, Christian 147 1
Dayhoff, Jacob 163 1
Dayhoff, James 139 1
Dayhoff, James W 172 1
Dayhoff, Jas M 116 3
Dayhoff, John 147 1
Dayhoff, Joshua T 165 1
Dayhoff, Mary J 147 1
Dayhoff, Peter 172, 176 1
Dayhoff, Peter 26 2
Dayhoff, Peter Sr 176 1
Daymon, John 163 1
Deabus, Jacob 163 1
Deal, J 263 1
Deal, John 104 1
Deal, Joshua 104 1
Deall, Geo 7 2
Dean, Alice R 107 3
Dean, Alice R 156 1
Dean, Cralton H [sic] 152 1
Dean, Elizabeth 152, 159, 163 1
Dean, Emily A 82 3
Dean, Emily O 152 1
Dean, G W 209 3
Dean, Geo A 156, 165 1
Dean, Geo W 156 1
Dean, George L 179 1
Dean, H 3 1
Dean, Harriet S 159 1
Dean, Hezekiah 152, 159, 164 1
Dean, J W 164. 171 1
Dean, Jacob 163, 171, 177 1
Dean, Jacob 186 2
Dean, James H 282 2
Dean, John 164, 172, 179, 200 1
Dean, John 186 2
Dean, John A 165 1
Dean, Josephine 156 1
Dean, Laura V 169 1
Dean, Luke V 169 1
Dean, Margaret 179 1
Dean, Martha 171 1
Dean, Mary A 165 1
Dean, Mary C 152 1
Dean, Mary V E 82 3
Dean, Robert 172, 177, 179 1
Dean, Robt 160 2

Dean, Samuel 159 1
Dean, Samuel J 179 1
Dean, W H R 71 3
Dean, Walter W 152 1
Dean, Wm 159, 183, 249 1
Deane, Mildred C 227 3
Deater, Fannie M 26 1
Deaver, Abraham 70, 144, 273 1
Deaver, Abraham 184 3
Deaver, Abraham 11, 27, 57, 185 2
Deaver, H T 186 3
Deaver, H T 211 2
Deaver, Henry 100 1
Deaver, Henry 28, 78 2
Deaver, Henry T 117, 144, 159, 264 1
Deaver, Henry T 228a 2
Deberry, Elgie 171 1
Debruler, Mary 171, 262 1
Decatur, Elvira formerly Farwell 152 1
Deck, Ella V 164 1
Deck, Geo A 166 3
Deck, Joseph 164, 169 1
Deck, Joseph 49 2
Deck, Lawrence E 164 1
Deck, Mary 169, 171 1
Decker, Mary E 184 2
Deeter, Harry 166 1
Deeter, John E 166 1
DeGarmendia Carlos M 148 1
Degarmendia, Corrinne F D 72 1
DeGarmendia, Gonzalo DeCórdoba 176 1
DeGarmendia, Pipilla 176 1
DeGatrmendia, Eva Myers 147 1
DeGrange 145 2
DeGrange, Charles A 148 1
DeGrange, Clayton O 150 1
DeGrange, Daniel 150 1
DeGrange, Daniel W F 150 1
DeGrange, David I 150 1
DeGrange, Elizabeth 152 1
DeGrange, Emma Frances 153 1
DeGrange, Garrett 172 2
DeGrange, Garrett D 153 1
DeGrange, Garrett G 157 1
DeGrange, Garrett S 147 1
DeGrange, Garrett S 160 2
DeGrange, Geo A 152 1
DeGrange, Gertrude V 150 1
DeGrange, H Clay 119 2
DeGrange, H Clay 176 1
DeGrange, Harlen W 148 1
DeGrange, Henry S 188 1
DeGrange, Henry S B 152 1
DeGrange, John 262, 275 2
DeGrange, John 160, 165 1
Degrange, John A 8, 165, 201 1
DeGrange, John P 166 1
DeGrange, John Peter 163 1
DeGrange, LeRoy 179 1
DeGrange, Mary Jane 148 1
DeGrange, Mary S 145 2
DeGrange, Mary S Leather 172 1
DeGrange, Peter 163, 176, 225, 263 1
DeGrange, Sallie 160, 172 2
DeGrange, Sarah A 179 1
Degrange, Urilla V 181 1
DeGrange, Urilla Virginia 150 1
Degrange, Wm Francis 183 1
Deheauline, Elizabeth 152 1
Dehlman, Lewis H 250 2
Deihl, Abraham S [sic] 159 1
Deihl, Hannah [sic] 159 1
Deiter, Cora High 148 1
Deitrich, Lewis J 31 3
Deitrick, Philip 176 1
Delaine, Joshua 264 2
DeLansmutt, Philip 144 2
Delaplaine, Alice A 144 1
Delaplaine, Catherine 147 1
Delaplaine, Charlotte 147 1
Delaplaine, E S 14 1
Delaplaine, Edw S 48, 129 1
Delaplaine, Edw S 166 2
Delaplaine, Eleanor Frances 153 1
Delaplaine, Ephraim 152 1
Delaplaine, Fannie B 68 1
Delaplaine, Geo B 68, 129 1
Delaplaine, J Howard 144 1
Delaplaine, Jamie H 153 1
Delaplaine, John 27 1
Delaplaine, Joseph 25, 116 1
Delaplaine, Joshua 116, 147 1
Delaplaine, Robert E 153 1
Delaplaine, Robert T 68 1
Delaplaine, Ruth C 129 1
Delaplaine, T C 156 1
Delaplaine, William T 68 1
Delaplaine, Wm T 153 1
Delaplane, Alice A 165 1
Delaplane, Charlotte 165 1
Delaplane, Chas P 165, 183 1
Delaplane, Daniel 185 2
Delaplane, E S 230 1
Delaplane, Edw 225a 2
Delaplane, Edw S 65, 70, 167 2
Delaplane, Emeline 183 1
Delaplane, Ephraim 164 1
Delaplane, Ephriam 39 2
Delaplane, Fanny 183 1
Delaplane, H James 164 1
Delaplane, Harry Frank 166 1
Delaplane, Hezekiah 159 1
Delaplane, Hezekiah 159 2
Delaplane, J A 282 2
Delaplane, Jacob 165 1
Delaplane, James M 165, 183, 264 1
Delaplane, James M 159 2
Delaplane, Janie H 252 2
Delaplane, John 164 1
Delaplane, John 54 2
Delaplane, John E 166 1
Delaplane, John H 163 1
Delaplane, Joseph 22 2
Delaplane, Joseph 164, 165, 183, 283 1
Delaplane, Joseph H 166 1
Delaplane, Joseph Sr 163 1
Delaplane, Joshua 164, 165, 283 1
Delaplane, Joshua 39, 54 2
Delaplane, Joshua Jr 196, 203 1
Delaplane, Joshua Jr [corrected from Sr] 163 1
Delaplane, Margaret M 171 1
Delaplane, Mary C 159 1
Delaplane, North H 175 1
Delaplane, Peter 176 1
Delaplane, Robert E 184 1
Delaplane, Robert L 255 2
Delaplane, Sarah 230 1
Delaplane, Sarah E 233 1
Delaplane, W T 65 2
Delaplane, William T 184 1
Delaplane, William T 20, 44 3
Delaplane, William T 3rd 165 1
Delaplane, Wm 176, 183, 184 1
Delaplane, Wm H 183 1
Delaplane, Wm T 183 1
Delashmutt, A 23 1
Delashmutt, A J 14, 177, 181 2
Delashmutt, Alvida B 144 1
Delashmutt, Andrew J 144, 152, 172 1
Delashmutt, Arthur 84, 258 2
Delashmutt, Arthur 144 1
Delashmutt, Arthur 122, 129, 209, 221 3
Delashmutt, Arthur 245 1
Delashmutt, B J 45 2
Delashmutt, B James 146 1
Delashmutt, Basil 146 1

Delashmutt, Basil 175 1
Delashmutt, Basil J 146 1
Delashmutt, Basil Jr 146 1
Delashmutt, Basil Sr 146 1
Delashmutt, Basil Sr 146 1
Delashmutt, Charlotte T 172 1
Delashmutt, E 164 1
Delashmutt, E E 52 1
Delashmutt, E L 14, 84, 96, 100, 124, 177, 181 2
Delashmutt, E L 39, 71, 87, 96, 98, 124, 185, 186, 209 3
Delashmutt, E L 57, 84, 144, 147, 152, 179 1
Delashmutt, E T H 109 1
Delashmutt, Elias 144, 146 1
Delashmutt, Elias E 152 1
DeLashmutt, Elias E 258 2
Delashmutt, Elias L 152 1
Delashmutt, Elizabeth 152 1
Delashmutt, Fannie S 165 1
Delashmutt, J Thomas 169 1
Delashmutt, John 163 1
Delashmutt, John A 144, 165 1
Delashmutt, John M 144 1
Delashmutt, Lynn O 169 1
DeLashmutt, Marian S 227 3
Delashmutt, Mildred L 146 1
Delashmutt, Philip 146, 172, 176 1
Delashmutt, Phoebe R 144 1
Delashmutt, R B 208 1
Delashmutt, Thomas J 85 1
Delashmutt, Wm R 57 3
Delauder, David W* 166 1
DeLauder, David W* 159 1
Delauder, Elias* 176 1
DeLauder, Henry H 159 1
DeLauder, Henry Hoffman 159 1
Delauder, James M 166 1
DeLauder, Lillie R 159 1
Delauder, Peter 176 1
Delauder, Robert S 179 1
Delauder, Samuel 179 1
Delauder, William H 166 1
Delaughter, Elias D 153 1
Delaughter, Elizabeth 164 1
Delaughter, Geo A 156 1
Delaughter, Henry Sr 159 1
Delaughter, Jacob 164 1
Delaughter, John 164 1
Delaughter, Minnie M 153 1
Delaughter, Samuel 164 1
Delauter, Ada 52, 213a 2
Delauter, Adah M 93 2
Delauter, Albert L 145 1
Delauter, Bertha E 40 2
Delauter, C 150 1
Delauter, Caleb U 148 1
Delauter, Clarence 148 1
Delauter, David 125, 150 1
Delauter, David 197 2
Delauter, David Jr 150 1
Delauter, David Sr 150 1
Delauter, David W 159 1
Delauter, David W-see "H" 150 1
Delauter, E C 14, 179 1
Delauter, E S 52 2
Delauter, E Stanley 153, 179 1
Delauter, E Stanley 174 3
Delauter, Elias 152 1
Delauter, Elias D 5 2
Delauter, G M 197 1
Delauter, Geo 214 1
Delauter, Geo N 2 2
Delauter, Geo S 20 2
Delauter, George 156 1
Delauter, George W 38 1
Delauter, Gladys R 242 2
Delauter, H K 6, 10, 11, 21, 28, 45, 56, 57, 72, 73, 94, 113, 148, 153, 159, 161, 166, 172, 189, 202, 207, 214 3
Delauter, H K 10, 15, 20, 31, 32, 40, 41, 45, 52, 58, 65, 67, 85, 87, 99, 102, 106, 116, 119, 122, 145, 150, 151, 167, 178, 189, 190, 211, 215, 218, 210a, 212a, 214a, 257, 268, 277, 283, 2
DeLauter, H K 4, 11, 19, 34, 41, 42, 52, 62, 63, 67, 68, 73, 97, 76, 85, 107, 111, 113, 120, 133, 146, 159, 166, 168, 176, 179, 210, 214, 235, 245, 237, 249, 260, 266, 272, 280 1
DeLauter, H Keefer 166, 189, 208 3
Delauter, H Keefer 73, 113, 163, 2
Delauter, H Keifer 28, 206 3
Delauter, H Keiffer 93 2
Delauter, H Kieffer 3, 56, 108, 128, 129, 140, 178 200, 206, 215, 257, 262 267, 271, 272, 278, 294, 295 2
DeLauter, H Kieffer 2, 3, 4, 11, 16, 21, 29, 46, 48, 58, 83, 208, 223, 224 3
DeLauter, H Kieffer 1, 19, 28, 48, 63, 74, 101, 107, 159, 186, 192, 203, 235, 246, 266, 270 1
Delauter, Harry D 199 2
Delauter, Ira Carlton 162 1
Delauter, Israel C 145 1
Delauter, Jacob 150, 163 1
Delauter, James H 123 1
Delauter, Jay K 85 2
Delauter, John 163 1
Delauter, John H 152 1
DeLauter, Leslie R 242 2
Delauter, Lillian C P 169 1
Delauter, Lola V 153 1
Delauter, Lydia E 150 1
Delauter, M H 169, 283 1
Delauter, Mahlon H 249 1
DeLauter, Marcy G 266 1
Delauter, N Lavier 280 1
Delauter, O V 2 2
Delauter, R S 169 1
Delauter, Rachel K 81 2
Delauter, Resta L 148 1
Delauter, Silas W 169 1
Delauter, Tracy H 28 1
Delauter, W M 40 2
Delauter, Wm M 62, 73, 85 1
Delauter, Wm M 188 3
Delawder, Elizabeth 152 1
Delawder, Geo W 156 1
Delawder, Rufus 156 1
Delawter, Bertha E Hoke 184 1
DeLawter, Beulah C 143, 145 2
Delawter, Elizabeth 218 3
DeLawter, H Keiffer 18, 32 2
Delawter, Isabelle 156 1
DeLawter, Marcie G 258 1
Delawter, William M 145 2
Delawter, William M 184 1
DeLawter, William T 143 2
Delawter, William T 184 1
DeLawter, Wm M 143 2
Deleaplaine, Wm 218 3
Dell, Eve D 152 1
Dell, Josiah 111, 171 3
Dell, T C 60 1
Delp, Anna C 165 1
Delp, Jacob 165 1
Delphey, Ethel H 41 2
Delphey, J Paul 238 2
Delphey, Paul 47 2
Delphy, Ann M 164 1
Delphy, J Paul 195 1
Delphy, John 164 1
Delphy, Paul 76, 140 2
Demming, Chas 163 1
Demming, James 163 1
Demuth, Florence T 155 1
Dennis, Fannie McP 52 1
Dennis, G R Jr 23 2
Dennis, Geo 67 2
Dennis, Geo R 23, 98 3
Dennis, Geo R 48, 71, 155 1
Dennis, Geo R 2 2
Dennis, Geo R Jr 6, 20 3
Dennis, Geo R Jr 42, 67, 120, 166, 250, 252, 253, 283 1

Dennis, Geo R Jr 2, 31, 34, 40, 65, 68, 72, 102 2
Dennis, George H 203 3
Dennis, George R 246 2
Dennis, George R 223 3
Dennis, George R Jr 10, 67, 172 1
Dennis, George R Jr 227a, 238, 268 2
Dennis, John M 155 1
Dennis, Mary M 67 1
Dennis, Mary McG 155 1
Dennis, Mary McGill 42, 166, 172 1
Dennis, Philip 176 1
Denny, Arthur A 145 1
Dentler, J A 201 1
Dere, L Z 254 2
Dern, Abraham 144 1
Dern, Bessie L 45 3
Dern, Carrie B 126 1
Dern, Ernest C 11 1
Dern, Isaac 100 2
Derr, A H 52, 73, 144 1
Derr, Abraham 82, 144, 147 1
Derr, Abraham 38 2
Derr, Abraham H 156 1
Derr, Abraham S 144 1
Derr, Abraham Sr 144 1
Derr, Alice V 152, 163 1
Derr, Ann Mary 144 1
Derr, Anna C 164 1
Derr, Anna L 144 1
Derr, Anna M 147 1
Derr, Bessie L 72 3
Derr, C E 179, 208 1
Derr, C E 227 3
Derr, C Edw 150 1
Derr, C H 150 1
Derr, C L 175 1
Derr, Catherine 147, 159 1
Derr, Charles H 224 2
Derr, Charles S 153 1
Derr, Chas E 147 1
Derr, Chas H 147 1
Derr, Cornelius 30 2
Derr, Cornelius E 147 1
Derr, Daisy M 222 3
Derr, Daisy M 26 1
Derr, Daniel 47, 59, 144, 150, 155, 159, 164, 165, 166, 171, 179, 193, 252 1
Derr, Daniel 87, 276 2
Derr, Daniel C 150, 165 1
Derr, David 152, 179 1
Derr, David 282 2
Derr, Elizabeth 147, 152, 163, 164 1
Derr, Ella M 153, 165 1
Derr, Ellen C 150 1
Derr, Elmer 222 3
Derr, Elmer S 166, 169, 180 1
Derr, Elmer S 220 3
Derr, Esther J 153 1
Derr, Eugene 152 1
Derr, Eugene L 153, 164, 164, 165, 172 1
Derr, Ezra 152, 153 1
Derr, Ezra Z 153 1
Derr, Fannie G 152 1
Derr, Freda 189 1
Derr, Frederick 195 3
Derr, Frederick 155 1
Derr, Geo B 147, 156 1
Derr, Geo N 156 1
Derr, Geo W 54, 179 3
Derr, Harold E 153 1
Derr, Harry 147 1
Derr, Harry S 144 1
Derr, Henry 159 1
Derr, Henry W 159 1
Derr, Isaac 26 2
Derr, Jacob 100, 163, 164 1
Derr, James C 262 2
Derr, John 26, 80, 113, 134, 148, 264 2
Derr, John 135, 144, 163, 164, 165, 171, 191, 205, 248, 253, 264, 271 1
Derr, John 2, 14, 18, 113, 209 3
Derr, John A 91 1
Derr, John A 140 3
Derr, John C 179, 226 3
Derr, John C 150, 165 1
Derr, John E 166, 235 1
Derr, John H 176 1
Derr, John J 165 1
Derr, John Jr 147 1
Derr, John L 164, 210 1
Derr, John of M 163 1
Derr, John P 164 1
Derr, John S 153 1
Derr, John Sr 164 1
Derr, John W 28, 282 2
Derr, John W 279 1
Derr, John W 176 3
Derr, L 60 1
Derr, Lewis E 169, 176 1
Derr, Luther Z 169 1
Derr, Margaret 171 1
Derr, Mary A 171 1
Derr, Mary Ann 144 1
Derr, Mary E 152 1
Derr, Mary L 172, 180 1
Derr, Mary Oneida 180 1
Derr, Philip 176 1
Derr, Philip 39 3
Derr, R Scott 144, 150 1
Derr, Samuel 116, 264 2
Derr, Samuel 159, 165, 177 1
Derr, Sarah A 179, 150 1
Derr, Sarah C 177, 180 1
Derr, Sohpa K [sic] 169 1
Derr, Sophia K 33 1
Derr, Sophia Kate 180 1
Derr, T C 60 1
Derr, Willis 147 1
Derr, Willis E 144, 169, 184 1
Derr, Wm H 152 1
Derry, Joseph C 166 1
Derry, Nettie E 147, 166 1
Dertzbaugh, Catherine 27, 175 1
Dertzbaugh, Catherine E 33, 147, 156 1
Dertzbaugh, Ellen J 156 1
Dertzbaugh, Emma I 153 1
Dertzbaugh, Frank M 195, 197 1
Dertzbaugh, G W 64 3
Dertzbaugh, G Wm 147 1
Dertzbaugh, George 156 1
Dertzbaugh, George V 156 1
Dertzbaugh, Harry B 153 1
Dertzbaugh, John 48 1
Dertzbaugh, Lewis R 27, 163, 183 1
Dertzbaugh, Wm H 33, 153 1
Dertzbaugh, Wm Lee 183 1
Despeaux, Frank H 155 1
Despeaux, Nannie S 155 1
Detrich, Frederick L 172 1
Detrich, Margaret Jane 172 1
Detrick John P 166 1
Detrick, D Wellington 150 1
Detrick, F L 166 1
Detrick, Harriet 209 2
Detrick, J Stoll 166 1
Detrick, John U 166 1
Detrick, L F 186 3
Detrick, Lewis 198 2
Detrick, Lewis F 91 1
Detrick, Lewis F 40 3
Detrick, Louis F 166 1
Detrick, Marian D 166 1
Detroit Fidelity & Deposit Co 293 2
Detroit Fidelity & Surety Co 44 1
Detroit Fidelity & Surety Co 119, 288 2
Detroit Fidelity & Surety Co 91 3
Detroit Fidelity and Surety Co 140 1
Deven, James A 134 2
Devilbiss, A V 172 1

Devilbiss, A W 156 1
Devilbiss, Abner C 96 1
Devilbiss, Abner L 79 3
Devilbiss, Adam 43 2
Devilbiss, Adam 133, 144, 156, 159, 164 1
Devilbiss, Adam A 143 2
Devilbiss, Adam A 144 1
Devilbiss, Adam W 145, 146, 156, 159, 171 1
Devilbiss, Albert V 172 1
Devilbiss, Alice V 147 1
Devilbiss, Ann E 144 1
Devilbiss, Barbara 146 1
Devilbiss, Basil 144 1
Devilbiss, Basil P 146, 156, 183 1
Devilbiss, C 179 3
Devilbiss, Casper 147 1
Devilbiss, Casper Sr 147 1
Devilbiss, Catherine 117 1
Devilbiss, Chas 147, 177, 181, 183, 196 1
Devilbiss, Chas W 82 1
Devilbiss, Clifton G 24 3
Devilbiss, Cordia 147, 148 1
Devilbiss, Cyrus F 144 1
Devilbiss, D M 3 2
Devilbiss, D M 73, 176 1
Devilbiss, D M Dr 242 2
Devilbiss, Darius 44 1
Devilbiss, David 47, 96, 116, 117, 147, 150, 156, 171, 213, 228, 239, 253 1
Devilbiss, David 219a 2
Devilbiss, David A 144 1
Devilbiss, David A 150 2
Devilbiss, David M 146, 150, 164 1
Devilbiss, David M 188 3
Devilbiss, David M 177 2
Devilbiss, Davis M 150 1
Devilbiss, E K 35 3
Devilbiss, Edw 147 2
Devilbiss, Edw 144, 179 1
Devilbiss, Edward T 1, 272 1
Devilbiss, Edwin 35, 83, 149, 153, 167, 176 3
Devilbiss, Edwin 58, 66, 76, 190, 218, 227, 212a, 238, 247, 259 2
Devilbiss, Edwin 38, 48, 63, 96, 97, 99, 101, 107, 109, 113, 123, 126, 144, 145, 153, 156, 162, 165, 169, 175, 192, 200 1
Devilbiss, Elizabeth 162 1
Devilbiss, Ephriam M 171, 177 1
Devilbiss, G C 60 3
Devilbiss, Gardeanis 116 1
Devilbiss, Geo 28, 101 2
Devilbiss, Geo 61, 157 1
Devilbiss, Geo A 133, 159 1
Devilbiss, Geo W 113 2
Devilbiss, Geo W 84, 156, 164 1
Devilbiss, George 222 2
Devilbiss, George 156, 169, 179 1
Devilbiss, George C 150 1
Devilbiss, George C 156 1
Devilbiss, George P 156, 184 1
Devilbiss, George W 156, 159 1
Devilbiss, Georgianna 144 1
Devilbiss, Grover C 3 3
Devilbiss, Grover C 245 1
Devilbiss, H A. 156 1
Devilbiss, H H 205, 265 1
Devilbiss, Harriet V 159 1
Devilbiss, Harry S 159 1
Devilbiss, Henry A 159 1
Devilbiss, Herbert 157 1
Devilbiss, Hilda M 28, 159 1
Devilbiss, Howard 42 1
Devilbiss, Howard H 61, 172, 89, 192 1
Devilbiss, Ida B 146 1
Devilbiss, Ida E 162 1
Devilbiss, Irving S 147 1
Devilbiss, Isaiah 229 2
Devilbiss, Isaiah 159, 162, 179 1
Devilbiss, Isiah 162 1
Devilbiss, Isiaih 229 2
Devilbiss, J 205 2
Devilbiss, J Clark 172 1
Devilbiss, J Clarke 6 1
Devilbiss, James H 144 1
Devilbiss, Jane R 126, 172 1
Devilbiss, Jennie 156, 165, 166 1
Devilbiss, Joanne 156 1
Devilbiss, John 163, 164 1
Devilbiss, John 27 2
Devilbiss, John H 150, 164, 172 1
Devilbiss, John L 164 1
Devilbiss, John of C 163 1
Devilbiss, John of C 179 3
Devilbiss, John of J 163 1
Devilbiss, Joshua 117 1
Devilbiss, Laura V 133, 169, 183 1
Devilbiss, Levi 26, 38, 150, 218, 225 2
Devilbiss, Levi 147, 164, 169, 177, 233 1
Devilbiss, Levi 53 3
Devilbiss, Levin 134 2
Devilbiss, Lizzie M 150 1
Devilbiss, Lottie R 159 1
Devilbiss, Lydia A 169 1
Devilbiss, Madelyn L 134 2
Devilbiss, Mahlon 157 1
Devilbiss, Margaret E 171, 172 1
Devilbiss, Maria 164 1
Devilbiss, Martin 147 1
Devilbiss, Martin L 60 3
Devilbiss, Martin L 162 1
Devilbiss, Mary 171, 172 1
Devilbiss, Mary A 172 1
Devilbiss, Maurice M 184 1
Devilbiss, Miranda 171 1
Devilbiss, Mollie L 176 1
Devilbiss, Myrtie C 153 1
Devilbiss, Preston F 176 1
Devilbiss, Preston S 144 1
Devilbiss, Reuben 144, 177 1
Devilbiss, Reuben 11 2
Devilbiss, Roger B 116 1
Devilbiss, Rufus 222 2
Devilbiss, S 124 3
Devilbiss, Samuel 96, 148, 179, 196, 263 1
Devilbiss, Samuel 209 3
Devilbiss, Samuel 203 2
Devilbiss, Samuel of J 163, 263 1
Devilbiss, Samuel of J 205 2
Devilbiss, Sarah 156 1
Devilbiss, Sarah M 179 1
Devilbiss, Solomon 11 2
Devilbiss, Solomon D 150 1
Devilbiss, Susanna 147, 179 1
Devilbiss, Thomas 210a 2
Devilbiss, Thomas 156, 159, 164 1
Devilbiss, Thomas 60, 75 3
Devilbiss, Thos 93, 113 2
Devilbiss, Thos 181, 271 1
Devilbiss, Thos L 181 1
Devilbiss, Thos N 181 1
Devilbiss, W S 227 2
Devilbiss, Warren G 183 1
Devilbiss, Wilbur 267 2
Devilbiss, William 229 2
Devilbiss, Willie S 147, 184 1
Devilbiss, Wm 156, 181, 183, 184 1
Devilbiss, Wm A 183 1
Devilbiss, Wm H 183 1
Devitt, Amelia 152, 156 1
Devitt, Amelia C 144 1
Devitt, Amelia K 150, 234, 239 1

Devitt, Annie M 144 1
Devitt, D D 106 3
Devitt, David 150 1
Devitt, David B 150, 152 1
Devitt, Edw I 150 1
Devitt, Elizabeth 150, 152 1
Devitt, Margaret 144, 176 1
Devitt, Margaret F 152, 172, 234
1
Devitt, Margaret V 144 1
Devitt, Martha F 239 1
Devitt, P M 150 1
Devitt, Philip H 176 1
Devitt, Wm I 176 1
Devoy, Ann 171 1
Devoy, Michael 171 1
Dewees, Wm 197 1
Dewers, Wm 283 1
Dialekton, Basilos 146 1
Dialekton, Geo A 146 1
Dicas, John 163 1
Dicas, Mary 163 1
Dicas, Sarah 163, 179 1
Dickensheets, Wm 183 1
Dickinson, Festus 40 1
Diehhnan, Henry C [sic] 159 1
Diehhnan, Lawrence L 159 1
Diehl, A 82 3
Diehl, Abraham G 44 1
Diehl, Adam 100 3
Diehl, Adam 144 1
Diehl, Barbara 144, 146 1
Diehl, Catherine 147, 171 1
Diehl, Clarence 167 2
Diehl, Elizabeth 152 1
Diehl, Frederick W E 155 1
Diehl, George 156 1
Diehl, Hannah 217 3
Diehl, Jacob 163 1
Diehl, Jacob 144 2
Diehl, Jacob H 171 1
Diehl, Jennie E 101 1
Diehl, John 28 2
Diehl, John 144, 163, 166, 203
1
Diehl, John 40 3
Diehl, John of M 163 1
Diehl, John T 164 1
Diehl, John W 196 3
Diehl, John W 171, 183 1
Diehl, John W 187 2
Diehl, Louisa 155 1
Diehl, Maria 156 1
Diehl, Marie 144 1
Diehl, Martin 146, 163, 171, 172
1
Diehl, Martin 38 3
Diehl, Mary 139 1
Diehl, Moses 54 3
Diehl, Moses 147, 152, 171 1
Diehl, Samuel 9 2
Diehl, Wm 152, 163, 171, 183, 264
1
Diehl, Wm 1, 39, 237 2
Diehl, Wm 217 3
Diehl, Wm S & 29 2
Diehlman, Lewis 250 2
Diehlman, Mary C 171 1
Diell, Andrew 144 1
Diell, Elizabeth [sic] 144 1
Dietrich, Lewis 237 2
Dietrich, Phillip 116 1
Diffendahl, John 276 2
Diffendahl, Samuel 38 3
Diffendal , John 100 1
Diffendal, C L 165 1
Diffendal, Felix A 155 1
Diffendal, J M 165 1
Diffendal, John 205 2
Diffendal, John 165 1
Diffendal, Juliet 165 1
Diffendal, Peter 205 2
Diffendal, Samuel 22, 96, 205
2
Diffendal, Samuel 26 1
Diffendall, John 171 1
Diffendall, Mary 171, 176 1
Diffendall, Peter 176 1
Diffendall, Samuel 176 1
Diffenderfer, Mabe J 189 1
Diffindall, Elizabeth 152 1
Diffindall, Samuel 152 1
Diggs, Edgar 49 2
Diggs, Edgar 177 1
Diggs, Esther 152 1
Diggs, Florence B 155 1
Diggs, Florence B 65, 75 2
Diggs, John 165 1
Diggs, John T 166 1
Diggs, John T 23 2
Diggs, Rachel Ann 177 1
Diggs, Susan 179 1
Diggs, William H 129 1
Diggs, Wm R 177, 184 1
Dihel,Frederick 155 1
Dill, Charles G 148 1
Dill, G T 67 1
Dill, Geo 55 1
Dill, Geo 54, 89 2
Dill, Geo H 171 3
Dill, Geo T 71, 164, 171, 176, 194,
245 1
Dill, Geo T 1, 28, 119, 177 2
Dill, Geo T 54, 167 3
Dill, George 220 2
Dill, George T 156 1
Dill, George T 227 2
Dill, J J 27 1
Dill, Jashua [sic] 30 1
Dill, John 7, 51, 63, 92, 93, 124,
150, 159, 165, 175, 177 2
Dill, John 14, 18, 38, 141, 167,
179 3
Dill, John 30, 44, 106, 131, 164,
193, 208, 260, 278 1
Dill, John T 91 1
Dill, Joshua 1, 8, 14, 15, 18, 26, 38,
81, 96, 212 3
Dill, Joshua 131, 144, 164, 165, 176,
204, 208, 228, 260 1
Dill, Joshua 7, 22, 26, 27, 28, 54, 92,
93, 96, 124, 129, 144, 159, 175, 177,
262, 290 2
Dill, Joshua J 156, 165 1
Dill, Josiah 167, 179, 185 3
Dill, Lewis 89 2
Dill, Lewis H 177 2
Dill, Lewis H 171 3
Dill, Lewis H 164 1
Dill, Lewis W 28 2
Dill, Louis H 167 3
Dill, Margrete 172 1
Dill, Mary E 172 1
Dill, Mary M 171 1
Dill, Philiphina 176 1
Diller, C H 129 2
Diller, C H 165 1
Diller, Charles H 15 3
Diller, Chas H 61 1
Diller, Eliza 165 1
Diller, Eliza A 152 1
Diller, J H 32 1
Diller, Jacob 14, 96, 138, 223a 2
Diller, Jacob 47, 76, 135, 165, 171
1
Diller, Jacob 41, 205 3
Diller, John 165, 171, 183 1
Diller, John 187 3
Diller, John A 100 1
Diller, John H 134 2
Diller, Margaret E 164, 165
1
Diller, Martin 171 1
Diller, Robert H 184, 198 1
Diller, Samuel 76 1
Diller, Wm H 183 1
Dillinger, Chas 229 1
Dillon, Bertha 146 1
Dillon, Bertha M 183 1
Dillon, John 146 1
Dillon, John J Jr 166 1
Dillon, Luke C 169 1
Dillon, Paul 146 1
Dillon, Wm C 169, 183 1
Dilworth, John 163 1
Dimain, Wm 218 3
Dinges, Guy M 162 1

Dinges, Isaac M 162 1
Dintaman, Daisy I 153 1
Dintaman, John A 153 1
Dintarman, Emily Irene 153 1
Dinterman, Alvey M 153 1
Dinterman, Anna L 41 2
Dinterman, Annie R 166 1
Dinterman, Charlotte 150 1
Dinterman, Charlotte C 145 1
Dinterman, Clarence L 148, 164 1
Dinterman, Clyde A 166 1
Dinterman, Ethel R 153 1
Dinterman, G H 156 1
Dinterman, G Harlan 108 2
Dinterman, G L 124 3
Dinterman, Geo B 156 1
Dinterman, Geo D 41 2
Dinterman, Geo D 179 1
Dinterman, Geo D 224 3
Dinterman, Geo H 156, 171 1
Dinterman, Geo H 41 2
Dinterman, Geo T 252 1
Dinterman, George 156 1
Dinterman, George D 156 1
Dinterman, George H 41 2
Dinterman, Harry E 156, 157 1
Dinterman, J 156 1
Dinterman, Jacob 164 1
Dinterman, Jacob D 8 2
Dinterman, Jesse H 166 1
Dinterman, Jessie P 250 2
Dinterman, JF 234 1
Dinterman, John M 166 1
Dinterman, John P 164 1
Dinterman, L B 27 1
Dinterman, L G 96, 107, 156, 197 1
Dinterman, Lincoln G 156, 179 1
Dinterman, Mary A 171 1
Dinterman, Phoebe 57 3
Dinterman, Rachel J 177 1
Dinterman, Roy C 156 1
Dinterman, Roy C 242 2
Dinterman, Susan 179, 184 1
Dinterman, Susan A M 179 1
Dinterman, Wm H 184 1
Disney, Eliza J 153 1
Disney, Eliza V 153 1
Disney, Marion 184 1
Disney, William H 184 1
Disney, Wm H 153 1
Diven, James A 197 1
Divine, James 163 1
Dixon, Agnes Virginia 145 1
Dixon, Alexander 144 1
Dixon, Amy Kump Mrs 106 2
Dixon, Annie R 144 1
Dixon, C Merle 217a 2
Dixon, Clara Estelle 148 1
Dixon, Dorothy 150, 159 1
Dixon, Eleanor M 153 1
Dixon, Eleanore 152 1
Dixon, Elizabeth M 153 1
Dixon, Ernest 153 1
Dixon, Fred L 55 1
Dixon, George W 157 1
Dixon, Haines 159 1
Dixon, Howard E 150 1
Dixon, J D 67 3
Dixon, James 51 2
Dixon, James B 166 1
Dixon, James E 166, 172 1
Dixon, James M 163 1
Dixon, James P 164 1
Dixon, James R 166 1
Dixon, Jane 164 1
Dixon, John 164 1
Dixon, John H 164 1
Dixon, Joshua 164, 171 1
Dixon, Josiah 185 3
Dixon, Julia A C 181 1
Dixon, L Frank 169 1
Dixon, Laura A 150 1
Dixon, Lola 148 1
Dixon, Margaret [?] 189 1
Dixon, Margaret E F 172 1
Dixon, Martha 67 3
Dixon, Martha 166 1
Dixon, Martha E 172 1
Dixon, Mary 171 1
Dixon, McDevitt C 150 1
Dixon, Rebecca 183 1
Dixon, Robert Lee 177 1
Dixon, Ruth 177 1
Dixon, Samuel 159 2
Dixon, Sidney E 172 1
Dixon, Sohpia [sic] 179 1
Dixon, Thomas 227 1
Dixon, Thomas 48, 213a 2
Dixon, Thomas 212 3
Dixon, Thomas E 177 1
Dixon, Thomas O 156 1
Dixon, Thos 191 3
Dixon, Thos 164, 181 1
Dixon, Thos E 279 1
Dixon, Thos. 171 1
Dixon, Vanburen 159, 182 1
Dixon, W E 67 2
Dixon, W E 19 1
Dixon, W H 171 2
Dixon, Wilmer R 148, 166 1
Dixon, Wm 183 1
Dixon, Wm E 150 1
Dixon, Wm H 201 1
Dixson, Chas H 51 3
Dobler, John J 43 3
Dodd, Edw M 162 1
Dodd, Ida M 162 1
Dodd, Robert S 177 1
Dods, John 163 1
Dods, Robert 57 2
Dods, Robert 163, 177, 179 1
Dods, Selkirg 179 1
Doefler, George 195 3
Doering, Alan C 172 1
Doering, Alvin C 144 1
Doering, Maggie E 144 1
Doering, Margaret E 172 1
Dofler, Bertha May 59 1
Dofler, George 146, 156 1
Dofler, Jacob 164 1
Dofler, Ruth 164 1
Dogan, John 163 1
Dohle, Henry 171 1
Dohle, Margaret 171 1
Dolan, Carrie L 148 1
Dold, Margaret W 173 1
Dolfield, Frederick 264 1
Doll, Adelia A 144 1
Doll, Alexander H 144 1
Doll, Ann E B 156 1
Doll, Arthur 34 1
Doll, Arthur H 76, 235 1
Doll, Arthur H 283 2
Doll, Arthur H 16 3
Doll, B Frank 144 1
Doll, Catherine 147 1
Doll, Charles H 148 1
Doll, Chas C 147 1
Doll, Chas D 126 1
Doll, Chas J 147, 156, 172, 179, 186 1
Doll, Clemetine E 148 1
Doll, Clifford H 147 1
Doll, Elizabeth W 182 1
Doll, Elizabeth Wisong 147 1
Doll, Ezra 222 3
Doll, Ezra 152, 153, 172 1
Doll, Ezra 132, 147 2
Doll, Frank A 31, 49, 104 2
Doll, Frank A 60, 176, 186 1
Doll, G F 60, 172 1
Doll, G J 96 1
Doll, G J 87, 100 3
Doll, G Joseph 156 1
Doll, Geo 156 1
Doll, Geo 46, 147 2
Doll, George 156, 159 1
Doll, George C 148 1
Doll, Gertrude B 157 1
Doll, Harriet 40 1
Doll, J E 149 2
Doll, Jacob 100 2

Doll, Jacob 91, 147, 157, 159, 164, 176 1
Doll, James A 67 2
Doll, James E 157, 172, 186, 248 1
Doll, John 163 1
Doll, John 53 3
Doll, Joseph 33 1
Doll, M E 87 3
Doll, M E 60, 125, 126, 155, 163 1
Doll, M E 30, 116, 189 2
Doll, M E of G 88 1
Doll, Mary 171 1
Doll, Mary L 147, 172 1
Doll, Melville E 172 1
Doll, Melvin E 159 1
Doll, Melvin E 15 2
Doll, Miriam T 104 2
Doll, Peter 46 2
Doll, Peter 126 1
Doll, Roger A 64 2
Doll, Roger A 33, 176 1
Doll, S V 60, 153 1
Doll, Samuel 156, 159 1
Doll, Samuel J 179 1
Doll, Samuel V 52, 172 1
Doll, Susannah 163 1
Doll, Virginia B 182 1
Doll, Washington W 144 1
Dollarhide, James 164 1
Dollinger, Charles 264 1
Domer, Charles H 51 3
Domer, Chas W 147 1
Domer, Daniel 156 1
Domer, George 156 1
Domer, George H 156 1
Domer, Marie E 52 2
Donald, James 172 1
Donald, Margaret 172 1
Donald, McDonald 171 1
Donnan, James Ward 166 1
Donne, Lydia A 169 1
Donnell, John 163 1
Donnelly, Bridget 146 1
Donnelly, Patrick 176 1
Donnelly, Simon 37 3
Donoghue, J 59 1
Donovan, Michael 171 1
Donsife, Charlotte 159 1
Donsife, F G 82 3
Donsife, G F 156 1
Donsife, Henry C 64 3
Donsife, Henry C 159 1
Donsife, Henry L 159 1
Donsife, Mary C 82 3
Donsife, Otho J 159 1
Donston, Ann M 144 1
Donston, Jacob 164 1
Dorcas, David 131 1
Dorcas, David F 138 2
Dorcas, Geo M 165, 168 1
Dorcas, Harry 125 2
Dorcas, Harry C 102 2
Dorcas, Harry C 3 3
Dorcas, Jacob 82, 91 3
Dorcas, Jacob 165 1
Dorcas, Katie V 168 1
Dorcas, William H 168, 184 1
Dorcis, John A 144 1
Dorcus, Anna R 145, 164 1
Dorcus, Chas W 147 1
Dorcus, Elsie 144 1
Dorcus, Elsie I 145, 183 1
Dorcus, Harry 55 1
Dorcus, Harry C 144, 189 1
Dorcus, Wm H 147, 165, 183 1
Dorff, George 156 1
Dorff, Mary 156 1
Dornheim, Marv J 8 1
Dorothy, Margaret 171 1
Dorsey, Alan G 253 1
Dorsey, Albert 144 1
Dorsey, Ann P 209 3
Dorsey, Ann P 144, 175 1
Dorsey, Ann PL 209 3
Dorsey, Aranina 144 1
Dorsey, Basil 44, 146, 159, 163 1
Dorsey, Basil E 156, 171 1
Dorsey, Basil of J 146 1
Dorsey, Benjamin L 30, 146 1
Dorsey, Byron S 215, 218 3
Dorsey, Byron S 43 2
Dorsey, C 81 3
Dorsey, Charles A 27 3
Dorsey, Claggett W 55, 147, 175, 205 1
Dorsey, Claggett W 67 2
Dorsey, Cordelia H 147 1
Dorsey, Dan 152 1
Dorsey, Edgar 152 1
Dorsey, Ely Jr 150 2
Dorsey, Ely Jr 1 3
Dorsey, Ely of Ely 152 1
Dorsey, Ely, Jr 152 1
Dorsey, Eugene 152 1
Dorsey, Evan 152 1
Dorsey, Frederick 279 1
Dorsey, Genevieve 73 1
Dorsey, George 156 1
Dorsey, H 112, 157 1
Dorsey, H 163, 212 3
Dorsey, H 9, 40, 66 2
Dorsey, H W 87 3
Dorsey, H W 120, 144, 183 1
Dorsey, H W 203 2
Dorsey, Hagar 159 1
Dorsey, Harriet J 210 3
Dorsey, Harriett 82, 146 1
Dorsey, Harriett W Jr 209 3
Dorsey, Harry G 10 3
Dorsey, Harry W 144, 146, 159 1
Dorsey, Harry W 39, 209 3
Dorsey, Harry W Sr 159 1
Dorsey, Harvey H 159 1
Dorsey, Henrietta 144, 177 1
Dorsey, Ignatius 57 2
Dorsey, Ignatius W 159, 162, 179 1
Dorsey, J W 176 1
Dorsey, J W 49 2
Dorsey, James E 67 1
Dorsey, Janet 181 1
Dorsey, Jennie L 199 2
Dorsey, Jennie L R 110 1
Dorsey, John 57 2
Dorsey, John 165, 166, 179, 186 1
Dorsey, John 40 3
Dorsey, John of J 163 1
Dorsey, John W 135 1
Dorsey, Joshua 163 1
Dorsey, Julia A 175 1
Dorsey, Kitty H 139 1
Dorsey, Lloyd 147, 159, 169 1
Dorsey, Lloyd 106, 207 3
Dorsey, Lloyd 43, 254 2
Dorsey, Lloyd Ann 169 1
Dorsey, Margaret 171 1
Dorsey, Margaret A 171 1
Dorsey, Mary 171, 172 1
Dorsey, Mary A 172 1
Dorsey, Mary H 172 1
Dorsey, Mary Matilda 171 1
Dorsey, Matilda 171, 172 1
Dorsey, Michael 171 1
Dorsey, Michael 154 2
Dorsey, Narciso 175 1
Dorsey, Nathan 175 1
Dorsey, Nellie 175 1
Dorsey, Nelson 175 1
Dorsey, Nicholas 139 1
Dorsey, Nicholas of L 175 1
Dorsey, Nimrod B 96 1
Dorsey, Ordella O 177 1
Dorsey, Philip 278 1
Dorsey, Philip A R 47 1
Dorsey, Pottinger 159, 176, 260 1
Dorsey, R 147 1
Dorsey, Randolph 177 1
Dorsey, Rebecca A 37 1
Dorsey, Rhoderick 44, 133, 177 1
Dorsey, Rhoderick 57 2

Dorsey, Richard 23, 70 3
Dorsey, Richard 133, 177, 181, 271, 283 1
Dorsey, Richard Dr 38 2
Dorsey, Richard G 177 1
Dorsey, Roderick 28, 34 2
Dorsey, Ruth 144 1
Dorsey, Samuel 34 2
Dorsey, Samuel T 146, 171, 179, 225 1
Dorsey, Susan L 179 1
Dorsey, Susan Laura 179 1
Dorsey, Susan M 179 1
Dorsey, Tabitha 181 1
Dorsey, Thomas W 181 1
Dorsey, Tristram S 175 1
Dorsey, Upton 152 1
Dorsey, Upton L 181 1
Dorsey, W H 196 3
Dorsey, Walter 96 1
Dorsey, Willard A 159 1
Dorsey, William B 276 2
Dorsey, William H 196 3
Dorsey, William R 294 2
Dorsey, Wm 67, 164, 184 1
Dorsey, Wm B 165, 175 1
Dorsey, Wm H 165, 185 1
Dorsey, Wm N 30 1
Dorsey, Wm R 44, 177 1
Dosh, H C 203 1
Dote, Morah N 172 1
Doterer, J Raymond 166 1
Dotrer, John 142 1
Dotrow, Geo 137 2
Dotrow, Henry 137 2
Dotson, Sarah 179 1
Dotter, Annie 155 1
Dotter, Francis 155 1
Dotterer, Bruce Bierly 146 1
Dotterer, Flora C 146 1
Dotterer, Franklin 155 1
Dotterer, Grace E 166 1
Dotterer, John 1 2
Dotterer, John 217 1
Dotterer, Josiah 165 1
Dotterer, Mary A 165 1
Dotterer, Minnie 171 1
Dotterer, Sannie E 146 1
Dotterer, William 55 3
Dotterer, Wm H 171 1
Doty, Annie O 147 1
Doty, Claude P 147 1
Doty, D C 54 2
Doty, Elmer W 183 1
Doty, John 282 2
Doty, Louise 172 1
Doty, Madora I 183 1
Doty, Madora Irene 173 1
Doty, Mary Alice 172 1
Doty, Walter C 183 1
Doty, Wm B 183 1
Doub, Abraham 144 1
Doub, Anna F 144 1
Doub, Annie M 165, 166 1
Doub, Bettie E 147 1
Doub, C S 188 2
Doub, C Staley 147, 169 1
Doub, Catherine 147, 172 1
Doub, Cornelius E 147 1
Doub, David 205 3
Doub, David of E 150 1
Doub, Eliza 35 2
Doub, Elizabeth 152 1
Doub, Elizabeth A 152 1
Doub, Elmer H 51, 153, 166 1
Doub, Eneas 186 3
Doub, Enos 144, 147, 152, 169, 191 1
Doub, Enos 101 2
Doub, Esther 79 1
Doub, Ezra 106, 147, 152, 171 1
Doub, Ezra 186 2
Doub, Ezra 18, 70, 165, 209 3
Doub, Ezra & 165 3
Doub, Florence W 155, 164 1
Doub, Geo 19 2
Doub, Geo L 113 2
Doub, Geo L 172 3
Doub, George 156, 164 1
Doub, George L 157 1
Doub, George W 26 3
Doub, Harriett E 159 1
Doub, Henry 147, 183 1
Doub, Isaiah 156, 159 1
Doub, Isiah 162 1
Doub, J 101 2
Doub, J Elmer 144 1
Doub, J Emuel [sic] 166 1
Doub, J Jonathan 150 1
Doub, J S 163 1
Doub, Jacob 38, 100, 137, 237 2
Doub, Jacob 163, 164, 249 1
Doub, Jacob 26 3
Doub, James 23 3
Doub, James E 188 3
Doub, James E 147 1
Doub, Joel 144, 165, 169, 191 1
Doub, John 163 1
Doub, John L 169 1
Doub, Johua 276 2
Doub, Jonas 191 1
Doub, Jonas A 165 1
Doub, Jonathan 26 1
Doub, Joseph 186 2
Doub, Joshua 40, 106, 156, 164, 253 1
Doub, Joshua 35 2
Doub, Joshua 93 2
Doub, Joshua 31 3
Doub, Joshus 224 2
Doub, Josiah 152 1
Doub, Josiah C 202 3
Doub, Josuah 185 3
Doub, Laura J 169 1
Doub, Lewis 152 1
Doub, Lewis P 169 1
Doub, Lola E 147 1
Doub, Lydia 169 1
Doub, M C 67 3
Doub, Margaret K 165 1
Doub, Mary Margaret 171 1
Doub, Merretta C 172 1
Doub, Sarah A 10 1
Doub, Valentine 47, 56, 162, 182, 196, 225 1
Doub, Valentine 11, 84, 100 2
Doub, Valentine 53 3
Doub, Valentine D 182 1
Doub, Virgil W 183 1
Doub, W H 9, 129 3
Doub, W W 50, 166 3
Doub, W W 265 2
Doub, William 54 3
Doub, William H 139 3
Doub, Wm 138, 197, 203, 218 2
Doub, Wm 129, 171 3
Doub, Wm 13 1
Doub, Wm H 37, 40, 58, 130, 164, 165, 182, 264 1
Doub, Wm H 35, 124, 177 2
Doub, Wm H 67 3
Doub, Wm W 183, 197 1
Doub, Wm W 56 3
Doudy, Harry W 159 1
Dougall, Charles R Jr 148 1
Dougall, Katherine L 148 1
Doughaday 40 1
Dougherty, Baxter C 166, 172 1
Dougherty, Baxter C 199 2
Dougherty, C Thomas 147 1
Dougherty, Charles F 172 1
Dougherty, Chas E 147 1
Dougherty, Idella E 197 3
Dougherty, J Frank 166 1
Dougherty, James 30 1
Dougherty, James D 176 1
Dougherty, James E 165 1
Dougherty, John 24 1
Dougherty, Lula M 110 1
Dougherty, Mary A 108 2
Dougherty, Minnie E 166, 172, 243

1
Dougherty, Nellie H 9 2
Dougherty, Raymond E 243 1
Dougherty, Sarah C 147 1
Dougherty, Sarah C E 179 1
Doughtery, C T 165 1
Doughtery, Chas E 165 1
Doughtery, F G 9 2
Doughtery, John 163 1
Doughtery, Margaret 163 1
Douglas, Martha I 64 2
Douglas, Samuel 22 2
Douglass, Wm 183 1
Douty, Henry W 52 1
Douty, James 38 2
Douty, James C 7 2
Douty, Sarah C 159, 179 1
Dove, Mary E 81 2
Dowell, John 163 1
Dowell, Joshua 182 1
Dowley, Edward 148 1
Downey, C A Lawrence 152, 155 1
Downey, C A Lawrence 129 2
Downey, Chas A 146 1
Downey, Cordelia H 22 2
Downey, Cordelia H 155, 159, 183 1
Downey, Elizabeth D 153 1
Downey, Fannie 48 1
Downey, Frank 50, 113, 166 3
Downey, Frank 155, 172, 183 1
Downey, Frank 245, 250 2
Downey, Frank J 153 1
Downey, Frank J 229a 2
Downey, Henry St George T 159 1
Downey, J W 60, 125 1
Downey, J W 20, 246 2
Downey, J Wm 27 1
Downey, Jesse 124 3
Downey, Jesse W 15, 188, 242, 245 2
Downey, Jesse W 187 3
Downey, Jesse W 37, 61, 147, 172, 183, 201 1
Downey, Jesse W Jr 165, 172 1
Downey, Jesse W Sr 155 1
Downey, Jno 132 3
Downey, John 225 2
Downey, M J 187 3
Downey, M Jane 155, 165 1
Downey, M Jane 196 3
Downey, Margaret J 172, 183 1
Downey, Margaret Jane 148 1
Downey, Mary W 110 1
Downey, Mary W 15 2
Downey, Michael 171, 172 1
Downey, N Jane 59 1
Downey, William 1, 9, 41, 42, 87, 124, 139, 186 3
Downey, William 27, 155 1
Downey, William 210a, 249, 250 2
Downey, Wm 19, 106, 187 3
Downey, Wm 37, 44, 59, 146, 147, 183, 219, 239 1
Downey, Wm 14, 19, 43, 57, 58, 166, 188, 197 2
Downing, Annie 144 1
Downing, Hannah 14 1
Downing, Joshua 122 3
Downing, Rebecca 81 2
Doyle, Catherine 147 1
Doyle, Wm 144 1
Drach, Adam 152, 279 1
Drach, Henry 144 1
Dracht, Margaret A 171 1
Draper, Cora V 150 1
Draper, Dewey G 150 1
Draper, Mae 173 1
Draper, Martin L 173 1
Draper, May H Lewis 173 1
Draper, Norman L 173 1
Draper, Stanley H 37, 150 1
Draper, Thomas 56, 173 1
Draper, Thos 133, 196 1
Drayer, Andrew 144 1
Drayer, Emanuel 152 1
Dresher, Jacob 165 1
Drew, Ella M 27 1
Dreyer, Arabella 147 1
Dreyer, Chas M 147 1
Drill, Andrew 163 1
Drill, Andrew 72 2
Drill, Annie J 175 1
Drill, Christian 152 1
Drill, Eve 152 1
Drill, Geo 152, 163 1
Drill, Geo 19 2
Drill, George 64 3
Drill, Harriet V 159 1
Drill, Henry C 159 1
Drill, Jacob 212 3
Drill, Jacob 152, 163, 228 1
Drill, Oliver B 175 1
Drinkhouse, Adam J 172 1
Droneberger, John 165 1
Droneburg, Claude T 168 1
Droneburg, Ernest H 177 1
Droneburg, Franklin Lee 177 1
Droneburg, Guy H 57, 111 3
Droneburg, Katie L 168 1
Droneburg, Reverdy 177 1
Droneburg, William B 4 3
Droneburg, William L 168 1
Dronenburg, Anna B 165 1
Dronenburg, Charlotte M 166 1
Dronenburg, Chas D 51 1
Dronenburg, Ella R 166 1
Dronenburg, Guy H 213a 2
Dronenburg, Henry 150 1
Dronenburg, Ida J 162 1
Dronenburg, Jacob 165 1
Dronenburg, Jacob 276 2
Dronenburg, James M 166 1
Dronenburg, John J 165 1
Dronenburg, John T 166 1
Dronenburg, John W 166 1
Dronenburg, Margaret 231 2
Dronenburg, Reverdy 15 2
Dronenburg, Wm L 166 1
Dronenburg, Wm U 183 1
Druen, Mary Virginia V 172 1
Drummond, James 163 1
Duball, Benjamin [sic] 146 1
Dubel, Ben L 147 1
Dubel, Bobbie D 10 2
Dubel, Cornelius 164 1
Dubel, H L 100 1
Dubel, Jacob 165 1
Dubel, John 164 1
Dubel, John 19 2
Dubel, John D 61 1
Dubel, John D 187 3
Dubel, John V 50 3
Dubel, Losson A 147 1
Dubel, Mary 165 1
Dubel, S H 165 1
Dubel, Susan V 165 1
Dubel, Tyson D 181 1
Duble, John D 40 3
Duble, Theresa E 181 1
Dublin, Wm Jr 26 2
Dubrow, Jerry M 113 2
Duckett, Thomas 70 3
Duddera, Wm 229 1
Dudderar Charles T 148 1
Dudderar, Albert 227a 2
Dudderar, Albert R 232 2
Dudderar, Albert R 176 1
Dudderar, B F 210a 2
Dudderar, B F 176, 183 1
Dudderar, Benj 150, 159 2
Dudderar, Benj E 146 1
Dudderar, Benj F 220 2
Dudderar, Benjamin 146, 147, 153 1
Dudderar, Benjamin F 146 1
Dudderar, Chas 80 2
Dudderar, Chas E 177 1
Dudderar, Clifton P 63, 146 1
Dudderar, Conrad 147 1
Dudderar, Conrad 214 2

Dudderar, D Hamilton 150 1
Dudderar, D W 265 1
Dudderar, Daisy A 62 1
Dudderar, Daisy Alton 150 1
Dudderar, Dallon 73 1
Dudderar, Daniel 150 1
Dudderar, Daniel H 21 1
Dudderar, David 22, 26, 117, 135, 147, 150, 163, 164, 260 1
Dudderar, David 150, 220, 221 2
Dudderar, David M 150, 183 1
Dudderar, David W 171 1
Dudderar, Dennis W 150 1
Dudderar, Dorcus 150 1
Dudderar, Emeline 165 1
Dudderar, F B 164 1
Dudderar, Ge 79 3
Dudderar, Geo 35, 70, 138, 181 2
Dudderar, Geo 146, 169, 201, 205 1
Dudderar, Geo W 84, 99, 159, 205 2
Dudderar, Geo W 205 3
Dudderar, Geo W 165, 177, 183, 191, 227 1
Dudderar, George T 156 1
Dudderar, George V 156 1
Dudderar, George W 294 2
Dudderar, George W 207 3
Dudderar, George W 19 1
Dudderar, Jacob 79 1
Dudderar, John 112, 131, 147, 152, 164, 171, 228 1
Dudderar, John 46, 137, 148, 150 2
Dudderar, John F 131, 165 1
Dudderar, John H 150, 179 1
Dudderar, John W 164 1
Dudderar, Juanita 148 1
Dudderar, Lucretia C 169 1
Dudderar, M 131 1
Dudderar, M Rosa 148 1
Dudderar, Maggie H 41 1
Dudderar, Margaret 171 1
Dudderar, Mary A 156 1
Dudderar, Mary B 153 1
Dudderar, Myra L 1 1
Dudderar, P 60 3
Dudderar, Peter 70, 99, 210a, 212a, 221 2
Dudderar, Peter 9 3
Dudderar, Peter 67, 96, 146, 150, 156, 176 1
Dudderar, Peter & 124 2
Dudderar, Peter T 68 1
Dudderar, Philip 46 2
Dudderar, Rachel P T 122 2
Dudderar, Randolph 177 1
Dudderar, Rosannah 177 1
Dudderar, Samuel 279 1
Dudderar, Susannah 179 1
Dudderar, W W 210a 2
Dudderar, W W 172 1
Dudderar, Warren E 41, 62 1
Dudderar, Warren E 226 2
Dudderar, William 79 1
Dudderar, Wm 27, 93, 150 2
Dudderar, Wm 110, 147, 183, 228 1
Dudderar, Wm S 30 1
Dudderar, Wm W 150 1
Dudderas, Albert R 220 2
Dudderer, Geo 184 2
Dudderer, John 164 1
Dudderow, Jacob 196 1
Dudderow, Washington 183 1
Dudderow, Wm 183, 208 1
Duderar, Albert 266 1
Duderar, John 160, 184, 195 3
Duderer, Joshua 165 3
Dudley, Alvin L 145 1
Dudley, George O 157 1
Dudley, Mildred 145 1
Dudrear Charles E 148 1
Dudrear, Loretta A 169 1
Dudrear, Mary A 172 1
Dudrear, W Irving 145, 183 1
Dudrow, Annie M 153, 184 1
Dudrow, Birdie J 146 1
Dudrow, C C 145 1
Dudrow, Caroline E 148, 153 1
Dudrow, Charlotte E 148 1
Dudrow, Christian 147 1
Dudrow, Cordelia 147 1
Dudrow, David 84 2
Dudrow, David 113 3
Dudrow, Elmer L 153 1
Dudrow, Fannie 155 1
Dudrow, Jacob 164 1
Dudrow, Jacob H 172 1
Dudrow, John 185, 195 3
Dudrow, Josiah 164 1
Dudrow, Mary Jane 172 1
Dudrow, Wm 155 1
Duen, James A 254 2
Duer, Robert 26 1
Duer, Samuel 57, 177 1
Duering, M E 148 1
Duffen, Elijah 152 1
Duffin, Elijah 118 1
Duffy, James 163 1
Dugan, C Nelson 195 2
Dugan, Frederick C 195 2
Dugan, Howard J 195 2
Dugan, Nancy 175 1
Dugan, Walter C 163 1
Duggan, John 163, 183 1
Duke, Elizabeth 156 1
Duke, Green H 156 1
Dukehart, C Edgar 172 1
Dukehart, Henry 159 1
Dukehart, John 9 1
Dukehart, John J 165, 166 1
Dukehart, Margaret 166 1
Dukehart, Mary A 171, 172 1
Dulaney, Margaret E 171 1
Dumas, H R 220 3
Dumm, Anna B 183 1
Dumm, Wm T 183 1
Dumm, Wm W 183 1
Dunawin, Catherine 147 1
Dunawin, Margaret 147 1
Duncan, Wm 175 1
Dungan, Levi 169 1
Dungan, Martha 169 1
Dunkehart, Catherine 159 1
Dunkehart, Henry 159 1
Dunkehart, Wm 159 1
Dunkin, Beulah I 148 1
Dunkin, Charles W 148 1
Dunkin, Guy C 148 1
Dunlap, Gibson 164 1
Dunlap, James 164, 183 1
Dunlap, John 179 1
Dunlap, Luther M 183 1
Dunlap, Rachel J 177 1
Dunlap, Samuel M 164 1
Dunlap, Wm G 179 1
Dunlap, Worthington 99 1
Dunlop, Geo T 159, 183 1
Dunlop, H 111 3
Dunlop, Henry 159 1
Dunlop, Henry 96, 126 3
Dunlop, James 275 2
Dunn, Edw 152 1
Dunn, J W 20 3
Dunn, John William 166 1
Dunn, Raymond 166 1
Dunne, John F 166 1
Dunnick, Michael 171 1
Dunning, Wm F 120 1
Dunott, Justus 166 1
Dunott, Mary Harrison Ritchie 166 1
Dunott, Thos J 220 3
Dunshee, Margaret E 181 1
Dunshee, Thos A 181 1
Dunsing, Daniel 222 1
Dunsing, Henry 159 1
Dunsing, Jacob 240 1
Dunsing, Samuel 240 1

Dunston, Anna M 164 1
Duphon, Samuel 184 3
Duphorn, John 116 1
Duphorn, Samuel 116 1
Dupuy, Alice 165 1
Dupuy, Joseph 144 1
Durberow, Margaret 214 2
Durbin, James 152, 165 1
Durbin, James 75, 81 3
Durbin, Nicholas 183 1
Durbin, William 254, 267 2
Durbin, William 1, 8, 38, 98, 202, 215 3
Durbin, William 9 1
Durbin, Wm 1, 18, 26, 87, 113 2
Durbin, Wm 37, 91, 195 3
Durbin, Wm 24, 37, 56, 116, 163, 183, 213, 219, 263, 278 1
Durbin, Wm Jr 64, 171 3
Durbin, Wm Jr 165, 185 2
Durborough, James R 164 1
Durborough, James R 211 2
Durborough, Margaret 164 1
Durborow, Margaret E 172 1
Durborow, Margaret E 198 2
Durst, Rebecca 177 1
Dusing, Callie L 148 1
Dusing, Daniel 150 1
Dusing, Joseph E 166 1
Dusing, Samuel D 166 1
Dusing, Thomas S 150 1
Dusinger, Martha 231 2
Dustin, Jonathan W 163 1
Dutor, Katherine E 155 1
Dutro, Elias 8 3
Dutro, George 156 1
Dutro, George 31 3
Dutro, Jacob W 175 1
Dutro, Nicholas 175 1
Dutro, Samuel 156 1
Dutrow, A Mary 177 1
Dutrow, A S 179 1
Dutrow, Ada R 179 1
Dutrow, Ada Rebecca 145 1
Dutrow, Agnes Cort 145 1
Dutrow, Agnes Corte 177 1
Dutrow, Andrew 144 1
Dutrow, Ann R 144 1
Dutrow, Annie R J 144, 177 1
Dutrow, B H 122 3
Dutrow, Bradley 116 3
Dutrow, Carrie H 160 2
Dutrow, Cordelia 164 1
Dutrow, Daniel T 20 3
Dutrow, David 171 1
Dutrow, Dora L 170 2
Dutrow, Dvid 137, 186 2
Dutrow, Eleanor M 153 1
Dutrow, Eliza A 153 1
Dutrow, Elizabeth 176, 179 1
Dutrow, Elsie R 145 1
Dutrow, Emma T 91 3
Dutrow, Fannie E 155 1
Dutrow, Fanny E 179 1
Dutrow, Franklin 112 1
Dutrow, Geo 155, 163, 179 1
Dutrow, Geo 137 2
Dutrow, Geo P 56 1
Dutrow, George 254 2
Dutrow, Granville M 157 1
Dutrow, Harold M 67 2
Dutrow, Hazel 83 3
Dutrow, Henry 144 2
Dutrow, Henry 159 1
Dutrow, Howard 91 3
Dutrow, I Myurtelin 132 2
Dutrow, I Myurtlin 172 1
Dutrow, Ida E 162 1
Dutrow, Ida V 177 1
Dutrow, J L 147 3
Dutrow, J W 163 1
Dutrow, Jacob 144, 163, 164, 171 1
Dutrow, Jacob 1 2
Dutrow, Jacob S 164, 172 1
Dutrow, Jacob W 166 1
Dutrow, James 163 1
Dutrow, James C 163 1
Dutrow, John 163, 171, 179 1
Dutrow, John 209 3
Dutrow, John L 45 3
Dutrow, John W 165 1
Dutrow, Jonathan D 166 1
Dutrow, Joseph L 171 3
Dutrow, Katharine E 145 1
Dutrow, Katie Lous 145 1
Dutrow, Lester G 172 1
Dutrow, Lewis 169 1
Dutrow, Lloyd T 112 1
Dutrow, Lucretia 177 1
Dutrow, Lucretia C 169 1
Dutrow, Lydia 144 1
Dutrow, M E Naomi 172 1
Dutrow, Mary 171 1
Dutrow, Mary Adele 172 1
Dutrow, Mary C 171 1
Dutrow, Mary E 144 1
Dutrow, Mary L 147, 172 1
Dutrow, Mary T 172 1
Dutrow, Milton G 172 1
Dutrow, Nannie E 44 3
Dutrow, Nicholas 159 1
Dutrow, Norman L 157 1
Dutrow, P M 19 3
Dutrow, Parthenia 44 1
Dutrow, Philemon 27 1
Dutrow, Philip 176 1
Dutrow, R C 169 1
Dutrow, R J 164 1
Dutrow, R Lee 172 1
Dutrow, R Lee 83 3
Dutrow, R O Lee 162 1
Dutrow, R P T 144 1
Dutrow, R S 177, 179 1
Dutrow, Rebecca E 179 1
Dutrow, Richard 177 1
Dutrow, Richard 2 2
Dutrow, Richard C 145, 155 1
Dutrow, Richard Claude 177 1
Dutrow, Richard J 147, 153 1
Dutrow, Richard J 23 3
Dutrow, Richard S 172 1
Dutrow, Richard S J 177 1
Dutrow, Robert I 155 1
Dutrow, Robert J 147 1
Dutrow, Ruth P 145, 177 1
Dutrow, Ruthy 163 1
Dutrow, S 120 3
Dutrow, Samuel 169, 171, 172, 177, 179 1
Dutrow, Samuel 23, 187 3
Dutrow, Samuel P 179 1
Dutrow, Susanna 179 1
Dutter, William 79 1
Dutterar, Geo 163 1
Dutterow, George 156 1
Dutterow, George B 37 1
Dutterow, Jacob 156, 186 1
Dutterow, Peter 156 1
Duttrow, Elizabeth 152 1
Duttrow, Geo B, 152 1
Duval, Grafton 129 3
Duvall, Ann R 144 1
Duvall, Anna Mary 145 1
Duvall, Annie E 144 1
Duvall, B D 55 3
Duvall, B F 19 3
Duvall, B W 19, 122 3
Duvall, Basil L 146 1
Duvall, Belle 70 1
Duvall, Benj 80 2
Duvall, Benjamin 146, 163 1
Duvall, Benjamin W 146, 156 1
Duvall, Benn S 210 1
Duvall, Bernard R 40 2
Duvall, Bettie C 210 1
Duvall, Betty C 83 3
Duvall, Chas A 147 1
Duvall, Chas E 147, 183 1
Duvall, Chas T 147 1
Duvall, Clara K 30 1

Duvall, Daniel 7, 69, 76, 78, 84, 93, 119 2
Duvall, Daniel 195 3
Duvall, Daniel 57, 84, 117, 147, 150, 156, 163, 176 1
Duvall, Daniel B 150, 283 1
Duvall, Daniel T 47 1
Duvall, David 150 1
Duvall, David 19 3
Duvall, Edwin B 284 2
Duvall, Edwin S 152 1
Duvall, Fannie L 155 1
Duvall, Gabriel 30 1
Duvall, Gabriel T 156 1
Duvall, Geo W 15 2
Duvall, Geo W 153 1
Duvall, George W 23 1
Duvall, Grafton 80, 101, 228a 2
Duvall, Grafton 117, 137, 156, 157 1
Duvall, H C 176, 270 1
Duvall, Harry C 159 1
Duvall, Henrietta P R 159 1
Duvall, Henry 159 1
Duvall, Henry C 179, 264, 279 1
Duvall, Henry C 171 2
Duvall, Herbert W 162 1
Duvall, I Ijams 64 3
Duvall, Ida O 162 1
Duvall, J Frederick 165 1
Duvall, J I 109, 156 1
Duvall, J Ijams 147 1
Duvall, Jemina A 109 1
Duvall, John C 165, 183 1
Duvall, John H 163 1
Duvall, John P 163, 165 1
Duvall, Kate H 165 1
Duvall, Leloyd T [sic] 150 1
Duvall, Lloyd 47 1
Duvall, Lloyd 203 2
Duvall, Lloyd etc 202 2
Duvall, Lloyd T 117, 144, 150, 169, 179, 248, 264 1
Duvall, Lloyd T 116 2
Duvall, Lloyd T 19, 81 3
Duvall, Lola M 169, 183 1
Duvall, Margaret R 183 1
Duvall, Mary 144 1
Duvall, Mary A 146, 172 1
Duvall, Rebecca 177, 183 1
Duvall, S G 52, 63, 145 2
Duvall, S G 131 1
Duvall, Samuel 70 3
Duvall, Samuel 113, 156, 165, 179 1
Duvall, Samuel 46, 185, 202, 203, 214 2
Duvall, Samuel G 160, 203 3
Duvall, Samuel G 152, 159, 177, 179 1
Duvall, Sarah A 179 1
Duvall, Sarah M 179 1
Duvall, Susan 147 1
Duvall, Susan V 179 1
Duvall, Thomas 88 1
Duvall, Thomas L 118 3
Duvall, Thos 182 1
Duvall, W E 199 3
Duvall, W H 146, 183, 265 1
Duvall, W H 55, 187 3
Duvall, W Luther 183 1
Duvall, Walter 30 1
Duvall, Walter H 49, 84, 254 2
Duvall, Wilbur H 65, 167, 202 3
Duvall, Wilbur H 30, 146, 183 1
Duvall, Wm 183 1
Duvall, Wm F 147 1
Duvall, Wm H 165 1
Duvall, Wm L 144 1
Duvall, Wm P 183 1
Duvall, Wm W 146 1
Dwen, Alice A 59 1
Dwen, James 59, 169 1
Dwen, James A 169 1
Dwen, James A 186 3
Dwen, James A 262 2
Dwen, James A [sic] 13 1
Dwen, Laura B 165, 169 1
Dwen, Laura V 165 1
Dwen, Lawrence 169 1
Dye, Clarence V 21 3
Dyer, Harry 150 2
Dyer, Joseph A 164 1
Dylan, John J Sr 166 1
E, Florence M 213 3
Eader, A L 41, 186, 194, 201, 219 1
Eader, A M 160 2
Eader, Abraham 189, 225 1
Eader, Ann C 189, 204 1
Eader, Bernard 54 2
Eader, Bernard J 188 1
Eader, Bernard J 11 3
Eader, Blanche L 188 1
Eader, Casper 189 1
Eader, Cecelia 205 1
Eader, Charles E 259 2
Eader, Charles E Jr 189 1
Eader, Charlotte E 189 1
Eader, Chas 189 1
Eader, Chas E 189, 208 1
Eader, Chas E 253 2
Eader, Daniel of John 191 1
Eader, David 196 1
Eader, David 100 2
Eader, David 18 3
Eader, Edw 171 2
Eader, Emma Mae 189 1
Eader, Fannie May 193 1
Eader, George 194 1
Eader, George D Sr 194 1
Eader, Hicks 201 1
Eader, Ida E 259 2
Eader, John 196 1
Eader, John D 40 1
Eader, Jonathan 40, 116, 156, 186, 189, 191, 196, 197, 205, 234, 237 1
Eader, Jonathan 84, 92 2
Eader, Jonothan 67 3
Eader, Lewis 189 1
Eader, Lewis B 193 1
Eader, Louis B 200 1
Eader, Manassas 201 1
Eader, Margaret 207 1
Eader, Maria Louisa 201 1
Eader, Mary 201 1
Eader, Mary Ann 194 1
Eader, P M 205 1
Eader, Pearl A 208 1
Eader, Pearl V 200 1
Eader, Peter M 203, 204 1
Eader, Peter M 44 3
Eader, Rondo C 204 1
Eader, Roy L 204 1
Eader, Sidney A 205 1
Eader, Solomon 205 1
Eader, Sophronia P 197 1
Eader, T E 62 2
Eader, Thomas 156 1
Eader, Thomas H H 201 1
Eader, Thomas S 194 1
Eader, Walter G 40, 203 1
Eader, Wm 93 2
Eader, Wm 208 1
Eador, Augustus 207 1
Eador, Thomas [sic] 207 1
Eagan, Mary Ellen 201 1
Eagle, Chas 189 2
Eagle, Cyrus W 189 1
Eagle, F L 208 1
Eagle, G M 6 1
Eagle, G Maynard 189 1
Eagle, Wm 129 2
Eagle, Wm 208 1
Earhart, David B 32 1
Earhart, Jacob 1 3
Earhart, Jonathan W 210 1
Earhart, Minnie C 180 1
Earley, Susan I 189 1
Early, Jane 197 1
Early, John 196 1
Early, Mary 196 1
Earnest, Mary E 201 1
Earnest, Peter 203 1

Earnest, Solomon 203 1
Earnest, Solomon P 201 1
Earnst, Elizabeth 192 1
Earnst, Esther 192, 205 1
Earnst, Solomon 205 1
Eastborn, Robinson 40 1
Eastburn, Robertson 204 1
Eastburn, Robinson 26 1
Easteday, Joseph 70 3
Easterday, Abraham 47, 186, 196 1
Easterday, Abraham 185 2
Easterday, Ada G 41 1
Easterday, Ada R 189 1
Easterday, Carroll E 189 1
Easterday, Catherine 189 1
Easterday, Charles I 192 1
Easterday, Chas 245 1
Easterday, Chas O 200 1
Easterday, Christian 189 1
Easterday, Christian Sr 189 1
Easterday, Clara M 186 1
Easterday, Conrad 189, 196, 257 1
Easterday, Conrad Sr 26 1
Easterday, Daniel 18 3
Easterday, Daniel J 171, 191, 189 1
Easterday, Dorothy E 192 1
Easterday, Effie J 192 1
Easterday, Effie J 113 2
Easterday, Eleanor E 58 3
Easterday, Elizabeth 192 1
Easterday, Ellen E 197 1
Easterday, Francis 193 1
Easterday, G E 60 1
Easterday, Geo 41 1
Easterday, Geo E 193, 194 1
Easterday, Geo H 205 1
Easterday, Geo W 40 1
Easterday, I 64 3
Easterday, Jacob 40, 47, 194, 196 1
Easterday, Joseph 117, 189, 192, 193 1
Easterday, Joseph 5 2
Easterday, Josephus 197, 200, 205 1
Easterday, Joshua L 197 1
Easterday, Julia Ann 197 1
Easterday, Lawrence 189 1
Easterday, Lewis 193, 200 1
Easterday, Lewis A 58 1
Easterday, Lewis C 200 1
Easterday, Magdalene 186 1
Easterday, Mary 196, 201 1
Easterday, Mattie E 200 1
Easterday, Maurice C 191 1
Easterday, Meadary M 194 1
Easterday, Noah 203 1
Easterday, Sarah A 23 3
Easterday, Sarah A N 205 1
Easterday, Sarah J 194 1
Easterday, Sarah S 205 1
Easterday, Solomon 84 1
Easterday, Susan C 197 1
Easterline, Catherine 196 1
Easterline, John 196 1
Eaton, C E 145 2
Eaton, Clinton E 201 1
Eaton, Harry A 195 1
Eaton, Letta Mae 200 1
Eaton, Mary J 201, 204 1
Eaton, Robert D 204, 205 1
Eaton, Rosa 145 2
Eaton, Rosa Belle 201 1
Eaton, Sarah A 205 1
Eaton, Virginia 207 1
Eaton, W H 82 3
Eaves, Florence Eliza 193 1
Eaves, Helen E 24 3
Eaves, Peter 150 2
Eaves, Peter 71 1
Eaves, Peter 27 3
Eaves, Walter Leo 193 1
Ebaugh, David S 276 1
Ebbert, John 120 3
Ebbert, John 211 2
Ebbert, John 171 1
Ebbert, John M 264 2
Ebbert, Michael 163 1
Ebbert, Philip 37 3
Ebbert, Samuel V 294 2
Ebbert, Valeerius 229 1
Ebbert, Valerous 106 3
Ebberts, Balerius 84 1
Ebberts, Joseph 25, 159 2
Ebberts, Joseph & 19 2
Ebberts, Joseph M 91, 150 1
Ebberts, Joseph W 201 1
Ebberts, Michael 201 1
Ebberts, Susannah 205 1
Eberhart, Geo 239 1
Eberly, John 205 1
Eberly, Susanna 71 1
Ebert, A H 171, 205 1
Ebert, Adam S 194 1
Ebert, Annie H 192 1
Ebert, Annie Neff 186 1
Ebert, Augustus 205 1
Ebert, Augustus F 186 1
Ebert, Augustus H 192 1
Ebert, Benjamin 188 1
Ebert, Caroline 188 1
Ebert, Charlotte 194 1
Ebert, Chas D 193 1
Ebert, Edw C 192 1
Ebert, Elizabeth 194 1
Ebert, Elizabeth M 186 1
Ebert, Emma 192 1
Ebert, Ephriam 192 1
Ebert, Fannie B 219 3
Ebert, Fanny V 37 1
Ebert, George A 193, 194 1
Ebert, Gustavus A 194 1
Ebert, Harry L 219 1
Ebert, Harry L 189 3
Ebert, Henry 171 1
Ebert, John 70, 188, 195, 196, 205, 214 1
Ebert, John 1 2
Ebert, John C 186 1
Ebert, John E 192, 202 1
Ebert, Joseph 192 1
Ebert, Mary B 53 1
Ebert, Mary Blanche 195 1
Ebert, Mary Ellen 201 1
Ebert, Michael 192 1
Ebert, Minnie F 201, 202 1
Ebert, S B 237 1
Ebert, Samuel 188 1
Ebert, Samuel B 205 1
Ebert, Valentine 207 1
Ebert, Valerius 196 1
Ebert, Wm A 193 1
Ebert, Wm A 219 3
Eberts, Geo 132 2
Eberts, George 194 1
Eberts, George A 194 1
Eberts, Harry L 162 1
Eberts, Joseph 195, 196 1
Eberts, Joseph M 93 2
Eberts, Joseph M 196 1
Eberts, Philip 195 1
Ebey, Christian 165 2
Ebey, John 196 1
Ebsworth, Thos 19 2
Ebworth, Daniel 19 2
Eby, Annie S 186 1
Eby, Charles C 189 1
Eby, Daniel 124 2
Eby, Daniel 191 1
Eby, Earl 191 1
Eby, Guy 191 1
Eby, Hugh 191 1
Eby, Lara E 204 1
Eby, Roy 191 1
Eby, Tason W 55 1
Ebye, Daniel 14 2
Ecard, John 277 1
Ecb, Joseph [sic] 24 1
Eccard, John 230 1
Eccard, Nathan 203 1
Eccard, Noah 72 3
Eccard, Simon P 72 3
Eccard, Simon P Sr 72 3
Eccard, Simon T Jr 199 2

Eccard, Ulrich 139 3
EChenson, Thomas 160 3
Echinrode, John 197 1
Echstem, C H 189 1
Eck, Joseph 201 1
Eck, Paul 220 2
Eck, Peter 207 1
Eck, Theodorus 207 1
Eckard, Henry 201 1
Eckard, Henry 26 2
Eckard, J W 196 1
Eckard, John 196, 283 1
Eckard, Michael 13 1
Eckard, Noah 201, 203 1
Eckenbrdoe, Vincent 214a 2
Eckenrode, C H 189 1
Eckenrode, Catherine 189 1
Eckenrode, Cora I 48 1
Eckenrode, E G 76, 194 1
Eckenrode, Etta M 189 1
Eckenrode, George 194 1
Eckenrode, H J 194 1
Eckenrode, J T 205 1
Eckenrode, J W 205 1
Eckenrode, Mary C 201 1
Eckenrode, Samuel W 205 1
Eckenrode, T H 189 1
Ecker, A Mehrl 194 1
Ecker, A Mehrle 63 1
Ecker, A Merhle 83 3
Ecker, A Merhle 223a 2
Ecker, A W 110, 193 1
Ecker, Albert J 62 1
Ecker, Albert W 15 2
Ecker, Albert W 186, 194, 201 1
Ecker, Albert W 197, 210 3
Ecker, Albury Wilson 189 1
Ecker, AW 206 3
Ecker, Claggett 205 1
Ecker, Claggett D 189 1
Ecker, Clyde W 68 1
Ecker, David 191 1
Ecker, David W 191, 228 1
Ecker, Elizabeth 73 1
Ecker, Ella V 192, 208 1
Ecker, Fred 75 3
Ecker, George 194 1
Ecker, George L 194 1
Ecker, Greenberry 194 1
Ecker, Hanson 192 1
Ecker, Ida B 186 1
Ecker, J Maurice 192 1
Ecker, Jacob 196, 201 1
Ecker, John 196 1
Ecker, Levi 200 1
Ecker, Levi 14 3
Ecker, Lizzie 191 1
Ecker, Margaret 201 1
Ecker, Margaret S 201 1
Ecker, Mary 191 1
Ecker, Mary Catherine 194 1
Ecker, Mary E 200, 201 1
Ecker, Noah 166 3
Ecker, Samuel 205 1
Ecker, Samuel 237 2
Ecker, Samuel 14 3
Ecker, Samuel B 205 1
Ecker, Sarah C 205 1
Ecker, Solomon S 118 1
Ecker, William 271 2
Ecker, Wm 196, 208 1
Ecker, Wm N 201 1
Eckes, James 203 1
Eckes, Nicholas 203 1
Eckinrode, John 197 1
Eckis, John 196 1
Eckis, Nicholas 196 1
Eckler, John 196 1
Eckler, Ulrick 196, 207, 278 1
Eckman, David S 96 1
Eckman, John 196 1
Eckstein, C H 24 1
Eckstein, C H 1, 54, 92, 195 2
Eckstein, C H 62, 65 3
Eckstein, Christian H 226 3
Eckstein, Christian T 201 1
Eckstein, Elizabeth 226 3
Eckstein, John 138 2
Eckstein, Mary K 189, 201 1
Edichelebergern, Grayson 186 3
Edmonston, Charles H 189 1
Edmonston, Eleanora F 194 1
Edmonston, Eleanora T 192 1
Edmonston, Geo H J 194 1
Edmonston, Roy 189 1
Edmunds, Harry C 209 2
Edmunds, Ida M 195 1
Edwards, Clarence B 10 1
Edwards, Earl S 19, 202 1
Edwards, Henry W 195 1
Edwards, James 14 3
Edwards, James F N 197 1
Edwards, James W 70 1
Edwards, John R 202 1
Edwards, Mary H 203, 207 1
Edwards, Philip C 203 1
Edwards, Richard H 204 1
Edwards, Robert E 204 1
Edwards, Stanford 271 2
Edwards, Susanna 205 1
Edwards, Susannah 204 1
Edwards, Thomas E 204, 207 1
Edwards, William R 208 1
Edwards, Wm Randolph 202 1
Ehrehard, Mary at Al 192 1
Ehrehart, Mary E 197, 201 1
Ehrenberg, Blanche Walker 188 1
Eichelberger Amanda 186 1
Eichelberger Grayson 41, 100 1
Eichelberger, A 208 1
Eichelberger, Abraham 186 1
Eichelberger, Abram J 186 1
Eichelberger, Adam L 186 1
Eichelberger, Amanda 186, 194 1
Eichelberger, Amy L 186 1
Eichelberger, Anna M 186, 204 1
Eichelberger, C D 92 1
Eichelberger, C D 30 2
Eichelberger, Cassandra 201 1
Eichelberger, Chas 181 2
Eichelberger, Chas 186 1
Eichelberger, Chas D 189, 278 1
Eichelberger, E C 82 3
Eichelberger, E J 1 1
Eichelberger, E S 48, 60, 201 1
Eichelberger, Edw 139, 181 2
Eichelberger, Edw S 72, 189 1
Eichelberger, Edw S 72 3
Eichelberger, Edw S 136, 160 2
Eichelberger, Edward 222 2
Eichelberger, Edward S 92, 192 1
Eichelberger, Effie G 186, 192 1
Eichelberger, Elizabeth 192 1
Eichelberger, Ella V 186 1
Eichelberger, Emma E 192, 194 1
Eichelberger, Frances M 193 1
Eichelberger, Frederick 197 2
Eichelberger, Frederick 40, 193 1
Eichelberger, G 106 3
Eichelberger, G M 137 2
Eichelberger, G M 8, 64, 202 3
Eichelberger, G M 58, 70, 78, 84, 106, 193, 196, 282 1
Eichelberger, Geo 155, 253, 263 1
Eichelberger, Geo 137, 185 2
Eichelberger, Geo D 99 2
Eichelberger, Geo M 1, 89, 137 2
Eichelberger, Geo M 57 1
Eichelberger, George M 58, 194 1
Eichelberger, Grayson 19, 50, 53, 87, 116, 129, 163, 167, 179, 186, 222 3

Eichelberger, Grayson 1, 14, 46, 51, 129, 186, 197, 231 2
Eichelberger, Grayson 44, 70, 71, 84, 96, 118, 192, 193, 194, 197, 201, 214, 260, 264, 271, 279 1
Eichelberger, Grayson M 207, 222 1
Eichelberger, H F 31 2
Eichelberger, J D 47 1
Eichelberger, J M 186 1
Eichelberger, J W 35 2
Eichelberger, J W 116, 193 1
Eichelberger, Jacob 197, 201 1
Eichelberger, Jacob H 197, 223, 240 1
Eichelberger, James M 192 1
Eichelberger, James M 196 3
Eichelberger, James W 186, 189, 196, 197 1
Eichelberger, Jane 197 1
Eichelberger, Janie B 196 1
Eichelberger, Joseph 1, 7, 19, 100, 131, 165 2
Eichelberger, Joseph 171, 223 3
Eichelberger, Joseph 193, 197, 203 1
Eichelberger, Louis E 186 1
Eichelberger, M G 186 1
Eichelberger, M J 223 1
Eichelberger, Marion E E 201 1
Eichelberger, Marion F 201 1
Eichelberger, Marion Gray 192 1
Eichelberger, Marion J 189 1
Eichelberger, Martin 7 2
Eichelberger, Martin 40, 196, 197, 207 1
Eichelberger, Martin 8, 167, 171 3
Eichelberger, Martin J 199 3
Eichelberger, Martin L 201 1
Eichelberger, Michael 223 3
Eichelberger, Michael F 125 1
Eichelberger, Michael F 28 2
Eichelberger, Odin P 203 1
Eichelberger, P M 253 1
Eichelberger, Peter 223 1
Eichelberger, Peter 186 2
Eichelberger, Russell G 204 1
Eichelberger, Samuel J 197 1
Eichelberger, Sarah M 205 1
Eichelberger, Virginia 207 1
Eichelberger, Wm A 208 1
Eichiltz, Samuel C 59 1
Eichleberger, Edward C 82 3
Eichleberger, G 64 3
Eichleberger, G M 184 3
Eichleberger, George M 96 3
Eichleberger, Grayson 207 3
Eichner, Amos E 186 1
Eicholtz, Adelina P 195 1
Eicholtz, Anderson 197, 205 1
Eicholtz, Anderson M 186 1
Eicholtz, Calvin 186 1
Eicholtz, Henry 195, 197, 205 1
Eicholtz, John 47 1
Eicholtz, Samuel 177 2
Eicholtz, Samuel 182, 187, 202 3
Eicholtz, Samuel 110, 197, 205, 214, 253, 257 1
Eicholtz, Sarah 205 1
Eigenbrode, C 263 1
Eigenbrode, Catherine L 31 1
Eigenbrode, Christian 189 1
Eigenbrode, Daniel 191, 196, 249 1
Eigenbrode, John 197, 277 1
Eigenbrode, Martha J 39 2
Eigenbrode, Martha J 208 1
Eigenbrode, Martha J & 39 2
Eigenbrode, R L 189 1
Eigenbrode, Vada E 12, 41 2
Eigenbrode, Wm H 208 1
Eighelberger, Grayson [sic] 13 1
Eikenbrode, Daniel 152 3
Eiker, Herbert R 195 1
Eiker, Ida F 195 1
Eiker, Walter E 195, 248 1
Eiler, Albert E 186 1
Eiler, Charles R 189, 201 1
Eiler, Conrad 189 1
Eiler, Conrad Sr 189 1
Eiler, Daniel J 119 1
Eiler, John 189, 197 1
Eiler, John W 205 1
Eiler, Joshua 197 1
Eiler, Lydian 119 1
Eiler, Mary C 207 1
Eiler, Mary E 201 1
Eiler, Peter 185 3
Eiler, Sarah L 207 1
Eiler, Scott W 165 1
Eiler, Usher J 207 1
Eiron, Elizabeth 192 1
Eiron, Michael 197 1
Eisenauer, Joe H 165 3
Eisenauer, John 165 3
Eisenauer, Joseph F 209 3
Eisenhart, William 171 3
Eisenhauer, Frank 116 2
Eisenhauer, J 171 3
Eisenhauer, J F 98, 176 3
Eisenhauer, J F 181 2
Eisenhauer, John 174, 176 3
Eisenhauer, John 201, 265 1
Eisenhauer, John 188 2
Eisenhauer, Joseph F 197 1
Eisenhauer, Joseph F 294 2
Eisenhauer, M 265 1
Eisenhauer, Margaret L 202 1
Eisenhauer, Mary B 197 1
Eisenhower, J Frank 198, 201 1
Eisenhower, John T 197 1
Eisenhower, John Thomas 198 1
Eisenhower, Joseph F Jr 197, 198 1
Eisenhower, Margaret 197, 198 1
Eisenhower, Mary B 201 1
Eisenhower, Rosa May B 198 1
Eissler, Daniel G 194 1
Eissler, Geo 106 2
Eissler, Geo 205 1
Eissler, George 194 1
Eissler, George 217 3
Eissler, George 271 2
Ekstein, C H 171 2
Elck, Dietrich 144 2
Elder, A T & 187 2
Elder, Aloysius 186 1
Elder, Anastasia 186 1
Elder, Caroline 189, 197 1
Elder, Catherine 189 1
Elder, Catherine 169 2
Elder, Francis P 193 1
Elder, Genevieve R 198 1
Elder, Harry 214a 2
Elder, Henry J 171 1
Elder, J A 2, 75, 187, 188 2
Elder, J Basil 189 1
Elder, J H 9 3
Elder, James 188, 227, 250 2
Elder, James 198, 200, 219, 245 1
Elder, James A 54, 203 3
Elder, James A 30, 46, 101, 129, 188, 198, 222, 217a, 221a, 242, 267 2
Elder, James A 59, 197, 205 1
Elder, James B 197 1
Elder, James M 111 2
Elder, Jas A 75 3
Elder, Jesse 89 2
Elder, Joachim 84 2
Elder, Joachim 37, 51, 197 1
Elder, John D 198, 205 1
Elder, John E 193 1
Elder, John F 197 1
Elder, John M 32 1
Elder, Joseph 196 1
Elder, Joseph E 200, 205 1

Elder, Joseph E & 29 2
Elder, Josephine 197 1
Elder, Lewis 91 1
Elder, Louis 200 1
Elder, Lucy 189 1
Elder, Mary 196, 197 1
Elder, Mary A 201 1
Elder, Mary Adele 186 1
Elder, Sarah B 205 1
Elder, Sarah B 18 2
Elder, Sarah E 198 1
Elder, Thomas 207 1
Elderdice, Hugh 195 1
Eldridge, Arthur 194 1
Eldridge, Elizabeth C 208 1
Eldridge, Erma 267 2
Eldridge, Geo C 201 1
Eldridge, George C 194 1
Eldridge, John 140 1
Eldridge, John 35 2
Eldridge, John W 125 2
Eldridge, Mary A 201 1
Eldridge, Rhoda 194 1
Eldridge, Valley G 194 1
Eldridge, William C 165 3
Eldridge, Wm C 208 1
Elefantis, Nikolas 203 1
Elgin, Anna 100 1
Elgin, Elisabeth K 25 2
Elgin, Emma F 192, 208 1
Elgin, Henry C 195 1
Elgin, Wm 164 1
Elgin, Wm S 208 1
Eli, Elliott 129 1
Eline, Annie Jessie 186 1
Eline, Annie V 186 1
Eline, Jacob 56 1
Eline, Jacob 220a 2
Eline, Leo 200 1
Elkins, Anna O 186 1
Elkins, Joseph 68 3
Elkins, Joseph E 186 1
Elkins, Joseph E 33 3
Elkins, Joseph E Sr 127 1
Elkins, Rebecca S 18 2
Eller, Joseph 13 1
Ellicott, George 194 1
Elliott, Amos A 197 1
Elliott, Chas M 189 1
Elliott, Eli 44, 196 1
Elliott, Geo 196, 208 1
Elliott, George 194 1
Elliott, Harry L 175 1
Elliott, James 197, 201 1
Elliott, James 69 2
Elliott, James H 197 1
Elliott, James W 197 1
Elliott, Joel 196 1
Elliott, John 196, 207 1
Elliott, Laura 208 1
Elliott, Mary C 201 1
Elliott, Mary E 201, 208 1
Elliott, Sarah 207 1
Elliott, Thomas 207 1
Elliott, Wm 208 1
Elliott, Wm W 208 1
Ellsworth, Amos 186 1
Ellsworth, Frederick 193 1
Elmer Trust Co 284 1
Elower, Geo V 197 1
Elower, John 197 1
Elsrodds, Frederick 193 1
Elsrodds, Frederick John 193 1
Elsrodds, John F 193 1
Elvin, John H 92 2
Ely, Charles E 189 1
Ely, Chas W 189 1
Ely, Daniel 25 2
Ely, David 191 1
Ely, Isaac H 195 1
Ely, Mary C 195 1
Ely, Mary D 189 1
Ely, Metta R 189 1
Ely, Sarah 205 1
Ely, Wm 208 1
Ely, Wm S 208 1
Emerson, George H 61 1
Emlet, Geo 201 1
Emlet, Mary 201 1
Emley, Daniel M 191 1
Emmert, Mazie P 28 3
Emmitt, Abagail 186 1
Emmitt, Joseph 196 1
Emmitt, Susanna 205 1
Emmitt, Wm 208 1
Employes Libility Insurance Corp 122 3
Ender, Pearl V 193 1
Engel, Chas 217 1
Engel, Daniel 279 1
Engel, David 203 1
Engel, Elizabeth 197 1
Engel, John 197 1
Engel, John R 197 1
Engel, John Sr 196 1
Engel, Joseph H 198 1
Engel, Joseph R 153 1
Engel, Peter 203 1
Engelbrecht, Effie Moore 197 1
Engelbrecht, Jacob 176 3
Engelbrecht, Jacob 197, 198, 208 1
Engelbrecht, Jacob E 160 1
Engelbrecht, L V 203 1
Engelbrecht, T M 176 3
Engelman, John 196 1
Engelman, Wm 196 1
England, C E 19 1
England, Evelyn Riggs 145 2
England, James 203 1
England, John W 197 1
England, Joseph 203 1
England, Mary E 201 1
England, Mary L 1 1
England, Nathan 64 3
England, Nathan 19, 23, 197 1
England, Nathan 254 2
England, Nathan J 19, 100, 147, 203 1
England, Nathan J 140 2
England, Nathanial 14 3
England, Walter A 267 2
Englar, Alfred 200 1
Englar, Basil 188 1
Englar, Carrie S 189 1
Englar, David 200 1
Englar, Elizabeth 196 1
Englar, Estella I 259 2
Englar, Henry 188 2
Englar, Hiram 200 1
Englar, J L 56 1
Englar, Jacob 184 3
Englar, Jacob 196, 200 1
Englar, Jacob 165 2
Englar, John 1, 57 2
Englar, John 196 1
Englar, John L 203 1
Englar, Leanna 200 1
Englar, Louis P 200, 203 1
Englar, Modica 26 1
Englar, N A 1 1
Englar, N O 187 3
Englar, Nathan A 203 1
Englar, Nathan L 100 2
Englar, O A 186 3
Englar, Philip 116, 203 1
Englar, S E 186 1
Engle, Abraham 186, 188 1
Engle, Anna Eve 186 1
Engle, Annie B 186 1
Engle, Annie C 186 1
Engle, C Elias 189 1
Engle, Calvin L 198 1
Engle, Charles W 189 1
Engle, Clara U 189 1
Engle, David 144 1
Engle, E J 60 1
Engle, F H 119, 183 1
Engle, Frances H 67 1
Engle, Francis 118 1
Engle, Francis H 193, 197 1
Engle, Francis H 159 2
Engle, Grace E 3 3
Engle, Ida M 195, 201 1
Engle, Jacob 196 1
Engle, Jesse 196 1
Engle, John 120, 196, 197 1

Engle, John A 193, 195, 197 1
Engle, John A 238 2
Engle, John D 189 1
Engle, John E 197 1
Engle, John M 186 1
Engle, John W 197, 198 1
Engle, Joseph 198 1
Engle, Joseph H 186 1
Engle, M L 83 3
Engle, Martha A 201 1
Engle, Mary Ann 201 1
Engle, Michael 201 1
Engle, Minnie E 208 1
Engle, Nathan 229 1
Engle, Nicholas 58 1
Engle, Peter 144, 197 1
Engle, Peter 19, 107 2
Engle, Sophia 183 1
Engle, Tacy 207 1
Engle, Walter 65 3
Engle, Wm H 208 1
Engle, Wm N 208 1
Englebrecht, Abraham L 186 1
Englebrecht, Ann M 186, 194 1
Englebrecht, B Kurtz 188 1
Englebrecht, Bettie M 188 1
Englebrecht, Conrad 189 1
Englebrecht, Frederick 37, 193 1
Englebrecht, Geo 176, 185, 222 3
Englebrecht, Geo 7 2
Englebrecht, Geo 40, 57, 70, 193, 196, 208 1
Englebrecht, George 194 1
Englebrecht, J L 58 2
Englebrecht, Jacob 193 1
Englebrecht, Jacob L 188 1
Englebrecht, Jeanette V 186 1
Englebrecht, Jeannette V 193 1
Englebrecht, John 177, 198 1
Englebrecht, John 163 3
Englebrecht, John C 196 1
Englebrecht, John Conrad 197 1
Englebrecht, John L 201 1
Englebrecht, John P 42 1
Englebrecht, John Philip 198 1
Englebrecht, L W 205 1
Englebrecht, Louisa F 196 1
Englebrecht, Margaret 71, 200, 201 1
Englebrecht, P M 87 3
Englebrecht, Philip M 189, 197, 203 1
Englebrecht, Salena V 197, 203, 205 1
Englebrecht, Susannah 208 1
Englebrecht, Wm 208 1
Englebright, Emma W 196 3
Engleman, Eden 106 1
Engler, Aaron 186 1
Engler, David 186, 203 1
Engler, H 67 3
Engler, Jennie M 27 1
Engler, John L 189 1
Engler, Joseph 81 3
Engler, Margaret Tabitha 202 1
Engler, S P 77 3
Engler, Sarah V 162 1
English, E F 198 1
English, Eloise Y 207 1
English, Eloise Y 69 2
English, George W 194 1
English, Grace L 88 1
English, J D 72 2
English, J D 197, 198 1
English, J D 167 3
English, J? [sic] D 204 1
English, James I 201 1
English, James J 195 3
English, Jane 150 2
English, Jane R 217 3
English, John D 186 3
English, Jonathan 152 1
English, Jonathan D 194, 197, 198 1
English, Levi 150 2
English, Mary 201, 204 1
English, Mary A 201 1
English, Mary C 196 1
English, Richard 18, 49, 57, 119, 136 2
English, Richard 197, 204 1
English, Thomas Dunn 207 1
Enis, Annie E 197 1
Ennis, John 197, 208 1
Ennis, Joseph 197, 228 1
Ennis, Joshua 197 1
Ennis, William 196 3
Ennis, Wm 15 2
Ennis, Wm 208 1
Enoch, J P 18 1
Enoch, John P 197, 201 1
Enoch, Matilda C 201 1
Enright, Ida M 197 1
Enright, James H 197 1
Enry, Samuel A 1 1
Ensor, Amy E 186 1
Ensor, E C 144 2
Ensor, E Clarence 192 1
Ensor, Ed 186 1
Ensor, Edw C 192 1
Ensor, Elijah 264 1
Ensor, Elijah C 181 1
Ensor, Harry A 186 1
Ensor, John 72 3
Ensor, Lottie T 72 3
Ensor, Luke C 77 3
Ent, Geo 7 2
Ent, Geo W 26 1
Ent, Geo W 195 3
Ent, George W 194 1
Enty, Elizabeth A 165, 192 1
Entz, E A 124 3
Eperly, Susannah 196 1
Ephraim, Ida M 203 1
Ephraim, Nathan 203 1
Ephriam, Nathan 15 2
Epperly, John 196 1
Eppley, Adam 54 2
Eppley, Adam 193 1
Eppley, Francis 193 1
Eppley, Francis Jr 193 1
Eppley, Virgie G 193 1
Equitable Surety Co of St Louis 189 2
Erb, A Lee 227 2
Erb, Elizabeth 192 1
Erb, Geo W 57 2
Erb, Jacob 192 1
Erb, Jacob 203 2
Erb, John 203 1
Erb, John 203 2
Erb, Perter 64 3
Erb, Peter 57 2
Erb, Peter 148 3
Erb, Peter Esq 203 1
Erb, Peter Sr 203 1
Erbe, Charles 57 1
Erbe, Mary Ann 202 1
Erdenbrecht, Catherine E 193 1
Erdenbrecht, Frederick 193 1
Ernest, Susan 205 1
Ernsberger, Lawrence 37 1
Ernst, Abraham 186, 196, 200 1
Ernst, Anna Mary 186 1
Ernst, Hannah 195 1
Ernst, Jacob 196 1
Ernst, Peter 26 1
Eroneesitch, Frederick [sic] 193 1
Erter, Magdalena 201 1
Ervin, John 139 1
Ervin, Samuel 196 1
Ervin, Wm T 139 1
Eschbach, Mary Susan 192, 201, 202 1
Eschbach, Mary T 201 1
Eschback, Edmund R 192 1
Estabrook, Emma H 192, 197 1
Estabrook, John O 197 1
Estabrook, Leon M 200 1
Estep, Carrie E 181 1
Estep, Richard C 204 1

Esterday, Louis A 200 1
Esterley, Clara May 200 1
Esterley, Lewis 200 1
Esterline, Sarah K 205 1
Esterline, Wm R 205 1
Esterly, Clara V 189 1
Esterly, Geo 101 2
Esterly, Geo W 83 3
Esterly, Irene 72 3
Esterly, Irene W 203 1
Esterly, J 81 3
Esterly, Joseph 152 3
Esterly, Phillip R 203 1
Esterly, Russell 72 3
Estham, John 137 2
Estip, C Elinor [sic] 204 1
Esworthy, Amos 214 1
Esworthy, Chas E 186 1
Esworthy, Daniel Leo 191 1
Esworthy, Francis J 189 3
Esworthy, Francis Jay 161 3
Esworthy, Gladys 18 2
Esworthy, John H 186 1
Esworthy, Margaret Clingan 204 1
Esworthy, Marie 191 1
Esworthy, Robert H 34 1
Etchision, H Dorsey 166 2
Etchison, A D 195 2
Etchison, A Hart 3, 45, 83, 107, 172, 197 3
Etchison, A Hart 64, 108, 143, 190, 232, 288 2
Etchison, A Hart 28, 63, 73, 133, 204, 220, 222, 233 1
Etchison, A L 28 1
Etchison, A P H 195 2
Etchison, Anna J 80 2
Etchison, Green S 205 3
Etchison, H D 82, 129, 174, 203 3
Etchison, H Dorsey 44, 63, 152, 165, 183, 195, 201, 232, 257 1
Etchison, H Dorsey 10, 32 3
Etchison, H Dorsey 9, 31, 35, 40, 65, 78, 80, 85, 134, 178, 198, 259, 291 2
Etchison, H M 265 1
Etchison, H N 209 3
Etchison, Hart 210a 2
Etchison, Henry 222 2
Etchison, Henry N 132 1
Etchison, Heppie E 152 1
Etchison, J 49 2
Etchison, James M 195 1
Etchison, Josephine 208 1
Etchison, L C 152 1
Etchison, Louis C 66, 76 2
Etchison, Louis C 126 1
Etchison, Louise C 9 2
Etchison, M F 208 1
Etchison, M K 195 2
Etchison, M R 9, 140, 143, 190, 288 2
Etchison, M R 201 1
Etchison, M R 107 3
Etchison, M Reiley 108 2
Etchison, Marjorie L 280, 284 2
Etchison, Marshall 172 2
Etchison, Marshall L 63, 215 1
Etchison, Mary 66 2
Etchison, Mary H 73, 120, 208 1
Etchison, Mary H 31, 40 2
Etchison, Mary H 32, 163, 174, 203, 212 3
Etchison, Mck R 110 1
Etchison, R Hart 9 2
Etchison, S M 195 2
Etchison, Sepsia 166 1
Etchison, Sybelle M 205 1
Etchison, William H B 245 2
Etchison, Wm P 208 1
Etvhison, H Dorsey 154 2
Etzler, A H 55, 72 3
Etzler, A H 194, 201, 245 1
Etzler, A M 54 2
Etzler, Albert W 86 1
Etzler, Alma E 186 1
Etzler, Alvey M 186 1
Etzler, Alvie M 8, 198 1
Etzler, Alvy M 201 3
Etzler, Anderson H 126, 186, 203 1
Etzler, Andrew 184 3
Etzler, Archibald 205 3
Etzler, Arthur 196 1
Etzler, Aubrey T 186 1
Etzler, Bassilliam 86 1
Etzler, Carl W 188, 189, 198 1
Etzler, Charles E 189 1
Etzler, Charles T 189 1
Etzler, Chas E 201 1
Etzler, Clay 201 1
Etzler, D Harry 56 1
Etzler, Daniel 186, 191, 196 1
Etzler, Daniel 70 3
Etzler, Daniel Sr 191 1
Etzler, Daniel W 191 1
Etzler, Dennis 171 1
Etzler, Dessie J 34, 186, 235 1
Etzler, Eliza C 192, 235 1
Etzler, Emma F 192 1
Etzler, Ethlyn M 186 1
Etzler, Ezra 196 1
Etzler, Ezra C 192 1
Etzler, F Elder 23 1
Etzler, Geo 138 2
Etzler, Geo W 171 3
Etzler, Geo W 41, 125, 194, 201 1
Etzler, George 32 3
Etzler, George Albert 194 1
Etzler, George W 84 1
Etzler, J W 194 1
Etzler, Jerimiah W 186 1
Etzler, John 196 1
Etzler, John (Ohio) 196 1
Etzler, John D 191, 198 1
Etzler, John H 198 1
Etzler, John N 137 1
Etzler, Joseph 88, 196, 201 1
Etzler, Joseph W 28, 78 2
Etzler, Joseph W 196, 197, 201, 271 1
Etzler, Joseph W 26 3
Etzler, Laura C 200 1
Etzler, Lester 189 1
Etzler, Letta R 200 1
Etzler, Magdalene 196, 201 1
Etzler, Mary 201 1
Etzler, Mary A 201 1
Etzler, Mary C 201 1
Etzler, Maurice 201 1
Etzler, Murray 208 3
Etzler, Nellie 107 1
Etzler, Olivia A 203 1
Etzler, Rosa M 186 1
Etzler, Roscoe E 189, 194, 204 1
Etzler, Ruth E 62 3
Etzler, W Paul 200, 204 1
Etzler, W R 107 1
Eury, Bessie A 19 1
Eury, Daniel A 191 1
Eury, David W 191 1
Eury, Harry E 205 1
Eury, John W 201 1
Eury, Mary 201 1
Eury, S A 85 1
Eury, S Benton 183 1
Eury, Samuel 57, 187 2
Eury, Samuel 41, 201, 205, 208 1
Eury, Samuel A 177, 205 1
Eury, Samuel Jr 205 1
Eury, Sarah 205 1
Eury, Susannah 205 1
Eury, Wm 208 1
Evans, Amos E 186 1
Evans, Ann Maria 89 2
Evans, David 192 1
Evans, Ephraim 152 3
Evans, Ezekiel 192 1
Evans, Fannie B 30 1
Evans, James 196 1
Evans, James H 277 2
Evans, James Hanson 91 3
Evans, John 135 1

Evans, Owen 196, 203 1
Evans, Rose E 163 2
Evans, Sarah 205 1
Evans, William E 186 1
Everhart, D B 215 3
Everhart, David G Jr 275 1
Everhart, David G Sr 191 1
Everhart, Eleanor L 191 1
Everhart, Frank 193 1
Everhart, Fred 84 1
Everhart, Geo P 40, 52 2
Everhart, Jacob 53, 184 3
Everhart, Jacob 193, 196 1
Everhart, Jacob 175 2
Everhart, Jacob 196 1
Everhart, John W 196 1
Everhart, Joseph 184 3
Everhart, L 176 3
Everhart, L 137 2
Everhart, Laurence 185 2
Everhart, Lawrence 200 1
Everhart, Lizzie Manda 200 1
Everhart, Lola B 193 1
Everhart, Mary 201 1
Everhart, Nannie M 191 1
Everhart, William 208 1
Everly, Jacob 197 1
Eves, Chas E 201 1
Eves, John 205 1
Eves, Mary 203 1
Eves, Mary Jane 201 1
Eves, Peter 203 1
Eves, Sarah A 205 1
Eves, Thomas C 203 1
Evilhear, Joseph 197 1
Evin, James 196 1
Evitt, Mary 208 2
Evitt, Mary 201, 208 1
Evitt, Woodward 208 1
Evitt, Woodward 45 2
Ewell, Clara Grove 198 1
Ewell, John R 198 1
Ewing, Annie M 186 1
Ewing, Charlotte P 189 1
Ewing, John A 186 1
Ewing, Parmalee D 189 1
Exner, Annie M 205 1
Exner, Sebastian 205 1
Eyenbrode, John 70 3
Eyler, A C 172 1
Eyler, Adam 186, 193 1
Eyler, Adam 197, 276 2
Eyler, Alice M 210a 2
Eyler, Alice M 208 1
Eyler, Amos 227 2
Eyler, Andrew 196 1
Eyler, Andrew J 197 1
Eyler, Ann Sophia 186 1
Eyler, Annie E 186 1
Eyler, Annie L 204 1
Eyler, Barbara E 186, 188, 189, 196, 204 1
Eyler, Benj 186 3
Eyler, Bertha M 160 2
Eyler, Bertha M 207 1
Eyler, Beulah 2 2
Eyler, Bruce W 205 1
Eyler, C C 112 2
Eyler, C Harry 189 1
Eyler, C R 189 1
Eyler, C Ruth 189 1
Eyler, Catherine R A 189 1
Eyler, Charles C 58 3
Eyler, Charles C 1 1
Eyler, Charles H 86 1
Eyler, Charles H 189 1
Eyler, Charles R 189 1
Eyler, Charles W 205 1
Eyler, Charles Wm 189 1
Eyler, Chas 152 1
Eyler, Chas 8, 195 2
Eyler, Chas A 189, 193, 197, 208, 244 1
Eyler, Chas H 201 1
Eyler, Chas H M 23 1
Eyler, Chas R 197 1
Eyler, Chrastian T 189 1
Eyler, Clarycann V 189 1
Eyler, Clemon H 189 1
Eyler, Clyde 28 3
Eyler, Daniel 128 2
Eyler, Daniel 186 1
Eyler, David 191 1
Eyler, David F 191 1
Eyler, Edgar J 192 1
Eyler, Edw R 189 1
Eyler, Ella M 192 1
Eyler, Ella Mae 140 1
Eyler, Ellis V 192 1
Eyler, Emma 194, 208 1
Eyler, Emma F 192 1
Eyler, Frederick 193 1
Eyler, Frederick 197 2
Eyler, Geo 196 1
Eyler, Geo F 194 1
Eyler, Geo S L 194 1
Eyler, George 192, 194 1
Eyler, Grace Steele 192, 204 1
Eyler, Henry 156 3
Eyler, Henry 237 1
Eyler, Ignatius 2 3
Eyler, J Albert 189 1
Eyler, J Mary S 85 1
Eyler, Jacob 197 1
Eyler, Jacob 26 2
Eyler, Jacob 184 3
Eyler, James B 192 1
Eyler, James W M 189 1
Eyler, Jeremiah 26 1
Eyler, John 193, 196, 197, 204 1
Eyler, John 50, 152, 165, 195 3
Eyler, John 159, 267 2
Eyler, John A 198 1
Eyler, John C 22 2
Eyler, John F 197 1
Eyler, John F 11 2
Eyler, John H 203 1
Eyler, John M L 197 1
Eyler, John of Jonas 196 1
Eyler, John Reuben 197 1
Eyler, John T 186 1
Eyler, John W 161 2
Eyler, John Wm 188, 203 1
Eyler, Jonas 196 1
Eyler, Joseph 129 2
Eyler, Joseph H 13 1
Eyler, Joshua 80 2
Eyler, Josiah 189, 201 1
Eyler, Lona C 179 3
Eyler, Louisa C 200 1
Eyler, Mamie Morgan 205 1
Eyler, Margaret 197 1
Eyler, Margaret S 202 1
Eyler, Marshall B 188 1
Eyler, Martha 189, 197 1
Eyler, Martin 191 1
Eyler, Mary 197, 201 1
Eyler, Mary 138 2
Eyler, Mary M 201 1
Eyler, Mary R 203 1
Eyler, Nancy 203, 207 1
Eyler, Nathaniel 25 1
Eyler, Nathaniel 128 2
Eyler, Nellie G 203 1
Eyler, Nora M 189 1
Eyler, Perry 194 1
Eyler, Peter 26 1
Eyler, Peter of J 203 1
Eyler, Philip 196 1
Eyler, R O 101 1
Eyler, Rachel 159, 196 1
Eyler, Reuben H 204 1
Eyler, Ross E 197 1
Eyler, Rudolph M 265 2
Eyler, Rudolph O 205 1
Eyler, Samuel 152 1
Eyler, Sarah 205 1
Eyler, Sarah E 23 1
Eyler, Sarah J 205 1
Eyler, Solomon J 205 1
Eyler, Susan E 192 1
Eyler, Sylvia 194, 205 1
Eyler, T F 4, 25, 119 1
Eyler, T F 15, 124, 290 2
Eyler, Thomas E 191 2

Eyler, Thomas F 207 1
Eyler, Thomas W 189 1
Eyler, Thos 51 2
Eyler, Thos F 197, 207 1
Eyler, Usher J 189 1
Eyler, Viola A 198 1
Eyler, Walter B 163 1
Eyler, Wm 198, 208 1
Eyler, Wm H 165 1
Eyler, Wm P 188, 197, 208, 244 1
Eyler, Wm T 92 1
Eyler, Zephaniah 209 1
Eyster, A 176 3
Eyster, Andrew 186 1
Eyster, Andrew 205 3
Eyster, Elizabeth S 193 1
Eyster, Ellen C 192 1
Eyster, Fannie M 193, 194, 243 1
Eyster, Geo E T 186 1
Eyster, Geo T 192, 194, 205 1
Eyster, Hall W 192 1
Eyster, Jacob 196 1
Eyster, Samuel H 189 1
F & D Co 262 2
F & M Nat Bk 20 2
F & M National Bank 205, 280 1
F & M National Bank 20 2
F & M National Bank 3, 197 3
F & M Nat'l Bank 24, 48 3
F & M Nat'l Bank 20, 200, 284 2
F & M Nat'l Bank 166 1
F & M Nat'l Bank. The 256 1
Fabule, F Marion 106 1
Fagan, Addie M 210, 214 1
Fagan, Chas 214 1
Fagan, Chas T 214 1
Fagan, George 223 1
Fagan, Lewis F 57 3
Fagan, Lewis L 210 1
Fagan, Ruth R 16 3
Fagan, Wm 89 2
Fagler, James 58 1
Fahner, John Jr 113 2
Fahrney, Besse Y 213 1
Fahrney, Bessie Y 225 1
Fahrney, Ella Z 221, 224 3
Fahrney, Gladys M 213 1
Fahrney, H Lawrence 213, 225 1
Fahrney, Harry P 206 3
Fahrney, Henry 112 1
Fahrney, Henry P 214, 225, 230 1
Fahrney, Henry T 214 3
Fahrney, Ida D 227 1
Fahrney, J W 220 3
Fahrney, J Welty 116 2
Fahrney, Mary B 234 1
Fahrney, Mary Ellen 220 3
Fahrney, Minnie T 208 1
Fahrney, P D 27 3
Fahrney, Patrick 18 1
Fahrney, Peter D 152, 227, 234 1
Fahrst, Jacob 228 1
Fahs, A R 264 2
Fahs, Julia E C 264 2
Fair, Jacob 8 3
Fair, John 128 2
Fair, John 228 1
Fairfax, John 229 1
Fairfax, Sarah C 229 1
Faks, Henry 32 1
Falconer, Eden 219 1
Falconer, Geo W 208 2
Falconer, Lucian 18 2
Falconer, Malcom 57 2
Falconer, Reuben 57 2
Falconer, Reuben 239 1
Falconer, W E 220a 2
Falconer, Wm E 32 3
Falconner, Alberta C 230 1
Falconner, Lucian K 230 1
Falconner, W E 230 1
Falk, Catherine E 214 1
Falk, Charles H 214 1
Falk, Chas H 214, 215 1
Falk, Christian 214 1
Falk, Christina 89 2
Falk, Clara E 214, 215 1
Falk, Elizabeth F 97 1
Falk, James 92 2
Falk, James H 97, 215 1
Falk, James H 265 2
Falk, James H 197 3
Falk, John 214 1
Falk, John A 214 1
Falk, John M 230 1
Falk, John M 106 2
Falk, John W 230 1
Falk, Matilda C 214 1
Fallen, John 228 1
Falner, John 80 2
Falsom, Ephriam 14 1
Family 9, 15, 20, 23, 25, 30, 31, 32, 41, 52, 58, 67, 72, 80, 84, 85, 96, 102, 107, 119, 131, 139, 145, 154, 160, 169, 211, 218, 224, 225, 238, 277, 286 2
Family 20, 72, 222 3
Family 23, 25, 27, 34, 52, 62, 76, 86, 101, 104, 109, 123, 148, 153, 169, 177, 205, 219, 230 1
Family bond 3, 6, 23, 43, 44, 45, 182, 96, 107, 124, 161, 176, 180, 199, 201, 206, 219, 227 3
Family bond 8, 43, 54, 58, 70, 220, 229, 254, 259, 262, 265, 268, 277, 283 2
Family bond 4, 48, 79, 112, 120, 157, 254, 272, 277, 283 1
Fant, Adelaide L 107 1
Farcht, Jacob 230 1
Farell, James R 58 1
Fargason, Wm 244 1
Farkuhar, Geo 143, 145 2
Farmers & Mechanics Nat 42 1
Farmers & Mechanics Nat Bk 148, 280 1
Farmers & Mechanics Nat'l Bank 107 3
Farmers & Mechanics Nat'l Bank 186 2
Farmers & Mechanics Nat'l Bk 21 3
Farmers and Mechanics Nat Bk 273 1
Farney, James H 229 1
Farney, James H Sr 229 1
Farney, Rebecca 229 1
Farnsworth, Charles L 215 1
Farnsworth, Edward D 215 1
Farnsworth, Eliza S 219 1
Farquahar, Elizabeth 229 1
Farquahar, Joseph 229 1
Farquahar, Wm P 183 1
Farquhar, Adlen 210 1
Farquhar, Geo 186 1
Farquhar, Geo A 205 3
Farquhar, George 217a 2
Farquhar, George A 254 2
Farquhar, Joe 205 3
Farquhar, Joel 195 3
Farquhar, John 210, 229 1
Farquhar, Joseph 229 1
Farquhar, Moses B 184 3
Farquhar, Ruth 195 3
Farquhar, William P 31 3
Farquhar, Wm 43, 197 2
Farquhar, Wm P 38, 185 2
Farquhar, Wm P 51 1
Farrell, Henry 123 1
Farrell, James 31 3
Farrell, James R 125 1
Farrell, Michael 71 1
Farrell, Michael 221 2
Farrell, Philip Fr 273 1
Farrell, W F 144 2
Farris, David H 70 1
Farris, John 228 1
Farwell, Elvira 152 1
Faubel, Catharine E 214 1
Faubel, Conrad 30 1
Faubel, F Marion 132, 214, 222 1
Faubel, Lawrence 214 1

Fauble, Ann R 210 1
Fauble, Ann Sophia 210 1
Fauble, Augustus D 234 1
Fauble, Catherine 159, 228 1
Fauble, David 214, 217, 228 1
Fauble, E B 48 1
Fauble, F Marion 15, 122, 160, 277 2
Fauble, F Marion 210, 217 1
Fauble, F Mason 55 1
Fauble, Horatio 10 1
Fauble, J Marion 238 2
Fauble, Jacob 135, 196, 228 1
Fauble, Jacob 39 3
Fauble, Jacob 262, 275 2
Fauble, Jacob Jr 228 1
Fauble, Jacob Sr 10 1
Fauble, John 112, 210, 214, 228 1
Fauble, John 221a 2
Fauble, John Sr 228 1
Fauble, Margaret 234 1
Fauble, Martha E 234 1
Fauble, Mary A 217 1
Fauble, Rufus E 80 2
Fauble, S M 8 2
Fauble, S M 253 1
Fauble, Wm 244 1
Faughman, Michael 23 3
Faulkner, Sophia 214 1
Favorite, Ada C 215, 219 1
Favorite, Alexzena 214 1
Favorite, Annie K 214, 234 1
Favorite, Catherine J 215, 282 1
Favorite, Chas H 214 1
Favorite, Cyrus O 214 1
Favorite, Edward L 12 1
Favorite, George 220, 223 1
Favorite, H G 234 1
Favorite, Helen M 220 1
Favorite, Henry 225, 234 1
Favorite, John W 220 1
Favorite, Joseph 228 1
Favorite, Marshall 234 1
Favorite, Mary 234 1
Favorite, Preston E 234 1
Favorite, Rebecca Ann 239 1
Favorite, Sarah 227, 240 1
Fawley, George W 240, 270 1
Fawley, Howard C 133, 227 1
Fawley, Ida Virginia 227 1
Fawley, John E 230 1
Fawley, Margaret L 133 1
Fawley, Samuel L 241 1
Fazer, Adam 210 1
Fazer, Adam 210 1
Feaga, C E 221 3
Feaga, Charles E 141 3
Feaga, Chas A 219 1
Feaga, Chas E 214 1
Feaga, Christiana 214 1
Feaga, E B 58 2
Feaga, Edmund P 219, 244 1
Feaga, Edwin 244 1
Feaga, Elizabeth A 219 1
Feaga, Geo 23 3
Feaga, Geo L 13 1
Feaga, George 44, 223 1
Feaga, Harry M 113, 223 1
Feaga, Henry M 45 3
Feaga, Hester A B 225 1
Feaga, Hester A R 225 1
Feaga, John J 230 1
Feaga, Joshua 229 1
Feaga, L E 62 1
Feaga, Luther E 207 3
Feaga, Lydia A M 219 1
Feaga, Mamie G 235 1
Feaga, Orsena P 237 1
Feaga, Uriah V 223 1
Feaga, Walter P 10, 278 2
Feaga, William 15 3
Feaga, William C 223, 235 1
Feaga, Wm 106 2
Feaga, Wm 229, 237 1
Feaga, Wm M 8, 113 2
Feaga, Wm M 203 3
Feaga, Wm M 51 1
Feagea, Geo 53 3
Feagler, Sarah C 71 3
Fearhake, A 244, 265 1
Fearhake, A Jr 96 1
Fearhake, Adolphus 197, 210, 219 1
Fearhake, Adolphus 137, 177 2
Fearhake, Agnes V 210 1
Fearhake, Elizabeth 219 1
Fearhake, Rosa 219 1
Fearhake, Susan 219 1
Feaser, Jacob 47 1
Feasler, Eve Ann 219 1
Feasler, John 116 1
Feaster, Ann Rebecca 228 1
Feaster, Daniel 217 1
Feaster, Daniel 212 3
Feaster, Daniel E 117 1
Feaster, Henry 225 1
Feaster, Jacob 207, 228, 229, 234 1
Feaster, Jacob 18, 290 2
Feaster, Jacob Jr 228 1
Feaster, Jacob Sr 228 1
Feaster, John 106 3
Feaster, John 240 1
Feaster, John H 229 1
Feaster, John Jr 57 1
Feaster, John Sr 229, 234 1
Feaster, John Sr 18 2
Feaster, Jonathan 225 1
Feaster, Leora E 233 1
Feaster, Mary Ann 229 1
Feaster, Mary Ann 234 1
Feaster, Sarah E 233, 234, 240 1
Feaster, Susannah 240 1
Feazer, Daniel 217 1
Feazer, Peter 238 1
Feelemyer, David 76 1
Feeley, Miriam W 166 3
Feeser, Adam 210 1
Feeser, Amos 233 1
Feeser, Geo 228 1
Feeser, Hettie 233 1
Feeser, Jacob J 230 1
Feeser, John 228 1
Feeser, Lydia A 233 1
Feete, Alva D 123 1
Feete, C H 10, 154 2
Feete, C H 9, 124, 215 1
Feete, Charles Floyd 215 1
Feete, Charles H 215 1
Feete, Chas 123 1
Feete, Chas H 225, 278 1
Feete, Chas H 161 3
Feete, Clara 161 3
Feete, Clara B 215 1
Feete, Harrison 13 1
Feete, Henry 13, 123, 225 1
Feete, Henry C 225 1
Feete, Henry Jr 225 1
Feezer, Catherine 214 1
Feezer, David 228 1
Feezer, Geo 228 1
Feezer, Jacob 228 1
Feezer, Jacob 137 2
Feezer, John J 233 1
Feezer, Laura V 214, 233 1
Feezer, Levi 233, 240 1
Feezer, Levi 218 3
Feezer, Levi 51 2
Feezer, Lydia Ann 233 1
Feezer, Martin 214 1
Feezer, Rachel A 219 3
Feezer, Samuel P 229 1
Feiser, Jacob 238, 240 1
Feiser, Jacob 68 3
Feiser, Laura M 233 1
Feiser, Levi 185 3
Feiser, P L 13 1

Feiser, Parma Lee 233, 238 1
Feiser, Peter 229 1
Feiser, Phoebe E 238, 239 1
Feiser, Rachel A 239 1
Feister, Jacob 125 1
Feitz, Carrie E 237 1
Feitz, Newell 237 1
Feldon, Holden S 33, 128, 182 3
Felker, Jacob 100 1
Fellers, Anna A 210 1
Fellers, Charles E 214 1
Fellers, Geo 214 1
Fellers, Guy R 210 1
Fellers, John D[?] 214 1
Fellows, Annie M 223 1
Fellows, Estelle M 239 1
Fellows, George W 223 1
Fellows, Ralph 239 1
Feltcher, John W 4 1
Felton, H 172 3
Felton, H S 31, 120, 229 1
Felton, H S 31 2
Felton, Holden S 6, 11, 16, 21, 48, 51, 73, 83, 140, 172, 180 3
Felton, Holden S 3, 9, 32, 36, 47, 67, 113, 119, 125, 136, 178, 189, 217, 234, 239, 241, 295 2
Felton, Holden S 28, 30, 31, 55, 63, 73, 97, 150, 168, 177, 194, 235, 243, 245, 257, 266 1
Felton, Holten S [sic] 157 1
Felton, Maud C 243 1
Felton, Thaddeus M 189 2
Felton, Thaddus M 243 1
Fenfrock, Henry 225 1
Fenfrock, John 225 1
Fenton, S 30 2
Fenwick, Helene 225 1
Ferguson, Amos 2 2
Ferguson, Amos E 210 1
Ferguson, Carrie 209 2
Ferguson, Effie 44 3
Ferguson, John 228 1
Ferguson, Rhoda K 210 1
Ferguson, Russell D 239 1
Ferree, Sarah 240 1
Ferrell, J C 230 1
Ferrell, James R 230 1
Ferrell, W F 230 1
Ferrell, Wm F 230 1
Fesser, John 189 1
Fessler, John 225, 228 1
Fessler, John 159 2
Fessler, John Jr 228 1
Fessler, John Sr 228 1
Fetrow, Frank 42 1
Fetterling, John 227a 2
Fick, Daniel 228 1
Fick, James M 229 1
Fick, John 228 1
Fick, Joseph H W 229 1
Fickel, Daniel 22 1
Fideliey & Deposit Co of Md 262 2
Fidelity & Casualty Co 124 3
Fidelity & Casualty Co 163 2
Fidelity & Casualty Co of N Y 204, 217, 282 1
Fidelity & Casualty Co of N Y 3, 28, 35, 58, 60, 166, 213 3
Fidelity & Casualty Co of N Y 89 2
Fidelity & Casualty Co of New York 3, 20 2
Fidelity & Casualty Co of New York 117, 243 1
Fidelity & Casualty Co, The 44 1
Fidelity & Dep Co 44 3
Fidelity & Dep Co of Balto 15, 28, 43 3
Fidelity & Dep Co of Md 195, 232 2
Fidelity & Dep Co of Md 10, 15, 23, 32 3
Fidelity & Deposit & Co 227a 2
Fidelity & Deposit & Co 8 1
Fidelity & Deposit Co 12, 32, 41, 43, 52, 87, 89, 93, 102, 119, 125, 139, 145, 148, 160, 169, 282, 284, 196, 202, 247 2
Fidelity & Deposit Co 42, 62, 73, 82, 97, 177, 179, 192, 200, 240, 254 1
Fidelity & Deposit Co 11, 24, 68, 83, 104, 113, 141, 148, 149, 180, 188, 196, 203, 207 3
Fidelity & Deposit Co Balto 150, 151 2
Fidelity & Deposit Co of Baltimore 62, 92, 183, 201, 214, 243, 278, 279 1
Fidelity & Deposit Co of Baltimore 31, 172, 175, 178, 188, 189, 202 2
Fidelity & Deposit Co of Baltimore Md 165 1
Fidelity & Deposit Co of Balto 91, 122, 174 3
Fidelity & Deposit Co of Balto 23, 235, 278 1
Fidelity & Deposit Co of Maryland 242 2
Fidelity & Deposit Co of Maryland 156, 202 3
Fidelity & Deposit Co of Maryland 8 1
Fidelity & Deposit Co of Md 2, 3, 11, 20, 21, 23, 33, 35, 56, 57, 65, 71, 72, 91, 98, 107, 111, 116, 149, 152, 156, 161, 169, 182, 188, 192, 197, 227 3
Fidelity & Deposit Co of Md 10, 16, 18, 20, 23, 31, 36, 54, 58, 59, 65, 66, 67, 68, 80, 85, 87, 93, 107, 112, 113, 125, 129, 139, 145, 153, 169, 198, 199, 205, 218, 220, 226, 227, 229, 217a, 227a, 229a, 238, 245, 246, 253, 254, 267, 277, 277, 283, 288, 290 2
Fidelity & Deposit Co of Md 1, 8, 10, 11, 33, 42, 45, 53, 55, 63, 74, 82, 83, 86, 92, 97, 107, 111, 113, 136, 156, 159, 179, 181, 202, 204, 214, 240, 241, 249, 253, 254, 260, 266, 272, 273, 282 1
Fidelity & Deposit Co of MD 167, 203 2
Fidelity & Deposit Co of Md, The 62 1
Fidelity & Deposit Co of Md, The 204 1
Fidelity & Deposit Co of Md, The 48 1
Fidelity & Deposit Co of N Y 111 3
Fidelity & Deposit Company 93, 129 2
Fidelity & Deposit Company 38, 135, 162 1
Fidelity & Deposit Company of Maryland 184 1
Fidelity & Deposit Company of Md 262 2
Fidelity & Deposit Company of Md 97 1
Fidelity and Casualty Co of N Y 293 2
Fidelity and Casualty Co of N Y 28, 92 1
Fidelity and Casualty Co of New York 28, 111 1
Fidelity and Casualty Co of NY, The 127 1
Fidelity and Casualty Company of N Y 140 2
Fidelity and Deposit Co 63, 99, 102 1
Fidelity and Deposit Co of Balto 227 2
Fidelity and Deposit Co of Maryland 109, 219 1
Fidelity and Deposit Co of Maryland 23 2
Fidelity and Deposit Co of Md 27, 166 3
Fidelity and Deposit Co of Md 59, 83 2

Fidelity and Deposit Co of Md 28, 110, 127, 130, 133, 140 1
Fidelity and Deposit Company 8 1
Fidelity and Deposit Company of Maryland 172 2
Fidelity and Deposit Company of Md 89, 206 3
Fidelity and Deposit Company of Md 106 2
Fidelity and Deposit Company of Md 63, 145, 230 1
Fidelity and Deposit of Md 220a 2
Fidelity and Depsit Co of Md 188 3
Fidelity and Guarrantee 224 2
Fidelity Deposit Co of Baltimore Md 176 1
Fidelity Deposit Co of Balto 166 3
Fidelity Deposit Co of Md 76 2
Fidelity Deposit Co of Md 106 3
Fidelity Deposit Co of Md 112 1
Field, Chas 205 2
Field, S P 67 2
Fields, John E 230 1
Figgins, A L 229 1
Figgins, Arthur H 210 1
Figgins, Eliza 210 1
Figgins, Eliza E 219, 229 1
Figgins, James 271 1
Figgins, James L 229 1
Figgins, James M 229 1
Fike, T S 144 1
Fike, Tobias S 243 1
Filby, Helen Nevada 225 1
Filker, Jacob 10 1
Filler, C E 129 1
Filler, D H 240 1
Filler, Daniel 219 1
Filler, Daniel H 217 1
Filler, Elizabeth 219 1
Filler, Floyd D 217 1
Filler, Harvey C 225, 240 1
Filler, Hilton E 225 1
Filler, Joseph 244 1
Filler, Mary C 16, 31 2
Filler, Mary C 244 1
Filler, Mary S 18 2
Filler, Oda B 182 2
Filler, Oda C 93 1
Filler, Rebecca 243 1
Filler, Rita B 235 2
Filler, Sarah E 240 1
Filler, Solomon 240, 244 1
Filler, Solomon A 240 1
Filler, Thomas 217 1
Filler, Thos F 240, 243 1
Filler, Willie H 235 2
Filler, Wm 244 1
Filler, Wm E 31 2
Filler, Wm E 244 1
Filling, Catherine 214 1
Findlay, Ellen 219 1
Fink, Bernard J 215 1
Fink, Bessie M 230 1
Fink, Chas R 150 1
Fink, Clarence J 215, 238 1
Fink, Cordelia C 214 1
Fink, Edward 133, 219 1
Fink, Elizabeth 223 1
Fink, Emanuel 228, 240 1
Fink, Emanuel 169 2
Fink, Emmanuel 219 1
Fink, Geo T 223 1
Fink, Henry S 71 1
Fink, John 14, 171 3
Fink, John 27, 137 2
Fink, John 279 1
Fink, John A 51 1
Fink, John Jr 27, 185 2
Fink, John Jr 67, 228, 230 1
Fink, John Jr 14 3
Fink, John Sr 228, 263 1
Fink, Joseph 71 1
Fink, Joseph C 223, 230 1
Fink, Leah 233 1
Fink, M F 219 1
Fink, Margaret E 37 1
Fink, Philip 215. 238 1
Fink, Pius J 238 1
Fink, R E 219 1
Fink, Richard 223 1
Fink, Richard E 239 1
Fink, Richard R 26 1
Fink, Samuel 66, 227a 2
Fink, Samuel 238, 240 1
Fink, Sarah A 150 1
Fink, Susan R 239, 240 1
Fink, W L 19 2
Finley, James 228 1
Finney, Charlotte 214 1
Finneyfrock, Georgiana 225 1
Finneyfrock, Henry J 225 1
Finneyfrock, Ira F 240 1
Finneyfrock, Samuel 240 1
Finnyfrock, Chas 123 1
Finnyfrock, Harvey 123 1
Fior, D 98 3
Fireman's Fund Indem Co 12 3
Firestone, Elizabeth 196 3
Firestone, James M 229 1
Firestone, Joshua 231, 234 1
Firestone, Martin L 229 1
Firestone, Mary 234 1
Firestone, William A 231, 266 1
Firestone, Zachriah T 196 3
Firor, Anna C 244 1
Firor, Anna Mary 196 1
Firor, Benjamin 213, 217 1
Firor, Calvin S 213 3
Firor, Charles F 217 1
Firor, Daniel 230, 249 1
Firor, David 244 1
Firor, David F 276 2
Firor, David S 217 1
Firor, Edw 244 1
Firor, Guy 244 1
Firor, Henry 275 2
Firor, Henry 263, 271 1
Firor, Henry N 225 1
Firor, J Edw 13 1
Firor, Jacob 185 3
Firor, Jacob 7, 19, 26, 159, 165, 262, 275 2
Firor, Jacob 51, 117, 125, 196, 229, 230, 253 1
Firor, James H 51, 230, 263 1
Firor, Jas H 190 2
Firor, John 229 1
Firor, John 231 1
Firor, Joseph T 229 1
Firor, Joseph T 276 2
Firor, Margaret 229 1
Firor, Martin D 217 1
Firor, Mary Elizabeth 234, 235 1
Firor, Mary S 234 1
Firor, Uriah 229 1
Firor, Wm 229 1
Firor, Wm J 213 1
Firor, Wm L 225, 244 1
Firor, Zacharias U 2 2
Fischer, Adam 210 1
Fischer, Daniel 33 3
Fischer, Geo 253 1
Fischer, Geo J 210 1
Fischer, John 228 1
Fischer, William 294 2
Fiser, P L 11 1
Fish, Ann Cecelia 210 1
Fish, James H 13 1
Fish, John B 228 1
Fishback, Beulah W 257 1
Fishback, Charles F 257 1
Fisher, A B 223 1
Fisher, Abraham 6 1
Fisher, Abram 210, 243 1
Fisher, Agnes 210 1
Fisher, Albert B 210, 223 1
Fisher, Allen G 230 1
Fisher, Andrew 210 1

Fisher, Archie 11 3
Fisher, Archie 270 1
Fisher, Chas 61 1
Fisher, Clarence H 88 1
Fisher, David 205, 217, 227 1
Fisher, Edw L 235 1
Fisher, Elizabeth 219 1
Fisher, Elsie 102 2
Fisher, Elva 57 3
Fisher, F C 209 2
Fisher, Frederick 222 1
Fisher, Frederick 93 2
Fisher, G William 207 3
Fisher, Geo C 223 1
Fisher, Geo W 233, 243 1
Fisher, George C 42 3
Fisher, Harriet F 28 1
Fisher, Harry 222 1
Fisher, I M 196 3
Fisher, Irvin J 217 1
Fisher, Isaac 227, 243 1
Fisher, Isaac M 227 1
Fisher, J M 237, 252 1
Fisher, J Roger 210 1
Fisher, Jacob 217, 231 1
Fisher, James 231 1
Fisher, James H 189 1
Fisher, Jeremiah 52 1
Fisher, Jeremiah 58 2
Fisher, John 92 2
Fisher, John 23, 207, 217, 227, 243, 263, 278 1
Fisher, John M 156 3
Fisher, John M 230, 278 1
Fisher, John M 231, 290 2
Fisher, John N 29 2
Fisher, John W 230 1
Fisher, John W 233 1
Fisher, Katherine C 32 2
Fisher, Laura W 210 1
Fisher, Lester 222 1
Fisher, Lydia Ann 233 1
Fisher, Margaret 219 1
Fisher, Martha E 235 1
Fisher, Martin 234 1
Fisher, Mary B 244 1
Fisher, Mary C 214 1
Fisher, Mary Catherine 235 1
Fisher, Mary E 234 1
Fisher, Michael 205, 234, 235 1
Fisher, Moses 5 2
Fisher, Nathaniel 234, 237 1
Fisher, Nathaniel 1, 22, 28 2
Fisher, Newton A 217 1
Fisher, Newton F 188 3
Fisher, Rebecca 61 1
Fisher, S Agnes 223 1
Fisher, Seth 40 1
Fisher, T S 210, 223 1
Fisher, Thomas 243 1
Fisher, Thomas E 243 1
Fisher, Thos J 243 1
Fisher, W L O 163 2
Fisher, W L O 28 1
Fisher, William L O 175 2
Fisher, Willis E 210, 233, 244 1
Fisher, Willis E 116 2
Fisher, Wm 139 2
Fisher, Wm 214 1
Fisher, Wm F 227, 235 1
Fister, Drusilla 217 1
Fitch, Mortimer C 71 3
Fitez, John D 230 1
Fitterling, Henry 228 1
Fitterling, John 228 1
Fitz, D 70 3
Fitzgerald, Cornelius C 116 3
Fitzgerald, Emily C 219 1
Fitzgerald, John 229 1
Fitzgerald, John F 229 1
Fitzgerald, Naomi E 243 1
Fitzgerald, T J Allen 243 1
Fitzhugh, Amelia 14 2
Fitzsimmons, James I 230 1
Fitzsimmons, James T 207 3
Fitzsimmons, John Ignatius 230 1
Fitzsimmons, Sophia C 241 1
Fitzsimmons, William J 259 2
Fizzle, Nimrod 128 2
Flack, Adam 213 1
Flack, Barbara 213 1
Flack, Geo 159 2
Flack, Geo 213, 260 1
Flack, George 51 1
Flack, George 26 3
Flack, Mary of Ohio 234 1
Flaharty, Margaret A 234 1
Flair, Amanda R 240 1
Flair, Amanda R 30 2
Flair, Simon Peter 240 1
Flanagan, Edith 140 1
Flanagan, Hugh 225 1
Flanagan, James 225 1
Flanagan, John 228 1
Flanagan, Malachi 234 1
Flanagan, Margaret E 235 1
Flanagan, Millard 225 1
Flanagan, Rosanna 13 1
Flanagan, Thomas 239, 243, 244 1
Flanagan, Thos 234 1
Flanagan, Wm 228 1
Flanegan, Thomas 8 1
Flanigan, Adam 230 1
Flanigan, Emma E 230 1
Flanigan, Ernest 54 2
Flanigan, Hugh 225 1
Flanigan, John M O 230 1
Flanigan, Noah 210 1
Flannagan, Margaret 235 1
Flannagan, Noah E 237 1
Flannagan, Ralph G 237 1
Flannigan, Adam H E 210 1
Flannigan, Catherine 214 1
Flannigan, James W 214 1
Flannigan, Lycurgus 210 1
Flannigan, Martha E[?] 237 1
Flannigan, Noah 215 1
Flannigan, Wm 148 2
Flather, Geo W 140 1
Flaut, Catherine 214 1
Flautt, Christian 214 1
Flautt, G R 166 3
Flautt, Gilmore 150 1
Flautt, Gilmore 196 3
Flautt, Gilmore R 172, 223 1
Flautt, Gilmore R 169 3
Flautt, Gilmore R Jr 223 1
Flautt, H R 48 1
Flautt, Hannah 214 1
Flautt, Harry R 208 3
Flautt, Hazel V 223 1
Flautt, Walter L 208 3
Flax, Bertha 213 1
Flax, Catherine 213 1
Flax, J Norman 213 1
Fleagel, Benjamin J 235 1
Fleagel, Martha [sic] 229 1
Fleagle, Elizabeth K 161 3
Fleagle, John 220 3
Fleagle, John A 229, 235 1
Fleagle, Maria A 230, 234 1
Fleagle, Milton 235 1
Flegle, John 57 2
Fleischman, Earl F 214 1
Fleischman, John L 214 1
Fleishman, Caroline L 214 1
Fleishman, Earl F 230 1
Fleishman, John Henry 230 1
Fleishman, John L 230 1
Fleming, Alice 210 1
Fleming, Arthur 210, 240 1
Fleming, Arthur 192 3
Fleming, Arthur E 239 1
Fleming, Catherine M 243 1
Fleming, Charles E 215 1
Fleming, Charlton 214 1
Fleming, Chas David 240 1
Fleming, Chas F 92 1
Fleming, D J (Rev) 217 1
Fleming, Elizabeth 219, 229 1
Fleming, Ellen B 225 1
Fleming, Harriet 234, 239, 240 1
Fleming, J Alfred 210 1

Fleming, John 50, 192 3
Fleming, John 171 2
Fleming, John 228, 253 1
Fleming, John C 13 1
Fleming, Joseph 195 3
Fleming, Joseph 228, 240 1
Fleming, Joseph D 210 1
Fleming, Joseph P 228, 243, 264 1
Fleming, Mary Jane 234 1
Fleming, Matthew 235 1
Fleming, Minnie 166 2
Fleming, Nicholas H 237 1
Fleming, Reuben 239 1
Fleming, Robert 239 1
Fleming, Robert 19, 186 2
Fleming, Robert Jr 239 1
Fleming, Ruth E 243 1
Fleming, Sallie 56 1
Fleming, Samuel 192, 202 3
Fleming, Samuel 210, 219, 240, 243 1
Fleming, Samuel of A 228 1
Fleming, Sarah 210, 240 1
Fleming, Sarah E C 240 1
Fleming, Thomas 243 1
Fleming, Thomas 224 2
Fleming, Thomas A 210 1
Fleming, Thomas H 243 1
Fleming, Thomas Lee 240 1
Fleming, Thos H 1 2
Fleming, Thos H 240, 243 1
Fleming, William 241 2
Fleming, Wm 235 1
Fleming, Wm H 243 1
Fleming, Wm R 26 1
Fleming, Wm R 224 3
Fleming, Wm W 237, 244 1
Flemming, Joseph P 13 1
Flemming, Robt 149 2
Flemming, Susannah 240 1
Flemming, William 6 3
Flemming, Wm R 38 2
Flemming, Wm W 1 2
Fleshman, Charles 214 1
Fleshman, Elizabeth 214 1
Fleshman, John H 62 1
Fleshman, Lewis H 62 1
Fletcher, David T 233 1
Fletcher, Ernest F 219 1
Fletcher, Louisa 233 1
Fletcher, Martha 235 1
Fletcher, William 268 2
Fletcher, Wm 41 1
Flickinger, Alice C 210 1
Flickinger, Andrew 210 1
Flickinger, Barbara 213 1
Flickinger, Catherine 239 1
Flickinger, Clarence L 239 1
Flickinger, Eli B 38 1
Flickinger, Howard D 210, 237 1
Flickinger, John 110, 115, 234, 238 1
Flickinger, John 40 2
Flickinger, John 215 3
Flickinger, John [?] 230 1
Flickinger, John P 13 1
Flickinger, Manzella 235 1
Flickinger, Minnie 108, 115 2
Flickinger, Nathaniel M 237 1
Flickinger, Peter 238 1
Flickinger, Raymond 239 1
Flickinger, Raymond 108, 115 2
Flickinger, Raymond 45 3
Flickinger, Rufus 239 1
Flickinger, William [?] 230 1
Flight, Elizabeth 225 1
Flight, Henry 225 1
Flight, John 228 1
Flin, Michael 220 1
Flinn, Ella J 220, 234 1
Flinn, Fannie M 222 1
Flinn, Lillie L 233 1
Flock, George 96 3
Flohr, James E 18 1
Flohr, John 14 3
Flohr, John 229 1
Flohr, John R 233, 279 1
Flohr, Josiah 229 1
Flohr, Leonard 233, 244 1
Flohr, Leonard J 174 3
Flohr, Wm 229, 244 1
Flook, A D 235 1
Flook, Albert A 230 1
Flook, Alden A 237 1
Flook, Alden A 235 1
Flook, Allen 219 1
Flook, Anna 210 1
Flook, B F 96 3
Flook, Barbara 213 1
Flook, Beulah 235 1
Flook, C F 257 1
Flook, C F 139, 189, 199, 229a 2
Flook, C F 82 3
Flook, Catherine 214, 229 1
Flook, CF 62 1
Flook, Cyrus 15, 190, 199 2
Flook, Cyrus F 215, 265 1
Flook, Cyrus F 12, 40, 258 2
Flook, Cyrus F 43, 44, 189 3
Flook, Cyrus T 144 1
Flook, D C 244 1
Flook, D Charles 217 1
Flook, D Charles Jr 14 1
Flook, D Chas 22, 23, 217, 219 1
Flook, D F 30 2
Flook, D F 156 1
Flook, Daniel 11, 100, 165 2
Flook, Daniel 214, 229, 234 1
Flook, Daniel B 217 1
Flook, Daniel P 229 1
Flook, David 229 1
Flook, Dawson F 122 2
Flook, Dawson F 230 1
Flook, Dawson Y 230 1
Flook, Dorothy P 73 3
Flook, Elizabeth E 215 1
Flook, Elizabeth S 219 1
Flook, Ella M 235, 237 1
Flook, Elmer D 219 1
Flook, Emma J 219 1
Flook, Ezra D 41 2
Flook, H Vincent 225 1
Flook, Harry 106 2
Flook, Henry 225 1
Flook, Indiana L 227 1
Flook, J 263 1
Flook, J E 225 1
Flook, J E 167 3
Flook, J Ridgely 113 3
Flook, Jacob 225, 228, 248 1
Flook, Jacob 126 3
Flook, Jacob 7 2
Flook, Jacob H 57 1
Flook, Jacob of J 70, 200, 228, 229 1
Flook, James E 210 1
Flook, John 35, 87, 134 2
Flook, John 225, 228, 229 1
Flook, John 53, 192 3
Flook, John H 229 1
Flook, John L 219 1
Flook, John of H 229 1
Flook, John P 229, 230 1
Flook, John P 71 3
Flook, John W 234, 237, 240 1
Flook, Joseph D 229, 230 1
Flook, Joshua 229, 234 1
Flook, Joshua M 230 1
Flook, Lawson F 262 2
Flook, Lewis E 288, 294 2
Flook, Lola V 241 1
Flook, Magdalene 234 1
Flook, Maria L 235 1
Flook, Martin 65, 106 2
Flook, Martin H 240 1
Flook, Martin L 240 1
Flook, Mary 234 1
Flook, Mathias 213 3
Flook, Max K 235 1
Flook, Mildred F 219 1
Flook, Millard F 235 1
Flook, Myrtle E 235 1

Flook, Naomi B 237 1
Flook, Nina D 36 2
Flook, Nina H 217 1
Flook, Oliver J 237 1
Flook, Oscar L 101 1
Flook, Oscar P 106 2
Flook, Philip E 230 1
Flook, S M 55 1
Flook, Sarah E 240 1
Flook, Sarah V 240 1
Flook, Staley L 235 1
Flook, Staley M 241 1
Flook, W S 244 1
Flook, Wilbur S 219 1
Flook, Wm 51 2
Flook, Wm 210 1
Flook, Wm S 244 1
Flook, Wm Sniveley 217 1
Flooke, Jacob 228, 229 1
Flooke, Jacob of J 238 1
Flooke, Jonas E 230 1
Flooke, Matthias 234 1
Flooke, Perry C 238 1
Flora, Anna M 233 1
Flora, Charles E 233 1
Flora, Joseph S 230 1
Flora, Lewis C 233 1
Flora, Valaria 230 1
Flore, Frederick 222 1
Florence, Annie C 210 1
Florence, Kavanaugh P 210 1
Florence[?], Annie C 240 1
Florence[?], Sebastian B 240 1
Flory, Peter 238 1
Flower, Barbara 213 1
Flowers, B C 125 1
Flowers, B F 39 2
Flowers, Benjamin C 275 2
Flowers, Mary A 234 1
Floyd, Anna B 141 3
Floyd, Annabelle 184, 238 2
Flynn, Catherine 214 1
Flynn, Elias 209 2
Flynn, Elias W 16, 35 2
Flynn, Mary 234 1
Fockler, Daniel 172 2
Fogle, A 166 2
Fogle, A C 233 1
Fogle, A C 82 3
Fogle, Abraham 234 1
Fogle, Adam 210 1
Fogle, Alice 210 1
Fogle, Andrew 210 1
Fogle, Archie T 145 2
Fogle, Archie Thomas 211 1
Fogle, Bessie A 220 1
Fogle, C H 2 2
Fogle, C Noelington 200 1
Fogle, Calvin C 32 3
Fogle, Calvin E 244 1
Fogle, Carlton 214 1
Fogle, Catherine 214, 230 1
Fogle, Charles 210 1
Fogle, Charles C 215 1
Fogle, Charles H 220, 235 1
Fogle, Chas H 235 1
Fogle, Chas H of M 5 2
Fogle, Christian 214 1
Fogle, Clayanna 219 1
Fogle, Daniel 217 1
Fogle, David 217, 237 1
Fogle, David 40 3
Fogle, David E 217 1
Fogle, Effie A 220 1
Fogle, Effie W 32 3
Fogle, Elias 219 1
Fogle, Elizabeth 219, 229 1
Fogle, Elizabeth J 28 1
Fogle, Elsie M 74, 219 1
Fogle, Emanuel 219 1
Fogle, Emanuel 247 2
Fogle, Emma Jane 219 1
Fogle, Ernest 235 1
Fogle, Geo 25 1
Fogle, Geo 187 3
Fogle, Geo F 205 1
Fogle, Geo P 223 1
Fogle, George 59, 244 1
Fogle, Goldie M 86 1
Fogle, Grant 223 1
Fogle, Hazel L 235 1
Fogle, Henry 225 1
Fogle, Henry 1, 18 3
Fogle, Henry Sr 225 1
Fogle, Henson T 235 1
Fogle, Ira A 219 1
Fogle, Isaac H 229 1
Fogle, J Herman 233 1
Fogle, J T 230 1
Fogle, J T 82 3
Fogle, Jacob 42 3
Fogle, Jacob 203 1
Fogle, John 225, 229, 234 1
Fogle, John 81 3
Fogle, John 19, 132, 159, 224a, 294 2
Fogle, John C 205 1
Fogle, John E 214, 229, 230 1
Fogle, John H 229, 244 1
Fogle, John M 229 1
Fogle, John of H 229 1
Fogle, John of J 73 1
Fogle, John T 58, 172, 229 1
Fogle, John W 230, 235, 238 1
Fogle, Joshua 230 1
Fogle, Laura E 233 1
Fogle, Lavinia C 233 1
Fogle, Lennie M 108 2
Fogle, Lillie May 20 3
Fogle, Lucinda A 243 1
Fogle, Lydia Ann 243 1
Fogle, M 5 2
Fogle, M Grace 112 2
Fogle, M Kathryn 200 1
Fogle, Madie 161 2
Fogle, Martha E 215, 235 1
Fogle, Mary 225 1
Fogle, Mary E 235, 237 1
Fogle, Mary H 189 1
Fogle, Mathias 62 2
Fogle, Mathias 196, 234, 250 1
Fogle, Mathias of H 234 1
Fogle, May H 219 1
Fogle, Michael 234, 235, 237 1
Fogle, Michael 2, 31, 138, 214a 2
Fogle, Michael W 58, 265 1
Fogle, Nettie 280 2
Fogle, Nicholas 185 3
Fogle, Nicholas 28 2
Fogle, Nicholas 144, 171, 217, 228, 229, 237 1
Fogle, Nicholas Jr 237 1
Fogle, Nicholas Sr 237 1
Fogle, Norman F 233 1
Fogle, Norris 82 1
Fogle, Pauline S 211 1
Fogle, Peter 214, 217 1
Fogle, Philip 238 1
Fogle, Rachel A 230 1
Fogle, Raymond G 223 1
Fogle, S J 230 1
Fogle, Samuel 240 1
Fogle, Sarah Ann 240 1
Fogle, Susan 240 1
Fogle, T R 240 1
Fogle, Thomas R 243 1
Fogle, Thomas W 243 1
Fogle, Thos W 243 1
Fogle, W 82 3
Fogle, William 275 2
Fogle, William 42 3
Fogle, Wm 100 2
Fogle, Wm 177, 210 1
Fogle, Wm H 219, 234, 244 1
Fogle, Wm H of A 166, 171 2
Fogle, Wm Jr 187 3
Fogle, Wm of H 244 1
Fogle[?], John M 234 1
Fogler, C C 143 2
Fogler, Henry 225 1
Fogler, Henry 84 2
Fogler, Henry Sr 84 2
Fogler, Martha 214 1
Fohr, Philip 10 1
Folger, Catherine 214 1
Folk, Edw L 233 1

Folk, Lucy F 233 1
Folkerth, Christopher 214 1
Folkerth, Michale [sic] 214 1
Foller, Henry 225 1
Folmer, Gaynelle A 229 2
Fonsten, John 93 2
Ford, Benjamin D 55 1
Ford, George Dewey 223 1
Ford, Hattie J B 106 2
Ford, Helen A 210, 244 1
Ford, Hugh 214 2
Ford, Isaac 165 1
Ford, Jennie 187 3
Ford, John L 230 1
Ford, Kate J 172 1
Ford, Madelyn V 223 1
Ford, Mary 234 1
Ford, Mary R 140 2
Ford, Mattie J B 239 1
Ford, Mattie J B 110 2
Ford, Mattie J B Keller 235 1
Ford, Raymond 67, 151 2
Ford, Raymond G 239 1
Ford, Raymond G 110, 116 2
Ford, Raymond I 210, 244 1
Ford, Robert 58 1
Ford, William M 223 1
Foreman, Albert J 240 1
Foreman, Anne Elizabeth 210 1
Foreman, Dennis C 240 1
Foreman, G W 264 1
Foreman, Geo 227 1
Foreman, Geo W 223 1
Foreman, George W 171 3
Foreman, George W 243 1
Foreman, H C 223 1
Foreman, Henry 239 1
Foreman, Henry 139 2
Foreman, Jacob E 167 3
Foreman, John Mc 230 1
Foreman, Mary Ann 161 3
Foreman, Rose C 230, 239 1
Foreman, Valentine 243 1
Foreman, William E 210 1
Foreman, Wm 244 1
Foreman, Wm H 244 1
Forest, Charles L 238 2
Forman, John 163 3
Formwald, Jacob 224 3
Formwald, John 224 3
Formwall, John 222 3
Formwalts, Jacob 228 1
Forney, Anna M 210 1
Forney, Bessie May 230 1
Forney, Chas E 210 1
Forney, David 228 1
Forney, Elizabeth 219 1
Forney, H C 265 2
Forney, James 230 1
Forney, John 91 1
Forney, John D 228 1
Forney, John G 230 1
Forney, Mary Helen 225 1
Forney, Patrick 231, 240 1
Forney, Samuel J 252, 257 1
Forney, Susannah 228 1
Forney, Walter S 240 1
Fornwalk, John 220 3
Forrest G Moler 8 1
Forrest, Charles L 210a 2
Forrest, Charlotte E 214 1
Forrest, Daniel 210 1
Forrest, Daniel 32 3
Forrest, Daniel 188 2
Forrest, Daniel W 217, 234, 240 1
Forrest, David A 217 1
Forrest, Edwin S 219 1
Forrest, H Jonathan 57 2
Forrest, Jacob 228 1
Forrest, Jeremiah 228, 229 1
Forrest, Jerimiah 129 3
Forrest, Jerimiah C 205 3
Forrest, John Q 228 1
Forrest, Jonathan 14 2
Forrest, Lilly M 233 1
Forrest, Maria S 234 1
Forrest, Nelson 116 1
Forrest, Otho L 217 1
Forrest, Samuel W 228 1
Forrest, Solomon 217, 228, 240 1
Forrest, Thelma M 87, 107 3
Forrest, Theodore 219 1
Fortney, David 177, 258 2
Fortney, David 217 1
Forvence, James 44 1
Fossett, Irwin W 239 1
Fossett, Roberta V 239, 243 1
Fossett, Talmage W 239 1
Fossett, Walter J 243 1
Foster, Annie E 214 1
Foster, Chas K 214 1
Foster, Clarence E 214 1
Foster, Elizabeth 214 1
Foster, James M 230 1
Foster, John 11 3
Foster, John Sr 171 3
Foster, Katie M 232 1
Foster, Sarah 240 1
Fouche, Clarence M 243 1
Fouche, Ellen L 243 1
Fouche, Frances R 225 1
Fouche, Harry W T 225 1
Fouche, Temple 243 1
Founce, Jacob 215 3
Founsten, John 110 1
Fouston, John 185 2
Fout 139 2
Fout, Ann E 210 1
Fout, Ann Rebecca 223, 229 1
Fout, Barbara 213 1
Fout, Blanch A 213 1
Fout, Boltzer 213 1
Fout, Bowyer B 231 1
Fout, C Will 290 2
Fout, Catherine C 223 1
Fout, Charity A R 234 1
Fout, Charles 214 1
Fout, Charlotte 214 1
Fout, Chas B 122 3
Fout, Chas W 241 1
Fout, Cora L 172 3
Fout, Daniel J 217 1
Fout, Edith C 219 1
Fout, Elizabeth 225, 237 1
Fout, Emma F 126 1
Fout, Geo 213 1
Fout, Geo C 223 1
Fout, Geo L 217 1
Fout, George 223, 225 1
Fout, George 37 3
Fout, George W 223 1
Fout, Grafton 31 3
Fout, Grafton 118 1
Fout, Greenbury 213, 223 1
Fout, Guy L 113 3
Fout, H 140 2
Fout, Henry 144, 225 1
Fout, Jno H 81 3
Fout, John 1 2
Fout, John H 213, 225, 229 1
Fout, John H 223 3
Fout, John William 231 1
Fout, Lauretta C 233 1
Fout, Lewis 91 1
Fout, Lewis 137 2
Fout, Lewis F 217 1
Fout, M W 213 1
Fout, M W 28 2
Fout, Magdalena 244 1
Fout, Margaret 234 1
Fout, Margaret A 189 3
Fout, Marie D 147 1
Fout, Marshall 165, 234, 235 1
Fout, Marshall 32 3
Fout, Mary C 235 1
Fout, Mary E 214 1
Fout, Mary H 239 1
Fout, Mary Jane 223 1
Fout, Mary M 234 1
Fout, Matilda M 147 1
Fout, Michael W 137, 234 1
Fout, Murray H 4 3
Fout, O T 234, 239 1

Fout, Otto T 13, 237 1
Fout, Peter 60, 70 1
Fout, Peter 124 2
Fout, Rachel 239 1
Fout, Rachel V 239 1
Fout, Ralph D 213 1
Fout, Raymond C 239 1
Fout, Sarah B 235 1
Fout, Sarah Blanche 241 1
Fout, Stephen S 126 1
Fout, Travers W 56 1
Fout, Wm 70 2
Fout, Wm 237, 241 1
Foutt, Catherine 237, 244 1
Foutt, Otho 237 1
Foutt, Peter 237 1
Foutz 71 3
Foutz, Catherine 236 2
Foutz, Chas 214 1
Foutz, David 11 2
Foutz, Ethel C 219 1
Foutz, Geo P 183 1
Foutz, George 14 3
Foutz, Grafton 34 1
Foutz, Issac 236 2
Foutz, John H 226 3
Foutz, Joseph 14 2
Foutz, M W 96, 160 3
Foutz, Michael W 181 2
Fowler, A May 73, 211, 213 1
Fowler, Alice 210 1
Fowler, Ann Eliza 238 1
Fowler, Dora C 217 1
Fowler, Gilbert 223 1
Fowler, Henry 225 1
Fowler, James 207 1
Fowler, Mary 225 1
Fowler, Mary E 223 1
Fowler, Perry 238 1
Fowler, Perry 238 1
Fowler, Zadock 88 1
Fowley, Howard C 203 3
Fox, Adolphus 196 1
Fox, Anna 30 1
Fox, Baltzer 22 2
Fox, Baltzer 210, 213, 234 1
Fox, C T 72 1
Fox, C V 124 3
Fox, Calvin C 48 1
Fox, Calvin O C 219, 230 1
Fox, Caroline M 219 1
Fox, Caroline T 166 2
Fox, Carrie E 215 1
Fox, Catherine 214 1
Fox, Catherine A 222 1
Fox, Catherine D 225 1
Fox, Charles L 215 1
Fox, Charles L H 215 1
Fox, Charles R 215, 222 1
Fox, Chas 240, 279 1
Fox, Chas B 210 1
Fox, Chas L 72 2
Fox, Chas T 126 1
Fox, Clara Louisa 214 1
Fox, Clayton A 217 1
Fox, Cyrus 275 2
Fox, E A 4 1
Fox, Elvira F 215 1
Fox, Emily J 229 1
Fox, Emily L 219 1
Fox, Ephriam 39 2
Fox, Ernest A 214 1
Fox, Ernest A C 219 1
Fox, Esther L 235 1
Fox, Flora B 222 1
Fox, Florence E 217 1
Fox, Francis 72 1
Fox, Franklin C 271, 222, 229 1
Fox, Franklin C 2 3
Fox, Frederick 196 1
Fox, Geo 47, 196, 222 1
Fox, Geo 7, 68, 87 2
Fox, Geo L 203 3
Fox, Geo P 70, 79, 223 1
Fox, Geo T 32 1
Fox, Geo T 19 2
Fox, George 56, 191, 223, 253 1
Fox, George 226, 258 2
Fox, George 26 3
Fox, George P 224a 2
Fox, George P 38, 212 3
Fox, George W 20 3
Fox, H C 33 1
Fox, Henry 38, 122 3
Fox, Henry 33, 225 1
Fox, Henry 226 2
Fox, Henry C 197, 225 1
Fox, Henry C 113 3
Fox, Henry C 242, 247 2
Fox, Henry J 225 1
Fox, Henry K 219 1
Fox, Henry K C 254 2
Fox, Howard 225 1
Fox, Irving A 227, 243 1
Fox, J Howard 78 1
Fox, Jacob 40, 212 3
Fox, Jacob 117, 186, 215, 223, 228, 229, 234 1
Fox, Jacob 119 2
Fox, James 69 2
Fox, James 229 1
Fox, James B 229 1
Fox, Jeremiah 230, 234 1
Fox, Jesse R 30 1
Fox, Jesse R 15 3
Fox, Jno E 70 3
Fox, John 223, 225, 228, 229 1
Fox, John 70, 113 3
Fox, John 224a 2
Fox, Joseph 138 2
Fox, Joseph J 230 1
Fox, Joseph J Sr 72 1
Fox, Julia A 215, 230 1
Fox, Lena A 233 1
Fox, Leslie W 30 1
Fox, Letha A 227 1
Fox, Lewis M 42 1
Fox, Littleton C 42, 219, 229 1
Fox, Littleton C 132 2
Fox, Maggie 106 2
Fox, Martin G 235 1
Fox, Mary 234 1
Fox, Mary Ann 235 1
Fox, Mary E 42, 83, 235 1
Fox, Mary M 234 1
Fox, Melvin T 215 1
Fox, Pearl C 199 2
Fox, Robert E 215 1
Fox, Samuel C 222 1
Fox, Sarah A 235 1
Fox, Sarah S 240 1
Fox, Sarah S 242 2
Fox, Singleton 240 1
Fox, Susan 240 1
Fox, T C 92 1
Fox, T C 153 2
Fox, Thos 223 1
Fox, Thos C 243 1
Fox, Thos C 107 2
Fox, Viola Man 42 1
Fox, Wm J 72 1
Fox, Wm O 219 1
Fox, Zelphia C, Jr 42 1
Foxx, Jesse 171 2
Foy, Kathryn 214 1
Frailey, Carson P 215 1
Frailey, Clara M 79 1
Frailey, Clarence G 215 1
Frailey, Thos E 243 1
Frailey, Thos J 215 1
Fraizer, Henry 64 3
Fraley, Annie Laura 214 1
Fraley, C J 239 1
Fraley, Chas 172 3
Fraley, Chas H 214 1
Fraley, Christiana V 233 1
Fraley, Clarence 235 1
Fraley, Clarence G 44 3
Fraley, Estella C 239 1
Fraley, Francis M 234 1
Fraley, Frank W 99 1
Fraley, J Baker 230 1
Fraley, J Samuel 230 1
Fraley, John 228 1
Fraley, John H 201 1
Fraley, L H 214, 229 1

Fraley, L H 56 3
Fraley, Lewis 214 1
Fraley, Lewis H 233, 234 1
Fraley, Lewis H 20 3
Fraley, Mahlon A 234 1
Fraley, Mary A 229 1
Fraley, Mary Ann 234, 235 1
Fraley, Oscar 223 3
Fraley, Oscar D 235 1
Fraley, Susan E 8 2
Fraley, Thos J 31 2
Frame, J Henry 230 1
Frame, Richard 239 1
Francis, George 223 1
Franer, James 26 1
Franer, V H 195 3
Frank, George 223 1
Franklin, Alice May 210 1
Franklin, Calvin L 215 1
Franklin, Charles 30 1
Franklin, Eliza Ann 243 1
Franklin, James 63 2
Franklin, John 214 3
Franklin, Joshua 270 1
Franklin, Noah J 187 3
Franklin, Thomas S 243 1
Franklin, Zephaniah 244 1
Frasher, Joan [sic] 120 1
Fray, Carl W 215 1
Frazier, Annette P 210 1
Frazier, C A [?] 18 1
Frazier, Clifford A 214, 217 1
Frazier, Clifford B 4 1
Frazier, Clifford L 126 1
Frazier, David 2 3
Frazier, David 8 2
Frazier, David 217 1
Frazier, E D 217 1
Frazier, Edw H 223 1
Frazier, Geo 76, 228, 237 1
Frazier, Geo 214 2
Frazier, Geo W 179, 223, 229, 278 1
Frazier, George W H 56 1
Frazier, H C 35, 211 2
Frazier, H C 117, 279 1
Frazier, Harriet S 56 1
Frazier, Henry 76, 225, 228, 243, 271, 279 1
Frazier, Henry 208, 214 2
Frazier, Henry 96 3
Frazier, James 240 1
Frazier, Jeremiah 237 1
Frazier, John 177 1
Frazier, John H 40 1
Frazier, John S 57 2
Frazier, John S 230, 243 1
Frazier, John Stone 228 1
Frazier, John T 229, 264 1
Frazier, Levi 23 1
Frazier, Mary 234 1
Frazier, Mary F 230 1
Frazier, Otho 237 1
Frazier, Selena M 240 1
Frazier, Stanley F 240 1
Frazier, T O S 240 1
Frazier, Thomas 243 1
Frazier, Victoria A 225 1
Frazier, Wm 229 1
Fream, Aaron 99 1
Frean, Aaron 210 1
Frean, Elizabeth 210 1
Freaner, Wm 224a 2
Frear, Jane 228 1
Frebush, Philip 238 1
Frederick County Nat'l Bank 234 2
Frederick, Jacob 144 2
Frederick, Nelson 237 1
Free, Dewit T 217 1
Free, Harry 85 2
Free, Mary G 28 1
Freed, Edwin 76, 217, 219 1
Freed, Emma J 229 1
Freed, Fannie 67 1
Freed, Fannie M 219 1
Freed, J D 229 1
Freeman, Edw D 67 2
Freese, Mary M 172 2
Freeze, Geo 244 1
Freeze, Geo 185 2
Freeze, George 223 1
Freeze, Howard W 229 1
Freeze, J M 244, 265 1
Freeze, J M 160 3
Freeze, Jacob 234 1
Freeze, Jennie N 230 1
Freeze, John 25 1
Freeze, John D 164 1
Freeze, Joseph 229, 244 1
Freeze, Joseph 51, 287 2
Freeze, Joseph C Jr 231 1
Freeze, Joseph C Sr 231 1
Freeze, Josiah 230 1
Freeze, Jossiah[sic] 234 1
Freeze, Lloyd M 229 2
Freeze, Mary 223 1
Freeze, Michael 234 1
Freeze, Susan 230 1
Freeze, W J 265 1
Freeze, Wilbur R 231 1
Freeze, William J 229 1
Freeze, William Jet al 2 3
Freeze, Wm 80 2
Freeze, Wm J 244 1
Freit, Christian 214 1
Freitt, Elizabeth Ann 240 1
Freitt, Sarah 240 1
French, Annie E 210 1
French, F J 222 1
Frerie, A W 229 1
Frerie, Anthony W 210 1
Frerie, Charles C 215 1
Frerie, Charles W F 215, 230 1
Frerie, J A W 229 1
Frerie, J Frank 210 1
Frerie, John F 230, 235 1
Frerie, Mary F 235 1
Freshman, John W 210 1
Freshour, A J 55 3
Freshour, Amanda E 214, 230 1
Freshour, Ann S 223 1
Freshour, Anna 210 1
Freshour, Catherine 214, 223, 243 1
Freshour, Charles E 214 1
Freshour, Chas 214 1
Freshour, Chas E 234 1
Freshour, Chas H 210 1
Freshour, Chas N 32 3
Freshour, Frederick 222 1
Freshour, Frederick 120 3
Freshour, Geo 137, 186 2
Freshour, Geo 223 1
Freshour, Geo C 223, 228 1
Freshour, Geo W 223 1
Freshour, Geo W 169 2
Freshour, George 31 3
Freshour, George 223 1
Freshour, Harry B 239 1
Freshour, Irmo[sic] 250 1
Freshour, Julia Ann 223 1
Freshour, Laura V 233 1
Freshour, M L 41 1
Freshour, Margaret 222, 234 1
Freshour, Martin L 123 1
Freshour, Martin L 32 3
Freshour, Mary C 223, 234 1
Freshour, Nancy 223, 234 1
Freshour, Richard H N 239 1
Freshour, Robert A 239 1
Freshour, Roy G 108 2
Freshour, U G 223 1
Freshour, Ulyses G 234, 243 1
Fresse, Catherine 214 1
Frey, Alfred M 210 1
Frey, D C 219 1
Frey, David R 230 1
Frey, E 210 1
Frey, Elizabeth 219, 220 1

Frey, Emory 49 1
Frey, Emory 199 2
Frey, Ephriam 219 1
Frey, Henry 219, 225 1
Frey, James 230 1
Frey, James L 230 1
Frey, John 219 1
Frey, John M 229 1
Frey, Joseph 229 1
Frey, Mary C 219 1
Frey, Mary E 234 1
Frey, Robert 244 1
Frey, Sophia M 229 1
Frey, Susan 229 1
Frey, Wm H 244 1
Frick, George 40 1
Friday, Frederick 222, 225 1
Friday, Frederick W 225 1
Friday, Henry 225, 240 1
Friday, John H 222 1
Friday, John M 229 1
Friday, Salome 229 1
Friday, Sarah E 240 1
Friend, Jennie Mrs 45 3
Fries, David H 70 3
Frieze, George 223 1
Frieze, Michael 223 1
Fringer, Jacob 228 1
Fringer, Jacob Jr 228 1
Fringer, Jacob Sr 229 1
Fringer, Nicholas 293 2
Frior, Jacob 149, 150 3
Frior, John 202 3
Frish, J Murray 18 1
Fritchie, Albert 228 1
Fritchie, Barbara 213 1
Fritchie, John C 76, 228, 229 1
Fritt, Edw 27 2
Fritz, Ada R 233 1
Fritz, Dorothy B 235 1
Fritz, Ira Kate 227 1
Fritz, Jack W 235 1
Fritz, James M 243 1
Fritz, Lewis A 233 1
Fritz, Margaret Smith 235 1
Fritz, Paul O 243 1
Fritz, Ralph S 233 1
Fritz, Virginia I 243 1
Frizell, E L 52 1
Frizzell, Enoch L 219 1
Frizzell, Wm B 219 1
Frizzle, Eli H 9 1
Frizzle, Nimrod 56, 219 1
Frobey, Robert E 222 3
Frock, Abraham J 211 1
Frock, Catherine Savilla 240 1
Frock, Daniel 38 2
Frock, Daniel 217 1
Frock, Levi R 211 1
Frock, Luther N 210 1
Frock, Michael 211, 217, 234 1
Frock, Michael Jr 234 1
Frock, Michael Jr 185 2
Frock, Michael Sr 185 2
Frock, Samuel E 210 1
Frock, Wm 234, 240 1
Frocks, J W 210 1
Fromke, A J 225 1
Fromke, August 210 1
Fromke, Augustus J 210 1
Fromke, H W 60 1
Fromke, Harry J 210, 225 1
Fromke, Henry W 225 1
Fromke, J A 210 1
Fromke, Margaret E 225 1
Fromke, Sophia 210 1
Fromke, W H 210 1
Fromwalt, John 87 2
Frost, Absalom 44 1
Frost, Eli 210, 239, 257 1
Frost, Eli 2 3
Frost, Eli 236 2
Frueger, Jacob 184 3
Frushour, C N 145 2
Frushour, Charles N 215 1
Frushour, Elsie R 108, 119, 274 2
Frushour, Geo C 106 3
Frushour, Geo W 135 1
Frushour, H A 179 3
Frushour, Henry 135 1
Frushour, Mary Alice 215 1
Frushour, Roy G 108, 119 2
Frushour, Roy G 284 1
Fry, Charles M 240 1
Fry, Chas E 214 1
Fry, Chas W 214 1
Fry, David 219 1
Fry, David H 219 1
Fry, David H 49 2
Fry, Edward F 219 1
Fry, Eli A 220, 230 1
Fry, Elizabeth 215 1
Fry, Emma R 219 1
Fry, Ernest W 58 3
Fry, Hattie L 58 3
Fry, Jacob H 214 1
Fry, Jonathan 11 1
Fry, Joseph C 230 1
Fry, Mary J 235 1
Fry, Mary O 169 3
Fry, Mary V 240 1
Fry, Matthew 234 1
Fry, Paul C 169 3
Fry, Robert 239 1
Fry, Samuel W 241 1
Fry, Sarah E 240 1
Fry, Scott L 219, 240 1
Fry, Stanley W 241 1
Fry, Wm E 169 3
Frye, Elizabeth R 93 1
Frye, Emory V 93, 102 1
Frye, Esther M 145 3
Frye, Katie C 237 1
Frye, Owen 237 1
Frye, Wm W 244 1
Fulford, Elizabeth 12, 58 3
Fuller, Frances 222 1
Fulmer, Annie 214 1
Fulmer, Charlotte 214, 225 1
Fulmer, Cora J 214 1
Fulmer, Ella S 219 1
Fulmer, Frederick G 97 1
Fulmer, Geo A 214, 225 1
Fulmer, George A 223 1
Fulmer, George E 219 1
Fulmer, Hammon F 225 1
Fulmer, John L 230, 240, 244 1
Fulmer, Lewis 233 1
Fulmer, M H 28 3
Fulmer, Marion C 230 1
Fulmer, Marshall H 223 1
Fulmer, Marshall H 3, 73 3
Fulmer, Mary M 235 1
Fulmer, Mollie R 235 1
Fulmer, Nora E G 278 1
Fulmer, Sarah 240 1
Fulmer, Wm 244 1
Fulrot, Henry 225 1
Fulton, Alexander 93 2
Fulton, Barbara 213 1
Fulton, C H 227 2
Fulton, Chas 219 1
Fulton, Chas E 100 1
Fulton, Chas H 229 1
Fulton, Emily J 219 1
Fulton, George 219 1
Fulton, H C 82 3
Fulton, H Clay 205 3
Fulton, H Clay 32, 223 1
Fulton, H K 262 2
Fulton, John 100, 118, 225, 229, 234 1
Fulton, Margaret 234, 239 1
Fulton, Mary A 100 1
Fulton, N A 57, 91 3
Fulton, N A 225, 235 1
Fulton, N A 23 2
Fulton, Newton A 32, 48 1
Fulton, Robert 26, 171 2
Fulton, Robert 32, 228, 234, 237 1
Fulton, Robt 171 2
Fulton, Solomon 11 2
Fulton, Solomon 117, 239 1
Fulton, Wm 93 2
Fultz, Albert M 113 3

Fultz, Mary S 235 1
Fultz, Wm H 235 1
Fundenburg 13 1
Fundenburg, Daniel 217 1
Fundenburg, David 217 1
Fundenburg, Elizabeth 219 1
Fundenburg, Esther 219 1
Fundenburg, Henry 70 3
Fundenburg, Henry 27 2
Fundenburg, Henry 219, 225, 263 1
Fundenfurg, Noah 32 1
Funk, Annie B 225 1
Funk, Annie E 210, 219 1
Funk, C A 242 2
Funk, Cora V 240 1
Funk, Edgar H 219 1
Funk, Elmer B 240 1
Funk, Georgiana S 243 1
Funk, Harry B 225 1
Funk, John B 46 3
Funk, Mary M 242 2
Funk, Silas C 240 1
Funk, Veniah B 243 1
Funk, Wilbur H 210 1
Funk, Wilbur Hamilton 244 1
Funk, Wm 132 2
Funk, Wm H 219 1
Funston, John 228 1
Funston, Sarah 228, 240 1
Furgueson, Annanïas 219 1
Furgueson, Eli 219 1
Furguson, Arthur J 210 1
Furguson, Carrie H 210 1
Furguson, Wm 244 1
Furney, Abraham 100 1
Furrey, Elijah 210 1
Furry, Abraham 210 1
Furry, Mollie M 240 1
Furry, Samuel B 240 1
Furshour, Chas E 75 3
Fuss, Asbury M 210 1
Fuss, Carrie V 210 1
Fuss, Charles R 217a 2
Fuss, Daniel 217 1
Fuss, Edw M 219 1
Fuss, Helen 169 1
Fuss, John 228, 229, 278 1
Fuss, John M 169 1
Fuss, John M 154 2
Fuss, Mary C 219 1
Fuss, Wm 229, 244 1
Fuss, Wm 8 2
Fute, C Floyd 124 1
Gabhart, John 184 3
Gabriel, Mariah L 245 2
Gabriel, Peter 212a 2
Gaines, Ruth Louise 278 1
Gaither, Bertha W 248 1
Gaither, Caroline A 249 1
Gaither, Edw 38, 45, 163 2
Gaither, Edw 253, 279 1
Gaither, Ephriam 1 3
Gaither, Ephriam 34, 279 1
Gaither, Francis S 82, 283 1
Gaither, Geo 138, 150, 159 2
Gaither, Geo 118, 229, 280 1
Gaither, George 229 2
Gaither, George 257 1
Gaither, H C 68 2
Gaither, Henry 41 1
Gaither, Henry 229 2
Gaither, Henry C 171 2
Gaither, Henry C 152, 260, 283 1
Gaither, J D 249 2
Gaither, J Dorsey 248 1
Gaither, Jesse S 177 1
Gaither, John 264, 266 1
Gaither, John 89 2
Gaither, John D 188 3
Gaither, John D 177, 271, 283 1
Gaither, John D 218, 250 2
Gaither, John W 175 1
Gaither, Juliet E 249 1
Gaither, Margaret 265, 271 1
Gaither, Martha 271 1
Gaither, Martha Sophia 271 1
Gaither, Nannie L 108 2
Gaither, R D 177 1
Gaither, Richard 271 1
Gaither, Richard D 177 2
Gaither, Sarah 57 1
Gaither, Stewart 156, 253 1
Gaither, Stewart 8, 124 3
Gaither, Stewart 14 2
Gaither, Stuart 279 1
Gaither, T H 260 1
Gaither, Thos H 283 1
Gaither, W M 49 2
Gaither, W M 125 1
Gaither, William 247 2
Gaither, Wm 245, 283 1
Gaither, Wm B 60 1
Gaither, Wm M 260, 265, 283 1
Galalpie, James 263 1
Gale, E P 189 1
Gale, Geo 245 1
Gale, Henry E 260 1
Gale, Mary E 260 1
Gall, Carl S 250 1
Gall, Henry L 272 1
Gall, Linnie 270 1
Gall, Lottie E 250 1
Gall, Lottie E 161 2
Gall, Mary J 272 1
Gallager, Daniel 135 1
Gallager, James A 26 3
Gallager, Michael P 26 3
Gallager, Richard 135 1
Gallagher, Aloysius J 245 1
Gallagher, Ann G 245 1
Gallagher, Richard 117 1
Gallagher, Thos P 196 3
Gallaher, Richard 174 3
Gallaher, T D 60 1
Gallet, John 42 3
Galley, Jacob 263 1
Galley, John 144 1
Galley, Peter 263 1
Galligher, Emanuel 253 1
Galligher, James 210a 2
Galligher, Richard 210 1
Gallion, Harriot 1 1
Gallion, John P 260, 264 1
Gallion, John P 246 2
Gallion, Wm 283 1
Galt, Elizabeth 253 1
Galt, Hy 22 1
Galt, John 263 1
Galt, Lucy H 246 2
Galt, Matthew 271 1
Galt, Moses 263 1
Galt, Samuel 82, 257, 271 1
Galt, Samuel 116, 137 2
Galt, Sarah 22 1
Galt, Sterling 46, 107, 116, 137, 186, 265 2
Galt, Sterling 82, 116, 257, 263 1
Galt, Wm 142, 263, 280 1
Galut, Wm [sic] 283 1
Galwith, Peter 70 3
Gambil, David 53 3
Gambill, A F 9 3
Gambill, David 53 3
Gamble, David 64 3
Gamble, David 252, 283 1
Gamble, Joseph 266 1
Gamble, Wm 283 1
Gambrill, A S 245 1
Gambrill, Alan E 253 1
Gambrill, Annie N 245 1
Gambrill, Antoinette F 67 3
Gambrill, Antoinette F 245 1
Gambrill, C S 245 1
Gambrill, C Staley 245, 250 1
Gambrill, Cyrus 250 1
Gambrill, Daniel 187 2
Gambrill, David 252 1
Gambrill, David 1, 137, 159, 169, 186, 214 2
Gambrill, J H 37 1
Gambrill, J H 51, 92, 143, 144, 166 2
Gambrill, J H 91 3
Gambrill, J H III 125 2

Gambrill, J H Jr 91 3
Gambrill, James H 72, 245, 266 1
Gambrill, James H 67, 165 3
Gambrill, James H 110 2
Gambrill, James H 3rd 266 1
Gambrill, James H Jr 266 1
Gambrill, James H Jr 110, 199 2
Gambrill, Jas H Jr 218 3
Gambrill, Joseph 279 1
Gambrill, Samuel 279 1
Gambrill, Staley Helfenstein 280 1
Gambrill, Wanetta M 280 1
Gambrill, Wm 279 1
Gambrill[?], Ann 263 1
Gandolfo, A H 59 1
Gannon, Albert B 266 1
Gannon, Cora I 284 1
Gannon, James M 266 1
Gannon, Mary E 283 1
Gannon, Wm H 283 1
Gant, Ada G 148 1
Gant, Madora M 273 1
Gantriss, James E 265 1
Garber, A B 249 1
Garber, Abraham 245 1
Garber, Abraham 39 2
Garber, Addison D 245 1
Garber, C A 164 1
Garber, C N 22 2
Garber, C N 249 1
Garber, Catherine 249 1
Garber, Cephas M 245 1
Garber, Charles E 245 1
Garber, Chas E 265 1
Garber, Christian 183 1
Garber, Christian 141 3
Garber, Christian 225a, 271 2
Garber, Christian N 249 1
Garber, Christian N 234 2
Garber, Earl R 254 1
Garber, Edw 249, 254 1
Garber, Elizabeth 253, 277 1
Garber, Emma J 254 1
Garber, Ephriaim [sic] 90 1
Garber, Ernest W 253, 254 1
Garber, Florence O 256 1
Garber, Geo 166 1
Garber, Geo 89 2
Garber, Geo W 82, 229, 254 1
Garber, Geo W 71 3
Garber, George W 257, 272 1
Garber, Glenn O 221 3
Garber, Glenn O 257 1
Garber, Hannah 260 1
Garber, Harry H 265 1
Garber, Isabelle 279 1
Garber, James E 265 1
Garber, John 263, 264 1
Garber, John 1, 18, 217 3
Garber, John 242 2
Garber, John H 265 1
Garber, John of S 253 1
Garber, Jonathan 70 3
Garber, Jonathan 263, 265 1
Garber, Kenley E 283 1
Garber, Lela C 270 1
Garber, Lelia C 277 1
Garber, Margaret 245 1
Garber, Margaret A 283 1
Garber, Margaret E 257 1
Garber, Margaret E 227 3
Garber, Mary A 254 1
Garber, Mary C 272 1
Garber, Paul C 277 1
Garber, Rachel 245 1
Garber, Rachel J 278 1
Garber, Rebecca 152 1
Garber, Soloman 54 3
Garber, Solomon 164, 263, 278, 279 1
Garber, Solomon 14 3
Garber, Wm 28 2
Garber, Wm 240, 279, 283 1
Garber, Wm H 283 1
Gardiner, Edith S 254 1
Gardiner, George 19 3
Gardiner, Margaret 196 2
Gardner, Alonza A 210 3
Gardner, Clement E 250 1
Gardner, Edith S 254 1
Gardner, Edith S 200 2
Gardner, Edw G 83 2
Gardner, Eliza T 270, 283 1
Gardner, Elizabeth L 254 1
Gardner, Emily T Wood 189 3
Gardner, Fannie M 256 1
Gardner, George C 257 1
Gardner, Isabelle 210 3
Gardner, John 129 3
Gardner, Lewis J 270 1
Gardner, Lorenzo S 270 1
Gardner, Margaret McP 250 1
Gardner, Mary A 257 1
Gardner, Ray V 254 1
Gardner, Roy 28, 147 1
Gardner, Roy 9 2
Gardner, Virginia 270 1
Gardner, W A 136 1
Gardner, W Arthur 68 1
Gardner, Wm 283 1
Gardner, Wm A 270 1
Gardner, Wm P 283 1
Garee, Alfred A 245 1
Garee, Gertrude 245 1
Garee, Isaac A 258, 262 1
Garee, Mildred 262 1
Garhame, James 30 1
Garmendia, Carlos de 254 1
Garmon, Ella E M 253 1
Garnand, Daniel 272 1
Garnand, Daniel 128 2
Garnand, Daniel S 252 1
Garnand, Daniel U 252 1
Garnand, George 257 1
Garnand, Ira H 262 1
Garnand, James U 252 1
Garnand, John 257 1
Garnand, John F 252 1
Garnand, Joseph 232 2
Garnand, Joseph C 28 3
Garnand, Mary L 272 1
Garnand, N P 272 1
Garnand, Noah Preston 262 1
Garnand, Wm 263 1
Garner, B W H 248 1
Garner, Henry 260 1
Garner, Mary E 272 1
Garner, Mary E 286 2
Garnhart, Catherine 249 1
Garret, Henry 100 1
Garrett, Barton 133, 248 1
Garrett, Barton 189 2
Garrett, E 120 3
Garrett, Erasmus 69 2
Garrett, Helen S 126 1
Garrett, John E 71 1
Garrett, Joseph B 265 1
Garrett, Warren 185 3
Garrett, Willard N 284 1
Garrett, William D 284 1
Garrett, William J 126 1
Garrett, Wm D . 72 2
Garrison, Wilbert A 284 1
Garrott, Ann 263 1
Garrott, Ann R 253 1
Garrott, Barton 264, 270, 271 1
Garrott, Barton B V 248 1
Garrott, Cora M 254 1
Garrott, E 26 1
Garrott, Edw 253, 263, 279 1
Garrott, Elizabeth 263, 279 1
Garrott, Emily A 234 1
Garrott, Erasmus 253, 254, 263, 264 1
Garrott, Erasmus F 253 1
Garrott, Erasueus 9 1
Garrott, George B 26, 254 1
Garrott, George B 200 2
Garrott, Hemima [sic] 265 1
Garrott, Henreanna 260 1

Garrott, J E 253 1
Garrott, John 264, 279 1
Garrott, John D 264 1
Garrott, John E 263 1
Garrott, John P 264 1
Garrott, Joseph 263 1
Garrott, Joseph 290 2
Garrott, Joseph 41 3
Garrott, Joseph B 59 1
Garrott, Lydia M 248 1
Garrott, Martha E 264 1
Garrott, Matilda 253. 264, 271 1
Garrott, Sarah 253, 279 1
Garrott, Wm E F 244 1
Garry, Catherine R 249 1
Garry, Michael 271 1
Garry, Rosanna 271 1
Gartrell, Alfred 129 1
Gartrell, Alfred G 245 1
Gartrell, Ann 245 1
Gartrell, Annie M 257 1
Gartrell, Chas G 172 2
Gartrell, Edw 253 1
Gartrell, Francis W 253 1
Gartrell, Geo W 257 1
Gartrell, Greenbury 257 1
Gartrell, Jesse 245 1
Gartrell, Lillie M 129 1
Gartrell, Lucy 257 1
Gartrell, Martha 272 1
Gartrell, Martha A 273 1
Gartrell, Maurice E 273 1
Gartrell, Richard 245 1
Gartrell, Singleton 279 1
Garver, Grayson H 257 1
Garver, Guy G 257 1
Garver, Sadie E 257 1
Garver, William 284 1
Garver, Wm 283 1
Garver[?], Abdil 245 1
Gasnell, Adam 260 1
Gasnell, Levin 260 1
Gassaway, Geo H 257 1
Gassaway, Harriet B 257 1
Gassnell, Hamilton G 260 1
Gassoway, Nicholas J 275 1
Gastley, Earl L 256 1
Gastley, Effie M 256 1
Gastley, Frank L 256 1
Gatton, Benjamin 248 1
Gatton, Benjamin F 248 1
Gatton, E M 254 2
Gatton, James H 248, 264 1
Gatton, Wm 248 1
Gatty, Henry 165 3
Gatz, Christian 249 1
Gatz, Mary Ann 249 1
Gaugh, Ada C 129 2
Gaugh, Adam 8 2
Gaugh, Addie C 246 1
Gaugh, Alice M 265 1
Gaugh, Daniel 128 2
Gaugh, Daniel 252 1
Gaugh, Elizabeth 264 1
Gaugh, Emma F 266 1
Gaugh, Geo 228 1
Gaugh, Glenn W 283 1
Gaugh, J W 252 1
Gaugh, Jacob H 266 1
Gaugh, John 264 1
Gaugh, John M 265 1
Gaugh, Jonathan 283 1
Gaugh, Jonothan 192 3
Gaugh, M A 129 2
Gaugh, M A 92 1
Gaugh, M C 129 2
Gaugh, Mamie E 235 1
Gaugh, Mamie S 210 1
Gaugh, Marshall A 143 2
Gaugh, Wilson A 283 1
Gaugh, Wm F 283 1
Gault, Jonathan 39 2
Gault, Samuel 253 1
Gaut, Flora 256 1
Gaut, Wm 210 1
Gaver, A W 72, 140, 257, 280 1
Gaver, A W 56, 68, 124 3
Gaver, A W 16 2
Gaver, Ada R 266 1
Gaver, Alford W 23, 63, 137, 245 1
Gaver, Alfred 40 2
Gaver, Alfred W 2, 18, 108 2
Gaver, Annie E 245 1
Gaver, C H 260 1
Gaver, Calvin L 249 1
Gaver, Caroline 249 1
Gaver, Carrie E 252 1
Gaver, Charles C 250 1
Gaver, Chas L 264, 271 1
Gaver, Cordelia 266 1
Gaver, Cordelia M 250 1
Gaver, Daniel 179 3
Gaver, Daniel 252 1
Gaver, David T 252, 266 1
Gaver, Elias 253 1
Gaver, Elias 54, 167 3
Gaver, Eliza C B 253 1
Gaver, Elizabeth 253 1
Gaver, F E 260 1
Gaver, Felton 253 1
Gaver, Florence C 256 1
Gaver, Floyd F[?] 276 1
Gaver, G E 234 1
Gaver, G W 247 2
Gaver, Geo 8 2
Gaver, Geo D 38, 265 1
Gaver, Geo D 15 2
Gaver, Geo W 257 1
Gaver, George 257 1
Gaver, George 42 3
Gaver, George 275 2
Gaver, George W 257 1
Gaver, Glenn 88 1
Gaver, H L 210, 234, 270 1
Gaver, H S 266 1
Gaver, Harman 8 1
Gaver, Harman L 41, 257, 260 1
Gaver, Harman L 84, 106 2
Gaver, Harmon L 100, 196 3
Gaver, Harry S 266 1
Gaver, Henrietta E 260 1
Gaver, Henry 260, 264, 265 1
Gaver, Herman L 135 1
Gaver, Herman L 258 2
Gaver, J 100 3
Gaver, J 257 1
Gaver, J L 260 1
Gaver, J O 265 1
Gaver, J W 67, 176 3
Gaver, J W 177 1
Gaver, J W 35 2
Gaver, J Wm 266 1
Gaver, Jacob 264 1
Gaver, James H 266 1
Gaver, Jeff 253 1
Gaver, Jennie E 266 1
Gaver, Jeremiah 15 2
Gaver, Jerome E 245, 266 1
Gaver, John 57 1
Gaver, John 210a 2
Gaver, John 31 3
Gaver, John C 250 1
Gaver, John D 71 1
Gaver, John P 253, 264, 271 1
Gaver, John T 160, 167 3
Gaver, John T 264, 266, 271, 283 1
Gaver, Jos W 159 1
Gaver, Jos W 254 2
Gaver, Joseph 252 1
Gaver, Joseph 192 3
Gaver, Joseph 35, 40, 52, 58, 122, 124 2
Gaver, Joseph 41, 197, 240, 253, 264, 265, 271 1
Gaver, Joseph L 135, 265 1
Gaver, Joseph T 19 1
Gaver, Joseph W 6, 55, 65, 160 3
Gaver, Joseph W 33, 48, 61, 152, 265, 266 1
Gaver, Kellsie A 268 1
Gaver, Laura E 141 3
Gaver, Lee J 61 1
Gaver, Lewis F 196 3
Gaver, Lewis F 260, 270 1

Gaver, Lewis F 227a 2
Gaver, Lillie R 291 2
Gaver, Lily R 255, 257 2
Gaver, Lula M 268 1
Gaver, M Lillian 245 1
Gaver, Margaret 271 1
Gaver, Margaret Caroline 256 1
Gaver, Martin D 265, 272 1
Gaver, Mary 257, 271, 272 1
Gaver, Mary L Floyd F[?] 257 1
Gaver, O F 276, 280 1
Gaver, O J 55 3
Gaver, Oscar F 148 3
Gaver, Oscar F 280 1
Gaver, Oscar S 116 2
Gaver, Otha J 42 3
Gaver, Otho J 249 1
Gaver, Peter 268, 276 1
Gaver, Philip A 197 3
Gaver, Raymond E 270, 279 1
Gaver, Samuel 279 1
Gaver, Sophia C 135 1
Gaver, Susan R 280 1
Gaver, Susn R [sic] 280 1
Gaver, T C 272 1
Gaver, T F 188, 271 2
Gaver, Tilghman 225 1
Gaver, Tilghman F 11, 72, 276 2
Gaver, Tilghman F 282 1
Gaver, W E 38 1
Gaver, W H 250 1
Gaver, Wm E 73 1
Gaver, Wm H 14, 264, 282 1
Gaver, Wm S 272 1
Gaver, Zona K 146 3
Gavire, Sophia 279 1
Gavis, Adam 40 2
Gaylor, Alice I 245 1
Gaylor, Daniel A 245 1
Gear, George 257 1
Gear, George 268 2
Gear, Peter 257 1
Geasey, Daniel 252 1
Geasey, Elizabeth 253 1
Geasey, Geo W 257 1
Geasey, Ida V 260 1
Geasey, John 8 2
Geasey, John 263, 265 1
Geasey, John A 38, 265 1
Geasey, Luther T 257 1
Geasey, Millard F 272 1
Geasey, Wm 283 1
Geasey, Wm H 283 1
Geates, Elizabeth 253 1
Geatley, Henry 37 1
Gebhardt, Geo 163 1
Gebhart, Frederick A 179 1
Gebhart, George 257 1
Gebhart, John G 179 1
Gedulick, Susanna 279 1
Gedultig, Catherine 249 1
Gedultig, Ezra 249 1
Gedultig, George 257 1
Gedultig, Henry 57 1
Gedultig, Jacob 257 1
Gedultig,[?] Henry 270 1
Geesey, Amelia M 265 1
Geesey, Augustus M 257 1
Geesey, C E 265 1
Geesey, Chas G 271 1
Geesey, Elias 253 1
Geesey, George 257 1
Geesey, Henry 260 1
Geesey, Ida V 12 2
Geesey, Jacob 91 1
Geesey, John 263 1
Geesey, John 275 2
Geesey, John A 113 3
Geesey, John A 238 2
Geesey, John T 265 1
Geesey, M F 113 3
Geesey, Mary A 271 1
Geesey, Thomas 39 2
Geesey, Thos 29 2
Geesey, William C 28 3
Geetheng, Adam 214 3
Geigas, Mathias 271 1
Geigas, Susannah 271, 279 1
Geiger, Eve Maria 253 1
Geiger, Leonard 270 1
Geisbert, Alexander H 245 1
Geisbert, Alice V 250 1
Geisbert, Ann 245 1
Geisbert, Bessie L 248 1
Geisbert, Charles G 58 3
Geisbert, Charles G 101 1
Geisbert, Chas G 73 3
Geisbert, Christian 249 1
Geisbert, Claude Wachter 250 1
Geisbert, Hester A 260 1
Geisbert, Jonathan 43 2
Geisbert, Margaret E 44 3
Geisbert, R H Jr 106 2
Geisbert, Roger H 248, 266 1
Geisbert, Sarah E 249 1
Geisbert, Stewart A 280 1
Geisbert, Stewart A Jr 280 1
Geisbert, Upton M 282 1
Geisburt, Ann 258 2
Geiselman, Geo K 84 1
Geiselman, Jesse 229 1
Geiselman, Laura V 283 1
Geiselman, M 58 1
Geiselman, Michel 213 3
Geiselman, Wm H 283 1
Geiser, Norman A 102, 167 2
Geisinger, Geo R 205 3
Geisinger, Jacob 180 3
Geisinger, John 53 3
Geisinger, Samuel 249 1
Geisinger, Samuel 1 3
Geisler, James E 266 1
Geisler, James W 266 1
Geisler, Jennie A 266 1
Geisler, Martha S 266 1
Geissinger, Samuel 280 1
Geitner, John 265 1
Gelenns Falls Indemnity Company 201 3
Gellelan, William 282 2
Gellwicks, Frederick 256 1
Gellwicks, J T 196 3
Geltier, D G 32 1
Gelwicks, Anne Carroll 246 1
Gelwicks, Emma 193 1
Gelwicks, Emma K 243, 265 1
Gelwicks, Emma K 254 1
Gelwicks, Geo 211 2
Gelwicks, Geo T 257, 265 1
Gelwicks, Harry R 257 1
Gelwicks, Isaac J 265 1
Gelwicks, J T 40 2
Gelwicks, J Thomas 265 1
Gelwicks, J Thomas 116 2
Gelwicks, J Thos 272 1
Gelwicks, James K 265 1
Gelwicks, John 5 2
Gelwicks, John T 278 1
Gelwicks, Joseph 5 2
Gelwicks, Joseph T 257 1
Gelwicks, Mary 189 3
Gelwicks, Mary B 265, 272 1
Gelwicks, Robert H 5 2
Gelwicks, Robert H 201 1
Gelwicks, Thos 199 2
Gelwicks, Thos 257, 278 1
George Hoffman 85 1
George, H Y 67 2
George, Harry Y 166, 270 1
George, Harry Y 75 2
George, Lena L 270 1
George, S W 215 3
Gephart, Catherine 257 1
Gephart, Charles Wm 250 1
Gephart, Franklin V 270 1
Gephart, Frederick A 256 1
Gephart, Geo 67, 195 3
Gephart, Geo 228 1
Gephart, Geo Jr 228 1
Gephart, Jacob 263 1

Gephart, John 5 2
Gephart, John 263, 264, 271 1
Gephart, John Jr 263 1
Gephart, John Sr 263 1
Gephart, Lewis 257 1
Gephart, Louisa V 270 1
Gephart, Mary 271 1
Gerbig, Robert H 111 1
Gere, John A 202 2
Gerith, Christian 249 1
Gerith, Henry 249 1
Gerlach, Dora E 252 1
Gerley, Thomas Jr 164 1
German, J A 219 1
Gernand, Andrew A 245 1
Gernand, Annie M 246 1
Gernand, Celeste 180 3
Gernand, Chas D 249 1
Gernand, D J 265 1
Gernand, D N 85 1
Gernand, D U 252 1
Gernand, Daniel 252 1
Gernand, Daniel 184 3
Gernand, Daniel J 245, 249 1
Gernand, David Ezra 246 1
Gernand, David J 252 1
Gernand, E Florence 82 1
Gernand, E J 253, 272 1
Gernand, E J 45, 72 3
Gernand, Ellen 89 2
Gernand, Eugene J 253 1
Gernand, Fannie E 249 1
Gernand, Frank D 246 1
Gernand, J A 117 1
Gernand, Jacob 25, 28, 119 2
Gernand, Jacob 171, 184, 185 3
Gernand, Jacob 192, 201, 205, 207, 263, 264, 283 1
Gernand, Joel 101 2
Gernand, Joel 252 1
Gernand, John 263 1
Gernand, John A 214 1
Gernand, Joseph 263 1
Gernand, Joseph 106, 134 2
Gernand, Joseph A 22 2
Gernand, Joseph C 119, 233 1
Gernand, Joseph C 91, 180 3
Gernand, Joseph G 253 1
Gernand, Julia A 265 1
Gernand, L J 20 3
Gernand, Mary E 252 1
Gernand, Wm 271, 283 1
Gernard, Joseph A 60 1
Gernard, Joseph C 72, 107 1
Gernth, Barbara 248 1
Gerrich, Mary E 272 1
Gerrich, Samuel A 272 1
Gerrick, John K 259 2
Gerrick, Mary E 126 1
Gerrith, Henry 14 2
Gerrith, John 263 1
Gerrith, Joseph 263 1
Gerther, Adam 82 1
Gertz, Fannie B 58 3
Gertz, Otho 58 3
Gesey, Ida N 110 1
Getsendanner, Daniel 214 3
Gettier, Daniel 186 2
Gettings, James 67 2
Gettings, Wm 67 2
Getty, Elsie 73 1
Getty, Elsie Birely 79 1
Getty, Elsie Birely 254 1
Getty, Elsie Birely 73, 79, 254 1
Getty, J Walter 79 1
Getz, Frederick 256 1
Getz, Mary 256 1
Getzendaned, Henry 184 3
Getzendanner, A E 100 3
Getzendanner, A V H 32 1
Getzendanner, Abraham 79, 90, 112, 245, 264 1
Getzendanner, Abram 117 1
Getzendanner, Alexander 156 1
Getzendanner, Almetta 44 3
Getzendanner, Almetta E 245 1
Getzendanner, Ann R 245 1
Getzendanner, Annie M 279 1
Getzendanner, C E 264 1
Getzendanner, Catharine A 249 1
Getzendanner, Catherine 264 1
Getzendanner, Charlotte E 249 1
Getzendanner, Chas 156 1
Getzendanner, Christian 10, 249, 263 1
Getzendanner, Christian 203 3
Getzendanner, Christian 169 2
Getzendanner, D Jr 186 3
Getzendanner, Daniel 1, 39, 40, 163, 209, 227 3
Getzendanner, Daniel 22, 28, 106, 197 2
Getzendanner, Daniel 58, 71, 117, 204, 249, 252, 263, 271 1
Getzendanner, Daniel C 51 1
Getzendanner, David 91, 150 1
Getzendanner, E E 67 3
Getzendanner, Edw 252 1
Getzendanner, Elizabeth 20 3
Getzendanner, Elizabeth 253, 257, 264 1
Getzendanner, F Marion 252 1
Getzendanner, Geo 257 1
Getzendanner, Geo 14 2
Getzendanner, H F 24, 100 3
Getzendanner, H F 92 1
Getzendanner, Hannah 260 1
Getzendanner, Harvey F 233 1
Getzendanner, Henry 260 1
Getzendanner, J 250 2
Getzendanner, J D 276 2
Getzendanner, J W 263 1
Getzendanner, Jacob 234, 263, 264 1
Getzendanner, Jacob 76 2
Getzendanner, Jacob R 263, 264 1
Getzendanner, John 87, 163 3
Getzendanner, John 14, 19, 185 2
Getzendanner, John 71, 263, 264 1
Getzendanner, John D 263, 272 1
Getzendanner, John D 1, 8, 247 2
Getzendanner, John J 264 1
Getzendanner, John M 249 1
Getzendanner, John W 264 1
Getzendanner, Jonathan 263, 264, 279 1
Getzendanner, L V 270 1
Getzendanner, Laura V 271, 272 1
Getzendanner, Louis D 22 1
Getzendanner, M E 41, 229, 270 1
Getzendanner, M E 1, 8, 30, 116 2
Getzendanner, M Eugene 272 1
Getzendanner, M Eugene 15 2
Getzendanner, Marshall A 271 1
Getzendanner, Martha V 272 1
Getzendanner, Mary A 271 1
Getzendanner, Mary Ann 272 1
Getzendanner, Mary E 272 1
Getzendanner, Mary V 245 1
Getzendanner, Michael J 271 1
Getzendanner, S J G 264 1
Getzendanner, S P 79 1
Getzendanner, Samuel 115 2
Getzendanner, Samuel 264, 279 1
Getzendanner, Samuel T 79 1
Getzendanner, Sarah 279 1
Getzendanner, Sarah 115 2
Getzendanner, T E 203 3
Getzendanner, William R 284 1
Getzendenner, Daniel 247 2
Geyer, Barbara 248 1
Geyer, James M 264 1
Geyer, John W 264, 279 1

Geyer, John W 237 2
Geyer, Samuel 279 1
Gibbons, Austin C 265 1
Gibbons, C N 205 2
Gibbons, Geo 265, 266, 272 1
Gibbons, Jacob 265 1
Gibbons, Jacob H 265, 266 1
Gibbons, Jacob N 265, 272 1
Gibbons, Mary E 265, 272 1
Gibbons, Sarah N 140 1
Gibbons, Thomas G 192 3
Gibbs, Sarah M 279 1
Gibson, Basil 243 1
Gibson, Clara T 252 1
Gibson, Daniel Cyrus 252 1
Gibson, Ellen A 19 1
Gibson, Richard 37, 70 3
Gibson, Richard 1 2
Gibson, Samuel 185 3
Gibson, Thomas 282 1
Gibson, Virginia D 282 1
Gibson, W Lacy 229 1
Gibson, Wm 270, 283 1
Giddings, Alice 264 1
Giddings, James 264 1
Giddings, Louisa 264 1
Giesinger, Sarah 279 1
Giessinger, Samuel L 279 1
Giessler, Wm 283 1
Gigeous, Orpha E 276 1
Gilbert, Alice V 245 1
Gilbert, Ben 179 1
Gilbert, Benjamin 129, 201, 225, 228 1
Gilbert, Birdie S 84 1
Gilbert, Chas W 248, 253, 279 1
Gilbert, Dovia A 252 1
Gilbert, E M 179 3
Gilbert, E M 15 2
Gilbert, E M 30 1
Gilbert, E Marshall 279 1
Gilbert, Edw W 254 1
Gilbert, Eli Marshall 183 1
Gilbert, Eliza A 253 1
Gilbert, Elizabeth 253 1
Gilbert, Ely 253 1
Gilbert, Ephriam W 253 1
Gilbert, G S 257 1
Gilbert, Geo A 113, 187 3
Gilbert, Geo A 140 1
Gilbert, Geo H 257, 271 1
Gilbert, George 290 2
Gilbert, George A 207 3
Gilbert, George H 257 1
Gilbert, Hammond 253 1
Gilbert, Henry 260, 271 1
Gilbert, Isaac 263, 285 1
Gilbert, Isaac 254 2
Gilbert, J Milton 245 1
Gilbert, Jeremiah 229, 263 1
Gilbert, John 225, 285 1
Gilbert, John B 263, 265 1
Gilbert, John B 14 2
Gilbert, John W 260 1
Gilbert, Joseph 253 1
Gilbert, Joseph 101 2
Gilbert, Joshua 171 2
Gilbert, Marshall 71 3
Gilbert, Martha J 272, 279 1
Gilbert, Melvinia L 271 1
Gilbert, Michael 271, 273 1
Gilbert, Oda C 172 1
Gilbert, Peter J 172 1
Gilbert, Raymond S 257, 280 1
Gilbert, Sarah C 279 1
Gilbert, Simeon H 253 1
Gilbert, Sophia 253, 279, 280 1
Gilbert, Vinnie C 282 1
Gilbert, W Ray 201 1
Gilbert, Wm H 279 1
Gilbert, Zippe 263, 285 1
Gilbert, Zippe 254 2
Gilds Or Glitz, John 264 1
Gilds, George 257 1
Gilds, John 264 1
Gilds, John N 272 1
Gilds, John W N 275 1
Gilds, Margaret M 272 1
Gilds, Margaretta M 275 1
Gilds, Nicholas A 275 1
Gilds, Wm 257 1
Gill, Andrew J 245 1
Gill, Kate A 245 1
Gill, Walter F 26 1
Gillehan, D C 179 3
Gillehan, John 221, 223 3
Gillelan, Carrie M 250 1
Gillelan, David S 252 1
Gillelan, Geo L 71 1
Gillelan, H M 252 1
Gillelan, H Maurice 260 1
Gillelan, J W 198 2
Gillelan, Jacob W 265 1
Gillelan, John 38 2
Gillelan, John T 250 1
Gillelan, Magdalena 271 1
Gillelan, Mary A 265 1
Gillelan, Ruth B 250 1
Gillelan, S D 188 2
Gillelan, Virginia 67 1
Gillelan, Wm 252, 283 1
Gillelan, Wm 28 2
Gillelann, Mary A 272 1
Gilles[?], Nancy 275 1
Gilliece, Owen J 213a 2
Gillilan, Geo 39 2
Gillilan, Margaret 165 2
Gillingham, James 264 1
Gillis, Howard H 178 2
Gillis, John H 266 1
Gillis, John Henry 266, 272 1
Gillis, Maggie E 272 1
Gillis, W E 272 1
Gillman, Judson 218 2
Gillmeyer, Catherine 249 1
Gillmyer, Catherine 256 1
Gillmyer, Francis 256 1
Gillson, Richard 222 3
Gilpin, Charles M 249 1
Gilpin, Chas M 250, 272 1
Gilpin, Maria L 272 1
Gilsan, C Albert 177 1
Gilsan, Mahala 44 1
Gilson, Basil C 172 3
Gilson, Basil C 260, 272 1
Gilson, Basil C 31 2
Gilson, C A 67, 271 2
Gilson, C A 57, 82, 91, 145, 189 3
Gilson, C A 23 1
Gilson, C Albert For, 21, 24, 51, 100, 206 3
Gilson, C Albert 111, 126, 144, 175, 250, 260 1
Gilson, C Albert 31, 72, 132, 170, 212a, 227a, 249, 255 2
Gilson, Chas 278 1
Gilson, D C 196 3
Gilson, Harriet E 260 1
Gilson, John 70 3
Gilson, John B 171 1
Gilson, John E 264 1
Gilson, Richard 264, 278 1
Gilson, Richard 64 3
Gilson, Richard 1 2
Gilson, S W 221a 2
Gilson, Samuel 184 3
Gilson, Sarah W 280 1
Gilson, Sarah W 31 2
Gilson, Thos N R 282 1
Gilson, William J 2 3
Gilson, Wm 245 1
Gingell, Anna P 260, 278 1
Gingell, Geo E 257 1
Gingell, George 257 1
Gingell, George 260 1
Gingell, Herbert L 257, 260 1
Gingell, Thomas R 260 1
Gintling, Susan M 279 1
Giorgetti, Rosalie 20 2
Girard Trust Company 167 2
Gisberts, Samuel T [sic] 279 1

Gist, Geo 100 2
Gist, Independent 262 1
Gist, Joshua C 262 1
Gist, Mary 271 1
Gist, Thos 69 2
Gitt, Annie L 188 3
Gittinger, Ann R C 245 1
Gittinger, Anna M 245, 253 1
Gittinger, Annie Kate 245 1
Gittinger, Bessie 270 1
Gittinger, Bessie R 250 1
Gittinger, C James 249 1
Gittinger, C James 19 3
Gittinger, Clara 27 1
Gittinger, E A 220 3
Gittinger, E A 8 2
Gittinger, E A 171, 249, 250, 277 1
Gittinger, E James 187 3
Gittinger, E James 100 1
Gittinger, Edw 39, 58, 124 2
Gittinger, Edw A 177 2
Gittinger, Edw A 75, 174 3
Gittinger, Edw A 197, 201, 254, 272 1
Gittinger, Edw A & 29 2
Gittinger, Edward 208 2
Gittinger, Eleanor H 253 1
Gittinger, Emela 265 1
Gittinger, Emma A 253 1
Gittinger, Emma R 254 1
Gittinger, F James 37 1
Gittinger, Frank H 199 2
Gittinger, Geo 7, 27, 166 2
Gittinger, Geo 72, 104, 139, 152, 164, 200 1
Gittinger, Geo M 245, 253, 254, 265, 271 1
Gittinger, Geo M of J 153 1
Gittinger, Geo W 245, 257, 272 1
Gittinger, George 6, 209 3
Gittinger, George 257, 263 1
Gittinger, George 96 2
Gittinger, George M 245 1
Gittinger, H M 107 3
Gittinger, H M 257 1
Gittinger, H V 217 3
Gittinger, Henry M 250, 265 1
Gittinger, Hugh V 260, 270 1
Gittinger, J Howard 19 1
Gittinger, J James 287 2
Gittinger, Jacob 263 1
Gittinger, James 166 2
Gittinger, James Z 263 1
Gittinger, John 263, 264, 265 1
Gittinger, John E 195 3
Gittinger, John Edward 265 1
Gittinger, Josephus 200 1
Gittinger, Laura C 270 1
Gittinger, Margaret 271 1
Gittinger, Margaret S 280 1
Gittinger, Mary E 257 1
Gittinger, S F 260 1
Gittinger, Samuel J 272, 280 1
Gittinger, Samuel L 265 1
Gittinger, Susan F 109 1
Gittinger, Z J 71 1
Gittinger, Z J 280 1
Gittinger, Z J 8, 181 2
Gittinger, Z J 165 3
Gittinger, Z James 109, 135, 171, 195, 201, 264, 277 1
Gittinger, Z James 64, 71, 160 3
Gittinger, Z James 8, 177 2
Gittinger, Z Jas 81 3
Gittings, Ann M 249 1
Gittings, Catherine 265, 270 1
Gittings, G Edw 257 1
Gittings, Geo 253 1
Gittings, Geo E 96 2
Gittings, Geo W 257 1
Gittings, George 257 1
Gittings, Henry C 57 1
Gittings, J 260, 271, 279 1
Gittings, J G 96 2
Gittings, J Willis 257 1
Gittings, James G 257 1
Gittings, Jeremiah 263 1
Gittings, Jeremiah Sr 263 1
Gittings, John 26 2
Gittings, John F 263, 271 1
Gittings, Josephus 265 1
Gittings, Levi 270 1
Gittings, Lewis 263 1
Gittings, Lloyd 137 2
Gittings, Lloyd 263, 270 1
Gittings, Mary Ann 271 1
Gittings, Mary C B 84 1
Gittings, Mary E 271, 272 1
Gittings, Mary P 264 1
Gittings, W S 160 3
Gittings, William T 195 3
Gittings, Wm 271, 272, 283 1
Gittings, Wm 166 2
Gittings, Wm T 100 2
Givens, Nina G 284 1
Givens, Walter 284 1
Glachen, Dennis 252 1
Gladen, John C 265 1
Gladhill, Barbara 248 1
Gladhill, C T K 57 3
Gladhill, Calvin C T K 250 1
Gladhill, Calvin T K 216 3
Gladhill, Caroline 249 1
Gladhill, Daniel 252 1
Gladhill, Daniel E 113 2
Gladhill, G Glenn 10 2
Gladhill, Glen 250 1
Gladhill, Habard 260 1
Gladhill, Howard J 260 1
Gladhill, Jacob S 208 1
Gladhill, James 39 2
Gladhill, James 249, 264 1
Gladhill, James S 19 1
Gladhill, James S 113 3
Gladhill, James S 110 2
Gladhill, John 264, 265 1
Gladhill, Lola M 235 1
Gladhill, Lydia A 265 1
Gladhill, Matilda 270, 272 1
Gladhill, Ray C 10 2
Gladhill, Ray C 99 1
Gladhill, Ray C 24 3
Gladhill, Sarah A 260 1
Gladhill, Sarah Agnes 280 1
Gladstone, John W 266 1
Gladstone, Statton V 266 1
Glass, Emma 54 3
Glass, Howard J 252 1
Glass, John M 54 3
Glass, John M 247 2
Glass, Mary I 161 2
Glatzkin, D J 70 2
Glaze, David 252, 260 1
Glaze, Elizabeth 253, 264 1
Glaze, John H 96 1
Glaze, Joseph 253, 264, 272 1
Glaze, Maria V 272 1
Glaze, Samuel 264 1
Glaze, Sarah A 279 1
Glaze, W O 253 1
Glaze, Wm 100 1
Glaze, Wm M 118 1
Glaze, Worthington O 23 2
Glaze, Worthington O 272 1
Glen Falls Indemnity Co 21 3
Glen Falls Indemnity Co 224 2
Glen Falls Indemnity Co 108, 224 2
Glen Falls Indemnity Co 28, 52, 63, 230 1
Glen Falls Indemnity Co of N Y 167 2
Glen Falls Indemnity Company 169, 257 1
Glen Falls Indemnity Company 51 3
Glenn Falls Indemnity Co 1, 101, 280 1

Glenn Falls Indemnity Co 83, 220 3
Glenn Falls Indemnity Co of N Y 11 3
Glenns Falls Indemnity Co 45, 166 3
Glenns Falls Indemnity Co 202 1
Glenns Falls Indemnity Co 283 2
Glenns Falls Indemnity Company 174 3
Glens Fall Indemnity Co 189 1
Glens Fall Indemnity Company 32 2
Glens Falls Ind Co 129 2
Glens Falls Indeminity Co 8, 34, 63, 107, 109, 136, 153, 219, 245, 248, 260, 266 1
Glens Falls Indemnity Co 45, 57, 58, 75, 83, 122, 174, 182, 201, 208, 223, 225 3
Glens Falls Indemnity Co 10, 20, 32, 36, 108, 112, 113, 151, 167, 175, 182, 191, 196, 200, 234, 259, 271, 278, 283, 284, 295, 2
Glens Falls Indemnity Co of N Y 46 3
Glens Falls Indemnity Co of N Y 125 2
Glens Falls Indemnity Company 206 3
Glens Falls Indemnity Company 184 1
Glens Falls Ins Co 119 2
Glens Falls Surety Co 49 2
Glessner, Alice A 79, 246 1
Glessner, Geo 159 2
Glessner, Geo & 28 2
Glessner, Geo E 278 1
Glessner, Geo W 257, 283 1
Glessner, George E 182 2
Glessner, Lucy 257 1
Glessner, M Elizabeth 257 1
Glessner, M J 283 1
Glessner, Mary 283 1
Glessner, Mary Jane 272 1
Glessner, Richard R 278 1
Glessner, Thomas H 79 1
Glessner, Wm 248 1
Glisan, Basil H 272, 279, 283 1
Glisan, Chas E 249 1
Glisan, F E 272 1
Glisan, Harry J 272 1
Glisan, John 23 1
Glisan, Mahala 279 1
Glisan, Mary E 272 1
Glisan, Orla 249 1
Glisan, Samuel 116 1
Glissam, John 226 2
Glissan, John 185 2
Glissan, John 14 3
Glissan, John 125, 275, 196, 264, 277, 279 1
Glissan, John B 175 1
Glissan, John Sr 205 1
Globe Indemnity Co 8, 73, 109, 169, 265 1
Globe Indemnity Co 6, 44, 152 3
Globe Indemnity Co 102, 259, 295 2
Globe Indemnity Co of N Y 163, 229, 215a, 255 2
Globe Indemnity Co of N Y 8, 14, 42, 67, 72, 74, 78, 119, 126, 137, 208, 227, 232, 243, 257, 279 1
Globe Indemnity Co of N Y 44, 62, 188 3
Globe Indemnity Co of N Y, The 183 1
Globe Indemnity Co, New York 1 1
Globe Indemnity Co, The 113 1
Globe Indemnity Company 11, 21, 58 3
Globe Indemnity Company 136, 215 1
Globe Indemnity Company 235 2
Globe Indemnity Company of New York 189 3
Globe Indemnity Company of New York 89 2
Gloninger, John R 273 1
Gloninger, Mary Walsh 273 1
Gloninger, Philip 277 1
Gloninger, Philip Sr 277 1
Gloyd, John 225a 2
Gochnauer, Carl O 250 1
Gochnauer, Carl P 250 ` 1
Godbee, Celeste M 250 1
Goettel, Jacob 263 1
Goff, Eli 260 1
Goff, Eugene E 253 1
Goff, Henry 260 1
Goff, Henry A 205 1
Gogel, Jacob F 264 1
Goings, James 264 1
Goings, Margaret 271 1
Goldenburg, Henry 238 1
Goldenburg, Henry 195 3
Golder, Virginia C 245 1
Goldsboro, Amy 202 3
Goldsboro, E Y 202 3
Goldsboro, Edward 38 3
Goldsboro, Ralston 202 3
Goldsborough, Amelia 245, 282 1
Goldsborough, Amy R 253, 279 1
Goldsborough, C D[?] 249 1
Goldsborough, C W 119 2
Goldsborough, C W 125 1
Goldsborough, Chas 57, 171 2
Goldsborough, Chas 129 3
Goldsborough, Chas 245, 249, 253, 271, 279, 283 1
Goldsborough, Chas H Dr 33 1
Goldsborough, Chas W 171, 249 1
Goldsborough, Chas W 181 2
Goldsborough, Chas W 218 3
Goldsborough, E R 33, 245 1
Goldsborough, E Y 23 3
Goldsborough, E Y 253, 260, 265, 271, 278, 272 1
Goldsborough, Edw 253 1
Goldsborough, Edw Y 249, 253, 264, 265 1
Goldsborough, Henrietta 33, 265 1
Goldsborough, John 249, 264, 265, 271 1
Goldsborough, John S 265, 278 1
Goldsborough, Julia A 264 1
Goldsborough, Julianna W 260 1
Goldsborough, M C 253, 265 1
Goldsborough, Margaret 264, 265, 271, 283 1
Goldsborough, Mary 265 1
Goldsborough, Mary 279 1
Goldsborough, Mary C 271, 272, 278, 283 1
Goldsborough, Nanie 265 1
Goldsborough, Nannie 260 1
Goldsborough, Nicholas W 275 1
Goldsborough, R H 33 1
Goldsborough, Robert H 278 1
Goldsborough, Sarah 279 1
Goldsborough, Wm 283 1
Golibart, Margaret R 273 1
Golibart, Mark J 273 1
Golly, Peter 186 2
Gombar, Chas 186 2
Gomber, Chas 234 1
Gomber, Chas 165 2
Gomber, Chas A 249, 271 1
Gomber, Chas A 252 2
Gomber, Chas A 252 2
Gomber, Ezra M 253, 263, 271 1
Gomber, Isaac E 179 1
Gomber, John 262, 263 1
Gomber, Margaret 271 1
Gomber, Minerva 271 1

Gomber, Sarah A 271 1
Gonsauck, John 271 1
Gonsauck, Margaret 271 1
Gonsauck, Mary 271 1
Gonso, Charlotte A 249 1
Gonso, Chas F 249 1
Gonso, Margaret 271 1
Gonso, Mary 271, 273 1
Gonzo, George 264 1
Gonzo, Henry 260 1
Gonzo, John F 260 1
Good, F G 169 2
Good, Mary J 284 1
Good, William F 284 1
Good, William F 72 2
Good, William I 115 1
Goode, Hazel Nellie 177 3
Goode, Silas S 177 3
Goodell, C F 149 2
Goodell, Chas 9 2
Goodman, Hannah 260 1
Goodman, J M 8 2
Goodman, Jacob 233 1
Goodman, Jacob Jr 263 1
Goodman, Jacob Sr 263 1
Goodman, Joseph 265 1
Goodman, Sarah 265 1
Goodmanson, Catherine 249 1
Goodmanson, M E 249 1
Goodmanson, Mary 272, 277 1
Goodmanson, Peter 252 2
Goodmanson, Peter 277 1
Goodwin, Ellen 203 3
Gordon, Beryl 276 1
Gordon, Carrie L 249 1
Gordon, Earl M 3 2
Gordon, Edna V 3 2
Gordon, Gerald E 278 1
Gordon, Grace 161 3
Gordon, J L 160 3
Gordon, John 188 2
Gordon, John 283 1
Gordon, Joseph 249 1
Gordon, Lydia 263, 279 1
Gordon, Mary 271 1
Gordon, Michael E 249 1
Gordon, Osceola 276 1
Gordon, Roy 279 1
Gordon, Roy M 278 1
Gordon, Russell 276 1
Gordon, Russell S 249 1
Gordon, Russell Samuel 278 1
Gordon, Samuel 279 1
Gore, Samuel 205 3
Gorman, Ida Elizabeth 262 1
Gorman, Jacob H 262 1
Gorssnickle, Albert E 14 1
Gorsuch, Geo C 282 1
Gorsuch, Harry P 283 1
Gorsuch, Sophronia 279 1
Gorsuch, Stephen 214 3
Gorsuch, Stephen 163 1
Gorsuch, T 1 1
Gorsuch, Thomas 59, 88, 91 1
Gorsuch, Thomas 46, 78, 228a, 287 2
Gorsuch, Thomas 9, 19 3
Gorsuch, Thos 118, 125, 197, 229, 234, 252, 282 1
Gorsuch, Thos 14, 39, 101, 138, 171, 198, 203, 2
Gorsuch, Thos & 159 2
Gorsuch, Wm B 171 1
Gorsuch, Wm McK 283 1
Gorsush, Thomas 23 3
Gosnell, Beal 131 1
Gosnell, Carrie B 265 1
Gosnell, Ellen H 63 1
Gosnell, Ida M 63, 254 1
Gosnell, Jesse A 265 1
Gosnell, Levin 270 1
Gosnell, Lucy Haller 270 1
Gosnell, Oscar R 24 3
Gosnell, Wm 38 2
Gosner, Catharine E 249 1
Gott, Eugenia 254 1
Goucker, Barbara 248 1
Gouker, Ann Elizabeth 250 1
Gouker, Atlee N 149 2
Gouker, Bertha O 282 1
Gouker, Curtis 250 1
Gouker, Daniel 252 1
Gouker, Gilbert 282 1
Gouker, Henry 260 1
Gouker, John 263 1
Gouker, Peter 277 1
Gouker, Teresa 277 1
Gould, Nelly Colbert 275 1
Goulding, Maria 271 1
Gourley, George W 257 1
Gouveneur, Mary D 272 1
Gouverneur, Mary D 279 1
Gouverneur, Samuel L 279 1
Govenar, Mary 129 2
Gover, Anna M 245 1
Gover, John W 264 1
Gover, Samuel G 210 1
Goves, Elizabeth O 253 1
Gow, Alexander Jr 246 1
Gow, Roselle Bischoff 246 1
Goyer, John 264 1
Gr Amer Ind Co 227a 2
Grabenhorst, Henry 245 1
Grabill, A W 23 2
Grabill, Abraham 186 3
Grabill, Abraham 263, 264 1
Grabill, Arnold 245 1
Grabill, Bertha M 248 1
Grabill, Dorothy 278 1
Grabill, Dorothy L 254 1
Grabill, Edward W 254, 278 1
Grabill, Esther M 254, 278 1
Grabill, G Frank 258 1
Grabill, Ida M 262 1
Grabill, John 263, 279 1
Grabill, John 39 3
Grabill, John 35, 111, 274 2
Grabill, John D 79 3
Grabill, Maria 283 1
Grabill, Maude E 248 1
Grabill, Minnie O 214, 258, 262, 273 1
Grabill, Moses 245, 271, 272, 273, 279 1
Grabill, Moses 1 3
Grabill, Moses Sr 271 1
Grabill, Peter 14 3
Grabill, Reuben 245 1
Grabill, Robert E 278 1
Grabill, Robert F 278 1
Grabill, Samuel 245 1
Grabill, Sarah 271, 279 1
Grabill, Sophia 272 1
Grabill, Walter L 258, 262, 273 1
Grabill, Wm 271 1
Grabill, Wm H 249, 279 1
Gracey, Cassandra B 264, 283 1
Gracey, John 264 1
Gracy, Cassandra 29 2
Graff, Anna 245 1
Graff, Chas B 249 1
Graff, Effie R 253 1
Graff, Eli G 253 1
Graff, Elizabeth 88 1
Graff, Elizabeth E 85, 249, 254 1
Graff, J Paul 266 1
Graff, John B 85 1
Graff, John P 238 2
Graff, John P 88, 245, 249, 254 1
Graff, John P C 266 1
Graff, Roger E 266 1
Graff, Sarah E 253 1
Graff, Sebastian 279 1
Graff, Theresa S 257 1
Graft, John 219, 266 1
Graham, Amos 245, 257 1
Graham, Amos Edgar 245, 270 1
Graham, Caroline 249 1
Graham, Catherine 257 1

Graham, Chas E 83 3
Graham, Edward McK 266 1
Graham, Francis 256 1
Graham, G A 37, 59 1
Graham, Geo 83 3
Graham, George A 257 1
Graham, George H 258 1
Graham, George H 35 3
Graham, J 25 1
Graham, James 52, 116, 276 2
Graham, James 32, 59, 264, 265, 283 1
Graham, John 111 3
Graham, John 163, 164, 182, 183 1
Graham, John 154 2
Graham, John W 266 1
Graham, Laura Barbara 270 1
Graham, Lillian S 258 1
Graham, Roy W 258 1
Graham, Thomas J 282 1
Graham, Thos 137 2
Graham, Wm 106 3
Graham, Wm 7, 70, 181 2
Graham, Wm 283 1
Graham, Wm Sr 283 1
Grahame, Ann Jane 263 1
Grahame, Anna J 245 1
Grahame, Grace J 250 1
Grahame, John 263 1
Grahe, Ella F 282 2
Grahe, Theodore 282 1
Graig, Ellen 235 1
Gram, G A 2 3
Gram, Geo A 258 2
Gram, James 258 2
Gram, John 8 3
Gram, Thomas 8 3
Grammar, Jacob 134 3
Grammer, David 84 2
Grammer, Henry 14 3
Grammer, Jacob 263 1
Grams, Ellis G 254 1
Grams, Florence May 76 1
Grams, John [?] 245 1
Grams, John N 264 1
Grams, John W 283 1
Grams, Maria 264 1
Grams, Mary Kate Huffer 254 1
Grams, Thos E 283 1
Grams, Wm 283 1
Grand Lodge of Md I00F 178 2
Grant, Benjamin 248 1
Grantham, Ezra Louis 97 1
Gratz, Chas P 249 1
Gray, Alice 74 1
Gray, Clarence I 266 1
Gray, Clyde I 258 1
Gray, Evan H 253 1
Gray, Grace M 266 1
Gray, Gracie M 258 1
Gray, Henrietta 260 1
Gray, Jacob M 266 1
Gray, James R 260 1
Gray, James T, Dr 31 1
Gray, L E 205 2
Gray, Laura E 96, 270 1
Gray, Nellie K 266 1
Gray, Nellie L 258 1
Gray, Ottis L 253 1
Gray, Wm F 260 1
Graybill, John 39 3
Grayham, Wm 116 2
Grayson, Bessie W 248 1
Greason, Geo A 257 1
Greason, Wath [wic] 283 1
Greason, Wm 116 2
Greason, Wm 283 1
Great Amer Ind Co 16 2
Great American Indemnity 235 1
Great American Indemnity Co 9, 22, 44, 45, 68, 93, 104, 140, 166, 198, 202, 235, 241, 248, 250, 252, 258, 280 1
Great American Indemnity Co 10, 52, 145, 193, 255, 259, 284, 288 2
Great American Indemnity Co 6, 11, 33, 35, 96, 98, 107, 122, 138, 141, 177, 189, 215 3
Great American Indemnity Co of N Y 215, 255 2
Great American Indemnity Company 230 1
Great American Indemnity Company 21, 35 3
Great American Indemnity Company, The 93 1
Greeg, A 257 1
Green, A S 221 3
Green, Amanda C 283 1
Green, Amanda E 286 1
Green, Annie M 245 1
Green, Carrie May 265 1
Green, Charles L 284 1
Green, Chas E 107, 283 1
Green, Chas H 249 1
Green, Cornelius T 249 1
Green, Elijah 270 1
Green, Enoch L 245 1
Green, Everett C 254 1
Green, Frank S 257 1
Green, Geo 81 3
Green, George B 257, 266 1
Green, Grover B 257 1
Green, H C T 159 2
Green, H T C 65 3
Green, James G 92 1
Green, Jennie 81 3
Green, John F 265 1
Green, John L M 266, 279 1
Green, John T 245 1
Green, Joseph D 163 1
Green, Leslie W 166, 197 3
Green, Lewis 265, 270 1
Green, Lewis P 283 1
Green, Mahlon B 273 1
Green, Marion K 87 2
Green, Mary 273 1
Green, Mary A 272 1
Green, Mary Ann 273 1
Green, Mary E 245 1
Green, Nellie H 254 1
Green, Peter 277 1
Green, Samuel 279 1
Green, Sarah I 265, 279 1
Green, Sarah V 279, 280 1
Green, Simon P 279 1
Green, Sophia L 279 1
Green, Stephen 279 1
Green, Stephen O 280 1
Green, W E 182 3
Green, William H 283 1
Green, Wm 283, 284 1
Green, Wm E 283 1
Green, Wm R 283 1
Green, Zachariah T 286 1
Greene, James B 265 1
Greenfield, Anna K 197 3
Greenholtz, Annie E 245 1
Greenholtz, C W 272 1
Greenholtz, Chas W 250 1
Greenholtz, M L 272 1
Greenholtz, Mary E 250 1
Greenholtz, Samuel 279 1
Greenhunt, Leopold[?] 270 1
Greenhunt, Pauline 270 1
Greenlay, James C 266 1
Greenlay, Jessie H 266 1
Greentree, John D 263 1
Greenwald, Mary R 273 1
Greenwald, Samuel H 279, 280 1
Greenwald, Susan C 279 1
Greenwalt, Christian 249 1
Greenwalt, Christian 282 2
Greenwalt, Wilson 249 1
Greenwood, Ann M 264 1
Greenwood, Barbara 59 1
Greenwood, Isaiah 248, 262 1
Greenwood, Joanna 262 1
Greenwood, John 164, 263, 264, 265 1
Greenwood, Joseph 263 1
Greenwood, Philip 211 2
Greenwood, Philip 37 1

Greeson, Wm 185 2
Gregg, James W 264 1
Gregg, Linda F 280 1
Gregg, Mary C 272 1
Gregg, Samuel 147 1
Gregg, Samuel U 272, 278 1
Gregsby, Pattie 84 2
Grendadam, Regina 278, 280 1
Grier, Robert S 119 2
Grier, Robert S 278 1
Griffin, Abraham 144 2
Griffin, B A 249 1
Griffin, Chas W 249 1
Griffin, Cleopatra 211 2
Griffin, David O 283 1
Griffin, James 264 1
Griffin, Jane E 283 1
Griffin, John N 249 1
Griffin, Joseph 172 2
Griffin, Joseph T 189 1
Griffin, L S 254 1
Griffin, Mary A 249 1
Griffin, Rachel J 192 3
Griffin, Thomas 282 1
Griffin, Wm H 283 1
Griffin, Wm H 172 2
Griffing, James 222 3
Griffis, Mordeca [sic] 249 1
Griffith, Chas A 38 2
Griffith, Chas A 271 1
Griffith, Chas O 278 1
Griffith, Elizabeth H 277 1
Griffith, Harriet Ann 260 1
Griffith, Harry L 277 1
Griffith, John 270 1
Griffith, Lebbens 270, 278 1
Griffith, Lydia 278 1
Griffith, Lydia 46 2
Griffith, Mordecai 271 1
Griffith, Mordecai 38 2
Griffith, P G M 278 1
Griffith, Philemon 277 1
Griffith, Philemon H 277 1
Griffith, Philip 278 1
Griffith, R A 229 2
Griffith, Rachel 278 1
Griffith, Rachel A 278 1
Griffith, Rachel J 270 1
Griffith, Ruth 278 1
Griffith, S W 270 1
Griffith, Samuel 279 1
Grim, Adam E 169 3
Grim, Alfred D 245 1
Grim, Benjamin 248 1
Grim, Daniel 248 1
Grim, Herman J 262 1
Grim, Israel 262, 266 1
Grim, Jonas 265, 266 1
Grim, Joseph 265 1
Grim, Samuel 279 1
Grim, Samuel B 279 1
Grim, Simon J 262 1
Grim, Simon L 266 1
Grimer, Jacob 224 3
Grimes, Agnes E 260 1
Grimes, Annie L 245 1
Grimes, Annie M 266 1
Grimes, Basil 248 1
Grimes, Christianna G 249 1
Grimes, Cornelius 57 2
Grimes, Edna K 106 2
Grimes, Elias 70 1
Grimes, Elias 37 3
Grimes, Elias 26 2
Grimes, Eliza Ann 253 1
Grimes, Elizabeth 283 1
Grimes, Ephriam 253 1
Grimes, Frances R 166 3
Grimes, Gassoway S 237 2
Grimes, Gertrude H 257 1
Grimes, Helen E 252 1
Grimes, Herman L 260 1
Grimes, Jaheiel 264 1
Grimes, James E 266 1
Grimes, Johiel 248 1
Grimes, John H 265 1
Grimes, John H 6, 20 3
Grimes, John H 89 2
Grimes, John M 263 1
Grimes, Joseph H 276 1
Grimes, Martha O 276 1
Grimes, Mary 271, 283 1
Grimes, Mildred V 241 1
Grimes, Oscar S 276 1
Grimes, Oscar S 20 3
Grimes, Robert A 266 1
Grimes, Sarah E 70 1
Grimes, W T 167, 210 3
Grimes, Warner T 147, 214, 283 1
Grimes, Warner T 7 2
Grimes, William 57 1
Grimes, William 6, 37, 201 3
Grimes, William Jr 195 3
Grimes, William Jr 67 1
Grimes, Wilson S 39 3
Grimes, Wm 159, 253, 263, 283 1
Grimes, Wm 66 2
Grimes, Wm G 245 1
Grimes, Wm H 116, 283 1
Grimes, Wm Jr 183, 283 1
Grimes, Wm Jr 46 2
Grimes, Wm T 118 1
Grimm, B E 265 1
Grimm, Beulah E 248 1
Grimm, John H 265 1
Grimm, Mildred L 42 1
Grinage, Esther E 83, 254 1
Grinder, Alonzo 279 1
Grinder, Eleanor 253 1
Grinder, Eli D 84 2
Grinder, Harriet 260 1
Grinder, Harriot 279 1
Grinder, J S 265 1
Grinder, John 263 1
Grinder, John S 260, 272 1
Grinder, John Scott 265 1
Grinder, John W 171 3
Grinder, John W 265 1
Grinder, Joseph S 272 1
Grinder, Magdalene 272 1
Grinder, Margaret L 260, 272 1
Grinder, Mary W 272, 273 1
Grinder, Michael 271 1
Grinder, R E 265 1
Grinder, Regina C 278 1
Grinder, Samuel 279 1
Grinder, Tolie 272 1
Gring, Emma A 283 1
Gring, Wm A 283 1
Grobp, Elizabeth 253, 263 1
Grobp, John 263 1
Grobp, John 275 2
Groch, Mary [sic] 271 1
Groff, Annie 33 1
Groff, C D 119 1
Groff, Catherine J 10 3
Groff, Charles B 250 1
Groff, Chas 42 1
Groff, Chas B 52, 245, 249, 265 1
Groff, David 192 3
Groff, David 252, 265, 282 1
Groff, Effie R 249 1
Groff, Eli 107 2
Groff, Eli G 214 3
Groff, Eli G 138 2
Groff, Eloise K 254 1
Groff, Eloise K 203 3
Groff, Emma C 250 1
Groff, Emma C 203 3
Groff, Emma K 254 1
Groff, Geo 131 1
Groff, Helen K 131 1
Groff, Henry 177, 221a 2
Groff, Joseph 100 2
Groff, Joseph 225, 265, 272, 275 1
Groff, Joseph 212 3
Groff, Joseph H 266 1
Groff, N C 60, 135 1
Groff, Nannie 41 1
Groff, Newton C 275 1
Groff, Sarah C 279 1

Groff, Sarah E 279 1
Groff, Susan 265 1
Groff, Wm 33 1
Groshon, Abraham 234, 245 1
Groshon, Abraham 51 2
Groshon, Annie V 245 1
Groshon, B F 44 3
Groshon, B Frank 254, 282 1
Groshon, Elias 107 2
Groshon, Elias 253 1
Groshon, Elias A 245 1
Groshon, Elias A 38 3
Groshon, Ellen A 254 1
Groshon, Geo 62, 138 2
Groshon, Geo S 177 2
Groshon, Geo S 257 1
Groshon, George W 257 1
Groshon, Hallie V 57 1
Groshon, John 257, 263, 264, 270 1
Groshon, John 195 3
Groshon, John 181 2
Groshon, life A 116 2
Groshon, Martin L 72 3
Groshon, Martin L 197 1
Groshon, Mary 271 1
Groshon, Meredith E 113 1
Groshon, Thos H 282 1
Groshon, Walter 283 1
Groshon, Wm J 283 1
Gross, Allen 245 1
Gross, Alma C 95 1
Gross, Charles 84, 120 1
Gross, Charles 1 3
Gross, Charles A 129 2
Gross, Chas 112, 249, 257, 260, 264 1
Gross, Clara N 58 3
Gross, Cora M 177 3
Gross, Edward L 177 3
Gross, Elizabeth D 52 1
Gross, Etta 245 1
Gross, Francis H 256 1
Gross, Geo 119, 150 2
Gross, Geo H 245 1
Gross, George 257 1
Gross, H B 172 1
Gross, H Boteler 87 3
Gross, H Boteler 33 1
Gross, H C 227a 2
Gross, Henry 249, 260 1
Gross, Henry Sr 260 1
Gross, Homer C 136 1
Gross, Howard A 3, 80 2
Gross, Howard A 49, 74, 180, 214 1
Gross, Howard A 3 3
Gross, Jacob 264 1
Gross, Josiah 260, 266 1
Gross, LC 256 1
Gross, Myra G 256 1
Gross, Roy L 266 1
Gross, W L 282 2
Gross, William L 55, 160 3
Gross, Wm 138, 195 2
Gross, Wm B 283 1
Gross, Wm L 51, 96 2
Gross, Wm L 188 3
Gross, Wm L 72, 95, 115, 175, 283 1
Grosse, Charles A 42 1
Grossnickel, Carrie M 96 3
Grossnickel, David 214 2
Grossnickel, Parker 71 3
Grossnickel, Russell H 102 2
Grossnickel, Russell H 278 1
Grossnickle, Albert E 245 1
Grossnickle, Alice M 246 1
Grossnickle, Annie M 246 1
Grossnickle, C 150 1
Grossnickle, C Elbert 250 1
Grossnickle, C Elbert 23 2
Grossnickle, C U 9 2
Grossnickle, C Upton 12 2
Grossnickle, Caleb A 252 1
Grossnickle, Caleb H 279 1
Grossnickle, Caleb T 250 1
Grossnickle, Carrie E 197 3
Grossnickle, Carrie M 73 1
Grossnickle, Catherine 249 1
Grossnickle, Chas 250, 282 1
Grossnickle, Chas C 272 1
Grossnickle, Chas E 187 3
Grossnickle, Chas E 265 1
Grossnickle, D 245 1
Grossnickle, D Roy 246 1
Grossnickle, Daniel 252, 260, 277 1
Grossnickle, Daniel 274, 286 2
Grossnickle, Daniel R 184 1
Grossnickle, David 250, 252, 277 1
Grossnickle, David 222, 238 2
Grossnickle, David 54 3
Grossnickle, Effie S 257 1
Grossnickle, Elias 7 2
Grossnickle, Elias 277 1
Grossnickle, Elias 41 3
Grossnickle, Ellen C 252 1
Grossnickle, Ellen E 253 1
Grossnickle, Elsie J 34 1
Grossnickle, Evelyn J 81 2
Grossnickle, G P 60 1
Grossnickle, Geo 277 1
Grossnickle, Geo F 139 2
Grossnickle, Geo O 257 1
Grossnickle, Geo O 125 2
Grossnickle, Hannah 260 1
Grossnickle, Jennie R 51 1
Grossnickle, John 7 2
Grossnickle, John 215, 249, 264, 277 1
Grossnickle, John M 282 1
Grossnickle, Jonathan 7 2
Grossnickle, Joshua B 252 1
Grossnickle, Joshua C 246 1
Grossnickle, Joshua R 265 1
Grossnickle, Leonard K 245 1
Grossnickle, Lillie L 257 1
Grossnickle, Mahlon 272 1
Grossnickle, Mahlon W 272 1
Grossnickle, Martha 206 3
Grossnickle, Martin 109 1
Grossnickle, Mary 271, 272, 277 1
Grossnickle, P C 253 1
Grossnickle, Parker C 143 2
Grossnickle, Parker C 252, 277 1
Grossnickle, Parker C 208 3
Grossnickle, Peter 260, 271, 277, 282 1
Grossnickle, Peter 186, 187, 207 3
Grossnickle, Peter 7 2
Grossnickle, Peter Jr 264, 277 1
Grossnickle, Peter of J 277 1
Grossnickle, Peter of P 277 1
Grossnickle, Peter of Peter 277 1
Grossnickle, Russell H 282 1
Grossnickle, Susan 52 1
Grossnickle, T F 272, 279 1
Grossnickle, Thos F 282 1
Grossnickle, Tilghman 181, 282 1
Grossnickle, Tilghman F 206 3
Grossnickle, Vernon M 208 3
Grossnickle, Vernon W 257, 272, 277 1
Grossnickle, Wm 277 1
Grottle, John 264 1
Grottle, Margaret 264 1
Grove, Adeline Wickham 245 1
Grove, Alice M 276 1
Grove, Amy B 175 2
Grove, Ann R 245 1
Grove, Anna F 266 1
Grove, Annie M 245 1
Grove, Annie M E 260, 279 1

Grove, B F 36 2
Grove, Benjamin F 248 1
Grove, Benjamin F 116 2
Grove, Carrie E 68 1
Grove, Catharine E 250 1
Grove, Catherine 249, 277 1
Grove, Catherine C 249 1
Grove, Chas B 272 1
Grove, Chas D 249, 252 1
Grove, Chas P 249 1
Grove, Chester L 248 1
Grove, Clara V 249 1
Grove, Cora E 250 1
Grove, D B 166 3
Grove, D R 271 1
Grove, Daniel 252 1
Grove, Daniel C 20 2
Grove, Daniel R 252, 279 1
Grove, Daniel T 215 3
Grove, David 252 1
Grove, DeWitt C 252 1
Grove, Edith M 254 1
Grove, Edw 270 1
Grove, Edw D 253 1
Grove, Edw G 116 2
Grove, Edw T 254, 272 1
Grove, Edward D 254 1
Grove, Eleanor C 249 1
Grove, Elias 253 1
Grove, Elias 253, 271, 277 1
Grove, Elizabeth J 266 1
Grove, Ella E 256 1
Grove, Ellen C 278 1
Grove, Esther C 284 1
Grove, Eugene A 254 1
Grove, F Henrietta 253 1
Grove, Fannie M 256 1
Grove, Frank H 256 1
Grove, Ge 64 3
Grove, Geo 65 2
Grove, Geo W 256, 271, 283 1
Grove, George 26 3
Grove, George W 257 1
Grove, Greenbury F 272 1
Grove, Greenbury S 249 1
Grove, Harry A 260 1
Grove, Helen L 266 1
Grove, Henrietta F 260 1
Grove, Hiram J 260, 271, 279 1
Grove, J Arthur 284 1
Grove, J Harry 11, 266 1
Grove, J Harry 56 3
Grove, Jacob 139, 167, 171, 205 3
Grove, Jacob 25, 76, 228, 263 1
Grove, Jacob 203 2
Grove, Jacob Randolph 265 1
Grove, James A 266, 272 1
Grove, James H Jr 101, 157 1
Grove, Jemima B 257, 265 1
Grove, Jesse L D 266 1
Grove, Jesse Lee Davis 254 1
Grove, Jessie B 249, 266 1
Grove, John 253, 273 1
Grove, John D 252, 256 1
Grove, John H 260, 265 1
Grove, John H 28, 217 3
Grove, John H 116 2
Grove, John H Jr 214 1
Grove, John M 250, 265 1
Grove, John Randolph 266 1
Grove, John W 245, 252 1
Grove, John W 116 2
Grove, Julia 254 1
Grove, Katie E 198, 272, 279 1
Grove, Laura A 270 1
Grove, Leonard 19 2
Grove, Leonard 263 1
Grove, Leonard S 249 1
Grove, Leslie W 249, 270 1
Grove, Lettie G 266 1
Grove, Lola V 270 1
Grove, Lulu V 270 1
Grove, M J 270, 271 1
Grove, Manassas J 249 1
Grove, Margaret 271, 272 1
Grove, Margaret E 272 1
Grove, Margaret J 252 1
Grove, Marietta 272 1
Grove, Marshall L 99 1
Grove, Martin N 271 1
Grove, Martin S 253, 271 1
Grove, Mary 271, 272 1
Grove, Mary F 272 1
Grove, Mary L 273 1
Grove, MJ 266 1
Grove, MJ 9 2
Grove, Nellie 260 1
Grove, Olive H 276 1
Grove, Oscar E 276 1
Grove, Patrick 54 2
Grove, Peter 277 1
Grove, Peter S 245 1
Grove, Rebecca 270, 278 1
Grove, Roscoe E 252 1
Grove, Samuel 11, 100 2
Grove, Samuel 243 1
Grove, Samuel E 265, 272 1
Grove, Sarah 279 1
Grove, Sarah A 249, 283 1
Grove, Valletta R 253 1
Grove, Violetta R 265, 282 1
Grove, W Jarboe 266 1
Grove, William 165, 167, 185 3
Grove, William 264 2
Grove, William A 14 3
Grove, William D 284 1
Grove, William F 245 1
Grove, William J 104, 260 1
Grove, Wm 14, 22, 51 2
Grove, Wm 252, 284 1
Grove, Wm A 283 1
Grove, Wm A 202, 215 3
Grove, Wm E 42 1
Grove, Wm J 58, 80, 169 2
Grove, Wm J 272 1
Grove, Wm T 167 3
Grover, Ann 171 1
Grover, Geo 27, 54, 76, 169 2
Grover, Geo 245, 256, 260 1
Grover, Geo 64 3
Grover, George 37, 249 1
Grover, John R 76 2
Grovnn, Wm 249 2
Grubb, George W 75 2
Grubbs, George W 257 1
Grubbs, James H 257 1
Gruber, Adam 245 1
Grumbine, Amy 245 1
Grumbine, Daniel N 13 1
Grumbine, David M 240 1
Grumbine, E Allan 33 3
Grumbine, Emma Amy 254 1
Grumbine, Emma S 254 1
Grumbine, Frank 10 3
Grumbine, Frank S 257 1
Grumbine, J Allen 240 1
Grumbine, John 181 2
Grumbine, John 88 1
Grumbine, M S 240, 263 1
Grumbine, Sarah S 10 3
Grumbine, Wm 137 2
Grumbine, Wm 96 1
Grundel, John 264 1
Grushon, B Frank 260 1
Grushon, Benjamin F 248 1
Grushon, Helen G 260 1
Grushon, John C L 229 1
Grushon, John W 266 1
Grushon, Lillian E 266 1
Grushon, Mildred V 266 1
Grushon, N Mae 248 1
Grushon, Nettie E 275 1
Guager, Nicholas 214 1
Gubben, Mary 271 1
Gue, Francis M 266 1
Gue, James C 266 1
Gue, Rachel E 278 1
Guess, Reuben 278 1
Guigeas, Mathias 58 1
Guirey, Mary C 245 1
Guiton, Abraham 245, 271 1
Guiton, Albert 245 1
Gump, George 263 1

Gump, John 263 1
Gump, Jonathan 263 1
Gump, Mary 271 1
Gundlach, Conrad 249 1
Gunn, John 263 1
Gunther, Mary 57 3
Gurley, Thomas 215a 2
Gurley, Thomas Sr 64 3
Gurley, Thos 26 1
Gurley, Thos 258 2
Gurley, Thos Jr 181 1
Gurshon, John 91 1
Gushour, Peter 277 1
Gusler, Wm T 198 2
Gustapon, Edw C 254 1
Gustopon, Ada T 254 1
Gutberlet, J Charles 129 3
Guthrie, Sue C 280 1
Guthrie, Wm G 71 1
Guy, Margaret M 272 1
Guyer, Samuel 67 3
Guyton, Daniel S 145 1
Guyton, Mamie A R 167 2
Guyton, Sarah 283 1
Guyton, Sopha E 145 1
Guyton, W L 18 1
Guyton, Wm 283 1
Guyton, Wm B 48, 283 1
Guyton, Wm L 283 1
Gveen, Nellie V 61 1
Gwinn, Priscilla 277 1
Gwinn, William P 135 3
H, Raymond 199 2
Haberkorn, Ada V 41 2
Haberkorn, Addie 3 2
Haberkorn, Mary E 41 2
Hackelton, James H 29 2
Hackelton, M W 29 2
Hackett, Emma 265 1
Hackett, Emma C 272 1
Hackett, John 49 2
Hackman, John 27 2
Hackney, Martin 38 2
Hackney, Mary B 38 2
Haddt, John C 64 3
Hadere, John 144 2
Hadere, Thos 144 2
Hafer, Catherine 9 2
Hafer, Ella 196 3
Hafer, Ella V 9 2
Hafer, Luther B 89 2
Hafer, Samuel 196 3
Haff, Abraham 1 2
Haffner, Bessie 58 2
Haffner, Catherine 38 2
Haffner, E E 12 2
Haffner, Jacob 26 2
Haffner, Lewis 58 2
Haffner, Michael 38 2
Haffner, Rosa 12 2
Haffner, S T 8, 218a 2
Haffner, Samuel T 264 2
Haffner, T S 124 2
Haffner, Walter 58 2
Hagaman, Sam c 51 2
Hagan, Adam 1, 214 2
Hagan, Adam 94, 111 3
Hagan, Benjamin 5 2
Hagan, Charles Mc 196 3
Hagan, Chas 161 3
Hagan, Chas M 39 2
Hagan, Dennis 11 2
Hagan, Elizabeth D 15 2
Hagan, Francis 5, 18 2
Hagan, Henry J D 40 1
Hagan, Henry J D 196 3
Hagan, Herman 39 2
Hagan, Ignatius 25 2
Hagan, J H D 66 2
Hagan, John 1, 6, 15, 40, 186, 224 3
Hagan, John 1, 29, 31, 46, 138, 159, 181, 197, 203 2
Hagan, John 48, 51, 67 1
Hagan, John C 29 2
Hagan, M E 39 2
Hagan, Mary E 39 2
Hagan, Mary M 39 2
Hagan, Michael P 39 2
Hagan, Mollie M 31 2
Hagan, Peter 156, 163 1
Hagan, Peter 46, 78, 197 2
Hagan, Richard P 39 2
Hagan, Wm M 58 2
Hagen, Rose C 30 1
Hahn, Abraham 1 2
Hahn, Adolph 2, 8 2
Hahn, Annie M 15 2
Hahn, C Earl 49 2
Hahn, C S 109 3
Hahn, Catherine 51 2
Hahn, Catherine A 7 2
Hahn, Charles S 9 2
Hahn, Chas Earl 9 2
Hahn, Chas N 98 3
Hahn, Chas N 182, 240 1
Hahn, Chas N 8 2
Hahn, Claude 63 1
Hahn, Claude S 86, 126, 172 1
Hahn, Clude S, 126 1
Hahn, Edgar A 16 2
Hahn, Edw O 15 2
Hahn, Elias 14 2
Hahn, Emma Jane 16 2
Hahn, Florence J 23, 198 2
Hahn, Frederick J 198 1
Hahn, H A 33 1
Hahn, H A 217 3
Hahn, H A 8, 166 2
Hahn, Hannah C 23 2
Hahn, Harvey L 23 2
Hahn, Henry 8, 26 2
Hahn, Henry A 52 1
Hahn, Henry A 23 2
Hahn, Hettye A 86, 120 1
Hahn, Hettye A 11 3
Hahn, Issac 275 2
Hahn, J A 37 1
Hahn, Jacob 1, 26, 93, 186, 203 2
Hahn, Jacob 183 1
Hahn, Jacob Jr 144 1
Hahn, John 203, 205 1
Hahn, John 29 2
Hahn, John D 42 1
Hahn, John H 29 2
Hahn, John M 32, 46 2
Hahn, John N 135 1
Hahn, Julia Koons 102 2
Hahn, Kenry W 41 2
Hahn, Margaret 34 1
Hahn, Margaret E 41 2
Hahn, Margaret H 10 2
Hahn, Maurice W 60 3
Hahn, Michael 38, 107 2
Hahn, Peter 144, 208 1
Hahn, Peter 38, 46 2
Hahn, Peter 167 3
Hahn, Preston 34 1
Hahn, Preston L 32 2
Hahn, Rose 221 3
Hahn, Rose Agnes 9, 49 2
Hahn, Sadie C 23 2
Hahn, Samuel 8 1
Hahn, Sarah E 52 2
Hahn, Solomon 51 2
Hahn, Susan A 37 1
Hahn, Washington 52 2
Hahn, William A 23 2
Hahn, William A 2 3
Hahn, William Adolph 34 1
Hahn, Wm 2 2
Hain, Philip 46 2
Haine, John 56 1
Haine, John 237 2
Haine, Wm 156 1
Haines, Abraham 70 1
Haines, Ada 3 2
Haines, Albert L 3, 18 2
Haines, Andrew 3 2
Haines, Anna 57 2
Haines, Annie E 12 2
Haines, Atlee 254 1
Haines, Benjamin W 5 2
Haines, Catherine 54 2
Haines, Clementine 9, 35 2
Haines, D Atlee 3, 12 2

Haines, Daniel	77	3	
Haines, Daniel	11, 57	2	
Haines, Daniel	294	2	
Haines, David	11, 38	2	
Haines, David	135	1	
Haines, Elizabeth	6	1	
Haines, Elizabeth	15	2	
Haines, Elizabeth A	15	2	
Haines, Ephriam	57	2	
Haines, Frances W	28	2	
Haines, Francis W	18	2	
Haines, Harvey B	3	2	
Haines, Henry	26, 27	2	
Haines, Henry	186	1	
Haines, Henry	1	3	
Haines, Israel P	51	2	
Haines, J C	51	2	
Haines, Jacob	26, 27	2	
Haines, Jacob L	28	2	
Haines, Joel L	26	2	
Haines, John	70	1	
Haines, John	218	3	
Haines, John	28, 38, 100	2	
Haines, John W	31	2	
Haines, Joseph	11, 26	2	
Haines, Joshua	49	2	
Haines, Josiah	27	2	
Haines, Lewis P	35	2	
Haines, Mary	39	2	
Haines, Mary E	31	2	
Haines, Michael	38	2	
Haines, Michael of John	38	2	
Haines, Mildred	117	1	
Haines, Mordecai	38	2	
Haines, Nathan	43, 197	2	
Haines, Reuben	49	2	
Haines, Richard	134	2	
Haines, Ruben	98	3	
Haines, Samuel	11, 26, 51	2	
Haines, Sarah	51	2	
Haines, Stephen	51, 218	2	
Haines, Stephen	56, 145	1	
Haines, Thomas	38, 54	2	
Haines, Uriah	27, 49	2	
Haines, William	231	2	
Haines, Wm	26, 38, 54, 57	2	
Haines, Wm H	57	2	
Haines, Wm M	57	2	
Hale, Geo	46, 214	2	
Hale, Geo	179, 201	1	
Hale, George	79	1	
Hale, George	31	3	
Hale, James D	35, 160	2	
Hale, Luther F	35	2	
Hale, Wm	214	2	
Haley, Lawrence	35	2	
Hall, Andrew	24	1	
Hall, Barbara A	51	2	
Hall, Barrick	70, 196	1	

Hall, Barrick	5	2
Hall, Barruch	18	2
Hall, Baruch	5	2
Hall, Benjamin	5, 57	2
Hall, Benjamin Sr	57	2
Hall, Blanche	5	2
Hall, Daniel I	33	1
Hall, Daniel R	12	2
Hall, David	165	3
Hall, Elizabeth	182	3
Hall, Elizabeth	14	2
Hall, Geo	44	1
Hall, Hester	22	2
Hall, J C	218a	2
Hall, J Thomas	39	3
Hall, Jacob	113	3
Hall, Joel	30, 51	2
Hall, Joel	153	3
Hall, Joel	58, 88, 156	1
Hall, John W	31	2
Hall, Josel	5	2
Hall, Joshua H	31	2
Hall, Julius	129	2
Hall, Levi (Col'd)	35	2
Hall, Louisa T	182	3
Hall, Mabel V	14	1
Hall, Mary	38	2
Hall, Mary Jane	54	2
Hall, Nicholas	75	3
Hall, Nicholas	14, 43	2
Hall, Nicholas Jr	43	2
Hall, Nicholas Sr	43	2
Hall, Peter	26	2
Hall, Sarah	51	2
Hall, Thomas H	54	2
Hall, Walter	57	2
Hall, William	165	3
Hall, Wm	58	2
Hallabaugh, Lucinda	35	2
Hallar, Annie C	1	1
Hallar, Eliza A	1	1
Hallar, H Kenneth	43	2
Hallar, John M	43	2
Hallar, Louisa	36	2
Hallar, Nettie	43	2
Haller, A D	23	2
Haller, Angeline D	2	2
Haller, Ann Elizabeth	3	2
Haller, Ann H	1, 29	2
Haller, Annie	58	2
Haller, Annie M	2	2
Haller, C Winston	32	2
Haller, Caroline	54	2
Haller, Carrie J	11	2
Haller, Charlotte E	8	2
Haller, Chas E	1	2
Haller, Chas W	91	3
Haller, Christopher	7	2
Haller, Clara	10	2

Haller, Cora E	10	2
Haller, Cyrus Winston	10	2
Haller, Daniel	11, 27	2
Haller, Daniel	18	3
Haller, Daniel	263	1
Haller, David H	129	1
Haller, David R	11	2
Haller, E F	23	2
Haller, Frank B	43	2
Haller, Geo	84	2
Haller, George Col'd	20	2
Haller, H H	196	3
Haller, H Kenneth	3, 32	2
Haller, H Noel	2, 23	2
Haller, H Noel	260	1
Haller, Hemma H	23	2
Haller, Henry	54	2
Haller, Ida M	32	2
Haller, Isaac H	71	3
Haller, J Fessler	32	2
Haller, Jacob	29	2
Haller, Jacob L	29	2
Haller, James Al	91	3
Haller, James L	32	2
Haller, Jesse H	225	1
Haller, Joel	220	2
Haller, John	38	2
Haller, John	27, 38, 46, 137	2
Haller, John	46	2
Haller, John	137	2
Haller, John M	32	2
Haller, Joseph	7, 11	2
Haller, Josephine	20	2
Haller, Josiah	81	3
Haller, Lucy	84	2
Haller, M H	13	1
Haller, Margaret K	40	2
Haller, Margaret L	39	2
Haller, Mary	38	2
Haller, Mary Louise	23	2
Haller, Meridith	32	2
Haller, Michael	93	2
Haller, Michael H	58, 225	1
Haller, Michael H	65	2
Haller, Nannie L	39, 43	2
Haller, Nettie M	270	1
Haller, Nicholas T	13	1
Haller, Peter	38	2
Haller, Peter Jr	38, 46	2
Haller, Ruth E	49	2
Haller, Ruth S	49	2
Haller, Samuel	51	2
Haller, Sarah C	252	2
Haller, Sarah M	29	2
Haller, T H	60, 224	3
Haller, T H	23	2
Haller, T H	186	1
Haller, T Stuart	10, 49	2
Haller, Thomas	195	2

Haller, Thomas 13 1
Haller, Thomas H 202 3
Haller, Thomas H 54 2
Haller, Thos 185 3
Haller, Thos 54, 198 2
Haller, Thos H 249 1
Haller, Thos H 54 2
Haller, Tobias 54 2
Haller, William L 137 3
Haller, Wm 139 2
Haller, Wm L 29 2
Haller, Wm S 58 2
Hallet, Daniel 23 3
Hallet, Michael H 31 3
Hallman, Charley 31 2
Hallman, Hannah 41 2
Hallman, Hannah A 23, 31 2
Hallman, James H 31 2
Hallman, John L S 31 2
Hallman, Moses 31, 41 2
Hallman, Rene 58 2
Hallman, Roger 41 2
Hallman, Wm H 58 2
Halls, Nichols 231 2
Halm, Freda J 40 2
Halm, Frederick J 18 2
Halm, Hazel R 18 2
Halm, Maria V 40 2
Hamaker, Ida C 25 2
Hambleton, John 27 2
Hamburg, Mary C 41 2
Hame, Caleb 30 1
Hamer, Frederick 139 1
Hamerick, Lewis M 40 2
Hamerick, Mary C 40 2
Hamerick, Phoebe A 46 2
Hamilton, Anna W 85 1
Hamilton, C H 90 1
Hamilton, Catherine 8 2
Hamilton, E M 200 1
Hamilton, Edw M 20 2
Hamilton, Edward M 6 3
Hamilton, Edward M 16 2
Hamilton, Elizabeth E 15, 29 2
Hamilton, Elsie M 16 2
Hamilton, Florence V 41 2
Hamilton, Francis A 18 2
Hamilton, Geo 29 2
Hamilton, Geo W 15, 20 2
Hamilton, Georgianna 30 2
Hamilton, Gilmore O 16 2
Hamilton, Grafton B 187 3
Hamilton, Grafton B 85 1
Hamilton, Grover 20 2
Hamilton, Grover C 191 1
Hamilton, Harry I 31 2
Hamilton, Henry A 18 2
Hamilton, Henry A 13 1
Hamilton, Henry I 41 2
Hamilton, J A 119 2
Hamilton, J H 30 2
Hamilton, James 175 2
Hamilton, James W 28 2
Hamilton, John 118 1
Hamilton, John 8, 29 2
Hamilton, John H 15, 29, 30, 245 2
Hamilton, John R 31, 49 2
Hamilton, Mary M 41 2
Hamilton, Mary V 85 1
Hamilton, Nathan 96 1
Hamilton, Randolph 15, 49 2
Hamilton, Roger 20 2
Hamilton, Thomas B 27 2
Hamilton, Virgie D 191 1
Hamm, Jacob 38 2
Hammaker, B F 60 1
Hammaker, B F 2 2
Hammaker, Barbara E 5 2
Hammaker, Benjamin F 5, 46 2
Hammaker, Ernest 235 1
Hammaker, F E 5 2
Hammaker, P N 61 1
Hammaker, P N 25, 102 2
Hammaker, Peter N 52 1
Hammaker, Peter N 46, 177 2
Hammaker, W F 68 3
Hammaker, Wilbur F 5 2
Hamman, Anna V 3 2
Hammer, Alice V 1 2
Hammer, George 19 2
Hammer, James 164 1
Hammer, James G 106 3
Hammer, Mary A C 40 2
Hammett, Chas E 12 2
Hammett, D C 119 1
Hammett, D Calvin 12 2
Hammett, Eleanor A 15 2
Hammett, John C 240 1
Hammil, Laura H 36 2
Hammond, Adelaide 3 2
Hammond, Ann Maria 2 2
Hammond, Ann Matilda 2, 12 2
Hammond, Anna 30 2
Hammond, Anna Wilson 2 2
Hammond, Annie 187 3
Hammond, Annie C 35 2
Hammond, Burgess 207 3
Hammond, Burgess 18 2
Hammond, Carl 7 2
Hammond, Carry E 8 2
Hammond, Charles 7 2
Hammond, Charles S 7 2
Hammond, Charlotte W 14 2
Hammond, Chas 75 2
Hammond, Chas C 8 2
Hammond, Cornelius 19 2
Hammond, Crafton 43 2
Hammond, D B 7 2
Hammond, D R 11 2
Hammond, D V 12, 54 2
Hammond, D V 207 3
Hammond, Daniel 12 2
Hammond, Dawson 7, 46 2
Hammond, Dawson 278 1
Hammond, Dawson V 12, 23, 28, 46 2
Hammond, Dawson W 2 2
Hammond, Dennis 11 2
Hammond, Denton 11, 14, 45 2
Hammond, Denton 125 1
Hammond, Denton 14 3
Hammond, Drusilla 12 2
Hammond, E 14 2
Hammond, E D 45 2
Hammond, Eden 14 2
Hammond, Edgar 56 3
Hammond, Edgar J 41 2
Hammond, Eliza A 19 2
Hammond, Elizabeth 14, 30, 39, 43 2
Hammond, Elizabeth 187 3
Hammond, Elizabeth M 14 2
Hammond, Elizabeth R 15 2
Hammond, Emma 41 1
Hammond, Ernest A 54 2
Hammond, Eugene 44, 56, 188 3
Hammond, Eugene 2, 16 2
Hammond, Eugene S 184 1
Hammond, Eugene S 3, 16 2
Hammond, Evan 43, 45, 65 2
Hammond, Evan V 185 3
Hammond, F Sidney 3, 16 2
Hammond, Frances E 18 2
Hammond, Francis S 18 2
Hammond, Frank A 40 2
Hammond, G 57 2
Hammond, G B 239 1
Hammond, G B 87 3
Hammond, Geo 253 1
Hammond, Geo W 19 2
Hammond, Grafton 11, 14, 19, 45 2
Hammond, Grafton B 14, 39 2
Hammond, Grafton D 20, 30 2
Hammond, H Virginia 264 1
Hammond, Harriet 23 2
Hammond, Harriet 249 1
Hammond, Henrietta Lee 23, 43 2
Hammond, Howard D 172 1
Hammond, J 59 1
Hammond, J A 29 2
Hammond, J H 102 3
Hammond, Jane Ida 32 2
Hammond, Jemima 31 2

Hammond, John 29 2
Hammond, John 79, 183, 249 1
Hammond, John W 28 2
Hammond, Linwood 40 2
Hammond, Lloyd N 35 2
Hammond, Luther Lee 12, 23 2
Hammond, Margaret 38 2
Hammond, Mary A 40 2
Hammond, Mary B 235 1
Hammond, Mary C 29, 39 2
Hammond, Mary E A R 39 2
Hammond, Mary R 227a, 229a 2
Hammond, Mary V 39, 40 2
Hammond, Matilda M 57 2
Hammond, Matilda S 41 2
Hammond, N W 57 2
Hammond, Nathan 11, 14 2
Hammond, Nathan 70 1
Hammond, Nathan of O 43 2
Hammond, Nathan of V 43 2
Hammond, Netta Lee 23, 43 2
Hammond, Nicholas 43, 46 2
Hammond, Nicholas W 28 2
Hammond, O 43 2
Hammond, Ormond 45 2
Hammond, Philip 46 2
Hammond, Philip J 46 2
Hammond, Priscilla 46 2
Hammond, R T 7 2
Hammond, Rezin 49 2
Hammond, Richard 46 2
Hammond, Richard T 57 2
Hammond, Robt L 40 2
Hammond, Ruther Virginia 49 2
Hammond, Serena 52 2
Hammond, Thomas 7, 54, 56, 66, 75, 226, 275 2
Hammond, Thomas 8, 70, 136, 184, 185 3
Hammond, Thomas 133 1
Hammond, Thomas H 46, 54 2
Hammond, Thomas J 106 1
Hammond, Thos 2, 7, 14, 18, 49, 57 2
Hammond, Thos 138 3
Hammond, Thos 278 1
Hammond, Thos J 14 2
Hammond, Upton 56 2
Hammond, V 43 2
Hammond, Vachael 56 2
Hammond, Vachel 38 2
Hammond, Walter C 57 2
Hammond, Walter C of G 57 2
Hammond, Washington 43 2
Hammond, Wm 26 1
Hammond, Wm L 58 2
Hamner, Jas 113 3
Hampson, Amanda E 3 2
Hamrick, Henry W 39 2
Hamrick, John 205 2
Hamrick, John L M 29 2
Hamrick, Lewis 39 2
Hamrick, Lewis J 29 2
Hamrick, Michael 39 2
Han, Chas S 220 3
Handley, Catherine 8 2
Handley, Charles F 52 2
Handley, Curtis O 47 2
Handley, Dennis 185, 197, 203 2
Handley, Dennis 179 1
Handley, Jacob 8 2
Handley, John 197 2
Handley, John J 234 1
Handley, Phillip M 47 2
Handley, Sarah P 52 2
Hane, Carl H 170 2
Hane, Carl H 101, 252 1
Hane, Cora E 58 2
Hane, Daniel 11 2
Hane, David 271 1
Hane, Geo F 56 3
Hane, Geo F 107 1
Hane, Geo F 30 2
Hane, George C 32 1
Hane, Gertrude E 20 2
Hane, Jacob 15 3
Hane, Jacob D 30 2
Hane, Jacob D 97, 194, 197 1
Hane, James Edw 31 2
Hane, John 207 3
Hane, John 28, 31, 258, 282, 294 2
Hane, Margaret 28, 39 2
Hane, Maria 11 2
Hane, William H 58 2
Hane, Wm 11, 57 2
Hanell, Margaret 218 2
Hanell, Margaret M 218 2
Hanes, Charles H 9 2
Hanes, Frances 106 2
Hanes, Mary M 9 2
Hanes, Maurice 20 3
Hanes, Susie A 20 3
Hankey, F W 18 2
Hankey, Frederick 18, 165 2
Hankey, Frederick N 18 2
Hankey, Frederick W 156 1
Hankey, Geo 253 1
Hankey, Geo E 20, 29 2
Hankey, Geo W A 23 2
Hankey, Henry W 23 2
Hankey, Isaac 9, 25 2
Hankey, Isaac L 25, 41 2
Hankey, Isabella 25 2
Hankey, J A 265 1
Hankey, J A 18, 184 2
Hankey, J T 290 2
Hankey, John 27 2
Hankey, John H 20 2
Hankey, Justina 29 2
Hankey, Macey 12 2
Hankey, Marcie E 25 2
Hankey, Marcie Edna 41 2
Hankey, Mary E 12, 49 2
Hankey, Peter 89 2
Hankey, Peter 264 1
Hankey, Roy 195 2
Hankey, Roy W 12, 18, 49, 184 2
Hankey, Sarah E 52 2
Hankey, Sarah E C 18 2
Hankey, Sarah I 184 2
Hanks, Charlotte 29 2
Hanks, Jason 29 2
Hanks, Jerry 29 2
Hanley, J Hickman 52 1
Hanmer, Charles F 8 2
Hann, Elizabeth 57 3
Hann, Elizabeth 14 2
Hann, Henry 189 1
Hann, Henry 7 2
Hann, James H 27 2
Hann, John 26, 27 2
Hann, John 18 3
Hann, John D 30, 217 1
Hann, Leslie J 230 1
Hann, Lola I 30 1
Hann, Mary L 145 2
Hann, Mary L E 140 2
Hann, Mathias 38 2
Hann, Philip 14 2
Hann, Wm 57 2
Hanna, Isaac S 276 2
Hanna, J Milton 30 2
Hanna, John 27 2
Hanna, John L E 43 2
Hanna, Lydia 57 2
Hanna, Nathan 43 2
Hanna, Sarah 51 2
Hanna, Wm 27, 51, 57 2
Hanshew, Chas H & 20 2
Hanshew, Elbert J 16 2
Hanshew, Geo P 20 2
Hanshew, George B 19 2
Hanshew, Henry 67 1
Hanshew, Jno T 28 2
Hanshew, John 214, 228, 282 1
Hanshew, Philip 19 2
Hanshew, Wm 163 1
Hanshew, Wm E 28 2
Hanson, A B 1 2
Hanson, Geo A 1, 250 2
Hanson, Michael 129 3
Hanssen, Emma 16 2
Hanstine, John M 29 2
Hansue, Elizabeth 20 2

Hansue, Geo P 20 2
Hantz, John 177 2
Hantz, John 138 2
Hantz, John 197, 205 1
Hanvey, Conner 101 1
Hape, David 19 2
Hape, Geo 19 2
Hape, John 28 2
Har ey, J E 171 3
Harbaugh , Henry 165 3
Harbaugh, Ada M 223a 2
Harbaugh, Alexius 29 2
Harbaugh, Alice M 55 1
Harbaugh, Alvey J 2 2
Harbaugh, Alvey J 67 1
Harbaugh, Ann 22 2
Harbaugh, Ann Elizabeth 1 2
Harbaugh, Anna Margaret 2 2
Harbaugh, C 22, 29 2
Harbaugh, C F 52 2
Harbaugh, C H 20 2
Harbaugh, Carlton J 15 2
Harbaugh, Caroline E 8 2
Harbaugh, Carrie A 10 2
Harbaugh, Catherine 7, 8, 14 2
Harbaugh, Cecelia 58 2
Harbaugh, Chas H 22 2
Harbaugh, Christian 174 3
Harbaugh, Christian 7 2
Harbaugh, Chritian 185 3
Harbaugh, Clarence N 8 2
Harbaugh, Cornelia A E 22 2
Harbaugh, Daniel 11 2
Harbaugh, Daniel W 61 2
Harbaugh, David 71 1
Harbaugh, David 11 2
Harbaugh, E 18 1
Harbaugh, E B 51 2
Harbaugh, Edgar H 41 2
Harbaugh, Edith I 25 2
Harbaugh, Elias 7, 14, 15, 22, 28 2
Harbaugh, Elias 47, 200, 253 1
Harbaugh, Elias 223 3
Harbaugh, Elias of Jacob 14 2
Harbaugh, Elijah 205 3
Harbaugh, Ephraim 182 3
Harbaugh, Ephriam 164 1
Harbaugh, Ephriam F 15 2
Harbaugh, F E 20 2
Harbaugh, Geo 14, 35, 100 2
Harbaugh, Geo 194, 264 1
Harbaugh, Geo M 19, 20, 22, 61 2
Harbaugh, Glenn I 49 2
Harbaugh, H 40 1
Harbaugh, Hamilton 11, 22 2
Harbaugh, Helen Z 227 3
Harbaugh, Henry 7, 22, 26, 27, 100 2
Harbaugh, Henry 181, 193 1
Harbaugh, Henry 53, 185 3
Harbaugh, Henry H 223 3
Harbaugh, Henry of C 22, 89 2
Harbaugh, Henry of J 22 2
Harbaugh, Hiram 18 1
Harbaugh, Hiram 29, 35 2
Harbaugh, Hiram R 208 2
Harbaugh, Isaac D 25 2
Harbaugh, J 22 2
Harbaugh, J D 27 2
Harbaugh, Jacob 7, 14, 26, 27, 29 2
Harbaugh, Jacob 84, 200 1
Harbaugh, Jacob B 56 2
Harbaugh, Jacob of L 28 2
Harbaugh, Jacob Sr 26 2
Harbaugh, James O 52 2
Harbaugh, James P 179 3
Harbaugh, Jeremiah D 28, 35 2
Harbaugh, Jesse M 41 2
Harbaugh, John 184 3
Harbaugh, John 196 1
Harbaugh, John 26, 27, 237 2
Harbaugh, John E 52 2
Harbaugh, John of C 29 2
Harbaugh, John W 7, 28 2
Harbaugh, Kennard P 54 2
Harbaugh, L 28 2
Harbaugh, Lavinia 35 2
Harbaugh, Leonard 35, 187 2
Harbaugh, Leonard & 14 2
Harbaugh, Leonard C 8, 35, 40 2
Harbaugh, Levi 28 2
Harbaugh, Lewis T 188 3
Harbaugh, Lizzie 35 2
Harbaugh, Lottie 32 2
Harbaugh, Lottie 45 3
Harbaugh, M G 32 3
Harbaugh, M L 112 2
Harbaugh, Margaret 45 2
Harbaugh, Margaret S 39 2
Harbaugh, Marion L 2 2
Harbaugh, Martha 39 2
Harbaugh, Martin L 41 2
Harbaugh, Mary A 35, 40 2
Harbaugh, Mary Ann 40 2
Harbaugh, Mary B 41 2
Harbaugh, Mary C 125 2
Harbaugh, Mary E 41 2
Harbaugh, Michael 8 2
Harbaugh, Oscar P 45 2
Harbaugh, Roland W 227 3
Harbaugh, Samuel 182 2
Harbaugh, Samuel T 11 2
Harbaugh, Sanford 264 1
Harbaugh, Sarah 150 2
Harbaugh, Sarah J 58 2
Harbaugh, Sarah V 52 2
Harbaugh, Savilla 19 2
Harbaugh, Simon W 51 2
Harbaugh, Solomon 185 3
Harbaugh, Stanford 42, 48, 208 2
Harbaugh, Susanna M 20 2
Harbaugh, T H 72 3
Harbaugh, Thomas H 54 2
Harbaugh, Upton E 56 2
Harbaugh, Walter H 58 2
Harbaugh, Wm H 58 2
Harbaugh, Wm H 67 1
Harbaugh, Wm K 15 2
Harbaugh, Yost 61 2
Harbine, Thos 76 2
Harbst, George 38 2
Harbst, Mary 38 2
Harbst, Michael 38 2
Harden, T W 165 1
Harden, Wm 165 1
Hardey, E F 9 2
Hardey, Edw F 58 2
Hardey, Edward F 16, 43 2
Hardey, Nettie E 43 2
Hardey, Wm S 58 2
Harding, Ann R 2 2
Harding, Anna 102 3
Harding, Anna M 3 2
Harding, Anna Trail 3 2
Harding, Basil 5 2
Harding, Christian 32 1
Harding, Christian 7, 165, 197 2
Harding, Christian 38 3
Harding, Columbus 57 2
Harding, Constance 3 2
Harding, Elias H 116 1
Harding, Elias H 247 2
Harding, J M 153 2
Harding, J W 102 3
Harding, James 13, 208 1
Harding, James 18 3
Harding, James 203 2
Harding, James M 6, 31, 39, 96 3
Harding, James M 27, 29, 38, 282, 290 2
Harding, James M 32, 71, 228 1
Harding, James N 195 3
Harding, John 153 3
Harding, John 40 1
Harding, John 5, 34, 45, 150, 224a 2
Harding, John L 19, 27, 92 2
Harding, John L 8 3
Harding, Lewis 35, 51 2
Harding, Lewis R 288 2
Harding, Lewis R 288 2

Harding, Margaret E 5, 150 2
Harding, Norman B 43 2
Harding, Oliver P 153 3
Harding, Philip 7, 46 2
Harding, R A 160 3
Harding, Richard 186 3
Harding, Sarah 51 2
Harding, Sarah A 29 2
Harding, Wm 57 2
Hardings, John T 64 3
Hardman, Annie F 2 2
Hardman, Barbara 46 2
Hardman, Geo 46 2
Hardman, Geo 93 2
Hardman, George 53 3
Hardman, Henry 22 2
Hardman, Mary A 93 2
Hardman, Philip 46 2
Hardman, Philip 46 2
Hardman, Philip 98 3
Hardt, Charlotte 46 2
Hardt, Charlotte 7 2
Hardt, Geo 7 2
Hardt, George 19 2
Hardt, J C 177 1
Hardt, J C 87 3
Hardt, James C 50 3
Hardt, John 4 1
Hardt, John 8, 39, 61, 93, 181 2
Hardt, John 2 3
Hardt, John & 89 2
Hardt, John C 41, 60, 71, 72, 106, 165, 193 1
Hardt, John C 22, 29, 30, 40, 84, 148 2
Hardt, John C 2, 42, 50, 196 3
Hardt, Peter Sr 46 2
Hardt, Wm M 50 3
Hardt, Wm M 30 2
Hardy, Clarence E 224 2
Hardy, John 29 2
Hardy, Lewis 35 2
Hardy, Lewis D 29 2
Hargate, Elizabeth 14 2
Hargate, John 57 2
Hargate, John 91 3
Hargate, Peter 70, 113, 195 3
Hargate, Wm H 57 2
Harget, Edw S 87 3
Harget, Elizabeth 46 2
Harget, John 51 1
Harget, John E 15 3
Harget, Peter 46 2
Hargett, A H 22, 58 1
Hargett, Abraham 1 2
Hargett, Abraham 1 2
Hargett, Abraham H 1 2
Hargett, Anna K 2 2
Hargett, Annie K 2 2
Hargett, Annie Keller 80 2
Hargett, Annie M 8 2
Hargett, Arthur L D 30 2
Hargett, Arthur V 52 2
Hargett, Catharine E 8, 9, 15 2
Hargett, Charles N 27 3
Hargett, Chas N 8, 30 2
Hargett, Clara L 9, 30 2
Hargett, Cornelia A 9 2
Hargett, Curtis 18, 39, 138 2
Hargett, D H 82, 191, 229, 240 1
Hargett, D H 54 2
Hargett, Dessie M 217 3
Hargett, Douglas 2, 268 2
Hargett, Douglas H 12 2
Hargett, E H 201 1
Hargett, Earl F 217 3
Hargett, Earlston L 15 2
Hargett, Edw T 15 2
Hargett, Elizabeth 15, 30 2
Hargett, Elsie A 10 1
Hargett, Emma C 52 2
Hargett, Emma L 15 2
Hargett, Emma M 12, 16 2
Hargett, Ernest 124 3
Hargett, Florence 58 2
Hargett, Francis A 18 2
Hargett, Frank C 18 2
Hargett, Geo F 15 2
Hargett, Grace T 20 2
Hargett, Grace T 53 1
Hargett, Henry N P 22 2
Hargett, J E W 82 3
Hargett, Jessie Matilda 32 2
Hargett, John 1, 28, 96 2
Hargett, John 177 1
Hargett, John 165 3
Hargett, John B 30 2
Hargett, John E 31, 52 2
Hargett, John E W 8, 30 2
Hargett, John L 30 2
Hargett, John W 28, 30, 264 2
Hargett, Joseph L 15 2
Hargett, Joseph Lee 32 2
Hargett, Margaret 41, 52 2
Hargett, Mary 38 2
Hargett, Mary C 18 2
Hargett, P L 15, 30, 52 2
Hargett, P L 55, 176 3
Hargett, P L 82 1
Hargett, Peter 33 1
Hargett, Peter L 31, 40, 46, 51 2
Hargett, R S 52 2
Hargett, Rebecca 49 2
Hargett, Richard S 41 2
Hargett, S 28 2
Hargett, S L 176 3
Hargett, S T 52, 119, 225 1
Hargett, S T 51 2
Hargett, S T 192 3
Hargett, Samuel 46, 51 2
Hargett, Samuel 249 1
Hargett, Samuel F 52 2
Hargett, Samuel L 12, 52, 214a 2
Hargett, Sarah J 52 2
Hargett, Schaefer T 40 2
Hargett, Schaeffer T 46, 52 2
Hargett, Schaeffer T 174 3
Hargett, Schaeffer T 97 1
Hargett, Schaffer T 31 2
Hargett, Schaffer T 119 1
Hargett, Shaffer T 12, 15 2
Hargett, Walter S 16 2
Hargett, Wm D 58 2
Hargett, Wm S 31 2
Hargis, Edw S 22 2
Harine, Catherine 9 2
Harkesheimer, Joseph 185 2
Harlan, J G W 43 2
Harlan, John M 28 2
Harlan, Nancy 43 2
Harley, Albert L 3 2
Harley, C F 8 2
Harley, Catherine 8, 45 2
Harley, Cornelius F 8 2
Harley, Daisy May 3 2
Harley, Elizabeth D 16 2
Harley, G W T 19, 45 2
Harley, Geo W T 96, 111 3
Harley, H T 19, 45 2
Harley, Henry 8 2
Harley, Henry T 23 2
Harley, J E 196 3
Harley, J E 8 2
Harley, Joseph S 45 2
Harley, Josephus E 23, 31 2
Harley, Josephus H 31 2
Harley, Joshua 27 2
Harley, Madeline Rebecca 3 2
Harley, Maggie M 16 2
Harley, Maggie W 43 2
Harley, Margaret M 153 1
Harley, Mary T 31 2
Harley, Mary Thedosia 40 2
Harley, Mary Theodisia 40 2
Harley, Minnie E 40 2
Harley, Narciso 43 2
Harley, Narcissa 8 2
Harley, Otho F 45 2
Harley, T E 45 2
Harley, W C 43 2
Harley, Willard 16 2
Harley, Wm A 40 2
Harley, Wm M 58 2
Harlin, James W 27 2
Harlin, Joshua 27 2

Harm, Luther E 37 1
Harm, Philip 116 1
Harman, Ada L 134 2
Harman, Anna M 2 2
Harman, Benjamin F 5 2
Harman, Charles W 9 2
Harman, Christian 7 2
Harman, Christian 88 1
Harman, Edna K 9 2
Harman, Frederick 54 3
Harman, Geo 185 3
Harman, Geo 117, 140 1
Harman, Geo 7, 22, 89 2
Harman, George 57 1
Harman, George I 63 1
Harman, John 26 3
Harman, M G 185 3
Harman, Margaret 38, 39 2
Harman, Nicholas 43 2
Harman, Ralph C 9 2
Harman, Winfield S 5 2
Harmis, Chas W 29 2
Harmis, George W 19 2
Harmis, Jacob 19, 29 2
Harmis, Jacob O 29 2
Harmis, Susan 19 2
Harmon, Christian 31 3
Harmon, Geo W 224 3
Harmon, Mary E 224 3
Harmon, May E 239 1
Harmon, Wm 29 2
Harn, Ambrose E 2 2
Harn, Charlotte 7 2
Harn, Ellen V 54 2
Harn, Emory G 16 2
Harn, Fannie 2 2
Harn, John 39 2
Harn, John H 31 2
Harn, Laura L 36 2
Harn, Mary 154 2
Harn, Matilda C 39 2
Harn, S W 7, 180 2
Harn, Singleton W 51 2
Harn, Thomas 51 2
Harn, Thomas W 54 2
Harn, Thos W 7 2
Harn, Wm 39 2
Harn, Wm A 51 2
Harn, Wm B 31, 45, 154 2
Harne, B F 30 2
Harne, G O 30 2
Harne, James O 30 2
Harne, James O 75 3
Harne, Thos W 177 2
Harner, A A 166 3
Harner, Adolphers 52 2
Harner, Adolphus 182 3
Harner, Frederick 115 2
Harner, H C 132 2
Harner, Harry C 52 2
Harner, J A 161, 206 3
Harner, J W 163 3
Harner, Jacob 106 3
Harner, Jacob 29 2
Harner, James E 36 2
Harner, Lola Routzahn 36 2
Harner, Sophia L 52 2
Harnwell, Anna J 49 2
Harnwell, Anna Jane 18 2
Harnwell, F W 49 2
Harnwell, Frederick W 18 2
Harnwell, Gaylord P 97 1
Harold, David D 12 2
Harold, Grace 12 2
Harp, Alice M 3 2
Harp, Bertha A 49 2
Harp, Bessie 215, 222 2
Harp, Bessie 68 1
Harp, Bessie D 62 1
Harp, Bessie D 31, 49 2
Harp, Bessie D 73 3
Harp, Catherine 7, 19 2
Harp, Claretta E 9 2
Harp, Daniel 11, 51, 172 2
Harp, Daniel E 25 2
Harp, Daniel V 208 1
Harp, Daniel V 11, 29, 39 2
Harp, Earl D 16 2
Harp, G F 9 2
Harp, Geo 164 1
Harp, Geo 93, 231 2
Harp, Geo S 20 2
Harp, George 19 2
Harp, Hannah 22 2
Harp, Hezekiah 23 2
Harp, Isaiah 25 2
Harp, Jacob 106 3
Harp, Jacob 19, 27 2
Harp, Jno 171 3
Harp, John 147, 156 1
Harp, John 7, 19, 29, 31 2
Harp, Josiah 19, 30 2
Harp, M D 38 1
Harp, Madeline 31 2
Harp, Markwood 166, 294 2
Harp, Markwood 213 3
Harp, Markwood D 40 2
Harp, Markwood D 218 3
Harp, Mary A 30, 39, 40 2
Harp, Mary Ann 11 2
Harp, Mary E 40 2
Harp, Paul K 2 2
Harp, Peter S 40 2
Harp, R S 66, 89, 163 2
Harp, R S 57, 72, 82 3
Harp, Reno 218 3
Harp, Reno 220, 221, 214a, 231 2
Harp, Reno S 10, 56, 57, 73, 75, 107, 180, 192, 199, 210, 213, 218, 226 3
Harp, Reno S 2, 9, 15, 31, 40, 49, 67, 72, 78, 93, 119, 128, 139, 145, 198, 199, 209, 215, 229a, 231, 235, 265, 277, 283, 284 2
Harp, Reno S 34, 41, 42, 62, 68, 76, 92, 99, 107, 111, 119, 123, 140, 150, 165, 188, 214, 219, 230, 240, 260, 272, 273 1
Harp, Roger C 23 2
Harp, Roscoe A 40 2
Harp, Roy B 3 2
Harper, Arbelon 2 2
Harper, Blanche S 9 2
Harper, Calvin 9 2
Harper, Charles R 9, 227a 2
Harper, Chas R 8 1
Harper, Earl J 16 2
Harper, Emma V 16 2
Harper, Ernest K 16, 271 2
Harper, Francis (cold) 18 2
Harper, Harry 16 2
Harper, Harry E 16 2
Harper, J Norman 47, 49 2
Harper, Lloyd 35 2
Harper, Maria (col'd) 39 2
Harper, Mary E 16 2
Harper, Phoebe 47 2
Harper, R R 165 3
Harper, Richard 84, 90, 125, 223, 264 1
Harper, Richard 179, 202 3
Harper, Richard 177 2
Harper, Richard K 49 2
Harper, Thomas 54 2
Harper, Wm 57 2
Harr, Isaish 25 2
Harr, Rebecca 49 2
Harriet, John 65, 76, 137, 197 2
Harriett, John 26 2
Harriett, John 256, 283 1
Harrington, A H 2 2
Harrington, A H 60, 61 1
Harrington, Adolphus H 99 2
Harrington, Eliza C 60 1
Harrington, F H 62 1
Harrington, Franklin H 48 1
Harrington, Franklin H 18, 110, 286 2
Harrington, Geo W 20 2
Harrington, Margaret A 39 2
Harrington, Mary C 2 2
Harrington, May Pearl 18 2
Harrington, Timothy 163 1
Harrington, Wm T 125 1
Harris, Alfred 3 2
Harris, Ann 1 2
Harris, Augustus 49 2

Harris, Chas G 6 3
Harris, Clarissa 22 2
Harris, Clarrissa 8 2
Harris, Dorothea 32 2
Harris, E F 210 3
Harris, Elizabeth 31 2
Harris, Ella 31 2
Harris, Ella M 16, 220 2
Harris, Ephriam G 15 2
Harris, Estelle May 3 2
Harris, Geo W 22 2
Harris, Gordon E 32 2
Harris, Gordon W 32 2
Harris, H R 164 1
Harris, Henry 138 2
Harris, Henry 41 1
Harris, Henry R 22 2
Harris, Henry R 84, 117, 118, 135, 219 1
Harris, Henry R 124 3
Harris, Ida 25 2
Harris, Jack M 32 2
Harris, James 20, 31, 214a 2
Harris, James 28 1
Harris, James H 16, 20, 31, 39, 54, 171, 231 2
Harris, James H 161 3
Harris, James H 34, 106, 179, 240 1
Harris, James Heinlein 32, 178 2
Harris, James Heinlein 189 3
Harris, James P 40 2
Harris, Jas H 55 1
Harris, John 27 2
Harris, John Jr 26 2
Harris, John P 31, 61 2
Harris, Laura V 31 2
Harris, Lutie Price 35 2
Harris, M Emma 39 2
Harris, Maggie M 45 2
Harris, Maria V 6 3
Harris, Mary M 40 2
Harris, Mary V 40 2
Harris, Matilda 38 2
Harris, Nathan 43 2
Harris, Nellie V 52 2
Harris, Orman I 45 2
Harris, Richard 49 2
Harris, S F 223 1
Harris, S Fenton 31 2
Harris, Samuel H 52 2
Harris, Thomas 54 2
Harris, Thos 54, 75, 171 2
Harris, Wm H 58 2
Harris, Wm M 40, 58 2
Harris, Wm M 58 2
Harris, Z G 116 2
Harris, Zachanah G 61 2
Harrison, Andrew T 3 2
Harrison, Ann R 29 2
Harrison, Augustus 1 2
Harrison, Carlton 15, 18 2
Harrison, Constance C 9 2
Harrison, Eugene L 15 2
Harrison, F M 51 3
Harrison, Fannie Estella 18 2
Harrison, G 223 3
Harrison, G W 179 1
Harrison, Geo W 19 2
Harrison, Gertrude B 248 1
Harrison, Grafton A 20 2
Harrison, J N Jr 139 1
Harrison, James H 32 2
Harrison, Joseph 26, 28 2
Harrison, Josiah 29 2
Harrison, Luther F 35 2
Harrison, Madge V 32 2
Harrison, Mary 61 2
Harrison, Mary M 35, 40 2
Harrison, Philip L 61 2
Harrison, Theodore 19 2
Harrison, Thomas P 106 3
Harrison, Wm F 189 1
Harrison, Wm H 58 2
Harrison, Z 263 1
Harrison, Zephaniah 61 2
Harritt, John 26 3
Harritt, John 196 1
Harritt, John 1, 165 2
Harritter, Conrad 7 2
Harritter, Jacob 7 2
Harry, Elizabeth 14 2
Harry, Emma I 45 2
Harry, Henry 129 3
Harry, Irving 40 2
Harry, Isaac R 25 2
Harry, Mary C 40 2
Harry, Oscar P 45 2
Harry, Parmenio R 25, 46, 154 2
Harry, William H 15 3
Harsbugh, Geo 14 2
Harsh, B B 189 3
Harshman, Aopha V 2 2
Harshman, Barbara A 5 2
Harshman, C 279 1
Harshman, Catherine 7 2
Harshman, Charitisn [sic] 176 1
Harshman, Charles D 1 1
Harshman, Chas E 5 2
Harshman, Chas W 15 2
Harshman, Christian 7, 8 2
Harshman, Clarretta V 8 2
Harshman, Clyde 66 2
Harshman, Clyde L 37 1
Harshman, Clyde L 12, 41 2
Harshman, Cornelius 8 2
Harshman, D 55 3
Harshman, D Caleb 12 2
Harshman, D L 15 2
Harshman, Daniel 68, 126 1
Harshman, Daniel 7 2
Harshman, Daniel C 12, 15 2
Harshman, Daniel H 12 2
Harshman, David L 12 2
Harshman, Emmert L 15 2
Harshman, Ezra 15 2
Harshman, Franklin 156, 277 1
Harshman, Franklin D 18 2
Harshman, Isaac 38 1
Harshman, J 55 3
Harshman, J E 58 2
Harshman, J Frank 32 2
Harshman, J T 61, 100, 164 1
Harshman, J T 169 2
Harshman, Jennie C 32 2
Harshman, John 5, 8, 29 2
Harshman, John 39 3
Harshman, John 197 1
Harshman, John T 2, 30, 39 2
Harshman, Jonathan 29 2
Harshman, Josa A 76 1
Harshman, L P 119 2
Harshman, Laura C 35 2
Harshman, Lawson 8 2
Harshman, Lawson T 35 2
Harshman, LCR 166 1
Harshman, Lynn J 18 2
Harshman, Melissa J 41 2
Harshman, Millard A 32 2
Harshman, Minnie C 39 2
Harshman, Mollie 230 1
Harshman, Naomi 96 2
Harshman, Ora 167, 197 3
Harshman, R D 35 2
Harshman, Ralph 58 2
Harshman, Roy H 35 2
Harshman, Russell D 220 1
Harshman, Samuel 210a 2
Harshman, U W 30 2
Harshman, Vada E 12 2
Harshman, Valentine 176 1
Harshman, Welty 242 2
Harshman, Wm 189 2
Harshman, Wm C 58 2
Harshman, Wm E 35 2
Harsman, Daniel [sic] 264 1
Harsnipe, Alice 1 2
Hart, A 100 1
Hart, David 11 2
Hart, Elias 14 2
Hart, Elias 117, 215 1
Hart, Ellis 14 2
Hart, Geo 37 1
Hart, Jacob 26, 262 2
Hart, John 144, 152 1

Hart, John 26, 203 2
Hart, John 8 3
Hart, John C 87, 179 3
Hart, Joshua 144 1
Hart, Margaret 14 2
Hart, R S 112 2
Hart, Reno S 219 1
Hart, Wm 57 2
Hartdagen, Jennie M 32 2
Hartdagen, Ruth G 32 2
Hartford Accident & Indemnity Co 20, 54, 145 2
Hartford Accident & Indemnity Co 28 1
Hartford Accident and Indemnity Co 44, 238 1
Hartig, Bessie 199 2
Harting, Geo Edw 46 2
Harting, George Edward 20 2
Harting, Peter J 46 2
Hartman, Abraham 1 2
Hartman, Ann 1 2
Hartman, Ann 1 2
Hartman, Annie C 2 2
Hartman, Charles F 41 2
Hartman, Claud J 16 2
Hartman, Daniel A 12 2
Hartman, Edward L 16 2
Hartman, John J 41 2
Hartman, John M 31 2
Hartman, Joseph V 56 2
Hartman, Mary C 31, 41 2
Hartman, Mary M 39, 43 2
Hartman, Mattie L 16 2
Hartman, Nicholas 43 2
Hartman, Russell F 12 2
Hartman, Valentine 2, 56 2
Harts, Francis 18 2
Hartsock, Asbury 2 2
Hartsock, Clarence L 60 1
Hartsock, Daniel 144, 226 2
Hartsock, David 11 2
Hartsock, David E H 12 2
Hartsock, Elizabeth 14, 28 2
Hartsock, Frank 134 2
Hartsock, Geo W 20 2
Hartsock, H D 67 3
Hartsock, H D 101 2
Hartsock, Henry 22, 27, 39, 43, 57 2
Hartsock, Henry 141 3
Hartsock, I S B 79 1
Hartsock, J 179, 245 1
Hartsock, J F B 29, 107, 223a 2
Hartsock, J P 104 1
Hartsock, J S 223a 2
Hartsock, J S B 27 1
Hartsock, James D 28 2
Hartsock, John 144, 179 1
Hartsock, John 11, 14, 27, 28, 38, 80, 154 2
Hartsock, John A 28 2
Hartsock, John L 28 2
Hartsock, Joseph 116 1
Hartsock, Joseph 27, 28, 38, 39, 57 2
Hartsock, Joseph H 118 1
Hartsock, Joseph H 28 2
Hartsock, Keefer 60 1
Hartsock, Lott 14, 101, 107 2
Hartsock, Lott 160 3
Hartsock, Lott 79, 205 1
Hartsock, Lottie 39 2
Hartsock, Lydia 35 2
Hartsock, Mamie 12 2
Hartsock, Mary 38 2
Hartsock, Mordechai 39 2
Hartsock, Ozola I 20 2
Hartsock, Sarah A 57 2
Hartsock, Theophilus 57 2
Hartsock, Washington 57 2
Hartsock, Wm 57 2
Hartsock, Wm T 2 2
Hartz, Joseph 27 2
Hartz, Matilda 27 2
Hartzell, Carrie B 74 1
Hartzell, Mary 38 2
Hartzock, Henry 58 1
Hartzock, John 27 2
Harves, Ruby 265 2
Harvey, Evelyn E 32 2
Harvey, Isaac 263 1
Harvey, James N 30 2
Harvey, Matilda S 123 1
Harward, Thomas N 54 2
Harwelil, Lewis 35 2
Harwelil, Marshall G 35 2
Harwetel, Hannah 23 2
Harwetel, Lewis 23 2
Harwood, McKendree N 40 2
Harwood, Thomas 137 1
Harwood, Thomas 288 2
Harwood, Thomas N 54 2
Haskin, George 282 2
Haskins, Geo 32 1
Haskins, George 32, 184 3
Haskins, George 268 2
Hasselbock, George 40 1
Hassler, Christian 7 2
Hathaway, Emma V 15 2
Hathaway, Orville D 15 2
Hatherly, Benjamin 5 2
Hatherly, Joshua 27 2
Hatherly, Lucy 35 2
Hatherly, Mary Ann 38 2
Hatherly, Otho 45 2
Hathway, Orville D 45 2
Haubert, Magdalene 38 2
Hauck, John 26 2
Hauck, John Jr 26 2
Hauer, Ann C 1 2
Hauer, Ann Catherine 1 2
Hauer, Ann S 2 2
Hauer, Chas A 9 2
Hauer, Chas N 8 2
Hauer, Clara E 8 2
Hauer, Daniel 11, 275 2
Hauer, Daniel 31, 165 3
Hauer, Daniel Jr 11 2
Hauer, Daniel Sr 18 2
Hauer, Geo 40, 123, 263 1
Hauer, Geo 11 2
Hauer, Geo M 19 2
Hauer, George 165 3
Hauer, Margaret 38 2
Hauer, Mary L 1, 51 2
Hauer, N D 65 2
Hauer, N D 26 1
Hauer, Nicholas D 213 1
Hauer, Nicholas D 1, 11, 19, 38, 43, 51 2
Hauer, Susan 1, 51, 52 2
Hauet, Mary l 40 2
Haugh Eli G 272 1
Haugh Wm 171 1
Haugh, A A 271 2
Haugh, Adam 70, 97 1
Haugh, Ann 26 2
Haugh, Anna Mary 31 2
Haugh, Catherine 8, 22, 28 2
Haugh, Chas 31 2
Haugh, E G 55, 197 3
Haugh, Eli 222, 214a 2
Haugh, Eli 179 1
Haugh, Eli G 16, 102, 241, 259 2
Haugh, Eli G 40, 265, 283 1
Haugh, Eli G 10 3
Haugh, Eli J 195 2
Haugh, Forrest D 32 2
Haugh, Geo B 31 2
Haugh, Henry 22 2
Haugh, Ida V 54 2
Haugh, Jacob 28 2
Haugh, Jesse M 31, 32 2
Haugh, John 57, 163, 172 1
Haugh, John 26, 28, 57, 111 2
Haugh, John A 31, 58 2
Haugh, John A 31 2
Haugh, John H 31 2
Haugh, John M 31, 46 2
Haugh, Josiah 8, 22 2
Haugh, Louisa 31 2
Haugh, Mollie 41 2
Haugh, Nannie Dora Delaplane 175 1
Haugh, Paul 46 2

Haugh, Paul 23 3
Haugh, Samuel C 219 1
Haugh, Susan 52 2
Haugh, Susan H 40 1
Haugh, Thomas 35 3
Haugh, Thomas F 54 2
Haugh, William 282 2
Haugh, William 9 3
Haugh, Wm 106 3
Haugh, Wm 28, 46, 57 2
Haugh, Wm H 58 2
Haugh, Wm H 75 3
Haugh, Wm H 47, 51 1
Haupt, Albert T 2, 31 2
Haupt, Alta G 2 2
Haupt, Amanda 3, 28 2
Haupt, Geo W 218 3
Haupt, Jacob 30 2
Haupt, Jacob 30 2
Haupt, Jacob A 31 2
Haupt, Jacob N 28 2
Haupt, Jonas 61 1
Haupt, Jonathan 30 2
Haupt, Josiah 30 2
Haupt, Lydia 240 1
Haupt, Lydia C 35 2
Haupt, Mary M 35, 40 2
Haupt, Maurice 2 2
Haupt, Maurice E 31 2
Haupt, Nicholas 163 1
Haupt, Nicholas 43 2
Hauptman, George 19 2
Hauptman, Gergtha 20 2
Hauptman, Mary M 38 2
Hauptman, Philip 38, 46 2
Hauptman, Philip 91, 191 1
Hauptman, Philip 23 3
Haurer, Daniel Jr 31 3
Hauser, Floyd C 125 2
Hauser, Frederick 80 2
Hauser, Joseph C 125 2
Hauser, Michael 163, 228, 253, 263 1
Hauser, Michael 80, 100, 107, 144 2
Hautz, John 28 2
Hautz, John 110 1
Hautz, John 28 2
Hautz, Sarah 28 2
Hautz, Sarah 28 2
Hauver, Albert A 33 1
Hauver, Albert L 3, 20 2
Hauver, Charlotte C 54 2
Hauver, Christian 7 2
Hauver, Chritian 167 3
Hauver, Clyde L 9 2
Hauver, E D 122 2
Hauver, Effie V 9 2
Hauver, Emma B 3 2
Hauver, Ephraim D 167 3
Hauver, Geo 19 2
Hauver, Geo Jr 19 2
Hauver, Grace F 20 2
Hauver, Hilda Mae 23 2
Hauver, Ira H 20 2
Hauver, Jacob 249 1
Hauver, John C 167 3
Hauver, Margaret E 9 2
Hauver, Margaret R 49 2
Hauver, N D 46 2
Hauver, Peter 7, 46 2
Hauver, Roy V 63 1
Hauver, Roy V 49 2
Hauver, Stanley E 3, 20 2
Hauver, T L 15 3
Hauver, Thaddeus L 54, 58 2
Hauver, William E 145 2
Hauver, Wm 58 2
Havner, Annie L 11 2
Havner, David 11 2
Hawes, Charles G 10 2
Hawes, Charles W 10 2
Hawes, Clyde V 9 2
Hawes, Ida B 49 2
Hawes, Mary J 9 2
Hawes, Richard W 49 2
Hawes, Ruby 268 2
Hawk, Andrew 5 2
Hawk, Barbara 5 2
Hawk, Elijah B 15 2
Hawk, Fannie M 15 2
Hawk, Geo 5, 46, 169 2
Hawk, Peter 46 2
Hawker, Allen W 38 2
Hawker, Andrew 197 2
Hawker, Edward P J 189 3
Hawker, G W 46 2
Hawker, Geo 138 2
Hawker, Geo 222 3
Hawker, Geo W 39 2
Hawker, Joseph W 32 2
Hawker, Margaret A 39 2
Hawker, Mary E 32 2
Hawker, Philip 46 2
Hawker, Philip 124 2
Hawker, Richard 32 2
Hawkins, Mary E 59 2
Hawkins, Thomas 54, 228a 2
Hawkins, Thos 277 1
Hawkins, William A 59 2
Hawkins, Wm L 59 2
Hawkwe, George W 209 3
Hawman, Peter 46 2
Hawman, Philip J 46 2
Hawn, Peter 217a 2
Hawn, Simon 189 1
Hawver, Susanna 51 2
Hay, George Thomas 84 1
Hay, Mary A 84 1
Hayden, Basil 137 2
Hayder, Isaac 138 2
Hayes 139 2
Hayes, Alan 235 2
Hayes, Albert 43 3
Hayes, Charlotte 32 2
Hayes, Elizabeth 14 2
Hayes, Geo R 59 1
Hayes, Herman Homer 23 2
Hayes, Ida L 280 1
Hayes, J Garrott 178 2
Hayes, J T 223 3
Hayes, James T 188 2
Hayes, James T 55 1
Hayes, John O 14 3
Hayes, John O 101 2
Hayes, Joseph 181, 186, 219a, 276 2
Hayes, Josephine 32 2
Hayes, Samuel 227 2
Hayes, Thomas C 218a 2
Hayes, Thos C 44 1
Hayes, W L 138 2
Hayes, Wm H 99 2
Haynes, John 214 2
Hays, Abraham 1 2
Hays, Allen 2 2
Hays, Andrew T 2 2
Hays, C S 39 2
Hays, Catherine S 30 2
Hays, Cyrus A 23 2
Hays, Cyrus S 52 2
Hays, Elizabeth 14, 30 2
Hays, F Leonard 280 1
Hays, Geo 54 2
Hays, Geo R 106 3
Hays, Geo R 19 2
Hays, Geo Thomas 28 2
Hays, George R 20 2
Hays, George W 19, 224a 2
Hays, Harriet D 27 2
Hays, Harriet V 22 2
Hays, Henrietta 22 2
Hays, Henry 51 2
Hays, Hilleary 22 2
Hays, J T 140 1
Hays, James T 205 3
Hays, James T 2, 14, 30, 31, 54, 250 2
Hays, James T 219 1
Hays, John 223, 280 1
Hays, John 51 2
Hays, John G 36 2
Hays, John O 71, 164, 200 1
Hays, John O 30 2
Hays, John O 41 3
Hays, Jos 54 3

Hays, Joseph 125, 225 1
Hays, Joseph 6 3
Hays, Joseph 14, 22, 30, 202 2
Hays, Joseph G 27, 28 2
Hays, Joseph K 109 1
Hays, Levin 35 2
Hays, Lucy G 36 2
Hays, Maria E 22, 39 2
Hays, Mary 27 2
Hays, Mary A M 28 2
Hays, May 40 2
Hays, S C 2 2
Hays, Samuel 19, 51 2
Hays, Samuel S 54 2
Hays, Sarah A 19 2
Hays, Sarah A 51 2
Hays, Sarah Weimer 31 2
Hays, Silas A 86 1
Hays, Susan C 52 2
Hays, T J 250 2
Hays, Thomas 22, 26, 54, 159 2
Hays, Thomas 167 3
Hays, Thomas C 54, 190, 221a 2
Hays, Thomas C 190 2
Hays, Thos 201 1
Hays, Thos 1 2
Hays, Thos C 12, 31, 52 2
Hays, Thos L 54 2
Hays, Washington 57 2
Hays, Watson 28 2
Hays, Wilson 5, 35, 57, 87 2
Hays, Wilson 184 3
Hays, Wilson L 57 2
Hays, Wm 51 2
Hays, Wm H 118 1
Hayward, Maria T 54 2
Hayward, Maria Tyler 96 3
Hayward, Thomas B 54 2
Hazen, George L 20 2
Head, John 27, 57, 116, 282 2
Head, John 279 1
Head, Wm 25 1
Head, Wm 150 2
Head, Wm B 82 1
Head, Wm B 57, 150 2
Heagey, Barbara A V 5 2
Heagey, C A 184 2
Heagey, C A 179 1
Heagey, C A 65 3
Heagey, G W G 32 2
Heagey, Henry F C 32 2
Heagey, J F R 85 1
Heagey, Jesse F R 32 2
Heagey, Jessie F R 222 2
Heagy, Anna M 8 2
Heagy, C A 80 2
Heagy, C A 27 3
Heagy, Charles A 8 2
Heagy, J F R 55 1
Heagy, Jesse F R 142, 233 1
Heake, Martin 39 2
Heaphy, Wm V 41 1
Heapley, George 38 3
Heard, Ezra 15 2
Hearn, Daniel Sr 11 2
Hearn, Josiah L 11 2
Heater, Chas E 49 2
Heater, John 29 2
Heater, Philip H 46 2
Heater, Richard 46 2
Heatwole, Helen K 23 2
Hebb, E T 209 3
Hebb, Edw 146 1
Hebb, Edw T 91 3
Hebb, Edw T 66, 84 2
Hebb, Edward T 39, 97 3
Hebb, Edward T 113 2
Hebb, Geo Wm H 19 2
Hebb, Peter S 46 2
Hebbard, Ebenezer B 14 2
Hebbe, Edw T 163 1
Hebbe, Edw T 19 2
Hebberd, Wm 96 2
Heck, Charles K 49 2
Heck, Elizabeth 15 2
Heck, Elizabeth G 49 2
Heck, Geo W 20 2
Heck, Hiram R 15 2
Heck, Jacob 37 3
Heck, Jacob 26 2
Heck, Jacob Sr 26 2
Heck, Peter 179 3
Heck, Peter 169 2
Heck, R Franklin 49 2
Heckathorn, Christian 19 2
Heckathorn, George 19 2
Heckathrone, Mary 39 2
Heckman, Harriot 279 1
Hedge, Charles W 241 2
Hedge, Frederick 124 3
Hedge, John 260 1
Hedge, Lilly J 241 2
Hedge, S A 52 2
Hedge, Solomon D 100 1
Hedges, Amanda S 2, 35 2
Hedges, Anna Marie 2 2
Hedges, Annie P 20 2
Hedges, Anova K 12, 18 2
Hedges, Bailey S 5 2
Hedges, C C 40 2
Hedges, Catherine 56 1
Hedges, Catherine 26 2
Hedges, Catherine 8 2
Hedges, Catherine M 11 2
Hedges, Charles H 10 2
Hedges, Charles W 10, 232 2
Hedges, Clinton E 10, 40 2
Hedges, Daniel A 11 2
Hedges, David L 12, 23 2
Hedges, David L 226 3
Hedges, Dorcas 11 2
Hedges, Eneas 14 2
Hedges, Eneas 263 1
Hedges, Enos 186 3
Hedges, Enos 11, 22 2
Hedges, F H 115 1
Hedges, Florence C 18 2
Hedges, Frank 162 1
Hedges, Frank H 52 2
Hedges, Frank H 197 1
Hedges, Frank H Jr 18 2
Hedges, Frank H Sr ? 18 2
Hedges, Frank L 12 2
Hedges, Gideon M 20 2
Hedges, Gillelan M 40 2
Hedges, H H 218a 2
Hedges, Harry L 23 2
Hedges, Harry Z 12, 16, 18 2
Hedges, Henry S 22 2
Hedges, John S 52 2
Hedges, John W 31, 40 2
Hedges, Joseph 25 1
Hedges, Joseph 26, 38 2
Hedges, Joseph A 39 2
Hedges, Joseph H 39 2
Hedges, L E 14 2
Hedges, L E 152, 195, 277 1
Hedges, Lewis A 35 2
Hedges, Lycurgus E 8, 35 2
Hedges, Margaret E 22 2
Hedges, Mary 38 2
Hedges, Mary Ann 40 2
Hedges, Mary D 41, 47, 52 2
Hedges, Mary E 40 2
Hedges, Mary M 179 1
Hedges, Mary M 39, 51 2
Hedges, S H 52 2
Hedges, Samuel H 2 2
Hedges, Shadrach 51 2
Hedges, Shadrack A 39 2
Heefer, H M 215a 2
Heerd, Annie 3 2
Heerd, Lewis 3 2
Heerd, Margaret E 11 1
Hefestay, Chas L 9 2
Hefestay, Minnie M 9 2
Heffner, Austin L 20 2
Heffner, Benjamin 257 1
Heffner, Benjamin 18 2
Heffner, Bessie 266 1
Heffner, Catharine 8 2
Heffner, Catharine M 8 2
Heffner, Catherine 7 2
Heffner, Chas H 30 2
Heffner, Donald 248 1
Heffner, Ella 16 2
Heffner, Ella 30 2

Heffner, Elmer U 36 2
Heffner, Frederick 18 2
Heffner, Frederick 38 3
Heffner, Frederick D 30 2
Heffner, George W 19 2
Heffner, Gertrude B 20 2
Heffner, Henry 22 2
Heffner, J P 113 2
Heffner, Jacob 18, 26 2
Heffner, John 8, 26 2
Heffner, John 184 3
Heffner, John D 30 2
Heffner, John H 31 2
Heffner, John J 56 2
Heffner, John P 30, 51 2
Heffner, John T 287 2
Heffner, Lewis C 35 2
Heffner, Louis W 248, 252 1
Heffner, Lulu 30, 36 2
Heffner, Lulu S 294 2
Heffner, Margaret 38 2
Heffner, Mary Ann 38 2
Heffner, Mary S 35 2
Heffner, Michael 18 2
Heffner, Minnie G 41 2
Heffner, Rosie Ellen 49 2
Heffner, S T 71 3
Heffner, Sallie J 31 2
Heffner, Samuel 7, 8, 51 2
Heffner, Samuel P 59 1
Heffner, Samuel P 9 3
Heffner, Samuel Peed 247 2
Heffner, Sarah E 30 2
Heffner, Susannah 51 2
Heffner, Vernon E Jr 56 2
Heffner, Vernon E Sr 56 2
Hefter, Elmer W 16 2
Heiberger, Stella 200 2
Heichler, Elizabeth 14, 22 2
Heichler, Henry 22 2
Heidecker, Henry 22 2
Heidelberger, Rebecca 49 2
Heider 71 3
Heidinger, Louisa 57 3
Heidlein, Frederick 124 3
Heidler, Augustus E 41 2
Heidler, Jacob 47 1
Heidler, Margerite 41 2
Heighdt, Benjamin M 102 3
Heighe, James C 31 2
Heim, Abigail 1, 7, 11, 35, 38, 92 2
Heim, Andrew 56, 90, 152, 257, 271 1
Heim, Jacob 262 1
Heim, Jacob B 51 1
Heim, Lewis A 35 2
Heim, Louis A 35 2
Heim, Nellie A 192 1
Heimer, Ann R 22 2
Heimer, Harriet K 47 2
Heimer, Henry 22 2
Heimer, Peter E 15, 47 2
Heimer, Roger C 47 2
Hein, Andrew 196 1
Heina, Jacob H 28 2
Heina, John D 28 2
Heiner, John 217 1
Heinlein, Bertha 245 1
Heinlein, Chas F 9 2
Heinlein, E H 80 2
Heinlein, Edw 40 2
Heinlein, Edw 253 1
Heinlein, Edw 199 3
Heinlein, Edw H 16, 18, 139 2
Heinlein, Edw H 199 3
Heinlein, Edward 16 2
Heinlein, Ella L 16 2
Heinlein, Ella L 16 2
Heinlein, F 4 1
Heinlein, Frederick 33, 159, 219 1
Heinlein, Frederick 18, 39, 210a 2
Heinlein, Geo 9, 92, 134 2
Heinlein, Geo 100 1
Heinlein, Geo 199 3
Heinlein, Geo W 9, 16, 18, 40, 80, 139, 160 2
Heinlein, Geo W 199 3
Heinlein, Geo W 4, 179, 245, 253 1
Heinlein, George W 14, 200 1
Heinlein, George W 217a, 218a 2
Heinlien, Edw H 4 1
Heintz, Catherine 29 2
Heintz, Jacob 29 2
Helfenstein, Annie E 2, 8 2
Helfenstein, Annie E 245 1
Helfenstein, Cyrus 96, 111 3
Helfenstein, Cyrus C 207 3
Helfenstein, Cyrus G 8 2
Helfenstein, Edw T 2, 8 2
Helfenstein, Ernest 16, 144, 145 2
Helfenstein, Ernest 55, 220 3
Helfenstein, Jonathan 26 2
Helfenstein, Mary 2, 144 2
Helfenstein, Mary G 16 2
Helfenstein, Mary Grace 16 2
Helfenstein, Nannie E 94 3
Helfrestacy, H A 23 2
Heller, Jacob 30 2
Heller, Mildred R 267 2
Helman, Clara E 31 2
Helman, Isabelle 25 2
Helman, J A 60 1
Helman, James A 31, 52 2
Helman, Maria L 52 2
Helman, Mary E 31 2
Helman, Samuel D 52 2
Hember, Samuel A 200 1
Hemler, David 11 2
Hemler, Ella M 189 3
Hemler, John D 11 2
Hemler, John T 52 2
Hemler, Peter 46 2
Hemler, Samuel A 11, 52, 238 2
Hemming, Fred 166 2
Hemminger, John D 189 2
Hemp, Abraham 3, 29 2
Hemp, Abraham 120, 147 1
Hemp, Abraham 71 3
Hemp, Abraham Jr 183 1
Hemp, Abram 219, 278 1
Hemp, Abram 32 2
Hemp, Albert A 254 1
Hemp, C E 254 1
Hemp, C Elgin 100 3
Hemp, C Elgin 186 1
Hemp, C Elgin 76 2
Hemp, Charles A 32 2
Hemp, Charles E 10 2
Hemp, Chas 8 2
Hemp, Chas A 34 1
Hemp, Chas A 36, 40, 58 2
Hemp, Clarence E 34 1
Hemp, Clarice 10 2
Hemp, Clayton R 8, 52 2
hemp, Douglass 266 1
Hemp, Effie V 58 2
Hemp, Elizabeth A 40 2
Hemp, Fred S 73 1
Hemp, Frederick 18, 22 2
Hemp, Helem B 3 2
Hemp, Helen R 291 2
Hemp, Henry 22 2
Hemp, Henry 22 2
Hemp, Henry Jr 53 3
Hemp, Henry Jr 40 1
Hemp, J W 205 1
Hemp, J Wm 40 2
Hemp, John 228 1
Hemp, John 8 2
Hemp, John T 254 1
Hemp, John W C 32 2
Hemp, Julia A 29 2
Hemp, Julian 6 1
Hemp, Lewis 176 3
Hemp, Lloyd E 36 2
Hemp, Louisa N 36 2
Hemp, Mary A J 40 2
Hemp, Mary C 40 2
Hemp, Mary H 40, 41, 46 2
Hemp, Maude 49 2

Hemp, Nettie E	10	2
Hemp, Peter S	19, 228	1
Hemp, Peter S	40	2
Hemp, R D	70	2
Hemp, R Douglas	3	2
Hemp, R Douglas	136	1
Hemp, Robert D	49	2
Hemp, Robt D	23	3
Hemp, Robt V	192	3
Hemp, Sarah	58	2
Hemp, Sarah A	52	2
Hemp, Virginia A	36	2
Hemp, William F	58	2
Hemp, Wm	229	1
Hemp, Wm	129	2
Hemp, Wm A	58	2
Hemp, Wm C	58	2
Hendein, G W	124	3
Henderickson, J D	107	3
Henderickson, John T	202	3
Henderickson, R A	107	3
Henderson, Andrew	1	2
Henderson, Annie M	2	2
Henderson, Eliza C	1	2
Henderson, Florence Bruner	42	1
Henderson, Harry L	23	2
Henderson, Louisa	233	1
Henderson, Louise H	131	1
Henderson, Pearl	23	2
Henderson, Robert	49	2
Henderson, Wm T	1	2
Hendley, Mary M	39	2
Hendrichson, Charles B	224a	2
Hendricks, Henry (col'd)	22	2
Hendricks, John H	30	2
Hendrickson, C B	169	1
Hendrickson, C V T	265	2
Hendrickson, Charles B T	77	2
Hendrickson, Chas B	52	2
Hendrickson, Chas B	156	1
Hendrickson, Chas B T	35	2
Hendrickson, Chasles B T	242	2
Hendrickson, D	169	1
Hendrickson, E	75	3
Hendrickson, E C	15	2
Hendrickson, Edgar A	25	2
Hendrickson, Ephriam	15, 30	2
Hendrickson, Ephrian	31	3
Hendrickson, Eprriam	32	3
Hendrickson, Ida F	15	2
Hendrickson, Ida Frances	25	2
Hendrickson, J D	52	2
Hendrickson, J D	201, 265	1
Hendrickson, J D	111	3
Hendrickson, John D	124	3
Hendrickson, John D	31, 242	2
Hendrickson, John R	30	2
Hendrickson, L A H	31	2
Hendrickson, Louise A H	36	2
Hendrickson, R A	172	1
Hendrickson, R Ames	9, 35, 36, 106	2
Hendrickson, W E	183	1
Hendrix, Alexander (Col'd)	1	2
Hendrix, Cora W	9	2
Hendrix, Cora Whip	31	2
Hendrix, Cora Whipp	31	2
Hendrix, Geo	9	2
Hendrix, J O	88, 239	1
Hendrix, J O	31	2
Hendrix, Nathan	96	2
Hendry, C E C	43	2
Hendry, Charles	8, 7	2
Hendry, Chas	197, 240	1
Hendry, Chas	1, 38, 57	2
Hendry, Chas	171	3
Hendry, Chas Jr	7	2
Hendry, Eleanore	8, 15	2
Hendry, M Walter	19	1
Hendry, Nathaniel B	43	2
Henesey, James	26	2
Henett, Belle	5	2
Henett, Harry T	5	2
Henley, Noah	43	2
Henley, Rosella	20	2
Henning, Fairy D	196	2
Henning, Ida Maude	25	2
Henning, John	26	3
Henry, Chas	203	3
Henry, Frederick	18	2
Henry, Isaac S	15	2
Henry, Philip	246	2
Henry, Rhoda	49	2
Henry, Savina	18	2
Henry, Wm	104	1
Henshaw, Amelia G	2	2
Henshaw, Amelia G	163	3
Henshaw, H E	276	2
Henshaw, Henry P	84	2
Henshew, J J	156	3
Henshew, John	192	1
Hentz, Jacob	205	1
Herbert, Anna A	36	2
Herbert, Annie	20	2
Herbert, Conrad A	10	2
Herbert, Geo W	20	2
Herbert, Harriet S	23	2
Herbert, Jesse	104	1
Herbert, Joseph	210	1
Herbert, Lloyd H	36	2
Herbert, Nancy Cora	43	2
Herbert, Roger E	43	2
Herd, J Ames	159	2
Hergesheimer, Geo P	19	2
Hergesheimer, James	29	2
Hergesheimer, James	156	1
Hergesheimer, Jas	91	3
Hergesheimer, Julia	29	2
Hergesheimer, Margaret J	19, 40	2
Hergessheimer, Joseph	165	3
Herickler, Henry	144	2
Hering, Daniel W	30	2
Hering, Joshua	30	2
Hering, Lloyd	19	3
Herley, J E	19	2
Herman, Chas	249	1
Herman, Chas	134	2
Herman, E A G	189	1
Herman, Elizabeth	155	1
Herman, Geo H	39	2
Herman, George	19	2
Herman, Michael	39	2
Hermange, Anthony	1	2
Hermange, Eleanore	14	2
Hermann, Elizabeth	16	2
Hermann, Elizabeth H	16	2
Hermonge, Peter	53	3
Herr, Clarissa	22	2
Herr, Henry	22	2
Herrett, William	212	3
Herrigan, J F	245	1
Herring, A	28	2
Herring, A E	11	2
Herring, Adam	1	2
Herring, Anna E	11	2
Herring, C	29	2
Herring, Caroline	8, 22	2
Herring, Caroline	156	1
Herring, Casper	7	2
Herring, Cora L	10	2
Herring, D R	11	2
Herring, Daniel	100	2
Herring, Daniel C	11	2
Herring, Daniel S	22	2
Herring, Edw C	14	2
Herring, Edw L	14, 22, 28	2
Herring, Geo	209	3
Herring, George	19, 226	2
Herring, George Edward	10	2
Herring, Henry	1, 22, 26, 66, 275	2
Herring, Henry	225	1
Herring, Jacob	26	2
Herring, Jacob	176	3
Herring, John	79	3
Herring, John	147	1
Herring, John	7, 26, 43, 257	2
Herring, John of A	1, 28	2
Herring, John of C	29	2
Herring, Joseph	26	2
Herring, Joshua	22, 39	2
Herring, Joshua W	229	1
Herring, Josiah T	28	2
Herring, Lloyd	28	2
Herring, Lloyd	198	2

Herring, Lloyd H 22, 28, 39 2
Herring, Lloyd H 22 1
Herring, Mary 39 2
Herring, Mary M 22, 39 2
Herring, Robert 28 2
Herring, Susan 51 2
Herring, Wm T 26 1
Herschmen, Christian 277 1
Herself 107 3
Hershberger, Gertrude 56 3
Hershberger, John 32, 172 2
Hershberger, John 56 3
Hershberger, John Jr 32 2
Hershberger, Joseph 56 3
Hershberger, Lillian A 58 2
Hershberger, T T 8 2
Hershberger, T T 165 1
Hershberger, Tilghman F 165 1
Hershberger, William S 113 3
Hershberger, Wm S 58 2
Hershel, Peter 46 2
Hershenheimer, Joseph 75 2
Hershides, Joseph T 30 2
Hershman, Catherine 7 2
Hershman, Christian 7, 27 2
Hershman, Jonathan 7 2
Hershman, Laura C 12 2
Hershperger, Catherine 7 2
Hershperger, Helen S 23 2
Hershperger, Henry 7, 22, 54 2
Hershperger, Julia 29 2
Hershperger, Mary E 58 2
Hershperger, T T 264, 271 1
Hershperger, Thomas H 54 2
Hershperger, Tilghman H 29 2
Hershperger, Tilghman T 54, 58 2
Hershperger, Wm H 54, 58 2
Hershperger, Wm S 22 2
Hershsides, Joseph T 30 2
Herspberger, Mary E 229a 2
Hersperger, Elizabeth S 16 2
Hersperger, Ella Kea 59, 81 2
Hersperger, Henry 184 3
Hersperger, T T 11 2
Hersperger, Tilghman 202 3
Hersperger, U Scholl 81 2
Hersperger, W Scholl 59 2
Hersperger, William 54 3
Hersperger, Wm S 244 1
Hersperger, Wm S 54, 171 3
Herston, Charles 7 2
Herter, Ignatius 6 1
Herwig, Amy 87 2
Herwig, Chas H 58 2
Herwig, Fanny A 93 1
Herwig, Giles E 177 3
Herwig, H A 58 2
Herwig, Henry A 2 2
Herwitt, Wm 22 1
Hess, Charles 37 3
Hess, Charles Jr 7 2
Hess, Chas 7 2
Hess, Daniel 26, 79, 110, 203, 228, 234 1
Hess, Daniel 128 2
Hess, David 11 2
Hess, Esther 7 2
Hess, Henry 186, 220a 2
Hess, Joseph 51 2
Hess, Mary B 41 2
Hess, William A 42 3
Hesser, Carrie M 59 2
Hesser, Charles 7 2
Hesser, Chas 70 1
Hesser, Eliza S 219 1
Hesser, Geo 219 1
Hesser, Geo 19, 52 2
Hesser, Geo J 19 2
Hesser, Sophia C 52 2
Hesser, William M 59 2
Hessler, Geo 87 3
Hessler, George 1 3
Hessler, Levi 19 2
Hesson, Abraham 26 2
Hesson, Andrew 225 1
Hesson, Andrew 57 2
Hesson, Andrew J 57 2
Hesson, Ann R 31 2
Hesson, Beltzer 106 1
Hesson, Cassandra T 10 2
Hesson, Clarence 55 1
Hesson, Ezra 39, 70 2
Hesson, Frank 18 2
Hesson, Grace 4 3
Hesson, Jacob 26, 132 2
Hesson, Jacob A 28 2
Hesson, James E 40 2
Hesson, John 26, 100 2
Hesson, John E 31 2
Hesson, John T 31 2
Hesson, Margaret 39 2
Hesson, Matilda 40 2
Hesson, Peter 1, 11, 26, 57, 93 2
Hesson, Wendell 57 2
Hesson, Wm 28, 57 2
Hessong, Ann Rebecca 2 2
Hessong, Caroline V 8 2
Hessong, Catherine 7 2
Hessong, Ezra 8 2
Hessong, John 237 2
Hessong, John E 2 2
Hessong, Thos 7 2
Hester, Richard 49 2
Hett, Henry 214 1
Hett, Naomi R 291 2
Hetterly, Harry M 56 2
Hetterly, Ira 137 2
Hetterly, Ira 165 3
Hetterly, Vernon F 56 2
Hetzner, Michael 38 2
Hewes, Edw 61 1
Hewett, Ann 1, 57 2
Hewett, Wm 57, 58, 63 2
Hewett, Wm 150 3
Hewitt, Wm 110, 125 1
Hibbard, Silas 160 3
Hibberd, Joseph 26, 63, 237, 288 2
Hibberd, Silas 106 1
Hibberd, Wm B 70 1
Hibberd, Wm B 38 2
Hibbert, Silas 184 3
Hibbus, Wm 137 1
Hichman, Geo 64 2
Hickey, Catherine 30 2
Hickey, J H 30 2
Hickey, James A 32 2
Hickey, James D 30 2
Hickey, James F 30 2
Hickey, James F 146 1
Hickey, John F 171 2
Hickley, Thomas J 24 1
Hickman, Bessie L 206 3
Hickman, Catherine 7 2
Hickman, Charles D 16 3
Hickman, Christiana S 10 2
Hickman, Geo 197 3
Hickman, Geo 57 2
Hickman, Geo H 210 1
Hickman, Geo H 166, 206 3
Hickman, Geo H 20 2
Hickman, Geo H C 20 2
Hickman, Grace P 23 2
Hickman, Harry C 23, 41 2
Hickman, John B 32 2
Hickman, John P 31 2
Hickman, John W 10 2
Hickman, John Wm 31 2
Hickman, Katherine E 62 1
Hickman, Laurence 32 2
Hickman, Lullu 197 3
Hickman, Lulu W 166 3
Hickman, Mary E 20, 41 2
Hickman, Roy S 31 2
Hickman, S L 179 3
Hickman, S T 146 1
Hickman, Sam 10 2
Hickman, Samuel L 51 2
Hickman, Sidney R 206 3
Hickman, Sidney R 41 2
Hickman, Wm 57 2
Hicks, William 225 2
Hicks, Wm 225 2
Hickson, Mary 38 2
Hider, John 29 2
Hider, Wm H 29 2
Higbee, E L 16 2

Higbee, Mary K 16 2
Higdon, Geo W 20 2
Higdon, Henry W 23 2
Higdon, Mary W 20 2
Higgins, Benjamin 5 2
Higgins, Harriet 22 2
Higgins, James 27, 43, 197 2
Higgins, James 152, 203 1
Higgins, James L 27, 237 2
Higgins, Maria 27, 39 2
Higgins, Uriah 182 3
Higgins, William 8, 182 3
Higgins, Wm 39 2
Higgins, Wm 30 1
Higgs, Wm 22 2
Hightman, Annie P 2 2
Hightman, Arthur T 102 1
Hightman, Bruce E 5 2
Hightman, C D 2 2
Hightman, C D 18 2
Hightman, Chas T 8 2
Hightman, Clarence M 3, 5, 47 2
Hightman, Daniel 30 2
Hightman, Daniel E 31 2
Hightman, Eliza 15 2
Hightman, G Lewis 19 1
Hightman, Geo E 2 2
Hightman, Harriet L 23 2
Hightman, Henry 271 2
Hightman, J 19 2
Hightman, J W 31 2
Hightman, Jacob 29 2
Hightman, John 71, 171, 187 3
Hightman, John 22, 29, 30 2
Hightman, John 23, 192, 197 1
Hightman, Joseph 15, 29, 30, 31 2
Hightman, Joseph 233, 244 1
Hightman, M M 8 2
Hightman, Martin L 40 2
Hightman, Martin L 205 3
Hightman, Mary E 30 2
Hightman, Phoebe E 47 2
Hightman, Stella Z 145 1
Hightman, Stella Z 3, 5, 47 2
Hightman, T Frank 2, 54, 294 2
Hightman, Thomas 40, 54 2
Hightman, Thos 197 1
Hightman, Thos 15, 29, 30, 93, 113 2
Hightman, William J 59 2
Hightman, William J Jr 23, 59 2
Hijams, David 184 3
Hilberd, Wm 69 2
Hilbert, Godfrey 228 1
Hilbur, William 1 3
Hilbus, Wm 185 2
Hildebrand, Amanda L 2, 35 2
Hildebrand, Ann M 1 2
Hildebrand, Annie B 2, 119 2
Hildebrand, Annie L 9 2
Hildebrand, B F 2, 119 2
Hildebrand, B F 219 1
Hildebrand, Benjamin F 5 2
Hildebrand, Chas 25 2
Hildebrand, Chas E 9 2
Hildebrand, Chas R 9, 12, 15, 20 2
Hildebrand, Chas R 240 1
Hildebrand, D M 35 2
Hildebrand, David 11 2
Hildebrand, David F 31 2
Hildebrand, David M 2, 12 2
Hildebrand, Deplhia [sic] 210 1
Hildebrand, Esta L 240 1
Hildebrand, Esther L 15 2
Hildebrand, Ezra 14, 27 2
Hildebrand, Frank 210 1
Hildebrand, Geo E 20 2
Hildebrand, Geo L 2, 12, 20, 25, 35 2
Hildebrand, Jacob 27 2
Hildebrand, John 27, 28, 29 2
Hildebrand, John T 249 2
Hildebrand, Joseph 100 1
Hildebrand, Joseph 27 2
Hildebrand, Joseph D 31 2
Hildebrand, Joshua H 28 2
Hildebrand, L 75 3
Hildebrand, L C 35 2
Hildebrand, L C 35 2
Hildebrand, Laura V 35 2
Hildebrand, Lewis A 35 2
Hildebrand, Lewis M 35 2
Hildebrand, Mary A 28 2
Hildebrand, Mary A 71 3
Hildebrand, Mollie Shafer 196 2
Hildebrand, Wm 29 2
Hildebrick, John T 177 2
Hildebridle, Jacob 98 3
Hildebridle, John 51 2
Hildebridle, John 84 1
Hildebridle, Solomon 51 2
Hilderbrick, Jacob 226 2
Hildt, John C 87 3
Hileary, John 100 2
Hill, Ambrose 23 2
Hill, B S 151 3
Hill, C H 208 2
Hill, C W 55 3
Hill, Charles E 15 3
Hill, Charles H 9 2
Hill, Chas V 15 2
Hill, Christopher 7 2
Hill, Daniel G 12 2
Hill, David 22 2
Hill, Earl L 92 2
Hill, Elizabeth 15 2
Hill, Eve C 27 2
Hill, Fannie 205 3
Hill, Hannah 38, 116 2
Hill, Harriet 23 2
Hill, Henry 7, 22 2
Hill, Henry (col'd) 22 2
Hill, Hilda E 92 2
Hill, Hilda E 24 3
Hill, J H 143 2
Hill, Jacob (col'd) 28 2
Hill, Jane 35 2
Hill, John 7, 27, 30 2
Hill, John 117 1
Hill, John H 31 2
Hill, Judson 65 3
Hill, L Cameron 31 2
Hill, Lewis 35 2
Hill, Lydia 35, 116 2
Hill, Margaret P 12 2
Hill, Mary 38 2
Hill, Mary Jane 40 2
Hill, Maxie A 52 2
Hill, R S 237 1
Hill, Robert C 49 2
Hill, Rosa C 49 2
Hill, Sallie M 52 2
Hill, Sarah E 52 2
Hill, William 167 3
Hill, William A 58 2
Hill, William J 9 2
Hill, Wm 57 2
Hill, Wm 27 2
Hill, Wm 264 1
Hilleary, Ann 1 2
Hilleary, Berry 69 2
Hilleary, Charlotte 9 2
Hilleary, Clarence W 9, 30, 51 2
Hilleary, Cornelia 7 2
Hilleary, Cornelius 27 2
Hilleary, Elizabeth 14, 57 2
Hilleary, Elizabeth L 30 2
Hilleary, Ellen MacGill 15 2
Hilleary, Geo T 22 2
Hilleary, Harry 189 1
Hilleary, Harry W 96 3
Hilleary, Harry W 9 2
Hilleary, Henry 22 2
Hilleary, Ida F 25 2
Hilleary, J H 57 2
Hilleary, J W 19, 51 2
Hilleary, James E 28 2
Hilleary, John 19, 26, 54, 197 2
Hilleary, John 263 1
Hilleary, John H 27, 275 2
Hilleary, John W 19, 30 2
Hilleary, John W 81, 106 3

Hilleary, Marshall 15 2
Hilleary, Mary 28 2
Hilleary, Mary E 39 2
Hilleary, Nannie 30 2
Hilleary, Perry 26, 66 2
Hilleary, Perry 6, 64 3
Hilleary, Perry 40 1
Hilleary, Rebecca 14, 49 2
Hilleary, Sallie 9, 54 2
Hilleary, Sallie Ann 51 2
Hilleary, Sally A 1 2
Hilleary, Sarah O D 51 2
Hilleary, Thomas 242 2
Hilleary, Thomas H 81 3
Hilleary, Thomas Sr 51 2
Hilleary, Thos 205 2
Hilleary, Thos 106 3
Hilleary, Tilghman 27, 54 2
Hilleary, Tilghman 144 1
Hilleary, Tilghman 106 3
Hilleary, Tilghman Jr 81 3
Hilleary, William 57 2
Hilleary, Wm 26 2
Hilleary, Wm 153 2
Hilleary, Wm B 51 2
Hilleary, Wm P 1, 54 2
Hillen, Thos 185 2
Hillen, Thos 278 1
Hilleray, J W 186 3
Hillery, Clement T 96 3
Hillery, Henry 213 3
Hillery, Hightman 137 1
Hillery, J W 137 1
Hillery, J W 165 3
Hillery, John H 120 3
Hillery, Thomas 58, 137 1
Hillery, William H 213 3
Hilliary, Harry 174 3
Hilman, Nancy 43 2
Hilt, John C 32 2
Hilt, Thomas 32 2
Hiltabidel, Elizabeth 15 2
Hiltabidel, Samuel 15 2
Hiltahide, Harry C 75 3
Hilterbrick, David 11 2
Hilterbrick, John 11 2
Hilterbrick, Mary 11 2
Hiltner, Annie M 9 2
Hiltner, Christian 9 2
Hiltner, Clarence E 10, 58 2
Hiltner, Howard S 23 2
Hiltner, Jacob 29 2
Hiltner, Martha E 29 2
Hiltner, Mary E 10 2
Hiltner, Robert S 58 2
Hiltner, Rosalind 23 2
Hiltner, Roy M 58 2
Hiltner, W H 48 1
Hiltner, William H 58 2
Hilton , Lillian 32 2
Hilton, James 26 2
Hilton, Lucy B 26 2
Hilton, Rachel E 107 3
Hilton, Roy M 234 2
Hilton, Wm 80 2
Himbrey, J William 2 2
Himbury, H M 39 2
Himbury, John B 29 2
Himbury, John W 39 2
Himbury, Mary A 39 2
Himes, Albert H 3, 36 2
Himes, Catherine 8 2
Himes, Charles H 32 2
Himes, Charles W 10 2
Himes, Daniel 133 1
Himes, Guilford S 3 2
Himes, John S 32, 58 2
Himes, Julie C 3 2
Himes, Lucy B 36 2
Himes, M E 217 1
Himes, Mary El 255 2
Himes, Myrtle 10 2
Himes, Nannie C 193 1
Himes, Peter 185 2
Himes, Peter 70 1
Himes, Peter 184 3
Himes, Samuel 245 1
Himes, V Andrew 129 3
Himnes, Samuel L 51 2
Hinckle, Gloria A 180 3
Hinckley, Elnora 221a 2
Hinds, Barbara 5 2
Hinds, John 38 2
Hinds, John 5, 19 2
Hinds, Martin 38 2
Hinea, Allen V 35 2
Hinea, Ellen R 16 2
Hinea, Emma E 58 2
Hinea, Eva M 15 2
Hinea, Henry 18, 22 2
Hinea, Henry A 29 2
Hinea, Henry Sr 22 2
Hinea, Jacob H 15, 30, 57 2
Hinea, John 29 2
Hinea, John F 16 2
Hinea, John H 29 2
Hinea, Levi 29 2
Hinea, Levi F 35 2
Hinea, Mary M 35, 41 2
Hinea, Wm 29, 57 2
Hinea, Wm C 58 2
Hiner, John 14, 46, 96, 254 2
Hiner, John 135 1
Hiner, Peter 46 2
Hines, Albert H 45 2
Hines, Chas W 44 1
Hines, David 163 1
Hines, David 46 2
Hines, Hashabiah 147 1
Hines, Henry 186, 188 2
Hines, John C 30, 46 2
Hines, John S 30 2
Hines, Oliver W 45 2
Hines, Peter 150, 163 1
Hines, Peter 46 2
Hines, Philip 46 2
Hines, Philip 150 1
Hines, Washington J 19 3
Hines, Washington J 30, 58 2
Hinkins, Nina E 219 1
Hinkle, Catherine 8, 19 2
Hinkle, Frank 42 1
Hinkle, George 19 2
Hinkle, John 88 1
Hinks, Alice C 58 2
Hinks, Carrie 51 2
Hinks, Geo M 71 1
Hinks, Geo M 51 2
Hinks, Samuel 51, 214a 2
Hinks, Susan 51, 225 2
Hinks, William H 224 2
Hinks, Wm H 58 2
Hinton, Rachel 49 2
Hipkins, Bessie Al 173 2
Hipkins, Bessie L 173 2
Hipkins, Rufus B 173 2
Hipkins, Walter L 266 1
Hirsch, John 22 2
Hirsh, Harman 22 2
Hirsperger, T T 22 1
Hissey, Charlie L 9 2
Hissey, Mary A 9 2
Hitchew, P L 209 3
Hitchew, William 64 3
Hiteshew, Catherine 7, 8 2
Hiteshew, Charles P 18 2
Hiteshew, Chas P 101 1
Hiteshew, Chas P 47, 115 2
Hiteshew, Daniel 100 1
Hiteshew, Elizabeth 15 2
Hiteshew, Floy M 193 1
Hiteshew, Floy May 18 2
Hiteshew, Isaac 25 2
Hiteshew, Israel 137 2
Hiteshew, Israel 37 1
Hiteshew, Jacob 263 1
Hiteshew, Margaret E 2, 40, 84 2
Hiteshew, Matilda I 46 2
Hiteshew, Matilda J 39 2
Hiteshew, P M 2, 80, 84 2
Hiteshew, P M 181 1
Hiteshew, P Merle 8, 40, 47 2
Hiteshew, Philip 7, 39, 46, 57 2
Hiteshew, Philip L 46 2
Hiteshew, Philip M 76 1

Hiteshew, Philip M 46 2
Hiteshew, Regina 49 2
Hiteshew, Wm 213 1
Hiteshew, Wm 57 2
Hiteshew, Wm H 57 2
Hiteshue, Wm 58 2
Hitler, Adelaide 23 2
Hitselberger, Carrie 31 2
Hitselberger, Carrie G 10 2
Hitselberger, James F 10 2
Hitselberger, John J 31 2
Hitselberger, John J 62 1
Hitselberger, Teresa L 31 2
Hitterbrick, Geo 283 1
Hitterbrick, Peter 283 1
Hiviling, Abraham 1 2
Hoar, Albert W 20 2
Hoar, Clifford 20 2
Hoar, Frank G 18 2
Hoar, Gertie M 20 2
Hoar, Ida A 25 2
Hoar, James W 18 2
Hoar, Nellie H 18 2
Hoar, Z W 4 1
Hobbs, Albert L 1 2
Hobbs, Benjamin 5 2
Hobbs, C R 43 2
Hobbs, Charles F 8 2
Hobbs, E Guy 18 2
Hobbs, Edw 49, 57 2
Hobbs, Edw 176, 260, 265, 283 1
Hobbs, Edw D 179 1
Hobbs, Edward 16, 78 2
Hobbs, Edward M 91 1
Hobbs, Eleanora 29 2
Hobbs, Elizabeth C 15 2
Hobbs, Esther E 31 2
Hobbs, Frances L 18 2
Hobbs, Harry 5 2
Hobbs, J Henry 32 2
Hobbs, James M 31 2
Hobbs, John 98, 179 3
Hobbs, John 117, 238 1
Hobbs, John 28, 29, 38 2
Hobbs, John T 29 2
Hobbs, Joseph 29 2
Hobbs, Katie 181 1
Hobbs, Kitty 34 2
Hobbs, Malachia 38 2
Hobbs, Malachias 38 2
Hobbs, Margaret A 41 2
Hobbs, Martha 8 2
Hobbs, Martha F 32 2
Hobbs, Mary M 39 2
Hobbs, Maude V 43 2
Hobbs, N W 20 2
Hobbs, N W 146 3
Hobbs, Norval W 43 2
Hobbs, Paul A 14 1
Hobbs, Philip R 46 2
Hobbs, Rhoderick D 58 2
Hobbs, Rodrick D 49 2
Hobbs, S 57 2
Hobbs, Samuel 52, 238 2
Hobbs, Sophia 46 2
Hobbs, Ulysis 207 3
Hobbs, Warner 57, 58 2
Hobbs, William 59, 220 2
Hobbs, William H 16 2
Hobbs, William Jr 59 2
Hobbs, Wm 34, 86, 150, 163 1
Hobbs, Wm 41, 57 2
Hobbs, Wm of S 57 2
Hoblitzell, G W 257 1
Hoblizell, G W [?] 130 1
Hockensmith, Chas R 30 2
Hockensmith, Daniel 11 2
Hockensmith, David 11 2
Hockensmith, Elizabeth 14 2
Hockensmith, Geo 19, 57 2
Hockensmith, Jacob 26 2
Hockensmith, John 67 1
Hockensmith, John 14, 26, 28, 30, 57, 294 2
Hockensmith, John Jr 77 3
Hockensmith, Rosie B 111 1
Hockensmith, Sarah 51 2
Hockensmith, Wm 28, 30, 57 2
Hockensmith, Wm 195 1
HodgeKiss, Thomas H 54 2
Hodges, Thelma 231 2
Hodgkiss, Thomas H 185 3
Hodgson, Mary Condon 46 3
Hodgson, Mary Condon 97, 204 1
Hoff, A 81 3
Hoff, Abraham 26 1
Hoff, Elizabeth 14, 56 2
Hoff, John 26 2
Hoff, Mary 39 2
Hoff, Oliver 22 2
Hoff, Peter 46, 137 2
Hoffenberg, William 66 2
Hoffenberg, William 66 2
Hoffman, Adam 1 2
Hoffman, Addison I 81 2
Hoffman, Ann R 1, 2 2
Hoffman, Anna M 210a 2
Hoffman, Anne E 36 2
Hoffman, Austin C 10 2
Hoffman, Barbara 5 2
Hoffman, C Frank 10 2
Hoffman, C Mason 9 2
Hoffman, C Mason 33 3
Hoffman, C W 118 1
Hoffman, Calvin O 9 2
Hoffman, Casper 22 2
Hoffman, Casper 87 3
Hoffman, Catherine 7, 8, 9, 45 2
Hoffman, Charles W 8 2
Hoffman, Chas 10 3
Hoffman, Chas W 32, 40, 57 2
Hoffman, Cornelius 40 2
Hoffman, David 12 2
Hoffman, David M 43 2
Hoffman, David O 55 1
Hoffman, David W 11 2
Hoffman, Edna I 16 2
Hoffman, Effie 270 1
Hoffman, Eleanore 14 2
Hoffman, Elizabeth 14, 16, 26 2
Hoffman, Elmer F 58 2
Hoffman, Ezra 25, 27 2
Hoffman, Ezra D 25 2
Hoffman, Francis 18 2
Hoffman, Francis A 14 2
Hoffman, Francis A 139 3
Hoffman, Frank 23 2
Hoffman, Frank M 18 2
Hoffman, Frank N 23 2
Hoffman, Fred M 9 2
Hoffman, Geo 176 3
Hoffman, Geo 5, 18, 19, 23, 66 2
Hoffman, Geo J 20 2
Hoffman, Geo W 19, 22 2
Hoffman, George 19 2
Hoffman, George 56, 125 1
Hoffman, George 26 3
Hoffman, Hannah 20 2
Hoffman, Hannh E 23 2
Hoffman, Henry 159, 163 1
Hoffman, Henry 22, 23, 40, 268 2
Hoffman, Henry W 18 3
Hoffman, Henry W 13, 116 1
Hoffman, Ida Virginia 25 2
Hoffman, Jacob 51, 263 1
Hoffman, Jacob 9, 26, 27, 28, 30 2
Hoffman, Jacob 37, 176, 214 3
Hoffman, Jenry 56 1
Hoffman, Jerome J 32 2
Hoffman, John 71 1
Hoffman, John 31 3
Hoffman, John 2, 19, 26, 27, 28, 258 2
Hoffman, John H 2, 14, 31 2
Hoffman, John S 31 2
Hoffman, John W 58 2
Hoffman, Lillie H 36 2
Hoffman, Lorin K 36 2
Hoffman, M 101 2
Hoffman, M 164 1
Hoffman, Mabert Gingell 245 1
Hoffman, Margaret A R 38 2

Hoffman, Margaret E 40 2
Hoffman, Margaret W 40 2
Hoffman, Martin 7 2
Hoffman, Mary 40 2
Hoffman, Mary A Nusz 222 2
Hoffman, Mary D 254 2
Hoffman, Mary H 9 2
Hoffman, Matilda 40 2
Hoffman, Mayme 40 2
Hoffman, Mazie 22 1
Hoffman, Michael 39, 41 2
Hoffman, Michael 225 1
Hoffman, Minerva C 58 2
Hoffman, Minnie M 41 2
Hoffman, Mollie M 58 2
Hoffman, Nelson 43 2
Hoffman, Oliver H 45 2
Hoffman, Oliver M 18 2
Hoffman, Peter 27, 165 2
Hoffman, Philip 129, 174 3
Hoffman, Robert L 10 2
Hoffman, Roy L 49 2
Hoffman, Russell I 36, 49 2
Hoffman, Samuel 171 2
Hoffman, Sophia 51 2
Hoffman, T A 117 1
Hoffman, T H 260 1
Hoffman, T H 28 2
Hoffman, Thos S 54 2
Hoffman, Thos W 13 1
Hoffman, W C 71 3
Hoffman, William 58, 222, 287 2
Hoffman, William 1, 14 3
Hoffman, William F 58 2
Hoffman, William N 264 2
Hoffman, Wilma M 58 2
Hoffman, Wm 147, 205 1
Hoffman, Wm 28, 58, 102, 203 2
Hoffman, Wm C 234 1
Hoffman, Wm C 22, 26, 57, 58, 252 2
Hoffman, Wm F 40, 58 2
Hoffman, Wm O 8, 30, 54 2
Hoffmaster, Arthur 227 3
Hoffmaster, E J 101 1
Hoffmaster, Maude Z 227 3
Hoffmaster, T A 169 1
Hoffmaster, T A 89 3
Hoffmeier, John W 227 3
Hoffmeier, Sallie M 54 2
Hoffmeier, T Franklin 54 2
Hoffner, Austin F 52 2
Hoffner, Rebecca 49 2
Hoffner, Samuel 49 2
Hoffner, Samuel T 52 2
Hoffner, Susan R 52 2
Hoffner, Ward C 52 2
Hogan, Bessie L 20 2
Hogan, Ella R 41 2
Hogan, G H 226 2
Hogan, Geo H 20 2
Hogan, George 225 2
Hogan, Mary V 41 2
Hogan, S Thomas 51 2
Hogan, Samuel 49 2
Hogarth, Annie M 2 2
Hogarth, Mary 58 2
Hogarth, Mary D 41 2
Hogarth, W H 56 3
Hogarth, W H 27 1
Hogarth, W H 2 2
Hogarth, William H 196 3
Hogarth, Wm H 58 2
Hogg, Samuel 152 1
Hogg, Samuel 102 3
Hogg, Samuel B 28 2
Hogg, Samuel R 96, 106, 111 3
Hogg, Samuel R 51 2
Hoggins, Richard 49 2
Hoke, Amanda S 40 2
Hoke, Bessie 205 1
Hoke, Bradley H 52 2
Hoke, Charlotte A J 10 2
Hoke, Clara A 9, 12 2
Hoke, David H 12 2
Hoke, Elizabeth 31 2
Hoke, George 19 2
Hoke, George B 222 2
Hoke, J L 30 1
Hoke, Jacob 29, 31, 39, 198 2
Hoke, Jacob 54, 163, 186 3
Hoke, Jacob L 30, 39 2
Hoke, Jacob Sr 29 2
Hoke, Joseph E 31 2
Hoke, Kreamer 31 2
Hoke, Lydia A 30 2
Hoke, Martin 40, 51, 52 2
Hoke, Martin 33, 59, 85 1
Hoke, Michael 238 1
Hoke, Michael 39, 287 2
Hoke, Norman Z 30 2
Hoke, Peter 203 3
Hoke, Samuel 51, 52 2
Hoke, Teresa J 66 2
Hoke, W Lee 9 2
Hoke, Wm H 29 2
Holbrunner, Adam 1, 7, 27, 211 2
Holbrunner, Adam 70 3
Holbrunner, Annie E 3 2
Holbrunner, C E 28 2
Holbrunner, Casper 7 2
Holbrunner, Casper M 8 2
Holbrunner, Catherine 27 2
Holbrunner, Charles W 9 2
Holbrunner, E E 187 3
Holbrunner, Eliza E 1 2
Holbrunner, Geo 7 2
Holbrunner, George 19 2
Holbrunner, Henry H 61 1
Holbrunner, Henry H 31 2
Holbrunner, Henry W 54 2
Holbrunner, J M 72 2
Holbrunner, John 7, 27, 28, 211 2
Holbrunner, John 8, 27 3
Holbrunner, John 228 1
Holbrunner, John M 19, 31 2
Holbrunner, John Sr 27 2
Holbrunner, L A 28 2
Holbrunner, Lucinda 28 2
Holbrunner, Maurice 9 2
Holbrunner, Susan E 52 2
Holbrunner, T Etta 54 2
Holbrunner, T M 205 1
Holbrunner, Thomas 76 1
Holbrunner, Thomas 236 2
Holbrunner, Thomas M 112 1
Holbrunner, Thos 229 1
Holbrunner, Thos 163 2
Holbrunner, Thos M 1, 119 2
Holbrunner, Wilson G 8 2
Holburner, Thomas M 91 3
Holdcraft, John H 32 2
Holdcraft, Paul E 32 2
Holder, M Frank 41 2
Holdrey, George 137 2
Holger, J W 124 2
Holl, Alfred 11 2
Holl, Cyrus 14 2
Holl, Daniel 11 2
Holl, David 11, 14 2
Holl, Eve 14 2
Holl, John 26 2
Holl, Julius 11 2
Holl, Margaret 11 2
Holl, Stephen 51 2
Holladay, George 19 2
Holland, Anna E 199 2
Holland, Benj F 52 2
Holland, Bertha A 52, 255 2
Holland, C E 15 2
Holland, Caroline 16 3
Holland, Caroline M 51 2
Holland, Charles S 52 2
Holland, Chas R 9 2
Holland, Chas S 23 2
Holland, Clifford E 97 1
Holland, Clifford E 239 2
Holland, Edith B 213 3
Holland, Ella 15 2
Holland, Florence M 18 2
Holland, Frank E 15, 18, 52 2
Holland, Geo 166 2
Holland, H Reid 30 2
Holland, Hanson 23 2

Holland, Irvin 49 2
Holland, John R 30 2
Holland, Mary M 15 2
Holland, Mida E 9 2
Holland, Norine 18 2
Holland, R M 110 1
Holland, Robert Lee 49 2
Holland, Samuel 186 3
Holland, Samuel 118 1
Holland, Samuel 51, 212a 2
Holland, Stannike M 52 2
Holland, Susan R 52 2
Holland, W M 62 2
Hollar, John 93 2
Hollar, Melvin E 47 2
Hollar, Phillip S Jr 47 2
Hollar, Phlilip S Sr 47 2
Hollenberger, Wm 57 2
Holley, Maurice 38 2
Holliday, Charlotte 8 2
Holliday, Mary C 40 2
Hollinger, John S 32 2
Holly, Maurice 38 2
Holmes, Caroline V 9 2
Holmes, Chas R 166 3
Holmes, James 9 2
Holmes, Lucy 9 2
Holmes, Lucy K 81 2
Holmes, Mary C 41 2
Holmes, Mary E 9 2
Holmes, Russell 213 3
Holsey, Dora B 58 2
Holsey, John 58 2
Holsey, William H 58 2
Holt, Charles B 9 2
Holt, Chas B 166 3
Holt, Cora M 9 2
Holt, Emma 166 3
Holt, Glenn P 166 3
Holt, Harry C 201 1
Holt, Luther E 9 2
Holter, Albert 14 1
Holter, Albert E 15, 41 2
Holter, Albert E 124, 131, 146 1
Holter, Albert E 41 2
Holter, Amos 14 1
Holter, Amos A 3, 58, 83, 169 3
Holter, Amos A 3, 112, 143, 161, 167, 196, 291 2
Holter, Amos A 19, 42, 68, 97, 124, 128, 146, 186, 189, 195, 207,278 1
Holter, Amos L A 96 3
Holter, Annie C C 86, 195 1
Holter, C E 46 2
Holter, Chas E 9 2
Holter, Chas H 57 3
Holter, Chas R 15 2
Holter, Daniel 11 2
Holter, Dorothy K 32 2
Holter, Edward F 41 2
Holter, Elizabeth 150 1
Holter, Elizabeth 58 2
Holter, Elizabeth J 15 2
Holter, Frances A 196 2
Holter, Frances S 97 1
Holter, Frances S 207 1
Holter, Frances S 112 2
Holter, G M 9 2
Holter, Geo B 104 1
Holter, Geo B 57 2
Holter, Grace B 86 1
Holter, Grace B 57 3
Holter, Harriet C 52 2
Holter, J K 110 1
Holter, John 64, 87 2
Holter, John M 255 2
Holter, John W 120 1
Holter, John W 15, 32 2
Holter, M Frank 15, 87 2
Holter, M R 169 2
Holter, Mahala F 46 2
Holter, Margaret E 41 2
Holter, Margaret Eliz 41 2
Holter, Margaret F 52 2
Holter, Oscar W 32 2
Holter, Peter 46 2
Holter, S M 9 2
Holter, Samuel Cl 79 1
Holter, Samuel W 52 2
Holter, W P 56 3
Holter, Wm 57, 58, 65, 85, 203 2
Holtz, A 8 1
Holtz, A B 41, 60, 82, 214, 265 1
Holtz, A B 46 2
Holtz, A B 42 3
Holtz, Albert B 2, 28, 30 2
Holtz, Albert B 275 1
Holtz, Birdie 59 2
Holtz, Carl 59 2
Holtz, Carl E 224 3
Holtz, Catherine 7 2
Holtz, Clarence 49, 85, 212a 2
Holtz, Clarence C 2, 23 2
Holtz, Clarence C 42 1
Holtz, Clarence C 10, 221 3
Holtz, Clarence P 107 1
Holtz, Clarence Z 16 3
Holtz, David C 30 2
Holtz, Geo N 72 3
Holtz, George N 135 1
Holtz, Harriet V 23 2
Holtz, Harriet W V 23 2
Holtz, Henrietta A 23 2
Holtz, J A 226 2
Holtz, Jacob 26, 28 2
Holtz, John 27, 28, 30, 38, 87 2
Holtz, John 239, 257 1
Holtz, John C 186 3
Holtz, John O 159 1
Holtz, John O 15 3
Holtz, John Oliver 30 2
Holtz, Katherine 59 2
Holtz, Kathryn D 224 3
Holtz, Michael 38 2
Holtz, Nicholas 47 1
Holtz, Nicholas 26, 43, 254 2
Holtz, Nicholas 224 3
Holtz, Willaim H 59 2
Holtz, Wm H 30 2
Holtz, Zoe M 61 2
Holtzapple, Elizabeth 14 2
Holtzapple, Howard 22 2
Holtzapple, Margaret 22 2
Holtzman, Christian 185 3
Holtzman, Christian 7 2
Holtzman, Elizabeth 14 2
Holtzman, Geo J 45 2
Holtzman, Wm 7 2
Holtzople, Clinton E 10 2
Holtzopple, Harry B 3 2
Holtzzople, John C 10 2
Holzopple, Annie M 3 2
Homer, John A 56 3
Homerick, Geo 27 2
Homerick, Mary 39 2
Honaker, Albert Clarence 36 2
Honaker, Charles Harris 16, 36 2
Honaker, Elbert Clarence 16 2
Honaker, Elbert J 16 2
Honaker, Helen E 113 1
Honaker, James G 16 2
Honaker, James Glenn 16, 36 2
Honaker, Leota Blanche 36 2
Honaker, Leota J 16 2
Honts, Emory M 16 2
Honts, Minnie M 16 2
Hood, Alexander W 1 2
Hood, Ann 2 2
Hood, Benjamin 195 3
Hood, Benjamin 5 2
Hood, Chester 149 2
Hood, Daniel 69 2
Hood, Ella V 58 2
Hood, Emeline 15 2
Hood, Ephriam 15 2
Hood, Geo 146, 183 1
Hood, Geo 27, 29 2
Hood, Geo A 72 2
Hood, Geo E 20 2
Hood, George 20, 22 2
Hood, Helen W 257, 259 2
Hood, Henry 22, 27 2
Hood, Henry 135 1
Hood, J F 35 2
Hood, James 22 2

Hood, James D 1 2
Hood, James M 30 2
Hood, James M 117 1
Hood, James M 55 3
Hood, John 27, 29 2
Hood, John 194, 248 1
Hood, John 185 3
Hood, Joseph 270 1
Hood, Laura 52 1
Hood, Laura V 36 2
Hood, M E S 82 3
Hood, Maggie A 70 2
Hood, Margaret A 70, 72 2
Hood, Margaret E S 30, 40 2
Hood, Margaret E S 32 3
Hood, Marqret E S 196 3
Hood, Rebecca 58 2
Hood, W H 112, 142, 179 1
Hood, W H 35, 257 2
Hood, William B 73 3
Hood, William H 290 2
Hood, Wm 175, 188 2
Hood, Wm Albert 58 2
Hood, Wm H 22 2
Hooff, Douglass 12 2
Hooff, Mary D 12, 41 2
Hoofman, Hannah 166 2
Hoofnagle, Maranda 41 2
Hook, Daniel 11 2
Hook, James 11, 26 2
Hook, James 116 1
Hook, James S 26 2
Hook, Jane 26 2
Hook, John B 26 2
Hook, Thomas 38, 119, 293 2
Hook, Thos 7 2
Hook, Thos 163, 244 1
Hook, Thos 195 3
Hooke, Thomas 213a 2
Hoope, J Henry 124 2
Hooper, Anna M 58 3
Hooper, C 32 1
Hooper, Catherine 96 3
Hooper, Charles 8, 238 2
Hooper, Charles A 8 2
Hooper, Chas 58, 280 2
Hooper, Chas 47, 71, 150, 271 1
Hooper, Chas 54 3
Hooper, J H 202 2
Hooper, J Harold 189 1
Hooper, James 91 1
Hooper, James O 8, 31 2
Hooper, John 28 2
Hooper, John H 54 2
Hooper, John S 32 2
Hooper, Joseph 186 2
Hooper, Lewis 58 2
Hooper, Lillie M 31 2
Hooper, Richard 189 2
Hooper, Susan E 58 2
Hooper, Thomas L 54 2
Hooper, Thos 28, 54, 138 2
Hooper, U G 41 2
Hooper, U G 58 3
Hooper, Ulysses G 31 2
Hooper, Virgin M 140 3
Hooper, Wm 28 2
Hooper, Wm & 218 2
Hooper, Wm H 58 2
Hoopes, Gertrude B 52 2
Hoopes, Samuel W 52 2
Hoover, Allen D 19 2
Hoover, Amanda E 11 2
Hoover, Augustus C 1 2
Hoover, Catharine 8, 19 2
Hoover, Catherine V 9 2
Hoover, Charlotte A 8, 107 2
Hoover, Christian 64 3
Hoover, Christian 7, 26 2
Hoover, Christian 164 1
Hoover, Chritian 179 3
Hoover, Daniel 196 1
Hoover, Daniel 7, 11, 38, 118 2
Hoover, Elizabeth 26 2
Hoover, Erasmus 14 2
Hoover, Francis 27 2
Hoover, Francis J 27 2
Hoover, Geo 19 2
Hoover, Geo 245 1
Hoover, Geo 54 3
Hoover, Geo A 55, 87 3
Hoover, Geo A 106, 140 1
Hoover, Geo A 11, 14, 19 2
Hoover, George 26 3
Hoover, George 290 2
Hoover, Gideon 19 2
Hoover, Howison E 23 2
Hoover, J 192 3
Hoover, Jacob 27 2
Hoover, Jacob 19, 26, 27 2
Hoover, Jacob 26 2
Hoover, Jacob 40 1
Hoover, Jacob 19 2
Hoover, Jacob G 14 1
Hoover, Jess 176 1
Hoover, Jesse 14, 27, 28, 223a 2
Hoover, Jesse 109 1
Hoover, John 219 1
Hoover, John 7, 26, 27, 28, 30, 129
2
Hoover, John F 23 2
Hoover, John O 32 2
Hoover, John of J 192 3
Hoover, John W 28, 51 2
Hoover, John W 123 1
Hoover, John W 14, 39 3
Hoover, Joshua 219 1
Hoover, Joshua 51 2
Hoover, Magdalene 38 2
Hoover, Melcho 38 2
Hoover, Philip T 32 2
Hoover, Samuel 51 2
Hoover, Samuel L 23 2
Hoover, Susannah 51 2
Hope, Cora M 32 2
Hope, John A Sr 32 2
Hopkins, Alice E 2, 23 2
Hopkins, Alice E 23 2
Hopkins, Alice W 196 3
Hopkins, Clayton O 27 1
Hopkins, D H H 12 2
Hopkins, David 76 1
Hopkins, Elizabeth F 41 2
Hopkins, H H 147, 185 1
Hopkins, H H 188 2
Hopkins, H M Dr 172 3
Hopkins, Howard H 23 2
Hopkins, Howard H 196 3
Hopkins, Howard H Jr 61 1
Hopkins, Howard N 82 3
Hopkins, J Stephenson Dr 41 2
Hopkins, James 146 1
Hopkins, John 27 2
Hopkins, Josiah D 203 3
Hopkins, Margaret B 82 3
Hopkins, Margaret D 148, 185
1
Hopkins, Margaret D 172 3
Hopkins, Margaret D 41 2
Hopkins, Margaret M 82, 172 3
Hopkins, Margaret M 41 2
Hopkins, Margaret M 44, 185 1
Hopkins, Mary M 41 2
Hopkins, Rebecca 70 3
Hopkins, Sara 51 2
Hopkins, Sarah 88 1
Hopkins, Thomas 51 2
Hopkins, Wm D 23 2
Hopkins, Wm D 44 1
Hopp, Catherine 10, 23 2
Hopp, Edw B 40 2
Hopp, Harry A 23 2
Hopp, John F 43 2
Hopp, Joseph 23 2
Hopp, Martha 40 2
Hoppe, Frederick 18 2
Hoppe, Henry 51 2
Hoppe, I Henry 4 1
Hoppe, J Henry 26, 38, 133 3
Hoppe, J Henry 51, 57 1
Hoppe, J Henry 7, 38, 159, 186, 226
2
Hoppe, Martha 205 2
Hopwood, Catharine A C 9 2
Hopwood, Christiana 29 2
Hopwood, Guy E 58 2
Hopwood, James 7, 29, 197 2

Hopwood, James W 29 2
Hopwood, Stella A 9 2
Hopwood, Wm H 58 2
Horan, Frances E 18 2
Horan, John A 18 2
Horch, Elias 14 2
Horch, Margaret 14, 38 2
Horine, A Adele 2 2
Horine, A J 195 2
Horine, Alice R 2 2
Horine, Alvey J 3 2
Horine, Annie V 3, 35 2
Horine, Baxter T 16, 108 2
Horine, C R 9 2
Horine, Carlton 30 2
Horine, Carlton R 9 2
Horine, Cyrus F 3 2
Horine, E F 272 1
Horine, E J 9, 51 2
Horine, E S 268 2
Horine, Elias 185 3
Horine, Elizabeth 14 2
Horine, Emma S 15 2
Horine, Evelyn M 9 2
Horine, Ezra 54 2
Horine, Ezra J 2, 35 2
Horine, Ezra S 16 2
Horine, George 32 2
Horine, George W 268 2
Horine, George W 42 3
Horine, Grover F 2, 32 2
Horine, Herbert L 2 2
Horine, Jacob 100 2
Horine, Joal 30 2
Horine, Joel 54 2
Horine, John 14, 138 2
Horine, John 279 1
Horine, John D 193 3
Horine, John H 32 2
Horine, Joshua D 2, 32 2
Horine, Louise T 200 2
Horine, Luther 54 2
Horine, Luther A 35 2
Horine, Luther A T 35 2
Horine, M L 16, 30, 35, 45 2
Horine, M L 43 3
Horine, Martin 102, 160 2
Horine, Martin L 41 2
Horine, Martin L 234 1
Horine, Mary E 41 2
Horine, Millard H 3 2
Horine, Newton 256 1
Horine, Sarah E 52 2
Horine, Susan R 35, 52 2
Horine, Tobias 54, 100 2
Horine, Tobias 117 1
Horine, Tobias Jr 54 2
Horine, Tobias Sr 100 2
Horine, W Atlee 16, 41 2
Horine, W Ross 2 2
Horine, Washington 268 2
Horine, Wm A 15 2
Horman, L E 225 1
Horman, Lewis E 35 2
Horman, Mary E 41, 58 2
Horman, W H 33 1
Horman, Walter W H 35 2
Horman, William H 58 2
Hormer, A J 196 3
Horn, Emma V 15 2
Horn, Ernest B 15 2
Horn, Helen M 15 2
Horn, Mary V 15 2
Hornblower, Delilah 57 2
Hornblower, Wm 57 2
Horner, Aima E 45 2
Horner, Alexander L 209 3
Horner, Andrew 1 2
Horner, Andrew A 12 2
Horner, Chas A 58 2
Horner, David W 11 2
Horner, Eli 1, 14 2
Horner, George F 14 3
Horner, J A 44, 134, 188, 222 3
Horner, J A 15, 31, 58, 70, 169, 189, 199, 227, 222a, 229a, 259, 288 2
Horner, J A 44, 62, 72, 82, 126, 189, 219, 225, 230, 238 1
Horner, Ja 102 2
Horner, John A 166, 180 3
Horner, John A 33, 52, 140, 270 1
Horner, John A 23, 283 2
Horner, John H 246 2
Horner, Newton N 14 2
Horner, O A 13 1
Horner, Oliver A 11, 45 2
Horner, Oliver H 205 3
Horner, Olivetta 58 2
Horner, Silas M 187 3
Horner, Winfield 11 2
Horner, Winfield G 58 2
Hornicker, Peter 46 2
Hornicker, Susannah 51 2
Horning, Jacob 30 2
Horning, Samuel 51 2
Hornstein, Elizabeth 52 2
Hornstein, Samuel 52 2
Horsey, Anna C 2 2
Horsey, Eliza D 14, 45 2
Horsey, Elizabeth Lee 16, 45 2
Horsey, Geo Peter 159 1
Horsey, George C 282 2
Horsey, M Ellen 104 1
Horsey, Mary Ella 39 2
Horsey, O 196 3
Horsey, Outerbridge 37, 159, 272 1
Horsey, Outerbridge 2, 14, 39, 45, 67, 129, 139, 159 2
Horsey, Outerbridge Jr 45 2
Horsey, Outterbridge 50 3
Horsey, Thomas S Lee 137 1
Hort, Joseph 171 2
Horton, Arthur 18 2
Horton, Charles Richard 10 2
Horton, Fannie 10 2
Horton, Floyd 18 2
Hoskin, George 186 3
Hoskin, James N 69 2
Hoskins, Geo 257, 271 1
Hoskins, Geo 101, 211 2
Hoskins, George 50, 186 3
Hoskinson, John N 27 2
Hoskinson, Violette 56 2
Hospelhorn, Catherine O 10 2
Hospelhorn, Henry 22 2
Hospelhorn, Henry Sr 22 2
Hospelhorn, James 186 1
Hospelhorn, James 64 3
Hospelhorn, James 29, 49, 195 2
Hospelhorn, John 224 3
Hospelhorn, John T 29 2
Hospelhorn, Joseph T 190 2
Hospelhorn, Rachel 49 2
Hosselbock, George 87 2
Hosselbock, John 27 2
Hossler, Chas H 58 2
Hossler, Ella R 58 2
Hossler, Elsie V 58 2
Hossler, William H 58 2
Hotchkiss, Thomas 117 1
Hott, Arbelon C 201 1
Hott, Arbelon C 150 2
Hott, DeWitt 150 2
Hotwell, Ilijach H 205 3
Houch, Charles S Jr [sic] 76 1
Houch, George 290 2
Houch, Susanna 225a 2
Houck, Agnes H 3, 32 2
Houck, Alice J 119 1
Houck, Alice J 3 2
Houck, Amy E 189 3
Houck, Ann E 1 2
Houck, Anna M 3 2
Houck, C E 32 1
Houck, Catherine 8 2
Houck, Catherine E 8 2
Houck, Charles S Jr 10 2
Houck, Charles S Sr 10 2
Houck, Chas 96 3
Houck, Chas 18 2
Houck, Chas S 3 2
Houck, Chas S Sr 32 2
Houck, Daniel E 11, 12 2
Houck, Daniel J 11 2

Houck, Daniel J 12 2
Houck, Edw 46 2
Houck, Elizabeth 8 2
Houck, Elizabeth G 15 2
Houck, Elizabeth G 55 3
Houck, Elizabeth Rodick 16 2
Houck, Ella V 27, 55 3
Houck, Ella V 15, 16, 66 2
Houck, Elmer J 209 2
Houck, Elmer T 51 3
Houck, Emma 1 2
Houck, Emma B 15 2
Houck, Emma C R 31 2
Houck, Emma V 55 3
Houck, Ettie 52 2
Houck, Ezra 37, 67, 70, 91, 131, 152, 156, 164, 171, 214, 249, 264 1
Houck, Ezra 8, 14, 19, 22, 29, 38, 43, 66, 96, 132, 148, 159, 165, 186, 224a, 258, 288, 290 2
Houck, Ezra 2, 9, 39, 165, 202 3
Houck, Ezra Jr 16, 66 2
Houck, Ezra Jr 70, 283 1
Houck, Ezta 101 2
Houck, Florence M 18 2
Houck, Frank A 18 2
Houck, G 165 2
Houck, Geo 202 3
Houck, Geo 40, 156, 171, 177, 253, 260, 263 1
Houck, Geo 171 1
Houck, Geo 8, 14, 20, 22, 29, 38, 43, 134, 137, 144, 197 2
Houck, Geo E 20 2
Houck, George 19, 224a 2
Houck, George 165, 184 3
Houck, George B 20 2
Houck, Harry L 31 2
Houck, Harvey U 18 2
Houck, Henry 81, 195, 205, 209 3
Houck, Henry 22, 27, 46, 150, 203, 221a, 223a 2
Houck, Henry 40, 47, 57, 58, 84, 91, 106, 146, 152, 171, 271 1
Houck, Henry J 22 2
Houck, Howard 235 1
Houck, Howard E 23, 40 2
Houck, Ida H 40, 218, 212a 2
Houck, Isaac 87 2
Houck, Isaac J 25 2
Houck, J 106 3
Houck, J L 106 1
Houck, J of J 106 3
Houck, Jacob 26 2
Houck, Jacob 14, 26, 184 3
Houck, Jacob J 1 2
Houck, James 56, 165 1
Houck, James 8, 14, 29, 32, 66 2
Houck, James 2 3
Houck, James Edward 32 2
Houck, James W 10 2
Houck, John 56, 58, 106, 116, 139, 197, 210, 253 1
Houck, John 1, 18, 22, 27, 38, 165 2
Houck, John 81, 160 3
Houck, John Jr 40, 58 1
Houck, John T 31 2
Houck, Josiah 30 2
Houck, Larkin 116 1
Houck, Larkin 185, 202 3
Houck, Lavinia 46 2
Houck, Lydia A 35 2
Houck, Mamie E 23 2
Houck, Margaret 3, 32 2
Houck, Margaret C 39 2
Houck, Marion F 11, 40 2
Houck, Mary 39 2
Houck, Mary J 40 2
Houck, Mary Jane 39 2
Houck, Mary M 39 2
Houck, Mary Theresa 3, 32 2
Houck, Michael 38, 40 2
Houck, Mildred R 20 2
Houck, Milton D 3 2
Houck, Nan Johnson 43 2
Houck, Nora 54 2
Houck, Peter 26, 38, 46 2
Houck, Peter Jr 46 2
Houck, Rhoda 209 2
Houck, Roda E 51 3
Houck, S Marion 35 2
Houck, Samuel Jr 19 2
Houck, Scott C 25 2
Houck, Singleton E 40, 52 2
Houck, Talbott K 12 2
Houck, Thelma W 10 2
Houck, Tolbert K 54 2
Houck, Willie 73 3
Houff, Catherine E 31 2
Houff, Henry 165 3
Houff, J M 107 2
Houff, Jacob J 31 2
Hough, Edgar C 101 1
Hough, Nellie M 101 1
Hough, W C 225a 2
Houpt, Anna M 1 2
Houpt, Daniel 11 2
Houpt, George 221a 2
Houpt, George P A 19 2
Houpt, Henry 214 3
Houpt, Henry 22 2
Houpt, Isaiah 39 2
Houpt, Jacob 7, 38 2
Houpt, Jonathan 11, 22 2
Houpt, Margaret 38 2
Houpt, Mary 39 2
Houpt, Nicholas 38, 43 2
Houpt, Samuel 51 2
Houpt, Solomon 43 2
House, Andrew 26 2
House, Ann Rebecca 1 2
House, Anna 19 2
House, Annie M 9 2
House, Arthur C 2 2
House, Benedict 19 2
House, Benjamin 5 2
House, Caleb T 7 2
House, Charles J 9, 107 2
House, Chas 18, 89, 102, 160 2
House, Chas E 9 2
House, Chas J 20 2
House, Chas T 20 2
House, Christiana 8 2
House, Daniel 11 2
House, Daniel 129 3
House, Daniel V 165 3
House, David 138 2
House, David B 51 2
House, David B 79 1
House, Eli P 7, 14 2
House, Elisha 57 2
House, Elitha 19 2
House, Elizabeth 14 2
House, Emma F 18 2
House, Eveline C 15 2
House, Franklin G 18 2
House, G J 248, 283 1
House, Geo E 20 2
House, Geo Jr 19 2
House, Geo Sr 19 2
House, George C 20 2
House, Greenbury D 41 2
House, Greenbury J R 14, 20 2
House, Grove R 20 2
House, Hannah 23 2
House, Helen E 9 2
House, J W 20 2
House, John 243 1
House, John 26, 28, 57 2
House, John W P 31 2
House, Joseph A 9 2
House, Kate W R 34 2
House, L B 211 2
House, Lawson 15 2
House, Leonard S 2 2
House, Levin 14 2
House, Levin B 35 2
House, Margaret J G 35 2
House, Martin W 40 2
House, Mary 38 2
House, Mary E 40 2
House, Mary M 41, 57 2
House, Maytue W E 81 3
House, N W E 26 1
House, Nellie B 9 2
House, Peregrine T R 46 2

House, Raym nd G 213 3
House, Raymond 62 1
House, Raymond G 20 2
House, Robt S 49 2
House, Stephen 51 2
House, W 122 3
House, William 293 2
House, Wm 19, 26, 57 2
House, Wm of Daniel 129 3
House, Wm Sr 57 2
House, Wm W 28 2
Householder, Kathryn K 116 2
Houser, Michael 14 3
Houser, Pansy 85 2
Houser, Samuel 152 1
Housile, Lucinda 35 2
Houston, James F 116, 263 1
Houston, Jas T 81 3
Houston, John 116 1
Houwser, S H 81 3
Houx, John 28 2
Hovermale, Frederick W 18 2
Hovermale, Howard B 23 2
Hovermale, Victoria E 23 2
Howard, Alexander (Col'd) 1 2
Howard, Ann 25, 49 2
Howard, Ann H 1 2
Howard, Annie M 27 1
Howard, Austin 172 2
Howard, Austin W 35 2
Howard, Austin W 145, 157 1
Howard, Benjamin C 102 3
Howard, Charles 7 2
Howard, Charles E 7 2
Howard, Charles S 9 2
Howard, Chas S 9 2
Howard, Chas S 44 1
Howard, Clarence L 26 1
Howard, Cornelius 7 2
Howard, Daniel Jr 214 2
Howard, Darcus 11 2
Howard, Dennis D 11 2
Howard, Dennis D 70, 145 1
Howard, Doris Mottley 18 2
Howard, E 90 1
Howard, Edw 117 1
Howard, Edw 7, 14, 22 2
Howard, Edward 79 1
Howard, Edward 258 2
Howard, Elijah 67 3
Howard, Elisha 171, 194, 245 1
Howard, Elisha 7, 11, 14, 100, 185, 203 2
Howard, Elizabeth 14 2
Howard, Ellen R 15, 58 2
Howard, Ellen R s 2
Howard, Ellwood 26 3
Howard, F Dorsey 9 2
Howard, Francis D 9, 18 2
Howard, Henry 22 2
Howard, Isaac 25 2
Howard, Isaac H 22 2
Howard, James 49 2
Howard, James Tony 31 1
Howard, James W 163 3
Howard, James W 38 2
Howard, John C 38 2
Howard, Juliet 26 2
Howard, Katie 99 1
Howard, London W 25 2
Howard, Lyndon W H 35 2
Howard, M L 137 1
Howard, Margaret 38 2
Howard, Martha 38 2
Howard, Martha E 219a 2
Howard, Mary 38 2
Howard, Mary C 99 1
Howard, Mary D 41 2
Howard, Richard 38, 49 2
Howard, Richard 184 3
Howard, Rishard 160 3
Howard, Ruth 57 2
Howard, Thomas 7 2
Howard, Thomas H 54 2
Howard, Thos 22 2
Howard, Thos H 14 2
Howard, Thos H 163 3
Howard, Tony 98 3
Howard, W G 75 3
Howard, Wm 14 2
Howard, Wm C 210 3
Howard, Wm G 57, 69 2
Howard, Wm H 41 1
Howard, Wm H 1, 7, 58 2
Howell, Catherine 8 2
Howell, Jacob 250 2
Howell, Mary 38 2
Howell, Stephen 8, 38, 51 2
Howie, John N 32 2
Howie, Mattie O 32 2
Howker, Geo 8 2
Howry, Abraham 1 2
Howry, Abraham K 1 2
Howser, Dennis 12 2
Howser, Michael 110 1
Howser, Nina E 6 3
Hoy, Alice 3 2
Hoy, Ann E 43 2
Hoy, Daniel Raymond 3, 56 2
Hoy, Epriam 32 1
Hoy, John 27 2
Hoy, John 142 3
Hoy, Nicholas 27, 38, 43, 234 2
Hoy, Nicholas 142 3
Hoy, Nicholas Jr 43 2
Hoy, Rachel 49 2
Hoy, Susan 52 2
Hoy, Vinton 56 2
Hoyle, Hilda B 59 2
Hoyle, Wilford Marlowe 59 2
Hrgate, Samuel 70 3
Hubbard, Alta Irene 33 3
Hubbard, Emma J 172 3
Huber, Henry F 113 3
Hudson, Alexander C 1 2
Hudson, Edw J 15 2
Hudson, Nora H 43 2
Hudson, Robert W 1 2
Hudson, Rose 15 2
Huebener, Robert 162 1
Huett, Wm 179 3
Huff, Peter 144 2
Huffer, Anna Mary O 3 2
Huffer, Arthur H 16 2
Huffer, Austin L 12, 41 2
Huffer, C M 174 3
Huffer, C M 52 2
Huffer, Catherine 8 2
Huffer, Charles J 10, 12 2
Huffer, Charles M 10 2
Huffer, Charles S 10 2
Huffer, Chas 32 2
Huffer, Chas M 210 3
Huffer, Chas M 30 2
Huffer, Clarence T 41 2
Huffer, Daisy D 10, 12 2
Huffer, Elizabeth C 32 2
Huffer, Ella E 15 2
Huffer, Ella E 126 1
Huffer, Emma E 16 2
Huffer, Emma T 32 2
Huffer, Garland A 10 2
Huffer, Geo C 169 1
Huffer, Geo C 8, 20, 29 2
Huffer, Geo S 15, 31 2
Huffer, Geo S 126 1
Huffer, Harrie G 23 2
Huffer, Harry E 23 2
Huffer, Harry G 169 1
Huffer, Howard 67, 218a 2
Huffer, J 181 2
Huffer, J L 165 3
Huffer, J Wm 32 2
Huffer, Jacob 8 2
Huffer, Jacob M 279 1
Huffer, Jacob M 23, 29, 30, 31, 46 2
Huffer, Jacob T 32 2
Huffer, John 85 1
Huffer, Joseph 106, 144 2
Huffer, Joseph 64 3
Huffer, Joseph C 29, 31 2
Huffer, Joseph D 96, 125 1
Huffer, Joseph D 15 3

Huffer, Joseph L 58, 270 1
Huffer, Joseph L 46 2
Huffer, L M 52 2
Huffer, Mammie L 16, 32 2
Huffer, Margaret Ellen 41 2
Huffer, Martin Luther 41 2
Huffer, Mary Courtney 126 1
Huffer, Mary K 23 2
Huffer, Mary M 20, 40 2
Huffer, Obrum C 31 2
Huffer, Ohrem 3 2
Huffer, Phoebe E 46 2
Huffer, Ruth E 10 2
Huffer, S J 52 2
Huffer, Samuel J 23, 41 2
Huffer, Samuel J 14 1
Huffer, Sarah E 52 2
Huffer, Wm 240 1
Huffman, Etta R 20 2
Huffman, Geo W 76 1
Huffman, George W 20 2
Huffman, John 26 2
Hugh, Ann 1 2
Hughes, Absalom 38 2
Hughes, Ann 2 2
Hughes, Ann Rebecca 1 2
Hughes, Anna W 2 2
Hughes, Ben 279 1
Hughes, Benjamin E 84 1
Hughes, Benjamin E 5 2
Hughes, Catherine S 5 2
Hughes, Chas R 23 2
Hughes, Clinton K 9 2
Hughes, Daniel 11, 14, 237 2
Hughes, Daniel 32 1
Hughes, Edw W 2 2
Hughes, Elizabeth J 15 2
Hughes, Emma C 15 2
Hughes, Eugene 5 2
Hughes, Frances 15 2
Hughes, Francis 31 2
Hughes, Geo 5, 57, 89, 101 2
Hughes, Geo 57, 137, 139, 196 1
Hughes, Geo L 23 2
Hughes, Geo W 206 3
Hughes, George 19 2
Hughes, George 96, 208 1
Hughes, George W 75 3
Hughes, Green Lee 19 2
Hughes, Harriet R 23 2
Hughes, James 27 2
Hughes, James A 30, 31 2
Hughes, John 19, 26, 27, 35, 45 2
Hughes, John 56, 70 1
Hughes, Levi 219 1
Hughes, Levy 35 2
Hughes, Mary B 38 2
Hughes, Otho W 45 2
Hughes, Richard 11 2
Hughes, Samuel 208 1
Hughes, Thomas 54 2
Hughes, Wm 210, 279 1
Hughes, Wm 195, 205 3
Hughs, George 226 2
Hugo, Doris J 57 2
Hull, Abraham 1 2
Hull, Alfred 1 2
Hull, Americus K V 15 2
Hull, Andrew 1 2
Hull, Andrew 212 3
Hull, Andrew Sr 1 2
Hull, Ann Maria 1 2
Hull, Annie F 2 2
Hull, Barrick 213 3
Hull, Benjamin 5 2
Hull, Catharine A 9 2
Hull, Christian 7 2
Hull, Cyrus 228 1
Hull, Cyrus 26 2
Hull, D J 48 1
Hull, Daniel J 55 3
Hull, Daniel L 9, 12, 58 2
Hull, Eliza 15 2
Hull, Emma A 16 2
Hull, Frederick L C 16 2
Hull, Geo J 2 2
Hull, H C 223, 235 1
Hull, H Clay 23, 29, 231 2
Hull, Harry C 23 2
Hull, Jacob 53 3
Hull, Jacob 51 1
Hull, Jacob 1, 26, 28 2
Hull, John 26, 38, 57 2
Hull, Julia C 29 2
Hull, Julius 11, 26 2
Hull, Julius 53 3
Hull, Julius C 131, 228 1
Hull, Lavinia E 23 2
Hull, M E 2 2
Hull, Magdalene 38 2
Hull, Margaret A 1, 39 2
Hull, Mary C 163 3
Hull, Peter 238 1
Hull, Peter 1, 26 2
Hull, Priscilla 46 2
Hull, Stephen 51 2
Hull, Tideman 279 1
Hull, Wm 46, 58 2
Hulton, Catherine 7 2
Hulton, Geo 19 2
Hulton, Mary 19 2
Humberg, Conrad & 46 2
Humbert, Dorothy 11 2
Humbert, George 19 2
Hume, R C 52, 232 2
Hume, R Caldwell 49, 265 2
Hume, Sara Cull 49, 265 2
Hume, Sarah Cull 232 2
Hume, Sarah W 229a 2
Humerick, Chas O 9, 40 2
Humerick, Edgar G 139 2
Humerick, John 155 1
Humerick, John 27 2
Humerick, Mary E 40 2
Humerick, Maude C 9 2
Humm, Edw 14 2
Humm, Jane R 29 2
Humm, Jane Rebecca 14 2
Humm, John W 32, 35, 49 2
Humm, Levi A 29, 35 2
Humm, Levi A 29 2
Humm, Lilly M 266 1
Humm, Robt D 49 2
Humm, William C 125 2
Humm, Wm 149 2
Humm, Wm 49, 149 2
Humm, Wm C 73 1
Humm, Wm C 32 2
Hummel, Jacob 210 1
Hummer, Alice Ann 3 2
Hummer, Andrew 1 2
Hummer, Arthur H 32 2
Hummer, Blanche A 32 2
Hummer, Edith M 49 2
Hummer, Henry 22 2
Hummer, John 234 1
Hummer, John 26 2
Hummer, John 28 2
Hummer, John 26, 28, 46 2
Hummer, John 46 2
Hummer, John F 32 2
Hummer, John Henry 22 2
Hummer, Joseph 49 2
Hummer, Joseph H 32 2
Hummer, Julia E 32 2
Hummer, Raymond M 49 2
Hummer, Susannah 51 2
Humphrey, Alice 193 2
Hunichen, Ida E 25 2
Hunt, A H 186, 227a 2
Hunt, A H 44 1
Hunt, A H 227a 2
Hunt, Anna G 92 2
Hunt, Asbury 223 1
Hunt, Asbury H 2 2
Hunt, Caroline M 189 3
Hunt, Caroline V 9 2
Hunt, David O 270 1
Hunt, Samuel 44 1
Hunter, John F 67 2
Hunter, Mary M 234 2
Hurd, Annie 3 2
Hurd, J 70 3
Hurd, Lewis 3 2
Hurd, Sophia 51 2
Hurd, Virginia 56 2
Hurley, Anna S 68 3

Hurley, Geo W W 19 2
Hurley, J E 234 1
Hurley, John 28 2
Hurley, John E & 219 1
Hurley, Levin 19, 35 2
Hurley, Mary A E 35 2
Hursh, Goldie M 20, 32 2
Hursh, John M 32 2
Husberger, William 81 3
Huss, Andrew L 3 2
Huss, Florence Café 3 2
Huston, James 163 1
Huston, James 11 2
Huston, James F 116 2
Huston, James F 139 1
Huston, James H 88 1
Huston, John 196, 217 1
Hutzel, John 46 2
Hutzel, Peter 46 2
Hutzel, Samuel 51 2
Hutzell, Alice A 3 2
Hutzell, Jacob 51 2
Hutzell, Jonas E 32 2
Hutzell, Vernon E 3, 32 2
Hyatt, Chas M 35 2
Hyatt, Edna E 30 2
Hyatt, Eli 205 2
Hyatt, Eli 186 3
Hyatt, Eli H 15 2
Hyatt, Eli W 191 1
Hyatt, Ely 14 2
Hyatt, Emma C 58 2
Hyatt, Ezra 14 2
Hyatt, J Bradley 5 2
Hyatt, James 63 2
Hyatt, James W 21 3
Hyatt, James W 56 2
Hyatt, John E 30 2
Hyatt, Kate A 34 2
Hyatt, Lloyd H What 86, 209 3
Hyatt, Lloyd H 35 2
Hyatt, Lydia A 35 2
Hyatt, Mollie 35 2
Hyatt, W E 61 1
Hyatt, Wm Asa 14 2
Hyatt, Wm E 58 2
Hyde, I 176 3
Hyde, John 30 2
Hyde, Jonathan 26 2
Hyde, Samuel 30 2
Hyde, Thos 179 3
Hyde, Wm J 57 2
Hyden, Annie R 240 1
Hyden, Basil 167 3
Hyden, J W 185 3
Hyder, Annie R 29 2
Hyder, Catherine 25 2
Hyder, Daniel M 12 2
Hyder, Henry 23, 187 2
Hyder, Henry 171 1
Hyder, Isaaac 64 3
Hyder, Isaac 165 3
Hyder, Isaac 25, 28, 29, 51, 138 2
Hyder, J W 71 3
Hyder, Jacob 203, 217 1
Hyder, Jacob 28, 51, 57 2
Hyder, Jacob W 31, 51 2
Hyder, James W 29 2
Hyder, John E 31 2
Hyder, John W 28 2
Hyder, Marshall 25 2
Hyder, Mary Ann 23 2
Hyder, Sarah 51 2
Hyder, Sarah C 51 2
Hyder, Wm H 30 1
Hydicker, Wilhelmina 57 2
Hydler, Henry 54 3
Hydler, Jacob 214 2
Hyland, Alicia 5 2
Hyland, Benoni 5 2
Hyland, Elisha R 37 1
Hymes, John 11 2
Hymes, John 28 2
Hymes, Samuel L 28 2
Hyndman, Roy I 196 3
Hynes, Edward P 195 3
Hyser, Ernest S 151 2
Hyter, Christopher 7 2
Ide, Floyd M 64 2
Ide, Walter B 64 2
Idimiller, Nicholas 84 2
Iferd, Everd R 62 2
Iferd, John W 62 2
Ifert, Abraham M 112 2
Ifert, Amanda A 62 2
Ifert, Amanda C 62 2
Ifert, Chas E 62 2
Ifert, Ira D 64 2
Ifert, J J 91 1
Ifert, John 62 2
Ifert, Mary C 62 2
Ifert, Susan E 62, 64 2
Ifert, Vada E 64 2
Ignatius Waters 58 1
Ijames, Jacob [sic] 19 1
Ijams, Eliza A 62, 64 2
Ijams, Jacob 63 2
Ijams, Jacob 25, 146, 177 1
Ijams, John 22, 183 1
Ijams, John 63 2
Ijams, Mary M 62 2
Ijams, Mollie M 63 2
Ijams, Plummer 70, 84, 146, 177, 257 1
Ijams, Plummer 63, 275 2
Ijams, Plummer Jr 63 2
Ijams, Richard 63, 64 2
Ijams,Harriet H 63 2
Iler, Amos 63 2
Iler, Ann S 62 2
Iler, Barbara 62 2
Iler, Conrad 62 2
Iler, Daniel 62 2
Iler, Daniel 219 1
Iler, Geo W 62 2
Iler, Isaac 63 2
Iler, John 62 2
Iler, Peter 63 2
Iler, Peter 62 1
Indemnity Ins Co of N A 25 2
Independence Indemnity 227a 2
Independence Indemnity Co 166, 219a 2
Independence Indemnity Co 20, 180, 214 3
Independence Indemnity Co 120, 257, 271 1
Independence Indemnity Co of Pa 101 1
Independence Indemnity Co of PA 166 2
Independent Indemnity Co 259 2
Independent Indemnity Co of Phila 190 2
Ingels, John 63 2
Ingels, Thomas 63 2
Ingle, Mary A 63 2
Ingle, Osborne 85 1
Ingle, Osborne 63 2
Ingler, David 63 2
Ingler, Philip 63 2
Ingman, Amelia 63 2
Ingman, Joshua 63 2
Ingman, William H 64 2
Ingram, Thomas 64 2
Irey, Edith E 231 2
Irons, Rebecca 64 2
Irvin, James 63 2
Irvin, Samuel 63 2
Irving, W W 64 2
Isanogle, Amanda C 62 2
Isanogle, Ann Eliza 62, 63 2
Isanogle, Bradley C 62 2
Isanogle, Bruce M 62 2
Isanogle, Chas 62 2
Isanogle, Chas W 62 2
Isanogle, Geo M 62 2
Isanogle, Geo W 62 2
Isanogle, Matilda 62 2
Isanogle, Michael 63 2
Isbell, F B 62 2
Isbell, Loreena V 62 2
Isenhour, Balthauer 41 1
Israel, Reuben 38 2
Ivell, Joseph W [sic] 8 1

Jackson, Adolphus 65 2
Jackson, Chas 69 2
Jackson, Chas A 18 2
Jackson, Christian H 78, 177 2
Jackson, David 72 2
Jackson, Edw 65 2
Jackson, Evon Whalen 177 3
Jackson, Frank 68 2
Jackson, John 69, 70 2
Jackson, John 82 1
Jackson, John (Col'd) 69 2
Jackson, Letitia 72 2
Jackson, Lewis 72 2
Jackson, Mary 72 2
Jackson, Matilda E 72 2
Jackson, Melvin E 177 3
Jackson, Oscar B 140 2
Jackson, Polly 72 2
Jackson, Richard 75 2
Jackson, Richard P 246, 247 2
Jackson, Russell 120 1
Jackson, Thomas E 45 3
Jackson, Wm 78 2
Jacob, Joel 137 2
Jacob, Mikesell 46 2
Jacobs, A L 133 1
Jacobs, Adam 65, 69 2
Jacobs, Adam L 65, 67 2
Jacobs, Ann M 65 2
Jacobs, Barbara B 66 2
Jacobs, Benjamin L 66 2
Jacobs, C Edwin 66 2
Jacobs, C S 14 2
Jacobs, Calvin 257 2
Jacobs, Cammelious 66 2
Jacobs, Caroline S 9 3
Jacobs, Catherine S 15, 66 2
Jacobs, Catherine T 27 3
Jacobs, Corban 38 2
Jacobs, Corbett 66 2
Jacobs, Corbin 156 1
Jacobs, Daniel 65, 67 2
Jacobs, David 69 2
Jacobs, Davis 69 2
Jacobs, Elizabeth 68 2
Jacobs, Elmer Clarence 67 2
Jacobs, Emanuel 111 2
Jacobs, Fannie T 249 1
Jacobs, Geo W 68 2
Jacobs, George 6 1
Jacobs, George 68 2
Jacobs, Goldie 99 2
Jacobs, Grace H 12 2
Jacobs, Henry 69 2
Jacobs, Ignatius 72 2
Jacobs, Jacob 69 2
Jacobs, Jemima L 70 2
Jacobs, Jemima L 65, 70 2
Jacobs, Joel 11, 69 2
Jacobs, Joel 129 3
Jacobs, John 69 2
Jacobs, Joseph M 69 2
Jacobs, Mary 69 2
Jacobs, Mary A 66 2
Jacobs, Mary Ann 69 2
Jacobs, Mary Ann E 72 2
Jacobs, Mary V 73 2
Jacobs, Matilda 72 2
Jacobs, Michael 72, 175 2
Jacobs, Michael 225 1
Jacobs, Robert M 75 2
Jacobs, Salome 76 2
Jacobs, Salome 76 2
Jacobs, Wm 7, 68 2
Jacobson, Karl 72, 75 2
Jacobson, Katie 72, 75 2
Jacobson, Nathan 72 2
Jaens, W M [sic] 169 1
Jaharias, Edith M 75 2
Jaharias, George 75 2
James 70 3
James, Charles C 66 2
James, Clara E 75 3
James, Daniel 38, 67 2
James, Daniel 160 3
James, E A 189 3
James, E Austin 161 3
James, E Austin 181, 201, 278 1
James, E Austin 16, 20, 175, 196 2
James, Edw 10 1
James, Edw 78 2
James, Eli 185 2
James, Elisha 67 2
James, Frank 145 2
James, Herbert H 49 2
James, Jane Staley 68 3
James, Joseph 69 2
James, Joseph 160 3
James, Joseph 152 1
James, Mahlon 72 2
James, Mary P 87 3
James, Rose M 75 2
James, S P 70 1
James, Sarah Pratby 67 2
James, Sir Pratby 76 2
James, Sirpratby 160 3
James, Wm H 78 2
Jamison, A L 70 2
Jamison, Alexius 65 2
Jamison, B I 39 2
Jamison, B I 188 1
Jamison, B I 161 3
Jamison, B L 227 2
Jamison, Baker 214, 234, 243 1
Jamison, Baker 141, 212 3
Jamison, Baker 38, 66 2
Jamison, Benjamin 66 2
Jamison, Brook I 120 3
Jamison, Brooke 10 3
Jamison, Brooke I 187, 191 3
Jamison, Brooke I 66, 72, 76 2
Jamison, Brooke J 66 2
Jamison, Cora G 66 2
Jamison, Elmo 182 2
Jamison, Elmo V Jr 67 2
Jamison, Elmo Vincent 67 2
Jamison, Francis 72 2
Jamison, Francis V 165 2
Jamison, H M 88 1
Jamison, Henrietta L 41 2
Jamison, Henry 65, 165 2
Jamison, Henry 23 3
Jamison, Henry M 70 1
Jamison, Ignatius 69 2
Jamison, J I 120 3
Jamison, J V 39 2
Jamison, J V 230 1
Jamison, J Vincent 70 2
Jamison, John 39, 66, 69, 72, 107, 119, 205 2
Jamison, John 209 3
Jamison, John H 219 1
Jamison, John H 66, 70, 72, 255 2
Jamison, John H 44 3
Jamison, John I 120, 207 3
Jamison, John I 70 2
Jamison, John I 59 1
Jamison, John J 106, 160 3
Jamison, John J 139 1
Jamison, John J 72 2
Jamison, John Jay 76 2
Jamison, John L 187 3
Jamison, John R 76 2
Jamison, Joshua 69 2
Jamison, Katherine 69 2
Jamison, Kitty 72 2
Jamison, Leonard 149 3
Jamison, Leonard 78 1
Jamison, Mary 72 2
Jamison, Nena M 66, 70 2
Jamison, Oswald 65, 75 2
Jamison, Oswald 88 1
Jamison, Robert 75 2
Jamison, Robert I 125 1
Jamison, S B 69 2
Jamison, Susan R 76 2
Jamison, Teresa 69, 76 2
Jamison, Teresa J 76 2
Jamison, Theresa 75 2
Janney, Geo W 70 1
Jarboe, Alexander 65 2
Jarboe, Catharine 66, 75 2
Jarboe, Charles 66 2
Jarboe, Eleanor 69 2

Jarboe, Elizabeth 67 2
Jarboe, Ellen S 67, 80 2
Jarboe, Francis 68 2
Jarboe, Henry 66, 69 2
Jarboe, J S 208 1
Jarboe, J S 197 2
Jarboe, James E 69 2
Jarboe, John 69, 63, 198 2
Jarboe, John S 70 1
Jarboe, John S W 58, 159 1
Jarboe, John S W 72, 177 2
Jarboe, Margaret 72 2
Jarboe, Margaret L 72, 76 2
Jarboe, Raphael 75 2
Jarboe, Samuel 113, 237, 242, 264 2
Jarboe, Samuel 91, 117 1
Jarboe, Samuel 185 3
Jarboe, Sarah 68, 76 2
Jarboe, Teresa 76 2
Jarboe, Thomas 165 1
Jarboe, Thomas 72, 181 2
Jarboe, Thomas R 76, 177 2
Jarboe, Thomas R 91 1
Jarboe, Thos 159 1
Jarboe, Thos R 67 1
Jarboe, Wm 79, 84, 163 1
Jarboe, Wm 69, 75, 78, 185, 202 2
Jarboe, Wm B 78 2
Jason, Amos L 67 2
Jeans, Annie 65 2
Jeans, Franklin L 78 2
Jeans, Gertrude 68 2
Jeans, Roscoe 75 2
Jeans, William E 78 2
Jeans, William M 78 2
Jeems, Mary Hester 72 2
Jeffery, Edw T 119 1
Jeffery, James C 112 1
Jenkins, Adeline 65 2
Jenkins, Chas 49, 197 2
Jenkins, Chas J 47 1
Jenkins, Elsie G 67 2
Jenkins, Helena 69 2
Jenkins, Henry 69 2
Jenkins, Henry 84, 225 1
Jenkins, Jenks B 70, 76 2
Jenkins, Job 69 2
Jenkins, John 172 1
Jenkins, Marshall 72 2
Jenkins, Mary 72 2
Jenkins, Seloma B 76 2
Jenkins, Theodore 38, 76 2
Jenkins, V 76 2
Jenkins, Wm of V 78 2
Jenks, Wm D 78 2
Jennings, Ada S 65 2
Jennings, Chas E 67, 70, 75 2
Jennings, Clinton W 209 2
Jennings, Ellen S 75 2
Jennings, Emiline 67 2
Jennings, Emiline 70 2
Jennings, Emma A 67 2
Jennings, James W 70 2
Jennings, James Wm 70 2
Jennings, Joseph O 65 2
Jennings, Orville M 75 2
Job, Wm 78 2
Jodon, John 69 2
Jodon, Zachariah 69 2
Johannes, Arthur W 65 2
Johannes, Ina B 69 2
Johannes, William A 65 2
Johannes, Wm A 69 2
Johns, Abraham 65 2
Johns, Mary P 65 2
Johnson, Abraham L 65 2
Johnson, Ada M 65 2
Johnson, Adeline R 69 2
Johnson, Albert J 65 2
Johnson, Alexander 65 2
Johnson, Alice H 49 2
Johnson, Amanda A 65 2
Johnson, Amanda E 66 2
Johnson, Amanda E 65, 66 2
Johnson, America 203 2
Johnson, Ann Maria 65 2
Johnson, Ann R 65 2
Johnson, Ann R 65 2
Johnson, Anna M 65, 171 2
Johnson, B T 38, 154 2
Johnson, Baker 66 2
Johnson, Benj 100 2
Johnson, Benjamin 7, 66 2
Johnson, Bradley P 137 2
Johnson, Bradley T 29, 124, 144, 171 2
Johnson, Bradley T 129, 167 3
Johnson, Bradley T 146 1
Johnson, C D 171, 271 1
Johnson, Caroline 66, 70, 274 2
Johnson, Caroline G 75 2
Johnson, Cassandra 66, 78 2
Johnson, Catharine 66 2
Johnson, Catharine V 66 2
Johnson, Catherine 68 2
Johnson, Catherine N 65 2
Johnson, Charles 66, 234 2
Johnson, Chas 65, 69, 76, 78, 87 2
Johnson, Chas 185 3
Johnson, Chas 25 1
Johnson, Chas W 205 3
Johnson, Chas W 123, 234 1
Johnson, Chas W 66, 280 2
Johnson, Clara 66 2
Johnson, Clara B 66 2
Johnson, Clara D 56 2
Johnson, Claud E 68 2
Johnson, Clinton 164 1
Johnson, David 220 3
Johnson, David 8, 75 2
Johnson, David L 70 2
Johnson, Dewitt C 67, 76 2
Johnson, Dorcas 67 2
Johnson, E Frank 67 2
Johnson, E M 160 2
Johnson, Edgar 67 2
Johnson, Edwin 106 1
Johnson, Edwin 66, 78 2
Johnson, Edwin L 65, 66 2
Johnson, Edwin M 78, 113 2
Johnson, Effie 67 2
Johnson, Effie M 67 2
Johnson, Eleanor M 19 3
Johnson, Eleanor M 23, 67 2
Johnson, Eleanora 67 2
Johnson, Eleanore 67, 75, 76 2
Johnson, Elias 67 2
Johnson, Elinor S 67 2
Johnson, Eliza V 165 1
Johnson, Eliza, J 67 2
Johnson, Elizabeth 67 2
Johnson, Elizabeth 67 2
Johnson, Ellen S 67 2
Johnson, Emily 67, 70 2
Johnson, Emily C 75 2
Johnson, Emma 78 2
Johnson, F 78 2
Johnson, Fayette 68 2
Johnson, Florence 68 2
Johnson, G Walter 68 2
Johnson, Geo 245, 271 1
Johnson, Geo 22, 68, 72, 78, 87, 144 2
Johnson, Geo H 46, 68, 154 2
Johnson, Geo W Jr 72 2
Johnson, George 101 2
Johnson, Giles L 67 2
Johnson, Giles Livers 72 2
Johnson, Grace Atkinson 14 1
Johnson, Grahame 67 2
Johnson, Hannah 68 2
Johnson, Hannah B 69 2
Johnson, Hannah R 70 2
Johnson, Harry 72 2
Johnson, Hazel L 65 2
Johnson, Helen Y 66, 69 2
Johnson, Henrietta 69 2
Johnson, Henry A 18 1
Johnson, Henry J 78 2
Johnson, Henry T 70 2
Johnson, Ira D 78 2
Johnson, J 184 3

Johnson, J 78 2
Johnson, J A 57, 67, 76 2
Johnson, J G 42, 85 1
Johnson, J G 75 2
Johnson, J Graham 65 2
Johnson, J Graham 97 1
Johnson, J I 113 3
Johnson, J T 67 2
Johnson, Jacob 39, 69, 70, 254 2
Johnson, Jacob 11 1
Johnson, Jacob of J 184 3
Johnson, James 25 1
Johnson, James 68, 75 2
Johnson, James T 1, 70, 262 2
Johnson, James T 133, 150 1
Johnson, Jane 72 2
Johnson, Jeannette 70 2
Johnson, Jeannette 62 1
Johnson, John 76, 227 2
Johnson, John A 78 2
Johnson, John H 70 2
Johnson, John K 202 3
Johnson, John L 70 2
Johnson, John P 67 2
Johnson, John Sr 69 2
Johnson, John W 65, 69 2
Johnson, Joseph 69, 70, 78 2
Johnson, Joseph A 69, 70, 75, 76, 282 2
Johnson, Joseph A 6, 37, 195 3
Johnson, Joseph A 104 1
Johnson, Joshua 194, 282 1
Johnson, Joshua 7, 66, 67, 75 2
Johnson, Julia 69 2
Johnson, Leonard 225 1
Johnson, Lewis O 56, 72 2
Johnson, Margaret 72 2
Johnson, Maria 72 2
Johnson, Maria (col'd) 72 2
Johnson, Martha 123 1
Johnson, Mary 72 2
Johnson, Mary C 72 2
Johnson, Mary E 72 2
Johnson, Mary E (col'd) 72 2
Johnson, Mary L 76 2
Johnson, Mary Louisa 123, 222 1
Johnson, Mary Louisa 65 2
Johnson, Mary T 72 2
Johnson, Milton 72 2
Johnson, Mollie 72 2
Johnson, Mollie B 72 2
Johnson, Otis 67, 171 3
Johnson, Patrick T L 76 2
Johnson, Paul G 45 1
Johnson, Paul T 202 3
Johnson, Peter 75 2
Johnson, Polly 75 2
Johnson, Rebecca 75 2
Johnson, Richard 75 2
Johnson, Richard P 75 2
Johnson, Robert 179 3
Johnson, Robert 75 2
Johnson, Robert B 165 3
Johnson, Robert P 75 2
Johnson, Robt 149 2
Johnson, Roger 75 2
Johnson, Roger 104 1
Johnson, Ross 78 2
Johnson, Ruth G 78 2
Johnson, Ruth G 75 2
Johnson, Samuel 76 2
Johnson, Samuel T 123 1
Johnson, Sarah 76 2
Johnson, T A 76 2
Johnson, T B 104, 171 1
Johnson, Thomas 65, 72, 76, 78, 226 2
Johnson, Thomas 106, 123 1
Johnson, Thomas 67, 165 3
Johnson, Thomas A 76 2
Johnson, Thomas B 76 2
Johnson, Thomas H 76 2
Johnson, Thomas P 76 2
Johnson, Thomas W 88 1
Johnson, Thomas W 69, 76 2
Johnson, Thos 113 2
Johnson, Thos 81, 202 3
Johnson, Thos B 52 2
Johnson, Thos W 163 1
Johnson, Virgie M 67 2
Johnson, W 40 1
Johnson, W W 78 2
Johnson, Walter G 65, 78 2
Johnson, William C 78 2
Johnson, William C 165 3
Johnson, Wm 2, 68, 72, 75, 76, 78 2
Johnson, Wm 26, 163, 245 1
Johnson, Wm B 66 2
Johnson, Wm C 179, 233, 249 1
Johnson, Wm C 9, 68, 76, 78 2
Johnson, Wm F 234 1
Johnson, Wm F 78 2
Johnson, Wm F 81 3
Johnson, Wm H 118 1
Johnson, Wm H 56, 66, 67, 78 2
Johnson, Wm of J 78 2
Johnson, Wm S 78 2
Johnson, Wm T 70 1
Johnson, Wm T 78 2
Johnson, Worthington 104, 139, 249 1
Johnson, Worthington 78 2
Johnson, Worthington R 271 1
Johnson, Worthington R 22, 72, 75, 101, 144 2
Johnson, Wyndham 72 2
Johnston, Abraham L 72 2
Johnston, Caroline 66 2
Johnston, Carrie 66 2
Johnston, Carrie 221 3
Johnston, Clarence A 66 2
Johnston, Edward C 66 2
Johnston, Edwin M 165 3
Johnston, Frances 68 2
Johnston, Harry 221 3
Johnston, Hugh K 269 2
Johnston, Jeanette 68 2
Johnston, Joseph 38 3
Johnston, Joseph P 68 2
Johnston, Louis 72 2
Johnston, Margaret 72 2
Johnston, Mary C 72 2
Johnston, Mary Catharine 73 2
Johnston, Mary L S 73 2
Johnston, William 38 3
Johnston, William H 72 2
joint property 87, 180 3
Joliffe, W N 22 1
Jones, A A 70 2
Jones, A M 23 2
Jones, Abraham 51, 116, 177, 181, 192, 263 1
Jones, Abraham 14, 27, 38, 65, 65, 220a, 237 2
Jones, Abraham 38, 64, 163 3
Jones, Ada Elizabeth 65 2
Jones, Albert 112 1
Jones, Albert 68, 128 2
Jones, Alfred 185 3
Jones, Alice 65 2
Jones, Alice K 65, 75 2
Jones, Anderson 70 2
Jones, Anna F 72 2
Jones, B A 30 2
Jones, Benj 53 3
Jones, Chares McA 19 1
Jones, Chas 102 3
Jones, Chas McA 72 2
Jones, Colonel W 66 2
Jones, Cornelius H 78 2
Jones, Daniel T 67 3
Jones, Daniel T 51, 59 1
Jones, Daphne 67 2
Jones, David 11 2
Jones, David J 58 1
Jones, David Morgan 107 3
Jones, David T 160 3
Jones, E L 171 1
Jones, E Medora 72 2
Jones, Edgar L 67 2
Jones, Edw 65 2

Jones, Elen Doll 67 2
Jones, Elizabeth 67 2
Jones, Elizabeth V 67 2
Jones, Ellen Dall 171 1
Jones, Elmer E 11 1
Jones, Emma A 70 2
Jones, Fracis S 132 3
Jones, Frances H 69 2
Jones, Francis 28, 210a 2
Jones, Francis 58, 171 1
Jones, Francis S 65, 68, 237, 286 2
Jones, Francis S 47 1
Jones, Francis S 14 3
Jones, Frank 68, 70 2
Jones, G Arthur 148 1
Jones, Geo W 68 2
Jones, George E 69 2
Jones, Griffith 39 2
Jones, H M 166 3
Jones, H M 225, 226 2
Jones, Harriett B 70 2
Jones, Harry C 70, 78 2
Jones, Helen Manion (Frances H) 69 2
Jones, Hezekiah 69 2
Jones, Hilleary 205 3
Jones, Hiram B 69 2
Jones, Howard 193, 247 2
Jones, Howard M 19 1
Jones, Howard M 15, 67 2
Jones, J 11, 69 2
Jones, J B 70 2
Jones, J Burgess 70 2
Jones, J Edward 70 2
Jones, J R 78 2
Jones, James A 45 3
Jones, James H 70 2
Jones, James W 70 2
Jones, Jane Rice 70, 293 2
Jones, John 70, 167, 171, 205, 212 3
Jones, John 19, 36, 69, 78, 169, 203, 226, 214a, 228a, 288 2
Jones, John 22, 84, 97, 263 1
Jones, John A 12 2
Jones, John A 28 1
Jones, John G 49, 287 2
Jones, John G 192 3
Jones, John G 230 1
Jones, John Jr 69 2
Jones, John of J 84 1
Jones, John of J 11, 69 2
Jones, John P 112, 133 1
Jones, John P 75, 225, 226 2
Jones, John Peter 70 2
Jones, John R 1 1
Jones, John R 43, 70 2
Jones, John S 2 2
Jones, John Wm 70 2
Jones, John Wm 70 2
Jones, Joseph 134 2
Jones, Joshua 69 2
Jones, Joshua 146, 171, 271 1
Jones, Joshua 69 2
Jones, Lavinia 70, 72 2
Jones, Leonard Hays 72 2
Jones, LeRoy 72 2
Jones, M 59 1
Jones, M C 65, 70, 172, 214a 2
Jones, M C 107 3
Jones, Margaret D 166 3
Jones, Margaret Doll 148 1
Jones, Martha 72 2
Jones, Martin L 72, 78 2
Jones, Mary Ann 75 2
Jones, Mary E 67, 72 2
Jones, Mary E 254 1
Jones, Mary Hays 72 2
Jones, Mary J 72 2
Jones, Mary M 72 2
Jones, Mary P 72 2
Jones, Mathias 202 3
Jones, Maurice 72 2
Jones, Maurice I 67 2
Jones, Maurice J 54 3
Jones, Mordecai 99 1
Jones, Moses (col'd) 72 2
Jones, Myrtle 102 3
Jones, Nathan 75 2
Jones, Nettie F 65, 70, 75 2
Jones, Patrick 75 2
Jones, Pauline V 76 2
Jones, Peter 75 2
Jones, Philip 76 2
Jones, Philip 41 1
Jones, R 218 2
Jones, Rachel A 19 1
Jones, Ralph 40, 78, 253 1
Jones, Ralph 69 2
Jones, Raphael 32 1
Jones, Raphael 75 2
Jones, Ruth S 70 2
Jones, Ruthanna 192 3
Jones, S Eleanor 72 2
Jones, Samuel E 259 2
Jones, Spencer E 22 1
Jones, Teresa 76 2
Jones, Thomas 65, 76 2
Jones, Thos 54, 139, 185, 203 2
Jones, Truman S 76 2
Jones, Validelta 77 2
Jones, Wesley N R 78 2
Jones, William 202 3
Jones, William 78 2
Jones, William P 275 2
Jones, Winter D 75, 172 2
Jones, Wm 67, 78 2
Jones, Wm 44, 51, 112, 225, 235 1
Jones, Wm A 183, 225 1
Jones, Wm D 176 1
Jones, Wm H 72, 78 2
Jones, Zachariah L 79 2
Jordan, J 70 2
Jordan, J L 82 3
Jordan, John 70 2
Jordan, John L 280, 282 2
Jordan, John L 176 3
Jordan, John L Jr 70 2
Jordan, John L Sr 70 2
Jordan, Julia 70 2
Jordan, William 282 2
Jordan, Wm H 116 2
Jordan, Z 199 3
Jorden, Catherine 70 2
Joseph, Rebecca W 75 2
Jourdan, Chas 159 1
Joy, Benedict 66 2
Joy, Elizabeth 66 2
Joy, Geo W 68 2
Joy, Helen S 96 3
Joy, Herbert L 44 3
Joy, Hezekiah 69 2
Joy, James 171, 211 2
Joy, James R 96 3
Joy, John T 23 3
Joy, Rosa M 68 2
Joy, Rosanna M 211 2
Joy, S F 66 2
Joy, Stephen 260 1
Joy, Thomas 69 2
Joyness, Lucy H 242 2
Judy, Henry W 185 3
Judy, Jacob 69 2
Judy, Sarah I R 76 2
Justis, Margaret 72 2
Justise, David 67 2
Justise, Margaret 67 2
Kaas, Martin J 222a 2
Kaas, Mary S 89 2
Kabrick, A V 101 2
Kabrick, John 101 2
Kabrick, M E 101 2
Kabrick, Mary E 108 2
Kaedle, Nelson B 110 2
Kaehler, Marietta 161 3
Kaes, Barbara 83 2
Kaes, Peter 83 2
Kaetzel, C T 93 2
Kaetzel, Emma B 89 2
Kaetzel, G Maurice 177 3
Kaetzel, Garland B 93 2
Kaetzel, Maurice 124 1
Kaetzell, J W 45 3
Kahle, Annie M 80, 113 2
Kahle, Samuel W 113 2
Kailor, David 138, 226 2

Kanaoff, Chas E 82 1
Kander, Jacob 100 2
Kane, Wm J 116 2
Kannouff, Ann Eliza 101 2
Kannouff, Jacob 101 2
Kannouff, John W 101 2
Kanode, Benton 43 3
Kanode, Charles E 89 2
Kanode, Chas E 84 2
Kanode, David E 128 3
Kanode, David E 101 1
Kanode, Elias W 98 3
Kanode, Ella Nora 89 2
Kanode, Geo J H 96 2
Kanode, Hester A M 84, 96 2
Kanode, Jacob 102, 159 2
Kanode, Jeremiah 102 2
Kanode, Martin R 110 1
Kanode, Mollie C 84 2
Kanouff, Chas E 59 1
Kanouff, Jacob 70 1
Kanouff, John 196 1
Kanouff, John Jr 100 2
Kanouff, John Sr 100 2
Kaplon, Abraham I 203 1
Kaplon, Myer 203 1
Kaplon, Myer 58 3
Karch, Andrew 26 3
Karn, Adam 53 3
Karn, Alice Campbell 110 2
Karn, Carah C 205 3
Karn, Carmen Philip 110 2
Karn, Chas B 85 2
Karn, Clarence 85 2
Karn, E L 258 2
Karn, Ellen S 89, 93 2
Karn, Ezra 198 2
Karn, Ezra L 89, 93, 101, 113, 115, 250 2
Karn, Ezra L 196 3
Karn, Franklin H 102 2
Karn, G Roscoe 85 2
Karn, Geo T 93 2
Karn, George C 102 2
Karn, Jeremiah P 102 2
Karn, John E 89, 101, 102, 250 2
Karn, Josephus 93, 102 2
Karn, Julia A 101, 102 2
Karn, Lewis H 106 2
Karn, Maggie A F 102 2
Karn, Mary A 107 2
Karn, Oscar P 102, 110 2
Karn, Oscar P 111 1
Karn, Susannah 113 2
Karn, Thomas E 115 2
Karner, Alonzo K 166 1
Karns, George 93 2
Karns, Lawson 106 2
Karsten, Russell S 44 1
Karster, Rachel M 112 2
Karster, Russell S 112 2
Kass, Ellen 89 2
Kass, Ellen R 101 2
Kass, John 101 2
Kass, Martha A 108 2
Kass, Martha A 196 3
Kass, Martin J 89 2
Katzdaffner, J 196 1
Kauffman, Betty L 116 2
Kauffman, Charles Morris 116 2
Kauffman, Geo L 93 2
Kauffman, Geo P 116 2
Kauffman, George J 93 2
Kauffman, Henry 96 2
Kauffman, Henry & 101 2
Kauffman, Jonathan 100 2
Kauffman, Ollie 214 3
Kauffman, Susie 116 2
Kauffman, William 20 3
Kauffman, William E 116 2
Kauffman, Wm C 116 2
Kaufman, Ann R C 81, 102 2
Kaufman, Caroline 84 2
Kaufman, Chas S 84 2
Kaufman, Conrad 84 2
Kaufman, Geo I 147 1
Kaufman, Geo T 147 1
Kaufman, George L 294 2
Kaufman, Jesse D 102 2
Kaufman, Jesse E 113 2
Kaufman, Sarah R 93, 113 2
Kaufman, Sigmund C 84 2
Kavinaugh, Samuel J 113 2
Kearney, James 100 2
Keasey, Thomas 115 2
Keech, C Va 85 2
Keech, Clara Susan 85 2
Keech, George T 85 2
Keedey, Clayton O 92 1
Keedy, C L 71 3
Keedy, C O 14, 96, 97, 104, 107, 112, 119, 153, 172, 177, 179, 210, 240, 253, 260, 265 1
Keedy, C O 18, 80, 85, 163 131, 181, 211 217, 218, 224, 210a, 218 a 2
Keedy, C O 55, 71 3
Keedy, Clayton 172 2
Keedy, Clayton O 27, 62, 100, 120, 126, 130, 133, 144, 188, 197, 200, 201, 227, 234 1
Keedy, Clayton O 72, 85, 107, 119, 217a, 264, 265, 267, 288 2
Keedy, Clayton O 72, 85, 107, 119, 217a, 264, 265, 267, 288 2
Keedy, Clayton O 20, 44, 56, 188, 196 3
Keedy, Irene 85 2
Keedy, Irene R 99 2
Keedy, Joseph E 61 1
Keedy, Mary A 107 2
Keefe, Brdiget 83 2
Keefer, A Kemp 81 2
Keefer, A Kemp 80, 81 2
Keefer, A Kemp 182, 201, 202 1
Keefer, Abram Kemp 40 2
Keefer, Adam 80 2
Keefer, Amanda E 81, 116 2
Keefer, Ann Margaret 80 2
Keefer, Annie M 80, 84 2
Keefer, Annr 80 2
Keefer, Arthur C 190 2
Keefer, Arthur C 190 2
Keefer, Bernard T 81 2
Keefer, Calvin L 84 2
Keefer, Charles H 160 3
Keefer, Charles H 82 1
Keefer, Chas 201 1
Keefer, Chas H 84, 159 2
Keefer, Chas H 59 1
Keefer, Chas W M 84 2
Keefer, Christian 84 2
Keefer, Christian 56, 70 1
Keefer, Christian 84 2
Keefer, Christian Jr 177 1
Keefer, Chritian 122 3
Keefer, Cora M 85 2
Keefer, David 101 2
Keefer, David 23 3
Keefer, E S 58 3
Keefer, Eliza 89 2
Keefer, Frank B 33 3
Keefer, Frank J 280 2
Keefer, Frederick 92, 101 2
Keefer, Frederick 271 1
Keefer, George 93, 128 2
Keefer, Glenn S 166 1
Keefer, Glenn S 116 2
Keefer, H C 39 2
Keefer, H M 40, 84, 227 2
Keefer, H M 70 1
Keefer, Harry C 29, 84, 96 2
Keefer, Henry 38, 84, 87, 96 2
Keefer, Henry 8, 100 3
Keefer, Henry 72, 263 1
Keefer, Hiram 214a 2
Keefer, Jacob 26, 38, 75, 84, 87, 96, 100, 101 2
Keefer, Jacob 70 1
Keefer, Jacob 1, 23 3
Keefer, James R 115 2
Keefer, Jane 101 2
Keefer, John 101 2
Keefer, John H 112 1
Keefer, John H 100 2
Keefer, John L 64 3
Keefer, Joseph 91 1

Keefer, Katherine E 104 2
Keefer, L E 163 2
Keefer, Laura F 106 2
Keefer, Lewis 106 2
Keefer, Lillie I 33 3
Keefer, Ludwick 106 2
Keefer, Lydia 113 2
Keefer, M 154 2
Keefer, Margaret 96, 111 2
Keefer, Margaret H 107 2
Keefer, Mary A 57 3
Keefer, Mary S 108 2
Keefer, Michael 38, 75, 76, 96, 100, 231, 258, 2
Keefer, Michael 18, 139 1
Keefer, Michael 100, 165, 185 3
Keefer, Michel 197 2
Keefer, O N 102 3
Keefer, Oliver 79, 110 1
Keefer, Oliver 41, 271 2
Keefer, Oliver H 101, 179 1
Keefer, Oliver H 45 3
Keefer, Peter 93 2
Keefer, Philip 111 2
Keefer, Philip N 111 2
Keefer, Saml 197 2
Keefer, Samuel 179 1
Keefer, Samuel 84, 106, 113 2
Keefer, Sarah 113 2
Keefer, Stella C 84 2
Keefer, Susan Louise 113 2
Keefer, Theodore 264 1
Keefer, Theodore P 115, 169 2
Keefer, Thomas E 115 2
Keefer, Thos 96, 113 2
Keefer, Truman F 166 1
Keefer, W F 245 1
Keefer, Wm 116 2
Keefer, Wm 64 3
Keefer, Wm F 116 2
Keeler, Jacob 82 3
Keenan, Charles H F 85 2
Keenan, Jacob H 85 2
Keenan, John L F 85 2
Keene, Louis 209 2
Keeney, Annie E C 48 1
Keeney, C C 46 3
Keeney, C C 85 2
Keeney, Charles Calvin 85 2
Keeney, David Ray 87 2
Keeney, Grace A 94 2
Keeney, Harry A 48 1
Keeney, Harvey L 112 2
Keeney, Helen N 94, 99 2
Keeney, Ira M 99 2
Keeney, John T 48 1
Keeney, Richard A 112 2
Keeney, Robert L 112 2
Keeney, Sampson 71 1
Keepers, Charles P 106 2
Keepers, G E 9 2
Keepers, Geo 5, 139 2
Keepers, George E 196 3
Keepers, James 131 1
Keepers, James 89 2
Keepers, John 100 2
Keepers, Lucy M 106 2
Keepers, Mary L 196 3
Keepers, Michael 100 2
Kefauver, Agnes 100 3
Kefauver, Albert C 16, 110 2
Kefauver, Anna L 40, 107 2
Kefauver, Catherine 84 2
Kefauver, Chas L 85 2
Kefauver, Chas R 96 2
Kefauver, Clarence C 112 2
Kefauver, D 79 3
Kefauver, D C 150, 171 1
Kefauver, D E 20 2
Kefauver, D Edw 87, 116 2
Kefauver, D H 87 2
Kefauver, Daisy V 106 2
Kefauver, Daniel 29, 39, 87, 93, 101, 112, 177 2
Kefauver, Daniel C 84 2
Kefauver, Daniel E 84 2
Kefauver, Elizabeth 110 1
Kefauver, Emma F 89 2
Kefauver, Eugene C 89 2
Kefauver, G 100 3
Kefauver, G H 96 2
Kefauver, Geo 40, 87, 202 2
Kefauver, Geo 55 1
Kefauver, Geo H 73, 157 1
Kefauver, Geo W 113, 295 2
Kefauver, Geo W 150, 235, 257 1
Kefauver, Geo W 33, 102, 169 3
Kefauver, George 93 2
Kefauver, George 41 3
Kefauver, George H 59 1
Kefauver, George H 106 2
Kefauver, Grace H 116 2
Kefauver, H A 6 1
Kefauver, H B 276 2
Kefauver, H Edw 71 3
Kefauver, H M 96 2
Kefauver, Harry J 56 3
Kefauver, Harry J 96, 108 2
Kefauver, Henry 91 1
Kefauver, Henry 84, 87, 89, 96 2
Kefauver, Henry A 112 2
Kefauver, Henry M 96 2
Kefauver, Irving S 46 3
Kefauver, J H 37, 164 1
Kefauver, J H 35 2
Kefauver, J Orville 106 2
Kefauver, Jacob 28, 93 2
Kefauver, John 100 2
Kefauver, John 100, 110, 156 1
Kefauver, John D 89 2
Kefauver, John of G 100 3
Kefauver, L E 192 3
Kefauver, L F 131 3
Kefauver, L F 184 2
Kefauver, L M 200 1
Kefauver, Laura S 106 2
Kefauver, Lena T 107 3
Kefauver, Leo L 40 2
Kefauver, Leslie F 106 2
Kefauver, Lewis F 84, 85, 106, 108 2
Kefauver, Lillie M 106 2
Kefauver, Lilly M 110 2
Kefauver, Lora L 106 2
Kefauver, Luther M 112 2
Kefauver, M E 20 2
Kefauver, Mahlon C 108 2
Kefauver, Manville E 108 2
Kefauver, Marcelene 107 2
Kefauver, Martha E 108 2
Kefauver, Martha O M 56 3
Kefauver, Martin E 20, 107 2
Kefauver, Maud L 75 3
Kefauver, May S 46 3
Kefauver, Millard F 116 2
Kefauver, Miriam Evans 96 2
Kefauver, Morgan M 107 2
Kefauver, Myrtle E 157 1
Kefauver, N E 49 2
Kefauver, N E Jr 219 3
Kefauver, Noah 85, 112 2
Kefauver, Noah F 167 2
Kefauver, Oliver H 110 2
Kefauver, Oscar C 56 3
Kefauver, Oscar C 108, 150 2
Kefauver, Peter 111 2
Kefauver, R A 112 1
Kefauver, Richard 87 2
Kefauver, Richard C 84, 112 2
Kefauver, Richard C 130, 200 1
Kefauver, Robert A 112 2
Kefauver, Ruth W 207 3
Kefauver, Samuel 100 1
Kefauver, Samuel M 113 2
Kefauver, Stella V 113 2
Kefauver, W Jacob 116 2
Kefauver, W S 30 2
Kefauver, W Scott 93, 116 2
Kefauver, W Scott 27 1
Kefauver, Wm 100 2
Kefauver, Wm D 116 2

Keffer, Katherine L 104 2
Kehlenberg, Geo T 80 2
Kehler, Delia 87 2
Kehler, Frederick W 87 2
Kehler, Henry 191, 1271 1
Kehler, Minnie 87 2
Kehley, Frederick 101 2
Kehley, John N 101 2
Kehn, John H 102 2
Kehn, Wm 102 2
Kehne, August 84 2
Kehne, Charles H 10 2
Kehne, Charles H 24 3
Kehne, Charles H 155 1
Kehne, Chas A 84 2
Kehne, Chas H 45 3
Kehne, Geo B 93 2
Kehne, Geo D 93 2
Kehne, Harrison N 166 3
Kehne, Joanna 84 2
Kehne, Laura V 82 3
Kehne, Lillie A 84 2
Kehne, Wm H 116 2
Keifer, Samuel 113 2
Keilholtz, Andrew G 222a 2
Keilholtz, Ben 30 2
Keilholtz, Benjamin 125 1
Keilholtz, Benjamin 83 2
Keilholtz, Carrie R 222a 2
Keilholtz, Carroll C 106 2
Keilholtz, Clara E 85 2
Keilholtz, G Andrew 85 2
Keilholtz, George D 106 2
Keilholtz, Grier J 85 2
Keilholtz, H J 83 2
Keilholtz, Henry J 107 2
Keilholtz, J A 83 2
Keilholtz, J D ? 83 2
Keilholtz, James 197 1
Keilholtz, John J 102 2
Keilholtz, L H 222 3
Keilholtz, Luther H 106 2
Keilholtz, Mary C 107 2
Keilholtz, Naomi R 102 2
Keilholtz, W Glen 102 2
Keilhotz, H J 83 2
Keim, Jacob 283 1
Kein, Jacob 26 2
Keins, Elizabeth A 101 2
Keins, Joseph 101 2
Keiser, Chas W & 116 2
Keiser, Maria 116 2
Keiser, Samuel 113 2
Keiser, Wm 116 2
Keith, William H 85 2
Kelbaugh, Annie V 81 2
Kelbaugh, Irving 92 3
Kelbaugh, Irving A 81 2
Keller, A C 219 1
Keller, Adam 11, 107, 208 2
Keller, Adam 13 1
Keller, Addie B 107 2
Keller, Albert J 94 2
Keller, Amanda E 81, 102 2
Keller, Amos R 102 2
Keller, Annie E 80 2
Keller, Annie M 80 2
Keller, Annie May 84 2
Keller, Annie V 80 2
Keller, Arba C 80 2
Keller, B H 100 2
Keller, Benj H 84 2
Keller, C E 90 1
Keller, C R 101 2
Keller, C T 116 2
Keller, Calvin R 84, 115 2
Keller, Caroline E 106 1
Keller, Carrie V 90 2
Keller, Catherine 84 2
Keller, Charles H 76 1
Keller, Chas 107 2
Keller, Chas E 84, 92 2
Keller, Chas F 100, 177 2
Keller, Chas H 84 2
Keller, Chas W 101, 110 2
Keller, Clara F 85 2
Keller, Conrad 72, 84 2
Keller, Conrad 18 3
Keller, Cordelia F 84 2
Keller, D Rupley 87 2
Keller, Daniel 87, 100, 106, 112 2
Keller, David 164 1
Keller, David 70 3
Keller, David 28, 87, 100, 106, 208 2
Keller, Della V 96 2
Keller, DeWitt C 87 2
Keller, E B 94 2
Keller, Earl R 87 2
Keller, Edgar B 90 2
Keller, Edgar M 179 1
Keller, Edw 67 3
Keller, Edw F 29, 89 2
Keller, Edw L 92 2
Keller, Elizabeth 89, 100 2
Keller, Elizabeth A 93 2
Keller, Ellen C 89 2
Keller, Emma G 116 2
Keller, Emory 189 3
Keller, Ethel N 87 2
Keller, Flora M 271 2
Keller, Francis J 92 2
Keller, Frank M 96 2
Keller, Fred 100 2
Keller, Fred W 115 2
Keller, Frederick 71, 186, 225 1
Keller, Frederick 8 3
Keller, Frederick 84, 92 2
Keller, Frederick C 91, 240 1
Keller, Geo R 115 2
Keller, Geo W 93 2
Keller, Geo W 76 1
Keller, Geo W M 93 2
Keller, George 14 3
Keller, George R 80 1
Keller, Gerald C 94 2
Keller, Grover P 97 2
Keller, Gulielma B 106 2
Keller, H 18 1
Keller, H S 106 2
Keller, H T 66 2
Keller, Hannah 96 2
Keller, Harry C 87 2
Keller, Harry D W 80 2
Keller, Harry N 96 2
Keller, Hattie L 97 2
Keller, Helen 96 2
Keller, Henry 37, 41, 59, 144, 214 1
Keller, Henry 89, 96, 100, 101, 153 2
Keller, Henry 26 3
Keller, Henry T 47 1
Keller, Henry T 100 2
Keller, Isaac 87 2
Keller, J 100 2
Keller, J Charles 102 2
Keller, J Chas 80 2
Keller, J H 214 2
Keller, J H 71, 96, 165, 171 3
Keller, Jacob 7, 26, 27, 100, 101, 132 2
Keller, Jacob 82, 92, 186, 196, 223 1
Keller, Jacob 102, 163, 184, 213 3
Keller, Jacob A 101 2
Keller, Jacob Sr 100 2
Keller, James D 102 2
Keller, James Dallas 81 2
Keller, Jno D 167 3
Keller, Jno H 129 3
Keller, Joel 100, 101, 112 2
Keller, Joel 31 3
Keller, John 7, 8, 58, 87, 100, 107, 147, 150, 197, 225, 223a 2
Keller, John 214, 264, 272, 279 1
Keller, John 212 3
Keller, John D 54, 89, 101, 116 2
Keller, John D 257 1
Keller, John D 188 3
Keller, John E 195 3
Keller, John F 27 1
Keller, John H 38, 41, 52, 58, 96, 123, 140, 205, 208, 229 1
Keller, John H 1, 15, 35, 38, 93, 101,

107, 144, 187, 208, 223a, 225a, 254, 267 2
Keller, John H 19, 41, 64, 67, 91, 113, 116, 186, 187, 209 3
Keller, John M 92 2
Keller, John of A 40 1
Keller, John of J 37 1
Keller, John of J 100 2
Keller, Jonathan 100, 101 2
Keller, Jonathan M 97 2
Keller, Joseph 248 1
Keller, Keller R 104 2
Keller, Kermit Al 94 2
Keller, Lamora Beall 80 1
Keller, Lemuel J 106 2
Keller, Lillie M 106, 110 2
Keller, Lizzie 87 2
Keller, Lucinda C 106 2
Keller, Margaret 107 2
Keller, Mary 100 2
Keller, Mary B 110 2
Keller, Mary E 87, 101, 107 2
Keller, Mary Jane 89, 107 2
Keller, Maude E 112 2
Keller, Melinda 107 2
Keller, Michael 107, 134, 137 2
Keller, Miriam J 83 3
Keller, Nancy 110 2
Keller, Nellie I 80 2
Keller, Nettie G 110 2
Keller, Newton 80 2
Keller, Newton W 271 2
Keller, O J 3rd 63 1
Keller, Otho J 110 2
Keller, Otho J Iii 28 1
Keller, Otho J Jr 110 2
Keller, Robert F 112 2
Keller, Rosina 112 2
Keller, S Elizabeth 113 2
Keller, Sarah 41 1
Keller, Sarah 96 2
Keller, Sophia 115 2
Keller, Sumner K 96 2
Keller, Sumner K 96 2
Keller, T C 80, 124, 134 2
Keller, T C 189 3
Keller, T C 124 2
Keller, Theopolis 115 2
Keller, Thomas H 79 1
Keller, Thomas J 115 2
Keller, Valletta S 37 1
Keller, Vallietta W 84 2
Keller, Virginia A R 93, 115 2
Keller, Willard 87 2
Keller, Willard C 116 2
Keller, William C 116 2
Keller, William H 116 2
Keller, Wm 87, 96, 101, 116 2
Keller, Wm 90, 118 1
Keller, Wm B 150 2
Keller, Wm G 116 2
Keller, Wm H 84, 89 2
Keller, Wm O 110 2
Kelley, Chas H 107 2
Kelley, James M 102, 267 2
Kelley, James M 15 3
Kelley, Jerome 238 2
Kelley, Jesse 102 3
Kelley, John A 102 2
Kelley, Joseph 101, 106 2
Kelley, Louisa A 102 2
Kelley, Mary D 107 2
Kelley, Patrick 32 1
Kelley, Patrick 267 2
Kelly, Emma E 89, 102 2
Kelly, Emma S 89 2
Kelly, Frances S 21 3
Kelly, Frederick 80 2
Kelly, Jacob 22 1
Kelly, James 164 1
Kelly, James 101, 188 2
Kelly, James W 101, 106 2
Kelly, John D 89, 113 2
Kelly, John F 228 3
Kelly, Lewis 106 2
Kelly, Lewis J 222 3
Kelly, M J 32 1
Kelly, Mary Jane 111 2
Kelly, Mary V 159 3
Kelly, Patrick 111 2
Kelly, Patrick 58, 144 1
Kelly, Raymond L 243 1
Kelly, Rodney R 15 1
Kelly, Sallie 113 2
Kemp, A 165 2
Kemp, A R 166 2
Kemp, A S 87 2
Kemp, Abraham 11, 19, 27, 43, 80, 92, 132, 144, 159, 185, 258, 288 2
Kemp, Abraham 32, 37, 47, 56, 57, 133, 234, 249, 260 1
Kemp, Abraham 8, 70, 81, 160, 165, 192, 202 3
Kemp, Abram 71 1
Kemp, Allen D 112 2
Kemp, Allen Duvall 85 2
Kemp, Ann 80 2
Kemp, Anna S 80 2
Kemp, Annie M 224 2
Kemp, Annie Mary 84 2
Kemp, B Kemp 89 2
Kemp, C Edwin 85 2
Kemp, C T 265 1
Kemp, C Thomas 27 1
Kemp, C Thomas 85 2
Kemp, C Thomas 27, 56 3
Kemp, C Thos 47, 55, 88, 165 1
Kemp, C Thos 61 2
Kemp, Caroline 91 3
Kemp, Caroline E 85 2
Kemp, Charles A 118 3
Kemp, Charles E 214a 2
Kemp, Charles W 118 3
Kemp, Charlotte V 85, 112 2
Kemp, Chas Edw 84 2
Kemp, Chas W 84 2
Kemp, Christian 56, 163, 171, 279 1
Kemp, Christian 84, 87 2
Kemp, Christina 30 1
Kemp, Clayton E 102 2
Kemp, Columbia A 84 2
Kemp, Conrad 84 2
Kemp, D C 42, 65 3
Kemp, D C 87 2
Kemp, D Chester 23 1
Kemp, D Chester 80, 87 2
Kemp, D Columbus 55 3
Kemp, D Columbus 87 2
Kemp, Daisy A 87 2
Kemp, Daisy A 73 1
Kemp, Daniel 26, 87 2
Kemp, Daniel 113 3
Kemp, Daniel 37, 163 1
Kemp, Daniel M 87 2
Kemp, Daniel of H 120 3
Kemp, Daniel S 87 2
Kemp, Danuel 38 3
Kemp, David 26, 27, 87, 132, 153, 258 2
Kemp, David 133 1
Kemp, David C 87 2
Kemp, Davis 84 2
Kemp, Dorotha 92 2
Kemp, Dorothy 87 2
Kemp, E Brent 101 1
Kemp, E Brent 83 2
Kemp, E Brent (see B Kemp) 89 2
Kemp, Edw 88 1
Kemp, Edward 89, 92 2
Kemp, Edward 92 2
Kemp, Emma 102 2
Kemp, Emma 89, 102 2
Kemp, Emma 89 2
Kemp, Florence V 92 2
Kemp, Frederick 207 3
Kemp, Frederick 51, 56, 156, 223, 260 1
Kemp, Frederick 92 2
Kemp, Frederick 92 2
Kemp, Gilbert 30 1
Kemp, Graham 72 2
Kemp, H 120 3
Kemp, Harriet 96 2
Kemp, Harry D 102 2
Kemp, Henry 30, 51, 116, 135, 163

1
Kemp, Henry 26, 63, 87, 93, 96, 116, 257, 258, 268 2
Kemp, Henry 8, 64, 70 3
Kemp, Henry Jr 18 3
Kemp, Isaac 111 2
Kemp, Jacob 100 2
Kemp, Jeannette 102 2
Kemp, John H 111 2
Kemp, John Milton 102 2
Kemp, John Q A 87 2
Kemp, Jonathan 100 2
Kemp, Joseph 275 2
Kemp, Joseph 37, 163 1
Kemp, Joseph 111, 275 2
Kemp, Lewis 38, 96, 100, 106, 107, 153, 250 2
Kemp, Lewis 27, 163, 196 1
Kemp, Lewis 106 3
Kemp, Lewis G 118 3
Kemp, Lewis G 112, 115 2
Kemp, Lewis George 106 2
Kemp, Macie T 178 2
Kemp, Martha S 87 2
Kemp, Martin C 294 2
Kemp, Mary 107 2
Kemp, Mary M 55, 279 1
Kemp, Mary M 10, 27, 56 3
Kemp, Mary M 108 2
Kemp, Mary Matilda 85 2
Kemp, Peter 61 1
Kemp, Peter 46, 80, 111 2
Kemp, R A & 195 2
Kemp, R S 112 2
Kemp, Rebecca C 112 2
Kemp, Rhodes R 112 2
Kemp, Robert 20 2
Kemp, Robert A 73, 245 1
Kemp, Robert A 10 3
Kemp, Robert Kathy 51 3
Kemp, Robt A 72 3
Kemp, Robt A 101, 217 1
Kemp, Roenna R 198 2
Kemp, Ruanna R 112 2
Kemp, S V 83 2
Kemp, Smetlzer 89 2
Kemp, Solomon 80, 84, 100, 226 2
Kemp, Susan M 89 2
Kemp, Thomas 115 2
Kemp, Wm 89 2
Kemp, Wm H 87 2
Kemp, Wm H C 118 1
Kenaga, David 87 2
Kenaga, David 112 1
Kenaga[?], David 164 1
Kendrick, Nathan 64 3
Kenley, Mavoureen W 172 3
Kennard, Catherine 85 2
Kennard, George R 93 2
Kennedy, Amelia 85 2
Kennedy, Amelia V 80, 115 2
Kennedy, Ann 80 2
Kennedy, David C 113 3
Kennedy, Ellen 89, 111 2
Kennedy, H J 113 3
Kennedy, J Harry 102 2
Kennedy, J Harry 265 1
Kennedy, John A 85, 89, 111, 115 2
Kennedy, Patrick 111 2
Kennedy, T F 111 2
Kennedy, T J 89 2
Kennedy, Thomas F 115 2
Kennedy, Thomas J 213 3
Kennedy, Thos F 111 2
Kenney, Cornelia A E 71 1
Kenny, Alexander 80 2
Kenzey, Henry 96 2
Kephart, Barbara 83 2
Kephart, David 87, 220a 2
Kephart, David 167 3
Kephart, Eliza 87 2
Kephart, Geo 57 1
Kephart, Geo 19, 87 2
Kephart, George 8, 38 3
Kephart, George 93, 221a, 246 2
Kephart, George 84, 171, 194 1
Kephart, George Jr 93 2
Kephart, Jacob 100 2
Kephart, John 100 2
Kephart, Margaret 87 2
Kephart, Peter 93 2
Kephart, Sarah 87 2
Kepler, A C 172 3
Kepler, Absalom P 160 3
Kepler, Amanda E 96 2
Kepler, Annie A 81, 115 2
Kepler, Bertie L 83 2
Kepler, Catherine R 108 2
Kepler, Charles L 108 2
Kepler, Clara V 101 2
Kepler, D Ralph 87 2
Kepler, D S 112 1
Kepler, D S 238 2
Kepler, Daniel C 116 2
Kepler, Daniel C 87 2
Kepler, Daniel S 52, 130, 152 1
Kepler, H B 56 3
Kepler, Henry M 96 2
Kepler, Homer D 92, 152, 157 1
Kepler, J Hanson 102 2
Kepler, J Luther 101 2
Kepler, John 101, 129 2
Kepler, John H 116 2
Kepler, John Jr 100 2
Kepler, John Sr 100 2
Kepler, Karl Knox 81 2
Kepler, L M 115 2
Kepler, Leland M 108 2
Kepler, Lloyd M 106, 113 2
Kepler, Lloyd M 172 3
Kepler, Martha J 87 2
Kepler, Martin H 108 2
Kepler, Martin Henry 108 2
Kepler, Martin L 85, 108 2
Kepler, Martin L 41 1
Kepler, Mary E 108 2
Kepler, Rachel 112 2
Kepler, Ruth E 33 3
Kepler, Sebastian 113 2
Kepler, Vincent S 115 2
Kepler, W F 102 2
Kepler, W J 102 2
Kepler, Wm 96 2
Kepler, Wm J 101, 116 2
Kepner, B E 113 3
Kepner, B Evard 83, 93, 110 2
Kepner, Grace Simmons 93 2
Kepner, Nancy E 110 2
Kepner, S F 87 2
Kepner, V S 241 2
Kepner, Wm 193 1
Kerchner, Katherine 18 2
Kerman, Edward 89 2
Kern, Adam 80 2
Kern, Belle 83 2
Kern, Frederika 80 2
Kernan, Mary Ellen 149 3
Kerrigan, J Ward 46, 93, 108, 161 2
Kerrigan, J Ward 229, 280 1
Kerrigan, J Ward 57, 189, 196, 228 3
Kerrigan, James M 107, 129 2
Kerrigan, Margaret 129 2
Kerrigan, Margaret D 108 2
Kerrigan, Mary A T 107 2
Kerry, William 184 3
Kersher, Alan Motter 89 2
Kershner, Elnathan 246 2
Kershner, Elnathan M 89 2
Kershner, Elnathan M 182 2
Kershner, Helen Swoope 89 2
Kesecker, Mary E 112 2
Kesecker, Robert T 112 2
Kesselring, Edith R 89 2
Kesselring, Geo L 93 2
Kesselring, George 93 2
Kesselring, John 101 2
Kesselring, Laura 106 2
Kesselring, Mary A R C 107 2
Kesselring, Mary M 101 2
Kesselring, Michael 93 2
Kesselring, Samuel 71 1
Kesselring, Samuel 113 2
Kesselring, Samuel W 113 2
Kesselring, Susan 113 2

Kessler, A 49 2
Kessler, A P 38, 65, 80, 214 2
Kessler, A P 71, 84, 96, 100, 112 1
Kessler, A P 9, 209 3
Kessler, A T 212 3
Kessler, Absalom P 9 3
Kessler, Albert 67 3
Kessler, Albina A 80 2
Kessler, Andrew 81, 209 3
Kessler, Andrew 78, 80, 113, 153, 166, 246, 264 2
Kessler, Andrew 112, 222, 229, 271, 278 1
Kessler, Andrew Jr 80 2
Kessler, Andrew Jr 205 1
Kessler, Andrew Sr 80 2
Kessler, AP 144 2
Kessler, Benjamin 83 2
Kessler, Boyd A 100 3
Kessler, C C 218 2
Kessler, Estelle M 218 2
Kessler, Floyd 260 1
Kessler, Francis A 143 2
Kessler, Geo 117 1
Kessler, Geo 76 2
Kessler, George 93 2
Kessler, Harriet 96 2
Kessler, Israel 80, 99 2
Kessler, Israel 239, 271 1
Kessler, Israel 96 3
Kessler, J H 143 2
Kessler, J H 160 3
Kessler, Jacob 76, 93, 100 2
Kessler, Jacob 18 3
Kessler, John 148, 159 2
Kessler, Jonathan 101 2
Kessler, Joshua 101 2
Kessler, Lloyd 100 3
Kessler, Lloyd A 179 3
Kessler, Lloyd A & 1 2
Kessler, Mary M 107 2
Kessler, Philemon C 111 2
Kessler, Rachel 100 2
Kessler, Samuel 113 2
Kessler, Sarah Ann 99 2
Kessler, Thomas B 115 2
Kessler, Wm A 80 2
Kester, Harry J 113 2
Kester, Henry 271 2
Kester, S Burton 113 2
Ketrow, George 93 2
Ketrow, Henry 96 2
Ketrow, Lewis D 51 3
Ketrow, Wm 229 1
Ketrow, Wm 116 2
Ketrow, Wm H 96 2
Ketter, George 93 2
Kettleman, Francis H 92 2
Key, Ann 80 2
Key, Chas G 101 2
Key, Frances S 80 2
Key, George 93 2
Key, Hiram 96 2
Key, James 101 2
Key, Jesse 100 2
Key, John 101 2
Key, John (cold) 100 2
Key, John H 102 2
Key, Reuben 112 2
Key, Sarah (Cold) 113 2
Key, Wm 96 2
Keyes, Daniel M 116 2
Keys, Catherine 84 2
Keys, Wm 116 2
Keyser, Benjamin 220 3
Keyser, Calvin C 85 2
Keyser, Chas D 85 2
Keyser, George H 94 2
Keyser, Harrison 220 3
Keyser, Idella Eliza 81 2
Keyser, Jacob 100, 111 2
Keyser, John 111 2
Keyser, John C 102 2
Keyser, L Frank 106 2
Keyser, Lewis 111 2
Keyser, Lillie V 106 2
Keyser, Marie D 83 3
Keyser, Mary L 85 2
Keyser, Mary R 112 2
Keyser, Mary R 3 3
Keyser, Matthias 107 2
Keyser, Murray D 106 2
Keyser, Oscar W 81 2
Keyser, Philip 111 2
Keyser, Richard 3 3
Keyser, Richard S 112 2
Keyser, Samuel 111 2
Keyser, Wm F 85 2
Keyser, Zephamiah 220 3
Kidd, Ann M 101 2
Kidd, Ann Matilda 80 2
Kidd, Charles W 85 2
Kidd, Chas 146 1
Kidd, Chas W 100 1
Kidd, Florence Fout 102 2
Kidd, Geo 80 2
Kidd, Howard 102 2
Kidd, J Brunner 102 2
Kidd, Jennie S 85 2
Kidd, John C 101, 102, 113 2
Kidd, Joseph 100 2
Kidd, Mary E 102 2
Kidd, Perry 102 2
Kidd, Sarah 100 2
Kidweiler, Geo L 9 2
Kidwell, George W 93 2
Kidwell, Ida May 102 2
Kidwell, Susan E 93 2
Kidwell, Wm G 189 3
Kidwiler, Ethel I 92 2
Kidwiler, Fannie A 102 2
Kidwiler, Frank S 92 2
Kidwiler, J A 220 2
Kidwiler, Jacob A 102 2
Kidwiler, John 9 2
Kidwiler, Ruth M 181 1
Kidwiller, Cecilia A 96 2
Kidwiller, Hezekiah 96 2
Kiefer, Henry 169 2
Kiefer, Jacob 169 2
Kieffer, Chas W H 87 3
Kielholtz, L Hl 72 3
Kierner, J H 201 1
Kiler, Isaac 28, 99 2
Kiler, Mary A 108, 115 2
Kiler, Sarah A 113 2
Kiler, Theodore 115 2
Kiler, Theodore G 108 2
Kilgore, J Mortimer 70 3
Kilgour, Elizabeth 209 3
Kimball, R N 18 2
Kimes, Claud A 85 2
Kimes, Claud W 85 2
Kimes, Katherine L 85 2
Kimkel, Jacob M 106 3
Kimkel, John 87 3
Kimmel, A 154 2
Kimmel, A X 67 3
Kimmel, Agnes 80 2
Kimmel, Anna M 101 2
Kimmel, Anthony 67 2
Kimmel, Anthony Z 80 2
Kimmel, C T 92 2
Kimmel, Chas 80 2
Kimmel, E J 80 2
Kimmel, Elton G 92 2
Kimmel, Frederick 92 2
Kimmel, G F 92 2
Kimmel, Geo J 93 2
Kimmel, James 246 2
Kimmel, John 101 2
Kimmel, John M 101 2
Kimmel, John P 101 2
Kimmel, Mary 80 2
Kimmel, N P 209 3
Kimmel, P J 209 3
Kimmel, Sadie E 116 2
Kimmel, W H 92 2
Kimmel, William W 116 2
Kimmel, Wm 80 2
Kimmell, Anthony G 89 3
Kimmell, John 279 1
Kindle, Moses 107 2
Kindley, G W 265 1
Kindley, G W 60 3
Kindley, G Wesley 192 3

Kindley, G Wesley 93, 116 2
Kindley, Geo F 57 1
Kindley, Geo F 102 2
Kindley, Geo F Jr 93 2
Kindley, George F Jr 60 1
Kindley, George F Sr 93 2
Kindley, John N 110 2
Kindley, John Newton 102 2
Kindley, Mary L 102 2
Kindley, Nellie B 110 2
Kindley, Sebastian 93, 113 2
Kindley, Sebastian 60 1
Kindley, W E 68, 218 2
Kindley, Wesley 102 2
Kindley, Wm 93 2
Kindley, Wm J 113, 116 2
King, Agnes Beatric [sic] 124 1
King, Albert E 81 2
King, Andrew 79 1
King, Ann Mary 106 2
King, Annie E 81 2
King, C W 3 3
King, Caroline 84 2
King, Caroline 84 2
King, Charles C 85 2
King, Chas W 100 2
King, Christian 106 2
King, Dorsey Edwin 87 2
King, E Dorsey 89, 113, 277 2
King, E Gertrude 96 2
King, Edward L 81 2
King, Eleanore 89 2
King, Emeline 89 2
King, Fannie 100 2
King, Frederick 92 2
King, Geo 106 2
King, H Richard 96 2
King, Henrietta 96 2
King, Henry 96, 106, 224 2
King, Isabella D 99 2
King, J Otis 87, 107 2
King, Jamcs A 96, 107 2
King, James H 102 2
King, Jas H 187 3
King, Jesse 100 2
King, Jesse W 100 2
King, John 110, 117 1
King, John 226 2
King, John (cold) 100 2
King, John W 3 3
King, Joseph 101 2
King, Joseph 139 1
King, L 254 2
King, Lola E 81 2
King, Ludwig 106 2
King, Margaret A 107 2
King, Maria S C 92 2
King, Mary E 102, 107 2
King, Mary F L 89 2
King, Mary Margaret 107 2
King, Mary S 107 2
King, Nettie 107 2
King, Ruth R 87 2
King, Sarah A C 113 2
King, Singleton 107, 113 2
King, Thomas R 119 2
King, W R 56 1
King, William H 96 3
King, Wm B 152 1
King, Wm H 208 2
King, Wm R 119 2
Kingh, John 100 2
Kingsbaker, Solomon 238 1
Kingston, Frederick 81 3
Kinkel, John 26 2
Kinley, George F 93 2
Kinna, Ann Rebecca 80 2
Kinna, Anna M 85 2
Kinna, Anna R 115 2
Kinna, Charles E 85 2
Kinna, Chas T 84 2
Kinna, Clay C 106 1
Kinna, Cornelia E 85 2
Kinna, James 42, 109 1
Kinna, James 23, 113 3
Kinna, James 101, 110, 181, 205, 237 2
Kinna, James & 165 2
Kinna, James K 67 1
Kinna, John L 85 2
Kinna, Lauretta 84 2
Kinna, Nathaniel 110 2
Kinna, Robert Lee 85 2
Kinna, Ruth K 161 2
Kinna, Sampson 37 1
Kinna, Sampson E 113 2
Kinna, Samuel J 272 1
Kinna, Sarah E C 113 2
Kinna, Susannah 113 2
Kinna, Thomas 115 2
Kinna, Thompson 101 2
Kinnaman, Harry R 102 2
Kinnaman, John W 102 2
Kinsel, Joseph 210 3
Kinsey, Christian 93 2
Kinsey, George 93 2
Kinsey, Spencer W 113 2
Kinter, John 26 1
Kintz, Charles F 85 2
Kintz, F 229 1
Kintz, Frederick 71 3
Kintz, Frederick 92, 197 2
Kintz, Jacob F 92 2
Kintz, L M 244 1
Kintz, Lewis M 92 2
Kintz, William F 116 2
Kinzer, Ann 80, 101 2
Kinzer, Ann 101 2
Kinzer, David 67 3
Kinzer, Jasper 80, 100 2
Kinzer, Jasper 67 1
Kinzer, Jasper N 100 2
Kinzer, John 67, 205, 229 1
Kinzer, John 22, 28, 43, 80, 100, 101, 113, 136 2
Kinzer, John 40, 57, 60, 67, 195, 209 3
Kinzer, Sarah 113 2
Kipe James W 101 2
Kipe, Florence A 38 1
Kipe, Nettie A 112 2
Kipe, Oliver G 38, 47 1
Kipe, Oliver G 215 2
Kipe, Robert T 112 2
Kipe, Samuel A 101 2
Kipe, Wm H 2 2
Kirby, John 101 2
Kirby, Mary A 107 2
Kirk, Ada M 93 2
Kirk, Ada M 189, 248, 250 1
Kirk, George T 93 2
Kirk, Hattie D 102 2
Kirk, Jacob E 102 2
Kirk, Katie D 104 2
Kirschman, M Elizabeth 92 2
Kirwan, Leona May 73 1
Kirzer, John 55 1
Kissler, Andrew 198 2
Kite, Mary 112 2
Kite, Robert 112 2
Kitzmiller, John 136, 216 3
Kitzmiller, John 216 3
Kitzmiller, Leonard 106 2
Klay, Adam 80 2
Klay, Geo 80, 113 2
Klay, Geo 275 2
Klay, George 93, 96 2
Klay, Henry 96 2
Klay, John 93, 100 2
Klay, Lemuel 93 2
Klay, Samuel 113 2
Klay, Zebulon 100 2
Klees, Geo 107 2
Klees, Martha A 107 2
Kleim, Barbara D 83 2
Kleim, Clara J 83 2
Kleim, David E 83 2
Klein, Andrew J 80 2
Klein, Ann R 80 2
Klein, C Cyril 85 2
Klein, C Samuel 85, 89 2
Klein, Catherine 84 2
Klein, CF 80 2
Klein, Charles E 85 2
Klein, Chas 85 2
Klein, Clara J 66 2
Klein, Daniel 87 2

Klein, David E 33 1
Klein, Elizabeth 89 2
Klein, Harman S 108 2
Klein, Jesse 85 2
Klein, L Blanche 85 2
Klein, Mary E 80, 108 2
Klein, Naomi 108 2
Klein, Samuel 113 2
Klice, Solomon 113 2
Klietz, Annie M 187 3
Kline, Absalom 30 1
Kline, Albert W 28 1
Kline, Ann 80 2
Kline, Ary R 81 2
Kline, Austin M 202 2
Kline, C Samuel 107 2
Kline, Calvin 160 2
Kline, Casper 106 1
Kline, Charles D 85 2
Kline, Charles G 283 2
Kline, Charles M 150 1
Kline, Charles M 106, 108 2
Kline, Charles N 85 2
Kline, Chas G 186 1
Kline, Chas G 119 2
Kline, Chas M 62 1
Kline, Chas S 89 2
Kline, Chas W 96 2
Kline, Clara G 85 2
Kline, Clara G 58 3
Kline, Cora M 115 2
Kline, Cora May 85 2
Kline, Daniel 87 2
Kline, Daniel C 87 2
Kline, David E 107 2
Kline, E Fred 75 3
Kline, E Frederick 89, 138 2
Kline, Edward 41 3
Kline, Edward D 92 2
Kline, Elizabeth 89 2
Kline, Elizabeth E 104 2
Kline, Elizabeth G 90 2
Kline, Emma J 81 2
Kline, Estella M 172 1
Kline, Frederick 92 2
Kline, Geo 19 2
Kline, George 93 2
Kline, Hanson T 96, 113 2
Kline, Harry 189 3
Kline, Harvey 87, 102 2
Kline, Harvey 28 1
Kline, Hattie V 102 2
Kline, Horace F 275 1
Kline, J R 101 2
Kline, Jacob 40, 101 2
Kline, Jacob R 102 2
Kline, James 100 2
Kline, John 140 1
Kline, John 101, 112 2
Kline, Julia A 102 2
Kline, Lola A 28 1
Kline, Lola R 106 2
Kline, M L 107 2
Kline, Margaret C 265 2
Kline, Marion J 116 2
Kline, Mary B 112 2
Kline, Mary C 108, 160 2
Kline, Mary Kate 108 2
Kline, Mary Louise 108 2
Kline, Mary M 107 2
Kline, Melvin W 85, 106 2
Kline, Michael 160 2
Kline, Michael Sr 107 2
Kline, Nicholas 187 3
Kline, Paul 89, 93, 111, 169 2
Kline, Paul 40, 41, 70, 129 3
Kline, Peter 111 2
Kline, Peter 18 3
Kline, Ralph 115 2
Kline, Ralph G 112 2
Kline, Rebecca 112 2
Kline, Richard F 85 2
Kline, Robert A 145 2
Kline, S C 33 1
Kline, Stella 232 2
Kline, Stephen J 113 2
Kline, Susan 113 2
Kline, Thomas 115 2
Kline, W A 172 1
Kline, William E 265 2
Kline, William H 42 3
Kline, Wm H 113, 116 2
Klinehart, Francis 92 2
Kling, Annie M 81 2
Kling, Annie N 84 2
Kling, Chas E 84 2
Kling, Fannie H 115 2
Kling, J H 144 2
Kling, J Harry 81, 102 2
Kling, John D 102 2
Kling, Mary 113 2
Kling, Roger L 102 2
Kling, Samuel T 113 2
Kling, T E 126 1
Kling, Thomas E 102, 115 2
Klingan, Lewis S 10 3
Klingensmith, Annie 81 2
Klingensmith, Annie E 81 2
Klipp, C H 272 1
Klipp, Charles E 85, 99 2
Klipp, Chas E 102 2
Klipp, Chas E 68 1
Klipp, Chas H 96 2
Klipp, David C 85 2
Klipp, Henry 96 2
Klipp, Ida A F 99 2
Klipp, Ida M 102 2
Klipp, John 175 2
Klipp, John W 102 2
Klipp, Maggie 102 2
Klipp, Margaret S 85, 99 2
Klipp, Minnie M 108 2
Klipp, Philip 175 2
Klise Wm 116 2
Klise, Jacob 101 2
Klise, Sarah 113 2
Klise, Solomon 113 2
Klise, WM 116 2
Kloninger, Philip 111 2
Klonninger, Philip Sr 111 2
Knight, Francis Z S 92 2
Knill, Ellen N 89 2
Knill, Leroy 89 2
Knill, Michael 89 2
Knill, Viola 278 1
Knill, Viola A 273 1
Knipple, Margaret V 87 2
Knizer, John 186, 209 3
Knock, Alice E H 81 2
Knock, C F Jr 81 2
Knock, C Fred 73 1
Knock, Chas F 85 2
Knock, Chas F Jr 85 2
Knock, Hannah T 96 2
Knock, Henry F 96 2
Knock, Lewis H 85 2
Knock, Thos H 96 2
Knode, Elsie G 139 3
Knode, Jacob 101 2
Knode, Jacob C 101 2
Knode, James 101 2
Knode, John T 101 2
Knode, Martin 101 2
Knode, William 23 3
Knode, William L 166 1
Knodle, Annie C 81 2
Knodle, Annie Clara 83 2
Knodle, Benton 83, 107, 115 2
Knodle, Margaret 107 2
Knodle, Martin L 107 2
Knodle, Theodore 115 2
Knodle, Violette B 115 2
Knott, Alexander 81 2
Knott, Alice F 81 2
Knott, Alphonse 81 2
Knott, Bendict V 101 2
Knott, Benedict 83 2
Knott, C Elizabeth 92, 110 2
Knott, Caleb 84 2
Knott, Charles 83 2
Knott, D Columbus 93 2
Knott, David A 113 2
Knott, F C 92 1
Knott, F C 56 3
Knott, F Columbus 92 2
Knott, F Columbus 96, 109, 225 1

Knott, F Columbus 55, 113, 126, 160, 221 3
Knott, John D 102 2
Knott, John S 101 2
Knott, Joseph S 106 2
Knott, Joseph T 102 2
Knott, Joseph W 101 2
Knott, Kathryn 10 2
Knott, Louise A 106 2
Knott, Mary E 90, 101, 107 2
Knott, Nan C 110 2
Knott, Nannie C 92 2
Knott, Ruth 23 3
Knott, Sarah A 113 2
Knouff, Anna 80 2
Knouff, Eleanore 89 2
Knouff, Geo 107 2
Knouff, Jacob 43, 100, 101 2
Knouff, John 64, 184 3
Knouff, John 30 1
Knouff, John 100 2
Knouff, John & 38 2
Knouff, Mary 107 2
Knouff, Mary Ann 107 2
Knox, Anastasia 93 2
Knox, David W 87 2
Knox, Geo E 93 2
Knox, Joseph 69 2
Knox, Margaret 107 2
Knox, Maria 87 2
Knox, William 31 3
Knox, Wm 24 1
Knox, Wm 81 3
Knox, Wm 7 2
Knoxe, James 107 2
Knoxe, Jane 107 2
Knoxe, Joseph 70 1
Knoxe, Margaret 107 2
Knoxe, Mary 107 2
Knoxe, Wm 116 2
Knoxe, Wm H 107 2
Knoxe, Zeremiah 118 2
Koehler, Henry 112, 163 1
Koehler, Henry Sr 84, 96 2
Koester, Alice H 80 2
Koester, Christiana 96 2
Koester, Henry 37 1
Koester, Henry 96 2
Kohelenburg, Wilhemina 116 2
Kohlenberg, Adam Jr 80 2
Kohlenberg, Edythe A 89 2
Kohlenberg, Evaline 80 2
Kohlenburg, Adam 87, 163 2
Kohlenburg, Adam 271 1
Kohlenburg, Daniel H 87 2
Kohlenburg, Dolly 87 2
Kohlenburg, Dottie 89 2
Kohlenburg, Edythe A 93 2
Kohlenburg, Evaline 89 2
Kohlenburg, G T 172 1
Kohlenburg, Geo P 93 2
Kohlenburg, Harvey 100 2
Kohlenburg, Henry 96 2
Kohlenburg, Justis 100 2
Kohler, Henry 169 1
Kohler, Henry 221a 2
Kohlhass Christian 84 2
Kohlhass, Benjamin 83, 84 2
Kohlhass, Chas 101 2
Kohlhass, Christian 84 2
Kohlhass, Harley M 113 2
Kohlhass, Henry 96 2
Kohlhass, Jane 101 2
Kohlhass, Sarah E 113 2
Kohlhass, Wm 116 2
Kohlweyer, Rosa L 112 2
Kohn, Geo 64 3
Kolb, Absalom 10 1
Kolb, Ada R 106 2
Kolb, Ann M 80 2
Kolb, Bettie R 106 2
Kolb, Calvin W 84 2
Kolb, Caroline V 85, 87 2
Kolb, Catherine 84 2
Kolb, Charles P M 172 1
Kolb, Charles W W 96 2
Kolb, Chas E 15 2
Kolb, Chas J 84 2
Kolb, Chas R M 116 2
Kolb, Chas W 84 2
Kolb, Clayton 107 2
Kolb, D F 59 1
Kolb, D O 56 3
Kolb, Daniel 32 1
Kolb, Daniel 87 2
Kolb, Daniel D 87 2
Kolb, Daniel Jr 59 1
Kolb, Daniel Jr 87 2
Kolb, Daniel S 87 2
Kolb, David 223 1
Kolb, David 11, 87, 116 2
Kolb, David D 116 2
Kolb, David F 87 2
Kolb, David F 87 2
Kolb, David H 54 3
Kolb, David H 39, 87, 93 2
Kolb, E E 106 3
Kolb, Edw A 101 2
Kolb, Elizabeth 89 2
Kolb, Fannie E 258 2
Kolb, Frederick 92 2
Kolb, Frederick A 58 1
Kolb, Geo 39, 57 2
Kolb, Geo W S 96 2
Kolb, George W 93 2
Kolb, Harriett E 85 2
Kolb, Helen Thomas 116 2
Kolb, Henry H 96 2
Kolb, Ida M 99 2
Kolb, Ivy M 99 2
Kolb, John 100, 101, 154, 159 2
Kolb, John M 84, 92 2
Kolb, John W 61 1
Kolb, John W 49, 84 2
Kolb, John W C 101 2
Kolb, Lewis 87 2
Kolb, Lewis A 59, 61, 92 1
Kolb, Lewis A 87, 106, 107 2
Kolb, Lillie G 106 2
Kolb, Margaret 107 2
Kolb, Martha Ellen 87 2
Kolb, Mary A 108, 116 2
Kolb, Mary C 116 2
Kolb, Mary E 92 2
Kolb, Michael 69, 100 2
Kolb, Nettie R 172 1
Kolb, Robert L 85 2
Kolb, T J 208 1
Kolb, Thos J 27 1
Kolb, W A 84 2
Kolb, William G 290 2
Kolb, William O 116 2
Kolb, William O 56 3
Kolb, William W 294 2
Kolb, Wilson W 179 3
Kolb, Wm 203 3
Kolb, Wm 82, 123 1
Kolb, Wm 84, 116, 195, 237 2
Kolb, Wm A 116 2
Kolb, Wm Augustus 116 2
Kolb, Wm G 116 2
Kolb, Wm Jr 14 2
Kolb, Wm O 106, 116, 166 2
Kolenburg, Adam 122 3
Koogle, Adam 152 1
Koogle, Adam 80, 100, 110 2
Koogle, Adam of C 84 2
Koogle, Alta H 80 2
Koogle, Amanda C 112 2
Koogle, Ann Maria 80 2
Koogle, Annie 93 2
Koogle, Annie E 87 2
Koogle, Bruce 230 1
Koogle, Bruce S 85 2
Koogle, C 84 2
Koogle, C R 87 2
Koogle, Calvin R 85 2
Koogle, Carlton E 85 2
Koogle, Catherine 240 1
Koogle, Catherine 84 2
Koogle, Chas W 154 2
Koogle, Christian 84 2
Koogle, Clara V 85 2
Koogle, Clarence 87 2
Koogle, Clarence B 93 2
Koogle, Cora M 85 2

Koogle, Daniel 11 2
Koogle, Daniel 214 1
Koogle, Daniel of C 80, 84, 87 2
Koogle, Daniel S 87 2
Koogle, Daniel S 19 1
Koogle, David 87 2
Koogle, David H 87 2
Koogle, E Lewis 138 2
Koogle, Edgar H 3, 113 2
Koogle, Edgar H 57 3
Koogle, Eli 84, 92 2
Koogle, Elizabeth 154 2
Koogle, Frances 84 2
Koogle, Francis 92 2
Koogle, Geo 8, 11, 25, 39, 72, 80, 84, 92, 101, 107, 124, 138, 169, 205 2
Koogle, Geo 41, 47, 73, 100, 106, 135, 144, 175, 203, 205, 223, 233, 234, 240, 271 1
Koogle, Geo 91, 187 3
Koogle, Geo F 87 2
Koogle, Geo W 93 2
Koogle, George 110, 226, 235 2
Koogle, George 58, 59, 61, 272 1
Koogle, George 40, 67, 106, 209 3
Koogle, J W D 87 2
Koogle, Jacob 71 3
Koogle, Jacob 39, 40, 107, 277, 280 2
Koogle, Jacob 67, 85 1
Koogle, John 106, 210, 234 1
Koogle, John 89, 84, 87, 100, 107, 124, 184, 188, 208, 247 2
Koogle, John 27, 42 3
Koogle, John & 132 2
Koogle, John D 152 1
Koogle, John E 113 2
Koogle, John W 14, 71 3
Koogle, John W 26 1
Koogle, Joshua D 113 2
Koogle, Lillie M 107 2
Koogle, Malinda 92 2
Koogle, Mary E 107 2
Koogle, Mary J 107 2
Koogle, Melinda 84 2
Koogle, Oliver C 110 2
Koogle, Paul W 85, 116 2
Koogle, Roy J 112 2
Koogle, Roy J 120 1
Koogle, Russell I 112 2
Koogle, Ruth E 101 1
Koogle, Selena S 113 2
Koogle, Sherman R 113 2
Koogle, Susan M 113 2
Koogle, Susannah 113 2
Koogle, Thomas W 115 2
Koogle, Viola M 85, 116 2
Koogle, Wm H 116 2
Kooken, Ruth H 16 2
Koon, Chas M 210 3
Koon, Henry 82 1
Koon, John 100 2
Koon, John E 150 2
Koon, John J 106 1
Koon, John Jr 185 3
Koon, John W 40 3
Koons, Ann M E 80 2
Koons, Clyde O 62 1
Koons, David 87 2
Koons, Edw 2 2
Koons, Edw C 101 2
Koons, Edw J 89 2
Koons, Elizabeth 89 2
Koons, Emma J 89, 102 2
Koons, Geo D 35 2
Koons, Geo U 201 1
Koons, George 93 2
Koons, Henry 228 1
Koons, Henry 160 3
Koons, Henry Sr 96 2
Koons, Isaac 99 2
Koons, Isaac 32 3
koons, J A 198 2
Koons, Jacob 96, 101 2
Koons, John 7, 8, 38, 46 2
Koons, John 1 3
Koons, John A 101 2
Koons, John A & 75 2
Koons, John Sr 100 2
Koons, Joseph 89 2
Koons, Joseph M 102 2
Koons, Joseph M 62 1
Koons, Lawrence R 99 2
Koons, Peter 57 1
Koons, Peter 93, 101 2
Koons, Peter D 4 1
Koons, Peter D Jr 89 2
Koons, Wm 116 2
Koons, Wm M 89 2
Koontz 120 3
Koontz, Abraham 93, 217a, 219a, 224a 2
Koontz, Abraham 120, 160 3
Koontz, Abraham 80 2
Koontz, Abram 100 2
Koontz, Alice B 93 2
Koontz, Alice C 80 2
Koontz, Catherine A 84 2
Koontz, Clara E 34 1
Koontz, Clark 124 3
Koontz, David 87, 100, 107 2
Koontz, Edw 115 2
Koontz, Edw 129 3
Koontz, Edward 89, 119 2
Koontz, Edward I 67 1
Koontz, Eliza J 89 2
Koontz, Elizabeth 89, 90 2
Koontz, Emma 35 2
Koontz, G A 4 1
Koontz, Geo 11, 137 2
Koontz, Geo 6, 32, 139, 156 1
Koontz, Geo 179, 185, 203 3
Koontz, Geo A 89 2
Koontz, George 96, 106 3
Koontz, George 26, 263 1
Koontz, George 93, 282 2
Koontz, George A 93 2
Koontz, George W 93 2
Koontz, Godfrey 25, 32, 70, 71, 90, 118, 131, 139, 144, 263, 271, 275 1
Koontz, Godfrey 98, 106, 116, 122, 124, 128, 129, 179, 209 3
Koontz, Godfrey 29, 38, 39, 67, 69, 80, 93, 96, 137, 165, 294 2
Koontz, H 96 2
Koontz, Henry 70, 135 1
Koontz, Henry 96, 113, 211 2
Koontz, Henry & 96 2
Koontz, Henry Jr 96 2
Koontz, Henry of H 96 2
Koontz, Henry of J 96 2
Koontz, Henry Sr 96 2
Koontz, Hy Jr 30 1
Koontz, Isabella E 99 2
Koontz, J 96 2
Koontz, Jacob 149 2
Koontz, James A 102 2
Koontz, James W 93 2
Koontz, John 100, 107 2
Koontz, John 13 1
Koontz, Magdalene 107 2
Koontz, Margaret 107 2
Koontz, Margaret C 96 2
Koontz, Milton 12 2
Koontz, Nellie M Mrs 90 2
Koontz, Peter 110 1
Koontz, R Hollis 34 1
Koontz, Upton 115 2
Koontz, William 18 3
Koontz, William R 90 2
Koontz, Wm 53, 179 3
Koontz, Wm 57, 107 2
Kopp, Annie 85 2
Kopp, Annie M 116 2
Kopp, Charles E 85 2
Kopp, Chas E 116 2
Kopp, Frederick 92, 116 2
Kopp, Marian 108 2
Kopp, Minnie 179 1
Kopp, Minnie 92, 108 2
Kopp, Wolfgang 116 2
Korrell, Amelia C 27 1
Korrell, C C 27 1
Korrell, Elizabeth 101 2

Korrell, Hilda 108 2
Korrell, John 19, 101 2
Kost, Ann Maria 93 2
Kost, George 93 2
Koster, Wm 116 2
Kouch, George 93 2
Kovack, Teresa L 10 2
Kramer, Frederick 39 3
Kramer, Frederick W 92 2
Krammer, Adam 80 2
Krammer, Ann Marg't 80 2
Krammer, Daniel J 87 2
Krammer, Frederick 80 2
Krammer, Frederick 38 3
Krammer, Margaret 80 2
Krantz, A E 61 1
Krantz, Adam 80, 89 2
Krantz, Alice E 81 2
Krantz, Bessie C 92 2
Krantz, Catherine 84 2
Krantz, Charles E 108 2
Krantz, Chas E 81, 108, 116 2
Krantz, Edw C 89, 92 2
Krantz, Elias 89 2
Krantz, Elmegia 116 2
Krantz, Fred 89 2
Krantz, Frederick 84, 92 2
Krantz, Frederick 44 3
Krantz, Frederick Biser 92 2
Krantz, Henry 89 2
Krantz, Henry C 108 2
Krantz, John H 92 3
Krantz, Julia A 102 2
Krantz, L V 92 2
Krantz, Laura V 106 2
Krantz, Mabel 169 2
Krantz, Margaret A 108 2
Krantz, Mary M 108 2
Krantz, Miriam K 106 2
Krantz, Nannie E 110 2
Krantz, W B 102 2
Krantz, W H 92 2
Krantz, Walter B 102 2
Krantz, Wm H 108, 116 2
Kratz, Edward 92 2
Kratz, Freda R 92 2
Kreglo, Charles W 85, 262 2
Kreglo, Chas 107 2
Kreglo, Chas W 73 1
Kreglo, Harriet E 96 2
Kreglo, Jacob 237 2
Kreglo, John 100 2
Kreglo, Jonas 7, 96 2
Kreglo, Mary F 85 2
Kreglo, Mary Louisa 107 2
Kreglo, Thomas E 262 2
Kreglo, Thos E 107 2
Kreglo, Wm 100 2
Kreh, C Herbert 113 1
Kreh, Charles 85 2
Kreh, Chas 85, 89 2
Kreh, Cora I 85 2
Kreh, E H 188 1
Kreh, Edw 230 1
Kreh, Edw H 89 2
Kreh, Elizabeth 89, 111 2
Kreh, Elizabeth M 89 2
Kreh, Eva M 89 2
Kreh, H D 75 3
Kreh, Henry J 271 2
Kreh, Howard L 85, 106 2
Kreh, John 89 2
Kreh, John F 111, 116 2
Kreh, Laura 89 2
Kreh, Lewis 89 2
Kreh, Lewis F 111 2
Kreh, Lewis T 106 2
Kreh, Louis 106 2
Kreh, Mary M 85 2
Kreh, Nelson C 113 1
Kreh, Peter 89, 111 2
Kreh, William H 116 2
Kreig, Jesse 58 2
Kreitz, Andrew J 81 2
Kreitz, Elmer 90 2
Krepp, John 84, 92 2
Krepps, Guilford L 169 3
Krepps, Mary A 210 3
Krepps, Mary A 279 1
Kresh, Nicholas 92 2
Krey, Henrietta D 10 3
Krieglo, Jonas 262 2
Krise, Abraham 111 2
Krise, Chas H 93, 209 2
Krise, Chole F 198 2
Krise, Daniel 87 2
Krise, Daniel O 116 2
Krise, David 101 2
Krise, Edw 18, 89 2
Krise, Edw E 89 2
Krise, Edward F 124 1
Krise, Elbridge F 101, 107, 113, 116 2
Krise, Elias 1, 89, 96 2
Krise, Elijah 5 2
Krise, Erias T 107 2
Krise, Geo 89, 198 2
Krise, Geo H 138 2
Krise, Geo W 199 3
Krise, George W 93 2
Krise, George W 196 3
Krise, H J 229 1
Krise, Harry E 96, 108 2
Krise, Haxel E 101 1
Krise, Hazel C 124 1
Krise, Hazel E 223a 2
Krise, Henry 96, 100, 107, 159, 103, 220a, 221a, 223a 2
Krise, Henry 50 3
Krise, Henry J 96 2
Krise, Jacob 58 1
Krise, Jacob 100, 186 2
Krise, John 91, 125 1
Krise, John 87, 100, 101 2
Krise, Margaret 100, 107 2
Krise, Maria 107 2
Krise, Mary 107 2
Krise, Mary Ann 107 2
Krise, Mary T 101 2
Krise, Minnie M 188 2
Krise, Minnie Myrtle 108 2
Krise, Peter 107, 111 2
Krise, Samuel 113 2
Krise, Samuel H 7 2
Krise, Solomon 35, 38, 100, 113 2
Krise, Solomon 32 1
Krise, Wilbur F 89 2
Krise, William 276 2
Krise, William Fred 116 2
Krise, Wm 116, 198 2
Krise, Wm C 116 2
Krise, Zelda Z 116 2
Krom, John 184 1
Krom, Wm 19 2
Krone, Mary Susan 107 2
Krouse, Valentine 115 2
Krug, Arthur 112 2
Krug, Daniel 87, 186 2
Krug, Daniel 57 1
Krug, Lewis T 87 2
Krug, Rufus 87, 112 2
Krunine, Henry 32 1
Krunrine, Henry 1 3
Kugler, John R 132 2
Kugler, Kathryn N 173 1
Kugler, Louis S 132 2
Kuhn, A Scott 80 2
Kuhn, Ann R 80 2
Kuhn, Barney 83 2
Kuhn, Christian 84, 93 2
Kuhn, Daniel 87, 93 2
Kuhn, Deaton 210, 240 1
Kuhn, Elizabeth 89, 96 2
Kuhn, Ernest R 102, 120, 153 2
Kuhn, Frederick 122 3
Kuhn, Gabriel 93 2
Kuhn, Geo 26, 84, 111, 116, 169 2
Kuhn, Geo 135, 228, 234 1
Kuhn, Geo A 224 3
Kuhn, George 30, 196 1
Kuhn, George 93 2
Kuhn, Henry 40, 47, 56, 91, 240 1
Kuhn, Henry 8, 64, 202 3
Kuhn, Henry 26, 51, 96, 177, 228a 2

Kuhn, John 100 2
Kuhn, John E 63 1
Kuhn, John E 102 2
Kuhn, John H 100, 102 2
Kuhn, John W 223 3
Kuhn, Joseph 93, 100, 262 2
Kuhn, Joseph 171 3
Kuhn, Joseph 228 1
Kuhn, Joseph L 118 2
Kuhn, Mary A 128 2
Kuhn, P T 212, 217 3
Kuhn, Philip 102, 111 2
Kuhn, Rebecca K 83 3
Kuhn, Samuel W 113 2
Kuhn, Susan 113 2
Kuhn, Wm 37 3
Kuhn, Wm 116 2
Kuhn, Zebulon 70 3
Kuhn, Zebulon 51, 57, 118 2
Kuhn, Zebulon 30 1
Kuhn, Zenbulon 91 1
Kuhns, Jacob 26 1
Kump, Anna Ruth 81 2
Kump, Emmanuel J 81 2
Kump, Erwin 106 2
Kump, Lewis H 106 2
Kunkel, Annie M 101 2
Kunkel, Chas E 101 2
Kunkel, J B 101, 131 2
Kunkel, Jacob 101 2
Kunkel, Jacob M 101, 165 2
Kunkel, John 106, 196 1
Kunkel, John 163 3
Kunkel, John 101, 165, 258 2
Kunkel, John B 101 2
Kunkel, John J 101 2
Kunkel, Mary C 107 2
Kunkel, Mary E 101 2
Kunkel, P B 245 2
Kunkel, Philip 6 3
Kunkel, Philip 39, 51 2
Kunkel, Philip B 82 1
Kunkle, Amelia F 80 2
Kunkle, Ann C 80 2
Kunkle, Ann M 80 2
Kunkle, Chas 187 2
Kunkle, J M 87 3
Kunkle, Jacob 181 2
Kunkle, John 84, 100, 101, 116, 181, 187 2
Kunkle, John 102, 120, 122, 207, 213, 222 3
Kunkle, John 106, 116 1
Kunkle, John J 80 2
Kunkle, Mary C 80 2
Kunkle, Philip 94 3
Kunkle, Philip B 193 1
Kurrens, Elizah 30 1
Kurry, William R 42 3
Kurtz, Abraham 186 2
Kurtz, John 38, 100 2
Kurzer, John 294 2
Kushar, Charles 84 2
Kussmall, Fannie L 107 2
Kussmall, Mary 107 2
Kussmall, P F 111 2
Kussmaul, C T 111 2
Kussmaul, Fannie 92 2
Kussmaul, Helen 92 2
Kussmaul, J S Mrs 111 2
Lach, Chas 106 3
Lagarde, Ernest 129 2
Lagarde, John 129 2
Lair, Moses 144 2
Lake, Virginia C 233 1
Laken, John S 177 1
Lakin, Abraham 27, 78, 119, 150 2
Lakin, Abraham 260 1
Lakin, Amy 255 2
Lakin, Anna 129 2
Lakin, B Ella 122 2
Lakin, Bertha E 139 2
Lakin, C E 76 2
Lakin, Cephus E 124 2
Lakin, D T 106 1
Lakin, Daniel 44 1
Lakin, Daniel 257 2
Lakin, Daniel Jr 82 1
Lakin, Daniel Jr 128 2
Lakin, Daniel Sr 128 2
Lakin, Daniel T 128 2
Lakin, Daniel T 71 1
Lakin, Elizabeth 129 2
Lakin, Elizabeth A C 129 2
Lakin, Elizabeth R 129 2
Lakin, F T 1 1
Lakin, Flora B 124, 131 2
Lakin, Francis T 131 2
Lakin, Geo 255 2
Lakin, Henry 76 2
Lakin, Henry D 134 2
Lakin, Henry D 100 3
Lakin, Jerry 131 2
Lakin, John 69, 137 2
Lakin, John F 119, 129 2
Lakin, John H 139 2
Lakin, John S 70, 76, 134, 139, 150 2
Lakin, John S 100 1
Lakin, Josephine 129 2
Lakin, Lizzie R 128 2
Lakin, Mary F 131 2
Lakin, Sarah 150 2
Lakin, Susan 150 2
Lakin, Susan J 154 2
Lakin, Susan J 219 1
Lakin, Susan Julia 151 2
Lakin, Susannah 154 2
Lakin, T L 139 2
Lakin, Terry L 166 2
Lakin, W F 214 2
Lakin, W H 60 1
Lakin, W H 71 3
Lakin, William 268 2
Lakin, William C 122 2
Lakin, Wm 64 3
Lakin, Wm 112, 177, 229, 249, 260 1
Lakin, Wm 29, 69, 72, 78, 124, 128, 129, 137, 139, 150, 154 2
Lakin, Wm H 104 1
Lakin, Wm H 154 2
Laley, Wm 165 2
Lalley, Charles E 125 2
Lalley, Della 125 2
Lamar, Angela 119 2
Lamar, Austin A 119 2
Lamar, B J 120 3
Lamar, B S 83 2
Lamar, B S 118 3
Lamar, Baker 205 2
Lamar, Baker J 78, 144 2
Lamar, Baker J 129 3
Lamar, Benoni S 122 2
Lamar, C Hayes 125 2
Lamar, Caroline 124 2
Lamar, Clarence H 20 2
Lamar, Elizabeth 129 2
Lamar, Emma 129 2
Lamar, Emma K 119 2
Lamar, Emma S 129 2
Lamar, Harriet A 20 2
Lamar, Holmes 129 2
Lamar, James 57 1
Lamar, John C 101 1
Lamar, John C 20, 51, 139 2
Lamar, Kate 142, 149 2
Lamar, Lena E 119 2
Lamar, Mary 144, 149 2
Lamar, Mary C 150 2
Lamar, Meta J 139 2
Lamar, Richard 87, 149 2
Lamar, Richard J 67 1
Lamar, Robt G 124, 149 2
Lamar, Samuel C 150 2
Lamar, Sarah E 150 2
Lamar, T J 35 2
Lamar, Thomas 153, 208 2
Lamar, Thomas 39, 81, 171 3
Lamar, Thos 189 1
Lamar, Thos 57 2
Lamar, Wiola 125 2
Lamar, Wm 19, 57 2
LaMatte, Daniel M 128 2
LaMatte, Laura M 128 2
Lamb, Abraham 119 2
Lamb, Michael 144 2

Lamb, Milton 144 2
Lambert, Arthur H 11 1
Lambert, Catherine 124, 137 2
Lambert, Clarence 128 2
Lambert, David F 128 2
Lambert, David J W 128 2
Lambert, Evelyn R 145 2
Lambert, Florence A 245 1
Lambert, Frederick 144 2
Lambert, Geo 128 2
Lambert, Georgetta J B 132 2
Lambert, Harriet 137 2
Lambert, J J 70 1
Lambert, John 189, 245 1
Lambert, John 137 2
Lambert, John A 137, 139 2
Lambert, John G 128 2
Lambert, John G 37 1
Lambert, John Jacob 140 2
Lambert, John W 139 2
Lambert, Joseph 11, 124, 138 2
Lambert, Margaret E 150 2
Lambert, Mary 144 2
Lambert, Mary Elizabeth 145 2
Lambert, Raymond 150 2
Lambert, Samuel 150 2
Lamberth, David 225a 2
Lamberth, Florence A 131 2
Lamberth, J Ralph 12 2
Lamberth, Joseph 138 2
Lamberth, Maggie V 197 1
Lambrecht, Geo 144 2
Lambrecht, Henry 144 2
Lambrecht, Magdalena 144 2
Lambrecht, Mary 148 2
Lambrecht, Michael 144 2
Lambrecht, Philip 38, 148 2
Lambright, Ann R E 119 2
Lambright, Anna R E 4 1
Lambright, Annie 19 1
Lambright, Arthur B 148 2
Lambright, Clara V 148 2
Lambright, Geo 134 2
Lambright, George 132 2
Lambright, George 215 3
Lambright, Henry 134 2
Lambright, James L 139 2
Lambright, John 204 1
Lambright, John W 4 1
Lambright, Michael 134 2
Lambright, Philip 134 2
Lambright, Philip H 148 2
Lamden, William S 265 2
Lamed, Augustus 154 2
Lampe, Allen 129, 153 2
Lampe, Arthur C 85 2
Lampe, Elizabeth M 129, 139 2
Lampe, Henry 144 1
Lampe, Henry R 129, 139, 147 2
Lampe, J Gernard 129 2
Lampe, J H 92 1
Lampe, J H 101 2
Lampe, J Henry 147 2
Lampe, J Henry 54 3
Lampe, John H 139 2
Lampe, Mary C 145 2
Lampe, Mary Eva 145 2
Lampe, Nettie 129 2
Lampe, Nettie L 147 2
Lampe, Wm E 145 2
Lanahan, Geo W 206 3
Land, Alan S Lee 246 2
Landauer, A M 67, 106 3
Landauer, A M 39 2
Landauer, Abraham M 119 2
Landauer, Chas R 67 3
Landauer, Grace S 172 1
Landauer, Irving M 119, 136 2
Landauer, Irving M 28 1
Landerkin, Augusta 119 2
Landers, Annie M 57 3
Landers, Annie M 119 2
Landers, Charles E 57 3
Landers, Daniel 26 2
Landers, Geo 150 2
Landers, George 132 2
Landers, George 117 1
Landers, Harriet A 134, 139 2
Landers, Henry 134 2
Landers, Jacob 134 2
Landers, Jacob 75 3
Landers, Jacob 177 1
Landers, Jesse 96 3
Landers, John 139, 150 2
Landers, John 275 1
Landers, Juliet 117 1
Landers, Robt 169 2
Landers, Sophia 132, 150 2
Landers, William 14 3
Landers, William 282 2
Landers, William C 262, 271 2
Landers, William C 165 3
Landers, Wm 46, 101, 132, 181, 237 2
Landers, Wm 106 1
Landers, Wm C 139, 150, 164, 183, 277 1
Landers, Wm C 138 2
Landers, Wm L 117 1
Landes, John 138 2
Landes, Louisa 138 2
Landeur, A M 30 2
Landis, C A 124 2
Landis, C Rubie 124, 134 2
Landis, Catherine 124 2
Landis, Chas 134 2
Landis, Henry S 134 2
Landis, Jacob 195 3
Landis, Jacob 147, 152, 263 1
Landis, Jesse 136, 138 2
Landis, Jesse 39 3
Landis, John B 21 3
Landis, W C 57, 198 2
Landis, Wm 87 2
Landis, Wm C 134 2
Landis, Wm L 28 1
Lane, Charles G 125 2
Lane, Charles S III 125 2
Lane, Elizabeth 154 2
Lane, J Clarence 43 3
Lane, John 137 2
Lane, John 39 3
Lane, John C 138 2
Lane, Joseph 137 2
Lane, Joseph E 137 2
Lane, Sarah 150 2
Lane, Wm 154 2
Lanebright, John 139 2
Langdon, John R 145 2
Langdon, Mary E 145 2
Langley, Charles W 125 2
Laniers, James 138 2
Lansdale, P S 108 2
Lansdale, P S 73, 91 1
Lansdale, T S 88, 195 1
Lansford, Sarah L 150 2
Lansinger, F W 43 2
Lansinger, Frances W 55 3
Lants, John [sic] 196 1
Lantz, Albert 119 2
Lantz, Charles 124 2
Lantz, Charles W 125 2
Lantz, Christian 124 2
Lantz, Christian 186 3
Lantz, Christian 193 1
Lantz, Cyrus 104 1
Lantz, Cyrus 124, 138 2
Lantz, Geo 49 2
Lantz, Grace A 143 2
Lantz, H G 139 2
Lantz, Isabella C 136 2
Lantz, John 84 1
Lantz, John A 139 2
Lantz, John B 138 2
Lantz, John R 138, 139, 140 2
Lantz, Joseph B 139 2
Lantz, Lela V 154 2
Lantz, Lelia Virginia 143 2
Lantz, M E 119 2
Lantz, Mary J 140 2
Lantz, Mary S 139, 145 2
Lantz, Roscoe S 154 2

Lantz, W S 139, 234 2
Lantz, Winfield S 154 2
Lanzell, Raymond A 149 2
Lapole, Elsie Robertson 129 2
Lare, Annie R 124 2
Lare, Chas E 132 2
Lare, Chas E E 124 2
Lare, Cordelia E 154 2
Lare, Edw 7, 132 2
Lare, George 132 2
Lare, George B 132 2
Lare, Harvey M. 126 1
Lare, Henry 132 2
Lare, Henry C 134 2
Lare, Maria 134 2
Lare, Wm 118 1
Lare, Wm 5, 19, 68, 154 2
Largent, James J 139 2
Largent, M J 139 2
Largents, W T 139 2
Larkin, Jacob 137 2
Larkin, John Sr 137 2
Larkin, Thos 137 2
Larkins, Abraham 215 3
Larkins, Daisy 134 2
Larkins, Gertrude 134 2
Larkins, Grayson 134 2
Larkins, Grayson 42 1
Larkins, Harry 134 2
Larkins, Maria 67 1
Larned, A 100 2
Larned, Augustus 119 2
Larned, Sarah 119 2
Lashley, Lynn C 76 1
Lashorn, Conrad 124 2
Lashorn, Mary 124 2
Late, Allie M 132 2
Late, Catherine 124 2
Late, E Wm 139 2
Late, Geo 122, 139 2
Late, George 91 1
Late, George F 132 2
Late, Jacob 144 2
Late, Jacob 37 3
Late, John 116 1
Late, John 137, 139 2
Late, Maria 144 2
Late, Maria 144 2
Late, Maria 50 3
Late, Michael 106, 122 3
Late, Michael 27, 137, 144 2
Late, Michael 116 1
Late, Michael L 145 2
Late, Michael Sr 144 2
Late, Virginia C 145 2
Latham, Joseph W 143 2
Latham, Louisa 143 2
Latimer, Elizabeth M 182 2
Lauderkin, F W 129 3
Lauderkin, T 96 3
Lauderkin, T W 129 3
Lauderkin, Thomas C 96, 129 3
Laundauer, A M 231 2
Laverty, Ann 119 2
Laverty, Robert 119 2
Lawarence, Ernest A 129 2
Lawless, Philip 148 2
Lawney, C A 129 2
Lawrence, A C 147 1
Lawrence, Adam 119 2
Lawrence, Ann Maria 119, 144 2
Lawrence, C A 279 1
Lawrence, C A 129 2
Lawrence, Charles 124, 125 2
Lawrence, Charles A 27 3
Lawrence, Chas 63, 129, 205 2
Lawrence, Chas A 124 2
Lawrence, Daniel 183 1
Lawrence, Elizabeth 119 2
Lawrence, Ella J 129 2
Lawrence, Emma W 129 2
Lawrence, Ernest A 125, 129, 215a 2
Lawrence, Ernest A 189, 205 1
Lawrence, Eugene 125, 129 2
Lawrence, Harry T 139 2
Lawrence, Henry 38, 119 2
Lawrence, Jacob 11 2
Lawrence, Jerome 139 2
Lawrence, John 138 2
Lawrence, Joseph 138 2
Lawrence, Martha E 18 3
Lawrence, Mary E 144 2
Lawrence, P D 175 2
Lawrence, Sarah M 57 1
Lawrence, Sarah M 150 2
Lawrence, Stephen D 150, 205 2
Lawrence, Wm 119 2
Lawson, Catharine E 124, 139 2
Lawson, Ephriam 129 2
Lawson, Gabriel L 132 2
Lawson, Gabriel U 132 2
Lawson, H Holland 132 2
Lawson, Harry 60 1
Lawson, Hugh 187 3
Lawson, J H 61, 278 1
Lawson, J H 8 2
Lawson, J U 209 3
Lawson, J U 270 1
Lawson, J Uriah 132 2
Lawson, James 139 2
Lawson, James D 51 1
Lawson, James D 138, 214 2
Lawson, James H 140 2
Lawson, James U 139 2
Lawson, James W 44 1
Lawson, John 124, 132, 139, 214 2
Lawson, John 51 1
Lawson, John H 2, 212 3
Lawson, John H 137, 139 2
Lawson, John M 140 2
Lawson, John W 139, 140 2
Lawson, Lillie J 143 2
Lawson, Marion W 145 2
Lawson, Mary T 154 2
Lawson, Mary V 132 2
Lawson, Roy V 140, 154 2
Lawson, Stella M 132 2
Lawson, W P N 56, 187, 188 3
Lawson, William P 72 1
Lawson, Wm 146 1
Lawson, Wm 8, 101, 102, 132, 139 2
Lawson, Wm F 154 2
Lawson, Wm L 138 2
Lawson, Wm P N 113, 139, 154 2
Lawyer, Elma Fike 243 1
Lawyer, M O 63 1
Lawyer, Martin 290 2
Lawyer, Metty M 189 3
Lawyer, Milton O 243 1
Layer, Anna M 264 1
Layer, John 140 2
Layer, W H 140 2
Layer, William H 154 2
Layman, Chas E 210 3
Layman, Geo 134, 138, 208 2
Layman, Geo 91 1
Layman, Geo H 150 2
Layman, Geo W 132 2
Layman, George 132 2
Layman, H A 138 2
Layman, Henrietta 143 2
Layman, Henry 117 1
Layman, Henry 134, 208 2
Layman, J 143 2
Layman, Jacob 138, 143 2
Layman, John 138, 208 2
Layman, John 117 1
Layman, Josephine 140 2
Layman, Leonard 101, 134 2
Layman, Leonard J 143 2
Layman, Lydia 134, 143 2
Layman, Lydia S 143 2
Layman, Margaret C 113 1
Layman, Mary A 144 2
Layman, Rosie M 40 1

Layman, Sarah C 150 2
Layman, Sarahetta 150 2
Layman, Sophia R 132 2
Layman, Wm 132, 143 2
Leab, Jacob 45, 163 1
Leach, Thomas 153 2
Lead, Jacob 137 2
Leah, Jacob 205 2
Leak, William 154 2
Leakin, Daniel 141 3
Leakin, David 137 2
Leakin, John 137 2
Leakin, Wm H 154 2
Leakins, James D 143 2
Leakins, John T 138 2
Leakins, Levin 220 3
Leakins, Louis A 143 2
Leakins, Margaret E 138 2
Leakins, Mary Ann 145 2
Leakins, Thomas 153 2
Leakins, Wm H 153 2
Leaman, Morris 225 2
Leaper, Charlotte 124 2
Leapley, Elizabeth 129 2
Leapley, Geo 67 3
Leapley, Geo 129 2
Leapley, Peter 129 2
Lease, Aceneth 119 2
Lease, Adam 47 1
Lease, Adam 119 2
Lease, Alma S 134 2
Lease, Amelia 119 2
Lease, Amos 119, 124 2
Lease, Andrew J 119 2
Lease, Anna M 119, 154 2
Lease, Asceneth 143 2
Lease, Austin R 145 2
Lease, Catherine 124, 128, 147 2
Lease, Charles 22, 124 2
Lease, Charles 67, 122 3
Lease, Charles E 124 2
Lease, Chas 75 3
Lease, Chas 138 2
Lease, Chas 82 1
Lease, Chas H 119 2
Lease, Chas M 124, 145 2
Lease, Chas W 119 2
Lease, Daniel 128 2
Lease, Daniel 6 3
Lease, Delilah 124 2
Lease, Dorsey 154 2
Lease, Dorsey R 192 1
Lease, E B 119 2
Lease, E S 119 2
Lease, Edw 132 2
Lease, Edw C 124 2
Lease, Edw S 143 2
Lease, Eliza 134 2
Lease, Eliza 134 2
Lease, Emma 154 2
Lease, Emory 32 3
Lease, Emory B 143 2
Lease, Fannie G 145 2
Lease, G 223 3
Lease, Geo 154 2
Lease, Geo D 144, 147 2
Lease, Geo E 37 1
Lease, George 58, 144 1
Lease, George 132 2
Lease, George D 132 2
Lease, George E 132 2
Lease, George E 116 2
Lease, George H 132 2
Lease, Gideon 124, 132 2
Lease, Gideon 122 3
Lease, H N 72 1
Lease, H W 10 3
Lease, Harvey R 149 2
Lease, Harvey R 134 2
Lease, Hazel B 134 2
Lease, Henry 69, 134 2
Lease, Henry 134 2
Lease, Henry 6, 8, 67 3
Lease, Henry 56 1
Lease, Howard 132 2
Lease, Howard M 38 1
Lease, Howard M 134 2
Lease, Jacob 49, 69, 89, 119, 137 2
Lease, Jacob 218 3
Lease, Jacob 26, 47 1
Lease, Jacob Jr 26 3
Lease, Jennie 283 2
Lease, Joacb 224 2
Lease, John 6, 8, 75 3
Lease, John 56, 82, 225 1
Lease, John 132, 137, 138, 144, 214a 2
Lease, John M 27 3
Lease, L E 144 2
Lease, Lewis 75 3
Lease, Luther E 143, 242 2
Lease, Margaret 153 2
Lease, Mary 133 1
Lease, Mary 145, 154 2
Lease, Mary D 116, 132 2
Lease, Mary E 145 2
Lease, Mary M 144 2
Lease, Michael 31 3
Lease, Michael 225 1
Lease, Michael 134, 144, 154, 203 2
Lease, Millard F 145 2
Lease, Minerva 144 2
Lease, Minnie M 145 2
Lease, Nicholas 132, 147 2
Lease, Oliver 124 2
Lease, Oliver D 144, 147 2
Lease, Olivia J 260 1
Lease, Oran C 134 2
Lease, Pearl 134 2
Lease, Philip 271 1
Lease, Rebecca 154 2
Lease, Reuben S 154 2
Lease, Reuben S 107 1
Lease, Robert 139 1
Lease, Robert 67, 122 3
Lease, Robert 22 2
Lease, Robt 149 2
Lease, Sarah E 106 2
Lease, T W 260 1
Lease, Thomas 144 2
Lease, Thomas U 15 3
Lease, Thomas W 218a 2
Lease, Upton 153 2
Lease, W L 65 2
Lease, W N 154 2
Lease, William 58 1
Lease, William H 268 2
Lease, Wm 133 1
Lease, Wm 132, 154 2
Lease, Wm H 67, 154 2
Lease, Wm J R 154 2
Lease, Wm M 119 2
Leasehold 91 3
Leaser, Daniel 137 2
Leaser, Joseph 137 2
Leaser, Mary 157 2
Leaser, Samuel 137 2
Leaser, Zacharias 157 2
Leashorn, Ezra 129 2
Leather, Annie L 139 2
Leather, Caroline 132 2
Leather, Catherine 129 2
Leather, Christina 124 2
Leather, E E 214 2
Leather, Edith C 134 2
Leather, Edw E 2, 129 2
Leather, Edward E 107 3
Leather, Geo 11, 129 2
Leather, Geo W 132, 143 2
Leather, George 132 2
Leather, Harriet S 134 2
Leather, Ira B 136 2
Leather, J Frank 139 2
Leather, J Sr 47 1
Leather, James 129, 171, 214 2
Leather, James L 138 2
Leather, John 100, 124, 137, 138, 220a 2
Leather, Luther J 143 2
Leather, Mary S 132 2
Leather, Mary S (see DeGrange) 145 2
Leather, Merle 134 2
Leather, Russell C 136 2
Leatherman, Adam 119, 144

2
Leatherman, Alfred J 119 2
Leatherman, Amanda E 119, 139
2
Leatherman, Amanda E 104 1
Leatherman, Annie K 131 2
Leatherman, C G 143 2
Leatherman, Cara M 215 1
Leatherman, Carlton 144 2
Leatherman, Carrie M 154 2
Leatherman, Carrie M 38 1
Leatherman, Catherine 124 2
Leatherman, Charles L 62, 225 1
Leatherman, Charles L 197 3
Leatherman, Chas 139 2
Leatherman, Clara F 119 2
Leatherman, Clarence G 143 2
Leatherman, D S 128 2
Leatherman, Daniel 197, 252
1
Leatherman, Daniel 82, 195, 215
3
Leatherman, Daniel 128, 132, 144
2
Leatherman, Elias 129 2
Leatherman, Elizabeth 139 2
Leatherman, Elroy E 26 1
Leatherman, Ettie O 129 2
Leatherman, F C 9 2
Leatherman, Flody 131 2
Leatherman, Floyd 139 2
Leatherman, Geo 8, 11, 19, 22, 66, 124,
138 2
Leatherman, Geo 84, 104, 109, 264
1
Leatherman, George 132 2
Leatherman, George 13, 85 1
Leatherman, Godfrey 132 2
Leatherman, Harry 119 2
Leatherman, Harry F 62 1
Leatherman, Harry F 139 2
Leatherman, Harry J 38 1
Leatherman, Harvey I 150 2
Leatherman, Henry 134 2
Leatherman, Ira 119 2
Leatherman, Isaiah 128 2
Leatherman, J 82 3
Leatherman, J C 6 1
Leatherman, J C 129 2
Leatherman, J N 129 2
Leatherman, Jacob 37, 79, 91,
152, 201, 230, 252, 264 1
Leatherman, Jacob 1, 14, 185
3
Leatherman, Jacob 27, 128, 129,
132, 138, 144, 148 2
Leatherman, Jacob H 139 2
Leatherman, John 129, 199
2
Leatherman, John 184, 213
3
Leatherman, John 41 1
Leatherman, John C 62, 228, 230
1
Leatherman, John C 20, 132 2
Leatherman, John C 3, 82, 192
3
Leatherman, John D 147 2
Leatherman, John W 139 2
Leatherman, John, 129 1
Leatherman, Joseph 137, 237, 258
2
Leatherman, Joseph 70 3
Leatherman, Josephine 139 2
Leatherman, Kate W 142 2
Leatherman, L E 128 2
Leatherman, Laura E 280 2
Leatherman, Levi C 128, 143
2
Leatherman, Lizzie A 143 2
Leatherman, Luther 139 2
Leatherman, Luther E 143 2
Leatherman, Luther E 45 3
Leatherman, Marshal L 143 2
Leatherman, Marshall 139 2
Leatherman, Marshall H 119 2
Leatherman, Martin E ? 145 2
Leatherman, Mary 144 2
Leatherman, Mary M 144 2
Leatherman, Nancy 148 2
Leatherman, Norma E 147 2
Leatherman, Norman 52 2
Leatherman, O F 31, 52 2
Leatherman, Orestes F 147 2
Leatherman, P R 143 2
Leatherman, Peter 176, 239
1
Leatherman, Peter 19, 22, 66,
124, 138, 148 2
Leatherman, Peter Jr 148 2
Leatherman, Robert D 143 2
Leatherman, Robert M 119 2
Leatherman, S B 81 3
Leatherman, Sarah A 150 2
Leatherman, Susan 119 2
Leatherman, Susan R 150 2
Leatherman, Theodore V 142 2
Leatherman, Vernon 33 3
Leatherman, Wm 150 2
Leatherman, Wm H 148, 154
2
Leathern, John 39 3
Leatherwood, Bradley C 11 1
Leatherwood, Bradley C 149 2
Leatherwood, Francis J 131 2
Leatherwood, Herbert 131 2
Leatherwood, Lois M 170, 190
2
Leatherwood, Rosa B 149 2
Leatherwood, Russell 190 2
Leatherwood, Samuel 150 2
Leatherwood, Samuel B 150 2
Leau, Adam 218 3
Leazer, Ann Maria 119, 150
2
Leazer, Daniel 128 2
Leazer, Daniel 13, 63 1
Leazer, Samuel 150 2
Lebhertz, Harry J 32 2
Lebherz, Grace Worman 43 2
Lebherz, Harry J 154 2
Lebherz, Joseph 171 3
Lebherz, William H 154 2
Lechlider, George 132 2
Lechlider, Julia R 140 2
Lechlider, Nancy 148 2
Lechlider, Peter 148 2
Ledgwedge, Margaret A 145 2
Ledwidge, John 209 2
Lee, C O'D 153 2
Lee, Charles O'Donnell 2 2
Lee, Chas O'Donnell 125, 139
2
Lee, Chas O'Donnell 272 1
Lee, Cora D 15, 45, 125 2
Lee, Gilbert T 139 2
Lee, Harriet 134 2
Lee, Jacob 137 2
Lee, John 66 2
Lee, John Edw 139 2
Lee, John R 139 2
Lee, John W (Col'd) 138 2
Lee, Joseph Jenkins 145 2
Lee, Josephine 139 2
Lee, Lola N 143 2
Lee, Maria 220 3
Lee, Mary Diggs 154 2
Lee, Matilda D J 125, 145 2
Lee, Percey W 46 3
Lee, Percy W 148 2
Lee, Sara T Rau 288 2
Lee, Thomas 243 1
Lee, Thomas M (col'd) 153 2
Lee, Thomas S 153 2
Lee, Thos 129, 154 2
Lee, Wm 45, 66, 153, 154 2
Leehan, M 186 1
Leekins, Wm 154 2
Leese, Thomas U 246 2
Lefere, Mary 144 2
LeFevre, Edw J 129 2
Legard, Ernest 139 2
Legard, Ernest 43 3
Legarde, Ernest 100 1
Legarde, Ernest 65 3
Legare, Earnest 196 3
Legg, E K 176 3

Legg, Ellen T 176 3
Legg, T H 189 1
Legore, Eliza 138 2
Legore, Geo R 132 2
Legore, Harry W 132 2
Legore, J W 55 3
Legore, James 138 2
Legore, James W 138 2
LeGore, James W 50 3
Legore, John 138 2
Legore, John H 138 2
Legore, Sue 32 1
Lehman, Samuel F 151 2
Leib, Joseph W 214a 2
Leich, Jacob 119 2
Leidert, Jacob 94 3
Leigh, Geo 165 2
Leighton, Harry Arthur 134 2
Leighton, Ruth Bliss 134 2
Leileich, Jacob 93 2
Leilich, Catherine E 125 2
Leilich, Jacob 38, 129, 138, 165, 177 2
Leilich, Jacob 32, 94 1
Leilich, John J 138 2
Leilich, Michael 59, 84 1
Leilich, Michael 254 2
Leilick, Jacob 165 2
Leister, David 9 1
Leister, David 128, 137 2
Leister, John 137, 171 2
Leister, John 26, 209 3
Leister, L 137 2
Leitner, Joseph of L 137 2
Leman, Thos T 154 2
Lemen, John O 5 2
Lemen, Nannie M 5 2
Lemen, T T 5 2
Lemen, W N 5 2
Lemen, Willoughby N 154 2
Lemon, John H 268 2
Lemon, Nicholas 147 2
L'Engle, E J 150 2
L'Engle, Sarah C 150 2
Lenhart, Annie M 125 2
Lenhart, Charles 125 2
Lenhart, Chester W 140 2
Lenhart, Clemon H 140 2
Lenhart, Geo 139 2
Lenhart, Helen C 127 1
Lenhart, Henry W 134, 143 2
Lenhart, Jesse M 140 2
Lenhart, John J 139, 143 2
Lenhart, John O 143 2
Lenhart, John W 139 2
Lenhart, Leander D 143 2
Lenhart, Lewis F 143 2
Lenhart, Lewis M 143 2
Lenhart, Luther Daniel 143 2
Lenhart, Melvin H 143 2
Lenhart, Raymond W 61 2
Lenhart, Roy J 127 1
Lenhart, Sarah 139 2
Lenhart, Sterling L 143 2
Lenhart, Wm 154 2
Lenier, Henry 111 3
Lenier, Jas D 111 3
Leonard, Edward 129 2
Leopold, J S 140 2
Leopold, James E 140 2
Leopold, John W 140 2
Leopold, Joseph Daniel 140 2
Leopold, Julia Ann 138 2
Leopold, Theophilus 138 2
Lerch, C 225 1
Lerch, Charles S 113 3
Lerch, Frank 134 2
Lerch, Frank W 131 2
Lerch, Geo 131 2
Lerch, Henry 134 2
Lerch, John 131 2
Lerch, Mary E 272 1
Lescallet, John 123 1
Lescallet, L A 203 1
Lescallette, John 51 2
Lester M 136 1
Lester, F 51 3
Lester, John 62 1
Lester, Louis M 143 2
Lester, Margaret H Dudley 145 2
Letherman, George 229a 2
Lettig, Geo 106 3
Leuber, Francis 131, 165 2
Leuber, Helen M 131 2
Levy, Arthur E 59, 70 1
Levy, C B 60, 186 1
Levy, C S 112 2
Levy, C S 54 3
Levy, C V 72, 144, 265, 279 1
Levy, C V 211 2
Levy, C V S 39, 164 2
Levy, C V S 119, 125, 150, 194, 295 1
Levy, C V S 75, 81, 205 3
Levy, Charles V 235 2
Levy, Charles V S 124 2
Levy, Charles V S 202 3
Levy, Chas 39, 46, 124, 188 2
Levy, Chas P 124, 144, 148, 172 2
Levy, Chas P 144, 194, 201 1
Levy, Chas P 79, 205 3
Levy, Chas V S 101, 124, 242, 258 2
Levy, Harry J 79 3
Levy, Harry V 79 3
Levy, John 80 2
Levy, John L 144 2
Levy, Jonathan 137 2
Levy, Margaret A 145 2
Levy, Mary Ann 144 2
Levy, Mary G 79 3
Levy, Mary G 144, 148 2
Levy, Mary Grace 124 2
Levy, Perry 81 3
Levy, Perry 101, 124 2
Levy, Perry J 148 2
Levy, Perry J 79 3
Levy, R H 124 2
Levy, Robertta H 148 2
Levy, Samuel 150 2
Levy, Thos S 124 2
Levy, W S 145 2
Levy, Wm S 144 2
Lewin, Celia 125 2
Lewin, Isaac 125 2
Lewis, Abraham 119 2
Lewis, Albert 119 2
Lewis, Alfred 107, 122, 153 2
Lewis, Alfred 75 3
Lewis, Alton 119 2
Lewis, Annie M 120 2
Lewis, B 169 2
Lewis, Basil 72, 122 2
Lewis, Beatrice May 122 2
Lewis, Benjamin S 128 2
Lewis, Bernard 58 1
Lewis, Bernard 107, 122, 171 2
Lewis, C F 124 3
Lewis, C J 59 1
Lewis, Carlton T 143 2
Lewis, Chas H 125 2
Lewis, Chas J 15, 78, 203 2
Lewis, Chas J 118, 152 1
Lewis, Clara E 128 2
Lewis, Claude 166 3
Lewis, Cloyd 129 2
Lewis, Cornelia A 122 2
Lewis, David 51 1
Lewis, David A 68, 145 1
Lewis, David O 128 2
Lewis, David R 166, 181 1
Lewis, Edna J 134 2
Lewis, Edw L 9 2
Lewis, Edw T 86 1
Lewis, Elizabeth 129 2
Lewis, Fairybelle E 167 2
Lewis, Florence M 131 2
Lewis, Frank N 43 2
Lewis, Geo J B 122 2
Lewis, George E 57 1
Lewis, Grace A 215 3
Lewis, Gracie A 172 2
Lewis, Grover C 120, 153 2
Lewis, H O 58 2

Lewis, Harry Lee 134 2
Lewis, Harry W 134 2
Lewis, J Hooker 150 2
Lewis, Jacob 138 2
Lewis, Jacob E 35 2
Lewis, Jeremiah 139 2
Lewis, John 119 2
Lewis, John R 154, 241 2
Lewis, John T 11, 68 1
Lewis, John T 290 2
Lewis, Laura 150 2
Lewis, Levi T 143, 144 2
Lewis, Madge A 145 2
Lewis, Madge A 21, 110 1
Lewis, Margaret Duvall 145 2
Lewis, Mary 119 2
Lewis, Mary A 144 2
Lewis, Mary C 92 3
Lewis, Mary Jane Elizabeth 145 2
Lewis, Mason L 134 2
Lewis, Minnie E 144 2
Lewis, Mollie F 134 2
Lewis, R R 213 2
Lewis, R Rush 129, 145 2
Lewis, R Rush 72 1
Lewis, Ralph F 155 2
Lewis, Richard C 160 3
Lewis, S A 123 1
Lewis, S A 128 2
Lewis, S A 141 3
Lewis, S B 181 1
Lewis, S J 161 3
Lewis, S W 169 2
Lewis, Sam 172 2
Lewis, Samuel 93, 150, 171 2
Lewis, Samuel A 32, 171, 179, 189 3
Lewis, Samuel A 151 2
Lewis, Samuel A 28 1
Lewis, Samuel B 156 1
Lewis, Samuel W 85 1
Lewis, Samuel W 150 2
Lewis, Sarah 9 2
Lewis, Sophia 150 2
Lewis, Thaddeus R 153 2
Lewis, Upton 132, 153 2
Lewis, Upton 9 3
Lewis, W E 154 2
Lewis, William F 84, 155 2
Lewis, Wm 89, 154 2
Lewis, Wm F 107, 154 2
Lewis, Wm L 60 1
Lewis, Wm T 137, 152 1
Lewis, Wm T 139, 154 2
L'Hedureaux, Joseph B 140 2
Liability Assurance Corp 68 3
Lichtenwaller, Abram [?] 30 1
Lichtenwalter, Abraham 40, 70, 79, 125 1
Lichtenwalter, Abram 26, 96 1
Lichty, Daniel A 83 2
Lickle, E D 217 3
Liday, Della R 143 2
Liday, Jack 140 2
Liday, Joseph 140 2
Liday, Leslie G 143 2
Liday, Mary C 145 2
Liday, Nicholas Jr 185 3
Liday, Sadie L 140 2
Lidie, Calvin 125 2
Lidie, Coleman J 125 2
Lidie, Coy 125 2
Lidie, Geo W 132 2
Lidie, Lydia A 143 2
Lidie, Sarah 132, 150 2
Lieb, J H 30 1
Liesch, Clara C 182 2
Ligget, John 138 2
Ligget, John E H 138 2
Ligget, Mary E 138 2
Liggett, John 198 2
Liggett, John H 139 2
Liggett, Julia A 8, 139 2
Lighder [sic], Henry 196 1
Lighder, Hannah 134 2
Lighder, Henry 134, 185 2
Lighder, Henry 213 3
Lighder, Henry 257 1
Lighder, Lawson 14 1
Lighder, Peter 134 2
Lighdert, Henry 134 2
Lighdert, Henry Sr 134 2
Lighdert, John (Ohio) 137 2
Lighter, Amanda E 144, 150 2
Lighter, Barbara 122 2
Lighter, Charlotte A R 124 2
Lighter, Chas D 124 2
Lighter, Chas H 143, 153 2
Lighter, Clarence F 124 2
Lighter, Daniel 89 2
Lighter, David 122 2
Lighter, Elizabeth 129 2
Lighter, Hazel N 124 2
Lighter, Henry 134, 144 2
Lighter, J K 148 2
Lighter, John 129 2
Lighter, John H 101, 122, 139, 144 2
Lighter, John H 42 3
Lighter, L C 139 2
Lighter, Lawson 143 2
Lighter, Martha J 145 2
Lighter, Mary 144 2
Lighter, Mary Jane 144 2
Lighter, Peter 144, 148 2
Lighter, Russell E 32, 33, 73 1
Lighter, Russell Lee 145 2
Lighter, S P 148 2
Lighter, Simon 129 2
Lighter, Simon P 150 2
Lighter, Virginia E 153 2
Lightner, Anna M 149 2
Lightner, Barbara 128 2
Lightner, Catherine S 140 2
Lightner, Clarence R 149 2
Lightner, Daniel J 128 2
Lightner, Frederick 41 1
Lightner, Frederick 131 2
Lightner, H M 134 2
Lightner, Harriet S 134 2
Lightner, Isaac 84 1
Lightner, Isaac 195 3
Lightner, Isaac 136 2
Lightner, Isaiah 51 2
Lightner, J D 131 2
Lightner, John 137, 138 2
Lightner, John E 140 2
Lightner, John H 41 1
Lightner, Johnathan C 41 1
Lightner, Joshua F 138 2
Lightner, Prestley J 138 2
Lightner, R S 131 2
Lightner, Rachel 137 2
Lightner, Robt H 149 2
Lightner, Wm 171 1
Lightner, Wm 138 2
Lilley, Samuel 91 1
Lilly, Amastasia 119 2
Lilly, Bertha J 142 2
Lilly, Catherine 124 2
Lilly, Elias 124 3
Lilly, Elias 152, 279 1
Lilly, Elias 129 2
Lilly, Geo W 189 1
Lilly, Helen Root 134 2
Lilly, Janatius 196 1
Lilly, Kelly J 142 2
Lilly, S L 2 2
Lilly, Samuel 150 2
Linah, Samuel L 35 2
Lincoln Nat Bank 76 1
Lincum, Mary 144 2
Lind, Abraham 147 2
Lind, D Walter 140 2
Lind, Jacob 106 3
Lind, Joseph R 140 2
Lind, Nicholas 147 2
Lind, Nicholas 137 2
Lindesy, Hamilton 187 3
Lindsay, Adam 144 2
Lindsay, Benjamin 137 2
Lindsay, Benjamin 52, 113 1
Lindsay, Benjamin 122, 137 2

Lindsay, C Irving 124 2
Lindsay, Clarence A 92, 135 1
Lindsay, Columbus 124 2
Lindsay, Columbus 147 1
Lindsay, Fannie M 27 1
Lindsay, Fannie M 140 2
Lindsay, G 119, 153 1
Lindsay, G 39 2
Lindsay, G 55 3
Lindsay, G M 33 1
Lindsay, Granville 84, 213 2
Lindsay, H 1, 38, 106, 176, 234, 272 1
Lindsay, H 55, 179, 182, 215 3
Lindsay, H 2, 8, 15, 20, 30, 72, 84, 128, 154 2
Lindsay, Hamilton 2, 9, 23, 41, 55 3
Lindsay, Hamilton 11, 19, 30, 39, 54, 66, 72, 89, 115, 122, 139, 166, 211, 213, 214, 225, 210a, 213a 2
Lindsay, Hamilton 27, 33, 41, 60, 67, 71, 72, 88, 92, 96, 100, 110, 125, 129, 132, 137, 147, 152, 165, 188, 194, 217, 229, 234, 252, 253, 257, 272, 279, 283 1
Lindsay, J Hamilton 283 1
Lindsay, John 137, 138, 139, 150 2
Lindsay, John 51 1
Lindsay, Joshua 107 1
Lindsay, Joshua L 140 2
Lindsay, Levi 138, 150 2
Lindsay, Lewis 138, 150 2
Lindsay, Margaret A 124 2
Lindsay, Margaret Ann 144 2
Lindsay, Russell H 46 3
Lindsay, S D 72 1
Lindsay, Sarah 150 2
Lindsay, Sarah E 124 2
Lindsay, Stephen A 150 2
Lindsay, T O 8 2
Lindsay, Thoma O 139 2
Lindsey, Benj 209 3
Lindsey, Grauntle 166 3
Lindsey, H 71, 106, 166, 187 3
Lindsey, Hamilton 102, 129, 187 3
Lindsey, Hamilton 227, 268, 276 2
Lindsey, Nicholas Sr 185 3
Linebaugh, Benjamin 122 2
Linebaugh, C 138 2
Linebaugh, Catherine 124 2
Linebaugh, Daniel 128, 144 2
Linebaugh, Ezra 129 2
Linebaugh, Howard 101 2
Linebaugh, John 137 2
Linebaugh, John H 128 2
Linebaugh, Jonathan 138 2
Linebaugh, Magdalene 144 2
Linebaugh, Samuel P 122 2
Lingetfelter, Wm 154 2
Lingg, Edna 145 2
Lingg, Geo B 134 2
Lingg, Henry M 134 2
Lingg, I H 145 2
Lingg, Joseph 134 2
Lingg, Margaret 144 2
Lingg, Margaret C 145 2
Lingg, Michael 144, 225a 2
Lingg, Rose E 149 2
Lingy, Henry 188 2
Link, Adam 119, 128 2
Link, D T 23 2
Link, Daniel 128 2
Link, Geo 119 2
Link, George 132 2
Link, Jacob 153 2
Link, Lewis 205 3
Link, Margaret A 132 2
Link, Thomas 153 2
Link, Thos 26, 186 1
Linn, Abraham 8, 70 3
Linn, Frank A 136 2
Linn, Henry 134 2
Linn, Ida E 136 2
Linn, Isaac 134, 136 2
Linthicum, Amanda S 119 2
Linthicum, Burwell H 122, 140 2
Linthicum, Cassidy 230 1
Linthicum, Cassidy 210 3
Linthicum, Cassidy 149 2
Linthicum, Charles M 124 2
Linthicum, Chas H 119 2
Linthicum, Edw F 129 2
Linthicum, Elinor 154 2
Linthicum, Elinore 124, 129 2
Linthicum, G Best 284 1
Linthicum, H F 154 2
Linthicum, James G 140 2
Linthicum, John L 138, 144, 149 2
Linthicum, John M 138 2
Linthicum, John W 154 2
Linthicum, Joseph N 154 2
Linthicum, Margaret 129 2
Linthicum, Margaret E 124 2
Linthicum, Mary 138, 149 2
Linthicum, Mary A 144 2
Linthicum, Philemon M 148 2
Linthicum, Rachel E 149 2
Linthicum, Robt 138 2
Linthicum, Robt E 149 2
Linthicum, Wm N 154 2
Linthicum, Wm T 154 2
Linton, Annie E 149 2
Linton, Barbara A 122 2
Linton, Benj 153 2
Linton, Benjamin 122 2
Linton, Charles E 42 1
Linton, Cornelius D 125 2
Linton, Edward 122 2
Linton, John T 137 2
Linton, Rachel 122 2
Linton, Raymond H 149 2
Linton, Roger W 125 2
Linton, Thomas O 153 2
Lippe, Geo 31 3
Lippe, J J 20 3
Lippe, John 18 3
Lipps, Alton J 153 2
Lipps, Annie 124 2
Lipps, Annie P 124 2
Lipps, Catharine E 124 2
Lipps, Catherine 124 2
Lipps, David 87 3
Lipps, Geo L 124 2
Lipps, J P 188 3
Lipps, John 197 1
Lipps, John 124 2
Lipps, John A C 124 2
Lipps, John G 138 2
Lipps, John H C 138 2
Lipps, Simon 215 3
Lipps, Thomas S 153 2
Lipps, Thos 124 2
Lipps, William D 153, 155 2
Lippy, Bessie 134 2
Lippy, Ellen 129, 144 2
Lippy, Harry 134 2
Lippy, I M 183 1
Lippy, Michael H 144 2
Lippy, Michael I 129 2
Lippy, Wm H 129 2
Lipscomb, Marian E 28 3
Lipscomb, Mary R 28 3
Lipscomb, Mary R 119 1
Lisean, John G 195 3
Lison, T Watkins 85 1
Litchenwalker, Abraham 110, 244 1
Litchenwalter, Abraham 27, 51, 169 2
Litchenwalter, Adam 11 2
Litchenwalter, Adam 253 1
Litener, Jacob 137 2
Lithbridge, Chas M 124 2
Lithbridge, Mary C 124 2
Litten, Catherine B 45 1
Litten, Catherine B 155 2
Litten, Sarah E 155 2
Litten, William A 155 2

Little, Agnes Lee 148 2
Little, Albert Mrs 109 1
Little, Anna M 90 2
Little, Chas J 124 2
Little, David 128 2
Little, Henry 134 2
Little, Henry A 134 2
Little, Henry E 163 2
Little, Jacob 93, 137 2
Little, Jesse 84 1
Little, John 1, 139 2
Little, John 84, 163, 186 1
Little, John L 39 2
Little, Joseph 22, 215a 2
Little, Maria 144 2
Little, Paul M 148 2
Little, Philomena 139 2
Littlefield, Fred 131 2
Littlefield, Minnie W 145 2
Littlejohn, Geo 211 2
Littlejohn, Geo 32 1
Littlejohn, Geo W 100 2
Littlejohn, George 132 2
Livers, Anthony 119 2
Livers, Arnold 144 2
Livers, Arnold 91, 152 1
Livers, Elizabeth M 129 2
Livers, Geo 129, 132 2
Livers, Geo 186 1
Livers, Ignatius 136 2
Livers, J F 237 2
Livers, James F 144 2
Livers, James I 71 1
Livers, Joseph 32 1
Livers, Joseph F 40, 42 1
Livers, Margaret 144 2
Livers, Mary 144 2
Livers, Mary H 132 2
Livers, Thomas 217a 2
Lizar, Nancy 150 2
Lizar, Solomon G 150 2
Lizer, Brickford 125 2
Lizer, Clara 125 2
ller, John 63 2
Lloyd, Alma C 119 2
Lloyd, Ernest C 119, 140 2
Lloyd, James 137 2
Lloyd, John R 140 2
Lloyd, John R 152 3
Lloyd, John R 71, 73 1
Lloyd, John W 140 2
Lloyd, John W 26 1
Lloyd, Nellie H 25 2
Loats, John 37, 73, 112, 193 1
Loats, John 49, 54, 119, 129, 138, 203, 237 2
Loats, John 186 3
Loch, Geo 57 1
Lochner, Alice J 154 2
Lochner, Barbara 122 2
Lochner, Charles H 125 2
Lochner, Ella F 44 1
Lochner, Harry 122, 125 2
Lochner, Julius 122, 147 2
Lochner, Julius F 125 2
Lochner, Julius F 23 3
Lochner, L 153 3
Lochner, Levin F 23 1
Lochner, Lewis 223 1
Lochner, Lewis F 143 2
Lochner, Mary 125 2
Lochner, Mollie R 145 2
Lochner, Nicholas 147 2
Lochner, R Angeline 194 1
Lochner, William M 154 2
Lochner, Wm H 73 1
Lochr, Frede ick 184 3
Lock, Cornelius H 217 3
Lock, Frederick 62, 132 2
Lock, Geo 22, 258 2
Lock, George 132 2
Lock, George 58 1
Lock, George 70, 165 3
Lock, John 144 1
Lock, John F 144, 159 2
Lock, John F 203, 237 1
Lock, John H 229 1
Lock, John H 159 2
Lock, Mary 144 2
Locke, Angeline 119 2
Locke, Frederick 185 3
Locke, Geo F 138 2
Locke, George 184 3
Locke, John 238 1
Locke, John F 138 2
Locke, John F 26 3
Locke, John H 138 2
Locket, Samuel 26 2
Lockhart, Margaret A 144 2
Logan, Mary 10 1
Logan, Patrick 149 2
Logan, Robt 149 2
Logsden, John 156 1
Logsden, John 137, 149 2
Logsdon, Joshua 137 2
Logsdon, Robt 149 2
Logue, Lewis 159, 234 1
Logue, Lewis 23, 165 3
Loher, Calvin 189 3
Lohr, Abraham 138, 139, 188 2
Lohr, Abraham 208 1
Lohr, Abram 119 2
Lohr, B Baltzer 122 2
Lohr, Calvin E 231 2
Lohr, Calvin S 19, 86, 101, 127, 153, 189, 243, 246, 270, 276 1
Lohr, Calvin S 10, 16, 154, 190, 220, 284 2
Lohr, Calvin S 21, 58, 169, 193 3
Lohr, Calvin S Agent 101 1
Lohr, Calvin S Anc 24 1
Lohr, Catharine 175 2
Lohr, David 122 2
Lohr, Elizabeth 129 2
Lohr, Harry C 119 2
Lohr, John 137, 138 2
Lohr, Joseph N 139 2
Lohr, Joseph Sr 137 2
Lohr, Lorena V 161 2
Lohr, Margaret A 139 2
Lohr, William E 154 2
Lond, Isaac 6 3
Lond, John A 6 3
Long, A 129 2
Long, A S 230 1
Long, Abraham 119, 128, 154 2
Long, Abraham 85 1
Long, Abrham S 119 2
Long, Absalom 119, 129 2
Long, Alice R 140 2
Long, Amanda 124 2
Long, Amy 125 2
Long, Anna 138 2
Long, Annie 154 2
Long, Annie M 132 2
Long, Benj F 122 2
Long, Benjamin F 233 1
Long, Blanche E 154 2
Long, Cahharine 124 2
Long, Calvin C 154 2
Long, Caroline 124 2
Long, Carrie F 154 2
Long, Catharine 124 2
Long, Charles 124 2
Long, Charles C 143 2
Long, Charles H 125 2
Long, Christopher 106 3
Long, Christopher 124, 137 2
Long, Christopher 240 1
Long, Clara E 125 2
Long, Clarence E 119 2
Long, Cynthiann 134 2
Long, Cyrus G 124 2
Long, Daisy 58 2
Long, Daisy H 140 2
Long, Daniel 57, 124, 128 2
Long, Daniel 279 1
Long, Edgar M 68 2
Long, Edw 89 2
Long, Edw A 129 2
Long, Edw P 139 2
Long, Edward P 125 2
Long, Elizabeth 129, 138 2
Long, Elizabeth S 149 2
Long, Emma C 129, 154 2
Long, F R 139 2

Long, Frank C 155 2
Long, Geo 46 2
Long, Geo 40 1
Long, Geo B 132 2
Long, Geo P 128 2
Long, Geo W 132 2
Long, George 57, 156 1
Long, Hannah M 145 2
Long, Harvey E 134 2
Long, Henrietta 138 2
Long, Henry 134, 144 2
Long, Henry M 188 3
Long, Isaac 124 2
Long, J A Dr 32 2
Long, J C 139 2
Long, J T 145 2
Long, Jacob 137, 138 2
Long, Jacob 196 1
Long, James 138, 148, 149 2
Long, James A 140 2
Long, James D 138 2
Long, James W 96 1
Long, James W 119, 139, 150, 138, 142 2
Long, James W 27 3
Long, John 137, 188 2
Long, John 62, 156, 164, 222 1
Long, John D 129, 144 2
Long, John D 48, 129 1
Long, John J 138 2
Long, John P 138, 139 2
Long, John S 119 2
Long, John S 118, 233 1
Long, John T 138, 139 2
Long, John T 41 1
Long, John T 42 3
Long, John W 119, 139, 144 2
Long, John W 118 1
Long, Jonas 137 2
Long, Joseph 118 1
Long, Joseph 87, 93, 137 2
Long, Joseph C 55 3
Long, Joseph H 139, 150 2
Long, Joseph I 140 2
Long, Joseph W 140 2
Long, Josephus 65 3
Long, Josephus 71 1
Long, Josephus 129, 138, 139 2
Long, Katie T 139 2
Long, L C 249 1
Long, Laura E 143 2
Long, Lawrence J 154 2
Long, Louise M 143 2
Long, Mabel 83 1
Long, Margaret C 144 2
Long, Margaret R 145, 148 2
Long, Maria 144 2
Long, Martin E 14 3
Long, Mary C 144 2
Long, Mary E 145 2
Long, Mary F 144 2
Long, Maston D 24 3
Long, Naomi O 14 1
Long, Norman L 122 2
Long, Olive S 3 3
Long, Patrick E 148 2
Long, Peter 143 3
Long, Philip H 148 2
Long, R E 253 1
Long, R E 290 2
Long, R E 2 3
Long, Raymond E 27 1
Long, Raymond E 149 2
Long, Raymond E 2, 20 3
Long, Rebecca 149 2
Long, Reuben 144 2
Long, Reuben 149 2
Long, Reuben A 149 2
Long, Robert 8, 165 3
Long, Roland E 134, 149 2
Long, Ruben 54, 152 3
Long, Russell 31 2
Long, Sam 230 1
Long, Samuel 235, 244, 270 1
Long, Samuel 143, 150 2
Long, Samuel 44, 141 3
Long, Sarah 124, 154 2
Long, Sarah B 150 2
Long, Sarah E 129, 139, 150 2
Long, Savilla C 150 2
Long, Susannah 150 2
Long, Verna J 140 2
Long, W H 208 1
Long, W Harvey 154 2
Long, Wilbur H 154 2
Long, William 116, 195, 199 3
Long, William H 155 2
Long, William V E 83 1
Long, Wilson A 154 2
Long, Wm 128, 148, 154, 208 2
Long, Wm D 31, 54, 154 2
Long, Wm F 154 2
Long, Wm H 56, 72 3
Long, Wm H 57, 119, 143, 154 2
Long, Wm V E 44 1
Long, Wm V E 124, 154 2
Longbrake, Harry F 28 3
Longerbeam, Mary H 149 2
Longerbeam, Robt O 149 2
Longley, Carrie V 129 2
Longley, Ernest F 129 2
Longman, Geo 138 2
Longman, George 132 2
Longman, Jacob 138 2
Longman, Jacob 184 3
Longman, Joshua 132 2
Longnecker Alfred Y 119 2
Longnecker, Jacob 138 2
Longnecker, John D 119, 151 2
Longnecker, Rebecca 138 2
Longnecker, Salomon 135 3
Longnecker, Sarah E 151 2
Longnecker, Solomon 55 3
Longwell, Jane 137 2
Loots, Chas A 151 2
Loots, Helen M 134, 140 2
Loots, John T 140 2
Loots, John Tolbert 151 2
Loots, Susan E 151 2
Loots, Susan E 151 2
Lorentz, Adam 152, 240 1
Lorentz, Elizabeth 129 2
Lorentz, Henry 46, 100, 129, 134 2
Lorentz, Henry 125, 263 1
Lorentz, Henry 26, 128 3
Lorentz, Jacob 138 2
Lorentz, Jacob 147, 245 1
Lorentz, John 138 2
Lorentz, Joseph 138 2
Lorenz, Ann Maria 119 2
Lorh, Calvin S 106 2
Lorigman, Jacob [sic] 163 1
Lortz, Jacob 139 2
Lortz, John G 138 2
Lortz, John H 139 2
Lortz, John L 138 2
Lortz, John W 140 2
Lortz, Sarah A 139 2
Lott, H 33 1
Loud, Helen 140, 149 2
Loud, John A 140 2
Loud, Roland J 149 2
Louge, Lewis 35 2
Lough, Chas W 153 2
Lough, Geo A 139 2
Lough, Geo W 65 3
Lough, J T 245 1
Lough, John Q 139 2
Lough, John Q 11 1
Lough, Mary A 139 2
Lough, U A 225 2
Lough, Uriah A 153 2
Loughran, Jerome A 97 1
Love, Robt 149 2
Love, Wm 154 2
Lovejoy, Sara C 151 2
Loveley, Emanuell 129 2
Loveley, Mary Ann 129 2
Lovell, Greenbury 132 2
Lovell, Isaac 210 1
Lovell, Isaac 30, 132 2
Lovell, Isaac 167, 179 3
Lovell, J Floyd 188 3
Loventz, Henry 250 2

Loventz, Wm 13 1
Low, Louise M 143 2
Lowe, Adelaide 252 2
Lowe, Adelaide E 158 3
Lowe, Adelaide V 133 1
Lowe, Adelaide V 81 3
Lowe, Alexander 57, 119, 154 2
Lowe, Christina 124 2
Lowe, E L 179 3
Lowe, E Lewis 81, 158 3
Lowe, E Lewis 217a, 252 2
Lowe, E Lewis 234 1
Lowe, Elizabeth 124, 129 2
Lowe, Henry 124 2
Lowe, J M 57 2
Lowe, James W 150 2
Lowe, John 30 1
Lowe, John 154, 237 2
Lowe, John M 81 3
Lowe, Joseph 59, 115, 210 1
Lowe, Joseph 235 2
Lowe, Mary 144 2
Lowe, Millard F 150 2
Lowe, Patrick 148, 163 2
Lowe, Patrick 59 1
Lowe, Patrick 202 3
Lowe, Philip 124, 129, 148 2
Lowe, Samuel 5 2
Lowe, Samuel A 150 2
Lowe, Samuel A 135, 214 1
Lowe, Sophia E 150 2
Lowe, Susan A 150 2
Lowe, Susan J 151 2
Lowe, Susan J 150 2
Lowe, Theodore 278 2
Lowe, Urith 153 2
Lowe, William Jr 160 3
Lowe, Wm 154 2
Lowe, Wm 279 1
Lowell, Adelaide V 217a 2
Lowell, Catherine E 125 2
Lowell, Charles 125 2
Lowell, Christiana 124 2
Lowell, Jacob 137 2
Lowell, John W 154 2
Lowell, Theodore W 125 2
Lowell, Wm 149, 154 2
Lowenstein, Clara 2 3
Lowenstein, Clara 125, 265 2
Lowenstein, D 2, 224 3
Lowenstein, David 46, 128, 199, 259, 277 2
Lowenstein, David 56, 124 3
Lowenstein, E 65 3
Lower, Solomon 150 2
Lower, Solomon 150 2
Lowery, Chas W 124 2
Lowery, Nancy 147 2
Lowery, Paul L 148 2
Lowery, Rachel A 124 2
Lowman, Amelia C 240 1
Lowman, Amelia C 119, 128 2
Lowman, Dennis C 128 2
Lowman, Harry A 134 2
Lowman, John 20 2
Lowman, Pearl May 134 2
Lowman, Samuel 128 2
Lowry, David S 148 2
Loy, Alice E 119 2
Loy, Alice K 279 1
Loy, C W 34 1
Loy, Eleanor M 129 2
Loy, Eliza Lycett 129 2
Loy, Elizabeth A 129 2
Loy, Emily I 129 2
Loy, Frederick 131 2
Loy, Henry 134 2
Loy, I N 9 2
Loy, Isaiah N 136 2
Loy, J Perkin 136 2
Loy, J Raymon 136 2
Loy, J W 144 2
Loy, John W 52, 208 1
Loy, John W 12 2
Loy, Martin D 144 2
Loy, Mary A 144 2
Loy, Park W T 129 2
Loy, Wm H 177 2
Loy, Wm H 229, 234 1
lrich, Ruth M Mrs 206 3
Luby, Alice 58 3
Lucas, Agnila 209 3
Lucas, Aquilla 119 2
Lucas, Charlotte L 262 2
Lucas, Dorothy E 3 3
Lucas, Jane (col'd) 137 2
Lucket, E H 71 1
Luckett, Ann E 119 2
Luckett, Chas Gill 147 2
Luckett, Chas McGill 124 2
Luckett, Clarissa 124 2
Luckett, Clarissa 88 1
Luckett, E H 119 2
Luckett, Elinor H 144 2
Luckett, Elinore 129 2
Luckett, Joshua 124 2
Luckett, Josiah 117 1
Luckett, Lloyd 150, 163 2
Luckett, Lucinda 143 2
Luckett, Lucinda M 144 2
Luckett, M B 133, 260 1
Luckett, M B 28, 129 2
Luckett, M B 81, 207 3
Luckett, M P 156, 160 3
Luckett, Mary B 144 2
Luckett, Mont Joy B [sic] 193 1
Luckett, Monutezoy B 87 3
Luckett, Morentjob 286 2
Luckett, Mount Joy 119, 144 2
Luckett, Mount Joy B 222 1
Luckett, Mt Joy B 143 2
Luckett, Mt Joy B 88 1
Luckett, Nelson 150 2
Luckett, Nelson 124, 147, 150 2
Luckett, Samuel 150, 154 2
Luckett, Serena 150 2
Luckett, WF 264 1
Luckett, Wm 154 2
Luckie, Edwina L 126 1
Lucus, John 137 2
Ludig, Daniel 128 2
Ludwick, Elsie M 119 2
Ludwig, Adolph 119 2
Ludwig, Albert E 119 2
Ludwig, Geo 257 1
Ludwig, Gertrude 132 2
Ludwig, Mary 144 2
Ludy, Cyrus M 139 2
Ludy, Daniel 100, 254 2
Ludy, David 128 2
Ludy, Jacob 101, 128, 138 2
Ludy, Joseph A 139 2
Ludy, Michael 138 2
Ludy, Nicholas 100, 137, 144, 147, 237, 254 2
Ludy, Nicholas 186 3
Ludy, Nicholas Jr 152 1
Ludy, Wm 128, 147 2
Ludy, Wm 84 1
Lueber, Francis 156, 176 1
Luft, Juliana 137 2
Lugembeel, Wm 137 2
Lugenbaugh, Jonothan 205 3
Lugenbeal, William 160 3
Lugenbeall, Peter 79 1
Lugenbeel, Charles H 125 2
Lugenbeel, Chas H 153 2
Lugenbeel, Elizabeth C 138 2
Lugenbeel, J S 144 2
Lugenbeel, John 11, 22, 137, 154, 181, 247 2
Lugenbeel, John 23, 142, 184 3
Lugenbeel, John 79, 96, 144, 163, 205 1
Lugenbeel, John H 138, 154 2
Lugenbeel, Laura V 125 2
Lugenbeel, Louisa 143 2
Lugenbeel, Margaret 144 2
Lugenbeel, Martha 148 2
Lugenbeel, Moses 80, 144 2
Lugenbeel, P 1 1
Lugenbeel, P 35 2
Lugenbeel, P J 21 1

Lugenbeel, Peter 128, 144, 148, 153, 221, 222, 227, 212a, 282 2
Lugenbeel, Peter 9, 41, 55, 160, 163, 209 3
Lugenbeel, Peter 37, 41, 60, 79, 100, 118, 125, 150, 245 1
Lugenbeel, Sarah 150 2
Lugenbeel, T E S 79 1
Lugenbeel, T E S 113 2
Lugenbeel, Thomas 222 2
Lugenbeel, Thomas E S 153 2
Lugenbeel, Thos 181 1
Lugenbeel, Thos E 37 1
Lugenbeel, Wi liam 184 3
Lugenbeel, William 185 3
Lugenbeel, Wm 27, 150, 154 2
Lugenbeel, Wm 205 1
Lugenbell, Peter 163 2
Luginsland, David 283 1
Luginsland, David 128 2
Luid, John 137 2
Luid, Judith 137 2
Lukenland, Catherine 124 2
Lulick, Jacob 55 1
Lung, Jacob 137 2
Lung, Susannah 150 2
Luther, M 23 2
Lutman, C Arthur 18 2
Lutman, Cecilia V 154 2
Lutman, Claud 129 2
Lutman, W Claude 40, 154 2
Lutman, W Claude 152 3
Lutman, William G 154 2
Lutman, Wm 40 2
Lutz, Francis A 137 1
Lutz, Frank 126 1
Lutz, Isaac A 150 2
Lutz, J Franklin 140 2
Lutz, Jennie 259 2
Lutz, John 138, 140, 177 2
Lutz, John Elmer 140 2
Lutz, John H 140 2
Lutz, John Lewis 139 2
Lutz, L W 139 2
Lutz, L Walter 145 2
Lutz, Martin L 145 2
Lutz, Mary E 138, 145 2
Lutz, Mary Maud 126 1
Lutz, Michael 9 3
Lutz, Paul E 140 2
Lutz, Sarah 150 2
Luug, Ann 119 2
Lycett, Thomas E 153 2
Lych, Edw A 203 2
Lydes, Thomas 153 2
Lydes, Thomas 153 2
Lyles, Bessie N 122 2
Lyles, Earl W 122, 129 2
Lyles, Ernest M 129 2
Lyles, Nepier 3 3
Lyles, Thomas 153 2
Lyles, Thos 51 1
Lynch, Ed 234 2
Lynch, Edw 76 2
Lynch, Edw A 129 2
Lynch, Edward A 268 2
Lynch, Eliza H 129 2
Lynch, Ellen 129, 154 2
Lynch, Eugene 203 2
Lynch, James A 254 2
Lynch, John 5, 136, 159, 223a 2
Lynch, John 71, 248 1
Lynch, John 171 3
Lynch, John A 1, 19, 39, 54, 70, 160 3
Lynch, John A 29, 38, 129, 139, 144, 153, 197, 222, 231, 264, 282 2
Lynch, John A 71, 117, 118, 135, 137, 197, 214, 264 1
Lynch, Martha D 144 2
Lynch, Theresa 153 2
Lynch, William 51, 58 1
Lynch, William 207 3
Lynch, William 258, 275 2
Lynch, Wm 176 3
Lynch, Wm 57, 76, 117, 260, 263, 264 1
Lynch, Wm 14, 27, 72, 75, 137, 139, 154, 203, 208, 214 2
Lynch, Wm B 154 2
Lynch, Wm F 129 2
Lynch, Wm S 129 2
Lynd, Joseph 137 2
Lynn, Abraham 119 2
Lynn, Abram 38 3
Lynn, Adam 153 2
Lynn, Eve 129 2
Lynn, Henry 137 2
Lynn, Joseph 70 3
Lynn, Joseph 138 2
Lynn, Lee E 143 2
Lynn, Lewis L (Louis) 143 2
Lynn, Louis 143 2
Lynn, Luther S 143 2
Lynn, Maria L 144 2
Lynn, Nicholas 210a 2
Lynn, Wm A 144 2
Lyon, Isaac 11 2
Lyon, Susanna 150 2
Lyons, Robert W 256 1
Lyons, Wm 154 2
Lyter, S Elma 52 1
Lytle, Catherine 59 1
Lytle, Catherine 124 2
Lyvers, Jane 139 2
Lyvers, Wm E 139 2
Lyzar, James A 139 2
Mace, Elsie L 210 1
MacGill Rachel E 206 2
MacGill, Amelia 205 2
MacGill, Chas G 166 2
MacGill, Jennie 191 2
MacGill, Rachel G 166 2
MacGill, Robt H 205 2
MacGill, Wm E 206 2
Mackall, Benjamin 78 2
Mackenzie, Charles 170 2
Mackenzie, Daniel A 170 2
Mackenzie, George H 190 2
Mackenzie, James E 190 2
Mackenzie, Sherwood A 170 2
Mackenzie, W B 190 2
Mackley J Roscoe 190 2
Mackley J William 190 2
Mackley, Chas M 270 1
Mackley, Chas M 190 2
Mackley, Chas M 166 3
Mackley, Edwin O 200 2
Mackley, Howard E 195 2
Mackley, J Wm 274 2
Mackley, James I 190 2
Mackley, Laura V 195 2
Mackley, Mary C 190 2
Mackley, Mildred 200 2
Mackley, S I 265 1
Mackley, Samuel 195 2
MacPherson, Harriet A 181 2
MacPherson, Thomas B 181 2
Macubin, James 85 1
Madary, Andrew 159 2
Madary, Nettie 202 2
Madary, Nicholas 159 2
Madden, Regina S 126 1
Maddox, Samuel 96, 159, 201, 270 1
Magaha, Allen R 189 2
Magaha, Clarence C 166 2
Magaha, Daisy M 196 2
Magaha, G Ernest 52 2
Magaha, George Wm 178 2
Magaha, Irvin Conard 178 2
Magaha, Joseph 189 2
Magaha, K Blanche 47 2
Magaha, L F 166 2
Magaha, Lee W 196 2
Magaha, Luther F 196 2
Magaha, Margaret 198 2
Magaha, William C 215 2
Magaha, Wm 166 2
Magalis, Amos 206 2
Magalis, Camille E 209 2
Magalis, Harman 209 2
Magalis, Richard M 190, 206 2
Magalis, Rosa 206 2
Mager, Daniel 117 1
Magers, Abdiel E 159 2

Magill, Clara Woods 167 2
Maginnis, Mary 197 2
Maginnis, Matthew 197 2
Magruder, A F 206 2
Magruder, C L 172 1
Magruder, Elias 186 2
Magruder, Ellen C 171 2
Magruder, John 26 1
Magruder, John 185 2
Magruder, John R 40, 104 1
Magruder, John R 186 2
Magruder, Maria V 197 2
Magruder, Mary L 125, 150, 199 2
Magruder, Mary Louisa 198 2
Magruder, Nathan 202 2
Magruder, Rufas H 199 2
Magruder, Rufus 150 2
Magruder, Rufus H 125, 205, 206, 217 2
Magruder, Rufus K 205 2
Magruder, Zachariah 150 2
Magruder, Zachariah C 151, 199, 217 2
Maguire, Paul E 213 3
Maher, Thomas F Jr 28 1
Mahn, Geo 177, 197 2
Mahnoey, Wm [sic] 194 1
Mahon, Bernard 163 2
Mahoney Charles W 167 2
Mahoney, Blanche 214 2
Mahoney, Blanche 11 1
Mahoney, Blanche Ahalt 14 1
Mahoney, Charles R 202 2
Mahoney, John F 167 2
Mahoney, John J 190 2
Mahoney, Lewis 195 2
Mahoney, Mary J 214 2
Mahoney, Nellie V 167, 202 2
Mahoney, W 203 3
Mahoney, W 179 1
Mahoney, William 139 3
Mahoney, William 71 1
Mahoney, Wm 84, 139, 177, 195, 197, 225, 260, 264 1
Mahoney, Wm 81, 113 3
Mahoney, Wm 5, 39, 137 2
Mahoney, Wm J 214 2
Mahoney, Wm M 214 2
Mahony, Wm [sic] 13 1
Mahugh, Edw [sic] 228 1
Main, Ada S 199 2
Main, Adam 26, 159 2
Main, Alta M 219 1
Main, Ann E 159 2
Main, Annie M 160 2
Main, Annie S 189 2
Main, Annie S 31 1
Main, Arthur 160 2
Main, Austin L 12 1
Main, C A 189 2
Main, C E 171 3
Main, C F 119 2
Main, Cameron 159 2
Main, Carrie 32 1
Main, Charles F 167 2
Main, Charlotte 165 2
Main, Charlotte M 165 2
Main, Chas 175 2
Main, Chas E 189 2
Main, Clara A 178 2
Main, Clayton E 166 2
Main, Clinton E 167 2
Main, Clinton S 195 2
Main, Clyde D 199 2
Main, Cora J 171 2
Main, Cornelia 166 2
Main, Cornelius M 166 2
Main, Daisy M 45 3
Main, Daniel 41, 71, 165, 174, 202 3
Main, Daniel 54, 175, 187, 208, 231 2
Main, Daniel 37, 72, 91, 152, 196 1
Main, Daniel A 169 2
Main, David 150, 169, 197, 198 2
Main, David I 159, 169 2
Main, David M 165, 169, 198 2
Main, Edw M 171 2
Main, Elijah 208 2
Main, Elizabeth 59 1
Main, Elizabeth 172, 175, 208 2
Main, Ernest L 9, 189 2
Main, Ernest L 11 3
Main, F J 187 2
Main, Frances E 41 1
Main, Frederick 159, 175, 211 2
Main, Frederick T 71 3
Main, Frederick T 119, 175 2
Main, Frederick W 214 2
Main, Frederick W 51, 194, 225 1
Main, Frederick Z 118 1
Main, G M 169 2
Main, Geo 150 1
Main, Geo 176 3
Main, Geo 159, 166, 175, 177, 198 2
Main, Geo A 178 2
Main, Geo C 178, 189 2
Main, Geo C 147 1
Main, Geo J 110 2
Main, Geo W 209 2
Main, George 196 1
Main, George Wm 178 2
Main, Gladys V 196 2
Main, Grayson E 225 1
Main, Harriet I 189 2
Main, Helen B 223 3
Main, Isaiah 184 2
Main, J F 150 2
Main, J Fred 190 2
Main, J W 9 2
Main, Jacob 187 2
Main, Jesse 69 2
Main, John 186, 188, 208, 209 2
Main, John A 186 2
Main, John C 178, 189 2
Main, John J 187, 208 2
Main, John W 189 2
Main, Jonathan 189 1
Main, Jonathan 169 2
Main, Jonathan C 165, 169, 172, 189, 198 2
Main, Joseph D 13 1
Main, Joseph D 189 2
Main, Joshua 19, 187, 188 2
Main, Joshua D 189 2
Main, Joshua H 40, 184, 190 2
Main, Joshua H 27 3
Main, Joshua T 189 2
Main, L A 198 2
Main, L H 124 3
Main, Lewis 209 2
Main, Lewis H 51 1
Main, Lewis H 22, 112, 195 2
Main, Lewis T 196 2
Main, Lulu 160 2
Main, Lydia A 177 2
Main, M G 189 2
Main, Margaret R 199 2
Main, Marion F 198 2
Main, Martha 188 2
Main, Martha M 199 2
Main, Mary 197 2
Main, Mary Ann 197 2
Main, Mary M 198 2
Main, Maurice G 6 3
Main, Maurice G 166 2
Main, Mollie 209 2
Main, Nora Virginia 167 2
Main, Pauline Ruth 93 1
Main, Philip Keefer 44 1
Main, Rachel 205 2
Main, Roger L 166 2
Main, Russell U 167, 196 2
Main, S 13 1
Main, Salome 209 2
Main, Sarah 187, 208, 209 2
Main, Sophia B 166 2
Main, Sophia E 209 2
Main, Susan A R 208 2

Main, Thomas 209 2
Main, W 186 2
Main, William H 160 2
Main, William I 215 2
Main, Wm 71 3
Main, Wm 27, 177, 214 2
Main, Wm F 188 2
Main, Wm H 51 1
Maine, Daniel 159 1
Maine, Ella M 182 2
Mainhart, Daniel 28 2
Major, Ida Pauline 196 2
Major, L E 265 2
Major, Leonard E 196 2
Majors, Elias 171 2
Majors, Greenbury 237 2
Malambre, Emiline H 177 2
Malambre, Geo 177 2
Malambre, Jacob 185 2
Malambre, John 177, 185, 187 2
Maler, E P [sic] J 210 1
Malloney, James 51 1
Malloy, Arthur H 161 2
Malloy, Arthur H 113 3
Malloy, Mary Frances 161 2
Malone, John 187 2
Malone, Minnie 206 2
Manahan, Arby R 163 2
Manahan, Bessie E 163 2
Manahan, Chas 124 2
Manahan, Chas F 166, 277 2
Manahan, Cyrus B 166 2
Manahan, D J 181 2
Manahan, Daniel I 165 3
Manahan, Daniel J 169 2
Manahan, David 169 2
Manahan, Dennis 169 2
Manahan, E L 181 2
Manahan, Francis M 215 2
Manahan, Geo 49 2
Manahan, Geo 124 2
Manahan, Geo M 182 2
Manahan, Geo W 160, 215 2
Manahan, Geo W 72 3
Manahan, Geo W 38, 62, 92, 250 1
Manahan, George W 90 1
Manahan, Henry 181 2
Manahan, Jonas 187 2
Manahan, Leo R 163 2
Manahan, Marie L 163 2
Manahan, Silas L 85 1
Manahan, Susannah 118 2
Manahan, Victor M 169 2
Manahan, Wm T 166 2
Manchey, Mary 197 2
Manford, Lottie F 195 2
Mangans, J F 199 3
Mangans, J H 199 3
Manhattan, Geo 112 2
Manion, Annie E 161 2
Manion, James O 191 2
Manion, Walter V 191 2
Manion, William V 69, 161 2
Mann, Ann M 160 2
Mann, Chas B 160 2
Mann, Luther 169 1
Mannaing, E D 187 2
Manning, Chas 96 3
Manning, Chas A 177 2
Manning, E J 96 3
Manning, Emily F 96 3
Manning, John 187 2
Manning, Patrick 187 2
Mannix, Margery 177 1
Manroe, Jonathan 186 2
Manroe, Richard M 186 2
Mans, Anna Mary 159 2
Mans, Nicholas 32 1
Mansfield, W A 154 2
Manson, Elijah 171 2
Manson, Eliza A 171 2
Manstadt, Cecilia 165 2
Manstadt, Charles F 165 2
Mantx, Chas 40 3
Mantz, Annie R 161 2
Mantz, Barbara A 175 2
Mantz, Barbara Ann 163 2
Mantz, C Casper 294 2
Mantz, Casper 44, 47, 59 1
Mantz, Casper 53, 70, 205 3
Mantz, Casper 27, 111, 165, 171, 175, 185, 247, 275 2
Mantz, Catherine 165 2
Mantz, Charles 294 2
Mantz, Charles 41, 226 3
Mantz, Chas 47, 70, 76, 82, 84, 106, 135, 139, 150, 208, 223, 238, 262, 263, 271 1
Mantz, Chas 9, 41, 129 3
Mantz, Chas 29, 80, 84, 87, 115, 132, 159, 171, 181, 186 2
Mantz, Curtiss 31 3
Mantz, Cyres 64 3
Mantz, Cyrus 31, 37, 70, 217 3
Mantz, Cyrus 51, 111, 171 2
Mantz, Cyrus 196, 249 1
Mantz, E 249 1
Mantz, Edw 271 1
Mantz, Edw 11, 171 2
Mantz, Edward M 41 2
Mantz, Eliza 171, 202, 203 2
Mantz, Elizabeth M 171 2
Mantz, Eller 172 2
Mantz, Emanuel Peter 172 2
Mantz, Ezra 116 1
Mantz, Ezra 224a 2
Mantz, Francis 175 2
Mantz, Francis M 175 2
Mantz, Frank 161, 182 2
Mantz, Gideon 279 1
Mantz, Helen 172 2
Mantz, Henry 161, 182, 199 2
Mantz, Henry 81 3
Mantz, Isaac 88 1
Mantz, Isaac 214 2
Mantz, John 186, 247 2
Mantz, John 87 3
Mantz, John A 40 1
Mantz, Lewis 116 3
Mantz, Louisa 165, 171, 195 2
Mantz, Madora W 199 2
Mantz, Maggie 199 2
Mantz, Nannie 199 2
Mantz, Nellie B 16, 41 2
Mantz, Nicholas 202 2
Mantz, Peter 54, 84, 197, 203 2
Mantz, Peter 185 3
Mantz, Peter 79, 271 1
Mantz, Peter Jr 203 2
Mantz, Peter Sr 203 2
Mantz, Silas 5 2
Mantz, W Levy 182 2
Mantz, William 161 2
Mantz, William 122 3
Mantz, Wm 176 3
Mantz, Wm 203 2
Maple, Alfred 107 3
Maples, A B Kemp 85 2
Maples, Annie K 108 2
Maples, S W 85 2
Maples, Sam W 108 2
Maran, J J 100 1
Marble, Danforth 169 2
Marble, Morris A 198 2
Marcilly, Emma 171 2
Marcilly, Zulma 171, 217 2
Marguam, Philip M 171 1
Marguette, Sarah 209 2
Maring, Frederick 175 2
Maring, Geo 175 2
Maring, John 175 2
Marino, Anthony 160 2
Marino, Catharina 167, 178 2
Marino, Giuseppe 178 2
Marino, Lucy 209 2
Marino, Samuel 209 2
Marino, Vincenza 160 2
Maris, Geo W 110 2
Maritt, Maria E (Col'd) 198 2
Mark, James 116 1
Mark, James 293 2
Mark, Peter 203 2
Markell, C 71 3

Markell, C E 78 1
Markell, Caroline 175 2
Markell, Chas 175, 187, 195 2
Markell, E C 2, 12, 25, 177, 178 2
Markell, E C 10, 56, 172 3
Markell, E C 110, 123, 144, 183, 245, 249 1
Markell, E C [?] 266 1
Markell, Edw C 52 1
Markell, Edw C 72, 92 2
Markell, Edwin 65, 66, 166 2
Markell, Edwin C 73, 91, 92, 126, 137, 166, 197 1
Markell, Edwin C 10, 27, 87 3
Markell, Edwin C 20, 31, 76, 96, 129, 172, 175, 189, 199 2
Markell, Elizabeth 172, 209 2
Markell, F 220 2
Markell, Frances 165 2
Markell, Frances C O 175 2
Markell, Frances Oakes 215 2
Markell, Francis 72, 124, 165, 175, 186, 187, 195 2
Markell, Francis 106 3
Markell, Francis 100, 239 1
Markell, Francis E 32 1
Markell, Frank 264 2
Markell, Frederick 26, 118 1
Markell, Frederick 175 2
Markell, Geo 46, 78, 124, 165, 171, 177, 187, 195, 197, 202, 208 2
Markell, Geo 60, 85, 186, 253 1
Markell, Geo 50, 106 3
Markell, Geo 50 3
Markell, George 90, 213 1
Markell, George 186 3
Markell, George 227 2
Markell, J R 138 2
Markell, Jacob 32 1
Markell, Jacob 23, 106 3
Markell, Jacob 27, 186, 187, 197, 208 2
Markell, John 30 1
Markell, John 38, 124, 209 3
Markell, John 65, 119, 163, 187, 197, 214, 228a 2
Markell, John J 186 2
Markell, John U 189, 199 2
Markell, John U 10 3
Markell, John Usher 200 2
Markell, L 179 3
Markell, L 208 2
Markell, Lewis 50, 106 3
Markell, Lewis 171, 187, 195, 197, 202 2
Markell, Louis 165, 195, 220 2
Markell, Mary 197 2
Markell, Mary G 189, 199 2
Markell, Mary K 195 2
Markell, Mary L 116, 200 2
Markell, Mary L 195 1
Markell, Mary L 172 3
Markell, Samuel 186, 208 2
Markell, Samuel 210 1
Markell, Sophia 209 2
Markell, Thomas 46 2
Markell, Thomas 26 3
Markell, Thomas M 9 3
Markell, Thos 186 2
Markell, Thos M 39, 208 2
Markell, Victor M 61 1
Markell, William 214 2
Markell, William A 215 2
Markell, Wm A 172 2
Marken, J R 208 2
Marken, Jacob 234 1
Marken, John 187, 208 2
Marken, John R 40 3
Marken, Joshua 187 2
Marken, Samuel 35, 208 2
Marken, Sue B 213 2
Marken, Victor M 213 2
Marken, Wesley 214 2
Marker, Bettie 163 2
Marker, Betty R 10 1
Marker, Charles W 229a 2
Marker, D D 170 2
Marker, Daniel 68, 100 1
Marker, Daniel 169, 195 2
Marker, David 203 2
Marker, Elizabeth A 178 2
Marker, Ezra 203 2
Marker, Fern 170 2
Marker, Geo Jr 137 2
Marker, Geo W 178 2
Marker, George 37 3
Marker, Howard C 163 2
Marker, John 26, 185, 187, 237 2
Marker, John 116 1
Marker, Lewis 195 2
Marker, Mary A 199 2
Marker, Michael 100, 197 2
Marker, Peter 175 1
Marker, Peter 89, 93, 100, 187, 197, 203 2
Marker, Rachel H 205 2
Marker, Sallie R 48 1
Marker, Vera V 163 2
Market, F A 81 3
Market, Peter 75 3
Markey, Bertha L 163 2
Markey, Chas E 169 2
Markey, D J 28, 115 2
Markey, D J 71 1
Markey, D J 31 3
Markey, David 37, 164, 214 1
Markey, David J 51, 67, 88, 112, 164, 219, 228, 249 1
Markey, David J 165, 169, 271 2
Markey, David J 9 3
Markey, Edith 172, 199 2
Markey, Emanuel S 107 1
Markey, F A 91 1
Markey, F A 1, 208 2
Markey, F J 22 1
Markey, Frederick 175 2
Markey, Frederick A 175 2
Markey, G H 169 2
Markey, Ida 166 3
Markey, Ida 208 2
Markey, Ida M 188 2
Markey, J H 19, 32, 126, 160 3
Markey, J H 39, 150, 175, 188, 238, 276 2
Markey, J H 60, 67, 104, 253 1
Markey, J Hanshew 188 2
Markey, John 144 1
Markey, John H 59 1
Markey, Lucy E 195 2
Markey, Manelia S 175, 199 2
Markey, Mary V 199 2
Markey, Susan 169, 208 2
Markey, William H 163 2
Markezy, D J 205 3
Markle, Magdalene 202 2
Markle, Nicholas 202 2
Marlow, Edw 171 2
Marlow, Geo 171 2
Marlow, Hanson 28, 171, 181 2
Marlow, Hanson 283 1
Marlow, Mary 164 1
Marlow, Mary 198, 211 2
Marlow, Mary O 172 1
Marlow, Mary O 214 2
Marlow, Mary Olivia 198 2
Marlow, Thomas 225 1
Marlow, Thomas J 211 2
Marlow, Thos 163 1
Marlow, Thos 11 2
Marlow, Viola 213 2
Marlow, Wm 164 1
Marlow, Wm G 211, 214 2
Marlowe, Ann R 171 2
Marlowe, Eliza 171 2
Marlowe, Hanson 96 3
Marman, Ann E 159 2
Marman, E C 43 3
Marman, Washington P 159 2
Marmon, Thos 81 3
Marquam, Philip W 119 2
Marquart, Michael 26 1
Marquertz, Geo 177 2
Marquette, Hamon V 209 2

Marquette, John M 190, 209 2
Marriot, A W 282 2
Marriott, A W 14, 43, 45, 54, 134, 197 2
Marriott, A W 12, 91, 106, 118 1
Marriott, A W 106 3
Marriott, Adella 159 2
Marriott, Alpheus W 251 2
Marriott, Alphwna W 102 3
Marriott, Chas W 166 2
Marriott, Howard M 209 2
Marriott, M L 209 2
Marriott, Susan A E 222 1
Marriott, Susan E 166, 209 2
Marrone, Carmelo 167 2
Marronne, Josephine 167 2
Marsden, Geo 178 2
Marsh, Edw James 157 1
Marsh, Elizabeth 185, 205 2
Marsh, Geo W P 19 3
Marsh, Harriet S 203 2
Marsh, Henry H 181 2
Marsh, Joel 185 2
Marsh, Julia A 189 2
Marsh, M Margaret 189 3
Marsh, M Margaret 203 2
Marsh, Margaret 157 1
Marsh, Mason R 245 1
Marsh, Mason R 197 2
marsh, Paul E 203 2
Marshall, Ann P 205, 231 2
Marshall, Ann Peed 160 2
Marshall, Belva 136 1
Marshall, Daisy L 169 2
Marshall, Harriet M 181 2
Marshall, J 41 1
Marshall, Maurice S 56 3
Marshall, Nannie 181 2
Marshall, R H 64 3
Marshall, R H 57, 80, 165 2
Marshall, Richard 49, 78, 165, 186, 247 2
Marshall, Richard H 71, 91 3
Marshall, Richard H 47, 70, 88, 91, 92, 163, 193 1
Marshall, Richard H 14, 181, 205, 246, 264, 267, 275 2
Mart, Charls S 167 2
Martell, Helen C 196 2
Martell, Jacob 187 2
Martell, Louis P 196 2
Martin, A B Iah 220 3
Martin, Abiah 160, 187 2
Martin, Adrian Arthur 161 2
Martin, Adrian L 160 2
Martin, Alexander 159 2
Martin, Ann E 159 2
Martin, Ann S 160 2
Martin, Anna E 177 1
Martin, Anna L 160 2
Martin, Anne B 159 2
Martin, Annie 169 2
Martin, Augustus A 159 2
Martin, Bessie A 172 2
Martin, Burnell D 160 2
Martin, C R 125 2
Martin, Catherine 165 2
Martin, Charles J 170 2
Martin, Charles R 167 2
Martin, Charles W 167 2
Martin, Daniel 128, 275 2
Martin, Daniel 275 2
Martin, David 18, 46, 159, 169, 197 2
Martin, David 201, 228 1
Martin, David C 187 2
Martin, David S 217 1
Martin, David W 170 2
Martin, Edw 119, 172 2
Martin, Elizabeth 185 2
Martin, Elizabeth E 58 3
Martin, Ella Cassandra 172 2
Martin, Emma A 172 2
Martin, Emma C 190 2
Martin, Emma C 88 1
Martin, F R 209 2
Martin, Fannie M 215 1
Martin, Geo 240 1
Martin, Geo 14, 38, 177 2
Martin, Geo T 177 2
Martin, Geo W 186, 190 2
Martin, George 82 1
Martin, George 177 2
Martin, Goldie M 241 2
Martin, Grace 172 2
Martin, Hallie 215 2
Martin, Hannah 214 2
Martin, Henrietta 181, 187 2
Martin, Henry 181 2
Martin, Howard 199 2
Martin, J P 160 2
Martin, J T 70 2
Martin, Jacob 185 2
Martin, Jacob C 215 2
Martin, James A 161 2
Martin, James P 160 2
Martin, Jennie C 188 2
Martin, Jeremiah 159 1
Martin, Jeremiah 115, 118, 144, 165, 188, 189 2
Martin, John 28, 159, 177, 186, 187 2
Martin, John 171, 212 3
Martin, John A 205 3
Martin, John A 1, 187 2
Martin, John A 118 1
Martin, John D 188 2
Martin, John T 190 2
Martin, John W 188 2
Martin, Joseph 28, 144, 187, 188 2
Martin, Joseph 110 1
Martin, Joseph E 188 2
Martin, Julia 172 2
Martin, Justice 101 2
Martin, Kai F 167 2
Martin, Maggie E 198 2
Martin, Mary C 190 2
Martin, Mary E 177, 199 2
Martin, Mary Jane 198 2
Martin, Mary M 197 2
Martin, Mathias 115 2
Martin, Mollie 197 2
Martin, Patrick F 203 2
Martin, Patrick F Jr 203 2
Martin, Paul K 241 2
Martin, Peter 203 2
Martin, Peter 71, 213 3
Martin, Richard 179 1
Martin, Richard C 205 2
Martin, Richard C 171 3
Martin, Richard C 52 1
Martin, Ross 172 2
Martin, Samuel J 209 2
Martin, Sarah M 172 2
Martin, Tobias 144 3
Martin, Tobias Washington 170 2
Martin, W J 107 3
Martin, W J 264 2
Martin, William C 215 2
Martin, William J 215 2
Martin, William J 56, 107 3
Martin, Wm 163 2
Martin, Wm H 159, 181 2
Martin, Wm J 110, 125, 253 1
Martin, Wm J 214 2
Martz, Barbara Ann 163 2
Martz, Bertha May 163 2
Martz, Chas C 181 2
Martz, Christopher C 166 2
Martz, Cyrus 96 2
Martz, Cyrus 40 1
Martz, Daniel 169 2
Martz, David S 169 2
Martz, Deborah 169, 214 2
Martz, Ella V 215 2
Martz, F M 163 2
Martz, Geo 169, 177 2
Martz, Geo D 22, 177 2
Martz, George 222 3
Martz, George D 219a 2
Martz, George S 178 2
Martz, George, Maj 13 1
Martz, Harriet 169, 177 2
Martz, Harriet E 181 2

Martz, Harvey D 163 2
Martz, Hazel L 219 1
Martz, J H 163 2
Martz, James 197 2
Martz, John 179 1
Martz, John 229a 2
Martz, John 8 2
Martz, John H 2, 119, 190 2
Martz, John W 190 2
Martz, Kiefer H 82 1
Martz, L J 203 3
Martz, Lewis 169 2
Martz, Lewis F 209 2
Martz, Lewis F 57, 62 3
Martz, Lewis J 145 1
Martz, Lewis J 206 2
Martz, Luta P 169 2
Martz, Luto O 195 2
Martz, Mary M 190 2
Martz, Mehrle E 178 2
Martz, Raymond E 246 1
Martz, Rosa 206 2
Martz, Samuel B 209 2
Martz, William 219a 2
Martz, Willie H 215 2
Martz, Wilson 19 3
Martz, Wm H 169, 214 2
Marvin, Eleanore 171 2
Maryland Casualty Co 9, 220a 2
Maryland Casualty Co 60, 180, 203, 227 3
Maryland Casualty Co 61, 176, 186 1
Maryland Casualty Co Balto 227 3
Maryland Casualty Co of Baltimore 198 2
Maryland Casualty Co of Balto 91 3
Maryland Casualty Co of Md 129 2
Maryland Casualty Company 172 2
Masell, Leatha 188 2
Maser, Elizabeth 175 2
Maser, Frederick 175 2
Maser, Geo W 178 2
Maser, Margaret E 178 2
Mash, Charlotte 166 2
Mash, Ephriam 166, 172 2
Mason, Benjamin 163 2
Mason, Elijah 172 2
Mason, John C 60 3
Mason, John S 147, 266 1
Mason, John S 189, 198 2
Mason, Mary 166 1
Mason, Mary A 163, 198 2
Mason, Titus L 189 2
Mason, Titus L 56 3
Mass Bonding & Ins Co 139, 182, 232, 280 2
Mass Bonding & insurance Co 22 1
Mass Bonding & Insurance Co 72 3
Mass Bonding & Insurance Co 2, 49, 124, 245 2
Mass Bonding and Ins Co 32 3
Mass Bonding Co 197 3
Mass Bonding Co of Boston 203 3
Massachusetts Bonding & Ins Co 277 2
Massachusetts Bonding & Ins Co 161, 179 3
Massachusetts Bonding & Ins Co 73, 265 1
Masser, Geo W 178 2
Masser, Jennie 178 2
Masser, Leslie A 200 1
Masser, Wm 178 2
Mateny, Erven H 184 2
Mateny, Guy 202 2
Mateny, Guy C 184 2
Mateny, Ida M 202 2
Mateny, Ida R 184 2
Mateny, Nellie M 202 2
Mateny, Nellie N 211 2
Mateny, Thomas C 211 2
MaThais, Jacob 139 3
Mathais, Jacob [sic] 24 1
Mather, Henry 217 3
Mathews, Daisy Porter 170 2
Mathews, Eveline 172 2
Mathews, Francis K 31 2
Mathews, Jacob 278 1
Mathews, Jesse 185 2
Mathews, Jesse 201 3
Mathews, Jonas 81, 165, 209 3
Mathews, Jonas 27 2
Mathews, Jonas 243 1
Mathews, Nicholas 52 1
Mathews, Samuel 70 3
Mathews, Wm 164 1
Mathias, C 96 3
Mathias, C 72 1
Mathias, C C 132 2
Mathias, C M 79, 107, 166 3
Mathias, C Mc 92 1
Mathias, C McC 208 3
Mathias, C McC 19, 222 1
Mathias, C McC 222 1
Mathias, Catherine 165 2
Mathias, Charles 107 2
Mathias, Charles McC 123, 135, 227, 233, 239 1
Mathias, Charles McC 75, 129, 217a, 218a, 246, 278, 283 2
Mathias, Charles McC 45, 46 3
Mathias, Charles McC 46 3
Mathias, Chas 153, 165, 205, 230, 257, 272, 280 1
Mathias, Chas 83, 91, 122 3
Mathias, Chas 2, 52, 62, 80, 116, 145, 166, 199, 218, 220 2
Mathias, Chas & 129 2
Mathias, Chas C 35 2
Mathias, Chas etc 205 1
Mathias, Chas M 113 3
Mathias, Chas M 92 1
Mathias, Chas Mc 15 2
Mathias, Chas Mc 62 1
Mathias, Chas McC 78, 89 2
Mathias, Chas McC 72 3
Mathias, Chas McC 28, 42, 63, 72, 97, 101, 120, 135, 225 1
Mathias, Chas McC Jr 46 3
Mathias, Daniel 169 2
Mathias, Elizabeth 186 2
Mathias, Elizabeth D 235 2
Mathias, Eve 171 2
Mathias, Frances 84 2
Mathias, Frances 18 3
Mathias, Francis 113, 165 2
Mathias, Geo 171, 185, 186 2
Mathias, Geo Jr 186 2
Mathias, J P 230 1
Mathias, J P T 277 2
Mathias, J P T 123 1
Mathias, J T 230 1
Mathias, Jacob 18, 26, 38, 92, 96, 1 to 47, 149, 186, 203, 221, 218a 2
Mathias, Jacob 134, 165, 167, 171, 176, 215, 222 3
Mathias, Jacob 56 1
Mathias, John 18, 185 2
Mathias, John 165, 222 3
Mathias, John P 92 1
Mathias, Joseph 141 3
Mathias, Joseph 185, 186 2
Mathias, Peter 37 3
Mathias, Theresa McE Trail 98 3
Mathias, Theresa T 120 1
Mathias, Theresa Trail 45 3
Mathias, Theresa Trail 233, 239 1
Mathias, Wm & 278 1
Mattas, Nick 202 2
Mattern, Jacob 203 2
Mattern, Philip 203 2
Matthew, Philip 1 3
Matthews, Eleanore 171 2
Matthews, Eli 231 2
Matthews, Elizabeth D 235 2
Matthews, Francis S K 190 2
Matthews, Henry 197 2

Matthews, Isabella 184 2
Matthews, Israel 184 2
Matthews, J A 181 2
Matthews, Jacob 137 2
Matthews, Jacob G 171, 195 2
Matthews, James 203 2
Matthews, John 171, 195 2
Matthews, John A W 6 1
Matthews, John A W 190 2
Matthews, Jonas 187, 254 2
Matthews, Jonas 139, 125 1
Matthews, Jonas 50 3
Matthews, Lewis 187, 195 2
Matthews, Nicholas 202 2
Matthews, Peter 203 2
Matthews, Philip 203 2
Matthias, Chas 126 1
Matthias, Chas McC 67 1
Matthias, Jacob 96, 116, 126, 183 1
Matthias, Peter 203 2
Matthias, Peter 96 1
Maugan, James W 85 1
Maugans, Abram 165 2
Maugans, Amos M 160 2
Maugans, Conrad 165 2
Maugans, David 169 2
Maugans, Jacob T 190 2
Maugans, John 72, 165, 187 2
Maugans, John H 139, 189 2
Maugans, Rebecca 205 2
Maugans, Russell H 206 2
Maugans, Samuel 169, 209 2
Maugans, Samuel 39 3
Maught, A C 198 2
Maught, A C H 106, 218 3
Maught, A C H 192 1
Maught, Abraham 113 3
Maught, Andrew 159, 188 2
Maught, Andrew C H 197 1
Maught, Andrew C H 268 2
Maught, Andrew C H 212 3
Maught, Annie M 161 2
Maught, C C 212 3
Maught, Charles C 167 2
Maught, Daniel 106, 113 3
Maught, Eliza A E 188 2
Maught, Elizabeth 171 2
Maught, Florence M 175 2
Maught, Henry 150 1
Maught, Henry 181, 197, 214 2
Maught, John 59 1
Maught, John 159, 186, 188 2
Maught, John 39, 53 3
Maught, John A 175 2
Maught, John W 188 2
Maught, Julia A S 188, 198 2
Maught, Mary 198 2
Maught, Mary Ann 197 2
Maught, Myra L 188 2
Maught, Samuel 41, 98, 195 3
Maught, Samuel 159, 195, 208, 214, 258, 268 2
Maught, Samuel 71, 79, 194 1
Maught, Sarah A 181 2
Maught, Thos 186 2
Maught, Wm 214 2
Maugins, Daniel 186 2
Maugins, David 5 2
Maugins, John 186 2
Maugins, John Jr 186 2
Maugins, Samuel 5, 186 2
Maulsby, Charlotte 165 2
Maulsby, H H 44 3
Maulsby, Henrietta 27 1
Maulsby, Henrietta 224 2
Maulsby, Henrietta H P 182, 215 2
Maulsby, Henrietta H P 119 1
Maulsby, Henry 215 2
Maulsby, Henry H 119 1
Maulsby, Henry H 21 3
Maulsby, Henry Hanson 182 2
Maulsby, Mary S 21 3
Maulsby, Mary S 182, 227a 2
Maulsby, W P 57, 227a 2
Maulsby, W P Jr 222 2
Maulsby, W P Jr 186 3
Maulsby, W P Sr 32 3
Maulsby, W T Jr 116 3
Maulsby, William 224, 229a, 237 2
Maulsby, William P 257, 276 2
Maulsby, William P 20 3
Maulsby, William P 14, 20 3
Maulsby, William P Jr 277 2
Maulsby, Wm 160, 166 2
Maulsby, Wm 264 1
Maulsby, Wm Jr 24 1
Maulsby, Wm Jr 8, 101, 171, 181 2
Maulsby, Wm P 94, 187 3
Maulsby, Wm P 27, 84, 100, 130, 156, 164, 165, 257 1
Maulsby, Wm P 254 2
Maulsby, Wm P Jr 129, 143, 215 2
Maulsby, Wm T 94 3
Maultsby, Mary S 182 2
Maurer, Mary L H 199 2
Maurer, Paul 184 3
Maus, Jacob 183 1
Mause, John D 246 2
Mause, Viola Catherine 242 2
Mause, Viola P 20 2
Maxell, Henry 8 2
Maxley, Annie 211 2
Maxley, E G 211 2
Maxley, Thos E 211 2
Maxley, Wm T 211 2
Maxwell, A H 188 2
Maxwell, Albert H 39 2
Maxwell, F A 188 2
Maxwell, Francis 51 2
Maxwell, H F 60 3
Maxwell, H F 188 2
Maxwell, HL 2 3
Maxwell, Jane M 188 2
Maxwell, S 98 3
Maxwell, Samuel 113, 282 2
Maxwell, Samuel E 100 1
Maxwell, Thomas 211 2
Mayberry, Albert G 159 2
Mayberry, Ellan 171 2
Mayberry, Israel 186 2
Mayberry, Justinian 40 1
Mayberry, Mary Ann 197 2
Mayberry, Thomas 211 2
Mayberry, Thomas 129 3
Maybery, Justinian 186 2
Mayfield, J Elvans 57 3
Maygunigle, Henrietta 181 2
Mayhugh, Ella 189 2
Mayhugh, John H 189 2
Mayn, Chas E 217 2
Mayn, Daniel 234 2
Mayn, Zachary T 217 2
Maynard, Basil 163 2
Maynard, Benj 280 2
Maynard, Benj 186 3
Maynard, Benjamin 71 3
Maynard, Benjamin 163, 222 2
Maynard, C F 209 2
Maynard, Clayonia F 166 2
Maynard, Clayonia S 221a 2
Maynard, Cloyonia 111 3
Maynard, D H 28, 171 2
Maynard, Dennis H 11, 177 2
Maynard, Dennis H 55, 117, 118, 125 1
Maynard, Dennis H 9 3
Maynard, E H 61 1
Maynard, E H 150 2
Maynard, Eleanore 171 2
Maynard, Eliza D 175 2
Maynard, Eliza M R 171 2
Maynard, Emma J 172 2
Maynard, Ephriam H 177 2
Maynard, Eveline 171 2
Maynard, F N 107 2
Maynard, F N 124 3
Maynard, Frank 218 2

Maynard, Frank A 250 2
Maynard, Frank N 175 2
Maynard, Frank N 76, 115, 116, 153 1
Maynard, G H 76 2
Maynard, Geo W 177 2
Maynard, George 242 2
Maynard, H 229 1
Maynard, H G 71 3
Maynard, H G 47 1
Maynard, H G 67, 163, 171, 181 2
Maynard, H G & 89 2
Maynard, Howard 144, 221 2
Maynard, Howard G 112 1
Maynard, Howard G 107, 181, 222 2
Maynard, Howard G 129 3
Maynard, Ida M 181 2
Maynard, J E 202 2
Maynard, J L 21 1
Maynard, J Newton 60 1
Maynard, J T 107, 250 2
Maynard, James H 118 1
Maynard, Joseph T 112 1
Maynard, Nathan 51, 163, 171, 202, 280, 294 2
Maynard, Nathan 82, 197, 219 1
Maynard, Nathan 40, 67, 82, 129, 171 3
Maynard, Nathan of S 186 3
Maynard, Nathat 222 2
Maynard, P G 79 3
Maynard, Ruth 211 2
Maynard, S 186 3
Maynard, S M 56 3
Maynard, S S 111, 124 3
Maynard, S S 211, 236 2
Maynard, S S 179, 229 1
Maynard, S S Dr 221a 2
Maynard, S Sollers 209, 217a 2
Maynard, SF 84 2
Maynard, Thomas 67, 176 3
Maynard, Thomas 150 1
Maynard, Thomas 211 2
Maynard, Thomas B 241 2
Maynard, Thomas G 39, 71 3
Maynard, Thos G 211 2
Maynard, Thos G 210 1
Mayne, Ada 205 2
Mayne, David 169 2
Mayne, David F 169 2
Mayne, Enos L 169 2
Mayne, Fannie M 175 2
Mayne, Susan 188 2
Maynihan, Cornelius 165 2
Mayruder, Elias L 57 1
Mc Aleer, Hugh Jr 64 3
Mc Bride, Edgar 107 3
Mc Gill, Jennie B 94 3
Mc Mathias, Chas Mc 70 2
Mc Sherry, James 64 3
Mc Sherry, James 140 3
Mc.Aleer, Hugh 26 2
Mc.Coffrey, A 46 2
Mc.Hagan, Chas 243 1
MC.Intyre, Edward 59 1
Mc.Kinstry, E 234 2
Mc.Pherson, Alexander 159 2
Mc.Pherson, John 226 2
McAbee, Chas 181 2
McAbee, Chas W 59 1
McAfee, Annie 161 2
McAfee, Archibald 159 2
McAfee, David 159 2
McAfee, Ignatius 159 2
McAfee, Reuben 206 2
McAfee, Robert H 206 2
McAfee, Rosa P 206 2
McAleer, Hugh 91, 102, 106, 158 3
McAleer, Hugh 76, 84, 139, 196, 197, 271 1
McAleer, Hugh 38, 43, 148, 210a, 294 2
McAleer, Hugh & 7 2
McAleer, John 186 2
McAleer, Michael 186 2
McAleer, Michael F 199 2
McAleer, Patrick 148 2
McAleer, U [sic] 249 1
McAlleer, Hugh 221 2
McAller, Hugh[?] 24 1
McAtee, Ignatius 167 3
McAtee, James 212 3
McAtee, James 185 2
McAuley, Ann C 159 2
McAuliffe, Anthony 159 2
McBride, A C 65 2
McBride, Albert H 161 2
McBride, Allan C 161 2
McBride, Allen 160 2
McBride, Amos M ? 161 2
McBride, Andrew 214, 242 2
McBride, Andrew C 160 2
McBride, Annie E 137 1
McBride, Annie E 160, 224a 2
McBride, Anthony 44 1
McBride, Anthony 134, 262 2
McBride, Austin A 161 2
McBride, Avis Halbert 161 2
McBride, Bertha 196 2
McBride, C A 2, 23 2
McBride, Clarence 196 2
McBride, Daniel 169, 198 2
McBride, Dorothy F 16, 172 2
McBride, E H 189 3
McBride, E H 2, 165 2
McBride, Ed 258 2
McBride, Edgar 91 3
McBride, Edgar 9, 65, 124, 262 2
McBride, Edgar H 82, 116, 122, 196 3
McBride, Edgar H 23, 111, 113, 124, 160, 172, 209, 224a, 255 2
McBride, Edgar H 73, 86, 92, 97, 112, 137, 179, 205, 244, 260, 266 1
McBride, Edw 11 1
McBride, Edw 100 2
McBride, Edward 226 2
McBride, Ellen A 215 3
McBride, Ellen A 172 2
McBride, Geo 72 2
McBride, Geo W 187 3
McBride, H 214 2
McBride, Henry 181 2
McBride, Henry C 181 2
McBride, James H 190 2
McBride, John 185 2
McBride, Katie 193 2
McBride, L E 19 1
McBride, Lewis 59, 84, 214 1
McBride, Lewis 82 3
McBride, Lewis 181, 188, 195, 2
McBride, Lewis W 196 2
McBride, Lewis W 3 3
McBride, Luther E 124 3
McBride, M F 294 2
McBride, Mary 198 2
McBride, Millard F 195 2
McBride, Oliver C 169 2
McBride, Samuel E 161 2
McBride, Sarah E 209 2
McBride, Wm of H 214 2
McBride, Zella E 161 2
McBridge, Edgar H 201 3
McCabe, Anna N 161 2
McCabe, Mary 85 2
McCafferty, John 38 2
McCaffery, M A 215 2
McCaffery, Mary H 200 2
McCaffrey, A B 160 2
McCaffrey, Aloysius 165 2
McCaffrey, Ann V 46 2
McCaffrey, Anna 197 2
McCaffrey, Anne 160, 165 2
McCaffrey, Bernard E 163 2
McCaffrey, Chas B 165 2
McCaffrey, Henry K 181, 215 2
McCaffrey, John 188 2
McCaffrey, M A 160, 181 2

McCaffrey, M Elizabeth 163 2
McCaffrey, M H 215 2
McCaffrey, Mary H 199 2
McCaffrey, Michael 197 2
McCaffrey, Michael 163, 213 1
McCaffrey, Michael A 199, 215a 2
McCaffrey, Wm H 160, 215 2
McCaffrey, Wm H 169 1
McCahan, Catherine 166 2
McCahan, Hannah 181 2
McCahan, John 185 2
McCahan, John E 166, 181, 189 2
McCahan, Lydia E 195 2
McCain, Benjamin 163 2
McCain, Elizabeth Apple 19 1
McCain, Sarah 163 2
McCall, Isabella 184 2
McCall, Marie S 46 3
McCallion, Catherine 165 2
McCallum, Bernard 36 2
McCannen, John 185 2
McCanner, Charlotte V 167 2
McCanner, Franklin G 167 2
McCanner, Hazel K 167 2
McCannon, Ann 185 2
McCannon, Eleanor G 214 2
McCannon, Eleanore G 171 2
McCannon, James 185 2
McCannon, Wm H 214 2
McCardell, A C 109, 155, 165 1
McCardell, A C 113 3
McCardell, A C 80 2
McCardell, A L 167 3
McCardell, A L Jr 161 2
McCardell, A Lee Roy 113 1
McCardell, A Leroy 146, 245 1
McCardell, A Leroy 161 2
McCardell, A Lorey 160 2
McCardell, Adrian C 160 2
McCardell, Adrian C 159 1
McCardell, Albert 126 1
McCardell, Albert N 213a 2
McCardell, Barbara H 163 2
McCardell, Edgar S 173 2
McCardell, Eleanor Clingan 161 2
McCardell, Laura C 51 1
McCardell, Laura C 213a 2
McCardell, Pauline R 173 2
McCardelll, A C 87 3
McCarmack, Catherine 165 2
McCarren, Chas D 169 2
McCarren, Dennis 169, 188 2
McCartney, Harriet 181 2
McCartney, John T 187, 197 2
McCartney, Mary 198 2
McCartney, Michael 117, 125, 126, 200 1
McCartney, Michael 46, 66, 197, 250 2
McCarty, Harriett 238 2
McCasket, Joseph 186 3
McCastery, Joseph 26 2
McCauley, Ann C 160 2
McCharn, Michael 197 2
McClain, David M 169, 215 2
McClain, David N 170 2
McClain, Harry I 182 2
McClain, John 203 2
McClain, Joshua 185 2
McClain, Margaret 196 2
McClain, Mary 169 2
McClain, Peter 203 2
McClain, Wm H 215 2
McClaine, Peter 1 2
McClane, John 28 2
McClane, John 200 1
McClane, Peter 27, 61 2
McClary, C R 72 3
McClary, Martha E 102 3
McClaskey, John 221a, 231 2
McCleaf, Andrew L 161 2
McClean, John 192 3
McCleary, Andrew 159 2
McCleary, Martha E 199 2
McCleary, P E 159 2
McCleery, Andrew 228 1
McCleery, Andrew 159, 181, 205, 208 2
McCleery, Andrew Jr 205 2
McCleery, Bertha K 106 2
McCleery, Bertha L 166 2
McCleery, Caroline 205, 217 2
McCleery, Caroline B 166 2
McCleery, Claud 203 2
McCleery, Claud R 166 2
McCleery, Claude 64 2
McCleery, Elizabeth S 172 2
McCleery, Geo B 166, 172, 199, 203 2
McCleery, George Beall 178 2
McCleery, Harriet 205, 217 2
McCleery, Henry 181 2
McCleery, Henry 26 1
McCleery, Martha 166 2
McCleery, Martha E 199 2
McCleery, Mary J E 203 2
McCleery, Mary L Lakin 178 2
McCleery, P B 205 2
McCleery, P B 88, 182 1
McCleery, Perry 264 1
McCleery, Perry 29 2
McCleery, Perry B 159, 203, 205, 214, 217 2
McCleery, Perry B 47 1
McCleery, Perry E 81 3
McCleery, Peter M 205 2
McCleery, Rebecca 177, 205 2
McCleery, Robt 205 2
McCleery, Robt W 205 2
McCleery, Wm 203, 214 2
McCleery, Wm D 166 2
McCleery, Z K 159, 205 2
McCleery, Zerniah H 217 2
McClellan, Gertrude B 178 2
McClellan, J B 83 3
McClellan, J Bernard 178 2
McClelland, Martha 199 2
McCloskey, John 39, 188, 223a 2
McClow, Minnie 199 2
McCluer, Mary T 197 2
McCoffrey, Michael 22 1
McCollister, G 31 2
McCollister, J G 161, 227a 2
McCollister, Mary C 31 2
McCollum, Wm 43, 136 2
McComas, George W 178 2
McComas, M Edna 200 2
McComas, Mary E 200 2
McComas, Nellie K 178 2
McCormick, Alice I 175 2
McCormick, Emma C 172 2
McCormick, Frank 175 2
McCormick, Geo 177 2
McCormick, Sarah J 209 2
McCourtney, Michael 30 1
McCoy, Jessie B 215 2
McCoy, Walter L 215 2
McCrea, Thomson 201 1
McCreary, James 171 1
McCreery, John T 187 2
McCreery, L M 187 2
McCroskey, J 43 2
McCuller, Susie E 209 2
McCullough, Deliah 169 2
McCully, Andrew 159 2
McCully, John J 107 2
McCurdy, I J 72 1
McCurdy, Ira J 73, 112, 156, 207 1
McCurdy, Ira J 76, 184 2
McCurdy, Ira J 10 3
McCurdy, Irwin P 205 3
McCurdy, Lucy E 184 2
McCurdy, Lucy E 34 1
McCuskey, Harriette J 208 3

McCuskey, John 188 2
McCutcheon, Henry 195 2
McCutcheon, Luther 195 2
McDade, Alexander 47 1
McDanel, Catherine 165 2
McDanel, Elizabeth 165 2
McDaniel, A S 1 1
McDaniel, Daniel 169 2
McDaniel, Jacob 192 1
McDaniel, James 179 1
McDaniel, John 37 3
McDaniel, Miranda 169 2
McDaniel, Samuel 208 2
McDaniel, William 144 3
McDannel, Milton S 199 2
McDannel, Nellie A 215 2
McDannel, Walter H A 215 2
McDannell, Wm 1 2
McDara, Michael 197 2
McDarmwell, Milton 152 1
McDermott, Gladys M 200 2
McDermott, Richard 282 2
McDevit, Clara M 172 3
McDevit, J 83 3
McDevit, J 98 3
McDevit, Joseph 52, 187, 219a 2
McDevit, Joseph P 188, 198 2
McDevit, Mary 198 2
McDevitt, Aery 208 2
McDevitt, Austin H 167 2
McDevitt, Austin Z 160 2
McDevitt, Catharine 166 2
McDevitt, Charles E 167, 193 2
McDevitt, Chas 165 2
McDevitt, Cornelius I 166 2
McDevitt, Earl W 10 1
McDevitt, Edward C 175 2
McDevitt, Fannie 166 2
McDevitt, Fannie R 175 2
McDevitt, Fannie R 45 3
McDevitt, Fannie R 111 1
McDevitt, Guy H 178 2
McDevitt, J P 41 3
McDevitt, J P 290 2
McDevitt, James 187, 188 2
McDevitt, James V 188 2
McDevitt, Jane 187 2
McDevitt, John 82, 197 1
McDevitt, John 165, 166, 188 2
McDevitt, John 42, 64 3
McDevitt, John W 190 2
McDevitt, Joseph 155, 159, 197 1
McDevitt, Joseph 31, 145, 187 2
McDevitt, Julia J 188, 198 2
McDevitt, Katie 193 2
McDevitt, Larue 10 1
McDevitt, M Belle 175 2
McDevitt, Martha 198 2
McDevitt, Naomi 202 2
McDevitt, Naomi V 160 2
McDevitt, Nora 193 2
McDevitt, Samuel T 208 2
McDevitt, Tina F 178 2
McDevitt, Wm 29, 165, 166 2
McDevitt, Wm 144, 197 1
McDivit, Joseph 215 2
McDivitt, Harry N 190 2
McDivitt, Joseph 190 2
McDonald, Alexander 188 2
McDonald, Daisie E 170 2
McDonald, Francis 175 2
McDonald, J Knight 188 2
McDonald, Jacob 188 2
McDonald, Jacob V 188 2
McDonald, John 186, 208 2
McDonald, John 197, 225, 260, 263 1
McDonald, Mary E 198 2
McDonald, Samuel 208 2
McDonald, Wm 214 2
McDonell, Bernard 175 2
McDonell, Henry 181 2
McDonell, Jacob 181 2
McDonell, John 165 2
McDonell, Katherine 165 2
McDonnel, Mary A 198 2
McDonnell, John 260 1
McDonough, Ettie M 189 2
McDonough, John E 189 2
McDuel, Henry 50 3
McDuell, Ann 159 2
McDuell, Ella 189 2
McDuell, Geo M 177 2
McDuell, Henry 181 2
McDuell, Henry 58 1
McDuell, James 198 2
McDuell, Janie 189 2
McDuell, John 187, 205 2
McDuell, Magdalean 198 2
McDuell, Magdalena 181 2
McDuell, Magdalene 198 2
McDuell, Mary E 200, 205 2
McDuell, Mary Ella 199 2
McDuell, Robert 14 3
McDuell, Robert 58, 197 1
McDuell, Robert 198 2
McDuell, Robert M 205 2
McDuell, Robt 159, 187, 205 2
McDuell, Robt M 177 2
McDuell, Wm H 205 2
McElfresdh, Edmund W Jr 173 2
McElfresh, Anna 211 2
McElfresh, Annie B 211 2
McElfresh, Caleb 43, 165 2
McElfresh, Casper M 165 2
McElfresh, Charles 229a 2
McElfresh, Chas 203, 247 2
McElfresh, Chas 196 1
McElfresh, E W Jr 206 2
McElfresh, Edmund W Jr 173 2
McElfresh, Edmund W Sr 173 2
McElfresh, Elizabeth O 165 2
McElfresh, Henry 165, 181 2
McElfresh, Henry 39 3
McElfresh, Jane 186 2
McElfresh, John 277 1
McElfresh, John 27, 165, 186, 187, 203 2
McElfresh, John H 32 1
McElfresh, John H 27, 111, 165, 186 2
McElfresh, John P 190, 191 2
McElfresh, Philemon A 203 2
McElfresh, Philip 165, 203 2
McElfresh, Rachel 181, 205, 206 2
McElfresh, Rachel E 173 2
McElfresh, Teresa 165 2
McElfresh, Theresa 186, 211 2
McElfresh, Thos S 211 2
McElroy, John 82, 152 1
McElroy, John 268 2
McFadden, Dennis 1 2
McFadden, Michael 198 2
McFarland, Annie (Sr Leone) 161 2
McFarland, Leona Sister 161 2
McFarland, Patrick 203 2
McGaha, I C 231 2
McGaha, J M 9 2
Mcgaha, Luther F 196 2
McGaha, W L 22 1
McGahn, Abigail 159 2
McGahn, Hannah 159 2
McGaith, John G 134 2
McGarey, Felix 150 2
McGary, John 185 2
McGee, Peter 203 2
McGee, Rebecca 205 2
McGee, Thomas P 211 2
McGerry, Catherine 165, 175 2
McGerry, Catherine 225 1
McGerry, Felix 225 1
McGerry, Felix 175, 197 2
McGerry, Frederick F 175 2
McGerry, James 27, 159, 175 2

McGerry, James 139 1
McGerry, John 175 2
McGerry, John F 165 2
McGerry, John F 225 1
McGhee, Grant 178 2
McGill, A M 60 1
McGill, And 205 2
McGill, Ann M 160 2
McGill, Ann Matilda 198 2
McGill, Arabella W 160 2
McGill, Caroline F R 173 1
McGill, Chas B 165 2
McGill, E W 203 2
McGill, J Wakefield 173 1
McGill, John 160, 211 2
McGill, Joseph 208 2
McGill, Lloyd T 161, 179 3
McGill, Mary D 198 2
McGill, Patrick 11, 26, 154, 203, 211, 275 2
McGill, Patrick Jr 26 1
McGill, Patrick Jr 165 2
McGill, Patrick Sr 165, 203 2
McGill, R H 135, 150 1
McGill, Sarah A E 208 2
McGill, Sarah E 160 2
McGill, Thos 160 2
McGill, Thos J 147, 211 2
McGinnis, Robert 205 2
McGinnis, Robt 205 2
McGlue, Eliza 171 2
McGorgon, John 185 2
McGorgon, Thomas 185 2
McGovern, John C 199 2
McGovern, Margaret 199 2
McGowan, Helen M 182 2
McGowan, Margaret 197 2
McGowan, Margaret 47 1
McGowan, P 192 3
McGowan, Patrick 203 2
McGrath, Anna Louise 161 2
McGrath, John 176 1
McGrath, John 149, 203 2
McGraw, John Henry 191 2
McGraw, William C 191 2
McGregiry, G H 224 3
McGregor, G H 225a 2
McGregor, Glenn 166 1
McGregor, Glenn H 65 2
McGregor, Sadie E 13 1
McGregory, Sadie E 224 3
McGruder, Rufus 246 2
McGuigan, J A 13, 166 1
McGuigan, James A 13, 61 1
McGuigan, Miranda V 13, 21 1
McGuinness, Loretta 161 2
McGuire, James 189 2
McHaffie, James 278 1
McHaffie, James 185 2
McHagan, Chas 166 2
McHagan, Chas & 243 1
McHagan, Lizzie R 166 2
McHenry, Allen 166, 175 2
McHenry, Benjamin 1 2
McHenry, Catherine 166 2
McHenry, Catherine J 175 2
McHenry, Frank 175 2
McHenry, Harry 182 2
McHenry, Harry 96 3
McHenry, Harvey 182 2
McHenry, Henry 1, 181, 197 2
McHenry, Margaret 198 2
McHenry, Mary 197 2
McHenry, T B 181 2
McHoffie , James 185 2
McHoffman, Statton 12 2
McInstry, Daniel 53 3
McIntyre, Edw 39, 198 2
McIntyre, Edward 64 3
McIntyre, Edward 46 2
McJintire, Edw [sic] 225 1
McKalb, John 70 1
McKaleb, John 104, 125, 163 1
McKaleb, John 137, 258 2
McKaleb, John & 137 2
McKechney, Ann R 159 2
McKeehan, Geo 177 2
McKeehan, James 177, 208 2
McKeehan, James J 1 2
McKeehan, John 177 2
McKeehan, Samuel L 96 1
McKeehan, Samuel L 208 2
McKeehen, James T 252 1
McKeenan, George 30 1
McKehan, Geo 137 2
McKehan, Geo 91 1
McKehan, George 184 3
McKehan, James J 186 1
McKehan, James L 185 3
McKehan, John 186 1
McKehn, S L 244 1
McKellip, James 186 2
McKellip, John 47 1
McKellip, John 186 2
McKellip, W A 39 2
McKenna, A J 119, 191 1
McKenna, A J 124 3
McKenna, A J 15 2
McKenna, Alexander J 119 1
McKensey, A G 146 1
McKensey, Sadie A 179 1
McKensie, J E W 48 1
McKenzie, Fannie 192 3
McKenzie, Folger 192 3
McKenzie, Guy H 199 2
McKenzie, John H 189 2
McKenzie, Malinda V 199 2
McKenzie, Matilda V 189 2
McKenzie, Thomas 211 2
McKenzie, Warner Wet al 192 3
McKierman, Peter 189 1
McKierman, Peter 203 2
McKiernam, Mary 198 2
McKiernan, Peter 203 2
McKinley, Jacob 75 2
McKinney, A G 215 2
McKinney, Carrie U 215 2
McKinney, D F 124, 129 3
McKinney, David F 169 2
McKinney, David Treggo 170 2
McKinney, Francis S 170, 215 2
McKinney, Grace L 215 2
McKinney, Mary E 124 3
McKinney, Mary E 169 2
McKinney, Nora Witter 202 2
McKinney, Walter A 215 2
McKinney, William H 170, 215 2
McKinney, Wm 169 2
McKinney, Wm H 67 2
McKinsey, Daniel 138 2
McKinsey, Geo H 40 1
McKinsey, James E 188 2
McKinsey, Threasa E 188 2
McKinsey, Wm 188 2
McKinsley, Erma B 132 3
McKinsley, W E 132 3
McKinstrey, Evan 40, 179 1
McKinstrey, Samuel 40 1
McKinstry, Evan 51 1
McKinstry, Mordecai C 72, 112 1
McKinstry, S 164 1
McKinstry, Samuel 59, 82, 125, 245, 248 1
McKinstry, Samuel 212a 2
McKissick, Ann E 214 2
McKissick, Cora A 172 2
McKissick, Eugene 172 2
McKissick, J S 214 2
McKissick, James 185 2
McKissick, James S 190 2
McKissick, John 185 2
McKissick, L 172 2
McKissick, Lewis P 196 2
McKissick, Margaret 197 2
McKissick, Roy 206 2
McKissick, William L 190, 206 2
McKissick, Wm 197, 214 2
McKleb, John 47 1
McKnight, Thomas 154 2
McKroskey, Andrew 171 1
McLain, Ammon 159 2
McLain, Georgianna 212, 217

3
McLain, Joshua 188 2
McLanahan, John 187 2
McLanahan, John A 187 2
McLanahan, Susanna 208 2
McLane, Anna L 190 2
McLane, Charlotte A 125 1
McLane, Daniel 169 2
McLane, Daniel 159 1
McLane, Geo 27, 169, 177, 197 2
McLane, George 159 1
McLane, Hiram 187 2
McLane, John 187, 223a 2
McLane, Joseph 190 2
McLane, Julia A R 190 2
McLane, Martha 190 2
McLane, Mary 197 2
McLane, R T 214 2
McLane, Rufus A 52 1
McLane, Simon 208 2
McLane, T L 71, 129, 171, 186, 195 3
McLane, T L 59, 71, 82, 96, 106, 164, 243 1
McLane, T L 39, 106, 187, 198, 271, 282 2
McLane, Thos 249 1
McLane, Torrance 190 2
McLane, Wm 214 2
McLaughlin, Chas A 166 2
McLaughlin, Chas P 195 2
McLaughlin, James 185 2
McLaughlin, John 116, 176 1
McLaughlin, Louisa 195 2
McLaughlin, Sally 124 1
McLean, Georgenna 181 2
McLean, Harry O 181 2
McLean, J L 144 2
McLean, John 18 1
McLean, T L 83 2
McLean, T L 4 1
McLean, Thomas L 125 1
McMahan, Elizabeth 172 2
McMair, Levinia 195 2
McMakin, Benjamin 163 2
McMakin, Benjamin F 163 2
McMakin, John H 163 2
McMakin, Samuel 208, 214 2
McMakin, Susannah 208 2
McMakin, Wm 214 2
McManus, Abbey 160 2
McManus, Katie 160 2
McMaster, Anne B 160 2
McMaster, Leroy 160 2
McMathias, C 169, 181 2
McMathias, C 4 1
McMathias, Charles 40 2
McMathias, Chas 115, 126, 189, 249, 272 1
McMathias, Chas 72, 206 3
McMathias, Chas 160 2
McMillan, Emma E 155 1
McMillan, Mary A 208 2
McMillan, Sameul 208 2
McMillen, Boyd 170 2
McMillen, John F 26 1
McMillen, Kenneth H 170 2
McMiller, Hugh 171 1
McMullen, Annie C 166 2
McMullen, Chas E 166 2
McMullen, Dennis 65 3
McMullen, Hannah 185 2
McMullen, Hugh 163 1
McMullen, James 163 1
McMullen, James 185 2
McMullen, Susan 208 2
McMulty, Mary A 199 2
McMurray, J A 140 1
McMurrman, Wm 209 3
McMurry, Lulu B 140 1
McNair, Alice A 160 2
McNair, Robt 160 2
McNair, S N 11 2
McNair, S N 252 1
McNair, Samuel M 209 2
McNealey, S V 84 1
McNear, Alexander 159 2
McNear, Samuel 159 2
McNeel, John 177, 208 2
McNeel, John 84, 109, 265 1
McNew, Irene V 284 2
McNiel, John 150, 163 1
McNulty, Albert A 200 2
McNulty, Caroline B 167 2
McNulty, Cornelius 38, 165 2
Mcnulty, Cornelius 30 1
McNulty, James 186 2
McNulty, James P 203 2
McNulty, Mary T S 200 2
McNulty, Patrick E 203 2
McParson, John 59, 133, 214 1
McParson, John Jr 133 1
McParson, Wm 133, 214 1
McParson, Wm S 32 1
McPherson, Alexander 197 2
McPherson, Catherine D 166 2
McPherson, Catherine S 165 2
McPherson, Edw 186 2
McPherson, Fannie R 175 2
McPherson, Horatio 186 2
McPherson, John 57, 91, 139, 263 1
McPherson, John 96, 153, 159, 185, 186, 205, 214 2
McPherson, John 91 3
McPherson, John 96 3
McPherson, John Jr 81 3
McPherson, John Jr 205 2
McPherson, Libby K 195 2
McPherson, Louise 196 2
McPherson, Margaret W 199, 205 2
McPherson, Margaret W 171 1
McPherson, Mary B 197 2
McPherson, R G 214 2
McPherson, Robt G 166, 205 2
McPherson, Thomas 211 2
McPherson, W S 181 2
McPherson, Wm 137, 159, 186, 197, 205 2
McPherson, Wm Jr 197 2
McQuade, Arthur J 160 2
McQuade, Emma 160 2
McQuaid, Patrick 203 2
McQuilkin, Abraham R 160 2
McQuilkin, Ellen G 172 2
McSheery, Clara L 166 2
McSheery, J Roger 40 2
McSheery, James 38 2
McSheery, James Jr 39 2
McSheery, Wm C 166 2
McSherry, Amon 67 1
McSherry, Caroline S 167 2
McSherry, Clara L 189 2
McSherry, Clinton 181 1
McSherry, Edw 89 2
McSherry, Edw C 111 2
McSherry, Eliza 187 2
McSherry, J Roger 8 1
McSherry, J Roger 199 2
McSherry, James 6, 19, 23, 79, 96, 176, 179 3
McSherry, James 15, 101, 111, 167, 171, 187, 188, 189, 213a, 221a, 234, 294 2
McSherry, James 24, 41, 48, 82, 88, 133, 150, 171, 201, 219, 225, 239 1
McSherry, James Jr 223a 2
McSherry, James Jr 64 3
McSherry, James M 117 1
McSherry, Liza S 171 2
McSherry, W C 106 2
McSherry, W C 55 1
McSherry, W Clinton 32, 167, 172, 234 2
McSherry, W Clinton 86, 136, 202, 235 1
McSherry, W S 187 2
McSweeney, Edw 172 2
Md Casualty Co 215 2
Md Casualty Co 20, 35 3
Md Casualty Co 150 2
Md Casualty Co 183 1
Md Casualty Co of Baltimore 133 1

Md Casualty Co of Baltimore 45 2
Md Casualty Co of Baltimore Md 78, 265 2
Md Casualty Co of Md 92 1
Md Casualty Co of Md 209 2
Md Casualty Co of Md, The 28 1
Md Casualty Company 202 1
Mead, Joseph 264 1
Meadows, Birdie 190 2
Meadows, Birdie L 163 2
Meadows, J Eugene 190 2
Mealey, Catherine E 166 2
Mealey, Chas E 166 2
Mealey, Chas E 272 1
Mealey, Effie 166 2
Mealey, Elizabeth 171 2
Mealey, Elizabeth 185 3
Mealey, Isaiah 185 3
Mealey, Isiah 171 2
Mealey, Israel 201 1
Mealey, M 70 3
Mealey, Michael 197 2
Mealey, Milton 198 2
Mealey, Milton 70, 81 3
Mealey, Milton 249, 271 1
Mealey, Roy E 166 2
Mealey, Susan 166 2
Mealey, Thomas M 211 2
Mealey, Wm 197, 214 2
Mealy, Isaiah 53 3
Mealy, Isarel 87 2
Measel, Clarence S 169 2
Measel, David L 169, 177 2
Measel, Geo 177 2
Measel, John 38 3
Measell, E B 100 3
Measell, Franklin 211 2
Measell, Geo J 178 2
Measell, Harvey 166 3
Measell, Harvcy C 178 2
Measell, Harvey E 190 2
Measell, Jacob 184 3
Measell, Jacob G 190 2
Measell, John 57 1
Measell, John 26, 187 2
Measell, Nicholas 38 2
Measell, Roy J 170, 190 2
Measell, Thomas A 211 2
Measell, Thos J 211 2
Medtart, Jacob 185 2
Medtart, Jacob 70 1
Medtart, Lewis 171, 263 1
Medtart, Lewis 14, 39, 205 3
Medtart, Lewis 18, 27, 185, 195 2
Medtart, Louis 1 2
Meek, John 189 2
Meeks, Benjamin W 21 3
Meeks, David B 170 2
Meghan, James 203 2
Mehaffe, W H 8 2
Mehaffie, Brooks M 163 2
Mehaffie, Florence M 175 2
Mehriling, George T 178 2
Mehring, Hezekiah D 283 1
Mehrling, Anna Mary 161 2
Mehrling, Annie E 280, 283 2
Mehrling, Betty 166 2
Mehrling, Carrie O 166 2
Mehrling, Casper 166 2
Mehrling, Charles B 167 2
Mehrling, Geo 170, 187 2
Mehrling, Henry 223 1
Mehrling, Hezekiah 271 1
Mehrling, John 189 2
Mehrling, John J 178, 202 2
Mehrling, John W 189 2
Mehrling, Lewis W 196 2
Mehrling, Mamie N 178 2
Mehrling, Nellie R 202 2
Meier, H F August]sic] 182 2
Meisling, Andrew J 172 2
Meisling, Elizabeth L 172 2
Meisling, Frederick G 175 2
Meisling, Hayes G 120 1
Meisling, Hayes G 182 2
Meisling, Joseph A 172 2
Meisling, Pearl M 182, 203 2
Meitzler, Benjamin 163 2
Melcalf, Mary 249 1
Meldrow, Henry S 181 2
Melgenovitch, Joseph 189 2
Melius, Conrad 165 2
Melius, Mary 165 2
Mellinger, Mary B 200 2
Melter, Lewis 160 3
Menchey, Daniel 153 3
Menchey, Elizabeth P 198 2
Menchey, Mary 198 2
Mentz, Catherine 174 3
Mentzer, Alice 160 2
Mentzer, Conrad 197 2
Mentzer, Francis 175 2
Mentzer, Franklin P 32 3
Mentzer, Geo 177, 197 2
Mentzer, George H 178 2
Mentzer, John 188 2
Mentzer, John H 190 2
Mentzer, John W 209 2
Mentzer, Lewis 175, 188 2
Mentzer, Martha 188 2
Mentzer, Michael 197 2
Mentzer, Samuel 208 2
Mentzer, Samuel B 209 2
Mentzor, John 169 1
Mercantile Trust Co 282 1
Mercer, A Owen 202 2
Mercer, A Owen 96 3
Mercer, Ada S 214 2
Mercer, Albert M 3, 23 3
Mercer, Albert M 178, 199, 283 2
Mercer, Alice A 215 2
Mercer, Ann M 159 2
Mercer, Edgar 220 2
Mercer, Edgar T 143, 172 2
Mercer, Edw 179 3
Mercer, Edw 253 1
Mercer, Eva B 172 2
Mercer, G H 56, 220 3
Mercer, G H 40, 65 2
Mercer, G Wilson 178 2
Mercer, Grace H 178 2
Mercer, Grayson 97 1
Mercer, Grayson 3, 51 3
Mercer, Grayson 172 2
Mercer, Grayson H 10, 23, 73, 96 3
Mercer, Grayson H 2, 32, 116, 178, 199, 215, 280, 291 2
Mercer, Grayson H 120, 197 1
Mercer, Hattie 172 2
Mercer, Hattie May 172 2
Mercer, Henry 243 1
Mercer, Henry D 181 2
Mercer, J Ezra 148 1
Mercer, J K 179 3
Mercer, James 186 2
Mercer, John 186 2
Mercer, Lavinia C 196 2
Mercer, Levania 215 2
Mercer, Margaret V 199 2
Mercer, Mattie 166 3
Mercer, Mattie M 199 2
Mercer, Melvin L 172 2
Mercer, Rachel B 181, 205 2
Mercer, Samuel B 208 2
Mercer, Susan 208 2
Mercer, Susannah 208 2
Mercer, Victor G 178 2
Mercer, William C 215 2
Mercer, William V 179 3
Mercer, Wm 89, 172, 214 2
Mercer, Wm C 178, 214 2
Mercer, Wm E 208, 214 2
Mercer, Wm F 215 2
Merchant, Ralph 153 1
Mercier, Annie R 160 2
Mercier, Dorsey F 172 2
Mercier, Edw 172 2
Mercier, Eli W 172 2
Mercier, Emma D 172 2

Mercier, Ethel K 206 2
Mercier, Richard 172 2
Mercier, Richard C 206 2
Mercier, Robt W 206 2
Meredith, Anne 160 2
Meredith, John T 82 1
Meredith, Simon 39 3
Merghart, Charlotte 165 2
Merghart, Conrad 165 2
Mericer, Robt W 160 2
Mering, Jacob 38 3
Merrick, William M 203 3
Merrick, Wm M 137 2
Merriett, Harriet 181 2
Merriman, Dorothy V , 100 3
Merring, Geo 28 2
Merriot, A W 154 2
Merritt, Caleb C 166 2
Merritt, Jacob 12 2
Merritt, Laura M 166, 196 2
Mesing, Geo Jr 57 1
Messenbaugh, John 186 2
Messenbaugh, Susannah 208 2
Messiner, Herrit l 254 2
Messinger, Samuel 38 3
Messler, John 185, 186 2
Messler, Susannah 208 2
Messner, Josiah G 189 2
Messuer, Josiah G 10 1
Metcalf, Kenneth L 78 2
Metcalfe, Calvin 166, 202 2
Metcalfe, Calvin R 190 2
Metcalfe, Calvin W 166 2
Metcalfe, Clinton 166, 167, 175, 199 2
Metcalfe, Francis A 175 2
Metcalfe, Frank E 175 2
Metcalfe, John 202 2
Metcalfe, John W 190 2
Metcalfe, Lizzie M 68 3
Metcalfe, Maggie 200 2
Metcalfe, Mary J 199 2
Metcalfe, Nicholas 223 1
Metcalfe, Nicholas H 202 2
Metcalfe, Rachel 205 2
Metcalfe, Rachel 205 2
Metcalfe, S Nicholas 167 2
Metcalfe, Thomas Franklin 211 2
Metger, John 112 1
Mettzler, Elizabeth 163, 172 2
Metz, C D 73 3
Metz, Charles D 245 1
Metz, Charles D 75 3
Metz, D O 201 1
Metz, Daniel O 48 1
Metz, Daniel O 12, 172, 202 2
Metz, Daniel O 45, 72, 135 3
Metz, David 272 1
Metz, Elizabeth B 172 2
Metz, Nicholas 188, 202 2
Metz, Nicholas 65 3
Metz, Phoebe 203 2
Metz, Thos G 12 2
Metzer, Wm 124, 205 3
Metzgar, Wm 159 1
Metzger, Alice M 161 2
Metzger, Amos 159 2
Metzger, Frederick 51 1
Metzger, Geo 1, 39, 177, 186 2
Metzger, Geo 106, 196, 201, 203, 210, 214, 219 1
Metzger, Geo & 107 2
Metzger, George 187 2
Metzger, George 31, 67 3
Metzger, George 37 1
Metzger, Jacob 186, 187 2
Metzger, John L 189 2
Metzger, John W 161 2
Metzger, Joseph B 161 2
Metzger, Lydia 195, 214 2
Metzger, Mosheim 199 2
Metzger, Sarah 208 2
Metzger, William 1, 8, 40 3
Metzger, William 280 2
Metzger, Wm 39, 70, 80, 214 2
Metzger, Wm 113 3
Metzger, Wm 58, 90, 150 1
Metzger, Wm & 165 2
Metzger, Wm M 113 3
Meyer, B E 236 2
Meyer, Chas T 68 1
Meyer, Edward F 145 2
Meyer, Ida P 68 1
Meyer, James W 104 1
Mezger, Geo 146 1
Michael, A 46 2
Michael, Abraham 159, 160, 187 2
Michael, Adam 116 1
Michael, Alice J 175 2
Michael, Andrew 78, 159, 185 2
Michael, Andrew 146 1
Michael, Ann M 160, 254 2
Michael, Anne C 159 2
Michael, Austin 30 1
Michael, Barbara 163 2
Michael, Beatrice V 215 2
Michael, C W 254 2
Michael, Catherine 165 2
Michael, Charles W 167, 271 2
Michael, Chas B 166 2
Michael, Chas S 209 2
Michael, Chas W 160 2
Michael, Christopher 165, 197 2
Michael, Christopher 23, 38, 163 3
Michael, Conrad 165 2
Michael, Conrad 58, 101, 163 1
Michael, Cora E 160, 167, 271 2
Michael, Daniel 91, 217 1
Michael, Daniel 39, 165 2
Michael, David 51 1
Michael, Dorothy 169 2
Michael, Elizabeth 171 2
Michael, Elmer F 241 2
Michael, Ernest 220 2
Michael, Ernest D 199 2
Michael, Eugenia 172 2
Michael, Ezra 100, 104, 146, 152, 156, 164, 183 1
Michael, Ezra 1, 101, 159, 171, 172, 177, 276 2
Michael, Ezra 75, 186, 187 3
Michael, Fannie M 241 2
Michael, Frank E 55 1
Michael, Frank E 175 2
Michael, Franklin 160 2
Michael, Frederick A 175 2
Michael, G J 214 2
Michael, G L 96, 107, 174 3
Michael, G S 197 2
Michael, Geisbert 177 2
Michael, Geo M 177 2
Michael, Geo M 14 1
Michael, Gilbert 185 2
Michael, Glen R 81 2
Michael, Grover 20 3
Michael, Grover L 44, 102 3
Michael, Grover L 92, 96, 101 1
Michael, Grover L 172, 222, 249, 265, 283 2
Michael, H Lavier 190 2
Michael, H N 171 2
Michael, Henry 163, 169, 171, 177, 181 2
Michael, Henry A 181 2
Michael, Henry of G 217 1
Michael, Henry of P 217 1
Michael, Henry S 1, 57, 181 2
Michael, Henry Sr 181 2
Michael, Hiram S 58 1
Michael, Isaac 78, 163, 181, 214 2
Michael, Isaac 32, 165 3
Michael, Isaac 60, 91, 104 1
Michael, Isaiah 184 2
Michael, J H 270 1
Michael, J L 201 1
Michael, Jacob 30 1
Michael, James 188, 209 2
Michael, James H 184, 188 2

Michael, Jesse 16 3
Michael, Jesse H 172, 190 2
Michael, John 57, 171, 187, 188, 202 2
Michael, John 10, 32, 70, 147 1
Michael, John Calvin 190 2
Michael, John F 165 2
Michael, John L 181, 199 2
Michael, John L 27, 42, 82, 96 3
Michael, John L 41, 240 1
Michael, Joseph 100 1
Michael, Lewis 195 2
Michael, M S 171 2
Michael, Margaret 197 2
Michael, Marian S 23 3
Michael, Marion 106, 203 1
Michael, Marion S 30, 196, 199 2
Michael, Marshall H 172 2
Michael, Mary Catherine 199 2
Michael, Mary E 142 1
Michael, Mary E 175, 200 2
Michael, May Carty 85, 190 2
Michael, Minerva 199 2
Michael, Oliver B 202 2
Michael, P S 174 3
Michael, Peter 169, 177 2
Michael, Ray A 166 2
Michael, Roy C 119, 145 2
Michael, Solomon H 209 2
Michael, Sophia J 209 2
Michael, Sophie R 258 2
Michael, Stanley 81 2
Michael, Stanley A 20, 217 3
Michael, Stanley A 200, 284 1
Michael, Susan E 190 2
Michael, William O 215 2
Michael, Wm 43, 57, 137, 181, 214 2
Michael, Wm 106 3
Michael, Wm H 179 3
Michaels, Andrew 56 1
Michel, Austin L 175 2
Michel, Christopher 106 3
Mickley, Eli 171 2
Mickley, Elizabeth C 171 2
Mikesell, Abraham 205 2
Mikesell, Geo 177 2
Mikesell, Jacob 203 2
Mikesell, Mary E 198 2
Mikesell, Peter 203 2
Mikesell, Rachel 205 2
Miles, A 96 3
Miles, Adeline 177 2
Miles, Albert 213a 2
Miles, Charles 70 1
Miles, Charles A 200 2
Miles, Charles Alton 167 2
Miles, Chas 165 2
Miles, Chas Jr 177 2
Miles, Elizabeth 177 2
Miles, Geo 214 2
Miles, Geo H 177 2
Miles, George H 22 2
Miles, Greenberry 177 2
Miles, Katie E 193 2
Miles, Marshall T 167, 200 2
Miles, Martha E 200 2
Miles, Ollie E 37 1
Miles, Pauline G 167 2
Miles, Wm 214 2
Millard, Chas 208 2
Millard, Oscar 208 2
Miller, A G 30 2
Miller, Abraham 159 2
Miller, Ada H 161 2
Miller, Adam 159, 160, 186 2
Miller, Adam 37, 79, 82, 101 1
Miller, Adam 38 3
Miller, Addison R 208 2
Miller, Adeline S 159 2
Miller, Albert A 160, 161 2
Miller, Albert C 161 2
Miller, Amanda C 160 2
Miller, Amelia Lewis 151 2
Miller, Andrew 159 2
Miller, Ann E 159 2
Miller, Anna 187 2
Miller, Annie E S 188 2
Miller, Anthony 159, 185 2
Miller, Augustus A 159 2
Miller, Bertha E 163 2
Miller, Blanche S 18 2
Miller, C E 177 2
Miller, C G 44 3
Miller, C J F 85 1
Miller, C W 41, 205 3
Miller, C W 8, 14, 84 2
Miller, C W 106, 150, 233, 238 1
Miller, Calvin 187 2
Miller, Calvin R 165 2
Miller, Caroline 166, 187 2
Miller, Caroline M 166 2
Miller, Carrie V 220a 2
Miller, Catherine 159, 165 2
Miller, Cecilia K 102, 167 2
Miller, Charles Frank 34 1
Miller, Charles W 100 1
Miller, Charles W 1, 124 3
Miller, Charles W 283 2
Miller, Chas 39, 54, 160, 175, 186, 188, 209 2
Miller, Chas 279 1
Miller, Chas E 172, 199 2
Miller, Chas H 188 3
Miller, Chas J 31 2
Miller, Chas J 71 1
Miller, Chas J F 67, 188 3
Miller, Chas J F 2, 85, 134, 188 2
Miller, Chas M 166 2
Miller, Chas S 166 2
Miller, Chas W 2, 179, 222 3
Miller, Chas W 8, 15, 49, 113, 159, 166, 171, 187, 198 2
Miller, Chas W 99, 230, 249 1
Miller, Christian 165 2
Miller, Clara B 68 3
Miller, Clara M 115 1
Miller, Conrad 165 2
Miller, Cora May 166, 167 2
Miller, D A 166 2
Miller, D C 100 3
Miller, D T 220 3
Miller, Daniel 11 1
Miller, Daniel 174 3
Miller, Daniel 122, 169, 171 2
Miller, Daniel B 214 2
Miller, Daniel B 61 1
Miller, Daniel C 14, 187 2
Miller, Daniel M 75 3
Miller, Daniel M 189, 209 2
Miller, David 150 1
Miller, David 38, 165, 169 2
Miller, David E 28 2
Miller, David S K 159, 188 2
Miller, Della A 170 2
Miller, Della B 175 2
Miller, E 44 1
Miller, Edna B 32 2
Miller, Edward H 18 2
Miller, Eli 47 1
Miller, Elias C 80 2
Miller, Eliza A 171 2
Miller, Elizabeth 44, 88 1
Miller, Elizabeth 171, 198 2
Miller, Elizabeth B 172 2
Miller, Elizabeth C 195 2
Miller, Ellen F 11 3
Miller, Elsie E 172 2
Miller, Emma C 172 2
Miller, Ethel Bayard 172 2
Miller, Eve E 198 2
Miller, Frank A 178 2
Miller, Frank D 51 1
Miller, Frank Z 175 2
Miller, Franklin N 175 2
Miller, Frederick 29, 51 2
Miller, Frederick 52, 159, 278 1
Miller, Frederick A 199 2
Miller, Frederick D 177 2
Miller, G W 117 1
Miller, Geo 8, 14, 28, 166, 177, 185,

203 2
Miller, Geo 165, 171, 214, 223, 252, 264, 279 1
Miller, Geo 176, 205, 222 3
Miller, Geo D 41 1
Miller, Geo D 137, 178 2
Miller, Geo E 14 2
Miller, Geo Ezra 177 2
Miller, Geo F 178 2
Miller, Geo L 209 2
Miller, Geo M 177, 188 2
Miller, Geo McClellan 178 2
Miller, Geo W 22, 28, 177, 280 2
Miller, Geo W 41, 91, 179 3
Miller, Geo W 51, 60, 135, 205, 210, 223 1
Miller, George 70, 184 3
Miller, George D 59 1
Miller, George E 202 2
Miller, George L 178 2
Miller, George W 41, 124, 195 3
Miller, George W 218a 2
Miller, Gervis S 172 2
Miller, Grace 166 1
Miller, Grace E 175 2
Miller, Grace M 178, 215, 280 2
Miller, H 15, 81 3
Miller, H 181, 187 2
Miller, H A 195 2
Miller, H C 159 3
Miller, H F 25 1
Miller, Harrisn 181 2
Miller, Harrison 150 1
Miller, Harrison 202 2
Miller, Harry M 182 2
Miller, Harvey E 182 2
Miller, Hattie 199 2
Miller, Henrietta F 182 2
Miller, Henry 181 2
Miller, Henry 44, 91 1
Miller, Henry 165 3
Miller, Henry 159 2
Miller, Henry A 179 3
Miller, Hiram E 60 1
Miller, Hiram E 15, 181 2
Miller, Hiram L 92 1
Miller, Hiram L 182 2
Miller, J 247 2
Miller, J A 270 1
Miller, J E 26 1
Miller, J G 165 1
Miller, J G 102, 217 3
Miller, J Harry 189 2
Miller, J L 28, 247 2
Miller, J M 46, 65, 76, 175, 178, 223a, 276 2
Miller, J M 101, 172 3
Miller, J M 52, 181 1
Miller, J Marshall 73, 96, 110, 119, 123, 129, 144, 152, 249, 283 1
Miller, J Marshall 2, 43, 87, 176, 188, 213, 226 3
Miller, J Marshall 2, 16, 31, 34, 35, 72, 166, 189, 190, 199, 214, 234, 280 2
Miller, J Matt 113 3
Miller, J W 42 3
Miller, J W 187 2
Miller, Jacob 72, 154, 159, 188, 202 2
Miller, Jacob 164 1
Miller, Jacob B S 176 3
Miller, Jacob C T 167 3
Miller, Jacob L 195 3
Miller, Jacob L 1, 210 1
Miller, Jacob L 189 2
Miller, Jacob T C 208 2
Miller, Jacob T C 117, 196 1
Miller, Jacob T C 153, 192 3
Miller, James W 188 2
Miller, Jennie S 214 2
Miller, Jennie Schley 189 2
Miller, Jno 88 1
Miller, Job 187 2
Miller, Job 9 3
Miller, Joe M 189 2
Miller, John 106, 223 3
Miller, John 11, 22, 27, 51, 54, 96, 100, 171, 177, 185, 186, 187, 188, 205, 236 2
Miller, John 106, 159, 195, 217, 228, 263, 283 1
Miller, John A 188 2
Miller, John C 3 2
Miller, John D 187, 188, 199 2
Miller, John D 279 1
Miller, John F 187 2
Miller, John F 31 3
Miller, John F D 189 2
Miller, John Franklin 175 2
Miller, John H 190 2
Miller, John M 91 1
Miller, John Marshall 4 3
Miller, John Marshall 177 2
Miller, John of H 15, 81 3
Miller, John of H 181, 187 2
Miller, John of J 247 2
Miller, John of Joseph 187 2
Miller, John S 186 2
Miller, John Sr 187 2
Miller, John Sr 186, 187 2
Miller, John T 178 2
Miller, John W 70, 139 1
Miller, John W 186, 188, 189, 198, 208, 214, 237 2
Miller, John W 186, 223 3
Miller, John W L 189 2
Miller, John W of John 177 2
Miller, Jonathan 43, 185 2
Miller, Jos E R 15 2
Miller, Joseph 106, 179 3
Miller, Joseph 19, 29, 39, 46, 93, 159, 185, 187, 195, 197, 214, to 27 2
Miller, Joseph 10, 110, 186, 192, 222, 245, 248, 263 1
Miller, Joseph 187 2
Miller, Joseph & 187 2
Miller, Joseph G 13, 58, 59, 85, 118, 142, 192, 264, 272 1
Miller, Joseph G 11, 14, 39, 154, 189, 219a, 290, 294 2
Miller, Joseph G 9, 15, 23, 40, 41, 124, 186, 209, 212, 214 3
Miller, Joseph H 188 2
Miller, Joseph Z 2 3
Miller, Joshua 181 2
Miller, Josiah 177 2
Miller, Julia A 189 2
Miller, Julia A C 188 2
Miller, Julia Ann 188 2
Miller, Julia D 191 2
Miller, Julia M 189 2
Miller, Justice 229 1
Miller, Justice 106 2
Miller, Justus 59 1
Miller, Katie Mae 178 2
Miller, Katie May 193 2
Miller, L Homer 85, 200, 224 2
Miller, Larken H 84 1
Miller, Laura F 206 2
Miller, Lavinia R 189, 195 2
Miller, Lavinna C 195 2
Miller, Leonard 159 2
Miller, Levi 186 2
Miller, Levi F 177, 197 1
Miller, Levi F 186 3
Miller, Levi F 159, 237 2
Miller, Levi O 181 2
Miller, Levi T 202 3
Miller, Lewis 227 1
Miller, Lewis M 189 2
Miller, Lizzie S 171 2
Miller, Lucinda C 195 2
Miller, Lucinda D 195 2
Miller, Luella M 190 2
Miller, M D 211 2
Miller, Mahlon 198 2
Miller, Margaret 177, 211 2
Miller, Margaret E 199 2
Miller, Margaret O 198 2
Miller, Marshall 52 1
Miller, Martin 197 2
Miller, Martin 18 3
Miller, Martin L 198 2

Miller, Mary 159, 197 2
Miller, Mary 249 1
Miller, Mary A 198 2
Miller, Mary A P 199 2
Miller, Mary Ann 198 2
Miller, Mary D 199 2
Miller, Mary E 189, 199 2
Miller, Mary G 40 1
Miller, Mary Grace 209 2
Miller, Mary K 199 2
Miller, Michael 197 2
Miller, Michael 62, 123 1
Miller, Michael H 135 1
Miller, Michael H 187 2
Miller, Milton V B 199 2
Miller, Minnie A 199 2
Miller, Minnie E 12, 199 2
Miller, Nathan 164 1
Miller, Nellie Glessner 246 1
Miller, Nettie M 202 2
Miller, Noah 202 2
Miller, O E 182, 215 2
Miller, Oliver E 163 2
Miller, Oliver Ellwood 202 2
Miller, Orpha M 18, 202 2
Miller, Oscar D 139 1
Miller, Peter 203 2
Miller, Peter Sr 203 2
Miller, Pheobe 188 2
Miller, Philip 221, 223 3
Miller, Philip 11, 115, 203 2
Miller, Philip 128, 240 1
Miller, Rachel 205 2
Miller, Ralph W 182 2
Miller, Raymond H 206 2
Miller, Roland 11 1
Miller, Ronald M 26 1
Miller, Roy L 206 2
Miller, S Francis 166 2
Miller, Samuel 37, 85, 107 1
Miller, Samuel 159, 208, 209 2
Miller, Samuel H 203 3
Miller, Sarah 181, 187, 208, 209 2
Miller, Sarah A C 183 1
Miller, Sarah A C 209 2
Miller, Sarah A E 160, 166, 209 2
Miller, Sarah C 209 2
Miller, Sarah J 209 2
Miller, Sarah V 209 2
Miller, Sarar A R 208 2
Miller, Simon 187 2
Miller, Solomon 169 2
Miller, Susan I 214 2
Miller, Susan L 209 2
Miller, Susan S 208 2
Miller, Susannah 159, 185, 208 2
Miller, T E 31 2
Miller, T E 194, 205, 214 1
Miller, T E P 135 1
Miller, T E R 128, 264, 290 2
Miller, T E R 41, 82 3
Miller, T E R Dr 211 2
Miller, Thomas 62 2
Miller, Thomas E R 152, 186 1
Miller, Thos 219 1
Miller, Vernon H 280 2
Miller, Virginia 214 2
Miller, Virginia B 213, 215 2
Miller, W S 19 3
Miller, Wash M 92 1
Miller, Washington M 60 1
Miller, William 220a, 221a, 223a, 264 2
Miller, William 217 3
Miller, William A 151 2
Miller, William E 215 2
Miller, William H 195 3
Miller, William H 31 1
Miller, William H S 202 2
Miller, William S 91, 160 3
Miller, Wm 37, 195 3
Miller, Wm 70, 110, 112, 135, 142, 147, 213, 217, 228 1
Miller, Wm 27, 138, 198, 214, 217, 224a 2
Miller, Wm E 163, 182, 215 2
Miller, Wm F 182, 215 2
Miller, Wm H 15, 22, 40, 214 2
Miller, Wm H 33, 152, 263 1
Miller, Wm H 176, 182 3
Miller, Wm M 104 1
Miller, Wm S 37, 79, 106, 118, 176, 186 1
Miller, Wm S 84, 107, 115, 143, 214, 215 2
Miller, Wm S 186, 220 3
Miller, Wm T 234 1
Miller, Wm T 199 2
Miller, Zachariah 217 2
Millet, Chas 276 2
Millet, Jos 53 3
Mills, C T 186 1
Mills, Clifton 189 2
Mills, John 181 2
Mills, John R 106 1
Mills, John R 189 2
Mills, Mary N 200 2
Mills, Nathaniel B 202 2
Mills, Richard 185, 205 2
Milyard, Christian F 166 2
Milyard, Elizabeth 171 2
Miner, Edwared E 172 2
Mines, Ann M 160 2
Mines, Eleanor W 172 2
Mines, Eliza 172 2
Mines, Harry 172 2
Mines, John L 209 3
Mines, Martha R 209 3
Mines, Martha R 160 2
Mines, Mary R 199 2
Mines, W W 222 2
Mines, William W 209 3
Mines, William W 215 2
Mines, Wm W 199 2
Mines, Wm W 160, 172, 199 2
Mines, Wm W 172 2
Minksell, Peter 26 2
Minnick, Bartholomew 163 2
Minnick, Carlton L 166 2
Minnick, Chas C 166, 172 2
Minnick, E 18 1
Minnick, Elizabeth C 172 2
Minnick, Ezra 6, 42, 100 3
Minnick, Ezra 152 1
Minnick, Ezra 89, 177, 188, 198 2
Minnick, Geo 177 2
Minnick, Joseph 188 2
Minnick, Mary M 198 2
Minnick, Pearl C 163 2
Minnick, Pearl Lena 203 2
Minor, Charles H 283 2
Minor, Jackson M 208 2
Minor, John L 171 3
Minor, Mary 188 2
Minor, Spence 208 2
Mirrman, Reese 24 1
Miss, Anna Mrs 239 2
Miss, Charles L 167 2
Miss, Chas 178 2
Miss, Earnest L 172 2
Miss, Mary G 172 2
Miss, William E 16 2
Mitchell, Abel 160 2
Mitchell, Ann M 159 2
Mitchell, Archie J 196 2
Mitchell, Edw 171 2
Mitchell, Edw Jr 171 2
Mitchell, Elizabeth 160 2
Mitchell, Gorman V 196 2
Mitchell, Horatio 181 2
Mitchell, John T 52, 117 1
Mitchell, John W 193 2
Mitchell, Joseph T 159, 187 2
Mitchell, Kate L 187 2
Mitchell, Kate Oxemhan 193 2
Mitchell, Lillie M 196 2
Mitchell, Mamie C 68 1
Mitchell, Mary Ann 211 2
Mitchell, Samuel (Col'd) 208 2
Mitchell, Theodore 211 2
Mitchell, Thomas 211 2
Mitchelll, Wm 160 2

Mixell, Francis 185 2
Mixell, Jacob 185 2
Mixell, Jacob 185 2
Moats, Chas A 192 3
Mobberly, E W 40 1
Mobberly, Edw L 171 2
Mobberly, Eldred W 171 2
Mobberly, Elizabeth 171 2
Mobberly, J C 160 2
Mobberly, James 185 2
Mobberly, Joseph 11, 187 2
Mobberly, Levi 214 1
Mobberly, Rachel 160 2
Mobberly, Roanne 171 2
Moberly, Charles R 167 2
Moberly, David 39 2
Moberly, David H 147 1
Moberly, E Elfreda 200 2
Moberly, John C 205 2
Moberly, Joseph 208 2
Moberly, Levi 58 1
Moberly, Marion S 200 2
Moberly, Mary 52 1
Moberly, Merhl S 200 2
Moberly, Rachel R 205 2
Moberly, Sallie S 126 1
Moberly, Thomas P 167 2
Mobley, Ann R 160 2
Mobley, Barbara R 200 2
Mobley, Clarence D 166 2
Mobley, Clyde A 167 2
Mobley, David H 160 2
Mobley, Edw 203 2
Mobley, Geo L 203 2
Mobley, Geo T 177 2
Mobley, Harriet L 182 2
Mobley, Howard S 181 2
Mobley, Howard V 199 2
Mobley, J O 42 3
Mobley, Joseph O 188, 257 2
Mobley, Mollie E 181 2
Mobley, Mollie H 199 2
Mobley, Pleasant V 203 2
Mobley, William J 215 2
Mobley, Wm J 166, 188, 215 2
Mock, Andrew 196 1
Mock, Elizabeth F 214 2
Mock, Frederick 175 2
Mock, Peter 144 1
Mock, Rachel 205 2
Mock, Wm T 214 2
Moffett, Benj Jr 171 2
Moffett, Benjamin 163 2
Moffett, Benjamin Jr 163 2
Moffett, Jacob F 163 2
Moffett, Mary P 163 2
Moffett, Raymond C 280 2
Moffett, Samuel 84 1
Moffitt, Benjamin 163 2
Moffitt, Elizabeth A 171 2
Moffitt, Geo M 178 2
Moffitt, Linda H 178 2
Mohler, Bertha T 222a 2
Mohler, Bessie L 205 2
Mohler, Forest G 66 2
Mohler, Jacob 186 2
Mohler, Jeremiah 8 2
Mohler, Leona 195, 198 2
Mohler, Mary E 198 2
Mohler, R B Hays 205 2
Mohler, Rebecca A 224 3
Mohler, Rutherford B 195 2
Mohler, Rutherford D H 198 2
Moler, Daniel G 169 2
Moler, Ella D 169 2
Moleson, Matthew 118 1
Molesworth, A R 153, 197 1
Molesworth, A R 87, 124 3
Molesworth, A R 189 2
Molesworth, Alfred 159 2
Molesworth, Ann 160 2
Molesworth, Annie 189 2
Molesworth, Annie A 172 2
Molesworth, Annie M 160 2
Molesworth, Archie 218 3
Molesworth, Archie R 20 3
Molesworth, Archie R 73, 107, 130 1
Molesworth, Archie R 195 2
Molesworth, Archley 18, 206 2
Molesworth, Archley 201, 272 1
Molesworth, Archley R 215 1
Molesworth, Archley R 160 2
Molesworth, Archley R 51 3
Molesworth, Carlton 169, 209, 213 2
Molesworth, Carlton L 172 2
Molesworth, Drusilla 61 1
Molesworth, Drusilla 169 2
Molesworth, E M 31, 257 2
Molesworth, Edith H 189 2
Molesworth, Edw 237 1
Molesworth, Edw M 177, 195 2
Molesworth, Edward M 172 2
Molesworth, Eli H 172 2
Molesworth, F Della 20 3
Molesworth, G C 160 2
Molesworth, Geo W 177 2
Molesworth, Gurney C 197 1
Molesworth, Gurney C 178 2
Molesworth, J W 198, 221a 2
Molesworth, Jennie 178 2
Molesworth, Jennie M 190 2
Molesworth, Jesse C 189, 195 2
Molesworth, Jesse W 160 2
Molesworth, John 118 1
Molesworth, John A 189, 247 2
Molesworth, John A 119, 245 1
Molesworth, John E 189 2
Molesworth, John J 189, 198 2
Molesworth, John Jr 189 2
Molesworth, John R 12, 189, 195 2
Molesworth, John W 189, 191, 198 2
Molesworth, Joseph 188 2
Molesworth, Jurney C 142 1
Molesworth, Lewis A 195 2
Molesworth, Lillie M 195 2
Molesworth, M 146 1
Molesworth, Margaret M 189 2
Molesworth, Mary A 198 2
Molesworth, Mary A D 198 2
Molesworth, Mary T 199 2
Molesworth, Mary V E 197 1
Molesworth, Mathias 198 2
Molesworth, Matthias 100 1
Molesworth, Sarah E 159, 209 2
Molesworth, Thomas 198, 211 2
Molesworth, Thomas E 211 2
Molesworth, Thos 172 2
Molesworth, Thos E 211 2
Molesworth, Vernon T 211, 213 2
Molewworth, Drusilla 211 2
Moling, Edw S 171 2
Moling, Wm 171 2
Momas, O B 166 3
Monath, August 194 1
Monath, Hallie L 182 2
Moncrief, Robt 205 2
Mondorff, Beatrice P 196 2
Mondorff, Laurence L 196 2
Mondorff, Lawrence L 166 1
Mondorff, Lawrence L 3 3
Monroe, W F 189 3
Montgomery Charles W 167 2
Montgomery, Alice A 160 2
Montgomery, Ann H 160 2
Montgomery, Caroline 166, 187 2
Montgomery, Chas N 166 2
Montgomery, Chas W 160 2
Montgomery, Clara V 166 2
Montgomery, Edgar L 209 2
Montgomery, Ella H 16, 215 2
Montgomery, Ella Horsey 45 2
Montgomery, Geo W 166, 178

2
Montgomery, George W 178 2
Montgomery, I Raynor 178 2
Montgomery, J J 152 1
Montgomery, James 63, 187, 188 2
Montgomery, James I 160, 189, 198 2
Montgomery, John 1, 164, 179, 229 1
Montgomery, John 203 3
Montgomery, John 38, 186, 187 2
Montgomery, John Sr 186 2
Montgomery, John T 113 3
Montgomery, John W 188 2
Montgomery, John, Jr 96 1
Montgomery, Julia 178 2
Montgomery, Lida M 189 2
Montgomery, Luther A 160, 166, 196 2
Montgomery, Mary 166 2
Montgomery, Millard F 198 2
Montgomery, Susan A 188, 209 2
Montgomery, Warrick E 215 2
Montz, A B 160 2
Montz, Arabella 160 2
Montz, Joseph 185 3
Moody, Levi 195 2
Mooers, F Burt 175 2
Mooers, V Florence 175 2
Mooney, Mary 214 2
Mooney, William 18 3
Mooney, Wm 22, 214 2
Moore, Annabelle 190 2
Moore, Barbara C 163 2
Moore, Burgess 57 2
Moore, Burgess L 163 2
Moore, Catherine J 166 2
Moore, Daniel M 169 2
Moore, Delbert 170 2
Moore, E K 91 3
Moore, E L 23 1
Moore, Edgar K 189, 206 3
Moore, Edgar K 183, 169 1
Moore, Edward L 166 1
Moore, Eliza 171 2
Moore, Emma C 173 2
Moore, Geo 177 2
Moore, Geo M 177 2
Moore, George S 178 2
Moore, Georgia A 178 2
Moore, Harry M 182 2
Moore, Ira V 146 1
Moore, J E 183 1
Moore, James 185, 187 2
Moore, James E 40 1
Moore, Jesse 81 3
Moore, Jesse S 190, 206 2
Moore, John 195, 209 3
Moore, John 166, 196 1
Moore, John 100, 197, 208 2
Moore, John C 166 2
Moore, John T 177 2
Moore, Joseph 205 3
Moore, Laura G 178, 196 2
Moore, Laura G 19 1
Moore, Mabel E 182 2
Moore, Mary C 163 2
Moore, Mattie E 170 2
Moore, Rebecca D 205 2
Moore, Robt 18 3
Moore, Robt F 206 2
Moore, Sarah E 208 2
Moore, Tobias 211 2
Moore, Wm 171, 187, 208 2
Moore, Wm 253, 271 1
Moore, Wm H 40, 163, 214 2
Moorefield, Daniel 234 2
Moorehead, A E 206 2
Moorehead, Hilda B 215 2
Moorehead, Wilbur T 215 2
Mooreland, Eliza G 171 2
Mooreland, Wm 208, 214 2
Mopps, Geo W 177 2
Mopps, Howard E 177 2
Mopps, Jim 177 2
Mopps, Mary M 177 2
Moran, Anna 161, 190 2
Moran, John A 161 2
Moran, John S 190 2
Moran, Margaret B 48 1
Moran, Margaret R 53 1
Moran, Wm F 48 1
Moran, Wm F 161 2
Morehouse, Amy R 259 2
Morelan, Noble 202 2
Moreland, John 38 2
Moreland, Mary 197 2
Moreland, Wm 165 2
Morelock, Michael 234 1
Morgan, Allen M 161 2
Morgan, Benton M 163 2
Morgan, Catherine 195 2
Morgan, Chas E 82 1
Morgan, Dale 163 2
Morgan, Ethel G 173 2
Morgan, G H 144, 211 2
Morgan, Geo 118 1
Morgan, Geo W 195 2
Morgan, Gerard 177 2
Morgan, I R 189 2
Morgan, J W 2 2
Morgan, James W 276 2
Morgan, Jennie 211 2
Morgan, John 187, 195 2
Morgan, John 125, 139 1
Morgan, John W 195 2
Morgan, Laura F 144 2
Morgan, Lee W 195 2
Morgan, Louisa 195 2
Morgan, Lyttleton B 195 2
Morgan, Mary E 144, 211 2
Morgan, Rufus R 21 3
Morgan, Thomas 134 2
Morgan, Thomas W 54, 211 2
Morgan, Thos 101, 214 2
Morgan, Thos W 43 2
Morgan, Thos W Sr 211 2
Morgan, W Robert 51 3
Morgan, William R 215 2
Morgans, David K 169 2
Morgenroth, Jacob 187 2
Morgenroth, Rosanna 187 2
Moritz, Jos 254 2
Morlock, James 223 1
Morlock, Michael 98, 135 3
Mornignstar, Philip H 203 2
Morningstar, Charles G 182 2
Morningstar, Clifton O 202 3
Morningstar, Geo 209 2
Morningstar, Geo F 14 1
Morningstar, Harry G 182 2
Morningstar, Helen M 177 1
Morningstar, Jesse 39, 169 2
Morningstar, John H 196 2
Morningstar, Levi 100 1
Morningstar, Levi 70 3
Morningstar, Lucy Ellen 196 2
Morningstar, Morris Earl 182 2
Morningstar, Philip Sr 203 2
Morningstar, Salome 208 2
Morningstar, Sarah A 209 2
Morningstar, Vincent 169 2
Morris, Clifford O 46 3
Morris, David 169 2
Morris, Fanny Mary 175 2
Morris, John M 129 1
Morris, Jonathan 40 1
Morris, Robert F 175 2
Morris, Samuel 70 1
Morris, William B 148 3
Morrison, Ada 34 1
Morrison, Ann 205 2
Morrison, Anne B 161 2
Morrison, David 109 1
Morrison, David 169, 186 2
Morrison, E G 70 1
Morrison, Edgar B 161 2
Morrison, Edw L 140 1
Morrison, Evelyn T 161 2
Morrison, Francanna 175 2
Morrison, Geo 214 2
Morrison, Harriet 169, 181 2
Morrison, J 13 1

Morrison, J G 26, 225 1
Morrison, James 185, 208 2
Morrison, James 56, 112 1
Morrison, James F 42 3
Morrison, Jane 185, 186 2
Morrison, Jeremiah 76, 185 2
Morrison, Jeremiah 240, 270 1
Morrison, Jeremiah G 208 2
Morrison, Jeremiah G 163, 263 1
Morrison, John 70 1
Morrison, John 185 2
Morrison, John M 84 1
Morrison, Lloyd 181 2
Morrison, Lorna B 195 2
Morrison, Mary 185 2
Morrison, Oliver 175, 202, 208 2
Morrison, Oliver 32 1
Morrison, Paul A 195 2
Morrison, Reuben 202, 205 2
Morrison, Robt 205 2
Morrison, Samuel 23 1
Morrison, Samuel 208, 214 2
Morrison, Sarah 214a 2
Morrison, Susan 208 2
Morrison, W D 224a 2
Morrison, William 2 3
Morrison, William 217a 2
Morrison, Wm 82, 125, 197, 225 1
Morrison, Wm 51, 178, 181, 185, 214 2
Morrison, Wm B 214 2
Morrits, Joseph 186 2
Morse, Edmund C 172 2
Morse, Ivy M 172 2
Morse, Mathew P 198 2
Morsell, Julia 190 2
Morsell, Julia P 190 2
Morsell, Mary 197 2
Morsell, William 171 3
Morsell, William 251 2
Morsell, Wm 93, 197, 214 2
Mort, Annie V 160 2
Mort, Baltzer 163 2
Mort, Charles P 28 1
Mort, Charles P 167, 184 2
Mort, Elizabeth 171 2
Mort, Ethel I 173 2
Mort, F B 208 1
Mort, Franklin 234 1
Mort, Frederick R 175, 214 2
Mort, Geo 208 2
Mort, Harrison M 167 2
Mort, Ida F 184 2
Mort, Margaret A 208 2
Mort, Mary M 175 2
Mort, Mathias 197 2
Mort, Peter 203 2
Mort, S F 144 1
Mort, Samuel 208 2
Mort, Spencer E 173 2
Mort, Susan 209 2
Mort, Susan M 215 2
Mort, Walter A 160 2
Mort, WilliamM 215 2
Mort, Wm 68, 272 1
Mort, Wm 214 2
Mort, Wm H 215 2
Mortimer, Aubrey Max 161 2
Mortimer, Bessie J 163 2
Morton, Elizabeth W 173 2
Morton, Roberta D 173 2
Morton, William Dare 173 2
Mortz, Ruth E 215 2
Mortz, Wm C 215 2
Mortz, Wm M 215 2
Moser, A S 32 2
Moser, Abraham 159, 165 2
Moser, Albert W 166 3
Moser, Alpha T 161, 202 2
Moser, Alpha T 136, 234 1
Moser, C E 199 2
Moser, Carrie E 9 2
Moser, Christian 165 2
Moser, Clarence 167 2
Moser, Cyrus 166 2
Moser, Daniel 169 2
Moser, Daniel J 129 2
Moser, Edgar C 189 2
Moser, Edward J 172 2
Moser, Elias 277 1
Moser, Elias 171 2
Moser, Elizabeth L 172 2
Moser, Elizabeth S 215 2
Moser, Ella M 161 2
Moser, Elmer J 196, 215 2
Moser, Enos 188 2
Moser, Everett V 90 2
Moser, Ezra 128, 129, 169, 171, 195, 208 2
Moser, Ezra J 9 2
Moser, Floyd T 161, 202 2
Moser, Geo 177 2
Moser, Harvey E 167 2
Moser, Henry 129 2
Moser, J H 208 1
Moser, Jacob 165, 195 2
Moser, Jacob & 29 2
Moser, Jacob A 190 2
Moser, Jacob L 189 2
Moser, John 71 1
Moser, John 165, 187, 195, 208 2
Moser, John E 189 2
Moser, John H 190 2
Moser, John P 189 2
Moser, John R 188 2
Moser, Jonathan 188 2
Moser, Joseph C 190 2
Moser, Joshua 187 2
Moser, L M 129 2
Moser, Lewis E 171 2
Moser, Lizzie S 196 2
Moser, Lucinda 195 2
Moser, Lydia 171 2
Moser, Mamie E 172 2
Moser, Margaret T 92 3
Moser, Mary E 159 2
Moser, Milly 199 2
Moser, Nannie L 202 2
Moser, Olivia C 202 2
Moser, Sampson H 209 2
Moser, Samuel 208 2
Moser, Sarah 208 2
Moser, William S 215 2
Moser, Wilmer W 202 2
Mosher, Jonathan 186 2
Mosoner, Margaret 197 2
Moss, B H 283 1
Moss, Joseph E 218a 2
Mossberg, Grover 178 2
Mossburg, Ann E 181 2
Mossburg, Chas H 169 2
Mossburg, Darcus E 169 2
Mossburg, Geo J 178 2
Mossburg, Henry W 181 2
Motherway, Mary H Shafter 73 3
Motter, Ada S 160, 184 2
Motter, Andrew 106 1
Motter, Anna F 159 2
Motter, Catherine 165, 208 2
Motter, Daniel 169 2
Motter, Elizabeth 197 2
Motter, Ella J 160, 190 2
Motter, Ella Johnson 268 2
Motter, Ellijay 184 2
Motter, G K 232 2
Motter, Geo 177, 187 2
Motter, George S 178 2
Motter, Grace 48 1
Motter, Guy E 32 2
Motter, Guy K 88, 183, 254 1
Motter, Guy K 2, 83, 102, 160, 184, 190, 196, 225a, 268 2
Motter, Harriet 124, 181 2
Motter, Harriet H 182, 199 2
Motter, Henry 56 1
Motter, Henry 181 2
Motter, Henry 177, 181 2
Motter, Henry 1 3

Motter, Henry D 181 2
Motter, I Taylor 48 1
Motter, Isaac 197 2
Motter, Isaac M 70, 184, 185 2
Motter, Issac M 224a 2
Motter, J 91 3
Motter, J C 71, 85, 119, 208, 210, 265 1
Motter, J C 8, 29, 30, 49, 54, 223a 2
Motter, J C 55, 116, 124, 160, 187, 196, 210 3
Motter, J E 88 1
Motter, J T 82 3
Motter, J T 188 2
Motter, J T 165 1
Motter, J Taylor 26, 189 1
Motter, J Taylor 57, 124 2
Motter, Jacob 187 2
Motter, Jacob 196, 279 1
Motter, Jacob 53, 96 3
Motter, James 46 2
Motter, John 4, 265, 253 1
Motter, John 19, 87, 165, 198, 211, 213, 210a 2
Motter, John C 27, 30, 41, 48, 55, 60, 71, 82, 85, 92, 100, 106, 110, 112, 123, 126, 139, 150, 152, 176, 186, 197, 217, 234, 257, 279 1
Motter, John C 2, 6, 19, 23, 27, 42, 43, 50, 55, 71, 79, 87, 91, 96, 106, 107, 160, 161, 166, 171, 179, 182, 196, 207, 209, 221 3
Motter, John C 8, 15, 20, 22, 29, 35, 39, 40, 49, 51, 65, 68, 72, 92, 99, 101, 107, 113, 116, 119, 122, 144, 154, 160, 172, 178, 189, 190, 208, 209, 214, 221a, 223a, 225a, 238, 250, 277, 290 2
Motter, John F 165 3
Motter, John S 67, 89 3
Motter, John S 214 2
Motter, Joseph 19 1
Motter, Joshiah 203 3
Motter, Joshua 1, 14, 28, 54, 57, 107, 165, 177, 187, 188, 195, 197, 208, 250, 254, 274, 280 2
Motter, Joshua 8, 26, 40, 41 3
Motter, Joshua 58, 71, 139, 164, 239, 264 1
Motter, Joshua 14 3
Motter, Josiah 71, 176, 223, 224 3
Motter, Josiah 239, 279 1
Motter, Josuah 106 3
Motter, L 77 3
Motter, L Edwin 196 2
Motter, L M 30 1
Motter, L M 102 3
Motter, Lewis 6, 171 1
Motter, Lewis 14, 19, 57, 58, 165, 169, 195, 250 2
Motter, Lewis 26, 106 3
Motter, Lewis M 23, 58, 95, 169, 264 1
Motter, Lewis M 111, 187, 195 2
Motter, Lewis M 64, 65, 71 3
Motter, Lewis N 39 3
Motter, Louis 78 1
Motter, M Louise 181, 199 2
Motter, Mary 195 2
Motter, Mary M 197 2
Motter, Michael 185, 197 2
Motter, Paul 208 2
Motter, Roger 65 2
Motter, Samuel 177, 208 2
Motter, Samuel 19 1
Motter, Samuel 40, 203 3
Motter, Valentine 213 2
Motter, Wm 238 1
Motter, Wm 177, 181, 214 2
Mottern, Jacob 187 2
Mottern, John 187 2
Moudy (Mowdy), John M 190 2
Moudy, John M Sr 190 2
Mount, Alice S 160 2
Mount, Elias 229 1
Mount, Harry 70, 215 2
Mount, Harry O 206 2
Mount, Maurice W 160 2
Mount, Rachel Priscilla 206 2
Mount, Wallace M 218a 2
Mount, Wm 214, 215 2
Mouse, Andrew 186 2
Mouse, Geo 177 2
Mouse, Jacob 177 2
Mouse, Levi 177 2
Mouse, Ludwick 195 2
Mouse, Nicholas 195 2
Movelock, Michael 213 1
Mowdy, John M 190 2
Moxley, Amanda C 160, 205 2
Moxley, Annie 160 2
Moxley, Evaleen 224 2
Moxley, Everett Linwood 283 2
Moxley, Hattie V 181 2
Moxley, J E 41 1
Moxley, John H 160 2
Moxley, Joseph 181 2
Moxley, R M 241 2
Moxley, Reuben M 205 2
Moxley, T Edw 147 1
Moxley, Wm T 160 2
Moxly, Ezekiel 113 2
Moyer, Charlotte 165 2
Moyer, Jacob 185 2
Moyer, John 165, 185, 208 2
Moyer, Susannah 208 2
Moylan, Charles E 10 3
Moyster, Anna[?] 239 1
Muck, Elizabeth 171 2
Muck, Harry C 196 3
Muck, Henry 181 2
Mulcahy, Dennis D 144 1
Mulfinger, Bessie 190 2
Mulfinger, John P 190 2
Mullan, Mary A 198 2
Mullegan, Ann C 159 2
Mullen, D H 188 2
Mullen, Hugh 156 1
Mullen, Hugh 38 2
Mullen, James 188 2
Mullen, John J 76 1
Mullen, Mary 188 2
Mullen, Mary A 181 2
Mullen, Mary V 200 2
Mullen, Mary Virginia 200 2
Mullen, Matilda B 188 2
Mullendore, Catherine 165 2
Mullendore, Cora 24 1
Mullendore, D M 65 3
Mullendore, Daniel L 65 3
Mullendore, David 57 1
Mullendore, David 169 2
Mullendore, E A C 65 3
Mullendore, E C 42 3
Mullendore, Jennie 24 1
Mullican, Geo T 198 2
Mullican, Hiram H 28 2
Mullican, James J 196 3
Mullican, M Irene 215 2
Mullican, Mary E 198 2
Mullican, Wm T 215 2
Mullin, Charlotte E 166 2
Mullin, Chas E 166 2
Mullin, Edw 171 2
Mullin, H H 19 2
Mullin, Hugh 26, 181 2
Mullin, James 171, 188 2
Mullin, John 188 2
Mullin, Michael A 110 1
Mullin, Wm 214 2
Mullinix, Annie E 161, 195 2
Mullinix, Clifton A 181 2
Mullinix, E E 166 2
Mullinix, Eldridge C 172 2
Mullinix, Elisha E 172 2
Mullinix, Gertrude E 178 2
Mullinix, John 117, 153 1
Mullinix, L C 71 1
Mullinix, L C 113, 166 2
Mullinix, L E 31, 113 2
Mullinix, L E 88, 201 1
Mullinix, Leonard C 195 2
Mullinix, Leonard C 205 3
Mullinix, Lilliam Burke 68 1

Mullinix, Lillie 189 3
Mullinix, Lillie 175 2
Mullinix, Lillie M 215 2
Mullinix, Lonzo E 27 1
Mullinix, Lorenzo E 195 2
Mullinix, W T 175 2
Mullinix, Wm F 215 2
Mullinix, Wm T 163, 215 2
Mumford, Ann V 160 2
Mumford, Chas E 48 1
Mumford, E Carlton 189 2
Mumford, Grace L 86 1
Mumford, James 186 2
Mumford, John W 189, 205 2
Mumford, Laura E 195, 198 2
Mumford, Martin J 198 2
Mumford, Mary 198 2
Mumford, Richard 198 2
Mumford, Richard W 205 2
Mumford, Stanley 211 2
Mumford, Thomas G 211 2
Mumma, Charles L 167 2
Mumma, Charles W 167 2
Mumma, Ethel M 167 2
Mumma, John R 197 3
Mumma, Lillian W 197 3
Munay, Lucy A 165 1
Mundey, Harry E 182 2
Mundey, John 42 3
Mundshower, Jacob 186 2
Mundshower, John 186 2
Munroe, Nathan 202 2
Munroe, Wm C 215 2
Munshour, J Lester 190 2
Munshower, Chas L 189 2
Munshower, Jacob 188, 282 2
Munshower, John W 188, 189 2
Munsing, Lewis 228 1
Murdock, Aaron (col) 159 2
Murdock, Ann 159 2
Murdock, Benj 171 2
Murdock, Benjamin 163 2
Murdock, Comfort Rebecca 166 2
Murdock, Eleanore 171 2
Murdock, Elinore 197 2
Murdock, Elizabeth 171 2
Murdock, Geo 177 2
Murdock, Geo W 177 2
Murdock, John 72, 264, 271 2
Murdock, Jonathan (Col'd) 186 2
Murdock, Mary C 72, 197 2
Murdock, Mary Catherine 199 2
Murdock, R B 102, 205 2
Murdock, R B 91, 197 3
Murdock, R B 8 1
Murdock, R Bruce 134, 188, 189 3
Murdock, R Bruce 188 1
Murdock, R Bruce 218a 2
Murdock, Richard B 163, 205 2
Murdock, Richard H 205 2
Murdock, Wm 214 2
Murgee, McSherry 154 2
Murphy, A Kate 190 2
Murphy, Amanda J 172 2
Murphy, Ann 214 2
Murphy, Anna Kate 161 2
Murphy, Baxter 190 2
Murphy, Chas 178 2
Murphy, Emory A 172 2
Murphy, French 209 2
Murphy, H Kate 24 3
Murphy, Henry 181 2
Murphy, Hezekiah 181 2
Murphy, J Glenn 190 2
Murphy, J Glenn 190 2
Murphy, James 185, 247 2
Murphy, James H 185 2
Murphy, James M 196 2
Murphy, James M 63 1
Murphy, James W 190 2
Murphy, John 209 2
Murphy, John 201 1
Murphy, John D 189 2
Murphy, John R 181 2
Murphy, Joseph 185, 190 2
Murphy, Joseph 272 1
Murphy, Joseph A 185 2
Murphy, Lena O 139 3
Murphy, Lillie May 196 2
Murphy, Margaret A 93 2
Murphy, Mary Elizabeth 120 1
Murphy, Mary M 198 2
Murphy, Mollie E 189 2
Murphy, Myrtle M 21 3
Murphy, Patrick 203 2
Murphy, Samuel T 198 2
Murphy, Sarah J 209 2
Murphy, Susan C 208 2
Murphy, William 222 2
Murphy, Wm 185, 214 2
Murphy, Wm 27 1
Murphy, Wm R 48, 201 1
Murphy, Wm[?] R 11 1
Murrary, Joshua T 198 2
Murray 140 2
Murray, Annie G 160 2
Murray, Annie M 178 2
Murray, Bridget M 163 2
Murray, Charles C 167 2
Murray, Daniel M Jr 145 2
Murray, Daniel M, Jr 21, 48 1
Murray, Ella E 34 1
Murray, Ella E 167 2
Murray, Harry 198 2
Murray, James 186 2
Murray, John 186, 197, 205 2
Murray, John 192 1
Murray, John Donalds 190 2
Murray, John J 160, 189, 198 2
Murray, John Jacob 190 2
Murray, Joshua 185 2
Murray, Joshua T 189 2
Murray, Lewis 195 2
Murray, Marshall I 198 2
Murray, Mary Ann 197 2
Murray, Matthew 277 1
Murray, Matthew 185 2
Murray, Rachel 123 1
Murray, Roscoe C 68 1
Murray, Silas E 167 2
Murray, Thomas G 211 2
Murry, Basil 163 2
Murry, Mary 163 2
Musante, John 195 2
Musante, Lazzro 195 2
Musante, Mary K 195 2
Musante, Paul 195 2
Musgrove 160 3
Musgrove, Donald G 215 2
Musgrove, James S 188 2
Musgrove, Maurice R 208 2
Musgrove, Sammie Lee 208 2
Musgrove, William G 215 2
Mushenheim, Wm 215 2
Musphe, Hezekiah 32 1
Mussear, Jesse H 165 3
Musser, Francis T 175 2
Musser, Henry 27 2
Musser, John B 1 2
Musser, Ralph E 205 2
Musser, Sarah E 205 2
Musser, Sarah Ellen 209 2
Musser, Susan 188 2
Musser, Susan R 175 2
Mussetter, Alexander 159 2
Mussetter, C 146 1
Mussetter, Catherine 165 2
Mussetter, Christopher 165 2
Mussetter, Christopher 84, 163 1
Mussetter, H P 180, 208 3
Mussetter, Henry 189 2
Mussetter, Henry P 63, 225, 220a 2
Mussetter, Henry P 61 1
Mussetter, Henry R 156 1
Mussetter, John 163 1
Mussetter, John 165, 205 2
Mussetter, Lemuel 156 1
Mussetter, Lewis 203 2

Mussetter, Mary V E 200 2
Mussetter, Michael 197 2
Mussetter, Philip 110 1
Mussetter, Philip 93, 203 2
Mussetter, Phoebe 203 2
Mussetter, Ruth 205 2
Mussetter, Samuel 112 1
MvCardell, A LeRoy 294 2
Myer Margaret C 198 2
Myer, B E 257, 272 1
Myer, B F 265 1
Myer, Geo 47 1
Myer, James W 272 1
Myerhouffer, Peter 203 2
Myerly, Jacob 38 3
Myerly, Jacob 186 2
Myers 70 3
Myers, A Maria C 197 2
Myers, Abraham 214 1
Myers, Abraham 22, 138, 159, 160 2
Myers, Adam 6 1
Myers, Alexina 160 2
Myers, Andrew 159, 197 2
Myers, Annie Catherine 28 3
Myers, Annie M 188 2
Myers, Arthur V 199, 209, 211, 215a, 278 2
Myers, Arthur V 113, 157 1
Myers, Ashby W 160 2
Myers, Barbara 163 2
Myers, Benjamin S 163 2
Myers, Bernard 166 2
Myers, Blanche E 163, 18 2
Myers, C F 30 2
Myers, Casper 39 2
Myers, Catherine 165, 211 2
Myers, Catherine 18 3
Myers, Charles A 196 2
Myers, Charles S 199 2
Myers, Chas 135, 122 1
Myers, Chas 189 2
Myers, Chas H 165 2
Myers, Chas J 165 2
Myers, Chas W 166 2
Myers, Christian 268 2
Myers, Christian 6 1
Myers, Christian H 166 2
Myers, Christopher 165 2
Myers, Christopher 70 1
Myers, Clara E 166 2
Myers, Clara V 163 2
Myers, Daniel 169, 178, 185 2
Myers, Daniel 25 1
Myers, David 117, 240 1
Myers, David 79 3
Myers, David 169, 17, 186, 208, 226 2
Myers, David A 170 2
Myers, David L 169, 258 2
Myers, Edith V 18 2
Myers, Edw I 178 2
Myers, Edward I 278, 284 2
Myers, Edward L 18 2
Myers, Ellen E 166 2
Myers, Ephriam 169, 171 2
Myers, Ernest 139 2
Myers, Ernest L 89, 110 2
Myers, Eula A 124 1
Myers, F M 148 1
Myers, F Ross 43, 110, 131, 140, 172, 175, 199, 211, 238, 259, 283 2
Myers, F Ross 3, 92, 161, 224 3
Myers, F Ross 93, 127, 155, 183, 186, 204, 275 1
Myers, Frank D 175 2
Myers, Frank M 175 2
Myers, G Ed 136 2
Myers, G Edw 92 1
Myers, G Edward 219 1
Myers, Geo 39, 160, 177, 197 2
Myers, Geo C F 178 2
Myers, Geo E 107, 177 2
Myers, Geo W 166, 178, 209 2
Myers, Geo W 272 1
Myers, Geo W 15, 71, 113, 124 3
Myers, Geo Wm 178 2
Myers, George Edward 178 2
Myers, George W 211 2
Myers, Grace A 98 3
Myers, H L 166 2
Myers, Harry L 10 2
Myers, Henry 144 3
Myers, Ida M 184 2
Myers, Iseral 160 3
Myers, Israel 184, 185 2
Myers, Israel 133 1
Myers, Israel 8 3
Myers, J B 175, 199 2
Myers, Jacob 159, 185, 186, 188, 197 2
Myers, Jacob D S 169 2
Myers, James 187 2
Myers, James F 178 2
Myers, James W 265 1
Myers, Jas B 16 2
Myers, Jesse 258 2
Myers, Jesse 41 3
Myers, John 6, 26, 138, 165, 169, 185, 186, 188 2
Myers, John 91 1
Myers, John & 166 2
Myers, John H 98 3
Myers, John J 189 2
Myers, John J 96 3
Myers, John N 189 2
Myers, John S 188 2
Myers, Joseph 106, 177, 185, 186 2
Myers, Joseph A 2 2
Myers, Laura V 196 2
Myers, Lewis C 165 2
Myers, M C 96 3
Myers, Magadne 197 2
Myers, Magdalene 197 2
Myers, Margaret 150, 197 2
Myers, Margaret C 94 3
Myers, Margaret L 175, 199 2
Myers, Margaret Vivian 199 2
Myers, Martha 178 2
Myers, Martin 223a 2
Myers, Mary 197 2
Myers, Mary E 3, 178, 199, 200 2
Myers, Mary K 175 2
Myers, Mattie B 28 1
Myers, Michael 70 1
Myers, Michael 197 2
Myers, N W 184, 188 2
Myers, Peter 203 1
Myers, Peter 57, 185 2
Myers, Robt E 205 2
Myers, Rosanna 188 2
Myers, Samuel 14 3
Myers, Samuel 19 2
Myers, Samuel 228 1
Myers, Samuel Wesley 209 2
Myers, Sarah 208 2
Myers, T Ross 126 1
Myers, Thomas F 211 2
Myers, Thomas J 66, 211 2
Myers, Thos 31, 65 2
Myers, Tilghman P 211 2
Myers, Trevania 211 2
Myers, Valentine 96 3
Myers, Valentine 213 2
Myers, Virgia M 205 2
Myers, William 208 1
Myers, Wm 188 2
Myers, Wm D 160 2
Nagel, Jacob 4 1
Naggio, Vincent 178 2
Nagle, George 224 2
Nagle, Julia A 224 2
Nahan, Daniel 221 2
Naiel, Cora Jane 220 2
Nail, Christian 220 2
Nail, Elizabeth A 222 2
Nail, Jacob H 59 1
Naile, David W 207 3
Nailer, H L 146 1
Naill, Christian 113, 120, 217a, 220a, 275 2
Naill, D H 272 1
Naill, Daniel 221 2
Naill, David 26 1
Naill, David 18 3

Naill, David W 220, 221, 247 2
Naill, David W 51, 144, 159, 279, 283 1
Naill, Elizabeth A L 222 2
Naill, H C 28 2
Naill, H C 209 3
Naill, H Clay 118 1
Naill, H Cloy [sic] 85 1
Naill, Henry 271 1
Naill, Henry C 85 1
Naill, Jacob 57, 138, 221, 226, 212a 2
Naill, Jacob 221 2
Naill, Jacob H 141 3
Naill, Jacob H 28, 35 2
Naill, Jacob N 215a 2
Naill, John E 215a 2
Naill, Nathaniel H 75 3
Naill, Peter 75, 141 3
Naill, Peter 212a 2
Naill, Sam 263 1
Naill, Samuel 253 1
Naill, Samuel 135 3
Naill, Samuel 26, 220 2
Naill, Washington 279 1
Naill, Washington M 215a 2
Naill, William 220 2
Naill, William A 220 2
Naill, Wm 279 1
Naill, Wm 113 2
Naille, Bessie M 209 2
Naille, Samuel 203 2
Nalle, Flora Virginia 131 1
Nallen, Inez 190 2
Nallin, N R 190 2
Nash, Ruby E 215a 2
Nash, Viola E 215a 2
National Surety Co 87 3
National Surety Co 265 2
National Surety Co of N Y 48 1
National Surety Co of N Y 124, 215 2
National Surety Company 81 2
National Surety Corp of N Y 120 1
National Surety Corporation 63 1
Naught, A C 159, 265 1
Naught, A C H 124 2
Naught, Andrew 200 1
Naught, Andrew 139 2
Naught, C C 58 2
Naught, Conrad W 5 2
Naught, Daniel 70 1
Naught, John 66, 137 2
Naught, John 125 1
Naught, Samuel 165, 189, 229 1
Naught, Samuel 138 2
Naught, Samuel 2 3
Naylor, Henry 227 2
Naylor, James 40 1
Naylor, James 18, 187 2
Naylor, Jmaes 226 2
Naylor, John W 118 1
Naylor, John W 227 2
Naylor, Mary L 210a 2
Naylor, O Roscoe 215a 2
Naylor, Oso 212a 2
Naylor, Otho 118 1
Naylor, Richard 213a 2
Naylor, William H 215a 2
Naylor, Wm R 62 1
Nayor, John 212a 2
Nazareans, Matilda 210a 2
Nead, John 154 2
Neagley, Walberger 215a 2
Neal, Bascom S 67 2
Neal, Leone Mae 67 2
Neal, Maria 210a 2
Neal, Sophia 214a 2
Neale, Anna C 218 2
Neale, Mary F 210a 2
Neale, Robert 213a 2
Neale, Sophria 214a 2
Neall, Geo W 48 1
Nealle, Eleanor 218 2
Nebinger, Arthur 218 2
Need, Henry 210a 2
Need, Jacob 210a 2
Need, Jane C 227, 215a 2
Need, Jane C 215a 2
Need, John 1, 25, 27, 28, 132, 138, 187, 227, 275, 276 2
Need, John 195, 213 3
Need, John 67, 71, 106, 238, 239 1
Need, Magdalene 210a 2
Need, Mary 210a 2
Need, William T 209 3
Need, William T 210a, 215a 2
Neel, J Guy 11 3
Neeswagner, Christian 122 3
Neff, Adam 218 2
Neff, Barbara 220 2
Neff, Henry 226 2
Neff, Jacob 32 1
Neff, Jacob 26, 157, 208, 218, 220 2
Neff, Jacob 31, 38 3
Neff, John 226 2
Neff, Malinda 210a 2
Neff, Melinda 210a 2
Neidhardt, Caroline 19 3
Neidhardt, J William 227 2
Neidhardt, Mary 227 2
Neidhardt, Mary L 210a 2
Neidhardt, Randolph 52 1
Neidhardt, Rudolph 210a 2
Neidhardt, William 215a 2
Neidhart, Wm 32 1
Neidig, Abraham 18, 218 2
Neidig, Abraham & 182 1
Neidig, Benjamin 18, 132 2
Neidig, Benjamin 156 1
Neidig, Emma B 222 2
Neidig, Grace 215a 2
Neidig, Isaac 226 2
Neidig, Jacob 227 2
Neidig, Mary J 226 2
Neidig, William 227 2
Neidig, William C 222, 215a 2
Neidig, William C 113, 202 3
Neidig, Wm C 100 1
Neighbors, Anna L 224 2
Neighbors, E D 165 1
Neighbors, Ella M 222 2
Neighbors, Ella M 167 3
Neighbors, Eutaw D 214a 2
Neighbors, Eutaw D 222 2
Neighbors, Fleet R 224 2
Neighbors, Grace 227 2
Neighbors, J Wm 227 2
Neighbors, Martha R 210a 2
Neighbors, Mary F 26 1
Neighbors, N O 54, 160 3
Neighbors, N O 212a, 214a 2
Neighbors, N O 59, 73, 130, 171 1
Neighbors, Nathan O 212a, 247 2
Neighbors, Nellie 227 2
Neighbors, R M 257 1
Neighbors, R M 210a, 212a 2
Neighbors, Roger 212a 2
Neighbors, Roger M 214a 2
Neighbors, Roger M 41 1
Neighbors, Sarah E 214a 2
Neighbors, Utah D 167 3
Neighbors, Vila B 227 2
Neighbours, Annie L 218 2
Neighbours, Chester W 227, 215a 2
Neighbours, E D 223, 243 1
Neighbours, E D 40 2
Neighbours, E D Dr 189 2
Neighbours, Ella 189, 195 2
Neighbours, Ella M 222, 224 2
Neighbours, Eutaw D 23, 52 2
Neighbours, Eutaw Dr 195 2
Neighbours, Fleet Bond 224 2
Neighbours, Fleet R 224 2
Neighbours, Grace 227, 215a 2
Neighbours, J W 150 2

Neighbours, John O 213a 2
Neighbours, John O Sr 210a, 212a, 214a 2
Neighbours, John W 227 2
Neighbours, Martha O 210a 2
Neighbours, Mary F 170, 218, 224 2
Neighbours, Mildred 189 2
Neighbours, N O 238 1
Neighbours, Nathan 208 2
Neighbours, Nathan O 187, 212a 2
Neighbours, R M 2 2
Neighbours, Roger M 213a 2
Neighbours, Roger N 107 2
Neighbours, Sarah 214a 2
Neighbours, Vilia B 215a 2
Neighbous, Nathan O 212a 2
Neighoff, Christian 290 2
Neihoff, Elizabeth 224 2
Neihoff, Gabriel 224 2
Neill, Alexander 45 2
Neill, Alexander 43 3
Neill, Horatio G 152 1
Neimier, John 227 2
Neiswanger, Christian 220 2
Neiswanger, Lewis 229 2
Nelson, Ann Catherine 218 2
Nelson, Benjamin 220, 247 2
Nelson, Benjamin E 220 2
Nelson, Burgess Jr 220 2
Nelson, Burgess Sr 220 2
Nelson, Cora 222 2
Nelson, Dorothy Wagner 229 2
Nelson, E Edward 222 2
Nelson, Edward 222 2
Nelson, Edward W Jr 222 2
Nelson, Elisha 57, 222 2
Nelson, Elisha 184 3
Nelson, Eliza 222, 213a 2
Nelson, Elizabeth M 222 2
Nelson, Ellen 75 3
Nelson, Ellen 222, 213a 2
Nelson, Emory 271 2
Nelson, Ethel F 180 3
Nelson, F J 92 1
Nelson, Frederick 222, 210a 2
Nelson, Frederick 238 1
Nelson, Frederick J 224, 227a 2
Nelson, Frederick J 171 1
Nelson, Henry 67, 75, 76, 197, 222, 225, 227, 212a, 214a, 218a 2
Nelson, Henry 39, 67, 160, 187 3
Nelson, Henry 1, 40 1
Nelson, J Emory 227 2
Nelson, J M 227 2
Nelson, James A 226, 227 2
Nelson, Jeanette M 1, 146 1
Nelson, John 25 1
Nelson, John 187, 226 2
Nelson, John 70 3
Nelson, John H 146, 213 1
Nelson, John H 227 2
Nelson, John W 227 2
Nelson, Joseph 227 2
Nelson, Joseph R 290 2
Nelson, Josephine 210a 2
Nelson, Lawrence A 227 2
Nelson, Lowell 224 2
Nelson, Lyman Haviland 229 2
Nelson, M 133 1
Nelson, M H 56 3
Nelson, Madison 137, 222, 210a, 286 2
Nelson, Markell 224 2
Nelson, Markell H 73 1
Nelson, Markell H 225, 214a 2
Nelson, Matilda 222 2
Nelson, Nathan 78, 211, 220, 222, 212a, 214a, 242 2
Nelson, Nathan 26, 53 3
Nelson, Nathan 84, 118 1
Nelson, R J 119 2
Nelson, Rebecca M 213a 2
Nelson, Robert 14, 75, 76, 225, 213a 2
Nelson, Robert 100, 135 1
Nelson, Robert 35 3
Nelson, Robert J 222 2
Nelson, Robert W 213a 2
Nelson, Roberts 290 2
Nelson, Robet 214a 2
Nelson, Robt 128 2
Nelson, Robt 39, 202 3
Nelson, Roger 213a 2
Nelson, Sarah 214a 2
Nelson, Sidney A 214a 2
Nelson, Sophia 214a 2
Nelson, Sophria E 214a 2
Nelson, Susan 202, 212a 2
Nelson, Susan R 60 1
Nelson, Susan R 214a 2
Nelson, Thomas 227 2
Nelson, Thos 18 1
Nelson, V J 225 2
Nelson, W B 187, 276 2
Nelson, Walter 220 2
Nelson, William B 102 3
Nelson, Wm 54 3
Nemier, Elizabeth 222 2
Nemier, John 222 2
Nemyer, John 226 2
Neson, William J 227 2
Ness, Henry 225 2
Ness, William Ernest 167 2
Nester, Ida M 226 2
Nester, James L 18, 283 1
Nester, James L 226 2
Nester, Luella Annan 19 1
Nestor, Cecilia M 287 2
Neughbours, E D Dr 189 2
Neumann, C Richard 161 2
Nevins, Thos 228 1
Nevitt, James 226 2
Nevius, Elizabeth M 222 2
Nevius, Louise 222 2
Nevius, Walter I 215a 2
Nevius, Walter I 222 2
New Amsterdam Casualety Co of N Y 290 2
New Amsterdam Casualty 67 1
New Amsterdam Casualty Co 11, 20, 33, 44, 72, 83, 111, 118, 172, 197 3
New Amsterdam Casualty Co 67, 73, 82, 88, 93, 97, 101, 110, 120, 140, 150, 162, 201, 210, 215, 235, 245, 273, 284 1
New Amsterdam Casualty Co 3, 65, 72, 76, 96, 102, 107, 112, 116, 132, 154, 160, 161, 178, 190, 215, 222, 225, 219a, 250, 259, 274 2
New Amsterdam Casualty Co Inc 172 1
New Amsterdam Casualty Co N Y 16 2
New Amsterdam Casualty Co of N Y 15, 18, 20, 25, 41, 46, 69, 70, 75, 80, 92, 107, 113, 142, 144, 163, 166, 190, 209, 220, 227a, 250, 255 2
New Amsterdam Casualty Co of N Y 14, 22, 25, 28, 30, 44, 55, 76, 110, 136, 140, 156, 162, 189, 197, 219, 235, 265, 272 1
New Amsterdam Casualty Co of N Y 44, 60, 100, 102, 129, 192 3
New Amsterdam Casualty Co, The 83 1
New Amsterdam Casualty Company 89, 119 2
New Amsterdam Casualty Company 33 1
New Amsterdam Casualty Company, The 107 1
New Amsterdam Casualty Company, The 126 1
New Amsterdam Casualty of N Y 176, 189 3
New Amsterdam Casulayty Co of N Y 220 3
New Amsterdam Caualty Co 68 3

New Amsterdam Co of N Y 44 3
New Amsterdam Co of N Y 155, 177 1
New Amsterdam Company of N Y 14 1
New Amsterdan Casualty Co 46 3
New Amsterdan Casualty Co 190 2
New Amsterday Casualty Co 49 2
New England Equitable Insurance Co of Boston, Mass 119 1
Newbrant, John 227 2
Newbrent, John 44 1
Newcomb, Mary E 101 1
Newcomber, Harry Robert 225 2
Newcomer, Ella B 215a 2
Newcomer, H R 33 1
Newcomer, J 223a 2
Newcomer, Jacob 27 1
Newcomer, John 163 2
Newcomer, S J 34 1
Newcomer, Samuel 214a 2
Newcomer, Samuel 13, 51, 253 1
Newcomer, Samuel Jr 214a 2
Newcomer, William H E 215a 2
Newell, Anna 64 2
Newey, John 226 2
Newman, A P 158 3
Newman, Alice T 172 2
Newman, Amie Parsons 72 3
Newman, Amy Parsons 218 2
Newman, Amy T 172 2
Newman, Francis J 54 2
Newman, Frank J 227 2
Newman, Grach H 54 2
Newman, J M 55, 72 3
Newman, J M 172 2
Newman, J M 30 1
Newman, J N 82 3
Newman, J S 67, 82, 96, 152, 179, 203 3
Newman, Jacob 82, 158 3
Newman, Jacob 9, 80 2
Newman, Jacob M 64 3
Newman, Jacob M 234 2
Newman, Jacob N 227 2
Newman, John S 52, 55, 86, 96, 159 1
Newman, John S 2, 54, 107, 125, 172, 189, 218, 224, 227, 229, 229a, 234, 242, 277, 286 2
Newman, John S 50, 72, 147, 158, 180, 206, 210, 220 3
Newman, Katie E 229 2
Newman, Parsons 147, 161, 167, 180 3
Newman, Parsons 3, 70, 73, 102, 136, hundred and 72, 218, 220, 227, 234, 257, 283 2
Newman, Parsons 42, 83, 155, 157, 162, 166, 179, 184, 204, 214 1
Newport, Adam 218 2
Newport, Adam 88 1
Newport, Chas C 159 2
Newport, Jacob 40 1
Newport, John 79 1
Newport, John 70 3
Newport, Mary Ann 210a 2
Newport, Mary M 218 2
Newport, Sophia 210a 2
Newton, William 205 3
Newton, William L 291 2
Neymer, John 226 2
Nichels, Jacob 215 3
Nichloas, Joseph 226 2
Nichodemus, Henry 88 1
Nicholas, Charles 213a 2
Nicholas, Chas 40 2
Nicholas, Chas S 222 2
Nicholas, Edw 40, 188 2
Nicholas, Edward 222 2
Nicholas, Edward 67 1
Nicholas, Franklin 224 2
Nicholas, George W 224 2
Nicholas, Jacob 228 1
Nicholas, James 214 2
Nicholas, John 67 1
Nicholas, John 214 2
Nicholas, Peter 197, 212a 2
Nicholas, Peter 47, 208, 228 1
Nicholas, Rebecca 213a 2
Nicholas, Robt C 47, 228 1
Nicholas, S H 67 1
Nicholas, Seth H 152, 201 1
Nicholds, Eugene 67 3
Nichols, Adam Luther 218 2
Nichols, Alice C 50 3
Nichols, Ann Virginia 218 2
Nichols, C E 288 2
Nichols, Chas 222 2
Nichols, Clayton 214a 2
Nichols, Edw 91 3
Nichols, Edw 118 1
Nichols, Edw 51, 54 2
Nichols, Edward 222 2
Nichols, Edward 160 3
Nichols, Eliza 222 2
Nichols, Elizabeth 222 2
Nichols, Frederick S 3, 35, 58 3
Nichols, Israel L 227 2
Nichols, J K 268 2
Nichols, Jacob 134, 195 3
Nichols, James 215a 2
Nichols, John 227 2
Nichols, John Morris 218 2
Nichols, John R 227, 254 2
Nichols, John R 40 3
Nichols, John T 67 3
Nichols, Mary M 214a 2
Nichols, Peter 22, 208 2
Nichols, Peter 215 3
Nichols, Ralph 250 2
Nichols, Seth 22 2
Nichols, Seth A 271 1
Nichols, Seth H 282 1
Nichols, Seth H 69, 214a 2
Nichols, Seth N 22 2
Nichols, William 215a 2
Nicholson, Ann R 218, 227 2
Nicholson, John T 227 2
Nickel, Albert 225 2
Nickel, Harry C 225, 210a 2
Nickel, Mary M 210a 2
Nickel, Mary V 225 2
Nickell, Adam & 80 2
Nickham, J D 124 3
Nickols, Catherine 220 2
Nickols, Israel L B 220 2
Nickols, Peter 14 2
Nickols, Seth 14 2
Nickum, Elizabeth 222 2
Nickum, Jacob 163 1
Nickum, Jacob 226 2
Nickum, John 100 3
Nickum, John 226 2
Nickum, Mary Ann 222 2
Nickun, Jacob 25 2
Nicodemis, Chas E 140 1
Nicodemus, A W 187 2
Nicodemus, Albert C 218 2
Nicodemus, Allen W 215a 2
Nicodemus, Ann Maria 218 2
Nicodemus, Annie T 218 2
Nicodemus, Asbury 165 1
Nicodemus, Asbury 218 2
Nicodemus, Augustus 68 2
Nicodemus, Augustus W 218 2
Nicodemus, Augustus W Jr 218 2
Nicodemus, B W 58 2
Nicodemus, Bessie M 220 2
Nicodemus, Beulah G 218 2
Nicodemus, Bradley 210a 2
Nicodemus, C S 222 2
Nicodemus, C S 102 1
Nicodemus, Carrie 222 2
Nicodemus, Charles 229, 210a 2
Nicodemus, Charles A 220 2
Nicodemus, Chas 162 1

Nicodemus, Chas E 65 3
Nicodemus, Chas E 153 2
Nicodemus, David 240 1
Nicodemus, Edward B 222 2
Nicodemus, Eleanor G 222 2
Nicodemus, Eleanor G 76 1
Nicodemus, Eli 19, 222 2
Nicodemus, Elizabeth 222 2
Nicodemus, Elizabeth K 218 2
Nicodemus, Emma E 215a 2
Nicodemus, Emma S 222 2
Nicodemus, Fanny A 153 2
Nicodemus, H Fulton 161 3
Nicodemus, H Fulton 210a 2
Nicodemus, H W 28 2
Nicodemus, Hattie B 229 2
Nicodemus, Helen D 89 2
Nicodemus, Henry 26, 38, 225, 226 2
Nicodemus, Henry 67, 88, 179, 248 1
Nicodemus, Henry C 225 2
Nicodemus, Herman O 225 2
Nicodemus, Isaac 218, 226 2
Nicodemus, Isaac 133, 146, 152, 169, 205, 240 283 1
Nicodemus, Isaac C 31 3
Nicodemus, Isaac E 220 2
Nicodemus, Isacc C 226 2
Nicodemus, Issac 221, 226, 210a 2
Nicodemus, J 264 1
Nicodemus, J C 6, 150 1
Nicodemus, J L 41 1
Nicodemus, Jacob 70 1
Nicodemus, Jesse 227, 277 2
Nicodemus, Jesse N H 227 2
Nicodemus, Jihn 226 2
Nicodemus, Jno V 70 2
Nicodemus, John 48, 116, 117, 118, 133, 171 1
Nicodemus, John 6, 35, 91 3
Nicodemus, John 218, 225, 226, 210a, 224a, 241 2
Nicodemus, John D 227, 210a 2
Nicodemus, John J 222 2
Nicodemus, John L 58, 82, 109, 165, 163 1
Nicodemus, John L 227, 212a, 249 2
Nicodemus, John V 11 3
Nicodemus, John V 227 2
Nicodemus, John Z 219 1
Nicodemus, Josephine B 220 2
Nicodemus, Kent 210a 2
Nicodemus, Kent C 219 1
Nicodemus, Kent C 222, 227 2
Nicodemus, Kent C 11, 33 3
Nicodemus, L B 229 2
Nicodemus, Leonora B 229 2
Nicodemus, Lester B 229 2
Nicodemus, Lillian 215a 2
Nicodemus, Lydia 229 2
Nicodemus, M L 22 1
Nicodemus, Mabel Jeannette 229 2
Nicodemus, Margaret 210a 2
Nicodemus, Martin 106, 234 2
Nicodemus, Martin L 225, 210a, 250 2
Nicodemus, Martin L 22 1
Nicodemus, Mary A 221 3
Nicodemus, Mary B 210a 2
Nicodemus, Nancy 212a 2
Nicodemus, Norma E 195 1
Nicodemus, P O 19 1
Nicodemus, Philip 79 1
Nicodemus, Robert F 218 2
Nicodemus, Roland J 225 2
Nicodemus, Susannah 214a 2
Nicodemus, T B 225 2
Nicodemus, V W 60 3
Nicodemus, Valentine 57 1
Nicodemus, Valentine 215a 2
Nicodemus, Vernon W 222, 215a 2
Nicodemus, Vernon W 20 3
Nicodemus, Walter L 215a 2
Nicodemus, WH 124 3
Nicodemus, William 214a 2
Nicodemus, William T 215a 2
Nicodemus, Wm H 113, 226 2
Nicodemus, Wm H 129 1
Nicodemus, Wm H 71 3
Nicodemus, Wm T 124 1
Niedhardt, Caroline 213a 2
Niedhardt, Joseph 213a 2
Niedhardt, Mary L 215a 2
Niedhardt, Rudolph 215a 2
Niedhardt, Rudolph A 213a 2
Nieghbours, Harold D 222 2
Niemeyer, Chas E 220 2
Nikirk, Amanda C 218 2
Nikirk, Amanda E 224 2
Nikirk, Annie E 46 3
Nikirk, Annie N 224 2
Nikirk, C Earl 220 2
Nikirk, Charles E 220 2
Nikirk, E Roy 218 2
Nikirk, Edgar 224 2
Nikirk, Edwin F 12, 23, 32, 49, 224 2
Nikirk, Edwin F 172, 189 3
Nikirk, Edwin F 153, 166, 208 1
Nikirk, Geo 192 3
Nikirk, George 224 2
Nikirk, George D 224 2
Nikirk, George L 224 2
Nikirk, Glen R 224 2
Nikirk, Harry S 33 1
Nikirk, Samantha 214a 2
Nikirk, Walter 218 2
Nikirk, Walter L 224 2
Nipple, Jacob 227 2
Nipple, John 227 2
Nipple, Martha 227 2
Nirkirk, Harry S 218 2
Nisdorff, Henry M 19 1
Niswanner, Elizabeth 222 2
Niswanner, George W 222 2
Nixdorf, Henry 134 2
Nixdorf, Henry 120 3
Nixdorf, Samuel 29 2
Nixdorff, Asbury 225 2
Nixdorff, Eliza P 222, 224 2
Nixdorff, George A 224 2
Nixdorff, George D 224 2
Nixdorff, H M 54 3
Nixdorff, Harry 225 2
Nixdorff, Henry 39, 195, 208 3
Nixdorff, Henry 1, 19, 39, 51, 67, 187, 195, 208, 211, 225 2
Nixdorff, Henry 58, 117, 263 1
Nixdorff, Henry & 137 2
Nixdorff, Henry C 152 1
Nixdorff, Henry H 32 1
Nixdorff, Henry M 41, 59, 79 1
Nixdorff, Henry M 50 3
Nixdorff, Henry M 225 2
Nixdorff, Henry N 57 2
Nixdorff, L M 225 2
Nixdorff, L M 4, 171 1
Nixdorff, L M 2 3
Nixdorff, Lewis 187, 224, 225, 214a 2
Nixdorff, Lewis M 4, 8, 19, 26, 71, 88, 171, 201 1
Nixdorff, Lewis M 51, 115, 195, 229 2
Nixdorff, Lewis M 50 3
Nixdorff, Lewis W 276 2
Nixdorff, Louis 165 1
Nixdorff, Louis 229 2
Nixdorff, Louis & 264 1
Nixdorff, Louis M 96 1
Nixdorff, Louis M 39 2
Nixdorff, Louis M Jr 222 2
Nixdorff, Samuel 58 1
Nixdorff, Samuel 1, 78, 185, 214a 2
Nixdorff, Susan 214a 2

Nixdorff, Thelma P 225 2
Nixdorff, William 217a 2
Nixon, John 188 2
Nixon, John A 166 3
Noel, Blasius 220 2
Noel, Emanuel 222, 210a 2
Noel, Mary B 210a 2
Noggle, Julia 227 2
Nogle, Allen 225 2
Nogle, Harry 227 2
Nogle, Harry W 225 2
Noland, Edward 229 2
Noland, Lawrence 229 2
Noland, Lloyd 210a 2
Noland, Mary E 210a 2
Noland, Patrick 229 2
Noll, John Adam 227 2
Noll, John Benton 227 2
Noll, Margaret May 227 2
Noonan, Catherine 226, 213a 2
Noonan, Fanny 224 2
Noonan, J J 226 2
Noonan, John 226 2
Noonan, Louis T 224 2
Noonan, Robert E 213a 2
Norris, A Henry 218 2
Norris, A Henry 18 1
Norris, A R 227 2
Norris, Alexander J 218 2
Norris, Amon 209 3
Norris, Amon 222 2
Norris, Amos 218 2
Norris, Amos 23, 35 3
Norris, Ann 227, 229 2
Norris, Anna 220 2
Norris, Anna J 214a 2
Norris, Basil 283 1
Norris, Basil 44 1
Norris, Basil 28, 186, 187, 205, 220, 226, 229, 210a, 212a, 215a 2
Norris, Basil 18 3
Norris, Benjamin 220 2
Norris, Benjamin F 220 2
Norris, Claud E 220 2
Norris, D A 101 2
Norris, E O 4 1
Norris, Edgar 2, 89, 227 2
Norris, Edw 39 2
Norris, Edward 214a 2
Norris, Edward O 222 2
Norris, Elizabeth 229 2
Norris, Elizabeth 222, 229 2
Norris, Elizabeth A 222 2
Norris, Ella T T 27 2
Norris, Elmer 210a 2
Norris, Emily 227 2
Norris, Ferderika H 224 2
Norris, Florence 228a 2
Norris, Frederika H 218 2
Norris, G D 35, 72 2
Norris, G D 203 3
Norris, G D 171 1
Norris, Geo 139 2
Norris, Geo B 61 1
Norris, Geo D 72, 188, 203 3
Norris, Geo D 2 2
Norris, Geo D 150, 152, 177 1
Norris, George A 224 2
Norris, George B 43 3
Norris, George D 209 3
Norris, George D 210a 2
Norris, George W 225 2
Norris, Henrietta 187, 225, 215 2
Norris, Henrietta 60 1
Norris, Henrietta 182 3
Norris, Henry 270, 283 1
Norris, Henry 225, 227 2
Norris, Henry A 227 2
Norris, Henry A 225, 227 2
Norris, Henry A 227 1
Norris, Henry M 225, 229 2
Norris, Howard L 225 2
Norris, Isabella V 226 2
Norris, Israel 23, 64, 195 3
Norris, Israel 218 2
Norris, Issabella 213a 2
Norris, James C 212a 2
Norris, James L 26 1
Norris, Jane C 220, 227 2
Norris, Jas L 81 3
Norris, Joe 220 2
Norris, Joel 159 3
Norris, Joel 30 1
Norris, Joel 165, 226 2
Norris, John 262 1
Norris, John 9 3
Norris, John 205, 226, 227, 229, 210a 2
Norris, John B 227 2
Norris, John G 222, 227 2
Norris, John T 13 1
Norris, Jonathan 40 1
Norris, Joshiah 203 3
Norris, Joshua 227 2
Norris, Katie O 9, 213a 2
Norris, Lafayette 214a 2
Norris, Lloyd 227, 229 2
Norris, Lloyd 229 2
Norris, Lot 226 2
Norris, Lott 229 2
Norris, Lydia 229 2
Norris, Martin L 210a 2
Norris, Mary 210a, 212a 2
Norris, Mary E 220, 225 2
Norris, Mary Lettie 225 2
Norris, Mary M 210a 2
Norris, Mary O 203 3
Norris, Matthias B 210a 2
Norris, Minnie T 224 2
Norris, N B 66 2
Norris, N E 215 2
Norris, Nancy L 222 2
Norris, Nelson 226 2
Norris, Nicholas 58, 116, 164, 171 1
Norris, Nicholas 138, 195 3
Norris, Nicholas 89, 212a 2
Norris, Nichols 222 2
Norris, Nimrod 195, 222, 226 2
Norris, Nimrod 18 1
Norris, Oso 212a 2
Norris, Otho 185, 186, 205, 210a 2
Norris, Otho 44, 57 1
Norris, Otho 9 3
Norris, Otto 229 2
Norris, Raphael 215a 2
Norris, Richard 213a 2
Norris, Richard H 213a 2
Norris, S H 2 2
Norris, Samuel J 126 1
Norris, Samuel W 214a 2
Norris, Sarah 222, 214a 2
Norris, Sarah N 214a 2
Norris, Susan 210a 2
Norris, Thomas 215a 2
Norris, Thomas T 226 2
Norris, Thos 19 2
Norris, Upton 18 1
Norris, Wilford G 213a 2
Norris, William 226, 215a 2
Norris, William H 203 3
Norris, William Lee 215a 2
Norris, WilliamM 195 2
Norris, Wm 137 2
Norris, Wm 44, 96 1
Norris, Wm 165, 185, 186 2
Norris, Wm 192 3
Norrise, Nicholas 118 1
Norrise, Thomas T [sic] 118 1
Northwestern Casualty & Insurance Co 104 1
Northwestern Casualty & Surety Co 201 1
Northwestern Casualty & Surety Co 189 3
Northwestern Casualty Co 72 3
Northwestern Casulty & Surety Co 166 3
Norwood, Abner 218, 215a 2
Norwood, Albert 218 2
Norwood, Ann 218, 215a 2
Norwood, Anna 226 2
Norwood, C F 23 1
Norwood, Charles 213a 2
Norwood, Charles A 196 3

Norwood, Charles A 220 2
Norwood, Chas 31, 226 2
Norwood, Chas 88 1
Norwood, Chas A 55, 155 1
Norwood, Chas A 189 2
Norwood, Chas A 71, 182 3
Norwood, F C 51, 56, 57, 75, 104, 176, 180 3
Norwood, F C 72, 78, 92, 97, 104, 123, 17, 144, 172, 179, 188, 191, 193, 260 1
Norwood, F C 31, 40, 79, 166, 220, 265, 283, 288 2
Norwood, Frank 23 1
Norwood, Frank 31 2
Norwood, Frank C 43, 50, 55, 71, 182, 188, 192, 196 3
Norwood, Frank C 189, 224, 227a, 232 2
Norwood, Frank C 28, 48, 52, 73, 96, 104, 106, 133, 147, 155, 193, 197, 201, 210, 257 1
Norwood, Garrison M 224 2
Norwood, Isaiah 226 2
Norwood, Israel 39 2
Norwood, Jeremiah 226 2
Norwood, John T 3 2
Norwood, Joshua 100 2
Norwood, L Virginia 224 2
Norwood, Oliver 218 2
Norwood, R N 129, 288 2
Norwood, R Nelson 213a 2
Norwood, Thomas 80, 93 2
Norwood, Thos 100, 237 2
Norwood, William H 215a 2
Notnagel, H E 212a 2
Notnagel, Peter S 212a 2
Notnagle, Adam 135 1
Notnagle, Catherine C 220, 227 2
Notnagle, Frederick 224 2
Notnagle, J Fred 48 1
Notnagle, J Leonard 118, 224 2
Notnagle, J William 227 2
Notnagle, Jacob 180 3
Notnagle, Jacob 62, 92, 135 1
Notnagle, Jacob 202, 227 2
Notnagle, John J 64 3
Notnagle, John J 37 1
Notnagle, John Leonard 214a 2
Notnagle, Mary 224 2
Notnagle, P S 40 2
Notnagle, Sophia 224, 214a 2
Notnalge, Adam 218 2
Nottnagle, Henrietta E 225 2
Noyes, Flora B 220 2
Noyes, John H 220 2
Nuce, George W 225, 226 2
Nuce, Harry E 225 2
Nuce, Ida M 226 2
Null Abraham 11, 35, 115, 116, 124, 186, 215a, 220a 2
Null, Abraham 56, 100, 139, 234, 239, 271 1
Null, Abraham 37, 81, 195, 221, 223 3
Null, Abraham B 223 3
Null, Ann C 218, 227 2
Null, C F 124 3
Null, Carrie M 213a 2
Null, Carroll F 210a 2
Null, Charles E 220 2
Null, Chas E 230 1
Null, Frances E 215a 2
Null, Geo 188 2
Null, George 224 2
Null, George W 42, 55 3
Null, Harry W 140 2
Null, Ida 218, 227 2
Null, J A Edw 224 2
Null, J A R 227 2
Null, James 226, 227, 250 2
Null, Jas 67 3
Null, John 226, 210a 2
Null, John J 227 2
Null, John W 215a 2
Null, Jonathan A R 218 2
Null, Jonothan 227 2
Null, Lillian M 229 2
Null, Mae L 224 2
Null, Maggie S 210a 2
Null, Mary 210a 2
Null, Michael 37 1
Null, Michale 38 3
Null, Rantha Raymond 213a 2
Null, Ray C 210a 2
Null, Richard C 213a 2
Null, Roy C 213a 2
Null, Samuel 26, 38 3
Null, Valentine 215a 2
Null, William C 227, 215a 2
Null, Wm N 119 1
Nunamaker, Philip 26 2
Nunemaker, Philip 233 1
Nunnamaker, Emma 172 3
Nunnemaker, John 212a 2
Nunnemaker, Philip 212a 2
Nusbaum, A W 218 2
Nusbaum, Abraham 70 1
Nusbaum, Abraham 218 2
Nusbaum, Abram 225 2
Nusbaum, Abram W 218 2
Nusbaum, Adam 32 1
Nusbaum, Adam 153, 218 2
Nusbaum, Adam 31 3
Nusbaum, Adam F 139, 218 2
Nusbaum, Ann 218 2
Nusbaum, Anna 221 2
Nusbaum, Annie 224 2
Nusbaum, Catherine 220 2
Nusbaum, Daniel 185 3
Nusbaum, David 249 1
Nusbaum, E H 225 2
Nusbaum, Edward H 222 2
Nusbaum, Ephraim T 222 2
Nusbaum, Frederick 71 1
Nusbaum, Frederick W 224 2
Nusbaum, Gail 187 3
Nusbaum, Geo 218 2
Nusbaum, George McC 224 2
Nusbaum, Henrietta 225 2
Nusbaum, Henry P 225 2
Nusbaum, Henry P 42 3
Nusbaum, Hettie B 225 2
Nusbaum, Howard 225 2
Nusbaum, Isaac 283 1
Nusbaum, Isaac 218 2
Nusbaum, Isaac L 226, 271 2
Nusbaum, Isaiah 113 2
Nusbaum, Isaiah 88 1
Nusbaum, John 218 2
Nusbaum, Lewis F 209 2
Nusbaum, Margaret 218 2
Nusbaum, Marshall S 271 2
Nusbaum, Martha V 222 2
Nusbaum, Mary E 139 2
Nusbaum, Mary N 226 2
Nusbaum, Matilda 210a 2
Nusbaum, Osie I 212a 2
Nusbaum, Rachel 218 2
Nusbaum, S 214a 2
Nusbaum, S A 218 2
Nusbaum, Samuel 28 2
Nusbaum, Samuel of S 214a 2
Nusbaum, Sarah 84 1
Nusbaum, Sarah J 225 2
Nusbaum, Thomas 225 2
Nusbaum, W L 126 1
Nussbaum, A 227 2
Nussbaum, Abraham 226, 213a 2
Nussbaum, Abraham 30 1
Nussbaum, Abran 226 2
Nussbaum, Ann 212a 2
Nussbaum, Anna 227 2
Nussbaum, Anne 227 2
Nussbaum, Daniel 221, 226 2
Nussbaum, David 221 2
Nussbaum, David E 221 2
Nussbaum, Edward 214a 2
Nussbaum, Edward H 215a 2
Nussbaum, Eleanor 227 2
Nussbaum, Eliza 214a 2

Nussbaum, Elizabeth 222, 227 2
Nussbaum, Exra 214a 2
Nussbaum, Frederick 214a 2
Nussbaum, Henry P 210a 2
Nussbaum, Isaiah 221 2
Nussbaum, J 214a 2
Nussbaum, J H 214a 2
Nussbaum, J W 210a 2
Nussbaum, Jacob 226, 227 2
Nussbaum, Jacob R 227 2
Nussbaum, Jesse 226 2
Nussbaum, John 226 2
Nussbaum, John 30 1
Nussbaum, John H 227 2
Nussbaum, John of A 227 2
Nussbaum, John W 227 2
Nussbaum, Mary 210a 2
Nussbaum, Matilda 227 2
Nussbaum, Mattie V 215a 2
Nussbaum, Philip 212a 2
Nussbaum, Phillip 221 2
Nussbaum, Rachel 213a 2
Nussbaum, Rebecca 213a 2
Nussbaum, Samuel 226, 213a 2
Nussbaum, Samuel A 214a 2
Nussbaum, Samuel of A 214a 2
Nussbaum, Samuel of J 214a 2
Nussbaum, Sarah E 214a 2
Nussbaum, Sarah P 221 2
Nussbaum, Simon 213a 2
Nussbaum, Soloman 214a 2
Nussbaum, Susan J 214a 2
Nussbaum, Walter A 215a 2
Nussear, Charles 210a 2
Nussear, Elizabeth 222 2
Nussear, J Maurice 227 2
Nussear, J Morris 227 2
Nussear, Jesse 138, 227 2
Nussear, Jesse H 227, 210a 2
Nussear, Jesse W 227 2
Nussear, Jessie 222 2
Nussear, Jessie H 196 3
Nussear, Mary 227 2
Nussear, Mary A 210a 2
Nussear, Mary C 210a 2
Nusz, Alice S 227 2
Nusz, Bertha D 11 3
Nusz, Clara 220 2
Nusz, Clementine 220 2
Nusz, Elmer 220 2
Nusz, Elmer L 222 2
Nusz, Emory G 242 2
Nusz, Eva M R 222 2
Nusz, Ffederick 224 2
Nusz, Fleeton E 212a 2
Nusz, Frede ick 184 3
Nusz, Frederick 37, 70, 184 3
Nusz, Geo 243 1
Nusz, Guy L 186 1
Nusz, Guy L 210a 2
Nusz, Guy W 217 3
Nusz, Hilda P 213a 2
Nusz, Joseph H 227 2
Nusz, Mary M 212a 2
Nusz, Millard M 120 1
Nusz, Millard N 172 1
Nusz, Mollie M 186 1
Nusz, Mollie M 210a 2
Nusz, Nera C 210a 2
Nusz, Peter E 212a 2
Nusz, Ralph 220 2
Nusz, Robert E 213a 2
Nuttall, John 185 2
Nuze, Minnie R 169 3
Nyman, Daniel G 81 3
Oarme, Mildred 223a, 225a 2
Obenderfer, A 48 1
Obenderfer, Eva M 219a 2
Obenderfer, F U 2 3
Obenderfer, F W 27, 33, 219, 249, 264 1
Obenderfer, F W 15 2
Obenderfer, Fred W 208 1
Obenderfer, Frederick 124 2
Obenderfer, Frederick 249, 256 1
Obenderfer, Frederick W 219a 2
Obenderfer, John W 208 1
Obenderfer, John W Sr 224a 2
Obenderfer, John William Jr 224a 2
Obenderfer, John Wm 219a 2
Obenderfer, John Wm Sr 222a 2
Obenderfer, Mary Blanche 222a 2
Obenderfer, Nellie M 224a 2
Obenderfer, S W 145 2
Obenderfer, Susan V 264 1
Obendorfer, John L 221a 2
Oberlander, Fred A 23 2
Oberlander, Frederick A 219a 2
Oberlander, Lucille G 32 2
Oberlander, Lucille S 219a 2
Oberlander, Lucy S G 272 1
Oberlander, Nellie N 219a 2
Obermyer, Leonard 223a 2
O'Brien, John A 124 3
O'Brien, John A 222a 2
O'Brien, John R 222a 2
O'brien, Luke 57 1
O'Brien, Mary 223a 2
O'Brien, Mary 225a 2
O'Brien, William M 225a 2
O'Bryan, Ada 217a 2
O'Bryan, John 221a 2
Ocker, Barbara 217a 2
Ocker, Christian 218a 2
Ocker, Christian 53 3
O'Connell, James 60 3
O'Connell, James 198 2
O'connor, Edna M 45 1
O'Connor, Emma M 51 3
O'Connor, James L 225a 2
O'Connor, Thomas 225a 2
O'Connor, Thomas F 225a 2
Oden, Amelia 217a 2
Oden, Dorsey L Jr 224a 2
Oden, Dorsey Lee 218a 2
Oden, E P 124 3
Oden, Edw 223a 2
Oden, Frederick N 223a 2
Oden, John W 221a 2
Oden, Martha C 221a 2
Oden, Melvin A 223a 2
Oden, Nettie Estella 224a 2
Oden, Rufus L 224a 2
Oden, Sarah G 224a 2
O'Donnell, Byron 217a 2
O'Donnell, Caroline 221a 2
O'Donnell, J C 221a 2
O'Donnell, Oliver 10 1
O'Donoghue, Mary K 223a 2
Oerter, Albert L 224a 2
Oerter, Sarah M 224a 2
Offerd, Florence 219a 2
Offith, Ann 214a 2
Offith, Mary 214a 2
Offith, Richard 214a 2
Offutt, Ann 217a 2
Offutt, Charles 218a 2
Offutt, Colomore 218a 2
Offutt, John M 223a 2
Offutt, Lucinda 223a, 224a 2
Offutt, Mary 218a 2
Offutt, Mary T 223a 2
Offutt, Richard 214a, 218a 2
Offutt, Richard A 223a, 224a 2
Offutt, Richard C 224a 2
Offutt, W Jerome 11, 68, 192, 193, 223 3
Offutt, W Jerome 3, 16, 49, 143, 13, 222, 234 2
Offutt, W Jerome 32, 109, 157, 172, 208, 258, 279 1
Ogborn, Benjamin 217a 2
Ogborn, Cabel 195, 205 3
Ogborn, Caleb 47, 53 1
Ogborn, Caleb 218a 2
Ogborn, Joel 217a 2
Ogborn, John W 14 2
Ogborn, John W 59, 196 1
Ogborn, W W 225a 2
Ogborn, William W 30 1

Ogborn, William W 218a 2
Ogborn, Wm 5 2
Ogborn, Wm W 59, 91 1
Ogburn, William W 1 3
Ogle, Allen 240 1
Ogle, Ann L 225a 2
Ogle, Annit S 221a 2
Ogle, Archie W 217a, 225a 2
Ogle, B P 222a 2
Ogle, Bemjaman [sic] 88 1
Ogle, Benjamin 199, 217a 2
Ogle, Benjamin 91 1
Ogle, Benjamin P 62 1
Ogle, Benjamin P 217a, 221a 2
Ogle, C Elizabeth 30, 218a 2
Ogle, Carrie G 28 1
Ogle, Catherine 218a 2
Ogle, Charles A 19 1
Ogle, Chas J 83 2
Ogle, D P 82 3
Ogle, E B 222a 2
Ogle, Ellen 223a 2
Ogle, Geo 58 2
Ogle, George 217a 2
Ogle, George W 220a 2
Ogle, Harriett 221a 2
Ogle, Helen D 179 1
Ogle, J H B 149 3
Ogle, J H B 221a 2
Ogle, James 221a 2
Ogle, James H B 221a, 223a 2
Ogle, James H R 222a 2
Ogle, Jane E 221a 2
Ogle, John 32 1
Ogle, John 221a 2
Ogle, John S 221a 2
Ogle, John S 94 3
Ogle, John S 99 1
Ogle, Lauretta V 223a 2
Ogle, Lewis C 223a 2
Ogle, Made R 217a 2
Ogle, Margaret 221a, 223a, 224a 2
Ogle, Mary 223a 2
Ogle, Mollie E 224a 2
Ogle, R L 30 2
Ogle, Rebecca 224a 2
Ogle, Richard 116 1
Ogle, Robert A 155 2
Ogle, Robert L 218a, 224a 2
Ogle, Robert L 154 3
Ogle, Robt L 177 2
Ogle, Sadie V 223a 2
Ogle, Samuel 91, 159, 283 1
Ogle, Samuel 150, 217a 2
Ogle, Samuel V 224a 2
Ogle, Thomas 225a 2
Ogle, Thomas A 214, 217a, 225a 2
Ogle, Thos 47 1
Ogle, Thos A 211 2
Ogle, Virgie L 217a 2
Ogle, Virgie Lee 217a 2
Ogle, W Bruce 218a 2
Ogle, W W 225a 2
Ogle, William D 220a 2
Ogle, Wm 54 3
Ogle, Wm F 8 1
Ogleton Ezra 250 2
Ogleton, James P 221a 2
Ogleton, John H 221a 2
O'Hara, James 100 3
O'Hara, John 222a 2
O'Hara, John L 222a 2
O'Haro, Henry L 220a 2
Ohler, Annie R 169 1
Ohler, Annie R 217a 2
Ohler, B L 284 1
Ohler, David 30, 218a, 219a 2
Ohler, Edw F 140 1
Ohler, Edwin 31 2
Ohler, Edwin F 166 3
Ohler, Edwin F 233, 280 1
Ohler, Edwin F 222a 2
Ohler, Eliza I 220a 2
Ohler, Elizabeth 219a 2
Ohler, Emanuel 221a 2
Ohler, Emma 169 1
Ohler, Emma B 217a 2
Ohler, Frederick 219a 2
Ohler, Geo A 113 3
Ohler, George 220a 2
Ohler, George A 220a 2
Ohler, George O 222a 2
Ohler, Henrietta C 220a 2
Ohler, Henry 220a 2
Ohler, I D 284 1
Ohler, Isaiah J 221a 2
Ohler, J R 224a 2
Ohler, J Rowe 233 1
Ohler, J Rowe 206 3
Ohler, Jacob 222a 2
Ohler, Jacob R 222a 2
Ohler, Jacob R 183 1
Ohler, James 107, 221a 2
Ohler, Jane 107 2
Ohler, John 221a 2
Ohler, John H 218a, 222a 2
Ohler, John I 222a 2
Ohler, John W 222a 2
Ohler, Joseph 218a, 221a 2
Ohler, Joseph 283 1
Ohler, Margaret 219a 2
Ohler, S G 179 3
Ohler, Sam'l G & 13 1
Ohler, Samuel 57, 181, 224a 2
Ohler, Samuel 40 1
Ohler, Samuel G 28, 38, 224 2
Ohler, Samuel G 59, 82, 239 1
Ohler, Solomon 224a 2
Ohler, Thomas 225a 2
Ohler, Vergie M Valentine 151 3
Ohler, Wm 210 1
Ohr, Henry 51 1
O'Kane, Margaret 223a 2
O'Keefe, Mary 223a 2
Oland, Catherine D 218a 2
Oland, Charles 218a 2
Oland, Charles F 219a 2
Oland, D T 52 1
Oland, David 218a 2
Oland, David 201 1
Oland, David 20, 166 3
Oland, Frederick 219a 2
Oland, Frederick 50 3
Oland, Henry 4 1
Oland, Kate D 218a 2
Oland, Laura D 44 1
Oland, Sharetts E 44 1
O'Leary, A D 88, 118 1
O'Leary, Augustine D 217a 2
O'Leary, Charles 218a 2
O'Leary, Helen M 12 2
Oler, David 6 3
Oler, Raymond Mrs 8 1
Oliver, Cornelius 218a 2
Oliver, Elsie M 218a 2
Oliver, Leslie L 218a 2
O'Neal, Charlotte E 218a 2
O'Neal, Geo W 112 1
O'Neal, George W 220a 2
O'Neal, Horace G 37 1
O'Neal, I C 32 1
O'Neal, Israel 57 2
O'Neal, J C 205 3
O'Neal, J C 84, 125 1
O'Neal, James 218 3
O'Neal, John W 220a 2
O'Neal, Julia M 220a 2
O'Neal, Louisa A 223a 2
O'Neal, Patrick 205, 218 3
O'Neal, Patrick 38, 93 2
O'Neal, Singleton H 224a 2
O'Neale, Ann 217a 2
O'Neale, John 221a 2
O'Neale, Sarah E 224a 2
O'Neall, Louisa A 223a 2
O'Neel, Horatio 177 2
O'Neil, Patrick 62 3
O'Neill, H G 154 2
O'Neill, Horatio 225 1
O'Neill, Israel 129 2
O'Neill, Israel C 24, 194 1
O'Neill, J C 171 2
O'Neill, Louisa A 224a 2
O'Neill, Patrick 57, 129, 137, 186, 197,

224a, 234 2
O'Neill, Patrick 116 3
O'Neill, Patrick 51, 76, 82, 163, 176, 197, 252, 271 1
O'Neill, Patrick 186 2
O'Neill, Philomena 43 3
O'Neill, Ptrick 203 2
O'Neill, Thomas 225a 2
O'Neill, Thomas Joseph 225a 2
O'Neill, Thos 57 2
O'Neill, Thos H 134 2
O'Neill, Walter 225a 2
Opel, Hilda Z 222 3
Opel, Thos 195 3
Oram, Edward B 219a 2
Oram, George W 220a 2
Oram, Mary A 219a, 220a 2
Orame, Thomas 225a 2
Ordeman, Catherine 218a 2
Ordeman, D T 81 3
Ordeman, D T 171 1
Ordeman, D T 220a 2
Ordeman, Daniel 171 1
Ordeman, Daniel 32 3
Ordeman, Daniel T 33, 72 1
Ordeman, Daniel T 116, 218a 2
Ordeman, David T 218a 2
Ordeman, Edith M 218a 2
Ordeman, Georgiana 220a 2
Ordeman, H D 81 3
Ordeman, Helen C 218a 2
Ordeman, Herman D 220a 2
Ordeman, John H 222a 2
Ordeman, Sarah 222a 2
Orderman, D T 85 1
Orderman, D T 55 3
Orderman, Daniel T 85, 92 1
Orderman, Daniel T 220a 2
Orderman, H D 138 2
Orem, Jacob 111 3
Orendorff, A F 209 1
Orendorff, Aloysius F 217a 2
Orendorff, Christian 218a 2
Orendorff, Corrinne E 220a 2
Orendorff, Esther 219a 2
Orendorff, Eve 218a 2
Orendorff, F H O 222a 2
Orendorff, Hunter H 220a 2
Orendorff, James A 222a 2
Orendorff, John A 221a 2
Orendorff, Joseph 248 1
Orendorff, Joseph 205, 219a 2
Orendorff, Julius W 222a 2
Orendorff, Peter 205, 219a 2
Orendorff, Peter 278 1
Orendorff, Samuel A 224a 2
Orlman, Jacob 113, 279 1
Orm, Jacob 116 2
Orme, Archibald B 177, 217a 2
Orme, Archibald D 217a 2
Orme, Etty 219a 2
Orme, Jacob 217a, 219a, 224a 2
Orme, Jacob 150 1
Orme, Malinda A 51 1
Orme, McComas 223a 2
Orme, Nathan 224a 2
Orme, William H 221a, 223a 2
Orme, Wm H 153 1
Ormwake, W T 224a 2
Orndorff, Aloysus F 71 1
Orndorff, John 224a 2
Orndorff, Peter 116 1
Orr, Samuel S 224a 2
Orrison, B F 221a 2
Orrison, C Albert 218a 2
Orrison, C Albert 206 3
Orrison, C E 218a 2
Orrison, Charles G 218a 2
Orrison, Chas 40 2
Orrison, Clayton E 218a 2
Orrison, Clayton K 218a 2
Orrison, David F 218a 2
Orrison, E P 107, 219a 2
Orrison, Emily R 206 3
Orrison, Harry M 218a 2
Orrison, John W 221a 2
Orrison, Louella 276 1
Orrison, Margaret J 219a 2
Orrison, Paul A 218a 2
Orrison, Rebecca 221a 2
Ortner, John 191 1
Ortner, John 221a 2
Ortz, Abraham 163 1
Orum, Edward B 220a 2
Osborn, Ada M 219a 2
Osborn, Ada M 279 1
Osborn, Cabel 87 3
Osborn, Cabell 106 3
Osborn, Caleb 279 1
Osborn, Caleb 100 2
Osborn, Edith 219a 2
Osborn, Eugene E 219a 2
Osborn, John C 221a 2
Osborn, Lucian R 223a 2
Osborn, Rebecca 224a 2
Osborn, William W 186 3
Osborn, Wm 58 2
Osborn, Wm W 229 1
Osborne, John 293 2
Osborne, John C 106 1
Osborne, Joshua 271 2
Osborne, W W 260 1
Osborne, Wm W 179 3
Osbourn, John C 87 2
Osburn, John 135 1
Osburn, Joseph 221a 2
Osburn, Laura S 113 1
Osburn, Robert D 224a 2
Osburn, Rosa C 224a 2
Osburn, Rosa C. 113 1
Osburn, Rosalie Warner 113 1
Osburn, Turner 225a 2
Osburn, William W 224a 2
Osfer, Van B 13, 21, 55, 213, 223 1
Osler, Charles 225a 2
Osler, Van B 70, 225a 2
Ossive, George H 220a 2
Ossler, Charles H 218a 2
Oster, Helen C 129 3
O'Toole, Adelaide E 217a 2
O'Toole, C Bernadette 217a, 225 2
O'Toole, C Bernadette 225a 2
O'Toole, Claude A 217a, 225a 2
O'Toole, Claude A 225a 2
O'Toole, J J 217 2
O'Toole, Joseph A 223a 2
O'Toole, Lillie B 223a 2
O'Toole, Marion Theresa V 223a 2
O'Toole, Thomas 225a 2
O'Toole, Vincent R 225a 2
Ott, Eli 188, 219a, 221a 2
Ott, Eli 183 1
Ott, Elizabeth 219a 2
Ott, Emma C 219a 2
Ott, Geo 56 1
Ott, George 220a, 221a 2
Ott, George M 220a, 221a, 225a 2
Ott, Jacob 221a 2
Ott, Jacob 110 1
Ott, Jennie 220a 2
Ott, John 217, 228 1
Ott, John 1, 107, 220a, 221a, 223a, 224a 2
Ott, John 37 3
Ott, John 224a 2
Ott, John T 165 1
Ott, John T 219a 2
Ott, Josephine 221a 2
Ott, Marrillas E 223a 2
Ott, Mary 223a 2
Ott, Mary A 221a 2
Ott, Mary C 220a 2
Ott, Michael 220a, 223a 2
Ott, Samuel 219a, 221a, 224a 2
Ott, Sophia 219a 2
Ott, Susan 224a 2
Ott, Thomas 225a 2
Ott, William 220a, 268 2
Ott, Wm 179 1

Ott, Wm 225a 2
Ottner, Mary 223a 2
Otto, Eli 40 1
Otto, Jacob 93 2
Otto, Jessamine F 234 1
Otto, John 271 1
Otto, John 221a 2
Otto, L Ann 221a 2
Otto, Lucenda A 223a 2
Otto, Thomas G 223a 2
Otts, John 213 1
Oucke, John 137 2
Ould, Alice R 217a 2
Ourand, David 218a 2
Oursler, Wm 56 1
Ovelman, Abraham 106 1
Ovelman, Abraham 221a 2
Ovelman, Geo 57, 93, 107, 131, 134, 160, 188 2
Ovelman, Geo 133 1
Ovelman, Geo R 106 1
Ovelman, Geo R [?] 32 1
Ovelman, George 100, 220a, 221a 2
Ovelman, George R 91 1
Ovelman, George R 220a 2
Ovelman, Henry 220a 2
Ovelman, Hiram W 220a 2
Ovelman, John 220a, 221a 2
Ovelman, Joseph 221a 2
Ovelman, Prudence 220a, 224a 2
Ovelman, Sarah W 8, 220a 2
Ovelman, William J 225a 2
Overholtzer, Lewis A 223a 2
Overholtzer, Martin C 205 3
Overland, Geo 228 1
Overton, John 221a 2
Overton, Mary E 221a 2
Owen, J W 25 2
Owens, Elizabeth 220a 2
Owens, Hugh 220a 2
Owens, Nimrod 194 1
Owens, Patrick 169, 215a 2
Owens, Washington 202 2
Owings, Christian 179 1
Owings, Christopher 218a 2
Owings, Chritopher 122 3
Owings, Cordelia 218a 2
Owings, Edward 219a 2
Owings, Edward C 219a 2
Owings, Elizabeth 219a 2
Owings, Hannah 225a 2
Owings, Mary 223a 2
Owings, N H 225a 2
Owings, Nathan 11 2
Owings, Nathan 159 1
Owings, Nathan H 218a 2
Owings, Nimrod 113 3
Owings, Nimrod 219a, 224 2
Owings, Nimrod 116 1
Owings, O H 63, 218a 2
Owings, O H 248 1
Owings, Patrick 148, 223a, 224, 253 2
Owings, Patrick 149, 160, 164 1
Owings, Rebecca M 218a 2
Owings, Samuel 223a 2
Owings, Samuel C 283 1
Owings, Sarah 224a 2
Owings, Thomas B 225a 2
Owings, Thos 14 1
Owings, Thos B 43 2
Owings, Thos C 22 2
Owings, Washington 225a 2
Oxley, C W 206 2
Oxley, Chas 172 2
Oxley, Robt O 206 2
Oxley, Robt W 172 2
Oyler, Samuel G 205 3
Oyster, George M Jr 220a 2
Oyster, Susan 224a 2
Pace, Edna G 245 2
Pace, Oscar Edward 245 2
Packard, John A 237 2
Padgett, D Z 72, 159 1
Padgett, Daniel Z 231 2
Padgett, George W 234 2
Padgett, Ida V 231, 236 2
Padgett, Jane G 238, 246 2
Padgett, John 231 2
Padgett, Robert 231 2
Padgett, Robert H 234, 246 2
Padgett, William 250 2
Page, Calvin 229a 2
Page, Calvin 176, 201, 234 1
Page, Calvin 8, 14 3
Page, Daisy L 231 2
Page, Dudley 82 1
Page, Dudley 229a 2
Page, Dudley Merrill 245 2
Page, Jno W 129 3
Page, John 160 2
Page, John W 111 3
Page, Nellie P 82 1
Page, Nellie Percy 245 2
Page, W Y 210a 2
Page, Walker Y 129 3
Paine, Wm 147 1
Painter, Elmer F 163 2
Paisley, Ray A 132, 250 2
Paisley, Willetta M 250 2
Palm, Agustua 227a 2
Palmer, Adam W 231, 227a 2
Palmer, Albert C 243 2
Palmer, Amanda B 227a 2
Palmer, Annie R 227a 2
Palmer, Bruce 62 1
Palmer, Bruce D 239 2
Palmer, Caroline 238 2
Palmer, Daisy M 73 1
Palmer, Daisy M 231 2
Palmer, Daniel 231 2
Palmer, Elmer E 232, 249 2
Palmer, Fenton L 227a 2
Palmer, G Lloyd 49, 199, 211, 234, 242 2
Palmer, Gordon 134, 225 2
Palmer, Gordon F 266 1
Palmer, Grayson E 242 2
Palmer, Guy C 238 2
Palmer, H C 203 1
Palmer, Harry 242 2
Palmer, Harvey J 235 2
Palmer, Howard 231 2
Palmer, Howard C 235 2
Palmer, Jacob 80, 187 2
Palmer, Jacob E 91 1
Palmer, James 201 1
Palmer, James 87 2
Palmer, James M 56 1
Palmer, James O 238 2
Palmer, James W 241 2
Palmer, John C 238 2
Palmer, John C 86 1
Palmer, John C 43 3
Palmer, John E 238, 239, 247 2
Palmer, John E 40 3
Palmer, John L 242 2
Palmer, Jonathan 51 2
Palmer, Jos M 50 3
Palmer, Joseph 25, 35 2
Palmer, Joseph 96, 204, 249, 263 1
Palmer, Joseph 18, 40 3
Palmer, Joseph M 193 1
Palmer, Joseph M 67, 177, 237 2
Palmer, Josephine 235 2
Palmer, Josephus 238 2
Palmer, Laura E 241 2
Palmer, Laura V 241 2
Palmer, Mamie D 234 2
Palmer, Manzella 238 2
Palmer, Martha E 242 2
Palmer, Mary C 243 2
Palmer, Mary E 43 3
Palmer, Mary E 238, 242 2
Palmer, Michael 249 1
Palmer, Millard J 242 2
Palmer, Naomi C 243 2
Palmer, Peter 129 3
Palmer, Peter 67, 72 2
Palmer, Samuel 247 2
Palmer, Sarah J 232 2
Palmer, Thomas 249 2
Palmer, Thos 39 2

Palmer, Upton W 145 2
Palmer, Wade 242 2
Pampell, Frederick W 234 2
Pampell, Henry 235 2
Pampell, Jerome 234 2
Pampell, P F 254 1
Pancoast, Frances E 234 2
Pancoast, John 231 2
Pancoast, John 37 3
Pancoast, Samuel 247 2
Pancoast, Samuel 116 1
Pancoast, Samuel & 100 2
Pancost, John 32 1
Pane, Margaret 242 2
Parish, S R W 93 2
Parker, Chas H 129 1
Parker, E 4 1
Parker, Edw 242 2
Parker, Elizabeth E 241 2
Parker, H 75 3
Parker, Katie 268 2
Parker, Lewis H 241 2
Parker, Lillie M 73 1
Parker, Maria L 242 2
Parker, William 250 2
Parkerhurst, Simon 218 2
Parmly, Kate D 199 2
Parosns, Ann R 227a 2
Parrish, Edgar M 232 2
Parrish, Lena K 87, 89 2
Parrish, N M 264 1
Parson, Mason 26 2
Parson, W I 246 2
Parson, W Irving 40 2
Parson, W Irving [sic] 25 1
Parsons, Amie P 147 3
Parsons, Irving 96 3
Parsons, L J 250 2
Parsons, Laura J 177 2
Parsons, W I 35 2
Parsons, W Irvin 250 2
Parsons, W Irving 29, 227a 2
Parsons, W Irving 60, 67, 152 1
Parsons, W Irving 19, 205, 224 3
Parsons, W M 60 1
Parton, George P 234 2
Parton, Natalie L 234 2
Passaro, Michael 120 1
Pateman, Elkana 100 2
Patterson, A M 25, 246 2
Patterson, A M 240, 260, 272 1
Patterson, A M 20 3
Patterson, Addie B 227a 2
Patterson, Albert M 44 1
Patterson, Albert M 227a 2
Patterson, Albert M 82 3
Patterson, Caroline H 229a 2
Patterson, Eleanor 231 2
Patterson, Mary E 242, 250 2
Patterson, Nan A 219 1
Patterson, Robert M 246 2
Patterson, William 231, 250 2
Patterson, William W 250 2
Patterson, Wm 69 2
Patterson, Wm W 38 2
Pattingall, Samuel 56 1
Paucoast, Cabell 70 3
Paxson, Rosalie H 246 2
Paxton, Jenny 237 2
Paxton, John 99 1
Paxton, Samuel C 32 1
Paxton, Samuel C 40 3
Paxton, William 250 2
Paxton, Wm 125, 210 1
Paxton, Wm 237 2
Payne, Appleton C 227a 2
Payne, Blanche Mrs 10 2
Payne, Ellen 242 2
Payne, Ellen V 232 2
Payne, Emma N 227a 2
Payne, J William 195, 238 2
Payne, J William 91 3
Payne, J Wm 6, 229 1
Payne, J Wm 238 2
Payne, John A 160 3
Payne, John W 238, 239 2
Payne, Joseph 160 3
Payne, Joseph 238 2
Payne, Joseph 57 2
Payne, Joseph 100 2
Payne, Joseph 187 2
Payne, Joseph 197 2
Payne, Joseph 18, 51, 257 1
Payne, Mary A 242 2
Payne, Reppid 195 2
Payne, Reppie B 238 2
Pazdersky, Joseph C 239 2
Pazdersky, Joseph W 239 2
Peace, G Horton 249 2
Peace, Vernon L 249 2
Peach, Lloyd 250 2
Peach, Milly 242 2
Peach, Oliver 245 2
Peach, William 250 2
Peaire, Annie E 68 1
Pearce, Frances T 234 2
Pearce, Joshua 237 2
Pearee, William 165 3
Pearl, Catherine B 246 2
Pearl, Charles C 32 2
Pearl, George W 234 2
Pearl, Howard N 172 3
Pearl, James 237 2
Pearl, James C 239 2
Pearl, John C 209 2
Pearl, John T 242 2
Pearl, John W 239 2
Pearl, Loretta 241 2
Pearl, Mabel B 254 1
Pearl, Margaret L 242 2
Pearl, Nancy W 234 2
Pearl, Robert Hayes 246 2
Pearl, Sarah 239 2
Pearl, Sarah E 28 3
Pearl, William 250 2
Pearre Thos O 25 1
Pearre, A Austin 227a 2
Pearre, A L 189 2
Pearre, Albert 232 2
Pearre, Albert L 260 1
Pearre, Albert L 227a 2
Pearre, Alexander 237a, 242 2
Pearre, Alexander 85 1
Pearre, Aubrey 229a 2
Pearre, Aubrey 42 3
Pearre, Aubrey Jr 231 2
Pearre, Aubrey Jr 85 1
Pearre, Cecilia 229a 2
Pearre, Charles 229a 2
Pearre, Charles C 229a 2
Pearre, Clementine V 229a, 249 2
Pearre, David 63 1
Pearre, Debotah 241 2
Pearre, Eleanor Gould 275 1
Pearre, Eliza 232 2
Pearre, Emma R 231 2
Pearre, Estelle 231 2
Pearre, Frankline A 234 2
Pearre, Geo 124 3
Pearre, Geo A Jr 260 1
Pearre, George A 287 2
Pearre, George A Jr 162 1
Pearre, Ida 112 1
Pearre, J W 238 2
Pearre, James 7, 54, 72, 93, 181, 237, 238, 247 2
Pearre, James 59, 119, 164, 183 1
Pearre, James W 29, 115 2
Pearre, James W 40, 41, 186 3
Pearre, James W 106, 243 1
Pearre, Joshua 237 2
Pearre, Louisa V 245 2
Pearre, Lucretia C 241 2
Pearre, Lydia R 241 2
Pearre, M S 126 1
Pearre, Marie D 242 2
Pearre, Mary 63 1
Pearre, Mary A 242 2
Pearre, O Truman 245 2
Pearre, Oliver 245 2

Pearre, Oliver 245 2
Pearre, Oliver H 242, 245 2
Pearre, Samuel 79 1
Pearre, Sarah 247 2
Pearre, Sarah 237 2
Pearre, Thomas C 196 3
Pearre, Thomas C 229a, 249 2
Pearre, Thomas O 249 2
Pearre, Thos 124 2
Pearre, W H H 231 2
Pearrell, Bertha A 228a 2
Pearrell, James R 228a 2
Pearson, Elizabeth 231 2
Pearson, Helen S 172 1
Pearson, Isaac E 209 3
Pearson, Mary Beckley 150 1
Peasnurr, Simon [sic] 118 1
Peck, Harriott 235 2
Peck, Margaret C 126 1
Peck, Margaret C 242 2
Peddicord, Anita W 227a 2
Peddicord, Anna M 227a 2
Peddicord, Arthur 235 2
Peddicord, Arthur A 227a 2
Peddicord, Charles W 235 2
Peddicord, Elizabeth 231 2
Peddicord, Greenbury 234 2
Peddicord, H A 205 1
Peddicord, Harry 9 2
Peddicord, Harry A 235 2
Peddicord, Helen E 97 1
Peddicord, Henry A 159, 208, 235 2
Peddicord, J 238 2
Peddicord, Jasper 54 3
Peddicord, Jasper 234, 238 2
Peddicord, John 54 3
Peddicord, John T 186 3
Peddicord, Lucy L 155 1
Peddicord, Mary 181 2
Peddicord, Mary E 205 2
Peiffer, W H 28 1
Peiffer, William H 78 1
Peit, John B 144 1
Penn, Elizabeth 234 2
Penn, Francis 234 2
Penn, Frank W 107 3
Penn, Harriet 235 2
Penn, Jesse 237, 242 2
Penn, Joseph 8 3
Penn, Joseph 237 2
Penn, Mary 247 2
Penn, Mary 242 2
Penn, Samuel 208, 247 2
Pennel, John S 31 3
Pennell, Harry E 219 1
Pennell, Harry E 3 2
Pennell, James P 238 2
Pennell, John S 238 2
Penner, Italine C 20 2
Pennybaker, Samuel 247 2
Pentz, Myrtle E 242 2
Pentz, W H 242 2
Peoples, Edwin T 232 2
Peoples, James 179 3
Peoples, William 250 2
Pepple, Elizabeth 237 2
Pepple, Joseph 237 2
Perkins, Josephine 221a 2
Perkins, Josphine 41 1
Perrell, Mary A 242 2
Perrill, Samuel 247 2
Perrill, Samuel Sr 247 2
Perrill, Thomas 249 2
Perry, Benjamin C 129 2
Perry, Catherine 238 2
Perry, E A D 165 1
Perry, Ed A 235 2
Perry, George W 3 3
Perry, George W 102, 239 2
Perry, H Clay 11 2
Perry, Henry 5, 235 2
Perry, J P 82, 165 3
Perry, Jacob 204, 279 1
Perry, Jacob S 238 2
Perry, Jacob S 106 1
Perry, James 19 2
Perry, James 55 1
Perry, James P 5, 11, 89, 235, 238, 242, 276 2
Perry, James P 177, 210 1
Perry, James P 27 3
Perry, Jas F 60 3
Perry, John J 238, 242 2
Perry, Jonathan 110 2
Perry, Josephine E 239 2
Perry, Martha A 242 2
Perry, Martha S 238 2
Perry, Moriah 242 2
Perry, Sarah A 250 2
Perry, Thos 144 2
Perry, William 250 2
Perry, William 59 1
Perry, William K 250 2
Perry, William T 250 2
Pery, Jacob S 119 2
Pery, James T 119 2
Peter Burket 280 1
Peter, E D 28 3
Peter, Wm B 85 1
Peterman, Elizabeth 231 2
Peters, Anna 227a 2
Peters, Charles 184, 203 3
Peters, Geo 89, 207, to 11 2
Peters, Geo 163 1
Peters, Geo L 68, 213 1
Peters, Geo W 31, 68, 238 2
Peters, Geo W 124 1
Peters, George 234 2
Peters, George L 234 2
Peters, George W 234, 242 2
Peters, George W 28, 94 3
Peters, Horace T 238 2
Peters, John 238 2
Peters, John A 238 2
Peters, Julia M 234 2
Peters, Julian M 239 2
Peters, Lewis 41, 79 1
Peters, Lewis 234 2
Peters, M Dixon 214 3
Peters, Mary H 238 2
Peters, Michael 242 2
Peters, Minnie D 242 2
Peters, Oliva 249 2
Peters, Thomas 249 2
Peters, Thos W 234 2
Peters, Trovilla E 249 2
Peters, W Scott 68 1
Peterson, Wm 200 1
Petrott, Francis 83 3
Petrott, Francis 32, 239 2
Petrott, Francis 234 2
Petrott, Francis 140 1
Petrott, Mary James 234 2
Petticord, H A 9 3
Petticord, Harriet 139 2
Petticord, Harry A 227a 2
Petticord, John T 238 2
Petticord, Mary L 227a 2
Pettingal, Clara I 229a 2
Pettingal, Eliza 231 2
Pettingal, Elizabeth 231 2
Pettingal, Robert 231 2
Pettingal, S H 229a 2
Pettingall, Elizabeth 246 2
Pettingall, Harry E 250 2
Pettingall, Raymond E 250 2
Pettingall, Robert 246 2
Pettingall, Samuel 247 2
Pettingall, Sarah 246 2
Pettingall, Winfield S 250 2
Pettit, Anna F 227a 2
Pettit, Henry M 227a, 238 2
Pettit, Jane N A 238 2
Pettit, William B 238 2
Peugnet, Charles P E 229a 2
Peugnet, Emily C 232 2
Peugnet, Emily G 229a 2
Pfeifer, Addie S 235 2
Pfeifer, Annie S 227a 2
Pfeifer, Della M 238 2
Pfeifer, Della M 231 2
Pfeifer, H Milton 235 2
Pfeifer, John T 238 2

Pfeil, Mary R 176 3
Pfoutz, Catherine 234 2
Pfoutz, David 155 1
Pfoutz, Geo 58 1
Pfoutz, Geo 165 2
Pfoutz, George 234 2
Pfoutz, Isaac 28, 138, 237, 242 2
Pfoutz, Isaac 164, 264 1
Pfoutz, Isaac 40 3
Pfoutz, Issac 236 2
Pfoutz, Jesse 28 3
Pfoutz, John 138, 237, 238, 242 2
Pfoutz, John S 247 2
Pfoutz, Martin 242 2
Pfoutz, Mary E 242 2
Pfoutz, Peter 264 1
Pfoutz, Samuel 70 3
Pfoutz, Samuel 247 2
Pfoutz, Sarah J 247 2
Pfoutz, Soloman 242 2
Pfoutz, Solomon 155 1
Phalen, Ella M 247 2
Phalen, Sara A 247 2
Phebus, A E 119 2
Phebus, B E 212a 2
Phebus, Ben 147 1
Phebus, Benj 225 2
Phebus, Benjamin E 228a 2
Phebus, Elmer McC 242 2
Phebus, Emmeline 229a, 245 2
Phebus, Frances M 234 2
Phebus, George T 234 2
Phebus, Harry G 228a, 234 2
Phebus, Harry T 234 2
Phebus, Margaret E 111 1
Phebus, Margaret V 116, 242 2
Phebus, Peter 245 2
Phebus, R E 141 3
Phebus, Roger E 242 2
Phebuss, Elizabeth 245 2
Phebuss, Peter 245 2
Pheeler, Clarence M 266 1
Phelps, Bernard O 239 2
Phelps, Clara A 231 2
Phelps, Dexter E 231 2
Phelps, Dexter E 113 1
Phelps, Emma H 239 2
Phelps, John Kenneth 239 2
Phelps, Milton J 242 2
Phelps, Robert W 246 2
Pheobus, William H 250 2
Philips, Catherine 231 2
Philips, Ely 231 2
Philips, Ida Allen 4 1
Philips, John 27 2
Philips, William 4 1
Phillip, L N 245 2
Phillips, Ann M E 241 2
Phillips, Bertha A 284 1
Phillips, C Lee 250 2
Phillips, Dora E 238 2
Phillips, Elizabeth 231 2
Phillips, Elmer N 232 2
Phillips, Hanson Lee 235 2
Phillips, Harry P 174 3
Phillips, J 189 1
Phillips, J Jane 237 2
Phillips, Jacob H 238 2
Phillips, Jason 62, 237 2
Phillips, John 27, 43 2
Phillips, John 51 1
Phillips, John 39 3
Phillips, John G 41 1
Phillips, John R 250 2
Phillips, Levy 247 2
Phillips, Lillie A 241 2
Phillips, Lilly A 232 2
Phillips, Lycurgus M 241 2
Phillips, Lycurgus N 60, 85, 264 1
Phillips, M Kathryn 90 1
Phillips, Mabel I 174 3
Phillips, Margaret E 242 2
Phillips, Mary P 246 2
Phillips, Milton J 27 1
Phillips, Milton T 241 2
Phillips, Nancy 245 2
Phillips, Noah 51, 116, 163, 164, 213 1
Phillips, Noah 1, 38, 237, 245, 247 2
Phillips, Sabvitte 247 2
Phillips, Samuel 247 2
Phillips, Walter L 250 2
Phillips, Walter P 250 2
Philpot, Benjamin 18, 28 2
Philpot, Blanchard 277 2
Philpot, Elizabeth 110 1
Philpot, G B 198 2
Philpott, Amelia 227a 2
Philpott, Barbara C 228a 2
Philpott, Barton 228a 2
Philpott, Barton Sr 228a 2
Philpott, Benj 228a, 250 2
Philpott, Benjamin 68, 228a 2
Philpott, Elizabeth 231 2
Philpott, Washington G 250 2
Phleeger, C A 56 3
Phleeger, C M 56 3
Phleeger, C M 178 2
Phleeger, C M 260, 277 1
Phleeger, Clarence M 234 2
Phleeger, Frederick K 217 1
Phleeger, Frederick K 234 2
Phleeger, Hermie Catherine 286 2
Phleeger, John 40, 237, 238 2
Phleeger, John 220 3
Phleeger, John E 61 1
Phleeger, John E 55 3
Phleeger, Susannah 238 2
Phleelger, C M 100 3
Phoebus, Benj F 231 2
Phoebus, Charles M 229a 2
Phoebus, Charles O 231 2
Phoebus, Elizabeth 231 2
Phoebus, Elizabeth C 231 2
Phoebus, Ellen 250 2
Phoebus, Elmer McC 232 2
Phoebus, Emeline 238 2
Phoebus, Jacob A 238 2
Phoebus, Roger E 232 2
Phoutz, George 14 3
Phoutz, Michael 242 2
Pickenbaugh, Henry 185 3
Pickens, James R 237 2
Pickens, John F 237 2
Pickens, Mary 237, 242 2
Pickens, Robert 246 2
Pickett, James M 42 3
Pickett, John 133 1
Pickett, Johnsey 237 2
Pickett, Johnzee 57 1
Pickett, Lulu 149 2
Pickett, Margaret 237, 242 2
Picketts, Margaret 153 1
Picking, Barbara 228a, 249 2
Picking, Chas 250 2
Picking, Esther 231 2
Picking, John 218a, 237 2
Picking, John 238 1
Picking, John B 70, 165, 213 3
Picking, John B 22, 137, 138, 237 2
Picking, John B 67 1
Picking, John D 219 3
Picking, John T 195 3
Picking, L 223 1
Picking, Leonard 223, 249, 264 1
Picking, Leonard 7, 89 2
Picking, Leonard 40, 54, 218 3
Picking, Mary A 237 2
Picking, Robt 146 1
Picking, Thomas 231, 249 2
Picking, Thos 197 2
Picking, William H 250 2
Pickings, Leonard 167 3
Pickung, John B 119 2
Pierce, Carrie B 239 2
Pierce, Clarence A 234 2
Pierce, George W 234 2
Pierce, Helen M 234 2
Pierce, Isiah 237 2
Pierce, Joseph D 239 2

Pigman, ALexina 227a 2
Pigman, B F 66 2
Pigman, B S 70 1
Pigman, Bean S 10 1
Pinckney, Judy 237 2
Pingley, Charles F 229a 2
Pingley, Edna M 229a 2
Piper, Hulett V 166 1
Pittenger, Charles M 229a 2
Pittenger, Hezekiah D 229a 2
Pittinger, Benj 231 2
Pittinger, Benjamin 228a 2
Pittinger, C M 265 2
Pittinger, Charles N 238 2
Pittinger, Clara E 250 2
Pittinger, Daniel 231 2
Pittinger, Elinor 9 2
Pittinger, Geo H 145 2
Pittinger, Hannah A 241 2
Pittinger, Hezekiah 235 2
Pittinger, Hezekiah B 235 2
Pittinger, J Newton 238, 242, 246 2
Pittinger, Jacob M 10 3
Pittinger, Jacob M 246 2
Pittinger, Jacob N 145, 238 2
Pittinger, Jennie 238 2
Pittinger, Jeremiah 237, 238 2
Pittinger, Jesse 238 2
Pittinger, John 60 1
Pittinger, John 228a, 231, 238 2
Pittinger, Joshua W 237 2
Pittinger, Lycurgus L 241 2
Pittinger, Maude C 238 2
Pittinger, Minerva 242 2
Pittinger, Phil 235 2
Pittinger, Phoebe 245 2
Pittinger, Rebecca 246 2
Pittinger, T A 242 2
Pittinger, Walter 145 2
Pittinger, William J 250 2
Pittinger, Wm 183 1
Pittinger, Wm 169 2
Pittinger, Wm & 25 2
Pittinger, Wm B 64 3
Pittinger, Wm B 135 1
Pittinger, Wm P 26 1
Pittman, James W 239 2
Pitts, Annie 227a 2
Pitts, Charles 229a 2
Pitts, Elizabeth 231, 237 2
Pitts, John 186, 237 2
Pitts, John L 106 3
Pitts, John L 26, 30, 196 1
Pitts, John L 14 2
Pitts, N H 186 2
Pitts, Nicholas H 25, 139 1
Pitts, Sussanna J 247 2
Pitzenberger, Abraham 25, 30 1
Pitzer, Allan M 44 3
Pitzer, Allen M 174 3
place Baltimore city 16 2
place Balto Co 290 2
place Montpelier, Vt 257 2
place Ohio 38, 137 2
place Reading, Pa 223a 2
place Texas 199 2
Place, Baltimore 120, 209 3
Place, Jefferson Co, VA 185 3
place, Ohio 38 2
Place, Ohio 234 1
Place, Wash Co? 99 1
Plain, David 56 1
Plaine, Catherine 229a 2
Plaine, Daniel 229a 2
Plaine, Daniel 220 3
Plaine, Daniel 112 1
Plaine, Jonathan 237 2
Plaine, Laura Clemson 241 2
Plaine, Lydia 237 2
Plaine, Nancy 247 2
Plaine, Stephen 30 1
Plate, B C 125 1
Plater, Aloise 227a 2
Plater, Hiram 129 3
Plato, Thomas W 249 2
Pletsch, Emma 241 2
Pletsch, Emma 232 2
Pletsch, L L 241 2
Pletsch, Lewis L 232 2
Pletsch, Louis 241 2
Plummer, A N 144 2
Plummer, Abner 236 2
Plummer, Abner M 30 1
Plummer, Abner M 38 2
Plummer, Arline C 227a 2
Plummer, Catharine A 229a 2
Plummer, Catherine 249 2
Plummer, Charity 251 2
Plummer, Charles Gordon 58 3
Plummer, E G 229a 2
Plummer, Edwin 229a 2
Plummer, Evan 231 2
Plummer, Hullvah 235 2
Plummer, Israel T 236 2
Plummer, Issac 236 2
Plummer, Jane 237 2
Plummer, Jesse 164 1
Plummer, Jesse 141 3
Plummer, Jesse 237, 250, 254 2
Plummer, Jonathan 237 2
Plummer, Mary W 242, 249 2
Plummer, P Louisa 245 2
Plummer, Rachel 65, 237, 246 2
Plummer, Richard 246, 247, 251 2
Plummer, Ruben M 246 2
Plummer, Ruben N 245 2
Plummer, Rufus 81 3
Plummer, Samuel 249 1
Plummer, Samuel 247 2
Plummer, Samuel U 247 2
Plummer, Samuel W 271 1
Plummer, Sarah 247 2
Plummer, Thomas 235 2
Plummer, Thomas G 249 2
Plummer, Thomas M 141 3
Plummer, Thomas M 249 2
Plummer, Thomas M 32 1
Plummer, Thos 250 2
Plummer, Ursula 249 2
Plummer, W B 236 2
Plummer, William 247, 250 2
Plummer, Wm 51, 65, 237 2
Plummer, Yate 251 2
Plummer, Zephaniah 251 2
Plunkard, Emma D 234 2
Plunkard, Guy I 234 2
Plunkard, Harry T 234 2
Plunkard, James 238 2
Plunkard, James S 238 2
Plunkard, Mary A 242 2
Plunkard, Mary B 242 2
Plunkert, Addie 240 1
Plunkert, Lewis 220 1
Plunkert, Paul A 222, 233, 240 1
Plunkett, Ellen A 232 2
Plunkett, James 232 2
Plunkett, John 232 2
Plus, Charles W 229a 2
Plush, Addie G 227a 2
Plymier, Barbara A 144 1
Plymier, Henry A 144 1
Pnacoast[sic], John 196 1
Poe, Jacob 279 1
Poe, Nelson 279 1
Poffenberger, Catherine 229a 2
Poffenberger, Daniel 106 3
Poffenberger, David 14 3
Poffenberger, G J 147 1
Poffenberger, Jacob 94 3
Poffenberger, John 106 3
Poffenberger, John 263 1
Poffenberger, Laura E 241 2
Poffinberger, Aaron 231, 237 2
Poffinberger, Alverda V 231 2
Poffinberger, Arthur R 227a 2
Poffinberger, Charles A 229a 2
Poffinberger, Charles E S 229a 2
Poffinberger, Charles V 246 2
Poffinberger, Clara E 229a 2
Poffinberger, Daniel 231 2

Poffinberger, Daniel E 231 2
Poffinberger, David F 231 2
Poffinberger, Edgar E 227a 2
Poffinberger, Elizabeth 231 2
Poffinberger, Elmer 235 2
Poffinberger, Elmer W 232 2
Poffinberger, Enock 231 2
Poffinberger, George 229a, 287 2
Poffinberger, George F 235 2
Poffinberger, George J 234 2
Poffinberger, Henry 235 2
Poffinberger, Hezikiah 235 2
Poffinberger, Isaac 19 2
Poffinberger, Isaih 242 2
Poffinberger, Issac 231 2
Poffinberger, J Mc 238 2
Poffinberger, Jacob 237, 238 2
Poffinberger, Jacob Jr 237 2
Poffinberger, John 231, 237 2
Poffinberger, John H 235 2
Poffinberger, John M 238 2
Poffinberger, Joshua 234, 237 2
Poffinberger, Margie E 242, 246 2
Poffinberger, Martha E 246 2
Poffinberger, Mary 242 2
Poffinberger, Otho J 238 2
Poffinberger, Reno B 246 2
Poffinberger, Roy E 232, 246 2
Poffingberger, Elizabeth 231 2
Poffinger, Isaac 111 2
Pole, Francis 234 2
Pole, Geo W 283 1
Pole, George W 213 3
Pole, Thomas 249 2
Pole, William 234 2
Polk, Thomas E 55 3
Polk, William 250 2
Polle, Gertrude L 232 2
Polly, Ann Mariah 237 2
Polly, John H 237 2
Polly, W A 195 1
Polson, Elias 229a 2
Pomeroy, W A J 227a 2
Pomroy, Annie E 227a 2
Ponder, Andrew 171, 205 3
Ponder, Andrew 167 3
Ponton, Grant A 242 2
Ponton, Mary 242 2
Pool, Clara 246 2
Pool, Hallie G 250 2
Pool, William S 250 2
Poole, A Lincoln 227a 2
Poole, Agnes G 238 2
Poole, Alvin S 30 1
Poole, Annie R 227a 2
Poole, Benjamin 101 2
Poole, Benjamin 152 1
Poole, Bessie M 238 2
Poole, Bessie M 219 1
Poole, Brice 228a 2
Poole, Brice 241 2
Poole, Carrie B 249 2
Poole, Catherine 229a 2
Poole, Charles E 229a, 241 2
Poole, Chas 247 2
Poole, Chas E 246 2
Poole, Chs E 249 2
Poole, Cornelius J 229a 2
Poole, Daniel J 235 2
Poole, Dennis 142 1
Poole, Dennis 231, 234, 241 2
Poole, Dennis 53 3
Poole, Ellijay 232 2
Poole, Emeline 242 2
Poole, Ephriam H 171 2
Poole, Ernest F 227a, 232 2
Poole, Esther 237 2
Poole, Etta M 235 2
Poole, Frederick 234 2
Poole, Geo W 214 1
Poole, Geo W 205 3
Poole, George 234 2
Poole, George W 234 2
Poole, Grace R 246 2
Poole, Hanson 229a 2
Poole, Harriet D 235 2
Poole, Harriett D 229a 2
Poole, Harry C 235 2
Poole, Henry 235 2
Poole, J M 56 2
Poole, J W 44, 206 3
Poole, James M 241 2
Poole, James W 2, 15 2
Poole, James W 104 1
Poole, Jarrett H 238 2
Poole, Jesse 204 1
Poole, Jesse F 190 2
Poole, Jesse H 161 3
Poole, John W 238 2
Poole, Joseph 27, 237 2
Poole, L H 211 2
Poole, Lemuel H 241 2
Poole, Luceja E 241 2
Poole, Lucy 241 2
Poole, Luke 241 2
Poole, M R 68 2
Poole, Mahala 242 2
Poole, Margaret R 249 2
Poole, Mary 117 1
Poole, Nehemiah 139 1
Poole, Peter 26 2
Poole, Rachel R 246 2
Poole, Rodney 228a 2
Poole, Roy S 249 2
Poole, Roy W 52, 246 2
Poole, S M 204 1
Poole, Salmon 247 2
Poole, Samuel 82 1
Poole, Samuel 26, 247 2
Poole, Sarah 247 2
Poole, Susanna 247 2
Poole, T 67 2
Poole, Thomas 171 2
Poole, Thomas E D 234, 249 2
Poole, Thomas E D 185 3
Poole, Thomas E D 106, 112, 117 1
Poole, Thomas E V 185 3
Poole, Thomas Ed 250 2
Poole, Thornton 249 2
Poole, Thos 271, 283 1
Poole, Thos 69, 231 2
Poole, Thos E 271 1
Poole, Thos E D 13 1
Poole, Vernie M 249 2
Poole, Victoria L 249 2
Poole, Walter 104, 263 1
Poole, Walter 26 2
Poole, Walter 202 3
Poole, Walter C 227a 2
Poole, William 250 2
Poole, William H 250 2
Poole, Wm 131 2
Poole, Wm H 179, 263 1
Poole, Wm H 231 2
Pope, John 237 2
Pope, T E 39 2
Pope, Thomas E 51 1
Pope, Thos E 177 2
Pope, Thos E 135 1
Pope, Wm 237 2
Popper, James 165 2
Porter, Alexander 227a 2
Porter, Annie E 227a 2
Porter, Catherine 229a 2
Porter, Elizah 30 1
Porter, Hattie E 239 2
Porter, James W 239 2
Porter, Jesse 227a, 237 2
Porter, John 237 2
Porter, John W 237 2
Porter, Margaret 237, 242 2
Porter, Martha J 242 2
Porter, Mary J 245 2
Porter, Phillip 245 2
Porter, Rebecca 246 2
Porter, Robert 245 2
Porter, Vernon C 227a 2
Porter, Wm M 249 1
Porterfield, Grace 234 2

Porteus, Stella M 250 2
Porteus, William 250 2
Portner, Benjamin 228a 2
Portner, Benjamin A 228a 2
Portner, Bnj R 228a 2
Portner, Issac 236 2
Ports, Emma C 247 2
Ports, Sylvanus M 247 2
Portser, Bess V 124 1
Posey, Malinda A 242 2
Posie, Chairly 229a 2
Pots, Arthur 234 2
Pottbery, Charles 229a 2
Pottbery, Charles 229a 2
Potterfield, E D 238 2
Potterfield, Elias 126 3
Potterfield, Elias 232 2
Potterfield, Grace 232 2
Potterfield, Jonah 238 2
Pottinger, J W 159 1
Potts Richard 34 1
Potts, A 208 3
Potts, Albert S 57 3
Potts, Amelia 227a 2
Potts, Ann L 227a 2
Potts, Ann R 227a 2
Potts, Arthur 69, 104, 165, 192, 197, 203 1
Potts, Arthur 227a 2
Potts, Arthur 64, 72, 124 3
Potts, E M 227a 2
Potts, Edith L 232 2
Potts, Eleanor M 231 2
Potts, Elinor 231 2
Potts, Elizabeth 250 2
Potts, Elizabeth C 231 2
Potts, Elnor 231 2
Potts, Elnor, M 267 2
Potts, G M 205, 234 1
Potts, G M 67 3
Potts, G M 227a, 231, 246 2
Potts, Geo 91 1
Potts, Geo 72, 181, 205 2
Potts, Geo M 64 3
Potts, Geo M 125, 165, 193, 271 1
Potts, Geo M 22, 144, 177, 231, 234 2
Potts, Geo W 32 1
Potts, George 101 2
Potts, George M 67 3
Potts, George M 234, 294 2
Potts, Henry 227a 2
Potts, John 32 1
Potts, John L 245 2
Potts, John Lee 237 2
Potts, Joseph H 238 2
Potts, Louise 227a 2
Potts, Luther 241 2
Potts, Nina Powell 246 2
Potts, Philip T 245 2
Potts, Ralph H L 247 2
Potts, Ralph H L 11 3
Potts, Richard 14, 66, 80, 171, 177, 197, 214, 227a, 231, 237, 245, 246, 247, 250 2
Potts, Richard 70, 84, 88, 91, 193, 205 1
Potts, Richard 1, 113 3
Potts, Richards 231, 275 2
Potts, Sarah Lee 247 2
Potts, Stella M 238, 247, 290 2
Potts, Stephen C 247 2
Potts, William 250 2
Potts, William H 241 2
Poulson, Cornelius 229a 2
Poulson, John 229a 2
Poulson, Racael 229a 2
Powder, Andrew 207 1
Powder, Andrew 227a 2
Powder, Jacob 57 1
Powder, Jacob 237 2
Powder, Jacob Jr 288 2
Powder, Jacob Jr 47 1
Powder, John 237 2
Powell, Albert L 241 2
Powell, Christian 229a 2
Powell, Daniel 231 2
Powell, Daniel C 247 2
Powell, E M 72 1
Powell, Edward 231 2
Powell, Ellen C 242 2
Powell, Elmer M 232 2
Powell, Geo H 171 1
Powell, Geo H 250 2
Powell, Geo W 242 2
Powell, George 229a 2
Powell, George H 229a, 234 2
Powell, George W 234 2
Powell, Hannah E 241 2
Powell, Henrietta 235 2
Powell, J M 231, 234 2
Powell, James 154 2
Powell, John M 56 3
Powell, Jonathan 237 2
Powell, Julia 231 2
Powell, Julia A 238 2
Powell, L C 6 1
Powell, L C 75 3
Powell, L Cramer 12, 52, 90 1
Powell, L Cramer 3 3
Powell, L Cramer 134 2
Powell, Lethe A 241 2
Powell, Lewis J 241 2
Powell, Luther 40 2
Powell, Luther C 2 3
Powell, Luther C 52, 92, 183 1
Powell, Luther C 36 2
Powell, Mae L 232 2
Powell, Malcolm S 242 2
Powell, Milton L 241 2
Powell, Myrtle 40 2
Powell, Raymond 40 2
Powell, Silas A 247 2
Powell, Susan 231 2
Powell, Susannah 209 3
Powell, Thomas 124 3
Powell, Walter S 232 2
Powell, William 250 2
Powell, William M 250 2
Powell, William W 250 2
Powell, Wm 32 1
Power, Adeline 237 2
Power, Hamilton H 238 2
Power, Joseph 237, 238 2
Powers, Eugene L 174 3
Powers, Frank 133 1
Powers, Frederick D 234 2
Powers, Howard M 15 2
Powers, Lethe 241 2
Powers, Mary C 234 2
Powers, Richard 15 2
Powers, Richard 133 1
PPlaine, Stephen 247 2
Pratby, S 70 3
Prater, Andrew 137 1
Pratt, John W 56 1
Pratt, Thomas 249 2
Pratzman, Jacob 237 2
Pratzman, Jacob Jr 237 2
Prendergast, Maude 18 2
Prestman, George 234 2
Preston, Chas 223 1
Preston, S B 264 1
Preston, Samuel 88 1
Preston, Samuel 187 2
Preston, Samuel B 35, 76, 187, 221a, 250, 276 2
Preston, Samuel B 96, 117, 195, 225, 279 1
Preston, Samuel B 32, 70 3
Preston, Samuel D 185 3
Preston, W T 197 1
Preston, William T 19, 199, 209 3
Preston, William T 250 2
Preston, Wm 238 1
Preston, Wm 13, 197, 223, 238 1
Preston, Wm 35, 76, 198 2
Preston, Wm T 71, 85, 88, 225, 279 1
Preston, Wm T 258 2
Price, Amos 227a 2
Price, Annie 227a 2
Price, Banj 185 2

Price, Ben 279 1
Price, Benj 185 2
Price, Benjamin 113 3
Price, Benjamin 26, 51 2
Price, C Casper 224 2
Price, Carroll 34 1
Price, Charles 229a 2
Price, Charles 238 2
Price, Charles H 229a 2
Price, Charles S 229a, 238 2
Price, Charles U 229a 2
Price, Chas Jasper 35 2
Price, Chas S 220 2
Price, Chas W 61 1
Price, Daniel 51 1
Price, Edna A 218, 224 2
Price, Elijah 228 1
Price, Elijah 231, 249 2
Price, Elijah 192 3
Price, Elisha 227a 2
Price, Ellen 231 2
Price, Ernest 232, 241 2
Price, Ernest G 232 2
Price, Ethel M 232 2
Price, Geo 100 2
Price, Geo W 234 2
Price, George 37 3
Price, George W 229a 2
Price, Helen U 145 3
Price, Henry J 226 3
Price, Job 237 2
Price, John 29 2
Price, John 223 1
Price, John E 238 2
Price, John E 272 1
Price, Joseph B 15 3
Price, Levi 15, 231, 237, 241 2
Price, Mary 237 2
Price, Mary A 250 2
Price, Mary C 229a, 238 2
Price, Minerva C 242 2
Price, Montgomery 232 2
Price, Nellie I 21 3
Price, Oliver R 242, 247 2
Price, Osborne I 28 3
Price, Perry 19 2
Price, Robert L 232 2
Price, Samuel W 247 2
Price, Sarah W 35, 229a 2
Price, Thomas 231, 249 2
Price, Warren 169, 183 1
Price, Warren 234 2
Price, William H 250 2
Prior, George W 234 2
Prior, Martin L 234 2
Probey, Robert E 116 3
Proby, Robert E 51 1
Proctor, Edith B 246 2
Proctor, Gertrude C 234 2
Proctor, Henrietta 230 1
Proctor, J F 58 2
Proctor, James F 250 2
Proctor, John W 241 2
Proctor, Joseph 238 2
Proctor, Laura V 241 2
Proctor, Rachel 31 2
Proctor, Rachel V 41 2
Proctor, Roger St G 246 2
Proctor, William J 250 2
Pront, Issac 236 2
Protzman, Henry 84 2
Protzman, Henry 91 1
Proughen, Barbara 228a 2
Prugh, Frederick 169, 242 2
Prugh, Frederick 242 2
Prugh, Mary 242 2
Pry, Ethel 241 2
Pry, Geo W 246 2
Pry, Helen E 169 3
Pry, John W 238 2
Pry, Luther C 241 2
Pry, Outerbridge L 238 2
Pry, Outerbridge L 1 1
Pry, Rhoda 246 2
Pryor, Albert L 189 1
Pryor, Alfred 71 1
Pryor, Benjamin F 228a 2
Pryor, C P 102 2
Pryor, Catherine 229a, 245 2
Pryor, George W 6 1
Pryor, Ira E 228a 2
Pryor, Isabella 236 2
Pryor, James W 229a 2
Pryor, Martin L 242 2
Pryor, Maurice S 4 3
Pryor, Peter C 245 2
Pryor, Rookley W 87 3
Pryor, Samuel 22 2
Pryor, Theophilus C 189 1
Pryor, Victor 242 2
Pumphrey, Mary 242, 249 2
Pumphrey, Rachel 84 2
Pumphrey, Vachel 249 2
Pumphreys, Carrie 234 2
Pumphreys, George B 234 2
Purcell, Thomas 213 3
Purcell, Thos 106 3
Purcell, Thos 137 2
Purdam, John F 238 2
Purdam, Joseph 257 1
Purdam, Joshua W 238 2
Purdam, Mary E 238 2
Purdham, Alma V 227a 2
Purdham, Benj F 228a 2
Purdham, Emory 227a 2
Purdham, Ernest S 229a 2
Purdham, John F 247 2
Purdham, Sarah 247 2
Purdham, Wm 228a 2
Purdman, S M 228a 2
Purdom, Wm H 52 2
Purdom, Wm L 52 2
Purdum, Anna 239 2
Purdum, Frank C 250 2
Purdum, Franklin E 239 2
Purdum, John 205 2
Purdum, John D 238 2
Purdum, John D 48 1
Purdum, John E 239 2
Purdum, John F 238 2
Purdum, Joshua H 238 2
Purdum, Joshua W 238 2
Purdum, Josiah W 135 1
Purdum, Josiah W 238 2
Purdum, Lucinda 238 2
Purdum, Martha B 238 2
Purdum, Olea 44 1
Purdum, U S 83 1
Purdum, William H H 250 2
Purdy, George W 234 2
Purdy, Mary B 234 2
Purdy, Singleton 40 1
Purdy, Singleton 247 2
Purzenet, Lawrence A 241 2
Pusey, George 234 2
Putman, Bessie O 228a 2
Putman, Charles C 138 3
Putman, Effie M 232 2
Putman, Gertrude 232 2
Putman, Glenn L 232 2
Putman, J Fred 10 3
Putman, John 39, 160, 238 2
Putman, K Gertrude 241 2
Putman, Katie G 241 2
Putman, L C 247 2
Putman, Lewis 89, 241 2
Putman, Lewis W 232 2
Putman, Luther C 241 2
Putman, Martin L 232 2
Putman, N H 229 1
Putman, Samuel 164 1
Putman, Samuel 247 2
Putman, Samuel J 238 2
Putmen, John 238 2
Putnam, Samuel 78 2
Pyfer, P H 94 3
Pyfer, P Henry 245 2
Pyfer, Phillip 245 2
Pyfer, Rachel 246 2
Pyle, John C 238, 242 2
Pyle, Maggie C 242 2
Pyles, Charlotte E 42 1
Pyles, Josephine W 206 3
Pyles, W W 89 2
Pyles, Wallace W 73 3
Pypher, Philip H 6 3
Qquynn, Allen G 82 1

Quay, John C 159 2
Quinlan, Romaine K 116 2
Quinn, A G 214 3
Quinn, Allen[?] G 272 1
Quinn, Alvin G 225a 2
Quinn, Caspar 40, 71 1
Quinn, Casper 14 3
Quinn, Hattie E 188 3
Quinn, John P 214 3
Quinn, R O 72 3
Quynn, A G 96, 100 3
Quynn, A G 91, 137, 171 1
Quynn, A G 282 2
Quynn, A G 84, 282 2
Quynn, Alan 39 3
Quynn, Alan G 43, 171, 229a 2
Quynn, Allen 197, 244, 256 1
Quynn, Allen 7 2
Quynn, Allen G 153 1
Quynn, Allen G 51, 87, 96, 107, 252, 253 2
Quynn, Allen G 253 2
Quynn, Allen G 113 3
Quynn, Allen G son of D H 252 2
Quynn, Allen George 252 2
Quynn, Arthur 252 2
Quynn, Casper 176, 263 1
Quynn, Casper 22, 26, 27, 43, 89, 111, 177, 186, 252 2
Quynn, Charlew W 188 3
Quynn, Chas 132, 253 2
Quynn, D H 252 2
Quynn, D Hauer 113 3
Quynn, D Hauer 252 2
Quynn, Daniel Hauer 252 2
Quynn, Emma S 253 2
Quynn, H G 19 3
Quynn, Harriet 252 2
Quynn, Harriett E 252 2
Quynn, Harry 205 2
Quynn, John 252 2
Quynn, John T 19, 179 3
Quynn, John T 252 2
Quynn, John T 118 1
Quynn, Katharine 252 2
Quynn, Mary 253 2
Quynn, Mary M 252 2
Quynn, Mary W 252, 253 2
Quynn, Mary Whiting 252 2
Quynn, Patrick 253 2
Quynn, Patrick 256, 263, 282 1
Quynn, Rachel M 196 2
Quynn, S Katherine 252, 253 2
Quynn, Susan E 253 2
Quynn, Thomas M 253 2
Quynn, William H 86 1
Quynn, William R 53 1
Quynn, Wm H 253 2
Qynn, Allen 252 2
Raabe, Sophie H 16 2
Rabe, Nora J 166 1
Rabe, Nora J 215 2
Rack, Adam 254 2
Radcliff, A A 271 2
Radcliff, Charles H 258 2
Radcliff, Dainl S 262 2
Radcliff, Della 262 2
Radcliff, Elizabeth 264 2
Radcliff, Horace 262 2
Radcliff, J Marshall 293 2
Radcliff, Joseph 275 2
Radcliff, Robbie 293 2
Radcliff, Robbie R 256 1
Radcliff, Upton 293 2
Radcliff, Upton 188 1
Radcliff, William 264 2
Radcliffe, A A 89, 167, 201 3
Radcliffe, A Atlee 255 2
Radcliffe, Horace 83 3
Radcliffe, James M 119 1
Radcliffe, Upton 35 2
Radcliffe, Upton 205 3
Rader, Christopher 184 3
Radford, Thomas 275 2
Radisel, George 64 2
Radley, Anna E 255 2
Ragan, Alice 287 2
Ragan, Norah 286 2
Ragan, Patrick 287 2
Ragan, William 294 2
Rager, Carroll A 259 2
Rager, Clara A 259 2
Rager, R A 32, 113 3
Rager, R A 8, 165 1
Rager, R A 143 2
Rager, Rufus A 116 2
Rager, Rufus A 41, 60, 82, 152, 175, 214 1
Railing, Adam 254 2
Railing, Christian 259 2
Railing, Elmer C 265, 280 2
Railing, G H 271 2
Railing, George H 259, 268 2
Railing, Henry 271 2
Railing, Louisa V 280, 283 2
Railing, Margaret V 265 2
Railing, Minnie I 283 2
Rainer, Geo 57 2
Rainer, George 57 1
Rainer, George 225a, 249 2
Rainey, Roy A 294 2
Rainey, William T 294 2
Raitt, Arenna 275 2
Raitt, John 275 2
Ramick, Mary 282 2
Ramick, Michael 70 3
Ramick, Michael 282 2
Ramsay, Margaret 283 2
Ramsberg, Clinton O 283 2
Ramsberg, George Jr 268 2
Ramsberg, Harvey C 271 2
Ramsberg, Jacob 211 2
Ramsberg, John S 80 2
Ramsberg, Joshua 214 2
Ramsberg, S E 214 2
Ramsberger, George 268 2
Ramsberger, Matilda A C 282 2
Ramsburg, Albert F 280 2
Ramsburg, Alexander 252 1
Ramsburg, Alexander 40, 255 2
Ramsburg, Alexander 220 3
Ramsburg, Amos W 254 2
Ramsburg, Anna 254 2
Ramsburg, Anna E 254, 280 2
Ramsburg, Annie C 283 2
Ramsburg, Annie E 255 2
Ramsburg, Benj 221 3
Ramsburg, Benj 171 2
Ramsburg, Benjamin 224 3
Ramsburg, Benjamin 282 2
Ramsburg, Camden J 113, 217 1
Ramsburg, Casper 258 2
Ramsburg, Catherine 258, 294 2
Ramsburg, Cave W 259 2
Ramsburg, Charles D 264 2
Ramsburg, Charles T 259 2
Ramsburg, Charlotte 258 2
Ramsburg, Chas J 147 1
Ramsburg, Chas L 166 1
Ramsburg, Chas T 283 2
Ramsburg, Chas W 208 3
Ramsburg, Christian 23 1
Ramsburg, Christian 69, 186, 220, 229, 258 2
Ramsburg, Claggett 259 2
Ramsburg, Clantha 259 2
Ramsburg, Clara A 294 2
Ramsburg, Clayton A 259 2
Ramsburg, Clayton R 259 2
Ramsburg, Clinton R 290 2
Ramsburg, Cora S 280 2
Ramsburg, D 179 3
Ramsburg, D C 40, 271 2
Ramsburg, D Casper 262 2
Ramsburg, Daisey 255 2
Ramsburg, Daisy C 262 2
Ramsburg, Daniel 202, 223, 224 3
Ramsburg, Daniel 220a, 254, 275, 282 2

Ramsburg, Daniel 26, 32, 58, 59 1
Ramsburg, Daniel J 262 2
Ramsburg, Daniel S 262 2
Ramsburg, Dano F 262 2
Ramsburg, Dennis 15, 77, 81, 165, 167, 171 3
Ramsburg, Dennis 29, 38, 262, 280, 282 2
Ramsburg, Dora E 262 2
Ramsburg, Dorothy 184 1
Ramsburg, E B 188 3
Ramsburg, Edith M 140 3
Ramsburg, Edith U 135 3
Ramsburg, Edward 264 2
Ramsburg, Edward F 264 2
Ramsburg, Elias 27, 288 2
Ramsburg, Elias B 254, 265, 277 2
Ramsburg, Elias B Jr 274 2
Ramsburg, Elizabeth 264, 271 2
Ramsburg, Ellen 30 2
Ramsburg, Elmer K 293 2
Ramsburg, Elsie A 197 1
Ramsburg, Elsie S 45 3
Ramsburg, Elsie Sponseller 283 2
Ramsburg, Emanuel 126 1
Ramsburg, Emanuel L 264, 286 2
Ramsburg, Emory 286 2
Ramsburg, Emory R 58 3
Ramsburg, Emory R 34, 136, 271 1
Ramsburg, Emory R 277 2
Ramsburg, Ezra 186 3
Ramsburg, F C 80 2
Ramsburg, F C 156 1
Ramsburg, F D 290 2
Ramsburg, Foster 62 3
Ramsburg, Frances 291 2
Ramsburg, Frederick 258, 267, 275 2
Ramsburg, Geo 102 3
Ramsburg, Geo 204, 228, 257 1
Ramsburg, Geo L 259 2
Ramsburg, Geo P 87 2
Ramsburg, Geo W 191 1
Ramsburg, George 268 2
Ramsburg, George 8, 96 3
Ramsburg, George L 268 2
Ramsburg, George P 290 2
Ramsburg, Gideon G 268 2
Ramsburg, Grayson H 280 2
Ramsburg, H 27 1
Ramsburg, H B 176 1
Ramsburg, H E 100 1
Ramsburg, Hannah E 271 2
Ramsburg, Hanson 125, 253 1
Ramsburg, Hanson 70 3
Ramsburg, Harriet P 271 2
Ramsburg, Harry E 283 2
Ramsburg, Harvey E 10, 262 2
Ramsburg, Harvey E 189 3
Ramsburg, Harvey E 32, 197 1
Ramsburg, Henry 57, 112, 197, 257 1
Ramsburg, Henry 28, 214, 220, 271, 275 2
Ramsburg, Henry A 271 2
Ramsburg, Henry B 271, 291 2
Ramsburg, Henry T 113, 283 2
Ramsburg, Howard P 271 2
Ramsburg, Irvin J 140 3
Ramsburg, Israel 186, 214 2
Ramsburg, Israel 84, 263 1
Ramsburg, J 275 2
Ramsburg, J H, 106 1
Ramsburg, J P 276 2
Ramsburg, J S 30, 43, 96 2
Ramsburg, Jacob 202 3
Ramsburg, Jacob 39, 154, 254, 267, 275, 276 2
Ramsburg, John 37, 54, 124 3
Ramsburg, John 30, 51, 87, 101, 214, 222, 254, 264, 275, 276, 288 2
Ramsburg, John 117, 131 1
Ramsburg, John F 199 3
Ramsburg, John H 85 1
Ramsburg, John H 264, 276, 277 2
Ramsburg, John of J 275 2
Ramsburg, John R 195 3
Ramsburg, John S 99, 130 1
Ramsburg, John S 113, 271, 277 2
Ramsburg, John S 188 3
Ramsburg, John W 112 1
Ramsburg, John W 28, 110, 258, 277 2
Ramsburg, John W 224 3
Ramsburg, Jonas 101 2
Ramsburg, Joseph 179 1
Ramsburg, Joseph 181, 186 2
Ramsburg, Joshua 134 2
Ramsburg, Josiah 276 2
Ramsburg, Josiah 279 1
Ramsburg, L 258 2
Ramsburg, L P 106 1
Ramsburg, L. 56 1
Ramsburg, Lewis 70, 111, 160, 207 3
Ramsburg, Lewis 57, 70, 76, 118, 131, 137, 210, 219 1
Ramsburg, Lewis 11, 134, 148, 264, 276, 280, 288, 290 2
Ramsburg, Lewis of M 290 2
Ramsburg, Lewis P 290 2
Ramsburg, Lewis S 280, 290 2
Ramsburg, Lewis S 196 3
Ramsburg, Lilliam V 265 2
Ramsburg, Louis 275 2
Ramsburg, Luther W 136 1
Ramsburg, Lydia 280 2
Ramsburg, M 290 2
Ramsburg, M O 76 2
Ramsburg, Mabel G 284 2
Ramsburg, Mable G 294 2
Ramsburg, Malinda A C 282 2
Ramsburg, Margaret B 283 2
Ramsburg, Margaret D 295 2
Ramsburg, Maria C 282 2
Ramsburg, Marshall O 255, 277, 280, 283 2
Ramsburg, Mary 282 2
Ramsburg, Mary 159, 179 1
Ramsburg, Mary A 275, 282 2
Ramsburg, Mary A 275 2
Ramsburg, Mary Ann F 283 2
Ramsburg, Mary C 262 2
Ramsburg, Mary E 283 2
Ramsburg, Maud C 268 2
Ramsburg, Mehrle H 294 2
Ramsburg, Michael 282 2
Ramsburg, Milton D 166 1
Ramsburg, Minnie C G 283 2
Ramsburg, N A Fulton 283 2
Ramsburg, N D 172 2
Ramsburg, Nelson 101, 280, 286 2
Ramsburg, Nelson D 286 2
Ramsburg, Newton 195 3
Ramsburg, Othetto T 264 2
Ramsburg, Peter 287 2
Ramsburg, Philip 179 1
Ramsburg, Rebecca 288 2
Ramsburg, Robert M 195 3
Ramsburg, S 126 3
Ramsburg, S 32, 249 1
Ramsburg, S E 262 2
Ramsburg, S L 189 3
Ramsburg, S Laura 291 2
Ramsburg, S T 76 2
Ramsburg, Sabastian 184 3
Ramsburg, Samuel 260 1
Ramsburg, Samuel 58, 260 1
Ramsburg, Samuel 199 3
Ramsburg, Samuel 282, 290 2
Ramsburg, Sarah E 101 2

Ramsburg, Savilla E 290 2
Ramsburg, Sebastian 113, 144, 150, 268, 290 2
Ramsburg, Sebastian 215 3
Ramsburg, Sebastian 76, 112, 116, 156, 234 1
Ramsburg, Sebastian Jr 56, 177, 245 1
Ramsburg, Sebastian Jr 237 2
Ramsburg, Singleton 290 2
Ramsburg, Singleton E 291 2
Ramsburg, Stephen 134, 258, 275, 290 2
Ramsburg, Stephen 56, 82, 84 1
Ramsburg, Steven 18, 37 3
Ramsburg, Susan 290 2
Ramsburg, Susan E 290 2
Ramsburg, Susan L 159, 179 1
Ramsburg, Susie I 259 2
Ramsburg, U B 65 3
Ramsburg, Uriah 8, 159 2
Ramsburg, Urias D 293 2
Ramsburg, Virgie M 255 2
Ramsburg, W H 209 2
Ramsburg, W L 80, 290 2
Ramsburg, Walter 214 1
Ramsburg, Walter L 62 3
Ramsburg, Washington 276 2
Ramsburg, Washington Z 294 2
Ramsburg, William 287 2
Ramsburg, William H 217 3
Ramsburg, William H 262, 271, 294 2
Ramsburg, William L Jr 295 2
Ramsburg, William L Sr 295 2
Ramsburg, William S 293, 294 2
Ramsburg, Wm 35, 128 2
Ramsburg, Wm 219 1
Ramsburg, Wm H 61 1
Ramsburg, Wm H 218 3
Ramsburg, Wm L 62 1
Ramsburg, Wm L 277 2
Ramsburgh, Elias B 111, 283 2
Ramsburgh, Henry 93 2
Ramsburgh, Henry B 271, 283 2
Ramsburgh, Henry B 161 3
Ramsburgh, J Richard 265 2
Ramsburgh, John S 135 1
Ramsburgh, Julia M eta 271 2
Ramsburgh, Mabel 283 2
Ramsburgh, Mabel E 93, 271, 274 2
Ramsburgh, Mary C 283 2
Ramsburgh, Mary Catherine 283 2
Ramsburgh, Robert M 288 2
Ramsgurg, D C 212a 2
Ranck, Dorothy S 272 2
Ranck, Henry H 272 2
Ranck, James B 272 2
Randall, Allen W 254 2
Randall, Nichols 286 2
Randall, Vachel W 286 2
Randle, Mary N 283 2
Randolph, S H 212a 2
Raney, John 275 2
Rankin, Evelyn W 265 2
Rankin, Harper 265 2
Rankin, Harper 221 3
Rannals, Hannah 271 2
Ranneberger, Florence V 267 2
Ranneberger, Philip 18, 153 2
Rapp, John H 277 2
Rapp, Mary E V 277 2
Rate, Susan 290 2
Rath, Amos A 29 2
Rau, Amelia 254 2
Rau, R M 254 2
Rau, R M 102 3
Rau, Rudolph M 291 2
Rau, Rudolph M 288 2
Rau, Sallie E 102 3
Rau, Sallie T 254, 291 2
Rau, Sara T 291 2
Rau, W O 148 3
Rau, William O 230 1
Rauh, Gladys E 102 1
Rawson, Arthur J 284 2
Rawson, Marianna S 284 2
Ray, Alice C 294 2
Ray, Elizabeth 108 2
Ray, Harvey J 271 2
Ray, Henry F 271 2
Ray, W S 160 2
Ray, Weldon 271 2
Ray, William S 294 2
Ray, Wm S 214 1
Ray, Wm S 19 3
Raylor, J Howard 113 3
Raymer, Elizabeth R 265 2
Raymer, Elmer E 265 2
Raymer, Elmer E 35 3
Raymer, John 275 2
Raymer, John A 277 2
Raymer, Peter 275 2
Raymer, Simon P 277 2
Raymond, James 38, 45, 136 2
Raynor, John 290 2
Rea, Andrew J 254 2
Read, Edmund S 265 2
Read, Georgia Willis 278 1
Reagan, Mary Jane 283 2
Realing, Jacob S 275 2
Ream, M E 264 2
Reamer, Peter 179 3
Reaser, Jacob 214 2
Reaver, Franklin B 151 3
Reaver, Mary P 10 2
Reaver, Robert M 63 1
Rebert Ola H 259 2
Rebert, Clara H 259 2
Rebert, G Nevin 268 2
Rebert, Philip Nevin 268 2
Recher, Frederick 267 2
Recher, John C 267 2
Recher, Olive A 286 2
Reck, Chas 106 1
Reck, Dennis D H 262 2
Reck, Jeremiah 225 2
Reck, Ralph 262 2
Recker, F M 267 2
Recker, Frederick 267 2
Recker, John 208, 276 2
Recker, Jonathan 22 2
Recker, Jonothan 276 2
Recker, Josiah 276 2
Reckerd, Jonathan 93 2
Reddick, Celius B 172 1
Reddick, Celius W 280 2
Reddick, Clarence W 286 2
Reddick, Claude D 280 2
Reddick, Edith A 278 2
Reddick, James E 280 2
Reddick, James S 278 2
Reddick, John 115 2
Reddick, John 8 3
Reddick, John Jr 280 2
Reddick, Laura 159 3
Reddick, Laura J 280 2
Reddick, Leonard 115, 280 2
Reddick, Orra R 286 2
Reddiick, Leonard 213 3
Reddle, Ernest A 161 3
Redick, Leonard Jr 213 3
Redman, Alan R 255 2
Redman, Chas A 255 2
Redmond, Annie V Mrs 46 3
Redmond, George 268 2
Redmond, Robert A 291 2
Redmond, Vernon A 291 2
Redwood, John 221a 2
Reece, Jacob 263 1
Reecher, Henry 271 2
Reed, A W 182 1
Reed, A W 276 2
Reed, Amos 264 1
Reed, Charles C 271 2
Reed, Elizabeth 276 2
Reed, Emma 265 2
Reed, Enos D 106 3
Reed, Francis C 264 1

Reed, H A 271 2
Reed, Howard W 291 2
Reed, Isaac 106 1
Reed, Jacob 275, 276 2
Reed, John 276 2
Reed, Laura E 169 2
Reed, Mary Ann 282 2
Reed, Mary E 271 2
Reed, Rachel A 288 2
Reed, Samuel H 291 2
Reed, Stephen A 283 2
Reed, Thomas 176, 185 3
Reed, Thomas S 117, 171 1
Reeder, Charles E 259 2
Reeder, Chas N 277 2
Reeder, Daniel 262 2
Reeder, David 262 2
Reeder, J G 262 2
Reeder, John W 277 2
Reeder, Josephus 277 2
Reeder, Martin A 282 2
Reeder, O J 262 2
Reeder, Raymond N 259 2
Reeder, Sophia 290 2
Reeder, Walter 72 3
Reeder, Walter 167 2
Reeder, Wilford 290 2
Reel, Michael 282 2
Reel, Otho 282 2
Reel, William 294 2
Reely, James 125 1
Reese, Adam 254 2
Reese, Andrew 254 2
Reese, Carrie M 258 2
Reese, Catherine 258 2
Reese, Charles H 269 2
Reese, David 254 2
Reese, Edna Marie 155 2
Reese, Ella E 294 2
Reese, Gula 269, 271 2
Reese, H C 291 2
Reese, Harvey E 271 2
Reese, Jacob 24 1
Reese, Jacob 18, 38, 139, 176, 207 3
Reese, Jacob 7, 92, 93, 254, 276 2
Reese, John 185 3
Reese, John 38, 226, 276 2
Reese, Roger M 269 2
Reese, William H 258, 294 2
Reeser, Donald A 265 2
Reeser, Elmira M 265 2
Reeser, William D 294 2
Reeser, William E 294 2
Reever, John Wilbur 278 2
Reever, Ullrich 293 2
Rehmert, Elizabeth C 68, 70 2
Reich, A Virginia 255 2
Reich, Annie 255 2
Reich, B F 8, 96 2
Reich, B F 27, 104, 172 1
Reich, B F 71, 87 3
Reich, B G 97 1
Reich, Ben F 144, 171, 210 1
Reich, Benj 218, 12 2
Reich, Benj 230 1
Reich, Benj F 9 1
Reich, Benj F 8, 107 2
Reich, Benj F 55, 180, 188 3
Reich, Benjamin F 23, 30, 68, 92, 101, 155, 234 1
Reich, Benjamin F 23, 83, 246, 257, 286, 294 2
Reich, Benjamin F 196 3
Reich, Christian 258 2
Reich, John 116 1
Reich, John 275 2
Reich, John 1, 35 3
Reich, John H 276 2
Reich, Julian 57 2
Reich, Juliana 276 2
Reich, Lillian M 280 2
Reich, Lucy 9 1
Reich, Lucy 287 2
Reich, Margaret 282 2
Reich, N 286 2
Reich, Nellie 286 2
Reich, Nelly Lee 286 2
Reich, Phebe 275 2
Reich, Philip 14, 57, 276, 282, 287, 290 2
Reich, Philip 90, 147, 214, 222, 234 1
Reich, Philip V 287 2
Reich, Phoebe 160, 287 2
Reich, Raymond 23 1
Reich, Raymond E 294 2
Reich, Raymond Eugene 288 2
Reich, Sophia 255, 290 2
Reich, Sophia J 255 2
Reich, William 287, 294, 295 2
Reich, William G 287, 294 2
Reich, Wm 214, 234 1
Reich, Wm 8, 22, 30 2
Reicht, B F 20 3
Reicht, Benjamin F 287 2
Reicht, William 290 2
Reick, John 276 2
Reick, Philip 35 3
Reid, Eve M 264 2
Reid, James B 277 2
Reid, Margaret M 221a, 246 2
Reid, Matthias 283 2
Reid, Maurice E 295 2
Reid, Rachel A 293 2
Reid, Thomas S 76, 264, 293 2
Reid, Upton S 293 2
Reid, Vincent 101 1
Reid, W Edward 295 2
Reiff, Alvin V 262 2
Reiff, David D 262 2
Reifsnider, Catherine 258 2
Reifsnider, Chas T 271 2
Reifsnider, David 137, 159 2
Reifsnider, Frank 293 2
Reifsnider, Honovia E 271 2
Reifsnider, Jesse 1 1
Reifsnider, jno 167 3
Reifsnider, John 46, 113, 150, 163, 275, 276 2
Reifsnider, John 6, 195 3
Reifsnider, John 6, 30, 40, 58, 91, 106, 131, 152, 164, 195, 234, 264 1
Reifsnider, Robert B 288 2
Reifsnider, Robert R 291 2
Reifsnider, Samuel D 291 2
Reifsnider, Virginia 293 2
Reigart, Catherine 287 2
Reigart, Philip 287 2
Reigh, Mary 282 2
Reightler, J M 18 2
Reiley, Elen Jane 264 2
Reiley, James McKay 290 2
Reiley, Sallie M 290 2
Reilley, Elenor 264 2
Reinecker, Margaret 282 2
Reineivald, Charles 259 2
Reineivald, Irene D 259 2
Reisler, Annie M 255 2
Reisler, Jacob 275 2
Reisler, Owen 275 2
Reisler, T J 229 1
Reisler, Thomas J 32 3
Reissler, Margaret 282 2
Reissler, Thomas J 282 2
Reitermier, Chas 200 1
Reitmyer, Conrad 258 2
Reitnaner, Jacob 116 1
Remby, Margaret 282 2
Remby, Peter 287 2
Remsberg, Abbie McC 173 2
Remsberg, Albert S 254, 283 2
Remsberg, Alverda G 255 2
Remsberg, Alverta K 271 2
Remsberg, Amos Al 255 2
Remsberg, Annie A 268 2
Remsberg, Annie E 255, 283 2
Remsberg, Arthur R 267 2
Remsberg, C Garnet 272 1
Remsberg, Calvin E 284 2

Remsberg, Charles H 259 2
Remsberg, Charlotte M 255, 274 2
Remsberg, Chas J 272 1
Remsberg, Clara E 259 2
Remsberg, Daisy R 262 2
Remsberg, E Earl 293 2
Remsberg, Elizabeth B 293 2
Remsberg, Emory C 265 2
Remsberg, Ercelle M 196 2
Remsberg, F C 134, 280 2
Remsberg, Foster C 3, 64, 267 2
Remsberg, Foster C 14, 252 1
Remsberg, Frank G 262, 269 2
Remsberg, George C 269, 271 2
Remsberg, Gerald 175 2
Remsberg, Gerald G 196, 259 2
Remsberg, Harold A 274 2
Remsberg, Harriet G 259 2
Remsberg, Henry C 271 2
Remsberg, Henry T 271 2
Remsberg, Hiram E 272 2
Remsberg, Ida M 274 2
Remsberg, J Harman 277 2
Remsberg, J Homer 259 2
Remsberg, J Vernon 278 2
Remsberg, John 159 2
Remsberg, John H 278 2
Remsberg, John W 89 2
Remsberg, Laura M 259 2
Remsberg, LeRoy C 262 2
Remsberg, Luther F 272 1
Remsberg, Mamie I 271 2
Remsberg, Marie Renn 255 2
Remsberg, Mary C 255, 267, 283 2
Remsberg, Mary E 283 2
Remsberg, May 255 2
Remsberg, Minnie F 284 2
Remsberg, Nannie M 286 2
Remsberg, Naomi D 167 2
Remsberg, Oscar 271 2
Remsberg, S C 9 2
Remsberg, Singleton E 272 1
Remsberg, Susan E 268 2
Remsberg, Viola T 293 2
Remsberg, W L 9 2
Remsburg, Albert S 255 2
Remsburg, Albert S 48 1
Remsburg, Alta F C 254 2
Remsburg, Ames A 255 2
Remsburg, Amos L 277 2
Remsburg, Asa 254 2
Remsburg, Calvin E 259 2
Remsburg, Charles A 258 2
Remsburg, Chas 264, 276 2
Remsburg, Chas J 286 2
Remsburg, Chas T 19 1
Remsburg, Christian 275 2
Remsburg, Daniel 164 1
Remsburg, Daniel S 264 2
Remsburg, E Earl 265 2
Remsburg, E M 62 1
Remsburg, Edward 264 2
Remsburg, Elbert L 277 2
Remsburg, Elias 264 2
Remsburg, Elias H 264 2
Remsburg, Elizabeth 264 2
Remsburg, Elmer 271 2
Remsburg, Emory R 265, 280, 283 2
Remsburg, Emory R 107, 270 1
Remsburg, Eva D 265 2
Remsburg, Eve 264 2
Remsburg, Ezra 75 3
Remsburg, F C 102 2
Remsburg, F C 23 1
Remsburg, F C 2 3
Remsburg, Florence F 277 2
Remsburg, Foster 227a 2
Remsburg, Foster C 27, 183, 214 1
Remsburg, Foster C 262 2
Remsburg, Frances E 267 2
Remsburg, Hannah M 255 2
Remsburg, Hanson 264 2
Remsburg, Harry M 271 2
Remsburg, Harvey 267 2
Remsburg, Helen A 283 2
Remsburg, Henry C 271 2
Remsburg, Hiarm E 267 2
Remsburg, Israel 228 1
Remsburg, Israel 51 2
Remsburg, J Homer 255 2
Remsburg, Jacob 8 3
Remsburg, John 153, 166, 276 2
Remsburg, John H 19 1
Remsburg, John J 277 2
Remsburg, John S 264 2
Remsburg, John W 277 2
Remsburg, Jos S 255 2
Remsburg, Joshua P 19 1
Remsburg, L Roy 16 3
Remsburg, Lizzie C 280 2
Remsburg, Luther W 265, 280 2
Remsburg, Martin S 254 2
Remsburg, Mary C 294 2
Remsburg, Mary E 271, 277 2
Remsburg, Morgan H 283 2
Remsburg, Oscar C 283 2
Remsburg, Roy 283 2
Remsburg, Samuel 272, 290 2
Remsburg, Sebastian 290 2
Remsburg, Sebastian 26 1
Remsburg, Singleton 15 3
Remsburg, Susan L 271 2
Remsburg, William H 15 3
Remsburgh, Henry B 126 3
Remsburgh, Henry B 274 2
Remsbury, Dennis 46 2
Remsgerb, George I 268 2
Remsgerg, Foster C 268 2
Rench, John H 290 2
Rench, Sarah M 290 2
Renedollar, Henry 271 2
Renell, Daniel P 254 2
Renenon, John [?] 248 1
Rener, Geo 154 2
Renn, Ada G 265 2
Renn, Alvey V 65, 278 2
Renn, Annie R 255 2
Renn, Asa B 255 2
Renn, Austin P 274 2
Renn, Barnard 257 2
Renn, Bernard 257 2
Renn, C C 219 3
Renn, Catherine 258 2
Renn, Charles C 255 2
Renn, Charles L 259 2
Renn, E C 165, 219 1
Renn, E Charles 274 2
Renn, E Chas 244 1
Renn, Eli C 58 2
Renn, Eli C 205 1
Renn, Eli Charles 265 2
Renn, Elmira 123 1
Renn, Elmira E 265 2
Renn, Eugene 255 2
Renn, F C 23 1
Renn, George 268 2
Renn, Ida F 274 2
Renn, Ida M 265 2
Renn, Irvin 278 2
Renn, Isaac 203 3
Renn, Isaac 274 2
Renn, Isaac 150 1
Renn, John H 100, 276 2
Renn, John L 58, 276, 277 2
Renn, John S 278 2
Renn, John S 101 1
Renn, John S Jr 265, 278 2
Renn, Louis G 283 2
Renn, Mary Virginia 283 2
Renn, Nannie M 286 2
Renn, Nannie N 259 2
Renn, Sarah A R 276 2
Renn, W H 265 2
Renn, W Homer 40 2
Renn, William H 107 3

Renn, Wm H 142, 157, 172, 207 1
Renn, Wm H 58 2
Renneberger, Lee 267 2
Renner, Abraham 254 2
Renner, Adam 254 2
Renner, Alonza 196 3
Renner, Amanda H 267 2
Renner, Anna E 264 2
Renner, Anna L 258 2
Renner, Annie L 255 2
Renner, Catherine R 277 2
Renner, Chas E 265 2
Renner, Christian 258 2
Renner, Christiana 258, 294 2
Renner, Daniel P 30 1
Renner, Denda I 32 2
Renner, Elias 264 2
Renner, Elizabeth 264, 265, 294 2
Renner, Elmer A 294 2
Renner, Emanuel 19, 138, 265, 276, 290 2
Renner, Emanuel 51, 165, 183 1
Renner, Emanuel 218 3
Renner, F C 274 2
Renner, Francis C 8, 267, 277 2
Renner, Francis C 171 1
Renner, George I 268 2
Renner, Hannah A 271 2
Renner, Herbert G 286 2
Renner, Isaac 215 3
Renner, Isaac 8, 169, 258, 274 2
Renner, J I 160 2
Renner, J P 201 1
Renner, Jacob 276 2
Renner, Jacob J 276 2
Renner, James I 32 2
Renner, James I 172 3
Renner, Jane Ann 278 2
Renner, Jason C 172 1
Renner, Jason C 278, 286 2
Renner, Jesse 237 1
Renner, Jesse I 9, 52, 267, 271, 278 2
Renner, Jesse I 28, 48 1
Renner, Jesse I 11 3
Renner, John 275 2
Renner, John 201 1
Renner, John A 258 2
Renner, John P 104 1
Renner, Joshua 210, 234 1
Renner, Joshua 39, 277 2
Renner, Levi 280 2
Renner, Michael E 264 2
Renner, Milton O 283 2
Renner, Minnie E 294 2
Renner, Newton D I 286 2
Renner, Rachael A 265 2
Renner, S 144 1
Renner, Susan 290 2
Renner, T C 19 2
Renner, Theodore E 283 2
Renner, Wilfred A 294 2
Renner, Wilfred A 171, 196 1
Renner, William 294 2
Renner, William H 294 2
Renner, William I 268, 294 2
Renner, Wm I 223a 2
Renner, Zacharias 296 2
Rennetal, Lena S 265 2
Rennisen, H 245 1
Rep, J Hamilton 277 2
Repp, Anna B 254 2
Repp, Christian 258 2
Repp, Christian 219 1
Repp, Chritian 119 2
Repp, Esther J 265 2
Repp, George 254 2
Repp, Henry 8, 18 3
Repp, Henry 137, 271 2
Repp, Henry Jr 70 3
Repp, Henry Jr 196 1
Repp, Henry Jr 96, 115 2
Repp, Henry Sr 271 2
Repp, J H 1 1
Repp, J Hamilton 254 2
Repp, Jacob H 210 1
Repp, Jacob M 82 1
Repp, Jacob M 8, 276 2
Repp, John 101 2
Repp, John 82 1
Repp, John S 3 3
Repp, John S 8, 171, 276 2
Repp, John S 183, 253, 260 1
Repp, Leslie Q 42 1
Repp, Marion H 278 1
Repp, Mary Ann 282 2
Repp, Oliver 258 2
Repp, Otto V 291 2
Repp, S F 219 1
Repp, Samuel 29, 254 2
Repp, Samuel 82 1
Repp, Samuel F[?] 278 1
Repp, Samuel I 283 1
Repp, Samuel T 166 1
Repp, Samuel W 291 2
Repp, W O 73 3
Repp, W O 3 2
Repp, Wesley 245, 260 1
Repp, Wesley 29, 238 2
Repp, Wesley 54, 70 3
Repp, Zoia[?] A 107 1
Resk, David 262 2
Resse, Jacob 222 3
Resser, Grace Motter 268 2
Retgering, Sophia 290 2
Reynolds, Elenor 264 2
Reynolds, Elizabeth A 290 2
Reynolds, Geo P 284 2
Reynolds, James W 70 1
Reynolds, James W 275 2
Reynolds, John Jr 183 1
Reynolds, Mary C 264, 282 2
Reynolds, Mary Katherine 284 2
Reynolds, Peter 287 2
Reynolds, Samuel 183 1
Reynolds, Solomon 290 2
Rheam, Esther A 264 2
Rheam, Henry U 264 2
Rheam, John & 137 2
Rhine, Catherine L 259 2
Rhinhart, David 214a 2
Rhinhart, Geo 237 2
Rhoades, Abraham 254 2
Rhoades, Daniel 262 2
Rhoades, Elizabeth C 259 2
Rhoades, Schaeffer L 140 1
Rhoades, Vernon & 240 1
Rhoades, Vernon T 140 1
Rhoads, H E 186 1
Rhoads, Harriet E 67 1
Rhoads, Harriett E 271 2
Rhoads, Paul B 246 2
Rhoads, Paul B Jr 21 3
Rhoads, S L 186 1
Rhoads, Vernon M 293 2
Rhoda, Wm C 186 1
Rhode, Ann R 254 2
Rhode, Catherine 258 2
Rhode, Daniel 275 2
Rhode, Eliza L 264, 265 2
Rhode, Jacob 275 2
Rhode, Jacob 185 2
Rhode, John 258, 275 2
Rhode, Margaret 57, 60 3
Rhode, Margaret 282 2
Rhode, Peter 258 2
Rhodenhoffer, Chas 277 2
Rhoderick, Anna W 255 2
Rhoderick, Charles C 283 2
Rhoderick, Clemma 268 2
Rhoderick, Dorothy Geisbert 280 1
Rhoderick, G C 52 1
Rhoderick, G Edgar 169 1
Rhoderick, Geo C 59 1
Rhoderick, Geo Sr 80 2
Rhoderick, George 283 2
Rhoderick, George C 55 1
Rhoderick, George C 268, 271

2
Rhoderick, George C III 268 2
Rhoderick, George C Jr 268 2
Rhoderick, George C Sr 268 2
Rhoderick, Ida V 274 2
Rhoderick, John 275 2
Rhoderick, L 117 1
Rhoderick, Laura 282 2
Rhoderick, Lewis 40 1
Rhoderick, M Theodore 282 2
Rhoderick, Mahlon 47, 76 1
Rhoderick, Martin N 282 2
Rhoderick, Mary E 283 2
Rhoderick, Melvin D 283 2
Rhoderick, Nahlon [sic] 58 1
Rhoderick, Wm C 9, 213a 2
Rhoderick, Wm C 235 1
Rhodes, A C L 31 2
Rhodes, Blanche G 41 1
Rhodes, Catherine 258, 268
2
Rhodes, Charles H 259 2
Rhodes, Christian 258 2
Rhodes, David 198 2
Rhodes, Edgar N 277 2
Rhodes, Elizabeth 264 2
Rhodes, Elizabeth C 97 1
Rhodes, Geo 84 1
Rhodes, Geo 111, 113 3
Rhodes, Geo 72 2
Rhodes, Geo J 171 3
Rhodes, Geo Josiah 71 3
Rhodes, Geo S 59 1
Rhodes, George 268 2
Rhodes, George J 268 2
Rhodes, Henry 133, 150 1
Rhodes, Henry G 258 2
Rhodes, J L 188 3
Rhodes, J L 160 2
Rhodes, J Lewis 277 2
Rhodes, J Lewis 3 3
Rhodes, Jacob 8 3
Rhodes, John 120, 207 3
Rhodes, John 185 2
Rhodes, John 152, 263 1
Rhodes, John S 277 2
Rhodes, John S 11 1
Rhodes, Margaret 282 2
Rhodes, Margaret E 294 2
Rhodes, Peter 51 2
Rhodes, Peter 8 3
Rhodes, Roscoe B 271 2
Rhodes, S Catherine 277 2
Rhodes, S T 8 2
Rhodes, Samuel 57, 101, 290 2
Rhodes, Samuel 23 3
Rhodes, Samuel D 290 2
Rhodes, Sarah M 277 2
Rhodes, William H 294 2
Rhodey, Hugh 37 3
Rhorback, Allen 196 3
Rhorback, Chas 169 2
Rhorback, Jacob 213 3
Rhorback, Jacob 182, 218a 2
Rice, A P 96 3
Rice, A T 217 3
Rice, Albert T 20, 254, 287 2
Rice, Alice L 255 2
Rice, Alta May 265, 283 2
Rice, Alva F 58 3
Rice, Andrew D 280 2
Rice, Ann M R 268 2
Rice, Benjamin 193 1
Rice, Benjamin 257 2
Rice, Bertha A 179 1
Rice, Bertha A 294 2
Rice, Caleb F 259 2
Rice, Carrie E 259 2
Rice, Charles A 167, 259, 283 2
Rice, Charles F Sr 260 2
Rice, Charles H 259, 271 2
Rice, Charles W 259, 280, 286 2
Rice, Charles W Jr 259 2
Rice, Chas 189 2
Rice, Chas A 230 1
Rice, Chas W 62 2
Rice, Clarence 72 1
Rice, Cornelius I 259 2
Rice, David 254 2
Rice, David S 20, 92, 262 2
Rice, David S 172, 276 1
Rice, David S 26 3
Rice, Dorsey L 259 2
Rice, E Smith 264, 267, 268 2
Rice, Edw 228 1
Rice, Edw S 5 2
Rice, Eli D 264, 265 2
Rice, Eli Daniel 265 2
Rice, Eliza J 265 2
Rice, Elizabeht 264 2
Rice, Ervin D 278 2
Rice, Ezra J 265 2
Rice, F H 148 1
Rice, Frances A 267 2
Rice, Frances E 277 2
Rice, Frances Elizabeth 21 3
Rice, Frances M 276 2
Rice, G J 113, 169 2
Rice, G J 32 1
Rice, Geo 56, 57, 133, 164, 189,
244 1
Rice, Geo 1, 159 2
Rice, George 32 1
Rice, George 179, 185 3
Rice, George 262, 268, 275 2
Rice, George B 268, 275 2
Rice, George E 268 2
Rice, George W 124 1
Rice, German William 217a 2
Rice, Grafton J 268 2
Rice, H E 33 1
Rice, H T 84 2
Rice, Hannah N 120 1
Rice, Harriet E 271 2
Rice, Henrietta 271 2
Rice, Hiram F 271 2
Rice, Howard D 260, 284 2
Rice, Ira C 274 2
Rice, J Albert 119 1
Rice, J D 243 1
Rice, J Munroe 288 2
Rice, Jacob D 277, 290 2
Rice, James 50 3
Rice, James 106 1
Rice, James 11, 275 2
Rice, James M 288 2
Rice, Jane 257 2
Rice, Jared C 275 2
Rice, Jeremiah 62 2
Rice, Jeremiah D 278 2
Rice, Joanna S 277 2
Rice, Job 276 2
Rice, John 257 2
Rice, John C 275 2
Rice, John C 50 3
Rice, John L 278 2
Rice, John Leroy 278 2
Rice, John W 210 1
Rice, Joseph Oliver 278 2
Rice, Joshua A 277 2
Rice, Joshua C 283 2
Rice, Josiah O 271 2
Rice, Keefer C 53 1
Rice, L A 1 1
Rice, L A 196 3
Rice, L A 227a 2
Rice, L Earl 291 2
Rice, LeRoy E 284 2
Rice, Levin 113 3
Rice, Levin 48 1
Rice, Levin 280 2
Rice, Lewis 254, 280 2
Rice, Lewis 55 3
Rice, Lewis 254 2
Rice, Lewis A 33, 52, 72, 79, 85, 162,
172, 270, 272 1
Rice, Lewis A 20, 70, 85, 125, 265,
280, 283, 293 2
Rice, Lewis E 294 2
Rice, Lewis Spencer 278 2
Rice, Lillie M 259 2
Rice, Louis A 280 2
Rice, Louis V 291 2
Rice, Lydia M G 280 2
Rice, M G 264 2
Rice, Manassas 283 2
Rice, Margaret 282 2

Rice, Margaret A 284 2
Rice, Margaret E 284 2
Rice, Maria E 283 2
Rice, Marian C 283 2
Rice, Martha 282 2
Rice, Mary E 265, 268, 283 2
Rice, Mary F 259, 283 2
Rice, Millard M 283 2
Rice, Milton G 267, 277, 283, 290 2
Rice, Minnie C 157 1
Rice, Minnie I 291 2
Rice, Minnie Irene 284 2
Rice, Morgan S 284 2
Rice, Nina M 286 2
Rice, P Luther 14 1
Rice, Perry 129 3
Rice, Perry 150, 189 1
Rice, Perry 19, 84, 262, 268, 287 2
Rice, Perry G 194 1
Rice, Perry G 268, 275, 282, 287 2
Rice, Perry G Jr 1 2
Rice, Perry G Sr 1 2
Rice, Perry Sr 46, 287 2
Rice, Pirson S 259 2
Rice, R C 287 2
Rice, R G D 171 1
Rice, R H 125 2
Rice, Robert Ross 278 2
Rice, Rosanna 264 2
Rice, Rosanna D 280 2
Rice, Roy J 19 1
Rice, Roy M 283 2
Rice, Ruben G D 288 2
Rice, Ruger R 52 1
Rice, Ruger R 58 2
Rice, Russell B 259 2
Rice, S Addie 4 1
Rice, Sallie F 291 2
Rice, Samuel 268, 290 2
Rice, Sarah J 36 2
Rice, Silas P 283 2
Rice, Simon C 265, 291 2
Rice, Susan C 290 2
Rice, Susan Elizabeth 291 2
Rice, T P 196 3
Rice, T P 33, 244 1
Rice, T P 66, 166, 227a 2
Rice, Thomas P 265, 282, 283, 293 2
Rice, Thomas P 48 1
Rice, Thomas P 196 3
Rice, Thos P 20, 254 2
Rice, Thos P 68, 172 1
Rice, Virginia B 278 2
Rice, W Calvin 294 2
Rice, W L 129 3
Rice, W L 48 1
Rice, Wade O 274 2
Rice, Walter 54 2
Rice, Walter L 179 1
Rice, Walter L 280, 294 2
Rice, William H 294 2
Rice, William P 268, 271 2
Rice, William T 294 2
Rice, Wm P 89 2
Rich, Ephriam 234 1
Richard, John 248 1
Richard, L J 280 2
Richard, Philip 186 3
Richard, Wm T 270 1
Richards, Geo 47 1
Richards, George 84 1
Richards, George 268, 282 2
Richards, George 35, 213 3
Richards, Jacob 282 2
Richards, Mary 282 2
Richards, Mathias 282 2
Richardson, Aaron 254 2
Richardson, Ann 254 2
Richardson, C G 111 3
Richardson, Catherine E 259 2
Richardson, Catherine E 254 2
Richardson, Charles H 260 2
Richardson, D 120 3
Richardson, David 64, 129 3
Richardson, David 262, 282 2
Richardson, David 32, 162, 163 1
Richardson, Davis 116, 177 1
Richardson, Davis 1, 27, 66, 100 2
Richardson, Dorsey 280 2
Richardson, John C 295 2
Richardson, Louisa 280, 294 2
Richardson, Pinckney A 215 3
Richardson, Sarah 290 2
Richardson, W 26 1
Richardson, William 120 3
Richardson, William 258, 294, 295 2
Richardson, William E 260 2
Richardson, Wm 1, 70, 51, 171 2
Richardson, Wm 27, 139, 201, 264 1
Richardson, Wm 227 3
Richea, Adam 254 2
Richerd, Jonothan 288 2
Richmond, Ephraim 22 1
Richmond, F 13 1
Richmond, Francis 177, 185 2
Richmond, Francis 56 1
Richmond, Francis 217, 218 3
Richmond, U H 22 1
Richmond, Upton H 293 2
Richmond, Upton H 22 1
Rickard, Lewis S 291 2
Rickard, Silas L 291 2
Rickards, Amanda C 254 2
Rickenbaugh, Henry 202 3
Rickerd, Catherine L 267 2
Rickerd, Charles P 259 2
Rickerd, Francis M 267 2
Rickerd, Jonothan 259 2
Rickerd, Katie 280 2
Rickerd, Lewis S 280 2
Rickerd, Rebecca J 288 2
Rickerds, Gertrude E 3 3
Rickerds, Mary J 282 2
Ricketts, Benjamin 2 2
Ricketts, Benjamin F 153 1
Ricketts, Bessie V 257 2
Ricketts, Derrick 67 3
Ricketts, Derrick G 265 2
Ricketts, Dorothy I 262 2
Ricketts, Edward G 265 2
Ricketts, Eli 265 2
Ricketts, Laura P 265 2
Ricketts, Lucy G 265 2
Ricketts, Mary Agnes B 283 2
Ricketts, Mollie C 283 2
Ricketts, Thema E 34 1
Ricketts, Warrington E 283 2
Riddle, George 268 2
Riddle, Mary A 268 2
Riddlemoser, A R 38 1
Riddlemoser, Amelia 254, 276 2
Riddlemoser, Amelia R 254 2
Riddlemoser, C A 38 1
Riddlemoser, Charles E 85 2
Riddlemoser, Charles S 283 2
Riddlemoser, Clementine A 254 2
Riddlemoser, Clinton 276 2
Riddlemoser, Clinton A 258 2
Riddlemoser, Emma F 85 2
Riddlemoser, Ephriam 165 2
Riddlemoser, J M 38 1
Riddlemoser, Jacob 276 2
Riddlemoser, James 254, 276 2
Riddlemoser, James L 276 2
Riddlemoser, James L 205 3
Riddlemoser, John B 213 3
Riddlemoser, Joseph 276 2
Riddlemoser, Martha J 254, 258, 283 2
Riddlemoser, Samuel D 290 2

Riddlemoser, W E 134 2
Ridegely, Thomas 293 2
Ridegley, Greenburg 268 2
Ridemour, Elmer T 265 2
Ridenbaugh, Mabel Lee Tedrick 92 3
Ridenbaugh, Manzella 283 2
Ridenbaugh, Mary V 120 1
Ridenbaugh, Samuel 290 2
Ridenbaugh, Sarah E C 291 2
Ridenour, Adam 27 2
Ridenour, Adam 176 3
Ridenour, Andrew 254 2
Ridenour, C R 150 1
Ridenour, Charles A 258 2
Ridenour, Cora 265 2
Ridenour, Cornelius R 260 2
Ridenour, Daniel 276 2
Ridenour, Earl 265 2
Ridenour, Elizabeth 264 2
Ridenour, Frederick 185 3
Ridenour, Homer D 277 2
Ridenour, Howard 271 2
Ridenour, J H 106 3
Ridenour, J R 40 2
Ridenour, Jacob 184 3
Ridenour, Jacob 185, 275, 276 2
Ridenour, Jacob H 26 3
Ridenour, Jacob H 264 2
Ridenour, Jacob Jr 185 2
Ridenour, Jacob R 277 2
Ridenour, John 41 1
Ridenour, Joseph 184 3
Ridenour, Joseph 185, 276 2
Ridenour, Key 271 2
Ridenour, Paul M 224 2
Ridenour, Sarah C 290 2
Ridenour, Solomon 14 2
Ridenour, W G 294 2
Ridenour, W W 294 2
Ridenour, William A 294 2
Rider, Axcxander 290 2
Rider, Fannie R 267 2
Rider, Francis 267 2
Rider, Frederick 137, 267 2
Rider, Frederick C 267 2
Rider, George 282 2
Rider, Mary Ann 267 2
Rider, Michael 214, 282 2
Rider, Michael 214 2
Rider, Sarah 290 2
Ridgaway, Carrie Wood 199 3
Ridgaway, Thomas N 199 3
Ridge, Charles E 265 2
Ridge, Cornelius 234 1
Ridge, Cornelius 26, 39, 258, 264 2
Ridge, Cornelius 184 3
Ridge, E U G 265 2
Ridge, Ephriam 26, 258, 264 2
Ridge, Greenbury 253 1
Ridgeley, Jacob 268 2
Ridgeley, Ruth 288 2
Ridgeley, Thomas 268 2
Ridgeley, William 288 2
Ridgely, Chas C 192 3
Ridgely, Ellen S 265 2
Ridgely, Evers R 265 2
Ridgely, Geo S 265 2
Ridgely, Greenbury 35 2
Ridgely, Hiram 271 2
Ridgely, Jacob 35, 275, 293 2
Ridgely, Jacob J L 276 2
Ridgely, John 137, 175, 237 2
Ridgely, Joshua 290 2
Ridgely, Joshua T 271 2
Ridgely, Robert J 288, 294 2
Ridgely, Sally 290 2
Ridgely, Samuel 290 2
Ridgely, Samuel L 67 3
Ridgely, Thomas 35 2
Ridgely, Wesley 294 2
Ridgely, Westel 294 2
Ridgely, William 275, 294 2
Ridgely, Wm 248 1
Ridgley, Minerva M 284 2
Ridgly, Charles M 259 2
Ridinger, Andrew 254 2
Ridinger, John 275 2
Ridout, Agustus 254 2
Ridout, Isaac 274 2
Ridout, Richard 274 2
Rieck, Lilly M 280 2
Riegel, David 271 2
Riegel, Henry E 271 2
Riegle, Susanna 290 2
Riehl, Betty 79 1
Riehl, Charles J 79 1
Riehl, Frederick 267 2
Riehl, William H 79 1
Riehle, Addie L 259 2
Riehle, Charles J 259 2
Rife, Jacob 275 2
Rife, Jacob 275 2
Rife, Sophia 275 2
Riffee, William 294 2
Riffle, Edw 55 1
Rigdon, Lavinia Helen 280 2
Rigert, Catherine 258 2
Riggles, Frederick W 267, 283 2
Riggles, Margaret E 283 2
Riggs, Asburg 254 2
Riggs, Asbury 276 2
Riggs, Bettie H 257 2
Riggs, Betty H 277 2
Riggs, Betty H 265 1
Riggs, Christopher 283 1
Riggs, Christopher M 288 2
Riggs, Christopher M 33 1
Riggs, Clara M 259 2
Riggs, Delilah A 254 2
Riggs, Edward B 214a 2
Riggs, Edward D 196 3
Riggs, Elizabeth D 265 2
Riggs, Geo H 265 2
Riggs, Geo H Dr 257 2
Riggs, Geo H Dr 102 3
Riggs, George H 255, 277 2
Riggs, Henry 64 2
Riggs, Isaac 274 2
Riggs, J C 256, 283 1
Riggs, James 5 2
Riggs, James Jr 276 2
Riggs, James Sr 276 2
Riggs, Jennie 277 2
Riggs, John Donald 277 2
Riggs, Joseph 257 1
Riggs, Joseph 276 2
Riggs, Joseph C 277, 288 2
Riggs, Ralph W 259 2
Riggs, Ruth 288 2
Right, Jesse 53 3
Righter, Henry 271 2
Rigler, David 262 2
Rign ey, John 70 3
Rigney, John 91 1
Rigney, John 80 2
Rigney, John 184, 213, 214 3
Rikehard, John 249 1
Riley, McKendrick M 283 2
Riley, Michael 195 3
Rimbey, C 82 3
Rimbey, Gertie 82 3
Rimbey, Samuel G 1 2
Rimby, Uriah 1 3
Rindhart, H A 107 3
Rindhart, Susan M 107 3
Rine, J W 276 2
Rine, John 276, 290 2
Rine, Samuel 290 2
Rinecker, Paul 287 2
Rinedollar, Henry 47 1
Rinedollar, Louisa 271 2
Rinehard, Geo 234, 263 1
Rinehart , Wm 118 1
Rinehart, Andrew 247 2
Rinehart, Daniel 262 2
Rinehart, David 31, 81 3
Rinehart, David 125, 177 1
Rinehart, David 11, 22, 69, 262, 274 2
Rinehart, Geo 91, 283 1
Rinehart, Geo P 125 1
Rinehart, George 268, 294 2
Rinehart, George 8, 31 3
Rinehart, George 294 2

Rinehart, George P 268 2
Rinehart, Harriett A 271 2
Rinehart, Hattie A 268 2
Rinehart, Ida N 126 1
Rinehart, Israel 57, 262, 274 2
Rinehart, Israel C 262 2
Rinehart, Lincoln W 262 2
Rinehart, Rebecca 294 2
Rinehart, Rebecca L 262 2
Rinehart, Susam M 268 2
Rinehart, Susanna H 268 2
Rinehart, W G 166 3
Rinehart, William 294 2
Rinehart, Wm 40 1
Rineman, John 249 1
Riner, Charles E 259 2
Riner, Geo 159, 211, 218 2
Riner, Geo 19 1
Riner, Geo 53 3
Riner, George 184 3
Riner, George 222, 242, 247, 268, 275 2
Riner, George 32, 58, 84 1
Ringel, John 277 2
Ringel, Nannie A 277 2
Ringer, Daniel 262 2
Ringer, David 262 2
Ringer, Elizabeth 262 2
Ringgold, Arnold 277 2
Ringol, Christopher 276 2
Ringol, John Y 276 2
Rinker, Alice V 254 2
Rinker, Fannie W 267 2
Rinker, J H 276 1
Rinker, J Henry 267 2
Riordan, Anna M 265 2
Riordan, Charles 262 2
Riordan, Charles P 265 2
Riordan, Cornelius 259 2
Riordan, Daniel T 262 2
Riordan, Daniel T 137 1
Riordan, Dennis J 262 2
Riordan, Ella N 265 2
Riordan, Julia A 277 2
Riordan, William J 277 2
Rippen, David 262 2
Rippeon, Carrie V 45 2
Rippeon, Frances E 267 2
Rippeon, Frances L 267 2
Rippeon, Harriet S 276 2
Rippeon, Howard C 271 2
Rippeon, Ida M 277 2
Rippeon, J Ervin 283 1
Rippeon, John 219 1
Rippeon, John T 276, 277 2
Rippeon, John Z 257 1
Rippeon, Mary A 283 2
Rippeon, May A 73 1
Rippeon, Woodrow W 271 2
Rippon, Jerome 277 2
Rippon, Mary Ann 277 2
Risk, David 117 1
Risk, Mary Ann 282 2
Ritchie, Adam 254 2
Ritchie, Albert 64, 119, 159, 187, 197, 208, 214, 254, 294 2
Ritchie, Albert 176, 205 1
Ritchie, Albert Dr 223a 2
Ritchie, Bettie H M 257 2
Ritchie, Betty H M 129 2
Ritchie, Clara W 88 1
Ritchie, John 64, 159, 181, 187, 257, 275, 288 2
Ritchie, John 109, 130, 164, 186, 205 1
Ritchie, Margaret J 283 2
Ritchie, Nancy 254, 286 2
Ritchie, Robert 66, 288 2
Ritchie, Robert 18 3
Ritchie, William Jr 294 2
Ritchie, William N 288, 294 2
Ritenour, Ethel 288 2
Ritenour, Russell M 288 2
Rites, Philip 287 2
Ritt, Elizabeth 264 2
Ritter, A 113 3
Ritter, Alfred 258 2
Ritter, Alfred 135, 272 1
Ritter, Catherine E 258 2
Ritter, Chas L 51 3
Ritter, Emma V 265 2
Ritter, Emma Virginia 51 3
Ritter, Geo P 156 1
Ritter, J A 82, 129 3
Ritter, J A 29, 80, 252 2
Ritter, J A 249 1
Ritter, J Alfred 1, 46 2
Ritter, J Alfred 197 1
Ritter, J Frederick 132 2
Ritter, John 165 2
Ritter, John & 185 2
Ritter, John A 179 3
Ritter, Margaret L 11 3
Ritter, William E 184 1
Ritter, William E 295 2
Rives, John J 197 3
Rizer, George H 268 2
Roach, Edward H 223a 2
Roach, Mollie 196 3
Roach, Thomas 293 2
Robbins, Douglas 41 2
Robbins, Frank A Jr 190 2
Roberson, Benjamin 257 2
Roberson, Benjamin F 257 2
Roberson, Charles A 259 2
Roberson, Hazel D 259 2
Roberson, James 189 1
Roberson, William E 118 3
Robert, John M 82 3
Robert, Roach 70 3
Roberts, Alfred G 254 2
Roberts, Annie H C 255 2
Roberts, Asia 255 2
Roberts, Charles 225a 2
Roberts, Chas B 67 2
Roberts, Edward F 282 2
Roberts, Eliza A 264 2
Roberts, Emma G 294 2
Roberts, Francis 245, 267 2
Roberts, Frank 87 3
Roberts, Geo 192 3
Roberts, George T 27 3
Roberts, Helen E 283 2
Roberts, Henry 283 2
Roberts, Isaac 274 2
Roberts, James 101 2
Roberts, James C 264 2
Roberts, James H 254 2
Roberts, John 192, 223 3
Roberts, John 11 2
Roberts, Lloyd 280 2
Roberts, Lulu 280 2
Roberts, M 160 3
Roberts, Marion E 282 2
Roberts, Mary 282, 294 2
Roberts, Mary C 282, 283 2
Roberts, Michael 282 2
Roberts, Minnie M 27 3
Roberts, Minnie M 283 2
Roberts, Nelly 286 2
Roberts, Rachel 288 2
Roberts, Richard 196, 283 1
Roberts, Richard 185, 275, 288 2
Roberts, Sterling 10 2
Roberts, William 192, 223 3
Roberts, William 224a, 245, 267, 280, 294 2
Roberts, William A 294 2
Roberts, Wm 176 3
Roberts, Wm 11, 69, 128, 205 2
Roberts, Wm H 213 1
Roberts, Wm W 92 1
Roberts, Woodward A 295 2
Robertson, Alexander 257 2
Robertson, Barbara 257, 275 2
Robertson, C H M 257 2
Robertson, James 275 2
Robertson, Robert H 171 2
Robins, Martha 282 2
Robinson, Belva G 274 2
Robinson, Charles O 259 2
Robinson, Damon 293 2
Robinson, Effie S 259 2
Robinson, Elmira J 277 2
Robinson, Elmira J 55 3

Robinson, Frederick 286 2
Robinson, Geo M 56 3
Robinson, George 268 2
Robinson, George N 268 2
Robinson, Ida B 274 2
Robinson, J F 277 2
Robinson, J Lewis 215 2
Robinson, James 7, 277 2
Robinson, James W 4 1
Robinson, James W 115, 277 2
Robinson, Jas W 55 3
Robinson, John 218 3
Robinson, Julia M 46 3
Robinson, Martha 282 2
Robinson, Mary L 283 2
Robinson, Nichols 286 2
Robinson, Pansy Lee 66, 286 2
Robinson, Samuel S 283 2
Robinson, Sylvia McGhee 178 2
Robinson, Thos 2 2
Robinson, Vincent 293 2
Robison, Alexaner 254 2
Robison, Isabelle 268 2
Robison, John 267 2
Robitzsch, John 275 2
Roby, Catherine 26 1
Rockwell, E H 58, 139, 194, 240, 260 1
Rockwell, E H 167 3
Rockwell, Elihn H 67, 264 2
Rockwell, Elihu H 209 3
Rockwell, Elihu H 179 1
Rockwell, Elijah 56 1
Rockwell, Elijah H 67 3
Rockwell, Elijah H 117 1
Rockwell, Elijah H 70, 117 1
Rockwell, Elizah H [sic] 11 1
Rockwell, Rachael 264 2
Roddy, Abraham 181, 198 2
Roddy, Abraham F 254 2
Roddy, Abraham S 194 1
Roddy, Abraham T 118 1
Roddy, B F 188 3
Roddy, Catherie E 259 2
Roddy, D F 199 2
Roddy, Daniel 262 2
Roddy, Daniel F 262 2
Roddy, Elizabeth C 161 2
Roddy, F A 24 1
Roddy, Francis A 262, 267 2
Roddy, Hannah M 254 2
Roddy, John 181 2
Roddy, John A 262 2
Roddy, John H 107, 144, 198, 277, 294 2
Roddy, John M 221a 2
Roddy, John N 44 1
Roddy, Laura G 221a 2
Roddy, M Adeline 267 2
Roddy, M Katherine 284 2
Roddy, Mary A 283 2
Roddy, Mary C 188 3
Roddy, William J 294 2
Roddy, William M 161 2
Rodeniser, John 165 2
Roderick, A Viola 210 3
Roderick, Augustus E 255 2
Roderick, C 276 2
Roderick, Clara V 214, 259, 294 2
Roderick, Daniel 280 2
Roderick, Dorsey 196 1
Roderick, Ellen 294 2
Roderick, Eula I 295 2
Roderick, G C 172, 188 2
Roderick, G C 56 3
Roderick, G C 118 1
Roderick, G C Sr 177 2
Roderick, G T 268 2
Roderick, Geo C 171 3
Roderick, Geo C 115 2
Roderick, Geo T 35 2
Roderick, George W 268 2
Roderick, Harry 294 2
Roderick, Harry M 259, 295 2
Roderick, Isabella M 268 2
Roderick, John S L 106 1
Roderick, Joseph 71 3
Roderick, Joseph 117 1
Roderick, Lewis 215 3
Roderick, Lewis 280 2
Roderick, Louise 36 2
Roderick, M D 56 3
Roderick, Mahlon 171, 186 3
Roderick, Mahlon 22 2
Roderick, Margaret 280 2
Roderick, William 275, 294 2
Roderick, William C 36 2
Roderick, William M 274 2
Roderick, William Mc 294, 295 2
Roderick, Wm 199 2
Roderick, Wm C 255 2
Rodgers, Lydia A 280 2
Rodgers, Nichols 286 2
Rodgers, Peter 51 2
Rodkey, Geo 150 2
Rodock, Geo S 38 1
Rodock, Geo S 253 2
Rodock, George 268 2
Rodock, George S 268 2
Rodock, John 268 2
Rodock, Moriah 268 2
Rodrick, Joseph 276 2
Rodrick, Margaret G 283 2
Rodrick, Nathan 70 3
Rody, Frank A 259 2
Roeder, Emma J 265 2
Roeder, George M 268 2
Roelke, Clara 94, 259 2
Roelke, David H 120 1
Roelke, Eugene A 268 2
Roelke, George A 268 2
Roelke, John R 9, 89 2
Roelke, John R 9 2
Roelkey, Chas L 199 3
Roelkey, Christian 258 2
Roelkey, Christian 23 3
Roelkey, D H Jr 262 2
Roelkey, Daniel 147 1
Roelkey, David H 262, 283 2
Roelkey, Edw 29 2
Roelkey, Edw 4 1
Roelkey, Edward 258 2
Roelkey, Elroy L 265 2
Roelkey, G F W 4 1
Roelkey, Geo 165 2
Roelkey, George A 294 2
Roelkey, Ginera L 223 3
Roelkey, Henry F W 271 2
Roelkey, John 172, 272 1
Roelkey, John 11, 29, 229a, 258, 276, 277 2
Roelkey, Joseph E 277 2
Roelkey, Justina 276 2
Roelkey, L Roy L 223 3
Roelkey, Leroy L 245, 259, 290 2
Roelkey, Lew M 265 2
Roelkey, Martha A 283 2
Roelkey, Peter 129 1
Roelkey, Susanna R 290 2
Roelkey, Wilhelmina 271, 294 2
Roelkey, William Y 276 2
Roesler, John C 275 2
Roessler, Eve C E 264, 275 2
Roger, Mary J 134 2
Rogers, A H 137 1
Rogers, Annie A 288 2
Rogers, C A 288 2
Rogers, C Arunah 277 2
Rogers, Charles A 259 2
Rogers, Charles R 67 2
Rogers, E W 277 2
Rogers, Eleanor 218 2
Rogers, Elenor White 265 2
Rogers, Flora M 267 2
Rogers, James 47 1
Rogers, James K 2 2

Rogers, James P 277 2
Rogers, James S 277 2
Rogers, Jane 218 2
Rogers, Jas S 163 3
Rogers, Mary A 277 2
Rogers, Mary C 288 2
Rogers, Mary Elizabeth 153 1
Rogers, Nora G 286 2
Rogers, Nora G 259, 286 2
Rogers, Philip W 259, 287 2
Rogers, Phillip W 267 2
Rogers, Rachel 288 2
Rogers, Richard J 288 2
Rogers, Rosia 288 2
Rogers, Ruben D 259 2
Rogers, Ruth W 287 2
Roha, Henry 177 2
Rohr, Catherine 258 2
Rohr, Daniel 258 2
Rohr, Daniel H 118 1
Rohr, Daniel H 1 2
Rohr, Elizabeth 264 2
Rohr, Geo 26 2
Rohr, Geo 163 3
Rohr, George 30 1
Rohr, Henry 271 2
Rohr, Jacob 56 1
Rohr, Philip 91, 163, 169 1
Rohr, Philip 185 2
Rohr, Philip 53, 81 3
Rohr, Susan 290 2
Rohrbach, Jacob 96 2
Rohrbach, Jacob 130 1
Rohrback, Allen 15, 187, 220 3
Rohrback, Allen 85, 176 1
Rohrback, Allen 43, 254 2
Rohrback, Anna Mary 42 1
Rohrback, Chas 73 1
Rohrback, Chas 72 2
Rohrback, Daniel 262 2
Rohrback, Ellen C 264 2
Rohrback, Ida 80, 129, 166 2
Rohrback, Ida R 126 3
Rohrback, Ida R 10, 90, 123, 130 1
Rohrback, Ida R 75, 274 2
Rohrback, J 67, 82, 113, 166, 189, 217 3
Rohrback, J 129, 240 1
Rohrback, Jacob 10, 15, 20, 24, 45, 50, 55, 58, 82, 91, 96, 124, 126, 141, 161, 166, 187, 192, 196, 197, 210, 220, 223, 226 3
Rohrback, Jacob 2, 8, 9, 15, 31, 40, 43, 65, 66, 70, 75, 76, 78, 80, 89, 93, 96, 101, 107, 125, 129, 147, 151, 153, 166, 175, 199, 205, 210a, 223a, 229a, 234, 235, 254, 258, 274, 278, 283, 291, 294 2
Rohrback, Jacob 10, 27, 28, 33, 52, 55, 61, 62, 67, 72, 73, 78, 79, 85, 86, 88, 90, 100, 101, 107, 110, 112, 119, 120, 123, 129, 144, 155, 159, 166, 169, 172, 176, 177, 179, 182, 183, 192, 193, 194, 197, 201, 230, 257, 265, 277 1
Rohrback, Jacob & 215 2
Rohrback, Jacob R 2 3
Rohrback, M N 165, 171, 273 1
Rohrback, M N 235, 242 2
Rohrback, M W 91 3
Rohrback, Margaret E 72 2
Rohrback, Martin N 90 1
Rohrback, Martin N 15, 278 2
Rohrback, Martin R 264 2
Rohrback, Otho 210a 2
Rohrback, W N 122 3
Rohrer, George 294 2
Rohrer, Jacob 38 2
Rohrer, Jacob Sr 92 2
Rohrer, John F 28 3
Rohrer, Philip 195 3
Roles, Eliza Ann 264 2
Roles, Rosewell 264 2
Rollings, Chas W 139 2
Rollings, John P 277 2
Rollings, Wm T 139 2
Rollins, Chas W 290 2
Rollins, Janie E 43 2
Rollins, Mariah 152 1
Rollins, Ruth A 227a 2
Rollins, Sarah Ann 290 2
Rollins, W T 290 2
Romig, John 275 2
Rooney, Clyde 172 2
Rooney, John D 276 2
Roop Joel 43 2
Roop, David 67 1
Roop, David 39, 40, 70 3
Roop, David R 280 2
Roop, Edith B 21 3
Roop, Jacob 27 2
Roop, Jacob Jr 43 2
Roop, John 254 2
Roop, Joseph 1 2
Roop, Lydia A 280 2
Roop, Samuel 290 2
Roos, Ann Maria 254 2
Root, Agnes 254 2
Root, C M 153 3
Root, Charles M 259 2
Root, Chas M 265, 283 2
Root, Chas W 104 1
Root, D 262 2
Root, Danial F R 262 2
Root, Daniel 7, 254, 262 2
Root, Daniel 107, 197 1
Root, Daniel 8 3
Root, Daniel of D 58, 203 1
Root, Daniel of D 262 2
Root, Daniel of Richard 70 3
Root, Edgar L 265 2
Root, George W 259 2
Root, Henry C 271 2
Root, Jacob 12, 100, 196, 225, 264 1
Root, Jacob 6, 18, 26, 39, 70, 171, 205 3
Root, Jacob 11, 22, 57, 111, 150, 226, 288 2
Root, Jacob & 214 2
Root, James W 276 2
Root, John 43 3
Root, John 144, 228, 275, 283 1
Root, John 107, 189, 198, 176, 277, 294 2
Root, Margaret 282 2
Root, Minerva A 283 2
Root, Rebecca 288 2
Root, Richard 288 2
Root, Richard 70 3
Root, Richared 282 2
Roper, J Gowen 83 1
Ropp, George 290 2
Ropp, George W 268 2
Ropp, Harvey C 192 3
Ropp, Henry 113 2
Ropp, Jane 277 2
Ropp, John H 268, 283 2
Ropp, Jos 53 3
Ropp, Mary E 283 2
Ropp, Oscar 283 2
Ropp, Ova T 192 3
Ropp, Paul H 277 2
Ropp, Susannah 290 2
Ropp, William G 295 2
Rose, Blanche G 277 2
Rose, Daniel W 262 2
Rose, Josephine C 277 2
Rose, Mary 282 2
Rose, R Belle 277 2
Rosenbaum, Ida C 287 2
Rosenbaum, Philip D 287 2
Rosencrantz, Paul B 287 2
Rosencrantz, S M B 287 2
Rosenour, Abe 2 2
Rosenour, Abraham 255 2
Rosenour, Abram 172 1
Rosenour, B 58 2
Rosenour, B 72 3
Rosenour, B Jr 214, 265 1
Rosenour, B Jr 44, 56 3
Rosenour, B Jr 199 2
Rosenour, Benj 255 2
Rosenour, Benjamin 234 1
Rosenour, Benjamin Jr 83, 85, 268, 271 2
Rosenour, Benjamin Jr 161 3

Rosenour, Gerson 58, 268 2
Rosenour, Gerson 72 3
Rosenour, Hannah 271 2
Rosensteel, Charles L 258 2
Rosensteel, James 171 1
Rosensteel, James A 277 2
Rosensteel, John H 283 2
Rosensteel, John H Jr 277 2
Rosensteel, John H Sr 278 2
Rosensteel, Joseph 19 1
Rosensteel, Joseph C 283 2
Rosensteel, Joseph C 72, 171 1
Rosensteel, Maria 282 2
Rosensteel, Marion H 277 2
Rosensteel, Mary E 283 2
Rosensteel, Mary W 283 2
Rosenstein, Benj 203 3
Rosenstock, Aaron 49 2
Rosenstock, Aaron 199, 255 2
Rosenstock, B B 182 2
Rosenstock, B F 85 2
Rosenstock, Benjamin 166 1
Rosenstock, Benjamin 41 2
Rosenstock, Benjamin B 169 3
Rosenstock, Benjamin B 44 1
Rosenstock, Ettie 255 2
Rosenstock, Isabel 274 2
Rosenstock, Isael 49 2
Rosenstock, Jacob 277 2
Rosenstock, Samuel 255 2
Rosenstock, Samuel H 49, 265, 274, 277 2
Roser, Adam 188 3
Roser, Adam 265 1
Roser, Guy 150 1
Roser, Guy C 1, 172 1
Roser, Guy C 166 3
Roser, Jacob A 277 2
Roser, Jesse 138 2
Roser, Jesse 153, 201 1
Roser, Ruth Olive 277 2
Ross, Adam 254 2
Ross, Ann G 39, 67, 175 2
Ross, Ann Graham 254 2
Ross, Blanch S 85 1
Ross, Blanch S 259 2
Ross, Blanche 101 1
Ross, Blanche 189 2
Ross, Blanche S 56 3
Ross, Blanche S 73, 257 2
Ross, C R 8 2
Ross, C W 67, 71, 75, 87, 96, 106, 171, 209 3
Ross, C W 8, 35, 175, 205, 220 2
Ross, C W Jr 41 1
Ross, C Walter 93 2
Ross, Caroline 113 3
Ross, Caroline 258 2
Ross, Charles 210a, 215a, 227 2
Ross, Charles E 259 2
Ross, Charles W 43, 82 3
Ross, Charles W 227, 220a, 221a, 258, 294 2
Ross, Charles W 82 3
Ross, Charles W Jr 259 2
Ross, CharlewsW 209 3
Ross, Chas 29, 30, 35, 39, 49, 51, 66, 78, 107, 153, 181, 203, 205, 209, 222 2
Ross, Chas 179, 186, 203, 225, 245, 265 1
Ross, Chas B 159 2
Ross, Chas P 9 1
Ross, Chas W 23, 26, 27, 38, 41, 47, 52, 72, 85, 91, 96, 101, 104, 106, 119, 125, 129, 152, 171, 197, 234, 238, 240, 272 1
Ross, Chas W 19, 23, 32, 54, 55, 79, 100, 102, 106, 116, 129, 179, 187, 196, 202, 203, 208, 223 3
Ross, Chas W 30, 40, 54, 75, 92, 101, 111, 116, 144,177, 213, 245, 250, 254, 258, 264, 267, 282 2
Ross, Christiana 254 2
Ross, Cornelia 85, 135 1
Ross, Cornelia R 52 1
Ross, Cornelia R 67 3
Ross, Cornelia R 135 1
Ross, Cornelia R 254, 258, 259 2
Ross, Cornelius 234 2
Ross, Elenor 264 2
Ross, Eliza 264 2
Ross, F McP 175 2
Ross, Fannie M P 267 2
Ross, G J 82 3
Ross, Geo 160 2
Ross, George (Col) 268 2
Ross, George J 259, 268 2
Ross, George J 15 3
Ross, Helen S 268 2
Ross, John W 294 2
Ross, Joseph 187 3
Ross, Letty 280 2
Ross, Matilda J 282 2
Ross, Peter 217 3
Ross, Peter 254 2
Ross, Priscilla W 193 3
Ross, R P 14, 85, 234 1
Ross, R P 20, 56, 187, 199 3
Ross, Richard 210a 2
Ross, Richard P 43, 55 3
Ross, Richard P 27, 96, 101, 119, 137 1
Ross, Richard P 8, 148, 189, 1 255, 259 2
Ross, Richard P Jr 257 2
Ross, Theresa K 259 2
Ross, Theresa K 162 1
Ross, W J 135 1
Ross, W J 67, 100, 116, 171, 203 3
Ross, W J 276 2
Ross, W W 203 3
Ross, William 37, 207 3
Ross, William 227, 264, 268, 294 2
Ross, William J 14, 220, 258, 262, 282, 294 2
Ross, William J 64, 71, 113, 122, 207 3
Ross, Wm 35, 43, 51, 66, 67, 70, 75, 80, 93, 100, 101, 165, 181, 203, 205, 218 2
Ross, Wm 19, 139, 197, 203, 240, 245, 249, 263, 275, 283 1
Ross, Wm 18 3
Ross, Wm J 54, 113, 129, 202, 215 3
Ross, Wm J 1, 35, 43, 49, 66, 67, 69, 75, 78, 80, 144, 148, 165, 177 2
Ross, Worthington 207 3
Ross, Worthington 35, 43, 93, 294 2
Rossman, Edw 84 2
Roteing, Cyril 259 2
Rotering, Cecil 259 2
Rotering, Charles 259 2
Roth, Amos A 254 2
Roth, Laura J 254 2
Rothenhoefer, Annie 259 2
Rothenhoefer, Charles F 259 2
Rothenhoefer, J L 280 2
Rothenhoefer, John L 278 2
Rothenhoefer, John L Jr 100 3
Rothenhoefer, John W 278 2
Rothenhoefer, Lawrence 280 2
Rothenhoefer, May L 3 3
Rothenhoefer, Robert Salter 234 2
Rouse, Peter 32 1
Rouser, John 217 3
Rout, Ernest G 202 2
Rout, James 276 2
Rout, Joseph 183 1
Rout, William H 276 2
Route, Isaac L 274 2
Routson, Benjamin 100 2
Routson, Edward C 288 2
Routson, Eli 213 1
Routson, Ellen 224 3
Routson, Fannie G 267 2
Routson, Joseph 288 2
Routson, Margaret M 284 2
Routson, Rosa May 288 2
Routson, Stoddard Smith 293 2

Routson, T Clyde 20 3
Routson, T Clyde 267, 284 2
Routson, T Clyde 284 2
Routson, Thomas Clyde 293 2
Routzah, Catherine 257 2
Routzahm, Adam 254 2
Routzahn 267 2
Routzahn Daniel H 15 2
Routzahn, A B 147 1
Routzahn, Adam 84 1
Routzahn, Adam 237, 254 2
Routzahn, Albert B 255 2
Routzahn, Albert B 249, 282 1
Routzahn, Albert R 72 1
Routzahn, Amanda M 276 2
Routzahn, Benjam 70 1
Routzahn, Benjamin 7, 26, 218, 254, 257, 262, 264, 275 2
Routzahn, Calvin 60 1
Routzahn, Catherine 258 2
Routzahn, Charles E 259 2
Routzahn, Charles M 259 2
Routzahn, Chas 264 2
Routzahn, Chas S 1/2 43 3
Routzahn, Clark O 295 2
Routzahn, Conrad 258 2
Routzahn, Cyrus 186 3
Routzahn, Cyrus 30, 147, 258, 276 2
Routzahn, Cyrus 27, 101, 104, 162 1
Routzahn, Cyrus 113 2
Routzahn, D H 78, 84 2
Routzahn, D H 57, 60, 191 1
Routzahn, D H 60, 67, 75, 196 3
Routzahn, Daniel 76, 135 1
Routzahn, Daniel H 33 1
Routzahn, Daniel H 262, 276 2
Routzahn, Daniel H 82 3
Routzahn, David 262, 282 2
Routzahn, Edw 37 1
Routzahn, Edward 71 1
Routzahn, Edward 264, 276 2
Routzahn, Edward 32 3
Routzahn, Edward C 265 2
Routzahn, Edward L 264 2
Routzahn, Eli 59, 229 1
Routzahn, Eli 116, 264 2
Routzahn, Eli 41 3
Routzahn, Elias 69, 276 2
Routzahn, Elias 252 1
Routzahn, Elias S 264, 265 2
Routzahn, Elizabeth 264, 265, 271, 276, 290 2
Routzahn, Elizabeth 224 3
Routzahn, Elizabeth 135 1
Routzahn, Elizabeth A 72 1
Routzahn, Ellen 264, 265 2
Routzahn, Elmer C 87 2
Routzahn, Enos 264 2
Routzahn, Enos S 265 2
Routzahn, Enos S Jr 265 2
Routzahn, Estella M 267 2
Routzahn, Eva M 294 2
Routzahn, Eve 264 2
Routzahn, Ezra 264, 280 2
Routzahn, Ezra 179, 187 3
Routzahn, Ezra 61 1
Routzahn, Ezra A 264 2
Routzahn, Foster S 267 2
Routzahn, Foster S 290 2
Routzahn, Franklin M 267 2
Routzahn, G H 62 3
Routzahn, Geo 84 2
Routzahn, George 254, 268 2
Routzahn, George 64, 213 3
Routzahn, George H 268 2
Routzahn, George L 268 2
Routzahn, H 64 3
Routzahn, H L 62, 79 1
Routzahn, H L 20, 30, 113 2
Routzahn, H M 188 2
Routzahn, Harman L 157, 265 1
Routzahn, Harriett A 264 2
Routzahn, Harry C 283 2
Routzahn, Henry 213 3
Routzahn, Herman 40 2
Routzahn, Herman L 213 3
Routzahn, Herman L 272, 276 2
Routzahn, Herman L 106 1
Routzahn, Hezekiah 271, 276 2
Routzahn, Hezekiah 58 1
Routzahn, Isaac 205 3
Routzahn, Isaiah 283 2
Routzahn, Isaih 274 2
Routzahn, J 124 3
Routzahn, J 276 2
Routzahn, J H 217 3
Routzahn, J L 124 3
Routzahn, J L 20 2
Routzahn, Jacob 76, 118 1
Routzahn, Jacob 69, 185, 254, 258, 280 2
Routzahn, Jacob 124 3
Routzahn, Jacob L 278, 280 2
Routzahn, John 58, 59, 106, 137, 164, 249 1
Routzahn, John 1, 35, 87, 264, 275, 276 2
Routzahn, John H 276, 280, 291 2
Routzahn, John J 276 2
Routzahn, John L 24, 32, 45, 51, 102, 213 3
Routzahn, John L 38, 51, 62, 63, 79, 235, 256, 257, 265 1
Routzahn, John L 20, 40, 41, 69, 106, 113, 166, 175, 210a, 264, 267, 272, 295 2
Routzahn, Jona 271 2
Routzahn, Jonathan 19, 157 1
Routzahn, Jonothan 79 3
Routzahn, Jonothan 264 2
Routzahn, Jos 54 3
Routzahn, Joseph 113, 264, 276, 277 2
Routzahn, Joseph 37, 59, 100, 137 1
Routzahn, Joseph L 15 2
Routzahn, Joseph L 275 1
Routzahn, Joseph L N 277 2
Routzahn, Joshua 115 2
Routzahn, Joshua 10 1
Routzahn, L 23, 79 1
Routzahn, Laura A 249, 257 1
Routzahn, Laura A 255 2
Routzahn, Lewis 254 2
Routzahn, Lucinda F 280 2
Routzahn, Ludwig 258 2
Routzahn, Ludwig 280 2
Routzahn, Ludwig 280 2
Routzahn, Ludwig 277 1
Routzahn, Ludwig 58, 69, 258, 280 2
Routzahn, Ludwig 58 2
Routzahn, Lydia 280 2
Routzahn, Margaret 283 2
Routzahn, Margaret C 262, 283 2
Routzahn, Mary A 282 2
Routzahn, Mary E 268 2
Routzahn, Noah 27 3
Routzahn, Oscar F 259 2
Routzahn, Oscar J 265 2
Routzahn, Oscar J 220 3
Routzahn, Otto M 259 2
Routzahn, Phillip 287 2
Routzahn, R Mary 283 2
Routzahn, Rebecca 224 3
Routzahn, Rebecca E 288 2
Routzahn, Robert H 295 2
Routzahn, Routzahn 264 2
Routzahn, S Elizabeth 265, 291 2
Routzahn, S Ethel 265 2
Routzahn, S Ethel 52 1

Routzahn, Sarah J 290 2
Routzahn, Silas 169 1
Routzahn, Simon D 280, 290, 291 2
Routzahn, Solomon 290 2
Routzahn, W Glenn 294 2
Routzahn, William S 87, 268, 295 2
Routzahn, Wm H 118 1
Routzawn, Daniel [sic] 112 1
Routzong, Adam 257 2
Routzong, Benjamin 257 2
Routzong, Conrad 258 2
Routzong, Daniel 262 2
Routzong, Daniel [sic] 32 1
Routzong, Jacob [sic] 228 1
Routzong, Jonothan 262 2
Routzong, Joseph 262 2
Routzong, Philip J 208 2
Rouzer, Abraham 254 2
Rouzer, Catherine 258 2
Rouzer, Daniel 185, 258, 262, 275 2
Rouzer, Daniel 64, 70 3
Rouzer, Daniel Jr 262 2
Rouzer, Daniel R 262 2
Rouzer, Eugenie G 265 2
Rouzer, H H 124 3
Rouzer, Henry 165, 167 3
Rouzer, Henry 262, 271 2
Rouzer, Horace D 277 2
Rouzer, J R 187, 206 3
Rouzer, J R 189 2
Rouzer, Jacob 275 2
Rouzer, John 46, 49, 80, 87, 132, 134, 181, 198, 276 2
Rouzer, John 10, 106, 117, 125, 139, 150, 183, 223, 264 1
Rouzer, John 14, 167, 179 3
Rouzer, John H 271, 277 2
Rouzer, John R 26, 59, 119, 125, 147, 229, 234, 265, 271, 272, 279, 283 1
Rouzer, John R 68, 69, 84, 271, 277, 287 2
Rouzer, John R 2, 160, 187 3
Rouzer, Margaret 254, 282 2
Rouzer, Martha E 277 2
Rouzer, Martin 139 1
Rouzer, Martin 282 2
Rouzer, Martin 171, 217 3
Rouzer, Peter 287 2
Rouzer, Robert B 277 2
Rouzer, William 262, 282 2
Rouzer, Wm 22, 134 2
Rouzer, Wm 253 1
Rouzser, E R 265 2
Row, Geo 169 2
Row, Jacob 40 1
Row, Jacob 38 3
Row, John 275 2
Row, Joseph 159 2
Row, Michael 282 2
Rowan, Catherine D 260 2
Rowe, Anna R 196 3
Rowe, B L 45 2
Rowe, Barbara 257 2
Rowe, Catherine 258 2
Rowe, Charles F 259 2
Rowe, Charles H 259 2
Rowe, Charles J 258, 283 2
Rowe, Chas 46, 169 2
Rowe, Chas F 50, 205 3
Rowe, Daniel 262, 275 2
Rowe, Daniel 26 3
Rowe, E Cora 258 2
Rowe, E H 71, 91, 92, 109, 119, 169 1
Rowe, E H 202, 205 2
Rowe, E L 30, 134, 175 2
Rowe, E L 27 3
Rowe, Edgar N 265 2
Rowe, Edw 219, 265 1
Rowe, Edw H 119 1
Rowe, Elgene L 224a 2
Rowe, Eli S S 264 2
Rowe, Elizabeth 282 2
Rowe, Enoch P 265 2
Rowe, Eugene 188 1
Rowe, Eugene 52, 148, 195, 199, 205, 227, 231 2
Rowe, Eugene E 1 1
Rowe, Eugene L 6, 15, 43, 65, 96, 107, 167, 187, 196, 205 3
Rowe, Eugene L 6, 27, 41, 171, 186, 192, 194, 197, 201, 230, 233, 257, 272 1
Rowe, Eugene L 35, 87, 153, 188, 209, 225a, 259, 265 2
Rowe, Eugene W 268 2
Rowe, Euguen [sic] L 171 1
Rowe, Eva M 283 2
Rowe, Frederick 267, 290 2
Rowe, Frederick A 267 2
Rowe, G W 210, 265 1
Rowe, Geo 11, 153, 188 2
Rowe, Geo 159 1
Rowe, Geo W 6 1
Rowe, Geo W 176 3
Rowe, Geo W 99, 258 2
Rowe, George 210a, 268 2
Rowe, George F 294 2
Rowe, George Sr 1 3
Rowe, George W 59, 194 1
Rowe, George W 224a, 268, 276 2
Rowe, George W 15 3
Rowe, Grace 16 2
Rowe, H J 258 2
Rowe, Hannah 271 2
Rowe, Harry 9, 257, 265 2
Rowe, Harry M 190 2
Rowe, Helen J 271 2
Rowe, Henry 188 2
Rowe, Howard M 271 2
Rowe, Howard S 271 2
Rowe, Isaac 11, 274 2
Rowe, Isaiah R 274 2
Rowe, J A 19 1
Rowe, J Henry 196 3
Rowe, J Henry 27, 163, 210 1
Rowe, J W 176 3
Rowe, Jacob 262, 268, 274, 275, 276, 282 2
Rowe, Jacob 228, 272 1
Rowe, Jacob 26, 165 3
Rowe, James A 39 2
Rowe, James C 257 2
Rowe, James H 197 1
Rowe, Jas A 163 3
Rowe, Joseph 275, 276 2
Rowe, Joshua 19 1
Rowe, Joshua 258, 264, 276 2
Rowe, Josiah 163 3
Rowe, Julia P 267 2
Rowe, L 60 1
Rowe, Margaret C 282 2
Rowe, Martha B 265 2
Rowe, Martha V 272 1
Rowe, Mary A O 223a 2
Rowe, Mary Garretta 283 2
Rowe, Michael 282 2
Rowe, Nathaniel 278 1
Rowe, Nathaniel 258 2
Rowe, R L 229 1
Rowe, Rosa A 210 3
Rowe, Samuel L 259 2
Rowe, Sarah 290 2
Rowe, William 294 2
Rowe, William T 294 2
Rowe, Wm L 58 2
Rowland, Helen D 277 2
Rowland, James L 277 2
Rowles, Geo W 88 1
Royal Indemnity Co 83 3
Royal Indemnity Co 227a, 257 2
Royal Indemnity Co of Md 56 3
Royal Indemnity Co of N Y 102 3
Royal Indemnity Co of N Y 115 1
Royal Indemnity Company 227 2
Royal Indemnity Company 90 1
Royer, Amanda J 277 2

Royer, Birdie K 257 2
Royer, Catherine 258 2
Royer, Charles O 260 2
Royer, John 257, 277 2
Royer, John T 257 2
Royer, Rufus A 19 3
Royer, Samuel 290 2
Royer, Thomas 290 2
Royston, Eppa C 265 2
Royston, M Margaret 265 2
Rozser, Enna K 265 2
Rsoe, Harvey R 262 2
Ruby, Milton 138 2
Rudd, Annie M 255 2
Rudenour, Sarah A 258 2
Rudisel, George 293 2
Rudisel, John 135 1
Rudisel, Ludwig 135 1
Rudisel, Tobias 293 2
Rudisell, Ludwick 125 1
Rudolph, Daniel 262 2
Rudolph, Peter 262 2
Rudy 267 2
Rudy, Amos W 255 2
Rudy, Ann R 254 2
Rudy, Anna Kate 255, 283 2
Rudy, Annie L 277 2
Rudy, Cassandra R 258 2
Rudy, Chas M 258, 276 2
Rudy, Clarence W 277 2
Rudy, Daniel 165 3
Rudy, Daniel 129, 134, 144, 148 2
Rudy, E C 293 2
Rudy, Edith R 86 1
Rudy, Edith R 277 2
Rudy, F F 258 2
Rudy, Frances L 267 2
Rudy, Frederick 163 1
Rudy, Frederick 175, 258, 267, 268 2
Rudy, George D 268 2
Rudy, George E 224, 268 2
Rudy, H T 209 3
Rudy, Hanson 96 2
Rudy, Hanson 187 3
Rudy, Hanson T 262, 271 2
Rudy, Hanson T 13 1
Rudy, J 75 3
Rudy, J E 271 2
Rudy, Jacob 13, 106 1
Rudy, Jacob 14, 26, 79, 215 3
Rudy, Jacob 237 2
Rudy, Jacob M 277 2
Rudy, Joshua 267, 276, 277 2
Rudy, Kate C 280 2
Rudy, Mary G 258 2
Rudy, Mary L 283 2
Rudy, Rhomer L 258 2
Rudy, Rose M 101 1
Rudy, Ruthie 255 2
Rudy, T C 106, 118 1
Rudy, T C 187 3
Rudy, T C 89, 271 2
Rudy, T Carlton 293 2
Rudy, T S 80 2
Rudy, Thomas C 186 3
Rudy, Thomas C 267 2
Rudy, Thos 107 2
Rudy, W Dana 255 2
Rudy, Walter Dana 295 2
Rudy, Walter R 119 2
Rudy, William E 267, 268 2
Rudy, William Edw 73 1
Rudy, William L 293, 295 2
Ruland, C 100 1
Ruland, Conrad 52 1
Ruland, Conrad 19 3
Rumeberger, Robert M 288 2
Rumeberger, Robert S 288 2
Rummel, Magdalene 275 2
Rummell, John F L 275 2
Rumpf, Elizabeth M 265 2
Rumsey, Jerry Thomas 277 2
Runkes, W G 277 2
Runkles, Albert H 290 2
Runkles, Albert H 112 1
Runkles, B A 294 2
Runkles, Belle 257 2
Runkles, Belle W 259 2
Runkles, Bessie 294 2
Runkles, Calvin D 258 2
Runkles, Charles A 259 2
Runkles, Eldred W 264 2
Runkles, Ellenor 264 2
Runkles, Ernest W 265 2
Runkles, Frank T 267 2
Runkles, Geo W 265 2
Runkles, Goldie N 220 2
Runkles, Ida V 274 2
Runkles, Isaac T 282 2
Runkles, Jacob 275 2
Runkles, Jennis 290 2
Runkles, John 275 2
Runkles, John B 290 2
Runkles, Joseph 276 2
Runkles, Joseph H 277 2
Runkles, Lucian O 107 1
Runkles, Martha D 265 2
Runkles, Mary 282 2
Runkles, Morgan 144 1
Runkles, Morgan 140 2
Runkles, Morgan P 52 1
Runkles, Samuel 237, 276, 290 2
Runkles, Samuel T 290 2
Runkles, W R 55 3
Runkles, Washington 294 2
Runkles, William 276, 290, 294 2
Runkles, William H 258, 294 2
Runkles, William O 294 2
Runkles, Wm M 101 1
Runkles, Wm O 234 2
Runnell, Magdalena M 282 2
Runner, Charity 258 2
Runner, Daniel 262, 275 2
Runner, Daniel P 6 1
Runner, Henry 275 2
Runner, John 258, 275 2
Rupley, F A 39 2
Ruppert, Mary W 284 2
Ruprecht, Guy F 268 2
Ruprecht, Joseph 278 2
Ruprecht, Louis F 280 2
Ruprecht, Mary Myers 284 2
Rusher, William 294 2
Russ, Catherine E 120 1
Russ, Clarence H 120 1
Russel, Isaac 30 2
Russell, Abel 254, 275, 288 2
Russell, Alexander 275 2
Russell, Anna 283 2
Russell, C L 125 2
Russell, Florence 267 2
Russell, Francis J 267 2
Russell, Henry 110 1
Russell, Henry 271 2
Russell, Isaac 1 3
Russell, Isaac S 276 2
Russell, James 187, 276 2
Russell, Jesse 275 2
Russell, John 275 2
Russell, John 249 2
Russell, John M 278 2
Russell, John Sr 275 2
Russell, Joshua 276 2
Russell, Marcella F 284 2
Russell, Mary T 283 2
Russell, Mary Theresa 284 2
Russell, Michael F 283 2
Russell, Robert G 275 2
Russell, Roberts 290 2
Russell, Samuel M 290 2
Russell, Sarah (Col) 290 2
Russell, T Edgie 196 2
Russell, Thomas J 278, 284 2
Russell, William 254, 294 2
Russell, William C 23 3
Russell, Wm 176, 229 1
Russell, Wm 154 2
Ruth, Chas M 277 2
Rutherford, Benj 159 1
Rutherford, Benj 169 2
Rutherford, Benjamin 257 2
Rutherford, George P 268 2

Rutherford, Robert R 288 2
Rutherfore, Charles 258 2
Rutson, Eli 19 1
Ruzer, Frank S 265 2
Ryan, Angie C 255, 257 2
Ryan, Barbara G 257 2
Ryan, Caroline F 267 2
Ryan, Frank C 255, 257, 267, 291 2
Ryan, John 275 2
Ryan, Matthew 282 2
Ryan, Samuel W 291 2
Rye, Henry 248 1
Rypma, Catharine A 258 2
Sadler, Geo 51 1
Safe Deposit & Tr Co of Balto 265 1
Safe Deposit & Trust Co 223a 2
Safe Deposit & Trust Co 227 3
Safe Deposit & Trust Co of Baltimore 11 1
Safe Deposit and Trust Co 109 3
Safe Deposit and Trust Co of Bal 11 1
Safe Depositi & Trust Co of Bal 52 1
Safert, Helen W 75 3
Safrit, Thomas H 75 3
Sager, Elmer 28 3
Sager, George 55 3
Sager, John 55 3
Sager, Mathias 59 1
Sager, Mathias 55 3
Sagle, Charles H 10 3
Sagle, Emma 10 3
Sagle, Peter 32 3
Sahm, Caroline 64 3
Sahm, Henry J 42 3
Sahm, Jacob 41, 64 3
Sahm, Jaob 41 3
Sahm, John J 41, 42 3
Sahm, Margaret 41 3
Sahm, Margaret R 58 3
Sahm, Mary 208 2
Sahm, Peter 71, 110, 125, 165, 229, 265 1
Sahm, Peter 1, 138, 195, 208 2
Sahm, Peter 2, 41, 64, 75, 98, 160, 195 3
Sain, Alan 38 3
Sain, John 5 2
Sain, John 38 3
Sain, John 247 2
Saire, John 5 2
Salem, Peter 276 2
Salm, John 185 2
Salmon, Catherine 9, 26 3
Salmon, Charles 9 3
Salmon, Charles 242 2
Salmon, Elizabeth 18 3
Salmon, Geo 18 3
Salmon, Geo 38 2
Salmon, George 14, 18, 26, 165 3
Salmon, George 276 2
Salmon, Sarah 81, 165 3
Salmon, W E 30 1
Salmon, W E 139 3
Salmon, William 81 3
Salmon, Wm 219, 239 1
Salmon, Wm E 59 1
Salmon, Wm S 124 3
Salomon, Chas 87 3
Salomon, Edward 18 3
Salter, Antonett F 3 3
Salter, Geo 52 2
Salter, George E 27 3
Salter, George W 27 3
Salter, Mary Ann 54 3
Salter, Nettie F 27 3
Saltkeld, John 37 3
Saltkeld, Lucy 37 3
Saltszgiver, John H 40 3
Saltzgiver, Magdalene 40 3
Sammeth, Linda 51 3
Sample, Annie M 230 1
Sample, Clayton E 11 3
Sample, Clayton E 230 1
Sample, George W 27 3
Sampson, Thomas 75 3
Samy, Daniel 37 3
Sander, Walter W 45 3
Sanders, Caroline B 89 2
Sanders, Caroline E 115 2
Sanders, Cora D 42 1
Sanders, D 41 3
Sanders, Geo 22 2
Sanders, Guy A 82 3
Sanders, Harry R 6 3
Sanders, Helen K 106 2
Sanders, Helen M 6 3
Sanders, Henrietta 31, 32, 75 3
Sanders, Hiram 33 3
Sanders, John 71, 106 3
Sanders, John 219a 2
Sanders, John of D 41 3
Sanders, John Sr 41 3
Sanders, Robert 41 3
Sanders, Samuel 71 3
Sanders, Sophie C 72 3
Sanders, Thomas 242 2
Sanders, Thomas 75 3
Sanders, Timothy 75 3
Sanders, W W 51, 72 3
Sanders, Wallis J 82 3
Sanders, Walter 169 2
Sanders, Walter 89, 269 2
Sanders, Walter W 72 3
Sanderson, F 82 3
Sanderson, W Raymond 71 3
Sanderson, William 82 3
Sanderson, William 258 2
Sanderson, William R 81 3
Sanderson, Wm 129 1
Sanderson, Wm R 11 1
Sandersonn, W Raymond 81 3
Sando, Edgar R 21 3
Sando, Frances H 21 3
Sands, Arabella 2 3
Sanford, Julian DeWitt 200 2
Sanford, Naomi Mussetter 200 2
Saniker, Emanuel 19 3
Sank, Elizabeth A 64 3
Sank, Plummer I 64 3
Sanks, Jemima W 43 3
Sannder, Ella M 79 3
Sannder, Lena B 79 3
Sanner, Charles V C 11 3
Sanner, Daniel W 79 3
Sanner, Ellen M 20 3
Sanner, Fannie O 20, 24, 79 3
Sanner, John 58, 84, 163 1
Sanner, Keefer Alonzo 48 3
Sanner, Lena 11 3
Sanner, Susan 79 3
Sanner, Vernon L 79 3
Sanner, Vincent 71, 79 3
Sanner, Vincent 96 2
Sanner, Vincent 234 1
Sanner, Virgie E 11 3
Sappington, C B 177, 218, 222 2
Sappington, Charles B 10 3
Sappington, Charles W 10 3
Sappington, Chas B 15 2
Sappington, Claire E 45 3
Sappington, Claire E 18 2
Sappington, Cora L 24 3
Sappington, Ct 75 3
Sappington, E U 75 3
Sappington, Ernest F 21, 28 3
Sappington, Eva E 35 3
Sappington, F B 67 2
Sappington, F B 23, 48, 57, 135, 139, 147, 179, 204 1
Sappington, F B 44, 67, 72 3
Sappington, F B, Jr 23 1
Sappington, F V 179 3
Sappington, Fannie E 24 3
Sappington, Fannie R 23 3
Sappington, Frances 23 3
Sappington, Frances B 23 3
Sappington, Francis 18, 132 2
Sappington, Francis 132 2
Sappington, Francis B 274 2
Sappington, Francis B 3, 23, 24, 50 3

Sappington, Francis B 28, 125, 181 1
Sappington, Francis B Jr 24 3
Sappington, Frank B 41 1
Sappington, Frank B 80 2
Sappington, Frank R 6 1
Sappington, G R 61, 76, 82, 88, 106, 272 1
Sappington, G R 15, 38, 218, 222, 290 2
Sappington, G R 71, 75, 81, 120, 186, 196 3
Sappington, Geo K 30 2
Sappington, George K 28 3
Sappington, George R 274 2
Sappington, Grace G 273 1
Sappington, Grace R C 284 1
Sappington, Greenbury 27 3
Sappington, Greenbury R 70 1
Sappington, Greenbury R 27, 171 3
Sappington, Greenbury R 150, 282 2
Sappington, Henry 267 2
Sappington, Irene L 35 3
Sappington, J M 71 3
Sappington, J M 27 3
Sappington, James 230 1
Sappington, James C 27, 44, 45, 56 3
Sappington, James M 1 1
Sappington, James M 44 3
Sappington, James of S 68 3
Sappington, James W 293 2
Sappington, Jas C 57 3
Sappington, L C 179 3
Sappington, Louisa 50, 75 3
Sappington, M Angela 35 3
Sappington, Myrtle S 21 3
Sappington, Nettie 10 3
Sappington, Nettie M 125 2
Sappington, R 122 2
Sappington, R C 262 1
Sappington, R C 71 3
Sappington, R Frank 68, 71, 72 3
Sappington, S 68 3
Sappington, Sallie R 72 3
Sappington, Sarah E 71 3
Sappington, Sidney 59, 125 1
Sappington, Sidney 140 3
Sappington, Sidney 71 3
Sappington, Sidney 169, 235 2
Sappington, Sydney 171 3
Sappington, Sylvester 81 3
Sappington, T 8, 271 1
Sappington, T P 66, 177 2
Sappington, T P 209 3
Sappington, Thomas 222, 226, 227a, 274, 286, 294 2
Sappington, Thomas 57, 70, 88, 106, 139, 181, 271 1
Sappington, Thomas 1, 14, 23, 64, 70, 75, 120 3
Sappington, Thomas Jr 75 3
Sappington, Thomas M 27 3
Sappington, Thomas P 61, 82 1
Sappington, Thomas P 71, 75, 196 3
Sappington, Thomas P 229a 2
Sappington, Thomas R 45 3
Sappington, Thos 70, 75, 81, 91, 98, 163, 179 3
Sappington, Thos 7, 11, 28, 38, 51, 56, 100, 115, 124, 247 2
Sappington, Thos 147, 159, 176 1
Sappington, Thos P 72 3
Sappington, Thos P 1 1
Sappington, Thos P 15, 106, 218 2
Sappington, Thos P Dr 272 1
Sappington, W 242 2
Sappington, W A 72 3
Sappington, William 81 3
Sappington, William C 120 3
Sappington, William C 286, 294 2
Sappington, Wm 227a 2
Sappington, Wm A 60 1
Sappington, Wm C 88, 106, 125, 176, 181 1
Sappington, Wm C 75, 179 3
Sappington, Wulliam 1 3
Sauble, Lillian G 45 1
Sauble, P G 160 3
Sauble, Peter G 196 3
Sauerwein, Carrie F 9 3
Sauerwein, Charles D 12 3
Sauerwein, Christopher 9 3
Sauerwein, John C 9 3
Sauerwein, Margaret E 12 3
Sauerwine, C 77 3
Saum, Abraham 1, 2 3
Saum, Barbara 6 3
Saum, Barbara & Mary 6 3
Saum, Frederick 23 3
Saum, Frederick 64 3
Saum, Isaac 35 3
Saum, Mary 64 3
Saum, Mary Barbara 53 3
Saum, Peter 35, 64 3
Saunders, John 38 3
Saunders, Walter 115 2
Saur, Miriam Coblentz 28 3
Sausser, Clara W M 200 2
Sautman, Catherine 9 3
Savage, Patrick 271 1
Savage, Patrick 64 3
Savoy, Barbara 6 3
Savoy, Richard 67 3
Saxten, B W 55, 82 3
Saxten, B W 19 1
Saxten, Benjamin W 156 1
Saxten, Frances Mae 267 2
Saxten, John 40 2
Saxten, John A 55, 82 3
Saxten, Mary Jane 55 3
Saxten, William 82 3
Sayes, Ida M 96 2
Sayler, C E 169 2
Sayler, Daniel Jr 1 2
Sayler, Florence M 24 3
Sayler, Geo 177, 186 2
Sayler, Grace R 46 3
Sayler, Hannah 32 3
Sayler, Henry 32 3
Sayler, Isaac S 248 1
Sayler, Jacob 1 2
Sayler, John W 46 3
Sayler, Laura V 209 2
Sayler, Mildred L 24 3
Sayler, Oscar 46 3
Sayler, Reuben 187 2
Sayler, Ruben 32 3
Saylor, Benjamin F 6 3
Saylor, C E 67 3
Saylor, Caroline 19 3
Saylor, Chas 144 1
Saylor, Chas 54 2
Saylor, D P 165, 215 3
Saylor, Daisie F 190 2
Saylor, Daniel 14, 70 3
Saylor, Daniel K 42 3
Saylor, Daniel P 171, 191 1
Saylor, Daniel P 15, 70, 165 3
Saylor, Daniel P 258, 262 2
Saylor, Dasie F 189 1
Saylor, E 30 1
Saylor, E C 32 1
Saylor, E R 72 3
Saylor, Elizabeth 19, 38 3
Saylor, Elizabeth A 21 3
Saylor, Emmanuel 19 3
Saylor, Ezra 18, 19 3
Saylor, Geo 218 3
Saylor, Geo 144, 159, 283 1
Saylor, Geo W 218 3
Saylor, George 18, 31 3
Saylor, George C 27 3
Saylor, Harry A 58 3
Saylor, Henry 159 1
Saylor, Henry 15, 31, 32, 38, 41 3
Saylor, I W 68 3
Saylor, J M 139 2
Saylor, Jacob 1 2
Saylor, Jacob 263 1

Saylor, Jacob 14, 40 3
Saylor, Jacob A 43 3
Saylor, James M 28 1
Saylor, Jno 70 3
Saylor, John 82, 84, 183, 271 1
Saylor, John 38, 42, 43, 55, 70 3
Saylor, John H 42 3
Saylor, Laura V 51 3
Saylor, M L 250 1
Saylor, M Luther 6, 79 3
Saylor, Margaret 55 3
Saylor, Mary A 54 3
Saylor, Mary C 27, 58 3
Saylor, Oscar 45 3
Saylor, Reuben 68 3
Saylor, Reuben 11, 28, 40, 237 2
Saylor, Robert J 6 3
Saylor, Rosa J 68 3
Saylor, Ruben 32, 40, 41 3
Saylor, Sarah 71 3
Saylor, Sarah 171 1
Saylor, Sarah C 72 3
Saylor, Sarah E 72 3
Saylor, Sarah K 15 3
Saylor, Sidney Ann 32, 71 3
Saylor, Simon P 19 3
Saylor, Solomon 18, 70 3
Saylor, Solomon 22, 124 2
Saylor, Susannah 70 3
Saylor, T R 147 2
Saylor, Thomas 172 3
Saylor, Thomas R 1 1
Saylor, Thomas R 167, 190, 200 2
Saylor, Thos 189, 200 1
Saylor, Vernon S 21, 79 3
Scaeffer, Marshall E 75 3
Scarff, Grace I 28 3
Scarff, J Fenton 28 3
Scarff, Mary 55 3
Scarff, P D 207 1
Scely, Emmaline 50 3
Scely, Lyman 50 3
Scencil, Edward C 20 3
Schaaf, Margaret 39 3
Schade, Christian 11 3
Schade, H E 31 2
Schade, William Osborne 11 3
Schaefer, D F 70 1
Schaefer, Frederick 55 3
Schaefer, Henry 55 3
Schaefer, Peter 67 3
Schaefer, Ruth James 67 2
Schaefer, Susanna 39 3
Schaeffer, Adam 38 3
Schaeffer, Alan D 56 3
Schaeffer, Amos 161 2
Schaeffer, Ann R 50 3
Schaeffer, Catherine 8 3
Schaeffer, Constance L 83 3
Schaeffer, D F 137 2
Schaeffer, Daniel 267 2
Schaeffer, David 18 3
Schaeffer, David F 14, 15, 23, 165 3
Schaeffer, David F 189, 237, 263 1
Schaeffer, David F 26 2
Schaeffer, David K 15 3
Schaeffer, E C 51 2
Schaeffer, Edward T 110 2
Schaeffer, Frederick D 23 3
Schaeffer, George F 26 3
Schaeffer, Jacob 38 3
Schaeffer, James E 82 3
Schaeffer, John 245 1
Schaeffer, John 38 3
Schaeffer, John F D 42 3
Schaeffer, Luther 50 3
Schaeffer, M A 42 3
Schaeffer, Mace B 15, 56 3
Schaeffer, Margaret A 26 3
Schaeffer, Margaret C 15, 55 3
Schaeffer, Maria E 55, 56 3
Schaeffer, Martha E 56 3
Schaeffer, Peter 8 3
Schaeffer, Roy C 81 2
Schaeffer, Thomas M 75 3
Schaeffer, William C 82 3
Schafer, John H 67 3
Schafer, John R 67 3
Schafer, John Sr 171 3
Schafer, Robert 67 3
Schafer, Theodore C 133 1
Schafer, Thomas 67 3
Schaff, Daniel 53 3
Schaff, Jacob 39 3
Schaff, Michael 53 3
Schaffer, Charles M 43 3
Schaffer, David 264 1
Schaffer, Ella M 60 3
Schaffer, Florence E 119 1
Schaffer, Franklin E 58 3
Schaffer, Grayson R 55 3
Schaffer, Harry P 72 3
Schaffer, J A 65 3
Schaffer, James A 57 3
Schaffer, James Arthur 46 3
Schaffer, Johnathan A 43 3
Schaffer, Marshall E 58 3
Schaffer, Mary D 57 3
Schaffer, Nicholas G 43, 60 3
Schaffer, Peter 65 3
Schaffer, Sterling R 69 2
Schaffer, Thomas H 122 3
Schaffer, Wm A 122 3
Schaffler, Charles Edward 65 3
Schamel, Elias N 230 1
Schamel, Eliza Marcella 21 3
Schamel, Harry S 21, 46 3
Schamel, J W 230 1
Schamel, John Walter 46 3
Schamel, Samuel T 72 3
Schamel, Sarah C 72 3
Scharer, John 38 3
Schdodel, Charles 3 3
Schebits, Henry 32 1
Scheel, Anna C 45 3
Scheel, Christian Edw 12 3
Scheel, Emma A 45 3
Scheel, Fannie P 24, 65 3
Scheel, Henry G 32 3
Scheel, J A 45 3
Scheel, John G 45 3
Scheel, Mary M 45 3
Scheel, Philip A 65 3
Scheep, Philip F 45 3
Scheetz, John T 45 3
Scheley, Edw 37 1
Schell, Ada E 46 3
Schell, Benjamin F 192 1
Schell, Benjamin F 6 3
Schell, Catharine A 9, 40 3
Schell, Charlotte 18 3
Schell, Chas D 144 2
Schell, Clara M 82 3
Schell, Enos 18 3
Schell, G Ed 92 1
Schell, G Edw 48 1
Schell, Harriett 45 3
Schell, Harry F 32 3
Schell, J E 188 3
Schell, Jesse P 46 3
Schell, Jessie P 45 3
Schell, John 131 2
Schell, John E 211 2
Schell, John E 119, 215 1
Schell, John E 45, 206 3
Schell, John E Jr 215 1
Schell, John Ed 213 1
Schell, John G 32 3
Schell, Joseph 240, 249, 279 1
Schell, Joseph 257, 258 2
Schell, Joseph 18, 40 3
Schell, Kate 48 3
Schell, Kathleen S 73 1
Schell, S C 9 3
Schell, S C & 215 2
Schell, William H 82 3
Schenck, John M 38 3
Scherrer, Daniel 15 3
Schields, John 40 3
Schietneck, Charles M 10 3
Schietneck, Frances 10 3
Schildknecht, Ann Sophia 68 3
Schildknecht, Anna E 33 3
Schildknecht, C N 210 1

Schildknecht, Calvin E 11 3
Schildknecht, Calvin E 210, 244 1
Schildknecht, E 82 3
Schildknecht, Edith 11 3
Schildknecht, Harlan A 33 3
Schildknecht, Harlan A 87 2
Schildknecht, Henry 31, 42, 53 3
Schildknecht, Henry A 32 3
Schildknecht, Jacob 42 3
Schildknecht, John P 32 3
Schildknecht, Josiah 257 1
Schildknecht, Louise M 51 3
Schildknecht, Roy C 68 3
Schildknecht, Roy C 41 2
Schildknecht, Susan 31 3
Schildknecht, Willaiam 82 3
Schildknecht, Wm 110, 159 2
Schildknect, J 124 3
Schildknect, Theodore E 75 3
Schildknect, William 75 3
Schildknect, Wm 106 3
Schildnect, Henry A 65 3
Schildnect, Henry L 65 3
Schilds, Henrietta 39 3
Schildt, Elizabeth E 21 3
Schildt, Elmer P 21 3
Schildt, Rhoda E 21, 68 3
Schildtnecht, Joshua 110 1
Schildtnecht, Josiah M 177 2
Schilenk, Charles T 10 3
Schilipp, John G 153 2
Schill, George B 26 3
Schill, Louisa M 51 3
Schill, Robert G 51 3
Schilling, John 195 2
Schiltnecht, Mary 53 3
Schindlar, Daniel 14 3
Schindlar, David 14 3
Schindler, Ann C 14 3
Schindler, David 14, 15, 18 3
Schindler, David 32 1
Schindler, Elizabeth 18 3
Schindler, Hamilton F 14 3
Schindler, John 264 2
Schindler, John 56, 240 1
Schindler, Maggie E 15 3
Schindler, Margaret E 56 3
Schinlder, Ann C 14 3
Schisler, Jacob 37 3
Schisler, Mary 37 3
Schissler, Adam 1 3
Schissler, Ann M 1 3
Schissler, Catherine 1 3
Schissler, Hiram 37 1
Schissler, Jacob 1 3
Schissler, John 228 1
Schissler, John 38, 184 3
Schissler, John A 39 3
Schissler, Margaret 1 3
Schiswell, Joseph N 221a 2
Schlane, Henry 165 2
Schlasinger, D 41 1
Schleigh, Daniel R 14 3
Schleigh, Mary A 55 3
Schleigh, Mary A 197 2
Schleigh, Mary Ann 14 3
Schlenk, Leila 51 3
Schlenk, Leila C 10 3
Schley, Agnes 4, 23 3
Schley, Alfred 2 3
Schley, Annie P C 56 3
Schley, B T 47 1
Schley, Benjamin H 6 3
Schley, Buchanan 82 3
Schley, David 14 3
Schley, David 99, 249, 256 1
Schley, David 177 2
Schley, E Louisa 21 3
Schley, E Margaret 19 3
Schley, E Margaret 47 1
Schley, Edw 165 2
Schley, Edw 163, 201, 225 1
Schley, Edward 1, 18 3
Schley, Effie 96 2
Schley, Eve M 18 3
Schley, Fairfaw 67 3
Schley, Fairfax 23, 32, 41, 50 3
Schley, Fairfax 1 2
Schley, Fairfax Dr 119 2
Schley, Florence 23 3
Schley, Frank 23 3
Schley, Fred A 124 3
Schley, Frederick 110 1
Schley, Frederick 23, 37, 38, 106 3
Schley, Frederick 185 2
Schley, Frederick A 8, 23, 39, 120 3
Schley, Frederick A 111, 185, 249 2
Schley, Frederick A 70, 139, 163, 283 1
Schley, Frederick A. 70 1
Schley, G 19 3
Schley, George 82 3
Schley, Gilmer 166 2
Schley, Harriet H 32 3
Schley, Henry 18, 32, 38, 54, 106, 120 3
Schley, Henry 99, 163 1
Schley, Henry 1 2
Schley, J T 78 2
Schley, Jacob 137 1
Schley, James M 23 3
Schley, Jane S 45 3
Schley, Jane S 67 2
Schley, Jeorgianna M 14 3
Schley, John 14, 18, 38, 41 3
Schley, John 129 2
Schley, John F 46 3
Schley, John R 44 3
Schley, John T 54, 64 3
Schley, John T 38 2
Schley, John T 163, 263 1
Schley, L V 179 3
Schley, Lilian K 51 3
Schley, Lillian F 44, 51, 72 3
Schley, Louis H 50 3
Schley, M H 23 3
Schley, M Sophia 6 3
Schley, Mary 54 3
Schley, Mary 82 1
Schley, Mary Helen 55 3
Schley, Mary M 56 3
Schley, Mary M 75 3
Schley, Mary M 85, 253 1
Schley, N Wilson 45 1
Schley, N Wilson 21 3
Schley, S A 205 1
Schley, Steiner 96 1
Schley, Steiner 119 2
Schley, Steiner 23, 32, 72, 192 3
Schley, T 19 3
Schley, Thomas 75 3
Schley, Thos 165, 253 1
Schley, William 184 3
Schley, William H 82 3
Schley, Wm 135 1
Schlossen, Peter G 75 3
Schlosser, Elizabeth 18 3
Schlosser, Geo 43, 57 2
Schlosser, Geo 109, 159, 163, 217 1
Schlosser, Geo 18, 208 3
Schlosser, George 1, 26, 195 3
Schlosser, George 264 2
Schlosser, Henry 31 3
Schlosser, Peter 171, 222 1
Schlosser, Peter 18, 31, 53, 64, 202, 208 3
Schlosser, Peter 57, 110, 205, 237, 254, 264 2
Schlosser, Peter G 58 1
Schlosser, Peter G 26, 65 3
Schlossler, Elizabeth 18 3
Schluckbier, Peter 65 3
Schmidt, A Margaretha 2 3
Schmidt, A Margaritha 2 3
Schmidt, Abraham M 57 3
Schmidt, Annie M 28 3
Schmidt, Cora M 12, 20 3
Schmidt, Dora May 45 3
Schmidt, Edw J 233 1

Schmidt, Eunice M 21 3
Schmidt, F K 222 2
Schmidt, George E 28 3
Schmidt, George M 33, 58 3
Schmidt, Harry F Jr 33, 58 3
Schmidt, Harry Frederick 33 3
Schmidt, Harry Koehler 200 2
Schmidt, Jacob 119, 138, 165, 177 2
Schmidt, Jacob 265 1
Schmidt, Jacob H 233 1
Schmidt, Jacob Henry 45 3
Schmidt, John 39 3
Schmidt, John J 43 3
Schmidt, John J 278 2
Schmidt, Joseph H 21 3
Schmidt, Laura B 51 3
Schmidt, Mary Almanda 58 3
Schmidt, Mary V 57 3
Schmidt, Nettie 83 3
Schmidt, Samuel 226 2
Schmidt, William H 83 3
Schmidt, William S 12 3
Schmieg, Peter 106 3
Schmitz, August 2 3
Schmoll, Gladys S 219 1
Schnauffer, Catherine R 83 3
Schnauffer, Clara M 167 2
Schnauffer, L West 88, 200 1
Schnauffer, L West 63 1
Schnauffer, P M 1 1
Schnauffer, P M 210 3
Schnauffer, Patrick M 125 2
Schnauffer, Patrick M 22, 34, 120 1
Schnauffer, Patrick M 11 3
Schnauffer, Patrick N 227 2
Schnauffer, William 9, 83, 171 3
Schnauffer, William 41, 47 2
Schnauffer, William Jr 192 3
Schnauffer, William M 167 2
Schnauffer, Wm 12, 144 2
Schnauffer, Wm 56 1
Schnauuffer, Geo M 215 3
Schneider, Charles A 10 3
Schneider, Joseph G 37 3
Schneider, Louisa C 10 3
Scholl, Charles 8 3
Scholl, Charles E 11 3
Scholl, Christian 8 3
Scholl, Christian 61, 210 1
Scholl, Christian & 35 2
Scholl, Christina 9 3
Scholl, Daniel 15 3
Scholl, David 8 3
Scholl, Elias 18 3
Scholl, Elias 79 1
Scholl, Elizabeth 18 3
Scholl, Elizabeth E 82 3
Scholl, Ellis 84 1
Scholl, George 8 3
Scholl, Helen K 55 3
Scholl, Henry 72 2
Scholl, Henry 32 1
Scholl, Henry 31, 39 3
Scholl, Henry of J 38 3
Scholl, J 38 3
Scholl, Jacob 39 3
Scholl, Jacob of J 38 3
Scholl, Jemima 43, 50 3
Scholl, John 39, 53 3
Scholl, L V 163, 171 2
Scholl, Lewis 18, 54 3
Scholl, Lewis V 1, 8, 50, 196 3
Scholl, Louis V 112, 118, 144 1
Scholl, Louis V 50 3
Scholl, Margaret 15, 55 3
Scholl, Margaret W 54 3
Scholl, Maria S 54 3
Scholl, Mary 18 3
Scholl, William H 82 3
School, Daniel 37 1
School, Jennie 70 1
Schooley, John W 37 1
Schooley, John W 202 2
Schoppert, Edith V 21 3
Schreiner, Edw D 172 1
Schriner, Alice E 201 1
Schriner, John 40, 41 3
Schriner, Louisa E 40 3
Schriver, Edw 135 1
Schriver, John 144 2
Schriver, Mary 14 3
Schrock, Anne 38 3
Schrodel, Arie E 3 3
Schrodel, Caroline 42 3
Schrodel, Eleanor R 3 3
Schrodel, John 42 3
Schroder, Frederick 58 1
Schroder, Harry O 73 3
Schroedel, John 227 2
Schroedel, John 44 1
Schroeder, A A 72 3
Schroeder, Albert A 4 3
Schroeder, E T 190 2
Schroeder, Elizabeth 18 3
Schroeder, Elizabeth G 32 1
Schroeder, Elizabeth N Gilson 4 3
Schroeder, Frederick 71, 250 1
Schroeder, Frederick 218 3
Schroeder, Frederick 220a 2
Schroeder, G A 210 1
Schroeder, Geo 165 1
Schroeder, Geo A 19 2
Schroeder, George A 160 3
Schroeder, George T 57 3
Schroeder, H O 72 3
Schroeder, Henry 9, 32 3
Schroeder, Henry B 84 1
Schroeder, Herbert S 58 2
Schroeder, Herbert S 180 3
Schroeder, Herbert S 250 1
Schroeder, Mary A 57 3
Schroeder, Mary Jane 56 3
Schroeder, Ralph E 191 1
Schroeder, Sophia W 23 3
Schroeder, Sophie W 72 3
Schroyer, Bettie V 6 3
Schroyer, Catherine 8 3
Schroyer, Chas 217 1
Schroyer, Chas E 6 3
Schroyer, Elizabeth 18 3
Schroyer, Harry L 43 3
Schroyer, John 40 3
Schroyer, John 225 2
Schroyer, Joseph G P 43 3
Schroyer, Lawson 50 3
Schroyer, Robert L C 28 3
Schroyer, Williaminah 50 3
Schuack, David 14 3
Schubert, John 38 1
Schuetze, Charles W 56 3
Schuetze, Martha E 56 3
Schuler, Jacob 38 3
Schultz, Agustus 2 3
Schultz, Caroline 9 3
Schultz, Caroline A 10 3
Schultz, Conrad 9 3
Schultz, Geo 219 1
Schultz, Henry 31 3
Schultz, Joseph 197 2
Schultz, Louisa 50 3
Schultz, Louisa 171 1
Schultz, Mary M 56 3
Schultz, Mary Matilda 75 3
Schultz, Sophia 165 1
Schultz, Sophia H 37 1
Schultz, Theodore 110, 156, 171, 260 1
Schumann, Clara Jean 127 1
Schumann, Robert 127 1
Schuoler, Anna 102 2
Schwaber, John C 40 3
Schwallenburg, Frank 106 2
Schwalm, Elizabeth 19, 31 3
Schwalm, Heinrich 31 3
Schwarber, John William 73 3
Schwarber, Samuel D 73 3
Schwarts, Bessie Schaeffer 46 3
Schwartz, Clinton 72 3
Schwartz, Edgar L 72 3
Schwartz, Edward 102 3
Schwartz, Frances E M 46 3
Schwartz, Frederick 23 3

Schwartz, John S 46, 72 3
Schwartz, Laura A V 50 3
Schwartz, Pearl 72 3
Schwartz, Samuel 72 3
Schwartz, Samuel G 72 3
Schwearing, Mary C 56 3
Schweigart, Adam 1 3
Schweigart, Elizabeth 18 3
Schweigert, Adam 113 2
Schwier, Anna C 6 3
Schwigart, Adam 1 3
Schwigart, Adam Jr 1 3
Scoggins, Sarah J 82 3
Scoggins, Sarah Jane 72 3
Scoggins, William H 82 3
Scoggins, Wm 112 1
Scott, Caroline V 9 3
Scott, David 185 2
Scott, Elizabeth 19 3
Scott, G 81 3
Scott, Hannah 19 3
Scott, Helen A 83 3
Scott, Henry E 9 3
Scott, John 38 3
Scott, John 171 2
Scott, Mary 54 3
Scott, Mary M 286 2
Scott, Samuel 70 3
Scott, Thomas P 27 2
Scott, Walter 123 1
Scott, William 81 3
Scott, Wm 188 2
Seabold, Peter 215a 2
Seabold, Vincent 160 3
Seabold, Vincent 120 1
Seaboldt, Samuel 40 3
Seaboldx, John D 44 3
Seabrook, J A 265 1
Seachrist, George 26 3
Seachrist, Grace A 29 3
Seachrist, Richard M 29 3
Seacrist, Annie R 4 3
Seacrist, Chas 19 2
Seacrist, John W 45 3
Seacrist, Mary Ann 53 3
Seacrist, Raymond 45 3
Seacrist, Wm F 129 1
Seager, Catherine 10 3
Seager, George 10 3
Seaman, Christian 9 3
Seaman, Chritian 219 3
Seaman, Elizabeth 19 3
Seaman, Mary 56 3
Sears, Edw C 24 3
Sears, Edward C 51 3
Sears, Florence E 24 3
Sears, Fulton D 51 3
Sears, Ira T 24, 51 3
Sears, Lottie V 51 3
Sears, Sarah J 72 3
Sears, William H 72, 82 3
Sears, William T 82 3
Sears, Willie M 51 3
Sears, Wm H 135 1
Seaton, E J 18 3
Seaton, Elizabeth 18 3
Sebold, Annie R 3, 79 3
Sebold, Catharine A 9 3
Sebold, Elizabeth F 20 3
Sebold, John D 219, 225 1
Sebold, John D 44 3
Sebold, Louise 3, 79 3
Sebold, Louise 14 1
Sebold, Peter 64 3
Sebold, Samuel 46, 160 2
Sebold, V 82, 199 3
Sebold, V 33, 71 1
Sebold, Vicent 189 2
Sebold, Vincent 52, 107, 144, 160, 172, 178, 188, 199, 205, 210a, 283, 290 2
Sebold, Vincent 79, 151, 182, 221 3
Sebold, Vincent 62, 125, 165, 197, 217, 219, 225, 244, 254, 257 1
Sechrist, Anna R 83 3
Sechrist, William F 83 3
Seck, Detrick 186 1
Secon, Gideon 38 2
Seeberger, Carl F 9 3
Seeberger, Maria 56 3
Seedling, George 2 3
Seedling, Jonah 2 3
Seedling, Julia H 2 3
Seeger, Albert C 95 1
Seeger, Catherine T 129 3
Seeger, Chas 65 3
Seeger, Harry P 254 1
Seeger, Maria 65 3
Seeger, Peter 65 3
Seeger, Peter 90 1
Seeger, Philip 154 2
Seeger, Wardie M 83 3
Seevers, Wm R 90, 165 1
Seffer, G P 91 1
Sefton, Andrew 2, 81 3
Sefton, Charles F 2 3
Sefton, E B 232 2
Sefton, George B 2 3
Sefton, M F 81 3
Sefton, Martin T 84 1
Sefton, Mary Ann 55 3
Sefton, May G 58 3
Sefton, Washington 81 3
Sefton, William 81 3
Sefton, Wm 118, 225 1
Sefton, Wm 171 2
Sefton, Wm F 118 1
Segafoose, T A 215 2
Segalof, Charles 32 3
Segaloff, Charles E 11 3
Segaloff, Chas 83 1
Segaloff, Hanna 32 3
Segaloff, Henry 11 3
Segaloff, Samuel 11 3
Seger, Peter 254 2
Segesman, Joseph 37 3
Seguin, Francis 23 3
Seibert, Caroline 10 3
Seibert, George 27 3
Seibert, Rebecca S 67 3
Seidling, Arthur 56 3
Seidling, Geo 225 1
Seidling, Julia F K 56 3
Seidling, Mary V 56 3
Seigmund, Christian 8 3
Seiner, Ann Maria 1 3
Seiss, Annie R 5 2
Seiss, Annie R I 3 3
Seiss, Annie R I 32 2
Seiss, Cloyd W 73 3
Seiss, Daniel 183 1
Seiss, Daniel 70 3
Seiss, Daniel L 5 2
Seiss, Elias 25 2
Seiss, Elias 214 3
Seiss, F C Oscar 23 3
Seiss, Godfrey 27 3
Seiss, Godfrey 30 1
Seiss, John 42 1
Seiss, John 40 3
Seiss, John 25 2
Seiss, M Belle 5 2
Seiss, Margaret M 23 3
Seiss, Maria 54 3
Seiss, Mariah M 53 3
Seiss, Minnie Belle 3 3
Seiss, Ora M 58 3
Seiss, Raymon S 40 3
Seiss, Raymond 27 3
Seiss, Raymond S 54 3
Seiss, Samuel 70 3
Seiss, Samuel E 73 3
Selby, Cornelius 50 3
Selby, F Eugene 24 3
Selby, Gladys M 11 3
Selby, Hamilton 32 3
Selby, John D 44 3
Selby, Joseph 35 2
Selby, Lulu E 44 3
Selby, Robert 67 3
Self 96 3
Self 57 3
Self 79, 82, 183, 230, 265 1
Self, none required 189 3
Selig, Henry 33 3
Sell, Daniel 14, 15, 38 3
Sell, Daniel 128, 186 2
Sell, Henry 70 1

Sell, Peter 54, 65 3
Sellers, Emma K R 21 3
Sellers, Emma K R 271 2
Sellers, W H 271 2
Sellman, Annie M 279 1
Sellman, Beall 6 3
Sellman, Chas W 71 3
Sellman, F Made 24 3
Sellman, Florence May 242 2
Sellman, Gassaway 26 3
Sellman, Geo 263 1
Sellman, J B T 22 2
Sellman, Ruth 67 3
Sellman, Sarah E 71 3
Sellman, Savilla C 22 2
Sellman, William 26 3
Selsam, Catherine 9 3
Selsam, David 15 3
Selsam, John C 43 3
Selsam, John T 43 3
Selson, Daniel 14 3
Seltzer, Alma G 163 3
Seltzer, Earnest T 57 3
Seltzer, Elizabet 58 3
Seltzer, Mary H 57 3
Seltzer, Maurice 58 3
Sencindiver, Elizabeth G 68 1
Sensenbaugh M, A C 42 3
Sensenbaugh, A E 190, 229a 2
Sensenbaugh, A E 33, 196 3
Sensenbaugh, Alvey E 189 2
Sensenbaugh, Alvin 245 2
Sensenbaugh, Alvin E 4 3
Sensenbaugh, I D 190 2
Sensenbaugh, Irl D 4 3
Sensenbaugh, James 54 3
Sensenbaugh, James C 42 3
Sensenbaugh, John 40, 41 3
Sensenbaugh, John W 71 3
Sensenbaugh, Joseph 41 3
Sensenbaugh, Magdalene 54 3
Sensenbaugh, Simeon D 71 3
Sensenbaugh, Simon P 40 3
Senseney, Christian 8 3
Senseney, Hanson 8 3
Sentz, Abraham 70 1
Sentz, Peter 70 1
Serton, William 81 3
Settlemyer, Peter 65 3
Seufferle, Jacob 8 3
Sevier, Elizabeth 18 3
Sewall, D Ella 140, 149 2
Sewart, Benjamin 6 3
Sewell, Della 28 3
Sewell, Frank 32 3
Sewell, Geo 65 2
Sewell, Geo 275 1
Sewell, George M 28 3
Sewell, Hannah A 65 2
Sewell, Henry 32 3
Sewell, John N 28 3
Sewell, Mamie 58 3
Sewell, Nicholas 60 3
Seybert, Rebecca S 27 3
Shaaf, M F 224 3
Shade, Christian 34 1
Shade, Geo 133 3
Shade, Wm P 34 1
Shaefer, Mary E 55 3
Shaefer, Paul 55 3
Shaeffer, Grace L 81 2
Shafer, A T 278 2
Shafer, Adam 26 1
Shafer, Adam 26 3
Shafer, Allen D 27 1
Shafer, Alonzo C 3 3
Shafer, Barbara 6 3
Shafer, C 65 3
Shafer, Carrie E 1 1
Shafer, Charles H 10 3
Shafer, Charles T 75 3
Shafer, Charles W 9, 11, 15 3
Shafer, Chas 210 3
Shafer, Chas C 28 3
Shafer, Chas W 68, 137 1
Shafer, Clavin P 75 3
Shafer, Clemma V 166 1
Shafer, Conrad 110 1
Shafer, Conrad 8 3
Shafer, Daniel 9, 15, 27, 55, 224 3
Shafer, David 13 1
Shafer, Dorotha 282 2
Shafer, Dorothea 37 3
Shafer, E T 43 3
Shafer, E Talbot 19 3
Shafer, Earlston F 21 3
Shafer, Eddie R 52 1
Shafer, Edw C 198 2
Shafer, Edw C 55 3
Shafer, Edw C 52, 179 1
Shafer, Edward C 20, 43, 55 3
Shafer, Effie J 75 3
Shafer, Eliza E 20 3
Shafer, Elizabeth 19, 39 3
Shafer, Elmer E 73 1
Shafer, Elmer E 75 3
Shafer, Elva 11 3
Shafer, Emma R 278 2
Shafer, Eva E 222 2
Shafer, Eva S E 20 3
Shafer, Evelyn L 21 3
Shafer, Florence A 65 3
Shafer, Frederick 23 3
Shafer, G E 48 1
Shafer, Geo 84 1
Shafer, Geo 53 3
Shafer, George 8, 26, 27, 64, 65 3
Shafer, George C 28, 42 3
Shafer, George E 28 3
Shafer, George F 26 3
Shafer, Grace L 219 3
Shafer, Gustavius U 28 3
Shafer, Gustavius W 27, 28 3
Shafer, H 181 2
Shafer, Hamilton 89 2
Shafer, Hamilton 220 3
Shafer, Hamilton W 32 3
Shafer, Harry M 55 3
Shafer, Harry T 65 3
Shafer, Henry 32 3
Shafer, Henry 84, 163 1
Shafer, Hettie 11 3
Shafer, Ira H 35 3
Shafer, Jacob 8, 39 3
Shafer, Jacob 47 1
Shafer, James 102 2
Shafer, John 88, 163, 164 1
Shafer, John 8, 38, 160 3
Shafer, John A 39 3
Shafer, John E 42 3
Shafer, John Edward 43 3
Shafer, John F 75 3
Shafer, John H 40 3
Shafer, John H 41 1
Shafer, John P 44, 56, 65 3
Shafer, John R 42 3
Shafer, John R 59, 90, 112, 125, 235 1
Shafer, John Sr 160 3
Shafer, John W A 32, 43 3
Shafer, Joseph 58 1
Shafer, Joseph 19, 26, 40, 42 3
Shafer, Joseph E 75 3
Shafer, Julia A 43 3
Shafer, Julia M 278 2
Shafer, Julius C 28, 45 3
Shafer, Laura V 28 3
Shafer, Leslie E 28 3
Shafer, Leva C 227 1
Shafer, Lewis M[?] 28 1
Shafer, Lucy M 51 3
Shafer, M F 27 3
Shafer, M F 179 1
Shafer, M Stanley 57 3
Shafer, M Stanley 37 1
Shafer, Magdelina 53 3
Shafer, Malinda C 56 3
Shafer, Margaret 26, 40 3
Shafer, Martin T 55 3
Shafer, Mary 10, 53 3
Shafer, Mary E 28, 58 3
Shafer, Matilda 71, 169 1
Shafer, Matilda 54 3
Shafer, Maud 58 3

Shafer, Millard F 57 3
Shafer, Millard T 55 3
Shafer, Myrtle 273 1
Shafer, Newton R 82 3
Shafer, Noah 32 3
Shafer, Nora M 73 3
Shafer, Oscar L 235 1
Shafer, Oscar P 273 1
Shafer, P 41 1
Shafer, P H 19 3
Shafer, Peter 96, 101, 177 2
Shafer, Peter 8, 26, 32, 38, 53, 64, 186 3
Shafer, Peter 58, 229 1
Shafer, Peter H 43, 65 3
Shafer, Peter Srt 59 1
Shafer, Peter W 135, 144 1
Shafer, Peter W 27, 65 3
Shafer, Peter W 144 1
Shafer, Peter W 276 2
Shafer, Philip 197 2
Shafer, Philip 31 3
Shafer, Roy C W 60 3
Shafer, Roy H 20, 113 3
Shafer, Sarah M 32, 73 3
Shafer, Susie 65 3
Shafer, T W 206 3
Shafer, Theodore 75 3
Shafer, Theodore C 43, 75 3
Shafer, Thomas 75 3
Shafer, William F 58 3
Shafer, William G 27, 55, 57 3
Shafer, Wm G 179 1
Shaff, Abraham 2, 42 3
Shaff, Arthur 1 3
Shaff, Bessie M 230 1
Shaff, C W 259 2
Shaff, Catherine 9 3
Shaff, Charles H 15 3
Shaff, Charles K 11 3
Shaff, Chas K 32 3
Shaff, Clinton W 10, 11 3
Shaff, D C 42 3
Shaff, Daniel 171 2
Shaff, Daniel 15 3
Shaff, Daniel C 2 3
Shaff, David 153, 282 2
Shaff, Francis 270 1
Shaff, Francis 23 3
Shaff, Francis L 126 1
Shaff, George 26 3
Shaff, Grover C 29, 56 3
Shaff, Harry M 32 3
Shaff, Jacob C 55, 71 3
Shaff, Jacob L 9 3
Shaff, John 42 3
Shaff, John G 46 3
Shaff, John G 189 1
Shaff, John T 1 3
Shaff, Julia Ann 42 3
Shaff, Julia R 10 3
Shaff, Katherine E 11 3
Shaff, Lottie M 29 3
Shaff, Luther 26 3
Shaff, M E 71 3
Shaff, Margaret 55 3
Shaff, Mary C 56 3
Shaff, Mary E 58 3
Shaff, Maurice E 56 3
Shaff, Myrven E 20 3
Shaff, Stella M 73 3
Shaff, Susan 171 2
Shaff, Susan 42 3
Shaff, Susannah 55, 71 3
Shaff, William N 43 3
Shaff, Wm N 71 3
Shaffer, Carrie E 57 3
Shaffer, Charles C 11 3
Shaffer, Charles D 55, 82 3
Shaffer, Charles W 82 3
Shaffer, Chas D 15 3
Shaffer, Chas H 217 3
Shaffer, Conrad 93 2
Shaffer, Daniel 15 3
Shaffer, David 26 1
Shaffer, David 227 2
Shaffer, David F 40, 57 1
Shaffer, Edw C 188 3
Shaffer, Elizabeth 19 3
Shaffer, Eva S E 41 2
Shaffer, Frank 38 1
Shaffer, Geo 54, 78, 87 2
Shaffer, Geo C 72 3
Shaffer, George 26, 31 3
Shaffer, Grayson R 83 3
Shaffer, Harry E 37 1
Shaffer, Henry 84 2
Shaffer, J A 45 3
Shaffer, James C 45 3
Shaffer, John 37, 52, 271 1
Shaffer, John 37 3
Shaffer, John 220a 2
Shaffer, John E 280 2
Shaffer, John H 192 3
Shaffer, John R 258 2
Shaffer, Jones 208 1
Shaffer, Kate M E 11 3
Shaffer, Katie M E 97 1
Shaffer, Katie M E 48 3
Shaffer, Loretta F 51 3
Shaffer, M F 83 3
Shaffer, Margaret R 55 3
Shaffer, Martha E 150 2
Shaffer, Mary D 45 3
Shaffer, Mary E 83 3
Shaffer, Maurice E 51 2
Shaffer, Millard F 15 2
Shaffer, Millard S 51 3
Shaffer, Mollie J 19 1
Shaffer, Peter 37, 229 1
Shaffer, Peter 39 2
Shaffer, Peter 186 3
Shaffer, Peter Sr 65 3
Shaffer, Peter W 11 2
Shaffer, Peter W 19, 65 3
Shaffer, Philip 46, 208 2
Shaffer, Ruth 38 1
Shaffer, Samuel 70 3
Shaffer, Sarah 71 3
Shaffer, Susan 71 3
Shaffer, Susan Eliz 72 3
Shaffer, Susannah 71 3
Shaffer, T L C 51 3
Shaffer, Thos 229 1
Shaffer, Washington 197 2
Shaffer, Washington L 82, 83 3
Shaffer, William D 83 3
Shaffer, Wilmer O 82 3
Shaffer, Wm 263 1
Shaffer, Wm C 22 2
Shafner, Mary 64 3
Shaft, D 186 2
Shafter, Edw C 72 3
Shaine, Charles R 10 3
Shan, Jonothan 39 3
Shanahan, John 37 3
Shane, George 45 3
Shane, Joshiah 45 3
Shaner, Cora A 35 3
Shaner, Irvin S 35 3
Shaner, Wm 51 1
Shank John W 13 1
Shank, Adam of P 249 1
Shank, Alta S 57 3
Shank, Ann M 27 3
Shank, Anna D 3 3
Shank, Anne E 18 3
Shank, Benjamin 96 1
Shank, C M 119 1
Shank, Carlton P 11, 27, 56 3
Shank, Carr E 140 1
Shank, Carr E 10 3
Shank, Charles 55 3
Shank, Charles B 20 3
Shank, Charles E 11, 23 3
Shank, Charles M 10 3
Shank, Chas 40 2
Shank, Chas E 71 3
Shank, Chas E 277 2
Shank, Clara V 11 3
Shank, Clare V 45 3
Shank, David A 140 1
Shank, Edith H 43, 68 3
Shank, Eith [sic] 26 1
Shank, Ellen C 55 3
Shank, Elmer H 11 3

Shank, Era 197 2
Shank, Esta C 11 3
Shank, Estee 45 3
Shank, Estelle May 21 3
Shank, Estha C 45 3
Shank, Eva 20 3
Shank, Ezra 109 1
Shank, Ezra 159 1
Shank, Ezra 18, 64, 195, 213 3
Shank, Ezra 106, 150 2
Shank, Ezra 171, 204 1
Shank, Frederick A 23 3
Shank, G 113 2
Shank, G 55 3
Shank, G Edgar 11, 45 3
Shank, G Edgar 11 3
Shank, G W 82 3
Shank, Geo 14, 54, 202 3
Shank, Geo 11, 26, 128, 138, 187 2
Shank, Geo 19, 283 1
Shank, Geo H 64 3
Shank, Geo M 179 3
Shank, Geo P 198 2
Shank, Geo W 1, 11, 15, 177 2
Shank, Geo W 71, 205, 227 3
Shank, Geo W 140, 186, 217, 283 1
Shank, Geo W of G 113 2
Shank, George 26, 27, 40, 42 3
Shank, George D 27 3
Shank, George H 27 3
Shank, George R 1 1
Shank, George W 58, 84 1
Shank, George W 6, 18, 27, 55, 218 3
Shank, George W of G 55 3
Shank, Grace M 51 3
Shank, Henry 31 3
Shank, J 65 3
Shank, J C 65 3
Shank, J J 65 3
Shank, Jacob 32 1
Shank, Jacob 31, 38, 40, 43 3
Shank, James C 45 3
Shank, Jennie B 27 3
Shank, Jennie B 11 1
Shank, Jennie D 43 3
Shank, John 37, 38, 42, 53 3
Shank, John J 43, 45 3
Shank, John W 60, 85, 101, 197, 238 1
Shank, John W 44 3
Shank, Jos 54 3
Shank, Joseph 52 2
Shank, Joseph 85 1
Shank, Joseph L 179, 240 1
Shank, Joseph L 27, 71 3
Shank, Kate I 48 3
Shank, L C 65 3
Shank, Lissa L 30 1
Shank, Luther F 51 3
Shank, Margaret 10, 55, 71, 82 3
Shank, Martin L 57 3
Shank, Mary 11, 53, 54 3
Shank, Mary A 55, 56 3
Shank, Mary C 11 3
Shank, Melvin L 51 3
Shank, Michael 19, 40, 55 3
Shank, Michael 32, 37, 57, 71, 79, 123, 278 1
Shank, Michael 43, 150, 227a 2
Shank, Otho J 43 3
Shank, Peter 56, 228, 271 1
Shank, Peter 23, 40, 64, 65 3
Shank, Raymond R 23 2
Shank, Raymond R 43, 57, 68 3
Shank, Richard S 67 3
Shank, Ruben W 18 3
Shank, Russell R 11 3
Shank, Sarah 71 3
Shank, Sarah C 22 1
Shank, Susan 71 3
Shank, T B 67 3
Shank, Weldon B 13 1
Shank, William 40, 64, 82 3
Shank, William 274 2
Shank, Wm 74, 245 1
Shank, Wm 51 2
Shankle, Daniel O 16 3
Shankle, Dennis J 16 3
Shankle, Harry D 16, 57, 68 3
Shankle, Howard L 33 3
Shankle, Jonothan 42 3
Shankle, Ma tin L 57 3
Shankle, Martin L 42 3
Shankle, Ossie A 68 3
Shankle, Ossie Anna 242 2
Shankle, Raymond J 16, 33 3
Shanks, Ezra 195 3
Shannon, Mary 53 3
Shannon, Maude Palmer 83 3
Shannon, William E 83 3
Shapro, Evelyn Grove 24 3
Shapro, Frank M 24 3
Sharer, Andrew 1 3
Sharer, Belva 6 3
Sharer, Daniel T 20 3
Sharer, Ersia L 20 3
Sharer, George 2, 27 3
Sharer, John 26 3
Sharer, Mary M 27 3
Sharer, Newton 188 3
Sharer, Newton O 83 3
Sharer, William E 83 3
Sharetts, D A 179 1
Sharetts, David 162 1
Sharetts, David A 15 3
Sharetts, David A 159 1
Sharetts, Mary C 15, 57 3
Sharetz, Catherine 37 3
Sharetz, John 37 3
Sharpe, Alfred R 21, 161 3
Sharpe, Alice M 21 3
Sharpe, Edward H 21 3
Sharrer, Carrie M 11 3
Sharrer, Charles F 83 3
Sharrer, George 26 3
Sharrer, Newton O 41 2
Sharrer, Newton O 11 3
Sharrets, Edwin H 77 3
Sharrets, Mollie 20 3
Sharretts, D A 67 1
Sharretts, D Albert 198 2
Sharretts, David 235 2
Sharretts, David A 245 2
Sharretts, Gertrude H 77 3
Sharretts, Mollie B 245 2
Sharretts, S A 60 1
Sharretts, Upton A 77 3
Sharupp, Henry 31 3
Shauck, Daniel 14 3
Shaupp, Barbara 6 3
Shaver, Carrie E 72 3
Shaver, J Clyde 72 3
Shaver, Jesse C 72 3
Shaver, Samuel A 72 3
Shaw , Moss 7 2
Shaw, Benjamin F 6 3
Shaw, Charles R 10 3
Shaw, D Edw 163 3
Shaw, Esther Elizabeth 58 3
Shaw, Fannie M 6 3
Shaw, Francis 23 3
Shaw, Francis 183 1
Shaw, Francis 186 2
Shaw, Frank 26 1
Shaw, Geo 171 3
Shaw, Geo R 187 3
Shaw, Harry G 65 3
Shaw, Hezekiah 31 3
Shaw, Hugh 27, 66 2
Shaw, J T 144 2
Shaw, John G 40 1
Shaw, John W 23 3
Shaw, Lelia D 51 3
Shaw, Lilia L 56 1
Shaw, M F 144 2
Shaw, Mabel Florence 58 3
Shaw, Mary L 56 3
Shaw, Moser 134 3
Shaw, Moses 56, 97, 118, 139, 228, 278 1
Shaw, Moses 185, 205, 250 2
Shaw, S Edward 8 1

Shaw, Samuel E 10 3
Shaw, Thomas 93, 106 1
Shaw, William 38 3
Shaw, William C 56, 82 3
Shaw, Wm 139, 163 1
Shaw, Wm 53 3
Shawbaker, Ethel J[?] 235 1
Shawbaker, Jacob G 45 3
Shawbaker, Jacob M 45 3
Shawen, Daniel 171 3
Shawen, Daniel 290 2
Shawen, James 234 1
Shawen, Joseph 112 1
Shawen, Samuel T 71 3
Shawen, Sarah 70 3
Shea, Owen 62 3
Sheahan, Anantasia 2 3
Shealey, Frederick 23 3
Shealey, John 218a, 237 2
Shealey, Samuel 70 3
Shearer, A E 14 2
Shearer, Chas L 82 1
Shearer, Daniel E 16 3
Shearer, Florence M 24 3
Shearer, George D 24 3
Shearer, John 139, 237 1
Shearer, John 11 2
Shearer, Lewis 193, 228 1
Shearer, Lilly A M 50 3
Shearer, Ludwig 50 3
Shearer, Mary 1, 54 3
Shears , Ira T 139 2
Sheatenhelm, Jacob 38 3
Sheatenhelm, Mary 38 3
Sheeley, Baltzer 6 3
Sheeley, Ephriam 20 3
Sheeley, Ephriam S 6 3
Sheeley, Ida G 35 3
Sheeley, William H 83 3
Sheely, Bertha I 44 3
Sheely, Harry E 33 3
Sheely, Jacob 43 3
Sheely, John F 44 3
Sheely, John F 265 1
Sheely, John F P 43 3
Sheely, Oliver 33 3
Sheesley, Ludwig 215 3
Sheesly, Ludwig 275 2
Sheetenhelm, Barbara 6 3
Sheetenhelm, Bernard G 6 3
Sheetenhelm, Bernard G 113 1
Sheetenhelm, C E 67 3
Sheetenhelm, E V 43 3
Sheetenhelm, Elizabeth 21 3
Sheetenhelm, Ezra R 6, 21 3
Sheetenhelm, Ezra R 113 1
Sheetenhelm, G W 67 3
Sheetenhelm, George 227a 2
Sheetenhelm, J C 67 3
Sheetenhelm, John C 43 3
Sheetenhelm, R 181 2
Sheetenhelm, Reuben 26 1
Sheetenhelm, Reuben 67 3
Sheetenhelm, Reuben 124, 128, 138 2
Sheetenhelm, Ruben 6 3
Sheetenhelm, Thomas 75 3
Sheets, Abraham 2 3
Sheets, Abraham 116 2
Sheets, Charles E 12, 58 3
Sheets, Clifford J 62 3
Sheets, Daniel 15 3
Sheets, Daniel 29 2
Sheets, David 137 2
Sheets, Dorothy 148 3
Sheets, Eden 147 1
Sheets, Elizabeth 18 3
Sheets, Ella M 20, 28 3
Sheets, George 26 3
Sheets, George H 28 3
Sheets, George W 28 3
Sheets, Greenbury 18, 38 3
Sheets, Isaac 35 3
Sheets, Jacob 26, 37, 38 3
Sheets, John 38 3
Sheets, John 96 1
Sheets, John 7 2
Sheets, Leroy T 12 3
Sheets, Louise A 12 3
Sheets, M R 28 3
Sheets, Myrtlen R 20, 28, 58 3
Sheets, Oliver W 62 3
Sheets, Peter 64 3
Sheetz, Geo 159 2
Sheetz, Harvey 45 3
Sheetz, John 81 3
Sheffer, Amanda D 27 3
Sheffer, Amanda J 3, 55 3
Sheffer, Daniel 137 1
Sheffer, Daniel 14 3
Sheffer, George P 27 3
Sheffer, Harlan L 33 3
Sheffer, Jonas 70, 71 3
Sheffer, M E 203 2
Sheffer, M J 33 3
Sheffer, Martin L 55 3
Sheffer, Mathias J 57 3
Sheffer, Morrise 169 1
Sheffer, Sarah 70 3
Sheffer, William M 83 3
Sheffield, Andrew 2 3
Sheffield, Cresence 10 3
Sheffield, Cresentz 2 3
Sheffield, John 100 3
Sheffield, John J 44 3
Sheffield, Wilbur F Jr 184, 264 1
Sheffield, Wilbur F Jr 67, 228a, 260 2
Sheffield, Wilbur F Jr 161 3
Sheffield, Wilbur, Jr, 4 1
Sheffler, Daniel 64 3
Sheffler, Jonas 64 3
Sheffler, Philip 64 3
Sheilds, Jeffershon 53 3
Shelburn, Henry 31 3
Shell, B F 124 3
Shell, Elizabeth 18 3
Shell, John E 131 3
Shellhouse, Juliana 64 3
Shellhouse, Peter 64 3
Shellman, Catherine 8 3
Shellman, Daniel J 19 1
Shellman, Geo W 144 1
Shellman, Jacob 40 1
Shellman, Jacob Sr 39 3
Shellman, John 37 3
Shellman, Lewis E 51 3
Shellman, Mary E 58 3
Shellman, William 39 3
Shellman, Wm 40 1
Shelly, Frederick 23 3
Shelmerdine, John A 37 3
Shelton, Bessie 129 2
Shelton, D J 13 1
Shelton, Edgar L 6 3
Shelton, Hattie A 48 1
Shenk, Elon D 45 3
Shenk, John H 45 3
Shephard, William 254 2
Shepherd, Abjah 27 2
Shepherd, Amelia A 20 3
Shepherd, Clinton W 2 3
Shepherd, Edward C 20, 21 3
Shepherd, Edward C Sr 20 3
Shepherd, Emily 89 2
Shepherd, Leana E 58 2
Shepherd, Lula L 21 3
Shepherd, Thomas 75 3
Shepherd, William 40 1
Shepley, Daniel 27 3
Shepley, Daniel 27 3
Shepley, Daniel 231 2
Shepley, Ida C 35 3
Shepley, Lillian H 230 1
Shepley, M F 270 1
Shepley, M F 57, 122, 174, 180, 196 3
Shepley, M Paul 90 2
Shepley, Melvin F 199, 217a 2
Shepley, Orville R 104 2
Shepley, Phyllis M 90 2
Shepley, Robert L 92 2
Shepley, Thos C 165 2
Sheppard, Emily R 20 3

Sheppard, Thomas 234 2
Sheppard, Wadsworth 81 3
Shepperd, Amelia A 2 3
Shepperd, Edward C 2 3
Shepperd, Emma R 43 3
Shepperd, Job K 43 3
Shepperd, Wm 210 1
Sherald, Bessie 240 1
Sherald, William 240 1
Sherer, Andrew 116 1
Sherfey, Lavinia 51 3
Sheridan, Edward 20 3
Sheridan, Gertrude 20 3
Sheridan, John L 107 3
Sherman, Elizabeth 37 3
Sherman, Jacob 37 3
Sherwood, Abraham 1 3
Shewbridge, Clarence R 56 3
Shewbridge, Mary A 56 3
Shibbetts, Henry 32 3
Shibbetts, William 32 3
Shibbitts, Wm 84 1
Shields, Annie C 46 3
Shields, Annie E 43 3
Shields, Charles E 204 1
Shields, Cynthia Annn 32 3
Shields, Ebenezer 18 3
Shields, Henry 32 3
Shields, James H 43 3
Shields, Jefferson 57 1
Shields, Jefferson 39, 209 3
Shields, Jefferson 1, 51, 171
2
Shields, John T 43 3
Shields, John W 39 3
Shields, Margaret A 53 3
Shields, William 81 3
Shields, Wm 260 1
Shildt, Samuel 132 2
Shill, Harry W 67 3
Shill, Randolph G 67 3
Shilling, Bessie M 46 3
Shilling, John R 46 3
Shilling, Marie 167 3
Shilling, Murray 167, 171, 205 3
Shilling, Wm 112 1
Shilt, Samuel 187 3
Shilt, Saran C 72 3
Shingle, Lawrence 50 3
Shinnick, Jacob A 44 3
Shinnick, Ornsby W 44 3
Shipley, Ann G 1, 75 3
Shipley, Blanche E 6 3
Shipley, C M 60 3
Shipley, Carrie D 58 3
Shipley, Catherine E 12 3
Shipley, Charles 10 3
Shipley, Charles F 12 3
Shipley, Clara A 9 3
Shipley, Clarence 120 1
Shipley, D 138 2
Shipley, D 260 1
Shipley, Daniel 253 1
Shipley, Emily C 21, 27 3
Shipley, Emory 51 3
Shipley, F N 82 3
Shipley, Franklin N 120 1
Shipley, Frederick 150 2
Shipley, G W 200 1
Shipley, G William 12, 58 3
Shipley, G William 65 1
Shipley, Geo E 129 3
Shipley, Geo H 177 2
Shipley, Geo W 210 1
Shipley, George E 27 3
Shipley, George E 271 2
Shipley, George W 68 3
Shipley, Grant J 28 3
Shipley, Harry F 33 3
Shipley, Harry F 3, 16 2
Shipley, Henry 31 3
Shipley, Howell 51, 247 2
Shipley, Ida R 10 3
Shipley, Isaac 35 3
Shipley, J O S 9 3
Shipley, J W 187 3
Shipley, Jessie P 28 3
Shipley, John H 209 2
Shipley, L H 123 1
Shipley, Laura V 50 3
Shipley, Lewis H 247 2
Shipley, M Mae 58, 82 3
Shipley, Mahala 8 2
Shipley, Margaret 53 3
Shipley, Mary C 33 3
Shipley, Mary Simmons 60 3
Shipley, N O 1 3
Shipley, N O 177 1
Shipley, Nicholas H 186 2
Shipley, Nimrod O 75 3
Shipley, Osko 50 3
Shipley, Otto R 10 3
Shipley, Rachael 67 3
Shipley, Robert L 68 3
Shipley, Roy L 68 3
Shipley, Thomas C 43, 231 2
Shipley, Thomas C 253 1
Shipley, Thomas C 67, 75 3
Shipley, Thos 163 3
Shipley, Thos 183 1
Shipley, Thos 186 2
Shipley, Thos C 43 2
Shipley, William G 81 3
Shipley, William H 82 3
Shipley, Wm H 14 1
Shipley,Henen M 27 3
Shipp, Mathias 53 3
Shipton, Prudence E 64 3
Shiver, Clarissa 9 3
Shiver, Cornelius 9 3
Shiver, Michael 9 3
Shivers, George W 27 3
Shivers, John 41 3
Shivers, Susan 27, 72 3
Shockey, Mary J 231 2
Shoemaker, A 32 1
Shoemaker, A R 210 3
Shoemaker, Christian 8 3
Shoemaker, Christina 8 3
Shoemaker, Daniel 56, 271 1
Shoemaker, Daniel 8, 14, 15, 70
3
Shoemaker, Daniel 157, 250
2
Shoemaker, Daniel W 41, 65 3
Shoemaker, Daniel W 65 3
Shoemaker, Danuel 15 3
Shoemaker, David S 15 3
Shoemaker, Dennis 18 3
Shoemaker, Earl 224 3
Shoemaker, Elizabeth 18, 57, 60, 81
3
Shoemaker, Geo W 243 1
Shoemaker, Geo W 15 3
Shoemaker, George 26 3
Shoemaker, Harry C 33 3
Shoemaker, Henry 31 3
Shoemaker, Henry 46 2
Shoemaker, Henry R 189 3
Shoemaker, Jacob 38, 41 3
Shoemaker, Jacob 282 2
Shoemaker, John 8, 39 3
Shoemaker, John W 26, 39 3
Shoemaker, Joss 15 3
Shoemaker, Lotta M 83 3
Shoemaker, Magdalena 53 3
Shoemaker, Margaret 41, 54 3
Shoemaker, Mary 54 3
Shoemaker, Mary M 54 3
Shoemaker, Minnie R 33 3
Shoemaker, N 78 1
Shoemaker, Nicholas 60 3
Shoemaker, Nicholas 57 3
Shoemaker, Otho J 62 3
Shoemaker, Q G 196 1
Shoemaker, Robert G 65 3
Shoemaker, Russell W 140 2
Shoemaker, Sarah Helen 73 3
Shoemaker, Susannah 70 3
Shoemaker, Thos I 15 3
Shoemaker, Walter W 83 3
Shoemaker, William 81 3
Shoemaker, William L 83 3
Shoemaker, Wm 239, 244, 265 1
Shoemaker, Wm 54, 83 3
Shoemaner, William 38 3
Shoemanker, Robert G 54 3

Shoff, Abraham 64 3
Shoffner, Jacob 184 3
Sholl, Elias 202 3
Sholl, John 202 3
Sholl, Stephen 70 3
Shook, Ann R 1, 71 3
Shook, Barbara A 27 3
Shook, Daniel 15, 26 3
Shook, Daniel 71 1
Shook, Daniel H 71 3
Shook, Denver J 189 1
Shook, Edward 20 3
Shook, Frank C 33 3
Shook, Frank C 28 1
Shook, G S 71 3
Shook, Georgetta 27, 43 3
Shook, Grandison G 15, 27 3
Shook, Granison G 27 3
Shook, Harriet A 33 3
Shook, Helen M 237 1
Shook, Henry 71 1
Shook, Henry 18, 27 3
Shook, Henry 14 2
Shook, Jacob Daniel 45 3
Shook, Jacob J 41 3
Shook, John H 43 3
Shook, Lewis H 14 2
Shook, Samuel D 71 3
Shook, Susan C 72 3
Shook, Susannah 71 3
Shook, William A 20 3
Shook, William T 83 3
Shope, C B 54 3
Shope, Charles B 10 3
Shope, Edwin I 32, 50, 56 3
Shope, Ernest R 19 3
Shope, Horace A 32 3
Shope, Marie L 56 3
Shoppe, Edwin I 10 3
Shorb, Aaron N 2 3
Shorb, Albert J 46 3
Shorb, Augustine 2 3
Shorb, Charles A 9 3
Shorb, Charles Edw 83 3
Shorb, E Lee 86 1
Shorb, Elizabeth 81 3
Shorb, Ethel E 46 3
Shorb, Frances A 58 3
Shorb, Geo W 56 3
Shorb, George W 2 3
Shorb, Helen M 58 3
Shorb, J 164 1
Shorb, J A 57 2
Shorb, Jacob 87 3
Shorb, Jacob 38 3
Shorb, James 137 2
Shorb, James 165, 228 1
Shorb, James A 67 1
Shorb, James A 18, 40 3
Shorb, James A 258, 282 2
Shorb, Jessie 206 3
Shorb, John 209 3
Shorb, John 84, 278 1
Shorb, Joseph Edward 46 3
Shorb, Joseph L 9, 46 3
Shorb, Joshiah 203 3
Shorb, Joshua 7, 177 2
Shorb, Joshua 19 1
Shorb, Joshua & 214 2
Shorb, Margaret 54 3
Shorb, Maria 57 3
Shorb, Mary 56 3
Shorb, Mary Genevieve 58 3
Shorb, Mattie V 58 3
Shorb, Peter 65 3
Shorb, Rose 65 3
Shorb, Susan C 2, 72 3
Shorb, William 81 3
Shorb, William J 83 3
Shorb, Wm 156 1
Short, Anne E 72 3
Short, John 116, 144 2
Short, John 175 1
Short, Joshua 58 1
Short, Sarah Eyler 72 3
Shorter, Francis 23 3
Shorter, Robert 68 3
Shorter, Roy H 68 3
Shortz, Elizabeth 19 3
Shote, Geo B 191 1
Shott, Jacob 64 3
Shotts, Henry 31, 38 3
Shotts, Jacob 37 3
Shotts, John 38 3
Shotts, Philip 64 3
Shoup, Elizabeth 18 3
Shourb, James 27 2
Shover Peter 64 3
Shover, Jacob 1, 27 2
Shover, Magdelina 53 3
Shover, Reuben 124 2
Shover, Sophia 70 3
Show, Henry 32 3
Showe, Rosalie 196 2
Showen, David 100 2
Shower, Sarah A 72 3
Showl, Stephen 70 3
Showman, H B 166 3
Showman, H B 58 2
Showman, J B 165 1
Shreeve, Jesse 183 1
Shreiner, Edward D Jr 20 3
Shrew, Levi 263 1
Shrew, Wm 263 1
Shriner, Abraham H 1 3
Shriner, Alice E 27 3
Shriner, Amanda S S 3 3
Shriner, Anna and Cornelius 3
3
Shriner, Anthony 1 3
Shriner, Basil 6 3
Shriner, Bruce I 24 3
Shriner, Carl L 3, 24 3
Shriner, Chas 185 3
Shriner, Cornelius 8, 53, 185
3
Shriner, Cornelius 57 1
Shriner, Cornelius 154 2
Shriner, Cornelius H 8 3
Shriner, E A 15, 55, 82 3
Shriner, E D 55 3
Shriner, E H 125 1
Shriner, Ed D 56 3
Shriner, Edw 81 3
Shriner, Edw 13 1
Shriner, Edw A 153 1
Shriner, Edw A 51 2
Shriner, Edw D 51 2
Shriner, Edw D Jr 119, 172
1
Shriner, Edward A 1, 8 3
Shriner, Edward A 276 2
Shriner, Edward D 20 3
Shriner, Edward S 170 2
Shriner, Ezra W 274 2
Shriner, F Earle 131 2
Shriner, Fannie M 24 3
Shriner, G W 201 1
Shriner, Geo 31, 37 3
Shriner, Geo B 177, 195 2
Shriner, Geo B 64 3
Shriner, Geo W B 55, 205 3
Shriner, George 14, 26, 37 3
Shriner, George 254 2
Shriner, George W B 27 3
Shriner, Henry 14, 26, 37 3
Shriner, Henry Jr 64 3
Shriner, Henry Sr 31 3
Shriner, Jacob 8 3
Shriner, Jacob 264 2
Shriner, Joanna 31 3
Shriner, M 179 1
Shriner, Mary 56 3
Shriner, Mary C 27 3
Shriner, Mary P 55 3
Shriner, Maurice E 3 3
Shriner, Micahel [sic] 110 1
Shriner, Michael 53 3
Shriner, Michael 93, 228a, 254, 275
2
Shriner, Michael 171 1
Shriner, Nannie 172 1
Shriner, Nannie G 20, 56 3
Shriner, Nannie G 144 1
Shriner, Peter 64 3
Shriner, Peter 254 2
Shriner, Philip 64 3

Shriner, Rosa B 145 2
Shriner, Rowe A 67 3
Shriner, Sarah 280 1
Shriner, Thelma W 145 2
Shriner, Thelma Walden 131 2
Shriver, A 26 1
Shriver, Abraham 1 3
Shriver, Andred 14 3
Shriver, Benjamin 57, 60 3
Shriver, Charles 8, 14 3
Shriver, Chas 27, 96 2
Shriver, Chas 39, 53 3
Shriver, Chas C 50 3
Shriver, Clifford W 11 3
Shriver, Cornelius 150 2
Shriver, David 44 1
Shriver, David 14 3
Shriver, David Sr 15 3
Shriver, E A 54 3
Shriver, E F 265 2
Shriver, E F Mrs 226 3
Shriver, Ed 8, 199 3
Shriver, Edw 14, 22, 27, 100 2
Shriver, Edw 41, 67, 117, 179, 190
or, 201, 223, 260, 264, 271, 282 1
Shriver, Edw 67, 81, 96, 129 3
Shriver, Edward 258, 275, 287 2
Shriver, Edward 91 1
Shriver, Edward 1, 156, 207 3
Shriver, Eleanor 20 3
Shriver, Ella M 67 3
Shriver, Ernest R 11 3
Shriver, Eve Barbara 18 3
Shriver, G J 50 3
Shriver, Geo B 44 1
Shriver, Geo J 24 1
Shriver, Harriett M 11 3
Shriver, Henry 32 3
Shriver, Isaac 139 3
Shriver, Isaac 25, 125, 217 1
Shriver, Jacob 183 1
Shriver, Jacob 258 2
Shriver, James A 67 1
Shriver, John 57, 60 3
Shriver, John H 50 3
Shriver, Lewis 50 3
Shriver, Lewis P 83, 271 2
Shriver, Lewis P 50 3
Shriver, Louisa E 50 3
Shriver, Margaret E 57 3
Shriver, Michael 57 2
Shriver, Naomi N 125 1
Shriver, Nathanial 60 3
Shriver, Nathaniel 57 3
Shriver, Norman J 11 3
Shriver, Olina 67 1
Shriver, Peter 163 1
Shriver, Thomas 70, 75 3
Shriver, William 214 3
Shriver, William E 81 3
Shrob, James A 165 2
Shroder, Francis T 23 3
Shroder, Mary J 23 3
Shroeder, Frederick 23 3
Shroeder, H B 181 2
Shroeder, John 38 3
Shroeder, John 37 3
Shroyer, Elizabeth 18 3
Shroyer, George D 28 3
Shroyer, John 159 1
Shroyer, John 106 3
Shroyer, Lawson 40 3
Shry, Charles A 10 3
Shry, Charles W 33 3
Shry, Effie C 79 3
Shry, Ernest 10 3
Shry, Florence F 45 3
Shry, Helen T 10, 33 3
Shry, J Atlee 33 3
Shry, Jas E 79 3
Shry, John W 45 3
Shry, Verina 79 3
Shry, Vernia A 79 3
Shryock, Christian 8 3
Shryock, Christina 8 3
Shryock, Florence R 24 3
Shryock, Grayson E 24, 83 3
Shryock, Jacob D 34 1
Shryock, Valentine 8, 79 3
Shryock, William H 83 3
Shuck, Julia A 41 2
Shuff, Adelaide G 2 3
Shuff, Albert 72 3
Shuff, B L 161 3
Shuff, Bej 212a 2
Shuff, Ben L 255 2
Shuff, Benj 227a 2
Shuff, Benj L 18 2
Shuff, Benjamin L 41, 72, 108,
265, 284 2
Shuff, Benjamin L 73, 82, 114
3
Shuff, Benjamin L 116, 245, 254
1
Shuff, Charles E 58 3
Shuff, Laura M 51 3
Shuff, Lauretta G 74 1
Shuff, Luretta G 79 1
Shuff, M F 161 3
Shuff, M F 18, 260 1
Shuff, M F 40 2
Shuff, M F Jr 19, 186, 203, 254, 280
1
Shuff, M F Sr 57 3
Shuff, M T 82 3
Shuff, Mary Julia 254 1
Shuff, Millard F 265 1
Shuff, Millard F 173, 178, 283 2
Shuff, Millard F 24, 51 3
Shuff, Minnie V 58 3
Shuff, Rebecca 82 3
Shuff, Ruth 51 3
Shuff, Sarah Ann Rebecca 72 3
Shuff, William 82 3
Shuff, William H 82 3
Shuff, Williard 144 2
Shuffler, Barbara 9 3
Shuffler, Charles 9 3
Shuffler, George T M 28 3
Shuh, Elizabeth 18 3
Shull, C J 83 3
Shull, Rosa V 83 3
Shultz, Charles W 57 3
Shultz, David 14, 37 3
Shultz, Davil 14 3
Shultz, Edward 31 3
Shultz, Ferdinand 23 3
Shultz, George 26, 27 3
Shultz, John 37 3
Shultz, Joseph 37 3
Shultz, Joseph C 40, 41 3
Shultz, Maggie H 57 3
Shultz, Sarah B 73 3
Shultz, Sophie K 75 3
Shultz, Theodore 75 3
Shumaker, Daniel 196 1
Shumaker, John Sr 38 3
Shumaker, Otho J 250 1
Shumpstine, Frederick 134 3
Shunk, Fanny 23 3
Shunk, Joseph 64 3
Shupp, Henry 56 1
Shupp, Henry 53 3
Shupp, Mathias 53 3
Shutt, Adam 1 3
Shutt, John 39 3
Shutt, John H 64 3
Shutt, Peter 1, 39, 64 3
Shutt, Samuel 39 3
Shylock, Valentine 275 2
Shylock, Wilson 57 2
Shyrock, Christian 8 3
Shyrock, Henry 8 3
Shyrock, Jacob D 8, 38 3
Sias, John 39 3
Sibley, Ann 75 3
Sibley, Thomas 75 3
Sidwell, Henry 171 1
Sidwell, Reuben 67 3
Sidwell, Sarah A 67 3
Sidwell, Thomas W 75 3
Siebert, Caroline 67 3
Siedling Johanna 27 3
Siedling, Annie M 2, 27 3
Siedling, George 27 3
Siedling, George F C 27 3
Siedling, Johanna C 43 3

Siedling, Julia H F 43 3
Sier, Charles E 12 3
Sier, Claude 11 3
Sier, Joseph B 45 3
Sier, Nettie B 11 3
Sier, Sarah L 73 3
Sies, John 184 3
Siess, A Scott 165 1
Siess, Benjamin 189 1
Siess, Daniel 26 3
Siess, Daniel 25 2
Siess, George 26 3
Siess, Godfrey 26 3
Siess, John 26, 54 3
Siess, Maria 54 3
Siess, Paul 64 3
Siever, Elizabeth 18 3
Siffer, John 13 1
Sifford, A J 41 3
Sifford, Annie J 138 2
Sifford, C A 9 2
Sifford, Christian 13, 84, 125, 277 1
Sifford, Christian 111 2
Sifford, Elizabeth D T 57 3
Sifford, J E 41 3
Sifford, John 11, 19, 46, 49, 69, 107, 119, 129, 203, 237, 250, 262 2
Sifford, John 51, 57, 112, 117, 131, 203 1
Sifford, John 41, 42, 128, 165, 202, 208, 209, 217, 218 3
Sifford, John E 112 1
Sifford, Mary Z 57 3
Sifton, Martin F 79 1
Sifton, William 254 2
Sigafoos, Benjamin F 6 3
Sigafoos, Carroll H 6 3
Sigafoose, Armstead H 82 3
Sigafoose, Chas H 283 2
Sigafoose, Julia A 45 3
Sigafoose, L 223 1
Sigafoose, L E 107, 166, 197 3
Sigafoose, L E 210 1
Sigafoose, Lawrence 45 3
Sigafoose, M W 166 3
Sigafoose, N W 197 3
Sigifoose, William S 82 3
Sigler, Alice T 191 2
Sigler, Aller Louise 46 3
Sigler, Amanda E 2, 82 3
Sigler, Caroline F 36 2
Sigler, Charles S 2, 11 3
Sigler, Clarence M 20 3
Sigler, Daniel 15, 71, 82 3
Sigler, Daniel 19 1
Sigler, Elizabeth 15, 20 3
Sigler, Geneva F 27 3
Sigler, Geo 19 1
Sigler, George 31 3
Sigler, Harry L 73 3
Sigler, Henry 9, 31, 39 3
Sigler, J J 72 3
Sigler, J L 27 3
Sigler, Jacob 128 2
Sigler, Jacob 41 3
Sigler, John 214 1
Sigler, John 39, 201 3
Sigler, John H 45 3
Sigler, John J 46 3
Sigler, John L 144 2
Sigler, John L 205 3
Sigler, John M 45 3
Sigler, John M 238 2
Sigler, John R 48 1
Sigler, John W 11 3
Sigler, Lloyd 27, 50 3
Sigler, Martha C 72 3
Sigler, Mollie 62 3
Sigler, Oliver C 38 1
Sigler, Oliver C 62 3
Sigler, Samuel C 72, 73 3
Sigler, Sarah 71 3
Sigler, William H 2, 82 3
Sigmund, Godliep 240 1
Sigmund, Gotleib 24 1
Sigmund, Gottliep J 217 1
Silance, James H 42 3
Silance, James W 44 3
Silbey, Jane 32 3
Silby, John 24 3
Silcox, Sarah B 272 1
Silkirk, Mae 82 3
Silkirk, William E 82 3
Silvey, Hugh 31 3
Sim, J T 224 2
Sim, J Thomas 43 3
Sim, Mary W 43, 56 3
Simmers, John J 58 3
Simmers, Minerva V 58 3
Simmons, A H 40 1
Simmons, A Howard 1, 39 3
Simmons, A Howard 171 2
Simmons, Abraham H 185 3
Simmons, Albert 1 3
Simmons, Albert H 19 3
Simmons, Ann E 42 3
Simmons, Baker 237 2
Simmons, Baker 31 3
Simmons, Baker H 242 2
Simmons, Blanche W 6 3
Simmons, C F 147 2
Simmons, Charles 14 3
Simmons, Charles E 9, 11 3
Simmons, Charles S 9, 71 3
Simmons, Chas S 67 3
Simmons, Chester J 192 3
Simmons, Edmund 20 3
Simmons, Effie H 19 3
Simmons, Eleanor P 70 3
Simmons, Eliza P 20 3
Simmons, Elizabeth 1, 21, 44 3
Simmons, Elizabeth A 19 3
Simmons, Elizabeth G 9 3
Simmons, Emory 18 2
Simmons, Florence E 113 3
Simmons, Frances H 221a 2
Simmons, Georgiana 15 2
Simmons, Georgiana 27 3
Simmons, H Emery 67 3
Simmons, Harry S 33 3
Simmons, Horace C 41 3
Simmons, I E 71 1
Simmons, J Lee 60 3
Simmons, James 38, 39, 212 3
Simmons, James 13 1
Simmons, James 249 2
Simmons, James 242 2
Simmons, James E 19 3
Simmons, James F 67 3
Simmons, James H 42 3
Simmons, James L 42 3
Simmons, James L C 46 3
Simmons, James S 152, 257 1
Simmons, James S 39, 40, 42, 67, 71 3
Simmons, James W 40 3
Simmons, Jas H 111 3
Simmons, Jesse 41 3
Simmons, John 38, 40, 41, 113 3
Simmons, John 71, 234, 253 1
Simmons, John 5, 15, 19, 69, 72, 76, 80, 93, 119, 147, 205, 229a 2
Simmons, John A 9, 41, 67 3
Simmons, John A 1, 5, 101, 119, 144, 250, 249 2
Simmons, John A 96, 119 1
Simmons, John E H 38, 39, 75 3
Simmons, John E H 257 1
Simmons, John F 44 1
Simmons, John H 58, 162 1
Simmons, John H 11 2
Simmons, John H 39, 67, 94 3
Simmons, John S 40 3
Simmons, Lewis 63 1
Simmons, Louis 8 2
Simmons, Martha E 20, 58 3
Simmons, Martha M 9, 55 3
Simmons, Mary A 41, 55 3
Simmons, Mary B 67 3
Simmons, Mary Ellen 195 1
Simmons, Mary M 54 3

Simmons, Mary P 56 3
Simmons, Minerva V 33 3
Simmons, Nanny W 60 3
Simmons, R E 229 1
Simmons, R E 150, 237 2
Simmons, R E 71 3
Simmons, R Emory 67 3
Simmons, Richard E 60, 67 3
Simmons, Richard F 11, 21 3
Simmons, Richard F 96 1
Simmons, Robert H 58 3
Simmons, Ruth C 46 3
Simmons, S C 144, 280 1
Simmons, S C 54 3
Simmons, S C 7, 19, 72, 2
Simmons, S F 177 1
Simmons, Samuel T 52, 60 1
Simmons, Samuel T 40 3
Simmons, Serena 71 3
Simmons, Simon C 71 3
Simmons, Sophia 57, 60 3
Simmons, Sophie 71 3
Simmons, Susan E 67 3
Simmons, Susannah 70 3
Simmons, T O 96 1
Simmons, Theresa 67 3
Simmons, W W D 116 2
Simmons, Wm 5, 78 2
Simmons, Wm A 15 2
Simmons, Wm A 195 1
Simmons, Wm H D 83 3
Simms, Alexious 1 3
Simms, Andrew T 3 3
Simms, Henry 79 1
Simms, Joseph 1 3
Simms, Mable V 3 3
Simms, Martha 54 3
Simon, Susannah 70 3
Simons, Walter M 83 3
Simpson, Anna Florence 4 3
Simpson, Anne 1 3
Simpson, Basil J F 125 1
Simpson, Catey 8 3
Simpson, Charles 8 3
Simpson, Charles B 9 3
Simpson, Charles R 59 1
Simpson, Chas 70, 167 3
Simpson, Chas B 59 1
Simpson, Chas B 276 2
Simpson, Delilah 14 3
Simpson, F Loraine 68 3
Simpson, F Loraine 58 2
Simpson, F Lorraine 225 1
Simpson, Geo B 50 3
Simpson, James C 43 3
Simpson, Joanna 40, 67 3
Simpson, John 40 3
Simpson, Lea M 4 3
Simpson, Lorain 184 1
Simpson, Mabel V 67 3
Simpson, Maggie R 83 3
Simpson, Mary 9 3
Simpson, Matilda 53 3
Simpson, Myra L 43 3
Simpson, Nancy 57, 60 3
Simpson, Nettie E 224a 2
Simpson, R W 75 3
Simpson, Rachael 67 3
Simpson, Rachael V 68, 75 3
Simpson, Reizin R 67 3
Simpson, Rezin 53, 167 3
Simpson, Richard 64, 67 3
Simpson, Richard E 57 3
Simpson, Richard W 67 3
Simpson, Robert L 67 3
Simpson, Sophie 70 3
Simpson, Thomas W 75, 79 3
Simpson, Thomas W 96 1
Simpson, Thomas W & 207 3
Simpson, Thos A 83 3
Simpson, Thos W 67, 81 3
Simpson, Thos W Dr 72 2
Simpson, Virginia 79 3
Simpson, W M 9 3
Simpson, Walter A 4 3
Simpson, Warfield 70, 81, 207 3
Simpson, William 81 3
Simund, Andrew 196 1
Sin, J Thomas 21 1
Sin, Thomas 96 1
Sin, Thos 47 1
Sine, Charles W 11 3
Sine, Ethel V 208 1
Sine, Ethel V 11 3
Singafoose, Ann 195 3
Singer, Charlotte A 40 3
Singer, Eve 37 3
Singer, Frederick 31 3
Singer, Hannah 31 3
Singer, Jacob 37, 70 3
Singer, John 31, 40 3
Singer, Samuel 70 3
Singer, Samuel 40 1
Sink, George 26 3
Sink, John 37 3
Sink, Joseph 37 3
Sink, Peggy 37 3
Sink, Rosannah 37 3
Sinn, C E 19 3
Sinn, C Edw 142, 149 2
Sinn, Catherine 9 3
Sinn, Edw 29, 54, 80, 124, 142, 149 2
Sinn, Edward 19, 42 3
Sinn, J T 54 2
Sinn, J Thomas 218, 213a 2
Sinn, J Thomas 2, 43, 65 3
Sinn, J Thos 257 1
Sinn, Jacob O 65 3
Sinn, John 159 2
Sinn, John R 112 1
Sinn, John T 29, 283 2
Sinn, John T 9, 42, 111, 137, 160 3
Sinn, Lucy Ann 75 3
Sinn, Mary A 56 3
Sinn, Mary E 96, 284 2
Sinn, Nyra E 284 2
Sinn, Pamelia F 65 3
Sinn, Thomas 79 1
Sinn, Thomas 26, 38, 39, 75, 81, 152 3
Sinn, W E 21 1
Sinn, Walter E 16, 161, 191, 242, 284 2
Sinn, Walter E 49, 86, 90, 101, 192, 127, 250 1
Sinn, Walter E 12, 35, 107, 174, 210 3
Sins, Thomas 63 2
Sipes, Henry A 32 3
Sipes, Jane A 32, 44 3
Six, Beatrice R 11 3
Six, Benj A 77 3
Six, Bertha M 97 1
Six, C A 48 1
Six, Charles A 11 3
Six, Chas A 20 2
Six, Ewd 139 1
Six, George 125 1
Six, Henry 14 3
Six, James G 77 3
Six, John 41 3
Six, John of Philip 64 3
Six, Leonard 50, 184 3
Six, Philip 64 3
Six, Philip 144 1
Six, Sarah Ann 41 3
Six, Uriah 41, 77 3
Skaggs, Laura F 51 3
Skaggs, Leonard 50 3
Skeggs, Henry 47 1
Skeggs, Henry E 51 3
Skifes, John 26 2
Skiles, Hopkins 50 3
Skiles, Letitia 50 3
Skinner, Avis C 45 3
Skinner, Avis C 172 2
Skinner, Charles M 10 3
Skinner, Charlotte M 10 3
Skinner, Henry S 171 3
Skinner, James W 45 3
Skunk, John 53 3
Slabaugh, Michael 38 2
Slack, Cornelius 14, 39 3
Slack, John 39 3

Slagel, Daniel L 16 3
Slagel, Laura H 16 3
Slagen, Katharyn M 178 2
Slagen, Norman A 177 1
Slagle, Annie C 82 3
Slagle, Annie M 3, 43 3
Slagle, C 19 1
Slagle, Charles 1 1
Slagle, Charles 8 3
Slagle, Daniel 27 3
Slagle, Daniel L 50, 57 3
Slagle, Eli 265 2
Slagle, Eli K 20 3
Slagle, Elizabeth 82 3
Slagle, Frederick 23 3
Slagle, George 31 3
Slagle, George C 51 3
Slagle, George W 27 3
Slagle, Henry 31 3
Slagle, James A 43 3
Slagle, John 129 2
Slagle, Laura E 58 3
Slagle, Laura H 51 3
Slagle, Mahlon L Sr 58 3
Slagle, Margaret G 73 1
Slagle, Mary C 55 3
Slagle, Mary M 57 3
Slagle, Samuel S 58 3
Slagle, W 82 3
Slagle, William 64, 82 3
Slagle, William J 20, 82 3
Slater, James E 45 3
Slater, Samuel H 20 3
Slater, Susan 45 3
Slatter, Emma V 20 3
Slaybaugh, Solomon 71 3
Slaymaker, Alexander 240 1
Slegle, Peter 19 2
Slemmer, Martha Kemp 87 2
Slemmer, William 74 1
Slemmer, Wm R 87 2
Sliance, J Vernon 42 3
Slick, A 156 3
Slick, Abednego 28 2
Slick, Carrie P 12 3
Slick, Jacob 37 3
Slick, John 37 3
Slick, Peter 37 3
Slifer, Amanda E 2 3
Slifer, Annie 171 2
Slifer, Arba L 3 3
Slifer, Asemeth 1 3
Slifer, Catherine 8, 28 3
Slifer, Charles E 9 3
Slifer, Chas E 23 1
Slifer, E 57 1
Slifer, Edna M 75 3
Slifer, Eliza A 55 3
Slifer, Emanuel 79, 88, 233 1
Slifer, Emanuel 8, 19, 40 3
Slifer, Emanuel 22, 100, 271 2
Slifer, Emmanuel 13 1
Slifer, Etta O 42 3
Slifer, Ettie O 65 3
Slifer, Ezra 8, 19, 38, 39, 40, 205 3
Slifer, Ezra 22, 26, 88, 248, 264, 271 1
Slifer, Ezra 258 2
Slifer, Francis T 23 3
Slifer, Frank 9 3
Slifer, George G 8 1
Slifer, George W 28 3
Slifer, Jacob 1, 64 3
Slifer, Jacob 13, 25, 51, 244 1
Slifer, John 1, 39, 40, 44, 64 3
Slifer, John 6 1
Slifer, John E 101 2
Slifer, John H M 42 3
Slifer, John M 65 3
Slifer, John Sr 37, 38 3
Slifer, Joshua 171 2
Slifer, Mary M 196 2
Slifer, Mary M 3 3
Slifer, Maud L 23 3
Slifer, Maurice 230 1
Slifer, Milton 40 2
Slifer, Milton B 9 3
Slifer, Milton V 55 3
Slifer, Otho J 13 1
Slifer, Peter 8, 38, 214, 228 1
Slifer, Peter 37, 64, 65 3
Slifer, S 54 3
Slifer, Samuel 64, 70, 81, 202 3
Slifer, Samuel 208 2
Slifer, Samuel 13, 229, 244 1
Slifer, Samuel T 2 3
Slifer, Samuel T 197 1
Slifer, T S 154 2
Slifer, Thomas A 75 3
Slifer, William 81 3
Slifer, Wm 217 1
Slifer, Wm 81 3
Slifer, Wm 128 2
Sliger, Milton B 19 3
Slingluff, Alverta 137 1
Slingluff, Charles the 38 3
Slingluff, Jesse 137 3
Slingluff, Jesse W 38 3
Slingluff, Louis P 137 1
Sliver, Ezra 19 1
Sloan, James 33 1
Slothower, John D 70 3
Slothower, Magdalene 54 3
Slothower, Stephen 70 3
Slowther, George 106 3
Sluckenbier, Peter 84 1
Slusher, Geo 14 2
Sluss, Andrew 1 3
Sluss, John 57, 276 2
Sluss, John 40 1
Sluss, John 42, 54, 148 3
Sluss, John 276 2
Sluss, Michael 19, 38, 111, 150, 223a, 225a, 268, 271, 275, 276, 282, 294 2
Sluss, Michael 54 3
Sluss, Michael 110, 139, 228, 243 1
Slyder, John 210 1
Small, William 81 3
Smallwood, Hanson 249 1
Smallwood, John W 75 3
Smallwood, Joseph R 46 3
Smallwood, Maggie R 46 3
Smallwood, Margaret R 58 3
Smallwood, Sallie 249 1
Smallwood, Thomas H 75 3
Smay, John 37 3
Smelser, Clara 212a 2
Smelser, Michael 116 1
Smeltser, John 234 2
Smeltz, Margaret 54 3
Smeltzer, Charles A 10 3
Smeltzer, Daniel 14 3
Smeltzer, Daniel B 14 3
Smeltzer, David 53 3
Smeltzer, Franklin D 82 3
Smeltzer, Henry 31, 106 3
Smeltzer, Henry R 196, 201 1
Smeltzer, Henry R 271 2
Smeltzer, Henry Sr 271 2
Smeltzer, James 2 3
Smeltzer, John 46 2
Smeltzer, John 116 1
Smeltzer, Mary 53 3
Smeltzer, Michael 53 3
Smeltzer, Sarah A 71 3
Smeltzer, William H 82 3
Smiley, Alberta M 46 3
Smiley, John W 46 3
Smith Edw J 28 1
Smith, A E 51 2
Smith, A Leonard 3 3
Smith, A Margaret Ann 2 3
Smith, Absalom 71 3
Smith, Absalom 2, 71 3
Smith, Ada 44 3
Smith, Ada V 254 1
Smith, Adam 1, 8, 23, 37, 64, 165, 184 3
Smith, Adam 100 1
Smith, Albert 2 3
Smith, Albert C 2, 55 3
Smith, Albert M 65 3
Smith, Albert R 83 3
Smith, Albert S 10 3

Smith, Alexious E 2, 179 3
Smith, Alfred 42 3
Smith, Alice C 24, 58 3
Smith, Alice M 3 3
Smith, Alice McP 3 3
Smith, Alice V 3, 4 3
Smith, Allen R 14 1
Smith, Alvy J 9 3
Smith, Andrew 1, 26 3
Smith, Andrew H 3 3
Smith, Ann 195 2
Smith, Ann 1 3
Smith, Ann L 33 3
Smith, Ann M 38 3
Smith, Ann R 3 3
Smith, Ann Rebecca 2 3
Smith, Anna Belle 3 3
Smith, Anna K 45 3
Smith, Anna Mary 28 3
Smith, Annie 82 3
Smith, Annie E 20 3
Smith, Annie G 3 3
Smith, Annie M 23 3
Smith, Annie R 126 1
Smith, Anthony 71 3
Smith, Arlene E 11 3
Smith, Aubrey J 3 3
Smith, Audrey 44 3
Smith, Avie C 12 3
Smith, B V 153 1
Smith, Barbara A 49 1
Smith, Barbara M 6 3
Smith, Basil 31 3
Smith, Benj 62 2
Smith, Benj 37, 38, 67 3
Smith, Benjamin 129 2
Smith, Benjamin 6 3
Smith, Benjamin F 6 3
Smith, C C 60, 278 1
Smith, C F 31 2
Smith, C H 153 1
Smith, C L 265 1
Smith, C P 100 3
Smith, C S 150 1
Smith, C T 188 3
Smith, Calvin 41 3
Smith, Calvin H 12 3
Smith, Calvin P 10 3
Smith, Carrie May 12 3
Smith, Carrie R 11 3
Smith, Carroll L 12 2
Smith, Catharine 8, 9, 26 3
Smith, Catherine W 58 3
Smith, Charles 217a 2
Smith, Charles 8, 9, 14, 75 3
Smith, Charles C 9, 10, 43, 55 3
Smith, Charles C 242 2
Smith, Charles D 6 3
Smith, Charles Dr 9 3
Smith, Charles E 9, 27, 67 3
Smith, Charles F 57 3
Smith, Charles G 9 3
Smith, Charles Hammond 35 3
Smith, Charles J 10 3
Smith, Charles J 224a 2
Smith, Charles L 9 3
Smith, Charles M 10, 56 3
Smith, Charles M 190 2
Smith, Charles M Sr 124 1
Smith, Charles Munroe 11 3
Smith, Charles W 11, 28, 44 3
Smith, Charles W 23 2
Smith, Charlotte 8 3
Smith, Charlotte P 27, 24, 148, 16 1
Smith, Charlotte P 196, 227, 260, 286 2
Smith, Charlotte P 58, 169 3
Smith, Charlotte P ' [sic] 92 1
Smith, Charolette 207 3
Smith, Chas 19, 51, 154 2
Smith, Chas 49, 271 1
Smith, Chas 41 3
Smith, Chas C 15, 54 3
Smith, Chas E 42, 81 3
Smith, Chas F Jr 16 2
Smith, Chas H 240 1
Smith, Chas H 82 3
Smith, Chas J 14 1
Smith, Chas J 51 3
Smith, Chas W 67, 72, 97 1
Smith, Chas W 65 3
Smith, Christian 76, 107, 115, 169 1
Smith, Christian 8, 9, 10, 18, 67, 89, 188 3
Smith, Christian 2, 11, 14, 15, 27 2
Smith, Christopher P 10 3
Smith, Chritopher 96 3
Smith, Clara Alice 11 3
Smith, Clara J 9, 44 3
Smith, Clara V 56, 83 3
Smith, Clarence E 56, 72 3
Smith, Clarence J 10 3
Smith, Claude R 51 3
Smith, Clement F 10 3
Smith, Clifford Alvey 12 3
Smith, Clifford S 10 3
Smith, Clifton E 71 1
Smith, Clinton E 28 3
Smith, Clyde W 83 3
Smith, Conrad 188 2
Smith, Cornelia V 41 3
Smith, Corrilla H 39 3
Smith, Corvilla H 9 3
Smith, Cyrus F 10, 27 3
Smith, D Sidney T 9, 233 1
Smith, D Sydney 55 3
Smith, Daisy F 16 3
Smith, Daniel 65 2
Smith, Daniel 14, 15, 39 3
Smith, Daniel 37, 71, 82, 204, 205, 225 1
Smith, Daniel E 16 3
Smith, Daniel G 31 3
Smith, Daniel L 14, 32 3
Smith, Daniel of G 32 3
Smith, Daniel of J 19 3
Smith, Daniel P 16, 35 3
Smith, David 191 1
Smith, David 8, 14 3
Smith, David J 67 1
Smith, David S K 55 3
Smith, Debbie 16 3
Smith, Della V 30 2
Smith, Donald L 51 3
Smith, Donald R 15 3
Smith, Drucilla 139 1
Smith, Drusilla 6 3
Smith, E J 2, 125, 227a 2
Smith, E J 162 1
Smith, E L. 19 1
Smith, E T 3 3
Smith, Earl E 20 3
Smith, Ed J 227a, 232 2
Smith, Edgar A 20 3
Smith, Edith J 188 3
Smith, Edw 85 2
Smith, Edw J 76, 80, 106, 113, 129 2
Smith, Edw J 169 3
Smith, Edw J 27, 42, 61, 92, 97, 101, 107, 162, 172, 177, 179, 197, 198, 217 1
Smith, Edward A 44 3
Smith, Edward J 3, 44, 57, 58, 169, 207, 224 3
Smith, Edward J 49, 52, 99, 146, 177, 241 1
Smith, Edward J 85, 167, 196, 227, 260, 262, 286 2
Smith, Eli 19, 54 3
Smith, Eli 264 2
Smith, Elias 124 2
Smith, Elias 19 3
Smith, Elijah 20 3
Smith, Eliza 18 3
Smith, Elizabeth 18, 19, 20, 38, 41 3
Smith, Elizabeth R 10 3
Smith, Ellen 19 3
Smith, Ellen T 19 3
Smith, Ellen V 20 3
Smith, Elmer 82 3
Smith, Elmer 209 2
Smith, Elmer C 46 3
Smith, Elmer J 79 1

Smith, Elmer J 196 3
Smith, Elouise E 11 3
Smith, Elsie M 3 3
Smith, Emanuel 64 3
Smith, Emanuel 186 1
Smith, Emanuel T 19 3
Smith, Emily A M 61 1
Smith, Emily N M 21, 44 3
Smith, Emily N M 42 1
Smith, Emma J 2, 20 3
Smith, Emma L 2, 9 3
Smith, Emory L 107, 137 1
Smith, Emory L 10 3
Smith, Ernest 82 3
Smith, Ernest T 26 1
Smith, Esther J 21 3
Smith, Ezra 78, 214, 224a 2
Smith, Ezra 18, 19, 42, 54, 81, 216 3
Smith, Ezra 51, 118, 126 1
Smith, Ezra M 165 3
Smith, Ezra of J 19, 41 3
Smith, Ezra of J 84 1
Smith, F B 222, 224 2
Smith, F B 224 2
Smith, F F 75 3
Smith, F F Dr 124 2
Smith, F Lester 24, 166 3
Smith, F Lester 178 2
Smith, F O 56 3
Smith, Fannie M 85 2
Smith, Floyd H 58 3
Smith, Frances M 51 3
Smith, Franklin 223 1
Smith, Franklin 166, 247 2
Smith, Franklin B 54 2
Smith, Franklin B 110 1
Smith, Franklin B 9, 23 3
Smith, Franklin E 55 3
Smith, Franklin P 55 3
Smith, Fred A 24 3
Smith, Frederick 100 1
Smith, Frederick 23, 64 3
Smith, Frederick 264 2
Smith, Frederick L 24 3
Smith, Freeda E 56 3
Smith, Frisby L 23 3
Smith, G 32, 41, 54 3
Smith, G Arthur 46 3
Smith, G B 229a 2
Smith, G Baxter 3, 29 3
Smith, G D 139 2
Smith, G E 9 3
Smith, G F 14 1
Smith, G L 67 3
Smith, G T 81 3
Smith, Galen 99 1
Smith, Gaynell Y 217 3
Smith, Genevieve Rose 30 1
Smith, Geo 8, 11, 14, 19, 27, 58, 63, 132, 166, 195, 203, 214, 247 2
Smith, Geo 32, 37, 117, 152, 156, 177, 197, 198, 205, 219, 234, 240, 249, 264, 282 1
Smith, Geo 39, 50, 53, 64, 91, 186 3
Smith, Geo B 120 1
Smith, Geo E 50 3
Smith, Geo F 72 3
Smith, Geo H 119 1
Smith, Geo H 51 3
Smith, Geo L 186 2
Smith, Geo L 72, 223 3
Smith, Geo M 24 1
Smith, Geo W 1, 54 2
Smith, Geo W 41, 47, 72, 79, 172 1
Smith, Geo W 23, 71, 81 3
Smith, Geo Wm 15 2
Smith, Geo Wm 9, 54, 67 3
Smith, Geo Wm 32, 175 1
Smith, George 8, 9, 10, 18, 26, 27, 40, 43, 67, 89 3
Smith, George 58, 76, 169, 197 1
Smith, George (German) 31 3
Smith, George C 28 3
Smith, George D 28 3
Smith, George D 259 2
Smith, George E 27, 28 3
Smith, George E 227a 2
Smith, George F 27 3
Smith, George J 26, 27 3
Smith, George Jr 1, 26 3
Smith, George L 6, 24, 165 3
Smith, George M 41 3
Smith, George of J 26 3
Smith, George of Sol 10 1
Smith, George S 26 3
Smith, George W 26, 28, 43, 165 3
Smith, George William 15 3
Smith, George Wm 27 3
Smith, Georgianna L 27 3
Smith, Gertrude 127 1
Smith, Gertrude K 81 2
Smith, Grace M 35 3
Smith, Grace P 15 3
Smith, Grace Price 28 3
Smith, Granville M 55 3
Smith, Grayson O 21 3
Smith, Grover C 107 2
Smith, Guide A 28 3
Smith, H 31 3
Smith, H Bertha 3 3
Smith, H H 30 2
Smith, H L 82 3
Smith, H M 165 2
Smith, H T 27 3
Smith, Hannah 32, 42 3
Smith, Harmon L 72 3
Smith, Harmon R 136 1
Smith, Harriet 32 3
Smith, Harriet J 6 3
Smith, Harry B 33 3
Smith, Harry G 205 3
Smith, Harry M 58 3
Smith, Harry R 239 1
Smith, Harvey R 75 3
Smith, Hattie P 28 3
Smith, Henry 7, 208 2
Smith, Henry 1, 26, 31, 163 3
Smith, Henry 88 1
Smith, Henry C 32 3
Smith, Henry C 271 2
Smith, Henry G 82 3
Smith, Henry of H 31 3
Smith, Henry W 1 3
Smith, Herman E 33 3
Smith, Hester I Feaga 237 1
Smith, Hiram 195 2
Smith, Hiram 32 3
Smith, Horace 189 2
Smith, Horace H 172 1
Smith, Horace H 58 2
Smith, Horice H 82 3
Smith, Houck 33 3
Smith, Howard L 60 3
Smith, Howard L 25 2
Smith, Howard S 175 1
Smith, Ida E 10 3
Smith, Ida Elizabeth 35 3
Smith, Ida M 43 3
Smith, Ida Mae 82 3
Smith, Ina I 35 3
Smith, Ira 3 3
Smith, Ira O 35 3
Smith, Isiah S 150 1
Smith, J 19, 26, 39, 41, 43, 72, 3
Smith, J Alton 11 3
Smith, J F 176, 220 3
Smith, J F 215 2
Smith, J G 39 2
Smith, J G F 83 3
Smith, J G F et al 215 1
Smith, J H 23, 165 2
Smith, J J 14, 262 2
Smith, J J 8, 23 3
Smith, J M 55 1
Smith, J M 217 3
Smith, J P 82 3
Smith, Jacob 18, 31, 37, 38, 39, 41, 43, 64, 70, 171, 224 3
Smith, Jacob 78, 100, 163, 165, 238 1
Smith, Jacob 268 2
Smith, Jacob B 42 3
Smith, Jacob G 44 3

Smith, Jacob H 41 3
Smith, Jacob of John 223 3
Smith, Jacob of M 42 3
Smith, Jacob T 43 3
Smith, James 37, 39, 44, 64, 124 3
Smith, James 7, 19, 58, 93, 169, 186, 288 2
Smith, James C 32, 45 3
Smith, James H 140 1
Smith, James H 41, 45, 75 3
Smith, James H 189 2
Smith, James M 41, 43 3
Smith, James N 39 3
Smith, James R 41 3
Smith, James T 40, 75 3
Smith, James W 37 1
Smith, James W 19, 44, 58, 65 3
Smith, Jas M 56 3
Smith, Jennie 82 3
Smith, Jennie E 46 3
Smith, John 76, 78, 84, 125, 164, 169, 210, 228, 256 1
Smith, John 7, 27, 93, 100, 137, 138, 144, 220, 219a, 220a, 275, 290 2
Smith, John 31, 37, 38, 39, 41, 42, 53, 70, 120, 213, 223 3
Smith, John (German) 39 3
Smith, John A 88 1
Smith, John A 41, 199 3
Smith, John D 43, 46, 65 3
Smith, John F 42 1
Smith, John F 232, 288 2
Smith, John F 10, 43, 44, 45 3
Smith, John Francis 21, 44 3
Smith, John Francis 48, 61, 79, 85, 100, 117, 249 1
Smith, John Francis 160 2
Smith, John G 195, 253, 261 1
Smith, John G 9, 40 3
Smith, John H 71 3
Smith, John H 1 1
Smith, John H M 39 3
Smith, John H M 22, 163 1
Smith, John I 76 1
Smith, John J 22, 27, 93, 258, 262, 264 2
Smith, John J 106, 152, 197, 266 1
Smith, John J 9, 39, 40, 42, 43, 53, 67, 185 3
Smith, John Jacob 177 1
Smith, John Lee 45 3
Smith, John M 12, 56 3
Smith, John M 19 1
Smith, John N 10 3
Smith, John Newton 46 3
Smith, John of A 40 3
Smith, John of G 41 3
Smith, John of Henry 208 2
Smith, John of J 39, 43 3
Smith, John of L 39 3
Smith, John of M 23, 40, 41, 53, 153, 176 3
Smith, John of M 32 1
Smith, John of N 28 2
Smith, John of P 37 3
Smith, John of W 39 3
Smith, John of Wm 57, 60 3
Smith, John P 38 3
Smith, John S 32, 45, 113 3
Smith, John T 41, 42 3
Smith, John T 11, 51 1
Smith, John Thomas 42, 44 3
Smith, John W 43, 44, 72 3
Smith, Jonas 137, 144 2
Smith, Joseph 69, 214 2
Smith, Joseph 18, 31, 37, 38, 39, 42, 53, 149, 209 3
Smith, Joseph 57, 60, 96, 225 1
Smith, Joseph & 69 2
Smith, Joseph B 26 1
Smith, Joseph E 125 2
Smith, Joseph E B 45 3
Smith, Joseph L 126, 210 1
Smith, Joseph L 18, 38 3
Smith, Joseph L 119 2
Smith, Joseph M 75 3
Smith, Joseph Sr 37 3
Smith, Joshua 183 1
Smith, Joshua 38, 41 3
Smith, Joshua Jr 1 2
Smith, Joshua Jr 207 1
Smith, Joshua P 43 3
Smith, Josiah 44 3
Smith, Josiah F 138 2
Smith, Josiah S 138 2
Smith, Julia A 44, 82 3
Smith, Julian 39 3
Smith, Juliet G 41 2
Smith, K F 124 2
Smith, Kate F 85 1
Smith, Kate F 10, 75, 176 3
Smith, Kate K 9 3
Smith, Kathleen R 48 3
Smith, L 39 3
Smith, L C 65 3
Smith, L C 84 1
Smith, L R 65 3
Smith, Laura Matilda 51 3
Smith, Laura V 35, 51, 83 3
Smith, Leonard 203, 210, 225 1
Smith, Leonard 69 2
Smith, Lewis 244 1
Smith, Lewis 42 3
Smith, Lewis A 51 3
Smith, Lewis H B 51 3
Smith, Lewis M 51 3
Smith, Lottie M 51 3
Smith, Louis E 82 3
Smith, Louis F 51 3
Smith, Lucinda 50 3
Smith, Lucy A 51 3
Smith, Lucy A 198 1
Smith, Luther C 50 3
Smith, Lydia 50 3
Smith, M 23, 40, 41, 42, 53, 82, 153, 176 3
Smith, M E 19 3
Smith, M L 19, 176 3
Smith, M M 177 2
Smith, Mae 28 3
Smith, Maggie 82 3
Smith, Maggie 199 2
Smith, Maggie V 58 3
Smith, Malinda 53 3
Smith, Margaret 81 3
Smith, Margaret E 56 3
Smith, Margaret M 83 3
Smith, Margaret R 56 3
Smith, Margaret S 27 3
Smith, Maria 249 1
Smith, Maria 54 3
Smith, Maria Lee 85, 88 1
Smith, Maria Lee 288 2
Smith, Maria Lee 44 3
Smith, Maria V 57 3
Smith, Mariah Lee 44 3
Smith, Marian N 57 3
Smith, Marshall 56 3
Smith, Martha 53 3
Smith, Martha F 58 3
Smith, Martha Lee 48 1
Smith, Mary 1, 19, 21, 26, 37, 53, 54, 55, 75, 3
Smith, Mary A 41, 53, 54, 55, 56, 58, 81 3
Smith, Mary A E 47 1
Smith, Mary A E 54 3
Smith, Mary Ann 53, 55 3
Smith, Mary B 54, 57 3
Smith, Mary C 56, 57 3
Smith, Mary C 116 2
Smith, Mary C E 58 3
Smith, Mary C E 81 2
Smith, Mary E 247 2
Smith, Mary E 71, 198, 257 1
Smith, Mary E 9, 42, 54, 55, 56, 58 3
Smith, Mary E M 96 2
Smith, Mary Elizabeth 58 3
Smith, Mary J 140 1
Smith, Mary J 41, 56, 91 3
Smith, Mary M 56 3
Smith, Mary S 56, 57 3
Smith, Mary Virginia 57 3

Smith, Maryl M 53 3
Smith, Mathias 53 3
Smith, Mathias 264 2
Smith, Matilda 54 3
Smith, Matilda C 57 3
Smith, Matilda K 10 3
Smith, Matthias 205 1
Smith, Mattie 56 1
Smith, Maurice C 55, 56 3
Smith, Maurice C 277 2
Smith, Maurice L 55, 56 3
Smith, Mehrl W 56 3
Smith, Michael 53, 54 3
Smith, Michael A 57 3
Smith, Middleton 53 3
Smith, Middleton 195, 272 1
Smith, Middleton 11 2
Smith, Middletown 53 3
Smith, Mollie 57 3
Smith, Mollie E 16 3
Smith, Myra Lee 57 3
Smith, Myron 57 3
Smith, N 28 2
Smith, Nancy W 60 3
Smith, Nannie L 60 3
Smith, Naomi Elizabeth 250 1
Smith, Nettie A 41 2
Smith, Nora B 77 3
Smith, Nora B 28 1
Smith, Nora E 83 3
Smith, Norval L 217 3
Smith, Oda E 56 3
Smith, Ola B 57 3
Smith, P 37 3
Smith, P O 265 1
Smith, Paul M 235 2
Smith, Pearl A 65 3
Smith, Pearl L 73 3
Smith, Perry B 167 3
Smith, Perry G 65 3
Smith, Perry Otis 65 3
Smith, Peter 144 2
Smith, Peter 1, 19, 41, 64, 65, 70, 218 3
Smith, Peter 76 1
Smith, Philemon M 39 3
Smith, Philemon M 106, 112 1
Smith, Philip 26 3
Smith, Philip E 64 3
Smith, R Garland 87 3
Smith, R Paul 73 1
Smith, R V 180 3
Smith, Rachel 67 3
Smith, Rachel A 42 3
Smith, Raymond L 12 3
Smith, Rebecca 67 3
Smith, Rebecca 249 1
Smith, Rebecca F 67 3
Smith, Richard 27 2
Smith, Robert L 145 1
Smith, Robert V 72 3
Smith, Robt V 68 3
Smith, Roger W 97 1
Smith, Ross D 272 1
Smith, Ross V 58 3
Smith, S B 129 3
Smith, S B 225 2
Smith, Sallie T 72 3
Smith, Samuel 205 1
Smith, Samuel 8, 70, 71 3
Smith, Samuel D 54 3
Smith, Samuel L 72 3
Smith, Samuel W 70 3
Smith, Sara 18 3
Smith, Sara 214 1
Smith, Sarah 43, 70 3
Smith, Sarah 58 1
Smith, Sarah C 73, 188 3
Smith, Sarah E 55, 72 3
Smith, Sarah Ellen 72 3
Smith, Sarah L 82 3
Smith, Sevilla 72 3
Smith, Soloman of G 54 3
Smith, Solomon 70 3
Smith, Solomon of J 72 3
Smith, Staten 234 2
Smith, Stephen 221a 2
Smith, Susan E 26 1
Smith, Susannah 70, 71 3
Smith, Suzanna 54 3
Smith, T 75, 81 3
Smith, T 67 1
Smith, T Keller 44 3
Smith, Theodore 75, 82 3
Smith, Thomas 196 1
Smith, Thomas A 2, 19 3
Smith, Thomas A of T 75 3
Smith, Thomas J 75 3
Smith, Thomas Keller 46 3
Smith, Thomas T 75 3
Smith, Thos 210, 227, 279 1
Smith, Thos A 51 1
Smith, Thos A 75 3
Smith, Thos A 116 2
Smith, Ulysses E 77 3
Smith, Uriah 77, 188 3
Smith, Uriah L 179 3
Smith, V rnon T 35 3
Smith, Vernon J 44 3
Smith, Vernon T 82 1
Smith, Viola M 10 3
Smith, W 39 3
Smith, W C W 82 3
Smith, W H 27, 224a 2
Smith, W L 35 3
Smith, W R 1 1
Smith, W R 100 3
Smith, W T 224a 2
Smith, Warren P E 51 3
Smith, Wash 81 3
Smith, Washington 81, 82 3
Smith, Webster R 58 3
Smith, William 81, 82 3
Smith, William 219a 2
Smith, William A 82, 83 3
Smith, William Bernard 83 3
Smith, William C 83 3
Smith, William C W 44, 83 3
Smith, William Calvin 83 3
Smith, William E 27, 56, 81, 83 3
Smith, William H 9, 43, 81, 82 3
Smith, William H 295 2
Smith, William H of M 82 3
Smith, William J 83 3
Smith, William Jr 81 3
Smith, William K 83 3
Smith, William L 3, 9 3
Smith, William M 57 3
Smith, William of T 81 3
Smith, William P 20, 56 3
Smith, William S 82 3
Smith, William S Sr 81 3
Smith, William Sr 64, 81 3
Smith, William T 2 3
Smith, William Taylor 82 3
Smith, William W 83 3
Smith, Wm 11, 100 2
Smith, Wm 37, 110, 208, 278 1
Smith, Wm 57, 60, 207 3
Smith, Wm [?] 278 1
Smith, Wm A 76, 230 1
Smith, Wm A 65 3
Smith, Wm C 107 3
Smith, Wm E 38 1
Smith, Wm E 80 2
Smith, Wm G 82 3
Smith, Wm H 71 3
Smith, Wm H 67, 72, 85, 117 1
Smith, Wm Jr 64 3
Smith, Wm K 27 1
Smith, Wm L 83 3
Smith, Wm L 54 2
Smith, Wm M 28, 92 1
Smith, Wm M 85, 106 2
Smith, Wm T 118 1
Smith, Zephaniah 85 3
Smmers, Edgar M 44 3
Smoot, John H 150 1
Smothers, Frederick S 46 3
Smothers, Julia Ann 46 3
Smothers, Robert 67 3
Smouse, Florence 207 3
Smoyer, Sarah 70 3

Smucker 120 3
Snader, Ellwood E 265 1
Snader, John D 45 3
Snader, Minnie L 45 3
Snader, Philip 28 2
Snader, Philip 179 1
Snafner, Peter R 64 3
Snak, Michael 26 3
Snavely, Constance B 55 1
Snedegar, E Brent 21 3
Snell, Michael 53 3
Snerr, Barbara 6 3
Snerr, Henry 6 3
Snider, Anna M 3 3
Snider, Ellen M 50 3
Snider, Geo 217 1
Snider, Henry 8 3
Snider, I C 3 3
Snider, John 42, 71 3
Snider, John A 54 3
Snider, Louisa 50 3
Snider, Mary A 42 3
Snider, Nicholas 7 2
Snider, Oliver P 31 3
Snider, Wm A 27 1
Sniger, John 212 3
Snively, George 26 3
Snook, Adam 47, 78, 196 1
Snook, Adam 1, 116, 195 3
Snook, Adam 186 2
Snook, Adam Sr 1 3
Snook, Alvey B 97 1
Snook, Alvie B 120, 139 1
Snook, Alvie B 3, 10, 57 3
Snook, Ann 2 3
Snook, Carl 224 3
Snook, Carl W 45 3
Snook, Charles S 10 3
Snook, Charles S 277 2
Snook, Chas 61 1
Snook, Chas S 96, 106, 126, 133 1
Snook, Chas S 15, 56 3
Snook, Chas S 290 2
Snook, Daniel 15 3
Snook, Daniel 7 2
Snook, Daniel F 15, 56 3
Snook, Daniel J 15 3
Snook, Daniel W 15 3
Snook, Elizabeth 18 3
Snook, Elsie C 15 3
Snook, Eutaw M 28, 51 3
Snook, Florence A 86 1
Snook, Florence L 45 3
Snook, Frederick 23, 53 3
Snook, George M 28 3
Snook, Hallie F 33 3
Snook, Harry R 33, 72 3
Snook, J W 107 2
Snook, J W 61 1
Snook, Jacob 40 1
Snook, Jacob 18, 41 3
Snook, Jacob 282 2
Snook, Jacob H 42 3
Snook, John 215 2
Snook, John 1, 53 3
Snook, John H 96 1
Snook, John M 2, 42 3
Snook, John N 87 2
Snook, John S 31 2
Snook, John W 96, 238 2
Snook, John W 3, 45, 149 3
Snook, Josiah G 51 3
Snook, Karl W 58 3
Snook, Kathryn A 33 3
Snook, Lewis A 106, 169 1
Snook, Lewis A 51 3
Snook, Lottie M 51 3
Snook, Mary 53 3
Snook, Mary A 15, 56 3
Snook, Mary C 96 1
Snook, Mary E 33 3
Snook, Mary I 255 2
Snook, Scott 42 3
Snook, Simon 257 1
Snook, Simon R 72 3
Snook, Teresa Ann 75 3
Snook, William 82 3
Snook, William H 58 1
Snook, Wm 31 2
Snooke, Adam 171 2
Snooke, Margaret 53 3
Snoots, Dorothy L 217 3
Snoots, Luther D 72 3
Snoots, Marshall W 120 1
Snoots, Samuel Luther 72 3
Snoots, Alice C 156 1
Snouffer, A F 6 3
Snouffer, A P 129 3
Snouffer, A T 122 3
Snouffer, Archibald 2 3
Snouffer, B J 87 2
Snouffer, B J 122 3
Snouffer, Benjamin J 6 3
Snouffer, Christian 8 3
Snouffer, Cristena 8 3
Snouffer, David 242 2
Snouffer, Ed N 44 3
Snouffer, Elizabeth 19 3
Snouffer, Ellan 6 3
Snouffer, G A T 44, 62 3
Snouffer, G F 122 3
Snouffer, G F 80 2
Snouffer, Geo 88 1
Snouffer, Geo 185, 208 2
Snouffer, Geo A T 2 3
Snouffer, Geo W 89, 98 3
Snouffer, Geo W 150, 169 1
Snouffer, George To, 8, 26, 27, 28, 37, 62 3
Snouffer, George 14 1
Snouffer, George A T 28 3
Snouffer, George W 27, 118 3
Snouffer, Helen J 68 3
Snouffer, J B 163 2
Snouffer, J D 98 3
Snouffer, John 8, 37, 185 3
Snouffer, John 242 2
Snouffer, John A 44 3
Snouffer, John R 18 2
Snouffer, Joseph 19, 42 3
Snouffer, Joshepine L 44 3
Snouffer, L A 44 3
Snouffer, Mary S 57 3
Snouffer, Otho T 47, 67 1
Snouffer, Otho T 27, 62 3
Snouffer, Patrick M 83 3
Snouffer, Philip 42 3
Snouffer, R Ashby 28 3
Snouffer, Roger V L 68 3
Snouffer, Ruth M 68 3
Snouffer, Susie E 28 3
Snouffer, Wm 122 2
Snow, David 74 1
Snowden, Alice F 3 3
Snowden, Alice S 3 3
Snowden, Annie 67 3
Snowden, Eliza 96 3
Snowden, Greenbury 28 3
Snowden, James A 48 3
Snowden, Kitty 48 3
Snowden, Roy 67 3
Snowden, Sheridan 67 3
Snowden, Solomon 70 3
Snowden, Walter 83 3
Snurr, Ella 118 1
Snyder, Abraham 1 3
Snyder, Albert J 57 3
Snyder, Anna Mary 62 3
Snyder, C Bula 10 3
Snyder, Charles 43 3
Snyder, Charles E 10, 41 3
Snyder, Charles E 214a 2
Snyder, Charles G 11 3
Snyder, Chas 225 2
Snyder, Christian 8 3
Snyder, Daisy B 20 2
Snyder, Daniel 220 3
Snyder, Daniel P 41, 54, 220 3
Snyder, David M 15 3
Snyder, Eda E 51 3
Snyder, Elizabeth 19 3
Snyder, Ezra 144 2
Snyder, Ezra A 150 2
Snyder, Florence M 24 3
Snyder, Geo 40 3
Snyder, Geo 70 2
Snyder, George 26 3

Snyder, George H 27 3
Snyder, George W 28 3
Snyder, Harlan K 190 2
Snyder, Hattie J 68 3
Snyder, Henry 43 2
Snyder, Henry 31 3
Snyder, Herbert M 266 1
Snyder, Herman 31 3
Snyder, Herman M 96 3
Snyder, J 135 1
Snyder, J J 34 1
Snyder, Jacob 1, 31, 37, 39, 40, 42
3
Snyder, Jacob 238 1
Snyder, Jacob 43, 214a 2
Snyder, Jacob Henry 39 3
Snyder, Jerome R 57 3
Snyder, John 41 3
Snyder, John 136 2
Snyder, John E 43 3
Snyder, John H 15 3
Snyder, John J 24, 46 3
Snyder, Joshua 40 3
Snyder, Joshua L 40 3
Snyder, Levi H 51 3
Snyder, Lucy D 73 3
Snyder, Lydia A 152 1
Snyder, Lydia S R 79 3
Snyder, M A 27 3
Snyder, Mahala 42 3
Snyder, Margie S 79 3
Snyder, Martha 171 1
Snyder, Mary 27, 40, 54 3
Snyder, Mary E 28, 43 3
Snyder, Minerva A 283 2
Snyder, Minerva J 57 3
Snyder, Nicholas 38 3
Snyder, Nicholas 38 2
Snyder, Oliver P 62 3
Snyder, Peter 70 3
Snyder, Ralph R 68 3
Snyder, Roy D 113, 257 1
Snyder, Roy V 15 3
Snyder, Samuel 10, 70 3
Snyder, Samuel 283 1
Snyder, Samuel E 73 3
Snyder, Sarah A 72 3
Snyder, Seney A E 72 3
Snyder, Susannah 71 3
Snyder, V A 55 3
Snyder, V S 41 3
Snyder, Vernon A 79 3
Snyder, W D 119 2
Snyder, William 70 3
Snyder, William 277 2
Snyder, William J 8 3
Snyder, Wm D 16, 36 2
Snyder, Wm S 135 1
Snyder,Genry M 67 3
Snyer, Christian 208 2
Socks, Samuel 71, 72 3
Soelkey, Frederick W 23 3
Soelkey, Senea 23 3
Sohm, Peter 32 1
Sollers, Barbara 6 3
Sollers, Dennis 14 3
Sollers, Mary 53 3
Sollers, Mary E 53 3
Sollers, Sabritt 14, 116 2
Sollers, Sabritt 64, 163 3
Sollers, Sabritt 139, 181 1
Sollers, Sabvitt 1, 14 3
Sollers, Sarah D 71 3
Sollers, Thomas 14 3
Sollers, Thomas E 6, 70, 171
3
Sollers, Thomas E 150 1
Sollers,Sabritt 70 3
Solliday, Alice B 6 3
Solliday, Benjamin H 6 3
Solmon, Chas 100 2
Solomon, George 70 3
Solomon, Jesse G 45 3
Solomon, John 116 1
Solomon, Wm 72 2
Soper, Carlene 11 3
Soper, Dorthy V 11 3
Soper, Elias P 51 1
Soper, Emma C 21 3
Soper, Franklin T 21, 75 3
Soper, Lucy 50 3
Soper, Thomas F 75 3
Soter, George 28 3
Sotrm, Wmm M [sic] 124 1
Souder, Anthony 137, 225a 2
Souder, Anthony 82 1
Souder, Anthony 53, 64 3
Souder, Benjamin 6 3
Souder, D M 255 2
Souder, David 262 2
Souder, David 6 3
Souder, David M 131 2
Souder, David M 16 3
Souder, Fannie R 45 3
Souder, Fanny R C 109 1
Souder, George 70 3
Souder, Jacob 18, 37 3
Souder, John N 265 2
Souder, John N 45 3
Souder, John N 109, 137 1
Souder, Margaret 53 3
Souder, Martha 16 3
Souder, Michael 53 3
Souder, Peter 64 3
Souder, Peter 225a 2
Souder, Philip 64 3
Souder, Raymond D 28 3
Souder, Susan 70 3
Souders, George 64 3
Souders, Jacob 221 3
Souders, John 64 3
Souders, John T 64 3
Souer, Adam [sic] 37 1
Sounders, Kenley 215 3
Southgate, Samuel 70 3
Soutman, James W 41 3
Sovocool, Clara E 59 2
Sowder, David 96 3
Sowder, Joshua 76 2
Sower, Adam 1 3
Sower, Charles 8 3
Sower, John 37 3
Sower, Peter 37, 64, 81 3
Sowerman, Henry 31 3
Sowers, Adam 64 3
Sowers, Adam 84 1
Sowers, Annie E 3, 72 3
Sowers, David 14 3
Sowers, Eli 19, 64 3
Sowers, Eliza 43 3
Sowers, Geo H 19 3
Sowers, Harry 3 3
Sowers, Harry S 32, 48, 58, 73 3
Sowers, John 38 3
Sowers, Joseph 43 3
Sowers, Joshua 14 3
Sowers, Kenley M 48 3
Sowers, Kenly M 56 3
Sowers, Margaret L 58 3
Sowers, Mary 56 3
Sowers, Mary E 58 3
Sowers, Peter 116 1
Sowers, Philip 64 3
Sowers, Sarah J 72, 73 3
Sowers, Susan 19, 71 3
Sowers, William 81 3
Spahr, Abraham 2 3
Spahr, Alice C 3 3
Spahr, Harry Milton 57 3
Spahr, Lydia E 57 3
Spahr, Milton O 57 3
Spalding, Harold L 28 1
Spalding, Henry 223 3
Spalding, John O 42 3
Spangler, Daniel 14 3
Spangler, Milton H 215a 2
Spargo, Ida A 67 3
Spargo, John M 40 3
Spargo, Lillie M 50 3
Spargo, Rachael A 50, 67 3
Spargo, Rachel 40 3
Spargo, William 82 3
Sparke, Arthur W 52 1
Sparks, Ann Elizabeth 3 3
Sparrow, Flo M 14 1
Sparrow, John 49 2
Sparrow, John W 14, 192 3

Sparrow, Wilson L 64, 81 3
Spates, George P Jr 254 1
Spaulding, Francis 70 1
Spaulding, Francis 26, 75 2
Spaulding, Henry 109 1
Spaulding, Henry 75, 220a 2
Spaulding, Howard J 186 1
Spaulding, J C 72 1
Spaulding, Rosella Welch, 4 1
Speak, Charles E 11 3
Speak, Chas E 42 3
Speak, Elmer C 11 3
Speak, Ethel M 68 3
Speak, James William 45 3
Speak, John P 67 3
Speak, John T 42 3
Speak, John T Sr 42 3
Speak, Mae V 58 3
Speak, Robert L 68 3
Speak, Roy W 45, 68 3
Speakes, Roy W 44 3
Speaks, Elizabeth J 20 3
Speaks, Ethel M 45 3
Speaks, George W 27 3
Speaks, James L 44 3
Speaks, Mary E 27 3
Spear, Annie M 3 3
Specht, Agnes C 40 2
Specht, Alice V 23 3
Specht, Alonzo 115 1
Specht, Ann E 2, 15 3
Specht, Annie E 28 3
Specht, B 28 3
Specht, Conrad 8 3
Specht, David 163 1
Specht, David 15, 122 3
Specht, Francis T 23 3
Specht, George J 28 3
Specht, Grace N 218 2
Specht, Jacob 23 3
Specht, Joseph 106 3
Specht, Lewis 50 3
Specht, Marion E 50 3
Specht, Michael C 60 1
Specht, Walter L 218 2
Spechten, Barbara 6 3
Speck, G 102 3
Speck, J L 80 2
Speckhardt, William 83 3
Speed, Jos 53 3
Spencer, A 153 2
Spencer, Albertas 150 2
Spencer, Albertus 67, 81 3
Spencer, Ida B 35 3
Spencer, John 39 3
Spencer, John Thomas 42 3
Spencer, John W 223a 2
Spencer, Martha 53 3
Spencer, Mary 39, 54 3
Spencer, Mary E 153 1
Spencer, Robert 35 2
Spencer, Robert L 67 3
Spencer, Robert T 67 3
Spencer, Robt 153 2
Spencer, Virginia 223a 2
Spencer, William 81 3
Spencer, William L 81 3
Spencer, Wm 112 2
Sperry, Aidan J 32 2
Sperry, Ralph S 177 3
Spitler, Mathias 53 3
Spittle, Amelia J 50 3
Spittle, E May 3 3
Spittle, Lewis C 50 3
Spitzer, Alonzo A 2 3
Spitzer, Frank L 44 3
Spitzer, Julia J 44 3
Spohn, Elizabeth 19 3
Spohn, Jacob 26 2
Sponseller, Adam 30 1
Sponseller, Arthur T 3 3
Sponseller, Charles G 38 1
Sponseller, Clifton 68 3
Sponseller, Estelle E 21 3
Sponseller, Eugene 18, 63, 279 1
Sponseller, Eugene 21, 43, 100 3
Sponseller, George F 41 3
Sponseller, Harling E 21 3
Sponseller, J W 41 1
Sponseller, Jacob 41 3
Sponseller, Jacob C 118, 131 1
Sponseller, Jacob C 195 3
Sponseller, Jacob W 45 3
Sponseller, James B 45 3
Sponseller, John 84 2
Sponseller, John D 79 3
Sponseller, John R 45 3
Sponseller, Josaph A 45 3
Sponseller, Laura V 51 3
Sponseller, Louis M 21 3
Sponseller, Lucy E 45 3
Sponseller, Martha 79 3
Sponseller, Mattie I 45 3
Sponseller, Michael 53 3
Sponseller, Olive 176 3
Sponseller, Olive W 68 3
Sponseller, Pearl 68 3
Sponseller, Roy L 68 3
Sponseller, Vallandingham 79 3
Sponseller, W M 79 3
Sprengle, David 111 2
Sprenkle, David 14 3
Spriddle, Martin 54 3
Sprigg, Ann W 1 3
Sprigg, John 177 1
Sprigg, Thomas O 75 3
Spriggs, Alfred 51 3
Spriggs, Ann 1 3
Spriggs, Benjamin 6 3
Spriggs, James 51 3
Spriggs, Lewis 51 3
Spriggs, Margaret L 58 3
Spriggs, Sarah 6 3
Spriggs, Thresa 75 3
Spring, Bernice 16 3
Spring, Bernice E 208 1
Spring, David W 16 3
Spring, Ella B 208 1
Springer, Christopher C 73 1
Springer, Daniel 38, 75 3
Springer, David 26 2
Springer, Edwin 13 1
Springer, Edwin .238 2
Springer, Edwin 40 3
Springer, Flora M 28 3
Springer, George S 28 3
Springer, Grant R 28 3
Springer, Henry H 28 3
Springer, Katherine A 167 2
Springer, Milton G 28 3
Springer, Thomas 38, 64, 75 3
Springer, Thomas 220, 242 2
Springer, Thomas 37, 70, 279 1
Springer, Thos 22 1
Springer, Thos 197 2
Springg, Otho [sic] 88 1
Spuckler, Esther 20 3
Spurriec, John H 82 3
Spurrier, Alpheus 31 3
Spurrier, Anna 10 3
Spurrier, Beulah 73 3
Spurrier, Beulah 245 1
Spurrier, Catherine 10 3
Spurrier, Charles F 10 3
Spurrier, Clarence E 24 3
Spurrier, Frank E 24 3
Spurrier, George W 82 3
Spurrier, Gordon W 4, 184 1
Spurrier, Gordon W 161 3
Spurrier, Gordon W 67, 228a 2
Spurrier, Henry 28 2
Spurrier, Henry 31, 179, 209 3
Spurrier, Howard W 44 3
Spurrier, Jacob H L 46 3
Spurrier, James 28 2
Spurrier, John E 45 3
Spurrier, John H 44, 55 3

Spurrier, Joseph 125 1
Spurrier, Lucy B 66 2
Spurrier, Martha D 55 3
Spurrier, Mary E 45 3
Spurrier, Myurtlin 73 3
Spurrier, R S 245 1
Spurrier, Robet E 52 1
Spurrier, Roland 73 3
Spurrier, Sadie B 73 3
Spurrier, Sadie E 73, 75 3
Spurrier, Sarah J 44 3
Spurrier, Taylor A 75 3
Spurrier, Teresa A M 75 3
Spurrier, Thomas 31 3
Spurrier, W L 34 1
Spurrier, Walter L 83 3
Spurrier, William 82 3
Spurrier, Wm 82 1
SStevens, Charles 8 3
St ner, Mary 54 3
Stager, Allen A 11 3
Stager, Clarence J 11 3
Staley, Abraham 1 3
Staley, Addie E 68 3
Staley, Agnes 2 3
Staley, Alice A 50 3
Staley, Alice E 3 3
Staley, Alice G 50 3
Staley, Ann 1 3
Staley, Ann E 2, 81 3
Staley, Anna E 2 3
Staley, C A 2 3
Staley, Carl C 34 1
Staley, Catherine 9, 79 3
Staley, Catherine 67 2
Staley, Catherine P 28 1
Staley, Charles A 11 3
Staley, Charles E 55 3
Staley, Chas 198 2
Staley, Chas 14 1
Staley, Chas B 56 3
Staley, Chas B 25 1
Staley, Chas C 224 3
Staley, Chas M 1 1
Staley, Christina 8 3
Staley, Clara A 6 1
Staley, Conrad 64 3
Staley, Cora M 83 3
Staley, Cornelia 71 3
Staley, Cornelia of T 75 3
Staley, Cornelius 1, 11, 14, 38, 159, 177, 187 2
Staley, Cornelius 1, 2, 9, 15, 26, 40 3
Staley, Cornelius 85, 197, 253 1
Staley, Cornelius A 9, 10 3
Staley, Daniel 14, 38 3
Staley, Daniel 205 2
Staley, Daniel O 177 2
Staley, Daniel O 15 3
Staley, David 8, 15 3
Staley, David L 54, 64 3
Staley, Dennis 171 3
Staley, Edma A 20 3
Staley, Edward 27 3
Staley, Edward M 21 3
Staley, Elizabeth 18, 19, 165 3
Staley, Ella V 15 3
Staley, Elmer B 20 3
Staley, Ezra 19 3
Staley, Fleet 150 2
Staley, Frederick 23, 26, 64 3
Staley, G H 52, 166 2
Staley, G H 75 3
Staley, G H 135, 214, 253 1
Staley, Geo 62 1
Staley, George 26, 27, 39 3
Staley, George F 26, 165 3
Staley, Gideon 19 3
Staley, Glenna M 259 2
Staley, Grayson H 79 3
Staley, Grayson H 115, 196 1
Staley, H E 40, 144, 257 1
Staley, H E 2, 52, 58, 212a, 214a 2
Staley, H E 15 3
Staley, Harry E 33 3
Staley, Henry 47, 79, 252 1
Staley, Henry 26, 51 2
Staley, Henry 31, 64, 202 3
Staley, Hilda E 33 3
Staley, Hiram Z 33 3
Staley, Horace 20, 166, 206 3
Staley, Horace E 187, 197 3
Staley, Horace E 58 2
Staley, Horace E 152, 223, 245, 257 1
Staley, Horice E 196 3
Staley, Ira M 177 2
Staley, Ira McD 15 3
Staley, Irving E 11 3
Staley, J 204 1
Staley, J A 64 3
Staley, J E 6 1
Staley, Jacob 169 2
Staley, Jacob 26, 165 3
Staley, Jacob H 18, 40 3
Staley, Jacob Sr 38 3
Staley, Joanna 41 3
Staley, John 1, 141 3
Staley, John 38 2
Staley, John H 259 2
Staley, John W 40 3
Staley, Jonothan A 81 3
Staley, Joseph 38 3
Staley, Joseph E 15 2
Staley, Joshua 23, 40 3
Staley, Lauretta V 21 3
Staley, Lethe S 50 3
Staley, Lewis 40 2
Staley, Lewis H 50 3
Staley, Lewis M 50 3
Staley, Lewis V 50 3
Staley, Lottie E 50 3
Staley, Luther R 50 3
Staley, M E 65 3
Staley, Margaret 54 3
Staley, Martha June 56 3
Staley, Mary A 50, 56 3
Staley, Mary C 55 3
Staley, McDuell 189, 200, 205 2
Staley, Milton E 57 3
Staley, Moses 53 3
Staley, Peter 1, 26, 64, 203 3
Staley, Peter S 64 3
Staley, Phoebe 65 3
Staley, R C 171 3
Staley, R M 227 3
Staley, Reverdy T 10, 56, 68 3
Staley, Rhuanna 67 3
Staley, Robert M 33, 68 3
Staley, S M 81 3
Staley, Sarah 40 3
Staley, Susan 40, 81 3
Staley, T 75 3
Staley, Tobias 75 3
Staley, Victor A 79 3
Staley, Virgie M 57 3
Staley, W 150 2
Staley, W W 225 1
Staley, William A 26, 81 3
Staley, William H 81 3
Staley, Worthington 9 2
Staley, Worthington C 56, 83 3
Staley, Worthington C 23, 178 2
Stalling, Elizabeth L 39 3
Stallings, Charles T 8 3
Stallings, Elizabeth 18 3
Stallings, Emma M 102 2
Stallings, Joseph 39 3
Stambaugh, Chas R S 125 2
Stambaugh, F 171 3
Stambaugh, Fannie M 24 3
Stambaugh, Harry 91 3
Stambaugh, Harvey L 97 1
Stambaugh, Isabella L 35 3
Stambaugh, Ray Jacob 68 3
Stambaugh, Samuel 91 3
Stambaugh, William B 35 3
Stammers, John 37 3
Standard Accident Ins Co 3, 16, 36, 41, 43, 73, 182, 200, 234 2
Standard Accident Ins Co 89, 161 3
Standard Accident Ins Co 155, 157, 184, 254, 280 1

Standard Accident Insurance Co 237, 284 1
Standard Accident Insurance Co 114 3
Standard Accident Insurance Co 70, 257 2
Standard Accident Insurance Company 34 1
Standsbury, Abram 38 2
Stansberry, Cecilia 10 3
Stansburg, Jacob 38 3
Stansburg, M Philip 60 3
Stansbury, Abraham 1 3
Stansbury, Anna C 2 3
Stansbury, Geo F 183 1
Stansbury, Mary A 60 3
Stansbury, N Philip 2 3
Stansbury, Nicholas 159 2
Stansbury, Nicholas C 60 3
Stansbury, Noah Phillips 60 3
Stansbury, William 1 3
Stansbury, Wm 113, 159 2
Stansbury, Wm 278 1
Stansbury, Wm J 183 1
Stanton, Annie 3 3
Stanton, Chloe 9 3
Stanton, Harry W 32 3
Stanton, Henry 3 3
Stanton, Patrick 64 3
Stanton, Viola A 32 3
Star, Maurice T 245 2
Starfer, John 223 3
Starleper, Mildred 225 1
Starr, Ann H 2, 19 3
Starr, Anna 2 3
Starr, Charles G 32 3
Starr, Chas H 9 2
Starr, Edw 187 2
Starr, Edwin 44 1
Starr, Edwin 19, 70 3
Starr, Elizabert A 19 3
Starr, Henry C 32 3
Starr, J D 79 1
Starr, J W 65 2
Starr, J W 110, 183, 249 1
Starr, J W 9, 82, 113, 215 3
Starr, Jesse 55 3
Starr, Jesse W 38 3
Starr, Jesse Washington 43 3
Starr, John 189 2
Starr, John N 38 3
Starr, L N 55 3
Starr, Lugurgus N 1 1
Starr, Lycurgus 50 3
Starr, Lycurgus M 55 3
Starr, Lydia E 50 3
Starr, M F 27 1
Starr, M F 56, 72 3
Starr, M Scott 57 3
Starr, Matilda argaret C 55 3
Starr, Maurice F 68, 183, 186, 265 1
Starr, Maurice F 27 2
Starr, Maurice F 56, 57, 207 3
Starr, Maurice T 38, 55 3
Starr, Nellie F 57 3
Starr, Sarah Ann 82 3
Starr, W Scott 27 1
Starr, Winfield S 82 3
Starrr, Maurice F [sic] 191 1
Starry, George 31 3
Starry, George Sr 26 3
Starry, Henry 31 3
Starter, J Stanley 44 3
Staub, Andrew J 2, 41 3
Staub, Chas 282 1
Staub, David 14 3
Staub, Eleanor H 41, 190 2
Staub, Elizabeth H 82 3
Staub, Eugene D 188 2
Staub, Eugene D 42 3
Staub, F V 52 1
Staub, F V 66, 172 2
Staub, Frank 66 2
Staub, J C 170 2
Staub, J E 33 1
Staub, J Marshall 24 3
Staub, J Marshall 41, 161, 163, 190 2
Staub, Jacob 171 2
Staub, James E 33 1
Staub, John 190 2
Staub, John W 47 1
Staub, John W 83, 84, 87 2
Staub, Laura E 41 2
Staub, M Pauline 24 3
Staub, Margaret 54 3
Staub, Mary E 2 3
Staub, Meredith Van R 24 3
Staub, S V 24 3
Staub, S V 244 1
Staub, William H 82 3
Staub, William H 82 3
Stauffer, Amanda C 65 3
Stauffer, Ann R 2 3
Stauffer, Annie 3 3
Stauffer, B F 65 3
Stauffer, B J 171 2
Stauffer, B T 65 3
Stauffer, Benjamin F 6 3
Stauffer, Bess M 16 3
Stauffer, Catherine 9 3
Stauffer, Charles C 20 3
Stauffer, Chas E 97 1
Stauffer, Clara C 72 3
Stauffer, Clara Courtney 11 3
Stauffer, Courtney E 72 3
Stauffer, D M 49 2
Stauffer, D Murray 15, 16, 82 3
Stauffer, D V 71 3
Stauffer, Daniel 118 1
Stauffer, Daniel E 15 3
Stauffer, David 198 1
Stauffer, David M 83 3
Stauffer, David V 2, 15 3
Stauffer, Elias 19 3
Stauffer, Ellen S 20 3
Stauffer, Emma 20 3
Stauffer, Ezra 138 2
Stauffer, Frank N 203, 253 1
Stauffer, G W 71 3
Stauffer, Geo 175 2
Stauffer, Glenn O 11, 72 3
Stauffer, H C 160 3
Stauffer, Henry 112 2
Stauffer, Henry 6 1
Stauffer, Henry 31, 32, 40, 54 3
Stauffer, Henry Clay 54 3
Stauffer, Henry E 20 3
Stauffer, J D 71 3
Stauffer, J H 227 2
Stauffer, J H 71 3
Stauffer, J H 96, 119, 171 1
Stauffer, Jacob 19 3
Stauffer, James F 42 3
Stauffer, John 8, 9, 18, 39, 40, 70, 195 3
Stauffer, John 14, 128, 175 2
Stauffer, John 104, 123 1
Stauffer, John H 45, 65 3
Stauffer, John H 253 1
Stauffer, Joseph 37 3
Stauffer, Joseph 40 3
Stauffer, Joseph Jr 70 3
Stauffer, Joseph Sr 70 3
Stauffer, Katharine C 127 1
Stauffer, Lewis C 15 3
Stauffer, Matilda N 54 3
Stauffer, P B 65 3
Stauffer, Peter B 65 3
Stauffer, R Ward 127 1
Stauffer, S Theodore 72 3
Stauffer, Samuel 70 3
Stauffer, Simon 138 2
Stauffer, Simon W 71 3
Stauffer, Sophia 81 3
Stauffer, Theodore 171 1
Stauffer, Theodore 32 3
Stauffer, Theodore 112 2
Stauffer, W Nelson 237, 240 1
Stauffer, W Nelson 11, 45 3
Stauffer, W Q 65 3
Stauffer, W Wilson 20 3
Stauffer, Willie A 2, 15 3

Stauffer, Willie A W 83 3
Stauffer, Willie Anna 82 3
Stauffer, Wm 85 1
Staup, Ann C 3 3
Staup, Charles 139 3
Staup, Daniel 15 3
Staup, David 15 3
Staup, George W 67 3
Staup, James 15 3
Staup, John 188 2
Staup, John 15 3
Staup, John M 43, 139 3
Staup, John W 42 3
Staup, John W 109, 272 1
Staup, Leander J 15 3
Staup, Lewis H 71 3
Staup, Ruth Ann 67 3
Staup, Solomon 71 3
Staut, John 187 2
Steadman, Charles 11 3
Steadman, Mary G 11 3
Steadman, Mary G 11 3
Stealey, H 210a 2
Steel, Abraham W 194 1
Steel, Anna M J 145 1
Steel, Emma J 247 2
Steel, James H 88 1
Steel, Mabel 166 1
Steele, Ann M J 11 3
Steele, Charles E 11 3
Steele, Emma 227a 2
Steele, George 26 3
Steele, Mamie S 58 3
Steele, S L Mrs 3 3
Steele, Samuel L 58 3
Steffey, Thomas E 143 2
Steigers, William 81 3
Stein, David E 61 1
Stein, Elizabeth 134 3
Stein, Lewis 38 2
Steiner, Almedia 3 3
Steiner, Almeida S 2 3
Steiner, Ann Frances 62 3
Steiner, Christian 9, 18, 31, 70, 192 3
Steiner, Christian 84 1
Steiner, Clara H 10 3
Steiner, Daniel 125 1
Steiner, Daniel H 144 1
Steiner, David 14, 38, 73, 184, 203 3
Steiner, David 96 2
Steiner, Elizabeth 18, 31 3
Steiner, Florence May 189 2
Steiner, Francis F 76 1
Steiner, Geo T 82 3
Steiner, George Anna 2 3
Steiner, Georgianna 28 3
Steiner, H F 39, 75 2
Steiner, H F 104, 205 1
Steiner, Hannah 31 3
Steiner, Henry 211 2
Steiner, Henry 18, 31, 64, 67 3
Steiner, Henry C 14 2
Steiner, Henry C 31 3
Steiner, Henry H 31 3
Steiner, Henry Jr 106 3
Steiner, Henry Jr 7 2
Steiner, Henry R 64 2
Steiner, Henry R 10, 15, 72 3
Steiner, Henry R 55 1
Steiner, Jacob 5, 211 2
Steiner, Jacob 38, 71 3
Steiner, John A 31, 91 3
Steiner, John A 19, 59, 71 1
Steiner, John A 1, 38, 119, 184 2
Steiner, L H 119 2
Steiner, Lewis H 9, 41, 67 3
Steiner, Louis H 32 3
Steiner, Louise 15 3
Steiner, Louise H 72 3
Steiner, Mahlon R 56 3
Steiner, Margaret H 58 3
Steiner, Marian C 72 3
Steiner, Marian Colton 58 3
Steiner, Marietta 56 3
Steiner, Mary 55 3
Steiner, Mary E 55 3
Steiner, Oscar E 62 3
Steiner, Rachael 67 3
Steiner, Rachel 31 3
Steiner, Rebecca 67 3
Steiner, Rodney B 56 3
Steiner, Rodney V 56 3
Steiner, Stephen 195, 215 3
Steiner, Stephen 37, 115, 228 1
Steiner, Stephen 7 2
Steiner, Steven 70 3
Steiner, Susan 10, 71, 72 3
Steiner, William F 82 3
Steiner, Wm 57 1
Steiner, Wm R 55 3
Steinhaus, Annas E 4 3
Steinhaus, William H 4 3
Steir, Frederick 116 1
Steir, Frederick 23 3
Steir, Hamilton 22 1
Stekcet, Abraham [sic] 4 1
Stem, C N 2, 8, 139, 203, 236 2
Stem, C N 72, 104, 172, 265, 272 1
Stem, C N 32 3
Stem, C N 75 3
Stem, Calvin 56 2
Stem, Calvin E 57 3
Stem, Calvin M 15 2
Stem, Calvin N 206 3
Stem, Calvin N 40 2
Stem, Calvin N 126 1
Stem, Carlton 189 2
Stem, Carroll Ezra 12 3
Stem, David 14 3
Stem, David E 123 1
Stem, David E 113 2
Stem, David S 65 3
Stem, Effie Bell 12 3
Stem, Francis T 32 3
Stem, H W 126 1
Stem, Harry F 32 3
Stem, Henry 40 2
Stem, Henry 8, 40 2
Stem, Henry M 188 3
Stem, Henry W 32, 42, 44 3
Stem, J Ezra 111 2
Stem, Jacob 26, 229a 2
Stem, Jacob 67 3
Stem, John 42, 44, 64 3
Stem, Mary L 57 3
Stem, Matilda C 172 1
Stem, Peter 61 2
Stem, Peter 64 3
Stem, Samuel 196, 205, 225 1
Stem, Susan 72 3
Stem, Tillie C 75 3
Stembel, Frederick 23 3
Stembel, Frederik 137 2
Stemble, Frederick Sr 150 2
Stemble, John 282 2
Stemmell, Jacob 38 3
Stephany, Herman 31 3
Stephen, Rezin 57 1
Stephen, Wm T 23 2
Stephens, Chas 283 1
Stephens, Chas 69 2
Stephens, Chas W 166 1
Stephens, David 15 3
Stephens, Fannie V 15 3
Stephens, James 37, 38 3
Stephens, James 283 1
Stephens, John 226 2
Stephens, Joseph S 51, 57 3
Stephens, Louisa E 50 3
Stephens, Lynwood 51 3
Stephens, Mary A 57 3
Stephens, Mary C W 55 3
Stephens, Mary M 56 3
Stephens, Mazie H 51, 57 3
Stephens, Nancy 60, 70 3
Stephens, Nathan 70 3
Stephens, Samuel 70, 71 3
Stephens, Samuel Jr 70 3
Stephens, Samuel S 70 3
Stephens, Susannah 37 3
Stephens, Thomas 181 2
Stephens, Thos 187 2
Stephens, Wm H 19 1

Stephenson, Hannah 81 3
Stephenson, Henry 31 3
Stephenson, James 37, 42 3
Stephenson, Joseph 38 3
Stephenson, Joshua 164 1
Stephenson, Samuel 70 3
Stephenson, Thomas 159 2
Stephenson, Thos 240 1
Stephenson, Wesley 81 3
Stephenson, William 37, 81 3
Stephenson, William H 184 3
Sterling, H F 201 1
Sterm, Solomon 72 3
Stern, A 65 3
Stern, Aaron 2 3
Stern, Arthur 44, 72 3
Stern, Calvin M 112 1
Stern, Jacob 220 3
Stern, Jennie 44 3
Stern, John 37 3
Stern, Julia 65 3
Stern, Peter 165 3
Stern, Phillip 65 3
Sterrett, Jane 40 3
Stesart, Walter W 44 3
Steven, W B 205 3
Stevens John B 71 3
Stevens Theodore A 71 3
Stevens, Amy C 60 3
Stevens, Arnold 1 3
Stevens, Benjamin 6 3
Stevens, Blanche B 73 1
Stevens, C Dorsey 20, 75 3
Stevens, C Grayson 60 3
Stevens, Catharine 35 3
Stevens, Catherine E 175 1
Stevens, Charles 9, 10, 40 3
Stevens, Charles I 10 3
Stevens, Charles W 175 1
Stevens, Clagett Dorsey 12 3
Stevens, Clarecne T 20 3
Stevens, Clarence 91 3
Stevens, Clarence T 75 3
Stevens, Edgar T 12 3
Stevens, Elizabeth B 20 3
Stevens, Elsie M 24 3
Stevens, Elsie M 260 1
Stevens, F M 154 3
Stevens, Flavius J 23 3
Stevens, Frank 223a 2
Stevens, Frank M 24, 201 3
Stevens, Frank M 80 2
Stevens, Frank M 113 1
Stevens, Frank N 10 3
Stevens, Geo A 71 3
Stevens, George 28 3
Stevens, George A 27 3
Stevens, Harry B 27 3
Stevens, Horatio 31 3
Stevens, Isaac L 46, 60 3
Stevens, J D 72 3
Stevens, J H 67 3
Stevens, James 100 2
Stevens, James 135, 223, 245 1
Stevens, James 38 3
Stevens, James G 28, 46 3
Stevens, James L 38 3
Stevens, Joanna M 41 3
Stevens, John R 31, 41 3
Stevens, Laura E 67 3
Stevens, Margaret V 10 3
Stevens, Mary E 27, 60 3
Stevens, Mary Ruth 55 3
Stevens, Mildred Rice 60 3
Stevens, Nannie 46 3
Stevens, Nannie E 60 3
Stevens, Nellie O 75 3
Stevens, Nellie Orlean 12, 60 3
Stevens, Reuben 67 3
Stevens, Reuben G 67 3
Stevens, Rezin 67 3
Stevens, Rosie O 28 3
Stevens, S M 57 3
Stevens, Samuel 70 1
Stevens, Samuel 137 2
Stevens, Susan 23, 71 3
Stevens, T A 201 1
Stevens, T A 160 2
Stevens, Theodore 67, 91 3
Stevens, Theorore A 75 3
Stevens, William H 81 3
Stevenson, Abeland 185 2
Stevenson, Basil D 6 3
Stevenson, Caroline M 8 3
Stevenson, Edward 195 3
Stevenson, Edwin D 18 3
Stevenson, John 39 3
Stevenson, Joshua 37, 38, 39 3
Stevenson, Joshua J 40 3
Stevenson, Josiah 38, 185 3
Stevenson, Lucy Ann 50 3
Stevenson, Samuel 40 1
Stevenson, Samuel 70, 81 3
Stevenson, Wm H 22 1
Stevents, Eugene E 97 1
Stevins, Geo A 110 1
Steward, Alexander 1 3
Steward, John 1 3
Stewart, Agnes 205 3
Stewart, Banjamin 6 3
Stewart, Benj 195, 205 3
Stewart, Benjamin F 29 2
Stewart, Elia 83 3
Stewart, Ella S 21 3
Stewart, Emma 21 3
Stewart, Geo 2 2
Stewart, Harriet R 33 3
Stewart, Harriett 32 3
Stewart, Henry 40 3
Stewart, J 22 1
Stewart, J S 171 3
Stewart, Jacob 41 3
Stewart, Jane 81 3
Stewart, John 137, 159, 185, 203 2
Stewart, John 56, 139, 282 1
Stewart, John 26, 151, 184, 185 3
Stewart, John (Col) 40 3
Stewart, John E 46 3
Stewart, John S 139 1
Stewart, John S 39, 185 3
Stewart, John W C 44 3
Stewart, Johnn 40 3
Stewart, Jordan 37 3
Stewart, Joseph 40 3
Stewart, Luther F H 51 3
Stewart, Mabel Eaton 58 3
Stewart, Molly 30 1
Stewart, Rosie E 46 3
Stewart, Virginia 41 3
Stewart, Walter W 83 3
Stewart, William 23, 81 3
Stewart, William R 83 3
Stichell, Eva E 21 3
Stichell, Oscar 21 3
Stickel, Solomon 165 2
Stickell, Soloman 1 3
Stickley, Leonidas T 51 3
Stickley, Mary E 51 3
Stier, Achsah A L 32 3
Stier, Achsah L 3 3
Stier, Alma D 3 3
Stier, Cornelius 8 3
Stier, Frederick 23 3
Stier, H Douglas 60 3
Stier, Hamilton 116, 140 1
Stier, Hamilton 32 3
Stier, Henry 57, 171 1
Stier, J H 3 3
Stier, Jay Hugh 35 3
Stier, Marsaline A 58 3
Stier, Mary D 55 3
Stier, Nannie F 3, 60 3
Stier, Otto P 55 3
Stier, William H J 23 3
Stillion, J Frank 67 3
Stillion, Rebecca 67 3
Stilly, Elizabeth 18 3
Stilly, John 37 3
Stimmel, George W 27 3
Stimmel, Henry 31, 186 3
Stimmel, Henry H 32 3
Stimmel, John B 37 3
Stimmel, John B 123, 131 1
Stimmel, John W 46 3
Stimmel, John W 188 2

Stimmel, Savilla C 27, 72 3
Stimmel, William 20 3
Stimmell, David 14 3
Stimmell, Edward H 20 3
Stimmell, Henry 31 3
Stimmell, Jacob 37, 40 3
Stimmell, Jacob 32 3
Stimmell, Joel 37 3
Stimmell, John B 282 1
Stimmell, John B 42 3
Stimmell, John W 20 3
Stinchcomb, Reed C 79 3
Stinchcomb, Victor 79 3
Stinchecomb, B C 223a 2
Stine Stephen 56 1
Stine, Amos C 65 3
Stine, Arthue E [sic] 22 1
Stine, E A R 19 3
Stine, Elias 19 3
Stine, Elizabeth 18 3
Stine, Elizabeth A R 19 3
Stine, Eyster 57 3
Stine, Fannie C 24 3
Stine, Flora M 167 2
Stine, Florence M 24, 100 3
Stine, Foster L 65 3
Stine, George H 24, 28 3
Stine, Gladys V 135 3
Stine, Harriett 32 3
Stine, Henry 32 3
Stine, Henry 37 1
Stine, Jacob 56 1
Stine, Jacob 43 3
Stine, John 40 3
Stine, John F 19, 44 3
Stine, John H 32 3
Stine, Joseph H 45 3
Stine, Mertie C 45 3
Stine, P Lawson 44, 65 3
Stine, Samuel M 32 3
Stine, Sarah 43 3
Stiner, Adam 1 3
Stiner, Daniel H 15 3
Stiner, Ezra 18 3
Stiner, Henry R 290 2
Stiner, Jacob 41 3
Stiner, Louis H 290 2
Stiner, Mary 41 3
Stinger, Charles 8 3
Stip, Joseph 41 3
Stipe, Nellie S 129, 215 2
Stirder, Sarah 71 3
Stirrat, Annie N 265 2
Stitcher, John 39 3
Stitcher, Peter 226 2
Stitcher, Peter 64 3
Stitely Jacob of J 186 1
Stitely, Anna May Albaugh 8 1
Stitely, Annie A 82 3
Stitely, B P 38 1
Stitely, Bradley P 6 3
Stitely, Catherine L 16 3
Stitely, Clarence J 16 3
Stitely, David 252, 265, 283 1
Stitely, David R 15 3
Stitely, David W 16 3
Stitely, Edw L 240 1
Stitely, Edward 222 2
Stitely, Edward L 21 3
Stitely, Elzie R 72 3
Stitely, George M 6 3
Stitely, Isaac 71 1
Stitely, Isaac P 219, 252 1
Stitely, J of Jno 70 3
Stitely, J W 201 1
Stitely, Jacob 40 3
Stitely, Jacob 214 2
Stitely, Jacob John 70 3
Stitely, Jacob of J 41 1
Stitely, Jno 70 3
Stitely, John 70 3
Stitely, John F 8 1
Stitely, John H 70, 71 3
Stitely, Luther C 12 2
Stitely, M W 73 1
Stitely, Marshall W 21 3
Stitely, Sam'l A 10 1
Stitely, Samuel 71 3
Stitely, Samuel A 72 3
Stitely, Solomon S 70 3
Stitely, Thomas L 6 3
Stitely, Winfield S 82 3
Stitlely, Sarah 70 3
Stitley, Daniel R 24 3
Stitley, David W 35 3
Stitley, David W 245 1
Stitley, Edward E 43 3
Stitley, Frank 24 3
Stitley, G P 236 2
Stitley, George 26 3
Stitley, Harry El 43 3
Stitley, Isaac P 15, 20, 35 3
Stitley, Isaiah Q 26 3
Stitley, Jacob 6, 39 3
Stitley, Jacob E 43 3
Stitley, Jane 42 3
Stitley, Joel A 43 3
Stitley, John 39, 40 3
Stitley, John R 43 3
Stitley, John W 42 3
Stitley, Mary 40 3
Stitley, Norman E 24 3
Stitzel, Jacob 205 2
Stitzel, Wm 205 2
Stockesdale, Chas R 28 3
Stockman, Bertha M 83 3
Stockman, Charlotte 9 3
Stockman, Charlotte A 10 3
Stockman, Chas 82 1
Stockman, Christian 177 1
Stockman, Christian 64 3
Stockman, Clara 45 3
Stockman, Clara B 133, 166 1
Stockman, Daniel 15, 42, 89 3
Stockman, David 14, 165 3
Stockman, E J 85, 166 1
Stockman, E Russell 210, 249 1
Stockman, Elizabeth E 20 3
Stockman, Ella M 44 3
Stockman, Emmanuel 229 1
Stockman, Frederic J 60 3
Stockman, George 26 3
Stockman, George A 10, 28 3
Stockman, George E 27 3
Stockman, Grayson 44 3
Stockman, Henry 9, 32 3
Stockman, J N 210 1
Stockman, J N 32 3
Stockman, J S 71 3
Stockman, James H 44 3
Stockman, John 39, 42, 53 3
Stockman, John J 26 3
Stockman, John Jr 53 3
Stockman, John L 85 1
Stockman, John M 133 1
Stockman, John N 112 1
Stockman, John N 55 3
Stockman, John W 45, 65, 89 3
Stockman, Luther F 51 3
Stockman, Mary 53 3
Stockman, Mary Ann 54 3
Stockman, Nathaniel C 60 3
Stockman, Nettie B 65 3
Stockman, Philip 64 3
Stockman, Phoebe A 65 3
Stockman, Roy M 73 3
Stockman, Silas V 60 3
Stockman, Susan V 73 3
Stockman, Susanna O 8 1
Stockman, W D 52 1
Stockman, Walter C 20, 27 3
Stockman, Walter D 34 1
Stockman, Walter D 83 3
Stockman, William 26, 39 3
Stockman, William 58 1
Stockman, William D 15, 42, 82, 100 3
Stockman, William H 20 3
Stockman, Wm 28 2
Stockman, Wm 229 1
Stockman, Wm 51, 54 3
Stocks, James W 33, 46 3

Stocksdale, Amanda V 1 3
Stocksdale, Charles R 235 1
Stocksdale, Chas R 220 1
Stocksdale, Geo 229, 253 1
Stocksdale, Geo W 19 1
Stocksdale, George 271 2
Stocksdale, George W 1, 28, 42 3
Stocksdale, Nathan B 60 3
Stocksdale, T C 42 3
Stockslayer, Henry 8 2
Stocksleger, Amos 1 3
Stocksleger, Catherine C 1 3
Stoeelemyer, J M 32 3
Stoffel Peter 53 3
Stoffell, Peter 80 2
Stoffer, Peter 185 3
Stokes, Carrie 96 2
Stokes, Chas 206 3
Stokes, Chas L 43 3
Stokes, Chas L 238 2
Stokes, Florence V 24 3
Stokes, Frank M 24 3
Stokes, Geo 185 3
Stokes, George 26, 39, 40 3
Stokes, Harriet D 32 3
Stokes, Henry 26, 32, 203 3
Stokes, Henry 14, 28, 29, 223a, 282, 287 2
Stokes, Henry 59, 71, 110, 165, 279 1
Stokes, Henry W 33 3
Stokes, J Henry 32 3
Stokes, J Henry 140 1
Stokes, James 39 3
Stokes, Joshua 194 1
Stokes, Joshua 26, 39, 40, 43 3
Stokes, Josiah 171, 218 3
Stokes, Koshua 282 2
Stokes, R Y 122, 129, 186 3
Stokes, Richard H 67 3
Stokes, Robert 66 2
Stokes, Robert 32, 67 3
Stokes, Robert Y 67 3
Stokes, Robt 148 2
Stokes, Robt Y 202 3
Stokes, Wm 14 2
Stokes, Wm 32 3
Stoler, S G 57 3
Stoll, Catherine O 222a 2
Stoll, Lewis H 113 2
Stollemyer, Joseph 9 3
Stoller, Henry 163 1
Stoltz, Mary M 53 3
Stonckman, Elizabeth E 27 3
Stone, A B 72 1
Stone, Adam 1 3
Stone, B O 192 1
Stone, Catherine E 9 3
Stone, Charles W 10 3
Stone, Cordelia D 81 3
Stone, D E 166 1
Stone, D E 220, 254, 258 2
Stone, D E Dr 59 1
Stone, D E Dr 50, 187 3
Stone, D E Jr Dr 20 3
Stone, Daniel E 61, 110 1
Stone, Daniel E 16 3
Stone, Daniel E Jr 15 3
Stone, E D 19 3
Stone, Elizabeth D 15 3
Stone, Ephraim 171 3
Stone, F K 214, 253 1
Stone, Frederick A 116 2
Stone, Frederick K 101 2
Stone, Frederick K 23 3
Stone, Frederick K 264, 272 1
Stone, G H 50 3
Stone, G K 100 1
Stone, H F 227 3
Stone, Harriett 42 3
Stone, Henry 9 3
Stone, Howard G 33 3
Stone, Ida 106 1
Stone, Ida A 127 1
Stone, Ida A A/K/A 35 3
Stone, Ida E 16, 35 3
Stone, J LaRue 265 2
Stone, Jacob 1, 38 3
Stone, John 41, 215 3
Stone, John A 77 3
Stone, John C 106, 198, 272 1
Stone, John C 23 3
Stone, John T 272 1
Stone, Joseph D 42 3
Stone, Joseph W 38 3
Stone, K K 271 1
Stone, Kieffer V 127 1
Stone, Kieffer V 35 3
Stone, L P 50 3
Stone, Luther M 54 3
Stone, Lydia 279 1
Stone, Lydia A 272 1
Stone, Mamie J 50 3
Stone, Margaret A 19 1
Stone, Margaret A 55 3
Stone, Mary Ann 41, 154 3
Stone, O B 34, 38, 62 1
Stone, O B 72 3
Stone, O B 166 2
Stone, O B Dr 200 2
Stone, Otis 149 2
Stone, Otis B 90, 107, 140 1
Stone, Otis B 10 3
Stone, Otto A 10 3
Stone, Ruth G 68 3
Stone, S K 253, 271 1
Stone, Uriah 77 3
Stone, Walter Eugene 68 3
Stone, Washington 81 3
Stone, William H 81 3
Stone, Wm 155 1
Stone, Wm 54 3
Stonebraker, D K 159, 165, 263 1
Stonecipher, Annie V 4 3
Stonecipher, David 84 2
Stonecipher, Mary E 4 3
Stonecipher, Robert W 4 3
Stoner, A 26 3
Stoner, Abraham 41, 70 3
Stoner, Allie M 3 3
Stoner, Augustus 2 3
Stoner, Augustus 55 1
Stoner, Augustus 11 2
Stoner, Autrian 1 3
Stoner, D E 65 2
Stoner, Dallas A 15 3
Stoner, Daniel 169 2
Stoner, Daniel 147, 171 1
Stoner, Daniel 14, 15 3
Stoner, David 14, 19, 54, 55, 67 3
Stoner, David 189, 197, 201, 277 1
Stoner, David 30, 169, 188, 254 2
Stoner, David R 21 3
Stoner, David Sr 14 3
Stoner, Elizabeth K 21 3
Stoner, Elmer S 77 3
Stoner, Ephraim 15, 171 3
Stoner, Ephriam 59, 189, 201 1
Stoner, Ephriam M 67 3
Stoner, Ephriam W 54 3
Stoner, Ephriam W 277 1
Stoner, Esther 19 3
Stoner, Ezra 252 1
Stoner, Ezra 30 2
Stoner, Ezra R 21 3
Stoner, Ezra R 265 1
Stoner, F E 196 3
Stoner, F L 15, 16, 24, 28, 44, 51, 56, 57, 67, 71, 72, 82, 87, 91, 100, 102, 111, 113, 124, 141, 175, 176, 179, 182, 187, 188, 192, 203, 206, 215, 220 3
Stoner, F L 2, 5, 15, 18, 20, 31, 46, 52, 68, 75, 78, 87, 106, 132, 139, 163, 166, 199, 225, 271 2
Stoner, F L 11, 19, 52, 62, 68, 71, 88, 92, 119, 145, 147, 166, 169, 183, 186, 230, 233, 235, 245, 248, 254, 257, 260, 265, 282 1
Stoner, Florence 31, 199 2
Stoner, Florence E 139, 265 2
Stoner, Florence E 97, 120, 219, 222, 265 1

Stoner, Florence E 24, 28 3
Stoner, Florence M 92 1
Stoner, Florence W 15 2
Stoner, Frank 145 1
Stoner, Frank 66, 68, 96, 139, 154, 172, 178, 188, 198, 206, 214, 215, 222, 212a, 218a 2
Stoner, Frank & 4 1
Stoner, Frank L 8, 20, 22, 23, 35, 54, 62, 70, 72, 77, 96, 106, 139, 143, 166, 171, 181, 203, 222, 224, 225, 229, 213a, 214a, 227a, 229a, 238, 241, 242, 247, 258, 262, 267, 277, 282 2
Stoner, Frank L 18, 19, 24, 25, 30, 33, 38, 41, 42, 44, 60, 61, 86, 92, 97, 101, 112, 115, 120, 126, 132, 135, 144, 156, 147 150, 152, 156, 172, 179, 183, 186, 188, 193, 195, 197, 201, 214, 219, 222, 225, 230, 240, 254, 257, 266 1
Stoner, Frank L 19, 24, 35, 43, 50, 55, 57, 71, 83, 113, 124, 149, 166 3
Stoner, Frank M 225 2
Stoner, Frederick 228 1
Stoner, Harry L 23 2
Stoner, Henry 14 3
Stoner, J E 75 3
Stoner, Jacob 38, 41, 70 3
Stoner, James 144 1
Stoner, John 52, 155, 191, 196, 203, 225, 263, 277, 278 1
Stoner, John 7, 22, 63, 113, 254 2
Stoner, John 1, 14, 38, 39, 40, 81 3
Stoner, John of A 26 3
Stoner, John R 9, 43 3
Stoner, John T 134 2
Stoner, John T 43 3
Stoner, M A 2 3
Stoner, Magdalena 54 3
Stoner, Magdaline 54 3
Stoner, Martha J 55 3
Stoner, Martha Potts 57 3
Stoner, Martha R 43 3
Stoner, Mary 40 3
Stoner, Mary Gertrude 262 2
Stoner, Mollie E 208 1
Stoner, Pauline 246 2
Stoner, Rachael 70 3
Stoner, Rebecca 67 3
Stoner, S L 57 3
Stoner, S L 240, 249 1
Stoner, Samuel 70 3
Stoner, Samuel E 42, 72 3
Stoner, Sarah 70, 71 3
Stoner, Suannah 70 3
Stoner, Susan 70 3
Stoner, T M A 15 3
Stoner, Theodore 75 3
Stoner, Thomas 9 2
Stoner, Thomas M N 91 1
Stoner, Thos 229 1
Stoner, U Roy 72 3
Stoner, Upton 27, 150 2
Stoner, Upton 70, 77 3
Stoner, William 6 1
Stoner, Wm 1, 117, 163 1
Stoner, Wm 134 2
Stoner, Wm J 72 3
Stoner, Wm J 36, 148, 262 2
Stoner, Wm J 72, 155, 278 1
Stonesifer, Abraham 19 2
Stonesifer, Adam 212 3
Stonesifer, Andrew 2 3
Stonesifer, Annie E 58 3
Stonesifer, Charles E 2 3
Stonesifer, Daniel 14 3
Stonesifer, David 14 3
Stonesifer, Elizabeth 18 3
Stonesifer, Jacob 150 2
Stonesifer, Mahlon 58 3
Stonesifer, Mary E 57, 72 3
Stonesifer, Robert W 58 3
Stonesifer, Samuel 210 1
Stonesifer, Sarah J 72 3
Stoneslifer, Jacob 18 3
Stoneslifer, Jared 41 3
Stoneslifer, Mahlon [?] 210 1
Stonsifer, William J 81 2
Storm, Betty Culler 83 3
Storm, C Irving 162 1
Storm, Charles Irvin 11 3
Storm, Edw D 226 3
Storm, Edward 49 1
Storm, Edward B 189 3
Storm, Edward D 45, 74, 166, 260 1
Storm, Edward D 161 2
Storm, Edward D 161 3
Storm, Elizabeth 182 2
Storm, Em N 184 1
Storm, Fairy 150 1
Storm, Francis E 59, 61 1
Storm, Gracie 62 3
Storm, Harrie 172, 254 1
Storm, Harrie E W 150 1
Storm, Harrie E W 33 3
Storm, Harry E B 150 1
Storm, Isabella 35, 64 3
Storm, James 22, 134, 159, 275 2
Storm, James 18, 41 3
Storm, John T 67 3
Storm, Joseph 43 3
Storm, Leonard 50 3
Storm, M Elizabeth 11, 51 3
Storm, M Elizabeth 56, 149 2
Storm, Mary 64 3
Storm, Mary M 54 3
Storm, O Leonard 54 2
Storm, O Leonard 10, 62 3
Storm, P L 54 3
Storm, Peter 64 3
Storm, Peter L 38 2
Storm, Peter L 64 3
Storm, Richard P 35 3
Storm, Richard S 64 3
Storm, Sperry 33 3
Storm, W Bartgis 65 1
Storm, W M 62 1
Storm, William 218a 2
Storm, William B 35, 64 3
Storm, William M 101, 120, 137, 166, 177, 278 1
Storm, William M 41, 136, 140, 200, 238, 271, 277 2
Storm, William M 10, 11, 24, 196 3
Storm, Wm 62, 124 3
Storm, Wm 214 1
Storm, Wm 93, 172, 178, 203, 222 2
Storm, Wm 62 3
Storm, Wm B 27 1
Storm, Wm B 71 3
Storm, Wm C 92 1
Storm, Wm C 176 3
Storm, Wm M 92, 97, 120, 126, 147, 148, 156, 186, 188, 194, 215, 219, 222, 254, 257 1
Storm, Wm M 15, 41, 49, 54, 56, 76, 85, 96, 104, 139, 143, 149 2
Storm, Wm M 10, 45, 51, 57, 75, 226 3
Stormes, James 169 2
Storms, Leonard Jr 116 1
Storms, Peter 137 2
Storms, Rezin 67 3
Storms, Rosanna 67 3
Storn, William M 224a 2
Storr, Addie G 45 3
Storr, Andrew 34 1
Storr, Charles H 12 3
Storr, Elizabeth 20 3
Storr, Henry C 41 3
Storr, John 41 3
Storr, John D 20, 45 3
Stotelmyer, Asa P 239 2
Stottelmyer, Elizabeth C 21 3
Stottelmyer, John 169 2
Stottlemyer 139 2
Stottlemyer, Amanda 42 3
Stottlemyer, Cassianus 9 3
Stottlemyer, Clarence 23 3
Stottlemyer, Clarence B 10 3
Stottlemyer, Clarence W 57 3
Stottlemyer, D 192 3
Stottlemyer, Daniel 15 3

Stottlemyer, Danuel 15 3
Stottlemyer, David 14 3
Stottlemyer, Denton C 123 1
Stottlemyer, Effie Irene 33 3
Stottlemyer, Elizabeth 21, 44 3
Stottlemyer, Elizabeth C 33 3
Stottlemyer, Elmer C 44 3
Stottlemyer, Emmert 73 3
Stottlemyer, Emory 45 3
Stottlemyer, Franklin 23, 41, 71 3
Stottlemyer, G R 42 3
Stottlemyer, Gail P 28 3
Stottlemyer, Geo 57, 60 3
Stottlemyer, Geo R 14 1
Stottlemyer, George 14, 26 3
Stottlemyer, George R 28 3
Stottlemyer, H F C 38 1
Stottlemyer, Hannah 31, 57, 60 3
Stottlemyer, Harlan D 33 3
Stottlemyer, Harreit 32 3
Stottlemyer, Henry 33 3
Stottlemyer, Hiram 32 3
Stottlemyer, J 7 2
Stottlemyer, Jacob 129, 184 3
Stottlemyer, Jacob 203 1
Stottlemyer, James C 57 3
Stottlemyer, Jas C 60 3
Stottlemyer, Johanna 15 3
Stottlemyer, John 26, 38, 39, 41, 42 3
Stottlemyer, John 69 2
Stottlemyer, John M 40 3
Stottlemyer, John M 125, 228 1
Stottlemyer, John P 41 3
Stottlemyer, John R 195 2
Stottlemyer, John R 45 3
Stottlemyer, John W 43 3
Stottlemyer, John W II 44 3
Stottlemyer, Joseph 15, 40, 42, 43 3
Stottlemyer, L A C 10 3
Stottlemyer, Malinda 55 3
Stottlemyer, Marg J 55 3
Stottlemyer, Maria J 57 3
Stottlemyer, Mary E 32 3
Stottlemyer, Mary Jane 65 3
Stottlemyer, Nelson 57, 60 3
Stottlemyer, Pointon 65 3
Stottlemyer, Sophia C 73 3
Stottlemyer, Susan 41, 71 3
Stottlemyer, Susan E 195 2
Stottlemyer, Susannah 82 3
Stottlemyer, W H 40 3
Stottlemyer, W H 214 2
Stottlemyer, Wm H 82 3
Stottlemyer, Wm S 123 1
Stottlemyre, Franklin 196 3
Stottlemyre, George F 196 3
Stottlemyre, Mary E 57 3
Stottlemyre, Mary E 57 3
Stottlymyer, Daniel 15 3
Stottymeyer, John 235 2
Stouder, Michael [sic] 279 1
Stouffer, A T 91 3
Stouffer, B F 163 2
Stouffer, Henry E 97 1
Stouffer, J H 124 3
Stouffer, Jacob 116 1
Stouffer, John 171 3
Stouffer, Simon W 26 1
Stouffer, William 81 3
Stouffer, Wm J 81 3
Stouter, Esther H 28 3
Stouter, Felix 24 3
Stouter, Geo T 72 3
Stouter, George P 28, 43 3
Stouter, Helen J 44 3
Stouter, John M 43 3
Stouter, John N 38 1
Stouter, Joseph H 43 3
Stouter, Mary M 24 3
Stouter, Sarah C 72 3
Stouter, Sarah M 172 2
Stover, Absalom 41, 60 1
Stover, Absalom 2 3
Stover, Annie E 2 3
Stover, Catherine 8 3
Stover, Charles A 2, 11 3
Stover, Charles A 28 1
Stover, Chas A 73 1
Stover, Elizabeth 85 1
Stover, George R 2 3
Stover, John 38 3
Stover, John 22 2
Stover, Raymond R 11 3
Stover, Wilbur Q 11 3
Stover, Wm 112 1
Stow, John C 144 2
Stown, Fairybell 33 3
Stra effer, Michael 53 3
Straeffer, Daniel 18 3
Straeffer, Esther 18 3
Straeffer, John 117 1
Straeffer, John 53 3
Strafer, Daniel 15 3
Strailman, Carroll H 56 3
Strailman, Carroll H B 119 1
Strailman, Charles G 10 3
Strailman, Charles J D 11 3
Strailman, Elsie J 76 1
Strailman, Elsie Jane 21 3
Strailman, Geo 106 1
Strailman, George 110 1
Strailman, H M 197 1
Strailman, Helan M 10 3
Strailman, Henry M 186 3
Strailman, Ida V 35 3
Strailman, Julina V 44 3
Strailman, Margaret E 119 1
Strailman, Margaret E 56 3
Strailman, Mary S 10 2
Strailman, Roy F 44 3
Strailman, W Grayson 44 3
Strailman, Wm G 119 1
Strailman, Wm G 56 3
Strasberg, Josiah 42 3
Strasberger, Bradley T 6 3
Strasberger, Catherine 235 1
Strasberger, Daniel 71 3
Strasberger, Dudley 204 1
Strasberger, George R 28 3
Strasberger, John E 39 3
Strasberger, John F 217 1
Strasberger, John W 71 3
Strasberger, Leroy 27 3
Strasberger, Mary Jane 159 1
Strasberger, Nancy 71 3
Strasberger, Solomon 71 3
Strasburg, Charles W 19 3
Strasburg, Elizabeth 19 3
Strasburg, Susan 42 3
Strasburg, Wm 169 2
Strausberger, Dudley F 6 3
Strausberger, George R 6 3
Strausburg, Nicholas 60 3
Strawder, John T 12 2
Strawsberger, George W 27 3
Strawsburg, John W 196 3
Strawsburg, Nicholas 60 3
Stream, Annie P 3 3
Stream, George C 28 3
Streams, Charles 11 3
Streams, George S 28 3
Streams, Israel 35 3
Streams, Samuel 11 3
Streight, Clarence 45 3
Streight, John C 45 3
Strickberry, Dorthy 184 3
Stricklin, Samuel 64 3
Strickstruck, Catherine 9 3
Stride, Amanda A 3 3
Stride, Irvin G 3 3
Strider, Isaac 35 3
Strine, Annie S 3 3
Strine, Benjamin 6 3
Strine, Elias T 55 1
Strine, Elias T 44 3
Strine, Francis 19 2
Strine, George H 28 3
Strine, Harvey R 33 3
Strine, Howard B 33 3
Strine, John H 44 3
Strine, Laura M 51 3

Strine, Mary E 58 3
Strine, Paul R 58 3
Strine, Raymond L 3, 28 3
Strine, Sarah 71 3
Strobel, Milton C 72 3
Strobel, Sophie 72 3
Strohrmann, Edward F 20 3
Strokes, Joshua 125, 140 1
Strong, Gordon 51 3
Strong, John 37 3
Strong, Louise Snyder 51 3
Stroughton, Marjorie 151 2
Stroup, Annie B 3 3
Stroup, Annie B 291 2
Stroup, J O 291 2
Stroup, J Ord 3 3
Strouse, William F 83 3
Strube, Albert 2, 68, 83 3
Strube, Andrew 2 3
Strube, Arthur 23 3
Strube, Bertha R 6 3
Strube, Fannie 23 3
Strube, Frank 23 3
Strube, Lela M 67 3
Strube, Robert E 67 3
Strube, Rosanna 68 3
Strube, William H 83 3
Struder, John 13 1
Stuart, Abraham 1 3
Stuart, George W 28 3
Stubbs, Caroline 10 3
Studebaker, L: M 137 3
Study, Henry 242 2
Study, Jacob 100, 107 2
Study, John Jr 93 2
Study, Lloyd W 83 3
Study, William A 83 3
Stuff, Annie M 73 3
Stull, A 26, 40, 53 3
Stull, Adam 53 3
Stull, Adam 1, 26, 53, 219 3
Stull, Adam 113 2
Stull, Amanda R 67 3
Stull, Ann Rebecca 2 3
Stull, Benjamin 6 3
Stull, Benjamin R 6 3
Stull, Benton 6 3
Stull, Bernard 42 1
Stull, Bessie V 81 2
Stull, Blanche 50 3
Stull, Blanche F 6 3
Stull, Byron S 6 3
Stull, C L 25 1
Stull, C L 134 2
Stull, Calvin 50 3
Stull, Carrie H 10 3
Stull, Catherine 8 3
Stull, Cecilia T 82 3
Stull, Christopher 8 3
Stull, Ckarke E 21 3
Stull, Daisy A 24 3
Stull, Daniel Z 16, 19, 72 3
Stull, Daniel Z 134 2
Stull, Dennis 15 3
Stull, Dorothy 72 3
Stull, Edward J 20 3
Stull, Elgie M 33 3
Stull, Elizabeth 71 3
Stull, Ella 189 1
Stull, Ella Mae 21 3
Stull, Ella N 21 3
Stull, Emma T 156 1
Stull, Emory W 21 3
Stull, Eve E 19, 40 3
Stull, Everett R 6 3
Stull, F J 20 3
Stull, Fred J 24 3
Stull, Frederick A 40, 50 3
Stull, Frederick S 2 3
Stull, G Bernard 167 2
Stull, Geo 181 2
Stull, George 27, 39 3
Stull, George of A 26 3
Stull, Hanson 27 3
Stull, Harry C 33 3
Stull, Harry C S 45 3
Stull, Harry W 33, 163 3
Stull, Howard E 32 3
Stull, Howard I 33 3
Stull, Ira S 33 3
Stull, Jacob 40 3
Stull, Jacob of A 40, 53 3
Stull, John 234, 244 1
Stull, John 18 2
Stull, John 1, 8, 37, 39, 40 3
Stull, John A 68 3
Stull, John J 50 3
Stull, Joshua 59 1
Stull, Joshua 41, 26 3
Stull, L H 186 3
Stull, Lawrence 50 3
Stull, Leander D 50 3
Stull, Lewis 18, 19, 50 3
Stull, Louisa C 32 3
Stull, Louisa V 50 3
Stull, Lovis 50 3
Stull, Lucvetia S 50 3
Stull, Luther B 72 3
Stull, Mamie I 62 3
Stull, Maria 45 3
Stull, Mary 53 3
Stull, Mary E 55 3
Stull, Michael 54, 205 3
Stull, Michael 263 1
Stull, Minerva A 50, 55 3
Stull, Miriam MG 33 3
Stull, N W 189 3
Stull, Norman H 10 3
Stull, O Clayton 62 3
Stull, Oliver G 68 3
Stull, Parker D 16 3
Stull, R Clinton 67 3
Stull, Randolph G 55 3
Stull, Raymond L 68 3
Stull, Roger B 68 3
Stull, Ross S 72 3
Stull, Ruby M 33 3
Stull, Rudolph 91 3
Stull, Rulhanna M 82 3
Stull, S Newton 72 3
Stull, Sarah S 15 3
Stull, Sarah Sophia 71 3
Stull, Singleton T 72 3
Stull, Spencer C 73 3
Stull, Sterling A 82 3
Stull, Susanna 40 3
Stull, Susannah 71 3
Stull, Theodore 101 1
Stull, Theodore H 76 1
Stull, William 54 3
Stull, William A 55 3
Stull, William H 82 3
Stull, William M 166 3
Stull, William Mahlon 82 3
Stull, Wm 46, 188 2
Stull, Wm H 71 3
Stull, Wm H 15 2
Stull, Wm V 82 3
Stuller, Conrad 8 3
Stuller, Henry 8 3
Stultz, Annie V 4 3
Stultz, Annie V 183 1
Stultz, C A 169 2
Stultz, Cecilia 23 3
Stultz, Chas 132 2
Stultz, Elizabeth 19 3
Stultz, Frederick 23 3
Stultz, Henrietta 32 3
Stultz, Millard F 19 3
Stummel, John B 205 1
Stunkle, C H 23, 55 3
Stunkle, Chas F 51 3
Stunkle, EJ 20 3
Stunkle, Ella E 33 3
Stunkle, Fred J 240 1
Stunkle, Frederick 20, 23 3
Stunkle, Henry E 33 3
Stunkle, Ira 20 3
Stunkle, Lewis F 51 3
Stunkle, Mary E 55 3
Stunkle, Mary J 51 3
Stup David 14 3
Stup, A C 19 3
Stup, Ann E 2 3
Stup, Ann S 6 1
Stup, Ann S 42 3
Stup, Annie C 44 3

Stup, Archie F 51 3
Stup, Bessie M 72 3
Stup, Charles W 57 3
Stup, Charles W 172 1
Stup, Chas W 16 3
Stup, Clayton J 20 3
Stup, David 102 2
Stup, David T 260 1
Stup, David T 20 3
Stup, E L 41 3
Stup, Effie M 20 3
Stup, Eleanore 19 3
Stup, Elijah C 14 3
Stup, Elmer G 21 3
Stup, Elmer S 2 3
Stup, Elnaore 19 3
Stup, Emanuel D 20 3
Stup, Emma G 51 3
Stup, Esther 260 1
Stup, Grayson F 19 3
Stup, Harry E 51 3
Stup, Harry T 250 1
Stup, Helen Myers 250 1
Stup, Howard M 16, 56 3
Stup, J D 100 3
Stup, Jacob 39, 41 3
Stup, Jacob E M 43 3
Stup, Jesse B 57 3
Stup, John 39 3
Stup, John J 28 2
Stup, John J 42, 71, 81 3
Stup, Joseph 39, 71, 171 3
Stup, Joseph 71 1
Stup, Joseph 27 2
Stup, Joshua 42 3
Stup, Josiah E 44 3
Stup, Katie M 72 3
Stup, Leora E 51 3
Stup, Lewis E 51 3
Stup, Malissa T 57 3
Stup, Mary 193 2
Stup, Mary Ann 53 3
Stup, Mary E 57, 58 3
Stup, Minnie F 80 2
Stup, Ruth E 51 3
Stup, S E 56, 189 3
Stup, Samuel 28 2
Stup, Samuel 71, 171 3
Stup, Sarah A M 43, 72 3
Stup, Spencer 245, 260 1
Stup, Spencer 47, 124, 199 2
Stup, Spencer 35 3
Stup, Spencer E 120, 126 1
Stup, Spencer E 12, 18, 49, 81, 85, 286 2
Stup, Spencer E 20, 58, 202 3
Stup, Susan 14 3
Stup, W H 72 3
Stup, William D 81 3
Stup, William H 44 3
Stup, Wm H 72 1
Stup, Wm H 224 3
Stup,Charles W 148 1
Stupp, Ann Rebecca 1 3
Stupp, David 15 3
Stupp, Joseph 39 3
Sturchsomb, B S 116 1
Sturgis, Flavius S 23 3
Sturgis, John T 23 3
Stuttler, Henry 1 1
Styern, C Edw 42 1
Suck, Altie E 3 3
Suck, George E 3 3
Sueter, Henry 9 3
Sulcer, Effie F 21 3
Sulcer, Frank Scott 21 3
Sulivan, Cornelius 8 3
Sulivan, William 51 1
Sullivan, Catherine 8 3
Sullivan, Charles T 23 3
Sullivan, Daniel 176 3
Sullivan, David 228 1
Sullivan, Elizabeth S 46 3
Sullivan, Ellen May 20 3
Sullivan, Fannie K 23 3
Sullivan, Ida P 35, 43 3
Sullivan, J W 83 2
Sullivan, Jacob 9 1
Sullivan, James J 46 3
Sullivan, John W 43 3
Sullivan, Lutricia R 46 3
Sullivan, Nancy 60 3
Sullivan, William 8 3
Sullivan, Wm 213 1
Sulser, Catherine 27 3
Sulser, George P 27 3
Sulser, Henry C 41 3
Sulser, John H 41 3
Sultzer, Peter 64 3
Suman, Albert 18 3
Suman, Aron 1 3
Suman, Catherine 8 3
Suman, Catherine 1 3
Suman, Eleanore 18 3
Suman, Emma E 20 3
Suman, F 14 1
Suman, Frank 24, 56, 189 3
Suman, Frank 62, 219 1
Suman, I W 65 2
Suman, Isaac 132 2
Suman, Isaac S 219 3
Suman, John W 52 1
Suman, John W 44 3
Suman, John W 46 3
Suman, Manzella 44 3
Suman, S E 113 3
Suman, Sarah E 71 3
Summers, Abraham 1 3
Summers, Alice 4 3
Summers, Amanda C R 71 3
Summers, Andrew J 3, 44, 161 3
Summers, Anna R 3 3
Summers, Bertie 6 3
Summers, C 39, 40, 41 3
Summers, C D H 15 3
Summers, C T 58 2
Summers, C Thomas 145 1
Summers, C Thomas 11, 163 3
Summers, C Thos 189 1
Summers, Catherine 9 3
Summers, Charles K 10 3
Summers, Charles W 11 3
Summers, Chester F 21 3
Summers, Chester Mrs 33 3
Summers, Christian 8 3
Summers, Clara V 82 3
Summers, Clayton 60 3
Summers, Cleo Darner 179 1
Summers, Cora L 16 2
Summers, D W 179 3
Summers, David 35 2
Summers, David 252 1
Summers, David W 15, 43 3
Summers, David W 280 2
Summers, E 20 3
Summers, Edgar M 57 3
Summers, Edna M 154 2
Summers, Elmer E 33 3
Summers, Emma F 21 3
Summers, Emma K 57 3
Summers, Emma Kate (Emma F) 21 3
Summers, Eva 169 2
Summers, Fannie E 24, 45 3
Summers, Florence L 23 3
Summers, Foster L 24 3
Summers, Geo 163 1
Summers, Geo S 3 3
Summers, Geo S 239 2
Summers, Geo W 54 3
Summers, George W 27, 70 3
Summers, George W S 28 3
Summers, H C 58, 72, 161, 203 3
Summers, H H 124 3
Summers, H H 44 1
Summers, Harold C 6 3
Summers, Harry C 49 2
Summers, Harry C 126, 179, 210 1
Summers, Harry C 113 3
Summers, Helen R 11 3
Summers, Henry W 32 3
Summers, Hezekiah 31 3
Summers, Hezekiah D 112 1
Summers, Hezekiah D 3, 33 3
Summers, I J 260 1

Summers, Isaac 253 1
Summers, Isaac J 35 3
Summers, J 237 2
Summers, J 40, 42, 53, 70, 192 3
Summers, J E 230 1
Summers, J F 31 3
Summers, J George 1, 9 3
Summers, J George 37 1
Summers, J George 294 2
Summers, J W B 82 3
Summers, Jacob 13, 91, 159 1
Summers, Jacob 175, 187 2
Summers, Jacob 223 3
Summers, Jacob E 9, 42 3
Summers, Jacob of C 40, 41 3
Summers, Jacob of J 40, 42, 53, 70, 192 3
Summers, Jacob of J 13, 37, 234 1
Summers, Jacob of J 237 2
Summers, Jacob V 13 1
Summers, Jacob V 44 3
Summers, John 40, 54 3
Summers, John 189 1
Summers, John 40 2
Summers, John A 44 3
Summers, John C L 44, 57 3
Summers, John E 44 3
Summers, John F 44, 195 3
Summers, John G 42 3
Summers, John J 65, 71 3
Summers, John of C 39 3
Summers, John T 43 3
Summers, John W B 140 1
Summers, Jonas V 45, 50 3
Summers, Joshua 44 3
Summers, Joshua 35, 132 2
Summers, L E 9 1
Summers, Landis M 3 3
Summers, Laura E 44 3
Summers, Laura G 51 3
Summers, Lawson 13 1
Summers, Lawson H 50, 71 3
Summers, Lewis E 50 3
Summers, Louis 115 1
Summers, Margaret 31 3
Summers, Margaret M 65 3
Summers, Mary A 107 3
Summers, Mary E 28, 50, 57 3
Summers, Mary Ellen 208 1
Summers, Mary G 44 3
Summers, Mary M 53, 54 3
Summers, Minnie M 10 3
Summers, Myrtle G 57 3
Summers, Philip 64 3
Summers, Philip W 32, 65 3
Summers, Roy A 50 3
Summers, S M 71 3
Summers, Samuel 27, 70 3
Summers, Samuel 84 1
Summers, Samuel 54 2
Summers, Samuel M 35 2
Summers, Samuel T 71 3
Summers, Samuel T 13 1
Summers, Sarah J 71 3
Summers, Simeon P 71 3
Summers, Susie M 11 3
Summers, Theresa M 231 1
Summers, Thos 140 1
Summers, W Bay 208 1
Summers, W E 51 3
Summers, William H 35, 82 3
Summers, Wm H 71 3
Summers, Wm H 40 2
Summons, John F 160 3
Sumwaldt, Isaac H 67 3
Sumwaldt, Ruayon H 67 3
Sumwalt, Andrew J 1 3
Sunday, Daniel 196 3
Sunday, Harold Hedges 33 3
Sunday, Mary Stull 33 3
Sundergill, Bettie E 72 3
Sundergill, J Roy 44 3
Sundergill, J Roy 126 1
Sundergill, J Roy E 1 1
Sundergill, Nellie D 44 3
Sundergill, Stanley H 72 3
Sunin, Robert 67 3
Suter, Catherine 9 3
Suter, Charles W 11 3
Suter, Henry 32 3
Suter, John H 11 3
Suter, Samuel L 20 2
Sutton, James R 45 3
Sutton, Mary E 45 3
Swaedner, Daniel 11, 57, 58, 137, 179, 188, 196, 233 1
Swaedner, Daniel 129, 288 2
Swaedner, Daniel 70 3
Swaedner, David 195 1
Swaedner, John 54 3
Swaedner, Ruth A 210 1
Swaedner, Winfield 216 3
Swaedner, Wm 201 1
Swales, Baker 6 3
Swalm, Henry 37 1
Swamley, Asa 1, 14 3
Swamley, Daniel 14 3
Swank, Ada E 3 3
Swank, G B 282 1
Swank, G Philip 139 2
Swank, Geo M 283 1
Swank, Geo P 225 1
Swank, Geo P 188 3
Swank, George M 27 3
Swank, George P 27, 28 3
Swank, Ruth Coblentz 28 3
Swann, Jeannette L 46 3
Swann, Martin W 192 3
Swann, Martin W 199 2
Swann, William A 51 3
Swarmley, Asa 106 1
Swartley, Jerome R 35 2
Swartz, Harriet 181 1
Swartz, Harvey P 181 1
Swartz, Mary 56 3
Swartzbaugh, J W 176 3
Sweadner, D 19 3
Sweadner, Daniel 14, 35, 237 2
Sweadner, Daniel 1, 14, 71, 91, 205, 207, 209 3
Sweadner, Daniel 21 1
Sweadner, Daniel Sr 14 3
Sweadner, David 67, 91 3
Sweadner, John 54, 163, 218 2
Sweadner, John 6, 187 3
Sweadner, John 48, 61 1
Sweadner, Leland 51 3
Sweadner, Marcellus 51 3
Sweadner, Marcellus W 58, 72 3
Sweadner, Richard D 67 3
Sweadner, Ruth A 83 3
Sweadner, S A 2 3
Sweadner, S Leland 72 3
Sweadner, W T 83 3
Swearingen, Elizabeth 18 3
Swearingen, Frank V 24 3
Swearingen, Joseph 193, 217 1
Swearingen, Joseph 37 3
Swearingen, Joseph 150 2
Swearingen, Joseph Van 39 3
Swearingen, Margaret R 55 3
Swearingen, Maria 54 3
Swearingen, Ruth 18, 54 3
Swearingen, Ruth D 55 3
Swearingen, Van 39 2
Swearinger, Elizabeth 79 3
Swearinger, Hazel Morgan 24 3
Swearinger, Ruth D 67 3
Swearinger, Tabitha 75 3
Swearinger, Van 79 3
Swearinger, Van P 79 3
Sweeney, Daniel G 19 3
Sweeney, Daniel T 82 3
Sweeney, Elizabeth G 19 3
Sweeney, Estelle M 21 3
Sweeney, Eugenia S 75 3
Sweeney, Israel 35 3
Sweeney, John B 35 3
Sweeney, Joseph 37 3
Sweeney, Martin 129 2

Sweeney, Martin 54, 203 3
Sweeney, Mary Anna 54 3
Sweeney, Mary C 125 1
Sweeney, Timoth C 75 3
Sweeney, William R 82 3
Sweeney, Wm R 201 1
Sweet, Sudie V 73 3
Sweigart, Peter 64 3
Swigart, Daniel 14 3
Swisher, Ruth 63 1
Switzer, David 67, 137 3
Switzer, David 186 2
Switzer, Elizabeth 18, 77 3
Switzer, Hanner 18 3
Switzer, Israel 67 3
Switzer, Israel 228 1
Switzer, Jacob 77 3
Switzer, Job 77 3
Switzer, John 57 2
Switzer, Jonas 53 3
Switzer, Mathias 53 3
Switzer, Rudolph 67 3
Switzer, Ulrick 37, 77 3
Swomley, Annie L 82 3
Swomley, Asa 139 1
Swomley, Daniel 15, 106 3
Swomley, Daniel 225 1
Swomley, Daniel E 107 1
Swomley, E C 20 3
Swomley, Edgar M 20 3
Swomley, Ela J 56 3
Swomley, Elisha 20, 56 3
Swomley, Ella J 21 3
Swomley, Ella J et al 20 3
Swomley, H B 82 3
Swomley, Harry C 56 3
Swomley, Mahlon 53 3
Swomley, Mahlon J 56 3
Swomley, Maynard N 56 3
Swomley, W B 56 3
Swomley, William D 82 3
Swope, Catherine 8 3
Swope, Charles 182 3
Swope, David 8 3
Swope, Ezra 20 3
Swope, Harry I 44 3
Swope, Henry 32, 152, 207 3
Swope, Henry 14, 78, 271, 293 2
Swope, Henry 139, 175 1
Swope, Horace A 59 1
Swope, John 182 3
Swope, John E 44 3
Swope, John N 44 3
Swope, Jos 255 2
Swope, Lyndhurst T 50 3
Swope, Mary 54 3
Swope, Michael 55 1
Swope, Nellie 44 3
Swope, Samuel 150 2
Swope, Samuel 100 1
Swpoe[sic], Henry 37 1
Syfert, Mathias 53 3
Sylcurk, Margaret A 56 3
Sylvester, Hugh A C 33 3
Sylvester, Laura Graham 33 3
Synday, Daniel 198 2
Syper, John 37 3
Sypher, Charles A 57 3
Sypher, Joseph 84 2
Tabker, Oatis V 118 3
Tabler, Anna C 42 3
Tabler, Catherine A 91 3
Tabler, Christian 126 1
Tabler, Christian 113 3
Tabler, Christian 69 2
Tabler, Emily E C 129 2
Tabler, F E 107 3
Tabler, Florence M 40 2
Tabler, Francis E 98 3
Tabler, G W 40 2
Tabler, Geo F 91 3
Tabler, Geo F 2 2
Tabler, Geo F 52, 189 1
Tabler, Geo W 104 3
Tabler, George F 100, 107, 118 3
Tabler, George Wm 100 3
Tabler, Harriett I 107 3
Tabler, Ida T 104 3
Tabler, J H 48, 130 1
Tabler, Jeanne C 227a 2
Tabler, Jeanne Cook 107 3
Tabler, John 102, 214 2
Tabler, John H 107, 129 3
Tabler, John H 2 2
Tabler, John W 119 2
Tabler, John W 60, 119 1
Tabler, John W 91, 107, 118, 129 3
Tabler, Lewis 5 2
Tabler, Lewis 111, 113, 120 3
Tabler, Lewis H 111 3
Tabler, Louisa 111 3
Tabler, Margaret 113 3
Tabler, Mary 113 3
Tabler, Melvin T 104, 107 3
Tabler, Melvin T 130 1
Tabler, Mollie K 113 3
Tabler, Peter 120 3
Tabler, Robert L 98 3
Tabler, Ursula T 111 3
Tabler, William 111, 113, 118, 120, 129 3
Tabler, William B 41, 102 3
Tabler, Wm 159 2
Tabler, Wm 249 1
Tabler, Wm B 39 2
Tabler, Wm D 215 3
Tabler, Wm D 14 2
Talbert, Joseph 174 3
Talbert, Joseph 256 1
Talbortt, Sam'l[?] 24 1
Talbott, Andrew J 146 3
Talbott, Ann D 87 3
Talbott, Chas 159, 185 2
Talbott, Geo 87 3
Talbott, Geo E 113, 124 3
Talbott, Geo E 110, 156 1
Talbott, H T 111 3
Talbott, Henry O 111 3
Talbott, J Stover 68 3
Talbott, John 220, 231, 237, 288 2
Talbott, John 106 3
Talbott, Joseph 150 2
Talbott, Joseph 116 1
Talbott, Lillian B 111 3
Talbott, Mahlon 57 1
Talbott, Mary 87, 113 3
Talbott, Nicholas 205 2
Talbott, Samuel 6, 131, 137 1
Talbott, Samuel 106, 124 3
Talbott, Samuel 51, 57 2
Talbott, Susannah 124 3
Tall, George F 100 3
Tan, John 120 3
Tan, Philip 120 3
Taney, A 106 3
Taney, Alice Louise 113 3
Taney, Augestine 237 2
Taney, Augustina 30, 32 1
Taney, Augustine 44 1
Taney, Augustine 87 3
Taney, Augustine 14, 69, 181, 197 2
Taney, Clara E 96 3
Taney, E S 187 2
Taney, Edw S 59, 169, 196 1
Taney, Edw S 39 2
Taney, Edward A 87 3
Taney, Edward S 96 3
Taney, F B 6 1
Taney, Felix 181, 220a 2
Taney, Felix B 69 2
Taney, Felix B 82, 238 1
Taney, Felix B 98, 124 3
Taney, Felix R 133, 196 1
Taney, Frederick 98 3
Taney, Jacob 9 1
Taney, Joseph 26, 107, 129, 220, 210a, 213a, 293 2
Taney, Joseph 82, 116 1
Taney, Joseph 106 3
Taney, L B 87 3
Taney, Lelia 96 3
Taney, Mary C 98 3
Taney, Mary Lelia 113 3
Taney, Phelix B 106 3
Taney, Phillip Felix B 32 1

Taney, Roger B 84, 139 1
Taney, Roger B 26 2
Taney, Sarah 106, 124 3
Taneyhill, Aaron 87 3
Taneyhill, Addie 87, 124 3
Taneyhill, Sarah E 124 3
Taneyhill, Tyler 124, 126 3
Tanzer, Ann 87 3
Tanzey, Arthur 93, 96, 264 2
Tarney, Arthur 87 3
Tarr, Philip 176 1
Taryor, Wm H 67 3
Tasker, William 129 3
Taugstrum, Jeanette 106 3
Taulton, Frank A 98 3
Taulton, Franklin B 98 3
Tavenner, Betty L 89 3
Tavenner, Ella 89 3
Tavenner, Luther 122 3
Tavenner, Luther N 89 3
Tavenner, Otho H 89 3
Tavenner, Ruth Anna 122 3
Tayloer, C Warren 89 3
Taylor, Annie E 87 3
Taylor, Benjamin 120, 122 3
Taylor, Bernard 70 3
Taylor, Brucie 89 3
Taylor, C Warren 92 3
Taylor, Charles W 91 3
Taylor, Edward E 96 3
Taylor, Elizabeth 96, 106 3
Taylor, Eugene A 6 3
Taylor, Francis D 98 3
Taylor, Geo 197 1
Taylor, Geo W 206 2
Taylor, George W 100 3
Taylor, Griffin 100 3
Taylor, Griffin 72, 76, 107, 129 2
Taylor, Griffith 75 2
Taylor, Howard G 284 1
Taylor, J Hiram 11, 144 2
Taylor, J P 223a 2
Taylor, James H 107 3
Taylor, John 106 3
Taylor, John 29, 163 2
Taylor, John 163 2
Taylor, John F 165 3
Taylor, John H 241 2
Taylor, John K 231 2
Taylor, John T 55 1
Taylor, John T 6 3
Taylor, John W 106 3
Taylor, Jula V 129 3
Taylor, Katherine A 109 3
Taylor, Mary A 113 3
Taylor, Mary E 113 3
Taylor, Nancy 116 3
Taylor, Nancy 116 3
Taylor, P H 189 1
Taylor, Philepena 120 3
Taylor, Pruthy 120 3
Taylor, Reuben 61 1
Taylor, Robert M 122 3
Taylor, Ruth 122 3
Taylor, Sarah A 91 3
Taylor, Sarah Ann 124 3
Taylor, Sarah C 124 3
Taylor, Susan A R 100, 124 3
Taylor, Victoria C 128 3
Taylor, W A 188 1
Taylor, W H 82 3
Taylor, William H 129 3
Taylor, William Wilson 129 3
Taylor, Wm B 79 3
Taynan, John 214 3
Tedrick, Charles A 92 3
Tedrick, Charles Homer 92 3
Tedrick, Hannah J 102 3
Tehan, Eliza 106 3
Tehan, John 137 2
Tehan, John 106 3
Tehan, Mary 106 3
Tehen, John 131 2
Templin, Samuel S 124 3
Tener, Geo 51 2
Tenor, Philip 120 3
Thaler, Edw 159 1
Thaler, Edward 1 1
Thaler, Sophia 124 3
Thaler, W H 124 3
Tharp, Leonard C 153 1
The Aetna Casualty & Surety Co 41 2
The Aetna Casualty & Surety Company 283 2
The Aetna Casualty and Surety Company 219 3
The American Bonding Co of Balto 69, 124 2
The American Bonding Company of Bal 200 2
The American Fidelity Co of Mont 40 2
The American Surety Co of N Y 40 2
The Empire State Surety Co of N Y 153 2
The F & M Nat'l Bank 12 3
The F & M Nat'l Bank 255 2
The Fidelity & Casualty Co N Y 81 2
The Fidelity & Casualty Co of N Y 287 2
The Fidelity & Deposit Co of Md 2, 35, 40 2
The Fidelity and Casualty Co of N Y 59 2
The Glenns Falls Indemnity Co 175 2
The Great American Indemnity Co 73, 167, 249 2
The New Amsterdam Casualty Co of N Y 40 2
The New Amsterdam Casulaty Co 268 2
The U S Fidelity & Guaranty Co 35, 124 2
Theiss, Nola M 126 3
Theiss, Thomas M 126 3
Thomas John 56 1
Thomas, " Eliza 96 3
Thomas, (Snowden) Eliza 96 3
Thomas, A D Mrs 87 3
Thomas, A E H 102 3
Thomas, A M 9 2
Thomas, A S 166 2
Thomas, Abbie L 87 3
Thomas, Abraham 87 3
Thomas, Alfred V 96 3
Thomas, Alice 143 2
Thomas, Alice B 91 3
Thomas, Alpheus D 87 3
Thomas, Amanda 87, 96 3
Thomas, Amos 271 1
Thomas, Ann E 106 3
Thomas, Ann M 87 3
Thomas, Ann S 91 3
Thomas, Anna 166 2
Thomas, Anna M 124 3
Thomas, Anna Maria 124 3
Thomas, Anna Mary 87 3
Thomas, Anna May 172 3
Thomas, Anna S 87, 124 3
Thomas, Annie A 100 3
Thomas, Annie C 87 3
Thomas, Annie E 87 3
Thomas, Annie E M J 87 3
Thomas, Annie M H 87 3
Thomas, Arch'd 89 3
Thomas, Archibald 87 3
Thomas, Archie A 101 1
Thomas, Arie E 87 3
Thomas, Austin C 8 1
Thomas, B O 102, 199 2
Thomas, B O 71 1
Thomas, B O 11, 94 3
Thomas, B O Dr 108 2
Thomas, Barbara 89 3
Thomas, Barbara Ann 89 3
Thomas, Benjamin 61 1
Thomas, Benjamin 89 3
Thomas, Benjamin R 89 3
Thomas, Bennie R 89 3
Thomas, Bernard O 25 2
Thomas, Bessie B 91 3

Thomas, Bruce V 89, 100 3
Thomas, C C 87 3
Thomas, C C C 111 3
Thomas, C E 98, 118, 163 3
Thomas, C F 72, 248 1
Thomas, C F 124 3
Thomas, C Frank 96 3
Thomas, C K 120, 165, 186 3
Thomas, C K 143 2
Thomas, C Kate 110 1
Thomas, C Kate 91 3
Thomas, C Keefer 37 1
Thomas, C Kieffer 91 3
Thomas, C M 272 1
Thomas, C M 209 3
Thomas, C M 84, 149, 280, 290 2
Thomas, C M G C 107 3
Thomas, C R 76 2
Thomas, C S 107 3
Thomas, C Silas 87, 96, 111, 113, 192 3
Thomas, C Silas 30 1
Thomas, C Wm 113 3
Thomas, Calvin A 62, 76, 152 1
Thomas, Calvin A 91 3
Thomas, Caroline S 91 3
Thomas, Catherine 91, 129 3
Thomas, Catherine 76, 165, 270 1
Thomas, Catherine F 91 3
Thomas, Catherine F 27 1
Thomas, Cephas 91 3
Thomas, Cephas M 91, 107, 124, 227 3
Thomas, Cephas M 38, 100, 101 1
Thomas, Cephus 192 3
Thomas, Charles E 91 3
Thomas, Charles F 91 3
Thomas, Charles Silas 92 3
Thomas, Charles T 160 3
Thomas, Charles W 91 3
Thomas, Charlotte 91 3
Thomas, Chas 138, 214 2
Thomas, Chas E 89, 98, 185 3
Thomas, Chas F 98 3
Thomas, Chas F 119, 169 1
Thomas, Chas F 218 2
Thomas, Chas G 47 1
Thomas, Chas J 87 3
Thomas, Christian 91, 100, 129, 221 3
Thomas, Christian 118 1
Thomas, Christian 51, 96 2
Thomas, Clara E 218 2
Thomas, Clara E 91 3
Thomas, Clara L 96 3
Thomas, Clarence C 124 3
Thomas, Clayborn A 91 3
Thomas, Clifford L 91 3
Thomas, Clinto C 124 3
Thomas, Clinton C 107, 113 3
Thomas, Clyde B 91 3
Thomas, Clyde E 111 3
Thomas, Clyde E 143 2
Thomas, Conner M 48 1
Thomas, Conner M 113 3
Thomas, Cora B 96, 114 3
Thomas, Cordelia 107 3
Thomas, Corrilla K 91 3
Thomas, Curtis W 91 3
Thomas, D Guy 126 1
Thomas, D Guy 206 2
Thomas, D Guy 98 3
Thomas, D O 67 1
Thomas, D O 91, 160 3
Thomas, Daniel 9, 94 3
Thomas, Daniel B 94 3
Thomas, Daniel P 94 3
Thomas, David 24, 71 1
Thomas, David 41, 75, 89, 91, 94, 100, 106, 120 3
Thomas, David 28, 51, 96, 132 2
Thomas, David D 94, 106, 113 3
Thomas, David G 94 3
Thomas, David O 24, 47, 60, 91, 147, 194, 234 1
Thomas, David O 81, 94, 113, 186 3
Thomas, David O 143, 282 2
Thomas, E 94 3
Thomas, E Eugene Jr 96 3
Thomas, E M 106 1
Thomas, E M 111 3
Thomas, E N 82 3
Thomas, E P 12 2
Thomas, Edgar 16 3
Thomas, Edgar E 142, 145 1
Thomas, Edgar E 199 2
Thomas, Edgar E 11 3
Thomas, Edgar E A 196 2
Thomas, Edgar L 95, 107 3
Thomas, Edith U 107 3
Thomas, Edith Utz 96 3
Thomas, Edmund 91 3
Thomas, Edna F 96 3
Thomas, Edward 96 3
Thomas, Eli 100 3
Thomas, Eliza 96 3
Thomas, Elizabeth 89, 94, 96, 111 3
Thomas, Elizabeth A 106 3
Thomas, Elizabeth R 94, 96 3
Thomas, Elmer C 96 3
Thomas, Emily V 96 3
Thomas, Emma S 96, 113 3
Thomas, Eve 96 3
Thomas, Ezra 125 1
Thomas, Ezra 166 2
Thomas, Ezra 54 3
Thomas, Ezra M 42, 96, 100 3
Thomas, Ezra M 69, 290 2
Thomas, F G 94 3
Thomas, F G 56, 222 1
Thomas, F G 116 2
Thomas, Fannie W 98 3
Thomas, Fenton 32 3
Thomas, Frances 98 3
Thomas, Francis 7, 181, 186, 275 2
Thomas, Francis 75, 96, 106 3
Thomas, Francis 57, 88, 116, 165 1
Thomas, Franklin C 124 3
Thomas, Franklin C 101 1
Thomas, Franklin Chas 91 3
Thomas, Franklin J 98 3
Thomas, G 100, 106, 113, 120 3
Thomas, G B L 102 3
Thomas, G C 67, 106 3
Thomas, G L 72, 87, 91 3
Thomas, G L 34 1
Thomas, G L 259 2
Thomas, G L Jr 72 3
Thomas, G Lester 124 3
Thomas, G M 94 3
Thomas, G Pearl 111 3
Thomas, Geo 80, 96 2
Thomas, Geo 106, 113, 171 3
Thomas, Geo 72 1
Thomas, Geo C 124 3
Thomas, Geo D 100 3
Thomas, Geo E 100 3
Thomas, Geo F 124 3
Thomas, Geo H 213, 260 1
Thomas, Geo Henry 87 3
Thomas, Geo J 87 3
Thomas, Geo of G 100 3
Thomas, Geo of H 89, 91, 96, 102 3
Thomas, Geo of H 32 1
Thomas, Geo W 100 3
Thomas, George 100, 113 3
Thomas, George B 100 3
Thomas, George C 107 3
Thomas, George D 100 3
Thomas, George H 100 3
Thomas, George of G 214 3
Thomas, George of H 40, 100, 113, 120 3
Thomas, George of H 58 1
Thomas, H 40, 89, 91, 96, 102, 113, 120, 195 3

Thomas, Harriet S 166 2
Thomas, Harriett A 94, 102 3
Thomas, Harriett S 102 3
Thomas, Harry F 102 3
Thomas, Hattie C 87 3
Thomas, Helen C 94, 97 1
Thomas, Helen G 92 3
Thomas, Henry 18, 75, 102, 214 3
Thomas, Henry Nelson 102 3
Thomas, Henry of G B L 102 3
Thomas, Henry of John 102 3
Thomas, Hiram G 111 3
Thomas, Ida M 4 3
Thomas, Ida Mae 100 3
Thomas, J B 67 1
Thomas, J Clark 150 2
Thomas, J E 111 3
Thomas, J F 41 1
Thomas, J F 94, 161, 220 3
Thomas, J F 129, 189, 227 2
Thomas, J Fenton 10, 107 3
Thomas, J Fenton 60 1
Thomas, J L 113 3
Thomas, J M 96 3
Thomas, J Samuel 113 3
Thomas, J T 59 1
Thomas, J T 94 3
Thomas, J Travers 25, 84 2
Thomas, J Travers 87, 107 3
Thomas, Jacob 116, 117, 131, 156, 164, 263 1
Thomas, Jacob 106 3
Thomas, Jacob 57, 181 2
Thomas, Jacob A 192 3
Thomas, Jacob B 106 3
Thomas, Jacob D 60 1
Thomas, Jacob Jr 100 1
Thomas, Jacob L 111 3
Thomas, Jacob of J 37, 40 1
Thomas, James 268 2
Thomas, James 39, 106 3
Thomas, James 57 1
Thomas, James 134, 268 2
Thomas, Jeremiah 6, 107 3
Thomas, Jesse L D 124 3
Thomas, John 14, 102, 106, 113 3
Thomas, John 47, 59, 88, 116, 164 1
Thomas, John 83, 100, 137, 150, 165 2
Thomas, John B 122 2
Thomas, John B 8, 29, 122 2
Thomas, John B 47, 48, 100, 116, 165, 271 1
Thomas, John B 29 2
Thomas, John B 91, 106, 107, 118, 124, 163, 186 3
Thomas, John D 234 1
Thomas, John D 107, 118 3
Thomas, John F 176 3
Thomas, John Franklin 100, 107 3
Thomas, John G 113, 122 3
Thomas, John H 106, 120 3
Thomas, John Hanson 106 3
Thomas, John M 106 3
Thomas, John M 56 1
Thomas, John Morgan 107 3
Thomas, John of G 106 3
Thomas, John P 223 3
Thomas, John W 107, 124 3
Thomas, Jonathan D 120 3
Thomas, Jonothan A 89, 106 3
Thomas, Joseph 102, 106 3
Thomas, Joseph 106 1
Thomas, Joseph C 260 1
Thomas, Joseph G 107 3
Thomas, Joseph I 107 3
Thomas, Joseph L 260 1
Thomas, Joshua S 107 3
Thomas, Joshua S 271 2
Thomas, Josiah S 124 3
Thomas, Julia E 114 3
Thomas, Kate C 100, 111 3
Thomas, L 118 3
Thomas, L C 91 3
Thomas, L E 124 3
Thomas, L M 113, 139 3
Thomas, Lee C 87, 111 3
Thomas, Leonard 111 3
Thomas, Leven 8 3
Thomas, Levin 7 2
Thomas, Levin 24 1
Thomas, Levin 11, 122, 124 3
Thomas, Lewis 29, 205, 227, 221a 2
Thomas, Lewis E 271 2
Thomas, Lewis M 24, 56, 164 1
Thomas, Lewis M 268 2
Thomas, Lewis M 40, 111 3
Thomas, Lewis N 1 3
Thomas, Lewis O 143 2
Thomas, Lillian F 112 2
Thomas, Lillie J E 111 3
Thomas, Lloyd 57, 116, 144, 243 1
Thomas, Lloyd 111 3
Thomas, Lottie V 100 3
Thomas, Louis E 22 2
Thomas, Louis M 1 2
Thomas, Louisa E 111, 166 3
Thomas, Louisa Leiner 111 3
Thomas, M Lema 107 3
Thomas, Margaret 113 3
Thomas, Margaret 113 3
Thomas, Maria V 113 3
Thomas, Martha 42 3
Thomas, Mary 96, 100, 113 3
Thomas, Mary A 113 3
Thomas, Mary A R 113, 129 3
Thomas, Mary Ann 87 3
Thomas, Mary Anna 113 3
Thomas, Mary C 91, 107, 111, 113 3
Thomas, Mary C 23 2
Thomas, Mary Catherine 113 3
Thomas, Mary E 92 1
Thomas, Mary E 91 3
Thomas, Mary Ellen 91 3
Thomas, Mary G 114 3
Thomas, Mary I 100 3
Thomas, Mary J 106, 118, 120 3
Thomas, Mary L 102 3
Thomas, Mary V 87 3
Thomas, Mary Virginia 111, 113 3
Thomas, Maude L 96 3
Thomas, Michael 163 1
Thomas, Michael 89, 102, 113, 124 3
Thomas, Michael of H 195 3
Thomas, Milton F 113 3
Thomas, Milton F 136 1
Thomas, Minnie L 107 3
Thomas, Motter C 92 1
Thomas, Myra V 91 3
Thomas, Nancy W 106 3
Thomas, Noble V 111 3
Thomas, Nora E 92 3
Thomas, Noteley 234 1
Thomas, Notely 37, 87, 89, 124 3
Thomas, Notling 122 3
Thomas, O B 196 2
Thomas, Otha of L 118 3
Thomas, Otho 87, 89, 91, 118, 124, 185 3
Thomas, Otho 59 1
Thomas, Otho B al 199 2
Thomas, Otho V 58 2
Thomas, Otis 122 3
Thomas, P of G 113 3
Thomas, Peter 96, 106, 113, 120, 165, 171 3
Thomas, Peter of G 113, 120 3
Thomas, Peter of H 91 3
Thomas, Phebe 96 3
Thomas, Phebe J 120 3
Thomas, Philip 94, 120 3
Thomas, R D 216 3
Thomas, Rebecca 111, 122 3
Thomas, Richard 42, 67, 89, 91, 118, 122, 124, 185, 186 3
Thomas, Richard 146, 148, 150 1

Thomas, Richard W 122 3
Thomas, Robert H 122 3
Thomas, Roy Z 111 3
Thomas, Ruth D 199 2
Thomas, Ruth D 206 3
Thomas, Ruth D 72, 176 1
Thomas, S A 94 3
Thomas, S C 228 3
Thomas, S D 107 3
Thomas, S D 48, 96, 110, 189 1
Thomas, S D 52 2
Thomas, S F 100, 144 1
Thomas, S Fenton 210 1
Thomas, S G 214 1
Thomas, S S 89 3
Thomas, Samuel 89, 122, 124 3
Thomas, Samuel 18, 128 2
Thomas, Samuel C 91, 100, 124 3
Thomas, Samuel Cornelius 124 3
Thomas, Samuel D 124 3
Thomas, Samuel D R 106 3
Thomas, Samuel H 124 3
Thomas, Samuel S 91, 94, 124 3
Thomas, Sarah C 91, 124 3
Thomas, Sarah T 101 1
Thomas, Stephen A 91, 124 3
Thomas, Stephen A 117 1
Thomas, Stephen A 83 2
Thomas, Stephen N 2 3
Thomas, Steven A 91 3
Thomas, Sue E 124 3
Thomas, Susan 87, 111, 120, 124 3
Thomas, Susan A 100 3
Thomas, Susan M 124 3
Thomas, Susan N 71 3
Thomas, Susan R 107, 124 3
Thomas, Susannah 124 3
Thomas, Susie 87 3
Thomas, Susie M 113 3
Thomas, Thomas 60 1
Thomas, Thos L 8 2
Thomas, William 120, 122, 129 3
Thomas, William 288 2
Thomas, William H 129, 131 3
Thomas, William H 265, 288 2
Thomas, Wm H 111 3
Thomas, Zacariah G 100 3
Thomas, Zach G 230 1
Thomas, Zachariah G 22 2
Thomas, Zachary G 131 3
Thompson, Alcinda 87, 107 3
Thompson, Alice V 57 3
Thompson, Annie E 87 3
Thompson, Bushrod 89 3
Thompson, Byron W 93, 166 1
Thompson, Byron W 83 3
Thompson, Carl F 98 3
Thompson, Catherine 135 1
Thompson, Chas 75 2
Thompson, Chas W 98 3
Thompson, Emma I 99 2
Thompson, Feilder 98 3
Thompson, Florence S 166 3
Thompson, Francis I 98 3
Thompson, Francis M 98 3
Thompson, Frank C 98 3
Thompson, Fred 106 3
Thompson, George 100 3
Thompson, H Edith 102 3
Thompson, Henry 100 2
Thompson, Henry A 102 3
Thompson, Herbert 102 3
Thompson, Howard C 98 3
Thompson, Jacob 106 3
Thompson, James H 107 3
Thompson, John 106, 107, 124 3
Thompson, John 88, 217 1
Thompson, John 223a 2
Thompson, John F 107, 129 3
Thompson, John P 88, 109, 117, 208 1
Thompson, John P 106 3
Thompson, John P 197 2
Thompson, John R 107, 166 3
Thompson, John W 106 3
Thompson, Lloyd 137 1
Thompson, M V 87, 107 3
Thompson, Mary 152 1
Thompson, Mary B 113 3
Thompson, Mary Louise 107 3
Thompson, Mary V 107 3
Thompson, Meredith 152 1
Thompson, Michael J 113 3
Thompson, Moses M 113 3
Thompson, Myrtle L 36 2
Thompson, Nancy W 263 1
Thompson, Nathan 116 3
Thompson, Nettie G 129 3
Thompson, Nicholas 116 3
Thompson, Nicholas 51 1
Thompson, Nicholas 22 2
Thompson, Norman C 107 3
Thompson, Otho F 98 3
Thompson, Philip 98 3
Thompson, Racheal J 98 3
Thompson, Richard 217 1
Thompson, Samuel 124 3
Thompson, Smallwood 124 3
Thompson, Viola C 129 3
Thompson, William 133 1
Thompson, William 98 3
Thompson, William E 129 3
Thompson, William H 89, 129 3
Thompson, Wm 137 1
Thomsen, John 107 3
Thomson 179 3
Thomson, Andrew 87 3
Thomson, Mary L 113 3
Thomson, Nancy S 116 3
Thomson, William J 129 3
Thorp, George H 100 3
Thorp, Sarah J 100 3
Thorpe, Agnes H 87 3
Thrasher, Albert 129 3
Thrasher, B Albert 34 1
Thrasher, B Albert 126 3
Thrasher, Ben 126 3
Thrasher, Benjamin 89 3
Thrasher, Charlotte B 91 3
Thrasher, Elias 96 3
Thrasher, Ella V 96, 129 3
Thrasher, George W 100 3
Thrasher, John R 91 3
Thrasher, M A 122 3
Thrasher, M B A 122 3
Thrasher, Margaret A 113 3
Thrasher, Martha 113, 126 3
Thrasher, Nellie V 100 3
Thrasher, Robert K 122 3
Thrasher, S Albert 91 3
Thrasher, Thomas 89, 126, 207 3
Thrasher, Thomas 134 2
Thrasher, Thomas L 113 3
Thrasher, Thomas S 91, 122, 126 3
Thrasher, Thos 75 2
Thrasher, W J 122 3
Thrasher, William J 129 3
Thrasker, M T 122 3
Tice, Elizabeth 96 3
Tice, Henry N 102 3
Tierman, L 104 1
Tierney, John 217 1
Tierney, John J 172 2
Tierney, John J 107 3
Tiers, Edw W 177 2
Tiers, Edward Wm 96 3
Tilghman, Fannie L 100 3
Tilghman, George W 100 3
Timothy, James H 40 1
Timson, Richard 122 3
Tingstimn, William H 129 3
Tingstrum, Frederick 98 3
Tingstrum, Frederick A 98 3
Tingstrum, Peter 120 3
Tinney, Louisa 111 3
Tinney, Sarah R 124 3

Tinny, Franklin 111 3
Tinny, J M 111 3
Tipton, Ada M 87 3
Tipton, Ethel H 87 3
Tipton, Ethel R 124 3
Tipton, Susan M 124 3
Title Guaranty & Surety Co, The 237 1
Titlow, C A 111 3
Titlow, Daniel 56, 58 1
Titlow, Daniel 94 3
Titlow, Daniel 61, 197 2
Titlow, Elizabeth 96 3
Titlow, Geo 43, 165 2
Titlow, Geo W 111 3
Titlow, George 100 3
Titlow, George W 94 3
Titlow, Isaac 205 1
Titlow, John 106 3
Titlow, John 100 2
Titlow, Kate A 9 2
Titlow, Lewis S 94, 111 3
Titlow, Rebecca 122 3
Titus, B T 229 1
Titus, Blair 102 3
Titus, Blair S 129 3
Titus, E P 28 1
Titus, Helena 102 3
Titus, William R 129 3
Titus, Wm R 102 3
Titzel, Robert J 22 1
Tobery, Andrew G W 87 3
Tobery, G W 87 3
Tobery, John E 118 3
Tobery, Jonathan 100, 169 2
Tobery, Jonothan 186 3
Tobery, Otha J 118 3
Tobery, Teresa 87 3
Toby, Jonothan W 171 3
Todd, Ben 139 1
Todd, Benj 102 3
Todd, Benj 37 1
Todd, Benjamin 51, 57, 106 1
Todd, Harriett 102 3
Todd, James 106 3
Todd, James H 106 3
Todd, Jesse P 102 3
Todd, Joshua 61 2
Todd, Mary J 113 3
Todd, Rebecca 122 3
Todd, Samuel 57 1
Todd, Susan 203 3
Todd, Thomas 51 1
Todd, William H 71, 122 3
Todd, William Sr 129 3
Todd, Wm 40 1
Todd, Wm H 106, 137 1
Todd, Wm H 71, 203 3
Todd, Wm H 1 2
Toffer, James 181 2
Tofler, Peter 120 3
Tokar, Christiana 91 3
Tokar, Otto 91 3
Tollinger, A 100 3
Tollinger, Geo D 100 3
Tolls, Richard 26 2
Tomlin, Henri Ralf 63 1
Toms, A E 72 3
Toms, Abraham 87, 94, 129 3
Toms, Abraham of W 100 3
Toms, Abraham Sr 87 3
Toms, Amanda H 106 3
Toms, Anna C 278 1
Toms, Annie C 87 3
Toms, Austin W 87 3
Toms, Barbara E 89 3
Toms, Celia A A 92 3
Toms, Charles A 92 3
Toms, Claud E 107 3
toms, Cordelia 100 3
Toms, D 129 3
Toms, Daniel 94 3
Toms, David 113 3
Toms, E 27 1
Toms, E A 15, 44, 56, 57, 72, 75, 82, 87, 96, 107, 122, 134, 161, 166, 171, 176, 188, 192, 196, 197, 206, 207, 210, 216, 221, 222 3
Toms, E A 2, 5, 9, 12, 20, 25, 31, 41, 49, 54, 58, 70, 85, 87, 89, 102, 106, 108, 124, 128, 131, 148, 154, 189, 199, 206, 210a, 214a, 217a, 225a, 229a, 259, 267, 288 2
Toms, E A 14, 27, 33, 41, 52, 62, 67, 68, 72, 73, 78, 82, 85, 96, 97, 107, 110, 120, 123, 126, 133, 137, 140, 153, 155, 159, 179, 183, 186, 188, 189, 192, 198, 210, 214, 217, 219, 223, 230, 235, 237, 238, 249, 253, 254, 257, 266, 270, 272, 276, 283 1
Toms, E A etla 259 2
Toms, E D 10 3
Toms, E F 186 1
Toms, E Ray 65 2
Toms, E T 189 1
Toms, E V 96 3
Toms, Edgar 40 2
Toms, Edw A 171 1
Toms, Edw A 56, 138 3
Toms, Edward A 227 2
Toms, Edward A 15, 180 3
Toms, Este O 138 3
Toms, Ezra 42, 96 3
Toms, G Franklin 124 3
Toms, Geo D 257, 272 1
Toms, Geo D 96 3
Toms, Geo D 245 2
Toms, Gideon 100 3
Toms, Grace T 109 3
Toms, Herman E 102 3
Toms, Hiram 87, 89 3
Toms, Isaiah 14 3
Toms, Israel 14 3
Toms, J 237 2
Toms, J H 82, 87, 166 3
Toms, J S 113 3
Toms, Jacob 171 2
Toms, Jacob 225 1
Toms, Jacob 14 3
Toms, Jacob Jr 163 1
Toms, Jacob Jr 106 3
Toms, Jacob L 124 3
Toms, Jacob Sr 106 3
Toms, Jacob Sr 11 1
Toms, Jacob Sr 237 2
Toms, Jay W 107 3
Toms, John 106, 124 3
Toms, John E 106 3
Toms, John H 75, 107 3
Toms, Joseph 107 3
Toms, Keefer 109 3
Toms, Keefer S 124 3
Toms, Lester A 111 3
Toms, Lulu F 102 3
Toms, M F 96 3
Toms, Martha A M 129 3
Toms, Mary 113 3
Toms, Michael 113 3
Toms, Raymond 107, 111 3
Toms, Raymond W 122 3
Toms, Samuel 163, 164, 228 1
Toms, Samuel 26, 27 2
Toms, Samuel 19, 94, 124, 129 3
Toms, Samuel of J 237 2
Toms, Samuel of Wm 124 3
Toms, Sarah 209 2
Toms, Sarah A 122 3
Toms, Sarah A E 160, 209 2
Toms, Sarah A E 124 3
Toms, Sheridan 89, 92, 107 3
Toms, Sophia 171 1
Toms, Susan 87, 124 3
Toms, W 100 3
Toms, William 87, 129 3
Toms, Wm 28, 46 2
Toms, Wm 113, 124 3
Toms, Wm 37, 91, 156 1
Toner, Margaret A 21 3
Tony, P 125 1
Tony, Patrick 137 2
Toodle, George A 100 3
Toodle, Phyllis A 100 3
Toogood, Caleb 91 3
Toohey, Isabelle Sister 161 2
Toomey, Patrick 62 3
Tooney, P 70 1
Topper, A J 209 1

Topper, Anthony J 87 3
Topper, Catherine M 91 3
Topper, J Francis 107 3
Topper, Jacob I 107 3
Topper, Jacob L 23 2
Topper, Jacob L 19 3
Topper, James B 282 2
Topper, James Lewis Sr 107 3
Topper, John J 87, 91 3
Topper, Margaret Evelyn 107 3
Topper, Mary E 113 3
Torrance, James 106, 212 3
Torrance, Mary A 113 3
Torrence, James 124 2
Torrence, James 100 1
Torxell, Robert L 124 3
Torxell, Thomas W 113 3
Touder, Andrew 192 3
Towers, Adam 63 2
Town, Lola Mae 122 3
Town, R E 86 1
Town, Raymond E 122 3
Towne, Ann Minerva 87 3
Towne, Minerva D 113 3
Toy, H D 124 3
Toy, Samuel H 124 3
Tozer, Isaac 104 3
Tracey, Chas E 100 3
Tracey, George W 100 3
Tracey, Howard R 101 1
Tracey, Howard R 102 3
Tracey, John F 111 3
Tracey, Lorn E 111 3
Tracy, Peter G 120 3
Traell, Chas 159 2
Traell, Edw 159 2
Trago, William 129 3
Trail, Arthur 87 3
Trail, Bertha 87, 89, 102 3
Trail, Bertha 27 1
Trail, C B 257 1
Trail, C B 98 3
Trail, Chares E 207 3
Trail, Charles B 91 3
Trail, Charles Bayard 89 3
Trail, Charles E 91, 111 3
Trail, Chas 85, 260 1
Trail, Chas 8, 101, 138, 224a 2
Trail, Chas B 241 2
Trail, Chas E 142, 194, 279 1
Trail, Chas E 9, 65, 67, 96, 176 3
Trail, Chas E 78, 264 2
Trail, Chas R 40 1
Trail, E 187 2
Trail, Ed 224a 2
Trail, Edw 111 3
Trail, Edw 85, 183, 203 1
Trail, Edw 137, 165 2
Trail, Edward 253 1
Trail, Edward 94, 96, 106 3
Trail, Florence 87, 98, 102 3
Trail, Francis L 98 3
Trail, Grace 45 3
Trail, Grace 199 2
Trail, Grace W 58, 91, 100, 102 3
Trail, Grace W 129 2
Trail, Henry 87, 98, 102 3
Trail, Henry 27 1
Trail, James 106 3
Trail, James E 29 2
Trail, Lewis A 111 3
Trail, Lydia C 111 3
Trail, Oscar F 118 3
Trainor, Jessie Johnson 111 3
Trainor, Lee S 111 3
Trapnell, Edmonia S 96 3
Trapnell, Joseph 106, 129 3
Trapnell, Richard W 122 3
Trapnell, William 129 3
Trask, Elias 65 3
Travers, Ann 87, 129 3
Travers, Boyle 87, 89 3
Travers, Catherine 91 3
Travers, J 94 3
Travers, John H 91 3
Travers, William 129 3
Travis, Kate E Carmack 115 1
Travis, Le Grand H 111 3
Travis, Legrand H 135 1
Travis, Legrand M 100 1
Travis, Legrande H 115 1
Trayer, Anna A 87, 113 3
Trayer, Jacob 106, 160 3
Trayer, Jacob 119, 287 2
Trayer, Lynn L 259 2
Trayer, Mortimer P 113, 124 3
Trayer, Sarah 106, 124 3
Trayer, Thomas C 287 2
Trayer, Wm H 119 2
Trayer, Wm H 106 3
Treaner, Vincent H 196 3
Tregellas, John N 270 1
Tregellis, Joseph 47 1
Trego, E Youge 107 3
Trego, Eveline 96 3
Trego, John T 107 3
Trego, John T Jr 106 3
Trego, Margaret 143 2
Trego, Sarah R 124 3
Trego, W Edgar 143 2
Trego, William C 129 3
Trego, Wm 7, 117 1
Tregonning, George W 100 3
Tregonning, Lena J 124 3
Tregonning, Mae M 100 3
Tregonning, Samuel L 124 3
Treiber, Mary A 113 3
Treiber, William A 129 3
Treich, Charles S 215 2
Treich, Jeannette A 107 3
Treich, John B 106 3
Treissler, Geo 196 1
Tresselt, Emily 96 3
Tresselt, Frederick 96 3
Tressler, Charles W 91 3
Tressler, Elizabeth E 91 3
Tressler, Jacob 208 2
Tressler, Luther 145 2
Tressler, Samuel G 27 3
Trevitt, Laura M 197 3
Trianger, Geo 124 3
Tribby, Dottie L 129 3
Tribby, William W 129 3
Trice, Nellie L 118 3
Trice, Oliver O 118 3
Trimmer, Sanford 174 3
Triplett, John B 148 1
Tritapoe, Geo H 234 1
Tritapoe, Mary E 52 1
Tritapoe, S E 125 1
Tritt, Elizabeth 96 3
Tritt, John 96, 120 3
Tritt, Paul 120 3
Trittapoe, Nora M 116 3
Trittapoe, Ralph W 122 3
Trittapoe, Samuel E 124 3
Trittapoe, William M 116, 122 3
Trittipoe, William M 129 3
Tro xell, John 179 3
Trostle, Jacob D 75 3
Trostle, John D 144 3
Trout, Catherine 91 3
Trout, Charlotte 91 3
Trout, Chas H 91 3
Trout, Claude C 146 1
Trout, Enna V 96 3
Trout, G C 116 2
Trout, G Cleveland 238 2
Trout, Geo M 108 2
Trout, George W 166 3
Trout, Harry 166 1
Trout, Harry 199 2
Trout, J W 27 3
Trout, John 28 2
Trout, John 91 3
Trout, John 176 1
Trout, Rizpah 146 1
Trout, Samuel C 91 3
Troxel, Adam 87 3
Troxel, Catherine 91 3
Troxel, Elias 96 3
Troxel, Elizabeth 96 3
Troxel, Frederick W 98 3
Troxel, Harriett 102 3
Troxel, Jacob 120 3

Troxel, Jacob 87 3
Troxel, Jacob 220 2
Troxel, James 224 2
Troxel, Joe P 96 3
Troxel, John 163 1
Troxel, John 102, 106, 120 3
Troxel, Josiah 96 3
Troxel, Margaret 113 3
Troxel, Peter of J 120 3
Troxel, Samuel 91, 124 3
Troxell, A M 54 2
Troxell, Abraham 87 3
Troxell, Alan J 225 2
Troxell, Alan J 91 3
Troxell, Ann M 87 3
Troxell, C P 252 1
Troxell, Charles P 24, 91, 107 3
Troxell, Charles P 218a, 262 2
Troxell, Charles R 92 3
Troxell, Chas 30 1
Troxell, Chas B 33 1
Troxell, Chas P 2, 54 2
Troxell, Claiborne 91 3
Troxell, Clayton J 92 3
Troxell, David 87, 94, 106, 113 3
Troxell, David 240 1
Troxell, Edgar C 92 3
Troxell, Edith M 93 1
Troxell, Elizabeth 96 3
Troxell, Fred rick 184 3
Troxell, Frederick 98 3
Troxell, Geo 104 1
Troxell, Geo 208 2
Troxell, George 70, 96, 100 3
Troxell, Henry L 102 3
Troxell, J G 171 1
Troxell, J G Dr 2 3
Troxell, J G Dr 217a 2
Troxell, J M 188 2
Troxell, J W 91 1
Troxell, Jacob 196 1
Troxell, Jacob When 06, 184 3
Troxell, Jacob G 209 3
Troxell, Jacob G 200 1
Troxell, Jacob L 107 3
Troxell, James 87 2
Troxell, James W 107, 165 3
Troxell, James W 217 1
Troxell, Jno 120 3
Troxell, John 27, 159 2
Troxell, John 96, 106 3
Troxell, John G 187 3
Troxell, John H 102 3
Troxell, Johnson W 107 3
Troxell, Joseph 96, 176 3
Troxell, Joshua 186 3
Troxell, M D 98 3
Troxell, Martin D 113 3
Troxell, Mary 102 3
Troxell, Mary A 107 3
Troxell, Mary E 111, 113 3
Troxell, Mary M 107 3
Troxell, Mary R 129 3
Troxell, Maurice L 114 3
Troxell, Peter 228 1
Troxell, Peter of Jno 120 3
Troxell, Samuel J 124 3
Troxell, Thomas W 107, 111 3
Troxell, Thos W 116 2
Troxell, William 124 3
Troxell, William D 98 3
Troxell, William H 129 3
Troxell, Wm 30 1
Trozel, J 120 3
Trozier, W C 106 3
Trubill, Nicholas 70 3
Trubitt, Nicholas 81 3
Trucks, John 54, 134, 224a 2
Trucott, Geo 29 2
Truecott, H H 102 3
Truescott, Geo 177 2
Truett, Mabel G 113 3
Truly, Catherine 91 3
Trumbo, Conrad 91 3
Trumbo, Geo 91 3
Trump, Anna Mary 87 3
Trump, Frederick 106 3
Trump, Frederick 69 2
Trump, Henry 87 3
Trump, John Caspar 106 3
Trundle, Alice 106, 124 3
Trundle, Bertha T 189 3
Trundle, C Newton 92, 124 3
Trundle, C Newton 48 1
Trundle, David 94 3
Trundle, David 117 1
Trundle, David J 109 1
Trundle, David of O 185 3
Trundle, Emma I 96 3
Trundle, H Clayton 235 2
Trundle, H Clayton 137, 264 1
Trundle, Henry T 102 3
Trundle, John 235 2
Trundle, John A 264 1
Trundle, John A 106, 113 3
Trundle, John A 92 2
Trundle, Martha E 106 3
Trundle, Mary E 129 3
Trundle, Mary Matilda 92 3
Trundle, Mary N 124 3
Trundle, Nellie S 124 3
Trundle, O 185 3
Trundle, Otho W 81 3
Trundle, Resetta 94 3
Trundle, S H 106 3
Trundle, Samuel B 124 3
Trundle, Samuel H 124 3
Trundle, Sidney A 96 3
Trundle, Sophie E 124 3
Trundle, William D 129 3
Trundle, Wm H A 106 3
Trunell, H C 225 2
Truscott, George 100 3
Truscott, H R 100 3
Truscott, Hannah R 102 3
Tuck, Bessie L 101 1
Tucker, Andrew 87 3
Tucker, Anna M 113 3
Tucker, Caroline B 91 3
Tucker, Catherine E 129 3
Tucker, Charles A 91, 96 3
Tucker, Charles H 91, 94 3
Tucker, Chas A 129 3
Tucker, Clarence E 91 3
Tucker, Clinton 124 3
Tucker, Daniel 91, 94 3
Tucker, Edw F 58 2
Tucker, Edward F Jr 96 3
Tucker, Edward S 96 3
Tucker, Elizabeth 96 3
Tucker, Ella 129 3
Tucker, Ella M 96, 129 3
Tucker, Francis 129 3
Tucker, Gracie May 91 3
Tucker, Meloina R 113 3
Tucker, Rachel 122, 129 3
Tucker, Richard 122 3
Tucker, Sarah T 124 3
Tucker, Solomon 124 3
Tucker, Thelma Z 227 3
Tucker, William 87, 129 3
Tucker, William J 96, 129 3
Tucker, Wm 11 2
Tull, Eleanor 179 1
Tull, Eleanor H 114 3
Tull, Eleanor M 129 3
Tull, Elinor 260 1
Tull, Howard S 114 3
Tull, Howard V 149 2
Tull, Mary Esther 114 3
Tull, Wesley S 129 3
Tully, Aquilla 56 1
Turbitt, Nicholas 26 2
Turbitt, Nicholas 84 1
Turbitt, Nicholas 185 2
Turbull, Rebecca 122 3
Turbutt, Nicholas 8 3
Turnbull, Chas T 102 3
Turnbull, Harriett 213a 2
Turnbull, Harriett Virgin 102 3
Turnbull, Joshua 213a 2
Turnbull, Nettie H 5 2

Turnbull, Samuel 129 3
Turnbull, William 129 3
Turnbull, William 218a 2
Turnbull, Wm 56 1
Turnbull, Wm 154, 202 2
Turner, Ann R H 113 3
Turner, Catherine 106 3
Turner, Charles 91 3
Turner, George W 129 3
Turner, Harry G 102 3
Turner, Helen L 102 3
Turner, J Ray 129 3
Turner, James W 106 3
Turner, John 106 3
Turner, John R 129 3
Turner, Lewis G 189 3
Turner, Lewis W 113 3
Turner, Mark B 116 3
Turner, Mary B 113 3
Turner, Mary E 113 3
Turner, Mary J 113 3
Turner, Nannie E 116 3
Turner, Thomas 54 2
Turner, Thomas 126, 185 3
Turner, Thomas 88, 146 1
Turner, Thos 119, 171 2
Turner, Thos 195 3
Turner, Virginia H 128 3
Turner, William 129 3
Turner, William A 113 3
Turner, William A Jr 129 3
Turner, William A Sr 129 3
Turner, Wm D 129 3
Turner, Wm D 225 2
Tusing, Jacob 106 3
Tuttle Guar & Surety Co of PA 43 3
Twenty, Florence B 122 3
Twenty, George L Sr 100 3
Twenty, John C 100 3
Twenty, Roy L 122 3
Twigg, Bradford C 89 3
Tyeryar F F 98 3
Tyeryar, Eugene 67 3
Tyeryar, Frederick W 98 3
Tyeryar, Mary E 113 3
Tyeryar, R O 98 3
Tyeryar, Randolph 92 1
Tyler, Ann Maria 87 3
Tyler, Benjamin 116 1
Tyler, Catherine M 91 3
Tyler, D G 166 3
Tyler, E E S 96 3
Tyler, Edward S 96 3
Tyler, Eleanor M 102 3
Tyler, Eliza 96 3
Tyler, Eliza C 160 3
Tyler, Geo 113 3
Tyler, Geo L 87, 100 3
Tyler, Geo M 100 3
Tyler, George 148 1
Tyler, George 100 3
Tyler, George L 100 3
Tyler, Harriet M 104 3
Tyler, Harriett M 102 3
Tyler, Ira 55, 87, 100, 104 3
Tyler, John 137, 213a 2
Tyler, John 106 3
Tyler, Maria 113 3
Tyler, R Bradley 113 3
Tyler, Robert L 122, 160 3
Tyler, Samuel 41 1
Tyler, Samuel L 122 3
Tyler, Susan 40 1
Tyler, T B 101 2
Tyler, W 102 3
Tyler, W 165 2
Tyler, W Bradley Dr 129 3
Tyler, William 26, 37, 106, 195 3
Tyler, William 219a, 290, 294 2
Tyler, William B 294 2
Tyler, William Dr 129 3
Tyler, Wm 7, 14, 19, 27, 43, 57, 115, 154, 165, 175 2
Tyler, Wm 41, 47, 58, 82, 91, 115, 148, 164, 186, 193, 196, 229, 253 1
Tyler, Wm 38, 91, 192 3
Tyler, Wm B 84 1
Tyler, Wm B 1, 171 2
Tyler, Wm Bradley 177 2
Tymeson, Arthur A Sr 87 3
Tymeson, Clyde N 87 3
Tymeson, Goldie B 87 3
Tyson, B H 107 3
Tyson, Belva H 61, 73, 88, 195 1
Tyson, Belva H 108 2
Tyson, Bennet 2, 107 2
Tyson, Bennett 43 2
Tyson, E W D 33 1
Tyson, Elizabeth H D 33 1
Tyson, Elizabeth MD 96 3
Tyson, Elizabeth W D 96 3
Tyson, G Warren 100 3
Tyson, Henry 96 3
Tyson, Henry B 67, 80 2
Tyson, J B 67 2
Tyson, J T Harshman[sic] 28 1
Tyson, Jacob 61, 206 2
Tyson, Jacob 33 1
Tyson, Jacob B 33, 59, 253 1
Tyson, Jacob B 96, 100, 107 3
Tyson, Jonathan 91, 96 1
Tyson, Joseph V 2 2
Tyson, Katie 100 3
Tyson, Marcelene K 122 3
Tyson, Margaret 116 3
Tyson, Nathan S 116 3
Tyson, R A 72 1
Tyson, R S 73, 204 1
Tyson, R S 100 3
Tyson, R S Dr 108 2
Tyson, R S Dr 73 1
Tyson, Robert S 195 1
Tyson, Robert S 107, 122 3
Tyson, Robert S 155 2
Tyson, Robert S Dr 28, 76 1
Tyson, Robert Stafford Jr 122 3
U & S Fidelity & Guaranty Co 132 3
U S F & G 76, 88 1
U S F & G Co 3, 6, 21, 68, 77, 197, 210 3
U S F & G Co 81, 151, 219a 2
U S F & G Co 120, 166, 192 1
U S F & G Company 45 1
U S F & Guaranty Co 277 2
U S F & guaranty Co 163 2
U S Fid & G Co, Md 52 1
U S Fidelity ' Guaranty Co of Baltimore [sic] 30 1
U S Fidelity & Casualty Co 207 3
U S Fidelity & Deposit Co 73, 184 1
U S Fidelity & Deposit Co 149, 172 2
U S Fidelity & Fuaranty Co 220a 2
U S Fidelity & G Co 44 1
U S Fidelity & G Co 16 2
U S Fidelity & Guanranty Co 215a 2
U S Fidelity & Guar Co 48, 93, 133 1
U S Fidelity & Guarantee Co 166, 172 1
U S Fidelity & Guarantee Co 72, 98, 192 3
U S Fidelity & Guaranty 1, 166, 220, 262 1
U S Fidelity & Guaranty 41, 85, 125, 209, 220, 242, 295 2
U S Fidelity & Guaranty 12, 33, 45, 48, 51, 58, 161, 192, 193 3
U S Fidelity & Guaranty Co 3, 4, 10, 12, 21, 24, 28, 45, 51, 57, 58, 68, 82, 87, 96, 100, 113, 129, 134, 138, 161, 163, 169, 172, 188, 189, 192, 193, 197, 199, 203, 221, 223 3
U S Fidelity & Guaranty Co 1, 9, 10, 19, 22, 23, 28, 34, 41, 42, 45, 49, 63, 68, 72, 73, 74, 76, 78, 83, 86, 92, 93, 97, 113, 115, 120, 133, 135, 147, 148, 150, 153, 155, 166, 169, 172, 181, 183, 186, 193, 198, 205, 208, 210, 219, 220, 230, 231, 244, 252, 253, 254, 256, 257, 260, 262, 272, 280 1

U S Fidelity & Guaranty Co 2, 3, 9, 15, 20, 23, 25, 41, 46, 52, 58, 72, 81, 85, 94, 106, 108, 112, 119, 122, 125, 129, 140, 145, 148, 149, 150, 161, 167, 172, 175, 178, 182, 189, 190, 191, 193, 195, 196, 199, 200, 202, 203, 209, 215, 220, 220a, 221a, 222a, 225a, 227a, 229a, 231, 238, 239, 241, 250, 253, 259, 262, 265, 267, 278, 280, 284, 288, 294 2
U S Fidelity & Guaranty Co of Balt 156 1
U S Fidelity & Guaranty Co of Baltimore 131 2
U S Fidelity & Guaranty Co of Balto 188 3
U S Fidelity & Guaranty Co of Md 22, 230 1
U S Fidelity & Guaranty Co of Md 124, 125, 189 2
U S Fidelity & Guaranty Co, The 96 1
U S Fidelity & Guaranty Col 265 2
U S Fidelity & Guaranty Company 143, 274 2
U S Fidelity & Guaranty Corp 262 1
U S Fidelity & Guaranty Corp 283 2
U S Fidelity & Guranty Co 94 3
U S Fidelity & Guranty Co 227a, 229a, 268 2
U S Fidelity & Guranty Co [sic] 1 1
U S Fidelity and Guarantee Co 112 2
U S Fidelity and Guaranty 123 1
U S Fidelity and Guaranty Co 31, 65, 88, 99, 111, 124, 126, 127, 130, 140, 145, 169, 227, 248 1
U S Fidelity and Guaranty Co 172, 209, 215, 235, 291 2
U S Fidelity and Guaranty Co 33, 83, 113, 129, 167 3
U S Fidelity And Guaranty Co 148 1
U S Fidelity and Guaranty Co of Md 210 1
U S Fidelity and Guaranty Co, The 61 1
U S Fidelity and Guaranty Company 18, 32, 102, 161, 225a, 283 2
U S Fidelity and Guaranty Company 101, 107, 124, 153 1
U S Fidelity and Guaranty Company 3, 6, 48, 58, 113, 167, 210, 220 3
U S Fidelity and Guarnaty Co 267 2
U S Fidelity Co of Baltimore 188 2
U S Fidelity Co of Md 33 3
U S Fidelity Guaranty Co 127 1
U S Fidelity Guaranty Co 82 3
U S Fidelty & Guar Co 257 1
U S Fidelty and Guarantee Co 222 2
U S Indemnity & Guaranty Co of Balto 237 1
Ukefer, Abdiel 70 3
Ukefer, Abdiel & 223 1
Uley, Elizabeth 135 3
Ulrich, George W 137 3
Ulrich, John R 139 3
Ulrich, Mary E 137 3
Ulrich, Mary Jane 139 3
Ulrich, Samuel 286 2
Ulrici, Charles 134 3
Ulrick, Charles 134 3
Ulrick, George W 100 1
Ultz, Jacob Jr 139 3
Ultz, Jacob Sr 139 3
Ultz, Joseph Michael 141 3
Ultz, Michael 141 3
Umbaugh, Charles W 141 3
Umbaugh, John 124 2
Umbaugh, Michael 141 3
Umbaugh, Michael F 141 3
Umberger, Alice 208 3
Umberger, Amy l 65 1
Umberger, Estie I 63 1
Umberger, Harry L 145 3
Umberger, John W 102, 140 3
Umberger, Lewis T 145 3
Umberger, Lilly M 140 3
Umberger, Margaret 141 3
Umberger, Michael 141 3
Umberger, William T 145 3
Umkeefer, Fannie C 139 3
Umkeefer, John E 139, 140 3
Umkeefer, Lydia R 140 3
Umstead, Elisha 116 1
Umstead, Enoch 64 3
Umstead, Enoch 116 1
Umstead, John A 139 3
Umstead, Nicholas 37, 142 3
Unestead, Nicholas 26 1
Unger, James H 141 3
Unger, John M 141 3
Unger, Martha 141 3
Unger, Mary C 141 3
Unglebower, Goldie May 137 3
Unglebower, Joseph A 141 3
Unglebower, Margaret 141 3
Unglebower, Maurice A 137 3
Unglesbee, Jennie B 140 3
Unglesbee, John 139 3
Unglesbee, John 150 1
Unglesbee, Lewis E 140 3
Unglesby, John 64 3
Union Bridge Bank & Tr Co 247 2
Union Bridge Bank & Tr Co 45 1
Union Bridge Banking & T Co 189 3
Union Bridge Banking & Tr 270 1
Union Bridge Banking & Tr Co 111 2
Union Bridge Banking &Trust Co 3 2
Union Bridge Banking &Trust Co 203 1
United Fidelity and Guaranty Co 4 1
United Security Co 72 3
United Security Co of Balto Md 33 1
United Stares Fidelity & Guaranty 278 2
United Stated [sic] Fid & Guaranty Co 34 1
United Stated Fidelity & Dep Co 137 1
United States F & G Co 268 2
United States F & G Co 107 1
United States Fidelity & Guant Co 270 1
United States Fidelity & Guarant Co 284 1
United States Fidelity & Guaranty 4, 11, 34, 44, 53, 173, 90, 107, 111, 148, 210, 245, 246, 257, 266 1
United States Fidelity & Guaranty 4, 11, 33, 51, 68, 92, 122, 161, 169, 182, 189 3
United States Fidelity & Guaranty 10, 32, 36, 83, 87, 99, 136, 140, 145, 154, 178, 190, 196, 199, 200, 236, 242, 265 2
United States Fidelity & Guaranty Co 3, 23, 32, 52, 83, 89, 116, 134, 145, 167, 178, 196, 200, 225, 242, 277, 286 2
United States Fidelity & Guaranty Co 3, 11, 21, 28, 92, 161 3
United States Fidelity & Guaranty Co 31, 42, 52, 162, 172, 203, 205, 240, 270, 280 1
United States Fidelity & Guaranty Company, The 93 1
United States Fidelity & Guranty Co

30, 88, 177 1
United States Fidelity and Guaranty 166 1
United States Fidelity and Guaranty 106 2
United States Fidelity and Guaranty Co 127, 166 1
United States Fidelity and Guaranty Co 73 3
United States Fidelity and Guaranty Co 113 2
United States Fidelity and Guaranty Company 157 1
United States Fidelity and Guarnaty 18 2
United States Fidelity Co 10 1
United States Fidelity Inc Guaranty Co 85 1
United States Guaranty Co 104 2
United Surety Co 2, 58 2
United Surety Co 99, 235 1
United Surety Co of Baltimore 178 2
United Surety Co of Baltimore 147 1
United Surety Co of Baltimore City 147, 194 1
United Surety Co of Balto 160, 210 3
United Surety Co, The 79 1
United Surety Company 189 2
Unkefer, A 70 3
Unkefer, Abdial 196 1
Unkefer, Abdial 237 2
Unkefer, Abdiel 31, 39, 50, 70, 132, 136, 174 3
Unkefer, Abdiel 135 1
Unkefer, Abdiel 11, 14, 56, 119, 136 2
Unkefer, Fanny C 279 1
Unkefer, Frederick 136 3
Unkefer, John E 67, 132 3
Unkefer, John E 279 1
Unrich, Augusta 132 3
Unversagt, Jonas T 138 3
Unverzagt, Henry 138 3
Uphold, Emanuel 135 3
Upkraft, Mary 143 3
Upkraft, Mary 141 3
Upkraft, Robert 143 3
Upperman, Joseph 139 3
Urban, Carl A 134 3
Urner, Annie M 132 3
Urner, Calvin S 148 2
Urner, Calvin S 134 3
Urner, E W 118 1
Urner, E W 163, 238 2
Urner, Edward E 134 3
Urner, Elkana W 184 2
Urner, Frances H 265 1
Urner, Francis H 265 1
Urner, Francis Hammond 138 3
Urner, George 137 3
Urner, H 72 2
Urner, H 1 1
Urner, H 144 3
Urner, Hamilton 225 2
Urner, Hammond 2, 20, 23, 144, 148, 154, 184, 211, 222, 238, 242, 246 2
Urner, Hammond 52, 100, 133, 140, 150, 181, 202, 225, 235 1
Urner, Hammond 71, 75, 91, 96, 98, 129, 138, 141, 167, 182, 192 3
Urner, Hammond G 258 2
Urner, Hannah 138 3
Urner, John H 134 3
Urner, Jonas 222 2
Urner, Jonas 139, 144 3
Urner, M G 72, 126, 186, 225, 282, 283 1
Urner, M G 206 2
Urner, M G 71, 75, 98, 116, 122, 132, 139, 144, 161, 163, 186, 187, 3
Urner, M G Jr 72 1
Urner, M G Jr 98, 141, 206 3
Urner, M G Sr 56 3
Urner, M G Sr 1 1
Urner, M G Sr 131, 294 2
Urner, Mary C 141 3
Urner, Mary L 141 3
Urner, Milton 75 3
Urner, Milton 89, 153, 181, 188, 218 2
Urner, Milton G 1, 13, 14, 27, 30, 41, 51, 60, 67, 71, 96, 99, 100, 119, 123, 125, 126, 131, 133, 140, 150, 166, 181, 205, 219, 235, 243, 257, 265, 282 1
Urner, Milton G 2, 20, 23, 31, 35, 40, 70, 75, 92, 107, 112, 144, 148, 172, 181, 188, 189, 205, 227, 220a, 227a, 231, 242, 250, 271 2
Urner, Milton G 9, 15, 55, 71, 91, 129, 134, 141, 179, 182, 192, 195, 196, 209 3
Urner, Milton G Jr 141, 144, 145, 172, 196, 197 3
Urner, Milton G Jr 110, 189, 235 2
Urner, Milton G Jr 27, 123, 126, 140, 150, 181, 282 1
Urner, Milton G. 72 1
Urner, Mollie C 139 3
Urner, S Amos 92, 96, 100, 133, 175 1
Urner, S Amos 56, 139, 144 3
Urner, Samuel 192, 243 1
Urner, Samuel 56, 184, 222 2
Urner, Samuel 14, 64, 137, 138, 144 3
Urner, Samuel A 187 3
Urner, Susan C 126 1
Urner, W Grayson 145 3
Urvin, Wm T 47 1
Utermiethl, Naomi 87 2
Utt, John 263 1
Utterback, Charles L 135, 145 3
Utterback, E J 2, 56 3
Utterback, Edward J 135, 140 3
Utterback, Emma W 135 3
Utterback, Ida R Putman 138 3
Utterback, Lillie K 140 3
Utterback, William W 145 3
Utz, Barbara 133 3
Utz, Catherine 134 3
Utz, Charles M 134 3
Utz, Elizabeth B 135 3
Utz, John 139 3
Utz, John H 282 2
Utz, John S 22 1
Utz, Joseph 139 3
Utz, Margaret E 282 2
Utz, Rosa E 134 3
Utz, S S 134 3
Utz, Samuel P 144 3
Vaciliou, Wm N 127 1
Valentine, Addie Bruce 151 3
Valentine, C L 154 3
Valentine, C L 90 1
Valentine, Chas E 152 3
Valentine, E C 28, 151 3
Valentine, E C 107 2
Valentine, E F 56 3
Valentine, Ed G 153 3
Valentine, Edw G 153 3
Valentine, Edward G 149 3
Valentine, Elias F 149 3
Valentine, Ella C 149 3
Valentine, Ellsworth C 149 3
Valentine, Elmer 60 3
Valentine, Erwin F 149 3
Valentine, Esther 149 3
Valentine, Evan 57 3
Valentine, Evan 102 2
Valentine, Frederick 150 3
Valentine, G H 149 3
Valentine, G H 14 1
Valentine, G S 156 3
Valentine, Geo S 151 3
Valentine, George 152 3
Valentine, H C 159 3
Valentine, Hannah C 151 3
Valentine, Harry C 153 3

Valentine, Harvey E 151 3
Valentine, Hector 151 3
Valentine, Henry 152 3
Valentine, Henry Albert 151 3
Valentine, Jacob 123 1
Valentine, Jacob 152 3
Valentine, James E 152 3
Valentine, John 152 3
Valentine, John 107 2
Valentine, John A 149 3
Valentine, John W 152 3
Valentine, Josephine 152 3
Valentine, Josiah 152 3
Valentine, Lola C 149 3
Valentine, Martin E 151, 206 3
Valentine, Mary E 153 3
Valentine, Mary M 153 3
Valentine, Maxia 149 3
Valentine, Milton 214a 2
Valentine, Milton G 152 3
Valentine, Milton O 153 3
Valentine, Samuel 26, 156 3
Valentine, Samuel 221a 2
Valentine, Solomon 156 3
Valentine, Sylvester 156 3
Valentine, T H 153 3
Valentine, Thos H 153 3
Valentine, W J 159 3
Valentine, William 152, 159 3
Valentine, William 221a 2
Valentine, William A 271 2
Valentine, William A 159 3
Valentine, William J 156 3
Valentine, Wm 22 2
Van Fossen, Edgar A Jr 149 3
Van Fossen, Geo W 100 3
Van Horn, Bertha D 147 3
Van Horn, John 152 3
Van Horn, V D 152 3
Van Meter, Nettie V 159 3
Van Swearingen, Joseph 39 3
Vanella, Samuel 167 2
VanFossen, Bertha I 159 3
Vanfossen, Catherine E 159 3
VanFossen, Edgar A 149 3
Vanfossen, Edgar A 26 1
Vanfossen, Geo W 159 3
VanFossen, Geo W 102 3
VanFossen, Ida Mae 149 3
VanFossen, L 208 2
Vanfossen, Levi 63, 115, 282 1
VanFossen, S C 100 3
Vanfossen, Sarah Catherine 156 3
Vanfossen, Thomas D 156 3
Vanfossen, W H 100 2
Vanfossen, William 159 3
VanFossen, William E 159 3
VanFossen, Wm E Jr 159 3
Vanhorn, Ishmael 51 1
Vanmeter, William H 159 3
VanMeter, William H 159 3
VanOrder, Howard 172 2
Vansant, Abel 146 3
Vansant, Claudia M 146 3
Vansant, Clinton E 96 1
Vansant, J M 48 1
Vansant, James 146 3
Vansant, John 254 2
Vansant, Moses 153 3
Vansant, Oliver P 154 3
Vansant, Oliver P 154 3
Vansant, Susannah 153 3
Vansant, Wm H 153 3
Varden, Josiah (Rev) 152 3
Varden, Margaret A 152 3
Varner, Charlotte 148 3
Varty, C C 188 3
Veant, Christina 148 3
Venable, Annie E 230 1
Vercendiere, Victor 70 1
Vernon, C A L 169 1
Vernon, C L 169 1
Vernon, Charlotte A 148 3
Vernon, E C 169 1
Vernon, Emma E 149 3
Vernon, Eugenia C 149 3
Vernon, George W F 148, 149 3
Vernon, Henry H 152 3
Vernon, John A D 152 3
Vernon, Nathaniel 152 3
Vincendierc, Magnan 78 1
Vincendierc, V 88 1
Vincendierc, Victoria 88, 116 1
Vincendiere, Etrama PMD 149 3
Vincendiere, Victoire 158 3
Vincendiere, Victoria 149 3
Violet, S Mae 11 3
Virts, Amy V 146 3
Virts, Benjamin 147 3
Virts, Benjamin T 172 1
Virts, C Clifton 36 2
Virts, C Clifton 21 3
Virts, Charlotte E 148 3
Virts, Cornelius W 148 3
Virts, Della O 148, 153 3
Virts, Edgar C 148 3
Virts, Ella V 149 3
Virts, Emory L 153, 159 3
Virts, Harold C 151 3
Virts, Harvey G 146 3
Virts, Jacob 150 1
Virts, John 69 2
Virts, John A R 152 3
Virts, John R 152 3
Virts, John W 152 3
Virts, Leone Pauline 151 3
Virts, Lettie 119 1
Virts, Marshall L 153 3
Virts, Minnie A 153, 159 3
Virts, Minnie B 155 3
Virts, Richard A 155 3
Virts, Ryan J 149 3
Virts, W J 148 3
Virts, Wallis L 159 3
Virts, Walter K 153 3
Virtz, Ann Rebecca 146 3
Virtz, Bernard 147 3
Virtz, C Clifton 46 3
Virtz, Pauline Vivian 68 1
Virtz, Wallace L 146 3
Vodgis, Theodore C 166 1
Volger, Susan 156 3
Vollous, Ellen 149 3
Vollous, Joseph 149 3
Von Spoeckelsen, Thomas 158 3
VonEiff, Caroline R 262 2
VonEiff, Fannie S 262 2
Vore, Mary 153 3
Vore, Mordecai 153 3
Vore, Mortecai 159 3
Vore, William 159 3
Vore, Wm 153 3
Wachtel, Annie M 241 2
Wachtel, D J 27 3
Wachtel, Daniel 167, 171, 205 3
Wachtel, Elizabeth 171 3
Wachtel, Frank 182 2
Wachtel, G W 242 2
Wachtel, Geo 209 2
Wachtel, Geo W 92, 201, 203 1
Wachtel, Geo W 11, 39, 195, 199 2
Wachtel, George W 27, 176 3
Wachtel, Harlan S 241 2
Wachtel, Mary E 210 3
Wachtel, Soloman 205 3
Wachtel, W S 209 2
Wachtel, William S 161, 190, 242 2
Wachtel, William S 176, 210 3
Wachtel, Wm 32 2
Wachtel, Wm S 201, 250 1
Wachtel, Wm S 201 3
Wachtell, George W 42 3
Wachter, Ada S 160 3
Wachter, Albina C 161, 166 3
Wachter, Alcinda 161 3
Wachter, Allen T 161 3
Wachter, Amanda E 161 3
Wachter, Andrew J 67 1

Wachter, Andrew J 202 3
Wachter, Ann M 160 3
Wachter, Barbara 195 3
Wachter, Benton F 56 3
Wachter, C L 188 3
Wachter, Calvin W 202 3
Wachter, Catharine A 165 3
Wachter, Charles 213a 2
Wachter, Charles E 166 3
Wachter, Charles H 166 3
Wachter, Charles L 166 3
Wachter, Charles N 166 3
Wachter, Chas 35 2
Wachter, Clara 180, 182, 210 3
Wachter, Clara W 180 3
Wachter, Claude H 166 3
Wachter, D R 100 1
Wachter, Daniel 167 3
Wachter, Daniel H 167 3
Wachter, Daniel H Jr 167 3
Wachter, David E 167 3
Wachter, David F 167 3
Wachter, David M 167 3
Wachter, Denton 56 3
Wachter, Doctor 167 3
Wachter, Doctor R 202 3
Wachter, E E 167 3
Wachter, Edgar B 161 3
Wachter, Eliza H C 167 3
Wachter, Elizabeth B 185 3
Wachter, Elmer E 180, 182, 192, 199, 210 3
Wachter, Elmer Elroy 172 3
Wachter, Ezra C 172, 202 3
Wachter, Frank J Jr 174 3
Wachter, Frank J Sr 174 3
Wachter, G C 189 3
Wachter, Geo 154, 186, 187 2
Wachter, Geo 186, 195 3
Wachter, Geo 117, 119, 263 1
Wachter, Geo H C 286 1
Wachter, Geo M 134 2
Wachter, Geo of T 32 1
Wachter, Geo W 96 1
Wachter, George 176 3
Wachter, George M 58 3
Wachter, Granville L 188 3
Wachter, H M 179 3
Wachter, Harvey E 172 3
Wachter, Helen 180 3
Wachter, Helen Gosnell 203 3
Wachter, Hellen Rhoads 293 2
Wachter, Henry 167, 202 3
Wachter, Howard H 210 3
Wachter, Ida M 166 3
Wachter, Isaac 182 3
Wachter, Isacc 167 3
Wachter, Jacob 116, 147 1
Wachter, Jacob 185, 186 3
Wachter, Jacob M 195 3
Wachter, Jacob M 71 1
Wachter, Jane R 188 3
Wachter, Jennie M 206 3
Wachter, John 187 3
Wachter, John H 189 3
Wachter, John P 189 3
Wachter, Joseph 205 3
Wachter, Josephine 167 3
Wachter, Julia B 172 3
Wachter, L H 71 1
Wachter, L M 138 2
Wachter, Lewis 205 3
Wachter, Lewis 231 2
Wachter, Lewis F 1 2
Wachter, Lewis F of P 188 3
Wachter, Lewis M 192 3
Wachter, Lloyd W 172 3
Wachter, Loretta S E 192 3
Wachter, Louisa E 182, 192 3
Wachter, Lucy 213a 2
Wachter, Lucy E 166 3
Wachter, Luther H 192 3
Wachter, Mamie Sophia 207 3
Wachter, Martin 210 3
Wachter, Martin L 167, 195 3
Wachter, Martin L Jr 208 3
Wachter, Martin L Sr 208 3
Wachter, Mary A 196 3
Wachter, Mary C 166 3
Wachter, Mehrl 278 2
Wachter, Michael 156, 214, 249 1
Wachter, Michael 187, 192, 195 3
Wachter, Mildred I 87, 94 2
Wachter, Millard 210 3
Wachter, Muriah M 195 3
Wachter, Murray S 161, 189, 197 3
Wachter, N F 179 3
Wachter, Nathanietl T 42 1
Wachter, Newton E 167 3
Wachter, Noah 199 3
Wachter, P 188 3
Wachter, Phebe E 202 3
Wachter, Philip 160, 167, 202 3
Wachter, Philip 276 2
Wachter, Philip Jr 167 3
Wachter, Philip Sr 202 3
Wachter, Randolph F 203 3
Wachter, Ray A 186, 189 1
Wachter, Raymond S 166 3
Wachter, Ruth G 28 3
Wachter, Samuel 7, 18 2
Wachter, Samuel 234 1
Wachter, Samuel 205 3
Wachter, Sarah L E 206 3
Wachter, Spencer E 206 3
Wachter, Susan E 187 3
Wachter, Thos 82 3
Wachter, Uriah 81, 196 3
Wachter, Virgie M 208 3
Wachter, W A 179 3
Wachter, W S 147 1
Wachter, Wesley A 167, 202, 210 3
Wachter, William M 210 3
Wachter, William N 210 3
Wachter, Wm 40 2
Wachter, Wm S 206 3
Waddles, Edward S 172 3
Wade, Alice 160 3
Wade, Andrew 161 3
Wade, Clara V 192 3
Wade, Eli 61 1
Wade, Harriett A 160 3
Wade, Lena E 202 3
Wade, Lester V 192 3
Wade, M E 160 3
Wade, Peyton J 202 3
Wade, Sanders 206 3
Wade, Sarah A 205 3
Wade, William A 202 3
Wade, Wm H 91, 129, 221 3
Wadsworth, Adaline 160 3
Wadsworth, Adeline 15 2
Wadsworth, Edward F 160 3
Wadsworth, Frederick B 174 3
Wadsworth, Henry 174, 203 3
Waesche, Catherine 166 3
Waesche, Clinton 192 3
Waesche, J A 166 3
Waesche, J T 92 1
Waesche, J T 166 3
Waesche, James T 106, 195 1
Waesche, Leonard R 192 3
Waesche, Thomas R 207 3
Wagaman, Anna K 62 1
Wagaman, David 207 1
Wagaman, David A 24, 67 1
Wagaman, David B 167 3
Wagaman, David D 167 3
Wagaman, Harry A 210 3
Wagaman, John E 188 3
Wagaman, Richard 188 2
Wagaman, Samuel G 210 3
Wagaman, V A 75 3
Wagaman, William 210 3
Wageley, James R 186 3
Wageley, Violetta S T 186 3
Wagerman, John W 189 3
Wagerman, Virginia 189 3
Wagers, Barbara 163 3

Wagers, Elizabeth 49 2
Wagers, Elizabeth M 163 3
Wagers, James 119 2
Wages, Barbara 184 3
Wages, Elizabeth 171 3
Wages, James 184 3
Wages, Jemima P 186 3
Waggaman, Mary Jane 209 3
Waggaman, William 209 3
Wagner, Ada R 196 3
Wagner, Agnes 187 3
Wagner, Alice J 26 1
Wagner, Augustine 160, 196 3
Wagner, Barbara 163 3
Wagner, Catherine 187, 209 3
Wagner, D Wm A 167 3
Wagner, David 68, 116 1
Wagner, David 11 2
Wagner, David 8, 26, 167, 184, 195, 214 3
Wagner, Edmund 94 3
Wagner, Elizabeth 176 3
Wagner, Francis G 174 3
Wagner, Geo V 210 3
Wagner, George I 196 3
Wagner, Grafton G 176 3
Wagner, Grafton J 176 3
Wagner, Harry 215 2
Wagner, Henry 46, 70 2
Wagner, Howard M 176 3
Wagner, John 8, 184, 195 3
Wagner, John E S 187 3
Wagner, Joseph E 160 3
Wagner, Joseph I 187 3
Wagner, Laura A 192 3
Wagner, Laura R 192 3
Wagner, Margaret S 196 3
Wagner, Margarett 195 3
Wagner, Martin R 20 2
Wagner, Mary 195 3
Wagner, Mary 129 2
Wagner, Mary A 196 3
Wagner, Nettie M 199 3
Wagner, Nicholas 199 3
Wagner, Rebecca M 203 3
Wagner, Robert W 199 3
Wagner, Sally 205 3
Wagner, Sarah 184 3
Wagner, Thomas T 110 1
Wagner, Vernon W 176 3
Wagner, W H 139 2
Wagner, William 9, 209 3
Wagner, William 293 2
Wagner, William H 23, 192, 210 3
Wagner, William T 210 3
Wagner, Wm 11 1
Wagner, Wm 215 2
Wagner, Wm H 8, 22 2
Wagner, Wm H 41, 118, 123, 156, 240 1
Wagner, Wm H 203 3
Wahlen, John 138 2
Waille, Geo H 96 1
Wakenight, Mary C 196 3
Walch, Albert R 161 3
Walch, Rudolph C 161 3
Waldeck, John 185 3
Waldeck, Mary E 196 3
Waldex, John M 123 1
Waldez, Mary E 123 1
Walker, A J 5 2
Walker, Alice P 203 3
Walker, Annie M 161 3
Walker, Annie M 177 2
Walker, Arianna 161 3
Walker, Charles D 169 3
Walker, Charles E 169 3
Walker, Chas 188 1
Walker, Chas D 26 1
Walker, Cyrus 275 2
Walker, Cyrus 165 3
Walker, Dixon C 176 3
Walker, Edith M 188 3
Walker, Edw 197 2
Walker, Edward 171, 180 3
Walker, Edward W 44 3
Walker, Ella P 171 3
Walker, Elliott 210 3
Walker, Ernest A 210 3
Walker, Francis Wm Jr 174 3
Walker, Georgia 176 3
Walker, Grace 52 2
Walker, Hallie 188 3
Walker, Harmon A 180 3
Walker, Helen Stauffer 174 3
Walker, Henry 179 3
Walker, Horace T 44, 180 3
Walker, Isaac 6, 182, 185 3
Walker, Isaac 26, 40, 115 1
Walker, Issac 218a 2
Walker, J C 2, 82, 196 3
Walker, J C 96 2
Walker, J Calvin 188 3
Walker, J Calvin 83 2
Walker, J E 177 2
Walker, Jacob 40, 96, 104, 106, 207, 249 1
Walker, Jacob 9, 171, 182, 185, 195, 205 3
Walker, Jacob 78 2
Walker, James 8, 132 2
Walker, James 44 1
Walker, James 179 3
Walker, James E 96, 245 2
Walker, James E 43, 188 3
Walker, James E 85, 171, 234 1
Walker, Jesse 141 3
Walker, Jesse 163 2
Walker, Jesse C 187 3
Walker, Jesse C 245 2
Walker, John 61 1
Walker, John 205, 218a 2
Walker, John 184, 185 3
Walker, John A 185 3
Walker, John Arthur 185 3
Walker, John C 72, 100 1
Walker, John C 55, 187 3
Walker, John C 5, 124, 238, 290 2
Walker, John Calvin 189 3
Walker, Joseph 209 3
Walker, Joseph R 186 3
Walker, Laura A 192 3
Walker, Lewis 192 3
Walker, Lucy Ellen 192 3
Walker, Margaret 195, 205 3
Walker, Margie I 210 3
Walker, Mary 195 3
Walker, Mary A 195 3
Walker, Mary A E 209 3
Walker, Perry 202 3
Walker, Philip 202 3
Walker, Rebecca J 203 3
Walker, Richard W 203 3
Walker, Robert A 180 3
Walker, Robert Aldridge 192 3
Walker, Robert R 19 3
Walker, Samuel 205 3
Walker, Samuel 40 1
Walker, Samuel C 26 1
Walker, Samuel D 205 3
Walker, Stephen 205 3
Walker, Steven 37 3
Walker, W W 41 1
Walker, W W 171, 214a 2
Walker, William 9, 39, 209 3
Walker, William 276 2
Walker, William A 192, 210 3
Walker, William B 209 3
Walker, William G 210 3
Walker, William P 192, 210 3
Walker, William R 209 3
Walker, William W 64 3
Walker, Wm A 188 1
Walker, Wm R 67 1
Walker, Wm W 67, 195 3
Wallace, Albert R 179 1
Wallace, Charles 196 3
Wallace, Chas T 255 2
Wallace, Mary A 196 3
Wallace, Oliver 201 3
Wallace, Rebecca E 203 3

Wallace, Rebecca E 179 1
Wallace, Richard 184 2
Waller, Annie R 222a 2
Walling, Byron W 203 3
Walling, Henry J 179 3
Walling, James 27 2
Walling, James 186 3
Walling, John 275 2
Walling, Juiet C 186 3
Walling, Monro H 186 3
Walling, Reverdy R 203 3
Wallis, A Grafton 161 3
Wallis, Albert E 160 3
Wallis, Albert E 152 1
Wallis, Albert R 159 1
Wallis, Albert Resin 161 3
Wallis, Charles T 169 3
Wallis, Cora A R 58 3
Wallis, Elizabeth E 195 2
Wallis, Fannie Elizabeth 161 3
Wallis, J F 195 2
Wallis, James F 189 3
Wallis, Rosa M 169 3
Walsh, James 185 3
Walsh, Mary J 209 3
Walsh, Mary L 265 2
Walsh, Upton R 71 3
Walsh, William 209 3
Walsh, Wm 83 2
Walt, Upton R 208 3
Walt, Upton R 99 2
Walter, Albert 187 3
Walter, Albert J 161 3
Walter, Albert W 166 3
Walter, C A 169 3
Walter, C S 166 3
Walter, Charles F M 166 3
Walter, Chas A 166 3
Walter, Chas G 70 1
Walter, Edgar 161 3
Walter, F 187 3
Walter, Geo 161 3
Walter, Jacob 209 3
Walter, John 234 2
Walter, John 71, 96, 183, 207 1
Walter, John 54, 188 3
Walter, John S 187 3
Walter, John W 206 3
Walter, M M 187 3
Walter, Mary E 196 3
Walter, Mary E 183 1
Walter, Michael 195 3
Walter, Sarah C 210 3
Walter, Susan I 206 3
Walter, William 209 3
Walter, William F 196, 210 3
Walter, William H 209 3
Walterman, Joseph 96 1
Walters, Charles D 166 3
Walters, Charles G 166 3
Walters, Chas C 56 3
Walters, John 185 3
Walters, Joseph 185 3
Walters, Lois H 43 2
Walters, Nora M 268 2
Walters, Sarah 185 3
Walthen, Marghuerite 62 1
Waltman, Barbara 189 3
Waltman, J Elmer 189 3
Waltman, Jacob 184, 186 3
Waltman, Jacob Sr 184 3
Waltman, James Elmer 202 3
Waltman, Joseph 100 1
Waltman, Joseph 186 3
Waltman, Joseph H 187 3
Waltman, Joseph I 188 3
Waltman, Mary Ellen 197 3
Waltman, Mary J 195 3
Waltman, Michael 195 3
Waltman, Nancy Ann 199 3
Waltman, Peter 63 2
Waltman, Peter 202 3
Waltman, Peter T 186 3
Waltman, Peter Thomas 202 3
Waltman, Thos 195 3
Waltman, William 63 2
Waltz, Barbara A 174 3
Waltz, C A 201 1
Waltz, Claggett 203 1
Waltz, Eli 171 3
Waltz, Elizabeth 205 3
Waltz, Elizabeth B 172 3
Waltz, Emerson E 180 3
Waltz, Enoch I 71 1
Waltz, Francis W 174 3
Waltz, Homer E 180, 201 3
Waltz, Isaac 218 3
Waltz, Isaac G 174, 182 3
Waltz, Jess 128 2
Waltz, John T 70 1
Waltz, John T 186 3
Waltz, Martin 195 3
Waltz, Mary Eet al 180 3
Waltz, Oscar Twain 201 3
Waltz, Oscar W 172, 174 3
Waltz, Oscar W 201 3
Waltz, Rinehart 203 3
Waltz, Rinehart 159 1
Waltz, Ruth Irene 201 3
Waltz, Soloman 205 3
Waltz, Susan C 186 3
Waltz, Upton 71, 196, 249 1
Waltz, Upton 89, 165 2
Waltz, Upton R 65 3
Waltz, Upton R 29, 39, 143 2
Waltz, Upton R 213, 245 1
Wampler, Abraham 137, 147, 227a 2
Wampler, Abraham 228 1
Wampler, Abraham 184, 185, 192, 195, 207 3
Wampler, David 112 1
Wampler, David 129, 169 2
Wampler, James 28 2
Wampler, John 56 1
Wampler, John 184 3
Wampler, Ludwig 192 3
Wampler, Philip E 96 1
Wandel, Mary 195 3
Wanipler, Abraham 56 1
Wantz, Charles 189 3
Wantz, Charles L 189, 206 3
Wantz, David 250 2
Wantz, Ella M 172 3
Wantz, Frederick 37 3
Wantz, Geo F 206 3
Wantz, Howard 189 3
Wantz, Isadora F 182 3
Wantz, James Francis 189 3
Wantz, John R 189 3
Wantz, Robert 203 3
Wantz, Sallie E 189 3
Wantz, Sallie M 206 3
Ward, Berkeley 163 3
Ward, Henry C 163 3
Ward, John Clarence 1 2
Ward, Joseph 186 3
Ward, Minnie 196 3
Ward, Peris 163 3
Ward, Rachel 203 3
Ward, Sarah A 205 3
Ward, Washington 165 3
Warden, M Alma 196 3
Warden, Mary A 196 3
Wardenbaker, John 163 1
Ware, E Spencer 189 1
Wareheim, Henry 19 2
Warehime, Dorothy W 167, 201 3
Warehime, Oliver C 201 3
Warenfeltz, Catherine 165 3
Warfel, Clarence O 169 3
Warfield, A S D 139 3
Warfield, Alexander 91, 106, 217 1
Warfield, Alexander 26, 237 2
Warfield, Alexander 8, 160 3
Warfield, Alexander of J 160 3
Warfield, Annie E 187 3
Warfield, C E 94 3
Warfield, Caroline 176 3
Warfield, Catherine 165 3
Warfield, Charles G 165 3
Warfield, Charles H 165 3
Warfield, Chas D 277 1

Warfield, D Howard 198 2
Warfield, Delilahs 167 3
Warfield, E A 110 1
Warfield, Eliza A 160, 171
3
Warfield, Elizabeth 171 3
Warfield, Ella B 192 3
Warfield, F Howard 189 2
Warfield, Garrison 176 3
Warfield, Geo W 195 3
Warfield, George 207 3
Warfield, Henry R 179 3
Warfield, J 160 3
Warfield, James L 129 3
Warfield, Jas L 187 3
Warfield, Jesse 26 2
Warfield, Jesse 160 3
Warfield, Jno A 171 3
Warfield, John 188, 205 1
Warfield, John 50 3
Warfield, John A 39, 195, 205 3
Warfield, Joseph 160 3
Warfield, Joshua 26 2
Warfield, Joshua 177 1
Warfield, Kaleb 165 3
Warfield, L D 187 3
Warfield, Lewis 81 3
Warfield, Lloyd A 171 3
Warfield, Luther D 176, 192
3
Warfield, Mabel M 197 3
Warfield, Margaret W 195 3
Warfield, Mary 160, 195 3
Warfield, Nannie S 20 3
Warfield, Nanny S 83 3
Warfield, Nettie L 124 3
Warfield, Oneida M C 172 3
Warfield, Preston 202 3
Warfield, Richard D 171 3
Warfield, Robt L 49 2
Warfield, S D 160, 195 3
Warfield, Sarah 207 3
Warfield, Sharrett D 205 3
Warfield, Sophie 205 3
Warfield, Suratt D 50, 205 3
Warfield, Surratt 288 2
Warfield, Surratt D 78, 84, 91,
139 1
Warfield, Thomas 8, 167, 207
3
Warfield, Thomas 237 2
Warfield, Thomas J 207 3
Warfield, Tillman 165 3
Warfield, Wm 96, 176 3
Warfield, Zadock 84 1
Warhm, Henry 93 2
Warmer, Wm H 82 1
Warner, Adison W 160 3
Warner, Augustus 164 1
Warner, Bertha V 188 3
Warner, C A 52 2
Warner, Carrie M 52, 223a
2
Warner, Catherine 165, 187
3
Warner, Charles A 223a 2
Warner, Charles A 169 3
Warner, Charles D 177 3
Warner, Christian 165 3
Warner, Clarence W 206 2
Warner, D W 187 3
Warner, David M 171 3
Warner, E L 219 1
Warner, Elias 272 1
Warner, Emanuel 160, 171
3
Warner, Geo 93 2
Warner, Geo B 171, 187 3
Warner, George 110 1
Warner, George 176, 184 3
Warner, George Clarence 177 3
Warner, Gertrude 192 3
Warner, Grant D 219 3
Warner, J W 160 3
Warner, Jane E 177 2
Warner, John 184, 186, 187 3
Warner, John A 187 3
Warner, John E 188 3
Warner, John W 187 3
Warner, Johnnie 202 3
Warner, Joseph F 189 3
Warner, Leslie T 177 2
Warner, Lewis J 192 3
Warner, Louisa 192 3
Warner, Margaret 43 3
Warner, Martha E 272 1
Warner, Mary C 206 2
Warner, Phillip 202 3
Warner, Rachel V 203 3
Warner, Samuel J 165 3
Warner, Samuel W 58 3
Warner, W H 226 2
Warner, William H 209 3
Warner, Wm 83 2
Warner, Wm 30 1
Warner, Wm H 110, 205 1
Warner, Wm M 189 3
Warren, Dale E 191 3
Warren, Ester J 191 3
Warren, Joseph 188 3
Warren, Kenneth L 191 3
Warren, William E 191 3
Warrenfels, Hannah 179 3
Warrenfeltz, Adam 186 3
Warrenfeltz, Clara V 206 3
Warrenfeltz, Claude T 166 3
Warrenfeltz, Daniel 64, 186 3
Warrenfeltz, Daniel 101 2
Warrenfeltz, Daniel P 167 3
Warrenfeltz, Edgar C 242 2
Warrenfeltz, Edgar C 206 3
Warrenfeltz, Edgar L 197 3
Warrenfeltz, Elizabeth 171 3
Warrenfeltz, Ezra 171, 202
3
Warrenfeltz, Ezrra 165 3
Warrenfeltz, Frank 220 1
Warrenfeltz, H H 16 2
Warrenfeltz, H M 56 3
Warrenfeltz, H M 183 1
Warrenfeltz, H M 136 2
Warrenfeltz, Henry 25, 31, 206,
232, 277 2
Warrenfeltz, Henry M 28, 188, 196
3
Warrenfeltz, Henry M 280 1
Warrenfeltz, Hezekiah 43 2
Warrenfeltz, J Luther 55 3
Warrenfeltz, Jacob 184, 186
3
Warrenfeltz, Jacob 187, 197
2
Warrenfeltz, John 184, 180
3
Warrenfeltz, John G 188 3
Warrenfeltz, John W 189 3
Warrenfeltz, Jonas 186 3
Warrenfeltz, Jonas 187 2
Warrenfeltz, Josiah P 187 3
Warrenfeltz, L 65 3
Warrenfeltz, L M 20 3
Warrenfeltz, L M 30 2
Warrenfeltz, Luther H 192 3
Warrenfeltz, M F 171 3
Warrenfeltz, M M 171 3
Warrenfeltz, Marcellas P 196 3
Warrenfeltz, Margaret M 189, 197
3
Warrenfeltz, Marion H 196 3
Warrenfeltz, Marion M 171, 196
3
Warrenfeltz, Mary 184 3
Warrenfeltz, Mollie V 192, 197
3
Warrenfeltz, Paul W 197 3
Warrenfeltz, Peter 202, 205
3
Warrenfeltz, Phillip 202 3
Warrenfeltz, R W. 142 1
Warrenfeltz, Sarah A 187 3
Warrenfeltz, Soula J 206 3
Warrenfeltz, Uriah 202, 208
3
Warrenfeltz, Uriah 117, 229
1
Warthan, Mary J 32 3
Warthan, Mary Jane 196 3

Warthen, Catherine A 179 3
Warthen, Eva 189 3
Warthen, G W 145 2
Warthen, Geo 46 2
Warthen, George W 176 3
Warthen, Henry 176, 179 3
Warthen, Joseph B 189 3
Warthen, Louise P 197 3
Warthen, Mary Edith 197 3
Warthon, John F 185 3
Wasche, Geo 283 1
Washburn, Wm 58 1
Washington Loan & Trust 159 1
Washington, Annie 160 3
Washington, Lee 192 3
Washington, Maria 196 3
Waskey, Augustus 160 3
Waskey, Charles H 169 3
Waskey, Chas 224 2
Waskey, Christian 165 3
Waskey, Eli 124 3
Waskey, Eli C 171 3
Waskey, Elizabeth 185 3
Waskey, Jacob 165, 185 3
Waskey, Jane A 188 3
Waskey, John N 8 2
Waskey, John N 189, 209 3
Waskey, L C 171 3
Waskey, Levi C 206 3
Waskey, Mabel O 169 3
Waskey, Nevin T R 42, 48, 145 1
Waskey, Nevin T R 28, 216 3
Waskey, Nevin T R 85, 259, 284 2
Waskey, Perry 160 3
Waskey, Perry 29, 241 2
Waskey, Susan R 171, 206 3
Waskey, William A 209 3
Wass, Mary J 197 3
Wastler, Alma & 188 2
Wastler, Anna J 46 3
Wastler, Annie R 96 1
Wastler, Annie R 160 3
Wastler, Elias J 196 2
Wastler, Elias J 4 3
Wastler, Gertrude D 253 1
Wastler, Henry 179 3
Wastler, Henry 159 1
Wastler, Henry Sr 179 3
Wastler, John 7 2
Wastler, Marie 4 3
Wastler, Mary M 63 1
Wastler, Morris A 257 1
Wastler, Sarah 179 3
Wastler, Thaddeus A 188 2
Wastler, Thos 45 1
Wastler, Wm 154 2
Water, Benjamin 163 3
Water, L M 132 2
Water, Summerset 186 2
Waterman, Curtis H 166 3
Waterman, Elmer E 166 3
Waterman, Leo F 193 3
Waterman, Leo Thomas 193 3
Waterman, Mae Delores 193 3
Waterman, Marian R 63, 253 1
Waterman, Simon 70 1
Waters C C 72 3
Waters, Ann 160 3
Waters, Ann M 33 1
Waters, Anna 160 3
Waters, Annie M 160, 161 3
Waters, Burgess H 12 2
Waters, C 82, 56, 91, 126, 160, 161, 166, 188, 221 3
Waters, C C 9, 52, 58, 62, 70, 84, 134, 154, 166, 189, 198, 209, 214 2
Waters, C C 44, 72, 82, 85, 99, 100, 112, 165, 172, 194, 201, 225, 230, 235, 253, 265, 270 1
Waters, Charles C 238, 271, 290 2
Waters, Charles C 20, 43, 44, 166, 196 3
Waters, Charles C 72, 79, 85 1
Waters, Charles E 160, 166 3
Waters, Chas 129, 131, 172, 175, 195, 198, 218, 225 2
Waters, Chas 8 1
Waters, Chas & 172 2
Waters, Chas C 9, 19, 27, 61, 67, 72, 88, 96, 100, 106, 119, 123, 133, 135, 165, 192, 217, 233, 234, 239, 1
Waters, Chas C 12, 23, 30, 31, 84, 89, 96, 106, 119, 144, 268, 280 2
Waters, Chas C 9, 10, 27, 55, 65, 72, 122, 159, 167, 188, 206, 210 3
Waters, Drusilla H 207 3
Waters, Eleanor 203 3
Waters, Elizabeth 171 3
Waters, Emma J 172, 188 3
Waters, F Gordon 174 3
Waters, Guy P 197 3
Waters, Haratio 179 3
Waters, Harry W D 179 3
Waters, Hazel 57 1
Waters, Henry 213 2
Waters, Henry 180, 195 3
Waters, Henry G 40, 67, 116 1
Waters, Henry G 6, 26, 179, 184 3
Waters, Henry G 208 2
Waters, Horatio 203 2
Waters, Horatio 32, 196, 282 1
Waters, Horatio 14, 39, 179 3
Waters, Ignatius 53 3
Waters, Ignatius Jr 171 3
Waters, Isaac 182 3
Waters, J Clarence 172, 189 3
Waters, J F 188 3
Waters, James 186 3
Waters, James 131, 198, 214a 2
Waters, James A 172, 189 3
Waters, James K 67, 126, 140, 222 1
Waters, James K 27, 160, 186, 188 3
Waters, James K 1, 259 2
Waters, Jno C 166 3
Waters, Joab 184 3
Waters, John C 160, 188, 189 3
Waters, John S 161 3
Waters, Leah 192 3
Waters, Lucretia 192 3
Waters, Margaret 179, 196 3
Waters, Mary A 197 3
Waters, N M 47 1
Waters, Nathaniel M 60 1
Waters, Nathaniel N 179 3
Waters, R C 171 3
Waters, Rebecca 160 3
Waters, Richard W 203 3
Waters, Roberta L 19 1
Waters, Rosa L R 72 1
Waters, Rosa L R 166 3
Waters, S R 176 1
Waters, S R 66, 203 2
Waters, Samuel 111 1
Waters, Samuel 41 2
Waters, Silas 205 3
Waters, Somerset 7, 43 2
Waters, Summerset R 116 1
Waters, Thomas Leo 207 3
Waters, Thos 207 1
Waters, Tighman 207 3
Waters, UChas C 208 3
Waters, Ulysses 208 3
Waters, Ulysses 70 1
Waters, William Dr 209 3
Waters, Wm 1, 18 2
Watkins, C Herbert 210 3
Watkins, C T 210 3
Watkins, Estelle 210 3
Watkins, Iva E 79 3
Watkins, J G 110 1
Watkins, John L 238 2
Watkins, John Latimer 169 1
Watkins, John S 197 3
Watkins, Lewis A 192 3
Watkins, M 209 3
Watkins, Malissa B 197 3
Watkins, Marcie F 79 3

Watkins, Mary E 195, 209 3
Watkins, Melven E 36 2
Watkins, Melvin Eugene 197 3
Watkins, Myrtle May 197 3
Watkins, Sarah E 192, 209 3
Watkins, Silas B 205 3
Watkins, Vernon T 115 2
Watkins, Vernon T 208 3
Watkins, Veron T 215 2
Watkins, William E 210 3
Watkins, William S 209 3
Watkins, William T 209 3
Watson, Catherine 165, 202 3
Watson, George Benjamin 177 3
Watson, Henry H 179 3
Watson, James 62 3
Watson, John M. 104 1
Watson, Mary 209 3
Watson, Melissa E 12 2
Watson, Phineas 202 3
Watson, William 209 3
Watters, C C [sic] 253 1
Watters, Chas 181 2
Watts, George F 188 3
Watts, John W 188 3
Watts, Robert 203 3
Way, David 167 3
Way, Dorcas 167 3
Wayble, George E 177 3
Wayman, Francis B 174 3
Wayman, Henry 106 1
Ways (Wade), Sanders 206 3
Ways, Carl L 206 3
Ways, Sanders 206 3
Ways, William H 2, 209 3
Ways, William H 282 2
Ways, William H Sr 209 3
Ways, Wm 72 2
Ways, Wm 135, 183 1
Ways, Wm H 91 1
Weagley, Ella 147 1
Weagley, Ella L M 165, 172 3
Weagley, Ida M 210 3
Weagley, Thomas 207 3
Weagley, William F 210 3
Weagly, Charles W C 165 3
Weagly, Clinton B 169 3
Weagly, Louise A 208 3
Weagly, Louise A 113 2
Weagly, Viola E 169, 208 3
Weagly[?], Ella L M 234 1
Weakley, Eliza 201 3
Weakley, James 201 3
Weakley, James 165 1
Weakley, Otho 201 3
Weakley, Thomas 207 3
Wealand, Bernard 163 3
Wealand, Bernard Jr 163 3
Wealand, Catherine 165 3
Wealand, Elizabeth 163 3
Weamert, Elsie P 189 3
Weamert, James 189 3
Weaning, Alton D 161 3
Weaning, Hilda V 161 3
Weanling, Alta 189 3
Weanling, J Walter 189 3
Weant, E O 165, 214 1
Weant, Edward O 180 3
Weant, Hannah E 180 3
Weant, J W 205 3
Wear, Christianna 165 3
Weast, Charity E 196 3
Weast, Mary 196 3
Weaver, A E 139 2
Weaver, Addie C 153 1
Weaver, Casper 141 3
Weaver, Casper M 116 1
Weaver, Catherine 165 3
Weaver, Charles L 169 3
Weaver, Christian 128, 275 2
Weaver, Christian 194, 196, 271 1
Weaver, Christian 165, 179 3
Weaver, Daniel 167 3
Weaver, Ella O 172 3
Weaver, Geo 81 3
Weaver, George 176 3
Weaver, Harmon 179 3
Weaver, Harriett 179 3
Weaver, Henry 179 3
Weaver, Jacob 184 3
Weaver, John 156 1
Weaver, John Jr 184 3
Weaver, John Sr 184 3
Weaver, John W 15 3
Weaver, Joseph 196 1
Weaver, Mary 259 2
Weaver, Virginia Clary 169 3
Weaver, Wm H 203 3
Webb, Annie M 196 3
Webb, Asa 51 1
Webb, Caroline O 120 1
Webb, Ellen 186 3
Webb, Ernest C 73 3
Webb, Fannie 100 1
Webb, Frank B 174 3
Webb, Geo 57, 60, 209 3
Webb, Henry 186 3
Webb, Jennie V 188 3
Webb, Jessie G 174 3
Webb, John R 189 3
Webb, John T 186 3
Webb, Joseph 89 2
Webb, Joseph W 188 3
Webb, Mary 195, 209 3
Webb, Richard J 89 2
Webb, Thos 186 3
Webb, William 209 3
Webber, Jeannette A 3 2
Webber, R D 96 3
Webber, Robert D 75 3
Webber, Robt D 52 1
Weber, Caherine 165 3
Weber, Harmon 179 3
Weber, Harriet G 180 3
Weber, Joseph 100 2
Webster, A E 187 3
Webster, Allen P 176 3
Webster, Allen T 206 3
Webster, C G 187 3
Webster, C Harry 188 3
Webster, Charles H 166 3
Webster, Chas E 192 3
Webster, Chas H 192 3
Webster, Francis C 166 3
Webster, G A 176 3
Webster, Geo F 96, 176 3
Webster, Geo F 152 1
Webster, Geo S 176 3
Webster, Geo W 176 3
Webster, George 176 3
Webster, George A 206 3
Webster, George F 9, 207 3
Webster, George F 282 2
Webster, Hannah 179 3
Webster, Henry 179 3
Webster, Isabelle S 9 2
Webster, James T 186 3
Webster, John B 209 3
Webster, John T 186, 188 3
Webster, Joseph E 187 3
Webster, Laura V 192 3
Webster, Mary Ann 195 3
Webster, Mary V 197 3
Webster, Samuel 205 3
Webster, Samuel 163 1
Webster, Sarah 187 3
Webster, Susan M 206 3
Webster, Thankful 176, 207 3
Webster, Thomas 209 3
Webster, Thomas C S 207 3
Webster, Thos 69 2
Webster, William 209 3
Webster, Wm 27 2
Webster, Wm H 179 3
Weddle, Ann 205 3
Weddle, Annie 161 3
Weddle, B P 72 3
Weddle, Beulah M 169 3
Weddle, C Ray 169, 176 3
Weddle, Catherine 165 3

Weddle, Chas W 140 2
Weddle, Cyrus A 166 3
Weddle, Elizabeth 186 3
Weddle, Ella 82 3
Weddle, Evers 141 3
Weddle, Evers Fred 189 3
Weddle, G C 123 1
Weddle, G C 129 2
Weddle, Grayson C 9, 176 3
Weddle, James of L 187 3
Weddle, John D 186 3
Weddle, John M 56 2
Weddle, John M 169 3
Weddle, John P 35 3
Weddle, John W 188 3
Weddle, Joseph A 189 3
Weddle, L 187 3
Weddle, M L 82 3
Weddle, Mary E 188 3
Weddle, Samuel 205 3
Weddle, Sarah E 206 3
Weddle, Susan 187 3
Weden, Daisy M 189 3
Weden, Joseph A 189 3
Wedszen, Christopher 165 3
Weedon, Carl W 166 3
Weedon, Chas W 192 3
Weedon, Hiram 166 3
Weedon, James H 264 1
Weedon, Laura 192 3
Weeks, Hezekiah 179 3
Weeks, Rachel 179 3
Weems, James 186, 187 3
Wegner, Barbara Fout 202 1
Weidrick, Jacob 1 1
Weightnight, Mary C 196 3
Weinberg, David 167 3
Weinberg, George G 177 3
Weinberg, Jeanette 167 3
Weinberg, L Rae 192 3
Weinberg, Leo 22, 34, 48, 56, 73, 101, 123, 126, 150, 177, 183, 191, 195, 217, 235, 240, 249, 256, 276, 283 1
Weinberg, Leo 32, 56, 72, 82, 111, 129, 167, 176, 180, 182, 192, 203, 210 3
Weinberg, Leo 23, 40, 83, 93, 128, 172, 181, 199, 205, 277 2
Weinberg, Manuel M 46, 180 3
Weinberg, Manuel M 28, 44, 148 1
Weinberg, Manuel M 170, 234 2
Weinberry, M Hudson 197 3
Weinburg, Leo 290 2
Weiner, Geo 199 2
Weiner, Geo H 206 3
Weiner, Henry M 196 3
Weiner, Margaret G 161 2
Weiner, Michael 196 3
Weingberg, Jeanette 34 1
Weingerg, Leo 180 3
Weir, Maria 166 2
Weirick, Charles 165 3
Weirick, Mary A 196 3
Weise, Mary Ann 195 3
Weissinger, Leonard 192 3
Weist, Jacob 57 1
Weistling, Rachel 205 3
Weland, Elizabeth 165 3
Welch, Marcella O 67 3
Welder, Annie B 294 2
Welker, C A 179 1
Welker, Chas E 210 3
Welker, Emma E 172 3
Welker, John 37, 156 1
Welker, John 294 2
Welker, Martha E 48 1
Welker, William W 210 3
Weller, Anna S 166 3
Weller, Barbara 163 3
Weller, Byson M 188 3
Weller, Catherine 165, 184 3
Weller, Catherine Cordelia 169 3
Weller, Charles 166 3
Weller, Charles J 166 3
Weller, Charles M 166 3
Weller, Christian 115 1
Weller, Christian 27 2
Weller, D C 208 1
Weller, Daniel 163, 167 3
Weller, Daniel 47 1
Weller, David C 186 3
Weller, Elias 171, 184 3
Weller, Elias 91, 123 1
Weller, Frederick 123 1
Weller, Frederick 207 3
Weller, George 176 3
Weller, Henry 282 1
Weller, Henry 179 3
Weller, Henry A 179 3
Weller, Isaac 47 1
Weller, Isaac 7 2
Weller, Isaac 182 3
Weller, Jacob 115, 118, 181, 263 1
Weller, Jacob 124, 275 2
Weller, Jacob 8, 184, 185 3
Weller, Jacob & 208 2
Weller, Jacob BS 184 3
Weller, Jacob P 188 3
Weller, Joanna M 188 3
Weller, Joannah M 188 3
Weller, John 22 2
Weller, John 186, 208, 271 1
Weller, John When 84, 186 3
Weller, Joseph 128 2
Weller, Juliana 185 3
Weller, Martha E 197 3
Weller, Mary 185 3
Weller, Nathaniel 199 3
Weller, Nathaniel 131 1
Weller, O C 166 3
Weller, R B 140 2
Weller, Simeon A 206 3
Weller, Simon 59 1
Weller, Thomas 207 3
Weller, W O 182 3
Weller, William T 206 3
Weller, William W 210 3
Welling, Amos L 160 3
Welling, Catharine E 179 3
Welling, Jane 160 3
Welling, Susan 206 3
Wells, Alice M 136 1
Wells, John 6 3
Wells, Mary 124 3
Wells, Mary Clare 209 3
Wells, Vachael W 208 3
Welsh, C G 183 1
Welsh, Kate D 183 1
Welsh, Luther 192 3
Welsh, Luther 215a 2
Welsh, Maggie F 210 3
Welsh, Milton 192 3
Welsh, W F 210 3
Welsh, Warner 192 3
Welsh, Warner G 209 3
Welsh, Warner W 159 2
Welsh, William M 210 3
Welty, A T 160 3
Welty, Abraham 163 1
Welty, Abraham 160 3
Welty, Annie C 203 3
Welty, Barbara 186 3
Welty, Bernard 120, 163, 184 3
Welty, Bernard 196 1
Welty, Bernard J 15 2
Welty, Catherine M 174 3
Welty, Charles F 166 3
Welty, Florence I 208 3
Welty, Frederick 51 2
Welty, Frederick A 174 3
Welty, Geo W 205 3
Welty, Henry 179 3
Welty, J Bernard 139 1
Welty, Jacob 120, 163, 184, 186 3
Welty, John 7 2
Welty, John Jr 184 3
Welty, Jos 53 3
Welty, Joseph 1, 27, 46, 51, 195, 226 2
Welty, Joseph 164, 196, 243, 246 1

Welty, Joseph 120, 163, 186, 222 3
Welty, Joseph H 15 2
Welty, Margaret C 196 3
Welty, Paul C 166 3
Welty, Philip Hammond Sr 208 3
Welty, Rebecca A 203 3
Welty, Russell S 166 3
Welty, Samuel 160, 186, 205 3
Welty, Virginia Douglass 208 3
Welty, William E 210 3
Welty, Williams 209 3
Welty, Wm E 38 1
Weltz, Andrew 160 3
Weltz, Daniel 196 1
Weltz, Joseph 196 1
Weltz, Rebecca 160 3
Weltzheimer, Ann M 160 3
Weltzheimer, Lewis 41 1
Weltzheimer, Lewis 192 3
Wenn, John S 277 2
Wenner, C F 187 3
Wenner, Charles F 82 3
Wenner, Charles Fenton 165 3
Wenner, Chas F 234, 253 1
Wenner, Chas F 144 2
Wenner, E Minor 189 3
Wenner, G S 208 1
Wenner, Geo 138 2
Wenner, George S 176 3
Wenner, John S 189 3
Wenner, M S 186 3
Wenner, Martha R 176 3
Wenner, Mary K 197 3
Wenner, Mortimer S 188 3
Wenner, Robert J 203 3
Wenner, Russell S 203 3
Wenner, Sarah F 210 3
Wenner, Susan A 187 3
Wenner, W W 186, 187 3
Wenner, William B 166 1
Wenner, William E 197 3
Wenner, William V 210 3
Wenner, Wm B 177 3
Wenner, Wm W 144 2
Wenner, Wm W 187 3
Wenrich, Charles E 166 3
Wenrick, Maggie Lee 166 3
Wenschoff, Catherine 171 3
Wentz, Frederick 250 2
Wentz, George 176 3
Wentz, George 165 3
Wentz, H W 97 1
Wentzel, H N 107 1
Wenz, E Lewis 171 3
Wenz, George 171, 174, 176 3
Wenz, Lewis 31 3
Wenzell, June F 188 3
Werbel, Frederick 202 3
Werbel, Phillip 202 3
Werking, Dora E 188 3
Werking, Dove E 167 3
Werking, George 189 3
Werking, Harvey H 188 3
Werking, Henry 179 3
Werking, Henry 223a 2
Werking, Henry 52 1
Werking, J C 55 3
Werking, James C 179, 188 3
Werking, James H 167 3
Werking, John P 189 3
Werner, Lavinia 165 3
Werner, Sarah F 206 3
Werner, William B 75 3
Wertenbaker, Ann S 160 3
Wertenbaker, Catherine 192 3
Wertenbaker, Geo W 176 3
Wertenbaker, Jacob 184 3
Wertenbaker, John 184 3
Wertenbaker, John 27 2
Wertenbaker, Lewis 192 3
Wertenbaker, W O 42, 62, 68, 84, 147, 150 1
Wertenbaker, W O 49, 54, 81, 172, 178, 189, 265 2
Wertenbaker, W O 44, 107, 188 3
Wertenbaker, William 209 3
Wertenbaker, Wm 96 2
Wertenbaker, Wm O 186, 214, 260 1
Wertenbaker, Wm O 176 3
Wertheimer, Annie M 46 2
Wertheimer, Charles 28, 166, 169, 196 3
Wertheimer, Charles 27 1
Wertheimer, Charles Jr 166 3
Wertheimer, Charles W 196 3
Wertheimer, Chas 33, 60, 61, 72, 126, 166, 172, 223, 244 1
Wertheimer, Chas 8, 15, 46, 178 2
Wertheimer, Chas 55, 56, 87, 124, 166, 174, 192, 223 3
Wertheimer, Clotilva 166 3
Wertheimer, David 174 3
Wertheimer, David 60, 249 1
Wertheimer, Frances K 203 1
Wertheimer, Francis K 174, 196 3
Wertheimer, Francis K 70 2
Wertheimer, Frederick 174 3
Wertheimer, M 166 3
Wertheimer, Marcus 196 3
Wertheimer, Myre 196 3
Wertheimer, Philip 169, 174 3
Wertheimer, Rhodes 116 1
Wertheimer, Rose 203 3
Wertheimer, S K 166 3
Wertheimer, Samuel 174 3
Wertheimer, Sarah 206 3
West, Benj 37, 38 3
West, Benj 185 2
West, Benjamin 54, 69, 208, 211 2
West, Benjamin 116, 250 1
West, Benjamin 163 3
West, Chas A 197 3
West, Danj 64 3
West, Eleanor Arabella 171 3
West, Eliza H 172, 192 3
West, Elizabeth 41, 47 2
West, Erasmus 56 1
West, F McGill 192 3
West, G W 163, 179 3
West, G W 225 1
West, Geo W 54, 249, 258 2
West, Geo W 70 1
West, Geo W 111, 185, 195 3
West, George W 126 3
West, Gordon R 16 2
West, Henry J 179 3
West, J 225 1
West, J Ed 250 2
West, John D 189 3
West, John R 84 1
West, Joseph 163, 185 3
West, Joseph 142, 228 1
West, Joseph 208, 214 2
West, Laura E 217 3
West, Lavin 185 3
West, Leven 249 2
West, Levi 28 1
West, Levi 290 2
West, Levin 11, 12, 54, 68, 70, 76, 122, 144, 203, 231, 258 2
West, Levin 61, 144, 163, 189, 214, 225, 279 1
West, Levin 126, 171, 185, 192, 195 3
West, Leviu 179 3
West, Mable 129 3
West, Maggie M 197 3
West, Mary H 185, 195 3
West, P M 171 3
West, P M 122, 144, 160 2
West, Patrick 198 2
West, Patrick M 9 3
West, Samuel 206 3
West, Serenia 205 3
West, T M 171 3
West, Thomas 207 3
West, William 209 3
Westall, Henrietta V 189 3
Westall, James A 189 3

Westall, James A 45 2
Westcott, Mary 196 3
Westerman, John 186 3
Western Maryland Trust Co 151 2
Western Md Trust Co 249 2
Wetenbaker, John 171 1
Wetnight, David 205 3
Wetnight, Jacob 64 3
Wetnight, Mary Gardner 256 1
Wetnight, Samuel P 205 3
Wetnight, Simon P 214 1
Wetzel, Albert C 57 3
Wetzel, Bernard J 163 3
Wetzel, David F 45, 149 3
Wetzel, Elmer D 206 3
Wetzel, Hezekiah 187 3
Wetzel, Jacob 185, 187 3
Wetzel, Mary Ann 196 3
Wetzel, Mary I 197 3
Wetzel, Nellie G 163 3
Wetzel, Nora V 163 3
Wetzel, Samuel 206 3
Wetzel, Wm G 140 2
Wever, Caper 141 3
Weybright, Annie E 72 3
Weybright, Daniel Saylor 162 1
Weybright, John 192 3
Weybright, John S 72 3
Whalen, B H 107, 149 2
Whalen, Beal H 163, 182 3
Whalen, Ellen A 182 3
Whalen, Geo 214 1
Whalen, Geo A 235, 245 1
Whalen, George A 177 3
Whalen, Hannh V 205 3
Whalen, Isaac C 182 3
Whalen, John 149 2
Whalen, John W 187 3
Whalen, Mary E 239 1
Whalen, Nannie C 87 3
Whalen, Sallie 182 3
Whalen, Sally 205 3
Whalen, Susan J 187 3
Whalen, Thos S 239 1
Whaley, Mary W E 205 3
Whaner, Francis A 174 3
Wheeler, Gurney M 177 3
Wheeler, Joseph A 39 2
Wheeler, Walter C 215 2
Whimore, Mary 196 3
Whip, Daniel 214 1
Whip, David 256 1
Whip, David M 229 1
Whip, Franklin K 259 2
Whip, Geo 252 1
Whip, Geo W P 31 2
Whip, Lewis 229 1
Whip, Lewis C 112, 264 1
Whip, Lewis O 119, 172 1
Whip, Lloyd 139 1
Whip, Louis O 110 1
Whipp, Annie E 161 3
Whipp, Annie M 188 3
Whipp, Barbara 163 3
Whipp, C E 188 3
Whipp, Catherine 165 3
Whipp, Charles M 161 3
Whipp, Charlotte C 166 3
Whipp, Clarence M 197 3
Whipp, D M 169 2
Whipp, D P 271 1
Whipp, David 23 1
Whipp, David M 167, 176 3
Whipp, David M 214, 240 1
Whipp, David M 70 2
Whipp, David N 71 3
Whipp, Dorthy V 197 3
Whipp, E Milton 172 3
Whipp, Elsie 210 3
Whipp, Emanuel 171 3
Whipp, Emily 171 3
Whipp, F R 188 3
Whipp, Frank R 189 3
Whipp, Geo 70, 106, 113, 188, 198 2
Whipp, Geo 71 1
Whipp, Geo T 240, 264 1
Whipp, Geo T 176 3
Whipp, George 38, 176 3
Whipp, George 41 1
Whipp, George T 15, 32, 176, 196 3
Whipp, Harvey C 192 3
Whipp, Jacob 176, 186 3
Whipp, John 53, 120, 165, 185 3
Whipp, John 80 2
Whipp, John N 188, 189 3
Whipp, L O 264 2
Whipp, Learie E 259 2
Whipp, Lena S 193 3
Whipp, Lettie M 176, 196 3
Whipp, Lewis 70, 124, 129 2
Whipp, Lewis O 156, 240 1
Whipp, Lucy V 192 3
Whipp, Malissa V 172 3
Whipp, Mary 185 3
Whipp, Mary M 196 3
Whipp, Melissa V 197 3
Whipp, Peter 160, 202 3
Whipp, Samuel T 54, 186 3
Whipp, Samuel T 19 1
Whipp, Sarah M 205 3
Whisner, Charles D 166, 196 3
Whisner, H M 11 3
Whisner, Joseph P 196 3
Whisner, Margaret 196 3
Whisner, Michael 196 3
Whisner, Minnie T 196 3
Whit hill, John 188 3
Whitaker, H B 235 1
Whitaker, Susan E 39 2
White, Adalade 160 3
White, Alice A 161, 189 3
White, Amanda C 161 3
White, Ann E 160 3
White, Arthur 187 3
White, B Frank 163 3
White, Barbara H 23 2
White, Benj 187 3
White, Benjamin 163 3
White, Carriebelle Travis 111 3
White, Cherry Ford 169 3
White, Clara E 166 3
White, David G 172 3
White, Dorsey Grace 169 3
White, E W 85 1
White, Elizabeth 171 3
White, Elizabeth M 172 3
White, Ellen M 172 3
White, Emily J 171 3
White, F 209 3
White, F G 272 1
White, Fredeick 156 3
White, Frederick 24, 55, 79, 84, 194, 197 1
White, Frederick 1, 22, 150, 220a, 238, 254, 262, 267, 290 2
White, Frederick 19, 171, 179 3
White, Gene 172 3
White, H Walton 172 3
White, Harriett 172 3
White, Harry J 85 1
White, Henry A 171, 188 3
White, Isaac C 172 3
White, J C 70 2
White, J Furr 163 3
White, J Thomas 161 3
White, James W 220a 2
White, Jas W 81 3
White, Jerome S 186 3
White, John 56, 243 1
White, John 32, 185, 187 3
White, John 221a 2
White, John H 67 2
White, John J 188 3
White, John M 187 3
White, John T 19, 185, 187, 189, 206 3
White, John W 186, 187 3
White, John W 279 1
White, Joseph 188 3
White, Joseph C 189 3
White, Mary 195 3
White, Mary Jane 195 3
White, Mary L 189 3

White, Nathan S 179 3
White, Phillip P 202 3
White, Roscoe C 70 2
White, S A 209 3
White, Sarah Alice 205 3
White, Sarah J 187 3
White, Srah J 206 3
White, Susan 174, 206 3
White, W 226 2
White, W W 223 1
White, Walter E 166 3
White, William 167 3
White, William 171, 185, 209 3
White, William 267, 290 2
White, William Dr 209 3
White, William F E 209 3
White, William H 189, 210 3
White, William H 13 1
White, Wm 57, 84, 139, 148, 197, 213 1
White, Wm 187, 195 3
White, Wm 238 2
White, Wm H 210 3
White, Wm P P 171 3
Whitehill, Ambrose 23 3
Whitehill, Ann 160, 186 3
Whitehill, Barbara 163, 186 3
Whitehill, C W 163 3
Whitehill, Charles W 165 3
Whitehill, J C 163 3
Whitehill, J Reese 188 3
Whitehill, J W 165 3
Whitehill, James 40, 67, 186 3
Whitehill, James 57, 82, 117, 118, 139, 175, 264, 271 1
Whitehill, James 28, 69, 87, 197, 237 2
Whitehill, Jas 87, 195 3
Whitehill, John 110, 159 1
Whitehill, John C 185, 186, 195 3
Whitehill, Mary 195 3
Whitehill, Maximus 85 1
Whitehill, Naomi 188 3
Whiteing, Lee 275 1
Whitelock, George 120 3
Whiten, Benjamin 163 3
Whiten, Eliza A 163 3
Whitington, John 184 3
Whitington, Rebecca 203 3
Whitler, Ella 32 3
Whitmer, Martin L 196 3
Whitmore, Ann V 203 3
Whitmore, Annie E B 203 3
Whitmore, Benj 163, 195 3
Whitmore, Benj Sr 163 3
Whitmore, Benjamine 184 3
Whitmore, Cecilia S 189 3
Whitmore, Charles M 32 2
Whitmore, Christian 51 1
Whitmore, Christian 53, 165 3
Whitmore, Clinton M 189 3
Whitmore, D J 235 1
Whitmore, Daniel 167 3
Whitmore, David 165, 167, 174, 179 3
Whitmore, Ella A 189 3
Whitmore, Ellen C 172, 187 3
Whitmore, Emanuel D 205 3
Whitmore, Frank 189, 206 3
Whitmore, Frederick 174 3
Whitmore, Geo 265 1
Whitmore, Geo H 58 2
Whitmore, Geo H 257 1
Whitmore, Geo H 166, 176, 179 3
Whitmore, George H 207 3
Whitmore, Harvey V 189 3
Whitmore, Henrietta F 179 3
Whitmore, Henry 64 3
Whitmore, Isabella C 182 3
Whitmore, Isabelle 176 3
Whitmore, James H 189 3
Whitmore, John 179, 184, 186 3
Whitmore, John 22, 96, 203, 237 2
Whitmore, John 223 1
Whitmore, John H 189 3
Whitmore, John M 187, 199 3
Whitmore, John S 189 3
Whitmore, John T 189 3
Whitmore, Jonas 163, 184, 195 3
Whitmore, Joseph 165, 174 3
Whitmore, Laura V 192 3
Whitmore, Lawrence W 192 3
Whitmore, Mary 195 3
Whitmore, Mary C 196, 197 3
Whitmore, Mary M 167, 196 3
Whitmore, Minnie M 197 3
Whitmore, Nicholas 43 2
Whitmore, Nicholas 31, 199 3
Whitmore, Nicholas T 199 3
Whitmore, Oscar H 201 3
Whitmore, Pearl I 189 3
Whitmore, Rachel D 201 3
Whitmore, Randolph M 203 3
Whitmore, Rebecca 203 3
Whitmore, Simon 26 2
Whitmore, Simon P 165, 205 3
Whitmore, Simon T 174 3
Whitmore, Stiers 206 3
Whitmore, Suannah 184 3
Whitmore, Susannah 205, 206 3
Whitmore, T A 46 2
Whitmore, T Arnold 176 3
Whitmore, T Arnold 53 1
Whitmore, Thomas P 207 3
Whitmore, William H 197 3
Whitmore, Willie H 179 3
Whitmore, Wm 69 2
Whitter, Ella V 189 3
Whitter, H B 209 2
Whitter, John C 189 3
Whitter, Mary 209 2
Whitter, Susan E 207 3
Whitter, Thomas 207 3
Whitter, Willis D 209 2
Whittier, Gabriel 176 3
Whittier, John C 176 3
Whittle, Charity 184 3
Whittle, John 184 3
Whitton, Peter 202 3
Whyte, Violet H 12 2
Wickam, Lewis A 26 1
Wickham, Edith E 245 1
Wickham, Henry Wm 179 3
Wickham, John 116, 179, 184, 195 3
Wickham, John Jr 184 3
Wickham, Margaret 195 3
Wickham, Susan 205 3
Wickless, Annabelle O 29 3
Wickless, Antony F 161 3
Wickless, Antony J 161 3
Wickless, Augustine G 161 3
Wickless, C Carroll 169 3
Wickless, Charles A 169 3
Wickless, Chas A 161, 192 3
Wickless, Jerome D 161, 192 3
Wickless, Laura V 192 3
Wickless, Margaret 195 3
Wickless, William J 169 3
Wicoxon, Anna Mary 160 3
Widder, H B 152 1
Widerick, Christian 165 3
Wideriek, Elizabeth 171 3
Widrick, Christian 165 3
Widrick, Elizabeth 185 3
Widrick, George 176 3
Widrick, Jacob 31, 165, 176, 185 3
Widrick, John 185 3
Widson, Zachariah T 116 2
Wienberg, Leo 10, 43, 44, 50 3
Wienberg, Leo 234, 255, 265 2
Wiener, Annie E 192 3
Wiener, Bertha M 163 3
Wiener, Geo 192 3

Wiener, Lillie May 192 3
Wiener, Michael J 197 3
Wier, Catherine 165 3
Wierman, Daniel 167 3
Wiest, Frederick A 185 3
Wiest, Jacob 191, 256 1
Wiest, Jacob 184, 185 3
Wiest, Jacob 184 3
Wiest, Susan 185 3
Wiestling, Maria K 264 2
Wiestling, Maria K 196 3
Wiggington, Bessie 207 3
Wiggington, T omas H 207 3
Wight, Ira E 182 3
Wight, Ira E Jr 182 3
Wightman, Isabelle Hall 182 3
Wiilhide, H 187 3
Wiilhide, John of H 187 3
Wilbahn, Catherine 165 3
Wilcom, Annie 161 3
Wilcom, Isabelle 182 3
Wilcom, John J 189 3
Wilcom, Laurence R 182 3
Wilcom, William J 182 3
Wilcomb, Annie 188 3
Wilcomb, Jacob J 188 3
Wilcomb, John J 188 3
Wilcome, Jerome 188, 190 3
Wilcox, Martha E 106 2
Wilcoxen, A J 1, 91, 271 1
Wilcoxin, Andrew J 209 3
Wilcoxin, Margaret A 195 3
Wilcoxin, William 209 3
Wilcoxon, A J 28, 258 2
Wilcoxon, Andrew 85 1
Wilcoxon, Andrew 198, 276 2
Wilcoxon, Andrew J 1, 93 2
Wilcoxon, Andrew J 210 3
Wilcoxon, Clinton 160 3
Wilcoxon, Elizabeth C 172 3
Wilcoxon, G E W 160 3
Wilcoxon, Geo E 85, 253 1
Wilcoxon, Geo E 20, 176 3
Wilcoxon, Geo E Jr 21 3
Wilcoxon, Horathia 179 3
Wilcoxon, Isabelle 176 3
Wilcoxon, John 19, 159 1
Wilcoxon, John 7, 14, 171 2
Wilcoxon, John 187, 203 3
Wilcoxon, Martha E 187 3
Wilcoxon, Rebecca O 160 3
Wilcoxon, Ruth 203 3
Wilcoxon, Sarah 179 3
Wilcoxon, Wilbur 210 3
Wilcoxon, William 210 3
Wilcoxon, William 258 2
Wilcoxon, Wm 1, 7 2
Wilcoxon, Wm 19, 25, 91, 116, 253, 264, 272 1
Wilcoxon, Wm C 210 3
Wildersin, Joshua 46 2
Wildonger, George 176 3
Wile, George 176 3
Wile, George H 176 3
Wile, George Peter 176 3
Wile, Hannah 205 3
Wile, Henrietta 179 3
Wile, Jacob 184 3
Wile, Mary 176 3
Wile, Peter 47 1
Wile, Samuel 205 3
Wile, William 176 3
Wiles John J 26 3
Wiles, A C 166 3
Wiles, Albert 225 2
Wiles, Americus G P 160 3
Wiles, Annie M 179 3
Wiles, Birdie M 208 3
Wiles, C C 176 3
Wiles, Charles C 6, 169 3
Wiles, Charles I 169, 172 3
Wiles, Charles W 166 3
Wiles, Christian T 166 3
Wiles, Chritian T 174 3
Wiles, Clagett B 207 3
Wiles, Claggett B 214 1
Wiles, Coleman R 166 3
Wiles, Elizabeth 171, 184 3
Wiles, Ella E 171 3
Wiles, Ernest Floyd 172 3
Wiles, Estella M 172 3
Wiles, Fanny C Lare 174 3
Wiles, Flora E 174 3
Wiles, Flora L 174 3
Wiles, Frederick M 174 3
Wiles, G P 187 3
Wiles, Geo P of P 176 3
Wiles, Geo R 202 3
Wiles, Hamilton D 179 3
Wiles, Hanson A 174, 180 3
Wiles, Henry 229 1
Wiles, Henry 49 2
Wiles, Henry G 171 3
Wiles, Ida F 182 3
Wiles, Ida M 182, 192 3
Wiles, Ida May 180 3
Wiles, J M 214 1
Wiles, Jacob 40, 179, 182, 188 3
Wiles, Jacob E 187 3
Wiles, James 184, 207 3
Wiles, Jeanetta L 187 3
Wiles, John 207 3
Wiles, Lelah L 207 3
Wiles, Mary E 207 3
Wiles, Millard C 192 1
Wiles, Millard C 166 3
Wiles, Myrtlin I 250 1
Wiles, Oneida M 201 3
Wiles, Oscar C 201 3
Wiles, P 176 3
Wiles, P McClary 187 3
Wiles, Peter 202 3
Wiles, Rebecca 202 3
Wiles, Richard C 172 3
Wiles, Richard E 172 3
Wiles, Russell P 174 3
Wiles, Sarah R 174 3
Wiles, T J L 150 1
Wiles, T McClary 171 3
Wiles, T McCleery 207 3
Wiles, Thomas 207 3
Wiles, Thomas J L 171 3
Wiles, Thos 187, 202 3
Wiles, Thos 57 2
Wiles, Thos J 214 1
Wiles, Vernon C 208 3
Wiles, Walter S 160 3
Wilhelm, Adolph 160 3
Wilhelm, Leonard J 192 3
Wilhelm, Luther H 192 3
Wilhelm, Peter 202 3
Wilhide, Ada F 44 1
Wilhide, Amanda M 161 3
Wilhide, Arnold 163 3
Wilhide, Barbara 163 3
Wilhide, Beatrice 180 3
Wilhide, Benj 80 2
Wilhide, Benjamin 163 3
Wilhide, Benjamin 38 2
Wilhide, Catherine E 166 3
Wilhide, Charles 166 3
Wilhide, Claude W 161 3
Wilhide, Conrad 213 3
Wilhide, F N 163 3
Wilhide, F N 85 1
Wilhide, Frederick 260 1
Wilhide, Frederick 169 2
Wilhide, Geo 214 1
Wilhide, Geo E 176 3
Wilhide, Geo L 176 3
Wilhide, George L 28 1
Wilhide, George L 119, 161, 182, 278 2
Wilhide, Grace V 197 3
Wilhide, Harry 166, 180 3
Wilhide, Jacob 203 2
Wilhide, James 9 3
Wilhide, James E 189 3
Wilhide, John 164 1
Wilhide, John 163 3
Wilhide, John 227 2
Wilhide, John H 24 1
Wilhide, John L 84 1
Wilhide, John W 205 3
Wilhide, Joseph 225 1

Wilhide, Joseph 167 3
Wilhide, Joseph 197 2
Wilhide, Lloyd Ross 197 3
Wilhide, Luther J D 176 3
Wilhide, Mary 166 3
Wilhide, Mary 31 2
Wilhide, Michael F 197 3
Wilhide, Samuel 125 1
Wilhide, Samuel 8, 53, 205 3
Wilhide, Samuel 159 2
Wilhide, Susannah 205 3
Wilhide, W Z 230 1
Wilhide, Willie Z 225 1
Wilhide, Wm 166 3
Wilhide, Wm 30 2
Wilkerson, Dora 192 3
Wilkerson, Lucy 192 3
Willar, David T 4 1
Willar, J O 160 3
Willard, A D 15, 23, 31, 222, 238 2
Willard, A D 4, 42, 44, 82, 120, 194, 214, 235, 237 1
Willard, A D 10 3
Willard, Abraham 62 1
Willard, Alice N 161 3
Willard, Arthur 96, 160, 188, 209, 215 2
Willard, Arthur D 67, 78, 104, 119, 166, 172, 193 1
Willard, Arthur D 84, 107, 189, 227, 277 2
Willard, Arthur D 10, 43, 172 3
Willard, C B 119 2
Willard, C D 174, 217 3
Willard, C H 102 3
Willard, C N 213 3
Willard, C T 283 1
Willard, Carl B 169 3
Willard, Catherine R 73 3
Willard, Charles F 166 3
Willard, Chas F 166 3
Willard, Chas H 14 2
Willard, Clinton B 169, 220 3
Willard, Corinne E 195 1
Willard, D 19 1
Willard, D 184 3
Willard, D 51 2
Willard, D A 277 2
Willard, D C 100 3
Willard, Daniel 93 2
Willard, Dewalt 79, 104, 252 1
Willard, DeWalt 106, 165 3
Willard, DeWalt 22 2
Willard, DF 270 1
Willard, Edgar H Dr 166 3
Willard, Edw 283 1
Willard, Edw L 96 1
Willard, Emma V 172 3
Willard, Ezra 198 2
Willard, Ezra 67, 248 1
Willard, F V 179 3
Willard, Geo 45 2
Willard, Henry 184 3
Willard, Joel E 169 3
Willard, John 84 2
Willard, John 110, 125, 233, 234 1
Willard, John of D 184 3
Willard, Laurence C 169 3
Willard, Louisa 186 3
Willard, M P 124, 187 3
Willard, Mary A 102 3
Willard, Mary L 283 1
Willard, Mary V 197 3
Willard, Oscar 102 3
Willard, Peter 54, 93 2
Willard, Raymond A 229a 2
Willard, Ridgely 210 3
Willard, Ridgely A 207 3
Willard, Sarah 181 2
Willard, T H 271 1
Willard, T H 29 2
Willard, Thomas H 212 3
Willard, Thomas H 84 2
Willard, Thomas H 59 1
Willard, Thos H 215 3
Willard, Tilghman A 207, 210 3
Willard, William B 197 3
Willard, William C 161 3
Willard, Wm 244 1
Willard, Wm H 8 2
Willett, Sarah A 166 2
Willhide, Ann E 160 3
Willhide, Chas 187 3
Willhide, Conrad 165, 184 3
Willhide, Daniel 167 3
Willhide, Elizabeth M 210 3
Willhide, Emma 172 3
Willhide, Ephraim M 171 3
Willhide, Ezra 171 3
Willhide, F 179 3
Willhide, Frede ick 184 3
Willhide, Frederick 174 3
Willhide, Geo E 187 3
Willhide, Geo N 199 3
Willhide, George L 101 1
Willhide, Harvey W 188 3
Willhide, Henry 179 3
Willhide, Henry of F 179 3
Willhide, J L 186 3
Willhide, Jacob 185 3
Willhide, John 174, 179 3
Willhide, John L 187 3
Willhide, John Sr 184 3
Willhide, John W 187 3
Willhide, Joseph 165, 184, 187 3
Willhide, Josiah E 188 3
Willhide, L B 187 3
Willhide, Maggie 171 3
Willhide, Mary E 174 3
Willhide, N 67 3
Willhide, Nelson 179 3
Willhide, Niles N 199 3
Willhide, Samuel 205 3
Willhide, Samuel J 205 3
Willhide, Susan 187 3
Willhide, W Z 140 2
Willhide, William A 210 3
Willhide, Willie Z 136, 235 1
Willhide, Willie Z 25, 161 2
Willhise, Samuel 184 3
William, George 55 3
William, Gillelan 70 3
William, J T 7 2
William, James C 22 1
William, John 54, 185 3
William, John T 209 3
William, Williams 210 3
Williams, A H 152 1
Williams, A K 165, 177 1
Williams, A K 187 3
Williams, A K 58 2
Williams, Adolphus 160 3
Williams, Amon 161 3
Williams, Amy 179 3
Williams, Ann 160 3
Williams, Anthony K 161 3
Williams, Arthur 217 3
Williams, Benjamin 163 3
Williams, Charles A D 166 3
Williams, Charles G 259 2
Williams, Chas 63 2
Williams, Clara L 152 1
Williams, Columbia 206 2
Williams, Columbia M 166 3
Williams, Daniel 167 3
Williams, Douglas 166 3
Williams, Edgar G 209 3
Williams, Elizabeth A 161, 172 3
Williams, Ellis 72 1
Williams, G Ellis 249 2
Williams, George 176 3
Williams, George V 231 2
Williams, H 208 3
Williams, Harriett 179 3
Williams, Henrietta 67, 180 3
Williams, Henrietta M 180 3
Williams, Henry 72, 106, 110, 135, 140, 145, 152, 177, 197, 253 1
Williams, Henry 55, 67, 96, 102, 113, 176, 179, 180, 182, 187 3

Williams, Henry 8, 30, 111, 136, 205, 235, 267 2
Williams, Henry L 209 3
Williams, Henry O 179 3
Williams, Henry S 179 3
Williams, J C 188 3
Williams, J F 187 2
Williams, J H 156, 160 3
Williams, J H 59 1
Williams, J K 161 3
Williams, J W 30, 172 2
Williams, J W 152, 165 1
Williams, J W 100, 166, 188 3
Williams, J Windsor 28 1
Williams, J Wm 37 1
Williams, Jacob 51 1
Williams, Jacob 71 3
Williams, James 138 2
Williams, James H 188, 209 3
Williams, Jane E 187, 188 3
Williams, Jas H 179 3
Williams, Jennie I 188 3
Williams, John 27, 46, 101, 205 2
Williams, John 96, 196, 209 3
Williams, John 26 1
Williams, John E 166 3
Williams, John H 119, 250 2
Williams, John H 26, 37, 159 1
Williams, John H 81, 96, 187 3
Williams, John K D 172 3
Williams, John P 179 3
Williams, John T 43, 290 2
Williams, John T 187 3
Williams, John T 177 1
Williams, John T 59 1
Williams, John W 7 2
Williams, Joseph 185 3
Williams, M P 82 3
Williams, Margaret Janet 196 3
Williams, Maria 195 3
Williams, Martin 260 2
Williams, Mary C 196 3
Williams, Mary J 136 2
Williams, Mollie 197 3
Williams, Peter 185 3
Williams, Rebecca 91 3
Williams, Robert 203 3
Williams, Rosa May 163 3
Williams, S L 179 3
Williams, Soloman 205 3
Williams, Susan F 209 3
Williams, T Bayard 16 2
Williams, William 209 3
Williams, William A 209 3
Williams, Wm 159, 197 2
Williams, Wm Clay 209 3
Williamson, D M 48 1
Williamson, Eleanor 187 3
Williamson, Eleanor W 172 3
Williamson, Elinore W 124 2
Williamson, J A 188 3
Williamson, J A 208, 211 2
Williamson, J Alliene 189 3
Williamson, Jennie H 189 3
Williamson, Joseph A 187 3
Williamson, Julia P 172 3
Williamson, Mary 187 3
Williamson, Mary A 172, 207 3
Williamson, Mary W 189 3
Williamson, T M 224 2
Williamson, T M 163, 188 3
Williamson, Thomas N 172 3
Williamson, Thos 124 2
Williamson, Thos M 187, 207 3
Williamson, Warren R 209 3
Williar, A H 177 2
Williar, A H 160, 165 3
Williar, Abraham 40 1
Williar, Alfred P 160 3
Williar, Alonzo M 161 3
Williar, Andrew Sr 160 3
Williar, Bertha C 189 3
Williar, Cecilia Ann 165 3
Williar, Charles 160, 165 3
Williar, Charles A 169 3
Williar, Chas 9 1
Williar, D F 182 3
Williar, Ethel E 161 3
Williar, Frank E 189 3
Williar, Gilmer 161 3
Williar, Hiram A 179 3
Williar, Israel 182 3
Williar, Israel 194 1
Williar, Jacob 160, 186 3
Williar, Jacob F 160 3
Williar, Jacob O 189 3
Williar, John 160 3
Williar, John A 152 1
Williar, Lavinia 182 3
Williar, Margaret A 195 3
Williar, William K 179 3
Williard, A D 172 3
Williard, Abraham 160 3
Williard, Andrew 184 3
Williard, Ann M R 160 3
Williard, Arthur D 91 3
Williard, C H A 188 3
Williard, Catherine 165 3
Williard, D J 167 3
Williard, Daniel 167, 171 3
Williard, Dewalt 167, 199, 202, 215 3
Williard, E L 167 3
Williard, Edw L 172 3
Williard, Elias 171 3
Williard, Elizabeth 171 3
Williard, Ezra 160, 185, 195 3
Williard, Francis Virginia 174 3
Williard, Geo 171 3
Williard, Geo T 205 3
Williard, George 176 3
Williard, Harriett 179 3
Williard, Henry 176, 186, 195, 205 3
Williard, Jacob 184 3
Williard, Jno 185 3
Williard, Joel T 188 3
Williard, John 176, 184, 186 3
Williard, John D 185 3
Williard, John of Jno 185 3
Williard, Lewis A 192 3
Williard, Louisa 186 3
Williard, Maria 195 3
Williard, Martin O 171, 202 3
Williard, Nancy 199 3
Williard, P C 172 3
Williard, Peter 167, 171, 199, 202 3
Williard, Peter & 160 3
Williard, Rueben D 203 3
Williard, Susannah 205 3
Williard, Thomas H 199 3
Williard, W B 25 1
Williard, W H 179 3
Williard, Walter 167 3
Williard, William H 210 3
Willide, Frederick N 174 3
Willis, Ann 184 3
Willis, Elizabeth 171 3
Willis, Frances A 219 1
Willis, Francis A 174, 209 3
Willis, Henry 184 3
Willis, Herman Lee Sr 180 3
Willis, Jeremiah 37 1
Willis, Jermiah Y 184 3
Willis, John E 209 3
Willis, L C 209 3
Willis, Louis O 174 3
Willis, Louis Orndorff 192 3
Willis, Marguerite E 180 3
Willis, Peter 64 3
Willis, William B 192 3
Willis, William L 209 3
Willisms, Henry 72 1
Willmer, Fannie S 203 3
Willmer, Rabbi W 203 3
Wills, C Hampton 192 3
Wills, Charles E 166 3
Wills, Helena 108 2
Wills, Mary 87 3

Wills, Michael 195 3
Wills, Viola E 166 3
Wills, Wm 204 1
Willson, Catherine 165 3
Willson, Charles P 166 3
Willson, Daniel W 188 3
Willson, John 195 3
Willson, Julia A 188 3
Willson, Thomas P 91 1
Willson, William M B 209 3
Wilmner, Fannie S 210 3
Wilmner, Samuel H 210 3
Wilmner, Wolff 210 3
Wilson, Abraham 160 3
Wilson, Ann S 161 3
Wilson, Anna S 199 3
Wilson, August S 196 3
Wilson, B W 291 2
Wilson, Benk C 187 3
Wilson, C 193 3
Wilson, C L 183 1
Wilson, Caroline S When 66, 187 3
Wilson, Catherine Dora 166 3
Wilson, Charles S 169 3
Wilson, Charles S 217a 2
Wilson, Chas 185 3
Wilson, Chas 182 2
Wilson, Chas E 60 1
Wilson, Chas F 167 2
Wilson, Chas H 179 3
Wilson, Chas H 33 1
Wilson, Chas S 81 2
Wilson, Clara K 166 3
Wilson, Daniel B 180 3
Wilson, Daniel D 73 1
Wilson, Daniel D 166 3
Wilson, David 167 3
Wilson, E H 58 2
Wilson, Edmund F 171 3
Wilson, Edw J 82 1
Wilson, Etta C 32 2
Wilson, Evan 106 1
Wilson, Evan 139 3
Wilson, Evan 176, 199 3
Wilson, Frederick J 61 1
Wilson, Geo I 15 2
Wilson, George A 166 3
Wilson, Georgetta 176 3
Wilson, H E 220 2
Wilson, H E 210 3
Wilson, Hannah Mary 202 3
Wilson, Harriet M 180 3
Wilson, Harriett 179 3
Wilson, Harry E 180, 188 3
Wilson, Henrietta F 180 3
Wilson, Henry 238 2
Wilson, Henry B 88, 112 1
Wilson, Henry B 176, 179, 209 3
Wilson, Herman M 206 3
Wilson, Hetty L 179 3
Wilson, Ida C 182 3
Wilson, Irene M 182 3
Wilson, Isaac 100 1
Wilson, Isaac 184 3
Wilson, J R 150 1
Wilson, J R 2 2
Wilson, J T 186 2
Wilson, James 164 1
Wilson, James L 283 1
Wilson, James L 106, 185 3
Wilson, James W 206 3
Wilson, Jaob M 187 3
Wilson, Jesse B 188 3
Wilson, Jesse R 205 3
Wilson, John 31, 62, 101 2
Wilson, John 186, 187, 203 3
Wilson, John C 171 1
Wilson, John E 113, 188 3
Wilson, John J 40 1
Wilson, John J 186 3
Wilson, John Jr 197 1
Wilson, John Mc 161 3
Wilson, John W 189, 192 3
Wilson, Joseph 250 2
Wilson, Josephine 187 3
Wilson, L P 186 3
Wilson, Lidia J 209 3
Wilson, Lilly E 206 3
Wilson, Louis L 193 3
Wilson, Louis L 76 1
Wilson, Lucy I 192 3
Wilson, Lucy T 193 3
Wilson, Lydia I 192 3
Wilson, M Catherine 188 3
Wilson, M J 221a 2
Wilson, M R 2 2
Wilson, Margaret B 196 3
Wilson, Michael 195 3
Wilson, Milliard G 189 3
Wilson, N E 113 3
Wilson, N J 43, 83 2
Wilson, Nathaniel J 199 3
Wilson, Nettie V 210 3
Wilson, Ortha 201 3
Wilson, P L 113 2
Wilson, Peter L 290 2
Wilson, Peter Light 202 3
Wilson, Richard 169 2
Wilson, Robert 203 3
Wilson, Samuel 171 2
Wilson, Samuel 205, 206 3
Wilson, Samuel C C 206 3
Wilson, Sarah Ellen 205 3
Wilson, Sarah J 207 3
Wilson, Senie A 205 3
Wilson, Stella M 206 3
Wilson, Susannah 205 3
Wilson, Thomas 70, 201 3
Wilson, Thomas J 207 3
Wilson, Thomas M 207 3
Wilson, Thos J 238 2
Wilson, Virginia M 208 3
Wilson, Virginia May 169 3
Wilson, W M B 19 2
Wilson, W S 207 3
Wilson, William 222 2
Wilson, William G 209, 210 3
Wilson, William RH H 210 3
Wilson, William T 210 3
Wilson, Wm M B 171 3
Wilson, Wm O 72 2
Wilt, Claud A 35 3
Wilt, Claud A 34 1
Wilt, Claude A 45 2
Wimms, George W 188 3
Wimms, James 188 3
Winchell, Wm 43 3
Winchester, Hiram 177 2
Winchester, Nellie M 192, 200 1
Winchester, Paul 202 3
Windfield, Thos 106 1
Windson, E T 87 2
Windsor, A H 171 3
Windsor, Angeline 160 3
Windsor, Arnold 132 2
Windsor, Arnold H 160, 212 3
Windsor, Charles 212 3
Windsor, Columbus W 191 3
Windsor, Edmund L 171, 212 3
Windsor, Edna G 172 3
Windsor, Edward W 172 3
Windsor, Elizabeth 171 3
Windsor, Kavey 191, 212 3
Windsor, L T 203 3
Windsor, Robert B 203 3
Windsor, Robert B 14 2
Windsor, Robt B 53 3
Windsor, Z H 171 3
Windsor, Z T 112, 171, 249 1
Windsor, Zachariah T 96 2
Windsor, Zacharias T 212 3
Windsor, Zadock 212 3
Windsor, Zadock H 212 3
Windsox, Edward L 185 3
Windsox, James 185 3
Windsox, Zadock 185 3
Wineberg, Henry 180 3
Wineberry, Elias 172 3
Wineberry, Goldie E 197 3
Wineberry, M Hudson 197 3
Winebrener, Alice Feiser 161 3
Winebrener, Arie 161 3

Winebrener, Chas 140 1
Winebrener, Christian 10, 58 1
Winebrener, D C 14, 40, 154, 163, 189 2
Winebrener, D C 33, 59, 67, 117, 129, 229 1
Winebrener, D Charles 167 3
Winebrener, David 245 1
Winebrener, David 208 2
Winebrener, David C 76 1
Winebrener, David C 195 2
Winebrener, E J 201 1
Winebrener, E J Jr 192 1
Winebrener, Jacob 179 1
Winebrener, Miriam F 161 3
Winebrener, Philip Ritchie 167 3
Winebrener, Raleigh 175 2
Winebrener, S E 30 2
Winebrenner, Aria 203 3
Winebrenner, C 57 1
Winebrenner, Caroline 172 3
Winebrenner, Caroline M 166 3
Winebrenner, Christian 13, 117 1
Winebrenner, Christian 274 2
Winebrenner, Christian 166, 202 3
Winebrenner, Chritian 176, 179, 185 3
Winebrenner, D C 100, 104, 107, 165 1
Winebrenner, D C 2, 5, 87, 177, 188, 214, 268 2
Winebrenner, D C 9, 41, 56, 91, 166, 186, 199, 202, 219 3
Winebrenner, D C 3d 145 1
Winebrenner, D Chas 167 3
Winebrenner, D Chas 126 1
Winebrenner, David C 167, 176 3
Winebrenner, David C 3rd 167 3
Winebrenner, E J 166 2
Winebrenner, Edw J 172 3
Winebrenner, Edw J Jr 172 3
Winebrenner, Geo A 176 3
Winebrenner, Geo L 176 3
Winebrenner, Ida J 189 3
Winebrenner, Jacob 189 3
Winebrenner, Marshall H 197 3
Winebrenner, Marshall P 206 3
Winebrenner, Mary E 166, 210 3
Winebrenner, Mary Ellen 176 3
Winebrenner, Mary Louise 206 3
Winebrenner, Mollie E 166 3
Winebrenner, Phebe 202 3
Winebrenner, Philip 116 1
Winebrenner, Phillip 202 3
Winebrenner, R J 166, 202 3
Winebrenner, Raymond H 189 3
Winebrenner, Reverdy J 203 3
Winebrenner, S C 135 1
Winebrenner, Samuel C 206 3
Winebrenner, Samuel E 166, 206 3
Winebrenner, Susan 206 3
Winebrenner, Wm A 210 3
Winebrenner,3d David C 167 3
Wineburg, Leo 75 3
Winegardner, Geo F 177 3
Winegardner, Joseph L 177 3
Winehart, Israel C 77 3
Winfield, Creola 166 3
Winfield, Cyrus 166, 171, 207 3
Winfield, Ellen 171, 207 3
Winfield, Thomas 207 3
Winfield, Thomas L 207 3
Winkel, Marion 51 1
Winkler, James L 187 3
Winkler, Lucy M 187 3
Winnall, William 209 3
Winnebrenner, James T 186 3
Winnett, William 209 3
Winpigler, David W 196 3
Winpigler, Flora M 174, 189 3
Winpigler, Harriett 179, 185 3
Winpigler, Jesse I 188 3
Winpigler, John 185 3
Winpigler, John J 189 3
Winpigler, Mary E 188 3
Winpigler, Mary J 196 3
Winschoff, Edward 171 3
Winsnig, Augustus 160 3
Winsnig, Mamie D 160 3
Winter, Caroline 165 3
Winter, Columbia 196 3
Winter, David 167 3
Winter, Eliza B 165 3
Winter, Frederick 70, 174 3
Winter, Geo 186, 260 1
Winter, Geo 185 3
Winter, Geo of J 176 3
Winter, George 176 3
Winter, George 262 2
Winter, Henry 176, 185 3
Winter, Henry 228 1
Winter, J 176 3
Winter, Jacob 263 1
Winter, Jacob 176, 185 3
Winter, John 26 2
Winter, John 185 3
Winter, Joseph 184 3
Winter, Lewis 185 3
Winter, M Francis 196 3
Winter, Magdalene 195 3
Winter, Mary A 196 3
Winter, Samuel 176 3
Winter, Susanah N 196 3
Winter, Susannah 205, 206 3
Winter, Thomas 70 1
Winter, Thos 217 1
Winter, Thos 177 2
Winter, William 1 1
Winter, William 209 3
Winter, William B 165 3
Winterhalter, Mary M 16 2
Winters, Columbia 166 3
Winters, David 167, 171 3
Winters, Earhart 171 3
Winters, Erhart 171 3
Winters, Frederick 176 3
Winters, Geo 164, 177 1
Winters, Geo 14 2
Winters, George 184 3
Winters, Henry 124 3
Winters, John 184 3
Winters, Levi 192 3
Winters, Mary 196 3
Winters, Susannah 205 3
Winton, H B 39, 51 2
Wipigler, Edith M 174 3
Wire, Laura V 283 2
Wireman, Annie V 161 3
Wireman, Daniel 275 2
Wirt, Henry 14 3
Wirts, Jacob 112 1
Wirts, Jacob 187 3
Wirts, John 30 1
Wirtz, Jacob 185 3
Wirtz, Jacob 67, 117, 234 1
Wirtz, John 106, 185 3
Wirtz, John 248, 283 1
Wirtz, Peter 185 3
Wise, Amanda V 166 3
Wise, Ann E 28 2
Wise, Ann E 192 3
Wise, Charles E 166, 186 3
Wise, Floyd I 192 1
Wise, Henry 180 3
Wise, Henry A 180, 186 3
Wise, Jacob 185, 186, 202 3
Wise, John 186, 187, 202 3
Wise, John J 166 3
Wise, Joseph 186 3
Wise, Joseph 19, 27 2
Wise, L M 85 1
Wise, Levi O 202 3
Wise, Lewis O 192 3
Wise, Lewis O 28 2
Wise, Luther M 9 3
Wise, Luther M 72 2

Wise, Luther Melvin 192 3
Wise, Maranda 187 3
Wise, Mary E 147 1
Wise, Michael 205 3
Wise, Mollie 113 3
Wise, Peter 202 3
Wise, Philip 202 3
Wise, Stanley S 192 3
Wise, Valentine 208 3
Wise, Virginia M 208 3
Wiseman, Annie E 188 3
Wiseman, Daniel D 167 3
Wiseman, Daniel V 167 3
Wiseman, Enos 171 3
Wiseman, Geo 185 3
Wiseman, John 209 2
Wiseman, John 14, 185 3
Wiseman, John P 188 3
Wiseman, Martin L 167 3
Wiseman, Mary M E 167 3
Wiseman, Samuel 54, 205 3
Wiseman, William 171 3
Wisner, Amelia M 161 3
Wisner, Carrie I 166 3
Wisner, Charles E 166 3
Wisner, Christian 166 3
Wisner, Janie L 189 3
Wisner, Michael 174 3
Wisner, Michael 171, 254 1
Wisner, Samuel 9 2
Wisong, Isaac 184 3
Wisotskey, Eliza R 120 1
Wisotskey, J E 120 1
Wisotzkey, Belva L 189 3
Wisotzkey, John E 189 3
Wisotzkey, Laura M 193 3
Wisotzkey, O B 190 2
Wiss, Lewis 40 3
Wissinger, Geo 56 1
Wissinger, Geo 49, 137, 159 2
Wissinger, Geo & 71 1
Wissler, Cornelia A 166 3
Wissler, Geo E 166, 180 3
Wissler, Harry 199 3
Wissler, Harry W 180 3
Wissler, Nannie 199 3
Wissman, William 209 3
Wissong, Isaac 213 3
Wistler, Geo E 179 3
Wistler, Henry 179 3
Witherou, Elizabeth 171 3
Witherou, Harry A 209 3
Witherou, John 171, 209 3
Witherou, Margaret 196 3
Witherou, William H 209 3
Witherow, David 217a 2
Witherow, John 110, 117, 186, 196, 225, 240, 257 1
Witherow, John 37, 53, 185, 186, 187, 195, 196 3
Witherow, John 1, 11, 38, 84, 100, 134, 217a, 264 2
Witherow, John & 26 2
Witherow, John N 186 3
Witherow, John Ross 186 3
Witherow, Margaret 195, 196 3
Withers, A L 257 1
Withers, Chas B 125 1
Withey, Calvin 165 3
Withey, Louisa 165 3
Witmer Rosa Ann 196 3
Witmer, David C 167 3
Witmer, Ella D 183, 184 1
Witmer, Lydia A 167 3
Witmore, Corlius 165 3
Witmore, George H 2 3
Witmorre, Frederick C 165 3
Witter Harry B 272 1
Witter, Annie E 161 3
Witter, Edw H 92 1
Witter, H B 72, 188 3
Witter, H B 38, 123, 150, 223, 270 1
Witter, H B 2, 80, 102, 189 2
Witter, Harry B 180 3
Witter, Harry B 42, 201 1
Witter, Harry B 39, 235 2
Witter, Harry V 161 3
Witter, J A 214 3
Witter, J H 38 1
Witter, Jerledine D 197 3
Witter, John 260 1
Witter, John H 188 3
Witter, John M 235 2
Witter, John N 196 3
Witter, John WE 185 3
Witter, Mary C V 197 3
Witter, Mary C W 189 2
Witter, R B 188 3
Witter, Robert G 161 3
Witter, Willis D 180, 197 3
Wittler, Edw H 172 1
Witzer, Joshua S 72 2
Wivell, Anthony 277 1
Wivell, George 184 3
Wivell, Joseph 184 3
Wivell, Joseph 277 1
Wivell, Joseph 234 2
Wivell, Joseph Frank 189 3
Wivell, Mary Madeline 246 1
Wivell, William H 189 3
Wivill, George 13 1
Wivill, Joseph 13 1
Wivill, Joseph 83 2
Woerner, Sarah F 206 3
Woillard, Eliza 188 3
Wolf, Adam 209 3
Wolf, Addison E 161 3
Wolf, Andrew 160 3
Wolf, Andrew J 161 3
Wolf, Charles W 169 3
Wolf, Chas C 192 3
Wolf, Christiana 165 3
Wolf, Cora M 210 3
Wolf, Daniel 167 3
Wolf, Elmer P 161 3
Wolf, Eva B 62 1
Wolf, Franklin 174 3
Wolf, George 160 3
Wolf, Georgianna 176 3
Wolf, H Lee 57 3
Wolf, Harry 176 3
Wolf, Harry W 169 3
Wolf, Helen 42 1
Wolf, Henry Lee 180 3
Wolf, Ira L 182 3
Wolf, Jacob 165 3
Wolf, John 186 3
Wolf, Joseph 61 1
Wolf, Lewis H 167 3
Wolf, Lewis W 271 1
Wolf, Lloyd N 180 3
Wolf, Lula 161 3
Wolf, Mahlon K 192, 196 3
Wolf, Mary 186 3
Wolf, P L 161 3
Wolf, Roscoe G 167 3
Wolf, Samuel 156 1
Wolf, Samuel of J 37 1
Wolf, Upton 167 3
Wolf, Victor B 278 2
Wolf, Wade H 210 3
Wolf, William 209 3
Wolf, Wilmner 203 3
Wolfe, Abraham 195 3
Wolfe, Abraham 196 1
Wolfe, Abraham 208 2
Wolfe, Abraham L 161, 172 3
Wolfe, Abraham L 107 1
Wolfe, Adam 51 1
Wolfe, Adam 160 3
Wolfe, Amos R 205 2
Wolfe, Ann E 209 3
Wolfe, Annie R 161 3
Wolfe, C C 167 3
Wolfe, Cabell N 167 3
Wolfe, Charles C 169 3
Wolfe, Chas 40 2
Wolfe, Chas C 210 3
Wolfe, Chas J 189 3
Wolfe, Clifford W 210 3
Wolfe, D Upton 171 3
Wolfe, Daisy E 167 3
Wolfe, Daniel 41, 54, 167, 179 3
Wolfe, Daniel 61, 152 1

Wolfe, Daniel 8, 40 2
Wolfe, Daniel Jr 167 3
Wolfe, Daniel M 167 3
Wolfe, Daniel W 167 3
Wolfe, David 167, 195, 205 3
Wolfe, David 228, 234 1
Wolfe, David 169 2
Wolfe, David Jr 167 3
Wolfe, David Sr 167 3
Wolfe, Della 169 3
Wolfe, Eli 14 2
Wolfe, Eli 192 3
Wolfe, Eli R 171 3
Wolfe, Elizabeth 171 3
Wolfe, Emma S 172 3
Wolfe, Emma S 189 2
Wolfe, Geo 14, 100, 185, 275 2
Wolfe, Geo 196 1
Wolfe, Geo D 189 3
Wolfe, Geo H 82 1
Wolfe, George 176 3
Wolfe, George H 160, 176 3
Wolfe, George W 176 3
Wolfe, Guy 58 2
Wolfe, H L 32 3
Wolfe, H Lee 57, 179 3
Wolfe, Harry D 189 3
Wolfe, Harry E 169, 210 3
Wolfe, Helen R 189 3
Wolfe, Helen V 99 1
Wolfe, Henry 179, 205 3
Wolfe, Henry 207 1
Wolfe, Henry L 182 3
Wolfe, J 196 3
Wolfe, J M 159 2
Wolfe, Jacob 184, 186 3
Wolfe, James B 188 3
Wolfe, James K P 189 3
Wolfe, Jane C 58 2
Wolfe, Jas B 167 3
Wolfe, Jefferson M 189 3
Wolfe, Jno 186 3
Wolfe, John 30, 101, 113 2
Wolfe, John 214 1
Wolfe, John 81, 165, 186, 209 3
Wolfe, John W 189 3
Wolfe, Joseph 30, 40 2
Wolfe, Josiah 14 2
Wolfe, L H 179 3
Wolfe, Lavina 192 3
Wolfe, Levi J 205 3
Wolfe, Levina 14 2
Wolfe, Lewis 64 3
Wolfe, Lewis 275 2
Wolfe, Lewis W 152 1
Wolfe, Lewis W 100 2
Wolfe, Lewis W 160, 209 3
Wolfe, Lillie M 153 1
Wolfe, Lillie M 210 3
Wolfe, M K 199 3
Wolfe, M K 205 2
Wolfe, Margaret A 171 3
Wolfe, Martin 195 3
Wolfe, Mary 176, 195, 196 3
Wolfe, Mary A 176 3
Wolfe, Nancy A 199 3
Wolfe, Peter 202 3
Wolfe, Priscilla 176 3
Wolfe, Richard H 203 3
Wolfe, Roger B 210 3
Wolfe, Roger B 211 1
Wolfe, Sam 54 3
Wolfe, Samuel 167, 186, 203, 205 3
Wolfe, Samuel 217 1
Wolfe, Samuel 93, 208 2
Wolfe, Sarah 206 3
Wolfe, Sarah M 30 1
Wolfe, Susan R 205 2
Wolfe, Susannah 206 3
Wolfe, T M 179 1
Wolfe, Thomas H 189 3
Wolfe, Truman M 210 3
Wolfe, W N 40 3
Wolfe, Walter A 107, 167, 188, 210 3
Wolfe, Walter A 81, 102 2
Wolfe, William 42, 210 3
Wolfe, William H 209 3
Wolfe, William V 210 3
Wolfe, Wm 152 1
Wolfe, Wm N 186 3
Wolfe, Wm S 101 2
Wolfe, Zacharias W 176 3
Wollard, John 188 3
Woltz, John E 188 3
Wompler, David 48 1
Wonderlick, Joseph 184 3
Wood, A M 31 2
Wood, A M 188 3
Wood, A M 62, 73, 120, 263 1
Wood, Aaron 160, 161 3
Wood, Alban 18, 140 1
Wood, Alban M 45, 83, 161, 189, 208 3
Wood, Alban M 25, 67, 190, 247 2
Wood, Alban M 62, 97, 126, 144, 147, 172, 243, 278 1
Wood, Albin[?] M 273 1
Wood, Am 42 1
Wood, Amanda S S 188 3
Wood, Anna M 23 2
Wood, Annie 161 3
Wood, Annie L 27 3
Wood, Annie M 182 3
Wood, Annie M 2 2
Wood, Arron 71, 184 3
Wood, Basil 163 3
Wood, Basil 240 1
Wood, Basil T 163, 188 3
Wood, C W 123 1
Wood, Charles 166, 185 3
Wood, Charles D 3 3
Wood, Chas 144, 237 1
Wood, Chas 71 3
Wood, Chas 198 2
Wood, Chas B 107 2
Wood, Chas D 163 3
Wood, Chas D 169 2
Wood, Dona May 188 3
Wood, Doris H 189 3
Wood, Eliza W 62 1
Wood, Ella 97 1
Wood, Ellen 171 3
Wood, Elsie M 180 3
Wood, Elsie R 172 3
Wood, Emily Maude 189 3
Wood, Fannie E 179 3
Wood, George E 160 3
Wood, H Clay 197, 210 3
Wood, Harry 87, 166, 180, 208 3
Wood, Harry 56, 131, 166, 201, 240 1
Wood, Harry 20 2
Wood, Henry 179 3
Wood, Henry W 188 3
Wood, Ira Newton 182 3
Wood, Isaac N 61 1
Wood, Isaac N 182 3
Wood, J E 237 1
Wood, J E 67, 237 1
Wood, J E R 60, 146, 187 3
Wood, J E R 101 2
Wood, J E R 13 1
Wood, J N 123 1
Wood, Jacob G 187 3
Wood, James 184, 185, 187 3
Wood, James 188 1
Wood, James A 188 3
Wood, James E 185 3
Wood, James M 76 1
Wood, James R 188 3
Wood, James W 188 3
Wood, Jane A 186 3
Wood, Jesse L 188 3
Wood, Joel 275 2
Wood, Joel 185 3
Wood, John 185, 189 3
Wood, John 226 2
Wood, John H 203, 209 3
Wood, John Jr 189 3
Wood, John W 185, 187 3
Wood, John W R 188 3
Wood, Jonnathan 184 3
Wood, Jonothan 185 3
Wood, Jos 258 2
Wood, Joseph 100, 110, 144, 214, 249,

264, 271 1
Wood, Joseph 8, 23, 31, 32, 37, 50, 70, 182, 184, 185, 187, 203, 209 3
Wood, Joseph 132, 171, 198, 211, 226, 229a, 237 2
Wood, Joseph M 242 2
Wood, Joseph N 96 2
Wood, Joshia W 186 3
Wood, Lydia 192 3
Wood, Lydia A 182, 192 3
Wood, Lydia A 225 2
Wood, M P 106 3
Wood, M P 60 1
Wood, Mary 195, 196 3
Wood, Mary E 187, 197 3
Wood, Mary Louise 161 3
Wood, Melvin P 43, 182, 187, 196 3
Wood, Moses 196 3
Wood, Nettie R 278 1
Wood, Nettie R 225 2
Wood, Nettie Ruth 199 3
Wood, Nettie S 192 3
Wood, Pierce 26 2
Wood, Pierce 202 3
Wood, R V 188 3
Wood, Roberts 203 3
Wood, Roland T 172 3
Wood, Rosa E 210 3
Wood, Rufus 71 1
Wood, Ruth H 57 1
Wood, Ruth H 185, 203, 209 3
Wood, Shepherd 110 1
Wood, Sophia 187 3
Wood, Virginia A 179 3
Wood, Virginia Worthington 208 3
Wood, William 209 3
Wood, William H C 210 3
Woodcock, Allen T 166 3
Woodcock, Charles P 166 3
Woodcock, Charles S 166 3
Woods, Elias 96 2
Woods, Joseph F 189 3
Woods, Joseph R 189 3
Woods, Pearce 193, 194 1
Woodside, Daniel F 167 3
Woodside, Margaret 167 3
Woodside, Margaret 208, 282 1
Woodward, Alexander 161 3
Woodward, Baldwin 163 3
Woodward, Chas W 280 1
Woodward, Emma 210 3
Woodward, Horace 179 3
Woodward, Horace 137 2
Woodward, John J 187 3
Woodward, Lewis A 210 3
Woodward, Lydia Ann 163 3
Woodward, M A 218 2
Woodward, Milton A 187, 196 3
Woodward, Phoebe Helen 215a 2
Woodward, William A 161, 210 3
Woolf, John 184 3
Woolfe, Garrett 184 3
Woord, H M 227a 2
Wooten, Elizabeth C 205 3
Wooten, Singleton 205 3
Wooton, Elizabeth C 171 3
Wooton, Singleton 40 1
Wooton, William 209 3
Wootten, E 209 3
Wootten, W T 91 3
Wootton, William T 209 3
Working, Catherine 165 3
Working, Henry 11 2
Works, Nora A 199 3
Worley, James R 188 3
Worley, Joseph 184 3
Worman, A D 205 3
Worman, Andrew 160, 209 3
Worman, Andrew D 195 3
Worman, Emma F 179 3
Worman, Emma J 124, 172 3
Worman, Emma K 43 2
Worman, George M 176 3
Worman, Harry R 176 3
Worman, Henry C 179 3
Worman, Henry C 117 1
Worman, John 184 3
Worman, Julia 185 3
Worman, Margaret A 196 3
Worman, Mary 195 3
Worman, Mary A S 196 3
Worman, Mary Ann 195 3
Worman, Mary E 72 1
Worman, Mary E 195, 196, 209, 210 3
Worman, Mary Elizabeth 196 3
Worman, Mary M 124 3
Worman, Mary O 205 3
Worman, Mary W 172 3
Worman, Maximus J] 195 3
Worman, Moses 135, 139, 179 1
Worman, Moses 185, 195, 209 3
Worman, Noah 88 1
Worman, Noah 159, 186, 197 2
Worman, Sophie M 205 3
Worman, W D 195 3
Worman, W J 182 3
Worman, Wesley 209 3
Worman, William 42, 209 3
Worman, William D 209 3
Worman, William J 182, 205, 210 3
Worman, William M 209 3
Worman, Wm 148 2
Worman, Wm J 196, 224 3
Worman, Wm J 14, 29 2
Worten, Raphael 203 3
Worthing, Thomas 70 3
Worthingtn, Jane H 207 3
Worthington, A 199 3
Worthington, A Drucilla 97 1
Worthington, Alice S 160 3
Worthington, Ann H 160 3
Worthington, Arthur B 161 3
Worthington, C E 165 3
Worthington, Catherine 165, 208 3
Worthington, Charles E 59 1
Worthington, Charles E 165 3
Worthington, Charles of J 165 3
Worthington, Chas 185 3
Worthington, Chas 30 1
Worthington, Chas of J 171 2
Worthington, Chas of J 88 1
Worthington, Chas of J 205 3
Worthington, Clarke 188 3
Worthington, Elizabeth 172 3
Worthington, G C 55 3
Worthington, G H 112, 169, 253, 283 1
Worthington, G H 79, 188 3
Worthington, G H 52 2
Worthington, Glen H 41 1
Worthington, Glen H 2 3
Worthington, Glenn 41 1
Worthington, Glenn H 52, 282 1
Worthington, Glenn H 2, 43, 56, 161, 172, 176, 192, 219 3
Worthington, Glenn H 62 2
Worthington, H F 207 3
Worthington, Henrietta F 179, 187 3
Worthington, J 165, 205 3
Worthington, J 171 2
Worthington, J 165 1
Worthington, J D 30 1
Worthington, J Dorsey 185 3
Worthington, J H of J 165 3
Worthington, J Henrietta 187 3
Worthington, J T 120, 165 3
Worthington, J T 76 2
Worthington, James 88 1
Worthington, James 172, 192 3
Worthington, James 277 2
Worthington, Jas of Jno 185 3
Worthington, John 185 3
Worthington, John H 185, 186 3
Worthington, John H 106, 112, 159,

169 1
Worthington, John H 23 2
Worthington, John P 208 3
Worthington, John T 37 1
Worthington, John T 160, 185, 188, 199 3
Worthington, John W 75 3
Worthington, Julia 172, 192 3
Worthington, Julia A 56, 188 3
Worthington, Lavina 192 3
Worthington, Lavinia 165 3
Worthington, M J 165, 199 3
Worthington, Mary W 161 3
Worthington, N J 59, 144 1
Worthington, N J 165 3
Worthington, Nichlos 165 3
Worthington, Nicholas 186 3
Worthington, Nicholas C 199 3
Worthington, Nicolas J 199 3
Worthington, T G 160 3
Worthington, Thomas 70, 207 3
Worthington, Thomas C 207 3
Worthington, Thomas J 177 1
Worthington, Thos 271 1
Worthington, Thos 165 2
Worthington, Thos C 51 1
Worthington, Thos C 1 2
Worthington, Upton 139 1
Worthington, Upton 75, 165, 185, 186, 208 3
Worthington, Upton 171 2
Worthington, Wm 106 3
Worthy, Unice 192 1
Woster, Jacob 179 3
Woulfe, Maurice R [sic] 201 1
Woullard, Frank C 206 3
Woullard, Susan 206 3
Wren, Florence M 201 3
Wren, John R 14 2
Wren, Oliver 201 3
Wren, Robert S 42 3
Wright, A E (Mrs) 161 3
Wright, Annie E 283 2
Wright, Arthur H 174 3
Wright, Benjamin 163 3
Wright, C W 189 1
Wright, C W 163, 198 2
Wright, C W 50 3
Wright, Caroline K 203 3
Wright, Catherine 165 3
Wright, Catherine E 187 3
Wright, Catherine R 166 1
Wright, Charles T 169 3
Wright, Charles W 166 3
Wright, Chas 144 1
Wright, Chas W 210, 229 1
Wright, Chas W 166 3
Wright, Chas W 51, 64, 203, 277 2
Wright, Clara L 148 2
Wright, Clarence E 119 1
Wright, Clinton H 169 3
Wright, E C 76 2
Wright, Edward L 171 3
Wright, Emily 171 3
Wright, Eugene H 203 3
Wright, Francis L 174 3
Wright, Hugh E 166, 197 3
Wright, I Orville 166 1
Wright, Isaac 184 3
Wright, J B 210 1
Wright, James H 188 3
Wright, James Paul 189 3
Wright, Jese 139 3
Wright, Jess 22 1
Wright, Jesse 23, 81, 163, 184, 186, 187, 203 3
Wright, Jesse 19, 100, 137, 214, 247 2
Wright, Jesse 279 1
Wright, Jessie 205 3
Wright, Joel D 187 3
Wright, John 106, 185 3
Wright, John 129 1
Wright, Joseph 184 3
Wright, Lake 166, 197 3
Wright, Lawrence W 192 3
Wright, Lewis 51 2
Wright, Lewis W 79 3
Wright, Lulu 232, 241 2
Wright, Mabel I 228a 2
Wright, Madora 192 3
Wright, Margaret 186, 196 3
Wright, Mary 64 2
Wright, Mary 195 3
Wright, Mary E 189 3
Wright, Mary Elizabeth 197 3
Wright, Mary J 106, 197 3
Wright, Ocale 166, 197 3
Wright, Philip 71, 195 3
Wright, R Harold 41 2
Wright, Raymond W 188, 203 3
Wright, Reuben P 203 3
Wright, Rhoda W 255 2
Wright, Robert G 161, 203 3
Wright, Robert L 203 3
Wright, Samuel 163, 165, 184, 205 3
Wright, Sarah J 206 3
Wright, Sophia 205 3
Wright, Susannah 184, 205 3
Wright, Thos 186 2
Wright, William McK 197 3
Wright, Wm 176 3
Wright, Wm K 189 3
Wright, Wm McK 9 2
Wyant, Catherine 165 3
Wyant, Jacob 184 3
Wyant, Yost 165, 212 3
Wyatt, John 184 3
Wynkoop, James R 188 3
Wynkoop, Mary B 188 3
Wynn, Anna Mary 186 3
Wynn, John 186, 187 3
Yakey, John+ 215 3
Yakey, T S 72 2
Yandis, George 282 2
Yanitz, Susan 218 3
Yantis, Daniel 59, 181 1
Yantis, Daniel 163 3
Yantis, David F 213 3
Yantis, George 214 3
Yantis, Susan 218 3
Yardly, William 218 3
Yaste, Ann Amelia 212 3
Yaste, Catherine 213 3
Yaste, Cordelia B 213 3
Yaste, Dixon A 214 3
Yaste, Geo 215 3
Yaste, Geo 100 2
Yaste, Geo E 218 3
Yaste, George 39 3
Yaste, George E 214 3
Yaste, George Edward 214 3
Yaste, Jacob 215 3
Yaste, James T 212 3
Yaste, Minnie J 214 3
Yaste, Miriam J 242 2
Yaste, Mirian J 242 2
Yaste, Samuel 100 2
Yaste, Samuel 76 1
Yaste, Samuel 39, 213, 215, 217 3
Yaste, Sarah E 218 3
Yates, Alice 212 3
Yates, Catherine 213 3
Yates, David C 213 3
Yates, Edward 213 3
Yates, Gelia D 213 3
Yates, H N 213 3
Yates, Salome 218 3
Yatman, William 70 1
Yeager, Ann M 212 3
Yeager, Arthur Leon 217 3
Yeager, Charles 213 3
Yeager, Charles Lee 217 3
Yeager, Elizabeth 172 2
Yeager, Nannie May 217 3
Yeagle, Fannie B 56 3
Yeakey, Eliza 215 3
Yeakey, Jacob 215 3
Yeakle, A R 217 3
Yeakle, Edward C 213 3

Yeakle, Fannie B 217 3
Yeakle, Jacob 215 3
Yeakle, Joseph 215 3
Yeakle, Mary L 217 3
Yeakle, Mary L 110 1
Yeakle, Wm 215 3
Yearly, Alexander 41 1
Yearly, Alexander Jr 41 1
Yearly, Thomas C 59 1
Yeiser, Daniel 93, 202 2
Yeiser, George 214 3
Yeiser, Godleit 214 3
Yeiser, Godlieb 214 3
Yeiser, Golsiep 93 2
Yengle, Mary L 91 3
Yeomans, Agnes 260, 280 1
Yeomans, Richard 260 1
Yerk, Catherine 215 3
Yerk, John 215 3
Yieser, Daniel 214 3
Yinger, Charles F 213 3
Yinger, David 219 1
Yinger, Florence M 213 3
Yinger, John F 8, 19 1
Yinger, John F 215 3
Yinger, Lemar 213 3
Yinger, Lewis 217 3
Yinger, Lewis H 213 3
Yinger, Marion F 217 3
Yinger, Mary E 215 3
Yinger, Mary Lu 10 2
Yinger, Nicholas 217 3
Yingling, Abraham 212 3
Yingling, Benjamin 196, 262 1
Yingling, Daniel 137 2
Yingling, David 144 1
Yingling, David 213 3
Yingling, E L 219 3
Yingling, Edmund 218 3
Yingling, Edw 217 1
Yingling, Erie E 215 2
Yingling, Frederick 5, 262, 282 2
Yingling, Frederick 1 1
Yingling, Frederick 26, 64, 148, 217 3
Yingling, J T 56 1
Yingling, Jacob 197, 228 1
Yingling, Jacob 184, 215, 217 3
Yingling, John 215 3
Yingling, John 226 2
Yingling, John D 218 3
Yingling, John H 217 3
Yingling, John Peter 215 3
Yingling, John T 215 3
Yingling, John T 217 1
Yingling, Joshia 217 3
Yingling, Josiah 217 3
Yingling, Marg 217 3
Yingling, Margaret 217 3
Yingling, Mary 217 3
Yingling, Nora K 217 3
Yingling, Nora K 106 2
Yingling, Penelope 217 3
Yingling, Samuel W 240 1
Yingling, Sarah C 264 2
Yingling, Thos 66 2
Yingling, Vernon 215 2
Yingling, Vernon D 215 2
Yingling, Vincent D 215 3
Yingling, William G 218 3
Yingling, Wm G 283 1
Yingling, Zadock 218 3
Yingling, Zadock A 219 3
Yingst, Sarah 189 2
Yohn, William 288 2
Yon, Jacob 125, 194, 214, 228, 263 1
Yon, Wm 177 2
Yoner, Harriett 214 3
Yonkers, Bernard O 213 3
Yonkers, Genevieve 213 3
Yonkers, H W 213 3
Yonkers, Saranna 213 3
Yonkins, Arba W 217 3
Yonkins, Caroline S 217 3
Yonkins, John W 215 3
Yonkins, Martin L 217 3
Yonkins, Martin L 217 3
Yonson, Catherine 214, 217, 218 3
Yonson, Charles A 213 3
Yonson, Henry 207, 214, 215 3
Yonson, Jacob H 213, 215 3
Yonson, John 215 3
Yonson, Martin 217 3
Yonson, Mary A 217 3
Yonson, Peter L 217 3
Yonson, Victorius U 213 3
Yonson, William S 218 3
Yontsey, Sophia 218 3
Yontz, Nina N 192 3
Yontz, Samuel 84 2
York, Carnegia 224 3
Yose, George 214 3
Yost, Amelia 212 3
Yost, Mary 217 3
You, Jacob 215 3
You, Jacob 215 3
You, John 37 3
You, John 106 2
You, Wm 106 2
You, Wm 116 1
Young, Abraham 125 1
Young, Abraham 31 3
Young, Adam 212 3
Young, Alice I 212, 213 3
Young, Alvah 34 1
Young, Alvey D 214 3
Young, Andrew 212, 218 3
Young, Andrew Sr 212 3
Young, Ann 212 3
Young, Anna Margaret 212 3
Young, Austin U 216 3
Young, Barbara 213 3
Young, Beatrice 215 3
Young, Betty D 153 1
Young, Betty D 3 3
Young, C 215 3
Young, C T E 35 2
Young, C T K 140 1
Young, Calvin W 213 3
Young, Catherine 213 3
Young, Charles B 214 3
Young, Charles T K 33 1
Young, Charles T K 213 3
Young, Chas 68 2
Young, Chas B 218 3
Young, Chas T 92, 126 1
Young, Chas T K 144 2
Young, Chas T K 27 1
Young, Chas T K 227 3
Young, Christopher 214 3
Young, Clara A 215 3
Young, Clyde M 215 3
Young, Clyde N 213 3
Young, Conrad 213 3
Young, D 41, 215 3
Young, D 187, 203, 208, 231 2
Young, Daniel 181 2
Young, Daniel 39, 167, 213 3
Young, Daniel 6 1
Young, Daniel D 213 3
Young, Daniel H 213, 214 3
Young, Daniel J 27 1
Young, Daniel J 214 3
Young, David 217 3
Young, David F 212 3
Young, DeWalt 213 3
Young, Edgar 153 1
Young, Edgar R 215 3
Young, Effie I 212 3
Young, Elizabeth F 216 3
Young, Etta 42 1
Young, Eva M 214 3
Young, Florence I 213 3
Young, Genora 91, 218 3
Young, Genora, Mrs 91 3
Young, Geo 46 2
Young, Geo A 8 1
Young, Geo W 234 2
Young, George 214 3
Young, George W 38 3
Young, Hannah 214 3
Young, Harry A 215 3

Young, Harry W 214 3
Young, Henry 176 1
Young, Henry 37, 39, 53, 213, 214, 215 3
Young, Henry 165, 185 2
Young, Herman H 10, 214, 218 3
Young, Hezekiah 214 3
Young, Ida Alberta 6 3
Young, Ida M 215 3
Young, Ira J 64 2
Young, Ira J 215 3
Young, Isaac 55 3
Young, J H 218 3
Young, Jacob 215, 216 3
Young, Jacob 223, 228, 229 1
Young, Jacob 5, 181, 186, 188, 197, 275 2
Young, Jacob of C 13 1
Young, Jacob of D 40, 41, 215 3
Young, Jacob of D 58, 131 1
Young, Jacob of D 187, 203, 208, 231 2
Young, Jacob of P 215 3
Young, Jacob P 215 3
Young, Jacob S 215 3
Young, John 100, 163, 213, 215, 217 3
Young, John 163, 164, 223, 228, 238 1
Young, John 68, 87, 177, 197, 205 2
Young, John A L 215 3
Young, John H 37 1
Young, John H 39, 215 3
Young, John of C 6 1
Young, John of C 215 3
Young, John of D 215 3
Young, John of P 118 1
Young, John R 43, 71 3
Young, John R 115 2
Young, John W 215 3
Young, Jonas F 215 3
Young, Joseph N 215 3
Young, Joshua 212 3
Young, Julia M 215 3
Young, Kenneth W 216 3
Young, Laura 216 3
Young, Leila M 216 3
Young, Leonard 124 2
Young, Leonard 216 3
Young, Lewis 216 3
Young, Lucretia 213, 216 3
Young, Margaret 217, 218 3
Young, Margaret A 241 2
Young, Martin C 217 3
Young, Mary A 212 3
Young, Mary Ann 217 3
Young, Mary H 217 3
Young, McClintock 217 3
Young, Meredith S 175 2
Young, Nannie M 217 3
Young, Nellie Glisan 248 1
Young, Oliver H 217 3
Young, P 215 3
Young, Peter 39, 106, 215, 217 3
Young, Peter 139 1
Young, Philip 217 3
Young, R E 199 2
Young, R L 101 1
Young, Raymond O 216, 217 3
Young, Roger 192 3
Young, Roger E 288 2
Young, Rosetta G 213 3
Young, S Noah 215 3
Young, S Price 218 3
Young, Sallie E 218 3
Young, Samuel 218 3
Young, Samuel 96 2
Young, Samuel D 22 2
Young, Sarah 28 1
Young, Sarah E 218 3
Young, Sarah E 215 3
Young, Sarah Price 221 3
Young, Sarah Z 218 3
Young, Sophie E 218 3
Young, Stanley F 291 2
Young, Susan 218 3
Young, Susannah 218 3
Young, Thomas 212, 218 3
Young, Thos P 218 3
Young, Tilghman H 218 3
Young, W Meredith 283 2
Young, W Nash 234 1
Young, William H 218 3
Young, William R 218 3
Young, Wm 203 2
Young, Wm H 215 3
Young, Wm R 187 3
Young, Wm R 234, 240 1
Younkins, Arba W 68 1
Younkins, Cordelia 215 3
Younkins, John W 215 3
Younkins, Lizzie B 67 2
Younkins, Romer C 48 1
Younkins, Wm E 172 2
Yountsey Christian 217 3
Yountsey, C 217 3
Yountsey, Magdalena 217 3
Yountsey, Michael 217 3
Yourtee, George W 214 3
Yourtee, J E 79 1
Yourtee, John E 9 2
Yourtee, Laura E H 214 3
Youtsey, Christiana 213 3
Youtsey, George 214 3
Youtsey, John 213 3
Youtsey, Michael 217 3
Youtsey, Peter 217 3
Youtz, Samuel 137 2
Ysste, Leonard 217 3
Zacharias, Anna 219 3
Zacharias, C T 19 1
Zacharias, Catherine Z 220 3
Zacharias, Christian 231, 237 2
Zacharias, Christian 219, 220, 224 3
Zacharias, Christian T 224 3
Zacharias, Daniel 220, 222 3
Zacharias, Daniel Rev 220 3
Zacharias, Geo 220 3
Zacharias, Geo K 64 3
Zacharias, George 222 3
Zacharias, H C 106, 175, 213, 215 2
Zacharias, H C 27, 96, 189 3
Zacharias, H C 55 1
Zacharias, H Z 10 3
Zacharias, Horace C 181 2
Zacharias, Horace C 62, 265 1
Zacharias, Horace C 222 3
Zacharias, John 100 1
Zacharias, John 224 3
Zacharias, John F 223 3
Zacharias, Joseph 224 3
Zacharias, M 27 2
Zacharias, M P 91 1
Zacharias, Mathias 224 3
Zacharias, Matthias 57 1
Zacharias, Matthias P 220, 223, 224 3
Zacharias, R C 50, 67 3
Zacharias, Susan 222 3
Zacharias, Susannah 220 3
Zacharias, Tempie 96 3
Zacharias, Tempie E 55 1
Zacharias, Tempie E 222 3
Zacharias, William 227 3
Zadricks, Daniel 220 3
Zecher (Zecker), John Samuel 223 3
Zecher, D D 23 1
Zecher, Daniel D 1 1
Zecher, Elizabeth 3 1
Zecher, Emanda E 220 3
Zecher, F W 4 1
Zecher, Geo F 148, 225 1
Zecher, John 89, 228a 2
Zecher, John C 19 1
Zecher, John S 68, 240 1
Zecher, John S 161, 293 2
Zecher, Lee S 223 3
Zecher, Sallie Young 227 3

Zeck, Detrick 188 2
Zeck, Detrick 98, 160 3
Zeck, Detrick 192 1
Zeck, Edgar D 224 3
Zeck, Margaret M 224 3
Zecker, Amanda C 219 3
Zecker, D D 3 1
Zecker, Daniel D 220, 223 3
Zecker, Geo S 219 3
Zecker, George 223 3
Zecker, I C 3 1
Zecker, John 223 3
Zecker, John S 219 3
Zecker, John Samuel 223 3
Zecker, Margaret S 227 3
Zecker, William Carlton 227 3
Zedrick, Henry 222 3
Zedrick, Rebecca 222 3
Zedricks, Malinda 224 3
Zeek, Detrick 102 3
Zeighlr, Earl E 222 3
Zeigler, Amy R 224 3
Zeigler, Ann G 223 3
Zeigler, Charles C 220 3
Zeigler, Chas C 222, 223 3
Zeigler, Christian 220 3
Zeigler, Dennis 167 3
Zeigler, Elizabeth 221 3
Zeigler, Elizabeth A 221 3
Zeigler, Fannie L 221 3
Zeigler, Geo A 221 3
Zeigler, George Z 45 3
Zeigler, Grace M 224 3
Zeigler, Hannah 222 3
Zeigler, Henry 222 3
Zeigler, Henry L 156 1
Zeigler, J Walter 223 3
Zeigler, Jacob 61 2
Zeigler, Jacob H 220, 223, 224 3
Zeigler, Jacob Henry 223 3
Zeigler, Joanna 223 3
Zeigler, Katie 222 3
Zeigler, Lewis C 224 3
Zeigler, Mary Edna 227 3
Zeigler, Michael 224 3
Zeigler, Theresa I 227 3
Zeigler, Walter F 227 3
Zeiler, Elizabeth 221 3
Zeiler, George 222 3
Zeiler, Henry 222 3
Zeiler, J D 1, 29 2
Zeiler, John 181 2
Zeirold, Christian 219 3
Zeller, Henry 222 3
Zeller, Jacob 222 3
Zeller, Otelia 226 3
Zellers, Henry 222 3
Zellers, Loretta S 224 3
Zent, Harvey E 83 3
Zentmyer, Jacob 223 3
Zentmyer, Jacob 28 2
Zentmyer, Jacob 156 1
Zentmyer, Jacob Jr 159 1
Zents, Geo C 41 2
Zentz, A F 11 2
Zentz, A S 55 1
Zentz, Abraham S 219 3
Zentz, Adam R 219 3
Zentz, Adam R 242 2
Zentz, Annie D 220 3
Zentz, D W 172 1
Zentz, Daniel W 220 3
Zentz, David G 220 3
Zentz, E Monroe 226 3
Zentz, Effie G 220 3
Zentz, Geo C 222 3
Zentz, Harvey C 224 3
Zentz, Laura M 219 3
Zentz, Maggie W 224 3
Zentz, Minnie M 41 2
Zentz, Minnie M 222 3
Zentz, N M 172 2
Zentz, Newton 199 3
Zentz, Newton 181 2
Zentz, Newton M 226 3
Zentz, Robt F 219 3
Zepp, Harry R 254 1
Zepp, Leonard 224 3
Zepp, S D 254 1
Zerfass, Elizabeth 221 3
Zerganeston, J A 70 3
Zick, Catherine 12 2
Ziegler, David 217 1
Ziegler, Geo's Z 51 3
Ziegler, John 214 1
Zierold, August 219 3
Zimmerman, A J 175 1
Zimmerman, Aamanda M 219 3
Zimmerman, Abraham 227 3
Zimmerman, Albert D 224 3
Zimmerman, Albert F 219 3
Zimmerman, Albert J 221 3
Zimmerman, Albert S 221 3
Zimmerman, Albert T 219 3
Zimmerman, Alfred 280 1
Zimmerman, Alfred G 96, 224 3
Zimmerman, Alfred G 108, 163 2
Zimmerman, Alfred Glaze 220 3
Zimmerman, Alice O 219 3
Zimmerman, Alice V 219 3
Zimmerman, Alvey O 220 3
Zimmerman, Amanda D 219 3
Zimmerman, Andrew 219 3
Zimmerman, Andrew J 197, 219 3
Zimmerman, Ann C 79 1
Zimmerman, Ann R 219 3
Zimmerman, Annie 220 3
Zimmerman, Annie C 219 3
Zimmerman, Annie C 85 1
Zimmerman, Annie C 202 2
Zimmerman, Annie M 219, 227 3
Zimmerman, B F 189 2
Zimmerman, Barbara A 219 3
Zimmerman, Benj F 220 3
Zimmerman, Benjamin F 219, 228 3
Zimmerman, Benjamin F 259 2
Zimmerman, Benjamin J 219 3
Zimmerman, Benjamin M 219 3
Zimmerman, Bernard F 219 3
Zimmerman, C A 220 3
Zimmerman, C C 120 1
Zimmerman, C C 219 3
Zimmerman, C E 221 3
Zimmerman, C M 166 2
Zimmerman, C M 221 3
Zimmerman, Calvin 220 3
Zimmerman, Calvin C 142 1
Zimmerman, Calvin C 219, 220, 224, 227 3
Zimmerman, Caroline H 220 3
Zimmerman, Caroline R 226 3
Zimmerman, Catherine 220 3
Zimmerman, Cephas 144 1
Zimmerman, Cephas H 220 3
Zimmerman, Cephas H 169 1
Zimmerman, Charles 220 3
Zimmerman, Charles E 220 3
Zimmerman, Charles Ed 220 3
Zimmerman, Charles F 222 3
Zimmerman, Charles H 220 3
Zimmerman, Charles W 209 3
Zimmerman, Charlotte A 220 3
Zimmerman, Chas 214, 223 1
Zimmerman, Chas 222 3
Zimmerman, Chas A 220 3
Zimmerman, Chas E 219 3
Zimmerman, Chas E 265 2
Zimmerman, Chas W 48, 112 1
Zimmerman, Chas W 55, 221 3
Zimmerman, Chas W 46 2
Zimmerman, Christian 220 3
Zimmerman, Clara E 220, 227 3
Zimmerman, Cornelius T 220, 226 3
Zimmerman, Curtis T 220, 224 3
Zimmerman, D Ralph 35 2
Zimmerman, Daniel 222 3
Zimmerman, Daniel J 220 3
Zimmerman, Daniel P 10 1
Zimmerman, Daniel P 43, 206, 220

3
Zimmerman, David 220 3
Zimmerman, David D 227 3
Zimmerman, David E 220 3
Zimmerman, David M 220 3
Zimmerman, David R 220 3
Zimmerman, David Ralph 219 3
Zimmerman, E 89 3
Zimmerman, E E 206 2
Zimmerman, E J 58 2
Zimmerman, E R 55 3
Zimmerman, E Steiner 221 3
Zimmerman, Edna K 221 3
Zimmerman, Edna K Waesche 221 3
Zimmerman, Edw J Jr 221 3
Zimmerman, Edward 32, 223 3
Zimmerman, Edward D 221, 222 3
Zimmerman, Edward E 221, 224 3
Zimmerman, Edward J 65, 227 3
Zimmerman, Edwin D 219 3
Zimmerman, Elias 221, 222, 223 3
Zimmerman, Elias 59 1
Zimmerman, Elias 29 2
Zimmerman, Elizabeth 221, 226 3
Zimmerman, Elizabeth R 221 3
Zimmerman, Emma E 221 3
Zimmerman, Emma E D 221 3
Zimmerman, Emma V 221 3
Zimmerman, Ephraim B 206 3
Zimmerman, Ephraim I 221 3
Zimmerman, Estella H 226 3
Zimmerman, Eugene E 221 3
Zimmerman, Ezra R 221 3
Zimmerman, F M 220 3
Zimmerman, Fannie 221, 224 3
Zimmerman, Fannie J 221 3
Zimmerman, Florence M 244 1
Zimmerman, Florence N 221 3
Zimmerman, Frances C 227 3
Zimmerman, Francis M 221 3
Zimmerman, Frank W 272 1
Zimmerman, Frank W 222 3
Zimmerman, G Bernard 219, 221 3
Zimmerman, G C 219 3
Zimmerman, G E 79 1
Zimmerman, Geo 221, 222, 224, 227 3
Zimmerman, Geo 48, 112, 163, 176, 245 1
Zimmerman, Geo 8, 43, 138 2
Zimmerman, Geo F 205 2
Zimmerman, Geo F S 222 3
Zimmerman, Geo H 8 2
Zimmerman, Geo H 55, 222, 227 3
Zimmerman, Geo H 214, 230, 271 1
Zimmerman, Geo M 245 1
Zimmerman, Geo M 166 2
Zimmerman, Geo of N 219, 222 3
Zimmerman, Geo W 72, 192, 219, 223 3
Zimmerman, George 220, 222 3
Zimmerman, George 264 2
Zimmerman, George E 222 3
Zimmerman, George H 4 1
Zimmerman, George H 44 3
Zimmerman, George M D 222 3
Zimmerman, George W 222 3
Zimmerman, Gertrude L 221 3
Zimmerman, Gideon M 219, 220, 222 3
Zimmerman, Grace E 66, 296 2
Zimmerman, Grace E 221, 222 3
Zimmerman, H 67, 96, 224 3
Zimmerman, Harriet M 222 3
Zimmerman, Harry 222, 224 3
Zimmerman, Harry C 221 3
Zimmerman, Harry E 145, 148 1
Zimmerman, Harry E 222, 224, 228 3
Zimmerman, Harry W 221 3
Zimmerman, Harvey L 227 3
Zimmerman, Harvey R 222 3
Zimmerman, Helen A 226 3
Zimmerman, Helen E 220 3
Zimmerman, Helen V 220 3
Zimmerman, Henry 96, 222, 227 3
Zimmerman, Henry 274 2
Zimmerman, Henry 23 1
Zimmerman, Henry M 223 3
Zimmerman, Henry O 22, 248 1
Zimmerman, Henry O 227 3
Zimmerman, Hester C 221 3
Zimmerman, Horace J 24, 38 1
Zimmerman, Ida 220, 222 3
Zimmerman, Ila May 227 3
Zimmerman, Irene P 9 2
Zimmerman, Isaac C 226 3
Zimmerman, Isabelle R 226 3
Zimmerman, J 171, 223 3
Zimmerman, J 43 2
Zimmerman, J Leslie 224 3
Zimmerman, J M 50 3
Zimmerman, J N 9 3
Zimmerman, J N 211 2
Zimmerman, J Nicholas 2 3
Zimmerman, J P 282 2
Zimmerman, J W C 221a 2
Zimmerman, J Wesley 223 3
Zimmerman, Jacob 40, 219, 221, 223 3
Zimmerman, Jacob Alexander 223 3
Zimmerman, Jacob E 186 3
Zimmerman, James 221 3
Zimmerman, James A 223 3
Zimmerman, Jane 223 3
Zimmerman, Janie 66 2
Zimmerman, Jessie R 227 3
Zimmerman, John 106, 223, 226 3
Zimmerman, John 25, 38, 185 2
Zimmerman, John A 106 3
Zimmerman, John A J 223 3
Zimmerman, John H 222, 223 3
Zimmerman, John Henry 223 3
Zimmerman, John L 223 3
Zimmerman, John Nicholas 223 3
Zimmerman, John of J 223 3
Zimmerman, John of J 43 2
Zimmerman, John of N 223 3
Zimmerman, John P 222, 223, 227 3
Zimmerman, John P 56, 159 1
Zimmerman, John P 43, 131, 134, 282 2
Zimmerman, John T 87, 220 3
Zimmerman, John W C 227 3
Zimmerman, Jonathan T 223 3
Zimmerman, Jonathan T 79 1
Zimmerman, Jonothan A 96 3
Zimmerman, Joseph A 227 3
Zimmerman, Joseph D 223 3
Zimmerman, Joseph H 223 3
Zimmerman, Joshua 179, 271 1
Zimmerman, Joshua 237 2
Zimmerman, Joshua E B 223 3
Zimmerman, Joshua J 32 1
Zimmerman, Josiah B 71, 72, 223 3
Zimmerman, Josiah B 12 2
Zimmerman, Josiah J 222, 223 3
Zimmerman, Katherine C 104 1
Zimmerman, L C 226 3
Zimmerman, L M 165 3
Zimmerman, Laura C 84, 87 2
Zimmerman, Laura K 224 3

Zimmerman, Laura M S 224 3
Zimmerman, Laura V 224 3
Zimmerman, Leonard W 221, 224 3
Zimmerman, Lester C 224, 226 3
Zimmerman, Lester C 42 1
Zimmerman, Lewis F 221, 224 3
Zimmerman, Lula E 224 3
Zimmerman, Luther M 224 3
Zimmerman, M 176 3
Zimmerman, M 1 2
Zimmerman, M 37 1
Zimmerman, M A 254 2
Zimmerman, M C 221 3
Zimmerman, M C 136 1
Zimmerman, M Jr 13 1
Zimmerman, Margaret M 224 3
Zimmerman, Margaret R S 223 3
Zimmerman, Maria 221 3
Zimmerman, Maria A 224 3
Zimmerman, Martha 224 3
Zimmerman, Martha E 224 3
Zimmerman, Mary A 224 3
Zimmerman, Mary C 224 3
Zimmerman, Mary E 192, 224 3
Zimmerman, Mary Emma 219 3
Zimmerman, Mary J C 224 3
Zimmerman, Mary Jo 221, 224 3
Zimmerman, Mary M 223 3
Zimmerman, Mattie E 223a 2
Zimmerman, Maude A 249 2
Zimmerman, Mazepah A 222, 224 3
Zimmerman, Mazzeppa A 198 2
Zimmerman, Melvin H 222 3
Zimmerman, MF 35, 172 2
Zimmerman, Michael 37, 56, 57, 152, 196, 257 1
Zimmerman, Michael 67, 70, 87, 167, 195, 224, 227 3
Zimmerman, Michael 11, 87, 137, 169, 208 2
Zimmerman, Michael Jr 224 3
Zimmerman, Millard C 224 3
Zimmerman, Milton 286 1
Zimmerman, Milton F 224 3
Zimmerman, Milton S 63 1
Zimmerman, Milton S 159, 223 3
Zimmerman, Mollie 28 3
Zimmerman, Mollie V 219, 228 3
Zimmerman, N 219, 222, 223 3
Zimmerman, Nathan 37 3
Zimmerman, Nellie C 226 3
Zimmerman, Nellie E 222, 226 3
Zimmerman, Nicholas 226 3
Zimmerman, O I 179 3
Zimmerman, O T 71, 186 3
Zimmerman, Oliver T 219, 226 3
Zimmerman, Peter 222 3
Zimmerman, Peter T 226 3
Zimmerman, R C 96 3
Zimmerman, R Clinton 31, 160 2
Zimmerman, R Clinton 221, 224 3
Zimmerman, R D 93 2
Zimmerman, R E 83 3
Zimmerman, R E 175 2
Zimmerman, R E 63, 146 1
Zimmerman, R R 221 3
Zimmerman, Rachel A 223 3
Zimmerman, Ray B 226 3
Zimmerman, Rebecca 226 3
Zimmerman, Rhodela S 226 3
Zimmerman, Richard E 21, 24, 28, 51, 58, 83, 87, 98, 153 3
Zimmerman, Richard E 21, 73, 74, 102, 155, 186, 239, 250, 266 1
Zimmerman, Richard E 66, 67, 113, 172, 215, 235, 283, 295 2
Zimmerman, Rosanna 226 3
Zimmerman, Roscoe David 226 3
Zimmerman, Roy C 222, 226 3
Zimmerman, Roy V 192 3
Zimmerman, S G 116 3
Zimmerman, S J 244 1
Zimmerman, S J 221 3
Zimmerman, Samuel 135 1
Zimmerman, Samuel 222, 223, 227 3
Zimmerman, Samuel M 227 3
Zimmerman, Sarah C 227 3
Zimmerman, Soloma J 222 3
Zimmerman, Soloman 221, 222, 224, 227 3
Zimmerman, Solomon 135, 176 1
Zimmerman, Spencer 123 1
Zimmerman, Spencer 161, 196, 227 3
Zimmerman, Spencer E 119 1
Zimmerman, Susan 54 2
Zimmerman, Susannah 219, 227 3
Zimmerman, Susannah 219, 227 3
Zimmerman, Susannah A 227 3
Zimmerman, Susannah C 227 3
Zimmerman, Susie E 32 2
Zimmerman, T C 239 1
Zimmerman, Thadeus E 227 3
Zimmerman, Theodore C 226, 227 3
Zimmerman, Thomas L 227 3
Zimmerman, Thos H A 220, 227 3
Zimmerman, Thos L 222 3
Zimmerman, Tobias 155 1
Zimmerman, Tobias E 58 3
Zimmerman, Virginia E 228 3
Zimmerman, W H 37 1
Zimmerman, W H 1 3
Zimmerman, W M 96 3
Zimmerman, W P 221 3
Zimmerman, Walter C 161, 227 3
Zimmerman, William 54 3
Zimmerman, William 221a 2
Zimmerman, William D 58, 220 3
Zimmerman, William D 163, 199, 209 2
Zimmerman, William G 83 3
Zimmerman, William G 202 1
Zimmerman, William H 55 3
Zimmerman, William H 225a 2
Zimmerman, Wm 96 1
Zimmerman, Wm 85, 31 2
Zimmerman, Wm 224, 227 3
Zimmerman, Wm D 51, 222 3
Zimmerman, Wm D 19 1
Zimmerman, Wm E 219 3
Zimmerman, Wm G 215, 227 3
Zimmerman, Wm G 2, 199 2
Zimmerman, Wm G 19, 62, 230 1
Zimmerman, Wm H 222, 223, 224, 226, 227 3
Zimmerman, Wm H 38, 76, 91, 99, 135 1
Zimmerman, Wm H F 224 3
Zimmerman, Wm M 134 2
Zimmerman, Wm M 224, 227 3
Zimmerman, Wm N 222 3
Zimmerman, Wm Nicholas 227 3
Zimmerman, Wm W 224 3
Zimmerman, Z E 221 3
Zimmerman, Zachariah E 79 1
Zimmerman, Zachary 223 3
Zimmerman, Zachary E 219, 228 3
Zimmerman, Zoie L 140 1
Zimmernman, R Ralph 215 3

Zinkhan, Anna 68 3
Zinkhan, Geo C 68 3
Zittle, Alice Irene 219 3
Zittle, Horatio 223 3
Zittle, Jacob 223 3
Zittle, John H 223 3
Zittle, Wm 100 2
Zollekoffer, Daniel 184 3
Zollikoffer, Daniel 6, 53 3
Zollikoffer, David K 106 3
Zollinger, George 160 3
Zollinger, John 223 3
Zumbeum, Jacob 76 2
Zumbourn, Jacob 109 1
Zumbram, Jacob 220a 2
Zumbrum, Elizabeth 221 3
Zumbrum, Jacob 124, 150, 203 2
Zumbrum, Jacob 228, 260 1
Zumbrum, Jacob 221 3
Zumbrum, John 223 3
Zumpstein, Frederick 29 2
Zumstein, Frederick 119 2
Zurgable, Geo Thomas 222 3
Zurgable, George T 228 3
Zurgable, Henry T 222 3
Zurgable, Jacob W 223 3
Zurgable, M Barbara 223 3
Zurgable, Virginia G 228 3
Zurgables, Geo T 93 1

www.ingramcontent.com/pod-product-compliance
Lightning Source LLC
Chambersburg PA
CBHW080415270326
41929CB00018B/3034
* 9 7 8 0 7 8 8 4 2 5 7 8 3 *